Lecture Notes in Computer Science 1051
Edited by G. Goos, J. Hartmanis and J. van Leeuwen

Marie-Claude Gaudel James Woodcock (Eds.)

FME'96: Industrial Benefit and Advances in Formal Methods

Third International Symposium
of Formal Methods Europe
Co-Sponsored by IFIP WG 14.3
Oxford, UK, March 18-22, 1996
Proceedings

Springer
Berlin
Heidelberg
New York
Barcelona
Budapest
Hong Kong
London
Milan
Paris
Santa Clara
Singapore
Tokyo

Volume Editors

Marie-Claude Gaudel
Laboratoire de Recherche en Informatique, Université de Paris-Sud et CNRS
Bâtiment 490, F-91405 Orsay-cedex, France

James Woodcock
Computing Laboratory, Oxford University
Wolfson Building, Parks Road, Oxford OX1 3QD, United Kingdom

Cataloging-in-Publication data applied for

Die Deutsche Bibliothek - CIP-Einheitsaufnahme

Industrial benefit and advances in formal methods : proceedings / FME '96, Third International Symposium of Formal Methods Europe, Oxford, UK, March 1996. Marie-Claude Gaudel ; James Woodcock (ed.). Co-sponsored by IFIP WG 14.3. - Berlin ; Heidelberg ; New York ; Barcelona ; Budapest ; Hong Kong ; London ; Milan ; Paris ; Santa Clara ; Singapore ; Tokyo : Springer, 1996
(Lecture notes in computer science ; Vol. 1051)
ISBN 3-540-60973-3
NE: Gaudel, Marie-Claude [Hrsg.]; FME <3, 1996, Oxford>; GT

CR Subject Classification (1991): D.1-2, D.3.1,F.3.1, J.1

ISBN 3-540-60973-3 Springer-Verlag Berlin Heidelberg New York

Typesetting: Camera-ready by author
SPIN 10512716   06/3142 – 5 4 3 2 1 0   Printed on acid-free paper

Preface

This volume contains the proceedings of the Third Formal Method Europe Symposium. This series of Symposia aims to promote the interests of users, researchers, and developers of precise mathematical methods in software development, and to report advances in this field.

The FME Symposia are the successors of the four VDM symposia organised by "VDM Europe", an advisory board sponsored by the Commission of the European Union. After the last VDM symposium, VDM Europe became "Formal Methods Europe", with the mission of supporting the industrial use of formal methods for computer systems development. The first FME symposium was held in Odensee in April 1993, the second in Barcelona in September 1994; the scope of these symposia, which had already been widened to include Z, was extended to include all formal methods of software development.

This is emphasized this time by the fact that this symposium is co-sponsored by the IFIP Working Group 14.3 "Foundations of Systems Specifications", a recently created group which mainly works in the area of algebraic specifications.

FME'96 is being held at St Hugh's College in Oxford from 18 to 22 March 1996.

Like the previous FME symposia, this one focuses on industrial applicability. Its theme is *The Application and Demonstrated Industrial Benefit of Formal Methods, Their New Horizons and Strengthened Foundations.* Accordingly, three kinds of paper were solicited: reports on industry usage, research papers on existing methods (for instance extensions, innovative case studies, ...), and articles on stimulating theoretical research with strong potential applications.

Over the last few years, the use of formal methods has significantly progressed. These proceedings contain descriptions of applications to numerous and important areas: information systems, medical systems, aerospace and avionics, nuclear safety, energy, telecommunications, traffic modeling and transportation systems, etc.

103 papers were submitted, from 20 countries; 35 of them were accepted, roughly 8 on industry usage, 21 on existing methods, and 6 on theoretical research (some papers should be in two categories, thus these figures are not completely accurate). As can be seen in the following table of contents, the addressed topics cover the main existing methods plus several important and general problems such as: the role of formal methods in requirement analysis, user interfaces for formal methods, performance analysis, fault-tolerance, testing, reuse, and transformations.

The invited speakers are C.A.R. Hoare, from Oxford University, Terje Siversten, from the OECD Halden Reactor Project in Norway, and Jan Peleska, from JP Software-Consulting and the University of Bremen, reflecting the scope of the symposium, from foundations to industrial applications.

Moreover, the symposium will include 8 tutorials, some poster sessions, and an exhibition of formal-method tools.

The program committee of FME'96 is as follows: Egidio Astesiano*, Dominique Bolignano*, Gottfried Egger*, Hartmut Ehrig, Marie-Claude Gaudel*, René Jacquart*, Cliff Jones*, Bernd Krieg-Bruckner*, Peter Gorm Larsen*, Robert Milne, Peter Mosses*, Maurice Naftalin, Fernando Orejas*, Jan Storbank Pedersen*, Nico Plat*, John Rushby*, Jim Woodcock*.

We sincerely thank all the program committee members, especially those who managed to attend the selection meeting (the ones with * in the list above), and the referees listed on the next page for their care and advice.

Thanks are due to Michel Beaudouin-Lafon for providing the program used to collect the review forms. Evelyne Jorion, Bruno Marre, and Mountaz Zizi had to deal with a large number of submitted papers and reviews, and to prepare these proceedings. They did an excellent job and deserve special thanks for their contribution.

In addition, the following persons have played an essential role in the preparation of this symposium: Alejandro Moya, CEU, for his continued support; Peter Lucas, chair of Formal Method Europe; Hans-Jeorg Kreowski, chair of IFIP WG14.3 "Foundations of Systems Specifications"; and Alfred Hofmann, Springer-Verlag.

Thanks are also due to the organising committee of FME'96: Ana Cavalcanti, Anna Morris, Andrew Simpson and Maureen York from Oxford University; Bruno Marre and Mountaz Zizi from LRI, CNRS-Université de Paris-Sud.

FME'96 has been supported by the commission of the European Union, CRI, Formal Systems (Europe) Ltd, IFAD, Oxford University, Praxis plc, and Prentice Hall International.

Orsay, January 1996

Marie-Claude Gaudel
Jim Woodcock

External Referees

All submitted papers, whether accepted or rejected, were refereed by programme committee members and a number of external referees. This symposium would not have been possible without their voluntary and dedicated work.

Sten Agerholm
Marc Aiguier
Roswitha Bardohl
Michel Beaudouin-Lafon
Joffroy Beauquier
Michel Bidoit
Pierre Bieber
Robin Bloomfield
Frederic Boniol
Alexander Borusan
S. Brookes
Bettina Buth
Eric ten Cate
Jacques Cazin
Maura Cerioli
Ghassan Chehaibar
Christine Choppy
Ingo Classen
Tim Clement
Mirko Conrad
Patrice Cros
Werner Damm
Olivier Danvy
C.J. Dahl
Mourad Debbabi
Carlos Delgado-Kloos
Roger Duke
Heiko Dörr
Christian Engel
Andreas Fett
John Fitzgerald
David de Frutos-Escrig
Robert Geisler
F. Geurts
Reinhard German
Andrew Gordon
Wolfgang Grieskamp
Jan Friso Groote
Martin Grosse-Rhode
Jim Grundy
Ulrich Hannemann
Bo Stig Hansen
Kirsten Mark Hansen
Ian Hayes
Jifeng He
Maritta Heisel
Friedrich von Henke
Matthew Hennessy
Stephan Herrmann
Jan Hiemer
Michaela Huhn
Wil Janssen
Kurt Jensen
Gisela John
Stuart Kent
Marcus Klar
Torsten Klein
Tjabbe Kloppenburg
Peter Kluit
Kevin Lano
Frank Lattemann
Michel Lemoine
Jacques Loeckx
Rita Loogen
Michael Mac an Airchinnigh
Bernd Mahr
Bruno Marre
Javier Martinez
Jan de Meer
Pierre Michel
Kees Middelburg
Eugenio Moggi
Brian Monahan
Paul Mukherjee
Robert Nieuwenhuis
E.-R. Olderog
Florence Pagani
H. Partsch
Jan Peleska
Alfonso Pierantonio
Soren Prehn
Kees Pronk
Zhenyu Qian
Gianna Reggio
Leila Ribeiro
Willem-Paul de Roever
Bill Roscoe
Sadegh Sadeghipour
Ina Schieferdecker
Christel Seguin
N. Shankar
Hui Shi
Harbhajan Singh
Jeanine Souquieres
Mike Spivey
Mario Suedholt
Frans Ververs
Guy Vidal-Naquet
Walter Vogler
Frederic Voisin
Henrik Voss
Auke Woerlee
Virginie Wiels
Alan Williams
Burkhart Wolff
Eoin Woods
Elena Zucca

We apologise if we have inadvertently omitted a referee from the above list. To the best of our knowledge the list is accurate.

Tutorials

The tutorials form an important part of FME'96 symposium. Copies of the tutorial material will be distributed to all participants in the tutorials. We would like to thank all those who have kindly been willing to give these tutorials.
The tutorials are:

Formal Development of Object-oriented Systems in VDM++
by S. Goldsack and K. Lano, Dept. of Computing, Imperial College, UK.

Formal Development in B Abstract Machine Notation
by K. Lano and H. Haughton, Dept. of Computing, Imperial College, UK

A Tutorial on Action Semantics
by Peter D. Mosses, University of Aarhus, DK.

The Requirements State Machine Language and its Application to the Traffic Alert and Collision Avoidance System II (TCAS II).
by Mats P.E. Heimdahl, Michigan State University.

Tutorial on CSP and FDR
by Bill Roscoe, Oxford University.

The ProCoS Approach to the Design of Real-Time Systems: Linking Different Formalisms
by A.P. Ravn, Technical University of Denmark, Department of Computer Science, DK.

Tutorial on ACL2
by Matt Kaufmann, J.Strother Moore, and William D. Young, Computational Logic Inc.

An Introduction to Some Advanced Capabilities of PVS
by Sam Owre and John Rushby, Computer Science Laboratory, SRI International, Menlo Park, California, USA.

Table of Contents

Invited Lectures

Session 1: B

Session 2: Action Systems

Session 3a: Requirements

Session 3b: VDM

Session 4a: User Interfaces for Formal Methods

Session 4b: Z

Session 5: Distributed Systems (1)

Session 9: Architecture and Reuse

Session10: Transformations

Session 11: Model Checking (2)

How Did Software Get So Reliable Without Proof?

C.A.R. Hoare

Oxford University Computing Laboratory,
Wolfson Building, Parks Road, Oxford, OX1 3QD, UK

Abstract. By surveying current software engineering practice, this paper reveals that the techniques employed to achieve reliability are little different from those which have proved effective in all other branches of modern engineering: rigorous management of procedures for design inspection and review; quality assurance based on a wide range of targeted tests; continuous evolution by removal of errors from products already in widespread use; and defensive programming, among other forms of deliberate over-engineering. Formal methods and proof play a small direct role in large scale programming; but they do provide a conceptual framework and basic understanding to promote the best of current practice, and point directions for future improvement.

1 Introduction

Twenty years ago it was reasonable to predict that the size and ambition of software products would be severely limited by the unreliability of their component programs. Crude estimates suggest that professionally written programs delivered to the customer can contain between one and ten independently correctable errors per thousand lines of code; and any software error in principle can have spectacular effect (or worse: a subtly misleading effect) on the behaviour of the entire system. Dire warnings have been issued of the dangers of safety-critical software controlling health equipment, aircraft, weapons systems and industrial processes, including nuclear power stations. The arguments were sufficiently persuasive to trigger a significant research effort devoted to the problem of program correctness. A proportion of this research was based on the ideal of certainty achieved by mathematical proof.

Fortunately, the problem of program correctness has turned out to be far less serious than predicted. A recent analysis by Mackenzie has shown that of several thousand deaths so far reliably attributed to dependence on computers, only ten or so can be explained by errors in the software: most of these were due to a couple of instances of incorrect dosage calculations in the treatment of cancer by radiation. Similarly predictions of collapse of software due to size have been falsified by continuous operation of real-time software systems now measured in tens of millions of lines of code, and subjected to thousands of updates per year. This is the software which controls local and trunk telephone exchanges; they have dramatically improved the reliability and performance of telecommunications throughout the world. And aircraft, both civil and military, are now flying with the aid of software measured in millions of lines – though not all of it is safety-critical. Compilers and operating systems of a similar size now number their satisfied customers in millions.

So the questions arise: why have twenty years of pessimistic predictions been falsified? Was it due to successful application of the results of the research which was motivated by the predictions? How could that be, when clearly little software has ever has been subjected to the rigours of formal proof? The objective of these enquiries is not to cast blame for the non-fulfilment of prophecies of doom. The history of science and engineering is littered with false predictions and broken promises; indeed they seem to serve as an essential spur to the advancement of human knowledge; and nowadays, they are needed just to maintain a declining flow of funds for research. Nixon's campaign to cure cancer within ten years was a total failure; but it contributed in its time to the understanding on which the whole of molecular medicine is now based. The proper role for an historical enquiry is to draw lessons that may improve present practices, enhance the accuracy of future predictions, and guide policies and directions for continued research in the subject.

The conclusion of the enquiry will be that in spite of appearances, modern software engineering practice owes a great deal to the theoretical concepts and ideals of early research in the subject; and that techniques of formalisation and proof have played an essential role in validating and progressing the research. However, technology transfer is extremely slow in software, as it should be in any serious branch of engineering. Because of the backlog of research results not yet used, there is an immediate and continuing role for education, both of newcomers to the profession and of experienced practitioners. The final recommendation is that we must aim our future theoretical research on goals which are as far ahead of the current state of the art as the current state of industrial practice lags behind the research we did in the past. Twenty years perhaps?

2 Management

The most dramatic advances in the timely delivery of dependable software are directly attributed to a wider recognition of the fact that the process of program development can be predicted, planned, managed and controlled in the same way as in any other branch of engineering. The eventual workings of the program itself are internal to a computer and invisible to the naked eye; but that is no longer any excuse for keeping the design process out of the view of management; and the visibility should preferably extend to all management levels up to the most senior. That is a necessary condition for the allocation of time, effort and resources needed for the solution of longer term software problems like those of reliability.

The most profitable investment of extra effort is known to be at the very start of a project, beginning with an intensified study not only of the requirements of the ultimate customer, but also of the relationship between the product and the environment of its ultimate use. The greatest number (by far) of projects that have ended in cancellation or failure in delivery and installation have already begun to fail at this stage. Of course we have to live with the constant complaint that the customers do not know what they want; and when at last they say they do, they constantly change their mind. But that is no excuse for abrogating management responsibility. Indeed, even stronger management is required to explore and capture the true requirements, to set up procedures and deadlines for management of change, to negotiate and where necessary invoke an early cancellation clause in the contract. Above all, the strictest management is needed to prevent premature commitment to start programming as soon as possible. This can only lead to a volume of code of unknown and untestable utility, which will act forever after as a dead weight, blighting the subsequent progress of the project, if any.

The transition from an analysis of requirements to the specification of a program to meet them is the most crucial stage in the whole project; the discovery at this stage of only a single error or a single simplification would fully repay all the effort expended. To ensure the proper direction of effort, the management requires that all parts of the specification must be subjected to review by the best and most experienced software architects, who thereby take upon themselves an appropriate degree of responsibility for the success of the project. That is what enables large implementation teams to share the hard-won experience and judgement of the best available engineers.

Such inspections, walkthroughs, reviews and gates are required to define important transitions between all subsequent phases in the project, from project planning, design, code, test planning, and evaluation of test results. The individual designer or programmer has to accept the challenge not only of making the right decisions, but also of presenting to a group of colleagues the arguments and reasons for confidence in their correctness. This is amazingly effective in instilling and spreading a culture conducive to the highest reliability. Furthermore, if the review committee is not satisfied that the project can safely proceed to its next phase, the designer is required to re-work the design and present it again. Even at the earliest stage, management knows immediately of the setback, and already knows, even if they refuse to believe it, that the delivery will have to be rescheduled by exactly the same interval that has been lost. Slack for one or two such slippages should be built into the schedule; but if the slack is exhausted, alternative and vigorous action should be no longer delayed.

At the present day, most of the discussion at review meetings is conducted in an entirely informal way, using a language and conceptual framework evolved locally for the purpose. However, there is now increasing experience of the benefits of introducing abstract mathematical concepts and reasoning methods into the process, right from the beginning. This permits the consequences of each proposed feature and their possible combinations to be explored by careful and exhaustive mathematical reasoning, to avoid the kind of awkward and perhaps critical interactions that might otherwise be detected only on delivery. At the design stage, the mathematics can help in exploring the whole of the design space, and so give greater assurance that the simplest possible solution has been adopted. Even stricter formalisation is recommended for specifying the interfaces between the components of the design, to be implemented perhaps in different places at different times by different people. Ideally, one would like to see a proof in advance of the implementation that correctness of the components, defined in terms of satisfaction of the interface specifications, will guarantee correctness of their subsequent assembly. This can greatly reduce the risk of a lengthy and unpredictable period of integration testing before delivery.

At the final review of the code, judicious use of commentary in the form of assertions, preconditions, postconditions and invariants can greatly help in marshalling a convincing argument that a program actually works. Furthermore, it is much easier to find bugs in a line of reasoning than it is in a line of code. In principle, correctness of each line of reasoning depends at most on two preceding lines of reasoning, which are explicitly referenced. In principle, correctness of each line of code depends on the behaviour of every other line of code in the system.

Success in the use of mathematics for specification, design and code reviews does not require strict formalisation of all the proofs. Informal reasoning among those who are fluent in the idioms of mathematics is extremely efficient, and remarkably reliable. It is not immune from failure; for example simple misprints can be surprisingly hard to detect by eye. Fortunately, these are exactly the kind of error that can be removed by early tests. More formal calculation can be reserved for the most crucial issues, such as interrupts and recovery procedures, where bugs would be most dangerous, expensive, and most difficult to diagnose by tests.

A facility in formalisation and effective reasoning is only one of the talents that can help in a successful review. There are many other less formal talents which are essential. They include a wide understanding of the application area and the marketplace, an intuitive sympathy with the culture and concerns of the customer, a knowledge of the structure and style of existing legacy code, acquaintance and professional rapport with the most authoritative company experts on each relevant topic, a sixth sense for the eventual operational consequences of early design decisions, and above all, a deep sense of personal commitment to quality, and the patience to survive long periods of intellectual drudgery needed to achieve a thoroughly professional result. These attributes are essential. The addition of mathematical fluency to the list is not going to be easy; the best hope is to show that it will enhance performance in all these other ways as well.

3 Testing

Thorough testing is the touchstone of reliability in quality assurance and control of modern production engineering. Tests are applied as early as possible at all stations in the production line. They are designed rigorously to maximise the likelihood of failure, and so detect a fault as soon as possible. For example, if parameters of a production process vary continuously, they are tested at the extreme of their intended operating range. Satisfaction of all tests in the factory affords considerably increased confidence, on the part of the designer, the manufacturer, and the general public, that the product will continue to work without fail throughout its service lifetime. And the confidence is justified: modern consumer durables are far more durable than they were only twenty years ago.

But computing scientists and philosophers remain skeptical. E.W. Dijkstra has pointed out that program testing can reveal only the presence of bugs, never their absence. Philosophers of science have pointed out that no series of experiments, however long and however favourable can ever prove a theory correct; but even only a single contrary experiment will certainly falsify it. And it is a basic slogan of quality assurance that "you cannot test quality into a product". How then can testing contribute to reliability of programs, theories and products? Is the confidence it gives illusory?

The resolution of the paradox is well known in the theory of quality control. It is to ensure that a test made on a product is not a test of the product itself, but rather of the methods that have been used to produce it – the processes, the production lines, the machine tools, their parameter settings and operating disciplines. If a test fails, it is not enough to mend the faulty product. It is not enough just to throw it away, or even to reject the whole batch of products in which a defective one is found. The first principle is that the whole production line must be re-examined, inspected, adjusted or even closed until the root cause of the defect has been found and eliminated.

Scientists are equally severe with themselves. To test a theory they devise a series of the most rigorous possible experiments, aimed explicitly and exclusively to disprove it. A single test with a negative result may occasionally be attributed to impure ingredients or faulty apparatus; but if the negative outcome is repeated, parts of the theory have to be rethought and recalculated; when this gets too complicated, the whole theory has to be abandoned. As Popper points out, the non-scientist will often die with (or even for) his false beliefs; the scientist allows his beliefs to die instead of himself.

A testing strategy for computer programs must be based on lessons learned from the successful treatment of failure in other branches of science and engineering. The first lesson is that the test strategy must be laid out in advance and in all possible detail at the very earliest stage in the planning of a project. The deepest thought must be given to making the tests as severe as possible, so that it is extremely unlikely that an error in the design of the program could possibly remain undetected. Then, when the program is implemented and passes all its tests the first time, it is almost unbelievable that there could be any inherent defect in the methods by which the program has been produced or any systematic lapse in their application. This is the message of Harlan Mill's "clean room" strategy.

The earliest possible design of the test strategy has several other advantages. It encourages early exploration, simplification and clarification of the assumptions underlying use of the program, especially at edges of its operating range;

it facilitates early detection of ambiguities and awkward interaction effects latent in the specification; and it concentrates attention from the earliest stage on central problems of assuring correctness of the system as a whole. Many more tests should be designed than there will ever be time to conduct; they should be generated as directly as possible from the specification, preferably automatically by computer program. Random selection at the last minute will protect against the danger that under pressure of time the program will be adapted to pass the tests rather than meeting the rest of its specification. There is some evidence that early attention to a comprehensive and rigorous test strategy can improve reliability of a delivered product, even when at the last minute there was no time to conduct the tests before delivery!

The real value of tests is not that they detect bugs in the code, but that they detect inadequacy in the methods, concentration and skills of those who design and produce the code. Programmers who consistently fail to meet their testing schedules are quickly isolated, and assigned to less intellectually demanding tasks. The most reliable code is produced by teams of programmers who have survived the rigours of testing and delivery to deadline over a period of ten years or more. By experience, intuition, and a sense of personal responsibility they are well qualified to continue to meet the highest standards of quality and reliability. But don't stop the tests: they are still essential to counteract the distracting effects and the perpetual pressure of close deadlines, even on the most meticulous programmers.

Tests that are planned before the code is written are necessarily "black box" tests; they operate only at the outermost interfaces of the product as a whole, without any cognizance of its internal structure. Black box tests also fulfil an essential role as acceptance tests, for use on delivery of the product to the customer's site. Since software is invisible, there is absolutely no other way of checking that the version of the software loaded and initialised on the customer's machine is in fact the same as what has been ordered. Another kind of acceptance test is the suite of certification tests which are required for implementations of standard languages like COBOL and ADA. They do little to increase confidence in the overall reliability of the compiler, but they do at least fairly well ensure that all the claimed language features have in fact been delivered; past experience shows that even this level of reliability cannot be taken for granted.

Another common kind of black box test is regression testing. When maintaining a large system over a period of many years, all suggested changes are submitted daily or weekly to a central site. They are all incorporated together, and the whole system is recompiled, usually overnight or at the week end. But before the system is used for further development, it is subjected to a large suite of tests to ensure that it still works; if not, the previous version remains in use, and the programmer who caused the error has an uncomfortable time until it is mended. The regression tests include all those that have detected previous bugs, particularly when this was done by the customer. Experience shows that bugs are often a result of obscurity or complication in the code or its documentation; and any new change to the code is all too likely to reintroduce the same bug – something that customers find particularly irksome.

4 Debugging

The secret of the success of testing is that it checks the quality of the process and methods by which the code has been produced. These must be subjected to continued improvement, until it is normal to expect that every test will be passed first time, every time. Any residual lapse from this ideal must be tracked to its source, and lead to lasting and widely propagated improvements in practice. Expensive it may be, but that too is part of the cure. In all branches of commerce and industry, history shows dramatic reduction in the error rates when their cost is brought back from the customer to the perpetrator.

But there is an entirely different and very common response to the discovery of an error by test: just correct the error and get on with the job. This is known as debugging, by analogy with the attempt to get rid of an infestation of mosquitoes by killing the ones that bite you - so much quicker and cheaper and more satisfying than draining the swamps in which they breed. For insect control, the swatting of individual bugs is known to be wholly ineffective. But for programs it seems very successful; on removal of detected bugs, the rate of discovery of new bugs goes down quite rapidly, at least to begin with. The resolution of the paradox is quite simple; it is as if mosquitoes could be classified into two very distinct populations, a gentle kind that hardly ever bite, and a vicious kind that bite immediately. By encouraging the second kind, it is possible to swat them, and then live comfortably with the yet more numerous swarm that remains. It seems possible that a similar dichotomy in software bugs gives an explanation of the effectiveness of debugging.

The first tests of newly written code are those conducted by the programmer separately on isolated segments. These are extraordinarily effective in removing typographical errors, miskeying, and the results of misunderstanding the complexity of the programming language, the run-time library or the operating system. This is the kind of error that is easily made, even by the most competent and diligent programmer, and fortunately just as easily corrected in today's fast-turnround visual program debugging environments. Usually, the error is glaringly obvious on the first occasion that a given line of code is executed.

For this reason, the objective of the initial test suite is to drive the program to execute each line of its code at least once. This is known as a *coverage* test; because it is constructed in complete knowledge of the object under test, it is classified as an "open box" test. In hardware design a similar principle is observed; the suite of tests must ensure that every stable element makes at least one transition from high voltage to low and at least one transition from low voltage to high. Then at least any element that is stuck at either voltage level will be detected.

The cheapest way of testing a new or changed module of code in a large system is simply to insert the module in the system and run the standard suite of regression tests. Unfortunately, the coverage achieved in this way does not seem adequate: the proportion of code executed in regression tests has been reported to be less than thirty per cent. To improve this figure, a special test harness has to be constructed to inject parameters and inspect results at the module level. Unfortunately, for a module with many parameters, options and modes, to push the coverage towards a hundred percent gets increasingly difficult; in the testing of critical software for application in space, comprehensive testing is reported to increase costs by four times as much as less rigorously tested code. Equally unfortunately, total coverage is found to be necessary: more errors continue to be discovered right up to the last line tested.

In hardware design, exhaustive testing of stuck-at faults has also become impossible, because no sufficiently small part of a chip can be exercised in isolation from the rest. Nevertheless, quite short test sequences are adequate to identify and discard faulty chips as they come off the production line. It is a fortunate property of the technology of VLSI that any faults that are undetected by the initial tests will very probably never occur; or at least they will never be noticed. They play the role of the gentle kind of mosquito: however numerous, they hardly ever bite.

Returning to the case of software, when the program or the programmer has been exhausted by unit testing, the module is subjected to regression testing, which may throw up another crop of errors. When these are corrected, the regression tests soon stop detecting new errors. The same happens when an updated system is first delivered to the customer: nearly all the errors are thrown up in early runs of the customer's own legacy code. After that, the rate at which customers report new errors declines to a much lower and almost constant figure.

The reason for this is that even the most general-purpose programs are only used in highly stereotyped ways, which exercise only a tiny proportion of the total design space of possible paths through the code. Most of the actual patterns of use are explored by the very first regression tests and legacy tests, and beta testing enables the customer to help too. When the errors are removed from the actually exercised paths, the rate at which new paths are opened up is very low. Even when an anomaly is detected, it is often easier to avoid it by adapting the code that invokes it; this can be less effort and much quicker than reporting the error. Perhaps it is by this kind of mutual adaption that the components of a large system, evolving over many years, reach a level of natural symbiosis; as in the world of nature, the reliability and stability and robustness of the entire system is actually higher than that of any of its parts.

When this stable state is reached, analysis of a typical error often leads to an estimate that, even if the error were uncorrected, the circumstances in which it occurs are so unlikely that on a statistical basis they will not occur again in the next five thousand years. Suppose a hundred new errors of this kind are detected each year. Crude extrapolation suggests that there must be about half a million such errors in the code. Fortunately, they play the same role as the swarms of the gentle kind of mosquito that hardly ever bites. The less fortunate corollary is that if all the errors that are detected are immediately corrected, it would take a thousand years to reduce the error rate by twenty percent. And that assumes that there are no new errors introduced by the attempt to correct one which has already been detected. After a certain stage, it certainly pays both the customer and the supplier to leave such errors unreported and uncorrected.

Unfortunately, before that stage is reached, it often happens that a new version of the system is delivered, and the error rate shoots up again. The costs to the customer are accepted as the price of progress: the cost to the supplier is covered by the profit on the price of the software. The real loss to the supplier is the waste of the time and skill of the most experienced programmers, who would otherwise be more profitably employed in implementing further improvements in the functionality of the software. Although (surprisingly) the figures are often not officially recorded, the programmers themselves estimate that nearly half their time is spent in error correction. This is probably the strongest commercial argument for software producers to increase investment in measures to control reliability of delivered code.

5 Over-engineering

The concept of a safety factor is pervasive in engineering. After calculating the worst case load on a beam, the civil engineer will try to build it ten times stronger, or at least twice as strong, whenever the extra cost is affordable. In computing, a continuing fall in price of computer storage and increase in computer power has made almost any trade-off acceptable to reduce the risk of software error, and the scale of damage that can increasingly result from it. This leads to the same kind of over-engineering as is required by law for bridge-building; and it is extremely effective, even though there is no clear way of measuring it by a numeric factor.

The first benefit of a superabundance of resource is to make possible a decision to avoid any kind of sophistication or optimisation in the design of algorithms or data structures. Common prohibitions are: no data packing, no optimal coding, no pointers, no sharing, no dynamic storage allocation. The maximum conceivably necessary size of record or array is allocated, and then some more. Similar prohibitions are often placed on program structures: no jumps, no interrupts, no multiprogramming, no global variables. Access to data in other modules is permitted only through carefully regulated remote procedure calls. In the past, these design rules were found to involve excessive loss of efficiency; up to a factor of a hundred has been recorded on first trials of a rigorously structured system. This factor had to be regained by relaxing the prohibitions, massaging the interfaces between modules, even to the extent of violating the structural integrity of the whole system. Apart from the obvious immediate dangers, this can lead to even greater risk and expense in subsequent updating and enhancing of the system. Fortunately, cheaper hardware reduces the concern for efficiency, and improved optimisation technology for higher level languages promises further assistance in reconciling a clear structure of the source code with high efficiency in the object code.

Profligacy of resources can bring benefits in other ways. When considering a possible exceptional case, the programmer may be quite confident that it has already been discriminated and dealt with elsewhere in some other piece of code; as a result in fact the exception can never arise at this point. Nevertheless, for safety, it is better to discriminate again, and write further code to deal with it. Most likely, the extra code will be totally unreachable. This may be part of the explanation why in normal testing and operation, less than twenty per cent of the code of a large system is ever executed; which suggests an over-engineering factor of five. The extra cost in memory size may be low, but there is a high cost in designing, writing and maintaining so much redundant code. For example, there is the totally pointless exercise of designing coverage tests for this otherwise unreachable code.

Another profligate use of resources is by cloning of code. A new feature to be added to a large program can often be cheaply implemented by making a number of small changes to some piece of code that is already there. But this is felt to be risky: the existing code is perhaps used in ways that are not at all obvious by just looking at it, and any of these ways might be disrupted by the proposed change. So it seems safer to take an entirely fresh copy of the existing code, and modify that instead. Over a period of years there arise a whole family of such near-clones, extending over several generations. Each of them is a quick and efficient solution to an immediate problem; but over time they create additional problems of maintenance of the large volumes of code. For example, if a change is made in one version of the clone, it is quite difficult even to decide whether it should be propagated to the other versions, so it usually isn't. The expense arises when the same error or deficiency has to be detected and corrected again in the other versions.

Another widespread over-engineering practice is known as defensive programming. Each individual programmer or team erects a defensive barrier against errors and instabilities in the rest of the system. This may be nothing more than a private library of subroutines through which all calls are made to the untrusted features of a shared operating system. Or it may take the form of standard coding practices. For example, it is recommended in a distributed system to protect every communication with the environment, or with another program, by a timeout, which will be invoked if the external response is not sufficiently prompt. Conversely, every message accepted from the environment is subjected to rigorous dynamic checks of plausibility, and the slightest suspicion will cause the message to be just ignored, in the expectation that its sender is similarly protected by timeout.

A similar technique can be applied to the global data structures used to control the entire system. A number of checking programs, known as software audits, are written to conduct plausibility checks on all the records in the global system tables. In this case, suspicious entries are rendered harmless by a reinitialisation to safe values. Such audits have been found to improve mean time between crashes of an embedded system from hours to months. The occasional loss of data and function is unnoticed in a telephone switching application: it could hardly be recommended for air traffic control, where it would certainly cause quite a different kind of crash.

The ultimate and very necessary defence of a real time system against arbitrary hardware error or operator error is the organisation of a rapid procedure for restarting the entire system. The goal of a restart is to restore the system to a valid state that was current some time in the recent past. These warm starts can be so efficient that they are hardly noticeable except by examining the historical system log. So who cares whether the trigger for a restart was a rare software fault or a transient hardware fault? Certainly, it would take far too long to record information that would permit them to be discriminated.

The limitation of over-engineering as a safety technique is that the extra weight and volume may begin to contribute to the very problem that it was intended to solve. No-one knows how much of the volume of code of a large system is due to over-engineering, or how much this costs in terms of reliability. In general safety engineering, it is not unknown for catastrophes to be caused by the very measures that are introduced to avoid them.

6 Programming Methodology

Most of the measures described so far for achieving reliability of programs are the same as those which have proved to be equally effective in all engineering and industrial enterprises, from space travel to highway maintenance, from electronics to the brewing of beer. But the best general techniques of management, quality control, and safety engineering would be totally useless, by themselves; they are only effective when there is a general understanding of the specific field of endeavour, and a common conceptual framework and terminology for discussion of the relationship between cause and effect, between action and consequence in that field. Perhaps initially, the understanding is based just on experience and intuition; but the goal of engineering research is to complement and sometimes replace these informal judgements by more systematic methods of calculation and optimisation based on scientific theory.

Research into programming methodology has a similar goal, to establish a conceptual framework and a theoretical basis to assist in systematic derivation and justification of every design decision by a rational and explicable train of reasoning. The primary method of research is to evaluate proposed reasoning methods by their formalisation as a collection of proof rules in some completely formal system. This permits definitive answers to the vital questions: is the reasoning valid? is it adequate to prove everything that is needed? and is it simpler than other equally valid and adequate alternatives? It is the provably positive answer to these simple questions that gives the essential scientific basis for a sound methodological recommendation – certainly an improvement on mere rhetoric, speculation, fashion, salesmanship, charlatanism or worse.

Research into programming methodology has already had dramatic effects on the way that people write programs today. One of the most spectacular successes occurred so long ago that it is now quite non-controversial. It is the almost universal adoption of the practice of structured programming, otherwise known as avoidance of jumps (or gotos). Millions of lines of code have now been written without them. But it was not always so. At one time, most programmers were proud of their skill in the use of jumps and labels. They regarded structured notations as unnatural and counter-intuitive, and took it as a challenge to write such complex networks of jumps that no structured notations could ever express them.

The decisive breakthrough in the adoption of structured programming by IBM was the publication of a simple result in pure programming theory, the Bohm–Jacopini theorem. This showed that an arbitrary program with jumps could be executed by an interpreter written without any jumps at all; so in principle any task whatsoever can be carried out by purely structured code. This theorem was needed to convince senior managers of the company that no harm would come from adopting structured programming as a company policy; and project managers needed it to protect themselves from having to show their programmers how to do it by rewriting every piece of complex spaghetti code that might be submitted. Instead the programmers were just instructed to find a way, secure in the knowledge that they always could. And after a while, they always did.

The advantages of structured programming seem obvious to those who are accustomed to it: programs become easy to write, to understand, and to modify. But there is also a good scientific explanation for this judgement. It is found by a formalisation of the methods needed to prove the correctness of the program with the aid of assertions. For structured programs, a straightforward proof always suffices. Jumps require a resort to a rather more complex technique of subsidiary deductions. Formalisation has been invaluable in giving objective support for a subjective judgement: and that is a contribution which is independent of any attempt to actually use the assertional proof rules in demonstrating the correctness of code.

Another triumph of theory has been widespread appreciation of the benefits of data types and strict type-checking of programs. A type defines the outer limits of the range of values for a program variable or parameter. The range of facilities for defining types is sufficiently restricted that a compiler can automatically check that no variable strays outside the limits imposed by its declared type. The repertoire of operations on the values of each type are defined by simple axioms similar to those which define the relevant branch of mathematics. Strict typechecking is certainly popular in Universities, because of the help it gives in the teaching of programming to large classes of students with mixed abilities; it is even more widely beneficial in modern mass consumer languages like Visual Basic; and in very large programs which are subject to continuous change, it gives a vital assurance of global system integrity that no programmer on the project would wish to forego.

Another triumph of theoretical research has been widespread adoption of the principles of information hiding. An early example is found in the local variables of ALGOL 60. These are introduced by declaration and used as workspace for internal purposes of a block of code which constitutes the scope of the declaration; the variable name, its identity, and even its existence is totally concealed from outside. The concept of declaration and locality in a program was based on that of quantification and bound variables in predicate logic; and so are the proof methods for programs which contain them.

The information hiding introduced by the ALGOL 60 local variable was generalised to the design of larger-scale modules and classes of object-oriented programming, introduced into ALGOL 60 by SIMULA 67. Again, the scientific basis of the structure was explored by formalisation of the relevant proof techniques, involving an explicit invariant which links an abstract concept with its concrete representation as data in the store of a computer.

The value of a foundation in formal logic and mathematics is illustrated by the comparison of ALGOL 60 with the COBOL language, brought into existence and standardised at about the same time by the U.S. Department of Defence. Both languages had the highly commendable and explicit objective of making programs easier to understand. COBOL tried to do this by constructing a crude approximation to normal natural English, whereas ALGOL 60 tried to get closer to the language of mathematics. There is no doubt which was technically more successful: the ideas of ALGOL 60 have been adopted by many subsequent languages, including even FORTRAN 90. COBOL by comparison has turned out to be an evolutionary dead end.

7 Conclusion

This review of programming methodology reveals how much the best of current practice owes to the ideas and understanding gained by research which was completed more than twenty years ago. The existence of such a large gap between theory and practice is deplored by many, but I think quite wrongly. The gap is actually an extremely good sign of the maturity and good health of our discipline, and the only deplorable results are those that arise from failure to recognise it.

The proper response to the gap is to first congratulate the practitioners for their good sense. Except in the narrowest areas, and for the shortest possible periods of time, it would be crazy for industry to try to keep pace with the latest results of pure research. If the research fails, the industry fails with it; and if the research continues to succeed, the industry which is first to innovate runs the risk of being overtaken by competitors who reap the benefits of the later improvements. For these reasons, it would be grossly improper to recommend industry on immediate implementation of results of their own research that is still in progress. Indeed, Sir Richard Doll points out that scientists who give such advice not only damage their clients; they also lose that most precious of all attributes of good research, their scientific objectivity.

The theorists also should be accorded a full share of the congratulations; for it is they who have achieved research results that are twenty years ahead of the field of practice. It is not their failing but rather their duty to achieve and maintain such an uncomfortable lead, and to spread it over a broad front across a wide range of theories. No-one can predict, with any certainty or accuracy of detail, the timescales of change in technology or in the marketplace. The duty of the researcher is not to predict the future more accurately than the businessman, but to prepare the basic understanding which may be needed to deal with the unexpected challenges of any possible future development. Provided that this goal has been met, no researcher should be blamed for failure of early predictions made to justify its original funding of the research. Mistakes made by businessmen and politicians are far more expensive.

The recognition of the appropriate timescale to measure the gap between the theory and practice of a discipline is an essential to the appropriate planning of research and education, both to fill the gap by improving practice, and to extend it again by advancing the theory. I would recommend that the best researchers in the field should simultaneously try to do both, because the influence of practice on the development of theory is more beneficial and actually quicker than the other way round.

At the extreme of the practical end, I would recommend the theorist to alternate theoretical pursuits with much closer observation and experimentation on actual working programs, with all the mass of documentation and historical development logs that have accumulated in the last ten years. These systems are now sufficiently stable, and have sufficient commercial prospects, to justify quite practical research to answer questions that will guide recommendations for future beneficial changes in their structure, content or methods of development.

For example, it would be very interesting to find a way of estimating the proportional cost of cloning and the other over-engineering practices. By sampling, it would be interesting to trace a number of errors to their root cause, and see how they might have been avoided, perhaps by better specification or by better documentation or by better structuring of code. Is my conjectured dichotomy of error populations observed in practice? Any recommendation for improved formalisation or improved structure will probably be based on other people's research ideas that are up to twenty years old. Even so, they must be backed up by trial recoding of a range of existing modules, selected on the scientific principle of being the most likely to reveal the fallacies in the recommendation, rather than its merits. Strange to relate, it has been known for a business to spend many millions on a change that has not been subjected to any prior scientific trials of this kind.

Formal methods researchers who are really keen on rigorous checking and proof should identify and concentrate on the most critical areas of a large software system, for example, synchronisation and mutual exclusion protocols, dynamic resource allocation, and reconfiguration strategies for recovery from partial system failure. It is known that these are areas where obscure time-dependent errors, deadlocks and livelocks (thrashing) can lurk untestable for many years, and then trigger a failure costing many millions. It is possible that proof methods and model checking are now sufficiently advanced that a good formal methodologist could occasionally detect such obscure latent errors before they occur in practice. Publication of such an achievement would be a major milestone in the acceptance of formal methods in solving the most critical problems of software reliability.

I have suggested that personal involvement in current practices and inspection of legacy code may lead to quite rapid benefits, both to the practitioner and to the theorist. But this is not the right permanent relationship between them; in a proper policy of technology transfer, it is for the practitioner to recognise promising results of research, and take over all the hard work of adapting them for widespread application. In software, unfortunately, the gap between practice and theory is now so large that this is not happening. Part of the trouble is that many or most of the practitioners did not study formal methods or even computing science at University. This leaves a large educational gap, that can only be filled by programme of in-service education which will acquaint some of the best software engineers in industry with some of the important ideas of computing science. Since many of them have degrees in mathematics, or at least in some mathematical branch of science, they have the necessary background and ability: since they do not have degrees in computing, they need to start right at the beginning, for example, with context free languages and finite state machines, and simple ideas of types and functional programming.

Another high barrier to technology transfer is the failure of software engineering toolsets to include a modicum of support for formality – for example to allow mathematical notations in word processors, to incorporate typechecking for specifications, and hypertext techniques for quick cross-referencing between formal and informal documentation. Improved tools should concentrate first on very simple old techniques like execution profiles and selective compilation of assertions before going on to more advanced but less mature technology, such as model checking or proof assistance. The actual construction of industrial quality tools must be done in collaboration with the industrial suppliers of these tools. Only they have the knowledge and profit motive to adapt them, and to continue adapting them, to the rapidly changing fashions and needs of the marketplace.

For long-term research, my advice is even more tentative and controversial. It pursues a hope to complement the many strengths, and compensate the single weakness, of current theoretical research in formal methods. The strengths arise from the depth and the range of the specialisation of many flourishing research schools in all the relevant areas. For example, in programming language semantics, we have reasoning based on denotational, algebraic and operational presentations. Among programming paradigms, we have both theoretical studies and applications of functional, procedural, logical and parallel programming languages. Even among the parallel languages there is a great variation between those based on synchronous or asynchronous control, shared store or distributed message passing, untimed or with timing of various kinds; even hardware and software have different models.

Specialisation involves a deep commitment to a narrow selection of presentation, reasoning methods, paradigm, language and application area, or even a particular application. The whole point of the specialisation in formal methods is to restrict the notational framework as far as necessary to achieve some formal goal, but nevertheless to show that the restrictions do not prevent successful application to a surprisingly wide range of problems. This is the reason why specialist research into formal methods can run the risk of being very divisive. An individual researcher, or even a whole community of researchers, becomes wholly committed to a particular selection of specialisations along each of the axes: say an operational or an algebraic presentation of semantics, bisimulation or term rewriting as a proof method, CCS or OBJ as a design notation. The attraction of such a choice can be well illustrated in certain applications, such as the analysis of the alternating bit protocol or the definition of the stack as an abstract data type. The perfectly proper challenge of the research is to push outwards as far as possible the frontiers of the convenient application of the particular chosen formalism. But that is also the danger: the rush to colonise as much of the available territory can lead to imperialist claims that deny to other specialisms their right to existence. Any suggestion of variation of standard dogma is treated as akin to treason. This tendency can be reinforced by the short-sightedness of funding agencies, which encourage exaggerated claims to the universal superiority of a single notation and technique.

The consequences of the fragmentation of research into rival schools is inevitable: the theorists become more and more isolated, both from each other and from the world of practice, where one thing is absolutely certain: that there is no single cure for all diseases. There is no single theory for all stages of the development of the software, or for all components even of a single application program. Ideas, concepts, methods, and calculations will have to be drawn from a wide range of theories, and they are going to have to work together consistently, with no risk of misunderstanding, inconsistency or error creeping in at the interfaces. One effective way to break formal barriers is for the best theorists to migrate regularly between the research schools, in the hope that results obtained in one research specialisation can be made useful in a manner acceptable by the other. The interworking of theories and paradigms can also be explored from the practical end by means of the case study, chosen as a simplified version of some typical application. In my view, a case study that constructs a link between two or more theories, used for different purposes at different levels of abstraction, will be more valuable than one which merely presents a single formalisation, in the hope that its merits, compared with rival formalisations, will be obvious. They usually are, but unfortunately only to the author.

Since theories will have to be unified in application, the best help that advanced research can give is to unify them in theory first. Fortunately, unification is something that theoretical research is very good at, and the way has been shown again and again in both science and mathematics. Examples from science include the discovery of the atomic theory of matter as a unified framework for all the varied elements and components of chemistry; similarly, the gravitational field assimilates the movement of the planets in the sky and cannon balls on earth. In mathematics, we see how topology unifies the study of continuity in all the forms encountered in geometry and analysis, how logic explains the valid methods of reasoning in all branches of mathematics. I would suggest the current strength of individual specialisation in theoretical computing science should be balanced by a commitment from the best and most experienced researchers to provide a framework in which all the specialisations can be seen as just aspects or variations of the same basic ideas. Then it will be clear how both existing and new specialisations are all equally worthy of effort to deepen the theory or broaden its application. But the aim is no longer to expand and colonise the whole space but rather to find the natural boundaries at which one theory can comfortably coexist and cooperate with its neighbours. Closing a gap between one theory and another is just as important as closing the gap between theory and practice; and just as challenging.

8 Acknowledgments

I am very grateful to many programmers and managers working in industry, who have made available to me the benefits of their judgment and long experience. In particular, I would like to praise the leading practitioners of the state of the art in IBM at Hursley, in BNR at Maidenhead, and in Digital at Nashua. Many contributions to my thinking are due to members of IFIP WG2.3 on Programming Methodology, and to its chairman Cliff Jones, who made useful suggestions to the previous draft of the paper. Finally, thanks to those named in the paper, with apologies for lack of more formal reference.

A Case Study on the Formal Development of a Reactor Safety System

Terje Sivertsen
Institute for Energy Technology, OECD Halden Reactor Project
P.O. Box 173, 1751 Halden, Norway
e-mail: Terje.Sivertsen@hrp.no

Abstract. The EvalFM project was initiated in order to investigate the applicability of formal methods in the development of safety-critical software-based systems. The overall goal was to explore the strengths and limitations of these methods through practical experience on a realistic example. The present paper presents the main results from the project, related to a case study on the applicability of algebraic specification in the development of a reactor safety system.

1 Introduction

The recent years have witnessed the replacement of many conventional electromechanical process control systems with computer-based systems. This also includes the use of computers in safety-related tasks, e.g. in nuclear power plants and traffic control. The motivation behind this shift towards the use of programmable equipment is manifold. Important benefits are the possibilities for implementing more accurate trip criteria, the improved means for automatic surveillance, as well as simplification of calibration and functional testing during operation. There are however also more pragmatic concerns relating to decreasing availability of equipment and spare parts for the conventional systems and of personnel with appropriate technological expertise. Nevertheless, there has been a certain reluctance to use programmable equipment in safety systems. One reason for that has been the complexity of safety assessment and licensing of these systems, in particular of the embedded software.

Since 1977 the OECD Halden Reactor Project has been actively working in the field of software verification and validation [5]. The Halden Project is an international institution with participants from 19 countries. A main objective of the research activities is that the experiences and results from these activities can be utilized by member countries in real applications. An important part of the research activities within software verification and validation has been the applicability of formal methods in development of safety-related software systems [8]. One concrete achievement has been the establishment of a methodology for the practical application of algebraic specification in formal software development. The methodology allows for using the same language, tool and proof techniques both in specification and design, even down to a "concrete" specification. In the specification phase, the HRP Prover is used to verify and validate the specification, while in the design phase the same tool is used to verify the correctness of the design steps. The HRP Prover has been developed at the Halden Project to facilitate exploration of animation and theorem proving techniques in formal software development. A guiding principle in the development of the method and tool has been to avoid using heuristics which would complicate the comprehensibility of proofs and specifications. The adequacy of this principle becomes particularly clear when considering the possibilities of accomplishing a formal development of the theorem prover itself. In such an undertaking it is important that the proof techniques can be clearly stated in unambiguous terms and that it can be stated *a priori* how the proof will proceed, and why this indeed will be a sound way to proceed.

Only recently the application of formal software development methods have been seriously considered within the nuclear society. Much discussion and, to a certain degree, controversy arised from the verification and validation of the computer-based Darlington shutdown system [4]. The Darlington Nuclear Generating Station is a new station, consisting of four units 50 miles east of Toronto, Canada. The Darlington shutdown system design includes two independent triplicated shutdown systems. The development used the traditional four-step waterfall diagram, with verification and validation of the final implementation. The Atomic Energy Control Board (Canada) did however not achieve a sufficient level of confidence in the ability of the code to conform to the requirements, and eventually required that the existing functional specification should be replaced by a mathematically rigorous specification. It turned out that with the steps taken to meet the requirements, it was possible to achieve a licensable product. On the negative side, these steps involved considerable effort and difficulty. Following [6], formal methods were in effect used *a posteriori* to model what existed and to demonstrate that the code met the requirements.

There is today a growing consensus within the nuclear society that more practice on the use of formal methods is needed in order to evaluate their applicability [10]. Several independent studies suggest that there is a need for a systematic, rigorous effort in establishing design requirements to minimize errors in the final product [1]. Much of this motivation comes from the limited value of traditional methods. Following [7], "traditional software-development techniques usually do not provide the levels of dependability demanded by safety-critical systems, and the quality criteria are usually such that the amount of testing that is feasible cannot demonstrate that the desired goals have been achieved". There are several important aspects which make the application of software in safety-critical applications fundamentally different from their application in other areas. Safety-critical applications must work when needed, and it is not appropriate to wait for evaluation during use to bring the reliability up to an acceptable level. The realization of the potential benefits of computer-based control and safety systems for nuclear power plants[1] therefore requires *verifying* the reliability of these systems. Traditionally this has been done by means of simulation of the hardware design and exhaustive software testing. It appears however that the use of formal mathematics, in some form, is necessary in order to achieve substantial improvements in the development of dependable software. On this background, the Nuclear Regulatory Commission (USA) and other instances persuaded the OECD Halden Reactor Project to investigate the applicability of formal methods and in particular algebraic specification and the HRP Prover on a real example related to the control of a nuclear reactor. It was considered important to perform research which could contribute to a clarification of the role and limitations of formal methods when applied on the development of safety-critical software systems. Licensing authorities in general have a particular interest in representative applications of existing formal methods to make decisions on whether the use of formal methods should be required, which formal methods should be used, what is the appropriate way to use them, and what to require to be formally verified.

An example system was selected, based on the following criterion: it should be a realistic, preferably a real, safety-critical system related to nuclear power plant operation. Furthermore, the system should be of reasonable size to keep the effort needed reasonable. After consultation with Sydkraft (Barsebäck NPP) and ABB Atom in Sweden, it was decided to use the computer-based power range monitoring (PRM) system installed at Barsebäck NPP as an example system. The case study did not address ABB's implementation of the example system, but the development of a similar system using formal methods. The formal specification is based on the original customer's requirements document for the system, and is independent of ABB's implementation. The purpose of the PRM system that was of particular interest in this case study is the monitoring of the average power emission of the core. When high power emission is monitored, the system must trip the high level alarms. Based on the requirements document, the EvalFM project produced a formal algebraic specification of one out of four similar subsystems of the PRM system, utilizing a general mathematical tool-kit defined for the method. Finally, the subsystem was designed and implemented in a subset of Pascal.

2 The Structure of the PRM System

The PRM system belongs to class 1E, i.e. systems which automatically effectuate actions in relation to events that may jeopardize safety. PRM stands for Power Range Monitoring, which indicates that the main purpose of the system is to monitor the power emission of the core, represented by the neutron flux. The functioning of such a system is complicated by the fact that the neutron flux varies substantially between different parts of the core. In order to adequately monitor the power emission it is

1. Systems to control critical functions in NPPs are commonly called *reactor safety systems* or *reactor protection systems*.

important that the neutron flux is measured with a large number of distributed detectors.

The computations of APRM values (the average power emission in the core) are carried out in four different redundant computing units. The division into four redundant systems is in accordance with the general rule for reactor safety systems. To each of the four units a set of probes, each with four detectors, is connected. The number of probes per unit is either five or six. It is evidently important that the probes are distributed in a way which gives reliable values for the average power emission of the core. Each detector (LPRM) signal is amplified separately, while the adjustment of the amplification is done on a regular basis. The signals are compared to individual, adjustable low and high level alarms. Similar alarms are associated to the probes.

The plant operators select the detectors used by each unit for the computation of the APRM values. If the number of these detectors is below a minimum limit, an alarm indication will be given. Given the set of selected detectors, each unit will at regular intervals compute local APRM values. There are also requirements to the actual time performance of each unit. In order to predict the real-time behaviour of the system, the program execution is deterministic, i.e. the program is executed in a fixed cycle, independently of external events.

The PRM system is part of a larger system where all neutron monitoring systems are gathered. The customer's requirements document provides a very clear interface between the quoted equipment and the adjoining, existing system, and describes the system through a number of small, independent functional units. The specification of the system is greatly facilitated by the similarity of the four subsystems, and by the lack of two-way communication between them.

3 The Choice of Abstraction Level

It is well known that choosing an appropriate abstraction level is a particularly important decision in the creation of a formal specification. In this process, it is essential to capture the desired functionality without unduly biasing the design and implementation of the system. Nevertheless, it is far from obvious what characterises an appropriate abstraction level. The customer's requirements for the PRM system are stated in very concrete terms, which appears to be quite representative to safety critical systems, with a natural bias toward certain implementations. Furthermore, the requirements clearly reflect the fact that an analogue implementation of the system already existed at the time when the quotation was issued. The notation and language used suggest an implementation in terms of easily identifiable hardware components such as counters, majority selectors, etc. This tendency is further evidenced by the explicit requirements to e.g. power supplies to the amplifiers. When writing a formal specification based on the requirements document of the example system, it was necessary to abstract away irrelevant details, and otherwise make the requirements applicable as a basis for the specification and design of a software-based implementation. It is however important to note a requirements document typically is used as a basis for the derivation of other specifications for software, hardware, configuration, etc. In this process, experienced developers are usually well trained on treating the words and symbols in the requirements document as specifying functions on a more abstract level.

4 The Identification of Primitive Objects and State Variables

The first step in the specification of the PRM system is to identify the sets of "primitive" objects in the system. The requirements document provides a table describing the interface between the existing equipment and the quoted system:

LPRM Detectors - The components in the existing equipment are first of all 88 analog outputs, i.e. transducers which convert a physical measurement to an electrical signal with voltage between 0 and 10V. It is required that a sampler and A/D converter transforms this voltage to a number in the scale 0 - 125 (%). At this stage in the specification process, it is sufficient to identify these detectors as primitive objects, represented by a new type LPRM.

Probes - In the existing equipment there are also 22 probes, each including 4 specific LPRM detectors. At this stage, it is sufficient to identify the probes as another class of primitive objects, represented by a type PROBE.

For the purpose of the specification of the PRM system, the types LPRM and PROBE need not be further specified. The specification does not need to refer to any particular LPRM detector or probe, and an abstraction from the coded names can therefore be achieved. Such names do however make it easier to communicate the specification to the customer. This can be utilized by using coded names in the *animation* of the specification. The identification of instances might be necessary when directing the design toward a particular implementation, and is definitively necessary in the final implementation of the system.

When the primitive data types have been identified, the next step in the specification process is to identify the "state variables" and their types. These are entities which are essential to an adequate description of a particular state of the specified system, including adjustable parameters and entities representing parts of the "history" of the system. It might be difficult to identify all the variables initially; the need for some of them might be evidenced first in the process of defining the functionality of the system. Fortunately, the need to do some specification first does not jeopardize the formal development.

The values of the different variables are in the specification collected in terms sub(t_1, ..., t_n), where each t_i, $1 \le i \le n$, represents the value of a particular parameter or group (in the form of a compound term) of parameters. Our first task is to identify the parameters which should be represented, and to define the type of the representing terms. The adjustable parameters include the amplification factors for the LPRM signals, the selection of LPRM detectors to be used in the calculation of the APRM signal, the amplification of the APRM signal, and the various alarm limits. In addition to the adjustable parameters, we need to include parameters representing the previous values of the outputs from the subsystem, i.e. the alarms, the calculated APRM value, and values of relevance to the filtering of the APRM value and of the HC-flow (core cooling). The alarms of interest will be the low level and high level alarms associated to the LPRM detectors and the probes, and the alarms L1, H1, ..., H6 associated to the APRM and FLOW/FLUX values (see sections 5.3 and 5.4). We will treat all these alarms as a unit by specifying a data type 'SUB_ALARMS' with the following generator:

```
type SUB_ALARMS
generators
    sub_alarms: FUN(LPRM,BOOL)**2 x FUN(PROBE,BOOL)**2 x
                BOOL**7 -> SUB_ALARMS
```

The specification utilizes the parameterized type FUN(X,Y) of functions, specified in a mathematical tool-kit associated to the method.

In the case study, all functions common to the four subsystems are collected in the specification of a datatype SUB. For each of the four subsystems, it is straight forward to specify an enrichment providing additional functions specific to that subsystem. When the state variables common to the description of the state of the four subsystems have been identified, a generator 'sub' corresponding to the "record" of these variables can be declared:

```
type SUB
generators
    sub: FUN(LPRM,FLOAT) x SET(LPRM) x FLOAT**3 x
         SUB_ALARM_LIMITS x SUB_ALARMS x FUN(LPRM,FLOAT) x
         FLOAT**6 -> SUB
```

The specification utilizes the parameterized tool-kit types SET(X) of sets and FUN(X,Y) of functions. To select the different state variables, an appropriate number of selector functions are introduced:

selectors

amp, selec, aprm_amplific, scale_factor, limitation, alarm_limits, alarms, lprm, aprm, aprm_prev, filtered_aprm, filtered_aprm_prev, limited_hc_flow, filtered_hc_flow

For animation purposes, a constant 'initSUB' is defined in a separate module to keep a given value of the type SUB. In the examples below, only four LPRM detectors and one probe is considered in the animation.

Evaluating 'initSUB' with the HRP Prover gives (output is printed in italics):

> initSUB.

amp: *[(531K809->1.91),...,(531K812->2.54)]*

selec: *[531K809,531K810,531K811]*

aprm_amplific: *1.68*

...

filtered_hc_flow: *102.67*

If one primarily is interested in, say, the alarm limits, more detailed information on these can be given by using the selector 'alarm_limits':

> alarm_limits(initSUB).

lprm_l1limit: *[(531K809->10.0),...,(531K812->10.0)]*

lprm_h1limit: *[(531K809->110.0),...,(531K812->110.0)]*

l1limit: *5.0*

...

h6limit: *132.0*

In the specification of the PRM system, the signals from a set of LPRM detectors are represented by an element of the type FUN(LPRM,FLOAT). A constant 'signals' is defined to hold a given set of values of the LPRM detectors:

> signals.

... = *[(531K809->5.02),(531K810->36.2),(531K811->36.9),(531K812->34.9)]*

Note that 'initSUB' and 'signals' are used for animation only, and are not part of the specification of the PRM system.

5 The Evolution Towards a Complete Specification

The main task of the PRM system is to initiate shut-down of the reactor in the case of excessive power emission in the core. The interaction with the operator is essentially limited to the adjustment of parameters, and testing of the equipment. It is straight forward to specify separate adjustment routines for the parameters. By way of example, the adjustment of the amplification factor for a given LPRM detector can be specified with a function 'update_amp', taking as arguments the state of the system, the identifier for the LPRM detector of interest, and the new amplification factor:

update_amp: SUB x LPRM x FLOAT -> SUB

The function can easily be defined by using the function 'set_amp' generated for the selector 'amp', and the assignment function 'ass' defined for functions of any type:

update_amp(S,ID,V) == set_amp(S,ass(amp(S),ID,V)).

If we now want to update the amplification factor for detector '531K810' to 2.39, this is achieved by

> update_amp(initSUB,'531K810',2.39).

amp: [(531K809->1.91),(531K810->2.39),(531K811->2.27),(531K812->2.54)]

...

We will in the following discuss parts of the specification describing the main functionality of the quoted system.

5.1 LPRM-amplification

The relationship between the LPRM detectors and their values at a given time instant will be defined by a function from LPRM to FLOAT. To find the signal for a given LPRM detector reduces to applying this function on the identifier for this detector, using the mathematical tool-kit function 'apl'. Each LPRM signal is subject to an amplification by a factor defined by the operator, see the simplified diagram in Fig. 1.

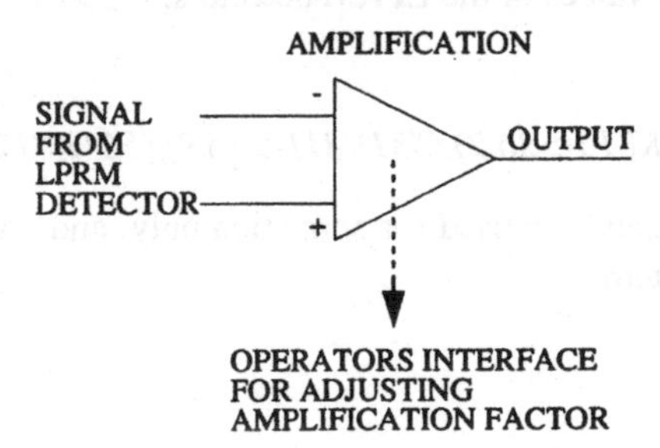

Fig. 1. Amplification of the LPRM signal.

The current amplification factors are given by the state variable selected by the function 'amp'. These factors are regularly changed in the calibration routines for the LPRM detectors. The amplification of a LPRM signal can be specified by a function which takes the current state variables, the given signals, and the identifier for the detector of interest, and returns the amplified signal from this detector. This gives a function 'amplified_lprm' declared

amplified_lprm: SUB x FUN(LPRM,FLOAT) x LPRM -> FLOAT

and defined

amplified_lprm(S,L,ID) == float_product(apl(L,ID),apl(amp(S),ID)).

The amplified signal from '531K810' is then given by

> amplified_lprm(initSUB,signals,'531K810').

... = *83.6217*

(Note that this would be a very high value for the amplified LPRM signal, since a value of about 60 would correspond to full power).

5.2 LPRM Trip Alarms

To each LPRM detector there is associated an adjustable low and high alarm limit, see Fig. 2.

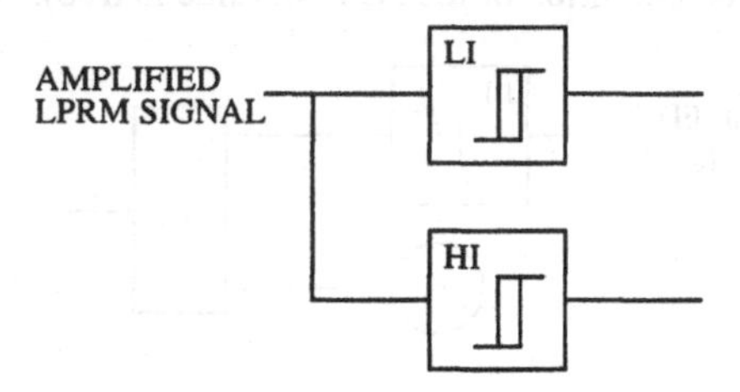

Fig. 2. Low and high LPRM alarms.

These limits can be represented as floating point numbers, and thus the relationship between the detectors and the alarm limits are represented by two selector functions yielding values of type FUN(LPRM,FLOAT).

In order to accomplish hysteresis, we need to compare the amplified LPRM signals not only with the given alarm levels but must also take into account the previous alarm output. Hysteresis about a high alarm limit is accomplished by not resetting the output value of the alarm to 'false' until the input value has dropped below the alarm limit minus the deadband value. Vice versa for low alarm limits. It is convenient to introduce two Boolean functions 'low_alarm' and 'high_alarm', each taking three arguments of type FLOAT and one argument of type BOOL:

- the present signal value;
- the alarm level;
- the deadband value;
- the previous alarm value.

The function 'low_alarm' is declared

```
low_alarm: FLOAT**3 x BOOL -> BOOL
```

and defined

```
low_alarm(V,L,DB,B) ==
        if B=true
        then float_less_than(V,float_sum(L,DB))
        else float_less_than(V,L)
        endif.
```

Particular care must be exercised with regard to the required use of the APRM value in connection with the low level alarms for the probes. The requirements document states that a relay should be falling if any of the detectors in a probe falls below the associated limit, if the APRM value exceeds it's H1 limit at the same time, see Fig. 3. (The input K is true if the stated condition of the APRM value is true).

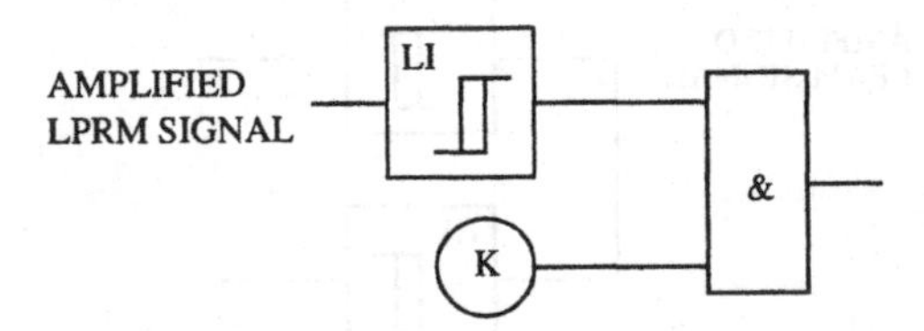

Fig. 3. Condition for low LPRM alarm.

However, the status of this alarm is needed in the determination of the detectors to be used in the calculation of the APRM value (see section 5.3). Apparently, this gives a cyclic definition of the LPRM L1 alarm and the APRM value, because both require the result provided by the other. Evidently, this problem relates to the use of the specification as a basis for the development of a digital system. The solution is easy to find by considering the temporal nature of the system, where the APRM value and other signals are calculated at regular intervals. The problem is therefore resolved by explicitly stating that the APRM value to be used in the calculation of the LPRM L1 alarm is the one calculated in the previous interval. This can be reflected in the specification by using either the previous APRM value or the previous APRM H1 alarm, both of which are represented in the state description of the system.

We will define a Boolean function 'lprm_l1' which returns 'true' if and only if the amplified LPRM value for a given detector is below the low alarm limit and the stated condition of the APRM value is satisfied. The deadband value for this alarm is set to 0.4. The function 'lprm_l1' is declared

lprm_l1: SUB x FUN(LPRM,FLOAT) x LPRM -> BOOL

and defined

```
lprm_l1(S,L,ID) ==
        and(low_alarm(amplified_lprm(S,L,ID),
                      apl(lprm_l1limit(alarm_limits(S)),ID),
                      0.4,
                      apl(lprm_l1alarm(alarms(S)),ID)),
            h1alarm(alarms(S))).
```

A function 'lprm_h1' for the high alarm limit can be defined in an analogous way. If we now try to evaluate this function for LRPM detector '531K809', we get

> lprm_l1(initSUB,signals,'531K809').

... = *true*

which means that the amplified signal from this detector is below the low alarm limit, and the most recent APRM signal did not exceed the H1 alarm limit.

5.3 APRM

The requirements document states that the detectors to be used in the calculation of the APRM value should be those selected by the operator, except those satisfying the condition for triggering the low level alarm. Otherwise there would be many false alarms during start up and low power operation, see Fig. 4. (The input B is true if the LPRM detector triggers the low level alarm).

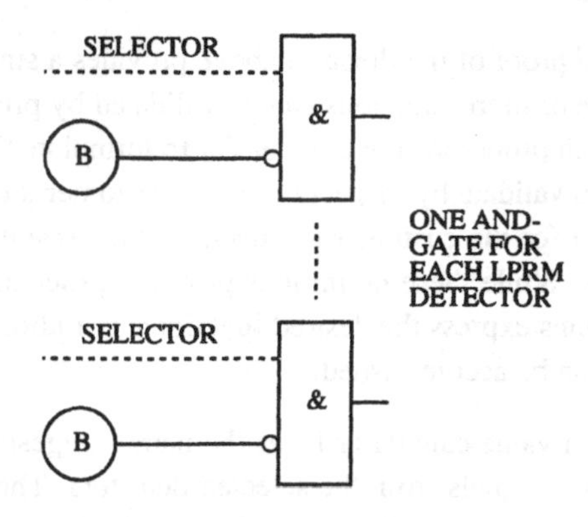

Fig. 4. The selection of LPRM detectors.

At any time, the set of detectors selected by the operator is represented by the state variable selected by the function 'selec'. By defining a filtering function 'exclude_low_lprm', we can easily find the subset of the operator selected detectors for which the amplified signals are not below the associated low alarm limits. This is specified with the function 'selected' declared:

selected: SUB x FUN(LPRM,FLOAT) -> SET(LPRM)

and defined

selected(S,L) == exclude_low_lprm(S,L,selec(S)).

Evaluating 'selected' gives

```
> selected(initSUB,signals).
... = [531K810,531K811]
```

The desired functionality of 'selected' can also be expressed by the theorem

I?selected(S,L) = and(I?selec(S),not(lprm_l1(S,L,I)))

Using the HRP Prover, this theorem can be proved by induction on the variable represented by selec(S), where 'selec' is one of the selectors for the type SUB:

```
> [selec(S)] in I?selected(S,L) = and(I?selec(S),not(lprm_l1(S,L,I))).
P(X14): X9?selected(sub(...,X14,...),X13)
        = and(X9?selec(sub(...,X14,...)),not(lprm_l1(sub(...,X14,...),X13,X9)))

P(emp)
P(X15) -> P(ins(X15,X16))
---------------------------------
P(X14)
```

Proof completed.

The formulation and proof of the theorem above provides a simple illustration on how the definition of one or more functions can be validated by proving desired properties of the functions. Such properties are often easier to formulate than explicit definitions, and may be easier to validate by inspection of the customer's requirements document. It may also be easier for the customer to understand the resulting theorems than constructive definitions. While these definitions provide "procedures' for calculating the functions, the theorems express the desired functionality indirectly, without describing how the functions can be accomplished.

The task of the mean value calculator is, as the name suggests, to calculate the mean value of the amplified signals from the selected detectors. The result is multiplied by an adjustable amplification factor represented by the selector function 'aprm_amplific'. The operations of the mean value calculator is therefore one summation, one division, and one multiplication, see Fig. 5.

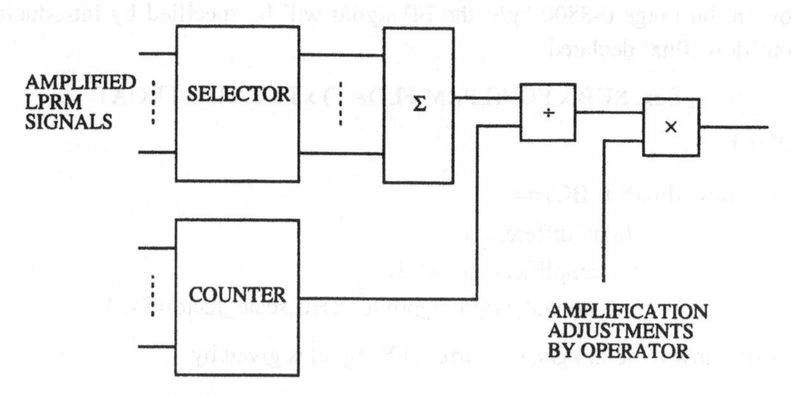

Fig. 5. Calculation of the amplified APRM.

We can specify the operation of the mean value calculator with the function 'amplified_aprm' declared

amplified_aprm: SUB x FUN(LPRM,FLOAT) -> FLOAT

and defined[1]

```
amplified_aprm(S,L) ==
        float_product(
          float_quotient(
            sum_of_amplified_signals(S,selected(S,L),L),
            integer_float(counter(S,L))),
          aprm_amplific(S)).
```

The function 'sum_of_amplified_signals' calculates the sum of the amplified signals of the elements in a set of detectors, while 'counter' returns an integer representing the number of selected detectors not having too low signal values.

5.4 FLOW/FLUX

The range of the HC-flow (core cooling) is 0-8800 kg/s, which can be expressed in percentages of full operating power. The requirements document does not explicitly provide the transition factor from kg/s to percentages, but indicates that it is a linear transition. In the calculation of the FLOW/FLUX (FF) signal, the HC-flow signal

1. The definition assumes no division by zero. This can be modified by introducing a conditional test on the value of counter(S,L).

should have an upper limit. In the requirements document, the FF signal is defined to be the difference between the APRM and the limited HC-flow. Given a value for the HC-flow in the range 0-8800 kg/s, the FF signal will be specified by introducing a function 'flow_flux' declared

```
flow_flux: SUB x FUN(LPRM,FLOAT) x FLOAT -> FLOAT
```

and defined

```
flow_flux(S,L,HC) ==
        float_difference(
            amplified_aprm(S,L),
            limited_hc(float_product(HC,scale_factor(S)))).
```

Given a HC-flow of 4843 kg/s, the current FF signal is given by:

```
> flow_flux(initSUB,signals,4843.0).
... = 37.9312
```

The requirements document defines a filtered FF signal by means of two Laplace transfer functions. These transfer functions give rise to a two-step and a one-step difference equation. Using bilinear transformation, we find the following difference equation for transfer function 2:

$$c(k+1) = \frac{r(k+1) + r(k) + (11/T - 1)c(k)}{11/T + 1}$$

Using this equation and the state variables representing the previous I/O values, transfer function 2 can be specified by introducing a function 'transfer2' declared

```
transfer2: SUB x FLOAT -> FLOAT
```

and defined in accordance to the one-step difference equation. In a similar way, we can introduce a function 'transfer1' corresponding to the two-step difference equation resulting from transfer function 1. The filtered FF signal can now be specified by introducing a function 'filtered_flow_flux' declared

```
filtered_flow_flux: SUB x FUN(LPRM,FLOAT) x FLOAT -> FLOAT
```

and defined

```
filtered_flow_flux(S,L,HC) ==
    float_difference(
        transfer1(S,amplified_aprm(S,L)),
        transfer2(S,limited_hc(S,float_product(HC,scale_factor(S))))).
```

5.5 APRM, FLOW/FLUX Trip Alarms

The requirements document states that in each of the four subsystems, there should be six high trip alarms and one low trip alarm for APRM and FLOW/FLUX. Note that some of these alarms are more appropriately implemented as indicators rather than as alarms. The alarm limits for the trip alarms should be adjustable (by authorized personnel) and are therefore included as state variables of the system. By way of example, the alarm limit for trip alarm H1 is given by the selector 'h1limit' applied on the state variable represented by the selector 'alarm_limits'. The deadband values for the APRM alarms are set to 1.0 and 2.0 for H1 and H2, respectively, otherwise 0.4. APRM alarm H1 can therefore be specified with a function 'h1' declared

```
h1: SUB x FUN(LPRM,FLOAT) -> BOOL
```

and defined

```
h1(S,L) == high_alarm(amplified_aprm(S,L),
                      h1limit(alarm_limits(S)),
                      1.0,
                      h1alarm(alarms(S))).
```

In a similar way, we can for the other trip alarms define functions 'l1', 'h2', 'h3', 'h4', 'h5', and 'h6'.

5.6 Output

The customer's requirements document provides a block diagram for the overall system, summarizing the output signals from the four subsystems. Common to the four subsystems are the LPRM alarms L1 and H1, the APRM alarms L1, H1, ... , H6, as well as the amplified LPRM signals and the APRM signal. The most recent values of these output signals are in the specification represented by the selector functions 'alarms', 'lprm', and 'aprm', respectively. It is convenient to introduce a function which calculates new values for the output signals, represented by a new value of type SUB. The function 'output' takes three arguments, one representing a state of the subsystem, one representing the LPRM values, and one representing the HC-flow.

The time from the actual moment when the FLOW/FLUX signal physically is exceeded until the alarm relay is activated is evidently of great significance. When it comes to formalization however, it remains to be demonstrated whether it is possible to include in the specification the given requirement that this time delay should be 50 ms or less, in such a way that every conceivable implementation always will execute with the given performance. Even if a global clock was included in the specification and a certain number of 'clock ticks' were associated to each operation, the final verification of the performance requirements would probably have to be done as a worst-case analysis directly on the chosen implementation and system configuration.

5.7 Validation Through Animation and Theorem Proving

It is essential that any implementation satisfying the formal specification also satisfies the customer's specification. Fortunately, the formal development of the implementation from the formal specification makes it possible to demonstrate *a priori* that the implementation satisfies the formal specification. The concern about the satisfaction of the customer's requirements therefore reduces to a validation of the formal specification against these requirements.

In the EvalFM project, the specification was assessed by means of animation and theorem proving. Both techniques were used in the process of writing the specification, and thereby contributed to a systematization of the development and assessment of the specification. Animation could be used incrementally at any level of the specification and design, and could be performed even when only small parts of the specification had been written. Animation also made it possible to elucidate the meaning of the specification, and thereby facilitated the communication between agents with widely varying technical background.

The assessment of the specification was also done by proving certain properties expected to hold. Many of these properties can be derived from the requirements document, and express desired relationships between the different functions. A complementary approach is, however, to present alternative definitions of the same function, and prove that they are equivalent. In both cases, theorem proving contributes in a practical way to the assessment of the specification. Both the animation and theorem proving involved in the assessment of the specification were performed by means of the HRP Prover.

6 Design and Implementation

As the use of formal reasoning was fundamental in the assessment of the specification, a similar approach was taken in the design of the system. By means of transformations, the specification could gradually be designed into an implementation, while the correctness of the design steps could be proved within the same framework. Because the design steps were written within the same notation, the intended relationship between them could be expressed by means of so-called abstraction functions. The correctness of the design steps were proved by means of the HRP Prover.

Several of the design steps involved in a formal development follow specific transformation rules, and can easily be automated. This also applies to the transformation from design to code. Because the design and implementation is given in two different notations, the correctness of the implementation can however not be proved directly by formulating abstraction functions and theorems expressing the desired relationship between the design and implementation. Instead, the design is systematically directed toward the implementation language until the design is sufficiently close to facilitate a more or less direct transformation. Alternatively, the implementation can be represented as an abstract syntax tree in algebraic specification. In that case, the correctness of the implementation can in principle be reduced to the correctness of the translation from the abstract syntax tree to the actual code. The development of an integrated environment for the methodology would include the establishment of correct transformation rules and a mechanism for performing (parts of) the actual transformation from design to code.

The development method based on algebraic specification and the HRP Prover allows for variation on the design of the specified system, both with respect to the implementation language, and to the efficient and safe use of the data structures provided by this language. This was also demonstrated in the EvalFM project, where two alternative designs were given which put different emphasis on the efficiency of the implementation. The case study demonstrates that the design of the example system could be directed to an efficient implementation in a safe subset of a specific programming language (in this case Pascal).

7 Further Work

The specification of the example system was written in a formal specification language without the support of any graphical presentation techniques. The comprehensibility of this specification could probably be improved by adopting such techniques, an approach which appears to be feasible because of the close correspondence between parts of the specification and the functional descriptions in the customer's requirements document. It is expected that the adoption of graphical techniques would make it easier to inspect the specification by domain experts with limited knowledge about formal methods. This is important, because part of the specification process is the interaction between the domain experts and the software developers. The adoption of graphical techniques would probably also make it easier for industrial organisations to integrate formal methods in their own development projects.

The application of graphical techniques to the case study is currently investigated in a co-operative project between OECD Halden Reactor Project and ENEA, Italy. One of the project assignments is to apply the IPTES methodology [2] on the PRM system. Much of the motivation behind the IPTES project was the observation that software developers are generally reluctant to using formal notations. The idea was to support widely used graphical notations with formal methods. As a concrete graphical notation, the IPTES project has used the SA/RT (Structured Analysis/Real Time), while high-level Petri nets and an executable subset of VDM (Vienna Development Method) have been chosen as the underlying formal notations. The strategy implemented in the

IPTES tools is to translate an SA/RT model into a high-level Petri net, and to use VDM for the formal analysis of the model.

The Pascal-program produced in the EvalFM project is utilized at the OECD Halden Reactor Project in investigations on the PIE method [9]. This method combines random testing with sensitive analysis, i.e. the analysis of how sensitive the revelation of a certain fault is to the choice of test data. A set of artificial faults, called *mutants*, are seeded into the program, which is executed back-to-back with an incorrupted program and with a large number of test data. The aim of the PIE analysis is to increase the confidence in a program in cases where no failures occur during testing.

An important extension of the case study would be to study the possibility of raising the abstraction level, combined with a consideration of a larger part of the system context. Through the research activities on formal process models, the Halden Project has been developing methods, principles and tools for formal representation of plant knowledge [3]. The goal of the work on formal process models has been to implement computerised support of the design and verification of control strategies. Examples are automatics and operating procedures. The approach has been to model process plants and plant automatics in a unified way to allow verification and computer aided design of control strategies. The methods are based on transforming as directly as possible the information in P&I diagrams and other plant knowledge into a knowledge base to be used in automated reasoning. The knowledge representation primitives must make it possible to utilise different types of knowledge according to what knowledge is available and to the different levels of abstraction used in solving the control problems. The scope of the EvalFM project was to take a detailed requirements document as a starting point, a situation which appears to be quite common in relation to nuclear power class 1E systems. The proposed extension would be particularly applicable if the project involved the production of a requirements specification, and not merely the formalisation of the existing specification. The practical impact on the development process would appear to be quite different in such an extension of the project.

The EvalFM project and many other case studies on the application of formal methods demonstrate that the practical usefulness of these methods depends on the availability of support tools, including powerful theorem provers for the development of proofs of safety invariants and correctness of design. A common objection to the use of formal methods has been that the supporting tools are themselves susceptible to programming errors. In addition comes the imperfectness of compilers, operating systems and computer hardware. The OECD Halden Reactor Project currently addresses these problems through the application of formal methods in the development of a new version of the HRP Prover.

8 Conclusions

The case example studied in the EvalFM project relates to the computer-based power range monitoring (PRM) system installed at Barsebäck NPP in Sweden. The purpose of the PRM system which was of particular interest in this context is the monitoring of the average power emission of the core, i.e. the average PRM (APRM) value. The project applied algebraic specification and the HRP Prover in formally specifying and designing one out of four similar subsystems of the PRM system. Based on the requirements document, a formal algebraic specification was written, utilizing a mathematical tool-kit associated to the method. The subsystem was designed and implemented in a safe subset of Pascal. The case study also investigated how the design could be varied to put stronger emphasis on efficiency. The results strongly indicate that formal methods can be utilized in the development of a real safety-critical system. At the same time, it is concluded that the potentials of formal methods are increased whenever the customer's requirements document allows a higher flexibility with respect to design and implementation. The development method based on algebraic specification supported in a natural way the implementation of a program which avoids potentially dangerous features of the Pascal language.

An important aspect of the specification process was the derivation of the abstract functionality from the technical descriptions provided by the customer. This would however be necessary whether or not a formal specification language was chosen, as the requirements document describes the desired system in a way which apparently suggests a specific, analogue hardware implementation. There are however important non-functional requirements for which the usefulness of algebraic specification, as well as of formal specification languages in general, is very limited. In the present case, this first of all relates to the given requirements to technical performance and accuracies.

The use of the HRP Prover formed an important part of the development of the case example. The tool supported the detection of syntactic errors in the specification, the execution of the specification as an early prototype of the system, proofs of properties of the specification, and proofs of the correctness of the design steps. All of these activities involve a large amount of symbolic manipulation, and the provision of a powerful theorem prover is therefore essential for the success of the method. Nevertheless, the isolated use of a theorem prover would probably not be sufficient in an industrial development project. Industrial use would presumably require a smooth integration of the tool in an application-oriented environment which included the theorem prover, relevant text editors, graphical user interfaces, transformation tools, etc. Furthermore, it would be essential to ensure that this environment were sufficiently reliable. For safety critical applications, this would suggest that several of the included tools, the theorem prover in particular, were formally developed.

The most important findings in the EvalFM project are summarized below. Since the purpose of the project was to evaluate established techniques, the reader should find many of them familiar. The findings are noteworthy first of all because of the particular character and importance of the application domain, i.e. the formal development of reactor safety systems.

- Formal specification can be facilitated by the use of some library of pre-defined data type specifications.
- Algebraic specification can be used in the design as well as in the specification, and allows for implementations in a wide variety of programming languages.
- The potentials of formal methods are increased whenever the customer's requirements allow for a higher flexibility with respect to design and implementation.
- Formal software development supports the implementation of programs which avoid undesired features of the chosen implementation language.
- There are important non-functional requirements for which algebraic specification provides little support, such as requirements to technical performance and accuracies.
- Whenever the customer's requirements are described in terms of an analogue implementation, certain modifications are necessary in order to use the requirements as a basis for the development of a digital system. The incompleteness or incorrectness of these modifications is the source of an important class of specification errors.
- Execution of the specification is an effective means for detecting specification errors and can be preformed incrementally during the production of the specification.
- Execution of the specification increases its comprehensibility, and thereby facilitates the communication between agents with widely varying technical background.
- Executable algebraic specifications appear to provide a sufficiently high abstraction level in most cases; the major limitation to the abstraction typically relates to the concrete nature of the customer's requirements.
- The assessment of an algebraic specification can be performed both by execution and by proving expected properties.
- Efficient use of theorem proving in specification and design requires that the specification language is supported by a powerful theorem prover. For safety-critical applications, parts of such a tool should probably be developed using formal methods.
- Algebraic specification supports a gradual design of the specification towards an implementation, and provides a framework for proving the correctness of the design steps.

- Industrial use of algebraic specification, as well as of formal methods in general, would require the provision of a reliable integrated environment.
- A large part of the effort involved in a formal development project is invested in the production and assessment of the specification. In most cases, only a minor part is invested in the actual implementation.

9 REFERENCES

[1] L. Beltracchi, NRC Research Activities, in: D.R. Wallace, B.B. Cuthill, L.M. Ippolito and L. Beltracchi (eds.), *Proc. Digital Systems Reliability and Nuclear Safety Workshop*, Sep. 13-14, 1993, NUREG/CP-0136, United States Nuclear Regulatory Commission, Washington DC (1994) 31-45.

[2] S. Bologna (ed.), *Special Issue: Incremental Prototyping Technology for Embedded Real-Time Systems*, Real-Time Systems **5**, 2/3 (May 1993).

[3] S. Bologna, T. Sivertsen and H. Välisuo, Rigorous Engineering Practice and Formal Reasoning of Deep Domain Knowledge - The Basis of Dependable Knowledge Based Systems for Process Plant Control, International Journal of Software Engineering and Knowledge Engineering **3** (1993) 53-98.

[4] R.H. Crane, Experience Gained in the Production of Licensable Safety-Critical Software for Darlington NGS, in: *Proc. Methodologies, Tools, and Standards for Cost-effective, Reliable Software Verification and Validation*, EPRI, Palo Alto, CA, USA (Jan. 1992).

[5] G. Dahll, T. Sivertsen, Halden Project Activities on Software Dependability, in: D. Ruan (ed.), *Intelligent Technologies for Man-Machine Interaction at the OECD Halden Reactor Project, Special Presentations of FLINS'94* (SCK-CEN Nuclear Research Centre, Belgium, 1994) 27-38.

[6] S. Gerhart, D. Craigen and T. Ralston, Experience with Formal Methods in Critical Systems, IEEE Software (Jan. 1994) 21-39.

[7] J. Knight and B. Littlewood, Critical Task of Writing Dependable Software, IEEE Software (Jan. 1994) 16-20.

[8] T. Sivertsen, Formal Methods and Their Applicability in the Development of Safety Critical Software, *Proc. IAEA Technical Committee Meeting on Advanced Control and Instrumentation Systems in Nuclear Power Plants: Design, Verification and Validation* (Helsinki/Espoo, Finland, 20-23 June 1994).

[9] J.M. Voas, PIE: A Dynamic Failure-Based Technique, IEEE Trans. Soft. Eng. **18** (Aug. 1992) 717-727.

[10] D.R. Wallace, B.B. Cuthill, L.M. Ippolito and L. Beltracchi (eds.), *Proc. Digital Systems Reliability and Nuclear Safety Workshop*, Sep. 13-14, 1993, NUREG/CP-0136, United States Nuclear Regulatory Commission, Washington DC (1994).

Test Automation for Safety-Critical Systems: Industrial Application and Future Developments

Jan Peleska

JP Software-Consulting and University of Bremen*

Abstract. Design, execution and evaluation of tests for safety-critical systems require considerable effort and skill and consume a large part of today's development costs. Due to the growing complexity of control systems, it has to be expected that their trustworthy test will become unmanageable in the future, if only conventional techniques, requiring a high degree of human interaction during the test process, are applied. In this article, we will focus on test automation for reactive real-time systems, with emphasis on Hardware-in-the-Loop tests analyzing the behaviour of combined software and hardware components. To illustrate possible approaches for this test problem, we describe a concept based on specifications written in Real-Time CSP. For the implementation of test generation and evaluation algorithms transition system representations are used, as can be obtained by Formal Systems' FDR tool. An industrial application of the method is presented and used for the evaluation of the benefits of formal methods-based testing in comparison with conventional techniques. Furthermore, we will indicate research topics in this field which are likely to become important for further improvements of the test process. Specifically, the benefits arising from an approach combining formal verification and testing will be discussed. Our presentation aims less at "promoting" a specific solution, but tries to illustrate the basic problems to be tackled with any formal method, when trying to develop test automation concepts to be applied in the context of reactive systems.

Keywords: CSP — FDR — reactive systems — refinement — test driver — test generation — test monitors — test oracles

1 Introduction

1.1 Objectives

The objective of this article is to outline some of the major problems to be tackled in the field of test automation. The growing demand for trustworthy, but at the same time manageable and cost effective test and verification methods on one hand and the growing number of publications and prototype tools focusing on

* Universität Bremen, Fachbereich 3, D-28334 Bremen, Germany, e-mail: jp@informatik.uni-bremen.de

automation techniques on the other hand lead to a rather optimistic view with respect to the progress to be expected for this field in the near future.

Since different types of systems require different test and verifications methods, we will focus on a specific class of applications, namely *safety-critical reactive real-time systems.* Obviously, this class is an important candidate for thorough testing. At the same time it offers good possibilities for test automation, because many safety critical systems have smaller size, simpler data structures and easier real-time requirements than arbitrary (and often huge and ill-designed!) application systems.

We will explain the main aspects of test automation referring to a real-world application which was tested by means of the VVT-RT *(Verification, Validation and Test for Reactive Real-time Systems)* test automation system developed by the author in cooperation with ELPRO LET GmbH and the Universities of Bremen and Kiel. It should be emphasized that the solutions sketched in this article are not necessarily considered to be optimal. Instead, our claim is that most of the problems encountered when solving the tasks of method development, tool construction and automated test execution are "universal" in the sense that any designer of alternative test automation methods and supporting tools should make sure to find solutions for them.

1.2 Why Testing ?

While it may be argued that the test of software code may become superfluous in the future, because programs may be derived from formal specifications by means of stepwise refinement accompanied by formal verification or by means of formally verified transformational techniques, we are convinced that testing will always remain mandatory for the analysis of behaviour *on system level*:

- Formal development and verification procedures will never cover the full range of software and hardware components, at least for medium-sized and large systems.
- As Brinksma points out in [2] in the context of *conformance testing*, manufacturers will not always disclose the implementation details of their products if external groups perform the product evaluation. As a consequence, (blackbox) testing will be the only means to investigate the correctness properties of such a system.
- While the correctness properties of formally verified software will not "wear out" during system operation[2], hardware components initially functioning correctly may fail after a period of operation which is only statistically predictable. As a consequence, safety-critical systems have to be analyzed in regular intervals using tests designed to detect "local" failures before they can impair the system functionality required by the user. For example, critical computer components in airborne systems have to perform continuous testing in all flight phases using their *Built-in Test Equipment (BITE)* [3].

[2] As long as the requirements remain constant over time!

– A psychological, but nonetheless even more important reason is that customers prefer to see a system in operation before paying the bill. An acceptance test with the real system will never be replaced by a document review of all the formal verification activities performed during system development.

1.3 Related Work

Testing and formal verification were originally investigated in different communities (see [15] for the conventional testing approach). Today, however, the link between these fields seems to be quite soundly established, and this has been mainly stimulated by the necessity to automize larger portions of the test process: Formal specification languages are mandatory for automatic test generation and evaluation.

Test automation concepts based on formal methods have been developed for most of the important system paradigms: Gaudel [7] investigates testing against *algebraic specifications*, Hörcher and Mikk in collaboration with the author [10, 11, 11, 12] focus on the automatic test evaluation against *Z specifications* and Müllerburg [14] describes test automation in the field of *synchronous languages*. Brinksma first presented the idea to apply the theoretical results about testing in *process algebras* to practical problems, with the objective to automize testing against LOTOS specifications [2]. Several authors already have addressed the question how to test reactive systems in an efficient way (see, e. g., [20, 21, 22]), but still this field seems to be less thoroughly explored than the test of non real-time or sequential systems.

1.4 Overview

This article is structured as follows: In Section 2, some of the basic concepts of hardware-in-the-loop tests for reactive systems are described. Section 3 introduces the reactive system which serves as an example to illustrate our concepts. The major steps performed during the test automation process for this system are described in Section 4. Section 5 presents the conclusions.

This article is complementary to [17], where a large part of the theoretical background assumed for the examples and discussions presented here is introduced.

2 The Concepts of Hardware-in-the-Loop Testing

Reactive Systems are characterized by their continuous interaction with the environment and often rely on specific environment behaviour as a premise for their correct operation. As a consequence, the environment behaviour has to be reflected in test configurations for reactive systems. For *safety-critical* reactive systems it is crucial to perform at least a large portion of the testing activities with the complete hardware/software configuration of the target system, in order to analyze the correctness of hardware/software cooperation. These considerations have resulted in ***hardware-in-the-loop tests*** being the most important testing technique for such systems. A hardware-in-the-loop test system consists of one or more computers connected to the target system by the interface designed for the "real" operational environment plus additional monitoring channels used to record or even manipulate internal states of the target system.

Let us look at the logical building blocks of a complete hardware-in-the-loop test automation system (Figure 1)[3].

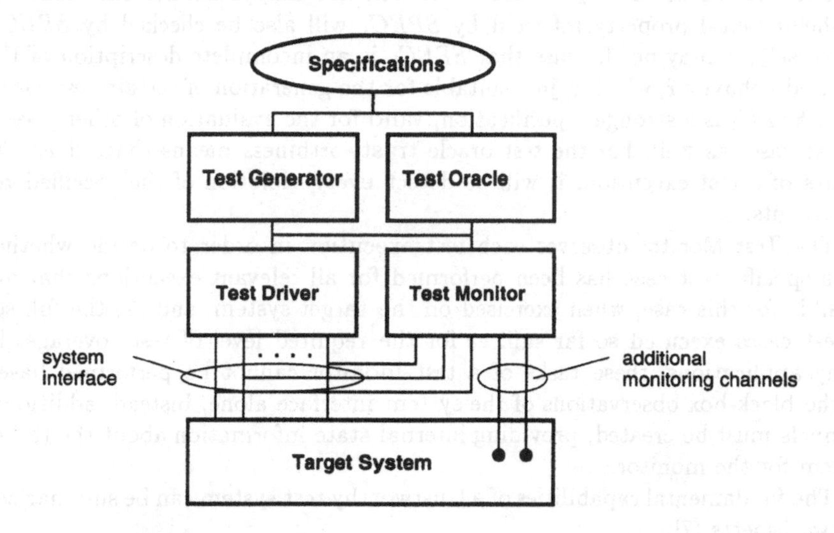

Fig. 1. Logical building blocks of a test automation system.

The Test Generator is responsible for the creation of test cases from specifications. The generator is called trustworthy, if for each possible implementation error violating the specified requirements a test case will be created which is capable of detecting this error. Observe that in the context of reactive systems, a test case is not simply a sequence of inputs and expected outputs: Since the target system may behave nondeterministically on the interface level, the same sequence of inputs may stimulate different responses of the target system, or may even be refused during repeated executions. Therefore we rather define a test case as a description of *execution rules*, specifying the full set of possible sequences of input and output events, together with *real-time assertions* which should be met when exercising the test case on the target system.

The Test Driver interprets the test cases provided by the test generator and controls their execution by writing data on input channels of the target system and collecting system outputs. In general, the target system is only required to behave according to the specification, as long as the operational environment

[3] Figure 1 is not intended to suggest a system architecture for a test system, it only represents logical components that should be present.

also behaves correctly. A test driver is therefore called trustworthy, if it exactly simulates the behaviour of the "real" environment during test execution.

The **Test Oracle** evaluates the observed test execution against a specification and decides whether the execution was correct. The specification document used for test evaluation, say, $SPEC_2$ is not necessarily the same as the specification $SPEC_1$ used for test generation: For example, $SPEC_1$ may be an explicit CSP specification, because the possibility to interpret explicit CSP processes is suitable for test generation. For the test oracle, it may be preferable to use trace assertions in $SPEC_2$. Moreover, it will not always be the case that every behavioural property reflected by $SPEC_1$ will also be checked by $SPEC_2$. Conversely, it may be the case that $SPEC_1$ is an incomplete description of the required behaviour, which is just suitable for the generation of certain test cases, while $SPEC_2$ is a stronger specification, valid for the evaluation of other classes of test cases as well. For the test oracle trustworthiness means that, given the results of a test execution, it will be detect every violation of the specified requirements.

The **Test Monitor** observes each test execution in order to decide whether (1) a specific test case has been performed for all relevant executions that are possible for this case, when exercised on the target system, and (2) the full set of test cases executed so far suffices for the required level of test coverage. In many applications, these tasks of a test monitor cannot be performed based on the black-box observations of the system interface alone. Instead, additional channels must be created, providing internal state information about the target system for the monitor.

The fundamental capabilities of a trustworthy test system can be summarized by two aspects [7]:

- *Unbias:* Correct target system behaviour is never rejected. For this property it has to be ensured that (1) the test generator only creates tests which should really be successfully executed according to the specification, (2) the test driver simulates the expected environment behaviour in a proper way and (3) the test oracle recognizes the test execution to be consistent with the specification.
- *Validity:* Only correct target system behaviour is accepted. For this property it has to be ensured that (1) the test generator is capable to create tests that can uncover each possible correctness violation, (2) the test driver simulates the expected environment behaviour in a proper way, (3) the test oracle recognizes the test execution to be inconsistent with the specification and (4) the test monitor detects whether the test executions so far have covered all relevant target system behaviours.

3 A Tramway Crossing Control System

In this section a *Tramway Crossing Control System (TCCS)* is informally described. The TCCS has been developed by ELPRO LET GmbH in Berlin, Germany [5] and tested and verified by JP Software-Consulting [18] using the VVT-RT test system. In the sections below we will describe some of the testing activities performed for the TCCS to illustrate the general problems to be mastered when testing reactive systems.

3.1 Overall System Function

The TCCS is sketched in Figure 2. Its basic objective is to control the signals SIG 1, SIG 2 and traffic lights TL 1, TL 2 to ensure safe operation of a two-track tramway crossing with a minimum amount of manual interaction.

The state of the signals have the following meaning: (1) OFF: tramways are not allowed to pass. (2) ON: tramways are allowed to pass.

The state of traffic lights have the following meaning: (1) OFF: the traffic on the streets is allowed to cross. (2) RED: the traffic on the streets is not allowed to cross. (3) YELLOW (STEADY): "prepare for RED" (4) YELLOW (FLASHING): the traffic on the streets is allowed to cross *on their own risk*, since safe operation of the TCCS cannot be guaranteed.

Approaching trains on track *i* are detected by means of a *track sensor* TS*i*-IN. This leads to a traffic light switching phase *off* → *yellow* → *red*, whereupon the signal SIG *i* on track *i* may be activated to indicate that the tramway is allowed to pass. The sensors TS*i*-X are used to control the entry of a tramway on track *i* into the crossing. The sensors TS*i*-OUT indicate that a tramway leaves the crossing.

The *Tramway Crossing Control Computer (TCCC)* collects the sensor information and controls signals and traffic lights. Apart from ensuring the safety requirements, the TCCC applies a control algorithm allowing several tramways to pass in a row before tramways are blocked again by the signals and the traffic on the street is allowed to pass. Conversely, the track sensor information is used to switch traffic lights to RED only if tramways are really approaching the crossing. Timeout mechanisms are applied to prevent tramways blocking the traffic on the street for too long and vice versa.

Additionally, the TCCC allows to run a simulation where the overall behaviour is triggered and observed via a *Simulation Control Panel (SCP)* accepting user input simulating sensor data.

For the operation of the TCCS, manual interaction is only required for maintenance, use of simulation control panel (e. g., to check repaired components) and for system startup, where it has to be ensured that normal operation is started only in absence of approaching trains.

3.2 Architecture of the TCCC

The architecture of the control computer is shown in Figure 3. The control algorithm deciding how to switch signals and traffic lights is implemented in the Control Module. To limit the complexity of this algorithm, the module does not directly handle the interfaces to the peripherals. Instead interface modules are

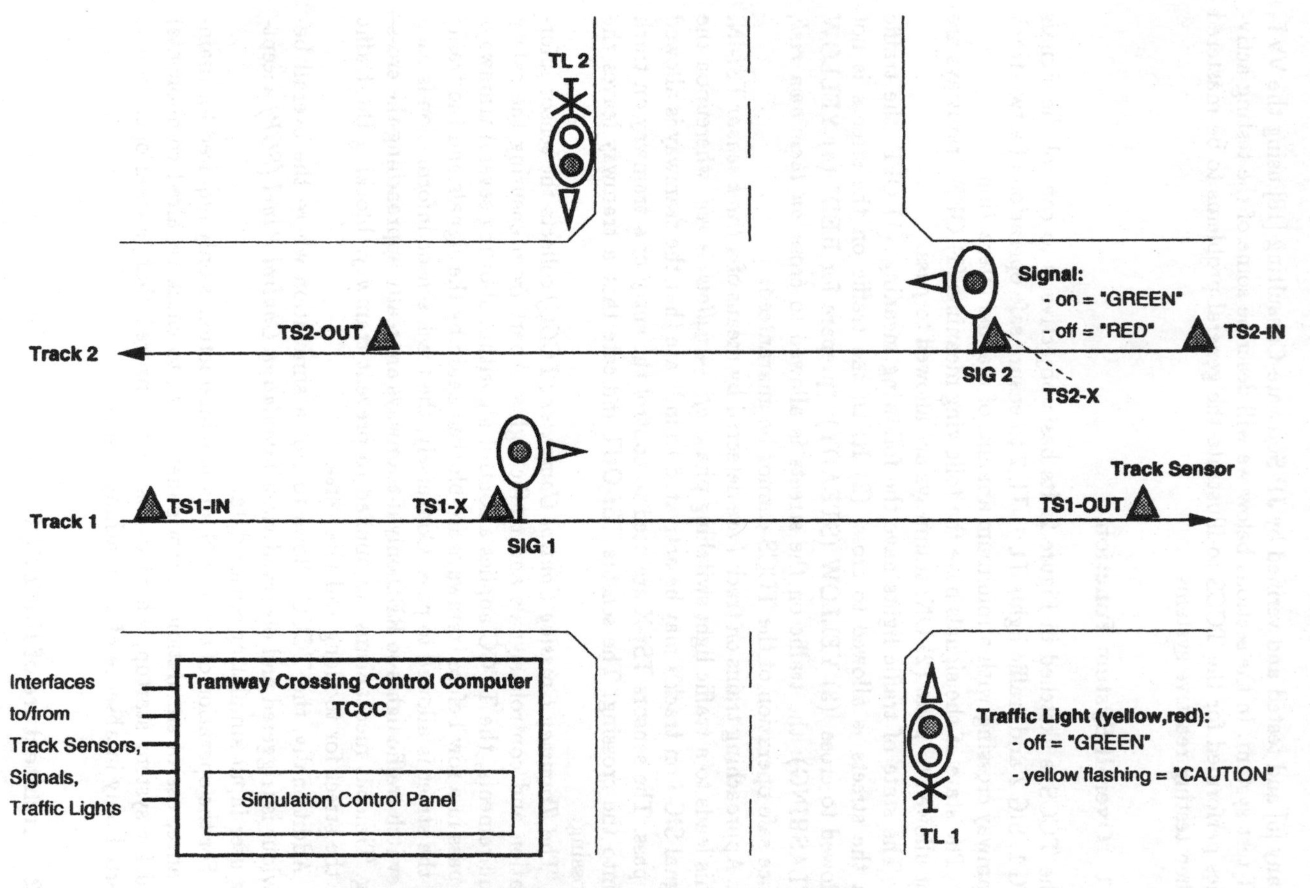

Fig. 2. Tramway Crossing Control System TCCS

inserted between peripherals and **Control Module** that transform input raw data into abstracted values and refine the logical commands issued by the **Control Module** according to the requirements of the TCCC output interfaces. For example, the **Track Monitor** receives raw signals from the track sensors. These signals are de-bounced and monitored with respect to steadiness over a certain time interval. After that they are accepted to be valid and passed to the **Control Module** as abstract events *in*1 (a train has passed track sensor TS1-IN), ..., *out*2 (a train has passed track sensor TS2-OUT). The **TL-Interface Handler** receives commands *red* = *On*/*OFF* and *yellow* = *ON*/*OFF* from the **Control Module**. These commands are transformed and multiplexed into the corresponding switching commands for both traffic lights. Moreover, the **TL-Interface Handler** monitors feedback lines from each traffic light indicating their actual status. To increase the reliability of the system, each lamp of a traffic light is equipped with a spare filament. This is automatically activated by the interface handler if the first one fails. The **SIG-Interface Handler** operates analogously.

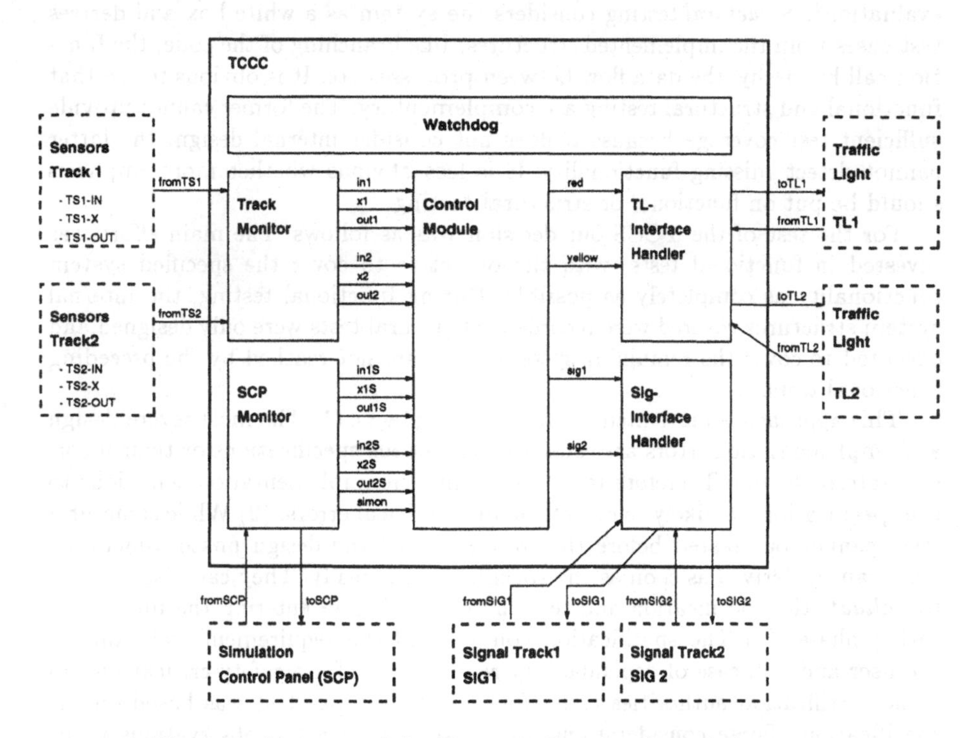

Fig. 3. Architecture of the Tramway Crossing Control Computer

The TCCC is controlled by a (hardware) **Watchdog**: if any of the interface or control modules detect a safety violation, the module directly triggers the watchdog to initiate a transition into a *stable safe state*, where the signals are automatically switched off and the traffic lights are switched to yellow-flashing.

This transition is completely performed by the watchdog hardware and does not require any cooperation of the software modules. The watchdog also detects hardware failures of the TCCC.

4 Test Automation for the TCCS

In this section we illustrate the concepts presented in Section 2 by describing the test automation process performed for the TCCS introduced in the previous section.

4.1 Functional Versus Structural Testing

For dynamic testing a basic distinction is made: *Functional* testing considers the target system as a black box and uses a specification of the required functionality *as far as visible at the system interface* for test generation, execution and evaluation[4]. *Structural* testing considers the system as a white box and derives test cases from the implemented structures, like branching of the code, the function call hierarchy, the data flow between processes etc. It is obvious to see that functional and structural testing are complementary: The former cannot provide sufficient test coverage because it does not consider internal design, the latter cannot detect missing functionality. It is less obvious whether more emphasis should be put on functional or structural testing.

For the test of the TCCS our decision was as follows: The main effort was invested in functional tests, with the objective to cover the specified system functionality as completely as possible. During functional testing, the internal system structures covered were recorded. Structural tests were only designed and executed to cover the remaining system structure not reached by the preceding functional tests.

This approach is motivated by the following facts: (1) The most severe design and implementation errors are caused by erroneous specifications or their incorrect interpretation. Therefore tests comparing the implementation behaviour to the specification are likely to detect the most critical errors. (2) While structural tests cannot be created before the completion of the design phase, functional tests can be derived as soon as the specification is ready. They can also be used to *validate* the specification and test the design before entering the implementation phase. (3) The specification contains all the requirements relevant for the user and – in case of dependability requirements for a safety-critical system – the certification authorities. Therefore the acceptance test was based on the specification. These considerations are consistent with the observations made in [20, 21, 11].

[4] To be more precise, the term *functional and behavioural testing* should be used, because in the context of reactive systems these tests have to analyze both the functionality (data transformations) and the behavioural properties (causal properties, synchronization and timing of events). However, the term *functional test* is so widely used that we do not wish to introduce a new term.

4.2 Selecting the Specification Language and the Correctness Relation

The expressive power of the specification language used as a basis for test automation and the correctness relation to be fulfilled by the test executions when compared to the specification should be carefully selected according to the nature of both the application to be tested and the implementation characteristics of the target system: If the specification language is too powerful, irrelevant test cases will be generated. If the correctness relation is too strict, valid implementations may be rejected. If the specification language or the correctness relation are too "coarse" they will not model the required system behaviour in a faithful way and therefore fail to capture erroneous executions of the target system.

For the test of the TCCS we selected *timed CSP* [9, 4] as the specification language, with *timed trace refinement* as the correctness relation. This relation requires that the test oracle should let a test execution pass as correct if and only if the timed trace observed during the execution is also a timed trace of the specification.

This decision was motivated as follows: (1) Though a PLC is used for the implementation of the TCCC and therefore IO-channels can be considered as "global variables", the event model of CSP is adequate for the TCCC, because the TCCC only reacts to *state changes* in the input channels. For outputs, it suffices to model the occurrence of an event "new value written on channel". (2) Using a timed specification language is mandatory for two reasons: First, complex and even safety critical timing requirements have been defined for the TCCS operation. Second, an untimed model would create test cases for sequences of events that could not really happen because of the timing requirements or could not be distinguished because they were equivalent in the timed trace model[5]. (3) The *timed failures* model of CSP would be too expressive for the following reason: Both the implementations of the TCCC and its peripherals never refuse inputs. Therefore a blocking situation at the system interface can never occur. Of course, the TCCC may refuse an expected output, but this situation is covered by timed safety conditions ("every expected output must occur before a timeout has elapsed") that are controlled by timed trace refinement.

4.3 Developing a Test Strategy

Even for a system of moderate complexity like the TCCC it has to be accepted that *exhaustive testing*[6] cannot be performed. Therefore a *test strategy* has to be developed which allows to test a smaller number of executions than needed for exhaustive testing and at the same time can be justified to analyze the "most important cases".

[5] Recall that two timed traces are equivalent if the second only permutes events which happen at the same time, e. g., $\langle(0,e),(1,f),(1,g),(2,h)\rangle$ is equivalent to $\langle(0,e),(1,g),(1,f),(2,h)\rangle$.

[6] i. e., testing every execution relevant to prove system correctness

Integration Test Strategies One heuristic approach is well known from practical testing: Perform detailed tests for isolated *units*. Then test the proper integration of an increasing number of units, ending up with the system test. For integration tests it is not necessary to cover the full functionality of each unit. Instead, only the correct *cooperation* between units has to be analyzed.

Using formal specification languages for testing has the advantage that such informal strategies can be precisely defined and formally verified. Our concept for such verifications is to exploit the compositional proof theory of CSP: From [8, 17] we know that the test concept implemented in the VVT-RT system ensures that an unbounded number of successful test executions "finally converges" to a refinement proof in the untimed CSP models. This also holds for the simple type of real-time requirements valid for the TCCS. As a consequence it is reasonable to justify a test strategy by means of the *compositional proof theory* of CSP in the following sense:

> Suppose every unit has not only been tested but *proven* to be a correct refinement of its associated specification. Furthermore assume that the correctness property investigated in each integration test has also been formally verified. Then prove that the full system is a correct refinement of its specification.

Adopting this approach has the further advantage that unit and integration tests can be combined with formal verification: It is often reasonable to verify the most critical units of a system formally, while less critical ones and the proper integration of the units are only tested. If the integration strategy is verified as recommended above, we know that the whole system will be *proven* to be correct as soon as every test has been carried out exhaustively or replaced by a refinement proof.

To illustrate this concept, let us look at an example from the TCCC, see Figure 3. Suppose we have performed detailed unit tests for the TL-Interface Handler and Sig-Interface Handler. As it is recommended for safety-critical systems, we did not test each unit in a separate "artificial" testbed, but in the full system configuration. What type of analysis, integration test or verification do we need to show that the combination of the two handlers will operate correctly in the TCCC? To analyze this question in a formal way, suppose *ATLIH* and *ASIGIH* are the timed CSP specifications of the required behaviour of the TL-Interface Handler and Sig-Interface Handler, respectively. Let *CM*, *TLIH*, *SIGIH*, *TL*1, *TL*2, *SIG*1 and *SIG*2 denote the CSP representations of the corresponding module, traffic light and signal implementations[7].

Having verified that the TL-Interface Handler implementation *TLIH* is a correct refinement of *ATLIH* when running in the real operational environment can

[7] Observe that these processes are in general unknown, we only need their existence to verify the integration test strategy.

be expressed by the refinement relation

$$
\begin{array}{l}
((CM \underset{\{\!|red,yellow|\!\}}{\|} (ATLIH \underset{\{\!|toTL1,fromTL1,toTL2,fromTL2|\!\}}{\|} (TL1 \,|||\, TL2))) \\
\quad \underset{\{\!|sig1,sig2|\!\}}{\|} (SIGIH \underset{\{\!|toSIG1,fromSIG1,toSIG2,fromSIG2|\!\}}{\|} (SIG1 \,|||\, SIG2))) \\
\quad \backslash (\Sigma - \{\!| \; red, yellow, toTL1, fromTL1, toTL2, fromTL2 \; |\!\}) \\
\sqsubseteq_{TT} \\
((CM \underset{\{\!|red,yellow|\!\}}{\|} (TLIH \underset{\{\!|toTL1,fromTL1,toTL2,fromTL2|\!\}}{\|} (TL1 \,|||\, TL2))) \\
\quad \underset{\{\!|sig1,sig2|\!\}}{\|} (SIGIH \underset{\{\!|toSIG1,fromSIG1,toSIG2,fromSIG2|\!\}}{\|} (SIG1 \,|||\, SIG2))) \\
\quad \backslash (\Sigma - \{\!| \; red, yellow, toTL1, fromTL1, toTL2, fromTL2 \; |\!\})
\end{array}
$$

Application of the hiding operator indicates that for the tests or formal verification of *TLIH* against *ATLIH* events outside the unit interface were disregarded. Similarly, the verification of the Sig-Interface Handler unit is expressed as

$$
\begin{array}{l}
((CM \underset{\{\!|red,yellow|\!\}}{\|} (TLIH \underset{\{\!|toTL1,fromTL1,toTL2,fromTL2|\!\}}{\|} (TL1 \,|||\, TL2))) \\
\quad \underset{\{\!|sig1,sig2|\!\}}{\|} (ASIGIH \underset{\{\!|toSIG1,fromSIG1,toSIG2,fromSIG2|\!\}}{\|} (SIG1 \,|||\, SIG2))) \\
\quad \backslash (\Sigma - \{\!| \; sig1, sig2, toSIG1, fromSIG1, toSIG2, fromSIG2 \; |\!\}) \\
\sqsubseteq_{TT} \\
((CM \underset{\{\!|red,yellow|\!\}}{\|} (TLIH \underset{\{\!|toTL1,fromTL1,toTL2,fromTL2|\!\}}{\|} (TL1 \,|||\, TL2))) \\
\quad \underset{\{\!|sig1,sig2|\!\}}{\|} (SIGIH \underset{\{\!|toSIG1,fromSIG1,toSIG2,fromSIG2|\!\}}{\|} (SIG1 \,|||\, SIG2))) \\
\quad \backslash (\Sigma - \{\!| \; sig1, sig2, toSIG1, fromSIG1, toSIG2, fromSIG2 \; |\!\})
\end{array}
$$

Now a rather lengthy algebraic calculation shows that this implies the desired refinement property for the integrated units,

$$
\begin{array}{l}
((CM \underset{\{\!|red,yellow|\!\}}{\|} (ATLIH \underset{\{\!|toTL1,fromTL1,toTL2,fromTL2|\!\}}{\|} (TL1 \,|||\, TL2))) \\
\quad \underset{\{\!|sig1,sig2|\!\}}{\|} (ASIGIH \underset{\{\!|toSIG1,fromSIG1,toSIG2,fromSIG2|\!\}}{\|} (SIG1 \,|||\, SIG2))) \\
\sqsubseteq_{TT} \\
((CM \underset{\{\!|red,yellow|\!\}}{\|} (TLIH \underset{\{\!|toTL1,fromTL1,toTL2,fromTL2|\!\}}{\|} (TL1 \,|||\, TL2))) \\
\quad \underset{\{\!|sig1,sig2|\!\}}{\|} (SIGIH \underset{\{\!|toSIG1,fromSIG1,toSIG2,fromSIG2|\!\}}{\|} (SIG1 \,|||\, SIG2)))
\end{array}
$$

provided that (1) the alphabets of *TLIH* and *SIGIH* are disjoint and (2) both specifications and implementations of the interface handlers behave identically at their interfaces $\{\!| \; red, yellow \; |\!\}$ and $\{\!| \; sig1, sig2 \; |\!\}$ shared with the Control Module *CM*. The nature of these premises suggests not perform an integration test, but simply an inspection for their verification: (1) is implied by the fact that the implementations of the two interface handlers do not share any resources (variables, IO-channels), as may be verified by a static analyzer. (2) is implied by the fact that the Control Module only outputs to the interface handlers, and – due to the interface concept using shared variables – such an output is never refused. As a consequence *TLIH* and its specification *ATLIH* act like $RUN_{\{\!|red,yellow|\!\}}$ and *SIGIH*, *ASIGIH* act like $RUN_{\{\!|sig1,sig2|\!\}}$ at the interface to *CM*.

Strategies Distinguishing Between Normal and Exceptional Behaviour A further important test strategy is to distinguish between *normal behaviour* and *exceptional behaviour* of the environment. It is often useful to start with tests only investigating the target system behaviour in presence of proper environment operation. The investigation whether the target system will react properly to abnormal environment behaviour is then tackled in a second test phase. This heuristic approach is also supported by theoretic considerations about dependable systems [19], so a test strategy separating normal and exceptional behaviour tests can be formally justified.

4.4 Preparing a Test Configuration

The application of various test strategies requires to test the target system in different environments, each one defined according to the specific restrictions of the actual testing stage. It is therefore desirable to generate each driver simulating a certain environment behaviour directly from specifications. Each test setup using a fixed environment is called a *test configuration*. We will now analyze the major steps required to construct such configurations.

Hardware-in-the-Loop Test Configuration To illustrate the architecture required for specific hardware-in-the-loop tests, let us suppose that we wish to set up a configuration for the test of the TCCC Control Module, without changing the TCCC structure depicted in Figure 3. Such a test configuration architecture is shown in Figure 4. The Environment Simulation Layer drives the test of the target component. The subordinate layers in the target system and the test system provide a *virtual data flow* between the two top-level layers. This will now be explained in more detail.

Defining Abstractions As pointed out in [11, 21], testing against specifications requires an *abstraction mapping* associating the concrete data and events generated by the target system with abstract objects in the specification. While Richardson [21] describes this task to be a "mapping of the name spaces", we think that more complex considerations are required in the context of reactive systems, because the abstraction is rather a *process* linking concrete and abstract layers. The mapping concept is more appropriate for tests involving data refinement. We will illustrate this observation using the TCCC test configuration introduced above.

For the purpose of testing the Control Module we think of the TCCC as divided into two layers: The Control Module represents the "visible" application layer, the other monitors and interface handlers are located in a subordinate layer supporting the Control Module communication.

The test driver part of the hardware-in-the-loop test system is subdivided into three layers: The Interface Driver Layer implements the low-level drivers needed to communicate raw data over the external interfaces $fromTR1, fromTR2, \ldots$ of the TCCC. These drivers have to be programmed (as far as not already available on

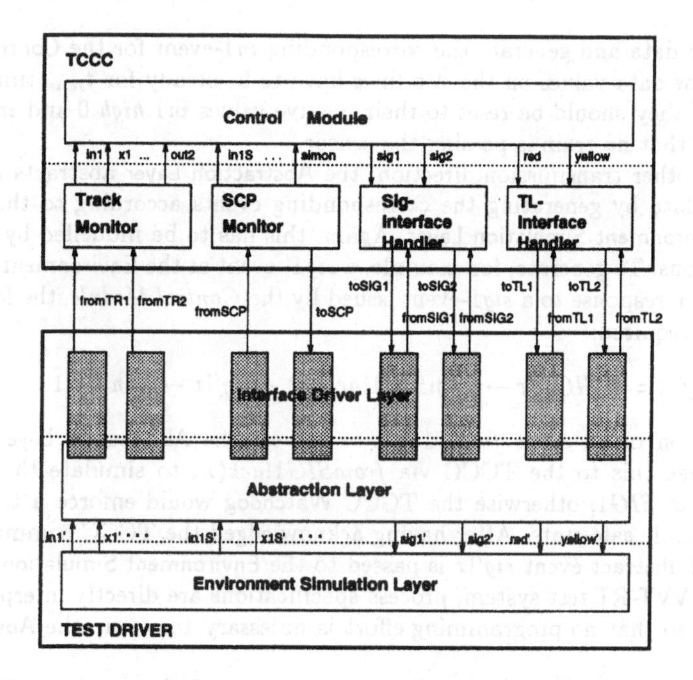

Fig. 4. Architecture of a configuration for testing the TCCC Control Module

the test system computer) according to the requirements of each interface. The driver layer interface offered to the Abstraction Layer is designed such that the parameters passed to and received from the Abstraction Layer can be associated in one-to-one fashion with the corresponding CSP events of the system interface, so on this level the mapping concept described in [11, 21] is appropriate.

The Abstraction Layer performs the required transformations to refine an abstract event sent by the Environment Simulation Layer into (sequences of) corresponding TCCS system interface events. Note however, that this is best defined by a real-time process specification instead of a simple mapping. If, for example, the Environment Simulation Layer requests the generation of an $in1$-event at the Control Module interface, this has to be transformed by the Abstraction Layer according to the process

$$\begin{aligned} GenIn1 = in1' &\rightarrow fromTR1!in1.high.1 \rightarrow fromTR!in1.low.0 \\ &\xrightarrow{t_{sens}} fromTR1!in1.high.0 \rightarrow fromTR!in1.low.1 \rightarrow GenIn1 \end{aligned}$$

$GenIn1$ is activated by the $in1'$-event issued by the Environment Simulation Layer. The process then generates two events $fromTR1!in1.high.1$ and $fromTR!in1.low.0$ which are transformed into the corresponding physical $fromTR1$-interface values by the Interface Driver Layer. The values $in1.high.1$ and $in1.low.0$ have to be transmitted on two digital lines transmitting the raw data of track sensor TS1-IN in the operational environment. In order to make the Track Monitor accept the sensor raw data and generate the corresponding *in*1-event for the Control Module, the raw data values on the two lines have to be steady for t_{sens} time units. After that they should be reset to their passive values *in*1.*high*.0 and *in*1.*low*.1 indicating that no train is passing the sensor.

In the other transmission direction, the Abstraction Layer abstracts received interface data by generating the corresponding events according to the inputs of the Environment Simulation Layer. Again, this has to be modelled by process specifications. To generate, for example, a *sig*1′-event at the Environment Simulation Layer in response to a *sig*1-event issued by the *Control Module*, the following process is required:

$$GenSIG1 = toSIG1?x \rightarrow fromSIG1!ack(x) \rightarrow sig'!x \rightarrow GenSIG1$$

On reception of an event $toSIG1.x, x = on, off$ the Abstraction Layer has to acknowledge this to the TCCC via $fromSIG1!ack(x)$ to simulate the correct operation of *SIG*1, otherwise the TCCC Watchdog would enforce a transition into the stable safe state. After having acknowledged the TCCC command, the associated abstract event $sig'!x$ is passed to the Environment Simulation Layer.

In the VVT-RT test system, process specifications are directly interpreted in real time, so that no programming effort is necessary to set up the Abstraction Layer.

Observe that the abstraction scheme has to be justified for each specific application, because the additional layers introduce a buffer and a time delay between the target component and the test driver. In case of the TCCC, the time delay and the additional level of buffering is unimportant, because the signal changes to be expected for each interface in the operational environment are much slower than the time needed to pass messages through the test system layers and the TCCC never refuses inputs. Furthermore note that the abstraction scheme described only holds for *deterministic* subordinate target system layers, as it is the case for the TCCC monitors and interface handlers. In case of nondeterministic behaviour, it would be uncertain whether an external stimulus (e. g., inputing a TS1-IN sensor signal at the *fromTS*1-interface with a nondeterministic Track Monitor) would really lead to the intended input at the target component interface (e. g., sending an *in*1-event to the Control Module). For these situations, additional monitoring channels have to be installed between the target system and the test system, so that the inputs really received and generated by the target component can be observed and used for test evaluation. In case of a high degree of nondeterminism it can be advisable to block the subordinate layer completely and use auxiliary channels to manipulate the inputs of the target system directly.

Specifying the Environment For the purpose of generating and driving tests we need a specification of the operational environment behaviour, while a specification of the target system is completely unnecessary for these activities: Any behaviour visible at the system interface and possible for the environment can be used for testing purposes, regardless of the intended behaviour of the target system. Even if the complete target system is required to operate in an arbitrary environment, environment specifications will be used to enforce the test strategies discussed above.

For the test of the TCCC using **VVT-RT**, the environment specification is an explicit timed CSP specification E, using untimed CSP syntax as accepted by Formal System's **FDR** tool [6] or a slightly restricted timed CSP syntax (see [16]) which is suitable for symbolic execution in real time. To allow test generation and symbolic execution, E is first transformed into a set of transition graphs [17] corresponding to each sequential process component of E. This transformation is performed by means of **FDR**. Real-time specification are pre-compiled into untimed specifications enriched by auxiliary timer events marking every "real" event associated with a time-depending refusal. The decomposition of E into several sequential components is performed for two reasons: First, to reduce the complexity of the transition graphs involved and facilitate their interpretation in real time. Second, to provide a basis for correct real-time simulation: In real-time specifications, the well-known semantic equivalence between distributed and non-deterministic sequential programs (see [1]) is no longer valid. As a consequence, a complete transition graph of a timed distributed program cannot be faithfully interpreted by one sequential test driver process. Instead, the test driver has to be implemented by parallel processes, each one interpreting the transition graph of a sequential environment component and cooperating with a scheduler observing the synchronization conditions between the sequential processes.

The transition graph representation of E will be executed in the **Environment Simulation Layer**. Note that if a configuration has to test the full target system, this layer directly receives and generates events of the system interface. In this case the **Abstraction Layer** is just the identity mapping, and only the correspondence of CSP events to interface driver calls is evaluated.

Let us consider the specification of normal environment behaviour, as it is used for the **Control Module** test configuration discussed above. A train number *trainNo* passing on track *trackNo* can be modelled as

$$\begin{aligned} &TRAIN(trackNo, trainNo) = WAIT\ 0 \,..\, t_0;\ inE!trackNo.trainNo \\ &\quad \rightarrow WAIT\ t_1 \,..\, t_2;\ xE!trackNo.trainNo \\ &\quad \rightarrow WAIT\ t_3 \,..\, t_4;\ outE!trackNo.trainNo \rightarrow TRAIN(trackNo, trainNo) \end{aligned}$$

$WAIT 0 \,..\, t_0$ denotes the nondeterministic choice of waiting for $0, 1, 2, \ldots$ or t_0 time units before entering the track near the crossing. $inE, xE, outE$ are auxiliary channels defined to control the generation of the track sensor events $in1, in2, \ldots$, as will be explained in the next specification. $WAIT\ t_1 \,..\, t_2$ denotes minimal, maximal and further durations to be tested for the time required by the train to drive from the IN-sensor to the X-sensor. Analogously, $WAIT\ t_3 \,..\, t_4$ denotes the durations to be tested for passing the track section starting with the X-sensor and ending with the OUT-sensor.

In normal operation, up to $maxTrains = 4$ trains may be located between the IN- and OUT-sensors. Trains will only pass an X-sensor if the corresponding signal is ON. Of course, trains cannot overtake each other. These conditions are modelled by[8]

$$
\begin{aligned}
&Ectrl1(inq, xq, sigState) = \\
&\quad (\#inq < maxTrains)\&inE.1?trainNo \rightarrow in1' \\
&\qquad\qquad \rightarrow Ectrl1(inq^\frown\langle trainNo\rangle, xq, sigState) \\
&\quad \Box(sigState = ON \wedge 0 < \#inq)\&xE.1!head(inq) \rightarrow x1' \\
&\qquad\qquad \rightarrow E1ctrl(tail(inq), xq^\frown\langle head(inq)\rangle, sigState) \\
&\quad \Box(0 < \#xq)\&outE.1!head(xq) \rightarrow out1' \\
&\qquad\qquad \rightarrow E1ctrl(inq, tail(xq), sigState) \\
&\quad \Box\, sig1'?z \rightarrow Ectrl(inq, xq, z)
\end{aligned}
$$

Each train generating an auxiliary inE-, xE- $outE$-event stimulates a corresponding $in1'$-, $x1'$-, $out1'$-event which is passed via abstraction layer and subordinate TCCC layers to the Control Module. $Ectrl2$ is specified accordingly. Finally, consecutive trains cannot pass the same sensor arbitrarily close:

$$INsensor(trackNo) = inE.trackNo?trainNo \xrightarrow{t_s} INsensor(trackNo)$$

$$Xsensor(trackNo) = xE.trackNo?trainNo \xrightarrow{t_s} Xsensor(trackNo)$$

$$OUTsensor(trackNo) = outE.trackNo?trainNo \xrightarrow{t_s} OUTsensor(trackNo)$$

The full environment specification is defined by

$$
\begin{aligned}
E = ((\, &|||_{trackId, trainId}\, TRAIN(trackId, trainId)) \\
&\underset{\{|inE, xE, outE|\}}{\|} (INsensor(1) \,|||\, Xsensor(1) \,|||\, OUTsensor(1) \\
&\qquad |||\, INsensor(2) \,|||\, Xsensor(2) \,|||\, OUTsensor(2))) \\
&\underset{\{|inE, xE, outE|\}}{\|} (Ectrl1(\langle\rangle, \langle\rangle, OFF) \,|||\, Ectrl2(\langle\rangle, \langle\rangle, OFF))
\end{aligned}
$$

Specifying the Target System Test oracles are based on specifications of the target system behaviour. For automatic test evaluation of the TCCC, VVT-RT supports two specification styles: (1) An explicit CSP specification $ASYS$ of the abstract system, written in the same style as the environment specification. (2) Implicit behavioural (timed) trace assertions $(E \underset{I}{\|} SYS) \setminus (\Sigma - I)$ **sat** $S(h)$. In this expression, $(E \underset{I}{\|} SYS) \setminus (\Sigma - I)$ denotes the environment E communicating via interface I with the target system SYS and every event of the complete event space Σ which is not an element of the interface I hidden. $S(h)$ is a predicate with free trace variable h, to be fulfilled by every trace of the target

[8] We use *communication guards*: in an expression $b\&c$, the communication via channel c is refused by the process, if the Boolean expression b evaluates to *false*. $\{| c, d, \ldots |\}$ denotes the set of channel events $\{c.x_1, c.x_2, \ldots, d.y_1, d.y_2, \ldots\}$, x_i and y_j are values of the channel alphabets of c and d, respectively.

system visible at the system interface I, when running in an environment as specified by E. Specification style (1) is mandatory if VVT-RT is used for the symbolic execution of the target system specification, if the test monitor should determine a measure for the test coverage achieved or if the system is to be applied for automatic *on-the fly* evaluation as *built-in test equipment*. If on-the fly evaluation is unnecessary, several explicit specifications describing different behavioural aspects and referring to different interface channels may be used. The implicit specification style (2) may only be used for offline evaluation of test results.

For the Control Module normal behaviour test configuration, E is the environment specification given above and the interface is defined by

$$I = \{\!| in1', x1', \ldots, red', yellow' |\!\}$$

For example, an explicit specification only capturing the untimed safety requirements *"whenever a signal is switched ON, the red light must be also ON"* looks like

$$SAFE = SF(false, false, false)$$

$$\begin{aligned} &SF(redIsOn, sig1IsOn, sig2IsOn) = \\ &\quad \neg\,(sig1IsOn \lor sig2IsOn)\&red'?x \rightarrow SF(x = ON, sig1IsOn, sig2IsOn) \\ &\quad \Box\, redIsOn\&sig1'?x \rightarrow SF(redIsSafe, x = ON, sig2IsOn) \\ &\quad \Box\, redIsOn\&sig1'?x \rightarrow SF(redIsSafe, sig1IsOn, x = ON) \end{aligned}$$

An implicit specification stating that the yellow phase should last for at least t_{yellow} time units could be written as

$$\begin{aligned} &S(h) \equiv_{df} \\ &\quad (\exists\, t_1, t_2, s \bullet h \restriction \{\!| yellow' |\!\} = s ^\frown \langle (t_1, yellow'.ON), (t_2, yellow'.OFF) \rangle) \\ &\qquad \Rightarrow t_{yellow} \leq t_2 - t_1 \end{aligned}$$

Validating the Specifications Since the test automation process is completely driven by the environment and target system specifications, their correctness is of great importance. It is not assumed that a formal higher-level document with all the required correctness properties might exist, so that the specification could be formally verified to be a refinement of the higher-level document. As a consequence the specification can only be *validated* by means of various heuristics. To this end, VVT-RT provides three techniques: (1) To validate the untimed safety- and liveness characteristics of the specification, the user can define refinement relations between the explicit specifications E, $ASYS$ and various user-defined auxiliary processes expressing the properties which should be present from the user's point of view. These refinement relations can be automatically verified using the FDR model checker. (2) $(E \underset{I}{\|} ASYS)$ may be symbolically executed using the interactive simulation component of VVT-RT. (3) Explicit specifications of E and $ASYS$ may be validated by creating a collection of redundant implicit specifications $S_i(h)$, that should all be satisfied by $(E \underset{I}{\|} ASYS) \setminus (\Sigma - I)$. Next, the explicit specifications E and $ASYS$ are used to generate traces h_j of $(E \underset{I}{\|} ASYS) \setminus (\Sigma - I)$. Using the second VVT-RT test oracle, these traces are evaluated against the implicit specifications: If $S_i(h_j)$ does not hold for a specific pair S_i, h_j, the explicit specifications E and $ASYS$ violate the assertion $(E \underset{I}{\|} ASYS) \setminus (\Sigma - I)$ **sat** $S_i(h)$, so either $E, ASYS$ or S_i contains a specification error.

4.5 Generating and Driving Test Cases

As indicated above, the VVT-RT system generates and drives test cases using the transition graphs associated with sequential environment processes. Each graph is executed by a separate process. The process determines its local readiness to engage into a certain set of events. A scheduler controls the synchronization requirements and marks all events which are ready for execution to be dispatched. For untimed and timed specifications different schedulers have to be used: The untimed CSP semantics allows events e to be interleaved by an arbitrary number of other events though e could be generated because every communication partner involved is waiting to engage into e . In contrast to this, the real time semantics requires that every event occurs as soon as all communication partners are ready for it and hidden events occur as soon as they are available [4]. This avoids unnecessary distinctions between different sequences of simultaneous events: These sequences are considered as equivalence classes, and one member of this class is sufficient to be covered by the test executions.

The test driver performs *on-the-fly* test generation, executing the transition graphs using a breadth-first strategy, as required for trustworthy failure detection [17]. Since for the test of the TCCC timed trace refinement is an appropriate correctness relation, the test driver operates with less complicated test cases than the untimed failures-divergence test driver specified in [17]: Both target system and environment never refuse inputs, therefore it is unnecessary to analyze the non-blocking properties of the target system for each trace length. Furthermore the test driver can choose any input to the target system but cannot influence the sequence of target system outputs by blocking the corresponding channels.

4.6 Evaluating the Test Results

Given the specification types described above, the implementation of test oracles in the VVT-RT system is straight forward: During test execution, the timed trace of all interface events is recorded. If explicit specifications have been provided, the trace is evaluated against a global (timed) transition graph derived from the specification. In case of failures, the correct prefix of the trace is displayed together with the erroneous event and possible correct alternatives. It is interesting to note that the CSP semantics allows easier evaluation algorithms as for example the CCS semantics [13]: Since CCS distinguishes between late and early branching, several transitions emanating from a state of a CCS transition graph may be labelled by the same event. This is not the case for CSP transition graphs. As a consequence, a test evaluation algorithm for CCS transition graphs has to apply backtracking techniques, since identical traces might be represented by different walks through the graph.

For the evaluation of the timed trace against implicit behavioural assertions, a component of the test tool developed by Hörcher and Mikk [11, 12] for the automatic evaluation of Z specifications is integrated into VVT-RT: Trace assertions are specified as Z schemas containing predicates over a free trace variable h : seq. The Z test tool automatically transforms the predicate parts of Z schemas into executable evaluation functions that are used to check the timed trace observed during a VVT-RT test execution.

5 Conclusion

In this article we have discussed several important aspects of test automation for reactive real-time systems. These aspects were illustrated by examples from tests performed for a tramway crossing control computer which is now in operation since 1995.

The test results were considered as successful [18] for the following reasons:

- Several errors were found by means of the test automation system VVT-RT, after the target system had been thoroughly tested in a manual way and passed the official acceptance tests performed by the certification authorities.
- The number of tests automatically performed and documented by the test system resulted in about 3600 pages of test documentation[9] which would otherwise have to be manually produced to document the same degree of test coverage without tool support.
- Though the test procedure using VVT-RT was performed for the first time and the formal specifications used for testing had to be explicitly produced for this purpose, the total costs of the automized tests were less than 30% of the costs estimated for an equivalent manual test.

Acknowledgements I would like to thank my friends and collaborators for their substantial contributions to the concepts and results presented in this article: Alexander Baer, Bettina Buth, Sabine Dick, Detlef Falkmeyer, Ute Hamer, Erich Mikk, Wolfgang Noack, Anders Ravn, Hans Rischel and Michael Siegel. This work was partially supported by the German Ministry of Education and Research BMBF, project UniForM.

References

1. K. R. Apt and E.-R. Olderog. *Verification of Sequential and Concurrent Programs.* Springer-Verlag, Berlin Heidelberg New York (1991).

[9] This corresponds to 98% branch coverage of the transition graph representing the specification.

2. E. Brinksma: A theory for the derivation of tests. In P. H. J. van Eijk — C. A. Vissers and M. Diaz (Eds.): *The Formal Description Technique LOTOS.* Elsevire Science Publishers B. V. (North-Holland), (1989), 235-247.
3. RTCA DO178B: *Development considerations in airborne computer systems.* (1993).
4. J. Davies: *Specification and Proof in Real-Time CSP.* Cambridge University Press (1993).
5. ELPRO LET GmbH: *Programmablaufplan - Bahnübergang.* ELPRO LET GmbH (1994).
6. Formal Systems Ltd.: *Failures Divergence Refinement.* User Manual and Tutorial Version 1.4. Formal Systems (Europe) Ltd (1994).
7. M.-C. Gaudel: Testing can be formal, too. In P. D. Mosses, M. Nielsen and M. I. Schwartzbach (Eds.): *Proceedings of TAPSOFT '95: Theory and Practice of Software Development.* Aarhus, Denmark, May 1995, Springer (1995).
8. M. C. Hennessy: *Algebraic Theory of Processes.* MIT Press (1988).
9. C.A.R. Hoare. *Communicating sequential processes.* Prentice-Hall International, Englewood Cliffs NJ (1985).
10. H. M. Hörcher and J. Peleska: The Role of Formal Specifications in Software Test. Tutorial, held at the FME '94.
11. H. M. Hörcher: Improving Software Tests using Z Specifications. To appear in J. P. Bowen and M. G. Hinchey (Eds.): *ZUM '95: 9th International Conference of Z Users,* LNCS, Springer (1995).
12. E. Mikk: Compilation of Z Specifications into C for Automatic Test Result Evaluation. To appear in J. P. Bowen and M. G. Hinchey (Eds.): *ZUM '95: 9th International Conference of Z Users,* LNCS, Springer (1995).
13. R. Milner: *Communication and Concurrency.* Prentice-Hall International, Englewood Cliffs NJ (1989).
14. M. Müllerburg: Systematic Testing: a Means for Validating Reactive Systems. In *EuroSTAR'94: Proceedings of the 2nd European Intern. Conf. on Software Testing, Analysis&Review.* British Computer Society, (1994).
15. G. J. Myers: *The Art of Software-Testing.* John Wiley & Sons, New York (1979).
16. J. Peleska: *Trustworthy Tests for Reactive Systems — Automation of Real-Time Testing.* In preparation, JP Software-Consulting (1996).
17. J. Peleska and M. Siegel: From Testing Theory to Test Driver Implementation. To appear in *Proceedings of the Formal Methods Europe Conference FME '96,* LNCS, Springer-Verlag, (1996).
18. J. Peleska: Testautomatisierung für diskrete Steuerungen, Anwendung: Bahnübergangssteuerung - Abschlußbericht Phase 1. Technical Report 06/95, JP Software-Consulting (1995).
19. J. Peleska: Formal Methods and the Development of Dependable Systems. Technical Report 07/95, JP Software-Consulting (1995).
20. D. J. Richardson, T. O. O'Malley and C. Tittle Moore: Approaches to Specification-Based Testing. In *ACM SIGSoft 89: Third Symposium on Software Testing, Analysis and Verification,* December (1989).
21. D. J. Richardson, S. Leif Aha and T. O. O'Malley: Specification-based Test Oracles for Reactive Systems. In *Proceedings of the 14th International Conference on Software Engineering, Melborne, Australia,* May (1992).
22. E. Weyuker, T. Goradia and A. Singh: Automatically Generating Test Data from a Boolean Specification. *IEEE Transactions on Software Engineering* Vol. 20, NO. 5, (1994).

Quantitative Analysis of an Application of Formal Methods

Juan Bicarregui[1] Jeremy Dick[2] Eoin Woods[3]

[1] Rutherford Appleton Laboratory, Oxfordshire, UK.
[2] Now at B-Core UK. Work done whilst at Bull Information Systems.
[3] Now at Sybase. Work done whilst at Bull Information Systems.

Abstract. This paper reports on the experience gained in the MaFMeth project, which undertook a formal development with tool support for several parts of the life cycle from requirements capture through to C code generation. We explore the hypotheses that formal methods enable the early detection of faults in design by examining the development process in the light of the stages at which faults were introduced and discovered.

1 Introduction

One of the major planks of the argument for formal methods is that they allow fewer design errors to be introduced in to software and allow remaining errors to be identified early in the development process, so minimising the cost of correcting them.

The process of formalising the specification encourages certain kinds of question to be asked of the requirements, raising issues which may not otherwise have been manifest until later in development. Having a machine-processable description at an early stage allows certain validation and verification activities not otherwise available, such as animation which serves to validate the specification against intended requirements, and proof of consistency which verifies the internal coherence of the specification. The ability to have precise discussion about the relationship of the specification to an implementation is an important enabling factor, since both descriptions are formalised, each design layer can be compared and verified against the layer above.

The longer a fault in design goes undiscovered, the more rework is necessary when it is found, and so the more expensive it is to correct. In the worst case, when a fault in the original specification is not found until after the product is delivered, in order to ensure the integrity of the product, the specification, design, implementation, testing, integration and delivery stages all have to be reworked. If that fault had been discovered early on the design phase, far less expense would have been involved in its rectification.

Very little quantitative evidence has been published to substantiate the supposed benefits of the formal approach. This paper reports quantitative aspects of the experience gained in the MaFMeth project[4] which used a combination of VDM and the B-Method and kept certain metrics with the aim of showing evidence for the early detection of errors and assessing the relative effectness of various activities in the overall process. These metrics amount to fault counts correlated against the activities during which the corresponding errors were introduced and discovered. For further descriptions of the system developed, the techniques used and a qualitative description of the problems encountered see [9], [10] and [1].

2 The Application

The project in question was the development of the second release of Groupe Bull's FlowBus™ product. FlowBus is an application integration product (of the type often known as "middleware") which allows applications to communicate in a number of ways via a single application programming interface. Its primary function is to provide distributed, multi-platform, inter-application message handling services involving message routing, storage, transformation and enrichment, all under administrator control, transparently to the applications.

FlowBus is intended to serve the needs of corporations with requirements driven by business in the area of inter-application communication, or wishing to restructure their business processes. Such environments are characterised by the need for extensive, flexible, inter-application communications that can be altered with the minimum of disruption. FlowBus is intended to provide the integration services to allow new applications, legacy applications and package software to be integrated to meet the needs of these environments.

FlowBus allows applications to communicate without explicit knowledge of each other's existence, form or function. Interaction between applications and FlowBus is via the sending and receiving of messages. Messages within FlowBus are typed and FlowBus routes messages between applications according to this type and possibly the message contents. FlowBus is also capable of message enrichment, transformation and conversion and is accessed using a single high-level API across all the supported platforms. Other FlowBus facilities include deferred message delivery (i.e. message queuing) and centralised administration facilities allowing large multi-platform FlowBus networks to be administered from a single workstation.

This development project was centred in the area of control and administration, particularly of queues. The *Queue Administration Tool* (QAT) is able to list the queues in the system, monitor the status of each queue and report it on demand, list the messages within a queue and view or update individual messages when required. When messages are updated, it must allow the administrator to reroute them given certain system-wide integrity constraints. The QAT is also

[4] The MaFMeth project is an application experiment funded under the EC ESSI programme. It is a collaboration between the Bull development centre (Hemel Hempstead), Bull S.A. (Paris), B-Core Limited (Oxford) and the Rutherford Appleton Laboratory.

capable of generating alarms when certain types of messages arrive on certain queues. Which combinations of message types and queues raise which alarms is configurable.

3 The Development Environment

The project was undertaken in a conventional system software development environment consisting of a department of some sixty software developers engaged in all aspects of system software supporting three Unix based software products. The development process used was relatively mature for a Unix system software development process, having been certified as ISO9001 (TickIt) [7] compliant for its quality management system and operating at a point close to level 3 of the SEI Capability Maturity Model [8]. Some use was being made of structured approaches, specifically the Yourdon Structured Method [11], although much of the development was still utilising a less rigorous approach using natural language augmented with informal diagrams. There was no general awareness or understanding of formal methods throughout the development staff.

The FlowBus project involved about twelve software developers, of whom three were involved directly in the development of the QAT subsystem's functional engine using formal methods[5]. Of these three staff, two had previous experience in applying formal methods, but one of these, the primary developer with responsibility for delivery of the finished component, had worked with formal specification only on trial projects and had not previously used formal approaches for product development. In particular he had no prior knowledge of the B Method or its associated tools which were critical to the development process used.

4 The Method

The development process adopted used was influenced by

1. the desire to cover as much of the development life cycle as possible by formal techniques in order to test the "faults discovered early" hypothesis;
2. the nature of the tool support available for each stage of development; and
3. the fact that the resulting code had to be closely integrated with other code both supplied by a third party as an existing package and developed in-house using more traditional techniques.

These three requirements immediately posed potential problems due to unavailability of a single tool supporting all the required features. In order to cover as much of the life-cycle as possible, from requirements capture to integration testing of code, and faced with the lack of a single tool providing all these facilities,

[5] Some consultancy on formal techniques used was also brought in under the ESSI project.

we found it necessary to use a number of different notations, each with their own forms of tool support.

The use of C as a target language was imposed by the development organisation. The B-Toolkit was chosen for its support of development from the design phase to C code generation. The decision to employ VDM rather than the Abstract Machine Notation (AMN) of the B method to capture the initial specification was motivated by three reasons:

- previous experience [2] that AMN encourages the specifier to think very much in terms of assignments to state variables, whereas VDM-SL facilitates the capture of the initial specification at a more abstract level;
- the desire to evaluate the diagrammatic approach to formal specification offered by the "VDM through Pictures" tool [3], and the style of specification imposed by this approach; and
- the desire to evaluate and take advantage of the ability to generate test cases from the VDM specification using the VDM Analysis Tool [4].

Naturally, using different notations introduced concerns about the training of staff and the co-existence and interaction of the various formalisms and tools however this could not be avoided if we were to cover the desired breadth of activities.

For the purpose of the assessing the development process, we identified 13 activities, with varying degrees of tool support. These are depicted in Figure 1. Measurements relating to these activities were taken for two purposes:

1. to compare a formal development process with a conventional one;
2. to compare the relative effectiveness of various stages of the formal process.

To meet the first of these objectives, the results of a number of development projects, all producing sub-products with similar characteristics, were compared[6]. The measurements were made according to the departments existing metrics programme which, for development projects, consists primarily of the following standard metrics being collected:

- number of faults per thousand lines of code found during unit tests and integration tests,
- number of faults per thousand lines of code found during validation test,
- number of faults per thousand lines of code found during customer use,
- person months of effort per thousand lines of code produced.

For these purposes a fault is recorded when a change is required to an design decision made at an earlier development stage. A design made and changed within one stage is not considered a fault.

---

[6] Though it would have made a more scientifically thorough trial, it was not considered economical to conduct a parallel development of the same component under the different methodologies.

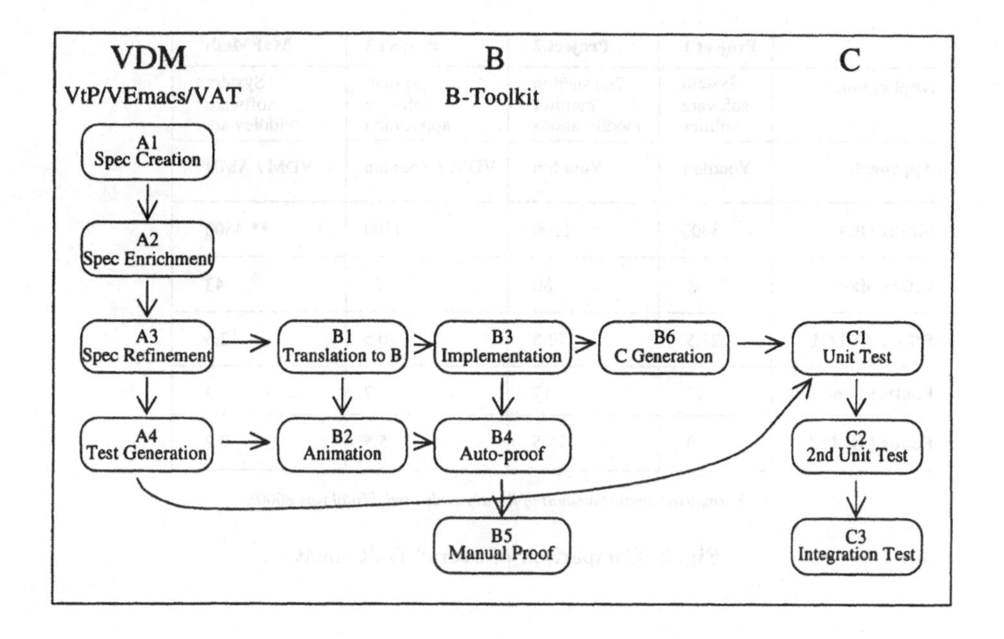

Fig. 1. Development activities identified in the MaFMeth project

To meet the second objective, counts of faults discovered were kept during each of the stages named above. Since some of the activities in the formal process took place in parallel, some faults were discovered at more than one stage. For this reason, each fault *discovery* was given a unique identity, and for each of these a record was made the stage it was first discovered, and the stage it was introduced. From these metrics, it was possible to estimate the effectiveness of each stage of the process in terms of the numbers of faults introduced and detected, though no attempt was made to assess the severity of each fault.

5 Overall Fault count

Despite the differing notations and the lack of integrated tool support described above, quantitative analysis of the overall fault count shows the approach to be very effective both in cost and quality.

Figure 5 compares data from this project with three others undertaken by the user partner using structured design.

The four projects were all developed in the same environment over a period of about 3 years and all used a similar development process apart from the technology involved. All projects were undertaken by engineers from the same development group and all were fragments of much larger developments. All, bar project 2, were new developments, whereas project 2 was a complex modification to an already heavily maintained system software component (hence, perhaps, the low productivity and quality of that development).

	Project 1	Project 2	Project 3	MaFMeth
Application	System software utilities	Transaction monitor modifications	System software application	System software middleware
Approach	Yourdon	Yourdon	VDM / Yourdon	VDM / AMN
Size (LOC)	3000	1100	1300	** 3500
Effort (days)	65	80	27	43
Effort / KLOC	21.5	72.5	20.5	12.5
Faults at unit test	27	17	7	3
Faults / KLOC	9	15.5	5.5	0.9

*** Normalised against amount of library code used. (Total was 8000).*

Fig. 2. Comparison of overall fault count

The LOC figure (Lines of Code) is clearly central to the metrics and for projects 1 to 3 refers to C language statements. For MaFMeth, in all 8000 lines of code were generated, however much of this arose from library components. The figure of 3500 lines of code is the developer's estimate of the amount of code that would have been produced to implement the same functionality without attempting any reuse. In fact, 1200 lines of implementation level B notation were produced to generate the final C code.

None of the effort figures include the learning and technology transfer time which is inevitable in applying new approaches.

The figures show that the MaFMeth project produced, on average, more code per day than any of the previous projects. Of course, this result must be tempered by the different application areas and the possible inaccuracy in the estimate of the equivalent number of lines of code. However, the improvement of nearly 100% is noteworthy.

Even more significant are the results concerning the number of faults at unit test. The unit testing used aimed at 100% functional black box test coverage and 100% branch level white box coverage. This was achieved by identifying test cases using techniques including equivalence partitioning, boundary value analysis and a judicious amount of error guessing! The MaFMeth project produced less than 20% of the faults of the next best project.

Unfortunately, no figures for faults found during validation testing and customer use are available.

6 Early detection of Faults

To explore the "faults found early" hypothesis, we analysed the process adopted according to the time taken, in terms of process stages, to discover faults in the system. We present this data using "Fault Grids" [5, 6] which display the faults found according to the stages at which they were introduced and detected.

6.1 Fault grids

Fault grids provide a means of presenting fault counts against process stages so as to

- highlight the effectiveness of each process stage in terms of the faults introduced and detected;
- assess the overall effectiveness of the process in terms of the number process stages between the introduction and discovery of faults.

The first requirement is to have a well-defined development process. Of interest here is the sequence (temporal and logical) of activities that make up the process. The temporal sequence of activities corresponds to the order in which the activities are carried out. The logical sequence corresponds the dependency of activities on each other; for instance, High-Level Design may be logically dependent on Requirements Capture, but not logically depend on Specification Animation (although animation may take place earlier).

For each fault found, a record is made of

- the activity that enabled the fault to be found;
- the estimate of which previous activity introduced the fault.

For each activity, a record is made of the cost of running that activity.

Figure 1 shows the general scheme for the presentation of fault counts. It shows a hypothetical but typical process consisting of 9 activities from specification through to production. The diagonal grid is used to record numbers of faults found during each activity against the originating activity. Thus, for example, the highlighted lines show that 2 faults were found during Integration Testing that were introduced during Design; adjacent top that we see that 10 faults originated from Coding were found at integration test.

Although hypothetical, the groupings of figures on the grid are typical. The group of figures near the top of the grid reflects the exploratory phases of development were requirements are understood and different specifications are proposed and assessed. The group in the middle correspond to those errors introduced in design and coding. The lonely "2" at the peak of the fault grid should cause concern; it took too long to find these faults!

The diagonals from top-left to bottom-right show the total number of faults introduced at each development stage, for example 3+2+10 faults were introduced during coding. The diagonals from top-right to bottom-left show the total faults found at each review state, here 3+8 faults were found at unit test.

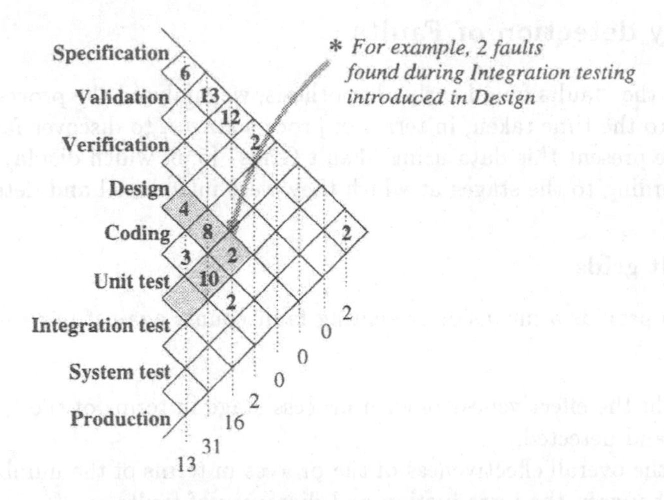

Fig. 3. Hypothetical example of fault grid

The vertical columns in the grid, indicated by the dotted lines, show faults that were found 1, 2, 3, etc. temporal stages down the process. The figures at the bottom of the grid show, therefore, that 13 errors were found after one stage, 31 after two, and so on. However, it may be more interesting to consider at how many logical stages were taken to discover faults. The logical ordering for our example process is shown in Figure 3. With this dependency between activities, for instance, Verification and Design is only one stage down the line from Specification.

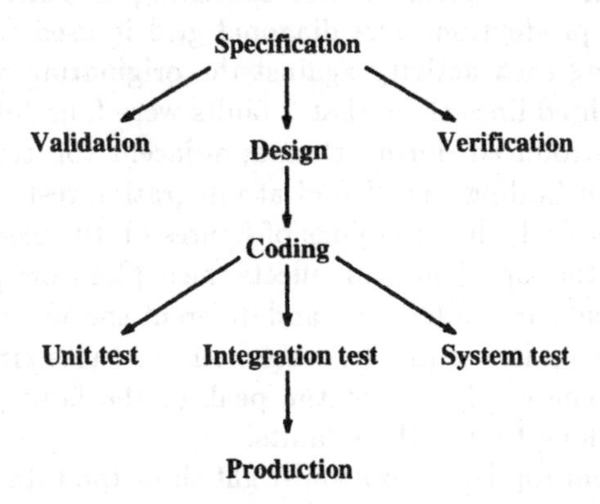

Fig. 4. Hypothetical activities dependences

The number of stages taken to discover faults in our hypothetical development are presented as bar charts in Figure 5. A comparison between the temporal and logical orderings may suggest that a change in the order of the activities would allow faults to be discovered more quickly. Here the activities Validation, Verification and Design all discovered a large number of faults and could all be done immediately aft the initial specification. Note how almost all faults are found after a single logical stage.

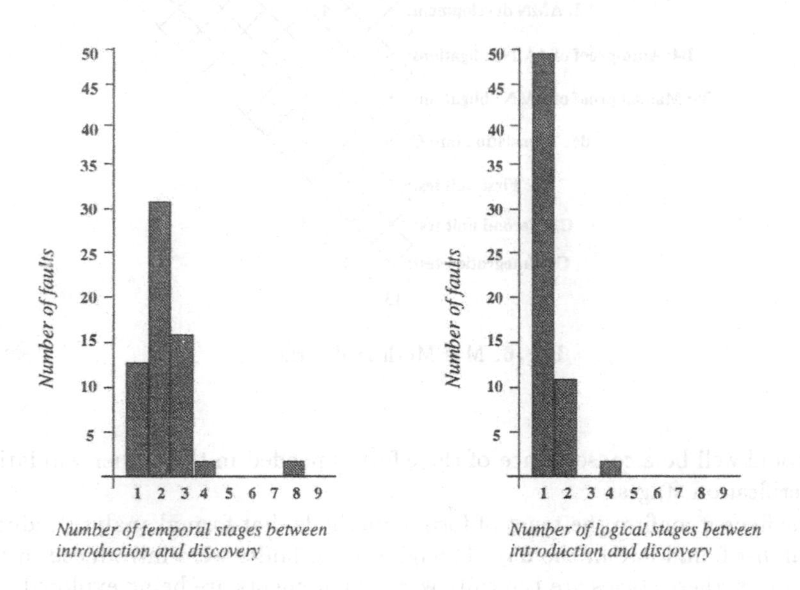

Fig. 5. Bar charts for number of stages between fault introduction and discovery

Of course, some caution must be exercised when considering these charts. Firstly, the columns do not represent the sum of like quantities, each step of the process is not equivalent in magnitude. Secondly, it is not meaningful to compare different project processes by their resulting bar charts as there may be a difference in the granularity of the process decomposition used in each project.

6.2 MaFMeth Results

Figure 6.2 shows the fault grid for the MaFMeth project[7].

Many faults found early. Significant is the tiny number of faults that were discovered during unit and integration testing. The single positive value in the lower part of the grid reflects that only three errors picked up by the testing stages.

[7] Note that in practice the three testing stages were amalgamated into one test suite

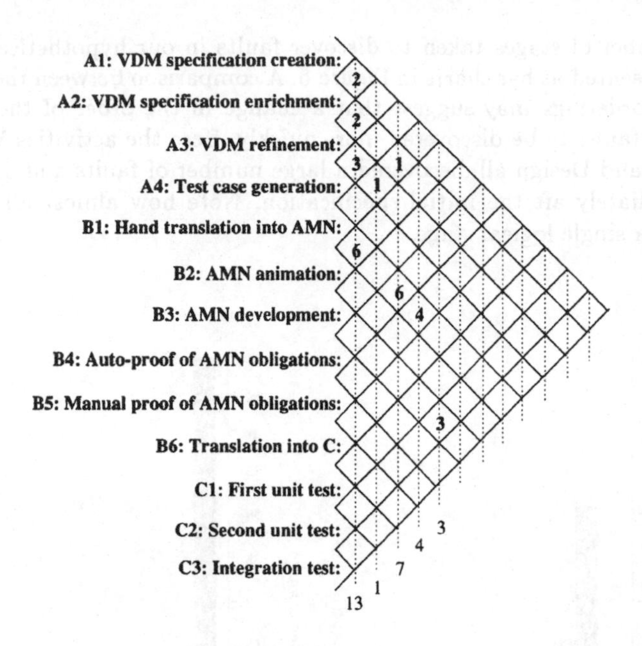

Fig. 6. MaFMeth fault grid

This could well be a consequence of the effort expended in the earlier validation and verification stages.

The figures confirm the tenet of formal methods that formal analysis reduces the number found late in the day. Though several faults were introduced in the early stages, these stages are typically were requirements are being explored and alternative approaches being tried in design. It can be seen as a good thing to introduce and discover faults here. In particular, no faults from the early VDM specifications persisted beyond stage B1.

Faults found quickly. The complete absence of any positive values on the right hand side of the grid is encouraging. It is revealing to note that nearly half the total number of faults were found immediately after their introduction. The number of stages taken to discover faults is summarised in Figure 7.

In this case there is no great difference between the two bar charts. What difference there is can be largely attributed to the temporal ordering of animation and proof stages (B 3,4 and 5). In fact, the logical independence of animation and proof was recognised in advance and these stages were actually carried out in parallel.

When faults were introduced. Highlighted by the diagonal 6,6,4 is the relatively large number of faults introduced by the manual activity of translation from VDM into AMN. 16 out of the total 28 faults were introduced at this stage.

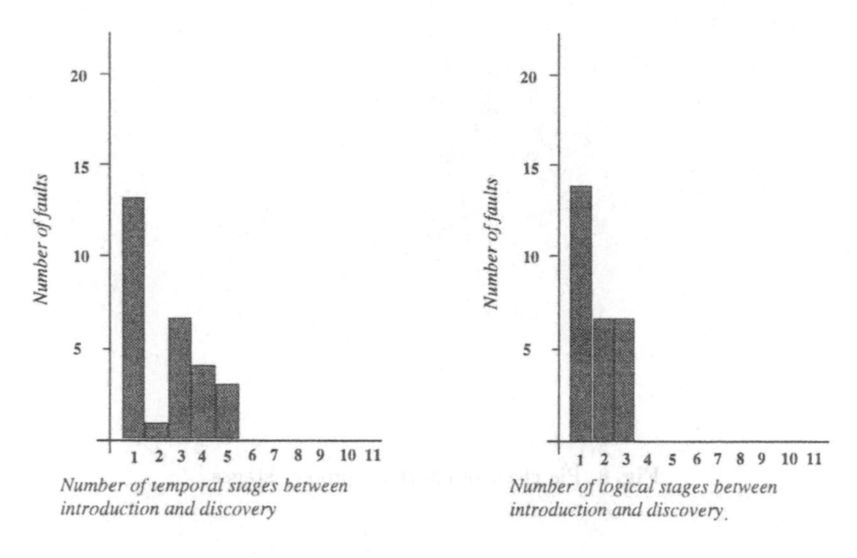

Fig. 7. Bar charts for MaFMeth

With hindsight, we realise that, although we had made a point of trying to keep this step as simple as possible, we were in fact simultaneously undertaking a change of data model, a change from implicit to explicit operation definitions, and the introduction of more structure into the specification [1]. It is clear that, in a tool supported development, the unsupported stages are likely to be the most error prone and it is imperative therefore to minimise the complexity of the unsupported stages.

It is sobering to note that all stages where development took place introduced faults!

7 Effort by stages

The distribution of effort by project stage is shown in Figure 8. As might have been expected, the bulk of the design effort was in the main development in B. A substantial component was also expended on the early specifications in VDM. Very little effort was required during the testing stage.

Some activities, for example the initial B specification and its animation, are grouped together as they were carried out simultaneously and no separate effort figures were kept.

The faults found can be plotted against these efforts as a histogram with the width of columns representing the relative effort expended in each stage. However, when inspecting this it must be remembered that some stages involved development whereas others purely involved review.

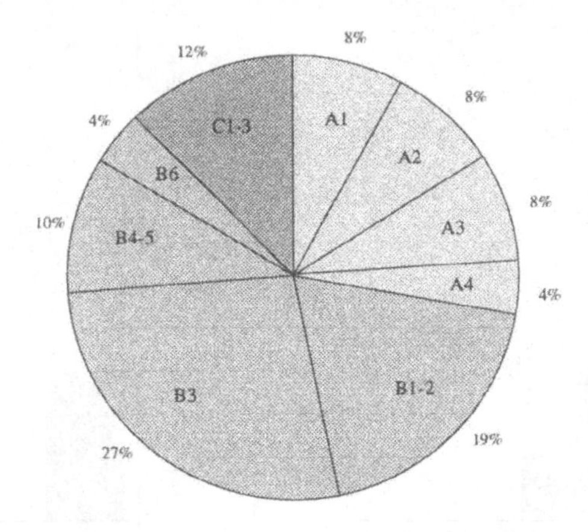

Fig. 8. Pie chart of effort by project stages

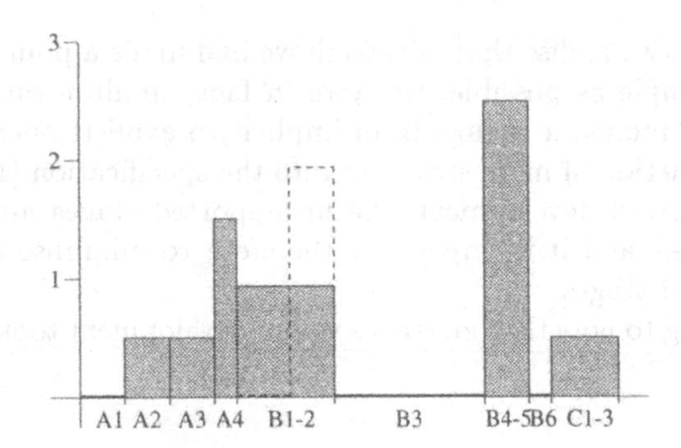

Fig. 9. Faults found per day by project stages

For stages B1-2, one cannot assess how much effort was expended in finding faults through animation and how much on development, but if one assumes that approximately one half of this effort was spent on each activity, then the dotted line applies.

Note how the most efficient fault finding occurs during test generation, animation and proof. Although this can perhaps be attributed to the fact that most faults were found before testing occurred, the test generation and proof stages allow a different perspective on the specification and highlight problems which might otherwise be invisible to the developer.

8 Conclusions

Conclusions drawn from this experiment should be moderated by the small size of the development and the correspondingly small number of faults detected. The development team was also small and staffed by self-selected individuals who, being keen to make a success of the experiment, were perhaps better motivated than average. It would not be wise therefore to extrapolate these results to larger projects. The lead partner will, however, be repeating the experiment with another development team.

An underlying assumption of the "Fault Grid" style of presentation is that activities in the development process are carried out in a linear fashion; it is difficult to present the results of performing activities in parallel, where the same faults may be discovered by more than one activity. Another feature of the "Fault Grid" presentation is that there is no record of faults found and introduced at the same stage. This is not considered to be a serious drawback, since, by their very nature, the cost of correcting such errors is low.

No attempt was made to moderate the effectiveness of fault finding by the severity of the faults found. Such an analysis could contribute to an estimate of the cost-effectiveness of each activity. None of the diagrams emphasise the fact that early fault detection saves money. It might be possible to estimate how much effort a process has saved in relation to how soon faults are discovered by keeping a record of how much effort is required to repair each faults found, and estimating how much effort would have been required to fix that fault if it had not been discovered until the last stage. The appropriate facts were not recorded in this project.

Unfortunately, due to some large-scale restructuring in the lead organisation, the code developed in this project never reached the production stage, and so no data is available on validation test and customer use. In particular, it remains unknown whether any types of error, perhaps peculiar to the use of formal methods, remained undetected by the development process.

Despite these qualifications, there is evidence in these results in favour of formal methods. Faults are inevitable and there detection is aided by formalisation. Amongst other things it is noted that all early stages, whether testing or development, found faults. It seems that any analysis , whether animation, PO generation, proof, or testing, is worthwhile. These activities are only possible once the objects involved are formalised.

This project has contributed to the beginnings of an accumulation of evidence for the benefits of formal methods. It has raised awareness of the need to gather such evidence for larger projects and suggested some techniques for doing so.

References

1. J.C. Bicarregui, J. Dick and E. Woods, Supporting the length of formal development: from diagrams to VDM to B to C Proceedings, 7th International Conference on: Putting into practice method and tools for information system design, Nantes (France), October '95, IUT de Nantes, H. Habrias (Editor) 1995.

2. J.C. Bicarregui and B. Ritchie. Invariants, frames and postconditions: a comparison of the VDM and B notations. In *Proceedings of Formal Methods Europe '93*, Lecture Notes in Computer Science, Springer-Verlag, 1993.
3. Jeremy Dick and Jerome Loubersac. A Visual Approach to VDM: Entity-Structure Diagrams. Technical Report DE/DRPA/91001, Bull, 68, Route de Versailles, 78430 Louveciennes (France), January 1991.
4. Jeremy Dick and Alain Faivre. Automating the generation and sequencing of test cases from model-based specifications. In J.C.P. Woodcock and P.G. Larsen, editors, *FME'93: Industrial-Strength Formal Methods*, pages 268–284, Formal Methods Europe, Springer-Verlag, April 1993. Lecture Notes in Computer Science 670.
5. J.Dick, Fault grids: another way of presenting fault counts, Software Reliability and Metrics Club Newsletter, Issue 16, July 1995, p 2-4. (published by the Centre for Software Reliability, University of Newcastle upon Tyne).
6. Des Maisey and Jeremy Dick, Measuring the quality of the development life cycle process, Submitted to SQM96, Software Quality Measurement.
7. U.K. Department of Trade and Industry, TickIT: Guide to Software Quality Management, System Construction and Certification using ISO9001/EN29001/BS5750 Part 1, February 1992, TickIT Project Office, 68 Newman Street, London, W1A 4SE, UK.
8. M.C. Paulk, W. Curtis, M.B. Chrissis, C.V. Weber, Capability Maturity Model for Software, Version 1.1, Carnegie Mellon University Software Engineering Institute Technical Report, CME/SEI-93-TR-24, February 1993.
9. E. Woods, The Development of a Software Subsystem Using VDM and B, University of Manchester, Board for Continuing Education, Department of Computer Science, MSc Thesis, 1995.
10. J. Dick and E. Woods, Lessons Learned Applying Formal Methods to System Software Development, submitted (July 1995) to IEEE Software.
11. Yourdon Inc., The Yourdon Systems Method: Model Driven Systems Development, Prentice Hall, Englewood Cliffs, NJ, USA, 1993, ISBN 0-13-285818-5

Applying the B Technologies to CICS

Jonathan Hoare[1]
Jeremy Dick, Dave Neilson and Ib Sørensen[2]

[1] IBM UK Limited, Hursley
[2] B-Core (UK) Ltd., Oxford Science Park

Abstract. This paper[3] reports on the experiences of IBM Hursley in using the Z notation and the B-Method [Abr95] [Abr93] in developing new function for IBM's CICS product[4] [IBM94].

A major constraint on the project was the need to produce code that not only corresponded to its required function, but also met a number of stringent non-functional requirements in areas such as integration, performance and maintenance.

The Z notation was used to capture the required function, and the resulting specification was hand-translated into AMN. The B-Toolkit, with project-specific extensions, was then used for the development down to PL/X code.

The success of this endeavour is discussed here. The use of Z and the B-Method were very successful in addressing the new functional requirements. Meeting the non-functional requirements, however, was more difficult.

1 Introduction

The application of mathematical methods to the development of IBM's CICS products began in 1982 with a collaboration between Hursley and the Programming Research Group at Oxford University on the use of the Z notation [Spi89] [Wor92] for the specification. Initially Z was used in the CICS code restructuring initiative [CN88] and since then it has been used for the specification of most new components of CICS as well as parts of the API [CNS89].

In this Z based development, whilst the specification stage was formal, the rest of the process did not change. The aim of IBM's use of the B-Method [NH94] is to reduce the effort in design and coding by extending the use of mathematical techniques and associated tools to cover these later stages, consequently allowing developers to concentrate on the creative aspects of software design.

The current project began in March 1993, when a site licence for the B-Toolkit [B-C93] was obtained for Hursley, and a collaborative contract was set up with B-Core (UK) Ltd..

[3] Parts of this paper are based on [Hoa95].

[4] CICS is a trademark of IBM Corporation.

2 The B-Method and B-Toolkit

The B-Method [NH94] [ALN+91] [Abr95] is a state-based method which uses the Abstract Machine Notation (AMN). Invented by J-R Abrial, the notation is based broadly on the same mathematics as Z (Zermelo set-theory and predicate logic), extended by a generalised notion of substitution. It contains a very small imperative programming language augmented by a number of specification constructs for expressing non-determinism. AMN semantics is compact and thus tractable for sizable developments.

AMN does not address concurrency. The aspects of systems addressed by the B-Method are similar to those of Z and VDM.

AMN admits three constructs: **MACHINES** which are expressed using only specification constructs, **REFINEMENTS** which may mix specification constructs with imperative statements, and **IMPLEMENTATIONS** in which all non-determinism is resolved through the use of imperative constructs only. Implementations are very easy to translate into commonly used programming languages.

The B-Method encourages software development in layers. Top level specifications are implemented in terms of lower level specifications, or designs which contain more detail. Thus the process of refinement decomposes abstract machines into smaller machines which are separately implementable through full information hiding. The verification conditions that must be proven for correct refinements are stipulated by the method.

The B-Toolkit [B-C93] provides a suite of programs that support the B-Method. These include a parser, typechecker, animator, proof obligation generator, proof tools and code translators. The three main products of a B development are code, design documentation and proof listings. The tools co-operate in a rigorously controlled programming environment driven by a dependency manager, which ensures the consistency of these three main products.

A major feature of the project reported in this paper is the extension of the B-Toolkit to accommodate the CICS development environment. These extensions are described in detail in Section 5.

The B-Method and B-Toolkit were selected as they were considered at the time to represent the only practical approach to formal refinement.

3 Approach

This project began with what has become standard practice in the CICS organisation: the production of an initial requirements document called the *Product Level Design* (PLD) that laid out the requirements which were to be addressed by the proposed component and included an abstract Z specification of the new function which was to be provided. Also included were details of some non-functional characteristics that needed agreement prior to the design phase.

In order to link into the B-Method, the Z specification in the PLD was rewritten in AMN, and the B-Toolkit animator was used to validate the hand translation. A certain amount of proof work was also carried out at the specification level at this stage.

An AMN design was then created to prototype the system against a model of the underlying API consisting of a set of C libraries. C code was generated from the prototype design, run and tested.

Satisfied with the overall design, the development team then proceeded to redevelop towards the final target language, PL/X, a PL/1-like IBM proprietary systems programming language. To achieve this, a new set of B-Toolkit system libraries had to be hand-coded in PL/X to form the target of the development.

Using a specially developed translator, PL/X was generated as the final code. This was subject to unit test, integration test and system test.

Figure 1 summarises the approach taken, showing the dependencies in the various activities undertaken.

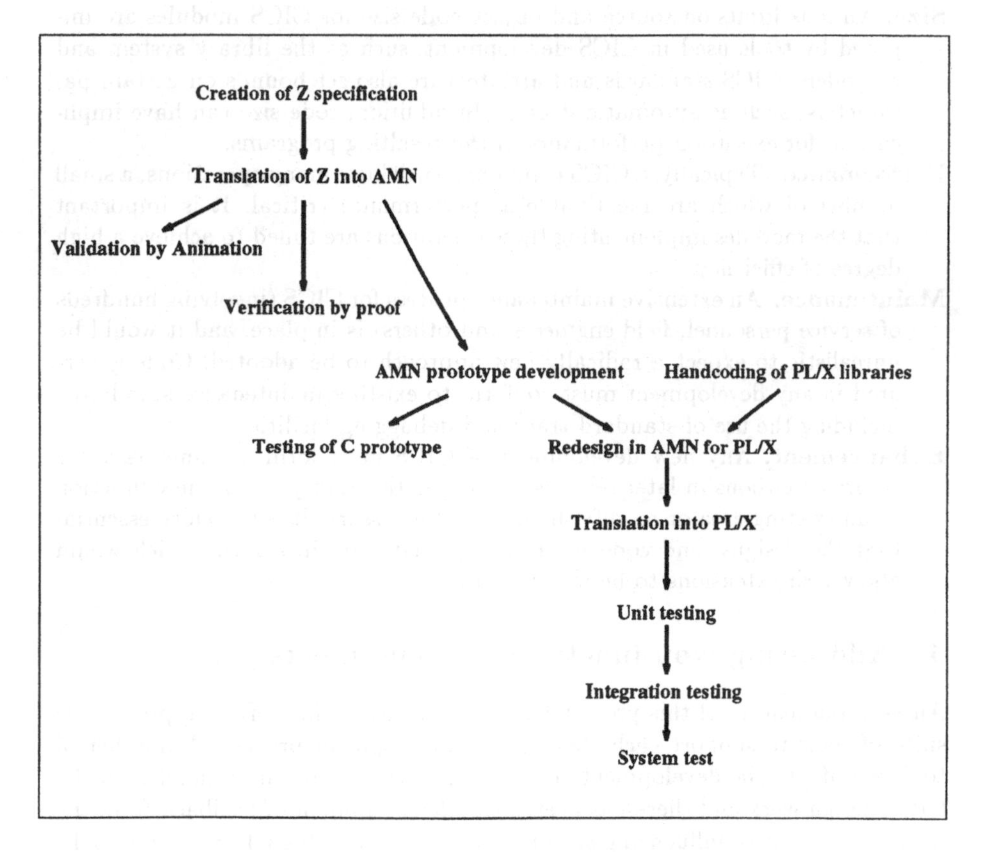

Fig. 1. The development approach adopted.

4 Non-functional Requirements

With an installed customer base of in excess of 30,000 licences, CICS is a mature product with a well established architecture and support infrastructure to which any further development must conform. For the application of a new method to CICS development, as described in this paper, this presents a number of challenges.

Several important non-functional requirements are not normally stated in the PLD, but are implicit for any new development. Amongst these are the following:

Architecture. The CICS architecture imposes a number of constraints, including the use of PL/X as the target language, CDURUN[5] definitions for interfaces between components, CICS storage management facilities (as opposed to native operating system functions), and the general use of CICS facilities for synchronisation and concurrency control.

Size. Various limits on source and object code size for CICS modules are imposed by tools used in CICS development, such as the library system and compilers. CICS standards and architecture also set bounds on certain parameters, such as automatic storage. In addition, code size can have implications for execution performance of the resulting programs.

Performance. Typically, a CICS component will have many operations, a small number of which are identifiable as performance critical. It is important that the modules implementing these operations are tuned to achieve a high degree of efficiency.

Maintenance. An extensive maintenance process for CICS (involving hundreds of service personnel, field engineers and others) is in place, and it would be unrealistic to expect a radically new approach to be adopted. Code generated in any development must conform to existing maintenance standards, including the use of standard trace and debugging facilities.

Enhancement. Any new development of CICS must form a sound basis for future extensions in later releases, including the ability to add new function to an existing area or modify the design if necessary. It is therefore essential that the designs, and code where appropriate, are in a form which would allow such extensions to be made readily.

5 Addressing Non-functional Requirements

An essential feature of this project has been the availability of a comprehensive suite of tools to support each stage of the development process. A number of tools specific to the development environment were created in parallel with the CICS design work and there has been a significant amount of feedback from the project in this area, influencing not only the evolution of the CICS specific tools, but also parts of the base toolkit.

This section describes those elements of the toolkit which were developed in order to meet specific non-functional requirements.

[5] A high-level language for the definition of CICS internal interfaces.

The PL/X translators and library coding tools.
An implicit non-functional requirement was that the IBM internal PL/X language should be used for the eventual code, and so an appropriate translator for AMN implementations was incorporated into the toolkit. This tool incorporated program transformation to improve the quality of the final code. A coding tool was also provided to assist in the production of the lowest level library modules.

Control Block generator.
The base B-Toolkit includes a utility called the base generator to produce a complex specification and its AMN implementation from a high level description of the encapsulated state, written in a special definition language. A similar facility was required for CICS whereby the software developer can give an abstract description of the control blocks needed in his design. The control block generator takes this description, and produces a specification which encapsulates access to the control block, together with a corresponding PL/X implementation. This was required in order to use the standard CICS facilities for storage management.

CDURUN generator.
The internal interfaces between CICS components (domains) are defined using a special language called CDURUN. In order for other parts of CICS to be able to use a new component it is necessary to produce a CDURUN definition for the top level interface. To meet this requirement a generator tool was written which produces a CDURUN definition and an AMN specification from a high level description of the interface. An output from this tool is also used to determine the action of the final CICS module construction tool.

Module construction.
The physical organisation of code into modules in the CICS environment often does not correspond to the layered logical structure of a B development. Instead, a vertical partitioning is used, in which all the PL/X code needed to implement a group of top-level operations is collected into a single compilable file or module. The CICS module construction tool performs this vertical partitioning for a B development by restructuring the B development tree. Such a vertical partitioning improves the performance of the final code by localising the flow of control.

Trace formatting.
For debugging purposes, particularly during maintenance, CICS standards require execution trace entries to be appended to a log file. An offline utility program is used to interpret the trace entries, allowing CICS' internal processing to be reconstructed. A facility was added to the B-Toolkit to add trace entries into the PL/X generated from AMN implementations, and to produce the corresponding trace interpretation code.

Dump formatting.
If an error occurs during CICS execution, or if explicitly requested, a storage dump is written to disk. For maintenance purposes, an offline utility program

is used to reconstruct the state of each CICS component at the time that the dump was taken. To meet this requirement, a facility was added to the B-Toolkit to generate code automatically for this utility.

Code annotation.

CICS maintenance requires code to be well annotated. The B-Toolkit translation process was extended by adding facilities that produce automatic annotation, hence increasing the traceability of program fragments back to AMN designs.

The GML markup tool.

The base B-Toolkit produces formatted output documents in the form of LaTeX source. IBM, however, uses its own proprietary markup language, GML [IBM89], for its documentation. It was therefore necessary to add an option to the toolkit to produce GML output instead of LaTeX.

The CICS specific tools were incorporated into the same dependency and configuration management environment as that of the base tools in the B-Toolkit.

Figure 2 shows the interaction of the tools specific to this project and the entities that they exchange. Processes appear as shaded diamond shapes; objects acted upon by those processes as rectangles. The rounded box marked 'Layered Design Process' embodies all the other work carried out within the base tools of the B-Toolkit.

The ease with which new tools could be added to the B-Toolkit was remarkable. This extensibility is achieved in such a way that all tools constitute a complete integrated development environment. The ability to so extend the B-Method and supporting tools is a direct consequence of working with a uniform syntax in all kernel tools.

6 Assessment of Results

The estimate at the outset of the project for the number of PL/X statements required to implement the specified function was 15 KPS[6], whereas the B development resulted in 20.4 KPS of PL/X. This last figure includes code that is replicated as a result of the vertical partitioning used during module construction, estimated to be approximately 35% ot the total. Normalising by this factor gives a figure of 13.3 KPS. Effort expended on the development amounted to 30 man-months (not including tool development).

The B development was structured into layers comprising 61 AMN constructs (abstract machines and implementations). The top layer specification contained 30 operations, fanning out into 324 distinct operations in the overall development. Four control blocks were used to define the concrete data structures, containing a total of 70 data fields. The generated PL/X comprised 8 modules.

Despite the complexity of the project, the B-Method proved highly satisfactory in meeting the functional requirements. Complete functionality was achieved down to running code, first in C in a simulated environment, and then

[6] 1000 program statements.

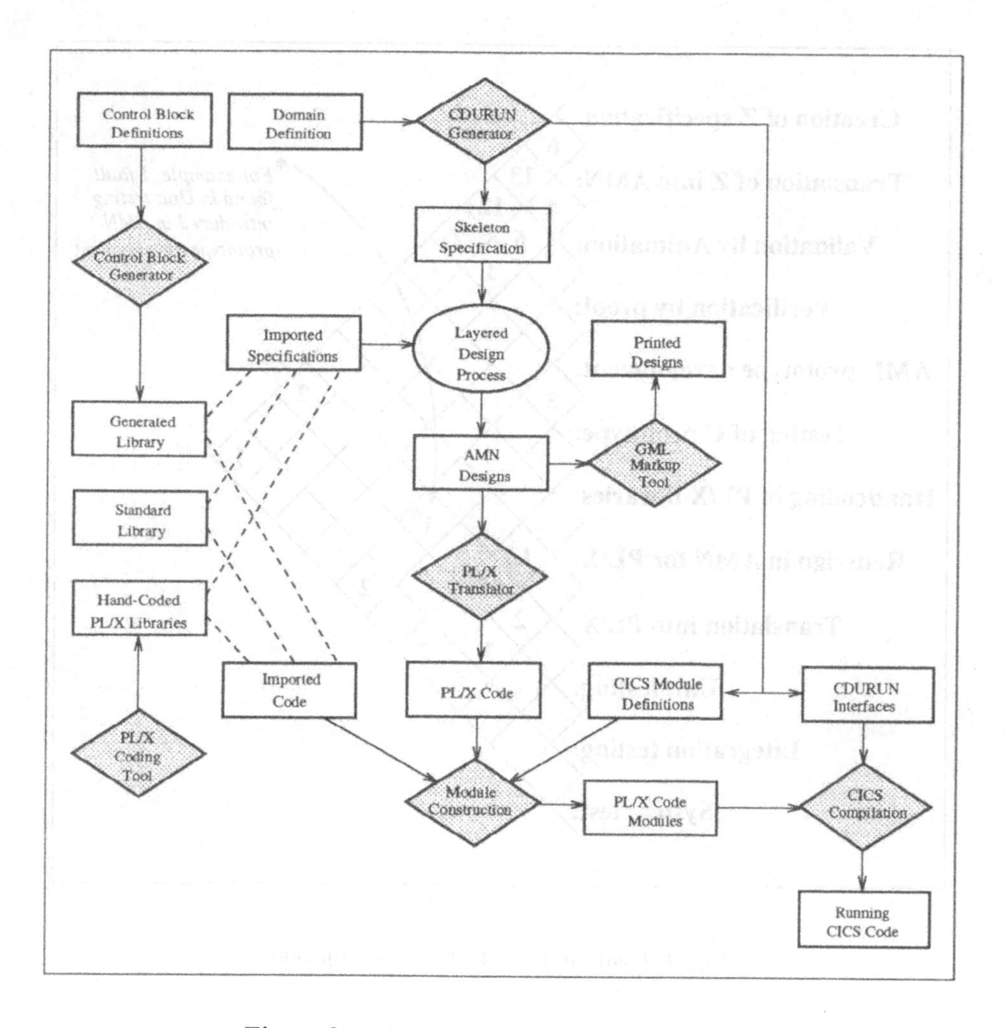

Fig. 2. Organisation of the CICS-specific tools.

in PL/X in the CICS environment. No data design errors were found in the AMN, no coding errors were produced in the code generated from AMN, and only easily correctable errors of omission in algorithmic design were encountered.

A summary of the numbers of faults found in each development activity is found in the Fault Grid [Dic95] in Figure 3.

The clusters of errors on the diagram reveal the activities that are prone to introducing errors. These are as follows.

- The creation of the original Z specification, which was carried out with no tool support apart from a type-checker. The bulk of these errors where found

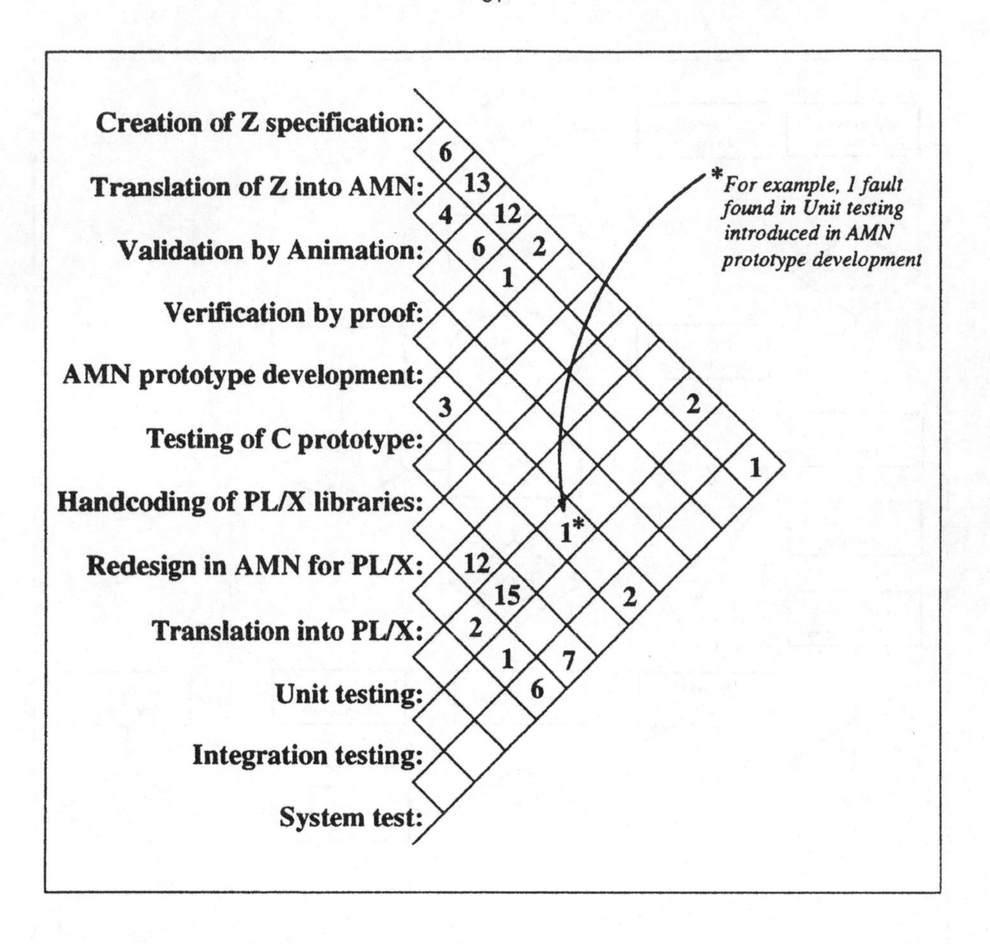

Fig. 3. Fault Grid for the CICS deveopment.

by animation and proof work performed on the AMN after translation. This underlines the importance of such tools in assessing the quality of a specification.

- The hand-coding of the PL/X libraries, which was carried out with limited tool support (in the form of the PL/X Coding Tool).

Note in particular the small number of faults found during testing of the that related to the original specification, three in total. The one fault at the peak of the grid (where the correction of errors is the most costly) was concerned with the invocation of an operation outside of its precondition.

The integration requirements of the CICS architecture were met successfully by the creation of three specific tools: the Control Block Generator, the CDU-

RUN Generator and the Module Construction tool.

The ability to produce code semi-automatically for dump and trace analysis tools was considered to be a distinct asset, and saved considerable effort in comparison with hand-coding. Also, the propagation of design annotations into the code, including traceability information, reduced programming effort.

In the final review, however, the code fell short of satisfying the non-functional requirements detailed below.

Size. The generated code exceeded acceptable limits for the CICS environment in several respects:

- The call-by-value parameter passing mechanism increases the requirement for automatic storage, and consequently causes the CICS architecture limits to be exceeded in some situations. More insight into how to use call-by-reference mechanisms is required before program transformation techniques can be used successfully to address this problem.
- Greater code size implies an increase in the number of variables, and a corresponding reduction in the ability of the PL/X compiler to make sensible use of base registers for optimisation purposes. This problem has been partly addressed by adding program transformations which remove many local variables used to pass values between operations.
- The volume of automatically generated annotation in the PL/X code made the source files too large for the CICS library system to handle. This problem could be addressed by finding the right balance in the amount of annotation generated.

Performance. The final code was not considered to be adequately efficient for certain critical operations. The reasons for this were:

- The hierarchical design adopted in the project is reflected in the structure of the final code. Where an operation has to access two distinct encapsulated data items through sub-operations, algorithmic control cannot descend below the lowest common ancestor of the two items. The effect of this is that control has to repeatedly descend and ascend through a series of layers to effect the operation, thus introducing inefficiency. It is possible that an alternative design could have been found to alleviate this problem. The addition of multiple refinement to the B-Method could also help in this area.
- Call-by-value is used in the generated code, sometimes making it necessary to copy quite large structures on calling functions, with consequent inefficiency. Program transformations applied at the code generation stage went some way to solving this problem by removing redundant parameter passing.
- Manual optimisation techniques, which would typically be used in association with traditional development, were not applied. Some of these techniques can be automated, but others, by their very nature, are not automatable, since they require an empirical approach. Manual post-hoc modification of generated code is undesirable in that it invalidates the AMN design, hence undermining many of the benefits of the method.

Maintenance / Enhancement. The code was not considered acceptable for maintenance and extensibility according to CICS standards, for the following reasons:

- The code, even with annotations, was not comprehensible enough to make it modifiable with confidence. Here, efficiency considerations in the use of in-line code to avoid function calls adversely affected readability.
- Modifications to the PL/X would have to be factored back into the AMN. For external logistical reasons, the decision was taken only to maintain the code at the PL/X source level.
- Logistical concerns raised issues regarding the longevity of the tools and the maintenance of relevant skills.

7 Recommendations

Given the stringent constraints imposed by the development environment, a compromise between traditional methods and the full B-Method would have been more suitable.

Our recommendation would be to use the base generators and libraries to produce an abstract executable prototype in which all major design decisions are cleanly expressed. Without the need to include implementation details of no relevance to the fundamental data or algorithmic design, there would be more freedom to remain abstract.

The prototype should be developed using the full B-Method from specification to low-level design, using typechecking and animation at every stage as a means of validation. Verification by proof should be carried out on selected modules.

When satisfied with the design, the development should be completed by traditional coding methods in compliance with the external requirements, working from the lowest level formal design of the prototype.

8 Conclusion

Never before have tool-supported formal methods been applied to this extent on an IBM project of such complexity. A major contributory factor in overcoming the considerable challenges encountered was the commitment of the project team working in close cooperation with the tool suppliers.

Whilst the meeting of non-functional constraints was a considerable challenge, overall the application of the B-Method in the CICS project was highly successful in addressing the functional requirements of the development.

Software engineering methods and tools often ignore the problem of non-functional requirements. Indeed, it is difficult to conceive of a generic tool sufficiently flexible in its approach to cater for the diversity of external constraints imposed by existing development environments.

For new developments, however, particularly those without such predetermined constraints, this project has demonstrated the feasibility of a tool-supported rigorous development, encompassing formal specification through to automatic translation into code.

References

[Abr93] J.R. Abrial. B-Technology technical overview. 1993.

[Abr95] J.R. Abrial. *The B-Book - Assigning Programs to Meanings.* 1995.

[ALN+91] J.R. Abrial, M.K.O. Lee, D.S. Neilson, P.N. Scharbach, and I.H. Sorensen. The B-method (software development). In W.J. Prehn, S.; Toetenel, editor, *VDM 91. Formal Software Development Methods. 4th International Symposium of VDM Europe Proceedings.*, volume 2, pages 398–405. BP Res., Sunbury Res. Centre, Sunbury-on-Thames, UK, Springer-Verlag, Berlin, Germany, October 1991.

The B-method is a formal software development process for the production of highly reliable, portable and maintainable software which is verifiably correct with respect to its functional specification. The method uses the abstract machine notation (AMN) as the language for specification, design and implementation within the process. AMN is a sugared and extended version of E.W. Dijkstra's (1976), guarded command notation with built-in structuring mechanisms for the construction of large systems. The method is supported over the entire spectrum of activities from specification to implementation by a set of computer-aided tools. (3 Refs).

[B-C93] B-Core (UK) Ltd. B-Toolkit User Manual. *(available from B-Core (UK) Ltd. on request)*, 1993.

[CN88] B. P. Collins and C. J. Nix. The use of software engineering, including the Z notation in the development of CICS. *Quality Assurance*, 14(3), September 1988.

[CNS89] B. P. Collins, J. E. Nicholls, and I. H. Sorensen. Introducing formal methods: The CICS experience with Z. *IBM Technical Report TR12.260*, 1989.

[Dic95] Dick, J. Fault grids: another way of presenting fault counts. *Software Reliability and Metrics Club Newsletter*, (16), 1995.

[Hoa95] J. P. Hoare. Application of the B-Method to CICS. In J. P. Bowen and M. Hinchey, editors, *Applications of Formal Methods.* Prentice Hall International, 1995.

[IBM89] IBM Corporation. *The IBM Publishing Systems BookMaster General Information. Manual GC34-5006*, 1989.

[IBM94] IBM Corporation. *CICS Family: General Information. Manual GC33-0155*, 1994.

[NH94] D. S. Neilson and Sorensen I. H. The B-technologies: A system for computer aided programming. In U. H. Engberg, K. G. Larsen, and P. D. Mosses, editors, *Proceedings of the 6th Nordic Workshop on Programming Theory*, pages 18–35. B-Core (UK) Ltd., BRICS Notes Series, Univ. Aarhus, Denmark, 17-19 October 1994.

[Spi89] J. M. Spivey. *The Z Notation: A Reference Manual.* Prentice Hall, Hemel Hempstead, 1989.

[Wor92] J. B. Wordsworth. *Software Development with Z: a Practical Approach to Formal Methods in Software Engineering.* Addison-Wesley, 1992.

Refining Action Systems within B-Tool

M. Waldén[1] and K. Sere[2]

[1] Åbo Akademi University, Department of Computer Science, FIN-20520 Turku, Finland, Marina.Walden@abo.fi

[2] University of Kuopio, Department of Computer Science and Applied Mathematics, P.O.Box 1627, FIN-70211 Kuopio, Finland, Kaisa.Sere@uku.fi

Abstract. Action systems is a formalism designed for the construction of parallel and distributed systems in a stepwise manner within the refinement calculus. In this paper we show how action systems can be derived and refined within a mechanical proof tool, the B-Tool. We describe how action systems are embedded in B-Tool. Due to this embedding we can now develop parallel and distributed systems within the B-Tool. We also show how a typical and nontrivial refinement rule, the superposition refinement rule, is formalized and applied on action systems within B-Tool. A derivation towards a distributed load balancing algorithm is given as a case study.

1 Introduction

Action systems are used to construct parallel and distributed systems in a stepwise manner as described by Back et al. [2, 4]. They are often developed using a poweful program modularization and structuring method called *superposition* [7, 9, 2]. In superposition some new functionality is added to an algorithm in the form of additional variables and assignments to these while the original computation is preserved.

Stepwise refinement of action systems is formalized within the *refinement calculus* [4] based on the weakest precondition calculus of Dijkstra [6]. A formalization of superposition as a refinement step within this calculus is put forward by Back and Sere [3]. Superposing one mechanism onto another often constitutes a large refinement step with many proof obligations. An example of verifying a complex distributed algorithm using superposition refinement is given in [13]. To get more confidence in the correctness proofs we need to use some mechanical tool. In this paper we show how superposition refinement of action systems can be performed using B-Tool.

The name B-Tool will in this paper refer to the B-Method and the B-Toolkit. The B-Toolkit [11] comprises a set of tools supporting a method of software development, the B-Method [1]. This method is succesfully used in many industrial projects applying formal methods. The B-Method is founded on the set theory and relies on an extension of the weakest precondition calculus of Dijkstra [6].

In this paper we show how action systems can be embedded in the B-Tool. We compare the refinement notions of the two systems, the action systems and the B-Method, and show how the superposition refinement rule formalized on action systems can be applied within the B-Tool. Since the superposition is a method for developing parallel and distributed systems, embedding the superposition method in the B-Tool makes it possible to develop parallel and distributed systems within B-Tool.

We will first briefly describe action systems and superposition refinement in section 2. In section 3, we give an overview of the B-Tool. In section 4, we show how action systems and superposition refinement are embedded in B-Tool. Finally, B-Tool is used for developing a load balancing algorithm of Hofstee et al. [8]. The first refinement step towards a distributed algorithm is given as an example. The complete derivation is reported in [14]. The load balancing algorithm within B-Tool is described in section 5. We conclude in section 6.

2 Action Systems and Superposition Refinement

We first consider the action systems framework together with its associated refinement calculus. We only give a very brief introduction here. More on these topics and further references can be found elsewhere [2, 3, 4].

2.1 Action Systems

An *action system* $\mathcal{A}$ is a statement of the form

$$\mathcal{A} \stackrel{\text{def}}{=} |[\ \textbf{var}\ x;\ x := x_0;\ \textbf{do}\ A_1\ \|\ \ldots\ \|\ A_m\ \textbf{od}\ ]| : z$$

on *state variables* $y = x \cup z$, where the variables z are the *global* variables and x are the *local* variables. Each variable is associated with some domain of values. The set of possible assignments of values to the state variables constitutes the *state space*. The initialisation statement $x := x_0$ assigns initial values to the state variables x.

Each action A_i is of the form $g_i \rightarrow S_i$ where the *guard* g_i is a boolean expression on the state variables and the *body* S_i is a statement on the state variables. We denote the guard g_i of A_i by gA_i and the body S_i by sA_i. Furthemore, we say that an action is enabled in a state when its guard evaluates to *true* in that state.

The behavior of an action system is that of Dijkstra's guarded iteration statement [6] on the state variables: the initialisation statement is executed first, thereafter, as long as there are enabled actions, one action at a time is nondeterministically chosen and executed. When all the actions are disabled the action system terminates.

If two actions are independent, i.e. they do not have any variables in common, they can be executed in parallel. Their parallel execution is then equivalent to executing the actions one after the other, in either order.

2.2 Refinement of Action Systems

The superposition method has been formalized as a program refinement rule within the refinement calculus for action systems. Let us now briefly describe this calculus.

Let S be a statement on the program variables x, z and S' a statement on the program variables x', z. Let the invariant $R(x, x', z)$ be a relation on these variables. Then S is *data refined* by S' using the data invariant R, denoted $S \leq_R S'$, if for any postcondition Q

$$R \wedge \text{wp}(S, Q) \Rightarrow \text{wp}(S', \exists x. R \wedge Q)$$

holds. Here wp is the *weakest precondition* predicate transformer [6]. Successive data refinements are modelled as follows: If $S_0 \leq_{R_1} S_1$ and $S_1 \leq_{R_2} S_2$ then $S_0 \leq_{R_1 \wedge R_2} S_2$.

Data refinement of actions is defined in a similar way, considering that the weakest precondition [6] for an action is defined as:

$$\text{wp}(A, R) \stackrel{\text{def}}{=} gA \Rightarrow \text{wp}(sA, R).$$

Let A be an action on the program variables x, z and A' an action on the program variables x', z. Let the invariant $R(x, x', z)$ be a relation on these variables. Then A is data refined by A' using R, denoted $A \leq_R A'$, if

$$\begin{array}{ll} \text{(A1)} & \{gA'\};\ sA \leq_R sA' \text{ and} \\ \text{(A2)} & R \wedge gA' \Rightarrow gA. \end{array}$$

Intuitively, (A1) means that A' has the same effect on the program variables that A has when A' is enabled and R holds and moreover, A' establishes R. The condition (A2) requires that A is enabled whenever A' is enabled provided R holds.

The superposition refinement of action systems is a special kind of data refinement and it is formally expressed as follows. Let $\mathcal{A}$ and $\mathcal{A}'$ be the two action systems:

$$\begin{array}{lll} \mathcal{A} & \stackrel{\text{def}}{=} & |[\ \textbf{var}\ x;\ x := x_0;\ \textbf{do}\ A_1\ \|\ \ldots\ \|\ A_m\ \textbf{od}\ ]| : z \text{ and} \\ \mathcal{A}' & \stackrel{\text{def}}{=} & |[\ \textbf{var}\ x, y;\ x, y := x_0, y_0;\ \textbf{do}\ A'_1\ \|\ \ldots\ \|\ A'_m\ \|\ B_1\ \|\ \ldots\ \|\ B_n\ \textbf{od}\ ]| : z. \end{array}$$

Let $g\mathcal{A}$ be the disjunction of the guards of the actions A_i, $g\mathcal{A}'$ the disjunction of the guards of the actions A'_i and $g\mathcal{B}$ the disjunction of the guards of the actions B_j. Then $\mathcal{A} \leq_R \mathcal{A}'$ using $R(x, y, z)$, if

$$\begin{array}{ll} \text{(S1)} & R(x_0, y_0, z), \\ \text{(S2)} & A_i \leq_R A'_i,\ \text{for } i = 1, \ldots, m, \\ \text{(S3)} & \mathit{skip} \leq_R B_j,\ \text{for } j = 1, \ldots, n, \\ \text{(S4)} & R \wedge \neg(g\mathcal{A}' \vee g\mathcal{B}) \Rightarrow \neg g\mathcal{A}, \\ \text{(S5)} & R \Rightarrow \text{wp}(\textbf{do}\ B_1\ \|\ \ldots\ \|\ B_n\ \textbf{od}, \mathit{true}). \end{array}$$

Informally, an action system $\mathcal{A}$ is correctly data refined by another action system $\mathcal{A}'$ using the data invariant R when

(S1) the initialisation in $\mathcal{A}'$ establishes R,
(S2) every action A_i is data refined by the corresponding A'_i using R,
(S3) every action B_j is a data refinement of the empty statement *skip* using R,
(S4) all actions in $\mathcal{A}$ are disabled whenever all actions in $\mathcal{A}'$ are disabled when R holds, i.e. the exit condition $\neg(g\mathcal{A}' \vee g\mathcal{B})$ of $\mathcal{A}'$ implies the exit condition $\neg g\mathcal{A}$ of $\mathcal{A}$ when R holds, and
(S5) the computation denoted by the actions $B_1, \ldots, B_n$ terminates provided R holds.

3 Overview of the B-Tool

A superposition refinement step is often large. In order to give more confidence in the correctness proof of a superposition step we want to use a mechanical tool. We will study B-Tool to see how it applies to action systems and how its proof rules agree with the superposition rule. The B-Toolkit [11] comprises a set of tools, which support a method of software development called the B-Method.

The B-Method is a mathematical method which gives a model oriented approach to software construction. The method is founded on set theory and relies on an extension of Dijkstra's weakest precondition calculus [6].

A program derivation in B-Method consists of a specification, possibly a number of refinements and an implementation. The *specification* is a high level description of a program under development and it usually involves a lot of nondeterminism. By the *refinements* the specification can stepwise be transformed into an implementation. This *implementation* represents the last refinement. It can directly be translated to executable code and it may not contain any nondeterminism.

Within B-Method the specifications, the refinements and the implementations are represented as Abstract Machines consisting of a context of global constraints and of operations on state variables. For specifying the operations B-Method uses the Abstract Machine Notation (AMN), which is a generalisation of Dijkstras guarded command notation. Every statement in AMN is a form of substitution. Each generated substitution S is defined as a predicate transformer which transforms a postcondition R into the weakest precondition for S to establish R, $\text{wp}(S, R)$.

The processing of Abstract Machines begins with syntax- and type-checking. Verification conditions needed for proving the specification consistency and the correctness of refinement steps can be automatically generated within the B-Toolkit. Furthermore, these verification conditions can be automatically or interactively proved using the so called autoprover or interprover, respectively. The provers are built on a mathematical library containing a collection of mathematical laws for the underlying set-theoretic notation. The autoprover first tries to discharge the proof obligations using the mathematical library. If the standard library is not enough, the user may supplement it with new necessary rules and then with the help of the interprover discharge the rest of the proof obligations.

```
MACHINE
  Machine_name(p)
CONSTRAINTS
  P
CONSTANTS
  c
PROPERTIES
  Q
VARIABLES
  x
INVARIANT
  R
INITIALISATION
  T
OPERATIONS
  Operation_name =  PRE L THEN S END ;
  :
END
```

Fig. 1. The syntactic structure of an abstract machine.

In addition to the above mentioned functions there are also facilities within B-Toolkit for generating code and documentation.

4 Embedding Superposition Refinement within B-Tool

We now show how action systems, their refinement, and the superposition refinement rule can be embedded in B-Tool.

4.1 Action Systems within B-Tool

Abstract Machine Specification We first look closer at how specifications are constructed within B-Tool. The syntactic structure of an abstract machine is given in Figure 1. An abstract specification, or abstract machine, in B-Tool is identified by a unique machine name. It can be supplied with parameters p for giving dimensional characteristics of the specification. The properties P of these parameters are given in the *constraints* clause. Furthermore, within the abstract machine we can introduce constants c which are defined in terms of the parameters and some given sets. The *properties* clause gives the definition Q of these constants.

The variables x in an abstract machine are defined in the *invariant* clause and initialised in the *initialisation* clause. The invariant R consist of a set of predicates including set-theoretical typing of each variable. The initialisation T is a substitution statement. A machine can also include variables of other machines to different extents.

An abstract machine has a number of operations. These operations are named procedures which might have parameters and/or be of resulting type. The operations are given in the form of substitutions using the AMN language. They are the interface of the machine. In Figure 1 the operation consists of a substitution S with a precondition L.

The internal consistency of the abstract specification in Figure 1 can now be proved in B-Tool by showing that the following five requirements are fulfilled:

$$
\begin{array}{ll}
\text{(C1)} & \exists p.P \\
\text{(C2)} & P \Rightarrow \exists c.Q \\
\text{(C3)} & (P \wedge Q) \Rightarrow \exists x.R \\
\text{(C4)} & (P \wedge Q) \Rightarrow \text{wp}(T, R) \\
\text{(C5)} & (P \wedge Q \wedge R \wedge L) \Rightarrow \text{wp}(S, R).
\end{array}
$$

The first three obligations are concerned with the consistency of the contextual information, i.e., the formal parameters, the constants and the variables. The fourth checks that the invariant is established initially and the fifth that each operation maintains the invariant.

Action Systems Let us now study how an action system can be embedded into this Abstract Machine specification. The AMN substitution $P \Rightarrow S$ is called the guarded substitution and is interpreted as guarding of the substitution S by the predicate P. The weakest precondition for the guarded substitution is defined as

$$\text{wp}(P \Rightarrow S, R) \stackrel{\text{def}}{=} P \Rightarrow \text{wp}(S, R).$$

This is, however, the same as the weakest precondition for the action $P \rightarrow S$. Hence, an action can be interpreted as a guarded substitution.

The syntax for a guarded substitution interpreted as an operation in B-Tool is:

Operation_name = PRE *true* THEN (SELECT P THEN S END) END ;

where the precondition has the value *true* and can be left out. The guarded substitution as an operation is then

SELECT P THEN S END .

Hence, we choose to represent each action in B-Tool by such an operation.

Let us now consider the following action system:

$$\mathcal{A} \stackrel{\text{def}}{=} |[\ \textbf{var}\ x;\ x := x_0;\ \textbf{do}\ A_1 \ [\!] \ A_2 \ [\!] \ A_3 \ \textbf{od} \ ]| : z$$

as well as its invariant $R(x, z)$ and its constraint $P(z)$. The invariant $R(x, z)$ describes the behaviour of the local variables x possibly in terms of the global variables z, while $P(z)$ gives the constraints of the variables z. We can now write the action system as the Abstract Machine specification *ActionSystem* as given in Figure 2. In the specification the global variables of an action system

$$\mathcal{A} \stackrel{\text{def}}{=} |[\ \mathbf{var}\ x;\ x := x_0;\ \mathbf{do}\ A_1\ \|\ A_2\ \|\ A_3\ \mathbf{od}\ ]|: z$$

```
MACHINE
  ActionSystem(z)
CONSTRAINTS
  P(z)
VARIABLES
  x
INVARIANT
  R(x, z)
INITIALISATION
  x := x0
OPERATIONS
  A1 = SELECT gA1 THEN sA1 END ;
  A2 = SELECT gA2 THEN sA2 END ;
  A3 = SELECT gA3 THEN sA3 END
END
```

Fig. 2. An action system and its embedding in an abstract machine.

are considered as parameters and, hence their constraints in $P(z)$ are given in the *constraint* clause. For the rest, the translation of action systems into AMN is straightforward.

A consistency proof of the specification is given using the autoprover in B-Toolkit verifying the proof obligations $(C1) - (C5)$.

4.2 Superposition Refinement within B-Tool

We will now study how the superposition rule can be interpreted within B-Tool. We begin by describing the Abstract Machine refinement in B-Tool.

Abstract Machine Refinement A refinement in B-Tool may either be a data refinement or an algorithmic refinement. Data refinement is achieved by a change of variables and the operations on them, while the algorithmic refinement allows the operations to be reformulated thereby making them more concrete without changing the state space. The refinement relation within B-Tool is transitive and monotonic.

If we have the machines N and M, where N refines M, then N and M must have identical operation signatures. This means that the corresponding operations in N and M must have identical names and, if the operations have parameters, these must also be identical. The machines N and M need, however, not contain the same variables. The machine N is produced by applying a syntactic construct, *Refinement*, to the machine M. The syntactic structure of an Abstract Machine refinement is given in Figure 3.

Although, a *Refinement* and a *Machine* resemble each other in many ways there are some differences. Firstly, a refinement has to state what it will refine, a machine or another refinement. Furthermore, the invariant R' of the refinement is an abstract relation that expresses the change of variables between the two

REFINEMENT
  Refinement_name
REFINES
  Machine_name
VARIABLES
  x'
INVARIANT
  R'
INITIALISATION
  T'
OPERATIONS
  Operation_name = PRE L' THEN S' END ;
  ⋮
END

Fig. 3. The syntactic structure of a refinement.

constructs, i.e. the relation between the variables x and x' in a data refinement. The operations of the refinement refer only to the variables x'.

In order to prove the refinement correct, a number of proof obligations are automatically created by B-Tool. The proof obligations created for the machine in Figure 1 and its refinement in Figure 3 are given below:

$$\begin{array}{ll} \text{(B1)} & (\exists(x,x').R \wedge R') \\ \text{(B2)} & \text{wp}(T', \neg\text{wp}(T, \neg R')) \\ \text{(B3)} & (\forall(x,x').(R \wedge R' \wedge L) \Rightarrow L') \\ \text{(B4)} & (\forall(x,x').(R \wedge R' \wedge L) \Rightarrow \text{wp}(S', \neg\text{wp}(S, \neg R'))). \end{array}$$

The first proof obligation asserts that the new invariant R' does not contradict the previous invariant R, while the second proof obligation checks that the new initialisation T' establishes a situation where the previous initialisation T cannot fail to establish the invariant R'. The last two obligations ensure the correctness of each operation. According to them the precondition L of operation S implies the precondition L' of S' when the invariants hold, i.e. the precondition is weakened. Moreover, an operation S' establishes a situation where the old operation S cannot fail to maintain R'. Due to the construction of the invariants, obligations (B2) and (B4) will also involve type-checking.

Superposition Step within B-Tool Let us now consider a superposition refinement $\mathcal{A}'$ of the action system $\mathcal{A}$ given above. We define $\mathcal{A}'$ as:

$$\mathcal{A}' \stackrel{\text{def}}{=} |[\ \textbf{var}\ x, y;\ x, y := x_0, y_0;\ \textbf{do}\ A'_1\ [\!]\ A'_2\ [\!]\ A'_3\ [\!]\ B_1\ [\!]\ B_2\ \textbf{od}\ ]| : z$$

and the invariant of the refinement as $R'(x, y, z)$. This refined action system can be embedded in an Abstract Machine refinement *RefActionSystem* as shown in

$$A' \stackrel{\text{def}}{=} \;|[\; \textbf{var}\; x, y;\; x, y := x_0, y_0;\; \textbf{do}\; A'_1 \,\|\, A'_2 \,\|\, A'_3 \,\|\, B_1 \,\|\, B_2 \;\textbf{od}\;]| : z$$

REFINEMENT
  RefActionSystem
REFINES
  ActionSystem
VARIABLES
  x', y
INVARIANT
  $R'(x', y, z) \wedge x' = x$
INITIALISATION
  $x', y := x_0, y_0$
OPERATIONS
  $A_1 =$ SELECT gA'_1 THEN sA'_1 END ;
  $A_2 =$ SELECT gA'_2 THEN sA'_2 END ;
  $A_3 =$ SELECT gA'_3 THEN sA'_3 END ;
  $B_1 =$ SELECT gB_1 THEN sB_1 END ;
  $B_2 =$ SELECT gB_2 THEN sB_2 END ;
  exit_cond =
    SELECT $\neg(gA'_1 \vee gA'_2 \vee gA'_3 \vee gB_1 \vee gB_2)$
    THEN *skip* END
END

Fig. 4. The refined action system and its embedding in a refinement machine.

Figure 4. The invariant R' includes the invariant R of the action system being refined.

In an action system refinement some variables x are left unchanged, these are the so called old variables. However, in B-Tool we cannot use the same variable names in the specification and the refinement. We, thus, rename the old variables to x' in the refinement and state the relationship $x' = x$ in the invariant of the refinement.

Furthermore, in B-Tool all the refinements use the same operation names, which means that all operations that will exist in the final refinement also have to exist in the first specification. Since we introduced the actions B_1, B_2 and *exit_cond* as operations in the machine refinement *RefActionSystem*, we also need to introduce corresponding operations in the machine specification *ActionSystem* as $B_i =$ BEGIN *skip* END for $i = 1, 2$, where we have skipped the precondition *true* as previously. We will return to *exit_cond* later.

We have expressed how an action system and its superposition refinement can be modelled as machines in B-Tool. Let us now consider the proof rule for superposition refinement of action systems. The five conditions (S1)-(S5) in the superposition rule are equivalent to refinement rules within B-Tool as will be shown below. We start by showing the equivalences for the first four superposition conditions. The treatment of the last condition (S5) is postponed.

(1) The condition (S1) is equivalent with the condition (B2), where

$$(S1): R'(x_0, y_0, z)$$
$$(B2): \mathrm{wp}((x', y := x_0, y_0), \neg\mathrm{wp}(x := x_0, \neg(R'(x', y, z) \wedge (x' = x)))),$$

because

$$\begin{aligned} &\mathrm{wp}((x', y := x_0, y_0), \neg\mathrm{wp}(x := x_0, \neg(R'(x', y, z) \wedge (x' = x)))) \\ \equiv\ &\mathrm{wp}((x', y := x_0, y_0), (R'(x', y, z) \wedge (x' = x_0))) \\ \equiv\ &(R'(x_0, y_0, z) \wedge (x_0 = x_0)) \\ \equiv\ &R'(x_0, y_0, z). \end{aligned}$$

(2) The condition (S2) corresponds to the condition $(B4[A_i])$, where

$$(S2): \quad A_i \leq_{R'} A'_i$$
$$(B4[A_i]): R'(x', y, z) \wedge (x' = x) \Rightarrow$$
$$\mathrm{wp}(A'_i, \neg\mathrm{wp}(A_i, \neg(R'(x', y, z) \wedge (x' = x)))).$$

B-Tool generates the following proof obligations from $(B4[A_i])$:
(i) $R'(x', y, z) \wedge (x' = x) \Rightarrow \mathrm{wp}(A'_i, \neg\mathrm{wp}(A_i, \neg(x' = x)))$
(ii) $R'(x', y, z) \wedge (x' = x) \Rightarrow \mathrm{wp}(A'_i, R'(x', y, z))$
(iii) $R'(x', y, z) \wedge (x' = x) \wedge gA'_i \Rightarrow gA_i$
These are, however, equivalent to the conditions (A1) and (A2) that define the data refinement between actions. The items (i) and (ii) correspond to (A1) and the item (iii) is the counterpart in B-Tool of condition (A2). Hence, (S2) corresponds to the condition $(B4[A_i])$.

(3) The condition (S3) corresponds to $(B4[B_i])$, where

$$(S3): \quad \mathit{skip} \leq_{R'} B_i$$
$$(B4[B_i]): R'(x', y, z) \wedge (x' = x) \Rightarrow$$
$$\mathrm{wp}(B_i, \neg\mathrm{wp}(\mathit{skip}, \neg(R'(x', y, z) \wedge (x' = x)))),$$

From $(B4[B_i])$ B-Tool generates the following proof obligations:
(i) $R'(x', y, z) \wedge (x' = x) \Rightarrow \mathrm{wp}(B_i, (x' = x))$
(ii) $R'(x', y, z) \wedge (x' = x) \Rightarrow \mathrm{wp}(B_i, R'(x', y, z))$
(iii) $R'(x', y, z) \wedge (x' = x) \wedge gB_i \Rightarrow \mathit{true}$
As above, these proof obligations correspond to the conditions $(A1)$ and $(A2)$ that are equivalent to $(S3)$ when instantiated appropriately.

(4) The condition (S4) corresponds to $(B4[\mathit{exit\_cond}])$, where

$$(S4): \quad R' \wedge \neg(g\mathcal{A}' \vee g\mathcal{B}) \Rightarrow \neg g\mathcal{A}$$
$$(B4[\mathit{exit\_cond}]): R'(x', y, z) \wedge (x' = x) \Rightarrow$$
$$\mathrm{wp}(\mathit{exit\_cond}', \neg\mathrm{wp}(\mathit{exit\_cond}, \neg(R'(x', y, z) \wedge (x' = x)))).$$

The operation *exit_cond* models the exit condition in an action system. The exit condition in the action system $\mathcal{A}'$ above is defined as $\neg(gA_1 \vee gA_2 \vee gA_3 \vee gB_1 \vee gB_2)$. The exit condition operation in the old action system $\mathcal{A}$ needs to be introduced as:

$$\mathit{exit\_cond} = \ \text{SELECT } \neg(gA_1 \vee gA_2 \vee gA_3) \text{ THEN } \mathit{skip} \text{ END}$$

From ($B4[\mathit{exit\_cond}]$) B-Tool generates the following proof obligations:
(i) $R'(x', y, z) \wedge (x' = x) \wedge g(\mathit{exit\_cond}') \Rightarrow (g(\mathit{exit\_cond}) \wedge (x' = x))$
(ii) $R'(x', y, z) \wedge (x' = x) \wedge g(\mathit{exit\_cond}') \Rightarrow (g(\mathit{exit\_cond}) \wedge R(x', y, z))$
(iii) $R'(x', y, z) \wedge (x' = x) \wedge g(\mathit{exit\_cond}') \Rightarrow g(\mathit{exit\_cond})$
These are easily seen to correspond to (S4).

The proof obligations (B1) and (B3) do not correspond to any of the conditions in the superposition rule. Since the invariant R is included in the invariant R' due to the superposition refinement, and the preconditions L and L' both have the value *true*, they trivially hold for the embedded action system.

Preliminary to relating the condition (S5) to a condition in the B-Method we present some additional constructs of the method.

Abstract Machine Implementation The Abstract Machine implementation is the only machine that allows loop-constructions in the operations. Since condition (S5) refers to a loop, we need to consider the implementation with a loop-construct to create a similar condition within B-Tool.

The loop-construct consists, apart from the loop, of an initialisation, an invariant, and a variant as follows:

$$T;\ \text{WHILE } P \text{ DO } S \text{ INVARIANT } R \text{ VARIANT } E \text{ END },$$

where P and R are predicates, T and S are AMN substitutions and E is an integer expression. The proof obligation created for such a loop with postcondition Q is the following:

$$\begin{array}{l}
(T1)\ \mathrm{wp}(T, R) \\
(T2)\ R \Rightarrow E \in \mathbf{N} \\
(T3)\ (\forall l.(R \wedge P) \Rightarrow \mathrm{wp}(S, R)) \\
(T4)\ (\forall l.(R \wedge P) \Rightarrow \mathrm{wp}(n := E, \mathrm{wp}(S, E < n))) \\
(T5)\ (\forall l.(R \wedge \neg P) \Rightarrow Q).
\end{array}$$

Here l denotes the variables modified within the loop. Following the obligations the initialisation T should establish the invariant R and the variant E should be an expression yielding a natural number. Furthermore, when the guard P of the loop holds, the body S should maintain the loop invariant R and decrease the variant E. Finally, the postcondition Q should hold when the loop terminates, i.e., when P does not hold anymore.

Termination of Auxiliary Actions Let us now proceed with the condition (S5): $R \Rightarrow \mathrm{wp}(\mathbf{do}\ B_1 \parallel \ldots \parallel B_n\ \mathbf{od}, \mathit{true})$. We need to find a variant such that the invariant R implies that the variant is a natural number and that the variant is decreased each time one of the actions in the loop is executed. These conditions are created as proof obligations for the WHILE-loop within B-Tool. We, thus, need to make a separate refinement step within B-Tool using a WHILE-loop to prove this condition.

In this refinement step the refined abstract specification has *true* as the invariant and *skip* as the initialisation and as the only operation. In the Abstract Machine implementation we then give a WHILE-loop with a variant E operating on some variables e. This operation generated from the action system $\mathcal{A}'$ is written as:

```
VAR x', y, e IN
  x' := x0; y := y0; e := e0;
  WHILE (gB1 ∨ gB2) DO
     IF gB1 THEN sB1
     ELSEIF gB2 THEN sB2
     END
     INVARIANT R'(x', y, z) ∧ R''(y, z, e)
     VARIANT E(e)
  END
END
```

The initialisation of the action system $\mathcal{A}'$ is the initialisation of the loop and the disjunction of the guards of the auxiliary actions is given as the WHILE-condition. Within the loop we represent the auxiliary actions with an *IF – ELSEIF*-substitution. Furthermore, the invariant $R'(x', y, z)$ of the Abstract Machine refinement is included in the invariant of the loop. The relation $R''(y, z, e)$ gives the definition of the variant and is also included in the invariant. A new expression $E(e)$ is created as the variant.

The condition (S5) in the superposition rule can now be translated into terms of proof obligations generated in B-Tool by:

(5) $\quad (S5) \equiv (T2) \wedge (T4).$

The proof obligations (T1), (T3), and (T5) do not directly correspond to any condition in the superposition rule. The obligation (T1) (and (T3)) is partly proved by proving the obligation (B2) (and $(B4[B_i])$), but additionally they check that the variant establishes the invariant $R''(y, z, e)$ in the initialisation and the operations. Since the postcondition of the action loop is considered to be *true* here, proof obligation (T5) holds trivially

5 Case study: Load Balancing Algorithm

As a case study we will formalize the load balancing algorithm of Hofstee et al. [8] within action systems and B-Tool. A first refinement step towards a distributed implementation of the algorithm is used to exemplify superposition refinement with B-Tool.

5.1 Load Balancing Algorithm

We consider a connected graph (V, E), where V is a finite set of nodes and E a finite set of edges on V. Let the nodes denote processes and the edges denote communication links between the processes. Each process is assumed to know the identities of its direct neighbours and the number of tasks it posesses, i.e. the load. Communication can only take place between nodes directly connected by an edge and it can go in both directions. Even so, the graph is considered to be a rooted directed tree, where the edges are directed towards the root. This assumption forces the load balancing to concentrate most of the tasks to the leaves of the tree and make it possible for the other nodes to transfer tasks from one branch to another.

The load balancing algorithm is given as an action system $\mathcal{B}$ below.

$$\begin{array}{ll} \mathcal{B} \stackrel{\text{def}}{=} & |[\ \textbf{var}\ load.i \in int\ \ \textbf{for}\ i \in V; \\ & \quad load.i := Load.i\ \ \textbf{for}\ i \in V; \\ & \quad \textbf{do}\ (bal\_load\_ij \parallel bal\_load\_ji)\ \ \textbf{for}\ (i,j) \in E\ \textbf{od} \\ &]|\!:\ top \in int \end{array}$$

Here *top* is a fixed positive number, the treshold, that states the preferable load of a process. In node i the number of tasks is denoted by $load.i$ and the initial value of the load is given by the constant $Load.i$. The indices i, j denote nodes. The actions are defined as follows:

$$bal\_load\_ij \stackrel{\text{def}}{=}$$
$$load.i < top \wedge load.j \geq top \rightarrow load.i, load.j := load.i + 1, load.j - 1$$

$$bal\_load\_ji \stackrel{\text{def}}{=}$$
$$load.i > top \wedge load.j \leq top \rightarrow load.i, load.j := load.i - 1, load.j + 1.$$

The total load of the system is stable after initialisation. If node i does not have enough tasks, i.e. its load is less than the treshold, and its father, node j, in the tree structure has a load greater or equal to the treshold, the action bal_load_ij is enabled and a task can be moved from node j to node i. On the other hand, if node i has too many task and its father, node j, has a load less or equal to the treshold, a task can be sent from i to j since the action bal_load_ji is enabled. Following this computation pattern no process is idle forever if there is enough work to be done.

We assume that the constraint $(top > 0)$ holds for the global variable *top* and that the constants $Load.i$ have the property $(\forall i \in V : Load.i \geq 0)$ in the load balancing algorithm. The following invariant then holds during the computation:

$$I_1 : (\forall i \in V : load.i \geq 0).$$

This is due to the fact that initially the load of a node i is assigned the value $Load.i$ and during the computation the load is only decreased if it is greater or equal to top, otherwise it is increased.

At termination each node either has a load greater or equal to the treshold *top* or a load less or equal to *top*:

$$(\forall i \in V : load.i \geq top) \vee (\forall i \in V : load.i \leq top).$$

```
MACHINE
  Load_Bal_1(top)
CONSTRAINTS
  top > 0
CONSTANTS
  Load1, Load2
PROPERTIES
  Load1 : NAT ∧ Load2 : NAT
VARIABLES
  load1, load2
INVARIANT
  load1 : NAT ∧ load2 : NAT
INITIALISATION
  load1 := Load1 || load2 := Load2
OPERATIONS
  init_12 =  BEGIN skip END ;

  bal_load_12 = SELECT load1 < top ∧ load2 ≥ top THEN
                        load1 := load1 + 1 || load2 := load2 − 1
                END ;
  init_21 =  BEGIN skip END ;

  bal_load_21 = SELECT load1 > top ∧ load2 ≤ top THEN
                        load1 := load1 − 1 || load2 := load2 + 1
                END ;
  exit_cond = SELECT  (load1 ≥ top ∨ load2 < top)
                      ∧ (load1 ≤ top ∨ load2 > top) THEN
                      skip
              END
END
```

Fig. 5. The load balancing algorithm represented in AMN.

It is now straightforward to give the action system as the Abstract Machine specification in Figure 5. There are, however, some restrictions for specifications in B-Tool. We are for example not allowed to use sequential composition in a specification. Instead we have to use parallel composition of substitutions. Since these substitutions have to refer to distinct variables, we cannot assign values to distinct elements in an array in parallel. Thus, these elements have to be considered as distinct variables and the replicator functionality is lost. In our machine we have, thus, restricted the graph to one with two nodes, node 1 and node 2. Node 2 is considered to be the root. It is, however, easy to extend the algorithm to contain more than two nodes [14]. The treshold *top* is given as a parameter and $(top > 0)$ as its constraint.

The operations *init_12* and *init_21* are only represented as *skip*-statements. They will later be introduced as actions in the refinement. Also the exit condition is given explicitely as an operation *exit_cond* for verification purposes.

5.2 A Superposition Refinement Step

We will now do a first refinement step towards a distributed load balancing algorithm using superposition. We add a new variable Q for representing communication links between nodes. The link $Q.i.j$ denotes the link from node i to node j. There is a link in both directions for each edge. Thus, for the edge (i,j) in the graph we have the links $Q.i.j$ and $Q.j.i$. We consider the link as a one place buffer and since we are not concerned with what is sent over the link at this stage, we can represent the link as a boolean variable. The link $Q.i.j$ is defined to be *true* if something is sent over the link and *false* otherwise. All links are initialised to *false*.

In the refined action system we split the change of loads into two phases. First, a node chooses which neighbour to change loads with. In the second phase the change of loads takes place. A node must not commit to change loads with more than one neighbour at a time. This can be expressed as in the predicate $F(i,j)$:

$$\begin{aligned} F(i,j) : (\forall k \in V : (i,k) \in E \vee (k,i) \in E : \neg Q.i.k \wedge \neg Q.k.i) \\ \wedge\ (\forall k \in V : (j,k) \in E \vee (k,j) \in E : \neg Q.j.k \wedge \neg Q.k.j). \end{aligned}$$

The predicate F states that the nodes i and j have to be free of any commitment, i.e., all their links have to be empty.

The refined action system $\mathcal{B}'$ is given below.

$$\begin{array}{lll} \mathcal{B}' \stackrel{\text{def}}{=} & |[& \mathbf{var}\ \mathit{load.i} \in \mathit{int}\ \ \mathbf{for}\ i \in V; \\ & & \quad\ \ Q.i.j \in \mathit{bool}\ \ \mathbf{for}\ i,j \in V; \\ & & \mathit{load.i} := \mathit{Load.i}\ \ \mathbf{for}\ i \in V; \\ & & Q.i.j := \mathit{false}\ \ \mathbf{for}\ i,j \in V (i \neq j); \\ & & \mathbf{do}\ (\mathit{init\_ij} \parallel \mathit{bal\_load\_ij}' \parallel \mathit{init\_ji} \parallel \mathit{bal\_load\_ji}')\ \ \mathbf{for}\ (i,j) \in E\ \mathbf{od} \\ &]|: & \mathit{top} \in \mathit{int} \end{array}$$

The new actions *init_ij* and *init_ji* describe the first phase of the change of loads, the commit, by setting the links $Q.j.i$ and $Q.i.j$, respectively, to *true* denoting that the loads are ready to be changed. Neither node i nor node j can be committed to any node for these actions to be enabled. The new actions are defined as follows.

$$\mathit{init\_ij} \stackrel{\text{def}}{=} \mathit{load.i} < \mathit{top} \wedge \mathit{load.j} \geq \mathit{top} \wedge F(i,j) \rightarrow Q.j.i := \mathit{true}$$

$$\mathit{init\_ji} \stackrel{\text{def}}{=} \mathit{load.i} > \mathit{top} \wedge \mathit{load.j} \leq \mathit{top} \wedge F(i,j) \rightarrow Q.i.j := \mathit{true},$$

where $F(i,j)$ is given above.

In the changed actions *bal_load_ij'* and *bal_load_ji'* where the loads are actually changed the corresponding links are set to *false* again stating that the changing of loads has been completed.

$$bal\_load\_ij' \stackrel{\text{def}}{=} load.i < top \wedge load.j \geq top \wedge Q.j.i \rightarrow$$
$$Q.j.i := false;\ load.i, load.j := load.i + 1, load.j - 1$$

$$bal\_load\_ji' \stackrel{\text{def}}{=} load.i > top \wedge load.j \leq top \wedge Q.i.j \rightarrow$$
$$Q.i.j := false;\ load.i, load.j := load.i - 1, load.j + 1$$

The following addition to the invariant I_1 of the action system $\mathcal{B}$ defines how the variables are used in the new action system $\mathcal{B}'$:

$$I_2 \stackrel{\text{def}}{=} I_{21} \wedge I_{22} \wedge I_{23}$$

where

$$I_{21} : (\forall i, j \in V : (i,j) \in E : Q.j.i \Rightarrow load.i < top \wedge load.j \geq top)$$
$$I_{22} : (\forall i, j \in V : (i,j) \in E : Q.i.j \Rightarrow load.i > top \wedge load.j \leq top)$$
$$I_{23} : (\forall i, j \in V : (i,j) \in E \vee (j,i) \in E : Q.i.j \Rightarrow (\neg Q.j.i \wedge$$
$$(\forall k \in V : ((i,k) \in E \vee (k,i) \in E) \wedge k \neq j : \neg Q.i.k \wedge \neg Q.k.i) \wedge$$
$$(\forall k \in V : ((j,k) \in E \vee (k,j) \in E) \wedge k \neq i : \neg Q.j.k \wedge \neg Q.k.j)))$$

The invariant I_{21} states that if there is something on the link from node j to node i, i.e. the value of $Q.j.i$ is *true*, then node j is overloaded and node i has a load lower than the treshold. A similar reasoning holds for the invariant I_{22}. Invariant I_{23} says that if there is something on the link from node i to node j then the link in the other direction has to be empty as well as all other incoming and outgoing links of nodes i and j.

We will now write the same refinement within B-Tool. The Abstract Machine refinement is given in Figure 6. The *sees* clause, *SEES Bool_TYPE*, is needed for reading boolean values. Since the operations in the machine refinement cannot involve variables of the machine being refined, we need to introduce new variables for the loads, *lload*1 and *lload*2. They are, however, stated to be equal to the old load variables in the invariant, $(lload1 = load1) \wedge (lload2 = load2)$. The invariant I_2 given above is also included in the invariant of the refined machine. The initialisation and the operations are created in the same way here as for the machine specification. For verification purpose we introduce the operation *exit_cond*.

The termination condition for the auxiliary actions are checked with a WHILE-loop in a machine implementation. The WHILE-loop for the load balancing algorithm is given in Figure 7. The disjunction of the guards of the operations *init_*12 and *init_*21 compose the guard of the loop. These operations are also included in the IF-substitution within the loop. The relation between the link variables Q and the variables $C1$ and $C2$ of the variant are added to the invariant. These relations give the definition of the function *BTS_BOOL* used for the variant, returning one for a parameter with the value *true* and zero otherwise.

```
REFINEMENT
  Load_Bal_2
REFINES
  Load_Bal_1
SEES
  Bool_TYPE
VARIABLES
  lload1, lload2, Q12, Q21
INVARIANT
  lload1 : NAT ∧ lload2 : NAT ∧ Q12 : BOOL ∧ Q21 : BOOL
  ∧ (lload1 = load1) ∧ (lload2 = load2)
  ∧ (Q21 = TRUE ⇒ lload1 < top ∧ lload2 ≥ top)
  ∧ (Q12 = TRUE ⇒ lload1 > top ∧ lload2 ≤ top)
  ∧ (Q12 = TRUE ⇒ Q21 = FALSE)
  ∧ (Q21 = TRUE ⇒ Q12 = FALSE)
INITIALISATION
  (lload1, lload2 := Load1, Load2) || (Q12, Q21 := FALSE, FALSE)
OPERATIONS
  init_12 =
      SELECT lload1 < top ∧ lload2 ≥ top ∧ Q21 = FALSE ∧ Q12 = FALSE THEN
                 Q21 := TRUE
      END ;
  bal_load_12 =
     SELECT lload1 < top ∧ lload2 ≥ top ∧ Q21 = TRUE THEN
                 Q21 := FALSE; (lload1 := lload1 + 1 || lload2 := lload2 − 1)
     END ;
  init_21 =
      SELECT lload1 > top ∧ lload2 ≤ top ∧ Q21 = FALSE ∧ Q12 = FALSE THEN
                 Q12 := TRUE
      END ;
  bal_load_21 =
     SELECT lload1 > top ∧ lload2 ≤ top ∧ Q12 = TRUE THEN
                 Q12 := FALSE; (lload1 := lload1 − 1 || lload2 := lload2 + 1)
     END ;
  exit_cond =
      SELECT  (lload1 ≥ top ∨ lload2 < top ∨ Q21 = TRUE ∨ Q12 = TRUE)
                  ∧ (lload1 ≥ top ∨ lload2 < top ∨ Q21 = FALSE)
                  ∧ (lload1 ≤ top ∨ lload2 > top ∨ Q21 = TRUE ∨ Q12 = TRUE)
                  ∧ (lload1 ≤ top ∨ lload2 > top ∨ Q12 = FALSE) THEN
                skip
      END
END
```

Fig. 6. Refinement of the abstract machine for the load balancing algorithm.

$$
\begin{array}{l}
\text{WHILE } (lload1 < top \wedge lload2 \geq top \wedge Q21 = FALSE \wedge Q12 = FALSE) \\
\quad \vee (lload1 > top \wedge lload2 \leq top \wedge Q21 = FALSE \wedge Q12 = FALSE) \\
\quad \text{DO} \\
\quad\quad \text{IF } (lload1 < top \wedge lload2 \geq top \wedge Q21 = FALSE \wedge Q12 = FALSE) \\
\quad\quad\quad \text{THEN } Q21 := TRUE;\ C2 \leftarrow BTS\_BOOL(Q21) \\
\quad\quad \text{ELSIF } (lload1 > top \wedge lload2 \leq top \wedge Q21 = FALSE \wedge Q12 = FALSE) \\
\quad\quad\quad \text{THEN } Q12 := TRUE;\ C1 \leftarrow BTS\_BOOL(Q12) \\
\quad \text{END} \\
\quad \text{INVARIANT } (lload1 : NAT \wedge lload2 : NAT \\
\quad\quad \wedge\ Q12 : BOOL \wedge Q21 : BOOL \\
\quad\quad \wedge\ C1 : NAT \wedge C2 : NAT \\
\quad\quad \wedge\ (Q12 = TRUE \Rightarrow C1 = 1) \\
\quad\quad \wedge\ (Q12 = FALSE \Rightarrow C1 = 0) \\
\quad\quad \wedge\ (Q21 = TRUE \Rightarrow C2 = 1) \\
\quad\quad \wedge\ (Q21 = FALSE \Rightarrow C2 = 0) \\
\quad\quad \wedge\ (Q21 = TRUE \Rightarrow lload1 < top \wedge lload2 \geq top) \\
\quad\quad \wedge\ (Q12 = TRUE \Rightarrow lload1 > top \wedge lload2 \leq top) \\
\quad\quad \wedge\ (Q12 = TRUE \Rightarrow Q21 = FALSE) \\
\quad\quad \wedge\ (Q21 = TRUE \Rightarrow Q12 = FALSE)) \\
\quad \text{VARIANT } (2 - (C2 + C1)) \\
\text{END}
\end{array}
$$

Fig. 7. The auxiliary actions of the load balancing algorithm.

Verification The autoprover was able to discharge most of the proof obligations generated for the load balancing algorithm. When a proof obligation cannot be discharged using the mathematical library of rules during the autoproof session, the user may supplement the library with further rules. In our case study the following kind of proof obligations could not be discharged. For the proof that the new guard implies the old, the autoprover need to use the invariant relation $(lload1 = load1) \wedge (lload2 = load2)$. Furthermore, the proof obligations for the *exit_cond*-operation need to be transformed using logical rules to bring the obligation into an expression which can be shown to be true. This proof can easily be done by hand-waving. The autoprover would only need to be supplied with these logical rules by the user. Finally, the proof obligation stating that the variant is a natural number was left unproved. Here it is again sufficient to explicitely give the definition of the variant, already given in the invariant, as an extra rule.

The proof obligations that are not discharged by the autoprover can first be discharged by the interprover. Then running the autoprover once again these obligations can be discharged by the autoprover as well using the user supplied rules. Thus, using B-Toolkit we were able to discharge all the proof obligations created for the superposition refinement step of the load balancing algorithm. Sample outputs produced by B-Tool are included in the full version of this paper [15].

6 Conclusion

We have described how an action system is turned into an Abstract Machine specification in B-Tool. We have construeted refinements which give rise to proof obligations that correspond to the conditions of superposition refinement within the action systems framework. We can, thus, do superposition proofs within B-Tool. Since superposition proofs are used for deriving parallel and distributed systems, we can now use B-Toolkit as a tool for deriving parallel and distributed systems.

By using B-Tool we gain some extra features. B-Tool can for example assist in finding the invariant for the system as well as help to find logical errors in the system. These shortcomings of an algorithm can usually be found by studying the proof obligations that cannot be automatically proved by the B-Toolkit.

There are, however, also drawbacks of using B-Tool for deriving action systems. The substitutions allowed in the specifications and refinements are very restrictive. For example a while loop cannot be introduced until the last refinement step. Even sequential composition is not allowed in the specifications. Furthermore, extra operations need to be introduced in order to be able to prove the superposition rule within B-Tool. The more complex action system we have the more complex these extra conditions will be.

We used a load balancing algorithm as a case study to exemplify how to use B-Tool for refining action systems. Most of the proof obligations created by B-Tool could be proved automatically and the rest were easily proved in an interactive way. Here we only study the very first refinement step. The complete derivation is reported in [14] .

We have also looked at other tools that could be used for refining action systems, such as the Synthesizer Generator [12] and the Refinement Calculator [10]. However, these tools still require introduction of the superposition rules in order to be applicable for superposition refinement of action systems. Furthermore, we have specified a program derivation editor [5] for strucuring and manipulating formal program derivations.

Acknowledgements

The authors would like to thank Michael Butler for fruitful discussions about the usage of B-Tool and the implementation of action systems. We would also like to thank Emil Sekerinski for the useful discussions concerning the algorithm and Wolfgang Weck for his comments on a previous version of this manuscript. The work reported here has been carried out within the Irene-project supported by the Academy of Finland.

References

1. J.-R. Abrial. The B Method for large software specification design and coding. In *Proc. of VDM'91 Vol. 2.* Springer-Verlag, 1991.

2. R. J. R. Back and R. Kurki-Suonio. Decentralization of process nets with centralized control. In *Proc. of the 2nd ACM SIGACT–SIGOPS Symp. on Principles of Distributed Computing*, pages 131–142, 1983.
3. R. J. R. Back and K. Sere. *Superposition refinement of reactive systems.* Series A–144, Reports on Computer Science and Mathematics, Åbo Akademi University, Finland, 1993. To appear in *Formal Aspects of Computing.*
4. R. J. R. Back and K. Sere. From action systems to modular systems. In *Proc. of FME'94: Industrial Benefit of Formal Methods.* LNCS 873, pp. 1 – 25, 1994.
5. M. Butler, E. Hedman, P. Nilsson, R. Ruksenas, M. Waldén and Y. Zhao. *Specification of a program derivation editor.* Series A–157, Reports on Computer Science and Mathematics, Åbo Akademi University, Finland, 1994.
6. E. W. Dijkstra. *A Discipline of Programming.* Prentice–Hall International, 1976.
7. N. Francez and I.R. Forman. Superimposition for interacting processes. In *Proc. of CONCUR '90 Theories of Concurrency: Unification and extension.* LNCS 458, pages 230–245, Amsterdam, the Netherlands, August 1990.
8. H. P. Hofstee, J. J. Lukkien and J. L. A. van de Snepscheut. *A distributed implementation of a task pool.* LNCS 574, pp. 338 – 348 , June 1991.
9. S. M. Katz. A superimposition control construct for distributed systems. *ACM Transactions on Programming Languages and Systems*, 15(2):337–356, April 1993.
10. T. Långbacka, R. Rukšėnas and J. v. Wright. *TkWinHOL: A tool for doing window inference in HOL.* Series A–160, Reports on Computer Science and Mathematics, Åbo Akademi University, Finland, 1995.
11. D. S. Neilson and I. H. Sorensen. *The B-Technologies: A system for computer aided programming.* B-Core (UK) Ltd., 1994.
12. T. Reps and T. Teitelbaum. *The Synthesizer Generator: A System for Constructing Language-Based Editors.* Springer-Verlag, NY,1988.
13. K. Sere. and M. Waldén *Verification of a distributed algorithm due to Chu.* Series A–156, Reports on Computer Science and Mathematics, Åbo Akademi University, Finland, 1994. Abstract appeared in *Proc. of The 13th Annual Symposium on the Principles of Distributed Computing*, Los Angeles, USA, page 391, 1994.
14. M. Waldén *Formal derivation of a distributed load balancing algorithm.* Series A–172, Reports on Computer Science and Mathematics, Åbo Akademi University, Finland, 1995.
15. M. Waldén and K. Sere. *Refining action systems within B-Tool.* Manuscript in preparation. Åbo Akademi University, Finland, 1995.

Integrating Action Systems and Z in a Medical System Specification

V. Kasurinen and K. Sere

University of Kuopio, Department of Computer Science and Applied Mathematics, P.O.Box 1627, FIN-70211 Kuopio, Finland

Abstract. Action systems and the specification language Z, are integrated and used to give different aspects of a single systems specification. The static part of the system under development, i.e., the state declarations together with their accompanying invariants, are first specified using Z. Then the reactivity and real time aspects of the same system are specified within the action systems framework making use of the Z definitions. Furthermore, Z style is used to specify the actions in the action system. We exemplify the proposed methodology through a case study on a medical system specification.

1 Introduction

This paper reports on work carried out on formal specification of a computer-based system that is used to train the reaction abilities of patients with severe brain damage. The system contains computer programs by which the patients carry out different tests that are designed to stimulate their eyes and ears. Systems of this type are new and no formal specifications for them exists to our knowledge. The system specified here is developed together with the neurological clinic of a Finnish university hospital. The patients who carry out the tests are in rehabilitation. The tests themselves are specified by the medical staff of the clinic.

Our system supports currently three reaction training tests. The formal specification of the system became important due to several reasons. First of all, there is the question of patients' integrity, because the system is used within health care: the system supports a data base on the test results of several patients. Furthermore, the test results themselves are interpreted and manipulated by the system, so the computation needs to be reliable. In addition, there is a family of related tests designed for different patient groups. All the tests are based on similar ideas, but the stimuli and the interpretation of the results vary. Hence, we wanted to create a high level specification of the systems that would be easy to adapt to the different needs.

The system consists of two parts: There is an interactive part where different stimuli appear on an ordinary computer screen at in advance determined times. A stimulus is either a picture that is drawn on the screen or a picture combined with a sound that comes from the loud speaker of the computer. This part also monitors the reactions the patient makes to different stimuli. The reactions are accepted via an ordinary keyboard. The other part takes care of the result data base. It also specifies the test to be carried out, stores the reactions, interprets them, and computes the results. The system has certain real-time requirements, partly constraining the appearances of stimuli and partly the time a patient has to make her reactions to different stimuli.

The two parts are completely different in nature. Therefore it was felt that a single formalism would not be optimal for the specification of the entire system. As a matter of fact, we started by developing the complete specification using the specification language Z [10, 11]. The Z formalism was very powerful when specifying the result data base and defining the different tests. It turned out, however, that this formalism was not very suitable for specifying the reactive behavior of the system.

The interactive, reactive part is specified within the action systems framework of Back et al. [2, 3]. Action systems is a formalism designed for the development of verified parallel and distributed systems. It has also been successfully applied in many reactive applications and furthermore, an extensive theory exists for the stepwise development of action systems from high level specification to an implementation as described by Back and Sere [1, 3].

All the operations and activities that have real time requirements are specified within the action systems formalism. We adopt the timed action systems formalism proposed by Fidge and Wellings [6]. That part of the activity that does not have timing constraints is specified within the Z framework.

We make contributions as follows:

- we show how two formalism are integrated in a single specification task,
- we propose a mixed style of specification, where activity is specified using both formalisms, and
- we develop a formal specification of a real world medical computer-based system.

We proceed as follows. In section 2, we define the state space of the system within the specification language Z. Also a couple of Z operations are defined to give a flavor of the interface between the medical staff and the system. These operations do not involve real time. We assume that the reader is familiar with the Z language. The action system specification for the interactive part is given in section 3 together with a short introduction to this formalism. The activity specified here is constraint by some real time requirements. We conclude in section 4.

2 The Z interface

The system we are about to specify consists of three basic components, the impulses, the reactions, and the tests. For a test, a number of impulses appear on the computer screen and the patient carrying out the test is given time to react, from a keyboard, to every impulse. Let us start by defining each component separately.

2.1 The impulses

The set of possible impulses is here left unspecified. We only assume that there is a set of distinct types of impulses in the system:

$[IMPULSE]$

A member of the set *IMPULSE* could be a circle, a square, or a triangle. The impulses appear in bursts of at most *burst* impulses.

$| \ burst : \mathbb{N}$

The time stamps that denote the appearances of the impulses on the screen are members of *AbsTime*

$$AbsTime == \mathbb{N}$$

Each appearance of an impulse has two features. First, two consecutive impulses can appear on a regular, irregular, or occasional time interval. Second, an impulse appears either on a defined or an undefined position on the screen.

If an interval is regular, then every two consecutive impulses always have the same interval between them. The set *RegularInterval* gives the possible intervals between regular impulses.

$$RegularInterval == \{di : AbsTime \mid di > 0\}$$

An occasional interval is such that its length has a lower bound and an upper bound. The set *OccasionalInterval* gives the minimum and maximum interval between two consecutive impulses.

$$OccasionalInterval == \{t1, t2 : AbsTime \mid t1 > 0 \land t1 < t2 \bullet (t1, t2)\}$$

Finally, an irregular interval in our system is retrieved from a set of three possible interval lengths. The set *IrregularInterval* defines the possible irregular intervals between impulses.

$$IrregularInterval == \{t1, t2, t3 : AbsTime \mid t1 > 0 \land t1 < t2 \land t2 < t3 \bullet (t1, t2, t3)\}$$

For example, if a regular interval is 8, the impulses arise at intervals of 8 time units. If an irregular interval is $(8, 10, 12)$, this denotes that after the first impulse the next one should arise either 8, 10 or 12 time units later. If an occasional interval is $(6, 60)$, it means that between every two impulses there is at least 6 and at most 60 time units.

Next we need to specify the screen coordinates of the position where an impulse appears:

$[Coordinates]$

The screen coordinates and the impulses form the set *ScreenInstance*.

$ScreenInstance == \{si : Coordinates \times IMPULSE\}$

There is a component in the set *ScreenInstance* that models an empty screen. This is defined as a constant *empty_screen*:

$| \ empty\_screen : ScreenInstance$

Moreover, when the position of an impulse is *defined*, the values of the screen coordinates are given by *defplace*:

$| \ defplace : Coordinates$

If there is a sound stimulus connected to an impulse, sound precedes the impulse at a regular interval on some positive number of time units.

$SoundInterval == \{sct : AbsTime \mid sct > 0\}$

2.2 The reactions

The reactions that a patient makes correspond to keypressings from an ordinary keyboard. For every reaction, i.e., set of keypressings, we store the time it has taken for the patient to make her reaction is terms of *AbsTime*. The value 0 denotes no reaction to a stimulus. At most *burst* reactions will be stored. The set *Reactions* contains the recorded reactions during a test.

$Reactions == \{la : \operatorname{seq} AbsTime \mid \#la \leq burst\}$

Let us look at an example. A sequence

$$\langle\, 3, 0, 2, 0, 0, 0\, \rangle$$

denotes that a patient has reacted by pressing some key for the first and third impulse. There has been no reaction for the second, fourth, fifth and sixth impulses.

2.3 The tests

The system presently supports three tests. In this paper two of them, test 1 and test 2, will be specified. Both tests contain three phases, A, B, and C. These are defined in *TestNumber*:

$TestNumber ::= T1A \mid T1B \mid T1C \mid T2A \mid T2B \mid T2C$

Every test phase comes with a set of parameters that will be called test limits. These parameters give particular values to the different types of interval between impulses and sound interval. Furthermore, they give the type of an impulse used, *basim*, and the time it stays on the screen. The schema type *TestLimit* specifies the possible test limits.

TestLimit
basim : *IMPULSE*
defint : *RegularInterval*
unint : *IrregularInterval*
ocint : *OccasionalInterval*
sotime : *SoundInterval*
deftime : *AbsTime*
defsotime : *AbsTime*

$defsotime < sotime$

$deftime < defint - sotime$
$deftime < first(unint) - sotime$
$deftime < first(ocint) - sotime$
$deftime > 0$

where the intuition behind the predicate is illustrated in Figure 1.

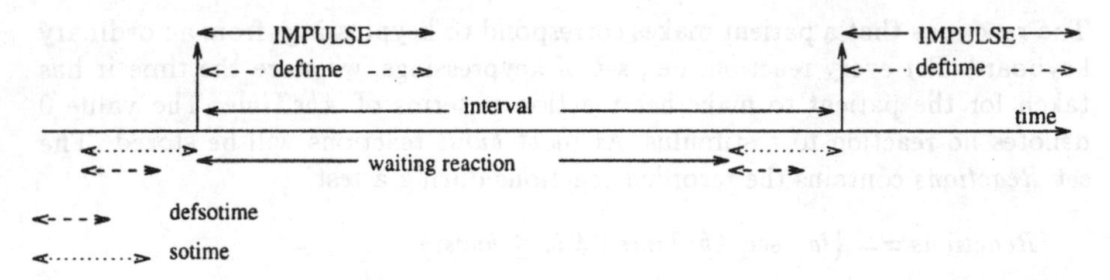

Fig. 1. Test parameters. The concept 'interval' denotes either a *defint* interval, an *ocint* interval, or an *unint* interval. The period when a patient is supposed to make a reaction is illustrated with 'waiting reaction'.

The predicate states that *sotime*, the time between a sound and the accompanying impulse, should be less than the entire interval. The parameter *defsotime* denotes time when sound is on before next impulse appears. After an impulse appears on the screen, it disappears *deftime* time units later. If a test does not include sound, a patient can make her reaction at any time between the impulses. The intuition of the test parameters for a test without sound is illustrated in Figure 2.

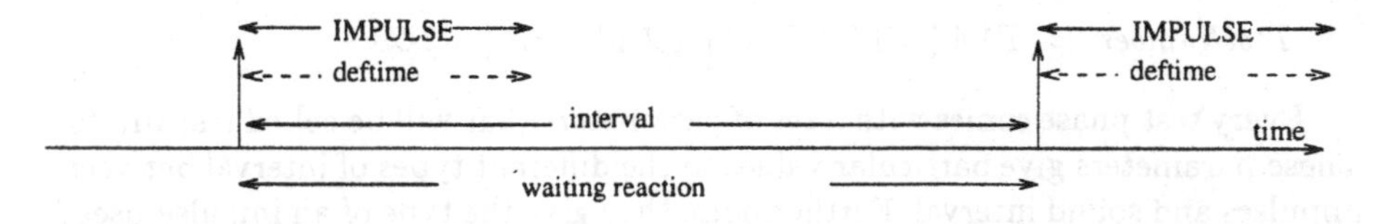

Fig. 2. Only the parameters *defint*, *ocint*, and *unint* are meaningful for defining 'waiting reaction' period, when the test does not have a sound signal.

A reaction is not taken into consideration in the following cases:

- It is made at the same time when an impulse appears.
- It is made at any time between a sound signal and the accompanying impulse.
- It is made at the same time when the sound signal is set on.

For example, a member of a valid set of test parameters *TestLimit* can be as follows: *defint* = 12, *unint* = (10, 12, 15), *ocint* = (10, 20), *sotime* = 2, *deftime* = 6, and *defsotime* = 1. The test parameters are interpreted as follows:

- If the test is without a sound signal, the first impulse appears at time stamp 0. Because *deftime* is 6, the impulse disappears at time stamp 6. If the interval is regular it is possible to make a valid reaction between times 1 and 9. A new impulse arises at time 10. In an interval is irregular, it is possible to make a reaction between time stamps 1 and 9, 1 and 11, or 1 and 14, because the next impulse appears either at time stamp 10, 12, or 15, respective. If an interval is occasional, a lower bound of 'waiting reaction' period is 1, and a upper bound can varies from 9 to 19.
- If the test has a sound signal included, the sound appears at time stamp 0 and it is on until time stamp 1, because *defsotime* is defined to be 1. The first impulse appears at time stamp 2. Because *deftime* is set to 6, the impulse disappears at time stamp 8. When the interval is regular, a valid reaction must be made between time stamps 3 and 11. At time 12, a new sound signal appears. In the case the interval is irregular, it is allowed to make a reaction between the time stamps 3 and 9, because a new sound signal appears at the earliest at time 10. It is also possible to make at time 10, because it might be so that the sound appears only at the time stamp 14. At the latest , the reaction can be made at the time stamp 14, because the last possible time for a sound in an irregular interval is 15. If the interval is occasional, the reaction must come at earliest at time 3 and the upper bound can varies from 9 to 19.

The global variable *testlimit* keeps track of the set of parameters currently in use.

$$testlimit : TestLimit$$

2.4 Global functions

We finally define a set of global functions. First of all, the features of an impulse depend on the test number.

The function *defso* returns the interval between an impulse and its preceding sound, if any (only test 2 includes sound).

$$defso : TestNumber \nrightarrow AbsTime$$

$$\begin{array}{l} \forall\, tn : TestNumber \bullet \\ \quad (tn \in \{T1A, T1B, T1C\} \Rightarrow defso(tn) = 0) \\ \quad \wedge \\ \quad (tn \in \{T2A, T2B, T2C\} \Rightarrow defso(tn) = testlimit.sotime) \end{array}$$

The function *generate_impulse* when given a test number returns the corresponding screen coordinates for the designated impulse (*testlimit.basim*).

$$
\begin{array}{|l}
generate\_impulse : TestNumber \rightarrow\!\!\!\!\!\!\rightarrow ScreenInstance \\
\hline
\forall\, tn : TestNumber \bullet \\
\quad (tn \in \{T1A, T1B, T1C\} \Rightarrow \\
\qquad generate\_impulse(tn) = (defplace, testlimit.basim)) \\
\quad \wedge \\
\quad (tn \in \{T2A, T2B, T2C\} \Rightarrow \\
\qquad (\exists\, i : Coordinates \bullet generate\_impulse(tn) = (i, testlimit.basim)))
\end{array}
$$

Finally, the impulse interval, regular, irregular, or occasional, defines the time units between impulses, therefore, one of the interval parameters *defint*, *ocint*, or *unint* in *testlimit* is set to be the center of attention in a test phase. The function *defimptime* accepts a test number and outputs a time.

$$
\begin{array}{|l}
defimptime : TestNumber \rightarrow\!\!\!\!\!\!\rightarrow AbsTime \\
\hline
\forall\, tn : TestNumber \bullet \\
\quad (tn \in \{T1A, T2A\} \Rightarrow defimptime(tn) = testlimit.defint) \\
\quad \wedge \\
\quad (tn \in \{T1B, T2B\} \Rightarrow \\
\qquad (\exists\, a, b, c, d : AbsTime \bullet \\
\qquad\quad (a, b, c) = testlimit.unint \wedge d \in \{a, b, c\} \wedge \\
\qquad\quad defimptime(tn) = d)) \\
\quad \wedge \\
\quad (tn \in \{T1C, T2C\} \Rightarrow \\
\qquad (\exists\, a, b, c : AbsTime \bullet \\
\qquad\quad (a, b) = testlimit.ocint \wedge c \in a \mathrel{..} b \wedge \\
\qquad\quad defimptime(tn) = c))
\end{array}
$$

2.5 Operation schemas

We define two Z operations, *GiveTestNumber* and *GenerateResult*, for our system. These operations model the interface between the medical staff and the system.

The operation *GiveTestNumber* accepts as input the test phase.

$$
\begin{array}{|l}
\underline{\;GiveTestNumber\;} \\
tn? : TestNumber \\
\hline
\end{array}
$$

The operation *GenerateResult* is activated at the end of a test phase. Its sole purpose is to compute the number of reactions.

$$\begin{array}{|l}
\hline
\textit{GenerateResult} \\
\textit{reac?} : \textit{Reactions} \\
\textit{res!} : (\textit{RightReactions} \times \textit{WrongReactions} \times \textit{Reactions}) \\
\hline
\#\textit{reac?} = \textit{burst} \\
\textit{res!} = (\textit{checkanswer}(\textit{reac?}), \textit{burst} - \textit{checkanswer}(\textit{reac?}), \textit{reac?}) \\
\hline
\end{array}$$

Here an input *reac?* is generated by the action system. The types *RightReactions* and *WrongReactions* are defined as follows:

$$\textit{RightReactions}, \textit{WrongReactions} == \mathbb{N}$$

Furthermore, the function *checkanswer* computes the number of right answers for a test phase. It accepts a test result, a member of the set *Reactions*, and returns the number of acceptable reactions.

$$\begin{array}{|l}
\textit{checkanswer} : \textit{Reactions} \nrightarrow \mathbb{N} \\
\hline
\forall\, at : \textit{Reactions};\ rt : \textit{AbsTime} \bullet \\
\quad rt = \textit{head}\ at\ \land \\
\quad (\textit{tail}\ at = \langle\rangle\ \land \\
\qquad (rt \neq 0 \Rightarrow \\
\qquad\quad \textit{checkanswer}(\langle at \rangle) = 1)\ \land \\
\qquad (rt = 0 \Rightarrow \\
\qquad\quad \textit{checkanswer}(\langle at \rangle) = 0))\ \land \\
\quad (\textit{tail}\ at \neq \langle\rangle \Rightarrow \\
\qquad \textit{checkanswer}(\langle at \rangle) = \textit{checkanswer}(\langle rt \rangle) + \textit{checkanswer}(\textit{tail}\ at))
\end{array}$$

In the actual implementation, a sequence *reac?* has much more information than what is specified here. Therefore, the calculation of the results is also much more elaborate. Our objective here is to only show the style of a mixed specification.

3 An action system interface

The interactive part of the rehabilitation system is specified using the action systems framework enhanced with real time facilities. The specification language Z is used when individual actions are specified.

3.1 Actions and action systems

Actions An action is any statement in an extended version of Dijkstra's guarded command language [5]. This language includes (multiple) assignment, sequential composition, conditional choice, and iteration, and is defined using *weakest precondition* predicate transformers.

An action A is a guarded command of the form $g \rightarrow S$, where g is a predicate, and S is any statement. An action is said to be *enabled* in some state when its guard g is true in this state.

Action systems An *action system* has the form

$$\mathcal{A} ::= [\![\mathbf{var}\ x;\ y^* \bullet I;\ \mathbf{do}\ A_1 [\!] \dots [\!] A_m\ \mathbf{od}]\!] : z$$

The action system $\mathcal{A}$ is initialized by action I. Then, repeatedly, an enabled action from $A_1 \dots A_m$ is nondeterministically selected and executed. The action system terminates when no action is enabled, and aborts when some action aborts.

The *local* variables of $\mathcal{A}$ are the variables x and the *global* variables of $\mathcal{A}$ are the variables y (exported) and z (imported). The local and global variables are assumed to be distinct. Each variable is associated with an explicit type. The *state variables* of $\mathcal{A}$ consist of the local variables and the global variables. The actions are allowed to refer to all the state variables of an action system.

Action systems are similar to the Unity logic of Chandy and Misra [4] and are also related to Lamports Temporal Logic of Actions [9]. However, contrary to these approaches we make no assumptions about fairness.

Parallel composition of action systems Consider two action systems $\mathcal{A}$ and $\mathcal{B}$:

$$\mathcal{A} ::= [\![\mathbf{var}\ x;\ y^* \bullet I;\ \mathbf{do}\ A_1 [\!] \dots [\!] A_m\ \mathbf{od}]\!] : z$$

$$\mathcal{B} ::= [\![\mathbf{var}\ u;\ v^* \bullet J;\ \mathbf{do}\ B_1 [\!] \dots [\!] B_n\ \mathbf{od}]\!] : w$$

where x, y, z, u, and w are distinct variables.

We define the *parallel composition* $\mathcal{A} \parallel \mathcal{B}$ of $\mathcal{A}$ and $\mathcal{B}$ to be the action system

$$\mathcal{C} ::= [\![\mathbf{var}\ x;\ y^*;\ u;\ v^* \bullet I;\ J;\ \mathbf{do}\ A_1 [\!] \dots [\!] A_m [\!] B_1 [\!] \dots [\!] B_n\ \mathbf{od}]\!] : z \cup w.$$

Thus, parallel composition will combine the state spaces of the two constituent action systems, merging the global variables and keeping the local variables distinct. The behavior of a parallel composition of action systems is dependent on how the individual action systems, the *reactive components*, interact with each other via the global variables that are referenced in both components. We have for instance that a reactive component does not terminate by itself: termination is a global property of the composed action system. More on these topics can be found in [1].

Timed action systems A *timed action system* $\mathcal{T}(\mathcal{A})$ is a parallel composition of an action system $\mathcal{A}$ and an action system $\mathcal{C}$ that contains actions to move time forward. The enabledness of an action in $\mathcal{A}$ might depend on time, but none of its actions is allowed to modify time. Moreover, an action in the action system $\mathcal{C}$ is enabled only when there are no enabled actions in $\mathcal{A}$.

Hence, we have that

$$\mathcal{T}(\mathcal{A}) ::= [\![now : Time \bullet \mathcal{A} \parallel \mathcal{C}]\!]$$

This way of specifying time within action systems was suggested by Fidge and Wellings [6].

3.2 An action system specification

Let us now give an action system specification of the interactive part of our case study.

The global variable *now* denotes the time as read from a clock.

$Time \mathrel{\widehat{=}} [now : AbsTime]$

The variable *kp* turns to *true* when a patient has made a keypressing:

$KeyPress \mathrel{\widehat{=}} [kp : \mathbb{B}]$

The variable *next* keeps track of the time when the next impulse should appear on the screen:

$NextTime \mathrel{\widehat{=}} [next : AbsTime]$

The behavior of the patient is stored in the sequence *reac*.

$Reaction \mathrel{\widehat{=}} [reac : Reactions]$

The action system specification of the rehabilitation program is a parallel composition of three separate action systems *SCREEN*, *REGISTER* and *LOUDSPEAKER*:

$SYSTEM ::=$
$[\![SCREEN \parallel REGISTER \parallel LOUDSPEAKER]\!] : Time, KeyPress$

The reactive components communicate with the environment via the variables *kp*, and *now*. The variable *kp* is set to true when a patient makes her reaction. Moreover, there is a clock system *C* that moves time forward. The global variable *now* that models time is initially set to zero, and it is replaced by $now + 1$ only when there are no enabled actions in *SYSTEM*. The enabledness of all the actions in *SYSTEM* depends on *now* as described below.

First, we specify the action system *SCREEN*, which generates impulses on the screen. The variable *scr* represents a state of the screen. The variable *l* keeps track of the length of *reac*. In addition to exported variable *next*, there is another exported variable *prev* keeps track of the time when the previous impulse appeared on the screen.

$SCREEN ::=$
$[\![$**var** $scr : ScreenInstance;\ NextTime(next^*);\ prev^* : AbsTime;\ l : \mathbb{N} \bullet$
$InitScreen;$
do
$l < \#reac < burst \wedge now = next \longrightarrow ShowImpulse;\ CountNext$
$[\!]$
$now = prev + testlimit.deftime \longrightarrow ClearScreen$
od
$]\!] : reac, now$

The operation *InitScreen* initializes variables *next*, and *prev* using the function *defso*. The schema *InitScreen* is as following, and it is illustrated in Figure 3.

$$\begin{array}{|l}
\textit{InitScreen} \\
\hline
scr;\ NextTime;\ prev;\ l \\
\hline
scr = empty_screen \land l = -1 \land \\
next = defso(tn?) \land prev = defso(tn?)
\end{array}$$

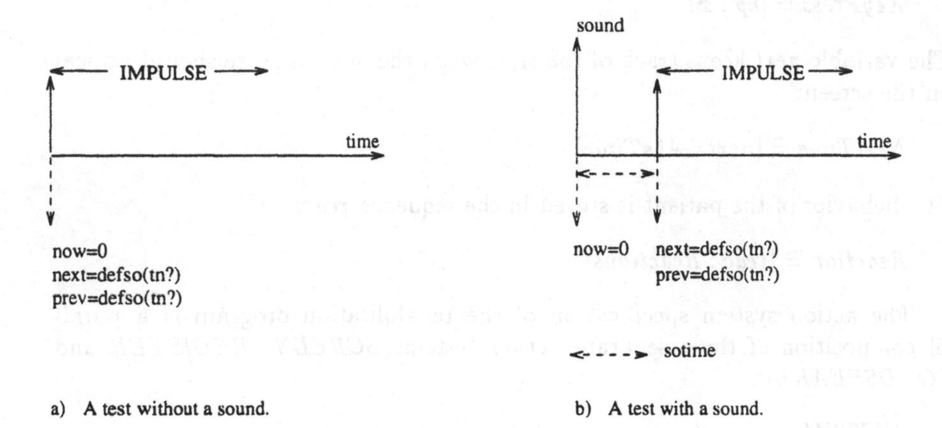

Fig. 3. Test initialization. The initial values of the variables *next* and *prev* are given by the function *defso*.

The operations *ShowImpulse* and *ClearScreen* are as follows:

$$ShowImpulse \mathrel{\widehat{=}} [\Delta(scr) \mid scr' = generate\_impulse(tn?)]$$

$$ClearScreen \mathrel{\widehat{=}} [\Delta(scr) \mid scr' = empty\_screen]$$

The operation *ShowImpulse* is enabled when time has reached *next* and the variable *reac* has been updated to reflect the result of the previous impulse. The operation *ClearScreen* makes an impulse to fade away when it is taken *testlimit.deftime* time units after the impulse appeared. The operation *CountNext* below calculates time of the next appearance of an impulse.

$$\begin{array}{|l}
\textit{CountNext} \\
\hline
\Delta(NextTime, prev) \\
\hline
next' = next + defimptime(tn?) \land \\
prev' = next \land l' = l + 1
\end{array}$$

The situation after the operations *ShowImpulse*, and *CountNext* is illustrated in Figure 4.

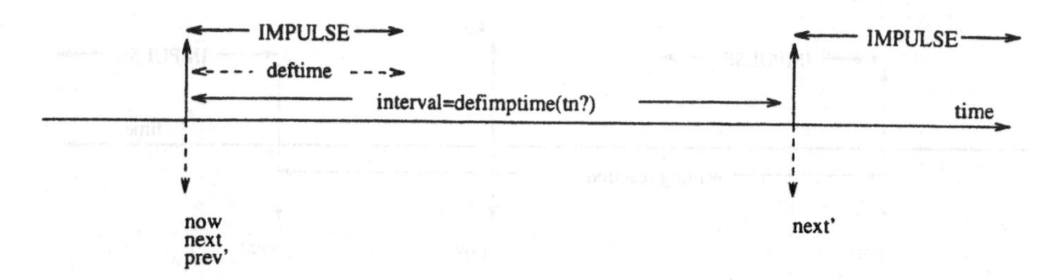

Fig. 4. The impulse appears, and time of the next impulse appearance is calculated.

The action system *REGISTER* generates the exported variable *reac* from the keypressings of a patient. The variable *kp* below is global and its value is set to *true* from outside of the system. The variable *reg* is set *true* when a patient has made a reaction in allowable period.

$REGISTER ::=$
$[\![$**var** $reg : \mathbb{B};\ Reaction(reac^*) \bullet$
$InitRegister;$
do
$kp \wedge \neg\, reg \wedge now < next - defso(tn?) \longrightarrow StoreReaction$
$[\!]$
$\neg\, kp \wedge \neg\, reg \wedge now = next - defso(tn?) \wedge now > 0 \longrightarrow StoreEmpty$
$[\!]$
$reg \wedge now = next - defso(tn?) \longrightarrow StartAgain$
od
$]\!] : next, now, prev, kp, tn?$

Here the initialization is defined as follows:

$$InitRegister \mathrel{\widehat=} [KeyPress;\ reg;\ Reaction \mid reg \wedge reac = \langle\rangle]$$

When the first reaction to an impulse is observed, i.e., the value of *kp* is *true*, and the time has not reached $next - defso(tn?)$, which it the time to generate the next stimulus, the value of the variable *reg* becomes *true*. The operation *StoreReaction* then records the reaction.

$$StoreReaction \mathrel{\widehat=} [\Delta(reg, Reaction) \mid reg' \wedge reac' = reac \frown \langle now - prev\rangle]$$

Both situations, i.e., a test with and a test without sound is are illustrated in Figure 5, and Figure 6.
If there has been no observable reaction to a stimulus, *kp* is *false* and time is already $next - defso(tn?)$, the operation *StoreEmpty* concatenates *reac* and an empty time stamp 0.

$$StoreEmpty \mathrel{\widehat=} [\Delta(Reaction) \mid reac' = reac \frown \langle 0\rangle]$$

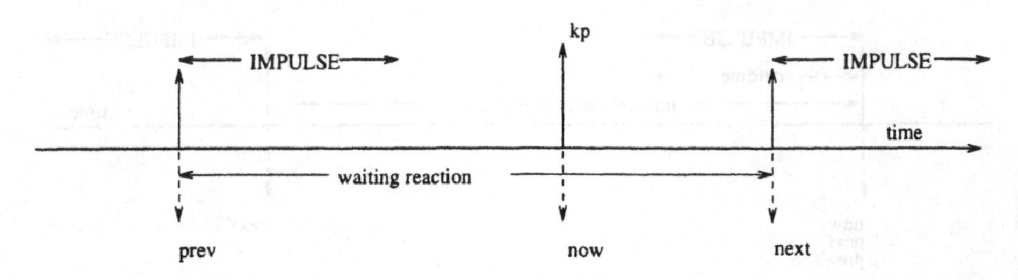

Fig. 5. There is no sound signal before the appearance of an impulse.

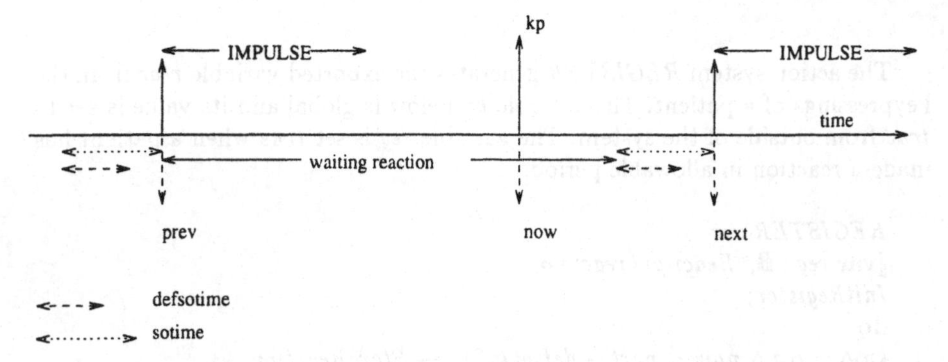

Fig. 6. There is a sound signal before the appearance of an impulse.

Finally, only the first keypressing to an impulse is registered. Therefore, immediately prior the next impulse, the operation *StartAgain* resets the variable *reg* to *false*.

$StartAgain \mathrel{\widehat{=}} [\Delta(reg, KeyPress) \mid \neg\, reg']$

The action system *LOUDSPEAKER* inserts a sound signal to the test. There is only one variable *sound* to denote if a sound signal on or off.

$LOUDSPEAKER ::=$
$[\![\mathbf{var}\ sound : \mathbb{B} \bullet$
$InitLoudSpeaker;$
$\mathbf{do}$
$now = next - testlimit.sotime \wedge defso(tn?) > 0 \longrightarrow SoundOn$
$[\,]$
$now = next - (testlimit.sotime - testlimit.defsotime) \wedge sound \longrightarrow SoundOff$
$\mathbf{od}$
$]\!] : next, now, tn?$

The initialization and the operations are straightforward:

$InitLoudSpeaker \mathrel{\widehat{=}} [sound \mid \neg\, sound]$

$SoundOn \mathrel{\widehat{=}} [\Delta(sound) \mid sound']$

$SoundOff \mathrel{\widehat{=}} [\Delta(sound) \mid \neg\, sound']$

The value of *testlimit.sotime* gives the interval between a sound and its accompanying impulse. The value of *testlimit.defsotime* gives the time a sound is on. This is illustrated in Figure 7.

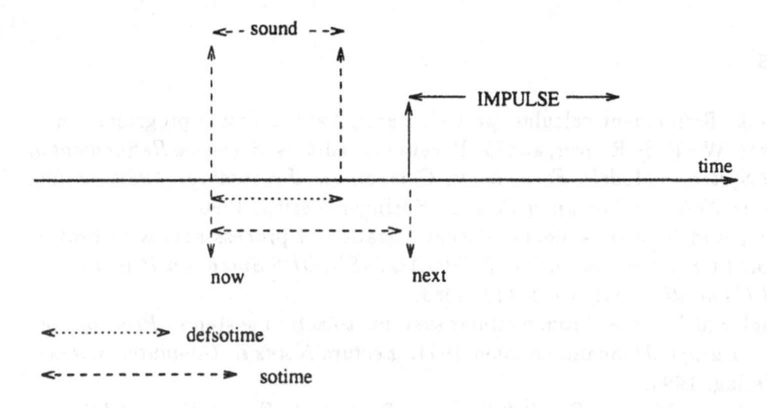

Fig. 7. Sound signal precedes an impulse.

4 Concluding remarks

We have formally specified a system that train the reaction abilities of different groups of patients suffering from severe brain damage. Our specification was based on existing programs and on the available documentation on these. It was, however, found important for the security and future development of such programs to redo the informal specifications and hence, a formal way of specifying this type of systems was attempted.

We found the idea of integrating Z and the action systems framework very natural to work with. The action systems could easily refer to variables and functions defined using Z. The concurrent and real time aspects are very naturally specified via the actions.

This work is part of our research on integrating formal methods and the system design process. We are particularly interested in the interplay between informal and formal methods in the definition phase when creating a requirements specification for a system [7, 8].Furthermore, the *refinement calculus* for action systems as described by Back and Sere [1, 3] can be directly used for further development of the system.

Acknowledgments

The authors like to thank the personnel at the neurological clinic of the University Hospital in Kuopio, and at the Brain Research and Rehabilitation Center of Finland for cooperation within the development of the Rekku system. We also thank Michael Butler and Marina Waldén for helpful comments on Z specification. The research is supported by the Academy of Finland and Tekes, The Technology Development Center of Finland.

References

1. R. J. R. Back. Refinement calculus, part II: Parallel and reactive programs. In J. W. de Bakker, W.-P. de Roever, and G. Rozenberg, editors, *Stepwise Refinement of Distributed Systems: Models, Formalisms, Correctness. Proceedings. 1989*, volume 430 of *Lecture Notes in Computer Science*. Springer-Verlag, 1990.
2. R. J. R. Back and R. Kurki-Suonio. Decentralization of process nets with centralized control. In *Proc. of the 2nd ACM SIGACT-SIGOPS Symp. on Principles of Distributed Computing*, pages 131-142, 1983.
3. R. J. R. Back and K. Sere. From modular systems to action systems. *Proc. of Formal Methods Europe'94*, Spain, October 1994. *Lecture Notes in Computer Science*. Springer-Verlag, 1994.
4. K. M. Chandy, J. Misra. *Parallel Program Design: A Foundation*. Addision-Wesley, 1988.
5. E. W. Dijkstra. *A Discipline of Programming*. Prentice-Hall International, 1976.
6. C. Fidge, A. Wellings. *An action-based formal model for concurrent, real-time systems*. Software Verification Research Center, Technical report 95-1, January 1995.
7. V. Kasurinen. *Informal and Formal Requirements Specification*. Manuscript, University of Kuopio, Department of Computer Science and Applied Mathematics, 1995.
8. V Kasurinen, K. Sere. Data Modelling in ZIM. To appear in *Proc. of Methods Integration Workshop*, Leeds Metropolitan University, 1-2 April 1996.
9. L. Lamport. *A Temporal Logic of Actions*. Research Report No. 57, DEC System Research Center, 1990.
10. B. Potter, J. Sinclair and D. Till. *An Introduction to formal specification and Z*. Prentice Hall, Englewood Cliffs NJ, 1991.
11. J. B. Wordsworth. *Software Development with Z*. Addison-Wesley, Wokingham, England, 1992.

Formalizing Anaesthesia: a case study in formal specification

Rix Groenboom[1], Erik Saaman[1], Ernest Rotterdam[2], and Gerard Renardel de Lavalette[1]

[1] Research Institute for Mathematics and Computing Science, University of Groningen, P.O. Box 800, NL 9700 AV Groningen, the Netherlands. E-mail: {rix,erik,grl}@cs.rug.nl

[2] University Hospital Groningen, Department of Medical Information Sciences, P.O. Box 30001, NL 9700 RB Groningen, the Netherlands. E-mail: ernest@fwi.uva.nl

Abstract. We report on the formalization of knowledge for a support system in the field of anaesthesiology. It is a case study in the use of the formal specification method we are developing. The method consists of guidelines (using concepts from object-oriented design methods), language (AFSL, Almost Formal Specification Language) and tools (type-checker, graphical representation of signatures).

Keywords: Case study, Development process, Linking formal and informal methods, Medical systems, Object-orientation.

1 Introduction

This paper reports on the project FAN (Formalization of ANaesthesia) which aims at formal specification of the domain knowledge that is needed to construct support systems for anaesthesiology. The specification is written in the formal specification language AFSL [26, 27], with modularization, parameterization, and sub-typing. The support systems to be based on FAN include diagnosis and monitoring systems.

This case study is part of a larger research effort concerning the use of formal specification languages (the Formal System Analysis-project). The FSA-project uses several cases to develop a method (consisting of guidelines, a language and tools) that is suited to formalize so-called open (i.e. ill-structured) knowledge domains. We will not compare several methods and languages, since we have only applied one method for our formalization.

1.1 Overview of paper

First, in section 2, we introduce our view on formalizing informal knowledge domains, in comparison with related work in this area. In section 3, we outline the problem: support of anaesthesia. We continue in section 4 by briefly explaining the language and method that are used for the FAN-project. Then we present the formal specification in section 5. Section 6 mentions the trajectory of the FAN-project including some of the design decisions. In the final section we draw some conclusions.

2 Formalizing the informal

2.1 Open versus closed knowledge domains

The FSA-project focuses on the formalization of *open* knowledge domains. Some characteristics of open knowledge domains are: ill-structured, unstable, and informal. Examples of open knowledge domains abound in e.g. cognitive science, linguistics, and medicine.

In contrast, *closed* problems are concerned with well documented, understood, and implemented problems. Examples are communication protocols and digital hardware. The literature on formal methods is often geared to closed problems: the proceedings of FME '93 [32] and FME '94 [19] contain hardly any case studies in open problems. Research is reported in railway applications, controllers and protocols. All these are fairly technical applications, involving systems that already have been implemented (and thus formalized in one way or another). For validation and proving correctness of implementations, the formalization of these domains is obligatory (cf. hardware and protocol verification).

In our opinion, the use of formal specification in ill-structured domains is an important field of research. The application of formal methods can be effective and help in the better understanding of the knowledge domain.

2.2 Related work

Knowledge-based systems An area that deals with formalization of open knowledge domains is the development of knowledge-based systems. Several methods for developing knowledge-based systems are available, examples are the KADS model of expertise [31] and the compositional method DESIRE [16].

The KADS-method gives guidelines for dividing problems into layers, and gives standard problem solving techniques for several kinds of problems. A drawback of this method is that it only prescribes the steps and layers that should be distinguished. The result is an informal description of the knowledge domain. Recently, formal specification languages have been developed for specifying and implementing complex reasoning systems which offer more possibilities for a formal specification of the knowledge domain (good overviews can be found in [5] and [30]).

Cognitive sciences Another source of open knowledge domains is cognitive science. An early case study of the FSA-project was the specification of SOAR. SOAR [15] is both a cognitive architecture based on Newell's theory of Human Problem Solving [20], and a computer program based on this architecture. An extensive formalization in Z is presented in [17], but this is in fact a specification of the program SOAR, not a high-level formalization of the theory behind SOAR. The specification in [2] comes closer to this. A more elaborate description of our view is in [11].

Linguistics In the field of linguistics much research is done on mathematization. With respect to formal specification of linguistic theories, we mention another case study of the FSA-project, which is concerned with the specification of a parser for natural language based on the Minimalist Program [1]. This work resembles the formalization in first-order logic and Prolog of Chomsky's theory of Government and Binding [29].

Medicine In the field of medicine much effort is invested in the production of implementations of medical systems. An example of this is [3], which gives many computer programs that perform clinical computations. More general work is done by Fieschi [6], this research focuses on expert system applications but is too restricted for our purposes.

3 Support in anaesthesia

Problem domain The context is: anaesthesia during thorax operations. At the Department of Anaesthesiology of the University Hospital Groningen a database system (Carola, documented in [8]) monitors the measurements performed during thorax operations. Based on this infrastructure, research is done to construct a system that can support anaesthetists during thorax operations [9].

Two essential ingredients are needed for the construction of a support system: computerized measurements and a formalization of medical knowledge. The measurements can be obtained from the Carola database and therefore we focus on the formalization of knowledge about these measurements.

We identify two types of anaesthesiological knowledge. The first is structural knowledge: knowledge about the concepts and their relations as present in anaesthesiology. Secondly, we identify medical facts as factual knowledge. In the model that we present, the factual knowledge is stored in a knowledge base. There is no ready-to-use model for anaesthesia available, and thus no formal model either. The research within FAN consists of defining a model for anaesthesia and formalizing it.

The factual knowledge stored in the knowledge base applies to the perfusion period. This is a critical period of a thorax operation. During the perfusion period a heart-lung machine takes over the functioning of heart and lungs.

Required functionality The aim of the FAN-project is to develop what is called a *support system* for anaesthetists. We do not call the envisioned system a decision support system since we aim at something different from what is commonly indicated by this term. As we perceive it, a typical decision support system computes which of a number of alternative options is best (according to particular criteria). The support system that we have in mind helps the anaesthetist by giving him better insight in the situation of the patient and by structuring the decisions that have to be taken.

The support we want to provide includes diagnosis (based on the measurements, the system infers possible diagnoses), simulation (the system enables the simulation of the application of a therapy), and treatment advice (the system advices the anaesthetist which therapy is applicable). A more detailed description of the functionality can be found in [24].

4 Formalization method and language

We outline the principles used in the FSA-project.

- Formal method: use of a formal specification language.

- Property oriented specification: the specification paradigm that is used is property based (as opposed to model based approaches).
- The formal specification language AFSL. It is inspired on the specification language COLD [4]. AFSL will be explained in somewhat more detail below. For FAN we use the static, declarative sub-language of AFSL.
- Graphical representation: to represent the signature of the specifications graphically we use a graphical notation based on the graph-visualization program da Vinci [7].
- Object-Oriented modeling technique: for the construction of the specification we use several ideas from the object oriented paradigm, viz. sub-typing and inheritance.

We discuss briefly the guidelines, language, and tools.

4.1 Guidelines

We present the guidelines used in the FAN project. The motivation is based on FAN and other case-studies; document [27] addresses these issues. Other sources of inspiration for the method were found in the literature on Object-Oriented Analysis, e.g. [25]. A specification is constructed in three parts: a dictionary, a signature, and an axiomatization. These three parts represent various aspects of a specification: intention, structure, and content.

Dictionary This is a list of concepts accompanied by *descriptions*. A description explains in informal terms what is covered by the concept. Additional (optional) parts are *examples*, *motivation* and *additional information* for each concept.

Signature The first step towards formalization is choosing the identifiers (names in the final specification) and their types for the concepts in the dictionary. Names can only refer to sorts, individual objects and functions. Individual objects have a sort name as type, and functions have the type $S_1 \times \ldots \times S_n \rightarrow S$ where $S_1, \ldots, S_n, S$ are sort names. The semantics of the names are (initially) given by informal axioms (stated in natural language). Diagrams play an important role in the construction of the signature.

Axiomatization The formalization is completed by adding axioms. The axioms must be such that the properties described in the dictionary and the corresponding informal axioms are satisfied.

4.2 Language

For presentation of the formal model, we use two types of representation. The first is a formal specification language, AFSL, with a formally defined syntax and semantics. The second way of presenting the model is the use of a graphical notation. The graphical notation is an additional representation, used to obtain a better overview over the specification. The meaning of this representation is explained in terms of the corresponding AFSL constructs. We discuss the two formats in turn.

AFSL: Almost Formal Specification Language The language AFSL is being developed as part of the FSA-project. It is an extension of first-order logic and is inspired on the specification language COLD [4]. AFSL is designed to support the guidelines that were mentioned in 4.1. Basically, AFSL is a language for writing first-order predicate logical theories (i.e. sets of axioms). To make predicate logic more appropriate for software specification, the language is extended by several constructs. A full account of AFSL can be found in [26]. We highlight some of the features of AFSL:

- AFSL is a typed first-order specification language, with equality and built-in sorts for boolean values, integer and real numbers, characters and strings. Functions may be partial. Predicates are regarded as boolean-valued functions. The language has a loose semantics, i.e. the semantics of a specification is not a single model but a class of models.
- Parameterized modules. Module definitions may contain parameters. Import of a module has the same effect as the textual substitution of the module text with the proper instantiations of the parameters.
- Sub-typing relation on sorts (denoted as <<<). When a function is defined on a type, it is also defined on its sub-types (inheritance). We allow multiple super-types.
- No overloading. Objects/functions with the same name should have the same semantics. To enforce this, the language does not allow for 'ad-hoc' overloading of object and function names. The only way to re-use a name is using sub-type polymorphism (a name is inherited from sorts higher in the sub sort hierarchy) or parameter polymorphism (a name is defined in a parameterized module, and imported via an instantiation of that module).
- Informal axioms. Axioms can be stated informally (as an intermediate step in the formalization process). Formal terms can be used in informal axioms by quotation; as such, they can be recognized and processed (e.g. type-checked) by software tools.

The syntax of AFSL is almost self explanatory. When necessary we explain constructs on the fly.

Graphical representation Diagrams are used to give overviews of larger parts of the signature definition. They contain information on object/function names, their types, and sub-typing relations. These diagrams, generated automatically from the specification text, proved to be an important instrument in the formal specification development process.

4.3 Tools

When working with large specifications the use of tools becomes inevitable. Within the FSA-project several tools have been developed, and for the FAN-project we used and experimented with the following tools:

- A parser and type-checker, implemented in the functional programming language SML [18] (the implementation is done by Indra Polak and the second author).
- The graph visualization system da Vinci of the University of Bremen (see [7]) for the construction of the diagrams.

– To manipulate the large number of files (every module is a separate file) we used AWK programs and UNIX shell scripts for the extraction of LaTeX and AFSL files from a general file-format (containing formal specification and documentation).

5 Formalizing anaesthesia

As stated in section 3, the desired functionality of the support system includes different tasks. Within FAN we additionally we distinguished the following phases:

Phase 1	Phase 2	Phase 3	Phase 4
Formalizing domain ontology and measurement data	Formalizing causal and has-part relations	Formalizing inference mechanism	Formalizing tasks and applications

The first phase introduces the objects of the specification. The second and the third phase focus on the relations between objects and the inference of propositions about objects, respectively. In the fourth phase we concentrate on the several tasks that can be performed using the inference mechanism, examples of those tasks are diagnosis and therapy advice. Currently, the FAN-specification includes phase 1 and 2. It is recognized that later phases may require extension of the specification of earlier phases. Method, language, and tools allow for easy accommodation of such extensions.

The division is inspired on the different layers in KADS [31]. In the KADS-terminology, the result of the first phase is the specification of the domain-layer, the second and third phase specify the inference layer, and the task layer corresponds with the last phase. Besides this 'horizontal' division, we also made a 'vertical' division that was already described above: we identify a so-called 'structural model' and a 'knowledge base'. The model presents the structural knowledge and the knowledge base contains the factual knowledge (the actual interpretations and relations).

The following examples of factual knowledge illustrate the type of knowledge that has to be formalized:

Cardiac output is equal to heart rate times stroke volume ($CO = HR \times SV$).

During the perfusion period, disconnection is unacceptable and airway obstruction is undesirable.

A too-high Mean Arterial Blood-pressure can cause Edema.

In subsections 5.1 – 5.4, we discuss specification of a structure for representing this kind of factual knowledge. In subsection 5.5, we use this structure to formalize the given examples of factual knowledge.

5.1 Overall characteristics of the specification

The complete specification consists of about 80 modules, with over 3000 lines of specification. The library modules for AFSL consist of a group of general modules, specifying algebraic structures and standard functions on the built-in sorts of AFSL (50 modules with 1100 lines). The FAN related modules consist of three groups. In the first we identify the domain ontology and measured data, a second group of modules specifies relations between measurements (in total 30 modules with 1600 lines) and the third is the knowledge base that contains the formalized knowledge (currently divided in 2 modules containing 1200 lines). The knowledge base will grow further since it currently contains only a sample of the knowledge that is actually needed. The general and structure parts of the specification are expected to keep their current size.

5.2 Algebraic structures

Modules for the definition of algebraic structures, like fields, groups and orderings, follow the definition in the Larch-library [13]. The absence of overloading forced us to select carefully the names and properties of operators which are fixed for the whole specification.

5.3 Domain ontology and measured data

When working in an ill-structured domain like anaesthesia, a precise definition of the ontology is of vital importance. The distinction between terms like disease, syndrome, sign, and symptom must be made explicit. Besides this, much of the data is obtained via measurement of physical quantities. Therefore, the structural model must incorporate both the domain ontology and measured data. Some preliminary design decisions include:

- The patient is not modeled explicitly: measurements are assumed to be from the same patient.
- Measurement data are assumed to be available at any moment in time (no sampling). We use a 'default' value when a signal is not known.
- For discretizations of measurements, we use five values: too-low, decreased, normal, increased, too-high.

To structure the domain ontology, we identify three classes of sorts: value sets (contain basic values), courses of value (model basic values that vary of time), and parameters (the collection of all known properties of a patient).

The three value sets are:

QuantityS	(physical quantities)
QualityS	(discrete values)
BoolS	(the two boolean values)

The next layer consists of courses of value (functions from time-points to a value set):

SignalS = **TimePointS** → **QuantityS**
DiscreteSignalS = **TimePointS** → **QualityS**
ConditionS = **TimePointS** → **BoolS**

For parameters we distinguish three types: magnitudes, levels, and phenomena. *Magnitudes* represent parameters with numerical values (typically measurement data, for example blood-pressure). More discrete parameters, like anaesthesia-depth or ventilation, are modeled as *levels* with five discrete values. The 'yes/no-parameters', e.g. the presence of 'high-blood-pressure', are modeled by *phenomena*. Phenomena will form the basis for phase 2 and 3 of the specification, in particular the inference relations.

A second subdivision concerns different modalities or worlds-of-reasoning, we model these by introducing three different *worlds*. Besides the *actual* (current) value of a parameter we also want to refer to the *target* (medically ideal) value of a parameter and the *default* value for the case that the measurements are not available.

Parameters are modeled as clusters of three course-of-values (one for each world-of-reasoning):

MagnitudeS = **WorldS** → **SignalS**
LevelS = **WorldS** → **DiscreteSignalS**
PhenomenonS = **WorldS** → **ConditionS**

Later we will introduce some additional attributes for parameters. To specify courses and parameters, we use the parameterization and sub-typing mechanisms of AFSL. We will discuss the construction of the sort **ParameterS** from the built-in sorts and library modules.

Value sets The sort **BoolS** is an AFSL primitive. Qualities are defined as an enumerated sort **QualityS** with 5 elements:

```
MODULE QualityM

SORT    QualityS

OBJ     TooHigh    : QualityS
OBJ     Increased  : QualityS
OBJ     Normal     : QualityS
OBJ     Decreased  : QualityS
OBJ     TooLow     : QualityS

IMPORT Enum5M[QualityS, TooLow, Decreased, Normal,
                         Increased, TooHigh]

END MODULE
```

The import of **Enum5M** forces that the five objects are distinct and introduces a linear ordering on the elements.

We specified a model for quantities including but not limited to the SI-quantities (Système International). The medical field uses many units other the those of the SI. Therefore conversion relations between different units must be specified. We model physical dimensions, units and quantities as follows:

```
MODULE QuantityM
  SORT   DimensionS
  OBJ    Time    : DimensionS
  OBJ    Length  : DimensionS
  (...)
  SORT   UnitS
  OBJ    Second  : UnitS
  OBJ    Meter   : UnitS
  (...)

  SORT   QuantityS

  FUNC   Quant: RealS, UnitS -> QuantityS
  FUNC   Dim  : QuantityS -> DimensionS
  (...)

  END MODULE
```

So, **Quant(10,Second)** is a quantity of 10 seconds and **Dim Quant(10,Second) = Time**. The full specification, reported in [21], contains also arithmetical operations on dimensions and units, and scaling functions on units. SI is also formalized in Z [14], where the typing mechanism of Z is extended to allow for type checking on physical units.

An interesting part of the SI specification is concerns the modeling of time. Since AFSL has no standard language construct for temporal expressions, time must be modeled explicitly (as in the other case studies [12] and [28]). Elements of **TimeS** represent a quantity of time. Elements of **TimePointS** denote a particular point in time and **TimePeriodS** models time-periods.

```
MODULE TimeM

SORT   TimeS <<< QuantityS
DECL   time  : TimeS
AXIOM  Dim(time) = Time

SORT   TimePointS
SORT   TimePeriodS
DECL   tp     : TimePointS
DECL   tper   : TimePeriodS

FUNC   Begin : TimePeriodS -> TimePointS
FUNC   End   : TimePeriodS -> TimePointS
AXIOM  Begin(tper) =< End(tper)
(...)

END MODULE
```

Using this specification, we can introduce several derived concepts, e.g.:

```
FUNC   Duration : TimePeriodS -> TimeS
FUNC   Contains : TimePeriodS,TimePointS -> BoolS
```

Course of values An important notion is time-dependent value, modeled as a function from time points to a value set. We collect them in the sort **CourseS** and distinguish three sub-sorts, depending on the value set involved.

Since AFSL is a first order language, we cannot define function types directly. So, we introduce the abstract sort **FunctionS[ArgS,ResultS]** of functions from **ArgS** to **ResultS**. Associated with these functions is a (partial) operation **.** which models function application.

```
MODULE FunctionM[ ArgS, ResultS ]

SORT ArgS
SORT ResultS
SORT FunctionS[ArgS,ResultS]

DECL arg  : ArgS
DECL func : FunctionS[ArgS,ResultS]

FUNC .    : FunctionS[ArgS,ResultS], ArgS -> ResultS PARTIAL

END MODULE
```

The sorts **ArgS** and **ResultS** are the parameters of the module. Observe that AFSL supports implicit quantification in axioms (here for **func1** and **func2**).

The module **CourseM[XS]** introduces the parameterized sort **CourseS[XS]** as a subset of the functions of **TimePointS** to **XS** to the arbitrary sort **XS**.

```
MODULE CourseM[XS]

SORT   XS

IMPORT TimeM
IMPORT FunctionM[TimePointS,XS]

SORT   CourseS[XS] <<< FunctionS[TimePointS,XS]
(...)

END MODULE
```

We use **CourseM** for defining **SignalS** (with **QuantityS** substituted for **XS**), for defining **DiscreteSignalS** (substituting **QualityS** for **XS**), and for defining **ConditionS** (with **BoolS** substituted for **XS**). Note that the definition of **CourseM** is more general and in the next paragraph we will re-use this module to define a fourth time-dependent sort.

Parameters With every parameter three courses of values are associated: the default course, the target course and the actual course. To select the different courses, we introduce the sort **WorldS** containing **Actual**, **Target**, and **Default**.

```
MODULE ParameterM[ XS ]
   SORT   XS
   IMPORT CourseM[XS]

   SORT   WorldS

   OBJ    Actual   : WorldS
   OBJ    Target   : WorldS
   OBJ    Default  : WorldS

   SORT   AnyParameterS

   FUNC   Description : AnyParameterS -> StringS
   FUNC   Observable  : AnyParameterS -> BoolS

   SORT   ParameterS[XS] <<< AnyParameterS

   FUNC   Course : ParameterS[XS], WorldS -> CourseS[XS]

   END MODULE
```

The function **Description** gives the full medical name of a parameter. Observable parameters can be observed by the physician possibly with the aid of measurement equipment, e.g. the body-temperature is observable.

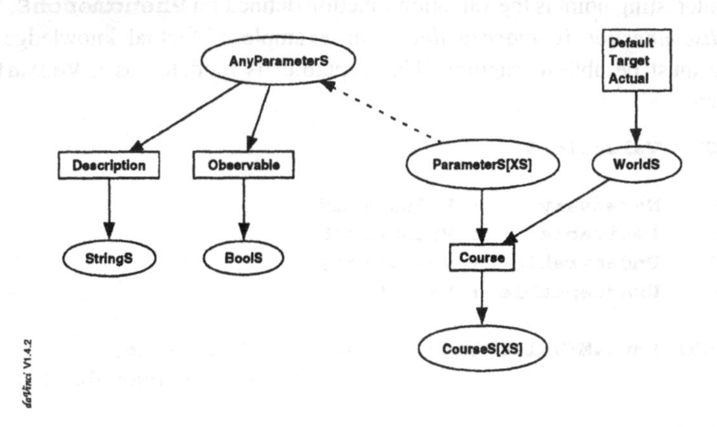

Fig. 1. Diagram of the module **ParameterM**.

A graphical representation of this module is given in figure 1. The abstract sort **ParameterS[XS]** is a subset of **AnyParameterS** (indicated with the dotted arrow). **ParameterS[XS]** therefore inherits the functions **Description** and **Observable** as defined on **AnyParameterS**. On **ParameterS[XS]** we define the function **Course** with a two arguments: a parameter and a world.

We obtain the three parameter sorts by importing this module with the correct instantiation for **XS**. We introduce the names **MagnitudeS**, **LevelS**, and **PhenomenonS** as abbreviations (using the keyword **ALIAS**):

```
MODULE FANParameterM

IMPORT QualityM
IMPORT QuantityM

IMPORT ParameterM[QuantityS]
IMPORT ParameterM[QualityS]
IMPORT ParameterM[BoolS]

ALIAS  MagnitudeS  === ParameterS[QuantityS]
ALIAS  LevelS      === ParameterS[QualityS]
ALIAS  PhenomenonS === ParameterS[BoolS]

FUNC   Discrete : MagnitudeS -> LevelS PARTIAL
(...)

END MODULE
```

From the module **FANParameterM** we omitted some additional axioms concerning the dimension and units on magnitudes and the corresponding quantities. The partial function **Discrete** gives the level corresponding with a magnitude according to a discretization.

An interesting point is the valuation function defined on **PhenomenonS**. We mentioned *disconnection is unacceptable* as an example of factual knowledge that the structure must be able to capture. 'Unacceptable' is modeled as a **Valuation** of phenomena:

```
SORT   ValuationS

OBJ    Necessary    : ValuationS
OBJ    Desirable    : ValuationS
OBJ    Undesirable  : ValuationS
OBJ    Unacceptable : ValuationS

IMPORT Enum4M[ValuationS, Necessary, Desirable,
                          Undesirable, Unacceptable]

IMPORT CourseM[ValuationS]
FUNC   Valuation: PhenomenonS -> CourseS[ValuationS]
```

It may be surprising that the result of the valuation function is a time dependent value. In general, the valuation of a certain phenomenon is not constant during an operation. Consider the phenomenon "low body temperature" (e.g. body temperature is below 25°C); under normal conditions this is unacceptable, while during the perfusion period it is necessary. By making the valuation a time-dependent function we can specify this as:

```
DECL   tp : TimePointS
OBJ    LowBodyTemp: PhenomenonS

AXIOM  PerfusionPeriod Contains tp        ==>
       Valuation(LowBodyTemp).tp = Necessary

AXIOM  Not (PerfusionPeriod Contains tp) ==>
       Valuation(LowBodyTemp).tp = Unacceptable
```

Operations on parameters Given the parameters as a data structure for our model, we define operations on parameters. First we define operations on value sets. Then we define a general lifting scheme to introduce operators on course-of-values and parameters based on those on the value sets (e.g. logical and numerical operators).

On **QuantityS** we define the arithmetical operations and a linear order, imposing some restrictions on the dimensions of the operands. On elements of **QualityS** we define the (linear) ordering **=<**. The operators on **BoolS** are as usual.

The second type of operation is the discretization of quantities to qualities. We define the function **Discretize** to perform the discretization of a quantity according to four bounding quantities:

```
FUNC Discretize : QuantityS, QuantityS, QuantityS, QuantityS,
                  QuantityS -> QualityS
```

The axiomatization of this function is straightforward: the first four arguments indicate the bounds for the five discretizations, the last quantity is to be discretized. Using this discretization, we also defined an relative discretizer which discretizes a quantity using four scaling factors and a reference quantity as bounds.

Now we want to lift these functions from the level of value sets to the level of course of value and parameters. An ad-hoc way is via overloading, but that is not allowed in AFSL. We prefer a solution based on parameterization, illustrated below for binary functions.

```
MODULE Course2LiftM[XS,YS,ZS,Oper]

  SORT   XS
  SORT   YS
  SORT   ZS

  IMPORT CourseM[XS]
  IMPORT CourseM[YS]
  IMPORT CourseM[ZS]

  DECL covx : CourseS[XS]
  DECL covy : CourseS[YS]
  DECL tp : TimePointS

  FUNC  Oper : XS, YS -> ZS
  FUNC  Course2[Oper] : CourseS[XS], CourseS[YS] -> CourseS[ZS]
```

```
AXIOM (covx Course2[Oper] covy).tp = (covx.tp) Oper (covy.tp)

END MODULE
```

This module introduces the binary function **Course2[Oper]** (given a function **Oper** from **XS**, **YS** to **ZS**) and defines it point-wise. An example of the use of this scheme is the definition of multiplication on signals, given the multiplication on quantities (**Course2[*]**):

```
IMPORT Course2LiftM[QuantityS,QuantityS,QuantityS,*]
```

The scheme for lifting operators to **ParameterS** is similar.

5.4 Relations between phenomena

The previous subsection was concerned with the definition of parameters. They are used to model properties of a patient and to classify measured values. A different type of knowledge has to do with relations between parameters. Physiological knowledge often concerns quantitative relations between magnitudes: the $CO = HR \times SV$ example mentioned above. Diagnostic knowledge mainly concerns qualitative relations between phenomena. The discretization functions discussed above bridge the quantitative and the qualitative values. For modeling qualitative relations we distinguish:

- Causal relations. For example "A Too-high Mean Arterial Blood-pressure can cause Edema".
- Has-part relations. If a disease has several symptoms and signs, then these symptoms and signs have a has-part relation with the disease. An example: "Symptoms of an increased or higher level of Stress are increased or higher levels of Mean Arterial Blood-pressure and Heart Rate".

Associated with each relation is a 'strength'. The possible strengths are facultative, obligatory, and pathognomonic. Facultative denotes a positive correlation between two phenomena, obligatory indicates an implication, and pathognomonic is used to indicate a bi-implication between two phenomena.

For the formalization of relations there are two options. We can model relations directly as boolean functions (stated as axioms using the logical operations) or we can objectify them by introducing special sorts for links. We have chosen for the last option for the following reasons:

- Anaesthetists tend to reason about relations as objects. The presence or absence of a causal relation (for example some kind of reflex) is an information item itself.
- When relations are objects, it is easier to classify them, for example by introducing an attribute for strength.
- Reasoning with the relations can now be described on a higher level of abstraction. The relations are then parameters of the rules.

To model this, we introduce the sorts **CausLinkS** and **HasPartLinkS**. Additionally we decided to regard the objects denoting links to be of type **PhenomenonS**:

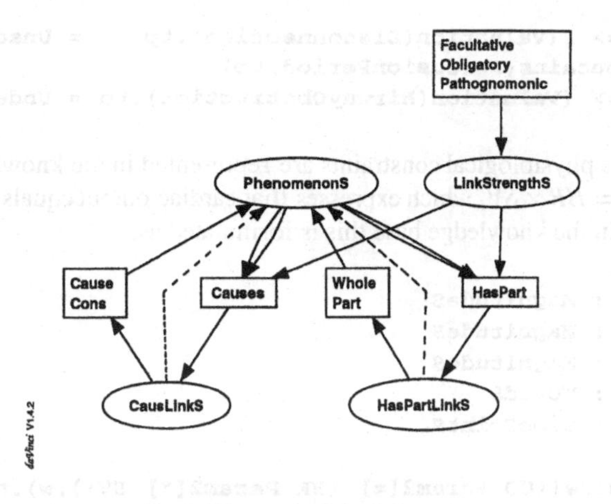

Fig. 2. Diagram of the link-sorts.

```
SORT    CausLinkS       <<< PhenomenonS
SORT    HasPartLinkS    <<< PhenomenonS
```

Objects of both **CausLinkS** and **HasPartLinkS** are constructed from two phenomena and a **LinkStrenghtS** (notice that Caus-links and Has-part-links are themselves phenomena):

```
FUNC Causes   : PhenomenonS, PhenomenonS, LinkStrengthS
                -> CausLinkS      PARTIAL
FUNC HasPart  : PhenomenonS, PhenomenonS, LinkStrengthS
                -> HasPartLinkS PARTIAL
```

Besides the constructor functions, we also have for each link-type two destructor functions (**Cause/Cons** and **Whole/Part**, see figure 2).

5.5 Knowledge base

The knowledge base contains the formalization of knowledge obtained from interviews and knowledge from physiological handbooks. The knowledge items are expressed in the signature provided by the model. Most of the expressions are straightforward, like our example:

> During the perfusion period, disconnection is unacceptable (...) and airway-obstruction is undesirable (...)

This is represented in the knowledge base as:

```
OBJ     Disconnection        : PhenomenonS
OBJ     AirwayObstruction    : PhenomenonS

AXIOM   Contains(PerfusionPeriod,tp)
```

```
        ==>  (Valuation(Disconnection).tp     = Unacceptable)
AXIOM   Contains(PerfusionPeriod,tp)
        ==> (Valuation(AirwayObstruction).tp = Undesirable)
```

Furthermore, the physiological constraints are represented in the knowledge base. One equation is $CO = HR \times SV$, which expresses that cardiac output equals heart rate times stroke volume. In the knowledge base this is formulated as:

```
OBJ    CO : MagnitudeS
OBJ    HR : MagnitudeS
OBJ    SV : MagnitudeS
DECL   w  : WorldS
DECL   tp : TimePointS

AXIOM Course((CO Param2[=] (HR Param2[*] SV)),w).tp
```

Note that we use the lifted, point-wise defined versions of = and *.

As an example of the specification of causal relations, we can formalize "A Too-high Mean Arterial Blood-pressure can cause Edema" as:

```
OBJ    PArtM   : MagnitudeS
OBJ    Edema   : PhenomenonS
AXIOM Course(
         Causes( (Discrete(PArtM) Param2[=] Param0[TooHigh])
               , Edema
               , Facultative),w).tp
```

The has-part relation "Symptoms of an increased or higher level of Stress are increased or higher levels of Mean Arterial Blood-pressure and Heart Rate" can be formalized as:

```
OBJ    Stress : LevelS
AXIOM Course(
         HasPart( Stress Param2[>=] Param0[Increased]
                , (Discrete(PArtM) Param2[>=] Param0[Increased])
                  Param2[Or]
                  (Discrete(HR)    Param2[>=] Param0[Increased])
                , Obligatory),w).tp
```

For a concise definition of the knowledge base we use abbreviations, for example:

```
FUNC EveryWhere : PhenomenonS -> BoolS
AXIOM EveryWhere phen
      <=>
      FORALL w,tp (Course(phen,w).tp)
```

The law $CO = HR * SV$ can now be re-formulated as:

```
AXIOM EveryWhere (CO Param2[=] (HR Param2[*] SV))
```

6 The FAN-project

The FAN-project went through several stages which we briefly discuss.

De Geus and Rotterdam [9] developed the Carola-database system and investigated the use of constraint satisfaction techniques for diagnosis. This thesis also contains the first attempts at formalizing anaesthesia for decision support. Two types of knowledge are identified: arithmetical constraints (mainly on physiological variables) and qualitative knowledge. A small implementation in a rule-based language RL was presented for arithmetic constraints [10]. The second type of knowledge is concerned with qualitative knowledge, and in [9, pp. 229] it is stated that:

> It seems most appropriate to represent knowledge with a language that can capture the different aspects of knowledge uniformly.

A first attempt to develop such a language is given in [22]. This report presents an ad-hoc formalism, baptized LaFAn (Language for Formalization Anaesthesia). LaFAn was used to give a first formalization of interviews of anaesthetists. It was hard to give a good definition of LaFAn since it was not stable. The main reason for this is that one first needs a proper theory of anaesthesia before being able to define a language to reason about it. To overcome these problems, we decided to take a new path: a general purpose formal specification language to formalize the concepts of anaesthesia. The formalization was carried out as part of the FSA-project. We started to work on the formalization of the model using the language and method proposed in the FSA-project. The two main tasks, viz. to define a model and to formalize it, were dealt with simultaneously.

The first result of the FAN-project was a specification written in the non-modular version of AFSL. One major drawback of this specification was that it did not provide a clear view on the underlying model. To improve this, a graphical representation technique was introduced.

Report [23] contains a reformulation of the model. The modular version of AFSL and a graphical notation are used to present the specification in a modular way. The overwhelming number of identifiers (function and sort names), all necessary to describe the model in full detail, forced us to use the parameter mechanisms of AFSL extensively. To enforce the use of these possibilities, a radical decision was taken: *No overloading allowed.* Other restrictions were to remove the parts that had to do with therapy advice and prediction/simulation. This way the formalization became more rigorous and less complex.

The final report of the FAN-project [21] contains the type-checked version of the FAN-specification, with automatically generated diagrams. The knowledge with respect to diagnosis is separated from the knowledge that is needed to interpret measurements. Furthermore, the aspect of data sampling is not treated.

Still the project needs further development. Especially the validation of the formal model is important. The FAN-project was mainly devoted to the development of the model and the formalization. Given these descriptions, we need to validate the knowledge that we have formalized.

6.1 Other phases

The report on FAN [21] contains the formal specification, structural model and knowledge base, of the first two phases. The next step is the formalization of the inference mechanisms, in particular to infer diagnoses based on the measured data. Further steps may consist of:

- The formalization of more factual knowledge in terms of the developed model. This includes the analysis of more interviews and the incorporation of physiological models from literature.
- The validation of the specification using a prototype. The functionality of this prototype is to infer simple diagnoses from the measured data. In view of the declarative nature of the specification, a declarative programming language is best suited to implement a prototype.

We think that the construction of a prototype based on the first three phases is important for the validation of the specified knowledge. After validation the fourth phase (design of required functionality of the support system) is feasible.

7 Conclusions

We have presented an overview of the specification process of a model for anaesthesiology. This model is intended as a basis for the specification and construction of a support system.

With the specification we are able to express arithmetical constraints as well as other declarative knowledge. Furthermore the specification gives a structured presentation of the concepts that we found important in the knowledge domain. The final version of the specification of the model and the knowledge base is available in [21].

We summarize some of the lessons that we have learned from this formalization case:

- The use of a special purpose language, like LaFAn, is not very productive in a large and not fully explored domain like anaesthesiology. In such a domain, first a proper formal model has to be constructed. A general purpose language, like AFSL, is suited for the description of such a model. Only when that model is stable, one can think of designing a special purpose language.
- The use of a first order language, with sub-typing and parameterized modularization (offering a poor man's second order facility) and no overloading, like AFSL, leads to a dilemma. On the one hand, overloading was not added to AFSL in order to improve the clarity of specifications by avoiding semantically different functions with identical names. It is our impression that this design decision on AFSL definitely had a beneficial effect on the overall structure of the specification. On the other hand, there are situations where overloading is common and considered to be natural. E.g. in the case of lifting an operation on some sort S to functions of type $S' \rightarrow S$. In AFSL, lifting of an operation can be accomplished via a parameterized module, see e.g. **Course2LiftM**.

- Restructuring of the specification was mainly performed during the the definition of the signature of the specification. This led to the guideline to restructure at the signature level, before full axiomatization takes place. The use of a graphical notation is useful, especially when defining the signature.
- A property-oriented way of specification seems a proper way of formalizing an open knowledge domain. Additional attributes can easily be given to objects, without conflicting with earlier introduction.
- Subtype and parameter polymorphism help to reduce the number of similar concepts. In earlier versions, magnitudes, levels and phenomena were not subsets of a common sort. The introduction of `Parameters[XS]` allows a uniform treatment of parameters. Furthermore, such abstractions make it possible to re-use specifications. An example is the specification of the mathematical structures and course of value.

Acknowledgments

We acknowledge Indra Polak for implementing parts of the type checker. We thank B. Ballast, G. Massée, J. de Jong, and P. Hennis for the possibility to interview them. Three anonymous referees are acknowledged for their comments on an earlier version of this paper.

References

1. N. Chomsky. A minimalist program for linguistic theory. Technical report, MIT Occasional Papers in Linguistics, 1992.
2. R. Cooper, J. Farringdon, J. Fox and T. Shallice. Levels of description in specifying Soar. In: *Proceedings EuroSoar-5*, 1991.
3. D. John Doyle. *Computer Programs in Clinical and Laboratory Medicine.* Springer Verlag, 1989.
4. L.M.G. Feijs and H.B.M. Jonkers. *Formal Specification and Design.* Cambridge Tracts in Theoretical Computer Science 35. Cambridge University Press, 1994.
5. D. Fensel and F. van Harmelen: A Comparison Of Languages Which Operationalize And Formalize KADS Models of Expertise, *The Knowledge Engineering Review*, vol 9(2), 1994.
6. M. Fieschi. *Artificial Intelligence in Medicine.* Chapman and Hall, 1990. Original title: Intelligence Artificielle en Médecine des Systèmes experts (translated by D. Cramp).
7. M. Fröhlick and M. Werner. *daVinci V1.4 User Manual.* Department of Computer Science, University of Bremen, January 1995.
8. A.F. de Geus. *The Carola Database – User Manual.* Department of Anaesthesiology, University Hospital Groningen, 1990.
9. A.F. de Geus and E.P. Rotterdam. *Decision Support in Anaesthesia.* PhD thesis, Department of Anaesthesiology, University of Groningen, 1992.
10. F. de Geus, E. Rotterdam, S. van Denneheuvel, and P. van Emde Boas. Physiological modeling using RL. In M. Stefanelli, A. Hasman, M. Fieschi, and J. Talmon, editors, *Proceedings of AIME '91*, pages 198 – 210. Springer Verlag, 1991.
11. R. Groenboom and G.R. Renardel de Lavalette. Formal Specification and Soar: does cognitive science need formalisms. In: *Proceedings of workshop Euro-Soar6*, 1992.

12. R. Groenboom, R.M. Tol, and E. Saaman. Formal specification and design of a simple real time kernel. In A. Nieuwendijk, editor, *Proceedings Accolade '94*, pages 87 – 102. Dutch Gradute School in Logic, Amsterdam, 1995.
13. John V. Guttag and James J. Horning, with S.J. Garland, K.D. Jones, A. Modet, and J.M. Wing. *Larch: Languages and Tools for Formal Specification.* Springer-Verlag Texts and Monographs in Computer Science, 1993.
14. I.J. Hayes and B.P. Mahony. Using units of measurement in formal specifications. *Formal Aspects of Computing*, 7: 329 – 347, 1995.
15. J.E. Laird, A. Newell, and P.S. Rosenbloom. SOAR: An architecture for general intelligence. *Artificial Intelligence*, 33(1): 1 – 64, 1987.
16. I. van Langevelde, A. Philipsen, and J. Treur. Formal specificartion of compositional architectures. In: *Proceedings of the 10th European Conference on Artificial Intelligence (ECAI-92)*, Vienna, 1992.
17. B.G. Miles. *A specification of the Soar cognitive architecture in Z.* Technical report CMU-CS-92-169, Carnegie Mellon University Pittsburgh PA, 1992.
18. C. Myers, C. Clack, and E. Poon. *Programming with Standard ML.* Prentice Hall, 1993.
19. M. Naftalin, T. Denvir, and M. Bertran (eds). *FME '94: Industrial Benefit of Formal Methods.* LNCS 873, Springer Verlag, 1994.
20. A. Newell and H.A. Simon. *Human problem solving*. Prentice-Hall, 1972.
21. G.R. Renardel de Lavalette (ed). *Formalization of Anaesthesia. Report on the FAN-project.* Technical Report, Department of Computing Science, University of Groningen, (in preparation).
22. E.P. Rotterdam. *Anesthesiekennis in Lafan*. Technical report R93026, Department of Medical Information Science, University of Groningen, 1993. (In Dutch).
23. E.P. Rotterdam. FAN: Formalizing anaesthesiology in AFSL. Technical Report R9406, Department of Medical Information Science, University of Groningen, 1994.
24. E.P. Rotterdam. *Desired Functionality of a Support System.* In: [21].
25. J. Rumbaugh et. al. *Object-Oriented Modeling and Design*. Prentice Hall, 1991.
26. E. Saaman. *User manual AFSL.* Department of Computing Science, University of Groningen, (in preparation).
27. E. Saaman and G.R. Renardel de Lavalette. *Object-Oriented Formalization*, Manuscript, Department of Computing Science, University of Groningen, 1995.
28. E. Saaman, P. Politiek, and K. Brookhuis. Specification and Design of InDeter-1. Technical report, Traffic Research Centre, University of Groningen, 1994. Deliverable 9 (321A).
29. E.P. Stabler. *The logical approach to syntax.* MIT Press, Cambridge, 1992.
30. J. Treur and T. Wetter (eds). *Formal Specification of Complex Reasoning Systems.* Ellis Horwood, 1993.
31. B.J. Wielinga, A. Th. Schreiber, and J.A. Breuker. KADS: A modelling approach to knowledge engineering. *Knowledge Acquisition*, 4(1), March 1992.
32. J.C.P Woodcock and P.G. Larsen (eds). *FME '93: Industrial-Strength Formal Methods.* LNCS 670, Springer Verlag, 1993.

A New System Engineering Methodology Coupling Formal Specification and Performance Evaluation

J. Martins J.-P. Hubaux

Swiss Federal Institute of Technology
TCOM Laboratory, Telecommunications Services Group
EPFL-DE-TCOM-GST, CH-1015 Lausanne
martins@tcom.epfl.ch and hubaux@tcom.epfl.ch

Abstract: This paper proposes a new methodology for system engineering. It provides an integrated approach covering formal specification and performance evaluation. Therefore it associates the advantages of formal techniques that allow formal proof and automatic implementation with the benefits of performance evaluation. The basic idea is to abstract the relevant features of the system in the formal specification (structure, functional description), enhance it with relevant information for performance modeling (quality of service, operating load, processing architecture and processing constraints), and map them into a performance evaluation environment. In this paper, we develop the suitable extensions for the formal language SDL and apply them to an example: Transmission Control Protocol (TCP).

Keywords: System Engineering, Formal Specification, System Analysis, System Design, Performance Evaluation, Simulation.

1. Introduction

Performance is becoming a critical aspect of emerging broadband technology. Therefore, the use of powerful performance modeling techniques becomes of prime importance. Their goal is to obtain some notion of how the system will perform under a given set of conditions. Besides, they facilitate analysis of proposals for new services or technology because they are more tractable and less expensive than field trials for evaluating alternatives. Performance evaluation facilitates comparing alternative designs and finding which is the best according to the chosen set of criteria. Even if there are no alternatives, it helps in determining how well the system would perform and whether any improvements need to be made.

Formal description techniques intend to describe the structure and the behavior of systems. Their purpose is to produce correct and unambiguous descriptions, that should ultimately produce efficient implementations. The input to the formal specification is a set of requirement statements and a conceptual overview of the proposed system. The output is a formal representation that captures the functional description of the proposed system. A formal specification should abstract from implementation details in order to give an overview of the system, to postpone implementation decisions, and to allow all valid implementations. It makes use of neither design nor implementation concepts; it defines rather a model that represents the significant properties and functionality of the system, which can be controlled through validation, verification and conformance testing.

Traffic and queueing theorists have long been using protocol specifications to make a heuristic model of the system and then analyzing the model. When system specifications exist, the question arises whether a more direct path to performance analysis cannot be found. Our scope is to provide a methodology that steadily integrates formal specification and performance evaluation (Figure 1). Formal specification handles the logical consistency of the system than performance modeling handles the operational consistency of the system. An efficient system should be logically error free, but it should also be performing enough to achieve its service.

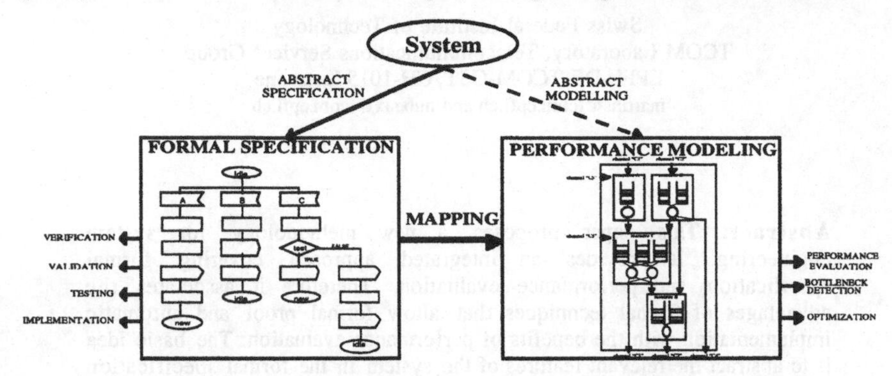

Figure 1: Performance evaluation and formal specification integration

Our methodology appeal consists in taking benefice of the similarities between the formal specification and the performance modeling. Both techniques share some common modeling that can be reused with each other.

Moreover, combining the formal specification and the performance evaluation allows to verify and improve the efficiency of the system. Formal specifications provide the basic input for the system validation, verification, automatic implementation and conformance testing. Therefore reusing a formal specification saves time because it reuses the expertise developed for formal modeling, and it avoids modeling errors because formal specifications can certify the logical consistence of the system.

2. System Engineering

System engineering aims at handling the complexity of systems in an organized way. Achieving this purpose requires supplying a methodology working at different levels, each focusing on certain aspects of the system.

■ The *analysis* consists in understanding and modeling the system and the domain within which it operates; it includes abstracting important real-world features, focusing on what has to be done, independently of how it is done.

■ The *design* consists in providing a high-level strategy for solving the problem and building a solution. It includes decisions about the organization of the system into hardware and software components and major policy decisions.

■ The *implementation* discusses the specific details for building the system.

Classical system engineering methodologies support analysis-design-implementation approach; however in many cases, analysis is refined in two models (Figure 2).

● The *requirement specification* aims to delimit the system, define the functionality of the system, and capture the customer requirements. It includes the definition of the service interfaces (which services, what quality of service, which cost) and of the information exchanged for a given service (which messages, which workload). This model is easy to understand and formulate from both the customer and the provider perspective, so they can talk to each other and see if we are building the correct system. This control is usually referred as the *verification* process.

• The *analysis specification* aims to structure the system independently of its implementation environment. It consists of the specification of the information held in the system, of the behavior that the system will adopt and of the details from presenting the system to the outside world. It is formed from the requirement specification. During the analysis, the system will be entirely partitioned into objects to obtain a robust and extensible structure. In practice it means that the functionality should be allocated to different components. When the system contains a large number of components, it is seldom possible to get a clear overview, so they are structured in subsystems. The task of a subsystem is to package the components so that complexity is reduced. The subsystem also works as handling units for the organization; all components that have a strong mutual functional and geographical coupling will be placed in the same subsystem. The analysis specification serves at least three purposes; at an early stage to specify, validate and verify the functionality and the system properties, then to provide a firm basis for design and implementation, and after implementation, to document the functional properties.

• The *design specification* aims at adapting the analysis specification to a particular implementation environment. The analysis specification was developed assuming ideal conditions that we must at this stage adapt to reality. The abstract vision of the analysis specification is suited because it provides a generic structuring that serves as basis for many alternative designs, and because it avoids the complexity introduced when looking at the implementation. On the other hand, design specifications provide physical designs of the system that will implement the specified functionality. This can be seen as mapping the abstract system defined in the analysis specification to a concrete system made up of hardware and software components. The design specification is an abstraction of how the system really is built. Its final structure will reflect how the implementation environment has affected construction.

• The *product implementation* consists of the software and hardware realization. It is the tail end of the system development; it provides the final product that will be used by customers. It should therefore satisfy and conform earlier phases of the system development. The control of its conformance towards the original analysis specification is usually referred as the *testing* or *conformance testing* process.

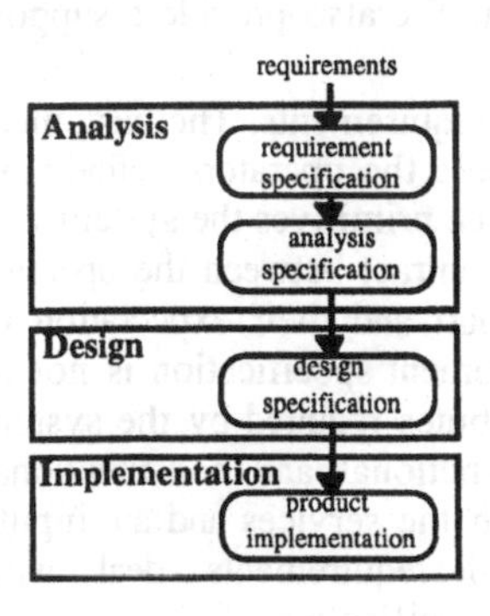

Figure 2: Classical system engineering approach

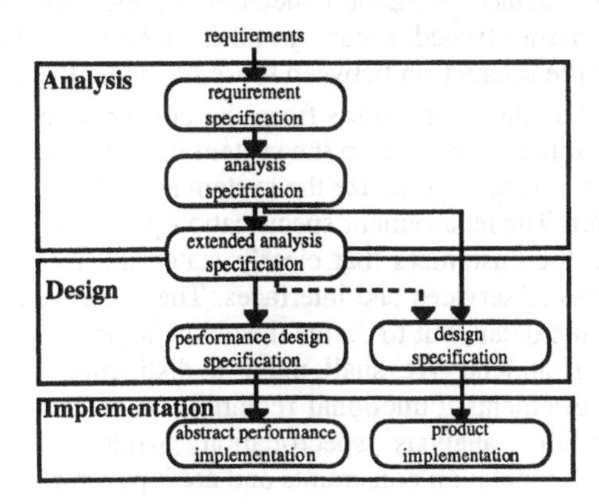

Figure 3: Our methodology decomposition

2.1. Our System Engineering Approach

Our approach is organized according to the basic decomposition in three planes: analysis, design and implementation, for which we define seven models (Figure 3).

- The *extended analysis specification* aims at refining and integrating some of the topics usually covered by the design specification. The additional features are given in a highly abstract notation; that is, we are not interested to really apprehend the nature of the implementation but only those features that affect the non-functional aspects of the system (e.g., performance, cost, user perception). In classical system engineering, improving performance requires simulating the critical parts of the system, or performing prototyping to get an early opinion of what the system will look like, but this is a risky method since we can easily do unrealistic simplifications. Prototypes and simulations always aim to highlight particular issues. General conclusions on other issues therefore cannot be drawn from a prototype, nor from a rudimentary simulation that do not highlight these issues. Using an extended analysis specification has the advantage to combine the robustness of the analysis specification and to be close enough from the design to cover almost all the issues of the system. Moreover, computing the performance evaluation at that abstract level allows comparing alternatives of designs.
- The *performance design specification* aims at adapting the extended analysis specification to a particular performance evaluation environment. This can be seen as mapping the abstract model defined in the extended analysis specification to a concrete system made up of software.
- The *performance abstract implementation* provides an executable software that mimics the behavior of the system. Executing it would provide statistical results that once being analyzed bring to an end optimization of the system. Simulations promote identifying bottlenecks and determining critical performance parts of the system that require further design or specification.

2.2. Our System Engineering Methodology

Our methodology integrates methods from the formal world and from the performance evaluation world. Formal methods are used for the requirement specification, the analysis specification, the validation process and the verification process, then the performance evaluation methods are used to determine some of the non-functional properties (speed, accuracy and availability) of the system. We also provide a support for the interaction between those methods (Figure 4).

Our methodology starts from the customer and operator requirements. The customers what they expect from the system in terms of service, while the operators define how they intend to organize the system and what type of service primitives the system will offer. The requirement specification plays the role of a contract between the operator and the customers that clearly states the role of each part and their expectation in terms of services and interfaces. The scope of the requirement specification is not to define detail, but to define the essential properties or attributes required by the system environment. We shall make a distinction between functional and non-functional requirements. Functional requirements are concerned with the services and are inputs for the analysis specification, while non-functional requirements deal with implementation constraints and are inputs for the design specification.

Usual methods to conceive earlier iterations of the requirement specifications are natural languages, i.e., English, French, ... However, to capture and to analyze needs and expectations, so that they can be mapped in rigid requirement formulas, involves using formal methods. Nevertheless, before formalizing a requirement specification, it can be iterated as many times because expressing the requirements helps to understand the needs better. The formalization of the requirement specification enjoins using a formal method. There are many formal methods available nowadays, however, the most common ones are those standardized: SDL (ITU), LOTOS and Estelle (ISO).

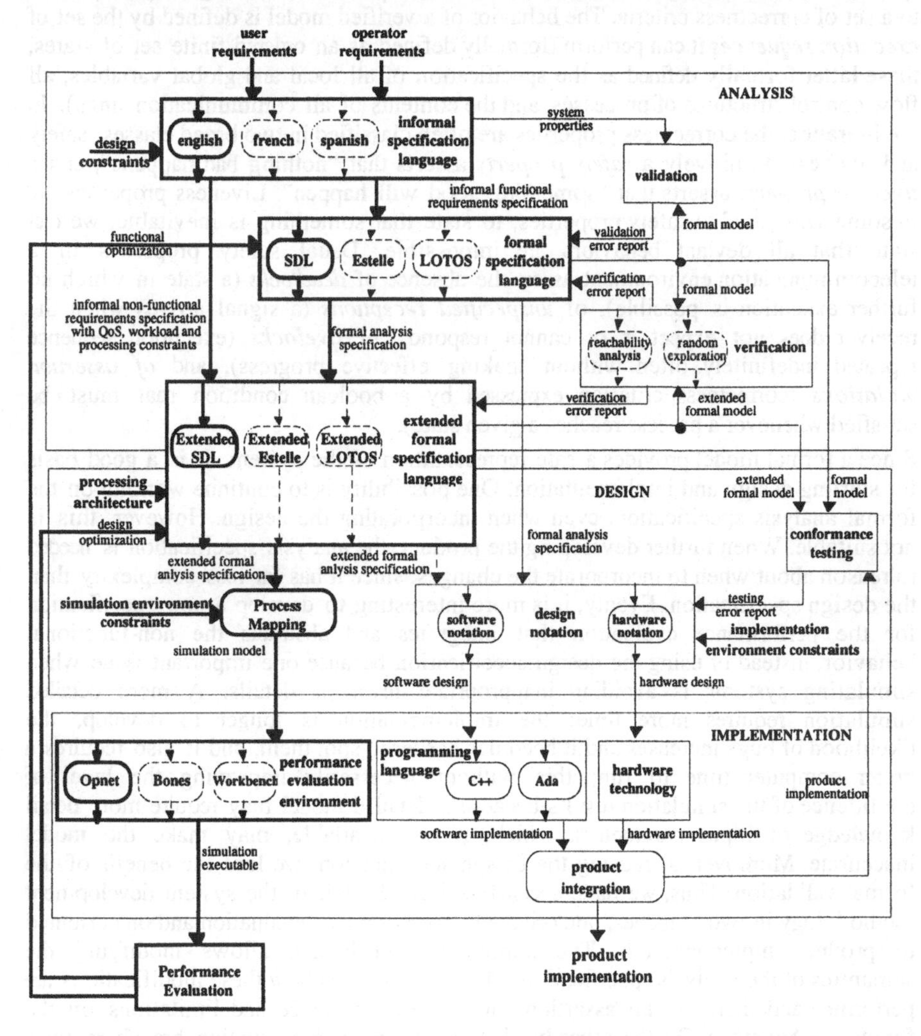

Figure 4: Integration methodology

Formalization provides a model which by successive refinements will meet the analysis specification, and which significant properties and functionality can be verified through validation and verification. As there is no clear agreement on these notions, we define them according to [20]:

* The *verification* is the process that compares a formal specification with the specification of what the system is intended to do, namely the services and system properties that the system provides to its users. A proof is performed to verify that

behavior of the system corresponds to its required properties; however, the verification is an informal control that checks the general structure and property assertions of the requirement specification, and puts them in confrontation with the informal requirements of the customers.

* The *validation* is the process that increases the confidence in the correctness of the system. The validation process checks if a formal specification is logically consistent to a set of correctness criteria. The behavior of a verified model is defined by the set of *execution sequences* it can perform (formally defined as an ordered finite set of states, these latter formally defined as the specification of all local and global variables, all flow control structures of processes, and the contents of all communication links). In the literature, the correctness properties are often classified in two broad classes: safety and liveness. Intuitively a *safety property* asserts that "nothing bad happens", and a *liveness property* asserts that "something good will happen". Liveness properties are in some sense dual to safety properties; to state that something is inevitable, we can state that all deviant behaviors are impossible. Usual safety properties in a telecommunication environment assert the absence of *deadlocks* (a state in which no further execution is possible), of *unspecified receptions* (a signal arrives when the receiver does not expect it or cannot respond), of *livelocks* (execution sequence repeated indefinitely often without making effective progress), and *of assertion violations* (correctness criterion expressed by a boolean condition that must be satisfied whenever a process reaches a given state).

Since a formal model provides a safe representation of the system, it is a good basis for starting design and implementation. One possibility is to continue working on the formal analysis specification, even when incorporating the design. However, this is not suitable. When further developing the product, the analysis specification is needed to reason about when to incorporate the changes, since it has far less complexity than the design specification. Evenly, it is more interesting to develop a new specification for the performance evaluation that integrates and abstracts the non-functional behavior, instead of using the design specification because one important issue when simulating systems is avoiding inappropriate level of details. A more detailed simulation requires more time: the implementation is longer to develop, the likelihood of bugs increases and it becomes harder to spot them, and it also requires a grater computer time to run; this without necessarily improving the level of confidence of the simulation results because a detailed model may require more detail knowledge of input parameters, which, if not available, may make the model inaccurate. Moreover, at reusing the design specification, we loss the benefit of the formal validation. Thus, we have decided to split the tail of the system development methodology in two branches, one oriented to performance evaluation and one oriented to product implementation. The implementation branch allows modifying the semantics of the analysis specification. There are no rules how these modifications are performed and there are no assertions about their influence and limitations on the functional behavior. On the other hand, the performance evaluation branch remains consistent with the original formal analysis specification semantics.

Each design alternative may be characterized by non-functional properties such as execution speed or memory requirements. Such properties may be important for the system performance. Non-functional properties should therefore be put dawn in the extended analysis specification, to ascertain that the right kind of design is chosen from the functionally equivalent alternatives. In order to conserve the benefit from the formal analysis specification we should describe these design alternatives within a formal method. Unfortunately nowadays current formal methods lack of expressive power to describe non-functional properties. However, equivalent developments can be done for the other languages. Therefore, it is necessary to extend the formal method with a quantification of the interaction between the system and its environment (workload), a definition of the performance settings (quality of service), a description of processing resources, and a description of the processing constraints. The extended formal method should conserve the original semantics, and when no other solution is available modify it, but limiting its effect on the original method. Our approach is generic, nevertheless, in further developments, we will focus on the extension of SDL and we will provide the methodology according to the particularities of this language.

The extended analysis specification abstracts from real implementation considerations, but it includes information that clearly belongs to design. For this reason, we have located the extended formal methods in an intermediate position, half in the analysis and half in the design. Its input is the analysis specification and its output is an extension that embraces part of the design. Its output has been steered for performance evaluation purpose, but it can also be used as input for the design specification.

The performance design specification adapts the extended analysis specification to a performance evaluation environment. There are many tools available nowadays, however, we choose OPNET because its structure is close to the one of SDL.

The performance abstract implementation provides an executable software code that has to be computed in order to provide some statistical results that should further be analyzed. The performance analysis is a complex task that requires, first to develop a set of performance experiments that allow to evaluate the selected metrics, then to acquire high confidence on statistical results by running simulations, and finally to develop a systematic analysis method that allows to determine bottlenecks and to provide them as outputs for functional and design optimizations, in case the system fails to satisfy the performance requirements.

On the other branch of the methodology, the design specification translates the analysis specification in a set of suited formalisms for the implementation taking in consideration the particularities of the system under design. The achieved set of models is then implemented as a set of independent components that are aggregated to achieve the final product. The product should still be checked for conformance. Testing consists in comparing the implementation with its analysis specification and determining if the product respects the original statements made about the system.

2.3. Related Work

Analyzing the quantitative performance and establishing the functional correctness of communication protocols directly from their formal specification has long been an objective of research in protocol engineering. Most efforts to date have concentrated on verifying [7], validating [20], and testing [16] functional correctness. Nevertheless, performance evaluation is equally desirable to derive measures such as potential throughput, response time, or to determine bottlenecks. The performance of a communication system is a complex interaction between the physical processing resources employed, the protocols involved and the workload on the system. A performance model should take all these factors into consideration. Furthermore, quantitative analyses involve time, and formal specification standards (Estelle, SDL, LOTOS) originally left the concept of time open to interpretation. Much effort has been invested during the last decade in the area of integrating time, probabilistic information and processing description in formal specifications. Many performance models are based on existing algebraic model extensions: some concern time [14, 12, 2] and some concern stochastic extensions [15, 10, 18].

There are also many extensions applying on finite state machines. For instance, in [3], authors propose an extension of the language Estelle that allows the description of performance aspects as time delays, resource usage and stochastic behavior. They introduce the concept of resource and associate it to process instances. They also define a delay clause that forces the process to hold for a duration before to complete a transition and provide them with a stochastic attribute. Finally they introduce the principle of process interaction through queues and associate a service delay to each queue. In [22], authors propose a hybrid model combining EFSM and QN. They enhance the ESTELLE specification by specifying transition time and by adding a set of external variables that describe the resource demands. In [11], authors present a method to derive semi-Markov models of the protocol execution directly from its state transition graph. In [5], Dembinski suggests how the Estelle semantics may be reinterpreted within a queueing network. In [1], authors propose an extension of SDL, called Timed SDL or TSDL. The principle is to extend SDL transitions with stochastic and time information. In [9], the proposed method enhances the formal specification with performance submodels which finally yield to a combined model that is quantitatively assessable and encloses the original formal description. The principle of this method is to enhance EFSM with "places" that serve as interfaces to the environment. They assume input places for message to be received and output places for messages to be forwarded. Places may be limited in capacity. The idea behind the introduction of places is to connect each input place to the output of a queueing network and to connect each output place to the input of a queueing network. Performance evaluation is then performed on the basis of the queueing network obtained by this association. In [17], authors consider an extension of SDL incorporating the concepts of mission, resource, delay, scheduling mechanism, and random decision. In [21], Wohlin proposes a methodology that transforms SDL descriptions into descriptions combining formal description and performance evaluation. In [8], the authors propose a method to extend a formal specification, based on finite state machine, with the description of the traffic source and a queue that serves as the interface between the source and the protocol. This queue is designed with a capability of storing messages that the protocol cannot immediately transmit, thereby smoothing the message flow but potentially introducing delay.

Other specification formalisms have also been proposed in the literature. In [13], author proposes a method to capture the Quality of Service or Network Performance requirements. The principle of the method is to map SDL specifications to a global state transition system. Then states and transitions are described in terms of logic formulae over state positions. In [6] authors present the most important classes of nets, gives their analysis possibilities and shows how they can be used to model and analyze communication and cooperation protocols.

3. Applying the Methodology to SDL

3.1. SDL - Analysis Specification

The basic idea of SDL [19] is to describe a system as communicating processes. A *process* is an extended finite state machine (EFSM), that is either processing data or if no data is available for processing, is dormant in a state (the *state* defines what actions a process is allowed to take, which events it expects to happen, and how it will respond to those events). When data becomes available the machine starts processing and continues until all the possible processing has been accomplished, then it goes dormant in the same state or in an other one. The processing performed depends solely on the state in which the machine was last dormant, on the data that becomes available and on the local conditions. Several items of data may become available during the machine processing of previously available data, and a queue is associated with the machine to pile up the data as it arrives. The usual representation is by means of a graph consisting of nodes, each indicating a state and arcs, these later indicating transitions. Each *transition* has a trigger condition to indicate the data and local conditions that if available, would activate the transition.

Communication between processes is performed asynchronously, by way of connection paths (channels or signal-routes), by discrete signals. A system contains blocks interconnected by way of channels. The *channels* are the links through which the *blocks* communicate with each other or with the environment. A channel can be unidirectional or bi-directional. A bi-directional channel can be considered as two independent unidirectional channels. The channels are typed, meaning that they can only contain messages of certain types called *signals*. A block can contain either a substructure of blocks, or one or several processes interconnected by *signal-routes*. The signal-routes are the links through which processes can communicate with each other inside a block, and with the block boundary.

In SDL a concept of time is defined. All processes in the system may acquire the value of the current real time. Furthermore, to model time-outs, SDL is equipped with timers; the timer mechanism stimulates a process as a function of the defined time by placing a timer signal in the input queue of the process.

3.2. Extended SDL - Extended Analysis Specification

Performance Evaluation requires a consistent representation of the system under analysis to achieve a confident evaluation. For this reason, the first question that we should answer when reusing an SDL specification for performance evaluation purpose, is to determine the level of confidence of the model. SDL is composed from abstract communication media and extended finite state machines, while a real-system is composed from physical components and communication networks. Consequently, the SDL representation sustains some differences towards the real-systems; some differences concern the nature of the components, than some address the functioning of the components. Therefore creating a consistent representation that should be reused for performance evaluation should eliminate as much of these differences as possible. It implies defining some SDL extensions that restrict the scope of these differences.

3.2.1. Modeling Processing Time

A basic assumption in SDL is that the system is fast enough to process the offered load. In a real-system this assumption is disabled because each signal transfer and each transition of a process take some time and require some processing resource. To map the formal SDL model, the real-system should be fast enough to meet the traffic load and response time without destroying the validity of the SDL descriptions.

Extended SDL provides a new transition concept that specifies processing duration. Each transition specifies zero, one or several delay clauses that force the transition to pause and model processing duration. The associated execution model stipulates that all the actions before a delay clause are executed immediately, then the execution is suspended for the specified duration; when completed, the automaton resumes its execution until the next delay specification.

<delay>::= **delay** <delay identifier> ({<delay item>}*)<end>

<delay item>::= <time expression> | {(<flag expression>)<bit rate expression>}

A *delay* specifies the pause duration during a transition. A delay may be expressed in seconds (<time expression>) or as a bit rate (<bit rate expression>), in which case the duration is calculated as the ratio between the signal length and the bit rate. In this latter case a flag should be set to TRUE. Each delay is identified by a name that distinguish it from other delay statements in the same process.

Another important performance evaluation feature that is not considered within SDL specifications is the specification of the physical distance covered by a communication link. In reality however, there may be large physical distances. This means that, in real systems, the transmission of information between two equipments may be delayed. Therefore, Extended SDL specification provides a special type of channels that allow modeling propagation delays.

All the temporal extensions of Extended SDL remain consistent with the SDL formal model. During the validation of the SDL model we will check the sequence of states and events of the system. Each validation state is defined by the aggregation of the state values of all the processes, of the content of all the communication links and of the variable values. However, there is no variable indicating the current time, that is, the functionality is verified independently of the time. In that sense, an Extended SDL specification is identical to the SDL specification because the sequence of events and states remains unchanged.

3.2.2. Modeling Unreliability

SDL systems may suffer from specification errors, but the abstract representations they provide do not suffer from physical errors. SDL assumes that processes and communication links always operate according to their specifications. It is not assumed that processes will stop or that communication links will distort the content of signals. But in the real world, errors manifest themselves as faults in operation of processes and communication. Hardware errors, physical damage and noise are caused by physical phenomena outside the realm of SDL. However, their effect is often handled explicitly in SDL specifications. One must consider what may happen, how it can be detected and how damages may be limited. One must consider what a process should do if it never gets a response to a request or if it gets an erroneous response.

Since communications have a considerable influence on the performance, it is vital to provide a realistic model of the communication links. In SDL, communication links (*channels* and *signal-routes*) convey the sequence of signals from the initiating port in that order to the end port, without introducing any distortion to the conveyed information. In channels, the transfer delay is non-deterministic (default) or negligible (*no-delay*); signal-routes always have a negligible delay. From a performance evaluation point of view, negligible and non-deterministic delays are unsuitable because performance evaluation requires an exact knowledge of the temporal operating.

Besides, in real world, communication links often suffer from disfunctionments and errors that make information to contain errors or to be lost. Fortunately, SDL allows refining communication channels and modeling unreliability by means of channel substructures. However, proper handling of this aspect can be very complex and normally requires additional functionality in the SDL specification. There is no analogous mechanism to model unreliable signal-routes. Nevertheless, in SDL only the interfaces between the system specified and its environment are mandatory; all internal structures are purely a means to express the overall system behavior. Thus, specifying unreliable signal-routes is achieved by modifying the internal structure of the system and transforming the signal-route into a channel.

During performance evaluation, communications links are frequently specified as unreliable. For this reason, we decided to specify a macro that facilitates their specification. An unreliable channel macro may be used instead of a channel definition. When expanded, it should be seen as a channel substructure. Each direction is specified by a single process that generates errors and losses according to the specified distributions and that delays the signals by <time expression> units of time.

<unreliable channel macro>::= **channel** <channel name> [**nodelay**] <unreliable path>
[<unreliable path>] **endchannel** [<channel name>]<end>

<unreliable path>::= **from** <channel endpoint> **to** <channel endpoint> **with** <signal list> <end> [**transferdelay** <time expression><end>] [**error** <distribution definition><end>][**loss** <distribution definition><end>]

3.2.3. Modeling Processing Resources

The model of concurrence used in SDL assumes that processes behave independently and asynchronously. There is no relative ordering implied by the sending and reception of signals. This permits SDL processes to be implemented either truly in parallel on separate hardware or in quasi-parallel on shared hardware. Moreover we may distinguish between two ways of executing parallelism: the synchronous operating, where operations are performed under the control of a common clock, and asynchronous operating, where operations are performed independently and possibly at different times. In the other hand, quasi-parallelism implies that only one process is active at a time and that the active process will block operating of other processes as long as it is allowed to remain active. This will affect the response times of the blocked processes, and it remains an acceptable approximation of the SDL semantics as long as the delays it introduces are acceptable to the environment. This will affect the response times of the blocked processes, and it remains an acceptable approximation of the SDL semantics as long as the delays it introduces are acceptable to the environment. Quasi-parallelism implies a scheduling algorithm that is handled by an operating system. The SDL model should represent it as a layer that implements a quasi-parallel virtual machine on top of the physical machine.

The act of aligning the operations of different concurrent processes in relation to each other is generally called synchronization. Such alignment is necessary not only to achieve correctness in communication, but also to control the access to shared resources. In SDL synchronization is achieved by means of buffered communication in which the sender may produce infinitely many signals without waiting for the receiver to consume them, which mechanism is often referred as asynchronous communication. Therefore SDL synchronization is time independent, using an asynchronous medium with infinite buffer capacity. In practice however, the queue will be finite, so in the case of a full queue the sender will have to wait or signals will be lost. To avoid it, output from an SDL process must be delayed until the receiving buffer is ready. This deviation from the SDL semantics can hardly be avoided in a finite implementation; care is needed to reduce to a minimum the practical problems this may cause. The synchronization of SDL rests on a basic synchronization mechanism called mutual exclusion. Only one process at a time can get access to the input queue. Only one service at a time can get access to shared data within the process and only one process at a time gets access to reveled data. Mutual exclusion is generally needed in the access to shared resources.

SDL has an unbounded queue in the input port of each process and allows infinite data to be specified. Hence the designer must find ways to implement potentially infinite SDL systems using finite resources. In practice however, all resources in a real system are finite. They may be a maximum number of processes the operating system can handle or a maximum number of buffers for sending messages. The memory space is finite and even primitive data like integers are finite. This deviation from the SDL semantics can hardly be avoided in a finite implementation; care is needed to reduce to a minimum the practical problems this may cause.

SDL processes consist of a single processing resource with a single infinite queue that follows a FIFO discipline. Even though this modeling is sufficient to capture the nature of many processes, it does not hold for all real processes. Thus, Extended SDL provides a new model of processing architecture. The idea is to associate each process with a set of finite queues and a set of servers (Figure 5).

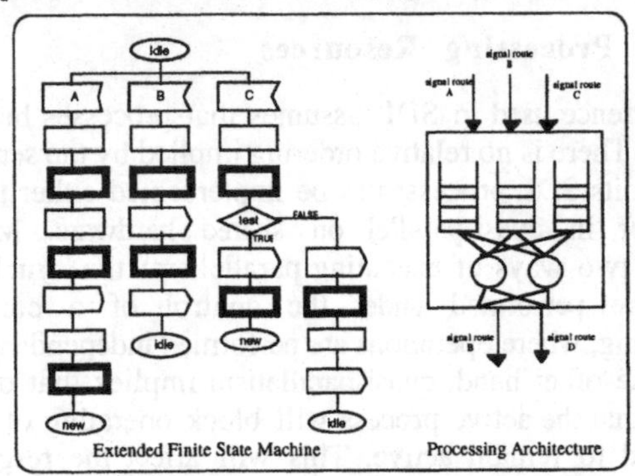

Figure 5: An Extended SDL process specification.

<process definition> ::= **process** {<process_name>|<process_identifier>} [<number of process instances><end>] [<formal parameters><end>] [<valid input signal set>] *[<resource definition>]* [<process body>] {<entity in process>|<signal route to route connection>}* **endprocess** [<process_name>|<process_identifier>]<end>

From a functional point of view, our extension may be seen as a macro that when expanded replaces a process by a set of processes (one for the modeling of the access, and a set for the modeling of multiple servers) (Figure 6). The access process manages the access to service of external signals, while each functional process models the functional behavior of the process specified in SDL. Thus, the extension may be seen as a modification of the specification but not as a modification of the semantics.

The access process defines where and how arriving messages should be stored. For instance, a process handling three priority data streams, can store them in three queues. Each signal arriving to the process will be analyzed and depending on its type and its parameters (associated variables) it decides in which queue it will be stored.

If an Extended SDL process specifies several servers, the expanded model instantiates the same number of process instances, each driving its server. At the completion of a transition, each process indicates to the access process that it is ready to receive the next signal by means of an exported variable.

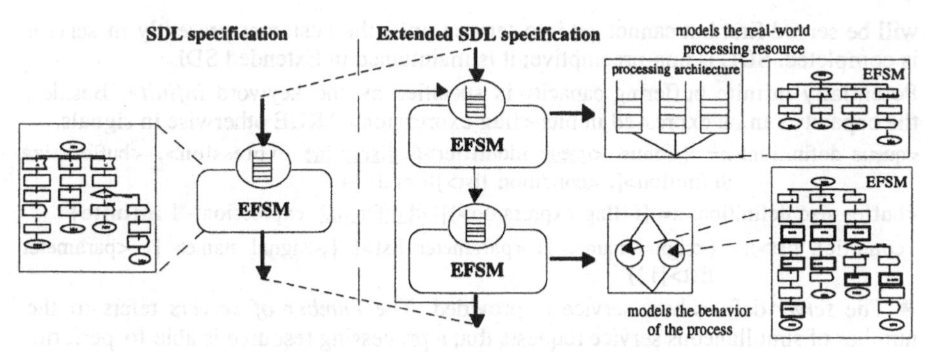

Figure 6: Extended SDL processing model

Our extension is based on existent SDL constructs. Therefore, we guarantee that we do not modify the semantics of SDL.

<resource definition>::= **resource** <process name><end> {<queue definition> <server definition>}+ **endresource** [<process name>]<end>

Each processing resource can be seen as customers arriving for service, waiting for service if it is not immediate and leaving the system after being served. It is divided in four components (Figure 7): input, queueing, server, and output.

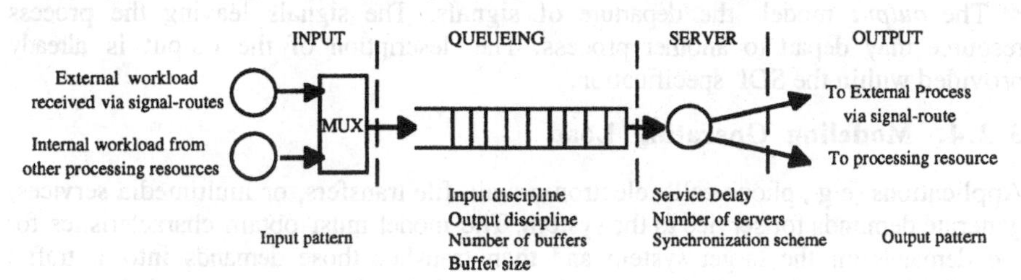

Figure 7: Processing resource

◆ The *input* models the arrival of signals to the resource. The signals entering the queue may come from other processes or may have been generated by the process itself. Extended SDL does not require a special description of the input because this information is already provided within the SDL specification.

◆ The *queueing* defines the storage policy. The *number of queues* models the number of distinct data-streams that handle the resource. Several queues are useful to separate signal-streams entering the system. Each queue is described by its *queueing discipline*, that refers to how the customers are inserted in the queues and selected for service when queues have formed and its *buffering capacity* (a limited buffering capacity may arise with signal losses). The most common queueing discipline is first in first out (FIFO). Other usual disciplines are last in first out, random service selection or priority based. A queuing discipline is identified by an integer that points to a library. Each queue identifies the signals that are allowed to enter the queue by a <condition list>. If no condition is specified, it means that all signals are allowed. A condition is formed from a signal name and optionally a list of parameter values if required. A priority discipline asserts that signals with the higher priority have to be served first. There are two general situations in priority disciplines: *preemptive*, where customers with higher priority are allowed to enter service immediately even if customers with lower priority are currently served, and *non-preemptive*, where high-priority customers will be served first but cannot get into service until the customer presently in service is completed. SDL is non-preemptive; it is maintained in Extended SDL.

Potentially infinite buffering capacity is specified by the keyword *infinite*. Besides, the capacity can be expressed in bits <flag expression> TRUE otherwise in signals.

<queue definition>::= {**queue** <queue identifier>(<discipline expression>, <buffer size definition>[, <condition list>])<end>}+

<buffer size definition>::= [(<flag expression>)]{<buffer size expression> | **infinite**}

<condition list>::= (<signal name> [: <parameter list>] {,<signal name> [: <parameter list>]}*)

◆ The *server* defines how service is provided. The *number of servers* refers to the number of simultaneous service requests that a processing resource is able to perform. The *service time* specifies the time required to serve a request. A potentially infinite number of servers is specified by the keyword *infinite*. Nevertheless an infinite number of servers only is an abstraction that helps to model particular processing configurations. Service is provided according to the automaton specification. The activities to proceed on each signal depend on the state of the process and on the attributes of the signal. Moreover, Extended SDL delay clauses model the processing time of specified actions.

<server definition>::= **service** ({<number of servers expression> | **infinite**})<end>

◆ The *output* models the departure of signals. The signals leaving the process resource may depart to another process. The description of the output is already provided within the SDL specification.

3.2.4. Modeling Operating Load

Applications (e.g., phone calls, electronic mail, file transfers, or multimedia services) generate demands for service to the system. The model must obtain characteristics for the demands on the target system and then translate those demands into a traffic model. This may be a difficult task because of the dynamic aspect of the service demands traffic. The workload characterization is a crucial part of the performance evaluation model because it is possible to reach misleading conclusions if the workload is not properly selected.

In SDL, the requests at the system's interface are qualitatively described, that is, each communication link identifies which signals are authorized to borrow the link, but there is no quantification. This information is insufficient to establish an adequate model of the workload. In the Extended SDL specification, we enrich the notion of system, by extending it to the original system and its environment. Extended SDL represents the environment by means of a block. Originally, the system corresponds with the environment by means of channels. In Extended SDL these channels connect the "system" to the "environment" block. The structure of the system remains unchanged, while the "environment" block is decomposed into a set of processes (Figure 8). There is exactly one process by channel connection. Each process describes quantitatively the statistical behavior of the interactions between the environment and the original system through a given channel. The information about the nature of the interactions was already contained in the original SDL specification. Thus, Extended SDL only enhances the description by specifying a statistical interarrival and length distribution for each valid signal. The arrival distribution mimics the temporal behavior of the customer producing system requests. The length distribution describes the temporal variation of the signal length. In performance evaluation, the length distribution is used to determine the processing delay of signals because the service rate of a processing resource often is expressed in bit/s. Other concerns are not specified in the extension. This extension introduces a set of new processes that model the behavior of the environment, but it does not modify the behavior of the system itself. Therefore we remain consistent with the SDL specification.

<env-block definition>::= **block** {<env-block name>} <end> {<channel to route connection> | <entity in block>}* **endblock** [<env-block name>]<end>

<env-process definition>::= **envprocess** <env-process name>:<channel identifier> <end> [<formal parameters><end>] [<valid input signal set>] {<entity in process>}* [<process body>] [<traffic definition>] **endprocess** [<env-process name>]<end>

<traffic definition>::= **traffic** <env-process name><end>{<workload definition>]}* **endtraffic** [<env-process name>]<end>

<workload definition>::= **workload** <signal name><end> < arrival attribute definition> <length attribute definition> [<signal attributes definition>]

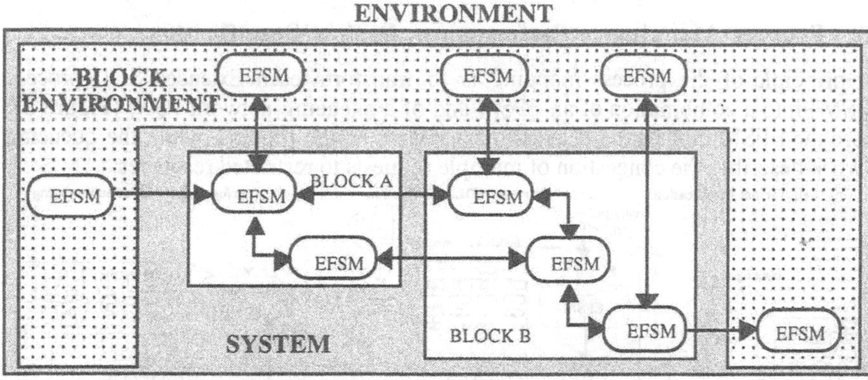

Figure 8: The Extended SDL specification.

3.2.5. Describing Quality of Service

A customer sees the system as a black-box to which it applies service requests and from which it gets an output. To achieve satisfactorily service, the customer requires some quality of service (QoS). In [4], the quality of service is defined as a set of user-perceivable attributes that make a service what it is. It is expressed in user-understandable language and manifests itself as a number of parameters, all of which have either subjective or objective values. Objective values are defined and measured in terms of parameters appropriate to the particular service concerned, and which are customer-verifiable. Subjective values are defined and estimated by the provider in terms of the opinion of the customers of the service, collected by means of user surveys. In performance evaluation, the quality of service monitors how the parameters evolve, and checks if the system fits the required values. A quality of service is satisfied when all its performance metrics are satisfied.

In SDL, the specification of the quality of service is missing. Thus, evaluating the performance implies to extend the specification with some static data, which in the performance evaluation environment can be expanded and reused. Since static data declarations do not evolve over time, the addition of the quality of service within Extended SDL does not modify the functional behavior of the specification.

<quality of service definition>::= **qos** <env-service name> <end> <metrics> {, <metrics>}* **endqos** [<env-service name>] <end>

<metrics>::=<delay criteria>|<ratio criteria>|<utilization criteria>|<jitters criteria>

<delay criteria>::= <delay keyword> **value** ({<min value>|<max value>}[,<optimum value>]) <end> **init** ({(<signal name>,<state name>,<process name>)}+) <end> **close** ({(<signal name>,<state name>,<process name>)}+)<end>

<ratio criteria>::=<ratio keyword> **value** ({<min value>|<max value>}[,<optimum value>])<end> **divisor** ({(<signal name>,<state name>,<process name>)}+) <end> **dividend** ({(<signal name>,<state name>,<process name>)}+)<end>

<utilization criteria>::=**utilization value**({<min value>|<max value>} [,<optimum value>])<end> **queue** ({(<queue name>,<process name>)}+) <end>

<jitters criteria>::=**jitters value** ({<min value>|<max value>} [,<optimum value>]) <end> **message** ({(<signal name>,<state name>,<process name>)}+)<end>

<ratio keywords>::=**throughput|reliability|availability|loss|error|resilience**

<delay keywords>::= **activation|release|transfer|response|turnaround|reaction**

3.3. Process Mapping - Performance Design Specification

The principle of the process mapping is to transform each Extended SDL process (EFSM) into a combination of an EFSM and of a queueing network (QN) (Figure 5), where the EFSM models the detailed mechanisms of the process, while the queueing network describes the congestion of multiple requests to restricted resources.

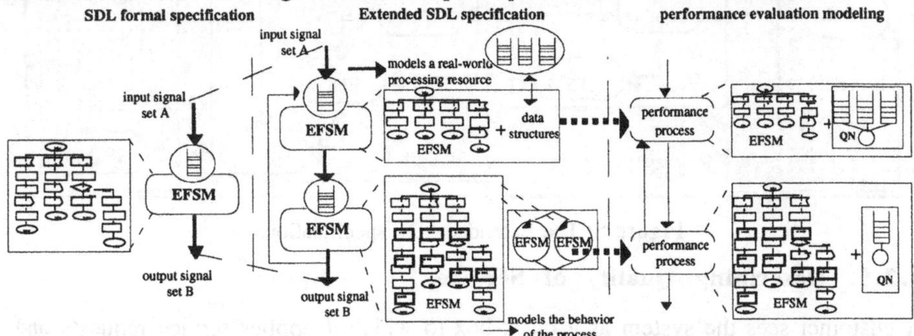

Figure 9: The process mapping technique.

Besides, the process mapping describes the nature and the way in which performance experiments will be conducted. There must be clear objectives of what is expected from the performance evaluation; we should be aware of the goals and limitations of the performance model. We will reuse the quality of service specification which defines what are the relevant metrics to evaluate.

The system may perform the service correctly, incorrectly, or refuse to perform the service. If the system performs the service correctly, its performance is measured by the time taken to perform the service (*response time*), the rate at which the service is performed (*throughput*), and the resource rate consumed during service (*utilization*). This last criterion gives an indication of the percentage of time a resource is busy for a given load. If the system performs the service incorrectly, an *error* is said to have occurred. It can be helpful to classify errors and to determine the probability of each class of errors. If the system is not able to perform the service, it is said to be *unavailable*. Two types of performance metrics need to be considered: punctual and global. Punctual metrics are evaluated over a given resource or set of resource, while global metrics are evaluated from end to end. There are cases where a decision that optimizes a punctual metric is different from one that optimizes a global metric.

Two types of performance metrics need to be considered: individual and global. Individual metrics reflect the utility of each user, while the global metrics reflect the system wide utility. The resource utilization, reliability, and availability are global metrics, while response time and throughput may be measured for each individual as well as for globally for the system. There are cases where the decision that optimizes individual metrics is different from the one that optimizes the system metric.

3.4. OPNET - Performance Abstract Implementation

There are many performance evaluation environments that suit for implementing performance modeling. By our study case we chose a commercial tool: OPtimized Network Engineering Tool (OPNET). OPNET is a simulation environment capable of developing and simulating communication networks with detailed protocol modeling and performance analysis. System behavior and performance are analyzed by performing discrete event simulations. Opnet expresses process models in a language called Proto-C, which is specifically designed to support development of protocols and algorithms. Proto-C bases on a combination of state transition diagrams, on a library of high level commands called kernel procedures, and on the general facilities of the C programming language. The state diagram description of a process defines a set of primary modes (states) that the process can enter, and the conditions that would cause the process to move from mode to mode. There are other important aspects of Proto-C; these include actions associated with each mode, variables and attribute declarations, and common expressions and functions. Proto-C defines two types of modes, called forced and unforced that differ in their execution timing. Unforced modes allow to pause between the enter executives and the exit executives. Forced modes do not allow to wait; therefore they cannot be used to represent modes of the system that persist for any duration. In other words, the exit executives of a forced mode are executed immediately upon completion of the enter executives. The last step consists in verifying whether the customer's quality of service is satisfied or not. When not, we should identify the bottlenecks of the system and optimize them.

4. A Case Study - Transmission Control Protocol

Transmission control protocol (TCP) is a transport protocol used among others on Ethernet networks. It provides a connection-oriented, reliable service to the application using it. Two stations using TCP must establish a TCP connection before starting to exchange data. During the exchange of data, TCP packetizes the customer data into segments, sets a time-out any time it sends data, acknowledges data received by the other end, reorders out-of-order data, discards duplicate data, provides end-to-end flow control, and calculates and verifies a mandatory end-to-end checksum. TCP is used by many popular applications, such as Telnet, FTP, or SMTP.

Figure 10: TCP illustration example.

In this example we focus on the exchange of data; we consider neither the establishment nor the release of TCP connections. Figure 10 shows the outline of the system. "Data Producer" is a customer which generates data that should be reliably transmitted to another customer: "Data Consumer". Between them, there is an unreliable network that generates errors. The TCP process prevents errors by implementing detection and resend mechanisms.

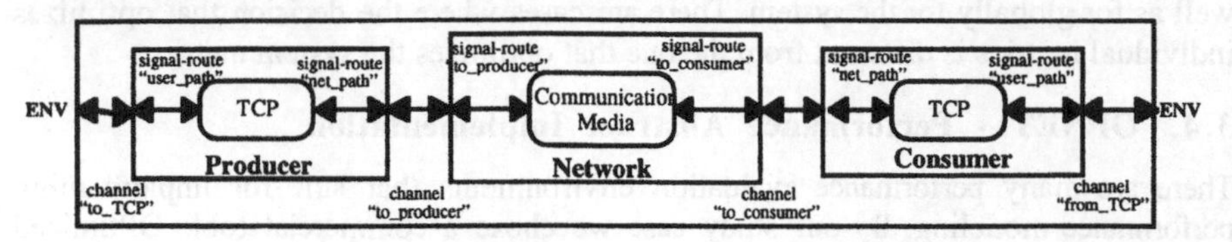

Figure 11: SDL specification of the TCP example.

Figure 11 shows the SDL specification. Customers are not considered. Data enter the system by the channel "to_TCP" and leave by "from_TCP".

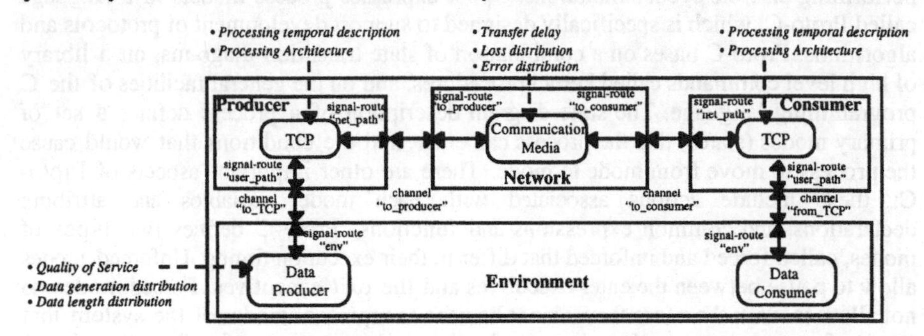

Figure 12: Extended SDL specification of the TCP example.

Figure 12 shows the Extended SDL outline. We enhance the SDL specification with the description of the consumers in terms of quality of service, and of workload (message interarrival and length distributions). We also enhance the description of the TCP processes by describing their processing architecture and their processing constraints. Finally, the network is described in terms of errors.

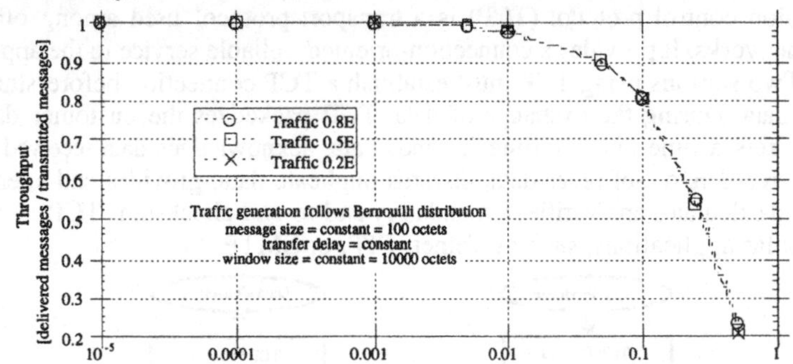

Figure 13: Throughput variation

The QoS states the performance expected from the connection between the "Data Producer" and the "Data Consumer". It embodies the limit values of the delay and of the throughput. These values allow determining if further optimization is necessary.

During performance experiments, the description of the workloads is used to mimic the generation of messages. Similarly, the processing architecture and the associated processing constraints are used to simulate the non-functional behavior of processes. Finally, the simulation of the system provides information on interesting performance metrics (e.g., resource utilization, delay, losses and throughput), both for end-to-end system and for subsets of the system.

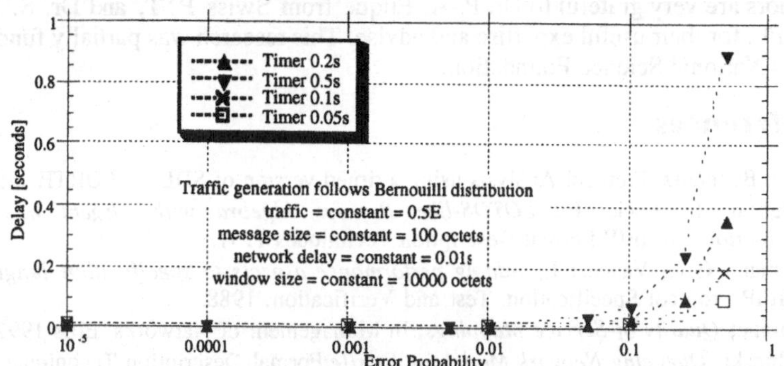

Figure 14: Delay variation as function of the retransmission timer

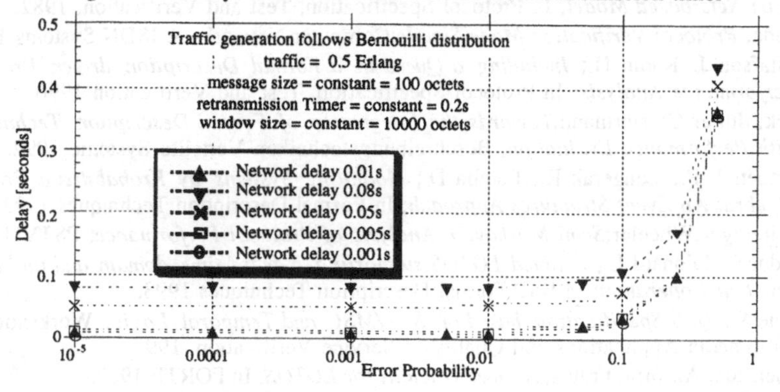

Figure 15: Delay variation as function of the network delay

We have computed simulations of the modeling of our TCP example. This modeling was obtained using our methodology, and was implemented on the tool Opnet. The simulation results (Figure 13, 14 and 15) are used to verify under which conditions the required quality of service is fulfilled.

5. Conclusion

We believe that modeling performance from formal descriptions is a powerful approach because it saves time by reusing the formal abstraction and avoids errors. Furthermore, it combines the power of formal techniques (validation and conformance testing) with the power of performance evaluation.

Our contribution proposes a methodology reusing the formal specification, enhancing it with performance information and mapping it to a performance modeling. Analyzing the simulation results of the performance modeling allows optimizing the system. We are convinced that our methodology is simple, powerful and generic. It is scalable, that is, it is applicable to simple as well as to complex systems. Besides, abstracting real systems first in SDL specifications, results in good validation possibilities that save time and avoid errors in developing a performance modeling. We have no doubt that our methodology can be automated.

6. Acknowledgments

The authors are very grateful to Dr. P.-A. Etique from Swiss PTT, and Dr. S. Znaty from EPFL, for their useful expertise and advise. This research was partially funded by the Swiss National Science Foundation.

7. References

[1]Bause, Buchholz, Protocol Analysis using a timed version of SDL, In FORTE 1991.

[2]Bolognesi T., Lucidi F.; *LOTOS-like Process Algebra with Urgent or Timed Interactions*; In IFIP Formal Description Techniques 1991.

[3]Bochmann G.v., Vaucher J., *Adding performance aspects to specification languages*, In IFIP Protocol Specification, Test and Verification, 1988.

[4]Cochrane; *Quality of Service Mappings*, In Management of Networks, Ellis 1992.

[5]Dembinski; *Queueing Network Model for Estelle*;Formal Description Techniques 1993.

[6]Diaz M., *Modeling and Analysis of Communication and Cooperation Protocol using Petri Nets based Model*, In Protocol Specification, Test and Verification, 1982.

[7]Gouda; *Protocol Verification Made Simple*;Computer Networks & ISDN Systems 1993.

[8]Gustafson J. Rudin H.; *Including a Queue in a Formal Description driven Protocol Performance Analysis*; In Protocol Specification, Test and Verification 1990.

[9]Heck,Müller-Clostermann,*Towards the Integration of Formal Description Techniques with Performance Evaluation*, Beschreibungstechniken Verteilte Systeme 1992.

[10]Katoen J.-P., Langerak R., Latella D.; *Modelling Systems by Probabilistic Process Algebra: An Event Structures Approach*; In Formal Description Techniques 1993.

[11]Kritzinger,Wheeler;*Semi-Markovian Analysis of Protocol Performance*; PSTV 1992.

[12]Leduc G. Léonard L.; *A timed LOTOS supporting a dense time domain and including new timed operators*; In IFIP Formal Description Techniques 1993.

[13]Leue S.; *QoS Specification based on SDL/MSC and Temporal Logic*; Workshop on Multimedia Applications and Quality of Service Verification, 1994.

[14]Quemada, Azcorra, Frutos, *A timed calculus for LOTOS*, In FORTE 1989.

[15]Rico,Bochmann; *Performance description and analysis for distributed systems using a variant of LOTOS*; Protocol Specification, Test and Verification 1991.

[16]Sidhu D.; *Protocol Testing: the first ten years, the next ten years*; In PSTV 1990.

[17]Sredniawa, Kakol, Gumulinski; *SDL in Performance Evaluation*; In SDL Forum 1987.

[18]Soerensen,Nordahl,Hansen;*From CSP to Markov Models*;Trans. Software Eng. 1993.

[19]UIT-T, Z.100; *CCITT Specification and Description Language*; UIT, 1993.

[20]West C., *Protocol Validation-Principles and Applications*, Computer Networks & ISDN Systems 1992.

[21]Wohlin C; *Performance Analysis of SDL systems from SDL Descriptions*, In SDL Forum III, 1991.

[22]Zhang, Chanson; *An Approach to Evaluating the Performance of Communication Protocols based on Formal Specifications*; Conference on Network Protocols 1993.

Formalizing New Navigation Requirements for NASA's Space Shuttle

Ben L. Di Vito

ViGYAN, Inc., 30 Research Drive, Hampton, Virginia 23666, USA

Abstract. We describe a recent NASA-sponsored pilot project intended to gauge the effectiveness of using formal methods in Space Shuttle software requirements analysis. Several Change Requests (CRs) were selected as promising targets to demonstrate the utility of formal methods in this demanding application domain. A CR to add new navigation capabilities to the Shuttle, based on Global Positioning System (GPS) technology, is the focus of this industrial usage report. Portions of the GPS CR were modeled using the language of SRI's Prototype Verification System (PVS). During a limited analysis conducted on the formal specifications, numerous requirements issues were discovered. We present a summary of these encouraging results and conclusions we have drawn from the pilot project.

1 Introduction

Among all the software developed by the U.S. National Aeronautics and Space Administration, Space Shuttle flight software is generally considered exemplary. Nevertheless, much of the quality assurance activity in early lifecycle phases remains a manual exercise in need of more precise analysis techniques. Software upgrades to accommodate new missions and capabilities are continually introduced. Such upgrades underscore the need recognized in the NASA community, and in a recent assessment of Shuttle flight software development, for "state-of-the-art technology" and "leading-edge methodologies" to meet the demands of software development for increasingly large and complex systems [12, p. 91].

Over the last three years, NASA's Langley Research Center (LaRC) has investigated the use of formal methods (FM) in space applications, as part of a three-center demonstration project involving LaRC, the Jet Propulsion Laboratory (JPL), and the Johnson Space Center (JSC). The goal of NASA's Formal Methods Demonstration Project for Space Applications is to find effective ways to use formal methods in requirements analysis and other phases of the development lifecycle. The Space Shuttle program has been cooperating in several pilot projects to apply formal methods to live requirements analysis activities such as the upgrades supporting the recent MIR docking missions, improved algorithms for the newly automated three-engine-out contingency abort maneuvers (3E/O), and the recent optimization of Reaction Control System Jet Selection (JS) [4, 6]. Other programs participating in the demonstration effort include the Cassini deep-space probe and the International Space Station [9, 7].

We focus in this paper on the formal methods-based analysis of a new Global Positioning System (GPS) navigation capability for the Shuttle. This work was performed in the context of a broader program of formal methods activity at LaRC [2]. The effort consisted of formalizing selected Shuttle software (sub)system modifications and additions using the PVS specification language and interactive proof-checker [13]. Our objective was to explore and document the feasibility of formalizing critical Shuttle software requirements.

The key technical results of the project include a clear demonstration of the utility of formal methods as a complement to the conventional Shuttle requirements analysis process. Although proof-based analysis was a goal of the project, the effort has thus far been limited to formalization of the requirements. Nevertheless, the GPS project uncovered anomalies ranging from minor to substantive, many of which were undetected by existing requirements analysis processes. These results corroborate the experiences of others in formalizing requirements [3, 1]. Dissemination of these techniques to the aerospace community should encourage further experimentation [14, 11]. Full details of the GPS study will appear in a forthcoming report [5].

1.1 Shuttle Software Background

NASA's prime contractor for the Space Shuttle is the Space Systems Division of Rockwell International. Loral Space Information Systems (formerly IBM, Houston) is their software subcontractor. Draper Laboratory also serves Rockwell, providing requirements expertise in Guidance, Navigation and Control.

Shuttle flight software executes in four redundant general purpose computers (GPCs), with a fifth backup computer carrying dissimilar software. Much of the Shuttle software is organized into major units called *principal functions*, each of which may be subdivided into *subfunctions*. Software requirements are written using conventions known as Functional Subsystem Software Requirements (FSSRs) — low-level software requirements specifications written in English prose with strong implementation biases, and accompanied by pseudo-code, tables, and flowcharts. Interfaces between software units are specified in input-output tables. Inputs can be variables or one of three types of constant data: *I-loads* (fixed for the current mission), *K-loads* (fixed for a series of missions), and physical constants (never changed).

Shuttle software modifications are packaged as Change Requests (CRs), that are typically modest in scope, localized in function, and intended to satisfy specific needs for upcoming missions. Roughly once a year, software releases called Operational Increments (OIs) are issued incorporating one or more CRs. Shuttle CRs are written as modifications, replacements, or additions to existing FSSRs. Loral Requirements Analysts (RAs) conduct thorough reviews of new CRs, analyzing them with respect to correctness, implementability, and testability before turning them over to the development team. Their objective is to identify and correct problems in the requirements analysis phase, avoiding far more costly fixes later in the lifecycle.

2 Overview of the Enhanced Shuttle Navigation System

GPS is a satellite-based navigation system operated by the U.S. Department of Defense (DoD), comprising a constellation of 24 satellites in high earth orbits. Navigation is effected using a receive-only technique. Dedicated hardware receivers track four or more satellites simultaneously and recover their signals from the code division multiplexing inherent in their method of transmission. Receivers solve for position and velocity, with a horizontal position accuracy of 100 meters for the Standard Positioning Service mode of operation.

The GPS retrofit to the Shuttle was planned in anticipation of DoD's phase-out of TACAN, a ground-based navigation system currently used during entry and landing. Originally, GPS was required for navigation only during the entry ¡flight phase after the disappearance of TACAN, but the scope has been broadened to cover all mission phases. As one of the larger ongoing Shuttle Change Requests (CRs), the GPS CR involves a significant upgrade to the Shuttle's navigation capability. Shuttles are to be outfitted with GPS receivers and the primary avionics software will be enhanced to accept GPS-provided positions and integrate them into navigation calculations. In particular, the GPS CR will provide the capability to update the Shuttle navigation filter states with selected GPS state vector estimates similar to the way state vector updates currently are received from the ground. In addition, the new functions will provide feedback to the GPS receivers and will support crew control and operation of GPS/GPC processing.

2.1 GPS Change Request

The GPS upgrade is being conducted according to a two-phase integration plan. First, a single-string implementation will be carried out involving only a single GPS receiver. After adequate testing, the full-up implementation involving three receivers will provide the operational configuration. Software requirements are structured to accommodate the three-receiver setup from the outset, requiring only minimal changes to go to the full-up version.

Figure 1 shows the integrated architecture for the enhanced navigation subsystem. GPS receivers are managed by the GPS Subsystem Operating Program (SOP), which acts as a device driver. The new principal function GPS Receiver State Processing accepts GPS state vectors, and selects and conditions a usable one for presentation to the appropriate navigation user. Another new principal function, GPS Reference State Processing, maintains reference states for the receivers and navigation functions. Inertial measurement units (IMUs) provide acceleration data and Redundancy Management (RM) functions maintain failure status information.

The GPS formalization focused on a few key areas because the CR itself is very large and complex. After preliminary study of the CR and discussions with the GPS RAs, we decided to concentrate on two major new principal functions, emphasizing their interfaces to existing navigation software and excluding crew I/O functions. The two principal functions, known as GPS Receiver State

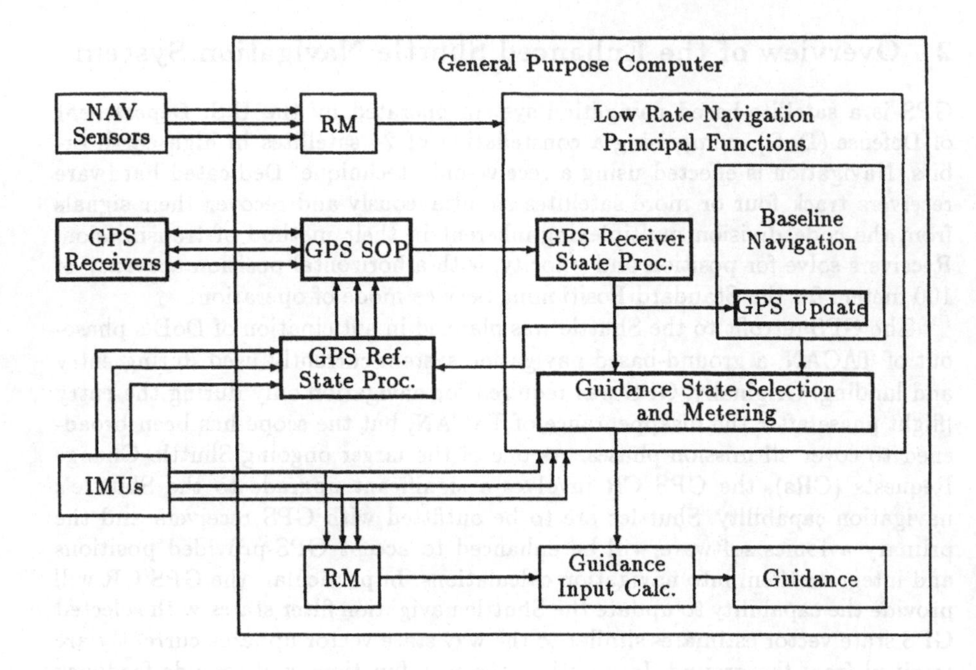

Fig. 1. Architecture for integrating GPS into navigation subsystem.

Processing and GPS Reference State Processing, select and modify GPS state vectors for consumption by the existing entry navigation software. As these functions are entirely new, we felt that concentrating on these areas would yield a high return on our formalization investment. Moreover, this choice obviated the need to model large amounts of existing Shuttle functionality.

The two chosen principal functions, in turn, are organized into several subfunctions each.

- GPS Receiver State Processing
  1. GPS IMU Assign
  2. GPS Navigation State Propagation
  3. GPS State Vector Quality Assessment
  4. GPS State Vector Selection
  5. GPS Reference State Announced Reset
  6. GPS Downlist Computation
- GPS Reference State Processing
  1. GPS External Data Snap
  2. IMU GPS Selection
  3. GPS Reference State Initialization and Reset
  4. GPS Reference State Propagation

The subset of the GPS CR represented here contains approximately 110 pages of requirements in the form of prose, pseudo-code, and tables. The entire CR is about 1000 pages long.

2.2 Characteristics of Application

The nature of the GPS CR application is that of a significant augmentation to a mature body of complex navigation functions. Interfaces among components are broad, containing many variables. Typical classes of data include:

- Flags to indicate status, to request services, and to select options among processing choices.
- Time values and time intervals both to serve as timestamps within state vectors and to control when operations should be performed.
- Navigation-related values such as positions and velocities.
- Arrays of all these types indexed by GPS receiver number.
- Various numeric quantities representing thresholds, tolerance values, etc.

Navigation state vectors are of the form $(\mathbf{r}, \mathbf{v}, t)$, where $\mathbf{r}$ is a position, $\mathbf{v}$ is a velocity, and t is the time at which the position and velocity apply. A position $\mathbf{r}$ or a velocity $\mathbf{v}$ is a three-element vector relative to a Cartesian or geodetic coordinate system. Usually the Shuttle uses an inertial coordinate system called the "Aries mean of 1950" system, abbreviated as "M50."

An important operation on state vectors is *propagating* them to a new instant of time. If we have a state vector $(\mathbf{r}, \mathbf{v}, t)$, and we have a measurement or estimate of the accelerations experienced by the vehicle over the (short) time interval $[t, t']$, we can propagate the state to a new state vector $(\mathbf{r}', \mathbf{v}', t')$ using standard techniques of physical mechanics. This type of operation is typically performed to synchronize state vectors to a common point in time.

Processing requirements within the CR are generally expressed in an algorithmic style using high-level language assignments and conditional statements. Within conditionally invoked assignments, the assumption is the usual procedural one that a variable not assigned retains its previous value, which may or may not have a meaningful interpretation in the current context. Flag variables are used to indicate when other (non-flag) variables hold currently valid data.

3 Technical Approach

The formal methods approach is loosely based on earlier work conducted by the inter-center team during 1993 on subsystems called Jet Select and Orbit DAP [10]. Those techniques were adapted to accommodate the needs of this new area of the Shuttle software. All work has been mechanically assisted by the PVS toolset. PVS (Prototype Verification System) is an environment for specification and verification developed at SRI International's Computer Science

Laboratory [13]. The distinguishing characteristic of PVS is a highly expressive specification language coupled with a very effective interactive theorem prover that uses decision procedures to automate most of the low-level proof steps.

3.1 State Machine Models

We have devised a strategy to model Shuttle principal functions based on the use of a conventional abstract state machine model. Each principal function is modeled as a state machine that takes inputs and local state values, and produces outputs and new state values. This method provides a simple computational model similar to popular state-based methods such the A-7 model [8, 15].

One transition of the state machine model corresponds to one scheduled execution of the principal function, e.g., one cycle at rate 6.25 Hz or other applicable rate. All of the inputs to the principal function are bundled together and a similar bundling of the outputs is arranged. The state variable holds values that are (usually) not delivered to other units, but instead are held for use on the next cycle.

The state machine transition function is a mathematically well-defined function that takes a vector of input values and a vector of previous-state values, and maps them into a vector of outputs and a vector of next-state values.

$$M : I \times S \rightarrow [O \times S]$$

This function M is expressed in PVS and forms the central part of the formal specification. We construct a tuple composed of the output and state values so only a single top-level function is needed in the formalization. Some values may appear in both the output list and the next-state vector, i.e., they are not mutually exclusive.

While the function M captures the functionality of the software subsystem in question, the state machine framework can also serve to formalize abstract properties about the behavior of the subsystem. The common approach of writing assertions about *traces* or sequences of input and output vectors is easily accommodated. For example, we can introduce sequences $I(n) = < i_1, \ldots, i_n >$ and $O(n) = < o_1, \ldots, o_n >$ to denote the flow of inputs and outputs that would have occurred if the state machine were run for n transitions. A property about the behavior of M can be expressed as a relation P between $I(n)$ and $O(n)$ and formally established, i.e., we can prove that the property P does indeed follow from the formal specification M using the PVS proof-checker.

3.2 Expression in PVS

Figure 2 shows the abstract structure of a Shuttle principal function rendered in PVS notation. Key features of this structure are:

- Principal functions use two kinds of variable data (input values, previous-state values) and three kinds of constant data (I-loads, K-loads, constants).

```
pf_result: TYPE = [# output: pf_outputs, state: pf_state #]

principal_function (pf_inputs, pf_state,
                    pf_I_loads, pf_K_loads,
                    pf_constants) : pf_result =

     (# output := <output expression>,
        state  := <next-state expression>
      #)
```

Fig. 2. PVS model of a Shuttle *principal function*.

- Executing a principal function produces output values and next-state values.
- All externally visible effects on variables are to be captured by this model.

The PVS definition assumes all input and state values have been collected into the structures **pf_inputs** and **pf_state**. Additionally, all I-load, K-load, and constant inputs used by the principal function are collected into similar structures. The **pf_result** type is a record that contains an output component and a next-state component. Each of these objects is, in turn, a structure containing (possibly many) subcomponents.

The output and next-state expressions in the general form above describe the effects of invoking the subfunctions belonging to the principal function. In practice, this can be very complicated so a stylized method of organizing this information has been devised. It is based on the use of a LET expression to introduce variable names corresponding to the intermediate inputs and outputs exchanged among subfunctions.

3.3 Deviations from CR/FSSR Requirements

In deriving the preceding specification method, we have tried to be faithful to the FSSR method of expressing requirements. A few deviations and omissions, however, should be noted.

- The concept of state variables is not explicitly mentioned in FSSR-style requirements. Their use has been inferred and a method has been provided for their specification to make the final requirements more clear.
- No provision was introduced to capture initialization requirements for state variables. This issue can be handled at the next higher level of modeling.
- Conditional assignments in algorithmic requirements occasionally leave variable values unspecified. We assign default values to such cases when it is clear that the variable's value on one branch of a conditional is a "don't care."

4 Formalizing the Requirements

Initially, the relevant portions of the CR were analyzed to determine the basic structure of the principal functions and how they are decomposed into subfunctions. Based on this organization, a general approach for modeling the functions and expressing the formal specifications in PVS was devised. A document on this prescribed technique for writing formal specifications for the GPS CR was written and sent to the Loral requirements analysts.

Next, the interfaces of the principal functions and their subfunctions were carefully scrutinized. Particular emphasis was placed on being able to identify the types of all inputs and outputs, and to match up all the data flows that are implicit in the tabular format presented in the requirements. While conducting this analysis and preparing to write the formal specifications, various minor discrepancies were detected in the CR and these were reported to Loral requirements analysts.

A set of preliminary formal specifications was developed for the principal functions known as GPS Receiver State Processing and GPS Reference State Processing, using the language of PVS. Assumptions were made as needed to overcome the discrepancies encountered. Enough detail was provided in the formal specifications to characterize the functions with high precision. In parallel with this activity, several Loral RAs have been learning formal methods and PVS and positioning themselves to carry out this work after the trial project is completed.

Formalization of the two principal functions in PVS has been completed and revised three times to keep up with requirements changes. Because of the breadth of this CR, convergence has been slow. Requirements changes have been frequent and extensive as the CR was worked through the review process. Our initial formal specification was based on a preliminary version of the CR, before the two-phase implementation plan was adopted. Subsequent versions were written to model the single-string GPS CR and its revisions. PVS versions were written for Mod B, Mod D/E and Mod F/G of the CR. (Revisions or modifications are denoted Mod A, Mod B, etc.)

Excerpts from the formalization are shown in Figures 3 through 8. The full formal specifications contain over 3300 lines of PVS notation (including comments and blank lines), packaged as eleven PVS theories.

Figure 3 shows a portion of the vector and matrix utilities needed to formalize operations in this application domain. Using a parameterized theory such as this made it easy to declare vectors of reals where the index type differs from one vector type to the next. Figure 4 illustrates the declaration of some typical types found in this application and how the vector types are incorporated. All the types needed are rather simple and concrete; structured types are all of fixed size. As is customarily done in PVS, vectors and arrays are represented by function types.

Figure 5 presents one of the subfunctions from GPS Receiver State Processing. The outputs are bundled together into a single record type and used as the result type for the PVS function used to model the Shuttle software subfunction. The definition of the function contains a single expression, a record constructor

```
vectors [index_type: TYPE]: THEORY
BEGIN

vector:          TYPE = [index_type -> real]

i,j,k:           VAR index_type
a,b,c:           VAR real
U,V:             VAR vector

zero_vector:         vector = (LAMBDA i: 0)
vector_sum(U, V):    vector = (LAMBDA i: U(i) + V(i))
vector_diff(U, V):   vector = (LAMBDA i: U(i) - V(i))
scalar_mult(a, V):   vector = (LAMBDA i: a * V(i))

 . . .

END vectors
```

Fig. 3. Vector operations organized as a PVS theory.

```
major_mode_code:    TYPE = nat
mission_time:       TYPE = real
GPS_id:             TYPE = {n: nat | 1 <= n & n <= 3}

receiver_mode:      TYPE = {init, test, nav, blank}
AIF_flag:           TYPE = {auto, inhibit, force}

M50_axis:           TYPE = {Xm, Ym, Zm}

IMPORTING           vectors[M50_axis]

M50_vector:         TYPE = vector[M50_axis]

position_vector:    TYPE = M50_vector
velocity_vector:    TYPE = M50_vector
GPS_positions:      TYPE = [GPS_id -> position_vector]
GPS_velocities:     TYPE = [GPS_id -> velocity_vector]

GPS_predicate:      TYPE = [GPS_id -> bool]
GPS_times:          TYPE = [GPS_id -> mission_time]
GPS_FOM_vector:     TYPE = [GPS_id -> GPS_figure_of_merit]
```

Fig. 4. Selected type declarations.

```
ref_state_anncd_reset_out: TYPE = [#
      GPS_anncd_reset_avail:    GPS_predicate,
      GPS_anncd_reset:          GPS_predicate,
      R_ref_anncd_reset:        GPS_positions,
      T_anncd_reset:            GPS_times,
      T_ref_anncd_reset:        GPS_times,
      V_IMU_ref_anncd_reset:    GPS_velocities,
      V_ref_anncd_reset:        GPS_velocities
      #]

ref_state_announced_reset(DT_anncd_reset,
                          GPS_DG_SF,
                          GPS_SW_cap,
                          R_GPS,
                          T_anncd_reset,
                          T_current_filt,
                          T_GPS,
                          V_current_GPS,
                          V_GPS) : ref_state_anncd_reset_out =

    (# GPS_anncd_reset_avail := GPS_DG_SF,
       GPS_anncd_reset       :=
         (LAMBDA I: IF GPS_DG_SF(I)
                    THEN (T_current_filt - T_anncd_reset(I)
                           >= DT_anncd_reset)
                    ELSE false
                 ENDIF),
       R_ref_anncd_reset     :=
         (LAMBDA I: IF GPS_DG_SF(I) THEN R_GPS(I)
                                    ELSE null_position ENDIF),
       T_anncd_reset         :=
         (LAMBDA I: IF GPS_DG_SF(I) AND
                    (T_current_filt - T_anncd_reset(I)
                      >= DT_anncd_reset)
                    THEN T_current_filt
                    ELSE null_mission_time
                 ENDIF),
       T_ref_anncd_reset     :=
         (LAMBDA I: IF GPS_DG_SF(I) THEN T_GPS(I)
                                    ELSE null_mission_time ENDIF),
       V_IMU_ref_anncd_reset :=
         (LAMBDA I: IF GPS_DG_SF(I)
                    THEN V_current_GPS(I)
                    ELSE null_velocity
                 ENDIF),
       V_ref_anncd_reset     :=
         (LAMBDA I: IF GPS_DG_SF(I) THEN V_GPS(I)
                                    ELSE null_velocity ENDIF)
    #)
```

Fig. 5. Sample subfunction of Receiver State Processing.

that gives values for each of the required outputs. In this case they are all structured objects with **GPS_id** as the index type. Therefore, lambda-expressions with the variable I ranging over **GPS_id** are used to construct suitable values.

To further illustrate the approach, consider the following example:

```
(LAMBDA I: IF GPS_DG_SF(I) THEN R_GPS(I) ELSE null_position ENDIF)
```

This expression evaluates to a function from $\{1, 2, 3\}$ to position vectors. For GPS receiver I, if its "data good" flag is set (**GPS_DG_SF(I)** holds), then use the position value **R_GPS(I)** derived from the input **R_GPS**, otherwise use a default position value.

In several cases, the subfunction requirements are fairly complex and it was necessary to introduce intermediate PVS functions to decompose the formalization. While this is a natural thing to do, it does cause some loss of traceability to the original requirements. Clarity and readability were judged more important, however, and such decompositions were introduced as needed.

Figure 6 shows the method of modeling principal function interfaces as records of individual values corresponding to Shuttle program variables. Because the interfaces at this level are quite broad, some of these lists become moderately long, on the order of 20 or 30 elements. In reality, these inputs and outputs are not actually "passed" in any programming language sense during execution; they are usually accessed as global variables and thus can be thought of as having the semantics of "call by reference." Consequently, our formalization must necessarily be viewed as a model of the software structure, and in some cases there are unpleasant artifacts of the difference between the model and the real system.

Figures 7 and 8 depict the top-level structure of the GPS Receiver State Processing model. Its interface types are given by the declarations shown in Figure 6. Its body is of the form

```
LET sf_1_out = subfun-1(...),
      . . .        . . .
    sf_n_out = subfun-n(...)
IN
   (# output := (# ... #),
      state  := (# ... #)
   #)
```

Each local variable assignment of the LET-expression represents the invocation of a subfunction and the storage of its intermediate results. Those values can be used directly as principal function outputs or passed to later subfunctions on the list. The final expression denotes the ultimate principal function result, which has the form of output values plus state values.

5 Results

The formalization step demonstrated that it is not difficult to bring the precision of formalization to bear on the type of requirements we examined. Expressing

```
rec_sp_inputs: TYPE = [#
      crew_deselect_rcvr:     GPS_predicate,
      earth_pole:             position_vector,
       . . .                   . . .
      V_GPS_ECEF:             GPS_velocities_WGS84,
      V_last_GPS:             GPS_velocities
      #]

rec_sp_state: TYPE = [#
      G_two_prev:             GPS_accelerations,
      GPS_DG_SF_prev:         GPS_predicate,
       . . .                   . . .
      V_last_GPS_sel:         velocity_vector,
      V_last_GPS_two:         velocity_vector
      #]

rec_sp_I_loads: TYPE = [#
      acc_prop_min_GPS:       real,
      acc_prop_thresh_GPS:    real,
       . . .                   . . .
      SF_vel:                 real,
      sig_diag_GPS_nom:       cov_diagonal_vector
      #]

rec_sp_K_loads: TYPE = [#
      acc_prop_min:           real,
      GPS_SW_cap:             num_GPS
      #]

rec_sp_constants: TYPE = [#
      deg_to_rad:             real,
      earth_rate:             real,
      G0:                     real,
      nautmi_per_ft:          real
      #]

rec_sp_outputs: TYPE = [#
      corr_coeff_GPS:         corr_coeff_vector,
      crew_des_rcvr_rcvd:     GPS_predicate,
       . . .                   . . .
      V_IMU_ref_anncd_reset:  GPS_velocities,
      V_ref_anncd_reset:      GPS_velocities
      #]

rec_sp_result: TYPE = [# output: rec_sp_outputs,
                         state:  rec_sp_state  #]
```

Fig. 6. Principal function interface types.

```
GPS_receiver_state_processing((rec_sp_inputs:    rec_sp_inputs),
                              (rec_sp_state:     rec_sp_state),
                              (rec_sp_I_loads:   rec_sp_I_loads),
                              (rec_sp_K_loads:   rec_sp_K_loads),
                              (rec_sp_constants: rec_sp_constants) )
                              : rec_sp_result =

 LET IMU_assign_out =
       IMU_assign(
          GPS_installed        (rec_sp_I_loads),
          GPS_SW_cap           (rec_sp_K_loads),
          nav_IMU_to_GPS       (rec_sp_inputs),
          V_current_filt       (rec_sp_inputs),
          V_last_GPS_two       (rec_sp_state) ),

     nav_state_prop_out =
       nav_state_propagation(
          acc_prop_min         (rec_sp_K_loads),
          acc_prop_min_GPS     (rec_sp_I_loads),
          . . .                . . .
          V_last_GPS_prev      (IMU_assign_out),
          V_last_GPS_sel       (rec_sp_state) ),

     SV_qual_assess_out =
       state_vector_quality_assessment(
          G_two                (nav_state_prop_out),
          GPS_DG_SF            (nav_state_prop_out),
          . . .                . . .
          V_GPS                (nav_state_prop_out),
          V_GPS_prev           (rec_sp_state) ),

     state_vect_sel_out =
       state_vector_selection(
          corr_coeff_GPS_nom   (rec_sp_I_loads),
          crew_deselect_rcvr   (rec_sp_inputs),
          . . .                . . .
          V_GPS                (nav_state_prop_out),
          V_GPS_sel            (nav_state_prop_out) ),

     ref_st_ann_reset_out =
       ref_state_announced_reset(
          DT_anncd_reset       (rec_sp_I_loads),
          GPS_DG_SF            (nav_state_prop_out),
          . . .                . . .
          V_current_GPS        (IMU_assign_out),
          V_GPS                (nav_state_prop_out) ),
```

Fig. 7. Principal function specification.

```
    GPS_downlist_out =
        GPS_downlist_computation(
            crew_deselect_rcvr    (rec_sp_inputs),
            DT_QA2                (SV_qual_assess_out),
            . . .                 . . .
            SF_vel                (rec_sp_I_loads),
            V_GPS_sel             (state_vect_sel_out) )

IN (# output := (#
      corr_coeff_GPS :=       corr_coeff_GPS      (state_vect_sel_out),
      crew_des_rcvr_rcvd := crew_des_rcvr_rcvd (state_vect_sel_out),
      . . .                   . . .               . . .
      V_IMU_ref_anncd_reset :=
                V_IMU_ref_anncd_reset              (ref_st_ann_reset_out),
      V_ref_anncd_reset :=  V_ref_anncd_reset    (ref_st_ann_reset_out)
      #),

     state := (#
      G_two_prev :=          G_two_prev           (SV_qual_assess_out),
      GPS_DG_SF_prev :=      GPS_DG_SF_prev       (SV_qual_assess_out),
      . . .                  . . .                . . .
      V_last_GPS_sel :=      V_last_GPS_sel       (nav_state_prop_out),
      V_last_GPS_two :=      V_last_GPS_two       (nav_state_prop_out)
      #)
   #)
```

Fig. 8. Principal function specification (cont'd).

the requirements in the language of an off-the-shelf verification methodology was straightforward. We found PVS effective for this purpose; we feel other languages would also fare well.

This much was unsurprising. What was more of a pleasant discovery was the number of problems found in the requirements as a simple consequence of carrying out the formalization. While many have claimed this as a benefit of formal methods, we can offer another piece of anecdotal evidence to support it. All of the errors identified so far have been due to carrying the analysis only to the point of typechecking. It was also our intention to take up some theorem proving as well, but this has had to wait for the requirements themselves to reach a firmer state of convergence.

Based on our initial results, some Shuttle RAs are optimistic about the potential impact of formal methods. Others in the Shuttle community are curious about the potential benefits of formalization. The RAs' feedback indicated our approach was helpful in detecting three classes of errors:

1. Type 4 — requirements do not meet CR author's intent.
2. Type 6 — requirements not technically clear, understandable and maintainable.
3. Type 9 — interfaces inconsistent.

An example of Type 4 errors encountered in the CR is o¡mission due to conditionally updating variables. Suppose, for example, one branch of a conditional assigns several variables, leaving them unassigned on the other branch. The requirements author intends for the values to be "don't cares" in the other branch, but occasionally this is faulty because some variables such as flags need to be assigned in both cases. Similar problems encountered are those due to overlapping conditions, leading to ambiguity in the correct assignments to make

Examples of Type 9 errors include numerous, minor cases of incomplete and inconsistent interfaces. Missing inputs and outputs from tables, mismatches across tables, inappropriate types, and incorrect names are all typical errors seen in the subfunction and principal function interfaces. Most are problems that could be avoided through greater use of automation in the requirements capture process.

All requirements issues detected during the formalization were passed on to Loral representatives. Those deemed to be real issues, that is, not caused by the misunderstandings of an outsider, were then officially submitted on behalf of the formal methods analysis as ones to be addressed during the requirements inspections. Severity levels are attached to valid issues during the inspections. This allowed us to get "credit" for identifying problems and led to some rudimentary measurements on the effectiveness of formalization.

Issue Severity	Mod B	Mod D/E	Mod F/G	Totals
High Major	1	0	0	1
Low Major	7	3	0	10
High Minor	19	40	6	65
Low Minor	8	0	2	10
Totals	35	43	8	86

Fig. 9. Summary of issues detected by formal methods.

Figure 9 summarizes a preliminary accounting of the issues identified during our analysis. The issues are broken out by severity level for the three inspections of the CR that took place during the formal methods study. A grand total of 86 issues were submitted for the three inspections. Of these issues, 72 of the 86 were of Type 9 (interfaces inconsistent). The rest were primarily scattered among Type 4 (requirements do not meet CR author's intent) and Type 6 (requirements not technically clear, understandable and maintainable). Note that many issues submitted at a given inspection remained unresolved in the next revision. These were not resubmitted, however, meaning all the issues cited in the table are distinct.

The meaning of the severity codes used in Figure 9 is as follows:

1. High major — Loral cannot implement requirement.
2. Low major — Requirement does not correctly reflect CR author's intent.
3. High minor — "Support" requirements are incorrect or confusing.
4. Low minor — Minor documentation changes.

As can be seen by these results, the added precision of formalization used early in the lifecycle can yield tangible benefits. While many of these issues could have been found with lighter-weight techniques, the use of formal specifications can detect them *and* leave open the option of deductive analysis later on. Thus, these results by themselves suggest a potential boost from the use of formal methods plus the promise of additional benefits if proving is ultimately attempted.

It is worth noting that most errors detected in the CR during the formalization exercise were not directly found by typechecking or other automated analysis activity, but were detected during the act of writing the specifications or during the review and preparation leading up to the writing step. Additional problems were found during the typechecking phase as well. When we reach the point of modeling higher level properties and carrying out proofs, we expect to see fewer errors still. This is consistent with general observations practitioners have about inspections and reviews. Light-weight forms of analysis applied early detect more problems and detect them quickly, but they are usually superficial. As more powerful analysis methods are introduced, we find more subtle problems, but they tend to be less numerous.

The next step in the application of formal methods to GPS, which was still in progress as of this writing, is to identify and formalize important behavioral properties of the processing of GPS position and velocity vectors. In particular, the feedback loop shown in Figure 1 involving the principal functions Receiver State Processing and Reference State Processing is fertile ground for investigation. Proving that suitable properties hold would offer a powerful means of further shaking out the requirements before passing them on to development.

Perhaps the most encouraging outcome of the study was a serious interest on the part of the requirements analysts to learn formal methods and continue the formalization activity themselves. Loral and JSC personnel received a training course at NASA Langley and intend to maintain and extend the GPS formal specifications during the implementation phase. Other CRs are being examined for potential evaluation as well. We are hopeful that this will lead to a continuing involvement by the NASA space community.

6 Conclusions

Experience with the GPS effort showed that the outlook for formal methods in this requirements analysis domain is quite promising. PVS has been used effectively to formalize this application, and the custom specification approach should be easy to duplicate for other areas. There are good prospects for continuation of the effort by Shuttle personnel. Some Shuttle RAs are optimistic about the potential impact of formal methods. Although the specification activity was assisted by tools, doing manual specification is also feasible here, albeit with reduced benefits.

PVS provides a formal specification language of considerable theoretical power while still preserving the syntactic flavor of modern programming languages. This makes the specifications fairly readable to nonexperts and makes their development less difficult than might otherwise be the case with specification languages whose features are more limiting. The scheme detailed here leads to specifications that RAs and others from the Shuttle community can and did learn to read and interpret without having to become PVS practitioners. Moreover, the mere construction of formal specifications using this method can and did lead to the discovery of flaws in the requirements. Future efforts can use the specifications as the foundation for more sophisticated analyses based on the use of formal proof. This additional tool provides the means to answer nontrivial questions about the specifications and achieve a higher level of assurance that the requirements are free of major flaws.

The methods outlined for formally specifying requirements were devised to meet the needs of the chosen CR. They are methods having fundamental utility that should lend themselves to other avionics applications. Tailoring a scheme for other uses or fine tuning it for the intended CR is easily accomplished. Alternative specification styles could readily be adopted. Experience in using the methods on live applications will help determine what direction future refinements should take.

In addition to specifications to capture the functionality of the principal functions, often it is desirable to formalize abstract properties about the long-term behavior of software subsystems. Formulating such properties is a way of assuring that certain critical constraints on system operation are always observed, allowing us to reason in a "longitudinal" manner by expressing what should be true about the software behavior over time rather than merely what holds at the current step. The specification framework sketched here can be extended easily to accommodate invariants or other property-oriented assertions.

The requirements analysis process used on the Shuttle program was originally put in place in the 1970s, and consists largely of manual, best-effort scrutiny whose effectiveness depends on the diligence of the analyst. Consider how formalizing requirements would help overcome several often-cited deficiencies of this process:

1. *There is no methodology to guide the analysis.*
   Formal methods offer rigorous modeling and analysis techniques that bring increased precision and error detection to the realm of requirements.
2. *There are no completion criteria.*
   Writing formal specifications and conducting proofs are deliberate acts to which one can attach meaningful completion criteria.
3. *There is no structured way for RAs to document the results of their analysis.*

Formal specifications are tangible products that can be maintained and consulted as analysis and development proceed. When provided as outputs of the analysis process, formalized requirements can be used as evidence of thoroughness and coverage, as definitive explanations of how CRs achieve their objectives, and as permanent artifacts useful for answering future questions that may arise.

Acknowledgements

The author is grateful for the cooperation and support of the requirements analysts and other staff members at Loral Space Information Systems: Larry Roberts, Mike Beims, and, in earlier phases of this work, David Hamilton and Dan Bowman. Their enthusiasm for the project made the work much more meaningful. Thanks are also due to John Kelly (JPL), John Rushby and Judy Crow (SRI), and Rick Butler (LaRC). This work was supported in part by the National Aeronautics and Space Administration under Contract No. NAS1-19341.

References

1. A. Arnold, M-C. Gaudel, and B. Marre. An Experiment on the Validation of a Specification by Heterogeneous Formal Means: The Transit Node. In *5th IFIP Working Conference on Dependable Computing for Critical Applications (DCCA-5)*, Champaign-Urbana, IL, 1995.
2. Ricky W. Butler, James L. Caldwell, Victor A. Carreño, C. Michael Holloway, Paul S. Miner, and Ben L. Di Vito. NASA Langley's Research and Technology Transfer Program in Formal Methods. In *Tenth Annual Conference on Computer Assurance (COMPASS 95)*, pages 135–149, Gaithersburg, MD, June 1995.
3. Dan Craigen, Susan Gerhart, and Ted Ralston. An international survey of industrial applications of formal methods; Volume 1: Purpose, approach, analysis and conclusions; Volume 2: Case studies. Technical Report NIST GCR 93/626, National Institute of Standards and Technology, Gaithersburg, MD, April 1993.
4. Judy Crow. Finite-State Analysis of Space Shuttle Contingency Guidance Requirements. Technical Report SRI-CSL-95-17, Computer Science Laboratory, SRI International, Menlo Park, CA, December 1995. Also forthcoming as a NASA Contractor Report for Task NAS1-20334.
5. Ben L. Di Vito and Larry Roberts. Using Formal Methods to Assist in the Requirements Analysis of the Space Shuttle GPS Change Request. Contractor report, NASA Langley Research Center, Hampton, VA, 1996. To appear.
6. David Hamilton, Rick Covington, and John Kelly. Experiences in Applying Formal Methods to the Analysis of Software and System Requirements. In *WIFT '95: Workshop on Industrial-Strength Formal Specification Techniques*, pages 30–43, Boca Raton, FL, 1995. IEEE Computer Society.
7. David Hamilton, Rick Covington, and Alice Lee. Experience Report on Requirements Reliability Engineering Using Formal Methods. In *ISSRE '95: International Conference on Software Reliability Engineering*, Toulouse, France, 1995. IEEE Computer Society.

8. K. L. Heninger. Specifying Software Requirements for Complex Systems: New Techniques and Their Application. *IEEE Transactions on Software Engineering*, SE-6(1):2–13, January 1980.
9. Robyn R. Lutz and Yoko Ampo. Experience Report: Using Formal Methods for Requirements Analysis of Critical Spacecraft Software. In *19th Annual Software Engineering Workshop*, pages 231–248. NASA GSFC, 1994. Greenbelt, MD.
10. Multi-Center NASA Team from Jet Propulsion Laboratory, Johnson Space Center, and Langley Research Center. *Formal Methods Demonstration Project for Space Applications – Phase I Case Study: Space Shuttle Orbit DAP Jet Select*, December 1993. NASA Code Q Final Report (Unnumbered).
11. National Aeronautics and Space Administration, Office of Safety and Mission Assurance, Washington, DC. *Formal Methods Specification and Verification Guidebook for Software and Computer Systems, Volume I: Planning and Technology Insertion*, July 1995. NASA-GB-002-95.
12. National Research Council Committee for Review of Oversight Mechanisms for Space Shuttle Flight Software Processes, National Academy Press, Washington, DC. *An Assessment of Space Shuttle Flight Software Development Practices*, 1993.
13. Sam Owre, John Rushby, Natarajan Shankar, and Friedrich von Henke. Formal Verification for Fault-Tolerant Architectures: Prolegomena to the Design of PVS. *IEEE Transactions on Software Engineering*, 21(2):107–125, February 1995.
14. John Rushby. Formal Methods and the Certification of Critical Systems. Technical Report SRI-CSL-93-7, Computer Science Laboratory, SRI International, Menlo Park, CA, December 1993. Also issued under the title *Formal Methods and Digital Systems Validation for Airborne Systems* as NASA Contractor Report 4551, December 1993.
15. A. John van Schouwen. The A-7 Requirements Model: Re-Examination for Real-Time Systems and an Application to Monitoring Systems. Technical Report 90-276, Department of Computing and Information Science, Queen's University, Kingston, Ontario, Canada, May 1990.

Combining VDM-SL Specifications with C++ Code

Brigitte Fröhlich[1] and Peter Gorm Larsen[2]

[1] University of Technology Graz, Münzgabenstr. 11/II, 8010 Graz, Austria
[2] IFAD (The Institute of Applied Computer Science), Forskerparken 10, 5230 Odense M, Denmark

Abstract. Experience shows that it is not economically feasible to formally specify all parts of a system in an industrial application. Either one already has a number of existing components which are trusted and therefore desirable for reuse, or components are so simple that there is no gain in formally specifying their behavior. In both cases it may be felt that it is not worth spending time on developing a detailed formal specification of the entire system. This raises the question what tools should be provided for the analysis of the entire system in which actual code is combined with specifications. In this paper we propose an approach which enables integration of code into a formal specification for prototyping facilities. The integration of code is supported by an extension to the IFAD VDM-SL Toolbox such that heterogeneous models can be interpreted.

1 Introduction

The successful introduction of formal methods into an industrial setting depends very much upon the choice of the parts of a given system that are subject to formal specification [14]. In the ConForm experiment it was concluded that formal specification is beneficial when either the functionality is simple but critical or the data structure or the functionality is complex [18]. The skill for selecting the most appropriate subsystems to be formally specified comes with experience in both formal specification and the given application domain. There is hardly any new input one can supply to meet this challenge. However, for tool developers supporting formal methods, it is a new challenge to enable users to gain insight in the interaction between the parts of the system which are being formally specified and the parts which simply are developed conventionally. With such a heterogeneous model of the system new problems arise.

There are a number of facilities, traditionally provided by operating systems or the programming languages, which for various reasons have been left out of conventional model-oriented specification languages such as Z and VDM-SL. These facilities include e.g. human-computer interfaces, input/output routines or the generation of random numbers. In this paper we will use as example the trigonometric functions which cannot appropriately be described in these specification languages because these kinds of primitives have not been included in Z and VDM-SL. Of course, as a tool developer one could extend the specification language to include all of these useful features. The main drawback of doing this directly is that this approach is static and requires the tool developer to re-compile the entire tool whenever a new feature is desired by another user. Therefore in this paper we advocate a dynamic approach which enables the user to supply the extensions (s)he is interested in for a particular application.

The motivation for the approach we are presenting here is to enable the user to interpret an executable part of a heterogeneous model. The combination we are dealing with includes the formal specification language VDM-SL and the programming language C++, but the approach presented here could just as well be used with other notations. The intention is to provide a prototyping facility by which one can determine how the parts that have been specified interact with the coded parts.

The Vienna Development Method (VDM) [16, 4] is one of the most mature formal methods, primarily intended for the formal specification and the subsequent development of functional aspects of software systems. Its specification language VDM-SL [7] is used during the specification and design phases of a software development project, and it supports the production of correct high quality software. VDM-SL is being standardized under the auspices of the International Standard Institution (ISO) [2]. It is currently a Committee Draft standard under ISO and it is expected that this draft will be accepted as a final standard soon.

A modular extension to ISO VDM-SL is supported by the IFAD VDM-SL Toolbox [10, 21, 12]. The Toolbox supports extensive type checking, LaTeX pretty-printing facilities, test coverage, code generation, interpretation and many debugging facilities. A large subset of IFAD VDM-SL is executable by the existing interpreter of the Toolbox. The work presented in this paper is an extension of the Toolbox. The main impact of the extension is on the interpreter as will be illustrated below.

The Toolbox has been implemented in C++ using a VDM library which provides a generic implementation of all the data types of VDM-SL. The code generator from the Toolbox also produces C++ code using this library. C++ is an object-oriented extension of C and this library uses inheritance to build a class hierarchy of general VDM values in C++ [13]. For historical reasons the objects from this VDM library have been called "Meta-IV values".[3]

After this introduction we will present a small example illustrating the basic idea underlying our approach. This is followed by a short introduction to the parts of the existing interpreter which are relevant for this work. Then the extensions to the interpreter to incorporate this approach are presented. Different alternative communication primitives are then discussed. Finally, some related work is mentioned and a few concluding remarks about future work and the applicability of this approach are given.

[3] "Meta-IV" was the name of the Danish dialect of VDM-SL before the standardization started.

2 Illustration of the Basic Idea

The combination of formal specifications and code written in C++ only becomes feasible by establishing a common framework combining them. The most basic problem is that the values in these two different worlds have different representations. For the two worlds to communicate, it is necessary to convert values from the specification world to the code world and vice versa. By means of small examples this section illustrates the idea of integrating code with a specification in order to obtain the required functionality.

The examples present the integration of trigonometric functions into a specification using the IFAD VDM-SL Toolbox. A specification of the trigonometric functions is most naturally formulated algebraically stating the relationship between the different trigonometric functions. An algebraic specification style is not supported by VDM-SL and implicit functions belong to the not executable subset of VDM-SL. Therefore the trigonometric functions cannot appropriately be described in the specification language with the intention to execute it. However, an implementation of these functions is part of almost every programming language.

2.1 Basic Idea

The aim of this approach is to be able to analyze the combination of specification and implementation. By combining code and specification our main intention is to provide a prototyping facility by integrating the execution of code into the interpretation of a specification. We enable definitions, made at the code level, to be integrated with a formal specification, such that their execution during the interpretation of a specification is enabled. Therefore we distinguish between the specification level, which refers to the Toolbox, and the code level which relates to the integration of code for the execution.

Figure 1 shows our approach of combining code and specification. The dashed boxes mark the different levels; the IFAD VDM-SL Toolbox represents the specification level and the code level corresponds to the code units. These code units are represented as "dynamic linked libraries" to the interpreter process. The bold boxes indicate the parts which the user has to develop additionally in order to combine code and VDM-SL specification.

For every unit of code, which may consist of one or more C++ files, an interface at the specification level as well as an interface at the code level must be developed by the user of the Toolbox. At the specification level a new kind of module, called *implementation module*, has been introduced. The module concept of the IFAD VDM-SL specification language provides a facility for the combination of multiple modules, which has been used for our approach.

An implementation module contains the corresponding type information for every definition of the C++ code to be integrated with the VDM-SL specification. For functions, this type information consists of a signature in VDM-SL and a VDM-SL type declaration for values. The implementation modules have to be imported by every module that accesses a function or value defined in code.

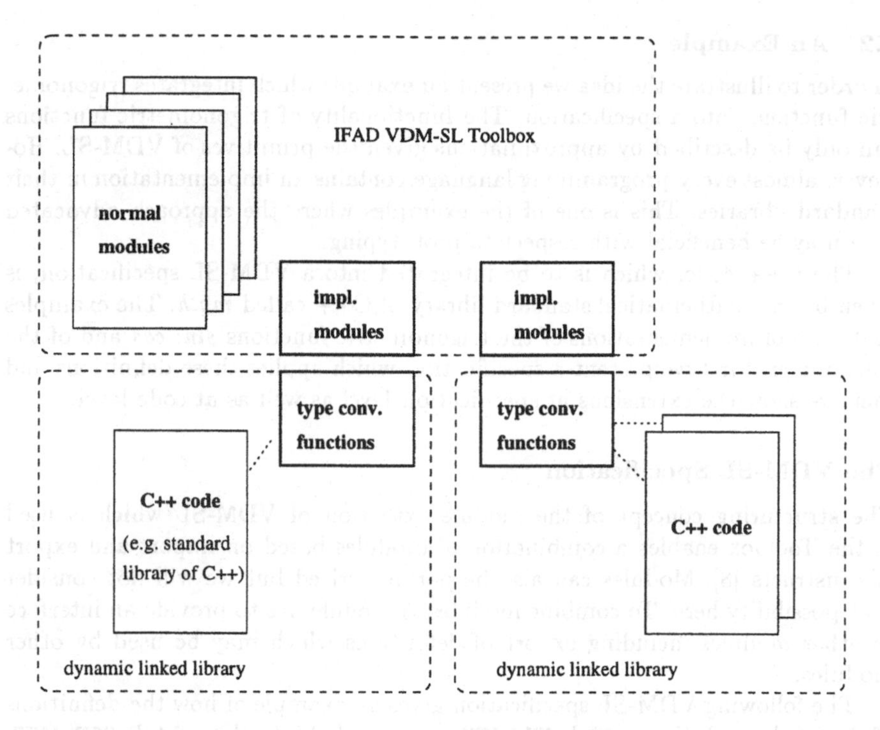

Fig. 1. Basic idea of combining code and specification in the Toolbox

The aim is to provide a prototyping facility by combining the interpretation of a specification with the execution of a module implemented in C++. As the C++ code and the IFAD VDM-SL interpreter have different representations for their types, a type conversion of values between those two worlds by the definition of type conversion functions is established. A type conversion function takes as argument values of the interpreter process, which are values of the VDM C++ class types (Meta-IV values), and converts these to values required by integrated code. The results of the C++ module are converted to Meta-IV values before being returned.

Our approach allows the integration of more than one dynamic library with a formal specification. The only requirement of the Toolbox is that an implementation module defined at the specification level exists for any dynamic linked library.

An important design decision has been to enforce the reuse of code and to support the reuse of specifications. The reuse of code is forced by establishing this prototyping facility. The type conversion functions contain all modifications to the code which are required in order to communicate with the interpreter process such that the C++ code used should not need to be modified for its integration into a specification. The reuse of formal specifications is accomplished by the implementation module which can be imported in every ordinary VDM-SL module.

2.2 An Example

In order to illustrate the idea we present an example which integrates trigonometric functions into a specification. The functionality of trigonometric functions can only be described by approximations given the primitives of VDM-SL. However, almost every programming language contains an implementation in their standard libraries. This is one of the examples where the approach advocated here may be beneficial with respect to prototyping.

The C++ code, which is to be integrated into a VDM-SL specification, is given by the mathematical standard library of C++ called *math*. The examples make use of implementations of the trigonometric functions *sin*, *cos* and of the constant *pi*. First we present a specification which applies these definitions and then we show the extensions at specification level as well as at code level.

The VDM-SL Specification

The structuring concept of the module extension of VDM-SL which is used in the Toolbox enables a combination of modules based on import and export of constructs [8]. Modules can also be parameterized but we will not consider that possibility here. To combine modules, a module has to provide an interface to other modules including export of definitions which may be used by other modules.

The following VDM-SL specification gives an example of how the definitions of the implementation module `MY_MATH` are imported into the module `USE_MATH`.

```
module USE_MATH

  imports
    from MY_MATH
      functions
        MyCos : real -> real;
        MySin : real -> real;

      values
        MyPI : real

   definitions
     functions
       CircCyl_Vol : real * real * real -> real
       CircCyl_Vol (r, h, a) = MY_MATH'MyPI * r * r * h *
                                                 MY_MATH'MySin(a)

end USE_MATH
```

The module `USE_MATH` imports the functions `MyCos` and `MySin` and the value `MyPI` from the implementation module `MY_MATH`. The function `CircCyl_Vol` evaluates the volume of a circular cylinder and makes use of the constant `MyPI` as well as the function `MySin`.

The Interface

As mentioned above, the interface between code and specification has to be provided at two different levels. The interface at the VDM-SL level specifies VDM-SL types of the implemented functions. The interface at the code level is based on the definition of type conversion functions, i.e. functions which establish type conversions between code and interpreter based on the VDM C++ library. Both interfaces must be developed by the user of the Toolbox in order to apply this prototyping facility. As the definitions of both parts are strongly related, we present both interfaces in two boxes below.

```
implmodule MY_MATH

  exports
    functions
      MyCos : real -> real;
      MySin : real -> real

    values
      MyPI : real


    uselib
      mymath.lib
end MY_MATH
```

```
#include "metaiv.h"
#include <math.h>

Generic MyCos(Sequence sq)
{
  double rad;
  rad = Real(sq[1]);
  return (Real( cos(rad) ));
}

Generic MySin(Sequence sq)
{
  double rad;
  rad = Real(sq[1]);
  return (Real( sin(rad) ));
}

Generic MyPI (Sequence sq)
{
  return(Real(M_PI));
}
```

The part between **implmodule MY_MATH** and **end MY_MATH** is the definition of an implementation module and constitutes the interface to VDM-SL. An implementation module always contains an export section which declares all constructs that are exported to the outside world. The constructs from the export section can be imported by other modules. The export section consists of the signatures for function definitions and the type information for value definitions related to the code. A value declaration in an implementation module relates either to a constant or variable definition in the code.

The **uselib** field contains a reference to the dynamic linked library where the code can be found. The relation between implementation module name **MY_MATH** and dynamic linked library **mymath.lib** is important for interpreting the specification later on.

The interface at the code level is developed in C++ and consists of some declarations and the definitions of the type conversion functions. The declaration part includes the standard mathematical library. The type conversion function converts the generic Meta-IV sequence value used by the interpreter to values accepted by the implemented code and vice versa. A generic VDM C++ type can have an underlying value of any VDM type. (e.g. the generic VDM C++ type `Sequence` represents a VDM-SL sequence which can contain arbitrary VDM elements.)

The interpreter process puts the arguments of the called function into a value of the generic VDM C++ type sequence and passes it to the type conversion function. It converts the elements of the sequence into values required by the integrated C++ code. The type conversion function `MySin` extracts the first element of the sequence and casts the generic type to the VDM C++ type `Real`, which is casted automatically to the C++ type `double`. After evaluating the `sin` at C++ level, the result is converted into a Meta-IV value and returned to the interpreter process.

In this case we used a C++ standard library as code, but it could also be a user-defined C++ package. Our approach is open to every kind of module developed in C++. The user is only required to develop an implementation module and to define type conversion functions. Type conversion functions and executable modules together form the dynamic linked library.

3 The Existing VDM-SL Interpreter

The IFAD VDM-SL Toolbox includes an interpreter for the execution of specifications for testing purposes. This interpreter supports a large subset of the VDM-SL specification language. In this work we extend the interpreter to include executions of functions which are implemented in C++ and integrated into a specification.

In order to understand the modifications of the interpreter, basic knowledge about certain parts of the existing interpreter is required. Before the interpreter is able to interpret an expression which makes use of definitions from a module it is necessary to translate each of the modules. The module translation takes as input an abstract syntax tree of the modules and creates a semantic representation for every module, which establishes the context for the interpretation of a construct in a given module. By initializing the specification, the global values of the semantic domain are initialized and parameterized modules are instantiated. The actual evaluation of an expression makes use of the context which has been incorporated in the previous steps.

3.1 Relation between Abstract Syntax and Semantic Values

The module translation establishes a related semantic value to an abstract syntax representation of a module. A module consists of an interface section and a definition section. Again, the module interface is separated in an import section, which lists all definitions used from other modules, and an export section which creates an interface to other modules. All the definitions in the export section will be visible outside the module. The translation of the interface section creates global values which form a semantic module value called `SigmaMO` together with the semantic values created by the definitions.

In most cases the semantic values of the definitions are strongly related to the abstract syntax representation. An explicit function definition is used to show this correlation.

$$\begin{aligned} \mathit{ExplFnDef} :: \mathit{nm} &: \mathit{Name} \\ \mathit{tp} &: \mathit{FnType} \\ \mathit{parms} &: \mathit{ParametersList} \\ \mathit{body} &: \mathit{Expr} \end{aligned}$$

The abstract syntax for an explicit function *ExplFnDef* consists of the function name, *nm*, the function type, *tp*, a list of the formal parameters, *parms*, and the body expression, *body*.

$$\begin{aligned} \mathit{ExplFN} :: \mathit{tp} &: \mathit{FnType} \\ \mathit{parms} &: \mathit{ParametersList} \\ \mathit{body} &: \mathit{Expr} \\ \mathit{env} &: \mathit{BlkEnv} \end{aligned}$$

Its semantic value *ExplFN* used in the interpreter is very similar to the abstract syntax. The semantic value of an explicit function definition consists of the function type, *tp*, the formal parameter list, *parms*, the function body expression, *body*, and a closure environment, *env*.

A closure model is used to establish the defining environment of locally defined functions. VDM-SL uses, like most programming languages, static scoping for functions evaluation, which means that a function is evaluated in its defining environment.

$$\begin{aligned} \mathit{SigmaMO} :: \mathit{explfns} &: \mathit{Name} \xrightarrow{m} \mathit{ExplFN} \\ \ldots &: \ldots \end{aligned}$$

For every created semantic value a representation in the module value is introduced. Usually this is a mapping from name to its semantic value as shown above for explicit function definitions. A semantic module value is integrated in the interpreter state as a mapping from module name to module value. The context for the evaluation of a specification, which consists of one or more modules, is established by the combination of all related module values.

3.2 The Evaluation Model

The IFAD VDM-SL interpreter uses an environment based evaluation model [19]. The main structure of the semantic domain is the environment (ENV_L) which is organized as a stack of function application environments (ENV).

$$ENV_L = ENV^*;$$

$ENV = BlkEnv^*$

When a function is called, it pushes a function application environment on top of the stack. A function application environment contains a number of ***block environments***. These block environments are created as a result of the introduction of a local identifier, for example in a let-expression. A block environment introduces a new scope within the current function application environment.

$BlkEnv = IdVal^*;$

$IdVal = AS`Name \times VAL$

The function application environment is organized as a stack of block environments. A block environment is a sequence of *IdVal* which relates a unique name to its semantic value.

The evaluation of a function application expression modifies the environment stack ENV_L in the following ways. The actual arguments are evaluated and a new and empty function application environment is pushed on top of the evaluation stack. Then their block environments are pushed onto the function application environment. These block environments contain bindings introduced by pattern matching and the bindings of a closure environment. One block environment is created by matching the function parameter against the evaluated arguments and pushing it onto the top of the function application environment.

During evaluation of the body of a function, all the identifiers must be defined either locally, which means in one of the block environments of the top function application environment, or defined globally. After function body expression evaluation the top function application environment is removed from the evaluation stack and the result value is returned.

The global outline of the specification of *EvalApplyExpr* is:

EvalApplyExpr : *ApplyExpr* $\xrightarrow{o}$ *VAL*

EvalApplyExpr (mk-*ApplyExpr* (*ftc-e*, *arg-le*)) $\triangleq$
 let *fct-v* = *EvalExpr* (*fct-e*),
   arg-lv = [*EvalExpr* (*arg-le* (*i*)) | *i* ∈ elems *arg-le*] in
 (*PushEmptyEnv*() ;
  PushBlkEnv(*fct-v*.*closenv*) ;
  let *benv* ∈ *PatternMatch* (*fct-v*.*parms*, *arg-lv*) in
  (*PushBlkEnv*(*benv*) ;
   let *res-v* = *EvalExpr* (*fct-v*.*body-e*) in
   (*PopEnvL*() ;
    return *res-v*)))

where *fct-e* is the function expression to be evaluated and *arg-le* the argument expressions to the functions. The result of evaluating *fct-e* is a semantic value, *fct-v*. This function value contains the parameters of the function, *parms*, and the body of the function, *body*.

4 Modifications to the VDM-SL Interpreter

The introduction of the concept of implementation modules to IFAD VDM-SL requires some modification of the IFAD VDM-SL specification language and the IFAD VDM-SL Toolbox. This section illustrates the extensions related to the specification language and the dynamic semantic specification.

4.1 Abstract Syntax

The implementation module *ImplModule* has been invented for the specification of an interface to VDM-SL .

$$
\begin{aligned}
&\mathit{ImplModule} :: \mathit{nm} &&: \mathit{Name}\\
&\qquad\quad \mathit{intf} &&: \mathit{ImplInterface}\\
&\qquad\quad \mathit{uselib} &&: \mathit{Name};
\end{aligned}
$$

$$
\begin{aligned}
&\mathit{ImplInterface} :: \mathit{imp}: \mathit{Name} \xrightarrow{m} \mathit{ImplImportSig}\\
&\qquad\quad \mathit{exp} : \mathit{ImplExportSig};
\end{aligned}
$$

$$
\mathit{ImplImportSig} :: \mathit{tps} : \mathit{Name}\text{-set};
$$

$$
\begin{aligned}
&\mathit{ImplExportSig} :: \mathit{val} &&: \mathit{Name} \xrightarrow{m} \mathit{Type}\\
&\qquad\quad \mathit{fns} &&: \mathit{Name} \xrightarrow{m} \mathit{FnType}\\
&\qquad\quad \mathit{ops} &&: \mathit{Name} \xrightarrow{m} \mathit{OpType}
\end{aligned}
$$

The abstract syntax of an implementation module consists of a module name, *nm*, an interface section, *intf*, and information related to the integrated code, *uselib*. A module interface consists of an import and an export section. The import section of an implementation module is restricted to importing type names. The type names are required, by the type checker, in case a user wants to refer to types defined in other modules. The export section mentions all constructs which can be imported by other modules.

The distinction between functions and operations is pragmatic in an implementation module. In VDM-SL a "procedure" which defines or modifies a state is called an operation. In the case of implementation modules the distinction is without meaning as the related definitions are C++ code.

4.2 Extensions to the Semantic Domain

The translation of an implementation module creates the semantic values from the definition in the export section. In addition, a reference to the C++ code library must be used such that it will be possible to refer to it when needed. The module translation of an implementation module establishes a relation between the implementation module and its related code. Related to the VDM-SL specification level the module name (`USE_MATH`) contains the necessary information for establishing the context for the interpreter as it refers to the module value (see Section 3.1). The interpreter process requires access to the dynamic linked library for executing the code. The `uselib` section of an implementation module contains the name of the dynamic linked library. This name is stored in the semantic module value, such that the interpreter process can access its operation during execution of a specification.

The semantic values of functions and operations, which consist either of an implicit or an explicit definition, are extended by *external* definitions. An external function is declared in an implementation module and is defined in the related code.

$$\begin{aligned} \mathit{ExtFN} :: \mathit{tp} &: \mathit{FnType} \\ \mathit{body} &: [\mathit{LOC}] \end{aligned}$$

The semantic value *ExtFN* of an external function consists of the function type, *tp*, and the function body, *body*. Because of the missing function definitions at the VDM-SL level neither a closure environment, nor a parameter list nor a function body expression exist. The interpreter implementation uses the memory location, where the function is stored, as representation of the function body. This concept is applied by the semantic value *LOC* of the function body.

Besides the introduction of new semantic values, the global values are extended by a new field for implementation modules. The translation of an implementation module creates a module value *SigmaIMO* and extends the state definition by a mapping from the module name to this value.

4.3 The Dynamic Semantic

The dynamic semantic specification is extended with a specification for applying external functions. If the interpreter needs to apply an external function, it evaluates the function expression and arguments first. The result of evaluating the function expression is a semantic value of type *ExtFN*.

The global outline of the specification *EvalApplyExt* is:

$$\mathit{EvalExtApply} : \mathit{ApplyExtExpr} \xrightarrow{o} \mathit{VAL}$$

$$\begin{aligned} &\mathit{EvalExtApply}\,(\mathsf{mk}\text{-}\mathit{ApplyExtExpr}\,(\mathit{fct\text{-}e}, \mathit{arg\text{-}le})) \triangleq \\ &\quad \mathsf{let}\ \mathit{fct\text{-}v} = \mathit{EvalExpr}\,(\mathit{fct\text{-}e}), \\ &\qquad \mathit{arg\text{-}lv} = [\mathit{EvalExpr}\,(\mathit{arg\text{-}le}\,(i)) \mid i \in \mathsf{elems}\ \mathit{arg\text{-}le}]\ \mathsf{in} \\ &\quad (\mathsf{let}\ \mathit{res\text{-}v} = \mathit{EvalExtBody}\,(\mathit{fct\text{-}v.body}, \mathit{arg\text{-}lv})\ \mathsf{in} \\ &\quad\ \ \mathsf{return}\ \mathit{res\text{-}v}\ ) \end{aligned}$$

where *fct-e* is the function expression to be evaluated and *arg-le* the argument expressions to the functions. The result of evaluating *fct-e* is a semantic value, *fct-v*.

Comparing with Section 3.2 the application of an external function does not require the creation of a function application environment in the interpreter. An external function is evaluated in the environment established by the execution of the related code.

The application of an externally defined function cannot be specified in an appropriate way because the C++ code is not explicitly modeled. The interpreter cannot make any assumptions about the functionality of the function because of the missing function body. Instead of interpreting a function body a function defined in a dynamic linked library is executed.

The dynamic semantic of the function *EvalExtBody* can be described in terms of the implementation but not in the specification. The meaning of the function *EvalExtBody* related to the semantic value of an external function is expressed in the implementation of the interpreter as

```
res_v = (*fct_v.body)(arg_lv);
```

where fct_v*.body* is a reference to a function in a dynamic linked library. A reference to a function can be executed in C++ after *dereferencing* it [22].

5 Different Communication Primitives

The implementation of the interpreter has to provide a facility to execute functions which are defined in code. In case a function from an implementation module is applied, the Toolbox process knows the name of the function and can calculate the actual arguments. Based on this information, communication between the Toolbox process and the executable code has to be assembled. The use of dynamic linking offers the required functionality and meets our implementation requirements.

5.1 Dynamic Linking

Static linking of the integrated code and the interpreter implementation would make the integrated code part of the interpreter process. Every time the code changes, a new creation of an interpreter process is required. This approach does not support our intentions of flexibility and efficient usage of this feature. The interpreter would combine internal specification and code. A separation of both seems to be desirable in order to enable a dynamic system implementation which supports the replacement of a specified module by its implementation. If the other parts of the specification are also executable, a kind of integration test for the implementation is provided by executing the specification [6].

Dynamic linking postpones the linking of components until execution time [1]. Functions defined in shared libraries are linked and loaded if their objects are accessed during run-time. Shared libraries are "transparent" to the process using them. This means that an object in a shared library is added to the address space at the time of execution. Further it does not restrict the types passed between the Toolbox process and the interface to code to a subset of VDM-SL types . However, the conversion functions have to transform the Meta-IV values into values which are used in the C++ code.

It is worth noting that the interface to code and the implemented code together form a shared library for each implementation module. The application of a shared library does not depend on process communication but requires operating system support [23]. The IFAD VDM-SL Toolbox is available for different operating systems which support dynamic linking in a similar way. The operating systems contain functions which provide a simple programmatic interface to handle dynamic linked libraries.

These programmatic interfaces always contain an `open` function which provides access to the library. It returns a reference to the shared library which can be used for later accesses to their objects. A `symbol` function retrieves the address binding for a function defined in the objects of the library. A reference to a shared object is deleted by a `close` function.

If the interpreter process has to evaluate an external function, it evaluates the arguments first. Afterwards the process retrieves the address binding of the function in the shared library. It should be mentioned that the interpreter searches for the type conversion function defined in the interface to code which, in turn, calls a function of the implemented code.

By accessing an object defined in a shared library a pointer is returned, which must be casted to a function type. The type checking of C++ prohibits a cast to a function type which has a variable number of arguments [9]. A solution for this problem is provided by the usage of Meta-IV values. The interpreter process passes a Meta-IV sequence value to the interface, where the length of the sequence is equal to the arity of the function. The effort related to the interpreter is to put the evaluated argument as Meta-IV values in a sequence. The type conversion functions must extract the values from the sequence and convert those into types required as arguments by the implemented code. The return value exchanged between the interface and Toolbox process is a generic Meta-IV value.

5.2 Alternative Communication Approaches

Other possible approaches establishing the communication primitives are Unix pipes. They provide a stream oriented communication medium between two different processes. A process can establish a pipe to exchange data with another process. As a pipe enables communication in one direction, two pipes would be required for bidirectional communication.

A disadvantage is that the stream oriented communication between interpreter and interface process will restrict types to a subset of the common VDM-SL types. There is also a considerable overhead for doing type conversions between the Toolbox process, the interface to C and the implemented code. An example of using pipes for interprocess communication in connection with the VDM-SL Toolbox is used in the IPTES Project [26]. In this case the data types are restricted to the VDM basic types and to sequences and tuples of it.

The interprocess communication facilities like message passing, shared memory or remote procedure calls would be required if the feature should support the integration of code whereas code and specification are stored on different machines. This case was not considered in this work but is supported in the IPTES Project.

6 Related Work

A number of researchers have worked on a common framework which can be used to combine different formalisms. This includes both theoretical work on the foundations [3] and more practical applications [27, 28]. Most of the existing work, however is focusing on how to combine different specification notations.

In our work we wish to enable a heterogeneous combination of a specification language and an implementation language. In this area related work can be found in the Larch community [17]. An approach of mixed evaluation of an algebraic specification and implemented parts in code is given in [5]. The execution is obtained by applying rewriting techniques to the algebraic specifications and direct evaluation of implemented parts.

The production of an executable model from a given VDM specification is presented in [25]. This work shows the integration of a VDM specification into the KIDS Toolbox which is used for executing the specification [20]. Another work in the VDM community which is somewhat related is the specification of library components in a programming language [11]. However, there is a large number of industrial applications of formal methods, where only a part of the system has been formally specified (e.g. [15]) which could benefit from the approach presented in this paper.

The idea of dynamically extending the functionality of a tool has already been used in the programming language community [24]. This concept is naturally a powerful feature which is desirable from a tool point of view.

7 Concluding Remarks

In this paper we have presented an approach enabling users to dynamically extend tools supporting the interpretation of formal specification. We believe that this approach will turn out to be valuable for practical applications where one wishes to gain insight into the interaction between parts of a system which have been formally specified whereas other parts simply have been developed conventionally. As specification languages get increasingly standardized and the supporting tools get more powerful we believe that a dynamic approach is essential.

Incorporating the ability to supply pre and post conditions for the different functions that are coded externally in C++ is considered as future work. It should then be possible to switch such conditions on or off during the interpretation. We also feel that more investigation is needed in order to determine what to do in the situation where the code for some reason fails to deliver an appropriate answer or result in a run-time error. We have not yet had time to properly work on the issue of such exception.

We feel that the most important work that needs to be done is to get feedback from industrial users of the IFAD VDM-SL Toolbox about this approach. We have already agreed with some of the users that they will get access to a beta version of this extension before it is released to everyone. Their feedback about the applicability of this approach will ultimately determine whether these new ideas will be adopted by other tool vendors to provide support for heterogeneous models of a system.

Acknowledgments

We would like to thank John Fitzgerald, Nico Plat and Paul Mukherjee for giving their remarks at an oral presentation of this work. We would also like to thank Peter Lucas and Werner Kerschenbauer for valuable remarks on an earlier version of this article. In addition we have had constructive remarks from our colleagues at IFAD. We are grateful to the support of the European Commission (Comett Grant) for Brigitte Fröhlich's stay at IFAD.

References

1. Silberschatz A., Peterson J., and Galvin P. *Operating System Concepts.* Addison Wesley, 1991.
2. D.J. Andrews, H. Bruun, B.S. Hansen, P.G. Larsen, N. Plat, et al. *Information Technology — Programming Languages, their Environments and System Software Interfaces — Vienna Development Method-Specification Language Part 1: Base language.* ISO, 1995.
3. E. Astesiano and M. Cerioli. Multiparadigm Specification Languages: A First Attempt at Foundations. In J.F.G̃roote D.J.Ãndrews and C.A. Middelburg, editors, *Semantics of Specification Languages*, pages 168–185, 25–27 October 1993, Utrecht Springer-Verlag 1994.
4. D. Bjøner and C.B. Jones, editors. *Formal Specification and Software Development.* Prentice-Hall International, 1982.
5. S. Kapplan C. Choopy. Mixing abstract and concret Modules: Specification, Development and Prototyping. In *12th IEEE-ACM International Conference on Software Engineering, Nice 1990*, pages 173–184, 1990.
6. Christine Choppy. Formal Specifications, Prototyping and Integrations Tests. In D. Simpson H.K. Nichols, editor, *ESEC'87 1.st European Software Engineering Conference, Strasbourg, 1987*, Lecture Notes in Computer Science 289, pages 172–179. Springer Verlag, September 1987.
7. John Dawes. *The VDM-SL Reference Guide.* Pitman, 1991.
8. Kees de Bruin. Towards an Interpreter for Full VDM-SL. Master's thesis, Delft University, June 1993.
9. Margaret A. Ellis and Bjarne Stroustrup. *The Annotated C++ Reference Manual.* Addison-Wesley Publishing Company, 1990.
10. René Elmstrøm, Peter Gorm Larsen, and Poul Bøgh Lassen. The IFAD VDM-SL Toolbox: A Practical Approach to Formal Specifications. *ACM Sigplan Notices*, 29(9):77–80, September 1994.
11. B. Fischer, M. Kievernagel, and W. Struckmann. VCR: A VDM-based Software Component Retrieval Tool. Technical Report 94-08, Technische Universität Braunsweig, November 1994.
12. The VDM-SL Tool Group. The IFAD VDM-SL Language. Technical report, IFAD, December 1994.

13. The VDM-SL Tool Group. The VDM C++ Library. Technical report, IFAD, October 1995.
14. Michael G. Hinchey and Jonathan P. Bowen, editors. *Applications of Formal Methods.* Prentice Hall, 1995.
15. Iain Houston and Steve King. CICS Project Report: Experiences and Results from the Use of Z in IBM. In S. Prehn and W.J. Toetenel, editors, *VDM'91 - Formal Software Development Methods*, pages 588–696. Springer-Verlag, October 1991.
16. Cliff B. Jones. *Systematic Software Development Using VDM.* Prentice-Hall International, Englewood Cliffs, New Jersey, second edition, 1990.
17. J.J. Horning J.V. Guttag and J.M. Wing. Larch in Five Easy Pieces. Technical report, Digital Systems Research Center, July 1985.
18. Peter Gorm Larsen, John Fitzgerald, and Tom Brookes. Lessons Learned from Applying Formal Specification in Industry. *Submitted to IEEE Software*, August 1995.
19. Peter Gorm Larsen and Poul Bøgh Lassen. An Executable Subset of Meta-IV with Loose Specification. In *VDM '91: Formal Software Development Methods.* VDM Europe, Springer-Verlag, March 1991.
20. Yves Ledru. Proof-Based Development of Specifications with KIDS/VDM. In M. Bertran M. Naftalin, T. Denvir, editor, *FME'94: Industrial Benefit of Formal Methods*, pages 214–232. Springer-Verlag, October 1994.
21. Paul Mukherjee. Computer-aided Validation of Formal Specifications. *Software Engineering Journal*, pages 133–140, July 1995.
22. B. Stroustrup. *The C++ Programming Language, 2nd edition.* Addison Wesley Publishing Company, 1991.
23. SUN-OS. Programmer's Overview Utilities & Libraries. Technical report, Sun Microsystems, Inc., 27 March 1990.
24. Larry Wall and Randal L. Schwartz. *Programming Perl.* O'Reilly and Associates, Inc, 1992.
25. M.-H. Liégeois Y. Ledru. Integrating REFINE prototypes in a VDM development framework. In *Constructing Programs from Specifications*, pages 236–258, 1991.
26. Nabil Zakhama. Run-Time Adaptation System - Target Code Procedures Activato (RTAS - TCPACT) - User's Guide. Technical report, Télésystèmes, March 1993. IPTES Doc.id.: IPTES-TS-53-V2.1.
27. Pamela Zave. A Compositional Approach to Multiparadigm Programming. *IEEE Software*, pages 15–25, September 1989.
28. Pamela Zave and Michael Jackson. Conjunction as Composition. *ACM Transactions on Software Engineering and Methology*, 2(4):379–411, October 1993.

Data Reification without Explicit Abstraction Functions

T Clement

Adelard**,
Coborn House,
3, Coborn Road,
LONDON E3 2DA,
U.K
e-mail: tpc@adtclem.demon.co.uk

Abstract. Data reification normally involves the explicit positing of an abstraction function with certain properties. However, the condition for one definition to reify another only requires that a function with such properties should exist. This suggests that it may be possible to carry through a data reification without giving an explicit definition of the abstraction function at all. This paper explores this possibility and compares it with the more conventional approach.

1 Introduction

An abstract type is a type name equipped with some operations, usually with parameters or results of other, previously defined, types. The *signature* of the abstract type gives the names of the operations and their types: for example, the abstract type *Set*, representing sets of integers, might have signature

$empty\colon \to Set$
$add\colon \mathbb{Z} \times Set \to Set$
$elem\colon \mathbb{Z} \times Set \to \mathbb{B}$

Because *empty* and *add* have results of type *Set*, they are said to be *constructors* of the type. The function *elem* is an *observer* because its result is of a predefined type. For technical reasons, it is convenient to consider only signatures with results of single types rather than tuples, so all operations are either constructors or observers.

In the model based approaches to formal specification, such as VDM or Z, an abstract type is defined by defining a set of values for the type name and defining the operations as (possibly partial) functions on this set and others corresponding to the predefined types. The signature is usually a part of these definitions rather than separate as above. It is possible to give many definitions of the same signature (which is why it will be convenient to separate it out here), and these will be distinguished by subscripting the type name and operation names. In

** This work was carried out while at the University of Manchester particular, when discussing reifications, the definitions of the specification will be identified by subscript S and those of the implementation by subscript $\mathcal{I}$.

One definition of abstract type T will implement another by data reification if the value of every term of the signature of type other than the abstract type (of *visible* type) is the same in both specification and implementation whenever it is defined by the specification. This will be the case if there exists a (possibly partial) function $\phi: T_{\mathcal{I}} \rightarrow T_S$ (an *abstraction function*) such that for all operations $op: T \rightarrow T$ in the signature the square

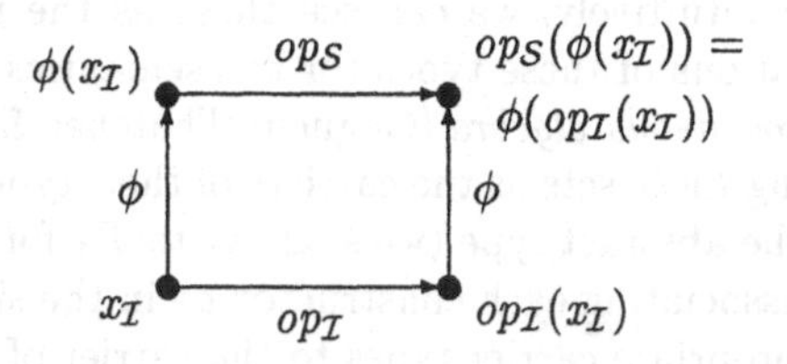

commutes whenever the upper path is defined. (A justification will be found in (Clement, 1993).) Using $\delta(t)$ to signify that term t is defined, we can write this *reification condition* for an operation formally as

$$\forall x \in T_{\mathcal{I}} \cdot \delta(op_S(\phi(x))) \Rightarrow \phi(op_{\mathcal{I}}(x)) = op_S(\phi(x))$$

If there is a parameter of a predefined type, this becomes

$$\forall x \in T_{\mathcal{I}}, y \in Y \cdot \delta(op_S(y, \phi(x))) \Rightarrow \phi(op_{\mathcal{I}}(y, x)) = op_S(\phi(x))$$

while for observations (with no parameters) it reduces to

$$\forall x \in T_{\mathcal{I}} \cdot \delta(op_S(\phi(x))) \Rightarrow op_{\mathcal{I}}(x) = op_S(\phi(x))$$

The traditional approach to data reification is to posit an implementation representation of the abstract type and definitions of the operations of the signature on it, and then to posit a function and prove that it has the desired properties. In the alternative, calculational, approach (Darlington, 1984; Morgan & Gardiner, 1990), the reification conditions are used as the defining properties of the operations. A more algorithmic definition working directly on the new representation can then be derived using conventional calculational techniques. However, it is still necessary to pick a set of values for the type and posit an abstraction function. Both are thus constructive approaches to showing the existence of an abstraction function. This raises the question of whether a non-constructive approach is feasible: if so, it may offer the advantage of not having to demonstrate that a posited function satisfies the reification conditions. In this paper we shall look at such an approach and assess its benefits and limitations.

In the next section, we shall present the basic idea for total operations. The techniques will be refined in Sect. 3 to deal with partial operations and abstraction functions. An extended example of the approach will be given in Sect. 4, and this will be compared with a more conventional approach to the same problem in Sect. 5. The last section will summarize and draw some conclusions. The paper assumes a familiarity with the basic definition of categories (this will be found in (Arbib & Manes, 1975)) but more specialized standard results will be summarized here for completeness.

2 Constructing Categories

We can construct an implementation of an abstract type with signature Σ in the following way. We first fix interpretations for all the visible types of the signature as sets: intuitively, we can see these as the interpretations fixed by the prior specifications of these types (or the semantics of VDM). We can then construct a *heterogeneous algebra* (Goguen, Thatcher & Wagner, 1978) for the signature by taking these sets as the carriers of their types and some arbitary set as the carrier of the abstract type (we shall write $T_{\mathcal{A}}$ for the carrier of type T in algebra $\mathcal{A}$), and associating each constructor *op* in the signature with a function $op_{\mathcal{A}}$ from the appropriate carrier types to the carrier of the abstract type. (The observer functions will be considered separately later.) The specification of the abstract type can be identified with one such algebra, where the abstract type carrier is the set corresponding to the model chosen in the specification, and the functions meet the specifications of the operations.

We define a morphism from algebra $\mathcal{I}$ to algebra $\mathcal{S}$ to be an indexed collection of functions

$$\phi = \{\phi_T\colon T_{\mathcal{B}} \rightarrow T_{\mathcal{A}} \mid T \text{ is a type in the signature}\}$$

For the visible types, we fix each function as the appropriate identity function: for the abstract type, any function satisfying the reification conditions on the constructors is allowed.

The algebras and morphisms together form a category. (Clearly, the identity function on the abstract type provides an identity morphism, and identities compose to give identities while composition preserves satisfaction of the reification condition.) The category is a subcategory of one which is well known in algebraic specification (see (Ehrig & Mahr, 1985), for example), where there is a free choice of carrier sets for all types in the signature, and for each function $op\colon T_1 \times \ldots T_n \rightarrow T$ the morphisms satisfy the condition

$$\phi_T(op_{\mathcal{I}}(x_1, \ldots, x_n)) = op_{\mathcal{S}}(\phi_{T_1}(x_1), \ldots, \phi_{T_n}(x_n))$$

(This is easily seen to specialize to the reification condition if all the ϕ_T functions for visible T are identities.)

The full category has *initial objects*: that is, objects with a (unique) morphism to every object of the category. One initial object (the *term algebra* $\mathcal{T}_\Sigma$, or $\mathcal{T}$ when the signature is clear from the context) is constructed by taking the set of terms of each type as the carrier of that type (the signatures that arise in algebraic specification have constructors of all types) and defining the function corresponding to an operation to map terms to the application of the operation to those terms. The morphism to any algebra $\mathcal{A}$ (to be written $\_^{\mathcal{A}}$) uses the functions of $\mathcal{A}$ to evaluate the term from the term algebra, so for any constant c in the signature $c^{\mathcal{A}} = c_{\mathcal{A}}$ and for any term $op(t)$, $(op(t))^{\mathcal{A}} = op_{\mathcal{A}}(t^{\mathcal{A}})$. This clearly satisfies the condition on morphisms. Any other object which is isomorphic to this is also initial.

The category we have just constructed also has initial objects. One can be produced using the construction above for the carrier of the abstract type, but using values from the other carriers rather than terms of the type as parameters. We shall call this the *relative term algebra*, and also denote it by $\mathcal{T}$ and the morphism to any other algebra by $\_^{\mathcal{A}}$. Since initial objects have a morphism to all objects, and the specification is one of the objects of the category, the relative term algebra defines an implementation of the type and its constructors. (Intuitively, an abstract type can be implemented whatever its specification by remembering in its values the values and operations used in their construction, since this gives enough information to define any observation.) In general, algebras isomorphic to this (and hence also initial) will give more interesting implementations.

For example, consider implementing sets with the signature of Sect. 1. Since they are predefined in VDM, the specification is trivial

$$empty_{\mathcal{S}} = \{\,\}$$

$$add_{\mathcal{S}}(n, s) \;\triangleq\; s \cup \{n\}$$

$$elem_{\mathcal{S}}(n, s) \;\triangleq\; n \in s$$

The carrier of the abstract type in $\mathcal{T}$ is terms of the form

$$add(n_1, add(n_2, \ldots add(n_n, empty)))$$

(which we can abbreviate as $add^n(n_1, \ldots, n_n, empty)$). The following definition describes an algebra which is more useful as an implementation.

$$Set_{\mathcal{I}} = X^*$$
$$empty_{\mathcal{I}} = [\,]$$
$$add_{\mathcal{I}}(x, s) \;\triangleq\; \mathbf{cons}(x, s)$$

(It is easy to see that it is isomorphic to the relative term algebra, but this could be verified by exhibiting a formal definition of the isomorphism.) This is a well-known implementation, of course, but the justification given by this approach is by appeal to abstract mathematics rather than by detailed calculation, and of course the abstraction function has not been made explicit.

We still need to derive an implementations of the observation *elem*. Following the calculational style of (Darlington, 1984), we use the reification condition to state an equality the implementation must satisfy

$$elem_{\mathcal{I}}(x, s) = elem_{\mathcal{S}}(x, \phi(s))$$

To find a definition of $elem_{\mathcal{I}}$ with no uses of ϕ satisfying this equation, we can consider cases of the structure of the set representation:

$$\begin{aligned}
\mathit{elem}_{\mathcal{I}}(x,[\,]) &= \mathit{elem}_{\mathcal{I}}(x,\mathit{empty}_{\mathcal{I}})\\
&= \mathit{elem}_{\mathcal{S}}(x,\phi(\mathit{empty}_{\mathcal{I}}))\\
&= x \in \mathit{empty}_{\mathcal{S}}\\
&= \mathbf{false}\\
\mathit{elem}_{\mathcal{I}}(x,\mathbf{cons}(y,s)) &= \mathit{elem}_{\mathcal{I}}(x,\mathit{add}_{\mathcal{I}}(y,s))\\
&= \mathit{elem}_{\mathcal{S}}(x,\mathit{add}_{\mathcal{S}}(y,\phi(s)))\\
&= x \in (\{y\} \cup \phi(s))\\
&= x = y \vee x \in \phi(s)\\
&= x = y \vee \mathit{elem}_{\mathcal{I}}(x,s)
\end{aligned}$$

The strategy is to express each value of the type as a term of the signature. (This is always possible, because the values are reachable by construction: the algebra has *no junk.*) We then apply the reification condition for the constructors, and use the definitions from the specification to deduce a simpler form of the equality. Recursion is introduced by using the defining equation again. The resulting equations clearly hold of the following VDM function definition, which expresses the expected implementation.

$$\begin{aligned}
\mathit{elem}_{\mathcal{I}}(x,s) \;\;\triangleq\;\; &\mathbf{cases}\ s\ \mathbf{of}\\
&\qquad\qquad [\,] \rightarrow \mathbf{false}\\
&\mathbf{cons}(y,s) \rightarrow x = y \vee \mathit{elem}_{\mathcal{I}}(x,s)\\
&\mathbf{end}
\end{aligned}$$

There are of course many implementations of specifications with signature Σ which are not isomorphic to T_Σ. To calculate more of them, we need to define other categories with definitions (including the specification) as objects and functions satisfying the reification conditions as morphisms, and with initial objects. The theory of algebraic specification tells us that the category of all algebras satisfying a given set of equations is known to have initial algebras, and this remains true when we restrict the category by fixing carriers of visible types. The equations are then only needed to restrict the possible choices for the abstract type, and should therefore only involve terms of that type. Any choice of equations satisfied by the specification will define an implementation, although some of these implementations will be of more interest than others.

The carrier of the abstract type in an initial algebra $\mathcal{I}_{\Sigma,E}$ in the category generated by signature Σ and set of equations E can be constructed from T_Σ by partitioning it into sets which are provably equal given the equations and the usual properties of equality. This clearly satisfies the equations, but "only just": no terms which do not have to be equal are equal. We say that there is *no confusion.* If we write $[t]$ for the set of terms equal to t, the operations are defined by $op_{\mathcal{I}}([t]) = [op(t)]$. This is well defined because equality is a congruence. We shall call the result the *quotient algebra* of Σ and E. It is initial because a morphism ϕ can be defined to any other algebra $\mathcal{A}$ satisfying E by taking $\phi([t]) = t^{\mathcal{A}}$. This is well defined because there is no confusion in the quotient algebra. It is obvious that for any term t, $t^{\mathcal{A}} = \phi(t^{\mathcal{I}})$: that is, that commutes.

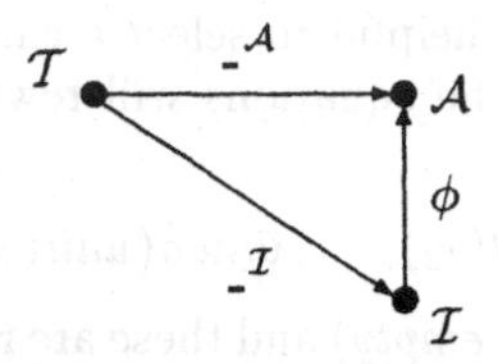

As an example of calculating an implementation using equations, we may take sets with the following signature:

$empty: \rightarrow Set$
$unit: X \rightarrow Set$
$union: Set \times Set \rightarrow Set$
$elem: X \times Set \rightarrow \mathbb{B}$

with specification

$Set_S = X\textbf{-set}$

$empty_S = \{\}$

$unit(x) \triangleq \{x\}$

$union_S(s_1, s_2) \triangleq s_1 \cup s_2$

$elem_S(x, s) \triangleq x \in s$

The constructor terms from this signature are *empty*, $unit(x)$ for all x in the carrier, $union(empty, unit(x))$, $union(unit(x_1), unit(x_2))$ and so on: they are isomorphic to the more familiar structure of binary trees with the values in the leaves only, *unit* corresponding to the leaf constructor and *union* to the binary tree constructor. To arrive at the sequence representation from this signature and set of definitions, we show that the equations

$union(empty, s) = s$
$union(s, empty) = s$
$union(s_1, union(s_2, s_3)) = union(union(s_1, s_2), s_3)$

hold of the specification (trivially in this case, as properties of $\cup$) and consider the category of algebras where these equations hold of the *union* function. The equations for sets equate terms containing *empty* with terms which do not (except for *empty* itself, which is in a partition of its own), and equate terms where the same elements appear in the same order as arguments to *unit* to each other irrespective of how these are distributed as arguments to *union*. In looking for isomorphic models, it is often helpful to select a canonical term from each partition and look at its form. The equations will rewrite any term to one of the form

$$union(unit(x_1), union(unit(x_2), \ldots, union(unit(x_n, empty))))$$

(deliberately putting back one *empty*) and these are readily seen to be isomorphic to sequences $[x_1, \ldots, x_n]$, giving the definition

$$Set_{\mathcal{I}} = X^*$$

$$empty_{\mathcal{I}} = [\,]$$

$$unit_{\mathcal{I}}(x) \triangleq [x]$$

$$union_{\mathcal{I}}(s_1, s_2) \triangleq append(s_1, s_2)$$

To derive the expected definition of $elem_{\mathcal{I}}$, we may begin again with the definition derived from the reification condition.

$$elem_{\mathcal{I}}(x, s) \triangleq elem_{\mathcal{S}}(x, \phi(s))$$

Considering cases of the value of s again, the derivation of $elem_{\mathcal{I}}(x, [\,]) = \mathbf{false}$ goes through as before and

$$\begin{aligned} elem_{\mathcal{I}}(x, \mathbf{cons}(y, s)) &= elem_{\mathcal{I}}(x, union_{\mathcal{I}}(unit_{\mathcal{I}}(y), s)) \\ &= elem_{\mathcal{S}}(x, \phi(union_{\mathcal{I}}(unit_{\mathcal{I}}(y), s))) \\ &= elem_{\mathcal{S}}(x, union_{\mathcal{S}}(unit_{\mathcal{S}}(y), \phi(s)))) \\ &= elem_{\mathcal{S}}(x, union_{\mathcal{S}}(unit_{\mathcal{S}}(y), \phi(s)))) \\ &= elem_{\mathcal{S}}(x, unit_{\mathcal{S}}(y)) \vee elem_{\mathcal{S}}(x, \phi(s)) \\ &= x = y \vee elem_{\mathcal{I}}(x, s) \end{aligned}$$

giving the same definition as above.

3 Partial Operations

Most abstract types have operations which are not defined everywhere on the type. For example, in the signature

$empty$: *Stack*
$push$: $\mathbb{Z} \times Stack \to Stack$
pop: $Stack \to Stack$
top: $Stack \to \mathbb{Z}$

we do not expect *pop* and *top* to be defined on *empty*. In VDM, such operations are defined as potentially partial functions, so abstract type definitions are *partial* (heterogeneous) *algebras* (Broy & Wirsing, 1982). The reification condition of Sect. 1 allows for a partial function to be implemented by one which is more defined. (This is reasonable in circumstances where all uses of a function are proved to lie in its domain, as they are in VDM.) It also allows the abstraction function itself to be partial.

As before, abstraction functions can be extended to provide abstraction morphisms on partial algebras by adding (total) identity functions for the carriers of the predefined types. The class of all partial algebras for a given signature and interpretation of the predefined types together with the abstraction morphisms again forms a category. Unlike the categories built on total algebras, there are in general no initial objects. However, the relative term algebra, which is of course total, is privileged in the sense that it has at least one morphism to every other algebra $\mathcal{A}$ and hence remains an implementation. (Once again, because it remembers everything about the construction of the value, it is not surprising that anything can be implemented using it.) We can construct this morphism as before by giving terms which are defined in $\mathcal{A}$ their value there. Those which are not are left unmapped. This is easily seen to satisfy the reification condition, and is the morphism we shall denote by $\_^{\mathcal{A}}$. However, it may also be possible to map undefined terms to some value in $\mathcal{A}$ while still satisfying the reification condition (one not in the domain of any operation in $\mathcal{A}$ will do), which is why there is not always an initial object. Similarly, when the category of algebras is restricted to one where the operations on the new type satisfy given equations, the (total) quotient algebra has a morphism ϕ to every other algebra $\mathcal{A}$ in the category: again, it maps the value $[x]$ to $x^{\mathcal{A}}$ (where $x^{\mathcal{A}}$ is defined) and again, this is well defined because equality is a congruence and the equations are satisfied by all the algebras. There is an issue here of what is meant by an algebra satisfying an equation when some terms may be undefined. We shall take the *strong* interpretation of equality: an instance of an equation will hold if the two sides are defined and have the same value or if both are undefined.

Equations were introduced in Sect. 2 to define restricted categories of algebras with new initial objects and hence generate more possible implementations. Now we want to introduce some further properties of algebras to generate implementations where some of the functions are partial. This will be done by using axioms of the form $U(t)$ to say that term t is undefined. For example, we might give $U(\mathit{pop}(\mathit{empty}))$ as an axiom on stacks. As with equations, the relative term algebra provides the basis for constructing an algebra which just meets any undefinedness requirement. The carrier for the abstract type is constructed by deleting from the set of terms all those which are demonstrably undefined: that is, those containing terms which are explicitly stated to be undefined. (Functions are strict in VDM.) For example, $\mathit{push}(x, \mathit{pop}(\mathit{empty}))$ and similar terms will be removed from the carrier as well as $\mathit{pop}(\mathit{empty})$. As usual, the operations just map values to the term which is the application of the operation to those values: where this is an undefined term the operation is undefined. There is a morphism ϕ to any algebra satisfying the undefinedness axioms, and thus with at least the same terms undefined. It is essentially that constructed from the relative term algebra, the difference being that the necessarily undefined terms do not appear in the carrier, rather than being left unmapped by the morphism. The algebra just constructed is thus an implementation of any other algebra with the same undefinedness properties.

Equations and undefinedness axioms can be combined. An initial algebra in the category satisfying all the axioms can be produced by taking the quotient algebra and deleting all sets of terms containing an undefined term from the carrier. Where a function would have given such a set as a result, it becomes undefined. The morphism to any algebra $\mathcal{A}$ satisfying all the axioms is defined as usual to map $[t]$ to $t^{\mathcal{A}}$ when these are defined. Such morphism definitions have the property that $t^{\mathcal{A}} = \phi(t^{\mathcal{I}})$, and hence ϕ satisfies the stronger reification condition $\phi(op_{\mathcal{I}}(x)) = op_{\mathcal{S}}(\phi(x))$ (where the equality is strong in each case). As before, we would usually look for a model isomorphic to the constructed one but based on more familiar structures to provide the actual implementation.

As an example, this construction can be applied to stacks. The stack operations are known to satisfy the equation

$$pop(push(x, s)) = s$$

This partitions the terms into two kinds of sets: those containing terms where no subterm has more *pop*s than *push*es, which each have a canonical term of form $push^n(x_1, \ldots, x_n, empty)$; and the rest, each containing a canonical term of the form $push^n(x_1, \ldots, x_n, pop^m(empty))$ (for $m > 0$ and $n \geq 0$). (The canonical terms are achieved by using the equation to cancel as many *pop*s as possible.) The sets of the second kind clearly contain terms which are undefined as a consequence of the U axiom above, and are deleted. The carrier is thus the sets of the first kind, and their canonical terms clearly show them to be isomorphic to the sequences $[x_1, \ldots, x_n]$. The empty sequence and **cons** operation are easily seen to correspond to *empty* and *push*. A legal *pop* on a canonical term can be cancelled with the preceding *push* to get a new canonical term with the first *push* of the old one removed, while *pop*(*empty*) is undefined, so *pop* corresponds to **tl**. This is the usual choice of model for stacks in VDM, constructed here from an algebraic specification.

There is a technical issue that arises when VDM is used to specify the abstract type as a partial algebra. The domain of a function is characterized by a precondition, and the semantics of the VDM standard (ISO, 1993) states that the function must be defined when the precondition holds, but is not necessarily undefined when it does not. However, the standard VDM reification condition is

$$\forall x \in T_{\mathcal{I}} \cdot \delta(\phi(x)) \wedge \textbf{pre-}op_{\mathcal{S}}(\phi(x)) \;\Rightarrow\; \phi(op_{\mathcal{I}}(x)) = op_{\mathcal{S}}(\phi(x))$$

which is also weaker and will be satisfied by any implementation constructed as described.

4 An Example

A more interesting example than those used above to illustrate the approach arises in the implementation of substitutions for the efficient unification algorithm described in (Boyer & Moore, 1972). The signature of the operations on substitutions needed by this algorithm is

empty: *Substitution*
update: *VarSymbol* × *Term* × *Substitution* → *Substitution*
_ • _: *Term* × *Substitution* → *Term*

where the constant *empty* is a substitution having no effect on any term, *update* adds a new binding of a term to a variable, and • applies a substitution to a term. The predefined type *VarSymbol* is an arbitrary set, while *Term* may be taken to be defined by

$$\begin{aligned} CT &:: op : FnSymbol \\ &\ args : Term^* \end{aligned}$$

$$Var :: v : VarSymbol$$

$$Term = Var \mid CT$$

We assume that a function $vars(t)$ yielding the set of variables in term t is predefined on *Term*.

Substitutions may be specified as maps which bind variables to the terms which will replace them when the substitution is applied.

$$Substitution_S = VarSymbol \xrightarrow{m} Term$$

where

$$inv\text{-}Substitution_S(\theta) \;\triangleq\; \forall v \in \mathbf{dom}\,\theta \cdot \theta(v) \neq \mathbf{mk}\text{-}Var(v)$$

The invariant ensures a unique representation for substitutions, a property that is usually desirable in abstract type specifications. The operations can then be specified by

$$empty_S = \{\,\}$$

$$\_ \bullet_S \_ : Term \times Substitution \rightarrow Term$$

$$\begin{aligned} t \bullet_S \theta \;\triangleq\; & \mathbf{cases}\ t\ \mathbf{of} \\ & \qquad mk\text{-}Var(v) \rightarrow \mathbf{if}\ v \in \mathbf{dom}\,\theta\ \mathbf{then}\ \theta(v)\ \mathbf{else}\ t \\ & mk\text{-}CT(f, args) \rightarrow mk\text{-}CT(f, \{i \mapsto args(i) \bullet_S \theta \mid i \in \mathbf{inds}\ args\}) \\ & \mathbf{end} \end{aligned}$$

$$\_ \circ \_ \ (\theta_1: Substitution, \theta_2: Substitution)\ \theta: Substitution$$
$$\mathbf{post}\ \forall t \in Term \cdot t \bullet_S \theta = t \bullet_S \theta_1 \bullet_S \theta_2$$

$$update_S : Variable \times Term \times Substitution \rightarrow Substitution$$

$$update_S(v, t, \theta) \;\triangleq\; \theta \circ \{v \mapsto t \bullet_S \theta\}$$

$$\mathbf{pre}\ v \notin \mathbf{dom}\,\theta \wedge v \notin vars(t \bullet_S \theta)$$

The composition operator $\_ \circ \_$ does not appear in the signature. It is defined only to assist in the definition of $updates_S$ and so is not subscripted. The strange definition of the function $updates_S$ reflects the needs of the unification algorithm, and is is partial in a way which means that substitutions are always idempotent. As a consequence, not all values of the type will be constructible. This is unusual (and in some ways undesirable) but will cause no particular problems in this development. The invariant needed to restrict $Substitutions_S$ to idempotent substitutions just adds complexity to the definitions.

If we can find some equations that the operations satisfy and determine which terms should be undefined, we shall have the basis for deriving a range of implementations. It turns out that if the precondition is taken to characterize undefinedness exactly, $updates_S$ is commutative.

$$updates_S(v_1, t_1, updates_S(v_2, t_2, \theta)) = updates_S(v_2, t_2, updates_S(v_1, t_1, \theta))$$

To prove this, it helps to name the intermediate results of the two orders of updating.

$$\theta' = updates_S(v_1, t_1, \theta) = \theta \circ \{v_1 \mapsto t_1 \bullet_S \theta\}$$
$$\theta'' = updates_S(v_2, t_2, \theta) = \theta \circ \{v_2 \mapsto t_2 \bullet_S \theta\}$$

We can then establish some useful lemmas characterizing the domain of the operation

Lemma 1.

$$\textbf{pre-}updates_S(v_1, t_1, \theta) \wedge \textbf{pre-}updates_S(v_2, t_2, \theta') \;\Rightarrow\; v_2 \notin \textbf{dom}\,\theta \wedge v_1 \neq v_2$$

Proof. *Obvious.*

Lemma 2.

$$\begin{array}{l} v_1 \neq v_2 \wedge \textbf{pre-}updates_S(v_1, t_1, \theta) \wedge \textbf{pre-}updates_S(v_2, t_2, \theta') \\ \Rightarrow\; v_2 \notin vars(t_2 \bullet_S \theta) \end{array}$$

Proof. *If $v_2 \in vars(t_2 \bullet_S \theta)$, then it will also be in $vars(t_2 \bullet_S \theta \bullet_S \{v_1 \mapsto t_1 \bullet_S \theta\})$. But this is contrary to the second precondition.*

Lemma 3.

$$\begin{array}{l} v_1 \neq v_2 \wedge \textbf{pre-}updates_S(v_1, t_1, \theta) \wedge \textbf{pre-}updates_S(v_2, t_2, \theta') \;\Rightarrow \\ \qquad v_1 \notin vars(t_2 \bullet_S \theta) \vee v_2 \notin vars(t_1 \bullet_S \theta) \end{array}$$

Proof. *If both $v_1 \in vars(t_2 \bullet_S \theta)$ and $v_2 \in vars(t_1 \bullet_S \theta)$ then the first substitution will leave occurrences of v_1 which will be replaced by terms containing v_2 by the second substitution. But this is contrary to the second precondition, which requires*

$$v_2 \notin vars(t_2 \bullet_S \theta') = vars(t_2 \bullet_S \theta \bullet_S \{v_1 \mapsto t_1 \bullet_S \theta\})\,.$$

Lemma 4.

$$v_1 \neq v_2 \wedge (v_1 \notin vars(t_2 \bullet_S \theta) \vee v_2 \notin vars(t_1 \bullet_S \theta)) \wedge$$
$$v_2 \notin \mathbf{dom}\,\theta \wedge v_2 \notin vars(t_2 \bullet \theta) \Rightarrow$$
$$\mathbf{pre}\text{-}updates_S(v_2, t_2, \theta')$$

Proof. *It is obvious that v_2 is not in the domain of θ', so the first conjunct of* $\mathbf{pre}\text{-}updates_S(v_2, t_2, \theta')$ *is satisfied. If $v_1 \notin vars(t_2 \bullet_S \theta)$, then*

$$t_2 \bullet_S \theta \bullet_S \{v_1 \mapsto t_1 \bullet_S \theta\} = t_2 \bullet_S \theta$$

and so $v_2 \notin vars(t_2 \bullet_S \theta')$. If $v_2 \notin vars(t_1 \bullet_S \theta))$, we observe that

$$vars(t_2 \bullet_S \theta \bullet_S \{v_1 \mapsto t_1 \bullet_S \theta\}) \subseteq vars(t_2 \bullet_S \theta) \cup vars(t_1 \bullet_S \theta)$$

so again $v_2 \notin vars(t_2 \bullet_S \theta')$. As a consequence, the second part of the precondition is also satisfied.

We can then establish that if one term is defined, the other is

Theorem 5.

$$\mathbf{pre}\text{-}updates_S(v_1, t_1, \theta) \wedge \mathbf{pre}\text{-}updates_S(v_2, t_2, \theta') \Leftrightarrow$$
$$\mathbf{pre}\text{-}updates_S(v_2, t_2, \theta) \wedge \mathbf{pre}\text{-}updates_S(v_1, t_1, \theta'') \Leftrightarrow$$
$$v_1 \neq v_2 \wedge (v_1 \notin vars(t_2 \bullet_S \theta) \vee v_2 \notin vars(t_1 \bullet_S \theta)) \wedge v_1 \notin \mathbf{dom}\,\theta \wedge v_2 \notin \mathbf{dom}\,\theta \wedge$$
$$v_1 \notin vars(t_1 \bullet \theta) \wedge v_2 \notin vars(t_2 \bullet \theta)$$

Proof. *The final formula is a conjunct of the first precondition and properties which have been shown equivalent to the second precondition in the lemmas. It is symmetric in its use of v_1 and v_2, so it is equivalent to the second formula too.*

We can complete the proof of commutativity by showing that when defined the terms are equal. The proof is by considering the values of the two substitutions at all variables in their common domain.

Theorem 6.

$$\mathbf{pre}\text{-}updates_S(v_1, t_1, \theta) \wedge \mathbf{pre}\text{-}updates_S(v_2, t_2, \theta') \Rightarrow$$
$$(updates_S(v_2, t_2, \theta')(v)) = (updates_S(v_1, t_1, \theta'')(v))$$

Proof.
We have

$$\begin{aligned} updates_S(v_2, t_2, \theta') &= \theta' \circ \{v_2 \mapsto t_2 \bullet_S \theta'\} \\ &= \theta \circ \{v_1 \mapsto t_1 \bullet_S \theta\} \circ \{v_2 \mapsto t_2 \bullet_S \theta \bullet_S \{v_1 \mapsto t_1 \bullet_S \theta\}\} \\ &= \theta \circ \{v_1 \mapsto t_1 \bullet_S \theta \bullet_S \{v_2 \mapsto t_2 \bullet_S \theta \bullet_S \{v_1 \mapsto t_1 \bullet_S \theta\}\}, \\ &\qquad v_2 \mapsto t_2 \bullet_S \theta \bullet_S \{v_1 \mapsto t_1 \bullet_S \theta\}\} \end{aligned}$$

Similarly

$$\begin{aligned} updates_S(v_1, t_1, \theta'') = \theta \circ \{&v_2 \mapsto t_2 \bullet_S \theta \bullet_S \{v_1 \mapsto t_1 \bullet_S \theta \bullet_S \{v_2 \mapsto t_2 \bullet_S \theta\}\}, \\ &v_1 \mapsto t_1 \bullet_S \theta \bullet_S \{v_2 \mapsto t_2 \bullet_S \theta\}\} \end{aligned}$$

It is enough, then, to show that the two substitutions

$$\begin{aligned}\theta_1 = \{&v_1 \mapsto t_1 \bullet_S \theta \bullet_S \{v_2 \mapsto t_2 \bullet_S \theta \bullet_S \{v_1 \mapsto t_1 \bullet_S \theta\}\},\\ &v_2 \mapsto t_2 \bullet_S \theta \bullet_S \{v_1 \mapsto t_1 \bullet_S \theta\}\}\\ \theta_2 = \{&v_2 \mapsto t_2 \bullet_S \theta \bullet_S \{v_1 \mapsto t_1 \bullet_S \theta \bullet_S \{v_2 \mapsto t_2 \bullet_S \theta\}\},\\ &v_1 \mapsto t_1 \bullet_S \theta \bullet_S \{v_2 \mapsto t_2 \bullet_S \theta\}\}\end{aligned}$$

are equal when the updates are defined, which can be done by considering their values at v_1 and v_2. We have

$$\theta_1(v_1) = t_1 \bullet_S \theta \bullet_S \{v_2 \mapsto t_2 \bullet_S \theta \bullet_S \{v_1 \mapsto t_1 \bullet_S \theta\}\}$$

Since the preconditions hold, $v_1 \notin vars(t_2 \bullet \theta)$ or $v_1 \notin vars(t_2 \bullet \theta)$. If $v_1 \notin vars(t_2 \bullet \theta)$, then

$$t_1 \bullet_S \theta \bullet_S \{v_2 \mapsto t_2 \bullet_S \theta \bullet_S \{v_1 \mapsto t_1 \bullet_S \theta\}\} = t_1 \bullet_S \theta \bullet_S \{v_2 \mapsto t_2 \bullet_S \theta\}$$

because the second substitution makes no difference. Similarly, if $v_1 \notin vars(t_2 \bullet \theta)$ then

$$t_1 \bullet_S \theta \bullet_S \{v_2 \mapsto t_2 \bullet_S \theta \bullet_S \{v_1 \mapsto t_1 \bullet_S \theta\}\} = t_1 \bullet_S \theta \bullet_S \{v_2 \mapsto t_2 \bullet_S \theta\}$$

still holds because the first substitution has no effect, and so its form is immaterial. In either case, we have $\theta_1(v_1) = \theta_2(v_1)$. The argument for $\theta_1(v_2) = \theta_2(v_2)$ is the same, with the rôles of v_1 and v_2 reversed.

The quotient model satisfying this equation groups all terms which have the same arguments to the series of *updates*, irrespective of order (since any ordering can be transformed into any other). This is isomorphic to the bag of (v_i, t_i) pairs.

Partial implementations turn out to be more interesting. Theorem 5 shows that we cannot bind the same variable more than once. In conjunction with commutativity, this can be defined by

$$U(update(v, t_1, update(v, t_2, \theta)))$$

The effect is to remove from the quotient model all sets containing terms with repeated variables. The remaining sets associate at most one term with any given variable, and their terms exhibit the bindings in all possible orders. They are isomorphic to partial functions from variables to terms. This is the same model as the specification, but the operations are defined differently. In the relative term algebra, updating θ by binding v to t gives $update(v, t, \theta)$. In the quotient model, the equivalence class of terms with the same bindings is mapped to the class including the new binding: in the isomorphic partial function model this corresponds naturally to adding a new pair to the function. The term *empty* is equivalent only to itself, and can be made to correspond to $\{\}$

$$empty_{\mathcal{I}} = \{\}$$

$$update_{\mathcal{I}}(v, t, \theta) \triangleq \theta \cup \{v \mapsto t\}$$

The $update_{\mathcal{I}}$ function is undefined if $v \in \mathbf{dom}\,\theta$: in the quotient algebra this corresponds to an operation with a deleted set as a result. We could make the domain explicit by writing

$$\textbf{pre-}update_{\mathcal{I}}(v, t, \theta) \triangleq v \notin \mathbf{dom}\,\theta$$

To arrive at the definition for substitution application based on this new representation of substitutions, we use the reification condition as usual.

$$t \bullet_{\mathcal{I}} \theta = t \bullet_{\mathcal{S}} \phi(\theta)$$

(Recall that this is now a strong equality.) We need to find a definition of $\bullet_{\mathcal{I}}$ with this property. Considering cases, applying the reification condition and unfolding gives

$$\begin{aligned}
\textbf{mk-}CT(f, args) \bullet_{\mathcal{I}} \theta &= \textbf{mk-}CT(f, args) \bullet_{\mathcal{S}} \phi(\theta) \\
&= \textbf{mk-}CT(f, \{i \mapsto args(i) \bullet_{\mathcal{S}} \phi(\theta) \mid i \in \textbf{inds}\, args\}) \\
&= \textbf{mk-}CT(f, \{i \mapsto args(i) \bullet_{\mathcal{I}} \theta \mid i \in \textbf{inds}\, args\})
\end{aligned}$$

$$\begin{aligned}
\textbf{mk-}Var(v) \bullet_{\mathcal{I}} \theta &= \textbf{mk-}Var(v) \bullet_{\mathcal{S}} \phi(\theta) \\
&= \textbf{if } v \in \mathbf{dom}\,(\phi(\theta)) \textbf{ then } (\phi(\theta))(v) \textbf{ else mk-}Var(v)
\end{aligned}$$

The first equation immediately suggests a definition of $\bullet_{\mathcal{I}}$ for compound terms, but the second needs work to remove the uses of ϕ. That in the condition can be removed using

Theorem 7. $\delta(\phi(\theta)) \Rightarrow \mathbf{dom}\,\theta = \mathbf{dom}\,(\phi(\theta))$

Proof. *By induction over θ. The induction principle for maps given in (Jones, 1990) is essentially*

$$\frac{P(\{\}) \quad x \notin \mathbf{dom}\, m; P(m) \vdash P(\{x \mapsto y\} \cup m)}{\forall m \cdot P(m)}$$

The base case is established by

$$\begin{aligned}
\mathbf{dom}\,(\phi(\{\})) &= \mathbf{dom}\,(\phi(empty_{\mathcal{I}})) \\
&= \mathbf{dom}\,(empty_{\mathcal{S}}) \\
&= \mathbf{dom}\,\{\}
\end{aligned}$$

while the inductive case is proved by

$$\begin{aligned}
\mathbf{dom}\,(\phi(\{v \mapsto t\} \cup \theta)) &= \mathbf{dom}\,(\phi(update_{\mathcal{I}}(v, t, \theta))) \\
&= \mathbf{dom}\,(update_{\mathcal{S}}(v, t, \phi(\theta))) \\
&= \mathbf{dom}\,(\phi(\theta) \circ \{v \mapsto t \bullet_{\mathcal{S}} \phi(\theta)\}) \\
&= \mathbf{dom}\,(\phi(\theta)) \cup \{v\} \\
&= \mathbf{dom}\,\theta \cup \{v\} \\
&= \mathbf{dom}\,(\{v \mapsto t\} \cup \theta)
\end{aligned}$$

The proof strategy is to rewrite the values as applications of constructors and use the reification condition and specification definitions to simplify just like the synthesis of $elem_{\mathcal{I}}$ in Sect. 2. It depends heavily on the stronger reification condition established in Sect. 3.

To simplify the expression in the **then** arm, observe that if v is in the domain of θ, it was put there by an *update*, and since the order of updates is unimportant, there is some θ' and t such that $\theta = update_{\mathcal{I}}(v, t, \theta')$. We may then show

Theorem 8.

$$\delta(\phi(update_{\mathcal{I}}(v,t,\theta))) \Rightarrow \phi(update_{\mathcal{I}}(v,t,\theta))(v) = (update_{\mathcal{I}}(v,t,\theta))(v) \bullet_{\mathcal{I}} (update_{\mathcal{I}}(v,t,\theta))$$

Proof.
Applying the stronger reification condition and unfolding, we have

$$\begin{aligned}\phi(update_{\mathcal{I}}(v,t,\theta))(v) &= update_{\mathcal{S}}(v,t,\phi(\theta))(v)\\ &= (\phi(\theta) \circ \{v \mapsto t \bullet_{\mathcal{S}} \phi(\theta)\})(v)\\ &= (\phi(\theta))(v) \bullet_{\mathcal{S}} \{v \mapsto t \bullet_{\mathcal{S}} \phi(\theta)\})\\ &= t \bullet_{\mathcal{S}} \phi(\theta)\end{aligned}$$

If $\phi(update_{\mathcal{I}}(v,t,\theta))$ is defined, we must have **pre-**$update_{\mathcal{S}}(v,t,\phi(\theta))$*, and so $v \notin vars(t \bullet_{\mathcal{S}} \phi(\theta))$. Hence*

$$\begin{aligned}t \bullet_{\mathcal{S}} \phi(\theta) &= t \bullet_{\mathcal{S}} \phi(\theta) \bullet_{\mathcal{S}} \{v \mapsto t \bullet_{\mathcal{S}} \phi(\theta)\}\\ &= t \bullet_{\mathcal{S}} update_{\mathcal{S}}(v,t,\phi(\theta))\\ &= (update_{\mathcal{I}}(v,t,\theta))(v) \bullet_{\mathcal{I}} (update_{\mathcal{I}}(v,t,\theta))\end{aligned}$$

Now the body of the variable case reduces to

$$\textbf{if } v \in \textbf{dom}\,\theta \textbf{ then } (\theta(v)) \bullet_{\mathcal{I}} \theta \textbf{ else } t$$

and there is a convenient definition with these properties to use as an implementation

$$\begin{aligned}t \bullet_{\mathcal{I}} \theta \;\triangleq\;& \textbf{cases } t \textbf{ of}\\ & \quad mk\text{-}Var(v) \rightarrow \textbf{if } v \in \textbf{dom}\,\theta \textbf{ then } (\theta(v)) \bullet_{\mathcal{I}} \theta \textbf{ else } t\\ & \quad mk\text{-}CT(f, args) \rightarrow mk\text{-}CT(f, \{i \mapsto args(i) \bullet_{\mathcal{I}} \theta \mid i \in \textbf{inds}\, args\})\\ & \textbf{end}\end{aligned}$$

5 Comparison

A more conventional development, positing implementation definitions and an abstraction function and then showing that the reification condition used here holds, is presented in (Clement, 1994) as a contrast with the usual VDM approach to reification: the relationship between the two is explored in more detail there. Here we want to compare that posit-and-prove development with the calculational development given here.

The most important practical consideration is the difficulty of constructing the proofs needed to justify the implementations. In the posit-and-prove approach, establishing that the reification condition holds involves a large amount of detailed reasoning using our intuition for how the implementation and the abstraction function work. In this particular development, the abstraction function is an iterated composition of the representation, and the arguments are based on how many iterations will be needed to guarantee that further iterations produce no change. Because the definitions involve substitutions, properties of the substitution operations are used widely throughout the proofs: these properties are taken as obvious in (Clement, 1994) but could be stated explicitly as lemmas and even proved from the specification.

In contrast, the approach using calculation presented here begins by establishing properties of the specification, independent of any implementation. The proof of commutativity is quite long, but only because the expanded formulae are quite large: the actual reasoning is exclusively concerned with the same kind of properties of substitutions that were used in the posit-and-prove approach (and which are again assumed). It was certainly easier to develop. The result of the proof is a theorem about the specification, which is potentially useful to definitions making use of the abstract type. This cannot be said of the reification condition proofs of the posit-and-prove approach (although useful lemmas may appear). The undefinedness property follows from one of the lemmas of the commutativity proof.

Once the properties have been determined, the term model has to be constructed and an isomorphic algebra found. This process has been presented informally, but the steps are formally defined and it would at least be possible to present a function connecting values in the quotient algebra with those in the implementation and show that it is an isomorphism. However, commutativity is well known to define bags and the effect of the undefinedness is reasonably clear so the less formal development here should be sufficiently convincing. In general, it seems more productive to exploit established results rather than prove everything ourselves. The final step is the synthesis of the observations: the proof here is very similar to that of the posit-and-prove development although it expresses a calculation rather than justifying a posited definition.

In practical terms, then, the calculational approach seems to have an advantage. This stems from avoiding an explicit definition of an abstraction function, since if one were to be posited as in the usual calculi, the calculation of the implementation of $update_{\mathcal{I}}$ would once again involve the details of how the implementation works.

A more philosphical question is to compare the amount and nature of the inspiration that was required to arrive at the implementation. This is, after all, what the calculational approach is meant to reduce. In the posit-and-prove approach, it leads to the posited implementation and abstraction function. In this case, the first informal idea is that recording the arguments to *update* will certainly be enough. Applying a substitution then means looking up each variable, and substituting the resulting term in the same way using the rest of the bindings. (This is already independent of the order in which the bindings are made.) A simplification of this process can be justified by observing that substituting using the whole substitution makes no difference, because the precondition means that the term cannot contain the variable it is bound to. It is this that suggests the definition of the abstraction function as an n-fold iteration.

The inspiration in the calculational approach is in the choice of properties. The undefinedness is an obvious consequence of the precondition (although its usefulness is less obvious at the start). Given that we need to be able to identify the implementation from the quotient algebra, it helps to restrict attention to simple algebraic properties like commutativity, but that still leaves a range of possibilities, some of which may be easier to discount than others. This is typical of calculational approaches: they define a spectrum of possible ways to proceed but some intuition for the expected final result of the calculation is necessary to decide which way to go. In this case, the commutativity might be suggested by the unification algorithm which motivates these definitions: it generates a series of updates, but could do so in any order. (It has to be said that in practice (Manna & Waldinger, 1981; Clement, 1991) the algorithm has been derived for a single order of updates rather than making this observation.) Failing that, the intuition for the posit-and-prove approach sketched above also tells us that the implementation of *update* is commutative and thus its specification should be, so at least the intuition needed for calculation is no harder to come by than that for posit-and-prove, even if there is limited evidence that it is easier.

On balance, then, the calculational approach seems to have advantages over posit-and-prove when it can be applied. In principle, it always can be, since any desired implementation can be given an algebraic definition, and it can then be confirmed that the properties hold of the specification. (These properties can be expressed in any language which allows us to construct objects with guaranteed morphisms to all others: a number are described in (Goguen & Burstall, 1992).) In practice, these algebraic definitions may need operations in their signatures which were not in the original specification. They could be added to the specification to allow their properties to be checked, but this extra work makes the approach look less attractive. It would be worth investigating examples of this kind, but for the moment the method looks more appropriate to cases where the implementations involve types with simple algebraic properties (although as we have seen the specifications can be quite complex).

6 Summary

We have presented a way of constructing implementations from specifications. They satisfy the VDM criterion that the implementation behaves like the specification whenever the specification is defined, but unlike the usual VDM approach do not require the explicit statement of an abstraction function. Instead, the approach makes use of properties of the specification, drawing heavily on the constructive aspects of the theory of algebraic specification. In the special case where operations and abstraction function are total, all the results presented are well known in the algebraic setting, and only the application to model based specification is novel. Partial algebras have also received some previous attention. The robust morphism introduced in (Broy, 1985) corresponds to the reification condition of Sect. 1 and the stronger condition satisfied by the calculated abstraction function corresponds to the weak morphisms of (Broy & Wirsing, 1982). (It is an accident of nomenclature that the weak morphism is stronger than the robust one!) However, their particular interest was in the identification of morphisms leading to algebras with initial or terminal algebras for specification rather than any application to implementation. (Both weak and robust morphisms give rise to categories with terminal algebras.) The morphisms with initial algebras that they define have the empty algebra as initial model in the absence of axioms saying that particular terms must be defined: this is in contrast to our approach where the quotient algebras are total unless terms are explicitly declared undefined. By applying algebraic techniques in a model based setting we have avoided the principal problem of algebraic specification, which is the need to give enough axioms to characterize the specificand uniquely: all we need here are enough properties to characterize the wanted implementation.

Another approach to the calculation rather than positing of abstraction functions is the *SETS* calculus of (Oliveira, 1992). There, the emphasis is on deriving abstraction functions (and invariants on the implementation) for structured types given abstraction functions and invariants for the component types. There seems to be scope for combining the two methods to construct complex specifications without writing down abstraction functions: it should be possible to combine their properties in much the same way that the functions themselves are combined in the *SETS* calculus. However, technical differences in the details of the reification conditions used would have to be resolved.

It is worth saying that none of the approaches to data reification is mechanical: each has some elements of intuition guiding the choice of definitions or properties and if the intuition is wrong then the formal development will fail to go through. In the case of posit-and-prove, it will be some reification condition that will fail to hold, and in the usual calculational approach, the defining property of an observation based on the reification condition may not lead to a definition with no use of ϕ. In this approach, a given set of properties may not lead to interesting models or convenient definitions of the operations.

How relevant is this work to industrial practice? Categories are thought of as abstract concepts even by mathematicians, and the computer industry does not usually rush to take up abstract mathematics. This is a mistake if the goal is to deliver more reliable software at lower cost. Reliability requires some kind of proof, and proof is expensive and becomes more so as proofs become larger. For this reason, the proofs in this development and in that described in (Clement, 1994) are rigorous rather than formal: only a top-level view of the proof is provided using phrases such as "by induction", and the reader is left to fill in the details. Not only are the proofs here shorter, but because they apply abstract ideas, some of the gaps can be filled in by reference to the standard literature rather than by detailed reasoning in the specific area of the application. They should thus be more convincing as well as less expensive.

References

M. A. Arbib and E. G. Manes. *Arrows, Structures, and Functors: The Categorical Imperative.* Academic Press, 1975.

R. S. Boyer and J. S. Moore. The sharing of structure in theorem-proving programs. In *Machine Intelligence 7*, pages 101–116. Edinburgh University Press, 1972.

M. Broy. Extensional behaviour of concurrent, nondeterministic, communicating systems. In *Control Flow and Data Flow: Concepts of Distributed Programming*, pages 229–276. Springer-Verlag, 1985.

M. Broy and M. Wirsing. Partial abstract types. *Acta Informatica*, 18:47–64, 1982.

T. Clement. Combining transformation and posit-and-prove in a VDM development. In *VDM'91: Formal Software Development Methods*, pages 63–92. Springer Verlag, 1991.

T. Clement. Notes on data reification. In *FME'93 tutorial material*, pages 151–190, 1993.

T. Clement. Comparing approaches to data reification. In *FME'94: Industrial Benefits of Formal Methods (LNCS 873)*, pages 118–133. Springer Verlag, 1994.

J. Darlington. The design of efficient data representations. In *Automatic Program Construction Techniques*, chapter 7, pages 139–156. Macmillan, 1984.

H. Ehrig and B. Mahr. *Fundamentals of Algebraic Specification*, volume 6 of *EATCS Monographs*. Springer-Verlag, 1985.

J. A. Goguen and R. M. Burstall. Institutions: Abstract model theory for specification and programming. *Journal of the ACM*, pages 95–146, 1992.

J. A. Goguen, J. W. Thatcher, and E. G. Wagner. An initial algebra approach to the specification, correctness and implementation of abstract data types. In *Current Trends in Programming Methodology*, volume 4, 1978.

International Standards Organisation. *Information Technology Programming Languages – VDM-SL First Committee Draft Standard CD 13817-1*, November 1993. Document Number ISO/IEC JTC1/SC22/WG19/N-20.

C. B. Jones. *Systematic Software Development Using VDM.* Prentice-Hall International, 2nd edition, 1990.

C. C. Morgan and P. H. B. Gardiner. Data refinement by calculation. *Acta Informatica*, 27:481–503, 1990.

Z. Manna and R. Waldinger. Deductive synthesis of the unification algorithm. *Science of Computer Programming*, 1:5–48, 1981.

J. N. Oliveira. Software reification using the SETS calculus. In *Proceedings of the 5th Refinement Workshop*, Workshops in Computing, pages 140–171. Springer-Verlag, 1992.

Formal and Informal Specifications of a Secure System Component: Final Results in a Comparative Study

T. M. Brookes[1], J. S. Fitzgerald[2], P. G. Larsen[3]

[1] British Aerospace (Systems and Equipment) Ltd., Plymouth, UK
[2] Centre for Software Reliability, University of Newcastle upon Tyne, NE1 7RU, UK
[3] IFAD (The Institute of Applied Computer Science), Odense, Denmark

Abstract. This paper presents the findings from the later phases of a study of the effects of introducing formal specification to the commercial-scale development of a small security-critical system component. The objectives and form of the study are briefly reviewed. Observations have been made of the effort profile across the project, compliance of the developed system with customer requirements and software characteristics. The results of these observations are presented. Conclusions and areas of further work are discussed.

1 Introduction

An important topic in any branch of practical engineering is how to improve the development process with the aims of decreasing time to market, reducing the overall development costs and ensuring that the product meets the customer's requirements. Numerous techniques, for example those of structured and object-oriented design, have been introduced in recent years with claims that they allow these objectives to be reached. Formal specification, the subject of this paper, can be viewed as a complementary technique which allows system requirements to be captured and expressed in a rigorous fashion.

The use of formal specification is currently mandated for high assurance security- and safety-critical systems [ITS91, MoD91a, MoD91b]. In these cases, the perceived expense of using formal specification can be justified as there is no other method of performing the project to the satisfaction of the regulatory authorities. But what are the true costs of using formal specification in such a project? The study described in [FBGL94] and [Fit95] sought to provide evidence on the costs and benefits of a modest degree of formal specification by comparing separate developments of the same system, one development using conventional practice, the other using the same techniques plus specification in VDM-SL supported by the IFAD Toolbox. A previous paper [FBGL94] described the differences in the two development paths' early phase of system design. This paper presents findings from the later software design, implementation and testing phases.

Section 2 briefly reviews the development process and the comparison already made of the early phases. Section 3 presents the new results from the later stages and compares the distribution of effort across the whole process. the overall observations of the project are discussed in Section 4. Section 5 describes the future direction of formal specification work in BASE and Section 6 briefly discusses the value of this kind of small comparative study.

2 Project Overview

2.1 Background

One important area of BASE business is the development of secure message handling systems. Such systems are typically developed to high levels of assurance assessed by a third party. Increasingly, the criteria for achievement of high assurance levels require some use of formal techniques. The study reported here was motivated by a desire to observe the consequences of introducing a modest degree of formal specification into a BASE development process in order to meet the criteria for high assurance levels.

The study was intended to assess:

1. the effectiveness of formal specification in terms of the additional development costs versus any benefits gained by reducing ambiguities, misunderstandings and rework, with a view to its possible introduction to all or part of the life cycle for other projects;
2. the problems and difficulties involved in the use of formal specification, so that future projects may learn from this experience; and
3. the training requirement needed to introduce formal specification into the design process.

It should be stressed that it was not an aim of this study to show the absolute worth of formal methods. In particular, it was not an attempt to prove that some costs or benefits stem directly from the formality of a notation.

2.2 The Trusted Gateway Development

The development of a *trusted gateway* was used as the baseline project for the comparison. The gateway considered is a simple device which is located in the communications path between systems at different security levels. Its purpose is to determine the classification of the messages which pass through it and to ensure that they only pass to a destination at the correct security level. It was an excellent system to consider as its behaviour could be well defined, was sufficiently simple as to be tractable with the effort available for the project, yet was sufficiently complex as to be non-trivial.

The trusted gateway was developed by two separate design teams who did not communicate, although they were aware of each other's existence. The first team used a conventional development methodology, Ward and Mellor [WM86] supported by the Teamwork[4] Computer Aided System/Software Engineering

[4] Teamwork is a Registered Trademark of Cadre Technology Inc.

tool set. The other team followed a similar design process, but used formal specification in VDM-SL [ABH+95] to support this design methodology. The formal specification was developed and tested using the VDM Toolbox from IFAD [ELL94]. The utilisation of tools and the details of the development process followed are described in [FLBG95].

The development was initiated by producing a customer requirement that was submitted to each of the design teams. In the first (system design) phase there was a divergence in the design as each of the groups interpreted the original specification. The two design processes were carefully logged: the results of their comparison are described in more detail in [FBGL94].

The second (software design) phase saw each system design and test plan developed to levels of greater detail. In the implementation and testing phases each version of the system was coded and tested using the test plan devised by its own design team. The test procedures from the other design team were then applied to compare the test coverage achieved by the two design approaches. The software produced was subjected to a final acceptance test by the customer. Areas where the performance was deficient were highlighted and examination of project records was used to pinpoint the decisions in the design process responsible for the introduction of that deficiency.

Training in the use of formal specification and the Toolbox was provided for the engineers involved in the design and monitoring activities. The Toolbox provided a means for preparing VDM specifications in the correct format, performed static checking, and could animate the VDM-SL specifications produced during the course of the design. IFAD and the Centre for Software Reliability at the University of Newcastle also participated in the comparative reviews of the design and progress.

3 Observations

This section presents the results of the observations made in the later design phases and across the project as a whole. The following points were assessed and used to compare the two design processes:

1. effort required to perform the design task (Section 3.1);
2. compliance of the system with the original specification(Section 3.2); and
3. performance of the system and tests in terms of code size, speed, and complexity (Section3.3).

A number of other observations on specification style, training, tool support and specification language syntax were also recorded (Sections 3.4 – 3.7).

3.1 Design effort

The tables below show how the effort expended on the project was distributed. Figure 1 shows the normalised number of hours spent in each phase assuming that the project was 100 hours in duration. The effort was provisionally allocated on a 40:40:20 hour split between systems design, software design and implementation. The column headed 'Allocated Time' indicates the time allocated to each phase at the start of the project. The columns headed 'Conventional' and 'Formal methods' show the time expended in the individual paths.

Figure 2 indicates the distribution of time among the phases in each path (note that the figures have been rounded to two places.)

Phase	Allocated Time	Conventional Method	Formal Method	*Excess F over C*
System Design	40	30	35	+ 17%
Software Design	40	40	33	- 17%
Implementation	20	17	13	- 24%
Totals	100	87	81	- 7%

Fig. 1. Normalised Number of Person Hours Spent in each phase

Phase	Conventional Method	Formal Method	*Ratio*
	% Project	% Project	*(C/F)*
System Design	34%	43%	0.77
Software Design	46%	41%	1.15
Implementation	20%	16%	1.25
Totals	100%	100%	

Fig. 2. Distribution of Project Time within each path

The system design phase required roughly 17% more effort in the formal path than for the conventional path when considered in terms of the overall project (which includes design reviews, etc.). The engineers in this phase had equal skills and experience. When the time spent in this phase is examined as a percentage of the project, there is a larger difference. In the formal path 43% of the time is spent in the system design phase as compared to only 34% on the conventional path; a more significant difference. Neither engineer was limited by available resources as both underspent the total project budget, by 25% in the conventional path, and 12.5% in the formal path.

In the software design phase the engineers were of different skill and experience, the engineer in the formal path having more experience. Although the formal path required less effort to complete, it was felt that this result was biased by the difference in the engineers. After comparing the work of the two engineers, and taking into account their different experience levels, there was not judged to be a significant additional effort which would be incurred if formal specification were used in the software design phase under normal conditions.

In the implementation phase, the engineers were again of similar age and experience. Both paths took the same amount of effort to complete the first version of the system. However, the conventional implementation required re-work to correct a problem discovered when the system was tested with the test suite developed on the formal path. This increased added about 15% to the cost of the phase. As a percentage of the overall project, the formal software implementation took 13% of the effort as compared to 17% in the conventional path.

Comparing the effort for the entire programme, the use of formal specification did not incur an overhead, in fact the overall effort required was slightly less. The difference is not felt to be significant. The effort distribution in the formal path exhibited higher costs in the early parts of the programme where system requirements are being analysed and understood, but that the additional effort is recovered in the later stages of the programme. This change in the effort profile is also typical of the introduction of structured design methods where system understanding is promoted before development.

3.2 Compliance with Customer Requirements

In the system design phase, the formal specification path detected a special condition, implicit in the requirement, which was not identified in the conventional path until the test suite developed for the formal path was run on the implemented system. In normal business, the error would not have been detected by testing, but would possibly have been detected by the customer[5]. Re-work was required in the conventional development process to correct this, adding the 15% extra effort to the implementation phase already discussed. No effort was used to correct the supporting design documentation, so this represents the very minimum additional cost. Had this system been developed for external evaluation, considerably greater time and effort would have had to be expended to correct and re-evaluate the design documentation.

3.3 Code Metrics

Complexity The routines which determine message security classification were compared to evaluate the relative complexity of the code developed on the two paths. This routine was chosen because it forms the kernel of the system, and in particular implements the security enforcing function.

The McCabe Complexity of the code was found to be 74 for this routine on the conventional path and 10 on the formal path. If the formal specification itself were treated as an implementation, its complexity would be estimated at 4.

[5] In BASE, this would be referred to as a *design error* because it led to the development of a product which did not meet the customer's expectations.

These figures would suggest that the formal path produced much simpler code in the main function than the conventional path. An investigation was conducted to see if the change to the code on the conventional path caused by the failure to pass the formal test suite had affected the code complexity. This showed that there had been a significant increase in the complexity (from roughly 10 to the 74 measured) when the code for the main function was re-written to correct the deficiency. The conventional development did not in itself produce complicated code, but problems may have been introduced when the routine was redesigned to correct problems discovered late in the testing process.

Size The number of lines of code in a routine is not a particularly helpful metric, although in this case, as both routines are trying to implement the same function, they are of some use. The code on the formal path was less than one fifth of the size of the code on the conventional path. The ratio of lines of comment to code, which is an indication of the maintainability of the final system as the code is probably better documented internally, was much larger on the formal path, albeit the number of lines of comment was smaller. The differences identified here cannot be attributed solely to the use of formal specification, and are believed to reflect the experience and ability of the software engineer.

Speed The speed of operation was tested by passing a large block of messages through the system. To minimise any machine-related errors, the software was installed on the same machine for each test, and all other software running was disabled. The results obtained are shown in Figure 3.

Phase	Formal Implementation	Conventional Implementation	*Ratio*
initialisation time (seconds)	70	17	4
processing rate (char per sec)	250	18	13.9

Fig. 3. Code Speed for the Different Implementations

The formal implementation spends roughly four times as long checking the system data, the classification definitions and start and end of message definitions, as the conventional implementation. However, when the system is processing messages it is almost fourteen times faster. Since the trusted gateway is designed to be set up once and then left to operate for a long period of time, the relative speed of initialisation does not matter in assessing system performance. The system developed in the formal path would thus be considered to be much faster than the conventional implementation. Note that speed was not given to either team as a design objective.

3.4 Specification Style: developing an implementation for a memory purging operation

To give an indication of the specification styles used by the BASE engineers, this section illustrates the evolution of the formal specification during the software development phase by considering the simple operation used to purge the trusted gateway's system memory. At the start of the system design phase, **Purge** was defined on the very abstract system design model, with no indication as to how the operation was to be implemented. The message is replaced by an empty sequence which would satisfy the requirements of the security policy model that there should be no remnant of the message left in the system after processing. The definition is shown below as recorded in the design documentation [6]:

```
This represents the clearing of the Message Data areas, which
is not strictly needed for the execution of the formal
specification in the IFAD Toolbox, but is included for clarity
of the overall formal specification.
\begin{vdm_al}

  operations


      Purge : () ==> ()

      Purge()==
              (
              ValidMessage := ""
              );

\end{vdm_al}
```

This specification was refined (in the informal sense) during the software design phase, where a specific algorithm recommended in the original customer specification is described. The algorithm writes characters over the location in the memory occupied by the message. The new definition is shown below, together with the designer's comments:

```
This operation performs a purge on the first 'length' characters
of 'buffer'. Each element of the buffer has the sequence FF
then 0 written to it eight  times followed by 246 once. This
sequence is repeated 4 times.

Note that the testing of this function in vdmde (the IFAD Toolbox)
is very time consuming due to the loops. It can be disabled if
```

[6] The LaTeX vdm_al commands are part of the interface of the IFAD Toolbox, and separate the VDM-SL formulae from the explanatory text.

```
required if the term length is replaced by 0 in the first for
loop. Also note that the characters written to the buffer are
not those required due to keyboard limitations.

Input Parameters    length
                    - The number of characters to be purged.
Returns             None
States Affected     buffer
                    - buffer has a wipe sequence written to it

\begin{vdm_al}

  Purge :  nat ==> ()
  Purge (length)==
  (
      for i = 1 to length do
      (
              for count1 = 1 to 4 do
              (
                      for count = 1 to 8 do
                      (
                              buffer := buffer ++ {i |-> 'A'};
                              buffer := buffer ++ {i |-> '0'}
                      );
                      buffer := buffer ++ {i |->'B'}
              );
              buffer := buffer ++ {i |-> '0'}
      ) -- i < length
  );

\end{vdm_al}
```

When this function has to be implemented in a high level language, the second version can be easily translated, whilst the first possesses insufficient detail to be used. The implementation in C is shown below.

```
/*************************************************************/
/* Function              : Purge                             */
/* This function will purge the data between the two pointers */
/* passed in                                                 */
/*                                                           */
/* Parameters   : (global) plus                              */
/*              LPSTR lpszCommence : point from which to     */
/*                                   commence purge          */
/*              LPSTR lpszFinish : stop purge                */
/*                                                           */
```

```
/* Return              :   void                              */
/*                                                           */
/*************************************************************/
void FAR PASCAL Purge(LPSTR lpszCommence, LPSTR lpszFinish)
{
  int iNumberChars, iLoop, iCount1, iCount;

  iNumberChars = lpszFinish - lpszCommence;

      for(iLoop = 1; iLoop <= iNumberChars; iLoop++)
      {
              for(iCount1 = 1; iCount1 <= 4; iCount1++)
              {
                    for(iCount = 1; iCount <= 8; iCount++)
                    {
                        _fstrcpy(lpszCommence, "A");
                        _fstrcpy(lpszCommence, "O");
              }
              _fstrcpy(lpszCommence, "B");
          }
          _fstrcpy(lpszCommence, "O");

      ++lpszCommence;
      }

  lpszCommence = lpszCommence - iNumberChars;

  /* clear */
  _fmemset(lpszCommence, 0, iNumberChars);

      //SendMessage(hMMI, STATUSMSG, IDS_PURGE, 0L);

}
```

The core of the implemented routine and the final VDM specifications are very similar. The code which has been added is primarily concerned with the implementation in the target hardware and operating system. A formal proof of correctness against the specification is hindered by the absence of an appropriate proof theory for the implementation language. However, informal examination of these structures would suggest that the implementation respects the formal specification.

3.5 Training

One objective of the study was to assess the training requirement needed to introduce formal specification into the design process. A basic one week course in the use of formal specification and the IFAD Toolbox was given, and was sufficient for imparting general specification skills. Overall, this is an encouraging result in that it suggests that the training overhead associated with the introduction of formal specification into a design process is typical of introducing a new technology into a company. The engineers, who had no background in formal methods, found it straightforward to apply. Consultancy from expert users was found to be essential when the engineers were starting to apply formal specification. This could be supplied either by experienced practitioners within the company, or by an outside consultant.

3.6 Tool Support

The formal path used the VDM Specification Language supported by a computer-based tool, the IFAD VDM-SL Toolbox, which allowed the specification to be type checked and animated. These facilities allowed engineers who were unfamiliar with the language to quickly learn how to write well-formed formal specifications.

It is important that the introduction of formal design into the development process be supported by computer based tool. Tool support was regarded as a practical necessity for the formal path to be followed at all. For a perspective on the practical use of the Toolbox, see [Muk95].

The use of animation allowed the system design to be examined early in the development process and let the engineers consider if the specified behaviour met expectations. The test cases used at this stage were carried forward through the programme and were eventually applied to the final system. This technique for demonstrating conformance to requirements could be applied by inexperienced engineers who have good domain knowledge but relatively little expertise in formal specification. For this reason it is believed to be a more attractive technique than formal proof.

3.7 Presentation of Specifications

VDM-SL was used in the formal path because of the availability of expertise and tool support for this language. In principle, any other model-oriented formal specification language susceptible to the same degree of type-checking and animation with sufficiently good tool support could have been used.

The Standard version of VDM-SL has an alternative ASCII syntax which does not use the mathematical symbols commonly found in formal specifications. The engineers expressed a preference for the the ASCII syntax, even though it is more verbose. This is probably due to their familiarity with programming languages and the IFAD Toolbox's use of the ASCII version of the language. In discussing formal specifications with colleagues unfamiliar with formal notation, the ASCII syntax was also preferred as a less intimidating alternative to the mathematical syntax.

4 Discussion

As indicated in the introduction, this study did not aim to show the absolute worth of formal specification. However, it does add to the body of evidence in the public domain on the costs and benefits of using formal techniques. In this section, we consider the main points which BASE have felt to be of relevance to them from the study. Recall from Section 2.1 that the study was intended to assess the effectiveness of formal techniques (costs and benefits), the problems and difficulties of adding formal techniques to the development process and the training requirement associated with formal specification. Each of these areas is considered in turn.

Effectiveness

The study indicated that adding formal specification can bring real benefits to a product development without incurring a prohibitive cost overhead when the costs are considered over the entire life cycle, providing it is applied where appropriate, and is applied in conjunction with other design methodologies which cater for large systems. The opportunity afforded for early error detection and resolution are expected to contribute to a reduction in time to market.

The development process clearly illustrated how the detection of errors late in the design process can lead to expense in making corrections and result in code which is poorly supported by the design documentation and is difficult to maintain. This is often stated in the literature as a driver to good systems design as a cost saver. Tests developed from a poor understanding of the system will not necessarily detect design flaws. These may be found for the first time by the customer.

It was felt that the major benefits of adding formal specification are seen in the better definition of the data used, and the identification of exception conditions. Defining data (in the system state and interfaces) in an implementation-independent manner allows this information to be passed through the various design stages without transformation, albeit with the addition of detail, until the system is implemented. The rigour required to define the data using a formal notation also forces the designer to question the customer (or to make and justify assumptions about the data) very early in the design process. It was noted that during the formal design of the trusted gateway considerably more time was spend in elucidating the data types which the system used and writing them down unambiguously (see [FBGL94]), possibly as a consequence of the use of a model-oriented specification language. The resulting formal definition can be included in the data dictionary entries used in the CASE tools.

Defining the required functionality is a more demanding activity because of the skill required to understand which parts of a design should be expressed formally and to be able to abstract the required functionality from requirements which are rarely clear, consistent and unambiguous.

Problems introducing formal specification

Formal specification did not make as valuable a contribution to the software design phase as was expected after the system design phase. This may have been because the example chosen was simple enough for the system design to be easily expressed as code, or it may be inherent in the method. Producing software from a formal specification is not simple even if the specification is executable: constructs used in the formal specification may not translate well into the target language leading to either an inefficient implementation, or a substantial amount of re-work to optimise the code design. One would expect that increasing local experience in designing efficient code from formal specifications would make this task easier, e.g. as well known implementation strategies are recorded for future use.

Training

It was originally felt that the same training would be appropriate for both systems and software engineers. However, after the experience of this project, we feel that short one- or two-day supplementary courses are needed to impart specialist skills. The systems engineers require skills in abstraction, functional specification and data specification. The software engineers require additional skills in refinement.

Training in the use of formal specification is essential for an engineer who is going to implement a formal specification. The ability to read a specification is not sufficient: the training must encompass the concepts behind the use of formal specification. In particular it should be stressed in training that the formal specification of an algorithm does not preclude many implementations from being used providing they are compatible with the formal specification. It is in this area that the skills of a software engineer will still be employed.

5 Outcome of the study

BASE has already applied formal specification to a sub-system in a larger secure system which required a high level of evaluation. The external authority which evaluates designs has indicated that the trusted gateway design using VDM-SL is could be evaluated to the new high level sought.

Guidelines are being developed recommending the use of formal specification techniques in the areas where this study has suggested they are beneficial, principally in the system design phase. However, it was also noted that formal specification should not be employed universally: each function should be considered on its own merits to assess whether or not the use of formal specification, with the attendant overhead, was justified.

Within the company, presentations have been given to the engineering community to disseminate the results of the trusted gateway study. With the existence of a small core of personnel who have some expertise with the use of formal specification, the aim is to spread the use into areas of projects where the use is beneficial. Formal specification will, at least initially, be applied where appropriate by reason of criticality, complexity of data or functionality.

6 Concluding Remarks

We have described the findings of the later stages of a comparative study in the development of a system with and without the use of formal techniques. One might conclude by asking how useful such a study is in increasing the exploitation of mathematically rigorous techniques in the development of software systems.

First, the object of the study was not to provide a "success story" for formalists. The trusted gateway project was aimed at one specific development process in BASE and geared to one area of application where the motivation to experiment with formal techniques already existed through the desire to reach specific levels of assurance. As an outcome of the trusted gateway development, it has become possible to develop some systems to a higher level of assurance than hitherto in BASE. Work is actively being pursued to widen the use of mathematically-based techniques where there is felt to be a genuine benefit in the company.

Although the trusted gateway development was a much more closely defined and monitored process than is usual in commercial software development, the sample size was one and a host of variable (human) factors were unaccounted for in the comparative analysis. To conduct a statistically significant "clinical trial" of formal methods would be beyond the means of most companies or even industrial sectors. We would suggest that adoption of formal methods is more likely to proceed via smaller-scale studies specific to the needs of particular groups, companies or sectors. The results of such studies will always be qualified, and rarely be generally applicable, but they will help in building a larger body of evidence which may be useful to those considering formal techniques for the first time, and certainly more useful than the unsupported claims which abound in some other areas of software engineering.

Acknowledgements

The authors would like to thank British Aerospace (Systems and Equipment) Limited for giving permission to publish many of the details of this work, as well as the engineers who participated in the study. We are grateful for the support of the European Commission (ESSI Grant 10670). JSF is grateful to the United Kingdom Engineering and Physical Sciences Research Council for support under an EPSRC Research Fellowship. All the authors are grateful to the anonymous referees for FME'96 for their helpful comments on an earlier draft of the paper.

References

[ABH+95] D.J. Andrews, H. Bruun, B.S. Hansen, P.G. Larsen, N. Plat, et al. *Information Technology — Programming Languages, their environments and system software interfaces — Vienna Development Method-Specification Language Part 1: Base language*. ISO, 1995.

[ELL94] René Elmstrøm, Peter Gorm Larsen, and Poul Bøgh Lassen. The IFAD VDM-SL Toolbox: A Practical Approach to Formal Specifications. *ACM Sigplan Notices*, 29(9):77–80, September 1994.

[FBGL94] J. S. Fitzgerald, T. M. Brookes, M. A. Green, and P. G. Larsen. Formal and informal specifications of a secure system component: first results in a comparative study. In M. Naftalin, B. T. Denvir, and M. Bertran, editors, *FME'94: Industrial Benefit of Formal Methods*, volume 873 of *Lecture Notes in Computer Science*, pages 35–44. Springer-Verlag, 1994.

[Fit95] J. S. Fitzgerald. The ConForm Project Home Page. World-wide web at URL:
http://www.cs.ncl.ac.uk/research/csr/projects/ConForm.html, 1995.

[FLBG95] J.S. Fitzgerald, P.G. Larsen, T.M. Brookes, and M.A. Green. *Applications of Formal Methods*, chapter 14 Developing a Security-critical System using Formal and Convential Methods. Prentice-Hall International Series in Computer Science, 1995.

[ITS91] Office for Official Publications of the European Community. *Information Technology Security Evaluation Criteria*, June 1991.

[MoD91a] United Kingdom Ministry of Defence, Directorate of Standardisation. *Safety Management Requirements for Defence Systems Containing Programmable Electronics*, 1991.

[MoD91b] United Kingdom Ministry of Defence,Directorate of Standardisation. *Procurement of safety-critical software*, 1991.

[Muk95] Paul Mukherjee. Computer-aided validation of formal specifications. *Software Engineering Journal*, pages 133–140, July 1995.

[WM86] P.T. Ward and S.J. Mellor. *Structured Development for Real-Time Systems*, volume 1-3. Yourdon Press, New York, 1985-1986.

Visual Verification of Safety and Liveness

Antti Valmari & Manu Setälä
Tampere University of Technology, Software Systems Laboratory
PO Box 553, FIN-33101 Tampere, FINLAND
email: ava@cs.tut.fi manu@cs.tut.fi

Abstract. An exceptionally user-friendly approach to computer-aided validation / verification of concurrent and reactive systems is presented. In it, the user needs not express his verification questions formally in detail. Instead, he specifies a point of view to the system by choosing a subset of its externally observable actions. An automaton abstracts and reduces the behaviour of the system according to the choice, and shows the result graphically on a computer screen. The resulting picture represents *all* executions of the system, as seen from the chosen point of view. Thus the information in it is as comprehensive as that obtained by ordinary verification. On the other hand, like ordinary testing, the method makes it possible for a system designer to get rapid feedback with ease, to "just try the system and see how it behaves". The article concentrates on practical and philosophical issues regarding the method and contains a detailed example.

Keywords: verification, process algebra, labelled transition system, reduction

1 Introduction

Embedded software systems, communication protocols, etc. are typically *reactive* and *concurrent*. A system is reactive if it is in continuous interaction with its environment. The desired behaviour of a reactive system is usually difficult to specify and sometimes even difficult to express, because the classical model of behaviour as a partial function mapping input to output does not apply. "Concurrency" means that the system consists of several co-operating autonomous units (often called *processes*). It is extremely difficult to ensure that the processes co-operate in the intended way in all possible situations. Consequently, reactive and concurrent systems are difficult to specify, design, and validate. The designers of embedded software, parallel algorithms, and protocols are painfully well aware of these problems.

The difficulties of ensuring the correct operation of concurrent and reactive systems have led to the development of several verification methods. Many of them consist of formulating and proving theorems about (a formal model of) the system. Although much of the theorem proving stage may be automated with modern theorem prover programs, these methods require significant human assistance in formulating the theorems, developing invariants and bound functions, guiding the theorem prover through difficult proofs, etc. It is clear that these methods can be beneficially used only by mathematically talented, mathematically oriented persons. Although there are significant examples of verifications of real systems by theorem proving [CGR93], it is questionable whether theorem proving can be taken into large scale industrial use in the near future.

Another group of verification methods is based on simulating (a formal model of) the system into all states it can reach. The simulation process can be fully automated. Therefore, these *state space* methods require less mathematical skills from the user than those based on theorem proving. Lots of examples of state space -based verification tools can be found in the surveys [Boc88, InP91, Fel93], and some tools have already reached the commercial stage, e.g. [FSE94]. However, the user has still the problems of formulating the verification questions and interpreting the results. When verifying "ad-hoc" properties (such as the absence of deadlocks) this is not difficult. The situation changes when the user wants to check, for instance, that a protocol implementation conforms to an informally given service specification.

The goal of the present work is to develop a verification approach which requires less mathematical skills from its user than current state space methods. Our approach is based on state space methods, and it has become possible because of recent developments in specification methods and verification algorithms for reactive systems. Its basic idea is that the user chooses a *point of view* to the system. In practice, this means that the user lists the actions of the system he is interested in. Then an automaton abstracts the behaviour of the system according to the selected point of view and displays the result in a computer screen in a graphical form. The user gets answers to his verification questions and other useful information simply by looking at this graphical representation.

Before discussing the technicalities of visual verification, we want to give the reader a good idea of what it looks like from the user's point of view. Therefore, in Sections 2 and 3 we discuss extensively the modelling and visual verification of a small but nontrivial system, namely Peterson's mutual exclusion algorithm for two customers [Pet81]. We pay special attention to the issues arising in the verification of the "eventual access" property. A much shorter version of this example appeared in [SeV94]. Section 4 is devoted to an informal discussion of the *Chaos-Free Failures Divergences* (*CFFD*) *theory* [VaT91, VaT95] underlying our visual verification method. The CFFD theory has been developed from the failures-divergences model for CSP [BrR85, Hoa85]. We investigate why the CFFD theory is much better suited for visual verification than the CSP and CCS theories [Mil89]. In Section 5 we turn into more philosophical issues. We analyse the role of visual verification in software engineering and try to give justification for the name "visual verification", although "visual validation" might have been a technically more correct term. We also compare visual verification to testing. The conclusions, including a brief discussion of whether the method scales up into the level of "real" systems, are in Section 6.

Compared to earlier verification methods based on abstraction (e.g. [MaV89]), the novelty of our approach is the high reliance on computer-generated graphical representations of abstracted behaviour, and the emphasis on after-analysis informal interpretation of the pictures instead of before-analysis formalisation of correctness requirements. The former is much easier but, as we will argue in Section 5, not essentially less reliable than the latter. Furthermore, we will see in Section 4.2 that the well-known semantic models typically used in abstraction-based verification are ill-suited for visual verification, because they either throw too much information away, or yield too big pictures. Visual verification of properties such as eventual access would not have been feasible without the recent development of the CFFD theory.

2 Example: Peterson's Algorithm

The CFFD theory underlying our visual verification method belongs to the large group of *process algebraic* theories. In them systems are modelled as collections of processes with synchronous communication (Ada-like rendez-vous). A process interacts with its environment by executing *visible actions* in *gates*. Each gate has a name, and a visible action occurring at a gate is denoted by the name of the gate. If two or more processes are connected to the same gate, then they have to execute the corresponding actions simultaneously. A process may also execute *invisible* or *internal* actions, which are not associated to any gate and cannot be synchronised to by other processes. Invisible actions are usually denoted by "τ". A process is often looked at as a *black-box* entity. That is, only the visible actions and their temporal orderings are considered important. This idea has made it possible to develop several powerful verification techniques and algorithms, which, in turn, are applied by visual verification.

The computer runs described in this article were performed using the *ARA* tool [VKCL93]. "ARA" is an abbreviation of "advanced reachability analysis". It can be used for analysing systems written in an extension of the specification language Basic Lotos [ISO89, BoB87]. Lotos is based on process algebras, and most of the analysis features of ARA are based on the CFFD theory. ARA was developed by VTT Electronics (VTT is a Finnish state-owned non-profit research and development organization).

2.1 First Model of Peterson's Algorithm

Peterson's algorithm is shown in pseudocode in Figure 1 almost exactly in the form it was given in [Pet81]. It consists of two processes, which communicate via three shared two-valued variables r_1, r_2 and t. Variable r_i ($1 \le i \le 2$) is used for indicating that customer i wants access to the critical section. Therefore, at line 1 r_i is set to **T** (= **true**), and again to **F** (= **false**) at line 5 when the customer exits the critical section. The purpose of t is to arbitrate between the customers if they simultaneously want access to the critical section. In line 2, each customer gives priority to the other by assigning its number to t. The notation "[*condition*] →" in line 3 denotes that a customer waits passively until the condition becomes valid. For instance, CUSTOMER_1 may proceed from line 3 to the critical section when either CUSTOMER_2 has not requested for the critical section ("$r_2 = \mathbf{F}$"), or CUSTOMER_1 has the priority ("$t = 1$"), or both.

In order to apply visual verification to the algorithm, it is necessary to express it in a formalism with gates, actions and synchronous communication. The use of ARA forced us to use Lotos in our experiments, but this choice has no fundamental significance. For simplicity, we represent the algorithm pictorially in this article. (The mapping from the pictures to Lotos is straightforward, and ARA can do the reverse mapping automatically.) Shared variables are not available. Therefore, we have to model r_1, r_2 and t by making them processes in their own right. Our first model of the algorithm thus consists of five processes, two representing the two customers, and three representing the shared variables.

$$\{ r_1 = r_2 = \mathbf{F} \wedge t = 1 \}$$

CUSTOMER$_1$	CUSTOMER$_2$
1: $r_1 := \mathbf{T}$	1: $r_2 := \mathbf{T}$
2: $t := 2$	2: $t := 1$
3: $[\, r_2 = \mathbf{F} \vee t = 1 \,] \rightarrow$	3: $[\, r_1 = \mathbf{F} \vee t = 2 \,] \rightarrow$
4: (* critical section *)	4: (* critical section *)
5: $r_1 := \mathbf{F}$	5: $r_2 := \mathbf{F}$

Fig. 1. Peterson's mutual exclusion algorithm

The statements of Peterson's algorithm are modelled by actions. For ease of reading, the names of the actions were chosen to reflect the effects of the corresponding statements. Thus the statements "r_1 := T" and "r_2 := T" at lines 1 of CUSTOMER$_1$ and CUSTOMER$_2$ are given the names $setr_1T$ and $setr_2T$, respectively. Similarly, *sett2* and *sett1* model line 2, and $setr_1F$ and $setr_2F$ model line 5. The tests at line 3 are represented by actions r_1isF, r_2isF, *tis1* and *tis2*. The comments on line 4 need not be modelled.

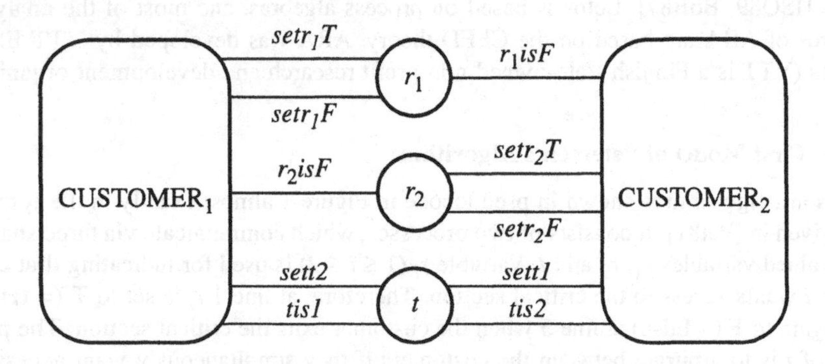

Fig. 2. Overall structure of the first model of Peterson's algorithm

The five processes are shown in Figure 2. The figure shows also which processes synchronize on each action.

Figure 3 shows the behaviours of processes CUSTOMER$_1$ and t in *labelled transition system* (*LTS*) form. An LTS is a graph-like structure with edges labelled by action names. It specifies what actions the corresponding process may perform and in which order. In Figure 3, the possible values "1" and "2" of variable t are represented by the two states of process t. (Another possibility would have been to store the value of variable t into a local variable of the corresponding process, but it would have made the presentation more complicated, because we would have had to introduce more notational conventions.) The state of t may be tested by trying actions *tis1* and *tis2*; exactly one of them is enabled at any instant of time. Action *sett1* takes t to the state corresponding to the value 1 independently of the state *t* happened to be in when *sett1* was executed. Action *sett2* works in a similar way.

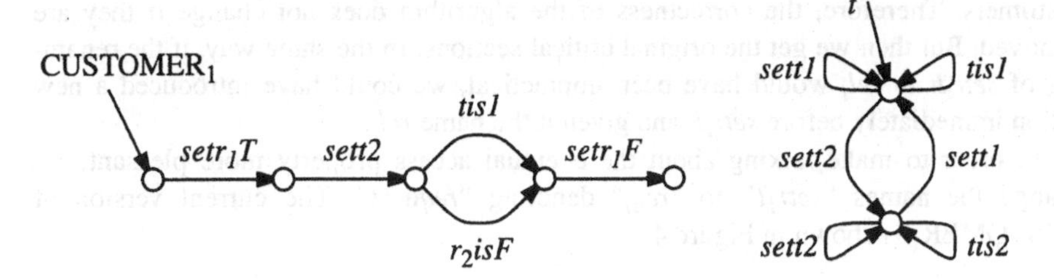

Fig. 3. LTSs of two processes of the first model

LTSs for the remaining processes can be obtained from those in Figure 3 by changing the names of actions in an obvious way.

Figures 2 and 3 model accurately Peterson's algorithm as it was given in [Pet81] and Figure 1. However, the model is in several ways unsuitable for verification. Therefore, in the next two subsections we modify it considerably.

2.2 Tuning the Model for Visual Verification

The purpose of Peterson's algorithm is to guarantee that at any instant of time, no more than one customer is in its critical section. We call this property *mutual exclusion.* Furthermore, the algorithm should guarantee the *eventual access* property: if a customer has requested access to the critical section, it should eventually be given permission to enter the section.

In order to analyse how well the model developed in the previous subsection satisfies the purpose of Peterson's algorithm, we have to recognise those actions which are important for the mutual exclusion and eventual access properties. Mutual exclusion holds if and only if CUSTOMER$_2$ is never in the state preceding action $setr_2F$ while CUSTOMER$_1$ is in the state preceding $setr_1F$. Talking about local states of processes is, however, a violation against the black-box view assumed by the verification algorithms used by visual verification. Fortunately, this problem is easy to solve: we make visible the actions preceding and succeeding the interesting states, and reason from the visible actions executed so far whether the customer is in its critical section. So, we should make actions r_1isF, r_2isF, *tis1*, *tis2*, $setr_1F$ and $setr_2F$ visible.

The name "$setr_1F$" is not, however, very informative from the verification point of view. Therefore, we give it a new name "rel_1", corresponding to the fact that with this action CUSTOMER$_1$ *rel*eases the critical section. Similarly, $setr_2F$ is re-baptized to rel_2.

According to the same logic we should next modify the names *tis1* and r_2isF to $enter_1$, but now we have a problem: two actions have to be mapped into one name without modifying the synchronisation structure of the model. Actually, Lotos has features with which this can be done, but again we prefer a solution which does not force us to introduce extra notational conventions. Namely, we introduce a new action immediately before rel_1 and call it $enter_1$, and similarly with CUSTOMER$_2$. The critical section of CUSTOMER_i is now interpreted to be the state between actions $enter_i$ and rel_i. Actions $enter_1$ and $enter_2$ will be used only for verification purposes, and they will not be synchronised to by other processes of the model than the corresponding customers. Therefore, the correctness of the algorithm does not change if they are removed. But then we get the original critical sections. In the same way, if the renaming of $setr_iF$ to rel_i would have been impractical, we could have introduced a new action immediately before $setr_iF$ and given it the name rel_i.

In order to make talking about the eventual access property more pleasant, we change the names "$setr_iT$" to "req_i" denoting "*req*uest". The current version of CUSTOMER_1 is shown in Figure 4.

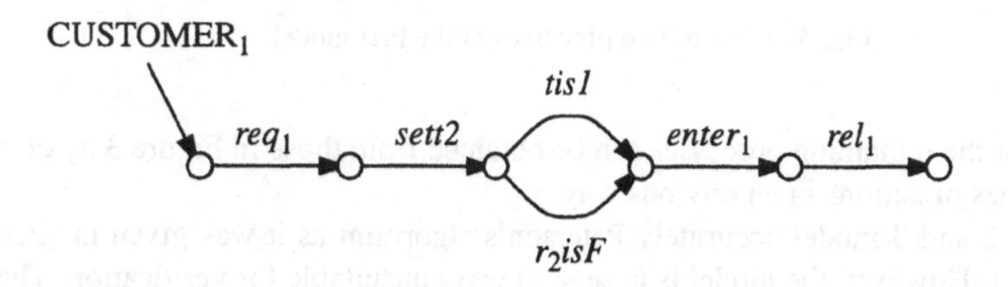

Fig. 4. Second version of CUSTOMER_1

The interesting actions regarding the mutual exclusion and eventual access properties are now called req_1, req_2, $enter_1$, $enter_2$, rel_1 and rel_2. We declare them visible and the others invisible.

Our model of Peterson's algorithm is now technically in a suitable form for visual verification. Unfortunately, it has some subtle but serious problems: it implicitly contains some unjustified assumptions. Therefore, an attempt to verify it using *any* verification method (visual verification or others) would yield incorrect results. In the next subsection we fix these problems.

2.3 Fixing Incorrect Implicit Assumptions

The model developed in Section 2.2 represents Figure 1 accurately, and is technically suitable for visual verification. However, it contains an implicit assumption which should not be made. Namely, in it customers try to get access to their critical sections only once. A verification conducted using it reveals whether the mutual exclusion property holds when the customers try to enter the critical sections for the first time, but it does not tell anything about what happens in subsequent times.

To fix this problem, we redirect the rel_i-actions to lead to the initial states. It is important to notice that the algorithm in [Pet81] did not contain this kind of return to initial state. Instead, its correctness proof took into account the possibility that it is repeated any number of times. That is, Peterson did not represent repetition formally in the algorithm, but informally in its correctness proof. This episode is an example of the fact that the use of a formal verification method forces the formalisation of details which may be difficult to recognise from the original problem description.

After this modification, the model can be used for the verification of the mutual exclusion property. Regarding the eventual access property, one problem still remains.

Namely, we have not specified what actions the customers *have to do* eventually, and what they *may choose to do not* if they don't want to. It is obvious that if one customer stays in its critical section forever, then the other customer cannot ever be granted access to its critical section without violating the mutual exclusion property. So, we have to require that if CUSTOMER_i has just executed $enter_i$, then it will execute rel_i sooner or later. In general, if a customer has started to execute its part of the mutual exclusion algorithm, it should execute it to completion (if it can).

On the other hand, a customer needs not ever request for access to the critical section if it does not want to. Therefore, the actions req_i are in a special position: the customers may legally forever refuse executing them, even if they are the only executable actions in the whole system. This difference between req_i and the other actions has not been encoded into our model. The CFFD theory includes the general assumption that if something can happen, then something will eventually happen. As a consequence, our current model of the customers specifies that a customer will eventually request for access to the critical section, if nothing else can happen. But under this assumption eventual access would be guaranteed even by an algorithm which first grants access to CUSTOMER_1, then to CUSTOMER_2, then again to CUSTOMER_1, and so on independently of who has requested for access.

Representing the difference between actions (or statements) which need and need not be performed is tricky. In temporal logics various *fairness* assumptions are used for this task. Fairness assumptions do not, however, work in the context of the CFFD theory (or almost any other process algebraic theory, for that matter), because they are not *compositional* in the sense required by the algorithms (see Section 4.2). Therefore, we model the difference using extra actions as follows.

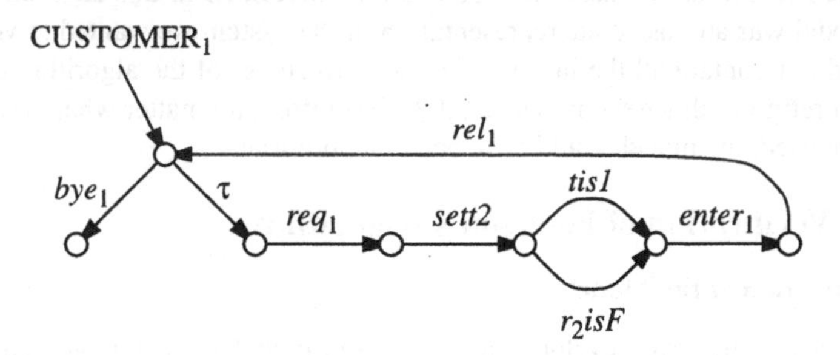

Fig. 5. Final version of CUSTOMER_1

When a customer is in its initial state, there are two possibilities: it will eventually request for access to the critical section, or it will not. This decision can be modelled by two actions starting at the initial state, one leading to the state immediately preceding action req_i, and the other leading to a deadlock state. These actions should be inaccessible to the other processes of the model, because otherwise they might force the decision by blocking one of the actions, which would be against the assumption that the decision is the customer's. So, it would be natural to make them invisible. However, the action leading to the deadlock is necessary for interpreting the verification results. Therefore, we give it the name bye_i, and require that only CUSTOMER_i is connected to it. The resulting model of CUSTOMER_1 is in Figure 5.

The overall structure of the final model is shown in Figure 6. In the figure, visible actions are shown as actions accessible outside the system.

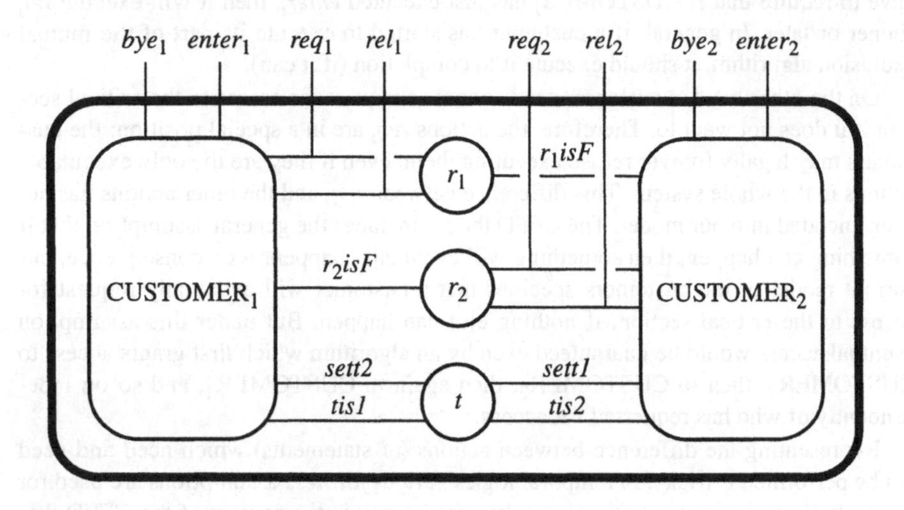

Fig. 6. Overall structure of the final model

At this point we would like to emphasize that it was not our visual verification method which forced us to make the modifications described in this subsection. The previous model was an inaccurate representation of the system we wanted to verify — it simply did not contain all the information the correctness of the algorithm depends on. (We will return to this issue in Section 3.2.) Therefore, no matter what verification method were used, the model would have been inappropriate.

3 Visual Verification of Peterson's Algorithm

3.1 Verification of the Model

In the previous section we developed a verification model for Peterson's algorithm. The ARA tool can be used to construct an LTS representing its behaviour, i.e. the joint behaviour of the processes of the system. It has 74 states and 140 transitions. So it is too big for manual inspection or to be shown here.

Like many other tools based on process algebraic theories, ARA contains a *reduction* algorithm which takes an LTS as input and produces a smaller LTS which behaves in the same way as the input LTS as far as the visible actions are concerned. When this algorithm is applied to the LTS obtained from our Lotos verification model of Peterson's algorithm, the result has 33 states and 51 transitions. It is thus much smaller than the input LTS, but still far too big for manual inspection.

With typical state space verification techniques, the next step would be an investigation of the properties of the LTS with some query or model checking tool; or a repetition of the LTS construction after adding assertions and other "on-the-fly" error-catching devices to the verification model; or the (automated) comparison of the LTS with another LTS representing the requirement specification of the system. (Actually, ARA was originally designed for the latter two kinds of verification.) The use of a query tool requires that the user can find the right questions and express them in the input language of the tool. Except for some simple properties such as mutual exclusion, the design of error-catching devices is difficult and error prone. For instance, the eventual access property has to be formulated using devices such as states which should or should not be visited infinitely many times during an execution. And, finally, LTS comparison requires that someone designs the LTS representing the requirements. In conclusion, all these techniques require that the user has a good idea of what he wants to know about the system, and that he can express it in a formal way.

With visual verification the user needs not know more at this stage than what actions are important regarding the properties he wants to check. For instance, the validity of the mutual exclusion property depends only on the relative ordering of entries to and exits from the critical sections. In terms of our verification model, this means that only $enter_1$, $enter_2$, rel_1 and rel_2 are important. Therefore, we continue by declaring them visible and the other actions invisible. Then we use ARA to construct and reduce the LTS of the model. The full LTS of the new model differs from the full LTS of the previous model only in that all bye_i- and req_i-transitions have been changed to invisible transitions, so the numbers of states and transitions are still 74 and 140. However, the reduced LTS has become much smaller, because more actions are invisible. It contains only 4 states and 5 transitions, and it is shown in Figure 7.[1]

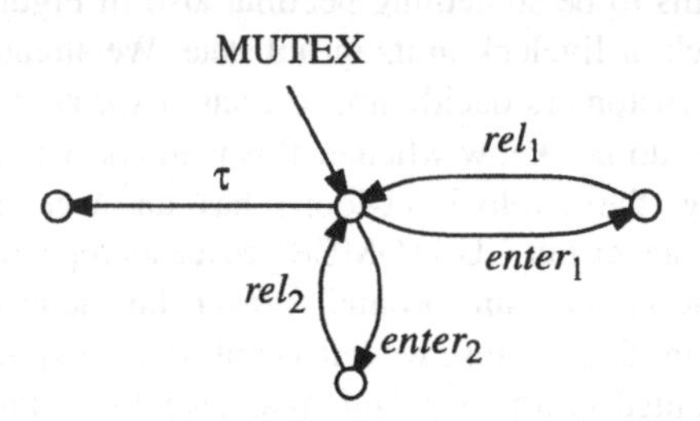

Fig. 7. A reduced LTS for verifying mutual exclusion

It is easy to see from Figure 7 that CUSTOMER_1 is in its critical section in the rightmost state and only in it, and CUSTOMER_2 is in its critical section in the bottommost state and only in it. The two customers are thus never in their critical sections simultaneously, and the mutual exclusion property is not violated.

However, if we investigate Figure 7 further, it may start to seem surprising. For instance, why is there a τ-transition leading to a deadlock? It is because we wanted that

1 ARA has a tool for showing small LTSs on computer screen. Figure 7 was designed with it. We had to redraw the figure because, to save space, ARA does not write action names next to the transitions; instead, it represents them by different colours. All LTS figures in this article were drawn according to the lay-out designed by ARA.

in our model, customers need not ever (or ever again) request for access to the critical sections if they do not want to. If both customers choose not to request for access, then nothing happens in the system, so it is in a deadlock. The reader may also miss a τ-transition before action $enter_1$, or a state where an $enter_1$-rel_1 cycle is possible but an $enter_2$-rel_2 cycle is not. The absence of such states and transitions will be explained after the introduction of CFFD-semantics in Section 4.1. We will explain there also why it is good and important that they are absent.

To verify that CUSTOMER_1 eventually gets access to the critical section if it requests for it, it is sufficient to leave visible the actions req_1 and $enter_1$. The resulting reduced LTS is shown in Figure 8. From it we see that the system is bound to execute $enter_1$ if it has executed req_1, so the eventual access property holds.

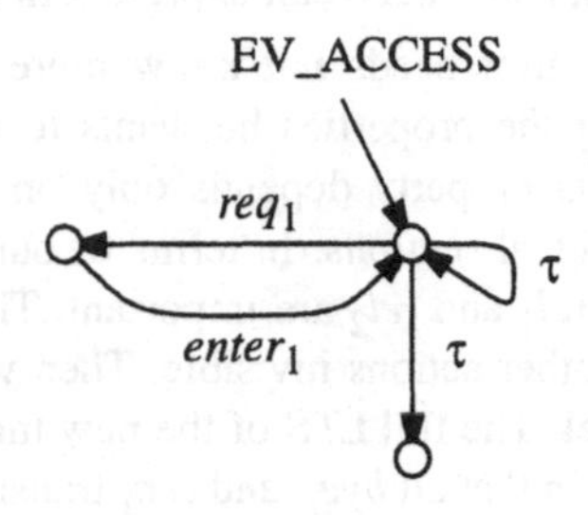

Fig. 8. A reduced LTS for verifying eventual access

However, there seems to be something peculiar also in Figure 8. According to it, the system may deadlock or livelock in its initial state. We already know that the system terminates if both customers decide not to request for access to the critical sections. Unfortunately, we do not know whether this is the *only* reason for the deadlock in Figure 8. Similarly, the livelock (τ-loop) has an acceptable explanation. If CUSTOMER_1 requests never but CUSTOMER_2 requests repeatedly for access to the critical section, then the system runs around forever, but none of the corresponding actions is visible in our model, because we left visible only req_1 and $enter_1$. So the infinite execution is represented by a τ-loop. But, again, we do not know whether there are also other reasons for the livelock. According to Figure 8, it is at least in theory possible that CUSTOMER_1 wants to request for access to the critical section, but cannot do that, because the system has deadlocked or livelocked.

In order to ensure that the deadlock and livelock in Figure 8 have only legal reasons, we analyse one more model. Its purpose is to check whether CUSTOMER_1 can request for access to the critical section if it wants to. We call this property *unprevented request.* Action bye_1 denotes that CUSTOMER_1 does not any more want to get access to the critical section. Therefore, we leave actions req_1 and bye_1 visible. Furthermore, in order to get rid of the τ-loop, we have to leave visible at least one of the actions of CUSTOMER_2 other than bye_2. Without knowing what would be the best one, we arbitrarily choose req_2. The resulting reduced LTS is shown in Figure 9.

From Figure 9 we see that deadlocks and livelocks cannot prevent CUSTOMER_1 from executing req_1, so the unprevented request property holds.

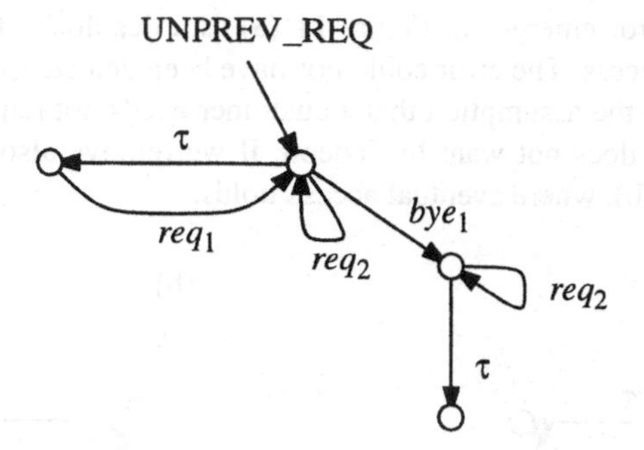

Fig. 9. A reduced LTS for verifying that CUSTOMER_1 may perform req_1 if it wants to

To complete our verification, we have to repeat the analysis of the eventual access and unprevented request properties with the roles of the customers reversed. As the result, we get figures which are otherwise the same as Figures 8 and 9, but all "1"s have been replaced by "2"s and vice versa.

3.2 Additional Checks

We have verified that our model has the mutual exclusion, eventual access and unprevented request properties. The development of our verification model was, however, rather complicated; we motivated two modifications to Peterson's original version by saying that otherwise certain kinds of errors cannot be detected. This raises the question: can we rely on the ability of even our final verification model to reveal errors? To test this, we do now some analysis runs with some errors introduced to Peterson's algorithm, and check that the errors manifest themselves in the reduced LTSs.

In our first check we remove the statements at line 2 of Figure 1. This should fool CUSTOMER_1 to think that it is its turn to enter the critical section although in reality it is not, leading to a violation of the mutual exclusion property. And it does, as can be seen from the leftmost state in the bottom row in Figure 10.

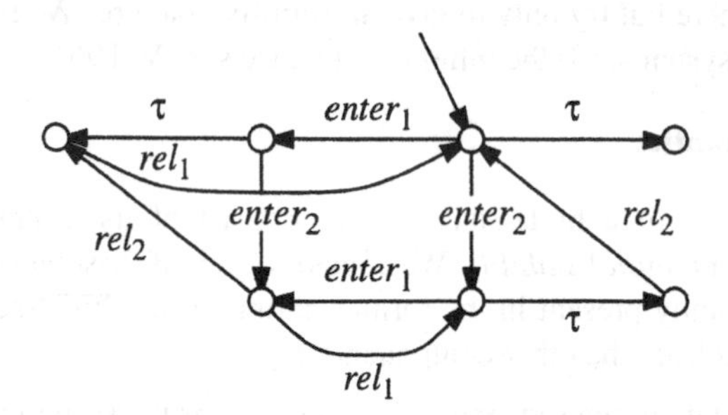

Fig. 10. A mutual exclusion verification picture of an incorrect algorithm

In the next check we remove the tests "$r_1 = \mathbf{F}$" and "$r_2 = \mathbf{F}$" from line 3 of Figure 1. After this modification, the algorithm forces the customers to enter their critical sections by turns. This error emerges in Figure 11 (a) as a deadlock after req_1, causing violation of eventual access. The error could not have been detected with a verification model not representing the assumption that a customer needs not request for access to its critical section if it does not want to. Indeed, if we remove also the bye_i-actions, then we get Figure 11 (b), where eventual access holds.

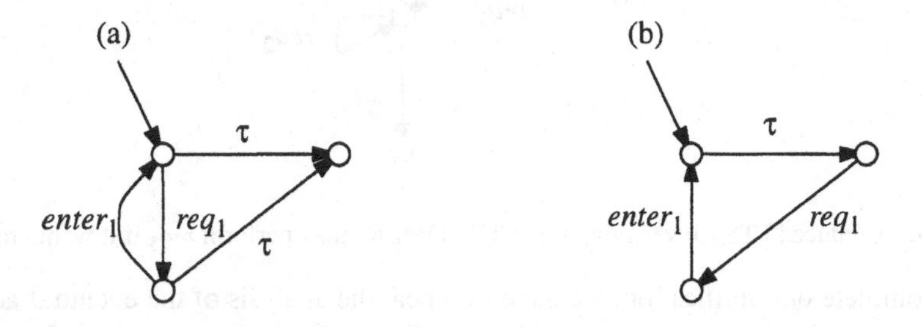

Fig. 11. Eventual access verification pictures of an incorrect algorithm when the customers (a) may (b) may not decide *not* to request for access to the critical section

4 Theoretical Basis of Visual Verification

It is obvious from Section 3 that the ability to reduce LTSs without modifying their visible-action-related (often called *externally observable*) properties is crucial to visual verification. Nothing can be modified without changing at least some of its properties — at least the number of states changes in a reduction (or otherwise we get no reduction). Of course, on the basis of reduced LTSs no conclusions should be made about properties which are not preserved in the reduction. Therefore, it is important to know exactly what properties are preserved.

The reduction algorithm in the ARA tool preserves the so-called *Chaos-Free Failures Divergences* (*CFFD*) *semantics* of systems. CFFD-semantics were first described in [VaT91], and their theory has been extensively studied in [VaT95]. We do not repeat the formal theory here but try only to give an intuitive picture. We restrict our discussion to finite-state systems; for the infinite-state case see [VaT95].

4.1 CFFD-Semantics

The CFFD-semantics of a finite-state system consist of its *traces*, *stable failures*, *divergence traces* and *initial stability*. We consider each of these in turn. (Actually, the traces are not explicitly present in the formal definition of CFFD-semantics, because they can be derived from the other components.)

A *trace* of a system is any sequence of visible actions the system may execute starting from its initial state. The system is allowed to execute invisible actions before, after, and between the visible actions, but they are not included into the trace. The execution need not be complete; even the execution consisting of doing nothing generates a trace, namely the *empty* trace containing zero visible actions. The empty trace is usually denoted by "ε". The traces of the model in Figure 8 are

ε,
req$_1$,
req$_1$ *enter*$_1$,
req$_1$ *enter*$_1$ *req*$_1$,
req$_1$ *enter*$_1$ *req*$_1$ *enter*$_1$,

and so on. The significance of the traces for verification should be apparent. For instance, mutual exclusion is violated if and only if the system has a trace where *enter*$_1$ and *enter*$_2$ occur without *rel*$_1$ in between, or *enter*$_2$ and *enter*$_1$ occur without *rel*$_2$ in between.

Stable failures carry information about deadlocks and the choices made or allowed by the system. A stable failure consists of two components. The first component is a trace of the system, and the second component is a set of actions. The interpretation of a stable failure is that it is possible for the system to execute the trace in such a way that the system ends up in a state where it can execute neither actions from the set nor invisible actions. For instance,

(*req*$_1$ *enter*$_1$ *req*$_1$, {*req*$_1$})

is a stable failure of the system in Figure 8, because it cannot execute *req*$_1$ or τ after cycling the *req*$_1$-*enter*$_1$-cycle $1^1/_2$ times; and

(*enter*$_1$ *rel*$_1$ *enter*$_1$ *rel*$_1$ *enter*$_2$ *rel*$_2$, {*enter*$_1$, *enter*$_2$})

is a stable failure of the system in Figure 7, because it can make the τ-move and end up in a deadlock any time it has returned into its initial state. However, (ε, {*req*$_1$}) is not a stable failure of the system in Figure 5, because in the initial state it can execute the invisible action τ, and after τ it can perform *req*$_1$. On the other hand, (ε, {*bye*$_1$}) is its stable failure.

A system can end up in a deadlock after executing the trace $a_1a_2...a_n$ if and only if ($a_1a_2...a_n$, Σ) is its stable failure, where Σ is the set of all visible actions of the system. In this way stable failures record the deadlocks of the system.

A *divergence trace* of a system is a trace such that, after executing it, the system may be able to execute invisible actions without limit. For instance, due to the τ-loop adjacent to the initial state of the LTS in Figure 8, ε and *req*$_1$ *enter*$_1$ are its divergence traces but *req*$_1$ is not. Divergence traces carry information about the livelock and progress properties of systems. For instance, the system in Figure 8 is guaranteed to perform *enter*$_1$ after *req*$_1$, but not the other way round, because it may run around forever in the τ-loop instead (and because it may deadlock).

The *initial stability* consists of only one bit of information. A system is initially stable if and only if its first action cannot be invisible. Initial stability is included into CFFD-semantics for technical reasons we cannot go into here (see [VaT91 or VaT95]). In many cases it can be omitted. Its only effect is that sometimes the reduced LTS may contain an apparently unnecessary initial τ-move, such as the one in Figure 11 (b).

The fact that CFFD-semantics preserve only the traces, stable failures, divergence traces and initial stability has sometimes surprising consequences. For instance, in Figure 7 the transition labelled *enter*$_1$ starts at the initial state, although CUSTOMER$_1$ performs four other actions before *enter*$_1$. This is because the four actions were declared invisible, and the reduction algorithm in ARA introduces invisible actions to reduced LTSs only where necessary for representing the stable failures, divergence traces and initial instability. Action $enter_1$ does not need a preceding τ-transition, because the only effect of such a transition would be the addition of stable failures such as (ε, $\{enter_2\}$) to the semantics, but they are already in the semantics because of the τ-transition leading to a deadlock.

An attempt to locate the execution of bye_2 in Figure 9 will yield another surprise. After bye_2, CUSTOMER$_2$ cannot ever perform req_2; before bye_2, nothing can prevent CUSTOMER$_2$ from executing req_2. In the leftmost state of Figure 9 bye_2 thus appears to have been executed, while in the initial state it appears not. But how can there then be a transition from the leftmost state to the initial state? The answer is that because bye_2 was declared invisible, the figure does not even try to show when it is executed. Instead, it shows whether it is possible for the system to refuse visible actions. At any state the system may invisibly refuse req_2 by choosing bye_2 instead. This is shown by τ-transitions leading to states where req_2 is not executable. The system refuses req_2 also if it has performed bye_2 some earlier time. CFFD-semantics do not reveal whether the decision between executing and refusing req_2 was made now or some earlier time. It shows only that after the visible actions shown, the system may be in a state where req_2 is executable, but it may also be in a state where it is not. Note that before executing bye_1, the system cannot enter a state where req_1 cannot be executed immediately or after some invisible actions. This is true about the model, preserved by CFFD-semantics, and apparent in Figure 9.

Similar reasoning explains why Figure 7 does not have a state where an $enter_1$-rel_1 cycle is possible but an $enter_2$-rel_2 cycle is not.

The user has also to be careful with the interpretation of divergences. CFFD-semantics do not distinguish τ-loops which can be exited from τ-loops which cannot. For instance, CFFD-semantics consider equivalent the two LTSs in Figure 12. The reader may dislike this feature of CFFD-semantics (so do we, because it makes more difficult the analysis of progress properties), but so far nobody has been able to find a compositional CFFD-like semantic model not suffering from this problem.

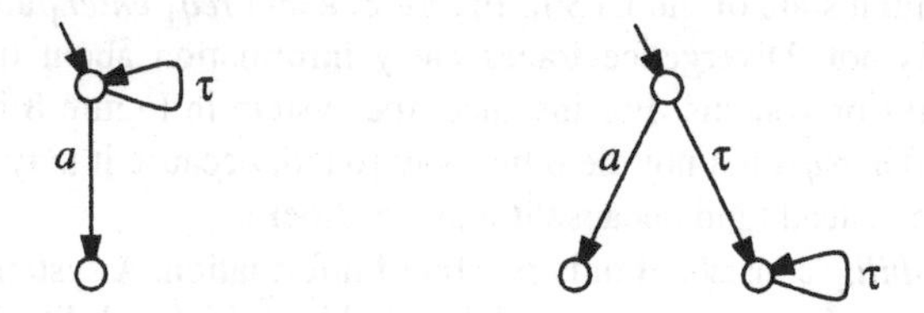

Fig. 12. Two CFFD-equivalent processes

In conclusion, difficulties in understanding reduced LTSs are often due to forgetting that CFFD-semantics allow throwing lots of information away. It is, however, crucial for visual verification that the LTS figures are as small as possible. Therefore, we have to make a compromise; we cannot afford to preserve information which is not really needed. In the next subsection we explain why we think that CFFD-semantics are a good compromise.

4.2 Why CFFD-Semantics?

Why did we choose CFFD-semantics for the basis of visual verification, and not one of the well-established semantic models, such as the *trace semantics*, *CSP-semantics* [BrR85, Hoa85], or Milner's *observation equivalence* [Mil89]?

The *trace semantics* of a system consist simply of its traces. They can be used for the verification of so-called *safety properties*, such as mutual exclusion. Actually, they are the best possible semantic model for verifying general safety properties. However, because they do not preserve deadlock and divergence information, they do not consider the system in Figure 8 any different from the system in Figure 13 (a), although the eventual access property holds in the former but not in the latter. Hence trace semantics do not preserve many of the properties we want to verify.

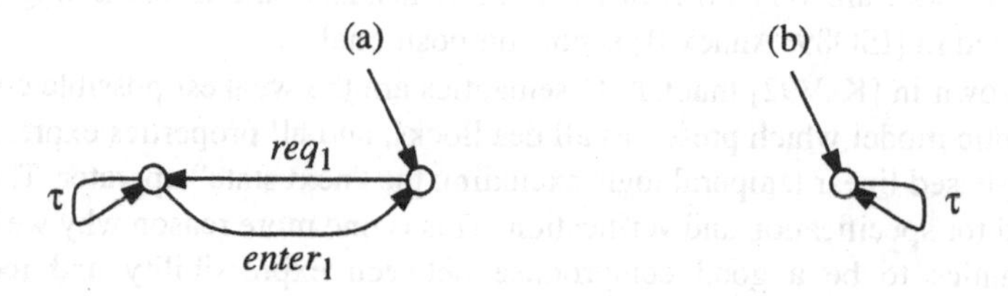

Fig. 13. A (a) trace equivalent (b) CSP-equivalent LTS to the LTS in Figure 8

CSP-semantics are very similar to CFFD-semantics; actually, the latter were developed from them. Because of reasons we cannot go into here, CSP-semantics do not preserve any information of a process after it has executed a divergence trace. Therefore, if CSP-semantics were used, the analysis of the eventual access property would have produced the LTS in Figure 13 (b) instead of Figure 8. Figure 13 (b) does not tell us anything about the eventual access property. CSP-semantics are thus not very useful if we may have livelocks in our systems. Because visual verification is experimental, intermediate models often contain livelocks even if we want the final models not to contain them. Furthermore, visual verification requires that only few actions are left visible, which causes "view-dependent" livelocks such as the one in Figure 8. In the absence of livelocks, CSP- and CFFD-semantics are almost the same, so it does not make any difference to use one instead of the other. ("Almost", because CSP-semantics do not contain the "initial stability" component.)

The "standard" version of Milner's *observation equivalence* does not preserve divergence information, so it, too, would be useless in the verification of eventual access. It is possible to add divergence preservation to observation equivalence. The result was investigated in [Elo94]. It was proven in [Elo94] that divergence-preserving observation equivalence preserves strictly more information than CFFD-semantics. Hence it can be used for the verification of all the properties which may be verified using CFFD-semantics, and more. However, the extra strength does not come for free. The more properties are preserved, the less an LTS can be reduced. If the semantics preserve properties we are not interested in, then the reduced LTSs are often unnecessarily big. For instance, with divergence-preserving observation equivalence the LTS in Figure 7 would have contained 33 states and 64 transitions, making it virtually unreadable. Similarly, Figures 8 and 9 would have grown to 10 and 10 states and 16 and 22 transitions. In the case of Figures 7 and 9 the numbers would have been the same with ordinary observation equivalence, because the LTSs shown in them do not contain divergences. So, divergence-preserving and ordinary observation equivalence do not seem to produce small enough reduced LTSs for visual verification.

One important reason for choosing CFFD-semantics was that they (like all the above-mentioned established semantic models) are *compositional*. That is, if we replace a component process in a system by a CFFD-equivalent process, then the resulting system is CFFD-equivalent to the original one. Compositionality gives us powerful weapons for fighting the *state explosion* problem (see e.g. [ChK93, GrS90, MaV89, Val93]), which all state space verification methods suffer from. Although it may sound surprising, compositional semantic models preserving required properties and not much more are very difficult to find. For instance, the Lotos testing equivalence described in [ISO89, Annex B] is not compositional.

It was shown in [KaV92] that CFFD-semantics are the weakest possible compositional semantic model which preserves all deadlocks, and all properties expressible in classic state-based linear temporal logic excluding the "next state" operator. This logic is often used for specification and verification. This is one more reason why we believe CFFD-semantics to be a good compromise between expressibility and reduction power.

5 Visual Verification in System Development

The basic difference between visual verification and classic state space verification is that the user of the former needs not specify his verification questions in great detail. Instead, he only lists the actions which are interesting regarding the property, and lets an automaton abstract away the uninteresting actions and represent the result in a graphical form. Then the user looks at the resulting picture and tries to decide whether the behaviour shown in it is acceptable.

Of course, if the user does not read the picture carefully, he may ignore some errors in the system. But the same may happen with classic verification methods if the user does not design and formalise verification questions carefully. With visual verification, the picture may warn him about problems he might not otherwise have even thought about. For instance, Figure 8 raised our concern about whether CUSTOMER_1 may be prevented from ever indicating that it wants access to the critical section. Similar feedback is more difficult to obtain with classic verification.

An ordinary test may be performed on software in two different ways. The user may compute the answer the program should produce before starting the test run, or he may just start the program and check the correctness of the output only after seeing it. The former approach is more systematic and the latter is more flexible. The former approach is often used in serious final testing, but it is almost certain that most programmers do test runs of the latter kind while developing programs.

Similarly, ordinary verification is good for checking the final result. However, when we are developing a system, it is useful to get some feedback about its behaviour without consuming too much effort for the designing of verification questions. Visual verification makes it possible to just "try the system and see what it does". On the other hand, the results of visual verification are different from the results of ordinary test runs in that they are comprehensive. No number of test runs can guarantee that the mutual exclusion property holds, but a single visual verification run may suffice.

The word "verification" is usually used to denote the act of checking that a system satisfies some specification. By "validation" people usually mean the act of checking that a system behaves as its designers or users want. Validation is by necessity informal, because at some stage the behaviour of the system has to be compared to the intuitive expectations living in the user's head. The user may write a formal specification expressing his expectations and verify that the system satisfies it, but then he has the problem of checking whether his specification agrees with his intuition. Therefore, no matter how we validate a system, there is always at least one informal step. With verification this step may be made easier, however, because the behaviour of the specification may be much easier to understand than the behaviour of the system, and verification guarantees that if the specification is acceptable, then also the system is.

In our visual verification method, the user does not write any document, formula or set of assertion statements expressing how he wants the system to behave. Instead, he asks an automaton to show the behaviour of the system from some point of view, and then accepts or rejects the result. Therefore, visual verification is not "verification" in the above sense of the word; "visual validation" would have been a technically more correct term.

The goal of validation is to get as much confidence as possible to the behaviour of the system. The obtained confidence level depends on many things, including the reliability of the formal steps (programmers of verification tools and even mathematicians make errors), and the difficulty of the unavoidable informal step. With ordinary verification the main concern is typically whether the user has found the right questions (and enough of them), and whether the representations of the questions as assertions, temporal logic formulas, etc. are accurate. With visual verification the main concern is typically whether the user interprets correctly the final LTS pictures. We believe that interpreting the pictures is no more difficult than writing temporal logic formulas, for instance. Therefore, we claim that the confidence level obtained by visual verification is not inferior to the confidence level obtainable by ordinary verification, and is far above the confidence level obtainable by performing test runs on the verification model. Quite the contrary, visual verification is sometimes better than ordinary verification, because a weird-looking picture may cause the user to realize problems he would not have otherwise even thought about.

So we believe that the confidence level obtained by visual verification is comparable to the confidence level obtained by ordinary verification. Furthermore, the reduction stage in visual verification is certainly formal. The term "visual validation" would have hidden the fact that the method is based on formal theory and automatic tools. Because of these reasons we chose the name "visual verification".

6 Conclusions

Visual verification makes it possible for system developers to get comprehensive information about the behaviours of their systems without having to pay much effort to the design of verification questions. In essence, ordinary verification answers the question

"Does the system behave in this way?", while visual verification answers the question "How does the system behave, as seen from this point of view?". Therefore, visual verification is much better suited for experimental use than ordinary verification. With it the system developer can play with his design ideas and get almost immediate feedback. If some picture looks peculiar, more information may be obtained by repeating the analysis with a different set of visible actions. We saw an example of this in Section 3.1, where we did an extra analysis to find out the reasons for the deadlock and livelock in Figure 8. We believe that due to these features, visual verification is easier to adopt by industrial system designers than ordinary verification.

Visual verification requires that the user is able to interpret the LTS pictures correctly. Ordinary verification requires that the user is able to recognise the essential features of the correct behaviour of the system and express them formally. Therefore, both approaches to verification require some skills from the user. In our opinion, mis-interpretation of LTS pictures is no more likely than insufficient or incorrect encoding of the expected correct behaviour. Furthermore, *all* formal verification methods require that all essential assumptions regarding the behaviour of the system are represented in its verification model in one way or another. We saw in Section 2.3 that important assumptions may be hidden in original system descriptions, so they may be easily missed. Because of these (and other) reasons, all verification methods are, in the end, unreliable. We believe that the results obtained by visual verification are in practice as reliable as those obtained by ordinary verification.

We used the recently developed CFFD semantic model in our visual verification method. This was not an arbitrary choice. We demonstrated in Section 4.2 that observation equivalence would have yielded too big pictures, and CSP-equivalence would have made impossible the analysis of systems with livelocks. So visual verification would not have been feasible with either of them. Visual verification of safety properties is possible with trace semantics, but if one wants to go beyond that, something like CFFD-equivalence is necessary.

An important question regarding the practicality of visual verification is whether it scales up into the level of "real" systems. Two issues may seem problematic:

- Will the reduced LTSs be small enough to be understandable?
- Will the LTS construction and reduction algorithms be able to process big enough systems?

In the case of Peterson's algorithm the reduced LTSs were certainly small enough. It is clear that to keep them small, the set of visible actions should be small and carefully chosen. It is therefore essential to concentrate on one aspect of the system at a time. For instance, in Section 3.1 we constructed one LTS picture for checking mutual exclusion, another one for eventual access, and yet another to ensure that the customer may not be prevented from requesting access to the critical section. We believe that this approach is applicable also with larger systems than Peterson's algorithm. Well-designed large systems contain several interfaces between system components, and they are likely to be amenable for visual verification. However, more experience has to be gathered before it can be said for certain how often in practice it is possible to obtain small enough LTSs.

The problem of too big systems hampers all state space verification methods, so here visual verification is not better or worse off than ordinary state space verification. The problem has been extensively studied and interesting results have been obtained. A proper discussion of them would be beyond the scope of this article, but let us mention that many of them are applicable in our context, such as compositional LTS construction [ChK93, GrS90, MaV89, Val93] and stubborn sets [WoG93, Val94]. See also [Val95] for a discussion of the state explosion problem in the context of CFFD-semantics.

In addition to Peterson's algorithm, we have applied visual verification to various versions of the alternating bit protocol [VKS96] and to a collision-avoidance protocol for the Ethernet, with good results. Capacity problems with the ARA tool have prevented us from analysing larger examples, but we are currently developing more powerful tools. One thing can be said for certain: a typical system designer can verify bigger systems and obtain more reliable results by visual verification than by just looking at his design.

Acknowledgements

The work of A. Valmari was partly funded by the Technical Research Centre of Finland (VTT) and the Technology Development Centre of Finland (TEKES) as part of the European Union ESPRIT BRA Project REACT (6021). The work of M. Setälä was funded by The Academy of Finland, project REFORM.

References

[Boc88] Bochmann, G. v.: *Usage of Protocol Development Tools: The Results of a Survey.* Proceedings of the 7th International Symposium on Protocol Specification, Testing and Verification (1987), North-Holland 1988.

[BoB87] Bolognesi, T. & Brinksma, E.: *Introduction to the ISO Specification Language LOTOS.* Computer Networks and ISDN Systems 14 1987 pp. 25–59. Also in: The Formal Description Technique LOTOS, North-Holland 1989, pp. 23–73.

[BrR85] Brookes, S. D. & Roscoe, A. W.: *An Improved Failures Model for Communicating Processes.* Proceedings of the NSF-SERC Seminar on Concurrency, Lecture Notes in Computer Science 197, Springer-Verlag, 1985, pp. 281–305.

[ChK93] Cheung, S. C. & Kramer, J.: *Enhancing Compositional Reachability Analysis with Context Constraints.* Proceedings of the first ACM SIGSOFT Symposium on the Foundations of Software Engineering, ACM Software Engineering Notes, 18(5) 1993, pp. 115–125.

[CGR93] Craigen, D., Gerhart, S. & Ralston, T.: *Formal Methods Reality Check: Industrial Usage.* Proceedings of Formal Methods Europe '93, Lecture Notes in Computer Science 670, Springer-Verlag 1993, pp. 250–267.

[Elo94] Eloranta, J.: *Minimal Transition Systems with Respect to Divergence Preserving Behavioural Equivalences.* Doctoral thesis, University of Helsinki, Department of Computer Science, Report A-1994-1, Helsinki, Finland 1994, 162 p.

[Fel93] Feldbrugge, F.: *Petri Net Tool Overview 1992.* Advances in Petri Nets 1993, Lecture Notes in Computer Science 674, Springer-Verlag 1993, pp. 169–209.

[FSE94] Formal Systems (Europe) Ltd.: *Failures Divergence Refinement User Manual and Tutorial,* version 1.4 1994.

[GrS90] Graf, S. & Steffen, B.: *Compositional Minimization of Finite State Processes.* Computer-Aided Verification '90 (Proceedings of a workshop), AMS-ACM DIMACS Series in Discrete Mathematics and Theoretical Computer Science, Vol. 3, American Mathematical Society 1991, pp. 57–73.

[Hoa85] Hoare, C. A. R.: *Communicating Sequential Processes.* Prentice-Hall 1985, 256 p.

[InP91] Inverardi, P. & Priami, C.: *Evaluation of Tools for the Analysis of Communicating Systems.* EATCS Bulletin 45, October 1991, pp. 158–185.

[ISO89] ISO 8807 International Standard: *Information processing systems – Open Systems Interconnection – LOTOS – A formal description technique based on the temporal ordering of observational behaviour.* International Organization for Standardization 1989, 142 p.

[KaV92] Kaivola, R. & Valmari, A.: *The Weakest Compositional Semantic Equivalence Preserving Nexttime-less Linear Temporal Logic.* Proceedings of CONCUR '92, Lecture Notes in Computer Science 630, Springer-Verlag 1992, pp. 207–221.

[MaV89] Madelaine, E. & Vergamini, D.: *AUTO: A Verification Tool for Distributed Systems Using Reduction of Finite Automata Networks.* Formal Description Techniques II (Proceedings of FORTE '89), North-Holland 1990, pp. 61–66.

[Mil89] Milner, R.: *Communication and Concurrency.* Prentice-Hall 1989, 260 p.

[Pet81] Peterson, G. L.: *Myths about the Mutual Exclusion Problem.* Information Processing Letters 12 (3) 1981, pp. 115–116.

[SeV94] Setälä, M. & Valmari, A.: *Validation and Verification with Weak Process Semantics.* Proceedings of Nordic Seminar on Dependable Computing Systems 1994, Lyngby, Denmark, August 1994, pp. 15–26.

[VaT91] Valmari, A. & Tienari, M.: *An Improved Failures Equivalence for Finite-State Systems with a Reduction Algorithm.* Protocol Specification, Testing and Verification XI (Proceedings of PSTV '91), North-Holland 1991, pp. 3–18.

[Val93] Valmari, A.: *Compositional State Space Generation.* Advances in Petri Nets 1993, Lecture Notes in Computer Science 674, Springer-Verlag 1993, pp. 427–457. (Earlier version in Proceedings of the 11th International Conference on Application and Theory of Petri Nets, Paris, France 1990, pp. 43–62.)

[VKCL93] Valmari, A., Kemppainen, J., Clegg, M. & Levanto, M.: *Putting Advanced Reachability Analysis Techniques Together: the "ARA" Tool.* Proceedings of Formal Methods Europe '93, Lecture Notes in Computer Science 670, Springer-Verlag 1993, pp. 597–616.

[Val94] Valmari, A.: *State of the Art Report: Stubborn Sets.* Petri Net Newsletter 46, April 1994, pp. 6-14.

[Val95] Valmari, A.: *Failure-based Equivalences Are Faster Than Many Believe.* Structures in Concurrency Theory, Proceedings, Berlin, Germany, May 1995, Springer-Verlag "Workshops in Computing" series 1995, pp. 326–340.

[VaT95] Valmari, A. & Tienari, M.: *Compositional Failure-based Semantic Models for Basic LOTOS.* Formal Aspects of Computing (1995) 7: 440–468.

[VKS96] Valmari, A., Karsisto, K. & Setälä, M.: *Visualisation of Reduced Abstracted Behaviour as a Design Tool.* To appear in Proceedings of Fourth Euromicro Workshop on Parallel and Distributed Processing, Braga, Portugal, Jan. 1996, IEEE publ., 8 p.

[WoG93] Wolper, P. & Godefroid, P.: *Partial-Order Methods for Temporal Verification.* Proceedings of CONCUR '93, Lecture Notes in Computer Science 715, Springer-Verlag 1993, pp. 233–246.

Graphical Development of Consistent System Specifications

Bernhard Schätz *
Heinrich Hußmann ‡
Manfred Broy *

*) Technische Universität München,
Arcisstraße 21,
80333 München, Germany
Email: broy@informatik.tu-muenchen.de,
schaetz@informatik.tu-muenchen.de

‡) Siemens AG,
Public Communication Networks, Advanced Development,
Hofmannstraße 51,
81359 München, Germany
Email: hussmann@oenzl.siemens.de

Abstract. While formal methods have promised essential benefits for the software development process, industrial development reality nevertheless relies mainly on informal and especially graphical description techniques. This article argues that formal techniques are indeed useful for practical application, but they should be put to indirect use. To demonstrate this approach, two pragmatic graphical description techniques, taken from the field of telecommunication, are analyzed regarding their information content and their application in the process of specification development; as a result these techniques are formally defined. Based on the formal definition, "safe" development steps and their graphical counterparts are introduced. This yields a graphical development method which relies on precise formal foundations.

1 Introduction

Informal graphical description methods have found wide-spread application in industry. Theoreticians have often criticized these methods for their lack of a precise definition of their conveyed information. However, for industrial practice the intuitive comprehendability of graphical methods makes them well-suited for a fast development of high-quality software. Formal approaches provide a high degree of semantic preciseness. In an industrial context, nevertheless, they can be applied only to a small number of carefully selected projects with specially trained personnel. This gap between theory and practice as well as ways to overcome it has recently attracted increasing scientific attention (see e.g. [12,2,8]).

This paper presents a method that combines semantic preciseness with a pragmatic graphical notation. To ensure the practical applicability of the method, the studied graphical notation has been derived from the specifications used in an industrial development project. This work neither reports on new theoretical insights nor on a completely new graphical specification method. Instead, it is shown how the state of the art in formal methods can be applied to analyze and improve an existing specification method. This way, precision of specification can be introduced into a given software development practice while still ensuring acceptance and usability by current development personnel. So the novel aspect of the work reported here is that in this case study the protagonists of formal methods did not try to revolutionize industrial practice, but instead tried to "phase in" with existing practice and to prepare a way for smooth evolution towards more powerful specification and development methods.

This paper is structured as follows: The remainder of this introductory section describes the industrial project in the context of which this work was carried out, as well as the theoretical background of the chosen formal semantics. In section 2, the graphical description techniques are introduced which have been taken from current (non-formal) development practice in this project. Afterwards, section 3 sketches how these notations can be supported by a formal semantics. The central part of this paper is section 4, which describes the new method proposed as the result of this study. This development method uses a slightly refined variant of the original graphical notations, but it defines a number of graphical development steps which ensure consistency of the developed specifications in the sense of formal semantics. Section 5 outlines the conception of a tool basing on these development steps. Section 6 concludes the paper with an outlook to further related work.

1.1 Industrial Background

The studied graphical description methods have been taken from a functional specification used in an industrial project (at Siemens AG, Public Communication Networks, Advanced Development). The specification deals with the high-level description of a system providing an Interactive Video Service to domestic customers. The complete project (which is a system development including hardware as well as software) has a size of approximately 100 person-years (carried out in a time span of approximately 2 years).

The Interactive Video Service.
The system developed in the studied project provides domestic customers with an interactive variant of television. For this purpose, the customer's TV set is connected with a so-called set-top box, which acts as an end system for a broadband communication network based on ATM (Asynchronous Transfer Mode) and advanced switching techniques. The set-top box of the Customer Premises Equipment ("CPE") not only receives information from the network (as in classical television) but also maintains a backchannel to control program sources by commands entered by the user with an infrared remote control. Content providers ("CP") offer video material for interactive access through the communication network, using powerful server computers.

The specification used as a reference example in this paper describes a "video-on-demand" service supported by such an infrastructure, where the customer can order video information interactively for immediate delivery over the communication network (in an individual data stream for each customer).

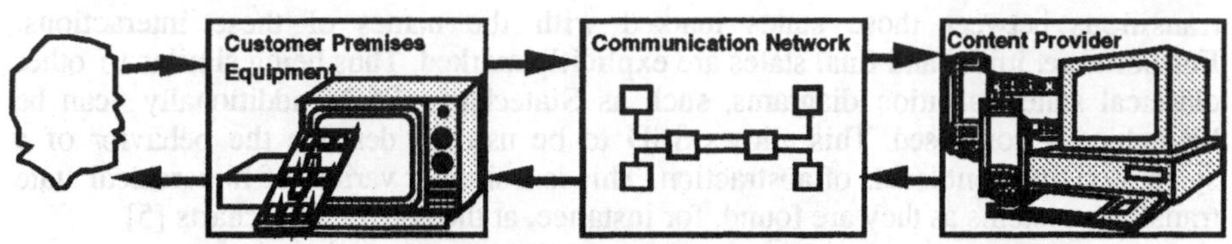

Fig. 1: The System Structure

1.2 Theoretical Background

To understand our approach requires a minimum of knowledge of the underlying formal concepts of Trace Theory. In [6], traces are introduced as a description of the system behavior:

"A communicating process is intended to interact with its environment at distinct points in time. Each individual interaction can be recorded as a value from a certain set $\mathcal{A}$ of event names (often called the alphabet of the process). An observation of the behavior of the process up to a given moment of time can be recorded as the sequence of events in which it has engaged so far. This is known as a *trace*..."

Thus, a trace can be understood as a finite sequence of symbols with each symbol denoting an action or event relevant for the system description. Given a certain set of symbols ("alphabet"), traces can be defined using the two constructors

- $\Diamond$: Denoting the empty sequence, i.e., the trace with no action occurred.
- $a \oplus t$: denoting the sequence with the action ``a´´ as its first element, and the trace "t" as its rest.

Furthermore, a function is introduced to filter out certain elements of a trace, leaving a trace consisting of parts of the original trace:

- $A © t$: Denoting the restriction of trace to elements from A according to the equations:

$$A © \Diamond = \Diamond$$
$$A ©(a\oplus t) = a\oplus (A ©t), \text{ if } a \in A$$
$$A ©(a\oplus t) = A ©t, \text{ if } a \notin A$$

Traces will be used as a semantic basis for the representation of system behaviors.

2 Graphical Description Techniques

The following graphical description techniques are used in the specification that was the starting point of this study:

Session State Diagrams

Extended Event Traces

Please note that the specification, being an informal one, also contains a significant amount of explanatory text ("prose"). The diagrams serve merely as illustrations which are explained in the accompanying text. It was the purpose of the work described here to give a more formal, self-contained meaning to the diagrams.

2.1 Session State Diagrams

Session State Diagrams (SSDs) are used to describe the global system from the user´s point of view. As implied by the name, the behavior of the system is described graphically using states. The interactions between user and system are described by transitions between those states marked with the names of these interactions. Furthermore, initial and final states are explicitly marked. Thus being similar to other classical state transition diagrams, such as Statecharts, SSDs additionally can be hierachically composed. This allows SSD to be used to describe the behavior of a system on different levels of abstraction. This is a simpler variant of hierarchical state transition systems as they are found, for instance, at the core of Statecharts [5].

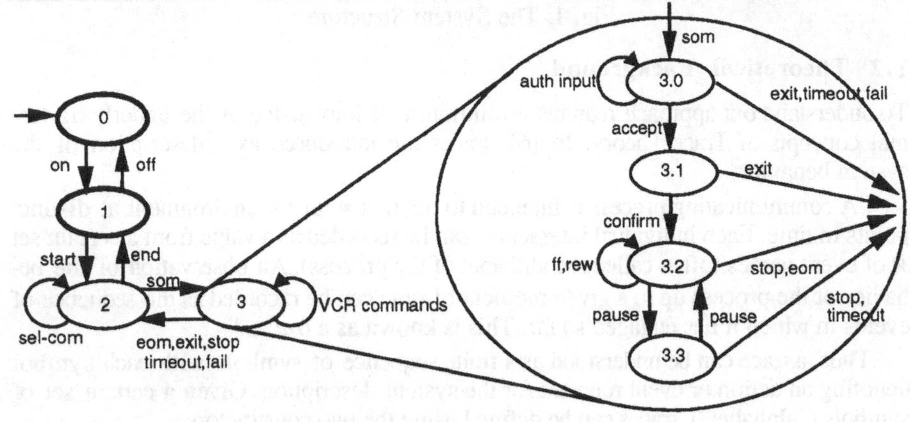

Fig. 2: System SSD and Refinement

Figure 2 describes the behavior of the "Interactive Video Service" as seen from an abstract point of view with the states "Not using IVS"(0), "Service Selection"(1), "Content Selection"(2) and "Content Transmission"(3); furthermore a more detailed view of the "Content Transmission" state is given.

2.2 Extended Event Traces

Extended Event Traces (EETs) are used for the description of the system from a more detailed, component oriented point of view. EETs describe parts from the course of interaction between two or more components; they are connected to a state of the system´s SSD. In general, EETs are seen as a sample collection of legal interactions without being necessarily complete. Concerning their graphical representation and their conveyed information EETs, on the whole, correspond to "Message Flow Diagrams" or "Message Sequence Charts" (see, e.g., [9]). Additionally, EETs allow the use of indicators for repeatable or optional sequences within an EET.

Figure 3 describes the interaction of the three components "CPE", "Network" and "CP" when setting up the connection between customer and provider.

These Event Traces are called "Extended", since they go slightly beyond the well-known syntax of Sequence Charts. In particular, Extended Event Traces may contain repetition indicators (marked "- * ") to designate parts of an event trace which can appear several times in sequence, or option indicators (marked "0 -") to designate optional parts. Due to these extensions, a single EET covers a number of cases which would traditionally be depicted in several Sequence Charts. See 3.3 for a more detailed discussion of repetition indicators.

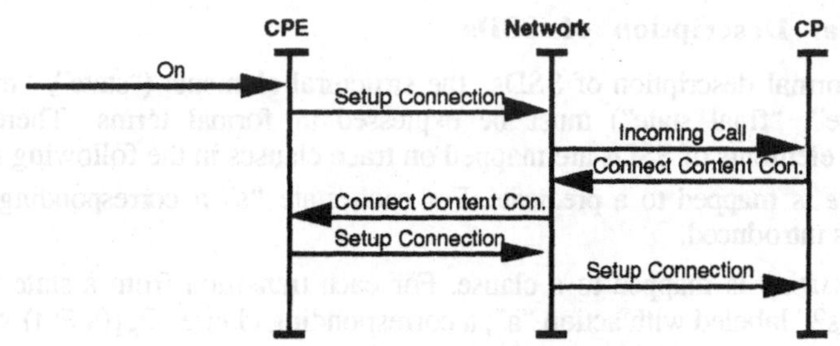

Fig. 3: EET of Connection Establishment

3 Formalization

The following section defines a formalization of the above introduced graphical notations. For the formalization of SSDs and EETs a common semantical model, the "trace model" is used (see [4] for a similar approach). This is necessary to allow the combination of both description forms into a coherent description formalism. The translation will give a precise meaning to SSDs and EETs to argue about the correctness of a development method described in section 4.

3.1 Traces by Clauses

Since SSDs and EETs will be embedded into a development method for system descriptions, it is necessary to find a coherent formal description form supporting common development mechanisms for both SSDs and EETs. As both description techniques are state based, it is reasonable to use a formalization based on states.[1] For the formal description of the system states are mapped on predicates. Each predicate characterizes the set of traces starting in the corresponding state. Transitions are represented by clauses over these predicates. Here, a simple form of clauses will be used consisting of predicates over traces. These clauses will either have the form

$$P_{s1}(a \oplus t) \Leftarrow P_{s2}(t)$$

denoting "An `a´ labeled transition leads from state s1 to state s2"[2], or the form

$$P_{s1}(t) \Leftarrow P_{s2}(t)$$

denoting "An unlabled transition leads from state s1 to states2".[3] Now, the behavior of the system given by such a set of clauses can be defined to be the set of traces characterized by those predicates that meet the conditions given by the corresponding clause set. Since several different predicates may be possible solutions for a clause set of this form, the strongest ("closest to false") solution will be chosen according to the *closed world assumption* (see, for instance, [10]).[4]

---

[1] While labelled transition systems (see, e.g., [11]) are an alternative representation, we chose trace semantics because of the simple refinement notion that will be used in section 4.5.

[2] Note that the orientations of the transition and of „⇐" are reversed.

[3] Here, „⇐" denotes the reverse implication.

[4] Otherwise, the trivial solution **True** would always fulfill the requirements for the predicates, characterizing all possible traces of the alphabet.

3.2 Formal Description of SSDs

To give a formal description of SSDs, the structural elements ("state", "transition", "initial state", "final state") must be expressed in formal terms. Therefore, the constituting elements of SSDs are mapped on trace clauses in the following manner:

- A *state* is mapped to a predicate. For each state "s" a corresponding predicate "P_s" is introduced.
- A *transition* is mapped to a clause. For each transition from a state "s1" to a state "s2" labeled with action "a", a corresponding clause "$P_{s1}(a \oplus t) \Leftarrow P_{s2}(t)$" is introduced.
- An *initial state* is mapped onto a clause relating the system predicate to the state. For each initial state "s", a corresponding clause "$S(t) \Leftarrow P_s(t)$" is introduced, with "S(t)" denoting the predicate describing the complete system behavior.
- A *final state* is mapped onto a clause for the empty trace. For each final state "s", a corresponding clause "$Ps(\langle\rangle)$" is introduced.

Table 1 shows parts of the formal description of the SSDs shown in Figure 2.

$S(t) \Leftarrow P_0(t)$	$P_2(\textbf{sel-com} \oplus t) \Leftarrow P_2(t)$
	$P_2(\textbf{timeout} \oplus t) \Leftarrow P_1(t)$
$P_0(\langle\rangle)$	$P_2(\textbf{som} \oplus t) \Leftarrow P_3(t)$
$P_1(\langle\rangle)$	
	$P_3(\textbf{eom} \oplus t) \Leftarrow P_2(t)$
$P_0(\textbf{on} \oplus t) \Leftarrow P_1(t)$	$P_3(\textbf{VCR-com} \oplus t) \Leftarrow P_3(t)$
$P_1(\textbf{off} \oplus t) \Leftarrow P_0(t)$	$P_3(\textbf{exit} \oplus t) \Leftarrow P_2(t)$

Tab. 1: Clausal Representation of Figure 3

Like in logic programming, the strongest family of predicates solving these implications is taken here.

3.3 Formal Description of EETs

To base the formal description of EETs on the same principle as of SSDs, implicit states within an EET after each interaction between two components are introduced. Figure 4 shows the EET for the "Content Selection Phase" together with the explicit depiction of those implicit states.

The mapping introduced above can be applied to EETs:

- An *implicit state* is mapped onto a predicate. For each state "i" a corresponding predicate "E_i" is introduced.
- A *transition* is mapped onto a clause. For each transition from a state "i" to a state "j" labeled with action "a", a corresponding clause "$E_i(a \oplus t) \Leftarrow E_j(t)$" is introduced.

- An *option indicator* is mapped onto a clause connecting the beginning of the optional sequence to its end. For an optional sequence with start state "i" and final state "j", a corresponding clause "$E_i(t) \Leftarrow E_j(t)$" is introduced.[5]
- A *repetition indicator* is mapped onto a clause connecting the end of the repeatable sequence with its beginning. For a repeatable sequence with start state "i" and final state "j", a corresponding clause "$E_j(t) \Leftarrow E_i(t)$" is introduced.

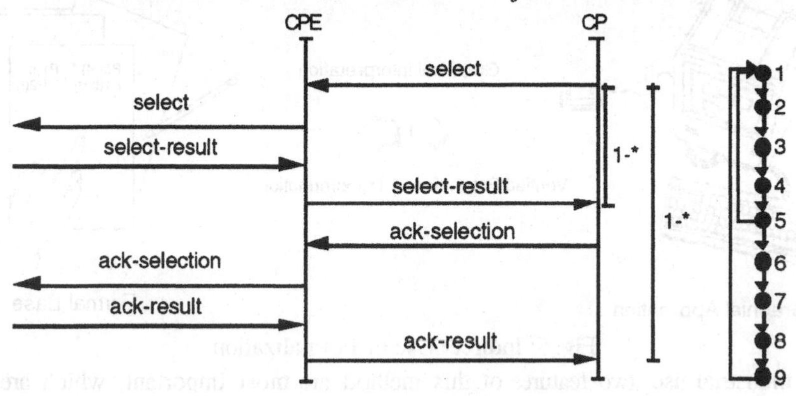

Fig. 4: EET of Content Selection and Explicit Depiction of Intermediate States

Table 2 shows the clausal description of the EET diagram depicted in Figure 4.

$E_1(\textbf{select} \oplus t) \Leftarrow E_2(t)$	$E_6(\textbf{ack-selection} \oplus t) \Leftarrow E_7(t)$
$E_2(\textbf{select} \oplus t) \Leftarrow E_3(t)$	$E_7(\textbf{ack-result} \oplus t) \Leftarrow E_8(t)$
$E_3(\textbf{select-result} \oplus t) \Leftarrow E_4(t)$	$E_8(\textbf{ack-result} \oplus t) \Leftarrow E_9(t)$
$E_4(\textbf{select-result} \oplus t) \Leftarrow E_5(t)$	$E_5(t) \Leftarrow E_1(t)$
$E_5(\textbf{ack-selection} \oplus t) \Leftarrow E_6(t)$	$E_9(t) \Leftarrow E_1(t)$

Tab. 2: Clausal Representation of Figure 4

4 Graphical Design Method for Consistent Specifications

It is not sufficient to simply translate the notations of an informal development method into a formal notation. The formal semantics makes sense only if some practical benefit is drawn from the introduced precision. On the other hand, the actual software developers and specifiers should be saved from direct contact with the formal notation (the clauses in our case). Therefore, we are now going to introduce a formal but graphical development technique.

Furthermore, a specification is not designed in a single step, but in several refining steps; each step is adding new details thus making an originally coarse-grained and abstract specification become sufficiently detailed. Thus, description techniques also have to be embedded into a development method, to offer a guide-line and help the developer making the necessary decision at the right time in the

[5] The formalization can be intuitively interpreted as „skipping from the start of the optional sequence to the end of it".

specification process. Such a development in general will lead to different specifications each covering different parts or aspects of the overall system. Therefore the method should support the development of "consistent" specifications, i.e., specifications which can be related in a sensible way to give rise to the complete system description without introducing contradictions or new ambiguities.

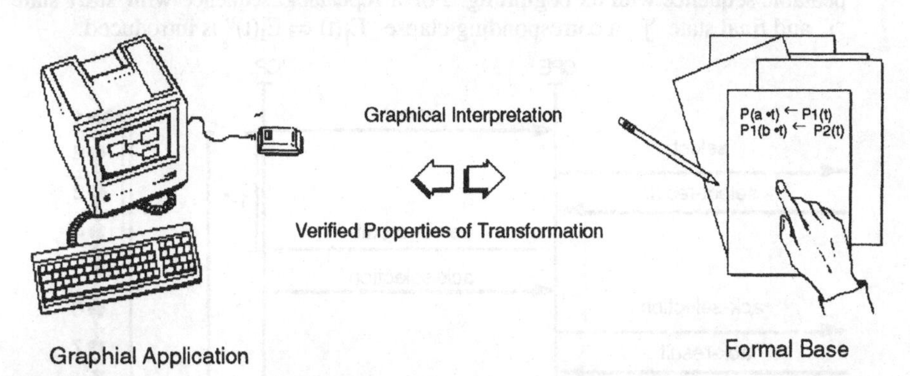

Fig. 5: Indirect Use of Formalization

For industrial use, two features of this method are most important, which are the *transparent use of formal methods*, and the *structured development of system descriptions*. In the following, after a short introduction to these concepts, the steps of this method are described. For the development of an SSD description, a more complex example will be given. Furthermore, the formal properties of the introduced transformations will be discussed. A possible conception for a corresponding development tool will close this section.

4.1 Transparent Use of Formal Methods

As argued in the introduction neither the informal nor the formal approach in its pure form is apt for industrial use, and only a combination of both aspects is adequate for the engineering process. The basic idea for combining the advantages of formal and graphical approaches is to use formality in a *transparent* way without the user's notice. One possible way for such an approach is the indirect use of formal description transformation ("refinement") rules. Here, the user of the method (the software developer) uses a fixed set of transformation rules for the derivation of graphical system descriptions (such as SSDs and EETs). Independently of this practical application, and once for all developments, a semantics specialist has used the formal interpretation of the graphical description techniques to prove that this set of transformation rules is "safe", in the sense that each transformation results in a formal refinement step[6]. This way, a "graphical development calculus" is introduced with verified "safe" operations on the description graphs.

This approach has advantages over an informal development of graphical specifications as well as over a purely formal development. The key point is that the notion of consistency of a - possibly compound - specification is well-defined, based on the

[6] The formal definition of the term „refinement" as used in our approach will be given in section 4.5.

formal semantics.[7] Moreover, a methodical guideline for the development of graphical specifications is offered, where the consistency is ensured step-by-step during the development. The next section describes this structured development method in more detail.

4.2 Development of System Descriptions

In 4.1 the design process was claimed to profit from restricting the legal design steps to controlled transformations according to the "graphical calculus". Furthermore, the use of the description techniques should be regulated to further the development process.

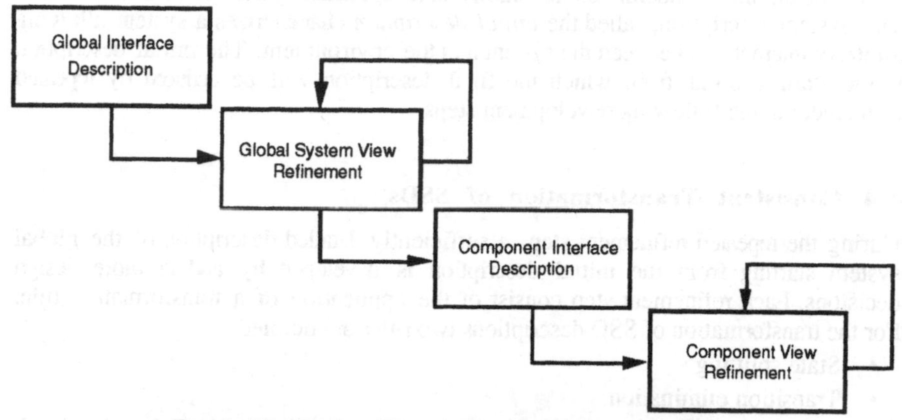

Fig. 6: The System Description Development Process

Thus, it is necessary to embed these description techniques in a structured development guideline to facilitate the design decisions by a clear separation of concerns during the development process. To meet this requirement, the description techniques are embedded in a development guideline based on the structured process found in formal specification development, consisting of four phases as depicted in Figure 6:

- Declaration of the syntactic interface of the global system,
- Refinement of the global view system description,
- Declaration of the syntactic interface of the components,
- Refinement of the component view system description.

A similar approach is used in other design methodologies, such as FOCUS [1]. The remainder of this section will deal with these development steps. Since it is obvious that such a straight-forward development process will in general not be possible in real world projects, sufficient support must be given for the revision of system descriptions. Section 5 will elaborate this question in more detail.

---

[7] In our approach, the consistency between a prior specification and the newly added details is defined in terms of a refinement relation between the original specification and the complete, more detailed specification.

4.3 The Global Syntactic Interface

To describe the syntactic interface of the system, the set of relevant interactions between system and system environment/user has to be defined. Furthermore for each interaction it has to be determined whether the action is controlled by the system or the system user. Actions controlled by the system are considered to be *output actions*, while actions controlled by the user are considered to be *input actions*. In the case of the Interactive Video Service, the set of input actions contains **Start Session, EXIT, FF, PLAY, REW, EXIT,** while the set of output actions contains actions like **End of Movie** or **End of Session**.

By declaring the syntactic interface of the global system, the description of the behavior of the most "liberal" or maximally underspecified system is also determined. This system description, called the *initial description* characterizes a system allowing arbitrary interactions between the system and the environment. The initial description is the starting point from which the final description will be deduced by repeated refinement in the following development steps.

4.4 Consistent Transformation of SSDs

During the repeated refinement steps a sufficiently detailed description of the global system starting from the initial description is developed by adding more design decisions. Each refinement step consist of the application of a transformation rule. For the transformation of SSD descriptions two rules are defined:

- State splitting
- Transition elimination.

While this rule set is *elementary* and consists of simple rules, it is, on the other hand, *complete* and thus allows the deduction of an arbitrary SSD beginning with the initial description.

State Splitting.

The first kind of transformation allows the introduction of new states by splitting an already existing state in two new states. The transitions of the two new states are determined in the following way.

- For any transition starting at the old state two corresponding transitions starting at each of the new states is introduced.
- For any transition ending at the old state two corresponding transitions ending at each of the new states is introduced.
- For any transition starting and ending at the old state two corresponding transitions starting and ending at the new states are introduced.
- For any transitions starting and ending at the old state two corresponding transitions starting at each one of the new states and ending at the other are introduced.

The following scheme considers incoming ("a1", "a2") and outgoing ("e1", "e2") transitions as well as feed-back ("i") transitions of the state "s" to be split.

$P_{r1}(a1 \oplus t) \Leftarrow P_s(t)$

$P_{r2}(a2 \oplus t) \Leftarrow P_s(t)$

$P_s(i \oplus t) \Leftarrow P_s(t)$

$$P_s(e1 \oplus t) \Leftarrow P_{t1}(t)$$
$$P_s(e2 \oplus t) \Leftarrow P_{t2}(t)$$

First, for each of the generated states s1 and s2, the corresponding transitions are introduced, by replacing s by s1 and s2, respectively, throughout the clauses for s.

$$P_{r1}(a1 \oplus t) \Leftarrow P_{s1}(t) \qquad P_{r1}(a1 \oplus t) \Leftarrow P_{s2}(t)$$
$$P_{r2}(a2 \oplus t) \Leftarrow P_{s1}(t) \qquad P_{r2}(a2 \oplus t) \Leftarrow P_{s2}(t)$$
$$P_{s1}(i \oplus t) \Leftarrow P_{s1}(t) \qquad P_{s2}(i \oplus t) \Leftarrow P_{s2}(t)$$
$$P_{s1}(e2 \oplus t) \Leftarrow P_{t2}(t) \qquad P_{s2}(e1 \oplus t) \Leftarrow P_{t1}(t)$$
$$P_{s1}(e1 \oplus t) \Leftarrow P_{t1}(t) \qquad P_{s2}(e2 \oplus t) \Leftarrow P_{t2}(t)$$

Furthermore, for each transition originally leading back into the split state, a corresponding transition from the first to the second state and vice versa is introduced.

$$P_{s1}(i \oplus t) \Leftarrow P_{s2}(t)$$
$$P_{s2}(i \oplus t) \Leftarrow P_{s1}(t)$$

Figure 7 shows the splitting of state "s" in the corresponding graphical description.[8]

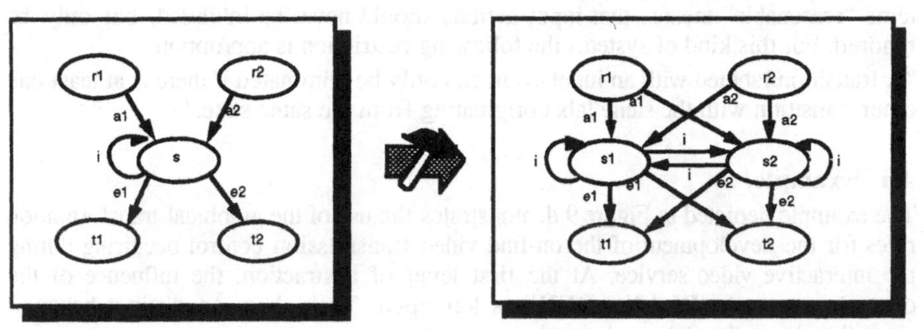

Fig. 7: Splitting of a State

Transition Elimination.

Although state splitting yields an additional structuring of the set of states, it does not restrict the set of possible system behaviors. Since the behavior of the system is essentially determined by the set of transitions, a possibility to reduce those transitions has to be introduced. This is done by simply removing a clause, in our example, for instance, the clause

$$P_{s1}(e1 \oplus t) \Leftarrow P_{s2}(t)$$

from the set of clauses describing the system. To restrict the behavior of a simple system of two states and three transitions, the set of clauses

$$P_{s1}(e1 \oplus t) \Leftarrow P_{s2}(t)$$
$$P_{s1}(e2 \oplus t) \Leftarrow P_{s2}(t)$$
$$P_{s2}(e3 \oplus t) \Leftarrow P_{s1}(t)$$

[8] The „hammer arrow" is used to indicate transformation steps which can be carried out mechanically.

can be reduced to the set

$P_{s1}(e2 \oplus t) \Leftarrow P_{s2}(t)$

$P_{s2}(e3 \oplus t) \Leftarrow P_{s1}(t)$

Figure 8 shows the same transformation on the graphical description level.

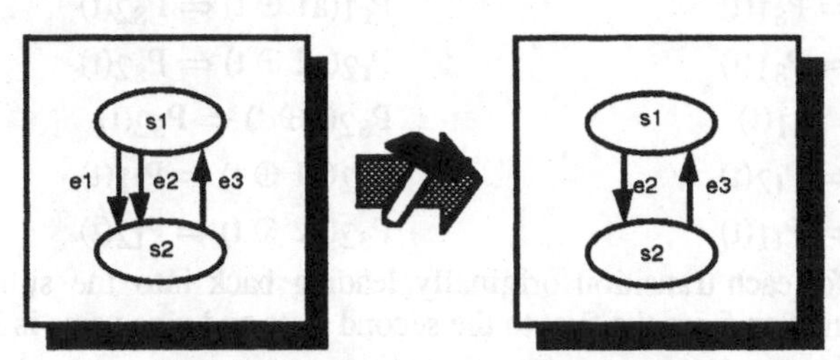

Fig. 8: Elimination of a Transition

Since not every set of states and transitions describes a "reasonable" system, the possibility of eliminating transitions should be restricted. In case of interactive systems "reasonable" means, that input actions should never be inhibited, but only be ignored. For this kind of systems the following restriction is appropriate:

"A transition labeled with an input event can only be eliminated if there is at least one other transition with the same label originating from the same state."

An Example.

The example depicted in Figure 9 demonstrates the use of the graphical transformation rules for the development of the on-line video transmission control occurring during the interactive video service. At the first level of abstraction, the influence of the control commands (**PLAY,...REW**) is left open. They show no distinct behavior since they leave the state unchanged.

The second level introduces a "pause"-state by splitting off a new state and elimination the appropriate transitions.[9] This leads to a more differentiated behavior of the system defining the system´s reaction given a **PAUSE** command including the ways to leave this "pause"-state.

Finally, the original state is split again, yielding a "stop"-state together with the corresponding transition eliminations. Again, this leads to a more detailed description of the system behavior clarifying underspecified questions of the interaction.

What looks obvious in this small example may become much harder to be checked in larger development steps: the transmission control can only be entered and exited by the originally defined actions making the refined specification fit in the overall specification; furthermore for each user interaction there is a well-defined system interaction yielding a precise system description.

4.5 Formal Properties of SSD Transformation

The upcoming proofs of the acclaimed propositions are only proof sketches to illustrate the proof ideas. For these sketches, *clause schemes* will be used for illustra-

[9] The eliminated interactions are depicted in a shaded font.

tion. Those clause schemes are terms with state predicates as their free variables. They are those terms that are build by conjunction of those clauses used to describe SSDs and EETs according to section 3. Thus, e.g., the conjunction of the clauses in Table 1 yields a clause scheme with free variables S (describing the system behavior), and $P_0,..,P_4$.

Since the clauses used here are all positive clauses, for a sufficient interpretation the *closed world assumption* has to be used, associating the *strongest* possible predicate P as solution of a term of the form

$$\exists P_{s1} \ldots P_{sn}.\ C(P, P_{s1},\ldots, P_{sn})$$

Here, P stands for the predicate characterizing the system behavior, $P_{s1},\ldots,P_{sn}$ are the state predicates denoting those states used in the formal description of the system, and

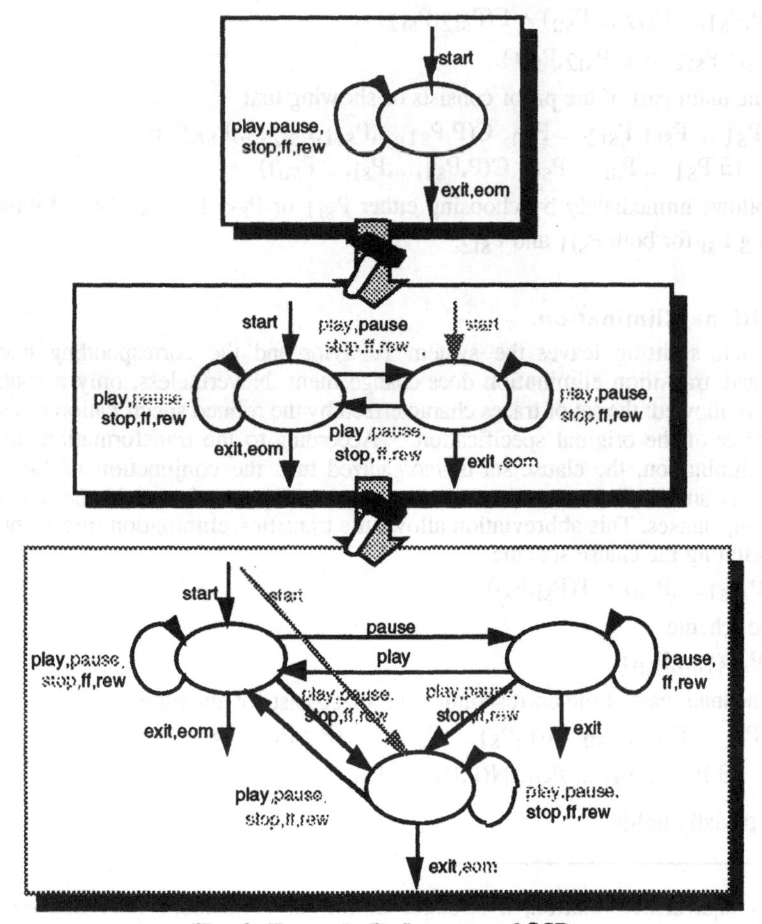

Fig. 9: Example Refinement of SSDs

C stands for the conjunction of the set of clauses used to described the system behavior.

State Splitting.

As already mentioned in 4.4, transformation by splitting a state si into states si1 and si2 does *not* change the behavior of the described system. More formally, it leaves the set of characterized traces unchanged.[10] According to the structure of the transformation, the clause set including the head clause is reorganized into the conjunction of the clause schemes N and F; here, F denotes the feedback clauses of the state to be split, i.e., those clauses describing transition with si as starting and ending state. N denotes the set of the remaining clauses. Using these abbreviations, state splitting can be seen as substituting the clause scheme

$N(P,P_{s1},...,P_{si},...,P_{sn}) \wedge F(P_{si},P_{si})$

with the scheme

$N(P,P_{s1},...,P_{si1},...,P_{sn}) \wedge F(P_{si1},P_{si1}) \wedge$

$N(P,P_{s1},...,P_{si2},...,P_{sn}) \wedge F(P_{si2},P_{si2}) \wedge$

$F(P_{si1},P_{si2}) \wedge F(P_{si2},P_{si1})$.

Thus, the main part of the proof consists of showing that

$$(\exists\, P_{s1} \ldots P_{si1}\, P_{si2} \ldots P_{sn}.\; C(P,P_{s1},...,P_{si1},P_{si2},...,P_{sn})) \Leftrightarrow$$
$$(\exists\, P_{s1} \ldots P_{si} \ldots P_{sn}.\; C(P,P_{s1},...,P_{si},...,P_{sn}))$$

"$\Rightarrow$" follows immediately by choosing either P_{si1} or P_{si2} for P_{si}. "$\Leftarrow$" follows by choosing P_{si} for both P_{si1} and P_{si2}.

Transition Elimination.

While state splitting leaves the system behavior and the corresponding trace set unchanged, transition elimination does change them. Nevertheless, only a controlled change is allowed: the set of traces characterized by the refined specification is a subset of the trace of the original specification.[11] According to the transformation structure of the elimination, the clause set is reorganized into the conjunction of the clause schemes N and T; T denotes the transition to be eliminated, and N the set of the remaining clauses. This abbreviation allows the transition elimination rule to be seen as substituting the clause scheme

$N(P,P_{s1},...,P_{sn}) \wedge T(P_{si},P_{sj})$

with the scheme

$N(P,P_{s1},...,P_{sn})$.

Thus, the main part of the corresponding proof consists of showing

$$(\exists\, P_{s1} \ldots P_{si} \ldots P_{sn}.\; N(P,P_{s1},...,P_{sn}) \wedge T(P_{si},P_{sj})) \Rightarrow$$
$$(\exists\, P_{s1} \ldots P_{si} \ldots P_{sn}.\; N(P,P_{s1},...,P_{sn})),$$

which trivially holds.

---

[10] This equivalence relation, a stronger notion of refinement than usually used, between two specifications (i.e.,predicates) S_1 and S_2 can be mathematically expressed as „$S_1 \Leftrightarrow S_2$“.

[11] This relation, corresponding to the usual refinement notion used with traces, between a specification (i.e., predicate) S_1 and S_2 can be mathematically expressed as „$S_2 \Rightarrow S_1$“.

4.6 Syntactic Interfaces of Components

Like the development of the description of the global system, the development of the component view starts with the determination of the syntactic interface of the components of the system. Hence, the set of relevant interactions between the components has to be determined as well as whether the actions is an input or an output action of the corresponding component.

As before, the determination of component interface again defines an initial description. To be consistent with the global description, however, the component description may not characterize arbitrary behaviors but must respect the global restrictions. Thus, arbitrary interactions between the components are only allowed within the global system states. According to the above schema, for each state s of the global system description and for each internal interaction i a corresponding clause

$$P_s(i \oplus t) \Leftarrow P_s(t)$$

is introduced. On the graphical level, this corresponds to an introduction of a feedback transition for every SSD state, labeled with all internal interactions.

Formal Property of Alphabet Change.
To change from the global system view to the component view, the set of relevant observed actions has to be changed. This transformation is referred to as "alphabet change". According to the transformation structure of the alphabet change, the clause set is reorganized into the conjunction of the clause schemes N and $F(P_{s1}) \wedge \ldots \wedge F(P_{sn})$; here, F denotes the conjunction of all newly introduced transitions labeled with internal actions i1,...,ik, and is of the form

$$P(i1 \oplus t) \Leftarrow P(t) \wedge \ldots \wedge P(ik \oplus t) \Leftarrow P(t).$$

N denotes the unchanged part of the clause set. This abbreviation allows the alphabet change to be seen as substituting the clause scheme

$$N(P_{s1}(A©.),\ldots, P_{sn}(A©.))$$[12]

with the scheme

$$N(P_{s1},\ldots,P_{sn}) \wedge F(P_{s1}) \wedge \ldots \wedge F(P_{sn}).$$

Thus, the main part of the corresponding proof consists of showing the proposition

$$\exists P_{s1} \ldots P_{sn}.\ N(P(A©.),P_{s1}(A©.),\ldots,P_{sn}(A©.)) \Leftrightarrow$$
$$\exists P_{s1} \ldots P_{sn}.\ N(P,P_{s1},\ldots,P_{sn}) \wedge F(P_{s1}) \wedge \ldots \wedge F(P_{sn}).$$

"$\Leftarrow$" follows immediately by restricting $P_{s1},\ldots,P_{sn}$ to the alphabet A. To proof "$\Rightarrow$", i.e., to obtain the same clause scheme, $F(P_{s1}) \wedge \ldots \wedge F(P_{sn})$ has to be inferred. This follows trivially using the following deduction:

True

$\Leftrightarrow (P(A©t) \Leftarrow P(A©t))$

$\Leftrightarrow (P(A©(i1 \oplus t)) \Leftarrow P(A©t))$

---

12 Here, the notation P(A©.) is used to denote the predicate Q with $\forall$ t. $Q(t) \Leftrightarrow P(A©t)$.

4.7 Refinement to Component View

The last step of the development process consists of the repeated refinement of the component view of the system. By construction, the formalizations of SSDs and EETs do not essentially differ. Therefore, from a formal point of view, no other transformations are needed for the refinement of EETs than in case of the refinement of SSDs. Since, however, the graphical description techniques differ essentially, an appropriate graphical representation of these rules must be offered. As the EETs are more restricted than SSDs concerning their expressiveness, a suitable extension of EETs should be offered for a homogeneous development method. Therefore, in this section the concept of *hierarchical EETs* is introduced, and appropriate transformation techniques are developed. Those transformation techniques are tailor-made for the communication sequence view offered by EETs in contrast to the state based view offered by SSDs and the formal description technique. Because of their similarity to the above described SSD transformation rules, the introduction of these transformations concentrates on the graphical level.

Hierarchical EETs.
As already mentioned above, EETs are much more restricted in their expressiveness compared to SSDs, since EETs do not allow to choose from a set of possible behaviors during a run of the system. To overcome this restriction EETs are enhanced by introducing a hierarchical notation and the possibility to describe the system behavior by sets of EETs.

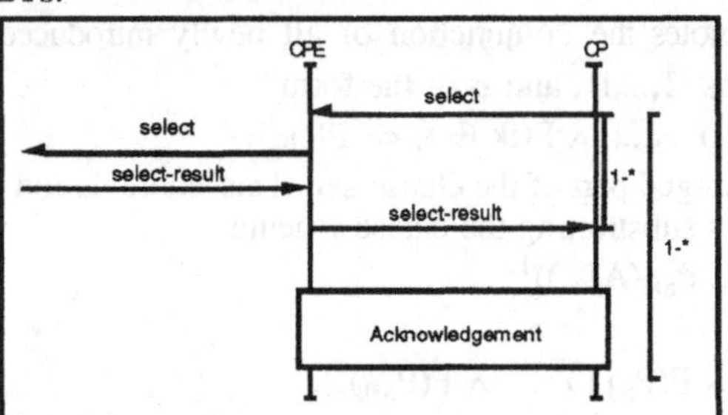

Fig. 10: Hierarchical EETs

Since an EET is already seen as a part of a larger description (i.e., the SSD), this notion is extended to make EETs legal subcomponents of another EET, too. This structuring allows hierarchical descriptions. By giving more than one EET for a certain phase of the system, each of the given possibilities becomes a legal behavior of the system. This is a standard interpretation commonly used with "Message Sequence Charts" and comparable description techniques. By combining both techniques, as suggested in current revisions of "Message Sequence Charts" (e.g., [9]) SSDs and EETs become equally expressive[13] and thus make a homogeneous description development possible, using the following three transformation rules.

---

[13] See [3], e.g., for the discussion of expressive power of comparable state-based formalisms.

Repetition splitting.

Those parts on an EET covered by a repetition/optionality indicator can be split into two identical copies chained to each other as depicted in Figure 11. Formally, the corresponding pairs of clauses of the form

$P_{s1}(a \oplus t) \Leftarrow P_i(t)$ and $P_f(e \oplus t) \Leftarrow P_{s2}(t)$.

are substituted by the clauses

$P_{s1}(a \oplus t) \Leftarrow P_{i1}(t)$, $P_{f1}(e \oplus t) \Leftarrow P_{i2}(t)$, and $P_{f2}(e \oplus t) \Leftarrow P_{s2}(t)$.

The corresponding repetition and optionality indicators

$P_i(t) \Leftarrow P_f(t)$ and $P_f(t) \Leftarrow P_i(t)$

are substituted by the clauses

$P_{i1}(t) \Leftarrow P_{f1}(t)$ and $P_{f1}(t) \Leftarrow P_i(1t)$,

$P_{i2}(t) \Leftarrow P_{f2}(t)$ and $P_{f2}(t) \Leftarrow P_{i2}(t)$,

as well as $P_{i1}(t) \Leftarrow P_{f2}(t)$ and $P_{f2}(t) \Leftarrow P_{i1}(t)$.

Furthermore, the corresponding part of the EET the indicator ranges over has to be split, too. This is done by substituting all the corresponding clauses

$P_r(a \oplus t) \Leftarrow P_s(t)$

by the corresponding pair of clauses

$P_{r1}(a \oplus t) \Leftarrow P_{s1}(t)$ and $P_{r2}(a \oplus t) \Leftarrow P_{s2}(t)$.

Comparable to the state splitting of SSDs, the indicator splitting does not change the behavior of the described system, but adds additional structuring.

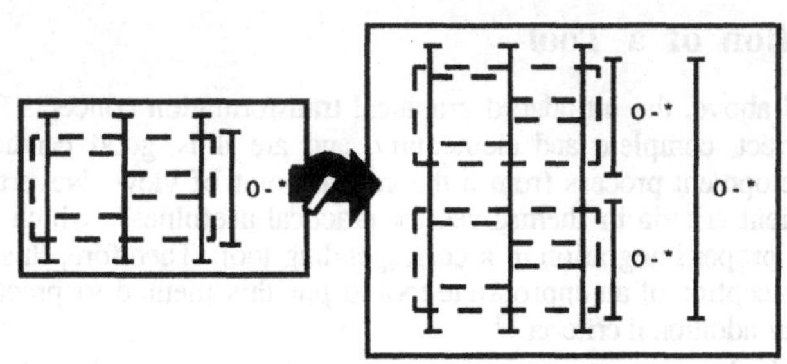

Fig. 11: Splitting of EET repetition

Subpart Splitting.

A second way of adding additional structure to the description without changing the system behavior is the splitting of subcomponents. Here, a subpart of a hierarchical system description is split up in two identical parts adding an alternative but identical behaviour.

On the level of the clausal description, the subpart splitting is carried out in similar fashion described in the case of the indicator splitting.

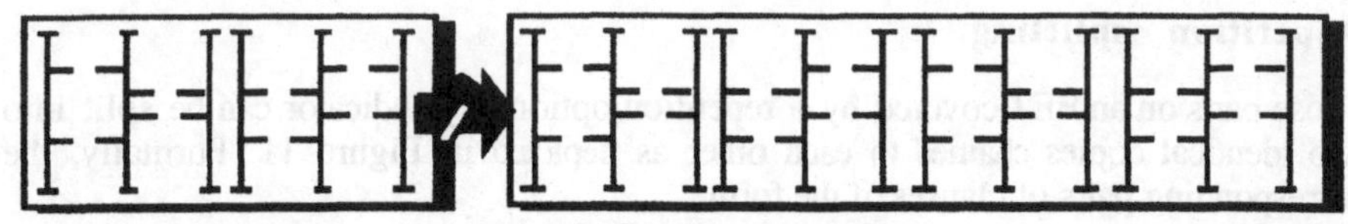

Fig. 12: Subpart Splitting

Indicator Specialization.

Finally, the indicators for repetition and optionality can be specialized in the following way:

- "0-*"-marked parts can be eliminated.
- "0-*"-marked parts can be substituted by corresponding "0-1"-marked parts.
- "0-*"-marked parts can be substituted by corresponding "1-*"-marked parts.
- "1-*"-marked parts can be substituted by corresponding unmarked parts.

All of these transformations are real behavior refinements and thus restrict the behavior of the described system.

Formal Properties.

Since all the above transformation rules given for EETs can be expressed with corresponding clause schemes as given for SSDs, the properties of the former can be deduced in equivalent fashion as the properties of the latter. For reason of brevity, the formal treatment of those rules will therefore be skipped here.

5 Conception of a Tool

As mentioned above, the introduced graphical transformation concepts for SSDs and EETs are correct, complete and elementary, and are thus good candidates for the described development process from a theoretical point of view. Nevertheless, those are not sufficient criteria in themselves for practical usefulness, which is depending essentially on proper integration in a corresponding tool. Therefore, this section will outline the conception of an appropriate tool to put this method to practical work by identifying four additional criteria:[14]

1. Although elementary transformation steps allow easy proofs of their properties, a development using these steps becomes cumbersome and is therefore of low practical use. A useful tool should hence allow us the combination of elementary steps to form more complex steps by offering "combinators" for the *creation of "macro steps"*. As indicated by example 4.4, state splitting is generally combined with transition elimination which should consequently be combined into one operation. This becomes even more obvious in the case of the development of EETs where the construction of a sequence of interactions consists of repeatedly splitting an option/repetition indicator, elimination of alternatives and the elimination of an option/repetition indicator.

[14] The next step of the cooperation is planned to include the realization of such a tool.

2. As mentioned in section 2.1, SSDs support a modular description of system behavior by allowing a refinement of SSD states by SSDs. Since descriptions of larger systems will often be developed in parallel in several groups, the envisaged tool should support such a *modularization of the system description* by offering techniques for splitting such descriptions into descriptions of subparts and re-combining them into a complete description.

3. The modular nature of SSDs also yields the possibility for views of the system behavior with different levels of abstraction. Thus this modularity is not only a useful technique for the development process, but also for the documentation and the communication of the system behavior. Thus, a suitable tool should offer a facility for the *generation of abstract views* of the system behavior by allowing to ignore irrelevant details. This may include the abstraction from certain actions, the unification of similar states, or the hiding of trivial actions and states.

4. So far, the described method only supports a top-down development process by repeated refinement of the system description. Since in practice this is hardly ever the case, support for the taking-back of erroneous design steps and the *revision of the system description* is indispensable for a practical tool. One simple revision concept might consist of the possibility to return to an earlier stage of the development process, substituting a previously taken erroneous design step by the correct one, and "replaying" the subsequently taken steps as far as possible, informing the user graphically about the inapplicability of "replayed" steps.

To guarantee the correctness of the development process using such a tool, all these described extensions must, of course, be proven correct in respect to the original method.

6 Concluding Remarks

We have described an approach to amalgamate a pragmatic software specification method taken out of daily industrial practice with a precise semantic background. The novel aspect of our approach is that we do not stop at a pure translation between informal and formal specifications but integrate both into a new development method that appears to the user as a structured graphical method. The formal background is then used to make the method much more elaborate in its methodical guidance. Moreover, the method offers an elegant way to ensure the consistency of a specification by construction. This seems to be superior to consistency tests as they have been defined in informal and formal methods up to now.

Of course, the described approach is not limited to the specific development method. The basic idea can be carried over to any other graphics-based method, including object-oriented methods. For example, [7] has exercised a quite similar approach for the complex method SSADM. The work that was presented here seems to be of a completely new kind compared to other activities in (formal or informal) system development. We have carried out here a piece of method development for a graphical method based on formal foundations. One can draw the conclusion that the analysis and improvement of practically used development methods can be a fruitful field of research (and also business!) for people with experience in both formal and informal development methods.

7 Acknowledgment

The authors would like to thank Alexander van der Vekens for contributions to an earlier version, and Konrad Slind for a careful reading of the article, as well as the reviewers for their helpful remarks.

8 References

[1] Broy, M., Dendorfer, C., Dederichs, F., Fuchs, M., Gritzner, T., Weber, R.: *The Design of Distributed Systems - An Introduction to FOCUS*. TUM-I9225, Technische Universität München, 1992.

[2] Bowen, J., Stavridou, V.: *The industrial take-up of formal methods in safety-critical and other areas: A perspective*. In: F. C. P. Woodcock, P. G. Larsen (eds), FME' 93, Lecture Notes in Computer Science Vol. 670, Springer 1993, pp. 183-195.

[3] Brauer, W.: *Automatentheorie*. Teubner, 1984.

[4] Facchi, C.: *Methodik zur formalen Spezifikation des IOS/OSI Schichtenmodells*. PhD-Thesis. Technische Universität München, 1995.

[5] Harel, D.: *Statecharts: a visual formalism for complex systems*. Science of Computer Programming **8** (1987) 231-274.

[6] Hoare, C.A.R.: *Mathematical models for Computer Science*. Working Material for Marktoberdorf Summer School 1994. Institut für Informatik, Technische Universität München, 1994.

[7] Hussmann, H.: *Formal Foundations for SSADM*. Habilitation Thesis, Technische Universität München, 1994.

[8] Hussmann, H.: *Indirect Use of Formal Methods in Software Engineering*. In: M. Wirsing (Ed): ICSE-17 Workshop on Formal Methods Application in Software Engineering Practice, Seattle (WA), USA. Proceedings, April 1995, pp. 126-133.

[9] International Telecommunication Union: *Message Sequence Charts*. ITU-T Recommendation Z.120. Geneva, 1994.

[10] Lloyd, J.W.: *Foundations of Logic Prograamming*. Springer, 1984.

[11] Milner, R. *CCS - A Calculus for Communicating Systems*. Springer Lecture Notes in Computer Science 83, 1983.

[12] Semmens, L.T., France, R.B., Docker, T.W.G.: *Integrated structured analysis and formal specification techniques*. The Computer Journal **35** (1992) 600-610.

Deduction in the Verification Support Environment (VSE)

Dieter Hutter, Bruno Langenstein, Claus Sengler,
Jörg H. Siekmann, Werner Stephan, Andreas Wolpers

Deutsches Forschungszentrum für Künstliche Intelligenz GmbH
Stuhlsatzenhausweg 3, D-66123 Saarbrücken, Germany
⟨*name*⟩@dfki.uni-sb.de

Abstract. The reliability of complex software systems is becoming increasingly important for the technical systems they are embedded in. In order to assure the highest levels of trustworthiness of software formal methods for the development of software are required. The VSE-tool was developed by a consortium of German universities and industry to make a tool available which supports this formal development process.
VSE is based on a particular method for programming in the large. This method is embodied in an administration system to edit and maintain formal developments. A deduction component is integrated into this administration system in order to provide proof support for the formal concepts.
In parallel to the development of the system itself, two large case studies were conducted in close collaboration with an industrial partner. In both cases components of systems previously developed by the industry were re-developed from scratch, starting with a formal specification derived from the original documents.
This paper focuses on the deduction component and its integration. We use a part of one of the industrial case studies in order to illustrate the important aspects of the deduction component: We argue that a close integration which makes the structure of developments visible for the theorem prover is necessary for an efficient treatment of changes and an indispensable structuring of the deduction process itself. Also we commend an architecture for interactive strategic theorem proving which has turned out to be adequate for applications in the context of formal program development. The last one of the three main sections addresses the important point of detecting bugs in implementations and specifications.

1 Introduction

The reliability of complex software systems is becoming increasingly important for the technical systems they are embedded in. Malfunctioning of software systems caused by design flaws or faulty implementations may lead to loss or garbling of data, breach of security, danger to life and limb, and, in almost all cases, severe economic losses.

Led by the *German Information Security Agency* (Bundesamt für Sicherheit in der Informationstechnik, BSI) a catalog of criteria for the evaluation of the security of information technology systems has been developed in Germany [IT-89]. In the assessment of a system's trustworthiness, the *development process* plays a major role. Requirements to the development process break down into aspects of (the formulation of) security and/or safety requirements, the overall structure of the system, and the implementation. The highest levels of quality require, to a varying extent, the use of *formal methods*. The BSI thus decided on the development of a tool to support the use of formal methods during all stages of the design process. Starting in 1991 the VSE system [BCC+92] was developed by a consortium consisting of Dornier/DASA, Friedrichshafen, the German Research Center for Artificial Intelligence (DFKI), Saarbrücken, the Gesellschaft für Prozeßrechner-Programmierung (GPP), München, the University of Karlsruhe, and the University of Ulm.

In August 1994 the first prototype was delivered, tested, and finally accepted by the BSI.

VSE is based on a particular method for *programming in the large*. This method is embodied in an *administration system* to edit and maintain formal developments. A *deduction component* is integrated into this administration system in order to provide proof support for the formal concepts.

This paper focuses on the deduction component and its integration. A part of an industrial case study called PERSEUS is used to illustrate the main ideas. The case study is part of an access control system for nuclear power plants. The task was to guarantee that only authorized staff is present in each area of the plant. The part we will be looking at is concerned with the manipulation of the rights of persons to enter different areas of the plant.

The paper is organized as follows. In the following section we give a survey of the VSE system and its underlying formal concepts. In section three we give a more detailed description of the part of the case study which is used in the following. We then discuss the integration of the deduction component into the administration system. We argue that a close integration which makes the structure of developments visible for the theorem prover is necessary for an efficient treatment of changes and an indispensable structuring of the deduction process itself. The next section describes what could be called interactive strategic theorem proving. This architecture has turned out to be adequate for applications in the context of formal program development. The last one of the three main sections addresses the important point of detecting bugs in implementations and specifications.

2 The VSE System

We begin with a survey of the VSE system introducing some underlying formal notions as well as the basic constituents of the systems in its technical realization. We will also mention the two industrial case studies that were carried out in the project.

2.1 The General Method

VSE is based on a method for the top-down development of ***structured, formal specifications*** and their ***stepwise implementation*** (refinement) using abstract intermediate layers represented by specifications.

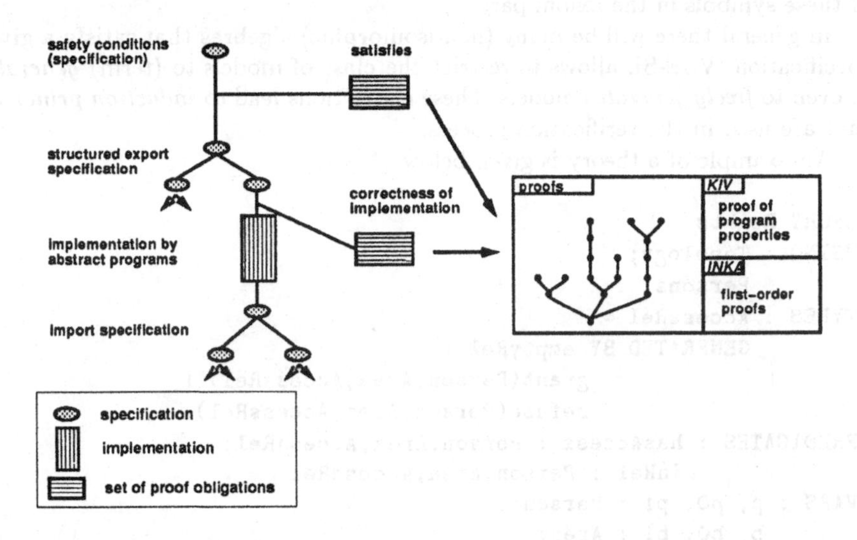

Fig. 1. The VSE Method

Refinement steps are specified by means of *abstract programs* that use concepts from the lower (import) level in order to implement the more abstract ones on the export level. The bottom layer is given by a collection of predefined concepts that can directly be realized in a target programming language. *Modularity* in this context means that sub-specifications can be implemented separately.

At each level, additional safety and/or security requirements can be formulated in addition to the system specification. These requirements are formalized in a separate specification which can be mapped onto the systems specification, such a connection is called a *satisfies*-link between the two.

Most of the development steps lead to so-called *proof obligations*. These formalized assertions are handed over to the deduction component where the actual verification takes place.

Figure 1 shows the general method for formal software development in VSE.

The concrete instance of this general method depends on the formal concepts used for modeling the desired system. Specification concepts covered in the current (first) version of the VSE system include *abstract data types* and *state transition systems*.

Abstract Data Types Abstract Data Types (ADTs) provide a view on a system as an *algebra*, given by a (typed) collection of sets of data objects and a (typed) collection of operations which manipulate these data.

Elementary specifications (of algebras), so-called *theories* are made up of a *signature* and a set of *axioms*. The signature part introduces the vocabulary of the data type. It consists of a set of types and a set of typed function and predicate symbols. VSE-SL allows full first-order logic to describe the semantics of these symbols in the axiom part.

In general there will be many (non-isomorphic) algebras that satisfy a given specification. VSE-SL allows to restrict the class of models to (term) *generated* or even to *freely generated* models. These restrictions lead to *induction principles* that are used in the verification process.

An example of a theory is given below:

```
THEORY Rights
 USING : Topology;
         Persons
 TYPES : AccessRel =
         GENERATED BY emptyRel |
                      grant(Person,Area,AccessRel) |
                      refuse(Person,Area,AccessRel)
 PREDICATES : hasAccess : Person,Area,AccessRel;
              inRel : Person,Area,AccessRel
 VARS : p, p0, p1 : Person;
        b, b0, b1 : Area;
        m : AccessRel
 AXIOMS : NOT inRel(p0, b0, emptyRel);
          inRel(p0,b0,grant(p0, b0, m));
          NOT inRel(p0, b0, refuse(p0, b0, m));
          b0 /= b1 OR p0 /= p1
          -> (inRel(p0, b0, m) <->
              inRel(p0, b0, grant(p1, b1, m)));
          b0 /= b1 OR p0 /= p1
          -> (inRel(p0, b0, m) <->
              inRel(p0, b0, refuse(p1, b1, m)));
          hasAccess(p, b, m) <->
          (b = extern
           OR visitor(p) AND inRel(leader(p), b, m)
           OR NOT visitor (p) AND
              (inRel(p, b, m) OR hasAccess(p, next(b), m)))
THEORYEND
```

The theory **Rights** corresponds to representation of the rights of persons to enter different areas of the plant. It refers to the (sub-) theories **Topology** (e.g. using the function **next**) which represents the topology of the plant and **Persons** (e.g. using the predicate **visitor**) modelling the different (types of) persons like staff members or visitors. Among other operations this kind of *enrichment* gives rise to a (horizontal) structure of abstract data type specifications.

In the refinement process functions and predicates from the export specification are implemented by (recursive) procedures that use function and predicate symbols from a given import specification. The relation between concepts from the export specification and parts of the implementation is given by a *mapping*. The theory underlying these concepts has been described in [Rei92b], [Rei92a].

Specification of State Transition Systems State transition systems are used to describe systems where the history of operations executed has an effect on the results produced. Here the operations cause *side effects* on a global system *state*.

State transition systems in VSE-SL are given by so-called *objects*. As an example, we present below a simple specification of a state transition system which is, like the theory presented in the last section, taken from the case study PERSEUS conducted in the VSE project.

```
OBJECT PlantAccess
 USING : Rights
 DATA : Matrix : AccessRel
 VARS : p, q : person;
        b : area
 OPERATIONS :
 PROC access(p : Person,b : Area) : bool
      ENSURES IF hasAccess (p, b, Matrix)
              THEN RESULT = T
              ELSE RESULT = F
              FI
 PROC setaccess(p : Person,b : Area,z : bool)
      MODIFIES Matrix
      ENSURES IF z = T
              THEN Matrix = grant(p, b, Matrix')
              ELSE Matrix = refuse(p, b, Matrix')
              FI
 INITIAL : leader(p) = leader(q) ->
          (hasAccess(p, b, Matrix) <->
           hasAccess (q, b, Matrix))
OBJECTEND
```

The *state space* is given implicitly through the items in the `DATA`-slot. The variables declared here are state-dependent and may be changed by the operations. Their types (sorts) are taken from the *theory* mentioned in the `USING`-slot. Additional local variables may be declared in a `VARS`-slot. The behavior of *Operations* is described by *pre- and postconditions*. In the postcondition a variable `x'` denotes the value of `x` prior to the execution of an operation. The preconditions form a complete case-distinction. In the `RESULT`-slot the value returned by an operation is specified. By an additional `REQUIRES`-slot one might restrict the situations in which the operations may be executed. These requirements have to be respected if an operation is used for example as an import operation in some implementation.

Consider the example of the procedure `setaccess`. `Matrix'` denotes the value of `Matrix` prior to the execution of the operation `setaccess`. Thus, in case the operation is called with `z` equal to `T` the new value of `Matrix` is computed from its current value by applying `grant` with additional parameters `p` and `b` on it.

The set of *initial* states (and perhaps also a global *invariant* of the system) is specified by first-order formulae. As with ADTs there are also *generic* state transition systems, and *unions* of such systems. Export operations of state transition systems are *implemented* in the VSE system by pieces of abstract programs that use operations from some import specification.

An introduction to state transition systems of this kind can be found in [RvHO91] while a comprehensive description of the syntax and semantics of state transition systems is given in [VSE94].

2.2 System Support

VSE is an integrated system that supports the user at all stages of the development process following the method outlined above. Basically there are two kinds of activities, *editing* and *proving*, that are in fact interleaved. This means that the user might edit (some part of) a specification, prove certain safety properties, edit an import specification and a refinement, prove the refinement correct, and then continue his work for example by a further refinement step.

The work is organized via a so-called *development graph* that displays the representation of a (partial) development to the user and allows him to continue his work at a node he wants to expand. The development graph also gives the user access to *status information* that is maintained by the administration system. This *correctness management* controls the work in the various development units and their proof obligations. It keeps track of dependencies between a proof and those parts of the specification which are used during the proof. Changing these parts of the specification will invalidate the related proofs while other proofs may not be affected.

The main system support w.r.t. editing specifications and implementations is *syntactical analysis* including type-checking. If a development step is completely edited and successfully checked, a *logical database* related to this step is created by the system. It is initialized by the axioms computed from the specifications involved and the proof obligations that correspond to the development step. The verification process then takes place in the context of this database where all kinds of logical information, like axioms, lemmata, and proofs are stored. When a branch of the development is completed, the actual code of the target language is generated by the system.

2.3 Case Studies

In parallel to the development of the system itself, two large case studies were conducted in close collaboration with Dornier. In both cases components of systems previously developed by Dornier were *re-developed* from scratch, starting with a formal specification derived from the original documents. The selection of the case studies was oriented along the specification paradigms supported by the VSE system.

The first case study deals with a system that controls the exchange of programs between radio stations, including the booking of leased communication lines. Within this case study, the kernel of the booking system was re-developed. It contains a complicated algorithm to re-schedule already booked transmissions in the case of conflicts. The booking system was modeled as an abstract data type, i.e. the booking system can be viewed as a structured collection of operations. The entire case study consists of about 5000 lines of specifications (including the security model), and 8000 lines of implemented source code.

The second case study named PERSEUS demonstrates the use of state transition systems. It is (part of) an *access control system* for nuclear power plants. Again the safety relevant kernel of the system, which supports the tracking and control of movements within a plant, was re-developed. This case study, which begun later, comprises currently about 3000 lines of specifications, which were partially implemented in 2000 lines of code.

2.4 Deduction

A distinguishing feature of the VSE system is that it offers deductive support for all formal concepts. This takes into account the experience that one of the main limiting factors for the application of formal methods in an industrial context is machine assistance for the construction of proofs.

Apart from *actualizations of generic* specifications, there are two major kinds of links in development graphs that lead to *proof obligations*, *satisfies-links* between systems specifications and additional *safety and/or security properties* and *refinement steps.* Safety and/or security properties lead to assertions in first-order predicate logic while in the case of refinements we have to prove assertions about programs. These are formulated in a variant of Dynamic Logic (DL), see [Pra76].

The deduction component is made up of two closely integrated provers: the KIV system (Karlsruhe Interactive Verifier) and the INKA system (INduction-prover KArlsruhe), see [HRS90] and [BHHW86]. KIV is mainly used for proofs in DL while INKA provides strategies for first-order assertions, in particular for inductive proofs. Both systems follow the paradigm of *interactive, strategic theorem proving.*

3 PERSEUS

As mentioned before we will use a part of the second case study PERSEUS to demonstrate the main features of the deductive component and its integration into the administration system. While in the first case study the safety requirements were concerned with the problem of exclusive use on lines, here the task was to guarantee that only authorized staff is present in each area of a nuclear power plant. A small part of the development graph concerning the access rights is given in Figure 2.

The part we will be looking at is concerned with the manipulation of an *access matrix* that encodes the rights of persons to enter different areas of the plant. Persons are either member of the staff or parts of visitor groups who are always escorted by a member of the staff (the so-called leader of a group). Visitors have same access rights to the areas as their leader (but may only enter an area together with their leader). In order to simplify matters staff members are always their own leader regardless whether they escort a visitor group or not.

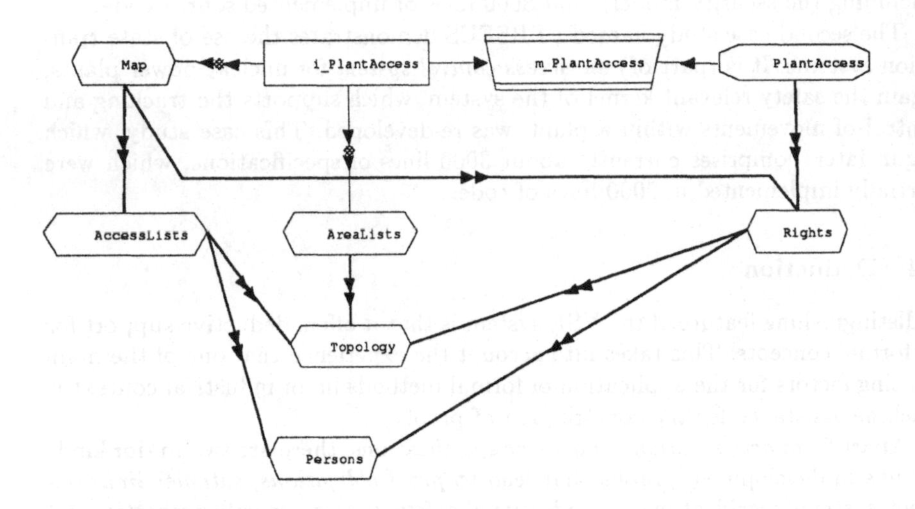

Fig. 2. A Development Graph

On the top-level we have the specification of an object **PlantAccess** which provides operations for looking up (**access**) and changing entries (**setaccess**) in the access matrix (**Matrix**). It uses *abstract data types* for matrixes (**AccessRel**), persons (**person**), and areas (**area**) given by the structured *theory* **Rights**.

In a typical refinement step we re-specify the theory **PlantAccess** on a lower specification level making some implementation decisions. For instance, we implement the access relation by a property list and define procedures **Get_access** and **Set_access** which operate on property lists and correspond to the functions **access** and setaccess specified in the theory **Rights**.

Next, we implement the access matrix in the theory **AccessLists**. A datatype **AccessList** is specified as a property list with persons as items and areas as values. An entry of a person p with value a denotes that p has access to a. Persons may occur several times in the property list specifying access rights to different areas.

```
THEORY AccessLists
 USING : Persons;
        Topology
 TYPES : AccessList = FREELY GENERATED BY
         nil |
         blst(getPerson : Person,getArea : area,rest : AccessList)
 FUNCTIONS : DEL : Person,Area,AccessList -> AccessList
 PREDICATES : in_list : Person,Area,AccessList
 VARS : b : area; p : person; l : AccessList
 ALGORITHMS : DEFPRED in_list(p, b, l) <->
              SWITCH l IN
              CASE nil : FALSE
              CASE blst : IF getPerson(l) = p
                          THEN IF getArea(l) = b
                               THEN TRUE
                               ELSE in_list(p, b, rest (l))
                               FI
                          ELSE in_list(p, b, rest(l))
                          FI
              NI;
 ...
THEORYEND
```

List of areas are defined in the theory **AreaLists**. Especially, the theory provides a function **higherAreas** of an area a which provides a list of all areas with higher security level than a.

```
THEORY AreaLists
 USING : Topology
 TYPES : areaList =
         FREELY GENERATED BY no_area |
                             add_area(first:area, rest:areaList)
 FUNCTIONS : higherAreas : area -> areaList
 PREDICATES : elem : area, areaList;
              _<_ : areaList, areaList
 VARS : b, b1, b2 : area;
        l, l1 : areaList
 ALGORITHMS : DEFPRED elem(b, l) <->
              SWITCH l IN
               CASE no_area  : FALSE
               CASE add_area : IF first(l) = b THEN TRUE
                               ELSE elem(b, rest(l)) FI
               NI;
              DEFPRED l < l1 <->
              SWITCH l IN
               CASE no_area  : l1 /= no_area
```

```
            CASE add_area : IF l1 = no_area THEN FALSE
                            ELSE rest(l) < rest(l1) FI
            NI
 AXIOMS : b2 elem higherAreas(b1) <-> (b2 > b1 OR b2 = b1)
THEORYEND
```

Based on the theories **AccessLists** and **AreaLists** the procedures **Get_Access** and **Set_Access** are defined which implement the functions **access** and **setaccess**. Thus, **Get_Access** implements the lookup whether a person is allowed to enter a specific area. It takes into consideration the access rights of visitors and an additional requirement that persons who have access to a specific area have also access to less secure areas. **extern** denotes the area outside the plant which is accessible by all persons.

```
FUNCTION Get_Access
 PARAMS : p_person : IN Person;
          p_area : IN Area
 RESULT : BOOL
 BODY   : DECLARE
           v_res: Bool:=F;
          IF p_area = extern THEN v_res := T
          ELSE IF visitor(p_person)
               THEN IF AccessToArea(leader(p_person),
                                    higherAreas(p_area)) = t
                    THEN v_res := T ELSE v_res := F FI
               ELSE IF AccessToArea(p_person,
                                    higherAreas(p_area)) = t
                    THEN v_res := T ELSE v_res := F FI
               FI
          FI;
          RETURN v_res
FUNCTIONEND
```

The procedure **Set_Access** grants or refuses (depending on the value of **p_entry**) a person access to a specific area.

```
PROCEDURE Set_Access
 PARAMS : p_person : IN person;
          p_area : IN area;
          p_entry : IN BOOL
 BODY : IF p_entry = t
        THEN IF NOT in_list(p_person, p_area, List)
             THEN List := blst(p_person, p_area, List)
             FI
        ELSE DelAccessToAreas(p_person, higherAreas(p_area))
        FI
PROCEDUREEND
```

In a next step we have to link both specifications, the theory **PlantAccess** and its implementation. This is done by so-called *Refinement steps* as it is shown in Figure 2. It consist of a *mapping* and a *module*. Modules, as the module **i_PlantAccess** below, contain slots for the import specifications, e.g. **Map** or **AreaLists**, the state dependent variables, e.g. **list**, and (references to) procedures that implement the abstract operations, e.g. **Get_Access** or **Set_Access**.

```
MODULE i_PlantAccess
 IMPORTSPEC : Map;AreaLists
 DATA : list : AccessList
 ELEMENTS : Get_Access, Set_Access, AccessToArea, DelAccessToAreas
MODULEEND
```

The theory **Map** provides the relation between the access relations and its implementation as a property list. Based on **AccessLists** the algorithm **list2rel** maps each access list into an access matrix:

```
THEORY Map
 USING : AccessLists;
         Rights
 FUNCTIONS : list2rel : AccessList -> AccessRel
 VARS : l : AccessList
 ALGORITHMS :
   DEFFUNC list2rel(l) =
           IF l = nil
           THEN emptyRel
           ELSE grant (getPerson(l), getArea(l),
                                        list2rel(rest(l)))
           FI
THEORYEND
```

The actual correspondence between the above procedures and the operations of the specification in **PlantAccess** is given by the mapping **m_PlantAccess**. In our case the access matrix is implemented by an access list while the operations **access** and **setaccess** are implemented by the procedures **Get_Access** and **Set_Access**.

```
MAPPING m_PlantAccess
 EXPORTSPEC : PlantAccess
 IMPLEMENTATION  : i_PlantAccess
 MAPS : Get_Access IMPLEMENTS access;
        Set_Access IMPLEMENTS setaccess;
        list2rel(List) IMPLEMENTS matrix
MAPPINGEND
```

4 Structural Deduction

Applying formal methods to industrial case studies results in thousands of lines of specifications which represent the logic database with the help of which various proof obligations have to be established. As mentioned above this specification is structured within a development graph (e.g. refer Figure 2 showing the development-graph of `PlantAccess`) and thus, the development graph represents also an structuring of the axiomatization. In Figure 2 doubled arrows indicate that the target theory of an arrow is (virtually) part of the specification of the source theory. This so-called theory-graph (the subgraph of the development graph wrt. double arrows) specifies which axiomatizations are part within a theory. E.g. `PlantAccess` uses the specification of `Rights` and thus, the axioms of `Rights` are visible within the theory of `PlantAccess`.

Proof obligations are always located at elements - e.g. mappings - of the development graph. They have to be established wrt. the specifications of theories accessible from this element via the arrows of the theory-graph. In case of `m_PlantAccess` the proof of some obligation may use the specifications of `i_PlantAccess`, `PlantAccess`, and the sub-theories visible in both. Hence, besides being a notion for structured specification the development graph represents also a structured database for the deduction system. Depending on the location of the proof obligation the corresponding subgraph of the development graph specify the axiomatization to be used for the proof.

Also each theory contains a set of lemmata formalizing properties on functions or operations which have been proven within the denoted subgraph. E.g. `Rights` may contain lemmata proven with the help of the theories `Rights`, `Topology`, and `Persons`.

4.1 Correctness Management

Verifying proof obligations with respect to the actual theories ensures the soundness of the corresponding development step. Since in general specifications contain errors which are usually detected during establishing the proof obligations there is an interleaved process of adapting the specification and proving theorems. In general changing the specification would invalid all proofs but with the help of the development graph the impacts of changing the specification can be restricted to specific parts of the graph while the soundness of proofs in other parts remains unaffected.

In general changing the axiomatization of a theory $\mathcal{T}$ will invalid the proofs (and thus also the lemmata) of all theories using T while underlying theories used by $\mathcal{T}$ are not affected. This work can be done without knowing a single proof just by a static analysis of the development graph. A more elaborated correctness management can be achieved by a dynamic analysis if we save for each lemma and proof obligation the set of axioms and lemmata used during the proof and build up a more elaborated dependency graph of lemmata and proof obligations.

Changing the implementation of a procedure (e.g. **Get_Access** in module **i_PlantAccess**) has no impacts to other parts of the theory-graph (e.g. the theories **PlantAccess** or **Map**) but will invalid lemmata in the implementation module **i_PlantAccess** and cause new proof obligations in the mapping **m_PlantAccess**. In order to reduce the amount of new proof obligations which occur after changing a procedure we use the implementation dependencies of the procedures in order to determine the subset of proof obligations which are affected by the change of the procedure.

4.2 Guiding Proofs

The first benefit of development graphs to the guidance of proofs is the reduction of search space by reducing the number of axioms and lemmata available during the proof. According to the theory-graph only a subset of the overall specification is available while establishing a proof obligation attached to an element of the graph.

Second, the development graph defines a partial ordering on theories and thus, also a partial ordering on functions and predicates defined within these theories which is used as a skeleton for a simplification ordering on formulas. E.g. **hasAccess** is defined within the theory **Rights** while **visitor** is specified within **Persons**. Thus, the system will orient appropriate equivalences as rewrite rules in order to replace occurrences of **hasAccess** in favor of **visitor** whenever possible.

Besides the explicit structure given by the development graph each axiomatization of a theory is structured again by itself. The axiomatization is build up by type declarations, specification of algorithms or procedures, arbitrary first-order formulas etc. Each of these types of specification result in a set of formulas which are part of the theory axiom. They differ in the way the deduction system uses them in order to guide a proof. E.g. algorithms (which are proved to be terminating) and type declarations are used to create induction schemes. Additionally, algorithms are used to refine the simplification ordering and to generate new simplification rules in order to enable symbolic evaluation.

Consider the freely generated datatype **areaList** inside the theory **AreaLists**. Its definition introduces a new (structural) induction scheme:

$$\Phi(no\_area) \wedge \forall x : areaList\ x \neq no\_area \rightarrow \Phi(rest(x)) \rightarrow \Phi(x)$$

$$\rightarrow \forall x : areaList\, \Phi(x)$$

Also the definitions of **elem** and **<** of the theory **AreaLists** which are proved to be terminating suggest (using their recursion orderings) induction schemes which are (in these cases) identical to the previous structural induction scheme. The algorithm of **list2rel** creates the simplification rules

$$list2rel(nil) \rightarrow emptyRel \text{ and}$$

$$list2rel(blst(p, a, tl)) \rightarrow grant(p, a, list2rel(tl))$$

5 Automation

Passive proof assistance where the system only *controls* the user (proof-checking) is not sufficient in situations where we are faced with proofs of thousands of deduction steps. On the other hand conventional fully automated theorem proving systems that carry out an exhaustive search following some complete (and therefore problem independent) strategy also turned out to be inadequate for our kind of applications. One reason for this is the limited possibility for user interaction where the activities of the user are restricted to certain preparations (formatting the input, choosing the search strategy and additional parameters) *before* the system is run.

Proof construction in VSE therefore follows the paradigm of *interactive strategic theorem proving*. A suitable representation of problem-specific knowledge which often is available in this context enables the system to exhibit an *active behavior*. It is this way that a routine generation of large and often technically complex proofs becomes possible. The main prerequisite for a strategic user interaction is an architecture that allows the user (and of course also the system) to analyze the *state of a proof*. In our architecture a proof state is given by a *partial proof tree*. The leaves of such a tree are open subgoals, lemmata or axioms. The basic activity is to refine a given subgoal by applying (backwards) proof steps thereby generating new subgoals. These proof steps are given by the general formalism and by local axioms. The user may also give more precise hints for a proof plan, which includes directives to apply a certain rule as the next step if the system gets stuck or he may replace hints. *Backtracking*, initialized either by the user or the system itself, allows proof steps to be undone and a previous situation to be restored. Thus, at each stage of the proof synthesis, the human user can revise the proof attempt specified so far or to give advice how to fill in the gaps of the proof tree.

Specifying, for instance, the mapping `m_PlantAccess` the system comes up with a proof obligation

$$\langle \texttt{Get\_Access(p, b, res)} \rangle \mathit{true}$$

which states that the procedure `Get_Access` terminates on all inputs *p*, *b*, and *res*. `Get_Access` uses a procedure `AccessToArea` which is defined as follows:

```
FUNCTION AccessToArea
 PARAMS : p_person : IN person;
          p_areaList : IN areaList
 RESULT : bool
 BODY : DECLARE
        v_res2: bool:=f;
        WHILE (NOT p_areaList = no_area) AND v_res2 = f DO
           IF in_list(p_person, first(p_areaList), List)
           THEN v_res2 := t
           ELSE p_areaList := rest(p_areaList) FI
        OD;
        RETURN v_res2
FUNCTIONEND
```

The deduction system reduces the proof obligation and comes up with a partial proof tree which contains a single open goal concerning the termination of the *while*-loop in `AccessToArea` (called by `Get_Access`). Now, it is up to the user to select an appropriate induction rule. After that the system continues and finish the proof automatically. During the proof several first order subgoals have to be proven like for instance,

$$\forall x : \mathit{areaList}\ x \neq \mathit{no\_area} \rightarrow \mathit{rest}(x) < x$$

This goal is proven automatically by induction. The system uses the knowledge of the termination ordering of < in the theory `AreaLists` in order to synthesize an appropriate induction scheme which results in this case in a structural induction. In case of

$$\mathit{rest}(x) = \mathit{add\_area}(\mathit{first}(\mathit{rest}(x)), \mathit{rest}(\mathit{rest}(x)))$$

we obtain an induction step. The system analyses the syntactical differences between the induction hypothesis

$$\underline{\mathit{rest}(x)} \neq \mathit{no\_area} \rightarrow \mathit{rest}(\underline{\mathit{rest}(x)}) < \underline{\mathit{rest}(x)}$$

and the induction conclusion

$$x \neq \mathit{no\_area} \rightarrow \mathit{rest}(x) < x.$$

These differences (which are underlined above) guide the prover in order to enable the use of the hypothesis [Hut90]. In this case the prover uses an axiom

$$\begin{aligned}\forall u, v : \mathit{areaList}\ u = \mathit{add\_area}(\mathit{first}(u), \mathit{rest}(u)) \wedge v = \mathit{add\_area}(\mathit{first}(v), \mathit{rest}(v))\\ \rightarrow (u < v) \leftrightarrow (\mathit{rest}(u) < \mathit{rest}(v))\end{aligned}$$

derived from the algorithm defined in the theory `AreaLists` to minimize the syntactical differences and we obtain:

$$x \neq \mathit{no\_area} \rightarrow \mathit{rest}(\mathit{rest}(x)) < \mathit{rest}(x).$$

Using the above precondition of the induction step the proof of the induction step is finished.

6 Fixing Bugs

So far, we have looked at the question of how to create proofs for *correct* theorems. In general, however, we will be confronted with errors in specifications, implementations, or both. Unless we have introduced "corresponding" errors in specifications and implementations, such errors will result in proof obligations which are not provable, i.e. we will reach open premises in the proof tree which can't be closed. As opposed to e.g. resolution based proofs, one can derive information about the potential problem by investigating the open premise and the path from the root of the proof tree to that premise.

As an example, consider the proof obligation for the `Set_Access` operation:

$$l = l' \vdash \langle \mathtt{Set\_Access}(p, b, z)\rangle (z = t \rightarrow list2rel(l) = grant(p, b, list2rel(l'))) \\ \wedge (z \neq t \rightarrow list2rel(l) = refuse(p, b, list2rel(l'))) \ ,$$

As mentioned before, *list2rel* maps access lists to the access matrix. This asserts that `Set_Access` will terminate, and afterwards the new value of the access relation, $list2rel(l)$, will correspond to the old value, $list2rel(l')$, with p granted or refused access to b according to the flag z.

While working on the proof, we will encounter an open goal

$$in\_list(p, a, l) \vdash list2rel(l) = grant(p, a, list2rel(l)) \ ,$$

since the implementation will add an entry only if it is not yet there (i.e. if $\neg in\_list(p, a, l)$ is true), while the specification does not treat that case separately. The goal is true if granting p access to a a second time (since if it is already in l, it will be in $list2rel(l)$ as well) has no effect. To prove this goal, we need axioms for the equality on relations. A quick look at the theory `Rights` reveals that such axioms have been forgotten.

Here, a sophisticated correctness management pays off. If we add the missing axioms to the theory `Rights`, the validity of the proofs for `m_PlantAccess` is not affected (since we only enlarge the axiom base, and our logic is monotonic). The change does, however, influence the correctness of an implementation of `Rights`. As a whole, it becomes invalid. The actual consequence of the change is a larger set of proof obligations, so that the existing proofs can remain valid. If we have to change the implementation as well to satisfy the additional proof obligations, even (some of) the proofs have to become invalid.

In general, an unprovable premise like the one above may hint at an error in any of the involved procedures or specifications, and a careful analysis is needed to find out the true reason for the problem.

A large number of bugs were uncovered during the verification process, in specifications as well as in implementations. In both case studies, bugs in specifications were more common, and were discovered when proving the security model or the correctness of an implementation. Also, aspects which were only vaguely described in the original documents and also difficult to formalize, proved to be those which significantly delayed the original projects. For the PERSEUS case study, for example, this included the treatment of visitor groups, the reaction to messages which are inconsistent with the current system state (e.g. staff members being detected in areas to which they have no access), and combinations of these problems (e.g. members of a visitor group who 'got lost'). The formal treatment of these parts uncovered intricate problems which had been overlooked in the original design.

7 Related Work, Current Research

In order to compare VSE to other methods and systems we recall the most important features of the system. The VSE methodology combines data type specifications with an abstract machine notation. Abstract machines are based on a notion of persistent states. The current version of VSE allows to specify operations causing state transitions as shown in section 2.1 . In that aspect VSE is similar to Z [Spi92] and systems like EHDM [RvHO91], VDM [Jon90], and the B Tool [ALN+91].

The methodology for developing abstract machines in B corresponds to that for state based systems in VSE . In VSE there is, however, a distinction between the problem of proving the *implementation* of a state based system correct, for which dynamic logic proof obligations are generated, and proving that one specification of a state based systems entails another. The latter is reduced to predicate logic proof obligations, and used to verify safety conditions and/or security models developed separately from a specification.

Reasoning about state based systems in the current version of VSE is restricted to invariance properties (given by a separate safety/security model) and the proof of refinements. However, the approach is compatible for example with Lamport's TLA, [Lam94]. Current work is concerned with an embedding of the specification technique into a temporal framework in order to cover for example eventuality properties and provide more general refinement concepts.

The data type part of VSE is based on abstract data types as compared to model based techniques like Z and VDM. Here and also in the case of abstract machines VSE supports algorithmic elements. In particular this concerns recursive definitions in constructive specifications and refinements. The correctness proof for an implementation, which usually involves assertions about the interplay between recursive procedures, also guarantees the consistency of the implemented data types relative to the consistency of the data types used for the implementation.

The algorithmic constructs allow for bridging the gap between concepts in abstract specifications and the concepts available in real programming languages. Proof support heavily relies on techniques for proving program properties and for guiding inductive proofs. In these aspects there is a different emphasis compared to Z-based systems.

From a more technical point of view considerable effort was made with respect to the integration of different proof techniques and the integration of the entire deduction component into a system for editing and storing formal developments.

Powerful proof support relies on special tailor-made calculi and an adequate representation of domain specific knowledge. The deduction component of the VSE system offers extensive proof support beyond the level of experimental or ad hoc systems. Up to now it is a heterogeneous system in that it combines two separated theorem proving systems. In the next version the various strategies will share a common deductive mechanism but still use different additional structures that allow for an efficient and highly automated proof generation.

VSE differs from systems with a loose integration of the deduction component or stands-alone deduction systems, like HOL, [GM93], or the Boyer-Moore prover, [BM79], not only by an automatic generation of proof obligations but also by offering a correctness management that maintains a consistent state of the development including the databases of logical objects. This correctness management is indispensable for an efficient treatment of changes. [BTo94]

With respect to both quantitative as well as qualitative aspects VSE is adequate for many industrial applications. However, this does not mean that no improvements are necessary. The VSE consortium is currently working on an enhanced version of the system to take notions like object orientation, concurrency, and real time into account.

Research at the DFKI is concerned with the extension of the formal basis of VSE and a further development of the deduction component. State transition systems as used in VSE are extended to cover *concurrent* and *embedded* systems based on an interleaving semantics. Temporal logics will be used in order to reason about these execution sequences.

With respect to the deduction component, we are working on a closer integration of KIV and INKA and a framework for proof planning which provides generic concepts and a more explicit representation of proof plans.

References

[ALN+91] J.R. Abrial, M.K.O. Lee, D.S. Neilson, P.N. Scharbach, and I.H. Sorensen. The B-method (software development). In W.J. Prehn, S.; Toetenel, editor, *VDM 91. Formal Software Development Methods. 4th International Symposium of VDM Europe Proceedings.*, volume 2, pages 398–405. BP Res., Sunbury Res. Centre, Sunbury-on-Thames, UK, Springer-Verlag, Berlin, Germany, October 1991.

[BCC+92] P. Baur, E. Canver, J. Cleve, R. Drexler, R. Förster, P. Göhner, H. Hauff, D. Hutter, P. Kejwal, D. Loevenich, W. Reif, C. Sengler, W. Stephan, M. Ullmann, and A. Wolpers. The Verification Support Environment VSE. In *Safety of Computer Control Systems 1992 (SAFECOMP'92)*, 1992.

[BHHW86] Susanne Biundo, Birgit Hummel, Dieter Hutter, and Christoph Walther. The Karlsruhe Induction Theorem Proving System. In Jörg H. Siekmann, editor, *Proceedings 8th International Conference on Automated Deduction (CADE), Lecture Notes in Computer Science (LNCS) 230*, pages 672 – 674, Oxford, England, 1986. Springer-Verlag, Berlin, Germany.

[BM79] R. S. Boyer and J Strother Moore. *A Computational Logic.* Academic Press, London, England, 1979.

[BTo94] The B-Toolkit. B-Core(UK) Limited, October 1994.

[GM93] M.J.C. Gordon and T.F. Melham. *Introduction to HOL.* Cambridge University Press, 1993.

[HRS90] Maritta Heisel, Wolfgang Reif, and Werner Stephan. Tactical Theorem Proving in Program Verification. In *Proceedings of the 10th International Conference on Automated Deduction*, volume 449 of *Lecture Notes in Artificial Intelligence (LNAI)*, pages 115–131. Springer-Verlag, Berlin, Germany, 1990.

[Hut90] Dieter Hutter. Guiding induction proofs. In Mark E. Stickel, editor, *Proceedings 10th International Conference on Automated Deduction (CADE), Lecture Notes in Artificial Intelligence (LNAI) 449*, pages 147–161, Kaiserslautern, Germany, July 1990. Springer-Verlag, Berlin, Germany.

[IT-89] IT-Sicherheitskriterien. Bundesanzeiger, 1989.

[Jon90] Cliff B. Jones. *Systematic Software Development using VDM.* Prentice Hall, 1990.

[Lam94] Leslie Lamport. The temporal logic of actions. *ACM Transactions on Programming Languages and Systems*, 16(3), 1994.

[Pra76] V. R. Pratt. Semantical Considerations on Floyd-Hoare Logic. In *Proc. 17th IEEE Symp. on Foundations of Computer Science*, pages 109–121, October 1976.

[Rei92a] Wolfgang Reif. Correctness of Generic Modules. In Nerode and Taitslin, editors, *Symposium on Software Technology and Theoretical Computer Science*, volume 620 of *Lecture Notes in Computer Science (LNCS)*. Springer-Verlag, Berlin, Germany, 1992. Tver, Russia.

[Rei92b] Wolfgang Reif. Verification of Large Software Systems. In Shyamasundar, editor, *Foundations of Software Technology and Theoretical Computer Science*, volume 652 of *LNCS*. Springer-Verlag, Berlin, Germany, 1992. New Dehli, India.

[RvHO91] J. Rushby, F. von Henke, and S. Owre. An Introduction to Formal Specification and Verification using EHDM. Technical report, SRI International, March 1991.

[Spi92] J. M. Spivey. *The Z Notation: A Reference Manual.* Series in Computer Science. Prentice Hall International, 2nd edition, 1992.

[VSE94] *Sprachbeschreibung VSE-SL*, 1994. Version 1.

Consistency and Refinement for Partial Specification in Z

Eerke Boiten, John Derrick, Howard Bowman and Maarten Steen

Computing Laboratory, University of Kent, Canterbury, CT2 7NF, U.K.
(Phone: +44 1227 827553, Email: {eab2,jd1,hb5,mwas}@ukc.ac.uk) *

Abstract. This paper discusses theoretical background for the use of Z as a language for partial specification, in particular techniques for checking consistency between viewpoint specifications. The main technique used is unification, i.e. finding a (candidate) least common refinement. The corresponding notion of consistency between specifications turns out to be different from the known notions of consistency for single Z specifications. A key role is played by correspondence relations between the data types used in the various viewpoints.

1 Partial specification

It is generally agreed that systems of a realistic size cannot be specified in single linear specifications, but rather should be decomposed into manageable chunks which can be specified separately. The traditional method for doing this is by hierarchical and functional decomposition. Nowadays, it is often claimed [11] that this is not the most natural or convenient (in relation to "perceived complexity") method – rather systems should be decomposed into different *aspects*. For each such *viewpoint* a specification of the system restricted to that particular aspect should be produced. Such *partial specifications* may omit certain parts of the system, because they are irrelevant to the particular aspect, and need not describe certain behaviours because they do not concern that specific viewpoint. Descriptions of this nature seem particularly appropriate for systems with various kinds of "users", each with their own view of the system. (Imagine, for example, the views of a library system that library managers, loan officers, clients, system operators, and programmers of the system would have.) Another reason for decomposing problems into aspects rather than subproblems is that different types of aspects have different specification languages that are best suited for them, for example dataflow diagrams for control flow, process algebras for "behaviour", data definition languages, et cetera.

There is one very serious problem in partial specification. Multiple viewpoints will describe what is intended to be the same system, and their descriptions will not in general be identical. Different viewpoints have different perspectives of

* This work was partially funded by the U.K. Engineering and Physical Sciences Research Council under grant number GR/K13035 and by British Telecom Labs., Martlesham, Ipswich, U.K.

the system, and they may even describe the system in different specification languages. This gives rise to an obligation to ensure that the partial specifications do not pose *contradictory* requirements: we need to check for *consistency*, potentially between descriptions in different languages and at different levels of abstraction.

One particular area in which viewpoint specification plays an important role is in *Open Distributed Processing* (ODP), an ISO standardisation initiative. The ODP reference model [9] defines five viewpoints for the specification of open distributed systems, with so-called *correspondence rules* as the links between the viewpoints (thus pinpointing the "is intended to be the same object" relationships). Our project 'Cross Viewpoint Consistency in Open Distributed Processing' aims to develop tools and techniques that enable the consistency of ODP specifications to be maintained. In previous papers [3, 5, 6] we have investigated techniques for consistency checking through unification in two of the main ODP specification languages: LOTOS [4] and Z [15]. The results obtained so far have convinced us that we need to explore further the nature of consistency checking and composition of partial specifications, and the role played by correspondence rules. This paper provides partial answers to these questions, mainly concentrating on the Z technique. Many of the issues raised will (thus) also be important to viewpoint specification in Z in general. The reader will be assumed to have a basic understanding of Z.

The next section presents a framework for consistency checking through unification, where the unification of specifications is a common refinement according to some refinement relation. Section 3 presents a number of general notions of consistency in Z. A concrete unification method for Z is then shown in section 4. We study mutual refinement in section 5, and conditions for a unified Z specification to be called consistent in section 6. In the final section we will draw some general conclusions and mention issues that need further research.

2 Consistency, unification, and refinement

We need to define what it means for a collection of viewpoint specifications to be consistent. Viewing the specifications as predicates over some universe, the logical definition of consistency is that it is impossible to derive both some proposition and its negation from the combined viewpoints.

In a context of specification and development of a concrete system, however, this abstract logical approach does not seem too useful. What *is* the universe we are quantifying over, and how do we map our specification language(s) to predicates over that universe? Would not a common semantic basis for possibly multiple languages necessarily be at such a low level that performing any kind of consistency proof becomes extremely complex [16]? What do we mean by "the combined viewpoints", will it always just be the logical conjunction of their formal interpretations, or do we need a more complex operator for combining viewpoints?

A more constructive view of consistency is one that is oriented towards system development. Instead of providing semantics for the specification languages, we encode our view of what specifications mean in *development relations*. Two specifications are in such a development relation if we consider one to be a correct development of the other on the way to an eventual implementation. A development relation may cross a language boundary, examples of such relations are semantics and translations, or it may not, in which case *refinement* relations form the main example, and equivalences another.

In such a framework, the consistency checking problem for a collection of viewpoint specifications is to find a specification which is a development of each of the viewpoint specifications according to the relevant development relations. Such common developments could also be called *unifications*. We are particularly interested in *least* unifications. In the special case where the development relation is a partial order (for example with refinement), a least unification is a *minimal* element in the set of unifications (where "minimal" is understood in the sense of fewest development steps done, least detail added, etc.) Such a least unification will be a most abstract specification that represents the viewpoints, which makes it a good choice to continue the unification process with. Suppose we wish to find a common development with yet another viewpoint. If the unification we chose is too concrete, we may have added details that make unification with the new viewpoint impossible. On the other hand, if we chose the most abstract one, we can be sure[2] that a unification with the new viewpoint, if it exists, can be found by unifying our previous unification with the new viewpoint. This guarantees that unifications of larger sets can be obtained by sequences of binary unifications.

In the examples we have looked at, it turned out that a lot of clarity was gained by being explicit about the overlap between the viewpoints. In many cases we can get away with assuming that equal names in different viewpoints refer to the same system object or function, but in some cases we cannot. A clear example of that is two objects with the same name but with different types: how do their types relate? Such relations between viewpoint specifications we will include explicitly as *correspondence relations* (as the name suggests, we think these may make up an important part of the correspondence rules in the ODP model). Unification and (existence of a) least common refinement will be with regard to a given correspondence relation.

In this way we have defined consistency as the existence of a least unification, with no additional tests. In practice, however, it is often convenient to generate a candidate least common development, i.e. some specification that *is* the least unification *if* one exists, and then to perform some consistency tests on it to determine whether it actually *is* a least unification. We will call such candidates "unifications" as well (using the term in a slightly sloppy sense). Finally note that it is strictly speaking incorrect to talk about *the* least unification of a

[2] Provided there are not multiple least unifications that are incomparable in the refinement ordering. Fortunately this will never occur with most known refinement relations, in particular Z refinement.

collection of viewpoint specifications, since for most specification languages and development relations there will be many equivalent ones.

3 General forms of consistency in Z

The language Z [15] is often used for viewpoint specifications, see for example [1, 10, 11], so there is a clear need for the investigation of consistency between partial specifications in Z, as most of the cited papers observe. What makes it particularly important for our project is that the ODP reference model [9] has adopted Z as one of the formal description techniques to be used as a viewpoint language, in particular for the *information* viewpoint.

Before going into the consistency *between* Z specifications in later sections, we briefly look at some ways in which a Z specification *on its own* can be considered inconsistent.

First, there are the direct contradictions, which all allow us to prove both P and $\neg P$ for some predicate P, or in other words (removing the quantification) which allow us to derive "false" from the specification. This is the simplest and most obvious definition of inconsistency in Z. The strong typing system of Z prevents quite a few classes of errors, but some kinds of contradictions can still be written, for example:

- Postulating that an empty set has an element:

  $| \; x : \varnothing$

- Abusing the fact that a function is a set of pairs:

  $$\begin{array}{|l} f : \mathbb{N} \rightarrow \mathbb{N} \\ \hline f = \{(1,2),(1,3)\} \end{array}$$

  (of course similar examples exist for all the different types of functions, including sequences).
- Inconsistent free types (a lot has been written on this, see [15, 2, 14]), for example $T ::= atom\langle\langle \mathbb{N} \rangle\rangle \mid fun\langle\langle T \rightarrow T \rangle\rangle$.

It is clear that inconsistencies of this type will also be inconsistencies if they occur in partial specifications.

A different type of possible inconsistency occurs when schemas have empty sets of bindings, for example (trivially)$D \mathrel{\widehat=} [x:S \mid \text{false}]$. As long as we do not assert that we have a value from D, this is not an actual inconsistency. In the states-with-operations interpretation of Z, described for example in [15, chapter 5], a schema with an empty set of bindings is probably a specification error. A special case of this condition is known as the *Initialisation Theorem*: the schema describing the initial state of an abstract data type should not be empty. Even though we will be adopting the states-with-operations approach to specification in Z, it is not clear at this point if we should mark empty schemas as inconsistencies in partial specifications, and whether we should distinguish between state schemas and operation schemas in that respect.

In the sequel we will see that (candidate) unifications of Z viewpoint specifications may satisfy all of the above notions of consistency, and still not retain the interpretations of the viewpoints. Before we can observe this, we have to show how to construct unifications.

4 A unification method in Z

In this (long) section we construct candidate least unifications for pairs of Z specifications, with the normal Z refinement relation as the development relation for both partial specifications. The unification will turn out to be a least common refinement provided two conditions hold of the viewpoint specifications.

We will concentrate on the unification of state and operation schemas, since we envisage the viewpoint specification style for Z to have those as its major elements. Other Z constructs are degenerate cases of these, or not expected to occur in more than one viewpoint. Operations change states, so we need to unify state schemas first. After that we can adapt and unify operation schemas.

4.1 Unification of state schemas informally

Let us (for now) take as the underlying interpretation of a state schema $D_1 \mathrel{\widehat=} [\, x{:}Apple \mid NotWormEaten\ x \,]$ that it allows us to choose from all apples, but we have to discard the worm-eaten ones. To unify this with $D_2 \mathrel{\widehat=} [\, x{:}Fruit \mid NotRotten\ x \,]$ we have to take the union of the base sets (which is *Fruit* in this case) and the intersection of the conditions (*NotRotten* and, if it is an *Apple*, also *NotWormEaten*). Thus, we interpret the type declaration as giving a "set we choose from", and unification extends the range of choice. The predicates on the other hand are interpreted as restrictions, which need to be combined in unification. Formally predicates and subtypes are of course equivalent, which suggests we should have disjunctions or conjunctions in *both* cases. For the examples we have dealt with so far [6, 7], however, this default interpretation seemed to capture the intuition much better.

So, suppose we have the following two state schemas (which, given the above interpretation, will *not* be normalised[3]). They have the same name (with a distinguishing index), which means that they are linked by an implicit correspondence rule.

D_1	D_2
$x{:}S$	$x{:}T$
$pred_S$	$pred_T$

According to our intuive view of state schemas, their unification should be [6]:

[3] The normalisation of a state schema changes the variables to be of their maximal type, and puts all other typing information in the predicate.

D

$x : S \cup T$

$x \in S \Rightarrow pred_S$
$x \in T \Rightarrow pred_T$

However, this is not type correct in general: $S \cup T$ is an error unless S and T have the same maximal type. A *disjoint* union of S and T would not be right either, since then values that S and T have in common would be considered different.

4.2 Totalised correspondence relations provide unions

So how do we resolve the situation that S and T may have values in common and may also be type-incompatible? The answer is to modify the second-best known implementation of disjoint union as a product[4] and to use correspondence relations.

(In order to keep this explanation simple, we venture outside the Z typing system for a moment.) If $\mathbb{1}$ is a type with a single element not in S or T, let us call it $\perp$, then we could define the disjoint union of S and T by

$$S + T = S \times \mathbb{1} \cup \mathbb{1} \times T$$

i.e. $S + T = \{(s,t) \mid (s \in S \wedge t = \perp) \vee (s = \perp \wedge t \in T)\}$. The smallest product set containing this set is $S_\perp \times T_\perp$, where $Q_\perp$ is the union of Q and $\mathbb{1}$. (Still a disjoint union, but of an appreciably simpler kind.) Now what we will do is construct particular subsets within $S_\perp \times T_\perp$, starting from $S + T$. The rules are simple: we can add tuples (s,t) for which $s \in S$ and $t \in T$, provided we then remove tuples $(s,\perp)$ and $(\perp,t)$ from the set. (The interpretation of this is that we no longer consider s and t different. Compare the interpretation of disjoint union: no element from the one set is equal to any element from the other.)

Let us call such sets *totalised correspondence relations*. Totalised correspondence relations over S and T are characterised by the fact that for each $s \in S$ there is a tuple (s,x) for some $x \in T_\perp$, and exactly one such tuple if $x = \perp$, and similarly for all $t \in T$. Totalised correspondence relations are linked in a one-to-one way with *correspondence relations* between S and T: for $tot\ R$ the totalised correspondence of R, we have $tot\ R = R \cup (S \setminus \operatorname{dom} R) \times \mathbb{1} \cup \mathbb{1} \times (T \setminus \operatorname{ran} R)$, and $R = tot\ R \cap S \times T$. In particular, the empty relation corresponds to the disjoint union. For any correspondence relation (given by the specifier), the totalised correspondence relation will provide the desired union of state spaces.

Here ends our brief excursion outside the Z typing system; we now give the formal definitions in Z. The main differences arise from the need to use explicit injection functions (into free types) where we used set unions above. The one-to-one correspondence also holds in Z, it just looks a bit more complicated.

[4] The best known one is $S + T = \{0\} \times S \cup \{1\} \times T$.

Definition 1 (Type with bottom) For any type S, we define the type $S_\perp$ by the following free type definition:

$$S_\perp ::= \perp_S \mid justS\langle\langle S\rangle\rangle$$

For all such types, a function *theS* is defined as the inverse of the injection *justS*:

$$\begin{array}{l} theS : S_\perp \twoheadrightarrow S \\ \hline \mathrm{dom}\, theS = \mathrm{ran}\, justS \\ \forall x{:}S \bullet theS\,(justS\, x) = x \end{array}$$

□

Definition 2 (Totalisation of a relation) The totalisation *tot R* of a relation R on two given types S and T is defined as follows:

$$\begin{array}{l} [S,T] \\ tot : (S \leftrightarrow T) \rightarrowtail\!\!\!\!\rightarrow (S_\perp \leftrightarrow T_\perp) \\ \hline \forall R : S \leftrightarrow T \bullet \\ \quad tot\ R = theS \mathbin{;} R \mathbin{;} justT \\ \qquad\qquad \cup \{x : S \setminus \mathrm{dom}\, R \bullet (justS\ x, \perp_T)\} \cup \{y : T \setminus \mathrm{ran}\, R \bullet (\perp_S, justT\ y)\} \end{array}$$

□

Totalised correspondences provide the possibility to specify anything between disjoint union (take the correspondence to be the empty relation) and union (take the correspondence to be the identity relation on the intersection). Moreover, they provide the opportunity to relate elements of types that cannot be directly related in Z even if they appear to be identical.

Example 3 (Union of enumerated types) If we have $S = a \mid b \mid c$ and $T = a \mid d$, we can form the obvious union where both a's are identified by taking the correspondence to be $\{(a,a)\}$. The totalised correspondence relation is then the set $\{(justS\ b, \perp_T), (justS\ c, \perp_T), (justS\ a, justT\ a), (\perp_S, justT\ d)\}$ which can be seen as a renaming of the set $\{b,c,a,d\}$.

□

If we provide a correspondence relation between S and T, which points out exactly which values in S correspond to which values in T, the totalised correspondence provides the required union of S and T. In many cases the specifier need not explicitly state what the correspondence relation is, the default correspondence relation defined below may give the desired result.

Definition 4 (Default correspondence) The default correspondence relation on schemas $D_1 \mathrel{\widehat=} [\,x{:}S \mid pred_S\,]$ and $D_2 \mathrel{\widehat=} [\,x{:}T \mid pred_T\,]$ is $\{(x,x) \bullet x \in S \cap T\}$ if $S \cap T$ is a well-typed expression (i.e. S and T have a common supertype); otherwise it is the empty relation.

□

(In another paper [3] we have described how the correspondence relation can be used to unify viewpoints that use different representations of the same data, using the same unification rules. In the current paper we concentrate on correspondence relations that are partial identity relations or other injective functions; the paper [3] shows that allowing general relations extends viewpoint unification with datatype implementation.)

4.3 State unification using correspondences

Let us assume that the correspondence relation between the types S and T is given by the relation $R \subseteq S \times T$. The inhabitants of the unified state schema will be the tuples of *tot* R.

$$
\begin{array}{l}
\textbf{schema } D \\
\hline
x_1 : S_\bot;\ x_2 : T_\bot \\
\hline
(x_1, x_2) \in \mathit{tot}\ R \\
\forall x : S \bullet x_1 = \mathit{justS}\ x \Rightarrow \mathit{pred}_S \\
\forall x : T \bullet x_2 = \mathit{justT}\ x \Rightarrow \mathit{pred}_T
\end{array}
$$

This looks like we are actually maintaining two values for the state variable x; however, due to (x_1,x_2) being in *tot* R it is the case that either exactly one of the two values is $\bot$ and thus invalid, or the two values are "equal" (since they are in R, and R only contains tuples of things we consider equal).

In the examples that follow, we will often observe isomorphisms between schemas: the schemas that get constructed often have additional clutter of constructor functions and their inverses, and renamings of all inhabitants of the schema usually exist that yield the intuitively desirable schemas. Such (injective) renamings of all inhabitants of a schema we call *isomorphisms*, they form a special case of data refinement in both directions, see section 5.

Example 5 (Union of enumerated types, continued) Continuing from example 3, suppose we have schemas $D_1 \mathrel{\widehat{=}} [\,x : S\,]$ and $D_2 \mathrel{\widehat{=}} [\,x : T\,]$ where the types are given by $S ::= a \mid b \mid c$ and $T ::= a \mid d$, and the correspondence relation by $R = \{(a,a)\}$ (the default correspondence would be empty). Their unification is given by the schema

$$
\begin{array}{l}
\textbf{schema } D \\
\hline
x_1 : S_\bot;\ x_2 : T_\bot \\
\hline
(x_1, x_2) \in \mathit{tot}\ R \\
\forall x : S \bullet x_1 = \mathit{justS}\ x \Rightarrow \mathrm{true} \\
\forall x : T \bullet x_2 = \mathit{justT}\ x \Rightarrow \mathrm{true}
\end{array}
$$

which (see example 3) is isomorphic to the schema $D \mathrel{\widehat{=}} [\,x : V\,]$ where $V ::= a \mid b \mid c \mid d$. Using the default would result in two different a's.

□

The next two examples do use the default correspondence.

Example 6 The schemas

$$
\begin{array}{l}
\textbf{schema } D_1 \\
\hline
x : \mathbb{Z} \\
\hline
-1 \leq x \leq 3
\end{array}
\qquad
\begin{array}{l}
\textbf{schema } D_2 \\
\hline
x : \mathbb{Z} \\
\hline
\exists z : \mathbb{N} \bullet x = z + z
\end{array}
$$

have the same type of component so their correspondence relation is the identity relation on that type. The schema that results from unification is

$$\begin{array}{|l} D \\ \hline x_1 : \mathbb{Z}_\perp ;\ x_2 : \mathbb{Z}_\perp \\ \hline (x_1, x_2) \in tot\,\{(x,x) \mid x \in \mathbb{Z}\} \\ \forall\, x : \mathbb{Z} \bullet x_1 = just\mathbb{Z}\, x \Rightarrow -1 \leq x \leq 3 \\ \forall\, x : \mathbb{Z} \bullet x_2 = just\mathbb{Z}\, x \Rightarrow \exists\, z : \mathbb{N} \bullet x = z + z \\ \hline \end{array}$$

The totalised identity relation on $\mathbb{Z}$ is the set $\{(just\mathbb{Z}\, x, just\mathbb{Z}\, x) \mid x \in \mathbb{Z}\}$, so this schema is isomorphic to

$$\begin{array}{|l} D \\ \hline x : \mathbb{Z} \\ \hline -1 \leq x \leq 3 \\ \exists\, z : \mathbb{N} \bullet x = z + z \\ \hline \end{array}$$

which, as it turns out, is the intersection (or rather: the *conjunction*) of the input schemas. This can be shown to hold in general: if the types of the components are identical, the union of the schemas is their conjunction for the default correspondence relation.

□

Example 7 Any similarity between this example and the previous one will be discussed in later sections. Schemas $D_1 \mathrel{\widehat{=}} [\, x : -1 \,..\, 3 \,]$ and $D_2 \mathrel{\widehat{=}} [\, x : \{z : \mathbb{N} \bullet z + z\} \,]$ have the identity relation on the intersection of their component types as the correspondence relation, i.e. {(0,0),(2,2)}. The schema resulting from their unification is isomorphic to $D \mathrel{\widehat{=}} [\, x : (-1 \,..\, 3) \cup \{z : \mathbb{N} \bullet z + z\} \,]$.

□

The final example shows that a schema with an empty set of bindings might fulfill a very useful role when we apply this state unification rule: it is the unit of state unification, modulo a trivial renaming.

Example 8 (The empty state) For the states $D_1 \mathrel{\widehat{=}} [\, x : \varnothing \,]$ and $D_2 \mathrel{\widehat{=}} [\, x : T \mid pred_T \,]$ there is only one correspondence relation possible, viz. the empty relation, the only subset of $\varnothing \times T = \varnothing$[5]. Totalising yields the set $\{x : T \bullet (\perp_\varnothing, just T\, x)\}$. (Note that the type $\varnothing_\perp$ has only one element, viz. $\perp_\varnothing$.) Thus, the unified schema is

[5] We are aware that for strict Z typing we have to state the types of the elements that the various empty sets do not contain.

$$\begin{array}{|l}
\multicolumn{1}{l}{D} \\ \hline
x_1 : \varnothing_\perp;\ x_2 : T_\perp \\ \hline
(x_1, x_2) \in \{x : T \bullet (\perp_\varnothing, \mathit{justT}\ x)\} \\
\forall x : \varnothing \bullet x_1 = \mathit{just}\varnothing\ x \Rightarrow \mathrm{true} \\
\forall x : T \bullet x_2 = \mathit{justT}\ x \Rightarrow \mathit{pred}_T \\ \hline
\end{array}$$

which is obviously isomorphic to $D \mathrel{\widehat{=}} [\, x : T \mid \mathit{pred}_T \,]$.

□

The significance of this is that we have a uniform way of treating state schemas across viewpoints: if a certain state schema is not defined at all in one viewpoint, we may regard it as defined to be an empty state space.

4.4 Unification of operation schemas

The unification of operation schemas proceeds in two steps. In the first step, all schemas get adapted to the unified state schemas. In the second step, operations that are defined in both viewpoints are unified using their pre- and postconditions.

In the presentation of these rules, we assume that the state has changed exactly according to the rule for state unification given above, i.e. that no renamings of the inhabitants have taken place. Note, however, that because these renamings are injective functions, we can freely translate back and forth between the isomorphic state spaces. In other words, in most concrete cases the expressions with lots of constructor functions etc., as we give them here, can be translated into something more intuitive, just as we did for state schemas in the examples.

An operation that was originally defined on the state D_1 by

$$\begin{array}{|l}
\multicolumn{1}{l}{Op_1} \\ \hline
\Delta D_1;\ \mathit{Decl}_1 \\ \hline
\mathit{pred}_1 \\ \hline
\end{array}$$

gets adapted to the new state schema by changing it to

$$\begin{array}{|l}
\multicolumn{1}{l}{\mathit{AdOp}_1} \\ \hline
\Delta D;\ \mathit{Decl}_1 \\ \hline
x_1 \in \mathrm{ran}\ \mathit{justS} \\
x_1' \in \mathrm{ran}\ \mathit{justS} \\
\mathbf{let}\ x == \mathit{theS}\ x_1\ ;\ x' == \mathit{theS}\ x_1' \bullet \mathit{pred}_1 \\ \hline
\end{array}$$

(and of course an almost identical rule is used for operations from the second viewpoint.) A very similar rule can be given for operations that do not change the state (i.e. that have ΞD in their declarations). The situation is only slightly more complicated if operations operate on multiple states – the rule above can then be applied repeatedly, and the only complication is the bookkeeping of which references to states have been updated to refer to changed states.

The unification of two viewpoint operations should exhibit possible behaviour of each of the viewpoint operations in each situation where the viewpoint operation was applicable. This requirement can be formalised using pre- and postconditions.[6] The unified operation should be applicable whenever one of the viewpoint operations is, i.e. its precondition should be the disjunction of the viewpoint operation preconditions. Moreover, when the unified operation is applied to a state satisfying one particular precondition, a state should result that satisfies the corresponding postcondition. Such an operation unification is also described by Ainsworth et al. [1], there called *union*, but they fail to mention that the union may not exist. The candidate least unification of operation schemas $AdOp_1$ and $AdOp_2$, both operating on the same state, is given by[7]

$$
\begin{array}{|l}
\textit{UnOp} \\
\hline
\textit{Decls};\ \Delta D \\
\hline
\text{pre } AdOp_1 \lor \text{pre } AdOp_2 \\
\text{pre } AdOp_1 \Rightarrow \text{post } AdOp_1 \\
\text{pre } AdOp_2 \Rightarrow \text{post } AdOp_2 \\
\hline
\end{array}
$$

where *Decls* is obtained by textually unifying the declarations of $AdOp_1$ and $AdOp_2$. That this schema only defines the desired unification under additional restrictions is clear from a little calculation. Note that the precondition of an operation Op with no input or output, operating on *State*, is given by

$$\text{pre } Op = \exists\, State' \bullet Op$$

We write pre_1 for pre $AdOp_1$ etc for clarity in the following calculation:

$$
\begin{array}{ll}
 & \text{pre } UnOp \\
\equiv & \quad \{ \text{ definition pre } \} \\
 & \exists\, State' \bullet (\text{pre}_1 \lor \text{pre}_2) \land (\text{pre}_1 \Rightarrow \text{post}_1) \land (\text{pre}_2 \Rightarrow \text{post}_2) \\
\equiv & \quad \{ \text{ pre}_1 \text{ and pre}_2 \text{ do not refer to } State' \ \} \\
 & (\text{pre}_1 \lor \text{pre}_2) \land \exists\, State' \bullet (\text{pre}_1 \Rightarrow \text{post}_1) \land (\text{pre}_2 \Rightarrow \text{post}_2)
\end{array}
$$

---

[6] Note that, unlike the precondition, the postcondition of a Z operation schema cannot be uniquely determined. For a schema $Op \mathrel{\widehat{=}} [\Delta D \mid pred]$ which (to avoid some semantic problems) satisfies the condition $pred \Rightarrow \text{pre } Op$, any condition P such that $\text{pre } Op \land P \Leftrightarrow pred$ will do as "the" postcondition, in particular *pred* itself. Thus any occurrence of post Op in the sequel should be taken to refer to *some* possible postcondition of Op.

[7] Wim Feijen pointed out the similarity between the conditions in this schema and those in the w(eakest)p(recondition)-calculus for the guarded command $P_1 \rightarrow Op_1 \,\Box\, P_2 \rightarrow Op_2$ where pre_i has the role of the guard.

$$\equiv \qquad \{ \text{ case analysis, } \exists\, State' \bullet \text{pre}_i \Rightarrow \text{post}_i \text{ holds } \}$$

$$(\text{pre}_1 \vee \text{pre}_2) \wedge \exists\, State' \bullet \text{pre}_1 \wedge \text{pre}_2 \Rightarrow \text{post}_1 \wedge \text{post}_2$$

$$\equiv \qquad \{ \text{ pre}_1 \text{ and pre}_2 \text{ do not refer to } State' \}$$

$$(\text{pre}_1 \vee \text{pre}_2) \wedge (\text{pre}_1 \wedge \text{pre}_2 \Rightarrow \exists\, State' \bullet \text{post}_1 \wedge \text{post}_2)$$

In other words, the precondition of the union is *only* the disjunction of the preconditions if both postconditions can be satisfied when both preconditions are. This is an essential condition which will form part of our consistency check. In fact, it is already a condition for the union to be a common refinement of the operations, and it is useful to give it a name.

Definition 9 Operations A and B, operating on the same state space *State*, are said to be *operation consistent* iff

$$\forall\, State \bullet \text{pre}\, A \wedge \text{pre}\, B \Rightarrow \exists\, State' \bullet \text{post}\, A \wedge \text{post}\, B.$$

□

4.5 Unification is least common refinement

Here we present what amounts to a correctness proof for the unification rules given above. The proof will be in three steps: showing that the adapted operations with the unified state form data refinements of the viewpoints; showing that unified operations are (operation) refinements of the adapted operations; and finally a proof that the unification is a *least* common refinement. The proof given below imposes extra conditions on the viewpoint specifications in two places: one is operation consistency as defined above, the other is *state consistency* which follows from analysis of the preconditions of the adapted operations.

First we show that the unified state with the adapted operations form data refinements of the viewpoints with operations. For that purpose we have to formally link the state schemas using a *retrieve relation*. For the unified state schema D and the state schema of the first viewpoint $D_1 \mathrel{\widehat=} [\, x{:}S \mid pred_S \,]$ the retrieve relation is given by the schema

```
┌─ Retr1 ──────────────────────────
│ D1; D
├──────────────
│ x1 = justS x
└──────────────────────────────────
```

There are two conditions to prove that this is a valid data refinement [15], making any universal quantifications implicit:

1. $\text{pre}\, Op_1 \wedge Retr1 \Rightarrow \text{pre}\, AdOp_1$
2. $\text{pre}\, Op_1 \wedge Retr1 \wedge AdOp_1 \Rightarrow \exists\, x' \bullet Retr1' \wedge Op_1$

The proof of the first property has a big hurdle in the middle of it. For simplicity we ignore the contribution of $Decl_1$ to the predicate $AdOp_1$ since it makes the same contribution to Op_1.

$\text{pre } AdOp_1$

$\equiv \quad \{ \text{ definition of pre } \}$

$\exists x_1'; x_2' \bullet AdOp_1$

$\equiv \quad \{ \text{ definition } AdOp_1 \}$

$\exists x_1'; x_2' \bullet D \land D' \land x_1 \in \text{ran } justS$
$\qquad \land x_1' \in \text{ran } justS \land pred_1[theS\ x_1/x][theS\ x_1'/x']$

$\equiv \quad \{ \text{ conjuncts independent of new state } \}$

$D \land x_1 \in \text{ran } justS$

$\land \quad \exists x_1'; x_2' \bullet D' \land x_1' \in \text{ran } justS \land pred_1[theS\ x_1/x][theS\ x_1'/x']$

$\equiv \quad \{ \textbf{ WISH: } x_2' \text{ always exists here; translation } x' := theS\ x_1' \}$

$D \land x_1 \in \text{ran } justS \land \exists x' \bullet D_1[theS\ x_1'/x] \land pred_1[theS\ x_1/x]$

$\equiv \quad \{ \text{ definition of pre } \}$

$D \land x_1 \in \text{ran } justS \land \text{pre } Op_1[theS\ x_1/x]$

$\Leftarrow \quad \{ \text{ definition } Retr1, \text{ substitution } \}$

$Retr1 \land \text{pre } Op_1$

Of course the crux of this proof is the step marked with **WISH**. It is clear that we need an extra condition here, the predicate really depends on x_2' through the conjunct D'. A correct x_2' may not exist in exactly one type of situation: $(x_1', x_2') = (justS\ x, justT\ y)$ and $(x,y) \in R$, $pred_S$ holds but $pred_T[y/x]$ does not hold. That is to say, the output value of the operation is linked by the correspondence relation to an "illegal" value, whereas the input value is linked to a legal one (and thus not excluded from the translated precondition $Retr1 \land \text{pre } Op_1$). At this point we will assume that the viewpoints are *state consistent* to prevent this problem:

Definition 10 The two state schemas $D_1 \mathrel{\widehat=} [\, x{:}S \mid pred_S \,]$ and $D_2 \mathrel{\widehat=} [\, x{:}T \mid pred_T \,]$ are *state consistent* with respect to the correspondence relation $R \subseteq S \times T$ iff

$$(x,y) \in R \Leftrightarrow (pred_S \Leftrightarrow pred_T[y/x])$$

□

This is a sufficient, but not a necessary condition; for a further discussion of related properties, see section 6. The second property is more easily proved:

$\exists x' \bullet Retr1' \land Op_1$

$\equiv \quad \{ \text{ definitions } \}$

$\exists x' \bullet D_1' \land D' \land x_1' = justS\ x' \land D \land D' \land pred_1$

$\equiv \quad \{ D \text{ and } D' \text{ independent of } x'; theS \text{ is inverse of } justS \}$

$(\exists x' \bullet D_1' \land theS\ x_1' = x' \land pred_1) \land D \land D'$

$\equiv \quad \{ \text{ one point rule for existential quantifier } \}$

$pred_S[theS\ x_1'/x] \wedge pred_1[theS\ x_1'/x'] \wedge D \wedge D'$

$\Leftarrow$ { first conjunct follows from D'; property of substitution }

$pred_1[theS\ x_1/x][theS\ x_1'/x'] \wedge x_1 = justS\ x \wedge D \wedge D'$

$\Leftarrow$ { definitions $AdOp_1$ and $Retr1$, add conjunct }

pre $Op_1 \wedge AdOp_1 \wedge Retr1$

Of course the proof for the second viewpoint is completely analogous.

The second step is to show that *UnOp* is a common refinement of $AdOp_1$ and $AdOp_2$. In this case, too, it suffices to give only one half of the proof. Because this step involves no change of state space, we only need to prove the two conditions for operation refinement [15], again omitting universal quantifications:

1. pre $AdOp_1 \Rightarrow$ pre $UnOp$
2. pre $AdOp_1 \wedge UnOp \Rightarrow AdOp_1$

The first is only true if the *operation consistency* condition holds, see the calculation of pre *UnOp* above (and then it is a one line proof). The second is easily proved using the fact that the predicate part of an operation schema A can be given as pre $A \wedge$ post A.

The final step of the least common refinement proof is showing that the unification is a *least* common refinement. This will be done by showing that an *arbitrary* refinement of both viewpoints is necessarily a refinement of the unification.

Suppose that state schema E with operation schema *Opp* also form a (data) refinement of both viewpoint specifications (D_1, Op_1) and (D_2, Op_2), and that the state of E is given by the (fresh) variable y. This means that two retrieve relations exists, let us assume they are given by $(i=1,2)$

```
┌─ Retr_i ──────────────────────
│ D_i; E
├───────────────
│ retr_i
└───────────────────────────────
```

The assumption that these are data refinements translates into assumptions we can use in proofs:

1. pre $Op_i \wedge Retr_i \Rightarrow$ pre Opp
2. pre $Op_i \wedge Retr_i \wedge Opp \Rightarrow \exists x' \bullet Retr_i' \wedge Op_i$

We now prove that, under these assumptions, (E, Opp) is a data refinement of $(D, UnOp)$. Thus we have to find some retrieve relation *RetrED* such that

1. pre $UnOp \wedge RetrED \Rightarrow$ pre Opp
2. pre $UnOp \wedge RetrED \wedge Opp \Rightarrow \exists x_1'; x_2' \bullet RetrED' \wedge UnOp$

Our choice for that retrieve relation is the following schema.

$$\begin{array}{|l}\hline \textit{RetrED} \\ D;\ E \\ \hline \textit{retr}_1[\textit{theS}\ x_1/x] \vee \textit{retr}_2[\textit{theT}\ x_2/x] \\ \hline\end{array}$$

(The main motivation for this particular choice is that it works.)

Now we prove the two properties. For the first we leave out universal quantification over y, the "concrete state".

$$\begin{array}{ll}
 & \forall x_1;\ x_2 \bullet \text{pre } Opp \Leftarrow \text{pre } UnOp \wedge RetrED \\
\equiv & \qquad \{\ \text{assuming operation consistency}\ \} \\
 & \forall x_1;\ x_2 \bullet \text{pre } Opp \Leftarrow (\text{pre } AdOp_1 \vee \text{pre } AdOp_2) \wedge RetrED \\
\equiv & \qquad \{\ \text{definition } RetrED\ \} \\
 & \forall x_1;\ x_2 \bullet \text{pre } Opp \Leftarrow (\text{pre } AdOp_1 \vee \text{pre } AdOp_2) \wedge D \wedge E \\
 & \qquad\qquad\qquad \wedge retr_1[theS\ x_1/x] \vee retr_2[theT\ x_2/x] \\
\Leftarrow & \qquad \{\ \text{calculus}\ \} \\
 & \forall x_1;\ x_2 \bullet \text{pre } Opp \Leftarrow (\text{pre } AdOp_1 \wedge D \wedge E \wedge retr_1[theS\ x_1/x]) \\
 & \qquad\qquad\qquad \vee(\text{pre } AdOp_2 \wedge D \wedge E \wedge retr_2[theT\ x_2/x]) \\
\equiv & \qquad \{\ \text{definition pre } AdOp_i \text{ (state consistency);} \\
 & \qquad\quad \text{translation } (x_1, x_2) := (justS\ x, justT\ y)\ \} \\
 & \forall x;\ y \bullet \text{pre } Opp \Leftarrow (\text{pre } Op_1 \wedge D_1 \wedge E \wedge retr_1) \\
 & \qquad\qquad\qquad \vee((\text{pre } Op_2)[y/x] \wedge D_2 \wedge E \wedge retr_2[y/x]) \\
\equiv & \qquad \{\ \text{definition } Retr_i\text{; assumptions}\ \} \\
 & \text{true}
\end{array}$$

The second proof is a quite complicated one. We are asked to prove that $\forall x_1;\ x_2;\ y \bullet P \Rightarrow (\exists x_1';\ x_2' \bullet Q)$ for certain predicates P and Q. The proof proceeds by first showing how $\exists x_1';\ x_2' \bullet Q$ can be rewritten as $\exists x' \bullet Q_1 \vee \exists x' \bullet Q_2$. Then we do a case introduction on P such that $P{=}(P_1 \vee P_2)$ and we show that $\forall x_1;\ x_2;\ y \bullet P_i \Rightarrow (\exists x' \bullet Q_i)$ follows from the assumption that E is a refinement of the i-th viewpoint, which then completes the proof.

$$\begin{array}{ll}
 & \exists x_1';\ x_2' \bullet RetrED' \wedge UnOp \\
\equiv & \qquad \{\ \text{definition } UnOp\text{, assuming operation consistency}\ \} \\
 & (\exists x_1';\ x_2' \bullet RetrED' \wedge AdOp_1) \vee (\exists x_1';\ x_2' \bullet RetrED' \wedge AdOp_2)
\end{array}$$

The simplifications of these disjuncts will be completely analogous so we show only one:

$$\begin{array}{ll}
 & \exists x_1';\ x_2' \bullet RetrED' \wedge AdOp_1 \\
\Leftarrow & \qquad \{\ \text{definition of } RetrED' \text{ and } AdOp_1\ \} \\
 & \exists x_1';\ x_2' \bullet D' \wedge E' \wedge (retr_1[theS\ x_1/x])' \wedge D \wedge x_1 \in \text{ran}\ justS
\end{array}$$

$$\wedge\ x_1' \in \operatorname{ran} justS \wedge pred_1[theS\ x_1/x][theS\ x_1'/x']$$

$$\equiv \quad \{ \text{ assuming state consistency, translate } x_1' := justS\ x' \ \}$$

$$\exists\, x' \bullet D_1' \wedge E' \wedge retr_1' \wedge D \wedge x_1 \in \operatorname{ran} justS \wedge pred_1[theS\ x_1/x]$$

$$\equiv \{ \text{ definition of } Retr_1 \ \}$$

$$\exists\, x' \bullet Retr_1' \wedge D \wedge x_1 \in \operatorname{ran} justS \wedge pred_1[theS\ x_1/x]$$

The antecedent (we called it P in the proof overview above) of the universal quantification can be rewritten in the form $P_1 \vee P_2$ as follows:

$$\operatorname{pre} UnOp \wedge RetrED \wedge Opp$$

$$\equiv \quad \{ \text{ assuming operation consistency } \}$$

$$(x_1 \in \operatorname{ran} justS \wedge \operatorname{pre} AdOp_1 \wedge RetrED \wedge Opp)$$

$$\vee \quad (x_2 \in \operatorname{ran} justT \wedge \operatorname{pre} AdOp_2 \wedge RetrED \wedge Opp)$$

Now we show that each of the disjuncts in the antecedent (P_i) proves one of the disjuncts in the consequent (Q_i). Again these two proofs are completely analogous, so only one is given.

$$\forall\, x_1;\ x_2;\ y \bullet x_1 \in \operatorname{ran} justS \wedge \operatorname{pre} AdOp_1 \wedge RetrED \wedge Opp$$

$$\Rightarrow \exists\, x' \bullet Retr_1' \wedge D \wedge x_1 \in \operatorname{ran} justS \wedge pred_1[theS\ x_1/x]$$

$$\Leftarrow \quad \{ \text{ assuming state consistency, translate } x_1 := justS\ x \ \}$$

$$\forall\, x;\ y \bullet \operatorname{pre} Op_1 \wedge D_1 \wedge E \wedge retr_1 \wedge Opp$$

$$\Rightarrow \exists\, x' \bullet Retr_1' \wedge pred_1 \wedge D_1$$

$$\equiv \quad \{ \text{ definition } Retr_1, \text{ assumption } \}$$

$$\text{true}$$

This concludes our proof that every common refinement of the viewpoints is a refinement of the unification, and thus the unification is indeed the least common refinement.

5 On mutual refinement

The previous section has shown how the unification is (with a few conditions) "the" least common refinement of the viewpoints, by proving that all common refinements are refinements of the unification. Obviously, in general multiple least common refinements exist – for example other unifications with *different* correspondence relations that fulfill the state and operation consistency conditions. One might think that the equivalence classes induced by mutual refinement contain only specifications that are equal modulo an injective renaming of the inhabitants of the schemas ("isomorphism"). This, however, is not the case.

Have another look at examples 6 and 7. The viewpoint specifications given there are actually semantically identical, their only difference is that some information has shifted from the type of x to the schema predicate. The source of difference in the examples is in the correspondence relation that was used. (Why we would choose different default correspondence relations for "identical" specifications will be discussed in section 7.) The question of whether these unified state schemas are refinements fully depends on what operations are defined in the viewpoints. In general the unification of example 6 will not be a refinement, because the state consistency condition is violated ($x{=}4$ is excluded by the first viewpoint predicate, for example). On the other hand, state consistency holds in example 7, so that is a correct refinement. However, if the only operation defined on both viewpoints is

$$\begin{array}{|l}
\hline Op_i \\
\Delta D_i \\
\hline x' = 2 - x \\
\hline
\end{array}$$

the unification is a refinement in example 6 as well. (If state consistency holds for the inhabitants of all operation schemas, i.e. in this case just 0 and 2, the unification is a refinement. See section 6 for a further discussion of this.) The unification of these two operations will (modulo renaming) be Op_1 in the situation of example 6, and Op_2 in example 7 – quite different operations, but *both* least common refinements. This may seem strange at first.

However, in general in Z any state schema with operations can be data-refined by either *embedding* the state space in a superset (unconditionally), or by *restricting* the state space to a subset *which is closed under all operations*. (In the example, {0,2} is indeed closed under $\lambda\, x \bullet 2{-}x$.) The operations will be unchanged in the first case, and restricted to the new state space in the latter case. This may result in severely restricted operations; to see this, consider that the rules for data refinement (if there is no initial state) are already satisfied if the retrieve relation is empty (if *Abs* is false, in the terms of [15]).

So, classes of specifications that are mutual refinements will be (perhaps unexpectedly) large. In the next section we will argue that *not* all of the least common refinements reflect our interpretation of viewpoints, and we will look for criteria for choosing among them.

6 Consistency for partial specification in Z

At this point we are able to assess what consistency means for partial specification in Z. First, we have to observe that our unification method does not generate internal inconsistencies in the sense of section 3. We only produce state and operation schemas, which do not lead to inconsistencies when contradictions occur (rather to uninhabited schemas). The free types we introduce are non-recursive. So we are confident that specifications unified with our method will be consistent, considered on their own, whenever the viewpoint specifications are.

Of course, as became clear in the proofs, a different consistency issue turns up in the case of partial specification: not within a specification, but between specifications. The unification may not always be a refinement of the viewpoints involved, and if it is not, no common refinement satisfying the given correspondence relation exists[8], so an inconsistency between the viewpoints has been found. The condition of operation consistency is clearly a necessary and sufficient one for consistency between viewpoints – however, it can only be checked for operations that operate on the same state, i.e. only when a state unification has been decided on. The choice of a correspondence relation is critical for finding a correct state unification, considering the role that the correspondence plays in determining state consistency.

Let us return briefly to the points in the proofs where we needed "state consistency". It was already claimed there that weaker conditions would also suffice in particular cases, and there is an example supporting that claim in the previous section. The condition we are looking for is that *if* a before-state is linked to a unified state by the state unification's retrieve relation, a possible corresponding after-state should *also* be linked to the unified state by that retrieve relation. State consistency guarantees that by making sure the correspondence relation does not link legal with illegal values. Another option would be to demand that all operations "respect" the correspondence relation, but this would give a quantification over all present and future operations. Also, that would make state unification dependent on operations, which seems to introduce a circular dependency.

So, now we know that state consistency is formally too strong, is it a problem to impose it as a condition on state unification? We should probably let our interpretation come to the rescue here. In general, in Z data refinement it is not necessary for every abstract state to be represented by a concrete state. However, in the examples we have considered so far, the data types defined in the viewpoints included *only* meaningful values that would be just as meaningful in the unification. For a unified state space *not* to represent some values of a viewpoint state space just seems wrong in our interpretation. This is exactly what state consistency prevents. Thus, state consistency may be *formally* too strong for checking that a unification is a refinement, in our *interpretation* it is the right condition even when it is not formally necessary. A methodological advantage of using the state consistency condition is that it greatly simplifies the unification process: state unification can be done independently of operation unification. Thus new operations may be added at any later point without introducing the risk of an invalidated state unification.

A certain way of guaranteeing state consistency is to define R not on $S \times T$ but on its subset $\{x:S \mid pred_S\} \times \{x:T \mid pred_T\}$.

To summarize: unification of internally consistent viewpoint specifications will result in an internally consistent (candidate) unification. In order to check whether the unification is indeed a common refinement, two types of conditions need to be checked. The *state consistency* condition is formally too strong, but we cannot do better without looking at the operations that have been defined,

[8] Observe that any two specifications are consistent for the empty correspondence relation.

and it conforms with our intuition of state unification. On each pair of operations that is unified we will have to check for *operation consistency*: if both preconditions are satisfied, can both postconditions be satisfied too? The choice of a correspondence relation is crucial for state consistency, and it indirectly also influences operation consistency.

7 Concluding remarks

One might have expected that using Z for partial specification would require a different specification style, a different interpretation, or even a different refinement relation. This paper has shown that for the most part, the states-with-operations style with standard interpretation and refinement will do just fine. Particular interpretations for viewpoint specification occur at two points only:

- Our motivation for imposing state consistency is supported by our interpretation. However, the formal condition of state unification being independent of the operations would lead to the same requirement.
- The notion of a *default correspondence* is clearly dependent on an interpretation of viewpoint specifications. Examples 6 and 7 show that there can hardly be a formal motivation: semantically identical specifications lead to different default correspondence rules. The correspondence relation is *the* parameter in unifying viewpoint specifications; note, however, that we could completely have left out our intuitive ideas about it by not defining a "default" correspondence at all.

The unification method we presented covers only a restricted part of Z: state and operation schemas, in which we have mostly disregarded input and output. These could easily be added to the unification rules. Unification rules for many other Z specification constructs (for example *Init* operations) can be obtained as degenerate cases of the state and operation rules.

This method for unifying two viewpoints has to be embedded in a larger scale unification method. This addresses how to proceed if unifications do not satisfy the consistency criteria – whether and how to choose different correspondence relations, how to determine that no sensible correspondence relation exists and thus viewpoints are fundamentally inconsistent, and how to deal with that [8]. Also, the method will have to be extended from two to an arbitrary number of viewpoints. Fortunately, the binary method appears to be associative up to isomorphism under realistic restrictions on the correspondence relations involved.

As it is presented now, the results of unification contain many complicated expressions due to occurrences of injection functions and "bottoms". We will fix this by adding a "renaming" component to our unification method, which maps *tot R* to some target data type, formalising the "isomorphisms" we appealed to in most of the examples in this paper. The "default" renaming will give the desired result immediately in most cases.

Acknowledgements

We would like to thank Ralph Miarka for his comments on a draft of this paper. The LaTeX code for this paper was generated using the MathSPad editing tool (http://www.win.tue.nl/win/cs/wp/mathspad/) with special stencils for oz.sty.

References

1. M. Ainsworth, A. H. Cruickshank, L. J. Groves, and P. J. L. Wallis. Viewpoint specification and Z. *Information and Software Technology*, 36(1):43–51, February 1994.
2. R. D. Arthan. On free type definitions in Z. In Nicholls [12], pages 40–58.
3. E. Boiten, J. Derrick, H. Bowman, and M.Steen. Unification and multiple views of data in Z. In J.C. van Vliet, editor, *Computing Science in the Netherlands*, pages 73–85, November 1995.
4. T. Bolognesi and E. Brinksma. Introduction to the ISO Specification Language LOTOS. *Computer Networks and ISDN Systems*, 14(1):25–29, 1988.
5. H. Bowman, J. Derrick, and M. Steen. Some results on cross viewpoint consistency checking. In Raymond and Armstrong [13], pages 399–412.
6. J. Derrick, H. Bowman, and M. Steen. Maintaining cross viewpoint consistency using Z. In Raymond and Armstrong [13], pages 413–424.
7. J. Derrick, H. Bowman, and M. Steen. Viewpoints and Objects. In J. P. Bowen and M. G. Hinchey, editors, *Ninth Annual Z User Workshop*, LNCS 967, pages 449–468, Limerick, September 1995. Springer-Verlag.
8. A.C.W. Finkelstein, D. Gabbay, A. Hunter, J. Kramer, and B. Nuseibeh. Inconsistency handling in multiperspective specifications. *IEEE Transactions on Software Engineering*, 20(8):569–578, August 1994.
9. ITU Recommendation X.901-904 — ISO/IEC 10746 1-4. *Open Distributed Processing - Reference Model - Parts 1-4*, July 1995.
10. D. Jackson. Structuring Z specifications with views. Technical Report CMU-CS-94-126, School of Computer Science, Carnegie Mellon University, Pittsburgh, PA 15213, 1994.
11. D. Jackson and M. Jackson. Problem decomposition for reuse. *Software Engineering Journal*, 1995. To appear.
12. J. E. Nicholls, editor. *Z User Workshop, York 1991*, Workshops in Computing. Springer-Verlag, 1992.
13. K. Raymond and L. Armstrong, editors. *IFIP TC6 International Conference on Open Distributed Processing*. Chapman and Hall, Brisbane, Australia, February 1995.
14. A. Smith. On recursive free types in Z. In Nicholls [12], pages 3–39.
15. J. M. Spivey. *The Z notation: A reference manual.* Prentice Hall, 1989.
16. P. Zave and M. Jackson. Conjunction as composition. *ACM Transactions on Software Engineering and Methodology*, 2(4):379–411, October 1993.

Combining Statecharts and Z for the Design of Safety-Critical Control Systems

Matthias Weber

Technische Universität Berlin
we@cs.tu-berlin.de

Abstract. In this report, we describe an approach that integrates a mathematical specification language with more traditional software design techniques to yield a practicable methodology for the specification of safety-critical control systems. To manage complexity and to foster separation of concerns, the system design model is divided into three views: the architectural view, specified with object and class diagrams; the reactive view, specified with statecharts; and the functional view, specified with Z. A systematic relationship between the reactive and the functional view entails proof obligations to guarantee semantic compatibility. We illustrate this approach with a case study on controlling a heavy hydraulic press.

1 Introduction

Formal methods have been seriously applied during the past years in various industrial and academic pilot projects as reported, for instance, in [3]. However, the breakthrough has not yet been achieved. Many companies involved in such projects are scaling down their use of formal methods to a level that is in accordance with their current industrial relevance. For instance, they have only small teams of highly trained research staff working on selected critical aspects of systems.

What are the reasons for the failure of formal methods to achieve broader acceptance? From our own experience and from our analysis of experience reports ([3, 8, 12], for instance), we believe that one major reason is that presently formal methods come with too broad a goal. Often, they aim at a superior and uncompromising methodological framework for the development of perfectly correct systems. They often presuppose idealized circumstances, and they have usually been developed in academic environments where such circumstances can be guaranteed. Also, such a monolithic approach does not leave much room for coexistence and interaction with other methodologies that are in standard use within an industrial development context. Still, research on such methods is necessary and has provided us with many useful techniques and results, but it is highly unlikely to lead to methods that will be quickly accepted in practice.

We believe that a more modest approach to the integration of formal techniques into the system design process will lead to a more immediate application of such techniques [7]. Starting out from existing and accepted conventional design methods which are amenable to the integration of mathematical techniques, one should investigate at which points during the design process mathematical techniques can be smoothly and usefully integrated. The rationale for the use of formal techniques at these points should be convincing to the experienced engineer. Once experiments and case studies have provided evidence that the formal elements introduced are accepted, one can start to investigate further possible anchor points for mathematical techniques. This investigation can then be based on the experience gained during the first phase and on the evolving formal literacy of the design team. Hence, in principle, by iterating this process, one obtains a method that has more and more formal elements. It is important to note, that we do not attempt to embed conventional techniques into a formal method but rather the other way around.

In this report, we sketch an approach that sets out to integrate a mathematical specification technique into a well-known engineering technique in order to yield a practicable methodology for the specification of safety-critical control systems. Our starting point is the statechart notation, which is currently gaining acceptance in industry for the specification of embedded systems. To cope with the growing complexity and the safety requirements of these systems, we propose an integration of the specification language Z into statecharts, Z being used to model the data structures and data transformations within the system.

The idea of combining statecharts and Z is certainly not new; for example [1] uses a combination of Z and timed statecharts in the context of an application from avionics. The next section explains key ideas of our approach. The remaining sections illustrate the approach by developing a control system for a heavy hydraulic press.

2 Specification Methodology

A widely used technique in modern software engineering is to model a system by a combination of different – but semantically compatible – "views" of that system. The primary benefit of such an approach is to keep very complex systems manageable and to detect misconceptions or inconsistencies at an early stage. In the approach presented here, we divide the modeling into three views: the architectural model of the system, the reactive model of the system, and the functional model of the system (Figure 1).

The *architectural model* of a system describes the relationships between the types of components used in the system as well as the actual configuration of the system components itself. For the description of this model, we adopt the object-oriented modeling paradigm [2, for instance]: We understand an embedded control system as a hierarchically structured collection of objects that change state and interact with each other throughout their lifetime. The relationships between object classes are described using well-known elements of class diagrams, i.e. diagrams displaying classes and their structural relationships, such as aggregation and inheritance.

The two other views are primarily concerned with the specification of the behavior of single components of the embedded control system. We make a

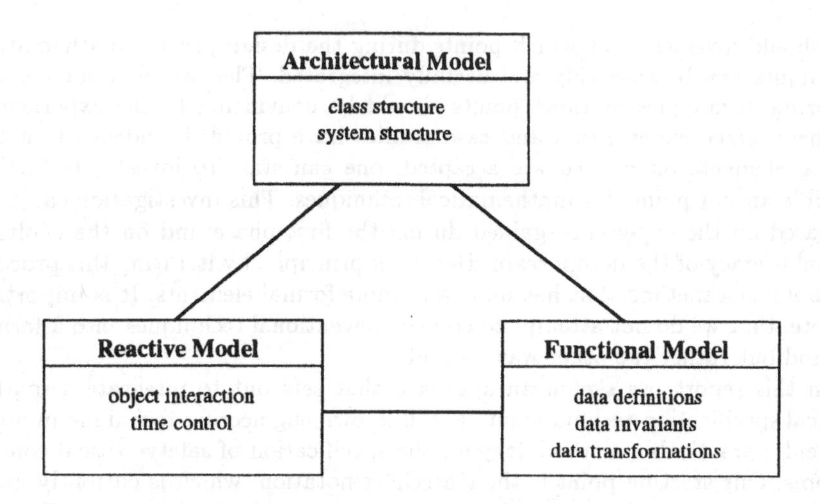

Fig. 1. The three modeling views of an embedded system

fundamental distinction with respect to the behavior of system components. The *functional model* of a component comprises data definitions, data invariants, and data transformation relations, in particular, for any component, its encompasses its local state and the input/output relation of its operations. Constraints, e.g. related to safety properties, about the components states can be derived based on these descriptions. The *reactive model* comprises the life-cycle of components, i.e. interactions with other components and the control of time during these interactions. Reactive behavior is modeled by specifying how, and under which timing constraints, operations from external objects are requested or supplied (or both) in the state changes of objects.

We specify reactive behavior using an appropriate variant of timed hierarchical state transition diagrams, i.e. with a variant of statecharts [5]. There are two reasons for this choice: firstly, statecharts have proven to be sufficiently expressive for modeling complex component interactions and time control, and secondly, the use of statecharts, or close variants of statecharts, is currently spreading in industry. This also enables us to use existing analysis and simulation tools for this notation.

Often, functional behavior in state-based systems is specified by textual or formal descriptions of pre- and postconditions and of data invariants. In our approach, we specify the functional behavior of objects using the state-based formal specification language Z [13]. There are two main reasons for using Z: firstly, in our view, Z has proven to be particularly useful for modeling complex functional data transformations; and secondly, both in academia and industry, Z has become one of the most widely used formal specification notations. Since we aim at a practical approach when modeling functionality, we try to stick to a constructive subset of Z, i.e. a subset that can be compiled into efficient code, whenever this is reasonable in a particular application. The use of a mathematical notation for modeling functional behavior enables us to prove abstract safety properties about the control system, such as provisions that the system may never enter certain hazardous states. Safety conditions imposed on data structures and data relationships should, of course, be specified using the full expressive power of the Z language.

Note that we are ***not*** arguing in favor of a monolithically formal approach. Rather, our goal is to systematically embed mathematical elements into industrially used engineering techniques. As will be seen, this leads to an approach some parts of which are "hard", i.e. fully precise, while others remain "softer", i.e. allow for a certain range of interpretations. In our view, such an approach leaves more room to be adapted to the actual circumstances in particular industrial application contexts.

3 The Case Study: Control of a Hydraulic Press

We consider a simple embedded control system, a controller for a heavy hydraulic press that is operated manually. Hydraulic presses are devices for pressing workpieces into a certain shape. The human operator, at the press, places the workpiece in the press and initiates the closing of the press. The plunger of the press moves down, presses the workpiece and subsequently moves up again. The workpiece can then be removed from the press and the entire process may be repeated.

Hydraulic presses are dangerous, since the worker operating the press may hurt himself by accidentally trapping his hand in the press. A typical safety device to prevent hand injuries are *two-hand controllers*, i.e. control units with two buttons, located about 1 meter apart, that must both be kept pressed while a potentially dangerous action is performed [4]. In addition, both buttons must be pressed within a small period of time (in our example 0.5 sec) in order to successfully initiate the closing of the press. The obvious intention behind two-hand controllers is to keep both of the worker's hands out of the danger area. If a button is released while the press is closing, the press will immediately stop and reopen. However, after a certain point is reached, which we call the *critical point*, the closing press can no longer be stopped physically, and hence cannot react to the release of a button. Finally, for reasons of reliability, the system should be capable of detecting sensor readings that are incompatible with the physical properties of the press. In such a situation, which might be due to a broken sensor or a failure in message transmission, the system should immediately stop the press.

This very simple embedded system is a good example to introduce and explain our approach, since it comes with interesting safety and real-time constraints, but is simple enough to not clutter the presentation with technical details. It should be obvious that the above informal specification is far too sketchy to adequately specify the required system behavior.

4 Architectural View

In the previous section, we have presented the informal requirements of the hydraulic press control case study. Since this is a very small example, the analysis and architectural design is straightforward. The results are summarized in the diagrams presented in Figures 2 and 4. For this example, we mostly use notations inspired from OMT [10] and Booch [2]. However, choice of notations is by no means essential and it should not be difficult for the experienced to adapt the information content of the following diagrams to his favorite notation.

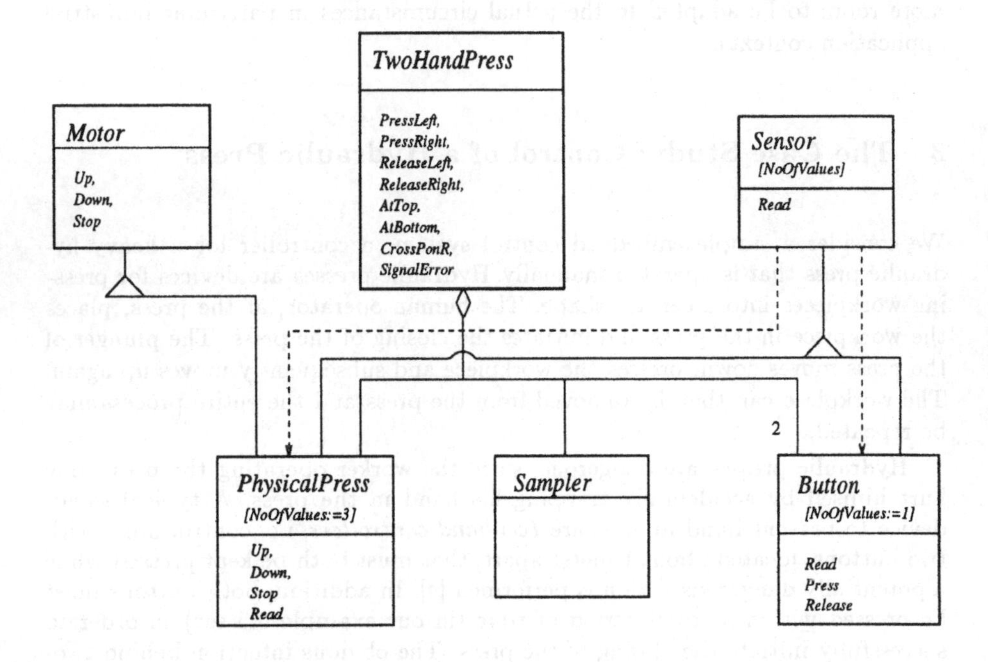

Fig. 2. Class diagram of the press system

The class diagram describes a two-hand press-object as consisting of four subobjects: two buttons to control the press, the physical press, and a data sampler. Aggregation is denoted by links adorned with a rhomb. Multiplicities can be specified explicitly along aggregation links. A button is a particular instance of a sensor. It offers an operation to read its (only) measured value. This value indicates whether the button is currently pressed. The parameter instantiation relationship is denoted by dashed arrows. In addition to being an instantiation, a button is also a specialization of a sensor, because it incorporates additional operations for pressing and releasing a button. The specialization (or inheritance) relationship is denoted by links adorned with a triangle. In the context of this case study, the physical press is modeled as an entity specializing both a sensor and a motor. In particular, besides an operation to read the current state of the press, it includes operations to move up, down and to stop. The physical press is also an instantiation of a sensor measuring three values. These values are further described below.

In Figure 2, the sampler and the control of the subobjects of the two-hand press together constitute the software part of the system. The press and the buttons model physical objects, connected to the control by communication lines. From a more traditional, software-centered point of view they would be represented as the environment of the software control component.

Since this is a rather simple system and it has a severe real-time requirement, our main architectural decision is to adopt a time-frame approach to specify its behavior (see Figure 3).

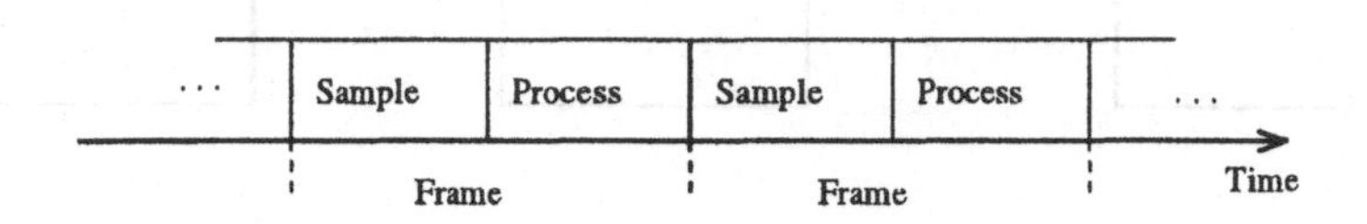

Fig. 3. Time-Frame Processing

More specifically, the idea is to let the sampler periodically read the current values measured by the physical press and the buttons and then, based on these values, to send control messages to the press control itself. The sending of these messages can be interpreted like events affecting control. The press control processes these messages and converts them into motor commands to move the press. In this sense the purpose of the sampler is to abstract from the low-level details of communication with the external devices and to offer an appropriate interface to the logical view of the controller. Of course, we must be concerned that the control does not miss a relevant input, i.e. the maximum time for the control to react to an input must be less than the length of sampling interval. The controller requests the operation of individual buttons using natural number indices, e.g. $Button[1].Read$ reads values from the first button.

The communication relationships between objects of this system are displayed in Figure 4.

Of course, there are many alternative approaches to this specific one, for example the two sensors could themselves be active processes interrupting the control by signaling events to it. However, the advantage of time-frame based processing is that we can more rigorously control the order of events. Furthermore, given the small number of sensors in this case study a concurrent solution would not be very realistic. In this example, all communications links denote synchronous communication. Asynchronous communication can be indicated by appropriate adornment of communication links.

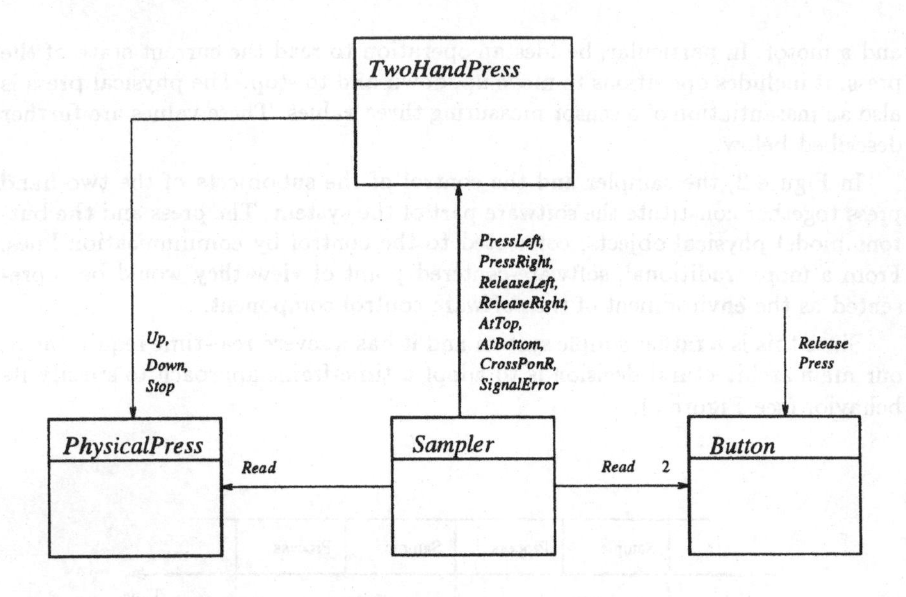

Fig. 4. Communication links of the press system

5 Reactive View

The top-level reactive behavior of the press control is described by the statechart in Figure 5. Initially, the control remains idle until the sampler signals that the

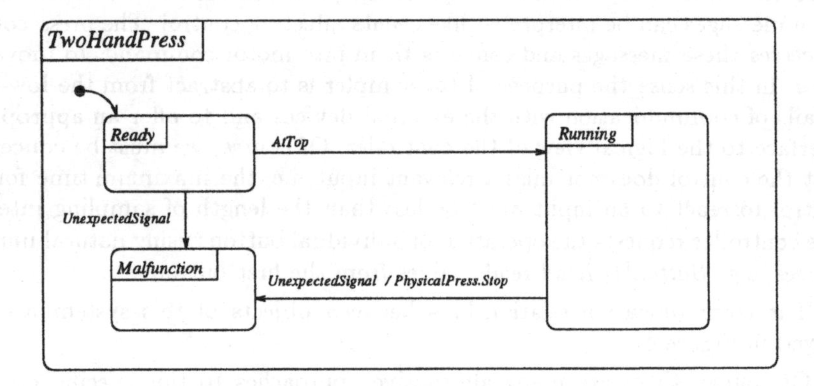

Fig. 5. Top-level reactive behavior of the controller

press is in default position, i.e. at the top. The control then enters the running mode. In case of a malfunction, the motor is stopped and a special error state is entered. A malfunction is recognized if the sensors deliver values that are not expected at any point of operation. *UnexpectedSignals* is an abbreviation for a group of transitions. We return to its definition below.

Following common conventions, we denote states by rounded boxes and indicate their names on the upper left corner. As usual, we use a dot-anchored kind of arrow to point to default substates to be entered when entering a complex state. In general we use two kinds of transitions, *operation transitions* and *timeout transitions*.

The arrows for operation transitions are in general adorned as follows:

ProvidedOperations[Condition]/RequestedOperations

If the object is in the source state and one of the indicated provided operations, separated by **or**, is requested from an external object, then, if the condition is satisfied, the indicated operations are requested from the indicated external objects and the object changes into the target state of the arrow. The condition is optional, an omitted condition acts as a condition that is always true. Requested operations are optional too: if no requested operations are indicated, the object just performs a change of the internal object state. The other form of transitions, the timeout transition, is explained below.

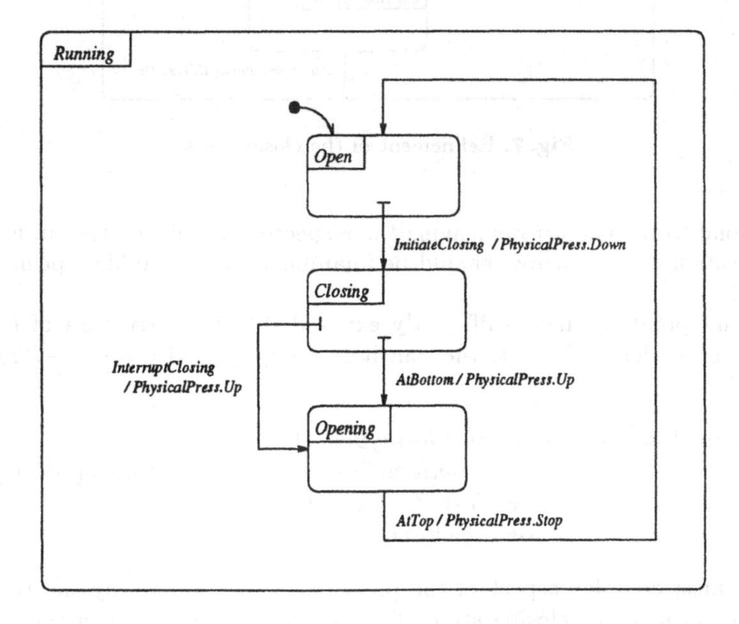

Fig. 6. Refinement of the running state

The running state is further refined in Figure 6. The press is operated in a continuous cycle of closing and opening. Entering the state *Closing* is associated to a motor command to move down. The open state and the label *InitiateClosing* are further refined below. The closing state may be left by either releasing one of the buttons, or by reaching the bottom of the press. Both cases lead to a motor command to move up. Opening then continues until the sampler signals the press being again at the top. Following a common convention about state diagrams, we use stubbed arrows to indicate transitions originating from substates of not yet sufficiently refined states.

The behavior of the control in the opening and closing states has not yet been refined to sufficient detail. First, we have to distinguish between those states in which the closing press above or below the *critical point*, i.e. the point below which the press can no longer be reopened before closing. This is clarified in the state diagram in Figure 7. The two arrows leaving the refined closing state

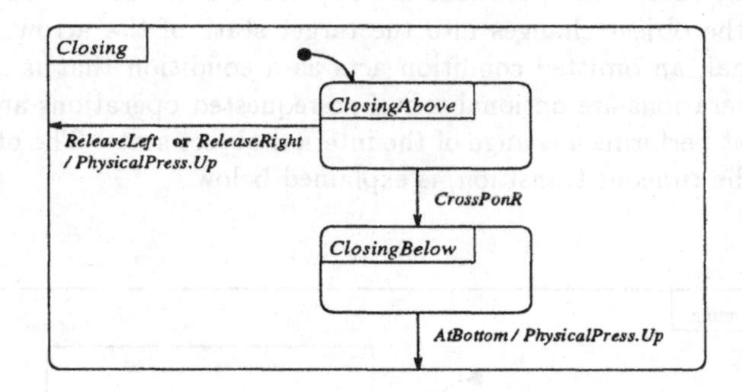

Fig. 7. Refinement of the closing state

correspond to the two arrows leaving the respective unrefined state in Figure 6. Identification of such arrows should be unambiguous by graphical position and by label.

At this point, we have sufficiently exposed the state structure of the two-hand press, to define precisely the transition group labeled *UnexpectedSignals* in Figure 5.

$$\begin{aligned} \textit{UnexpectedSignals} \equiv\ & \textit{AtTop}[\textit{ClosingBelow}] \\ & \textbf{or}\ \textit{AtBottom}[\textit{Ready} \lor \textit{Open} \lor \textit{ClosingAbove}] \\ & \textbf{or}\ \textit{CrossPonR}[\textit{Ready} \lor \textit{Open}] \\ & \textbf{or}\ \textit{SignalError} \end{aligned}$$

The most complex aspect of the press behavior is obviously the transition from the open to the closing state. This is described in detail in the state diagram in Figure 8 According to the logic of the two-hand press, in order to initiate the closing of the press, the two buttons have both to be released and subsequently both to be pressed within a specific time interval (*MaxDelay* milliseconds). Therefore, the safety state, which the system enters initially, can be left only when both buttons are released. Now when, e.g. the left button

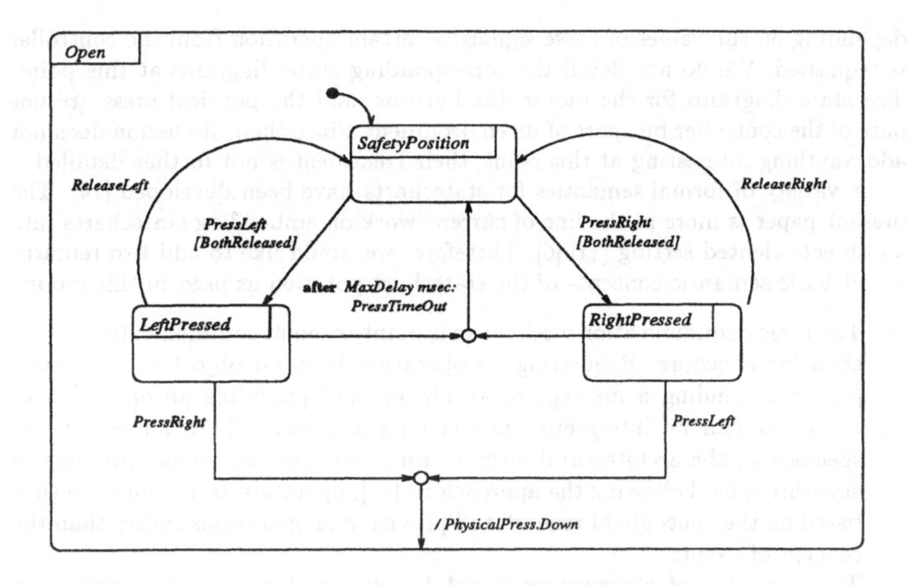

Fig. 8. Refinement of the open state

is pressed after both buttons were released, the right button must be pressed within a certain time interval, *MaxDelay* milliseconds, otherwise a timeout occurs and the system re-enters the safety state. If the right button is pressed soon enough, the system requests the motor to move the press down and enters the closing state.

The transition groups labeled *InitiateClosing* and *InterruptClosing* in Figure 6 can now be defined as follows:

$$InitiateClosing \equiv PressLeft \textbf{ or } PressRight$$
$$InterruptClosing \equiv ReleaseLeft \textbf{ or } ReleaseRight$$

This example has made use of the second kind of transition, the timeout transition. The respective arrows are adorned as follows:

$$\textbf{after } TimeExpression : InternalEvent / RequestedOperations$$

If the system has been in the source state of such an arrow for the time specified in the time expression, then it requests operations from other objects and changes into the target state of the arrow. As for operation arrows, the condition and requested operations may be omitted. Timeout transitions are a very simple, but often sufficient, means to deal with time constraints. If necessary, they could be generalized to timed transitions [9].

After modeling the reactive view of the global control of the hydraulic press system, we have yet to describe the reactive behavior of the sampler: After initialization, the sampler periodically samples the two button sensors and the press sensor. For each sensor, the current values of its signals are read, and, depending on the values of these signals, a certain operation from the controller is requested. We do not detail the corresponding state diagrams at this point. The state diagrams for the motor, the buttons, and the physical press are not part of the controller but part of its environment. Since their discussion does not add anything interesting at this point, their treatment is not further detailed.

A variety of formal semantics for statecharts have been developed [14]. The present paper is more in the line of current work on embedding statecharts into an object-oriented setting [11] [6]. Therefore, we would like to add two remarks about basic semantic concepts of the statechart notation as used in this report:

- The basic communication mechanism is point-to-point communication rather than broadcasting. Requesting an operation from an object can be interpreted as sending a message to an object, and providing an operation to an object can be interpreted as receiving a message from an object. As specified in the architectural view, communications can be synchronous or asynchronous. Following the approach in [11], operation transitions are thus based on the concepts of request and provision of operations rather than the concept of event.
- The execution of a transition is not timeless and external messages may arrive at any time. As a consequence, the system may not be able to immediately react to a message. Therefore, incoming messages must be queued and then worked off individually. By convention, if there is no transition for a particular message, then the system does not change state.

Further experience with case studies should guide the evolution of the notations and the semantics assumed here.

6 Functional View

Following common practice when presenting Z specifications, we first specify the state space of the hydraulic press control and then the effect of its operations on this space. The internal state space is essentially made up of appropriate *internal models* of the physical components. These models contain all information necessary for the control to decide on which action to take. In order to avoid naming confusion, we introduce a systematic naming convention: The internal model of a physical unit U is named *UModel*.

Press controller: State

First, we define the states of the button control. A button is an object that can be pressed or released.

$$Button ::= pressed \mid released$$

Remember, that the requirements of the press control described situations in which both buttons must be released first before they may be pressed again to initiate closing of the press. To model this information, we use the following set:

$DoubleRelease ::= required \mid notrequired$

We do not explicitly mirror the full substate structure of the press control from the reactive view, e.g. the various substates of open. Rather, in this functional view, we find it more convenient to model the buttons explicitly and later define in terms of our Z model the states of the state diagrams.

ButtonModel
$left, right : Button$
$release : DoubleRelease$

$(left = released \land right = released) \Rightarrow release = notrequired$

This schema describes the button model as consisting of the two buttons and a flag that indicates whether a release of both buttons is required. A logical constraint allows a release to be required only if at least one of the buttons is pressed.

We introduce an auxiliary schema for describing those situations in which the press is correctly triggered to start moving, i.e. both buttons have been pressed within the permitted delay after both have been previously released.

PressTriggered
$ButtonModel$

$left = pressed$
$right = pressed$
$release = notrequired$

Note, that in the functional view, we do not model real-time aspects, rather, these aspects are delegated to the reactive view.

Next, we define the press states. The press, without the buttons, may be ready, open, closing above or below the point of no return, opening, or in state of error.

$PressState ::= ready \mid open \mid closingabove \mid closingbelow \mid opening \mid error$

The internal model of the press is defined by:

PressModel
$press : PressState$

By means of the notions introduced so far, we can now specify the state of the press control as follows:

$$
\begin{array}{|l}
\hline
\textit{TwoHandPress} \\
\textit{PressModel} \\
\textit{ButtonModel} \\
\hline
\textit{PressTriggered} \Rightarrow \textit{press} \neq \textit{open} \\
\textit{press} = \textit{closingabove} \Rightarrow \textit{PressTriggered} \\
\hline
\end{array}
$$

This schema describes the press control as consisting of the press state and the button control all being subject to two constraining conditions related to functionality and safety: The first condition states that the press can be open only if it has not been triggered. The second condition states that above the critical point the press can be closing only if it has been triggered. These conditions must be satisfied for any state of the system

Note that the functional specification of the state space reexpresses information that is present in the state structure of the reactive view. For example, the definition of *PressState* is closely related, but not quite identical, to the states used in the reactive view. for example the state *Ready* can be defined by the following schema[1]

$$
\begin{array}{|l}
\hline
\textit{Ready} \\
\textit{TwoHandPress} \\
\hline
\textit{press} = \textit{ready} \\
\hline
\end{array}
$$

In general, our primary intention is to specify each view, so that it makes maximal sense by itself, e.g., in case of the functional view, we are interested in specifying clear and crisp data invariants. As in this example, this may well lead to redundancies. If desired, redundancy can be avoided by allowing, within the functional model, the use of states and operations *derived* from the reactive model. The development of a notation for such *derived functional models* is subject of current work.

Press controller: Operations

We now turn to the specification of the operations of the press controller. First, we specify the effect of pressing the left button. Local to the button model, the effect of this operation can be specified as follows.

[1] The relation between the reactive and the functional view are discussed in detail the next section.

$$\begin{array}{|l}
\textit{PressLeftLocal} \\
\Delta \textit{ButtonModel} \\
\hline
\textit{left} = \textit{released} \\
\textit{left}' = \textit{pressed} \\
\textit{right}' = \textit{right} \\
\textit{release}' = \textit{release}
\end{array}$$

This operation can be extended to the two-hand press state by specifying how the press state is affected by the pressing of the left button. There are two cases. If the right button has already been pressed and no release is required yet, then the press begins to close. If this is not the case, the press remains open.

$$\begin{array}{|l}
\textit{PressLeft} \\
\Delta \textit{PressModel} \\
\textit{PressLeftLocal} \\
\hline
(\textit{press} = \textit{open} \wedge \textit{right} = \textit{pressed} \wedge \textit{release} = \textit{notrequired}) \\
\qquad \Rightarrow \textit{press}' = \textit{closingabove} \\
(\textit{press} \neq \textit{open} \vee \textit{right} = \textit{released} \vee \textit{release} = \textit{required}) \\
\qquad \Rightarrow \textit{press}' = \textit{press}
\end{array}$$

This specification captures very succinctly the normal behavior of the operation to press the left button. The effect of pressing the right button can be specified analogously.

Next, we turn to the release operations. Again, we begin by specifying the effect of releasing the left button local to the button control.

$$\begin{array}{|l}
\textit{ReleaseLeftLocal} \\
\Delta \textit{ButtonModel} \\
\hline
\textit{left} = \textit{pressed} \\
\textit{left}' = \textit{released} \\
\textit{right}' = \textit{right} \\
\textit{right} = \textit{released} \Rightarrow \textit{release}' = \textit{notrequired} \\
\textit{right} = \textit{pressed} \Rightarrow \textit{release}' = \textit{required}
\end{array}$$

Note, that the release of a button may affect the release flag. Next, we extend this operation to the state of the two-hand press. The interesting case here is to capture the effect of releasing a button at a time when the press is closing and still above the point of no return.

$$\begin{array}{|l}
\hline
\textit{ReleaseLeft} \\
\Delta \textit{PressModel} \\
\textit{ReleaseLeftLocal} \\
\hline
\textit{press} = \textit{closingabove} \Rightarrow \textit{press}' = \textit{opening} \\
\textit{press} \neq \textit{closingabove} \Rightarrow \textit{press}' = \textit{press} \\
\hline
\end{array}$$

Analogously, we can specify the operation to release the right button.

After specifying the button operations, we now turn to the operations describing state changes resulting from signals received from the physical press. For example, the effect of the press indicating arrival at the top of the press can be specified as follows:

$$\begin{array}{|l}
\hline
\textit{AtTop} \\
\Delta \textit{TwoHandPress} \\
\hline
\textit{press} \in \{\textit{opening}, \textit{ready}\} \\
\qquad \Rightarrow \textit{press}' = \textit{open} \\
\textit{press} \in \{\textit{opening}, \textit{ready}\} \wedge (\textit{left} = \textit{pressed} \vee \textit{right} = \textit{pressed}) \\
\qquad \Rightarrow \textit{release}' = \textit{required} \\
\textit{press} \in \{\textit{closingabove}, \textit{closingbelow}\} \\
\qquad \Rightarrow (\textit{press}' = \textit{error} \wedge \textit{release}' = \textit{release}) \\
\textit{left}' = \textit{left} \\
\textit{right}' = \textit{right} \\
\hline
\end{array}$$

The first implication specifies the normal behavior, i.e. the signal is arriving during initialization or opening of the press. Note, in this case, the change of the release flag, i.e. after a arriving at the top, a full release of both buttons is required. The second implication specifies the abnormal behavior, i.e. the signal is arriving during closing of the press, in which case the press stops the motor and goes into the error state. The remaining operations *CrossPonR*, *AtBottom*, and *SignalError*. can be specified in a similar style.

Press controller: conditions

The condition that both buttons are released can be defined as follows:

$$\begin{array}{|l}
\hline
\textit{BothReleased} \\
\textit{TwoHandPress} \\
\hline
\textit{left} = \textit{released} \\
\textit{right} = \textit{released} \\
\hline
\end{array}$$

Press controller: internal events

Finally, we specify the sole internal event that arises in case the press is open, either one of the buttons was pressed, but the delay for pressing the other button has been exceeded. In this case, the event changes the system back into its safety position.

PressTimeOut

$\Delta TwoHandPress$

$press' = press = open$

$left = pressed \Leftrightarrow right = released$

$release = notrequired$

$release' = required$

$left' = left$

$right' = right$

This completes the functional view of the control. At this point, the reader may argue that this functional view of the system is redundant, since all behavioral aspects of this finite state system could have been adequately specified using statecharts alone. We would argue here that the functional view is useful in its own since it shows in a very explicit way that the internal models of the physical components satisfy important safety conditions. Admittedly, one could have expressed all details of the "button logic" with statecharts, but this would have definitely obscured the specification and the proof of its properties. Furthermore, this is a very small example, and, in our experience, the data space and the amount of data transformation tends to grow quickly in more complex control systems.

7 Consistency

The reactive and functional view of an embedded system can be checked against each other in many interesting ways: The basic idea is to systematically and consistently relate the state hierarchy and the transitions introduced in the statecharts with the state spaces and operations as defined by the Z schemas.

7.1 Relating states

A straightforward way to relate states between the two different views is to map every state diagram state S into an appropriate Z schema S_z describing this state, and then to formulate various proof obligations for this mapping to be adequate.

Assuming as given such a mapping for a particular component, the consistency conditions can be presented in three steps. For an arbitrary state S from the reactive model of this component, we distinguish between the following two cases:

- S is an elementary state, i.e. there is no decomposition of S in the reactive model. In this case, one has to verify that the associated Z state S_z is nonempty, i.e.

  Consistency: $\vdash \exists S_z$.
- S is a hierarchically composed state, i.e. in the reactive model S is decomposed into exclusive sub-states S_1, S_2, $\cdots$, and S_n $(n > 0)$ with associated Z-schemas S_z, S_{1z}, S_{2z}, $\cdots$, and S_{nz}. In this case, one has to check sufficiency, necessity, and disjointness of the decomposition.

  Sufficiency: $S_{1z} \vee S_{2z} \vee \cdots \vee S_{nz} \vdash S_z$.
  Necessity: $S_z \vdash S_{1z} \vee S_{2z} \vee \cdots \vee S_{nz}$
  Disjointness: $S_z \vdash \neg (S_{iz} \wedge S_{jz})$ for all $i, j \in \{1, \cdots, n\}$, where $i \neq j$.

Of course, the top-level statechart of a component must be related to the Z schema defining the full state space of the component.

7.2 Hydraulic press example

In case of the hydraulic press, the states from the state interaction diagrams can be defined in terms of the Z-model quite easily. We illustrate this for the substates of the open press (see Figure 8).

SafetyPosition
TwoHandPress

---

press = *open*
left = *pressed* ∨ *right* = *pressed* ⇒ *release* = *required*

The second condition states that in the safety position, if any button is pressed, a release is required before the press may begin to close.

The substate *RightPressed* can be defined as follows.

RightPressed
TwoHandPress

---

press = *open*
left = *released*
right = *pressed*
release = *notrequired*

The substate *LeftPressed* can be defined analogously. The composed state *Open* can be defined as follows.

Open
TwoHandPress
press = open

To ensure consistency between these definitions, we have to prove necessity of the OR-composition:

$$Open \vdash (SafetyPosition \lor LeftPressed \lor RightPressed)$$

Sufficiency and disjointness can be shown in a similar way. Similar definitions and consistency proofs can be given for the other states. The reader might object at this point, that one may always define composed states in such a way as to automatically satisfy the completeness proof obligation. While we admit that this is possible, we want to stress at this point, that our methodological guideline is to define composed states as naturally as possible from different points of view. In some cases, consistency between views may follow by construction, in others, e.g. the *Open* state, consistency must be ensured by a separate nontrivial reasoning.

7.3 Relating operations

In the functional view, we have defined a Z schema for each service, internal event, or guard in the statechart. Based on the association of a Z schema to each statechart box one can verify conformance between the statechart transitions and the Z definitions.

The idea is to consider an arbitrary state and an arbitrary operation and then to check for consistency with respect to the transitions leaving that state. More precisely, given an arbitrary operation Op and state S, we have to prove that each transition leaving S and labeled with Op, and possibly some condition, behaves as expected, i.e. results in the desired state. We furthermore have to prove, that if the operation or event Op occurs and neither one of the conditions of those transitions are true, the application of Op preserves this state.

First, we distinguish the case that no transitions labeled with Op are leaving S. In such a case, we have to show that application of S preserves this state.

Preservation: $S_z \land Op_z \vdash S'_z$.

S_z and Op_z are the Z schemata associated to S and Op.

It remains to deal with the case that the transitions $t_1, \cdots, t_n$ $(n > 0)$ are labeled with Op and guards $C_1, \cdots, C_n$ and move from S to states $S_1, \cdots, S_n$. We check for consistency of these transitions as follows:

Applicability: $S_z \vdash \text{pre } Op_z$.
Explicit Correctness: $S_z \land Op_z \land C_{iz} \vdash S'_{iz}$, for $1 \leq i \leq n$.

Implicit Correctness: $S_z \wedge Op_z \wedge \neg (C_{1z} \vee \cdots \vee C_{nz}) \Rightarrow S'_z$, if S_z is primitive.

C_{iz} and S_{iz} are the Z schemata associated with C_i and S_i. Note the applicability check, i.e. any state from which a transition labeled with *Op* is leaving must imply the precondition of *Op*. Note also, that implicit correctness has to be checked only for primitive states, as it induces implicit correctness for composed states.

Note that implicit correctness is trivial in those cases in which the disjunction of the guards is complete, for example in the frequent number of cases where $n = 1$ and $C_1 \Leftrightarrow true$.

7.4 Hydraulic press example

First, we consider the operation *PressLeft*. Apparently there are only two relevant transitions, giving rise to the obligations:

$SafetyPosition \wedge PressLeft \wedge BothReleased \vdash LeftPressed'$

$SafetyPosition \wedge PressLeft \wedge \neg\ BothReleased \vdash SafetyPosition'$

$RightPressed \wedge PressLeft \vdash ClosingAbove'$

Furthermore, the operation is inapplicable in two states only, namely:

$LeftPressed \vdash \neg$ pre $PressLeft$

$ClosingAbove \vdash \neg$ pre $PressLeft$

For the other primitive states, we have to prove preservation, e.g.:

$Opening \wedge PressLeft \vdash Opening'$

An orthogonal analysis can be done with the other press and release operations. Next, we turn to the control event *AtTop*. The transitions to be verified are:

$Ready \wedge AtTop \vdash SafetyPosition'$

$Opening \wedge AtTop \vdash SafetyPosition'$

$Running \wedge ClosingBelow \wedge AtTop \vdash Malfunction'$

Inapplicability is given in the states *Open* and *Error*. The other control events can be analyzed in a similar fashion.

Finally, there is one internal event *PressTimeOut*. The following transitions must be checked.

$LeftPressed \wedge PressTimeOut \vdash SafetyPosition'$

$RightPressed \wedge PressTimeOut \vdash SafetyPosition'$

Inapplicability is given in the the remaining states. All these properties amount to very simple checks of the given definitions. Nevertheless, checking these conditions is very helpful for debugging a specification.

8 Conclusions

The proposed combination of statecharts and Z for modeling embedded control systems proved to be both semantically and pragmatically interesting. It is important at this point, to conduct more experiments with the aim of identifying useful recommendations, guidelines, and heuristics for the process of developing such combined specifications. Parallel to that, tools for translating specifications into code should be developed or adapted. For statecharts, such tools are available. Concerning Z specifications, we would argue to stick to an operational modeling style, from which efficient code can be generated. This was straightforward in the hydraulic press example. The degree to which such a style can be reasonably adopted seems to depend on the particular application context.

References

1. L. M. Barroca, J. S. Fitzgerald, and L. Spencer. The architectural specification of an avionics subsystem. In *IEEE Workshop on Industrial-strength Formal Specification Techniques*, pages 17–29. IEEE Press, 1995.
2. G. Booch. *Object-Oriented Analysis and Design with Applications.* Benjamin Cummings, second edition, 1994.
3. D. Craigen, S. Gerhart, and T. Ralston. An international survey of industrial applications of formal methods. Technical Report NISTGCR 93/626, National Institute of Standards and Technology, Gaithersburg, MD 20899, 1993.
4. Zentralstelle für Unfallverhütung und Arbeitsmedizin. *Pressen – Sicherheitsregeln für Zweihandschaltungen an kraftbetriebenen Pressen der Metallbearbeitung.* Hauptverband der gewerblichen Berufsgenossenschaften, Langwartweg 103, 5300 Bonn 1, 2nd edition, 1978.
5. D. Harel. Statecharts: A visual formalism for complex systems. *Science of Computer Programming*, 8(3):231–274, 1987.
6. D. Harel and E. Gery. Executable Object-Modeling with Statecharts. In to appear, editor, *Proc. ICSE 18*, 1996.
7. M. Heisel, S. Jähnichen, M. Simons, and M. Weber. Embedding mathematical techniques into system engineering. In M. Wirsing, editor, *ICSE-17 Workshop on Formal Methods Application in Software Engineering Practice*, pages 53–60, 1995.
8. I. Houston and S. King. CICS Project Report: Experiences and Results from the Use of Z in IBM. In S.Prehn and W.J.Toetenel, editors, *VDM'91 Formal Software Development Methods*, volume 551 of *LNCS*, pages 588–596. Springer-Verlag, 1991.
9. Y. Kestens and A. Pnueli. *Timed and Hybrid Statecharts and their Textual Representation*, volume 299 of *LNCS*, pages 591 - 620. Springer-Verlag, 1992.
10. J. Rumbaugh et al. *Object-Oriented Modeling and Design.* Prentice-Hall, 1991.
11. B. Selic, G. Gullekson, and P. T. Ward. *Real-Time Object-Oriented Modeling.* John Wiley & Sons, 1994.
12. IEEE Software. *Safety-Critical Systems.* IEEE, January 1994.
13. M. Spivey. *The Z Notation, A Reference Manual.* Prentice Hall, 2nd edition, 1992.
14. M. von der Beeck. A comparison of statecharts variants. In *Symposium on Fault-Tolerant Computing*, LNCS. Springer, 1994.

Integrating Real-Time Scheduling Theory and Program Refinement

C. Fidge M. Utting P. Kearney I. Hayes

Software Verification Research Centre, Department of Computer Science,
The University of Queensland, Queensland 4072, Australia.

Abstract. We show how real-time schedulability tests and program refinement rules can be integrated to create a formal development method of practical use to real-time programmers. A computational model for representing task scheduling is developed within a 'timed' refinement calculus. Proven multi-tasking schedulability tests then become available as feasibility checks during system refinement.

1 Introduction

There has long been a gulf between formal methods for specifying and developing real-time programs and the needs of real-time programmers 'in the field'.

- Formal methods for specifying concurrent real-time systems typically make unrealistic simplifying assumptions. In particular, 'maximal parallelism' assumes that each task resides on its own processor and is thus never pre-empted. This is often justified by pointing to the ever-decreasing cost of hardware.
- Embedded systems programmers, on the other hand, constrained by the realities of power, cost and space limitations, try to implement as many tasks on the same processor as possible. Real-time scheduling theory is used to determine whether a given task set can meet its deadlines.

Consequently real-time programmers find that formal specification and development methods do not model their true concerns. If formal methods are to become a useful industrial tool for real-time programming this gap must be bridged.

In this paper we take a first step towards merging these two previously separate streams of activity by representing the computational model used by scheduling theory in a 'timed' refinement calculus. This makes already-proven schedulability results available as a basis for formal development of multi-tasking programs with hard real-time deadlines.

2 Background

2.1 Review of timed refinement

The *timed refinement calculus* [10, 11] is based on predicate transformer semantics with the specification language Z used as a convenient notation for expressing predicates. To make the calculus suitable for expressing parallel, reactive behaviours, it replaces the familiar pre/post-condition model with one based on environmental ***assumptions*** and desired ***effects***.

A specification statement

$$+\widetilde{v}: [A, E]$$

has three parts. Let $\widetilde{u}, \ldots, \widetilde{y}$ denote mutually disjoint sets of variables.

1. The set of variables $\widetilde{v}$ in the ***frame*** denote the observable variables which the specification constructs. Variables in $\widetilde{v}$ may appear in E but not A.
2. The assumption A defines knowledge the specification can use about the environment. It is a predicate on a set of variables $\widetilde{u}$ disjoint from $\widetilde{v}$.
3. The effect E is a predicate on variables in $\widetilde{u}$ and $\widetilde{v}$, typically defining the value of those variables in $\widetilde{v}$ in terms of those in $\widetilde{u}$.

Predicates are ordered in the underlying semantics by an entailment relation $\Rrightarrow$ [10, p.3].

Time is introduced into the calculus by a convention on the types of constructed variables. Each variable $v \in \widetilde{v}$ is actually a trace, or history, of values, one for each moment in time. The trace index is absolute time. For instance, a ***timed variable*** v of 'base' type V is declared as a function

$$v : \mathbb{A} \rightarrow V \,,$$

where $\mathbb{A}$ is the absolute time domain. Specifications thus define the values of each variable in the frame over all time.

The refinement relation $\sqsubseteq$ on such specification statements is defined using a handful of fundamental rules. Provisos are shown above the line and the refinement rule below.

Law R1: Weaken assumption [10, p.7]

$$\frac{A_1 \Rrightarrow A_2}{+\widetilde{v}: [A_1, E] \sqsubseteq +\widetilde{v}: [A_2, E]}$$

Law R2: Strengthen effect [10, p.7]

$$\frac{A \Rrightarrow (\forall \widetilde{v} \bullet E_2 \Rrightarrow E_1)}{+\widetilde{v}: [A, E_1] \sqsubseteq +\widetilde{v}: [A, E_2]}$$

Law R3: Introduce local constructions [10, p.9]

$$\frac{\text{variables in } \widetilde{x} \text{ are fresh}}{+\widetilde{v}: [A, E] \sqsubseteq |[\; +\widetilde{v} \cup \widetilde{x}: [A,\ [E;\ \widetilde{x}]] \setminus \widetilde{x} \;]|}$$

On the right-hand side the signature of schema E is extended to include declaration $\widetilde{x}$. (For brevity we omit types in these generic definitions.) The $|[\cdots \setminus \widetilde{x}]|$ construct declares local variables $\widetilde{x}$ that cannot be seen outside its scope [10, p.9].

Law R4: Introduce parallel composition [11, p.8]

$$\frac{A \Rrightarrow (\exists \widetilde{x};\ \widetilde{y} \bullet E)}{+\widetilde{x} \cup \widetilde{y}: [A, E] \sqsubseteq +\widetilde{x}: [A \wedge (\exists \widetilde{x} \bullet E), E] \parallel +\widetilde{y}: [A \wedge (\exists \widetilde{y} \bullet E), E]}$$

The $\parallel$ operator denotes parallel composition of specification statements [11]. The proviso prevents effect E from accidently strengthening assumption A when added to the assumptions of the two parallel components [10, p.8].

Laws **R1** to **R3** are variants of well-known refinement rules. Law **R4** allows a specification to be partitioned into parallel components where each component can assume properties effected by its siblings, as long as the properties do not reference the variables to be constructed by the component.

Significantly, the parallelism operator $\parallel$ is a 'true' concurrency operator. It is not directly suited to modelling the 'interleaved' concurrency found in uniprocessor multi-tasking applications.

2.2 Review of schedulability testing

Uniprocessor scheduling theory offers proven *schedulability tests* for verifying that a system design, with given timing characteristics, can be successfully scheduled under a particular scheduling policy and communication protocol.

To make analysis of complex real-time systems manageable, the theory uses an abstract computational model [1]. In this model a system consists of a set of *tasks*. Each task i *arrives* infinitely often, each arrival separated from the last by at least T_i time units. A *periodic* task arrives regularly with a separation of exactly T_i time units. A *sporadic* task arrives irregularly with each arrival separated from its predecessor by at least T_i time units.

At each arrival, task i issues a nominal *invocation request* for up to C_i units of processor time, its worst-case *computation time* [1]. (For simplicity the model assumes that only tasks consume time. Scheduling overheads such as context switching and shared resource locking are factored into the worst case computation time for each task.) To complete its workload, task i must have this request for processor time satisfied before some *deadline* D_i expires, measured relative to the arrival time of the task invocation. Usually D_i does not exceed T_i.

The scheduler places each task making a request in a notional *ready queue* [8]. It decides which task in the queue is currently *running* using the *priority* π_i of each ready task i and the particular scheduling policy it implements. In static-priority scheduling there is a fixed *base* priority associated with each task, although a higher *effective* (or *active*) priority may be temporarily allocated to the task at run time. In dynamic-priority scheduling a run-time metric is used to determine priorities during execution. Tasks of higher priority can pre-empt some task i, resulting in a degree of *interference* I_i to the progress of i.

So that communications overheads can be predicted accurately, the model assumes that all inter-task communication occurs through mutually-exclusive access to shared variables. This allows *a priori* knowledge of the worst-case *blocking time* B_i that task i may experience due to lower-priority tasks having locks on resources that it wishes to access, for a known locking protocol.

In general, schedulability tests can be divided into two classes, both based on analysis of worst-case scenarios. Tests that measure 'processor utilisation' check a bound on the total percentage of time that all tasks occupy the processor. For instance, the following test applies to a set of tasks under the *earliest deadline first* scheduling policy, using the *stack resource* locking protocol. Earliest deadline first scheduling is a dynamic-priority scheduling policy in which the task with the earliest *absolute* deadline from the current moment has the highest priority. The stack resource protocol [2] guarantees that task invocations begin executing only when all resources they may wish to access are free, and that each task invocation is blocked by a lower-priority task at most once.

Under these conditions a set of tasks $1..n$, ordered by increasing size of their deadlines, is schedulable if [2]

$$\forall i : 1..n \bullet \sum_{j \in 1..i} \frac{C_j}{D_j} + \frac{B_i}{D_i} \leqslant 1 . \tag{1}$$

The test checks, for each task i, that the processor utilisation by that task, plus that by higher-priority tasks that may pre-empt i, plus that by lower-priority tasks that may block i, is less than 100%. The first term is the processor utilisation by all tasks j of priority equal or higher than i. The second term is the degree of blocking that may be experienced. Under the stack resource protocol B_i is the execution time of the longest critical section executed by some task of lower priority than i.

Test 1 is a useful feasibility test in general; earliest deadline first scheduling is 'optimal' in the sense that if a task set is schedulable by any policy then it is schedulable by earliest deadline first.

The second class of tests works by precisely characterising system 'response times'. The worst case *response time* R_i for an invocation of task i defines how long it may take the task to complete its computation, measured from its arrival time. For instance, the following test applies to any assignment of base priorities to tasks [1], under a *static-priority* scheduling policy and using the *ceiling locking* protocol. A static-priority scheduler is one which makes the running task the one in the ready queue with the highest effective priority (favouring the currently running task in the case of ties to avoid unnecessary context switching). The ceiling locking protocol [8] is a special case of the stack resource protocol in which (a) each shared variable has an associated 'ceiling' value as great as the highest base priority of any task that may access it, and (b) each task that locks a variable has its effective priority set to that variable's ceiling value.

Under these circumstances, a set of n tasks, with a static assignment of *unique* base priorities, is schedulable if [1]

$$\forall i : 1..n \bullet R_i \leqslant D_i \quad \text{where} \quad R_i = C_i + B_i + I_i \tag{2}$$

$$\text{and} \quad I_i = \sum_{j \in hp(i)} \left\lceil \frac{R_i}{T_j} \right\rceil C_j .$$

Here $hp(i)$ is the set of tasks with higher base priorities than task i. For each task i the test checks that the response time R_i of the task does not exceed its deadline D_i. The worst case response time for i is the sum of its own worst case computation time C_i, plus its worst case blocking time due to lower-priority tasks B_i, plus the worst case interference due to higher-priority tasks I_i. Assuming use of the ceiling locking protocol B_i equals the longest critical section of any lower priority task accessing a shared variable with a ceiling as great as the priority of task i [1].

The interference term I_i determines how much pre-emption task i will experience during the interval of time defined by R_i due to higher-priority tasks j. For each task j this is its execution time C_j multiplied by the number of arrivals $\lceil R_i/T_j \rceil$ that j may have in R_i time units. Thus interference up to time R_i is defined in terms of the number of pre-emptions that may occur during the interval of time defined by R_i: the definition is recursive!

Fortunately, however, the equation can be solved iteratively [1]. Let R_i^x be the xth approximation to the value of R_i. Starting with $R_i^0 = 0$, equation

$$R_i^{x+1} = C_i + B_i + \sum_{j \in hp(i)} \left\lceil \frac{R_i^x}{T_j} \right\rceil C_j$$

converges to R_i. Evaluation stops either when the equation has converged, i.e., $R_i^{x+1} = R_i^x$, or, because $R_i^{x+1} \geqslant R_i^x$ for any x, iteration can stop as soon as $R_i^{x+1} > D_i$ in which case the test has failed.

3 A real-time multi-tasking refinement model

Our aim is to represent the computational model used by scheduling theory (Section 2.2) in the timed refinement calculus (Section 2.1) in such a way that proven schedulability results benefit the refinement process. To do this refinements must introduce those computational entities of interest in scheduling theory, namely tasks, protected shared variables and the scheduler itself, in order to capture the behaviour of a multi-tasking system.

This is illustrated in Figure 1. Boxes denote parallel specification components and arcs the flow of information, via the named variables. A top-level specification, defining values of output variables in terms of inputs, is refined to a description known to map to the scheduling behaviour of our target programming language.

The development procedure from top-level specification to multi-tasking system can be described in the following ten steps. A detailed example illustrating each step is given in the next section.

1. Requirements specification. This defines the functional requirement and its absolute time constraints, expressing the 'effect' variables $\widetilde{out}$ in terms of the 'assumption' variables $\widetilde{in}$.

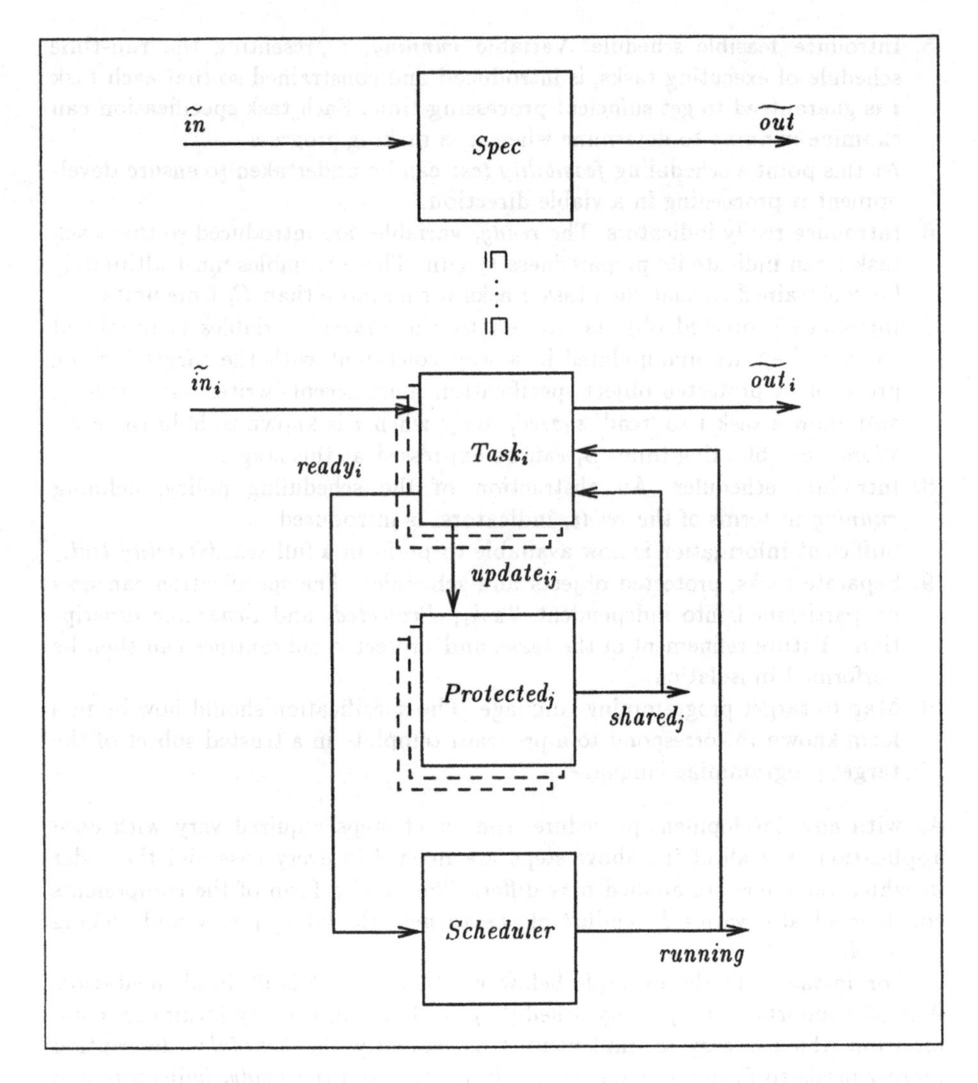

Fig. 1. Overview of the refinement procedure (for static-priority scheduling using the ceiling locking protocol).

2. Introduce shared variables. To allow for later system partitioning, new shared variables *shared*$_j$ are introduced. Typically this is done so that separate parts of the specification need not have input and output variables in common.
3. Introduce periodic and sporadic requirements. The functional requirements are re-expressed in forms corresponding to the notions of periodic and sporadic tasks. Interarrival times T_i and deadlines D_i are introduced here.
4. Introduce worst case execution times. For each task i a worst case execution time C_i is hypothesised.

5. Introduce feasible schedule. Variable *running*, representing the run-time schedule of executing tasks, is introduced and constrained so that each task i is guaranteed to get sufficient processing time. Each task specification can examine *running* to determine when it is making progress.
   At this point a scheduling ***feasibility test*** can be undertaken to ensure development is proceeding in a viable direction.
6. Introduce ready indicators. The $ready_i$ variables are introduced so that each task i can indicate its preparedness to run. These variables must ultimately be constrained so that each task i asks for no more than C_i time units.
7. Introduce protected objects. Access to the $shared_j$ variables is restricted so that they are manipulated in a way consistent with the target locking protocol. A protected object specification must accept 'writes' via $update_{ij}$, and allow a task i to 'read' $shared_j$, only when i is known to hold the lock. Worst case blocking times B_i can be expressed at this stage.
8. Introduce scheduler. An abstraction of the scheduling policy, defining *running* in terms of the $ready_i$ indicators, is introduced.
   Sufficient information is now available to perform a full ***schedulability test***.
9. Separate tasks, protected objects and scheduler. The specification can now be partitioned into independent $Task_i$, $Protected_j$ and *Scheduler* descriptions. Future refinement of the tasks and protected subroutines can then be performed in isolation.
10. Map to target programming language. The specification should now be in a form known to correspond to a program template in a trusted subset of the target programming language.

As with any development procedure, the exact steps required vary with each application. Not all of the above steps are needed in every case and the order in which the steps are applied may differ. The precise form of the components constructed also varies depending of the target scheduling policy and locking protocol.

For instance, in the example below we target an Ada 95 implementation. Ada 95 supports static-priority scheduling and ceiling priority locking, a combination which is easy to implement. Consequently the *Scheduler* description merely needs to form an imaginary ready queue from the $ready_i$ indicators and use this to set the value of *running* accordingly. Each $Protected_j$ definition is merely a 'merge' function that, when an $update_{ij}$ value appears, sets the value of $shared_j$ to be this new value. However, to allow such simple definitions, each $Task_i$ specification must be suitably well-behaved. The $ready_i$ indicator must always carry the effective priority at which $Task_i$ wishes to run, and i may make computational progress only when *running* indicates that it is executing. Furthermore, $Task_i$ may produce an $update_{ij}$ value, or examine the value of $shared_j$, only when it knows that it is the currently *running* task, and that its $ready_i$ priority is at least as great as the ceiling value for that shared object.

Other target implementations can be handled by our framework, however. For instance, earliest deadline first scheduling could be treated by including the (absolute) deadline of each $Task_i$ invocation in its $ready_i$ request. The *Scheduler* definition can then use these deadlines to determine which task to make *running*.

4 Example

We consider a version of the 'mine shaft' example that has proven to be a popular test-bed for real-time development methods [4]. The system aims to keep the level of ground water seeping into a mine shaft below a certain height as long as atmospheric conditions in the shaft are safe for operating electrical equipment.

4.1 Requirements specification

Firstly we introduce a discrete absolute time domain $\mathbb{A}$ and a type for durations $\mathbb{D}$ of time:

$$\mathbb{A} == \mathbb{N} \qquad\qquad \mathbb{D} == \mathbb{N} .$$

Input to the system consists of readings provided by two sensors. A water level sensor continuously provides depth readings.

Water

$H_2O : \mathbb{A} \to \mathbb{Z}$

The system will attempt to keep this reading below a certain mark.

$H_2Omark : \mathbb{Z}$

A methane sensor generates 'true' whenever the methane level in the mine becomes unsafe and 'false' whenever it falls back to a safe level again. The known rate of change of methane gas, and the callibration of the sensing equipment, guarantees that such values are generated no closer together than a fixed separation. At start-up time 0 some initial value is generated.

$CH_4sep : \mathbb{D}$

$CH_4sep > 0$

Methane

$CH_4 : \mathbb{A} \leftrightarrow \mathbb{B}$

$0 \in \operatorname{dom} CH_4$
$\forall x, y : \operatorname{dom} CH_4 \mid x < y \bullet$
$\quad x + CH_4sep \leqslant y$

Our goal is to pump the water out of the shaft whenever it becomes too deep. However the pump may run only when methane levels are low, for fear of causing an explosion. Also an alarm bell must ring while methane levels are dangerously high. The pump and alarm actuators are controlled by two variables,

$$Pump \mathrel{\hat=} [\, pumping : \mathbb{A} \to \mathbb{B}] \qquad Alarm \mathrel{\hat=} [\, ringing : \mathbb{A} \to \mathbb{B}] \ .$$

The system is allowed to take a certain amount of time to react to environmental changes.

$$\begin{array}{|l} react : \mathbb{D} \\ \hline react \leqslant CH_4sep \end{array}$$

Lambda expressions provide us with a convenient way to express properties of trace variables such as H_2O and CH_4:

$$\begin{array}{ll} deep_\delta & == \lambda\, t : \mathbb{A} \bullet t \geqslant \delta \wedge min\ H_2O(\!|\, t - \delta \mathinner{\ldotp\ldotp} t \,|\!) \geqslant H_2Omark \\ shallow_\delta & == \lambda\, t : \mathbb{A} \bullet t \geqslant \delta \wedge max\ H_2O(\!|\, t - \delta \mathinner{\ldotp\ldotp} t \,|\!) < H_2Omark \\ currCH_4 & == \lambda\, t : \mathbb{A} \bullet CH_4(max\ \mathrm{dom}(0 \mathinner{\ldotp\ldotp} t \lhd CH_4)) \\ danger_\delta & == \lambda\, t : \mathbb{A} \bullet t \geqslant \delta \wedge currCH_4(\!|\, t - \delta \mathinner{\ldotp\ldotp} t \,|\!) = \{\mathrm{true}\} \\ safe_\delta & == \lambda\, t : \mathbb{A} \bullet t \geqslant \delta \wedge currCH_4(\!|\, t - \delta \mathinner{\ldotp\ldotp} t \,|\!) = \{\mathrm{false}\}\ . \end{array}$$

For instance, $shallow_\delta$ is true at some time t only if the water level has been constantly below H_2Omark for the last δ time units. Similarly, $safe_\delta$ is true at t if, for the last δ time units, the most recent CH_4 value was always 'false'. (Function $currCH_4$ returns the most recent CH_4 value at any time t.)

The system is required to raise the alarm when the methane level is high, but not when it is low.

$$\begin{array}{|l} \hline \textit{ControlAlarm} \\ Methane;\ Alarm \\ \hline \forall\, t : \mathbb{A} \bullet (danger_{react}(t) \Rightarrow ringing(t)) \\ \qquad\qquad \wedge\ (safe_{react}(t) \Rightarrow \neg\ ringing(t)) \\ \hline \end{array}$$

If the methane level changed within the last *react* time units the value of *ringing* is unspecified.

Similarly, the pump must be switched on only when needed, and only when conditions are safe to do so.

$$\begin{array}{|l} \hline \textit{ControlPump} \\ Water;\ Methane;\ Pump \\ \hline \forall\, t : \mathbb{A} \bullet (deep_{react}(t) \wedge safe_{react}(t) \Rightarrow pumping(t)) \\ \qquad\qquad \wedge\ (shallow_{react}(t) \vee danger_{react}(t) \Rightarrow \neg\ pumping(t)) \\ \hline \end{array}$$

The full requirements specification is then

$$+\ ringing, pumping \colon \begin{bmatrix} Water & ControlAlarm \\ Methane & ControlPump \end{bmatrix} . \qquad (1)$$

4.2 Introduce shared variable

Both *ControlAlarm* and *ControlPump* use the CH_4 sensor variable. In order to achieve independent interfaces to the environmental inputs, we want to prevent the pump controller from directly using the methane sensor and instead have it access a shared variable set by the alarm controller to determine if conditions are safe or not.

In fact, a suitable variable already exists, *ringing*. For brevity we will use *ringing* as not only an 'output' variable, but also as the shared variable used for communication between the alarm and pump controllers.

Again some syntactic conveniences can be defined for referring to the state of this variable in the recent past:

$$noisy_\delta == \lambda\, t : \mathbb{A} \bullet t \geqslant \delta \wedge ringing(\!|\, t - \delta \,..\, t \,|\!) = \{\text{true}\}$$
$$quiet_\delta == \lambda\, t : \mathbb{A} \bullet t \geqslant \delta \wedge ringing(\!|\, t - \delta \,..\, t \,|\!) = \{\text{false}\}\ .$$

Since the pump controller will now use *ringing* to determine if methane levels are high, and it takes some time to update *ringing* whenever methane levels change, we need to shorten the available time to update the output variables in order to ensure that *pumping* is still always set correctly within *react* time units of environmental changes. Let *rt* and *pt* be tighter deadlines on how quickly *ringing* and *pumping* must be updated, respectively.

$$\begin{array}{|l} rt, pt : \mathbb{D} \\ \hline rt + pt \leqslant react \end{array}$$

Development proceeds by using the stronger update times and having the pump controller refer to shared variable *ringing* rather than the methane sensor.

$$\begin{array}{|l} \textit{ControlAlarm2} \\ \hline Methane;\ Alarm \\ \hline \forall\, t : \mathbb{A} \bullet (danger_{rt}(t) \Rightarrow ringing(t)) \\ \qquad \wedge\ (safe_{rt}(t) \Rightarrow \neg\ ringing(t)) \\ \hline \end{array}$$

$$\begin{array}{|l} \textit{ControlPump2} \\ \hline Water;\ Alarm;\ Pump \\ \hline \forall\, t : \mathbb{A} \bullet (deep_{pt}(t) \wedge quiet_{pt}(t) \Rightarrow pumping(t)) \\ \qquad \wedge\ (shallow_{pt}(t) \vee noisy_{pt}(t) \Rightarrow \neg\ pumping(t)) \\ \hline \end{array}$$

$$(1) \sqsubseteq \text{"by } \mathbf{R2}\text{"}$$

$$+ringing, pumping\text{:} \begin{bmatrix} Water & ControlAlarm2 \\ Methane\ ' & ControlPump2 \end{bmatrix} \qquad (2)$$

4.3 Introduce periodic and sporadic requirements

We will 'implement' the pump controller as a periodic behaviour and the alarm controller as a sporadic one. Interarrival times and deadlines for the sporadic s and periodic p requirements are introduced as follows.

$$\begin{array}{|l} T_s, D_s : \mathbb{D} \\ \hline D_s \leqslant T_s \\ T_s = CH_4sep \\ D_s \leqslant rt \end{array} \qquad \begin{array}{|l} T_p, D_p : \mathbb{D} \\ \hline D_p \leqslant T_p \\ rt + T_p + D_p \leqslant pt \end{array}$$

The second constraint on the right ensures that *pumping* is updated in time. Apart from the reliance on *ringing*, which may be *rt* time units out of date, two successive updates to *pumping* may be separated by period T_p plus deadline D_p in the worst case (i.e., where the first update occurs immediately after arrival in one period and the next occurs just before the deadline in the following period).

We define some convenient notations for referring to the sporadic and periodic arrival times, and the moment *before* the next arrival after some time t:

$$arrive_s == \mathrm{dom}\, CH_4$$
$$arrive_p == \{n : \mathbb{N} \bullet n * T_p\}$$
$$next_s(t) = \begin{cases} \infty, & t \geqslant max\, \mathrm{dom}\, CH_4 \\ max\{u : \mathbb{A} \mid u < (min\, \mathrm{dom}(0 \mathinner{..} t \lhd CH_4))\}, & \text{otherwise} \end{cases}$$
$$next_p(t) = max\{u : \mathbb{A} \mid u < \left\lceil \frac{t+1}{T_p} \right\rceil T_p\}\,.$$

The sporadic task arrives at each detected change in methane levels. The periodic task arrives every T_p time units. (There is no need to use T_s in defining $arrive_s$ in this example because CH_4 inputs are already known to be separated by at least this amount.)

It is also helpful to be able to assert that some timed variable v does not change its value at any of the absolute times in some, not necessarily contiguous, set A (where to be 'changed' a variable must have a different value than it had in the previous instant):

$$unchanged(v, A) = \forall t : A \bullet t \neq 0 \Rightarrow v(t) = v(t-1)\,.$$

We now re-express the controllers as behaviours that, following each arrival a, achieve their functional requirement by the time of their absolute deadline d, and update their output variables only at some time u between a and d.

Sporadic

$$Methane;\ Alarm$$

$$\begin{aligned}
&\forall a : arrive_s \bullet \\
&\quad \mathrm{let}\ d == a + D_s \bullet \\
&\qquad\quad (danger_{D_s}(d) \Rightarrow ringing(d)) \\
&\qquad \wedge (safe_{D_s}(d) \Rightarrow \neg\, ringing(d)) \\
&\qquad \wedge \exists u : a \mathinner{..} d \bullet unchanged(ringing, (a \mathinner{..} next_s(a)) \setminus \{u\})
\end{aligned}$$

Periodic

$$Water;\ Alarm;\ Pump$$

$$\begin{aligned}
&\forall a : arrive_p \bullet \\
&\quad \mathrm{let}\ d == a + D_p \bullet \\
&\qquad\quad (deep_{D_p}(d) \wedge quiet_{D_p}(d) \Rightarrow pumping(d)) \\
&\qquad \wedge (shallow_{D_p}(d) \vee noisy_{D_p}(d) \Rightarrow \neg\, pumping(d)) \\
&\qquad \wedge \exists u : a \mathinner{..} d \bullet unchanged(pumping, (a \mathinner{..} next_p(a)) \setminus \{u\})
\end{aligned}$$

(2) $\sqsubseteq$ "by **R2**"

$$+ringing, pumping : \begin{bmatrix} Water & Sporadic \\ Methane' & Periodic \end{bmatrix} \quad (3)$$

4.4 Introduce worst case execution times

Constants are introduced to represent the programmer's anticipated worst case computation times for the sporadic and periodic requirements.

$$\begin{array}{|l} C_s : \mathbb{D} \\ \hline C_s \leqslant D_s \end{array} \qquad \begin{array}{|l} C_p : \mathbb{D} \\ \hline C_p \leqslant D_p \end{array}$$

The actual computation time required upon each arrival is not yet known (and, indeed, will not be known until the final object code is generated!). At most, therefore, we can say only that at each arrival the notional invocation request will not exceed the worst case execution time.

$$\begin{array}{|l} invreq_s : \mathbb{A} \nrightarrow \mathbb{D} \\ \hline \operatorname{dom} invreq_s = arrive_s \\ max \operatorname{ran} invreq_s \leqslant C_s \end{array} \qquad \begin{array}{|l} invreq_p : \mathbb{A} \nrightarrow \mathbb{D} \\ \hline \operatorname{dom} invreq_p = arrive_p \\ max \operatorname{ran} invreq_p \leqslant C_p \end{array}$$

4.5 Introduce feasible schedule

There are three possible 'tasks' $\mathbb{T}$ that may occupy the processor in our system, the sporadic s and periodic p application tasks, and no activity at all:

$$\mathbb{T} ::= s \mid p \mid idle \; .$$

One of these is running at every moment in time:

$$Run \mathrel{\widehat=} [\, running : \mathbb{A} \rightarrow \mathbb{T} \,] \; .$$

Our overall constraint on the processor is that, for each invocation request, it gives the application tasks as many units of run time as they need.

$$\begin{array}{|l} \textit{Processor} \\ \hline Methane; \; Run \\ \hline \forall a : arrive_s \bullet \#(a \mathinner{..} a + D_s \lhd running \rhd \{s\}) = invreq_s(a) \\ \forall a : arrive_p \bullet \#(a \mathinner{..} a + D_p \lhd running \rhd \{p\}) = invreq_p(a) \\ \hline \end{array}$$

(3) $\sqsubseteq$ "by **R3, R2**"

$$\left[\!\left[\begin{bmatrix} ringing, \\ +pumping, : \\ running \end{bmatrix} \begin{bmatrix} Water & Sporadic \\ Methane' & Periodic \\ & Processor \end{bmatrix} \Big\backslash \; running \right]\!\right] \quad (4)$$

Here the scheduling model we are constructing first begins to benefit us. How can we be sure that the property of *running* specified in *Processor* is feasible? It is not obvious by inspection, especially in more complex examples. If it is infeasible then the above refinement step makes the effect 'false', i.e., we have refined to 'magic', and any further development effort would be wasted.

We require a feasibility test to guarantee that this is not the case. Test 1 from Section 2.2 is suitable. The programmer merely needs to supply anticipated values for the symbolic constants introduced above to see if the development is proceeding along a viable path. For instance, assuming $D_s = 15$, $C_s = 6$, $D_p = 20$ and $C_p = 10$, we can use test 1 to show that the requirement can be met for the sporadic behaviour because

$$\frac{C_s}{D_s} = \frac{6}{15} \leqslant 1 \,.$$

Similarly, the periodic behaviour can also be satisfied because

$$\frac{C_s}{D_s} + \frac{C_p}{D_p} = \frac{6}{15} + \frac{10}{20} \leqslant 1 \,.$$

(We have not yet introduced enough detail in the refinement to determine task blocking overheads, so these figures are omitted.)

Of course, this tells us only that a scheduler *exists* that will satisfy the requirement, not that the particular scheduling policy we will ultimately employ can do so.

4.6 Introduce ready indicators

Effective priorities $\mathbb{E}$ for tasks can be represented by natural numbers, with higher values denoting higher priorities,

$$\mathbb{E} == \mathbb{N} \,.$$

The lowest 'normal' priority is 1; we use 0 to indicate that a task is *not* ready.

In this example there are base priorities π_s and π_p for each of the two tasks, and a ceiling priority π_c for when they access the shared variable.

$$\begin{array}{|l} \pi_p, \pi_s, \pi_c : \mathbb{E} \\ \hline 0 < \pi_p < \pi_s \leqslant \pi_c \end{array}$$

It is considered more critical to note changes in methane than water levels, so π_s is higher than π_p.

Whenever a task is ready to run, its *ready* indicator records this with a value denoting the effective priority at which the task wishes to execute. The periodic task may run at its own base priority π_p, or the higher ceiling priority π_c while it is accessing shared variable *ringing*:

$$Ready_p \mathrel{\widehat{=}} [\, ready_p : \mathbb{A} \rightarrow \mathbb{E} \mid \operatorname{ran} ready_p = \{0, \pi_p, \pi_c\} \,] \,.$$

Our simple sporadic task does nothing but update the shared variable, so it always runs at the ceiling priority π_c, and π_s is not needed in this case:

$$Ready_s \mathrel{\widehat=} [\, ready_s : \mathbb{A} \rightarrow \mathbb{E} \mid \operatorname{ran} ready_s = \{0, \pi_c\} \,] \ .$$

$$(4) \sqsubseteq \text{“by } \mathbf{R3, R2}\text{”}$$

$$\left\| \begin{bmatrix} ringing, \\ pumping, \\ +running, : \\ ready_p, \\ ready_s \end{bmatrix} \begin{bmatrix} & Sporadic \\ Water & Periodic \\ & Processor \\ Methane \, , & Ready_s \\ & Ready_p \end{bmatrix} \Bigg\backslash \begin{matrix} running, \\ ready_p, \\ ready_s \end{matrix} \right\| \qquad (5)$$

4.7 Introduce protected objects

In this example we do not need to add any *update* channels, since *Periodic* does not attempt to write to *ringing*. Also, the *Sporadic* specification serves as both a sporadic requirement and custodian of the shared variable so a distinct *Protected* specification is unnecessary.

The task designs are completed by defining how access to the shared variable is controlled through manipulation of effective priorities. In doing so we further contrain the task definitions so that they always complete their work before some worst case response time, no greater than their deadlines.

$$\begin{array}{|l} R_s : \mathbb{D} \\ \hline R_s \leqslant D_s \end{array} \qquad \qquad \begin{array}{|l} R_p : \mathbb{D} \\ \hline R_p \leqslant D_p \end{array}$$

Our simple sporadic task does nothing but update shared variable *ringing*, so it always runs at effective priority π_c.

Sporadic2

$$\begin{array}{|l} Methane; \ Run; \ Alarm; \ Ready_s \\ \hline \forall\, a : arrive_s \bullet \\ \quad \exists\, r : a \mathinner{..} a + R_s \mid r = max \operatorname{dom}(a \mathinner{..} a + D_s \lhd running \rhd \{s\}) \bullet \\ \qquad (danger_{r-a}(r) \Rightarrow ringing(r)) \\ \quad\ \wedge (safe_{r-a}(r) \Rightarrow \neg\, ringing(r)) \\ \quad\ \wedge (\exists\, u : a \mathinner{..} r \bullet unchanged(ringing, (a \mathinner{..} next_s(a)) \setminus \{u\})) \\ \quad\ \wedge\, ready_s (\!| \, a \mathinner{..} r \, |\!) = \{\pi_c\} \\ \quad\ \wedge\, ready_s (\!| \, r + 1 \mathinner{..} \operatorname{next}_s(a) \, |\!) = \{0\} \end{array}$$

Time r is the (absolute) time at which a *particular* task invocation completes its work, defined to be the earliest time at which it has received $invreq_s(a)$ units of processor time (see schema *Processor* above). The task is ‘ready’ from time a until r. After this it will not request any more processor time until the next arrival.

The periodic task, on the other hand, must access the shared variable 'created' by the above schema. In doing so it may block task s if a CH_4 event occurs while the periodic behaviour p is accessing *running*.

$$\begin{array}{|l} B_s : \mathbb{D} \\ \hline B_s \leqslant C_p \end{array}$$

Activity of the periodic task following each arrival time a can be divided into two parts. We require that it first samples the value of the shared variable *ringing*, before some time x; to do so it must be ready at priority π_c. It then samples the value of H_2O and sets the value of *pumping*, before its worst case response time R_p has elapsed.

Periodic2

$$\begin{array}{|l} Water;\ Alarm;\ Run;\ Pump;\ Ready_p \\ \hline \forall\, a : arrive_p \bullet \\ \quad \exists\, r : a \mathinner{..} a + R_p \mid r = max\ \mathrm{dom}(a \mathinner{..} a + D_p \lhd running \rhd \{p\}) \bullet \\ \quad \exists\, x : a \mathinner{..} r \mid \#(a \mathinner{..} x \lhd running \rhd \{p\}) \leqslant B_s \bullet \\ \qquad (deep_{r-x}(r) \land quiet_{x-a}(x) \Rightarrow pumping(r)) \\ \qquad \land (shallow_{r-x}(r) \lor noisy_{x-a}(x) \Rightarrow \neg\, pumping(r)) \\ \qquad \land (\exists\, u : x \mathinner{..} r \bullet unchanged(pumping, (a \mathinner{..} next_p(a)) \setminus \{u\})) \\ \qquad \land ready_p(\!|\, a \mathinner{..} x \,|\!) = \{\pi_c\} \\ \qquad \land ready_p(\!|\, x + 1 \mathinner{..} r \,|\!) = \{\pi_p\} \\ \qquad \land ready_p(\!|\, r + 1 \mathinner{..} next_p(a) \,|\!) = \{0\} \end{array}$$

The new subscripts and arguments to *deep*, *quiet*, etc., reflect the more precise times at which these properties are tested. The alarm value is sampled within x time units of arrival a. The water sensor is sampled some time in the remaining $r - x$ time units, before the particular response time r.

$(5) \sqsubseteq$ "by **R2**"

$$\left\|\left[\begin{array}{l} ringing, \\ pumping, \\ +running, : \\ ready_p, \\ ready_s \end{array} \left[\begin{array}{l} Water \\ Methane \end{array}, \begin{array}{r} Sporadic2 \\ Periodic2 \\ Processor \end{array}\right] \Bigg\backslash \begin{array}{l} running, \\ ready_p, \\ ready_s \end{array}\right]\right\| \qquad (6)$$

4.8 Introduce scheduler

The scheduling policy can be introduced easily. At any time t it makes the running task the highest priority one in a notional ready queue formed from the *ready*$_s$ and *ready*$_p$ indicators.

Scheduler

$$\begin{array}{|l} Ready_p;\ Ready_s;\ Run \\ \hline \forall\, t : \mathbb{A} \bullet running(t) = highpri(t) \end{array}$$

Function *highpri* returns the highest priority ready task at time t:

$$highpri(t) = \begin{cases} idle, & ready_p(t) = ready_s(t) = 0 \\ p, & ready_p(t) > ready_s(t) \\ & \lor (ready_p(t) = ready_s(t) \neq 0 \\ & \quad \land t > 0 \land highpri(t-1) = p) \\ s, & ready_s(t) > ready_p(t) \\ & \lor (ready_s(t) = ready_p(t) \neq 0 \\ & \quad \land (t > 0 \Rightarrow highpri(t-1) \in \{s, idle\})) . \end{cases}$$

In other words, the highest priority ready task is *idle* if neither p or s is ready at time t. It is p if that task is ready with a higher effective priority than s, or both tasks are ready with the same priority and the task running at the last moment in time was p. An arbitrary decision has been made to favour s when both tasks become ready at the same priority at time 0 or following an *idle* period.

$$(6) \sqsubseteq \text{“by } \mathbf{R2}\text{”}$$

$$\left[\!\left[\begin{matrix} ringing, \\ pumping, \\ +running, : \\ ready_p, \\ ready_s \end{matrix} \begin{bmatrix} Water \\ Methane \end{bmatrix}, \begin{bmatrix} Sporadic2 \\ Periodic2 \\ Processor \\ Scheduler \end{bmatrix} \Big\backslash \begin{matrix} running, \\ ready_p, \\ ready_s \end{matrix} \right]\!\right] \qquad (7)$$

Again our refinement process benefits from scheduling theory. Although we claim the existence of worst case response times R_s and R_p above we now need to show that satisfactory values do indeed exist under this scheduling policy. Test 2 from Section 2.2 is suitable. For instance, given values of $T_s = 100$, $T_p = 25$ and $B_s = 5$, as well as the values for deadlines and computations times used in Section 4.5, we can determine that the sporadic requirement can be satisfied because

$$R_s = C_s + B_s = 6 + 5 = 11 \leqslant D_s .$$

There are no tasks of higher priority than s to pre-empt it, and the only lower-priority task that can block it is p, which can do so at most once. Hence the sporadic requirement will always meet its deadline of 15 time units from arrival.

To test the periodic requirement we note that no lower-priority tasks exist to block p, so 'B_p' is zero. But p can be pre-empted by s, so interference must be considered and

$$R_p = C_p + \left\lceil \frac{R_p}{T_s} \right\rceil C_s .$$

This recursive equation converges as follows:

$$R_p^0 = 0$$

$$R_p^1 = C_p + \left\lceil \frac{R_p^0}{T_s} \right\rceil C_s = 10 + \left\lceil \frac{0}{100} \right\rceil 6 = 10$$

$$R_p^2 = C_p + \left\lceil \frac{R_p^1}{T_s} \right\rceil C_s = 10 + \left\lceil \frac{10}{100} \right\rceil 6 = 16$$

$$R_p^3 = C_p + \left\lceil \frac{R_p^2}{T_s} \right\rceil C_s = 10 + \left\lceil \frac{16}{100} \right\rceil 6 = 16 .$$

Hence R_p is less than the deadline of 20 and we can conclude that the system is indeed schedulable! Intuitively this value is reasonable because, given the longer interarrival time of the sporadic task compared to the periodic one, s can preempt p at most once at any arrival of p.

4.9 Separate tasks, shared objects and scheduler

The task requirements and the scheduler can now be separated, for later individual refinement, by straightforward application of the refinement rules. Firstly the scheduler is separated from the tasks.

$$(7) \sqsubseteq \text{“by } \mathbf{R4, R2, R1, R2, R1}\text{”}$$

$$[\![\quad +\, running: \begin{bmatrix} (\exists\, running \bullet & \\ \quad Sporadic2 & , Scheduler \\ \quad \wedge Periodic2) & \end{bmatrix} \qquad (8)$$

$$\|$$

$$+ \begin{matrix} pumping, \\ ringing, \\ ready_p, \\ ready_s \end{matrix} : \begin{bmatrix} Water & \\ Methane & , \begin{matrix} Sporadic2 \\ Periodic2 \end{matrix} \\ Processor & \end{bmatrix} \qquad (9)$$

$$\backslash running, ready_p, ready_s \,]\!]$$

Part of the first 'strengthen effect' step eliminated *Processor* from the effect of the scheduler component by making use of knowledge about the tasks, specifically that they ask for exactly *invreq* time units at each invocation. (The proof relies on our scheduling policy model being deterministic; for particular task behaviours a unique *running* value is defined.) The first 'weaken assumption' step then removed unnecessary properties *Water*, *Methane*, *Scheduler* and *Processor* from the assumption of the scheduler component. The second 'weaken assumption' removed *Scheduler*, *Sporadic*2, *Periodic*2 and the unused existentially-quantified variables from the assumption of the tasks component.

Then the second component, the individual task requirements, is further refined to give three parallel components in total.

$$(9) \sqsubseteq \text{“by } \mathbf{R4, R2, R1, R2, R1}\text{”}$$

$$+\, ringing, ready_s: \begin{bmatrix} Methane \\ Processor \end{bmatrix}, Sporadic2 \qquad (10)$$

$$\|$$

$$+\, pumping, ready_p: \begin{bmatrix} Water & \\ Processor & , Periodic2 \\ Sporadic2 & \end{bmatrix} \qquad (11)$$

In both components the effect is strengthened to eliminate the 'non-constructed' variables. The assumption for the sporadic requirement was weakened to remove *Water*, *Sporadic*2 and *Periodic*2, and that of the periodic task to remove *Methane* and *Periodic*2. *Sporadic*2 remains as an assumption for the periodic task due to the role of *ringing* as a shared variable in this example. Both tasks retain assumption *Processor* so that they know they will receive as much processor time as needed.

4.10 Implementation

Our ultimate aim is to apply the above method to development of Ada 95 programs. This is feasible because the Ada 95 language design accounts for recent advances in schedulability theory [8]. The system above adheres to constructs supported by Ada 95 and can be mapped to the following program.

```
with Ada.Real_Time; use Ada.Real_Time;
pragma Task_Dispatching_Policy(FIFO_Within_Priorities);

protected Alarm is -- implements Sporadic2
   pragma Locking_Policy(Ceiling_Locking);
   pragma Priority(Interrupt_Priority'First); -- i.e., πc
   function danger return Boolean;
private
   procedure CH4high; pragma Attach_Handler(CH4high,...);
   procedure CH4low;  pragma Attach_Handler(CH4low,...);
   -- We assume blocked interrupts remain pending!
   ringing: Boolean := False; for ringing use ...;
end Alarm;

protected body Alarm is
   procedure CH4high is
   begin
     ringing := True
   end CH4high;
   procedure CH4low is
   begin
     ringing := False
   end CH4low;
   function danger return Boolean is -- part of Periodic2
   begin
     return ringing;
   end danger;
end Alarm;

task ControlPump is -- implements Periodic2
   pragma Priority(Priority'First); -- i.e., πp
```

```
end ControlPump;

task body ControlPump is
   H2Omark: constant Integer := H2Omark;
   H2O: Integer; for H2O use ...;
   pumping: Boolean := False; for pumping use ...;
   period: Time_Span := Tp;
   Next: Time := Clock; -- time "0"
begin
   loop
      delay until Next; -- arrival time
      pumping := not Alarm.danger and then H2O >= H2Omark;
      Next := Next + period;
   end loop;
end ControlPump;
```

Our *Scheduler* specification is implemented trivially by the compiler directive on the second line which requests static-priority, pre-emptive scheduling. Similarly, another compiler directive within protected object **Alarm** requests the ceiling locking protocol introduced in Section 4.7 above.

Our degenerate sporadic 'task', *Sporadic*2, is implemented by two interrupt-handling procedures **CH4high** and **CH4low**. (Ada 95 interrupt-handlers are parameterless, unlike the CH_4 variable which carried a boolean value.) The *Periodic*2 requirement is implemented as an iterative Ada task, with a function **danger** that gives it access to the shared variable **ringing**.

Input and output variables **H2O**, **ringing** and **pumping** are mapped to hardware-specific memory locations which are assumed to be continuously accessable by the environment. The hardware-specific interrupt handlers attached to the **CH4high** and **CH4low** procedures implement the CH_4 input.

Although not shown above, this program is still considered to be accompanied by the calculated timing constraints on each component. These must be retained until formally discharged. Real-time development is not considered complete until it has been shown, either experimentally or through further proof, that a call to function **danger** takes no more than B_s time units, that procedures **CH4high** and **CH4low** execute in under C_s time units, and that each iteration of **ControlPump** takes less than C_p time units (including context switching and interrupt handling overheads!).

We have not discussed in this paper how such computation times are determined, or how sequential code segments are generated. However, refinement rules that achieve both aims have already appeared [6], and extend the methodology above to do this.

5 Conclusion

We have shown how new results in real-time scheduling and refinement theories can be integrated. This was done by representing the computational model used by pre-emptive scheduling theory in a real-time refinement calculus. The refinement calculus then gained from proven schedulability results.

This work is part of the *Quartz* project, investigating formal methods for the development of hard real-time software. A number of major projects have goals similar to Quartz, especially the **safemos** [3], *ProCoS* [9] and TAM [13] projects, and Hooman's development method [7], but none makes use of scheduling theory. Previous modelling exercises used Z to define aspects of priority scheduling [5] and the priority ceiling protocol [12], but did not model absolute timing or define refinement methods.

Acknowledgements We wish to thank Andy Wellings for advice on scheduling theory, Graeme Smith for correcting errors in the paper, and the anonymous FME'96 referees for their comments. The Quartz project is funded by the Information Technology Division of the Australian Defence Science and Technology Organisation. Ian Hayes' participation in this work was funded by a University of Queensland Project Enabling Grant.

References

1. N. Audsley, A. Burns, M. Richardson, K. Tindell, and A. Wellings. Applying new scheduling theory to static priority pre-emptive scheduling. *Software Engineering Journal*, 8(5):284–292, September 1993.
2. T.P. Baker. Stack-based scheduling of real-time processes. *Real Time Systems*, 3(1):67–99, March 1991.
3. J. Bowen, editor. *Towards Verified Systems*, volume 2 of *Real-Time Safety Critical Systems*. Elsevier, 1994.
4. A. Burns and A. Wellings. *Real-Time Systems and their Programming Languages*. Addison-Wesley, 1990.
5. A. Burns and A.J. Wellings. Priority inheritance and message passing communication: A formal treatment. *The Journal of Real-Time Systems*, 3:19–44, 1991.
6. C. Fidge. Adding real time to formal program development. In M. Naftalin, T. Denvir, and M. Bertran, editors, *FME'94: Industrial Benefit of Formal Methods*, volume 873 of *Lecture Notes in Computer Science*, pages 618–638. Springer-Verlag, 1994.
7. J. Hooman. Extending Hoare logic to real-time. *Formal Aspects of Computing*, 6(6A):801–825, 1994.
8. Ada 9X Mapping/Revision Team Intermetrics. Ada 9X reference manual, draft version 5.0, June 1994.
9. H. Jifeng. *Provably Correct Systems*. McGraw-Hill, 1995.
10. B. Mahony. Using the refinement calculus for dataflow processes. Technical Report TR 94-32, Software Verification Research Centre, October 1994.
11. B. Mahony. Networks of predicate transformers. Technical Report TR 95-5, Software Verification Research Centre, February 1995.
12. M. Pilling, A. Burns, and K. Raymond. Formal specifications and proofs of inheritance protocols for real-time scheduling. *Software Engineering Journal*, 5(5), September 1990.
13. D. Scholefield. Proving properties of real-time semaphores. *Science of Computer Programming*, 24(2):159–181, April 1995.

Using a Logical and Categorical Approach for the Validation of Fault-Tolerant Systems

C. SEGUIN, V. WIELS
{seguin, wiels}@cert.fr

CERT-ONERA, 2 av. E. Belin, BP 4025, 31055 Toulouse cedex, France

Abstract. We propose a categorical and logical formalism and apply it in order to compositionally specify and verify the fault-tolerance mechanisms of the Modulor system. We claim that our approach is well-suited to the validation of real-sized critical systems.

1 Introduction

In this paper, we present how we have formally validated some fault tolerant mechanisms of the Modulor system, using a combination of a logical and a categorical approach. Through this experiment, we aim to demonstrate the interest of the approach for validating critical real-sized systems.

The Modulor system was developed at CERT jointly with the design of a flexible, massively parallel machine architecture. It supplies the programmers with ad-hoc software tools allowing to take advantage of the processor net of the machine. We were interested in validating the principle of the detection mechanism dedicated to the machine. The validation process was mainly influenced by the following system features.

- First, the whole system is *distributed and large* because it is composed of numerous replications of a basic set of processes; each set of processes runs on a processor and interacts with other sets of processes by communication channels building a net of processors. A *modular* approach allows control of the complexity of the validation induced by the size of the system.
- Next, the topology of the net of processors is *flexible* and changes during a runtime. In order to have general results, the validation results must be *generic*, i.e. independent of the net topology.
- Finally, the system provides *fault-tolerance* mechanisms. Consequently, the validation process must deal with *fault modeling.*

Before using the validation approach described in this paper, we have carried out validations based on CCS and model-checking principles (see [13]) and exhibited limits of these approaches for our purpose.

On one hand, logical formalisms such as TLA ([10]) or Unity ([2]) are expressive enough to easily specify distributed systems and their properties. However, these formalisms lack means of structuring specifications and fully automatic verifying tools. These gaps make the formal validation of a real-sized system difficult.

On the other hand, algebraic approaches such as CCS ([12]) or CSP([8]) offer composition and communication laws allowing structuring of specifications. Moreover, a lot of analysis tools are currently available (bisimulation analysis, model-checking of μ-calculus formulae,...). However the operational way of modeling systems makes the fault modeling cumbersome in our case. Each faulty state must be pointed out individually by performing a "fault-action" which triggers other actions describing the ad-hoc erroneous behavior. The specification is more concise using a descriptive approach since the features of the faulty states can be summed up by a few generic formulae once and for all.

The lack of means of expressing state properties also penalizes the description of the data properties. In case of fault tolerant systems, redundancy resources must be taken into account. In the case of the Modulor system, these resources evolve with time and we must deal with their generic properties. Operational approaches are not well-suited to express state invariants.

Our proposal aims to bridge the gap between the two trends: we wish to keep the expressiveness of the logical formalisms and the composition laws a la CCS. We have based our work on the categorical framework proposed by Fiadeiro and Maibaum [6]; each component of the system is described by a logical theory and the whole system results from the interconnection of the components by means of categories. We have defined a new logic to describe a component, mixing linear temporal logic ([11]), and dynamic logic ([7]). The linear temporal logic has proved to be well suited for expressing properties of concurrent and reactive systems; and the behavior of systems is easily described thanks to the explicit use of actions in the dynamic logic. Our logic is, in fact, a fragment of a particular μ-calculus [9] , but we have found an axiomatic sound and complete with respect to the proposed semantics [17]. This result makes the proofs easier on a component theory. The properties of the global system can be derived in a modular way in the categorical framework.

In section 2, we present the Modulor machine and its fault-tolerance mechanisms. The aim of section 3 is to introduce our formalism, using as a simple example the synchronization at the beginning of a phase. Section 4 finally gives the results we obtained about Modulor and shows the adequacy of the formalism for the specification and verification of fault-tolerant systems.

2 Modulor

The research project named Modulor[1] is directed towards the design and realization of a massively parallel, modular and dynamically reconfigurable computer, as well as the design and realization of the associated software tools. The architecture is a network of processors, and the physical reconfigurability of the hardware links connecting the processors allows us to satisfy two objectives:

[1] Modulor project has been mainly funded by DRET (Research Division of the French Defense Department).

- An optimal topology can be chosen for each application or each phase of the application. We limited our objectives to explicit, quasi-dynamic reconfiguration. We ask programmers to decompose their application into algorithmic phases. Each phase is a graph of communicating processes, written up to now in Occam, and necessitates a specific communication topology.
- Reconfiguration capabilities can be used to offer the dynamic redundancy needed for fault-tolerant computing (the likelihood of the occurrence of a faulty processor grows with the number of such processors).

Up to now, the interest of the approach has been validated by implementing algorithms ranging from numerical algorithms through to tree searching algorithms. More details about these experiments can be found in [4].

The development of a reconfigurable application is assisted by a set of software tools. A lot of them have been validated by practical experiments. Now, our main concern is to formally validate :

- the synchronization mechanisms for the phase initialization and completion.
- the fault-tolerance mechanisms.

2.1 Features of the net processors

We call "net processors" the processors required by an application. All the net processors are connected by oriented links. Considering one link, we call the source processor "father processor" and the target one "son processor". Among the net processors, we distinguish the host processor. It is connected to one of the net processors and is not supposed to break down. In this paper, we will base all our illustrations on the following configuration:

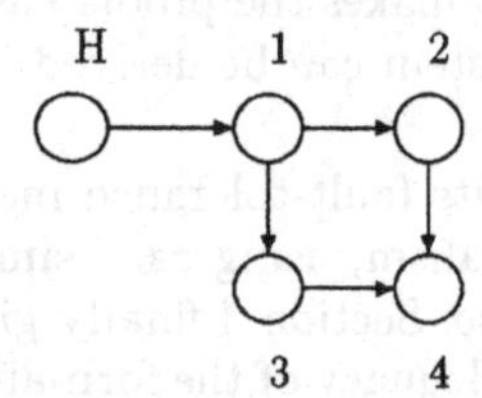

The process running on the host processor plays a supervisory role with respect to the execution of the computation phase: it chooses the type of the following phase in accordance with the results of the previous one and synchronizes the beginning and the end of each phase.

2.2 Synchronization mechanisms

A round of synchronization message exchanges occurs at the phase initialization. The used algorithm allows each processor [2] to receive the phase number, and then to begin the algorithmic phase with the suitable topology.

[2] For the sake of simplicity, we will identify a processor with the process that it is executing.

During the synchronization, the host processor sends the phase number to its son and it begins the execution of the phase. A net processor waits for a phase number from one of its fathers. Then it sends it to all its sons and waits for it from all its other fathers (if it has any) ; it can send and receive in parallel. Finally, when all the sendings and receivings are finished, it begins the execution of the phase.

A second rendez-vous takes place at the phase completion, which is the completion of each process. A communication tree exists for this synchronization (the root of this tree is the host processor). When a process has ended its computation, it waits for all its sons to send an *OK* message and then sends an *OK* message to its father.
After this ending synchronization, the supervisor physically modifies the communication links for the next phase. At this time, no process of the network must send messages, it is only waiting for a new phase to begin. All these mechanisms are only written with message exchanges.

Synchronization properties. The synchronization algorithm aims at triggering the computation of the phase and ensuring the consistent use of the exchanged data during the phase. Consistency is reached when a process does not receive synchronization messages while it is waiting for data messages.

So in the context of our application, we may express more precisely these requirements by:

- P1: each process receives at least one synchronization message before beginning the phase computation;
- P2: each process receives no more synchronization messages after entering the phase computation.

2.3 Fault-tolerance mechanisms

Fault tolerance is achieved by passive redundancy. So detection, isolation and recovery mechanisms have been implemented (fault detection, diagnosis and reconfiguration of the architecture in order to replay the phase). We detail the detection mechanism because it is this part we are interested in for the validation.

We assume that *a failure of the processor or of one of the communication links corresponds to a total stop of the processor.* Besides, every processor attempting to communicate with a faulty processor is blocked. We also assume the user's code has been already validated and then *we assume a maximum time for each phase execution.* So exceeding this limit is assimilated with an error, and means that a processor is faulty. The added mechanisms allow the deadlock to be detected when timers exceed the upper limit for the phase.

On each net processor of the net, the running process is divided into three processes (timer, server and phase) in order to control the state of the phase during its execution.

- The phase process is responsible for the execution of the phase. To achieve this execution, it communicates with the processors it is connected with. The phase process can break down at any time during the execution, or it can become blocked while trying to communicate with a processor that has broken down. The phase process regularly asks the server the current state of the phase. If the state is not correct, it stops its execution. If it can finish its execution correctly, it signals the correct end to the server.
- The server process updates the state of the phase (which becomes in error if a time-out has happened). The server also gives the state of the phase to the phase process. Finally, it stops the timer when the phase has ended correctly.
- The timer process initializes a timer at the beginning of the phase. When the execution of the phase is not finished in time (the process is locked, waiting for a communication with a locked or faulty processor), a time-out happens and the timer process unlocks the phase process if necessary. Otherwise, the timer process is stopped by the server process.

Detection Properties. We focus our experiment on the detection algorithm. We stated at least four requirements which express the correctness of this algorithm:

- P3: Every failure is detected: "Each time a processor is faulty, the host knows it".
- P4: The detection allows to resume communications between non-faulty processors: "All blocked processors will be released".

3 Specifying a component by means of the logic of actions and time

We have designed a logic to deal in the same formalism with the specification of a system behavior and the expected properties. This logic inherits the way of specifying the system actions from the dynamic logic and the expression of the properties from linear temporal logic. We first present the logic and then illustrate how to use it with the synchronization algorithm at the beginning of a phase.

3.1 Logic of actions and time

Syntax. For a given component of a system, let $\Delta_C = (CONST_C, ATT_C, ACT_C)$ be the component signature. $CONST_C$, ATT_C, and ACT_C are three disjoint and finite sets of name symbols denoting respectively the name of constants, attributes and actions of the component. We introduce the new action symbol τ which does not belong to ACT_C and denotes external actions of other components outside C.

From Δ_C, we inductively construct the set of the well-formed formulae relative to the component C:

- if $x \in ATT_C$ and $c \in CONST_C$, $x = c$ is a wff for C
- if A and B are wff for C and $\alpha \in ACT_C \cup \{\tau\}$ then $\neg A$, $A \rightarrow B$, $A \wedge B$, $A \vee B$, $A \leftrightarrow B$, T, F, $[\alpha]A$, $< \alpha > A$, OA, $\Box A$, $\Diamond A$, $A\, Until\, B$ are wff for C.

$\neg$, $\rightarrow$, $\wedge$, $\vee$, $\leftrightarrow$ are the connectives of the classical logic whereas $[\alpha]$, $< \alpha >$, O, $\Box$, $\Diamond$, *Until* are modal operators which have the following meaning :
$< \alpha > A$: it is possible to execute α reaching a situation in which A is true.
$[\alpha]A$: every execution of α leads to a situation in which A is true.
OA :at the next step of the execution, A will be true.
$\Box A$: now and in the future, A will always be true.
$\Diamond A$: A will be true.
$A\, Until\, B$: A will remain true until B becomes true.

We will give the semantics and an axiomatic for the connectives $\neg$, $\rightarrow$, the family of modal operators $[\alpha]$ and the temporal operators $\Box$, O and *Until*. The meaning of the other connectives, modal operators and the formulae T (true) and F (false) is given by the definitions above:

$T \equiv_{def} A \rightarrow A$ $\qquad$ $A \leftrightarrow B \equiv_{def} (A \rightarrow B) \wedge (B \rightarrow A)$
$F \equiv_{def} \neg T$ $\qquad$ $< \alpha > A \equiv_{def} \neg[\alpha]\neg A$
$A \wedge B \equiv_{def} \neg(A \rightarrow \neg B)$ $\qquad$ $OA \equiv_{def} \bigvee_{\alpha \in ACTC \cup \{\tau\}} < \alpha > A$
$A \vee B \equiv_{def} \neg A \rightarrow B$

Semantics The formulae of our logic are interpreted within an infinite sequence of states standing for a computation of a component. In order to deal explicitly with actions, we label the transitions from one state to its immediate successor in the sequence, by a subset of $ACT_C \cup \{\tau\}$. We do not assume any hypothesis about the parallelism but an interleaving semantics can be gained by labeling the transition by an unique name of $ACT_C \cup \{\tau\}$.

We chose a linear time semantics rather than a branching one as proposed by Fiadeiro and Maibaum, because it seems to be expressive enough for our purpose without requiring the complexity of a temporal logic such as CTL* [5] .

Model definition. A model M_C relative to the signature $\Delta_C = (CONST_C, ATT_C, ACT_C)$ of a component is a quintuplet $(W, \{R_\alpha | \alpha \in ACT_C \cup \{\tau\}\}, \Pi, D, I_{CONSTC}, I_{ATTC})$ where:

- W is a non empty set of worlds (or states)
- each R_α is a partial function over W. R_α(w)=w' also noted by wR_αw' means that the successor w' of w is reached by performing α.
- Π is the next-state function which associates with each world its successor in the computation. In order to relate time and action, we add the following constraint: $\Pi = \bigcup_{\alpha \in (ACTC \cup \{\tau\})} R_\alpha$, which expresses that a transition always results from performing at least one action.
- D is a domain of values
- I_{CONSTC} is the function of interpretation of the constants. The interpretation of the constants is time independent. $I_{CONSTC} : CONST_C \rightarrow D$

- I_{ATTC} is the function of interpretation of the attributes. This function is time dependent since the value of an attribute may change from one state to the other. $I_{ATTC} : ATT_C \times W \rightarrow D$

Satisfiability relation. The satisfiability relation $\models$ between pairs (M_C, w) and formulae is defined by the following rules :
$(M_C, w) \models (x = c)$ iff $I_{ATTC}(w, x) = I_{CONSTC}(c)$
$(M_C, w) \models \neg A$ iff $not((M_C, w) \models A)$
$(M_C, w) \models A \rightarrow B$ iff $(M_C, w) \models \neg A$ or $(M_C, w) \models B$
$(M_C, w) \models [\alpha]A$ iff $\forall w' \in W$, if $wR_\alpha w'$ then $(M_C, w') \models A$
$(M_C, w) \models OA$ iff $(M_C, \Pi(w)) \models A$ [3]
$(M_C, w) \models \Box A$ iff $\forall i \geq 0, (M_C, \Pi^i(w)) \models A$
$(M_C, w) \models A\, Until\, B$ iff $\exists i \geq 0$ such that
$(M_C, \Pi^i(w)) \models B$ and $\forall j < i, (M_C, \Pi^j(w)) \models A$

Satisfiability. A formula A is satisfiable if there is a model M and a world w of the set of world of M such that $(M, w) \models A$.
Validity. A formula is valid iff it is satisfiable in every world of every model.

Axiomatic The following system captures the semantics given in the previous section.

- Axioms of the propositional calculus and of the equality predicate
- Axiom of the propositional dynamic logic : $[\alpha](A \rightarrow B) \wedge [\alpha]A \rightarrow [\alpha]B$
  We recall the linkage definition between action and time:
  $OA \equiv_{def} \bigvee_{\alpha \in ACTC \cup \{\tau\}} <\alpha> A$
- Axioms of the propositional linear temporal logic :
  $\Box(A \rightarrow B) \wedge \Box A \rightarrow \Box B$ $\quad OA \leftrightarrow \neg O \neg A$
  $\Box(A \rightarrow OA) \wedge A \rightarrow \Box A$ $\quad A\, Until\, B \rightarrow \Diamond B$
  $\Box A \rightarrow A \wedge O\Box A$ $\quad A\, Until\, B \leftrightarrow B \vee (A \wedge O(A\, Until\, B))$

  Inference rules:
- R1 $\frac{\vdash A, \vdash A \rightarrow B}{\vdash B}$ (modus ponens)
- R2 $\frac{\vdash A}{\vdash \Box A}$ ($\Box$ necessitation)
- R3 $\frac{\vdash A}{\vdash [\alpha]A}$ ($[\alpha]$ necessitation)

Theorem. We have proved that the restriction of the proposed semantics to the pure propositional models is sound and complete with respect to the axiomatic below [17].

[3] As OA is defined by a combination of operators $<\alpha>$, the definitions of the relation Π and of the satisfiability relation for OA are not required; however we gave them for sake of readability.

3.2 Specification of a component

Each component C of a system can be described by a theory Φ_C of the logic of action and time presented above, using the object-oriented methodology proposed by Fiadeiro and Maibaum. The key point is the encapsulation principle allowing compositional specification and validation.

The component encapsulation

Principle. A component is defined by attributes and specific actions. Attributes are the state variables of the component; their values range over a set of constants. The actions are the "methods" related to the component. The encapsulation principle for a component C is stated as follows:

- the attributes and the actions of a component are only those whose names occur in the signature Δ_C;
- the possible values of an attribute range over the constants denoted by the names of $CONST_C$.
- Moreover, the scope of the effects of an action are local to the component; so, the attribute values of a component C can only be modified by the actions of ACT_C.

Indeed, the signature Δ_C is a way to circumscribe a component.

Modeling encapsulation in a theory Φ_C. To take into account the locality of the action effects, we add a locality axiom in each theory describing a given component. For a given component C and its signature $\Delta_C = (CONST_C, ATT_C, ACT_C)$, the locality axiom has the following pattern :

$$locusC : \bigvee_{\alpha \in ACTC} < \alpha > True \vee (\bigwedge_{x \in ATTC} (\bigvee_{c \in CONSTC} (x = c \wedge O(x = c))))$$

This axiom means that either an action of the component C is performed or the attributes keep their values in the next state.

Semantics point of view. Each time a transition is labeled by τ (i.e. by no action of the observed component), then the values of the component attributes remain unchanged after the transition.

According to the Fiadeiro and Maibaum's terminology, we call a model $M_C = (W, \{R_\alpha | \alpha \in ACT_C \cup \{\tau\}\}, \Pi, D, I_{CONSTC}, I_{ATTC})$ a Δ_C-locus with respect to the signature Δ_C iff:
$\forall (w, w') \in W$, if $wR_\tau w'$ and $R_\alpha(w)$ is undefined for all α of ACT_C,
then $\forall x \in ATT_C, I_{ATTC}(x, w) = I_{ATTC}(x, w')$

Let M_{locusC} be the set of models for C which are Δ_C-loci. We proved ([17]) that the locus axiom is exactly defined by the set of M_{locusC} :
$\forall M_C, \forall w, (M_C, w) \models locusC$ iff $M_C \in M_{locusC}$

We say a formula A is **loci-valid** and write $\models_{loci} A$ if
$\forall M_C \in M_{locusC}, (M_C, w) \models A$.

Description theory of a component We saw in section 2 that each computation phase on the Modulor machine begins with a synchronization of all the active processes of the phase. We present here the logical theory describing the behavior of one processor during this synchronization round.

Signature. For the description of a process, **three attributes** are needed: *ready_to_send, connect_to_j* and *connect_from_j*. The attribute *ready_to_send* takes the value *True* [4] when the process has received a number for the phase, it means it is now able to send it to its sons. The attributes *connect_to_j* and *connect_from_j* describe the connections that exist between the processors. They may take three values: 0 when the connection does not exist, 1 when the connection exists and 2 when the connection with the processor j exists and the number has been sent or received to or from the processor j.

The process can execute **three actions**: send the number to a process j *send_j*, receive the number from a process j *receive_j* and begin the phase *begin_phase.*

Theory. Let us now define the theory associated with a component. First we express the properties of the attributes. Their values range over subset of constants and cannot have simultaneously two different values. These properties are **integrity constraints** which must always be satisfied during a computation. In the case of the theory of a process in Modulor, we express this by the formula: $\Box(ready\_to\_send = True \oplus ready\_to\_send = False) \wedge \Box(connect\_from\_j = 0 \oplus connect\_from\_j = 1 \oplus connect\_from\_j = 2) \wedge (connect\_to\_j = 0 \oplus connect\_to\_j = 1 \oplus connect\_to\_j = 2)$ where $\oplus$ stands for the exclusive or.

In order to reason with initialized computation, we may add formulae describing the **initial state of the attributes**. For instance, we have:
$ready\_to\_send = False$

Then we define formulae to express the features of the actions. We determined four classes of formulae:

- **necessary preconditions** to perform an action; for example, the process can only receive the number from a process j if j is connected with it:
  $\Box(< receive\_j > T \rightarrow connect\_from\_j = 1)$
- **reactivity or fairness formulae** to guarantee the trigerring of enable actions. For example, we have:
  $\Box(ready\_to\_send = True \wedge connect\_to\_j = 1 \rightarrow \Diamond < send\_j > T)$
  to ensure the action will be done if the preconditions are satisfied.
- **weakest post-conditions** to describe the effects of the actions. For example, after the reception of the number from j, the attribute *ready_to_send* takes the value True and *connect_from_j* the value 2:
  $\Box([receive\_j](connect\_from\_j = 2 \wedge ready\_to\_send = True)$
- **frame axioms** which characterize what attribute values remain unchanged after an action. These axioms may be seen as specialization of the locus

[4] The two values *True* and *T* must be distinguished: *T* is a wff of our logic, *True* denotes a constant.

axiom: they express that an attribute value changes during a transition if and only if some actions are performed. For instance:
$\Box(connect\_from\_j = 1 \wedge O(connect\_from\_j = 2) \rightarrow < receive\_j > T)$

The behavior of a process during the synchronization can then be summarized (forgetting the frame axioms, the integrity constraints and the initialization) as follows:

Constants : $True, False, 0, 1, 2$
Attributes : $ready\_to\_send, connect\_from\_j, connect\_to\_j$
Actions : $send\_j, receive\_j, begin\_phase$
Axioms : $\Box([receive\_j](connect\_from\_j = 2 \wedge ready\_to\_send = True)$
$\Box(< receive\_j > T \rightarrow connect\_from\_j = 1)$
$\Box([send\_j]connect\_to\_j = 2)$
$\Box(< send\_j > T \rightarrow connect\_to\_j = 1 \wedge ready\_to\_send = True)$
$\Box(ready\_to\_send = True \wedge connect\_to\_j = 1 \rightarrow \Diamond < send\_j > T)$
$\Box(< begin\_phase > T \rightarrow \bigwedge_{j \in [0..5]}((connect\_to\_j = 0 \vee connect\_to\_j = 2)$
$\wedge(connect\_from\_j = 0 \vee connect\_from\_j = 2)))$

4 Combining components by means of categories

In this section, we present the category of object descriptions defined by Fiadeiro and Maibaum in [6], and we consider the descriptions given in section 2 as objects of this category. Our aim in this section is to explain that the categorical framework offers a well-suited structure for the combination of components. In the category of descriptions, interactions between objects are described by the morphisms of the category, and we will see that the characteristics of these morphisms have some consequences on the types of composition which can be achieved between the descriptions. A diagram is obtained by linking the descriptions of all the components with the morphisms representing the relationships between them. This diagram can finally be collapsed in an object of the category whose formulae specify the behavior of the whole system.

4.1 The category of descriptions.

First, we recall the definition of a category. A category is composed of two collections: the *objects* of the category and the *morphisms* of the category, and of four operations. Two of these operations associate with each morphism f of the category respectively its domain $dom(f)$ and its codomain $cod(f)$, both of which are objects of the category. One writes $f : C \rightarrow D$ to indicate that f is a morphism with domain C and codomain D. The other two operations are an operation which associates with each object C of a category a morphism I_C called identity morphism and an operation of composition which associates to any pair (f, g) of morphisms such that $dom(f) = cod(g)$ another morphism $f \circ g$. These operations are required to satisfy the following axioms:

$dom(I_A) = A = cod(I_A)$

$dom(f \circ g) = dom(g), cod(f \circ g) = cod(f)$
$I_A \circ f = f, f \circ I_A = f$
$(f \circ g) \circ h = f \circ (g \circ h)$

In this paper, we will consider the category of descriptions defined by Faideiro and Maibaum. The objects of this category are descriptions like the ones presented in section 2 (that is to say composed of a signature and of a set of formulae specifying the behavior of the processes described. We have changed the logic used to build the formulae but the structure of a description has been kept). The morphisms of this category are defined as follows:
Given object descriptions (Δ_1, Φ_1) and (Δ_2, Φ_2), a description morphism $\sigma : (\Delta_1, \Phi_1) \rightarrow (\Delta_2, \Phi_2)$ is a signature morphism $\Delta_1 \rightarrow \Delta_2$ such that:
$\models_{loci\Delta 2} \Phi_2 \rightarrow \sigma(F)$, for all axiom F of Φ_1
$\models_{loci\Delta 2} \Phi_2 \rightarrow \sigma(Locus_{(\Delta_1, \Phi_1)})$
where a signature morphism is defined by: given two object signatures $\Delta_1 = (CONST_1, ATTR_1, ACT_1)$ and $\Delta_2 = (CONST_2, ATTR_2, ACT_2)$, a signature morphism $\sigma : \Delta_1 \rightarrow \Delta_2$ consists of
for each c_1 in $CONST_1$ a constant symbol $\sigma(c_1)$ in $CONST_2$
for each a_1 in $ATTR_1$ an attribute symbol $\sigma(a_1)$ in $ATTR_2$
for each act_1 in ACT_1 an action symbol $\sigma(act_1)$ in ACT_2

From the definition of description morphisms, we know that the axioms of the source description are translated to theorems of the target description; but we can also infer the following property: given a morphism $\sigma : (\Delta_1, \Phi_1) \rightarrow (\Delta_2, \Phi_2)$,
$If \models_{loci\Delta_1} \Phi_1 \rightarrow F, then \models_{loci\Delta 2} \Phi_2 \rightarrow \sigma(F)$

All the properties of a specification can thus be exported along a description morphism. Moreover, the axiom of locality is translated to a theorem of the target description.

4.2 Combining two components.

In the introduction, we said we would like to keep composition laws a la CCS. Particularly, as we are dealing with concurrent and reactive systems, parallel composition and communication mechanisms (like the synchronization of CCS) would be very useful. In this section, we will see how these combinations can be achieved with the categories. In the categorical framework, morphisms are the tools to use to express relationships between components. The general principle to describe an interaction between two components is to create a common subcomponent in which they synchronize. Given two objects A and B, we create an object C and two morphisms f and g such that $f : C \rightarrow A$ and $g : C \rightarrow B$. It can be represented by the first scheme of the following figure.

Then, to get an object describing the combination of A and B with correspondence on the elements of C, we build the push-out of this diagram. The push-out of such a diagram consists of another object D of the category together with two morphisms $h : A \rightarrow D$ and $k : B \rightarrow D$ such that, on the one hand, the second scheme of the following figure commutes (i.e. $h \circ f = k \circ g$, i.e. only one copy of C is obtained in D); and on the other hand, D is minimal, i.e. for every commuting diagram (cf last scheme of the following figure) there is a unique morphism $j : D \rightarrow E$ such that $j \circ h = h''$ and $j \circ k = k''$.

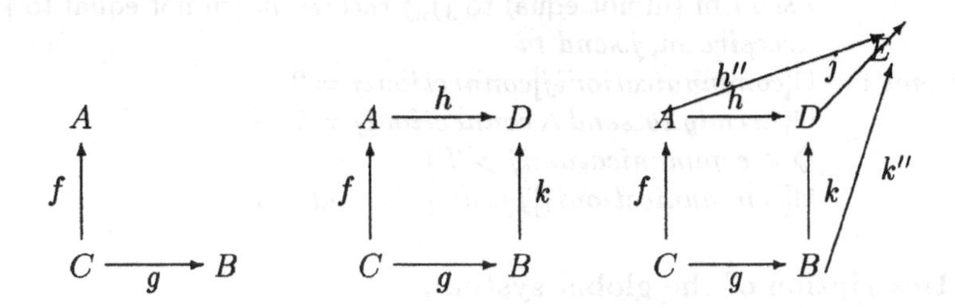

In the category of descriptions, the push-out corresponds to the parallel composition of two processes (A and B) with synchronization on the elements of the sub-component C. We are going to illustrate this method on the example of the composition of two processes of the Modulor machine.

Suppose we have the descriptions of two processes i et j and we want to describe the parallel composition of these 2 processes, taking into account that when Pi sends a message to Pj, this action corresponds, for Pj, to a reception of a message from Pi. It is sufficient to create a new object *channel* that contains one attribute and one action: *attr1* and *act1* and two morphisms between this object and Pi and Pj respectively.
Morphism ci: $attr1 \rightarrow connect\_to\_j, act1 \rightarrow send\_j$
Morphism cj: $attr1 \rightarrow connect\_from\_i, act1 \rightarrow receive\_i$
The role of the morphisms *ci* and *cj* is to indicate that *send_j* and *receive_i* must correspond to the same action in the object that will describe the parallel composition of the 2 processes (idem for the attributes).

When we compute the push-out of this diagram, we get the following diagram:

Proc i $\xrightarrow{\ i\ }$ Pij

ci $\uparrow$ $\qquad$ $\uparrow$ j

channel $\xrightarrow{\ cj\ }$ Proc j

The resulting description Pij is the following, where *connectionij* corresponds to the *attr1* in *channel* and *communicationij* to the *act1* in channel and where the attributes and actions that take no part in the interaction between Pi and Pj stay the same but are prefixed by i or j in order to avoid conflicts of names. We do not give the axioms that are not concerned by the interaction: they are the same that in the example of 3.2, just prefixing the attributes and axioms by i or j (for example, $\Box[i.receive\_m]i.connect\_from\_m = 2$).

$Constants: True, False, 0, 1, 2$
$Attributes: connectionij, i.ready\_to\_send, j.ready\_to\_send$
$i.connect\_from\_m, j.connect\_to\_m$
$i.connect\_to\_m$ (m not equal to j), $j.connect\_from\_m (m \neq i)$
$Actions:$ $communicationij, i.begin\_phase, j.begin\_phase$
$i.send\_m$ (m not equal to j), $j.receive\_m$ (m not equal to i)
$i.receive\_m, j.send\_m$
$Axioms:$ $\Box[communicationij]connectionij = 2$
$\Box(i.ready\_to\_send \wedge connectionij = 1 \rightarrow$
$\Diamond < communicationij > T)$
$\Box[communicationij]j.ready\_to\_send = True$

4.3 Description of the global system.

In order to describe a system, we have seen that each component must be first described individually, then all these components must be interconnected with morphisms and sub-components. A diagram is then obtained. For instance, in Modulor, the diagram is composed of the five processes interconnected by sub-objects and morphisms. In the previous paragraph, we built an object representing the parallel composition of two components (push-out). Now, we want to obtain the parallel composition of all the components of the diagram, i.e. we have to generalize the notion of push-out for an arbitrary diagram. This notion exists: it is the colimit of a diagram.

Push-outs and more generally colimits can be calculated in a category if this category is finitely cocomplete. Fiadeiro and Maibaum have proved that the category of descriptions is finitely cocomplete, but more generally, there are at least two ways to build a finitely cocomplete category: the Comma construction and the finding of an initial object, coproducts and coequalizers; these two ways can be found in [15] and they have been implemented in a tool [16].

Let us see how to build this description concretely. We call 0,1,2,3,4 the morphisms between the descriptions of the processes (host,1,2,3,4) and the global description *system*. All the attributes and actions of the processes will be translated through these morphisms to become attributes and actions of the system. But the correspondences imposed by the sub-objects (like *channel*) must be taken into account. So there is no actions *send_i* or *receive_j* left but only *communicationji*, and the same thing for the connections. The axioms of the resulting theory are:

$\Box[communicationij]connectionij = 2$
$\Box(i.ready\_to\_send \wedge connectionij = 1 \rightarrow \Diamond < communicationij > T)$
$\Box[communicationij]j.ready\_to\_send = True$
$\Box(< i.begin\_phase > T \rightarrow \bigwedge_{j \in [0,5]}((connectionji = 0 \vee connectionji = 2) \wedge (connectionij = 0 \vee connectionji = 2)))$

Comment: the genericity of our formalism must be noticed here. With the previous method, we build a description of the system which is itself an object of the category of descriptions and which may be reused as a component of an other diagram. We will see an example of this genericity in the next section.

5 Verification

In this section, we present how validation of a system specification can be achieved in the proposed hybrid framework. We first deal with the expression of the system properties and then describe our verification methodology.

5.1 Expressing properties.

By inheriting both from the linear temporal logic and the dynamic logic, our logic allows dual ways to express the properties of the system. If the stress is put on action, we may express properties in a mu-calculus fashion thanks to the predefined temporal operators instead of fix-point formulae and the actions operators (see e.g. the user manual of the Concurrency Workbench [3] for an outlook in the branching time case). And we can also express properties by means of state formulae combined by temporal operators (and this is often easier).

We give the following examples of properties for the synchronization algorithm.

- P1: each process receives at least one synchronization message before beginning the phase computation;
- P2: each process does not receive any more synchronization messages after entering the phase computation.

  These properties can be expressed by the formulae:
  $\Box(< begin\_phase > T \rightarrow ready\_to\_send = True)$
  $\Box([begin\_phase] \bigwedge_{j \in [0,5]}(\Box\neg < receive\_j > T))$

5.2 Verification strategy

Our hybrid framework suggests a strategy to break down the complexity of the proofs. We based the strategy on exploiting the structure of the composed system.

- For a given global property, we scan the constraint, attribute and action names occuring in the formula. We intend to select the smallest component description which may enable the proof. The order between theories is induced by the description morphisms used to interconnect components: we say (Δ_2, Φ_2) is greater than (Δ_1, Φ_1) if the descriptions are connected in the whole system by a morphism f: $\Delta_1 \rightarrow \Delta_2$. If the heuristic succeeds, we can put back the theorem in the wished theory by means of the morphisms.
- When this heuristic fails, or when the least description results from colimit computation, we try to decompose the property in elementary lemmas provable in more basic descriptions (and these lemmas are translated along the morphisms to the global description).

– In the worst case, we have to prove the property in the object which describes the global system.

Comments on the automation:

– The development of a tool assisting the computation of push-outs and colimits of diagrams is experimented in CERT ([16]).
– We have proved that our logic is decidable ([17]); the sizes of the elementary component descriptions enable us to use automatic decision procedure which are always inefficient when the size of the specification is too big.
– The decomposition of properties in sub-properties requires a priori a good knowledge of the application. However, the encapsulation of the components and the frame axioms lead to a common strategy to prove liveness or "until" properties: we are looking for the actions which may modify the values of particular attributes. This strategy can be formalized in proof plans as in Bundy's approach in order to automatize the complete proof process [1]. Moreover, the proposed normalization of component descriptions should make the task easier. We show in the following section how these ideas may be exploited to lead proofs.

6 Results about Modulor

We saw in the previous section how to specify the synchronization at the beginning of a phase. We did not write down the verification of the properties, but we will show an example of proof in this section.
We are now concerned with the detection mechanism of Modulor (see the description of the fault-tolerance software tools in section 2). We want to prove that this mechanism is correct. We decompose this verification in two parts:

– the fact that, locally (on a processor), if the process is blocked, this will be detected and there exists a time where the process will be released (local detection)
– the fact that, if there is a faulty processor somewhere in the net, the host processor will be blocked (propagation due to the synchronization at the end of the phase).

With these two parts, we prove the correction of the detection. Indeed: if a fault occurs somewhere in the net, the host processor will be blocked (propagation), this will be detected and the host will be released (local detection), so it will be able to start a diagnostic phase. The other processors will be either OK and waiting for a new phase to begin, or faulty (and this will be found by the diagnostic phase), or blocked and in this case it will be detected and the processor will be released (local detection again).

6.1 Local detection

We will just present the specification of the local detection, because it is the most interesting part: we take advantage of the modularity and genericity of the formalism for this specification. Indeed, in order to model this detection mechanism (see section 2) on a processor, we have to consider three processes: the phase process, the server and the timer. So we can consider each object *proci* as build from three smaller objects as shown by the following scheme:

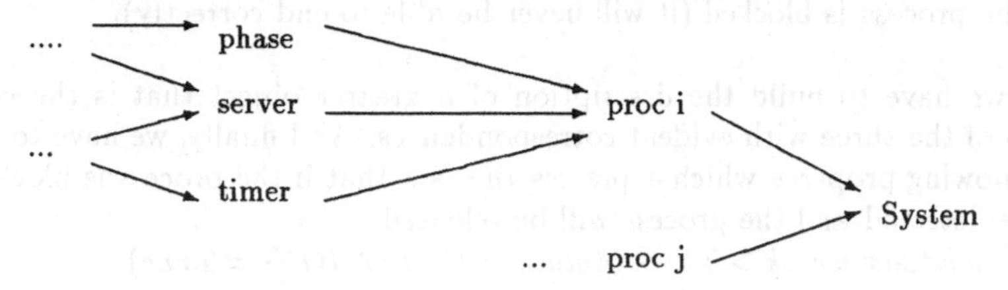

So we have two levels: from the three processes (phase, server, timer), we build the description of a processor in Modulor. This description is itself an object that can be combined with other objects (the other descriptions of processors) to build a description of the system. So here, we have a good example of the genericity of our formalism.
For the description of these three processes, we try to be as close as possible to the real implementation. When the phase process ends correctly, it notices this correct end to the server that stops the timer. When a fault occurs, a time-out happens in the timer, the timer warns the server that changes the state of the phase and finally the timer releases the phase process.

Description of the phase process.
The phase process represents in fact the behavior of the process during a phase; it contains the synchronization at the beginning of the phase (described in previous section), the synchronization at the end of the phase (see after), and the behavior during the phase: the computation itself that will not be described and the additional actions that allows to detect a fault. It is this last part we are interested in.
We suppose we have an attribute *end_ok* which takes the value *True* when the phase has ended correctly. The part we are interested in is described by the following axioms:
$\Box < send\_server\_ok > T \rightarrow end\_ok = True$
$\Box[release]BEG = True$
$\Box(faulty = True \leftrightarrow \Box \bigwedge_{a \in ACT} \neg < a > T)$
where BEG is an attribute that takes the value $True$ when the process is ready to begin a new phase.

Description of the server.
$\Box[time - out]state = False$
$\Box[receive\_ok] < stop - timer > T$

Description of the timer
$\Box(\Box\neg < send\_server\_ok > T) \rightarrow \Diamond < time - out > T$
$\Box < time - out > T \rightarrow (\Box\neg < send\_server\_ok > T)$

$\square[time - out] < release > T$
$\square[stop - timer]end\_timer = True$

Comment: the property $\square\neg < send\_server\_ok > T$ corresponds to the fact that the process is blocked (it will never be able to end correctly).

Then we have to build the description of a greater object that is the combination of the three with evident correspondences. And finally, we have to verify the following property which expresses the fact that if the process is blocked, it will be detected and the process will be released:
$(\square\neg < send\_server\_ok > T) \rightarrow \Diamond(state = False \wedge BEG = True)$

6.2 Propagation-Synchronization at the end.

In this paragraph, we want to show that, if there is a faulty processor somewhere in the net, the host processor will be blocked at least during the synchronization at the end of the phase. In order to specify this synchronization at the end, we adopt the same methodology as for the synchronization at the beginning of the phase: we describe the behavior of a process and then we build the description of the system (cf example in 3.2). We do not give details because it is the same kind of description (it must just be noticed that the connections are not the same because here we have a tree (cf 2.2, synchronization mechanisms)). The description of a process is the following:

$Constants : True, False, 0, 1, 2$
$Attributes : aconnect\_to\_j, aconnect\_from\_j, faulty$
$Actions : send\_ok\_j, receive\_ok\_j$
$Axioms : \square([receive\_ok\_j]aconnect\_from\_j = 2)$
$\square(< receive\_ok\_j > T \rightarrow aconnect\_from\_j = 1)$
$\square([send\_ok\_j]aconnect\_to\_j = 2)$
$\square(< send\_ok\_j > T \rightarrow \bigwedge_{m\in[0,5]}(aconnect\_from\_m = 2 \vee aconnect\_from\_m = 0) \wedge aconnect\_to\_j = 1$
$\square(faulty = True \leftrightarrow (\square \bigwedge_{a\in ACT} \neg < a > T))$

The last axiom shows how we model the fault: when a processor becomes faulty, it is not able to execute actions any more.

For the host, the description is the same, but an attribute *end_ok* must be added as well as the following axiom:
$\square(end\_ok \leftrightarrow \bigwedge_{j\in[0,5]}(aconnect\_from\_j = 0 \vee aconnect\_from\_j = 2))$

Description of the system. We do not give the description of the system, but it can easily be obtained in the same way as in the previous section.

Expressing properties. The property we want to verify is:
P4: if one of the processor is faulty, the host process will be blocked.

This property can be expressed by the formula:
$\square(1.faulty = True \vee 2.faulty = True \vee 3.faulty = True \vee 4.faulty = True) \rightarrow \square 0.end\_ok = False$

Verification. We are going to verify the property in the case where this is the processor 4 which is faulty. We use intensively the modularity of our formalism. Indeed, the proof is decomposed in four lemmas and each lemma can be verified on a single process. These four lemmas are:

- if proc4 is faulty then it does not send any message *ok* to proc2. This lemma must be verified on proc4 and can be expressed in the following way:
  $faulty = True \rightarrow \Box\neg < send\_ok\_2 > T$
- if proc2 does not receive any message *ok* from proc4, then it does not send any message *ok* to proc1. This lemma must be verified on proc2 and can be expressed in the following way:
  $\Box\neg < receive\_ok\_4 > T \rightarrow \Box\neg < send\_ok\_1 > T$
- if proc1 does not receive any message *ok* from proc2, then it does not send any message *ok* to the host. This lemma must be verified on proc1 and can be expressed in the following way:
  $\Box\neg < receive\_ok\_2 > T \rightarrow \Box\neg < send\_ok\_0 > T$
- if the host does not receive any message *ok* from proc1, then *end_ok* will always stay false. This lemma must be verified on the host and can be expressed in the following way:
  $\Box\neg < receive\_ok\_1 > T \rightarrow \Box end\_ok = False$

The first step is given by the axiom:
$\Box(faulty = True \leftrightarrow (\Box \bigwedge_{a \in ACT} \neg < a > T))$

The second and third steps have the same demonstration, so we just give it for the second one. We work inside the description of proc2. We have:
$(\Box(< send\_ok\_j > T \rightarrow \bigwedge_{m \in [0,5]}(aconnect\_from\_m = 2 \vee aconnect\_from\_m = 0) \wedge aconnect\_to\_j = 1)$
For proc2, the only j for which $aconnect\_from\_j$ is equal to 1 is proc1 ; and the only m for which $aconnect\_from\_m$ is different from 0 is 4. So the precondition for proc2 sending a message *ok* to proc1 is that $aconnect\_from\_4 = 2$. The only means for $aconnect\_from\_4$ to take the value 2 is to receive a message *ok* from proc4:
$\Box([receive\_ok\_4]aconnect\_from\_4 = 2)$ So we have proved the second step.

There is the last step left. It can be proved inside the description of the host. A similar reasoning as for the second step can be used to state that the only mean for $aconnect\_from\_1$ to take the value 2 is to receive a message *ok* from proc1. So if we suppose that the host does not receive any message *ok* from proc1, we know that $aconnect\_from\_1$ will always keep the value 1 and so, because of:
$\Box(end\_ok \leftrightarrow \bigwedge_{j \in [0,5]}(aconnect\_from\_j = 0 \vee aconnect\_from\_j = 2))$
end_ok will always stay false.
To get the complete proof in the global description of the system, we then translate the 4 properties along the morphisms (4,2,1,0 respectively) into the object *system* ; and due to the correspondence of
$4.send\_ok\_2$ and $2.receive\_ok\_4$
$2.send\_ok\_1$ and $1.receive\_ok\_2$

$1.send\_ok\_0$ and $0.receive\_ok\_1$,
we have

- $4.faulty = True \rightarrow \Box\neg < communication\_ok\_42 > T$
- $\Box\neg < communication\_ok\_42 > T \rightarrow \Box\neg < communication\_ok\_21 > T$
- $\Box\neg < communication\_ok\_21 > T \rightarrow \Box\neg < communication\_ok\_10 > T$
- $\Box\neg < communication\_ok\_10 > T \rightarrow \Box end\_ok = False$

So finally, we get: $4.faulty = True \rightarrow \Box end\_ok = False$
and the property of propagation is proved.

7 Conclusion

We proposed in this paper an hybrid formalism which improves the mixing of categories and logic proposed by Fiadeiro and Maibaum. We keep their categorical structure which has several advantages. At the specification level, the modularity induced by the categories allows to describe a big system more easily: each component is described independently (encapsulation); then the interactions between the components are specified; and finally, with composition laws a la CCS, we build a description of the system which is itself an object of the same category and can be reused. At the verification level, lemmas are verified locally on the components of the system (encapsulation) ; then these lemmas are translated along the morphisms to the global description. Thus, modular proofs can be achieved.

We add to this framework a logic well-suited for the design and verification of concurrent and reactive systems. Our logic inherits both from dynamic logic and temporal logic. So at the specification level, we have got on the one hand the notion of states which is very useful for the expression of properties and for the modeling of some static characteristics; and on the other hand, actions allow us to specify easily dynamic behaviors and to handle communications. Moreover, we gave a methodology to guide writing of specification in this logic. At the verification level, our logic is proved sound, complete and decidable and we hope this result makes easier the automation of proofs.

We applied this formalism to Modulor, a real-sized and fault-tolerant parallel machine. We thus realized our formalism was adapted to the specification and verification of such systems. As far as we know, there are few reports about the use of formal methods to validate fault tolerance mechanisms based on a passive redundancy approach. Most of the experiments deal with masking transient fault by active redundancy. In this context, we have only found logical proofs of correctness of vote or synchronization algorithms ([14]). The authors explain their logical approach is really expensive and can be applied fruitfully only to the most critical part of the system, to get generic results. Our modular way of specifying and validating can complement these approaches and extend their scope. Moreover, the logic proposed is well-suited for modeling passive redundancy: action and communication concepts are useful for modeling the behavior of a distributed system whereas the state notion caught in the logic makes easier the fault handling.

Acknowledgements We would like to thank P. Michel for his helpful comments.

References

1. A. Bundy, F. van Harmelen, J. Hesketh, and A. Smaill. Experiments with proof plans for induction. *Journal of Automated Reasoning*, 7:303–324, 1991.
2. K.M. Chandy and J. Misra. *Parallel Program Design. A Foundation.* Addison-Wesley, 1988.
3. R. Cleaveland, J. Parrow, and B. Steffen. The concurrency workbench. In *proceedings of the workshop on automatic verification methods for finite-state systems, LNCS 407*, pages 24 - 37, 1989.
4. V. David, Ch. Fraboul, J.Y. Rousselot, and P. Siron. Partitioning and mapping communication graphs on a modular reconfigurable parallel architecture. In *CONPAR'92*, Sept 1992.
5. E. Allen Emerson. Temporal and modal logic. In *Handbook of theoretical computer science*, pages 996–1071. Elsevier Science, 1990.
6. J. Fiadeiro and T. Maibaum. Temporal theories as modularisation units for concurrent system specification. *Formal Aspects of Computing*, 1992.
7. D. Harel. *Handbook of philosophical logic*, volume 2, chapter 10, Dynamic Logic, pages 497–604. 1984.
8. C.A.R. Hoare. *Communicating Sequential Processes.* Prentice Hall, 1985.
9. D. Kozen. Results on the propositional mu-calculus. *Theoritical Computer Science*, 27:333–354, 1983.
10. L. Lamport. The temporal logic of actions. Technical Report 79, SRC, 1992.
11. Zohar Manna and Amir Pnueli. *The temporal logic of reactive and concurrent systems.* Springer-Verlag, 1992.
12. Robin Milner. *Handbook of theoretical computer science*, chapter 19, Operational and algebraic semantics of concurrent processes, pages 1203–1242. Elsevier Science, 1990.
13. F. Pagani, C. Seguin, P. Siron, and V. Wiels. Verification experiments on a large fault-tolerant distributed system. In *Workshop AMAST "Model and Proof"*, Bordeaux, France, juin 1995.
14. John Rushby. Formal specification and verification of a fault-masking and transient-recovery model for digital flight-control systems. In J. Vytopil, editor, *Formal Techniques in Real-Time and Fault-Tolerant Systems*, number 571 in LNCS, Nijmegen, The Netherlands, January 1992. Springer Verlag.
15. D.E. Rydeheard and R.M. Burstall. *Computational Category Theory.* Prentice Hall, 1988.
16. J. Sauloy. Interconnexion de modules. Technical report, CERT-ONERA, DERI, 1992.
17. V. Wiels. Specification et verification de programmes paralleles tolerants aux fautes. Master's thesis, E.N.S.E.E.I.H.T, 1994.

Local Nondeterminism in Asynchronously Communicating Processes

F.S. de Boer and M. van Hulst

Utrecht University, Dept. of Comp. Sc.,
P.O. Box 80089, 3508 TB Utrecht, The Netherlands

Abstract. In this paper we present a simple compositional Hoare logic for reasoning about the correctness of a certain class of distributed systems. We consider distributed systems composed of processes which interact asynchronously via unbounded FIFO buffers. The simplicity of the proof system is due to the restriction to local nondeterminism in the description of the sequential processes of a system. To illustrate the usefulness of the proof system we use PVS (Prototype Verification System, see [ORS92]) to prove in a compositional manner the correctness of a heartbeat algorithm for computing the topology of a network.

1 Introduction

In [dBvH94] we have shown that a certain class of distributed systems composed of processes which communicate asynchronously via (unbounded) FIFO buffers, can be proved correct using a simple compositional proof system based on Hoare-logic. The class of systems introduced in [dBvH94] is characterized by the restriction to deterministic control structures in the description of the local sequential processes. An additional feature is the introduction of input statements as tests in the choice and iterative constructs. Such input statements involve a test on the contents of the particular buffer under consideration. Even in the context of deterministic sequential control structures this feature gives rise to *global* nondeterminism, because the choices involving tests on the contents of a buffer depend on the environment.

To reason about the above-mentioned class of distributed systems a buffer is represented in the logic by an input variable which records the sequence of values read from the buffer and by an output variable which records the sequence of values sent to the buffer. The communication pattern of a system then can be described in terms of these input/output variables by means of a global invariant. This should be contrasted with logics which formalize reasoning about distributed systems in terms of histories ([OG76, AFdR80, ZdRvEB85, Pan88, HdR86]). The difference between input/output variables and histories is that in the former information of the relative ordering of communication events on different buffers is lost. In [Fra92] these input/output variables are used in a non-compositional proof system based on a *cooperation test* along the lines of [AFdR80] for FIFO buffered communication in general. A compositional proof system based on input/output variables is given in [dBvH94] for the class of systems composed of deterministic processes as described above. However, the proof system in [dBvH94] allows only a decomposition of the pre/postcondition part of the specification of a distributed system. The global invariant, which is needed for completeness and which describes the ongoing communication behaviour of the system in terms of the input/output variables, does not allow a decomposition into local invariants corresponding to the components of the system. This is due to the global non-determinism inherent in the distributed systems considered in [dBvH94].

In this paper, we investigate *local* nondeterminism, that is, we restrict to distributed systems composed of processes which may test only their own private program variables. The resulting computational model is still applicable to a wide range of applications: For example, it can be applied to the description of socalled heartbeat algorithms like, for instance, the distributed leader election problem and the network topology determination problem. The latter problem we will discuss in some detail in this paper.

We show that when restricting to local non-determinism, a complete specification of a distributed system can be derived from *local* specifications of its components, that is, from specifications which only refer to the program variables and the input/output variables of the component specified. This additional compositional feature is very important because it allows for the construction of a *library* of specified components which can be reused in any parallel context. The proof system in [dBvH94] does not allow this because part of a local specification is the global invariant which specifies the overall communication behaviour of the entire system. Moreover, the relevance of a compositional reasoning pattern [dB94, dBHdR, dBvH95, HdR86] with respect to the complexity of (mechanically supported) correctness proofs of concurrent systems lies in the fact that the verification of the local components of a system can in most practical cases be mechanized fully (or at least to a very large extent). What remains is a proof that the conjunction of the specifications of the components implies the desired specification of the entire system. This latter proof in general involves purely mathematical reasoning about the underlying datastructures and does not involve any reasoning about the flow of control. This abstraction from the flow of control allows for a greater control of the complexity of correctness proofs.

We will illustrate the above observation by proving the correctness of a heartbeat algorithm for computing the network topology using the Prototype Verification System (PVS). As the formalization of the local reasoning is straightforward, our verification effort concentrates on the second, global part of the correctness problem, viz. the proof that the conjunction of the specifications of the components implies the desired specification of the entire system.

The specification language of PVS is a strongly typed, higher-order logic. Specifications can be structured into a hierarchy of parameterized theories. There are a number of built-in theories (e.g. reals, lists, sets, ordering relations, etc.) and a mechanism for automatically generating theories for abstract datatypes. Due to its high expressivity, the specification language can be invoked in many domains of interest whilst maintaining readable (i.e. not overly constructive) specifications. At the core of PVS is an interactive proof checker with, for instance, induction rules, automatic rewriting, and decision procedures for arithmetic. Moreover, PVS proof steps can be combined into proof strategies.

The reason to choose PVS is a pragmatic one: it allows a quick start, and, more importantly, its powerful engine allows one to disregard many of the trivial but tedious details in a proof, a virtue that is not shared by most of the currently available proof checkers/theorem provers. Much effort has already been invested in developing a useful tool for (automated) verification by means of PVS [CS95, Raj94].

The rest of this paper is organized as follows: In section 2, the programming language is defined. Section 3 explains the algorithm for computing the topology of a network. Then, in section 4, the proof system is introduced and its formal justification is briefly touched upon. The theorem prover PVS and the specification of the correctness of the algorithm in PVS are discussed in section 5. Finally, section 6 contains some concluding remarks and observations.

2 The programming language

In this section, we define the syntax of the programming language. The language describes the behaviour of asynchronously communicating sequential processes. Processes interact only via communication channels which are implemented by (unbounded) FIFO-buffers. A process can send a value along a channel or it can input a value from a channel. The value sent will be appended to the buffer, whereas reading a value from a buffer consists of retrieving its first element. Thus the values will be read in the order in which they have been sent. A process will be suspended when it tries to read a value from an empty buffer. Since buffers are assumed to be unbounded, sending values can always take place.

We assume given a set of program variables *Var*, with typical elements $x, y, \ldots$. Channels are denoted by $c, d, \ldots$. We abstract from any typing information.

Definition 1. The syntax of a statement S which describes the behaviour of a sequential process, is defined by

$$
\begin{aligned}
S ::= &\ \mathsf{skip} \\
|\ &\ x := e \\
|\ &\ c??x \mid c!!e \\
|\ &\ S_1; S_2 \\
|\ &\ []_i[b_i \rightarrow S_i] \\
|\ &\ \star[]_i[b_i \rightarrow S_i]
\end{aligned}
$$

In the above definition skip denotes the 'empty' statement. Assigning the value of e to the variable x is described by the statement $x := e$. Sending a value of an expression e along channel c is described by $c!!e$, whereas storing a value read from a channel c in a variable x is described by $c??x$. The execution of $c??x$ is suspended in case the corresponding buffer is empty. Furthermore we have the usual sequential control structures of sequential composition, guarded command and iterated guarded command (b denotes a boolean expression). In the example below, we only have need for simple guarded statements, which we will denote by if b then S_1 else S_2 fi and while b do S od.

In [dBvH94] we considered deterministic choice and iteration constructs which use input statements as tests. For example, the execution of a (conditional input) statement if $c??x$ then S_1 else S_2 fi consists of reading a value from channel c, in case its corresponding buffer is non-empty, storing it in x and proceeding subsequently with S_1. In case the buffer is empty control moves on to S_2. These constructs will in general enhance the capability of a deterministic process to respond to an indeterminate environment and in this respect they give rise to global nondeterminism in the sense that the choices of a process depend on the environment. Note that this is not the case in our present language, where processes can only inspect their local variables. Nevertheless many interesting algorithms described in the literature can be expressed in a programming language based on local nondeterminism. As an example we consider in the next section the algorithm for computing a network topology.

Definition 2. A parallel program P is of the form $[S_1 \parallel \ldots \parallel S_n]$, where we assume the following restrictions: the statements S_i do not share program variables, channels are unidirectional and connect exactly one sender and one receiver.

3 An example: Computing the network topology

We consider a symmetric and distributive algorithm for computing a network topology, which is described in [And91]. We are given a network of processes which are connected by bi-directional communication links, and each link is represented by two (unidirectional) channels, i.e. between any two processes S_i and S_j there is a channel from S_i to S_j iff there is a channel from S_j to S_i. Each process can communicate only with its neighbors and knows only about the links to its neighbors. We assume that the network is connected. A symmetric distributed solution to the network topology problem can be obtained as follows: Each process first sends to its neighbors the information about its own links and then each of its neighbors is asked for its links. After having obtained this information each process will know its links and those of its neighbors. This it will know about the topology within two links of itself. Assuming that we know the diameter D of the network, that is, the largest distance between two nodes, iterating the above D times will solve the problem.

To formalize the above algorithm we represent the network topology by a matrix $top[1:n,1:n]$ of BOOL, where n is the number of processes. $top[i,j]$ indicates whether there exists a link from process i to process j. Since we have bi-directional links we have for all processes i and j $top[i,j] = top[j,i]$. For each pair of linked processes i and j we have channels c_{ij} and c_{ji}. With respect to channel c_{ij} process i is the sender and j the receiver. The contents of each channel c is described by two variables $c??$ and $c!!$. The first variable $c??$ is local to the receiver and records all values that have been read; the second variable $c!!$ is local to the sender and records the sequence of values that were sent. Thus the input/output variables of process i are $c_{ji}??$ and $c_{ij}!!$, for all processes j such that i and j are linked. Processes communicate by sending and receiving their local views of the global topology. Each process has a local variable $lview_i$, which represents its (local) knowledge of the global topology top. Initially, $lview_i$ is intialized to the neighbors of process i, that is $lview_i[k,l] = true$ if and only if $k = i$ and $top[i,l] = true$. A local view received by a process i from one of its neighbors is stored in a local variable $nview_i$. These local views are combined by an *or*-operation on matrices, denoted by $\vee$, which is an obvious extension of the corresponding boolean operation on the truth values. The diameter of the network is given by D. The behaviour of process i is then described by the following statement:

```
S_i ≡ r_i := 0;
      while r_i < D
      do    j := 1;
            while j ≤ n
            do if top[i,j]
                 then c_ij!!lview_i
                 fi;
                 j := j + 1
            od;
            j := 1;
            while j ≤ n
            do if top[i,j]
                 then c_ji??nview_i;
                          lview_i := lview_i ∨ nview_i
                 fi;
```

```
            j := j + 1
          od;
          r := r_i + 1
     od
```

For a network of n processes the program for computing the network topology, i.e. the matrix *top*, is defined by $[S_1 \parallel ... \parallel S_n]$.

4 The proof system

In this section we provide a proof system for proving partial correctness and deadlock freedom of programs. To this end, we introduce correctness formulae $\{p\}P\{q\}$ which we interpret as follows:

> Any computation starting in a state which satisfies p does not deadlock, and moreover, if its execution terminates, then q holds in the final state.

Note that this interpretation is stronger than the usual partial correctness interpretation in which absence of deadlock is not required. The precondition p and postcondition q are formulae in some first-order logic. We omit the formal definition of this logic which is rather standard; here we only mention that p and q will contain besides the program variables of P the input/output variables $c??$ and $c!!$, where c is a channel occurring in P. These variables $c??$ and $c!!$ are intended to denote the sequences of values received along channel c and those sent along channel c, respectively. Logically they are simply interpreted as (finite) sequences of values (thus we assume in the logic operations like append, tail, the length of a sequence etc.).

To derive the correctness of a program P compositionally, we introduce local correctness formulae of the form $I : \{p\}S\{q\}$, where p and q are (first-order logic) assertions, allowed to refer to the variables of S only. The set of variables of a statement S consists of its program variables and those input/output variables $c??$ ($c!!$) for which c is an input channel of S (c is an output channel of S). The assertions p and q are called the precondition and postcondition, respectively, while the assertion I is called the invariant. The invariant I is a conjunction of implications of the form $Rc \rightarrow p$, where Rc denotes a predicate which indicates that the next execution step involves a read on channel c. An assertion $Rc \rightarrow p$ thus specifies that if control is about to execute a read on the channel c then p holds. The information in I will be used in the analysis of deadlock. Intuitively the meaning of a correctness formula $I : \{p\}S\{q\}$ can be rendered as follows:

> The invariant I holds in every state of a computation of S starting in a state which satisfies p and upon termination q is guaranteed to hold.

Note that the invariance of $I \equiv Rc_1 \rightarrow p_1 \wedge ... \wedge Rc_k \rightarrow p_k$ amounts to the fact that whenever control is at an input $c_i?x$, $1 \leq i \leq k$, p_i is guaranteed to hold. In other words, I expresses certain invariant properties which hold whenever an input statement (specified by I) is about to be executed. It is important to note that thus the predicates Rc_i are a kind of 'abstract' location predicates, in the sense that they refer not just to a particular location of a statement but to a *set* of locations.

Now we present the axioms and rules of our proof system.

The axiom for the assignment statement is as usual, apart from the addition of an arbitrary invariant; this is allowed because there is no communication, so none of the Rc will hold during execution of the statement.

Axiom 1 *(assignment)* $I : \{p[e/x]\}x := e\{p\}$

The output statement $c!!e$ is modeled as an assignment to the corresponding output variable $c!!$ which consists of appending the value sent to the sequence $c!!$. The operation of 'append' is denoted by '$\cdot$'. With respect to the invariant, a similar remark holds as for the assignment axiom.

Axiom 2 *(output)* $I : \{p[c!! \cdot e/c!!]\}c!!e\{p\}$

An input statement $c??x$ is modeled as a (multiple) assignment to the variable x and the input variable $c??$. The associated invariant states that when reading on c, the substituted postcondition should hold.

Axiom 3 *(input)* $Rc \rightarrow \forall v.\ p[v/x, c?? \cdot v/c??] : \{\forall v.\ p[v/x, c?? \cdot v/c??]\}c??x\{p\}$

We now give the rule for sequential composition; the rules for the choice and while statement can be obtained by extending in a similar way the usual rules for these constructs.

Rule 1 *(sequential composition)*

$$\frac{I : \{p\}S_1\{q\},\ I : \{q\}S_2\{r\}}{I : \{p\}S_1; S_2\{r\}}$$

So in order to prove that I is an invariant of $S_1; S_2$ one has, naturally, to prove that I is both an invariant of S_1 and S_2.

We have the following local consequence rule:

Rule 2 *(local consequence)*

$$\frac{I' \to I,\ p \to p',\ I' : \{p'\}S\{q'\},\ q' \to q}{I : \{p\}S\{q\}}$$

We introduce the expression c as an abbreviation of the expression $c!! - c??$. By $c!! - c??$ we denote the suffix of the sequence $c!!$ (i.e. the sequence of values sent) which is determined by its prefix $c??$ (i.e. the sequence of values read). Thus c represents the contents of the buffer, that is, the values sent but not yet read. The empty sequence we denote by ϵ.

In preparation of the parallel composition rule, we first observe that a possible deadlock configuration of a program P is characterized by: Every process is either done or about to execute a read on a channel for which the corresponding buffer is empty; moreover at least one process is not yet done. Suppose $P = [S_1 \parallel \ldots \parallel S_n]$ and each S_i has input channels $c_1^i, \ldots, c_{m_i}^i$. Hence we have the predicates $Rc_1^i, \ldots, Rc_{m_i}^i$ for each $i \in \{1, \ldots, n\}$. Furthermore assume a postcondition q_i for each of the S_i. Now we introduce a set of assertions $C(P)$, the disjunction of which characterizes all possible deadlock configurations of P:

$$C(P) = \{\textstyle\bigwedge_i p_i \mid p_i \equiv Rc_k^i \wedge c_k^i = \epsilon, \text{ for some } k \leq m_i, \text{ or } p_i \equiv q_i, \\ \text{and there exists } j : p_j \not\equiv q_j\}.$$

Note that each assertion $p \in C(P)$ characterizes a *set* of possible deadlock configurations.

Definition 3. Given some local postconditions $q_1, \ldots, q_n$, we define for local invariants $I_1, \ldots, I_n$ the assertion $DF(I_1, \ldots, I_n)$ as

$$\bigwedge_{p \in C(P)} \left(\bigwedge_{i=1}^{n} I_i \wedge p \to \textbf{false} \right)$$

The above assertion $DF(I_1, \ldots, I_n)$ expresses that the conjunction of the local invariants is inconsistent with any possible deadlock configuration, i.e. the assertion $\bigwedge_{i=1}^{n} I_i$ guarantees deadlock freedom.

Local correctness formulas then can be combined into correctness formulas of an entire program as follows:

Rule 3 *(parallel composition)*

$$\frac{I_i : \{p_i\}S_i\{q_i\}(i = 1, \ldots, n),\ DF(I_1, \ldots, I_n)}{\{\bigwedge_i p_i\}[S_1 \parallel \ldots \parallel S_n]\{\bigwedge_i q_i\}}$$

In the premise of the above rule the formula $DF(I_1, ..., I_n)$ is implicitly assumed to be defined with respect to the local postconditions $q_1, \ldots, q_n$. The compositional method of proving deadlock freedom incorporated in the above rule can be best understood by comparing it with the standard way of proving deadlock freedom using the *proof outlines*. For example in [AFdR80], given proof outlines of the components of a CSP program $P \equiv [S_1 \parallel \ldots \parallel S_n]$, absence of deadlock can be proved by first determining statically all possible deadlock configurations. Such a configuration consists of a n-tuple of local locations (one location for each component). Each possible deadlock configuration then is characterized by the conjunction of the assertions associated with its locations by the given proof outlines. Absence of deadlock then can be established by showing that the assertion associated with each possible deadlock configuration is equivalent to false. The main difference with our deadlock analysis lies in the use of the predicates *Rc* which do not refer to a specific location but represent a set of locations, namely all those locations where the corresponding process is about to execute a read on channel c. In our case then deadlock freedom can be established by showing that the conjunction of the local invariants, which provide information about the local states of processes when these are about to execute a read, is inconsistent with any possible deadlock configuration. This abstraction from specific locations, which is due to the restriction to local nondeterminism, allows for the simple compositional proof rule for parallel composition described above.

Apart from the above rule for parallel composition we also have the usual consequence rule for programs. With respect to reasoning about global states we moreover have for each channel c the following axiom of asynchronous communication:

$$c?? \leq c!!$$

where $\leq$ denotes the prefix ordering on sequences.

The formal justification of the proof system, i.e. soundness and (relative) completeness can be proved in a rather straightforward manner using a compositional semantics which associates with each statement S a meaning

$$\mathcal{M}(S) \in \Sigma \rightarrow \mathcal{P}(\Sigma \times Chan \rightarrow \mathcal{P}(\Sigma))$$

(Σ denotes the set of states, a state being a function which assigns values to the program variables and the input/output variables, and *Chan* denotes the set of channel names). Here $\langle \sigma', f \rangle \in \mathcal{M}(S)(\sigma)$, with $f \in Chan \rightarrow \mathcal{P}(\Sigma)$, indicates that σ' is the result of a terminating computation of S starting from σ, and every intermediate state σ'' just before an input on a channel c belongs to $f(c)$. In other words, $f(c)$ collects all the intermediate states which occur just before an input on channel c is executed. Formally we then define for $I \equiv \bigwedge_i Rc_i \rightarrow p_i$,

> $\models I : \{p\}S\{q\}$ iff for every pair of states σ and σ' and function $f \in Chan \rightarrow \mathcal{P}(\Sigma)$, such that $\langle \sigma', f \rangle \in \mathcal{M}(S)(\sigma)$ and p holds in σ, it is the case that q holds in σ' and p_i holds in every state $\sigma'' \in f(c_i)$.

The semantics of a program can be defined in terms of the meaning $\mathcal{M}(S)$ of its components by a straightforward 'translation' of the parallel composition rule of the proof system. Moreover it is rather straightforward to prove the correctness of the compositional semantics with respect to an operational semantics. More details can be found in the technical report [dBvH96].

5 Automated verification in PVS

In this section, we will show how the network topology determination algorithm can be specified and verified using PVS.

The specification to be proved is

$$\{\bigwedge_i (lview_i[i,l] = top[i,l] \wedge (j \neq i \rightarrow lview_i[j,l] = \ false))\}$$
$$[S_1 \parallel \ldots \parallel S_n]$$
$$\{\bigwedge_i lview_i = top\}$$

In words, if initially for every i, $lview_i$ is initialized to the neighbours of i, then the program $[S_1 \parallel \ldots \parallel S_n]$ terminates in a state in which for any i, $lview_i$ equals the actual network topology top .

Using the local proof rules, it is not difficult to derive the following local specification for each S_i (it is implicitly assumed that the indices j and k range over the neighbours of i):

$$\bigwedge_j Rc_{ji} \rightarrow (\bigwedge_k |c_{ik}!!| = r_i \wedge \bigwedge_{k<j} |c_{ki}??| = r_i \wedge \bigwedge_{k \geq j} |c_{ki}??| = r_i - 1\ ):$$
$$\{lview_i[i,l] = top[i,l] \wedge (j \neq i \rightarrow lview_i[j,l] = \ false)\}$$
$$S_i$$
$$\{q_i \wedge \bigwedge_j |c_{ij}!!| = |c_{ji}??| = D\}$$

For the moment, we do not consider yet the first part of the postcondition q_i, which we will consider in detail later in this section. The invariant informally states that when a process is ready to receive on channel c_{ji}, all its outgoing channels have length r_i, as well as its in-going channels from processes with index smaller than j, and the in-going channels from all processes from index j upward have length $r_i - 1$.

To derive the specification for $[S_1 \parallel \ldots \parallel S_n]$ we have to show first that the condition for deadlock freedom holds, so that we can apply the parallel composition rule. Then there remains to show that the conjunction of the q_i implies the global postcondition $\bigwedge_i lview_i = top$.

As to the first problem, we have to show for any $p \in C(P)$: $\bigwedge_i I_i \wedge p \rightarrow \ false$. The proof of this is far from trivial, and omitted for reasons of space. Essentially, it involves starting at some process waiting for an input, and tracking down the processes on which it is waiting until arriving at the first process again or at a terminated process, which in both cases leads to a contradiction. The intricacy of the proof stems from the fact that the processes may run 'out of phase' to a considerable degree.

In the rest of this section, we will focus on the second essential part of the proof, which involves an application of the global consequence rule. We now focus on the specification of this problem in PVS.

Specifications in PVS are organized in theories, which may depend on other theories via an importing mechanism. In particular, any theory may import from the set of built-in theories. As an example of this, in the theory **processes** below the type **nat** is (silently) imported. Theories may be parameterized, as in our case: the parameter n denotes the number of processes that participate in the algorithm. The first axiom below takes care that we are dealing with at least 2 processes. The type **process** is defined as a subtype of the natural numbers, i.e. the primitive type **nat**. The type **pairset** will be used further on in the definition of type **links**; it fixes the type of sets of 2-tuples of processes.

```
processes [ n: nat ] : THEORY
BEGIN

process   : TYPE = {m: nat | 1 <= m AND m <= n}

pairset   : TYPE = setof[[process,process]]
```

The variable declarations which follow below should be self-explanatory. The constraints on the type **links** express the properties that any network topology should possess: no channel should connect a process with itself (**nonrefl**), channels are bidirectional (more accurately: the existence of a channel implies the existence of the reverse channel) (**symmetric**) and any process should be connected to at least one process (**connected**) (we provide the definition of **nonrefl** only). The projection functions proj_1 and proj_2 are built-in accessor functions on tuples.

```
m,m1,k        : VAR nat

i,j,i1,j1,i2,j2  : VAR process

z, z1         : VAR [process,process]
```

```
p         : VAR pairset


nonrefl    : pred[pairset] =
             LAMBDA (p):
                (FORALL(z):
                   (member(z, p)) IMPLIES proj_1(z) /= proj_2(z) )


links     : TYPE = { p: pairset | nonrefl(p) AND
                                  symmetric(p) AND
                                  connected(p)    }


l         : VAR links
```

The following fragment should be self-explanatory.

```
%
% neighbors(l,i) yields the set of neighbors of process i in
% linkset l
%

neighbors: [links,process -> setof[process]] =
           LAMBDA (l,i): { j | EXISTS (z): member (z,l) AND
                               proj_1(z) = i AND proj_2(z) = j }



%
% path(l,i,j,m) = TRUE iff there exists a path of length m
% between i and j in linkset l
%

path   : pred[[links,process,process,nat]] =
         LAMBDA (l,i,j,m):
           (EXISTS(sp: sequence[process]):
                    i = sp(0) AND j = sp(m) AND
                    (FORALL (m0: nat): m0 < m IMPLIES
                    (member( sp(m0 + 1), neighbors(l,sp(m0)))) ))
```

The next two lemmas are useful in proving the larger lemmas below. Their proof in PVS requires minimal effort, while they provide more clarity in bigger proofs. **chain** states that if there exists a path from i to j of length $m+1$ then there exists a neighbor of i which has distance m to j.

```
chain    : LEMMA
             FORALL (m:nat):
               (path(l,i,j,m+1)
                 IMPLIES
                   (EXISTS (j1:process): member(j1, neighbors(l,i))
                    AND path(l,j1,j,m) ))


zeropath : LEMMA
             path(l,i,j,0)
               IMPLIES
                 i = j
```

The type `matrix` is used as representation for the data objects in our domain, viz. $lview_i$ and $nview_i$ in the algorithm. Each channel c_{ij} is described by the channel variables `inchan(i,j)` for c_{ij}?? and `outchan(i,j)` for c_{ij}!!.

```
matrix    : TYPE = [process,process -> bool]

index     : TYPE = {m:nat | m < n-1}

ix,ix2    : VAR index

chan      : TYPE = [[process,process],index -> matrix]

inchan    : chan

outchan   : chan
```

`topold(l,i)` yields the matrix with only the i-th row filled in according to the neighbor set of `i` with respect to `l`. Thus it corresponds to the value of $lview_i$ at the beginning of the algorithm.

```
topold    : [links,process -> matrix] =
```

```
LAMBDA(l,i): (LAMBDA(i1,j1):
               IF i = i1 THEN member(j1, neighbors(l,i))
               ELSE FALSE
               ENDIF )
```

Using the rules of the proof system for local correctness formulas it is straightforward to derive the following postcondition, for each i (note that any free variable is implicitly universally quantified over, so that **postcond** below expresses the conjunction over all i). Note that, because the postcondition directly relates the values of indexed channel variables (which are matrices), there is no need to introduce local variables. The postcondition, referred to as q_i above, is plainly expressed by

$$c_{ij}!![ix] = \left(\texttt{topold(l,i)} \lor \bigvee_{\substack{i2 \in \texttt{neighbors(l,i)} \\ 0 \leq ix2 < ix}} c_{i2,i}??[ix2]\right)$$

In words, the matrix that is sent out to any j in the ix-th (outer) loop equals the original topology of the sender, or-ed with all inputs from its neighbors so far (note that $\lor$ denotes the logical *or* lifted to matrices). Wrapping together all postconditions, this amounts to the following PVS expression:

```
postcond : AXIOM
           member(j,neighbors(l,i)) IMPLIES
             outchan((i,j),ix) =
                          (LAMBDA(i1,j1):(topold(l,i)(i1,j1) OR
                             (EXISTS(i2:process):
                              (EXISTS(ix2:index):
                               (member(i2,neighbors(l,i)) AND
                               ix2 < ix AND
                               inchan((i2,i),ix2)(i1,j1)))) ))
```

The next lemma **chansplit** which is used in the proof of **main** below was proven with induction on **k**. It expresses the following relation:

$$c_{ij}!![k+1] = \left(c_{ij}!![k] \lor \bigvee_{j2 \in \texttt{neighbors(l,i)}} c_{j2\ i}??[k]\right)$$

It reduces the matrix that has been sent over c_{ij} in the $k+1$-th (outer) loop to an expression consisting of matrices that were sent and received by i in the k-th loop.

```
chansplit: LEMMA
          forall(k):
          k < n-2
            IMPLIES
            (member(j,neighbors(l,i))
             IMPLIES
               outchan((i,j),k+1)(i1,j1) =
               (outchan((i,j),k)(i1,j1) OR
                (EXISTS(j2): member(j2,neighbors(l,i))
                  AND inchan((j2,i),k)(i1,j1) )))
```

Before coming to the main theorem, we show a few other helpful lemmas:

```
%
% lessdist is true iff there is a path between i and j with length
% smaller than or equal to k
%

lessdist : [links,process,process,nat -> bool] =
           LAMBDA(l,i,j,m):
            EXISTS(m1):(m1 <= m AND path(l,i,j,m1))


nextneigh : LEMMA
            (lessdist(l,i,j,m+1) AND i /=j )
               IMPLIES
                  (EXISTS(i2):(member(i2,neighbors(l,i))
                         AND  lessdist(l,i2,j,m)))


ldist1    : LEMMA
            lessdist(l,i,j,m) IMPLIES lessdist(l,i,j,m+1)


ldist2    : LEMMA
            (NOT lessdist(l,i,j,m+1))
```

```
          IMPLIES
             FORALL(j1): (member(j1,neighbors(l,i))
                               IMPLIES
                                (NOT lessdist(l,j1,j,m)))
```

We now come to the main theorem which states that the k-th output over channel c_{ij} is a matrix that equals topold(l,i1) with respect to row i1 if the distance in the network between i and i1 is less than or equal to k, and otherwise it yields FALSE on that row. In particular, it follows from this theorem (again using local reasoning) that after D executions of the loop, the value of $lview_i$ corresponds with the network topology *top*. The second conjunct may not seem too exciting, but is needed to keep the induction going.

```
main     : THEOREM
           k < n-1 IMPLIES
             ((lessdist(l,i,i1,k)
               IMPLIES
                FORALL (j): member(j, neighbors(l,i))
                    IMPLIES
                   (outchan((i,j),k)(i1,j1) = topold(l,i1)(i1,j1)))
             AND
             ((NOT lessdist(l,i,i1,k))
               IMPLIES
                FORALL (j): member(j, neighbors(l,i))
                    IMPLIES
                   (outchan((i,j),k)(i1,j1) = FALSE)) )

END processes
```

The proof of main is currently about 15 pages. Possibly this can be improved by defining some clever strategies (in fact macros of proof steps). Perhaps more interesting is to construct as general as possible a proof, so that it can be re-used in the light of small changes.

6 Conclusions

We have shown how the restriction to local nondeterminism gives rise to a simple compositional proof system based on Hoare logic for distributed systems composed of processes which interact asynchronously via unbounded FIFO buffers.

We used the theorem prover PVS in a non trivial application of the proof system to the correctness of a heartbeat algorithm for computing the topology of a network.

In general we believe that a fruitful line of research with respect to automated verification is the syntactic identification of classes of distributed systems which allow a simple compositional reasoning pattern.

References

[AFdR80] K.R. Apt, N. Francez, and W.-P. de Roever. A proof system for communicating sequential processes. *ACM-TOPLAS*, 2(3):359–385, 1980.

[And91] Gregory R. Andrews. *Concurrent Programming, Principles and Practice.* The Benjamin/Cummings Publishing Company, Inc., 1991.

[CS95] D. A. Cyrluk and M. K. Srivas. Theorem proving: Not an esoteric diversion, but the unifying framework for industrial verification. In *IEEE International Conference on Computer Design (ICCD) '95*, Austin, Texas, October 1995.

[dB94] F.S. de Boer. Compositionality and completeness of the inductive assertion method for concurrent systems. In *Proc. IFIP Working Conference on Programming Concepts, Methods and Calculi*, San Miniato, Italy, 1994.

[dBHdR] F.S. de Boer, J. Hooman, and W.-P. de Roever. *State-based proof theory of concurrency: from noncompositional to compositional methods.* Draft of a book.

[dBvH94] F.S. de Boer and M. van Hulst. A proof system for asynchronously communicating deterministic processes. In B. Rovan I. Prívara and P. Ružička, editors, *Proc. MFCS '94*, volume 841 of *Lecture Notes in Computer Science*, pages 256–265. Springer-Verlag, 1994.

[dBvH95] F.S. de Boer and M. van Hulst. A compositional proof system for asynchronously communicating processes. In *Proceedings MPC'95*, Kloster Irsee, Germany, 1995.

[dBvH96] F.S. de Boer and M. van Hulst. Local nondeterminism in asynchronously communicating processes. Technical report, Utrecht University, 1996. In Preparation.

[Fra92] N. Francez. *Program Verification.* Addison Wesley, 1992.

[HdR86] J. Hooman and W.-P. de Roever. The quest goes on: a survey of proof systems for partial correctness of CSP. In *Current trends in concurrency*, volume 224 of *Lecture Notes in Computer Science*, pages 343–395. Springer-Verlag, 1986.

[OG76] S. Owicki and D. Gries. An axiomatic proof technique for parallel programs I. *Acta Informatica*, 6:319–340, 1976.

[ORS92] S. Owre, J. Rushby, and N. Shankar. PVS: A prototype verification system. In *11th Conference on Automated Deduction*, volume 607 of *Lecture Notes in Artificial Intelligence*, pages 748–752. Springer-Verlag, 1992.

[Pan88] P.K. Pandya. *Compositional Verification of Distributed Programs.* PhD thesis, Tata Institute of Fundamental Research, Homi Bhabha Road, Bombay 400 005, INDIA, 1988.

[Raj94] S. Rajan. Transformations in high-level synthesis: Formal specification and efficient mechanical verification. Technical Report CSL-94-10, CSL, 1994.

[ZdRvEB85] J. Zwiers, W.-P. de Roever, and P. van Emde Boas. Compositionality and concurrent networks: Soundness and completeness of a proofsystem. In *Proc. ICALP'85*, volume 194 of *Lecture Notes in Computer Science*. Springer-Verlag, 1985.

Identification of and Solutions to Shortcomings of LCL, a Larch/C Interface Specification Language

Patrice Chalin, Peter Grogono and T. Radhakrishnan

{chalin,grogono,krishnan}@cs.concordia.ca
Concordia University, Department of Computer Science
1455 de Maisonneuve Blvd. West
Montréal, Québec, Canada H3G 1M8

Abstract. We present some of the more significant shortcomings of LCL, a Larch/C specification language used to document the interfaces of modules written in ISO C. We illustrate inadequacies in the definition and insufficiencies in the expressiveness of LCL by means of examples that cover dependencies between objects, the trashing of objects, and implicit parameter constraints in function specifications. A violation of the principle of referential transparency is also shown. We describe changes to the LCL language that overcome the identified shortcomings. Since most of the shortcomings are not particular to LCL, this paper will be of interest to language designers and users of other module interface specification languages.

1 Introduction

The Larch approach to specification promotes the modular development of programs and encourages the use of data abstraction. In Larch there are two specification tiers or levels. The *shared tier* contains specifications (called *traits*) written in the *Larch Shared Language* (LSL) [8]. A trait defines a multisorted first-order theory. The *interface tier* contains interface specifications written in a Larch interface language. There are several Larch interface languages. The most widely used are LCL, LCPP (an interface language for C++) and LM3 (an interface language for Modula-3). Each[1] interface language is specialized for use with a particular programming language. Using constructs and concepts from the programming language, an interface specification describes what resources are being provided by a module.

Specification languages can be used during the entire software development process to document requirements, designs and the interface specifications for modules and program components. One must be careful in choosing an appropriate specification language for the task at hand [9, 1]. The specialization of a specification language to a particular programming language is an important

[1] With the exception of the two generic interface languages GIL [3] and GCIL [14].

characteristic of *module interface specification languages* (MISL's). Most specification languages are general purpose languages. Among the most popular are VDM-SL [13] and Z [18]. These languages are best suited for design specification.

Much less attention has been given to MISL's by the research community than to design or wide-spectrum specification languages. To our knowledge, the only MISL's are the Larch interface languages and an adaptation of the language used with the Trace Assertion Method (TAM) [16]. Of the Larch interface languages, LCL would seem to be the most developed and used. Development of the TAM-based language is at a preliminary stage and a new release is in preparation [10].

MISL's are an excellent way of introducing formal methods into industrial settings [12]. It is particularly important to industry that start-up costs be minimized and that benefits be apparent even with small investments; we believe that MISL's can offer this. Some of the advantages of the use of MISL's are enumerated next[2].

MISL's can be immediately and 'unintrusively' integrated into current industrial development processes [21]. A company that has invested considerable resources in the creation and installation of their development processes (e.g. training of personnel and construction of tools) is more likely to welcome formal methods that can be used in conjunction with inhouse development standards.

One of the greatest challenges faced by industry is the maintenance of legacy code. Not only can MISL's be applied to new developments, they can also be integrated into the maintenance cycle of existing software systems. This is of great value since it means that formal methods can be retroactively brought into projects that were developed without formal methods.

MISL's can be *gradually* integrated into a project:

- they can be applied to isolated portions of a system (such as those aspects for which reliability is most critical),
- MISL's can be used with varying degrees of rigor: from merely documenting function signatures to providing complete behavioral descriptions for functions. In all cases one can reap benefits.

Tool support for most other classes of specification language is limited to type checking. More automated checks can be performed for MISL's. For example, LCLint, a tool for checking LCL specifications and C code, can be used to detect abstraction boundary violations, illicit access to global variables, and undocumented modification of client-visible objects [6]. As another example, Vandevoorde has developed a prototype program optimizer that makes use of the information derived from module interface specifications to perform optimizations that cannot be accomplished by the inspection of code alone [20].

This paper contributes to the evolution of LCL by documenting some of the more significant shortcomings of LCL 2.4[3]and by proposing solutions to the

[2] These advantages are not necessarily exclusive to MISL's—they may be shared by other classes of specification language.

[3] Version 2.4 is the latest public release of LCL.

identified shortcomings. The authoritative references for LCL 2.4 are the Larch book [8] and Tan's PhD thesis [19]. A basic understanding of LCL is assumed.

2 Dependencies Between Objects

In this section we introduce the concept of object dependency and describe how dependencies can arise. We argue that programmers rely on certain "desirable" kinds of dependency and that they tend to overlook other "less desirable" forms. Our examples will serve to illustrate that LCL lacks operations that would allow specifiers to document and reason about dependency relationships in interface specifications.

2.1 Definitions

In C, an object is a region of data storage consisting of a contiguous sequence of storage units [11, p. 2]. In LCL, the term is used in a more abstract sense (in particular because of the need to model objects that are instances of abstract types): an *object* is a container for values of a particular type [8, p. 59].

We say that an object x_1 ***depends on*** an object x_2 if changing the value contained in x_2 may affect the value contained in x_1. It is possible for x_1 to depend on x_2 without x_2 depending on x_1[4]. If x_1 depends on x_2 or x_2 depends on x_1, then we say that a dependency exists between x_1 and x_2. If x_1 is not dependent on x_2, then we say that x_1 ***is independent of*** x_2. The objects in a given collection are ***independent***, if each object from the collection is independent of every other object in the collection. Given an expression e that refers to an object—e is called an *lvalue* in C—we shall often lighten our prose by speaking of "the object e" instead of the more verbose but precise "the object referred to by e". Thus, for example, we may state that e_1 and e_2 are independent by which we mean that the objects that are denoted by the expressions are independent. As a consequence, we note that if e_1 and e_2 are independent then the expressions cannot be aliases.

Turning to the low-level model of C for an example, we understand that two objects with overlapping regions of storage are dependent on each other. Thus, objects of array, structure and union types depend on the objects that correspond to their members and *vice versa*. For example, given the following declarations

```
struct { int i; } s;
int a[10];
```

`s.i` and `s` depend on each other since these expressions refer to the same region of memory. Also, by definition, `s` and `s.i` are dependent on each other since changing the value of one will affect the value of the other. Similarly, a

[4] This kind of asymmetry may exist between instances of an abstract type.

depends on its members—e.g. **a[9]**. On the other hand, **a[0]**, **a[1]**, ..., **a[9]**, and **s.i** are independent. The dependency relationship that holds between an aggregate or union object and its members is one of the kinds of dependency that programmers rely on and actually take for granted.

When dealing with abstract types we can no longer appeal to the low-level concept of overlapping storage for an intuitive model of dependency. Whether a dependency exists between two instances of an abstract type will depend on the implementation of the abstract type [4].

2.2 Motivating Example: Error in the Larch Book

The purpose of this example is twofold: we wish to illustrate that there are legitimate uses of dependencies (beyond those mentioned in Section 2.1) and that there are certain kinds of dependency that are often overlooked by specifiers and implementors.

```
typedef struct {... char name[maxEmployeeName]; ...} employee;

bool employee_setName(employee *e, char na[]) {
    requires nullTerminated(na^);
    modifies e->name;
    ensures result = lenStr(na^) < maxEmployeeName
          ∧ (if result
             then sameStr(e->name', na^)
                  ∧ nullTerminated(e->name')
             else e->name' = e->name^);
}
```

Fig. 1. An Excerpt from **employee.lcl**

Our example (see Figure 1) is an excerpt from the Larch book **employee** specification [8, p. 65]. This specification is part of a small database program used to store and perform simple queries on employee records. Employee records are represented by the exposed type **employee** which is defined as a C structure. Of the functions provided for manipulating employee records we show only the function **employee_setName**. It can be used to assign a string to the **name** field of an employee record. Before calling **employee_setName**, a client must make sure that the parameter **na** is a null terminated string. The expressions $e^\wedge$ and e' denote the values contained in the object referred to by the subexpression e in the pre-state (the program state before function entry) and post-state (the state after function return) respectively. After the call, the name field of the given employee record will be set to the string contained in **na** if the string length is less than **maxEmployeeName**. Otherwise, the name field of the record is left unchanged. The function result is true if and only if the length of the string contained in **na** is less than **maxEmployeeName**.

Suppose that all of the employee records in a given database begin with either of the titles "Mr." or "Ms." and that the database maintainer wishes to remove the titles. He or she decides to write a program that will accomplish this task by accessing each employee record, say, as the variable **e**, and then performing the call

```
employee_setName(&e,e.name + 3)
```

Unfortunately the program crashes[5] and inspection of the implementation of **employee_setName** reveals the cause:

```
bool employee_setName(employee *e, char na []) {
    int i;

    for (i = 0; na[i] != '0'; i++)
      if (i == maxEmployeeName) return FALSE;
    strcpy(e->name, na);
    return TRUE;
}
```

The particular way in which **employee_setName** is being invoked causes the standard library function **strcpy** to be called with overlapping arguments (since **e->name** and **na** are part of the same array). The behavior of **strcpy** is undefined when it is called under such circumstances [11, §7.11.2.3]. The specification of **employee_setName** does not prohibit calls for which its arguments are dependent. It is possible that the specification inaccurately reflects the intent of its authors or that the source of error is the implementation: in either case the implementation is incorrect with respect to its specification. With appropriate (but small) changes, the implementation can be corrected by making use of the standard library function **memmove** instead of **strcpy** (since **memmove** may be called with overlapping arguments). The reader may wonder whether **memmove** can be specified in LCL; we address this question in Section 2.4.

We can trace the publication of the database program to the original technical report on LCL 1.0 [7]. The program was subsequently revised and published as part of the Larch book [8, §5.3]. To determine the effectiveness of LCLint at detecting certain classes of errors in LCL specifications and their implementations, David Evans applied LCLint to (among others) the database program. Evans writes:

> "The specifications [of the database program] had been checked by the LCL checker [a predecessor of the LCLint tool] ..., and the source code had been compiled and tested extensively. Since the code and specifications were written by experts, and checked copiously by hand prior to

[5] A sample program compiled with gcc version 2.6.3 and run under SunOS release 4.1.3 generates a segmentation fault.

publication, it was expected that not many bugs would be found." [5, p. 41]

The case study "did uncover two abstraction violations, and one legitimate modification error" [5, p. 50]. We have demonstrated an additional error in the database program which has also escaped the scrutiny of the original designers and subsequent reviewers.

This example illustrates that there are legitimate uses of dependencies (such as the dependency permitted between `*e` and `na` in `employee_setName`) beyond those mentioned in Section 2.1. It also illustrates that errors resulting from unexpected dependencies between arguments can easily be overlooked. We believe that this is true because developers have not been encouraged to think about dependencies that may exist among parameters or between parameters and global variables. A specification language that permits dependencies must have constructs that allow the description of dependency relationships as well as a semantic model that supports reasoning about dependencies: LCL is deficient in both these respects.

2.3 Example: *lookup*

The specification given in Figure 2 defines a global `struct` variable `as` consisting of an array of elements, `elts`, and the size of the prefix of `elts` that is in use. It also defines the function `lookup` which can be used to search for an occurrence of the given value `v` in `as`[6]. If `v` is present in `as`, then `*i` is set to the index of an element of `as` containing `v` and `as` is left unchanged; otherwise, `v` is added to `as` and `*i` is set to the index of the newly added value. The function result is true precisely when the value `v` occurs in `as` (before `lookup` is invoked). The predicate that follows the `else` in the ensures clause of `lookup` is not shown since it is not relevant to our discussion.

After a careful review, the reader may feel that the specification of `lookup` is accurate. It is actually inconsistent—there is no implementation that can satisfy it—since there are situations for which the postcondition cannot be satisfied. For example, suppose that `v` occurs in `as` and that `*i` is an alias for `as.size` or any of the elements of `as.elts` that are in use. Then the ensures clause states that the value of `*i` may change while requiring that the value of `as` remain unchanged; this constraint, in general, will be unsatisfiable in the presence of the described aliasing.

We can attempt to remedy the situation by strengthening the precondition of `lookup` so that `*i` is prohibited from being an alias for any of the subcomponents of `as` (see Figure 3). The resulting specification is less clear and more complex (this augments the risk of introducing errors into the specification) and less maintainable since the specification is now more sensitive to changes in the `AS` structure.

---

[6] We will at times use the term "`as`" to refer to the prefix of `as.elts` that is in use.

```
constant int N;
struct AS {int size; int elts[N];} as;

bool lookup(int v, int *i) struct AS as; {
  requires as.size^ < N;
  modifies *i, as;
  ensures    result = v ∈ prefix(as.elts^,as.size^)
         ∧ if result
           then  0 ≤ (*i)′ ∧ (*i)′ < as.size^
              ∧ as.elts^ [(*i)′] = v
              ∧ as′ = as^
           else /* v is inserted into as.elts */ ...;
}
```

Fig. 2. Specification of *lookup*

```
bool lookup(int v, int *i) struct AS as; {
  requires as.size^ < N  ∧  *i ≠ as.size
          ∧ (∀ j:int ((0 ≤ j ∧ j ≤ as.size^)
                             ⇒ *i ≠ as.elts[j]));

  ...
}
```

Fig. 3. Strengthened Precondition for *lookup*

More importantly, the specification is still inconsistent since it is possible for `*i` and `as` to satisfy the requires clause without being independent. In formulating the strengthened precondition we have relied on the following *false* assumption: if two distinct objects are instances of base types (`char`, `int`, etc.), then they must be independent. In C, as in some other imperative programming languages, this assumption can be invalidated by the use of union types. Type casting can also invalidate the assumption.

This example illustrates the need for new LCL language constructs which would allow specifiers to accurately and succinctly express the independence of objects.

2.4 Example: ISO C String Library Functions

It would be reasonable to expect LCL to be expressive enough to allow one to document the behavior of most ISO C standard library functions. Consider the task of writing specifications for the standard string copying functions `memcpy` and `memmove` [11, §7.11.2].

```
void *memcpy(void *s1, const void *s2, size_t n);
```

```
void *memmove(void *s1, const void *s2, size_t n);
```

Both functions can be used to copy **n** characters from the object pointed to by **s2** into the object pointed to by **s1**. There is an extra requirement for **memcpy**: the objects ***s1** and ***s2** must not overlap [11, §7.11.2]. It is impossible to write an LCL specification for **memcpy** since we cannot express the requirement that its arguments are independent of each other.

2.5 Dependencies and Abstract Types

The **fresh** operator is the only LCL operator, other than equality over objects, that allows specifiers to document dependency relationships between objects. An occurrence of the expression **fresh(***e***)** in the ensures clause of a function specification asserts that the object referred to by *e* is not aliased to any object that was visible to the client before function entry [8, p. 77]. By means of the next example, we highlight the need for LCL primitives that would allow for a more precise description of the dependency relationships that may exist between objects.

Most abstract type constructors yield instances of the abstract type that are independent of other client-visible objects. It is not uncommon, though, to find "quick" or "destructive" versions of some constructors that fail to guarantee the independence of the resulting abstract type instance; independence is sacrificed for sake of efficiency.

```
mutable type List;

uses List(int,List);

List mkList(void) {
  ensures  result' = empty ∧ fresh(result);
}
List concat(List x1, List x2) {
  ensures  result' = x1^ || x2^ ∧ fresh(result);
}
List fastConcat(List x1, List x2) {
  ensures  result' = x1^ || x2^;
}
```

Fig. 4. List specification.

For example, a list module might provide two versions of the concatenation operation—see Figure 4. Notice that the specification of **fastConcat** does not ensure **fresh(result)**. It would be more useful, for example, if we could assert that the only dependency created by **fastConcat** is between **result** and **x2**. This extra information would allow us to make better use of **fastConcat**, for example, in the optimization of a series of successive concatenations.

3 Implicit Constraints on Parameters

In LCL, the specifications of functions with parameters have implicit constraints, derived from the parameter declarations, that affect the meaning of the specifications. Unfortunately, most of these implicit constraints are either not documented or inadequately defined. The purpose of this section is to expose some of these implicit parameter constraints and to discuss the consequences of their inclusion in LCL.

3.1 Constraint for All Parameters

There is an implicit constraint that applies to all parameters in a function specification. It requires that the parameters be *defined*. This implicit constraint on parameters is not documented in the Larch book [8] nor in Tan's semantics [19]. We have only been able to find an explicit statement of the constraint in Evans's thesis:

> "LCL specifications denote if the values associated with parameters are defined. ... All other parameters [i.e. other than out-qualified pointer parameters] are assumed to be defined when the function is entered." [5, p. 36]

(The **out** parameter qualifier is discussed in Section 3.3.) For example, consider the function **empset_clear** from the Larch book **empset** specification [8, p. 73]:

```
void empset_clear(empset s) {
   modifies s;
   ensures s' = { };
   }
```

By the absence of a requires clause, no explicit requirements are placed on clients of **empset_clear**. Implicitly, though, it is assumed that on function entry, **s** is bound to a defined **empset** (as can be concluded from the informal description of **empset_clear**): "**empset_clear**, is provided for reinitializing an existing **empset**" [8, p. 76].

3.2 Parameters of Pointer Types

There is an additional constraint for parameters of pointer types. The implicit property requires that a pointer parameter reference an allocated object and that this object be defined. This constraint is not documented in the Larch book nor in Tan's semantics[7]. Evans writes:

[7] Tan documents the effect of the out parameter qualifier as applied to parameters of pointer types, but he fails to describe the implicit constraints derived from pointer parameters that are *not* qualified with out.

"Normally, if a parameter to a function is a pointer, it is assumed that the value it points to is defined and may be used in the body of the function." [5, p. 36]

We discuss some of the shortcomings associated with this implicit constraint.

Constraint is Overly Restrictive The implicit constraint for pointer parameters is overly restrictive since it prevents us from using certain useful implementation techniques. Consider the specification fragment

```
typedef struct node { ... } *List;
constant List emptyList = 0;
List mkList(int info, List tail) { ... }
```

in which the empty list is represented by a null pointer. The function `mkList` is meant to allow clients to construct a new list from a given integer and list. The implicit constraint for pointer parameters effectively prohibits us from representing the empty list by means of a null pointer, since, for example, we cannot call `mkList` with `emptyList` as an argument for `tail`. This is because all pointer parameters must refer to allocated objects and a null pointer "is guaranteed to compare unequal to a pointer to any object or function" [11, §6.2.2.3]—i.e., a null pointer can never refer to an allocated object.

Constraint is Ambiguous and Problematic From a given pointer parameter `p` we can access all of the objects `p+i` for `i` in the index set

$$I = \{\, i \mid \texttt{minIndex(p)} \le i \le \texttt{maxIndex(p)} \,\}$$

[8, p. 60]. With this in mind, there would seem to be two reasonable interpretations for the implicit constraint. Firstly, we can interpret the implicit constraint as applying to all of the objects that can be accessed via `p`: i.e. all objects `p+i` (for `i` $\in I$) would have to be allocated and defined. Such an interpretation renders the constraint too restrictive. For example, this would require that every member of a string (represented by a pointer into an array of `char`) be initialized before the string is passed as an argument, even if the string does not occupy the entire array. There is no reason to require that the string be initialized beyond the null character that terminates the string.

Another possible interpretation for the implicit constraint would require that all objects `p+i` (`i` $\in I$) be allocated but that only the object at `p` need be defined. Assuming $1 \in I$, how would a specifier express the additional requirement that `p+1` be defined? There are no LCL language constructs available to the specifier that would allow the expression of this property.

3.3 The out Parameter Qualifier

It is common in C for a function to return values to its caller by means of objects that are referenced by the function's pointer parameters; the **out** parameter qualifier serves to indicate which parameters are being used for this purpose [19, §4.3]. The specification of **add** given in Figure 5 illustrates the use of **out**. The **out** qualifier has the effect of partly "relaxing" the extra constraint that

```
void add(int m, int n, out int *sum) {
  modifies *sum;
  ensures  (*sum)' = m + n;
}
```

Fig. 5. Use of out in a function specification.

is usually applied to pointer parameters. An **out** qualified pointer parameter is still implicitly required to refer to an allocated object, but that object need not be defined [19, §4.3].

As a final remark, we highlight a contradiction in [19]: although Tan states that the **out** qualifier is applicable *only* to parameters of pointer types [19, §4.3], he also applies it to array parameters [19, §D.27]. Of course, this more liberal use of **out** is reasonable (and is accepted by LCLint), but it has not been documented. Array parameters are discussed in Section 3.4.

3.4 Parameters of Array Types

Although we have found no explicit description of it, there is an implicit constraint on array parameters that is similar to the one for pointer parameters. This would seem reasonable, due to the close relationship between pointers and arrays in C. In fact, someone familiar with C might think that it would be unnecessary to reformulate the implicit constraint for pointer parameters in terms of array parameters because the type of an array parameter is "adjusted to" a pointer type [11, §6.7.1]. In LCL, parameters of array types have a different semantics from those of pointer types [8, p. 60], [19, §7.3.1]—in particular, array parameters are not treated as pointer parameters.

The specification of **date_parse** [19, §D.28] given in Figure 6 provides evidence of the implicit assumption that array parameters refer to objects that have been *allocated* and whose contents are defined. In the specification, **cstring**'s are null-terminated arrays of **char**. If **indate** is a well-formatted date, then this date is parsed and returned in ***d**. The function **date_parse** makes use of the content of **indate**, hence **indate** must refer to allocated storage and its contents must be defined.

The implicit constraint over array parameters suffers from the same ambiguities and drawbacks as the constraint for pointer parameters discussed in

```
bool date_parse (cstring indate,..., out date *d)... {
  modifies ...;
  ensures  result = okDateFormat(getString(indate^))
        ∧ if result
          then (*d)' = string2date(getString(indate^))
          ...;
}
```

Fig. 6. Tan's **date_parse** Function

Section 3.2; i.e., it is not clear whether the implicit constraint requires that all or only some of the array elements be defined—either interpretation leads to difficulties.

3.5 Parameters of Other Types

Consider a function specification with the header

```
void f(int **i)
```

The implicit constraints require that `i` be defined and that `*i` be allocated and defined. Suppose that we further wished to constrain the parameter by requiring that `**i` be allocated and defined. We cannot document this extra property for lack of language primitives in LCL. Similar remarks can be made about parameters of other types (e.g. array of pointer, struct containing a pointer member).

3.6 Parameters *vs.* Global Variables

In designing a module one must decide on the mechanisms by which information will be communicated between the module and its clients. In particular, one must choose between information exchange by means of function parameters or global variables. A designer's freedom of choice is impeded (in favor of the use of function parameters) by the lack of expressiveness of LCL.

For example, given

```
int *gv;

void f(int *pv) { ... }
void g(void) int *gv; { ... }
```

one could not express, in the specification of **g**, a constraint on **gv** that would be equivalent to the implicit parameter constraint on **pv** in **f**. This is because, unlike for function parameters, implicit constraints are not imposed on variables (like **gv**) that are part of the global variable list of a function specification. It is also because there are no language constructs in LCL that express the property that a given object is allocated, or that it is both allocated and defined.

4 Trashing of Objects

The **trashed** operator can be used in the ensures clause of a function specification to indicate that a given object cannot be reliably accessed after the function returns. The **trashed** operator is typically used in the specifications of functions that deallocate memory or that dispose of instances of mutable abstract types. For example, after a call to the function **trashIntObj**

```
void trashIntObj(int *i) {
  modifies *i;
  ensures trashed(*i);
}
```

a client must not attempt to access the contents of `*i` "because referencing a trashed object can even cause the client program to crash" [8, p. 76]. Notice the presence of `*i` in the modifies clause: an object can be trashed only if it is listed in the modifies clause—although specifications in the LCL literature consistently mention trashed objects in the modifies clause, there is no explicit statement of this requirement. Hence, the modifies clause plays a dual role: it serves to identify those objects that may be trashed as well as those objects that may be preserved but whose values may be modified.

On the other hand, after the invocation of **changeVal**

```
void changeVal(int *i) {
  modifies *i;
  ensures true;
}
```

a client may still make use of `*i` (though no constraint is placed on the value contained in `*i`) [8, p. 76]. Thus, an object that is not explicitly trashed is implicitly preserved—i.e. *not* trashed. We will illustrate next that this aspect of the semantics of LCL can lead to contradictory interpretations for function specifications that should have the same meaning.

4.1 Referential Opacity

Consider the following specification of **trashOrChange**, which may nondeterministically choose between trashing and not trashing `*i`:

```
void trashOrChange(int *i) {
  modifies *i;
  ensures trashed(*i) ∨ ¬trashed(*i);
}
```

The predicate in the ensures clause is an instance of the law of excluded middle and hence, it is logically equivalent to **true**. One would expect to be able to simplify the ensures clause while preserving the meaning of the specification.

```
void trashOrChange(int *i) {
  modifies *i;
  ensures true;
}
```

The resulting specification of **trashOrChange** cannot trash ***i** because of the implicit constraint that ***i** be preserved.

We have illustrated a violation of the principle of referential transparency which states, in essence, that the only important property of an expression is its value and that we can, consequently, substitute equals for equals. Referential transparency is a fundamental principle of mathematical formalisms.

Not only do formal specification languages permit precise documentation, but they also provide the grounds for the formal analysis and transformation of specifications. Formal arguments are most often conducted within a proof system (rather than by direct application of a model theory). For example, in the Refinement Calculus [15], one can make use of "refinement laws" (which can be used as proof rules) to establish the correctness of an implementation with respect to its specification. As a consequence of the identified referential opacity, we note that laws, such as the strengthen postcondition law, do not hold for LCL [2].

5 Shortcomings Resolved

5.1 Dependencies Between Objects

The history of programming languages has been marked by a tendency to make languages more abstract. Increasingly, languages are based on programming concepts (i.e. *semantic objects*) that allow designers to think at a level of abstraction that is closer to the problem domain and further from the computer architectures on which the programs are being executed. In the programming language community, object dependencies tend to be frowned upon. High-level languages tend to severely restrict the kinds of dependency that can be created and low-level languages are characterized by the opposite. In the extreme, object dependencies are prohibited from high-level languages—as in logic or functional programming languages in which computation is based on values rather than objects (by definition, object dependencies cannot exist between values, only between objects). It is important to note that object dependencies *cannot be eliminated* from imperative programming languages that support abstract and indexable[8] types.

By suggesting the systematic adherence to certain programming conventions (e.g. with respect to mechanisms for the implementation and use of abstract types), LCL attempts to raise the level of abstraction at which C programmers think. In providing a semantics for LCL, there would seem to be a tension: although use of LCL promotes C programming at a higher level of abstraction, it is also necessary that the semantic model of LCL subsume that of C since

[8] E.g. array or dynamic types.

LCL is an interface specification language *for* C. The LCL semantic model must capture the behavior of as large a class of C programs as is possible. Hence arises the question: to what degree should dependencies be supported in LCL?

Usually, a model that supports descriptions from two levels of abstraction must be defined in terms of concepts that are from the lowest level. Hence, the semantic model for LCL must accurately capture the kinds of object dependency that can be created in C programs. Our approach to modeling dependencies is formally described in [2]. Of course, it is also necessary that the LCL language have an expressively complete set of constructs for describing dependency relationships. These constructs are introduced next.

In its full generality, the object dependency relation is a dynamic property. For example, dependencies between instances of abstract types implemented by shared realizations may change at run-time [4]. Modeling the object dependency relation as a dynamic property would complicate the semantics and would have important repercussions at the language level. It is not clear, at this point in our research, what language constructs would be best suited to supporting a dynamic dependency relation. The extent to which the dynamic quality of the dependency relation would be actually needed in documenting interface specifications is also unclear. Consequently, in this version of the semantic model the object dependency relation is represented by a static relation, that is, a relation whose value is independent of the program state.

We propose the introduction, in LCL, of two predicates:

- `depOn`(e, e') holds when the object referred to by e depends on[9] the object referred to by e'.
- `indep`($e_1, e_2, \ldots, e_n$) holds when the expressions e_1, e_2, ..., e_n denote objects that are independent.

The `depOn` predicate allows specifiers to describe any (static) dependency relation that can exist between objects. Although `indep` can be defined in terms of `depOn`, `indep` is more likely to be used in practice since we generally wish to specify that the objects in a given collection are independent (as opposed to characterizing a particular dependency relationship). For example, `indep` can be used to write concise and accurate specifications for the functions `lookup` and `memcpy`. Concretely, in the case of `lookup`, we capture the requirement that `as` and `*i` be independent by adding `indep(as,*i)` to the requires clause:

```
bool lookup(int v, int *i) struct AS as; {
  requires as.size^ < N ∧ indep(as,*i);
  ...
}
```

The last example of Section 2 required that we be able to strengthen the specification of `fastConcat` by ensuring that the only dependencies created by `fastConcat` are between `result` and `x2`. More precisely, we wish to ensure that

[9] The definition of dependence is given in Section 2.1.

result is independent of any client-visible object that is active in the pre- and post-states and that is also independent of **x2**. One way of rewriting the specification to include this property is as follows[10]

```
List fastConcat(List x1, List x2) {
  ensures ∀ void *x (
            ((*x)\activePre ∧ (*x)\activePost
            ∧ indep(*x,x2)) ⇒
               indep(result,*x))
         ∧ result' = x1^ || x2^;
}
```

(The \activePre and \activePost operators are discussed in the next section.) The ensures clause is somewhat intimidating. Frequent occurrence, in specifications, of properties like these may warrant the introduction of special notation that would allow us to say, e.g. "**fresh(result)** *except for* **x2**."

5.2 Implicit Constraints on Parameters

Constraints for All Parameters The values contained in objects are inevitably encoded in some medium—e.g. volatile storage. It may be the case that for a given object of type **T** some encodings—e.g. bit patterns—will not correspond to values of type **T**. We say that an object is ***well-defined*** with respect to a type **T** if it contains an encoding that corresponds to a value of type **T**; that is, if the object contains a ***valid representation*** of a value of type **T**. When we say, without qualification, that an object is well-defined, we mean that the object is well-defined with respect to its declared type.

Although the LCL literature is not clear about the logical foundations of LCL, we have chosen LL, the logic underlying LSL to be the logical base for LCL. LL is a first-order multisorted logic with equality in which all function symbols are interpreted as total functions and sorts do *not* have distinguished "undefined" values [2]. Hence, we cannot model undefined *values* in LCL—although we do model non-well-defined objects. The implicit constraint, discussed in Section 3.1, that "all parameters must be defined" becomes a fundamental consequence of the semantic model of LCL and is therefore no longer an implicit constraint.

New LCL Operators In Sections 3.2, 3.5 and 3.6, we noted that it is not possible in LCL to express the property that an object is allocated or that it is both allocated and well-defined. For this purpose we propose the introduction of the following boolean operators

```
__ \activePre,  __ \wellDefPre,
__ \activePost, __ \wellDefPost,
__ \activeAny,  __ \wellDefAny : T → Bool
```

[10] The notation that we are using for the declaration of the quantifier variable is not the notation of LCL 2.4.

The expression e`\activePre` holds when the object e is active (i.e. allocated) in the pre-state. e`\wellDefPre` holds when the object e is active and well-defined in the pre-state. The other operations provide similar predicates over the post and generic states. Note that the meaning of the trashed operator can be given in terms of \activePost

```
trashed(gv) ⇔ ¬ (gv\activePost)
```

Due to the problems discussed in Section 3, the implicit constraints for pointer and array parameters are dropped. The new operators can be used to express the necessary constraints. For example, the following specification of **f** requires that the object pointed to by **i** be allocated and that the global variable **gv** be well-defined. The function ensures that the post-state value of ***i** is well-defined and that it is equal to the pre-state value of **gv**.

```
void f(int *i) int gv; {
  requires (*i)\activePre ∧ gv\wellDefPre
  modifies *i;
  ensures  (*i)\wellDefPost ∧ (*i)′ = gv^;
}
```

Although this approach results in function specifications that are more verbose; elsewhere [2], we have suggested the use of Ada-like parameter qualifiers (**in**, **out**, **inout**) that would allow us to recover the original terseness.

5.3 Trashing of Objects

The semantics of function specifications, in LCL 2.4, is defined in such a way that under certain circumstances some objects are implicitly preserved. We now explain this aspect of the semantics of LCL 2.4 in more detail than in Section 4 and we reexamine the resulting violation of the principle of referential transparency.

The *modified set* of a function specification consists of those objects that are referenced by expressions occurring in the modifies clause. The *trashed set* of a function specification consists of those objects that are referenced by expressions occurring as arguments to the **trashed** operator in the ensures clause [19, §7.4.1]. For example, the modified and trashed sets for the following specification of **trashSome** are {*a, b, *c}, and {*a, b} respectively.

```
mutable type M;

void trashSome(int *a, M b, int *c) {
  modifies *a,b,*c;
  ensures  (*c)′ = (*c)^ + 1 ∧ trashed(b)
           ∧ (if (*a)^ != (*c)^ then
                then ¬trashed(*a) ∧ (*a)′ = (*c)^
                else trashed(*a));
}
```

As was indicated in Section 4, an object that is a member of the modified set may be either trashed or modified. An object in the modified set is implicitly preserved only if it is not a member of the trashed set. In the **trashSome** example, ***c** is implicitly preserved. Thus, the presence or absence of certain argument expressions (of the **trashed** operator) affects the meaning of the function specification. Since the meaning of a function specification depends on more than the truth or falsity of the ensures clause predicate, this clearly leads to a violation of the principle of referential transparency. To recover referential transparency we need only eliminate that aspect of the semantics that relies on the presence or absence of argument expressions to the **trashed** operator.

An obvious approach to achieving this would preserve the dual role of the modifies clause while eliminating the implicit constraint that objects in the trashed set are implictly preserved. As a consequence of this approach specifiers would have to explicitly indicate when objects are to be preserved. For example, the specification of **trashSome** would have to be rewritten as

```
void trashSome(int *a, M b, int *c) {
  modifies *a,b,*c;
  ensures  (*c)' = (*c)^ + 1 ∧ trashed(b)
           ∧ ¬trashed(*c)
           ∧ (if (*a)^ != (*c)^ then
              then ¬trashed(*a) ∧ (*a)' = (*c)^
              else trashed(*a));
}
```

(Notice the addition to the ensures clause of a predicate asserting that ***c** is not trashed.) In practice, very few functions trash the objects in their modified sets. For example, of the fifty-two functions given in LCL specifications in the Larch book, only two of the thirty-two expressions (that occur in the modifies clauses) are arguments to the **trashed** operator [8]. Thus, requiring an explicit statement of the fact that objects are preserved would (unnecessarily) lengthen specifications; function specifications that are less concise are more difficult to write, understand and maintain.

Fortunately there is a better solution. We suggest the introduction of a trashes clause which is syntactically like the modifies clause except for the leading **trashes** keyword. That is, the trashes clause is optional and when present, it may be followed by the **nothing** keyword, or by a list of lvalues (expressions denoting objects). A function may trash an object if and only if that object is referenced by an expression that occurs in the trashes clause[11]. Thus, the modifies clause recovers its intended role: it identifies which objects may have their values *modified*. The roles of the modifies and trashes clauses are *independent*; an expression may occur in both, in either or neither of the clauses. Under this scheme, the specification of **trashSome** would be identical to its original specification but with the addition of the clause **trashes *a,b**. Most function

[11] Actually, object dependencies must be taken into account for both the modifies and trashes clauses. Details are given in [2].

specifications will be written without a trashes clause, implying that no (client-visible) object may be trashed. For those few functions that do trash objects, these objects will be explicitly identified by listing them in the trashes clause.

6 Conclusion

The specialization of a specification language to a particular programming language is an important characteristic of module interface specification languages (MISL's). The only well-developed MISL's are the Larch interface languages and among these LCL would seem to be the most mature. We have argued that MISL's are an excellent way of introducing formal methods into industrial settings.

We have identified inadequacies and insufficiencies in the LCL language. In particular, by introducing the concept of object dependency we illustrate, by means of realistic examples, that there is a need for LCL language constructs that would allow specifiers to describe and reason about object dependencies. We argue that the meaning of a function specification is affected by implicit parameter constraints that have been poorly documented. These constraints are shown to be problematic—in particular, they are ambiguous and potentially overly constraining. We show that the current definition of the meaning of a function specification relative to trashed and non-trashed objects leads to a violation of the principle of referential transparency.

The version of LCL described in this paper differs from LCL 2.4, principally in that:

- new primitives have been added for describing object dependencies,
- the implicit constraints over pointer and array parameters have been dropped and new language primitives have been added that allow specifiers to assert whether or not an object is active or well-defined,
- a trashes clause has been added to function specification bodies.

These changes increase the expressiveness of LCL and allow us to overcome the identified shortcomings of LCL 2.4. In particular, we eliminate the instance of referential opacity. The shortcomings and solutions documented in this paper, as well as others that require a deeper understanding of the semantics of LCL, are described in detail in [2], which also includes a formal semantics for a core subset of LCL. Finally, we note that the identified shortcomings are not particular to LCL, they are shared by other module interface specification languages.

Acknowledgments

We thank Gary Leavens and David Evans for their comments on an earlier draft of this paper.

References

1. Jonathan Bowen and Mike Hinchey. Ten commandments of formal methods. *IEEE Computer*, 28(4):56–63, April 1995.
2. Patrice Chalin. On the language design and semantic foundation of LCL, a Larch/C interface specification language. CU/DCS TR 95-12, Computer Science Department, Concordia University, December 1995. Ph.D. Thesis.
3. Jolly Chen. The Larch/Generic interface language. S. B. Thesis, Department of Electrical Engineering and Computer Science, MIT, 1989.
4. George W. Ernst, Raymond J. Hookway, and William F. Ogden. Modular verification of data abstractions with shared realizations. *IEEE Transactions on Software Engineering*, 20(4):288–307, April 1994.
5. David Evans. Using specifications to check source code. TR 628, MIT LCS, June 1994. S.M. Thesis.
6. David Evans, John V. Guttag, James J. Horning, and Yang Meng Tan. LCLint: A tool for using specifications to check code. In *Symposium on the Foundations of Software Engineering*, December 1994.
7. John V. Guttag and James J. Horning. LCL: A Larch interface language for C. Technical Report 74, DEC Systems Research Center, July 1991.
8. John V. Guttag and James J. Horning, editors. *Larch: Languages and Tools for Formal Specification*. Texts and Monographs in Computer Science. Springer-Verlag, 1993.
9. C.A.R. Hoare. An overview of some formal methods for program design. *IEEE Computer*, 20(9):85–91, September 1987.
10. Michal Iglewski, Jan Madey, David Lorge Parnas, and Philip C. Kelly. Documentation paradigms. CRL TR 270, McMaster University, July 1993.
11. ISO/IEC 9899 : 1990 (E). *Programming languages—C*.
12. Ann Jackson and Daniel Hoffman. Inspecting module interface specifications. *Software Testing, Verification and Reliability*, 4:101–117, 1994.
13. Cliff B. Jones. *Systematic Software Development using VDM*. Computer Science Series. Prentice Hall International, second edition, 1990.
14. Richard Allen Lerner. *Specifying Objects of Concurrent Systems*. PhD thesis, Carngie Mellon University, May 1991. TR CMU–CS–91–131.
15. Carroll Morgan. *Programming from Specifications*. Computer Science Series. Prentice Hall International, 1990.
16. David Lorge Parnas and Yabo Wang. The trace assertion method of module interface specification. TR 89-261, Queen's University at Kingston (Dept. of Computing and Information Science), 1989.
17. S. Prehn and W.J. Toetenel, editors. *VDM'91: Formal Software Development Methods*, volume 551 of *Lecture Notes in Computer Science*. VDM Europe, Springer-Verlag, 1991. Volume 1: Conference Contributions.
18. J.M. Spivey. *The Z Notation: A Reference Manual*. Computer Science Series. Prentice Hall International, second edition, 1992.
19. Yang Meng Tan. Formal specification techniques for promoting software modularity, enhancing documentation, and testing specifications. TR 619, MIT LCS, June 1994. Ph.D. Thesis.
20. Mark T. Vandevoorde. Exploiting specifications to improve program performance. TR 598, MIT LCS, February 1994. Ph.D. Thesis.
21. Jeannette M. Wing and Amy Moormann Zaremski. Unintrusive ways to integrate formal specifications in practice. In *[17]*, pages 545–569, 1991.

Formal Specification and Verification of the pGVT Algorithm*

Balakrishnan Kannikeswaran, Radharamanan Radhakrishnan, Peter Frey, Perry Alexander, and Philip A. Wilsey

Computer Architecture Design Laboratory, Dept of ECECS, PO Box 210030, University of Cincinnati, Cincinnati, Ohio 45221–0030, phil.wilsey@uc.edu (513) 556–4779 (voice) (513) 556-7326 (fax)

Abstract. The time warp mechanism is a technique for optimistically synchronizing Parallel and distributed Discrete Event-driven Simulators (PDES). Within this synchronization paradigm lie numerous parallel algorithms, chief among them being an estimation of the Global Virtual Time (GVT) value for fossil collection and output commit. Because the optimistic synchronization strategy allows for temporary violations of causal relations in the system being simulated, developing algorithms that correctly estimate GVT can prove extremely difficult. Testing and debugging can also prove difficult as error situations are frequently not repeatable due to varying load conditions and processing orders. Consequently, the application of formal methods to develop and analyze such algorithms are of extreme importance. This paper addresses the application of formal methods for the development of GVT estimation algorithms. More precisely, the paper presents a formal specification for and verification of one specific GVT estimation algorithm, the pGVT algorithm. The specifications are presented in the Larch Shared Language and verification completed using the Larch Proof Assistant. The ultimate goal of this work is to develop a reusable infrastructure for GVT proof development that can be used by developers of new GVT estimation algorithms.

1 Introduction

Discrete event-driven simulation is an important modeling technique used across many disciplines including, to name a few: communication networks, weather prediction, molecular motion, and economic forecasting [8]. While widely used, desires for more accurate results stimulate a need for faster simulator throughput. In response to this need, the simulation community has turned, in part, toward the potential solutions offered by parallel processing (resulting in the emergence of the subfield of Parallel Discrete Event-Driven Simulation or PDES [9]).

* Support for this work was provided in part by the Advanced Research Projects Agency, contracts F33615–93–C–1315 and F33615–93–C–1316 monitored by Wright Laboratory and contract J–FBI–93–116 monitored by the Department of Justice. The authors also wish to thank Wright Labs and ARPA for their continuing support.

Parallel solutions for discrete-event driven simulation can be broadly classified as using either (i) a central event dispatch mechanism [2, 5] or (ii) a distributed event execution mechanism [9, 20]. Modifying sequential simulators for parallel execution using central event dispatch is reasonably simple, but provides only limited speedups. Parallel simulators using distributed control are able to exploit higher degrees of parallelism, but their implementation costs can be high. This is especially true in optimistically synchronized simulators where causality relationships can be violated and then repaired [9, 13]. Decisions about global progress and the satisfaction of termination conditions in such simulations can be difficult to make. Consequently, algorithms for such decisions are frequently difficult to develop, analyze, and test.

At the University of Cincinnati, we have been studying the acceleration of digital system simulation using the time warp optimistic synchronization strategy. As part of our investigations, we have implemented a time warp simulation called WARPED and released it for public use [17, 18]. The WARPED kernel required a five month development time and over half of that time was spent in the development and test of algorithms to solve two problems, namely: decisions about the global progress of the simulation (computing a value called Global Virtual Time, or GVT), and deciding when the simulation had terminated. The difficulty experienced in developing these sections of the WARPED kernel motivated us to consider the use of formal methods for our algorithm development.

This paper presents our experiences using formal methods to develop a specific GVT estimation algorithm called pGVT. In particular, we describe our development of a formal specification and proof for the pGVT algorithm. The algorithm is specified using the Larch Shared Language [11]. This formal specification is then used to prove the correctness of the algorithm by passing the specification through the Larch Prover[2] [10] and establishing that the system GVT increases monotonically. Similar endeveours with formal specification in the distributed environment are being actively pursued by many researchers[16, 21, 23].

The reminder of the paper is organized as follows: Section 2 provides some background information on time warp, the pGVT algorithm, and the WARPED project. Section 3 presents an overview of the Larch Shared Language and the Larch Prover. Section 4 presents the formal specification of the pGVT algorithm. Section 5 contains the proof that the pGVT algorithm works correctly. Sections 6 and 7 contain some concluding remarks and a discussion of assumptions and limitations.

2 Background

2.1 Parallel Simulation and Time Warp

In distributed discrete event driven simulation, a system is generally modeled as a group of communicating entities, referred to here as *Logical Processes* (or LPs). Each LP maintains a local clock that defines the simulation time for that

[2] Please note that in this paper the abbreviation LP does not denote Larch Prover.

LP and the LPs operate as distinct discrete event simulators, exchanging event information as necessary. Synchronization between the LPs can be either *conservative* [3, 9, 20] or *optimistic* [4, 9, 13]. Under conservative synchronization, events are processed by each LP only when it can guarantee that no causality (out of order) violation will occur. In contrast, an optimistically synchronized simulation does not strictly enforce causality constraints; instead, some mechanism to recover from a causality violation is defined. Time warp is an example of an optimistically synchronized parallel simulator.

In time warp any LP with an event to process is allowed to simulate without consideration of the progress of other LPs. Since some LPs will process ahead of others at any given (real) time, simulation time is referred to as *virtual time*, and a given object's simulation time at any given moment is called its *local virtual time* (or LVT) [9, 13]. Furthermore, since each LP simulates asynchronously, it is possible for an LP to receive an event from the past — violating the causality constraints of the simulation. Such messages are referred to as *straggler* messages. In order to recover, the LP receiving the straggler message must *rollback* to an earlier simulation time and reprocess the events in their correct order. To enable rollback, each LP must maintain a history of state and event information (Figure 1). During rollback, an LP must revert to an earlier state and cancel any output events sent while it was doing (possibly) erroneous look-ahead. This cancellation is performed by sending *antimessages* to other LPs who then remove the erroneous event message from their input queue (sometimes causing rollback).

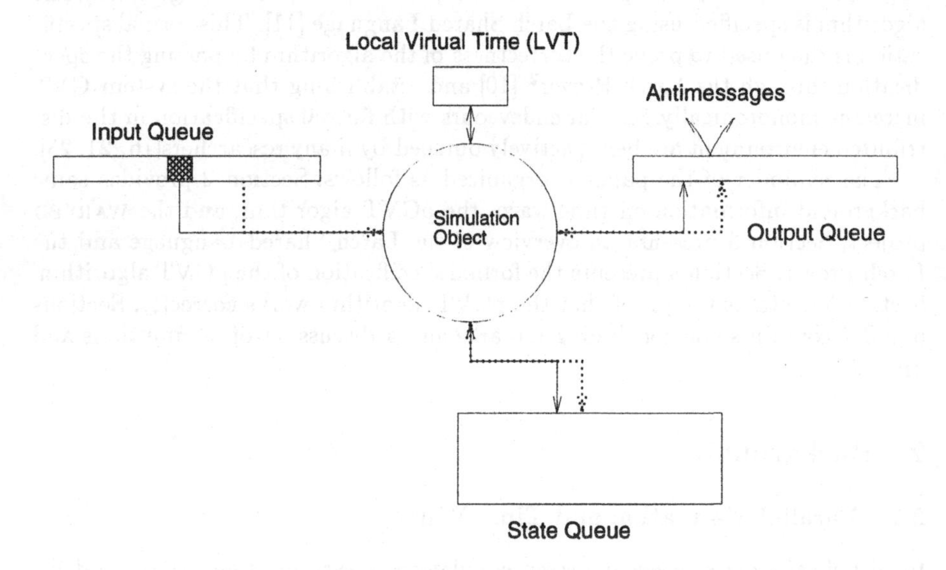

Fig. 1. A Time Warp Simulation Object

One important overhead associated with checkpointing state and event information is the memory space required for the saved data. This space can be freed only when global progress of the simulation advances beyond the (simulation) time at which the saved information is needed. The process of identifying and reclaiming this space is called *fossil collection.* The global time against which fossil collection algorithms operate is called the *global virtual time* (or GVT) and several algorithms for GVT estimation have been proposed [1, 6, 7, 15, 19, 24, 26]. In addition to its use for fossil collection, GVT is also useful for deciding when irrevocable operations (such as I/O) can be performed and, in some instances, when the simulation has completed.

2.2 The pGVT Algorithm

The pGVT algorithm [6, 7] is comprised of two functional elements: (1) the GVT management process; and (2) LGVT (local GVT) value calculation and reporting by the LPs. The GVT manager calculates, maintains, and broadcasts GVT information to LPs. Responsibility for LGVT management is distributed to each LP and is ideally organized to report new LGVT information to the central GVT manager only when failure to do so would inhibit advancement of estimates of GVT. Thus, LPs on the critical path will frequently report new LGVT information to the GVT managers, whereas LPs well in advance of the GVT will report less frequently [7]. This is described more formally below.

A single GVT manager calculates, maintains and broadcasts global GVT information to the LPs. As the LPs report their LGVT values to the GVT manager the information is saved and used to determine new estimates for GVT. When estimates of GVT increase, the GVT manager distributes (for purposes of this paper, broadcasts) this information to the LPs. Included in the GVT broadcasts, the GVT manager also computes and distributes the average rate of increase in the GVT estimates, called ΔGVT. ΔGVT is used by the LPs in determining when to report new LGVT information. More precisely, following the nth GVT broadcast, the GVT manager computes:

$$GVT' = min(\{LGVT\}) \tag{1}$$

$$\Delta GVT = \frac{\sum_{i=n-k}^{n} \Delta GVT_i}{k} \tag{2}$$

where $\{LGVT\}$ is the set containing all reported LGVT values, k is the sample size used for smoothing the ΔGVT values, and ΔGVT_i is the increase in the GVT value in the ith GVT broadcast. The ith discrete increment in the estimated GVT value is denoted ΔGVT_i and the average of the last k increases in GVT estimates is ΔGVT. From these calculations, the GVT manager then broadcasts an ordered pair, $\langle \Delta GVT, GVT' \rangle$, to each LP.

As previously indicated, each LP independently determines when to calculate and report new LGVT information. Ideally, the LPs will report new information only when failure to do so would hinder the advancement of GVT. Thus, messages to report GVT information by each LP are reduced for all LPs except those on the critical path of GVT advancement.[3] The LPs defining the critical path frequently report the GVT information and allow an accurate estimate of GVT. More formally, the LPs report GVT information as follows:

1. Each LP calculates GVT information and saves it in a buffer called LGVT (local GVT). LGVT is the smaller of the minimum timestamp of all unprocessed events in the event queue and the minimum timestamp of all unacknowledged output messages.
2. Each LP maintains a ratio of the (real) time for a message to be sent and acknowledged to the GVT manager (denoted by t_{mesg}) and the average (real) time between successive GVT updates (denoted by ΔRT_i). That is, if K denotes the aforementioned ratio, then on the nth GVT broadcast K is defined as:

$$K = \frac{t_{mesg}}{\frac{\sum_{i=n-k}^{n} \Delta RT_i}{k}} \tag{3}$$

   where k is the sample size for smoothing. K helps trigger the calculation of new LGVT information. Informally, $\lceil K \rceil$ is the number of ΔGVT cycles required to report new information to the GVT manager. Because the time required to report a value from a LP to the GVT manager may vary based on processor localities, K is computed locally.
3. Each LP recalculates and reports new LGVT information whenever:
   (a) The LP receives a straggler message with a timestamp smaller than the current LGVT value. The LP reports the new LGVT value (which will be lesser than or equal to the straggler message time) to the GVT manager before acknowledging receipt of the straggler message. When the GVT manager reports acknowledges the report, the LP acknowledges and processes the straggler message.
   (b) The broadcast GVT value approaches the current LGVT value. Reporting of new LGVT information is triggered following a just-in-time policy to ensure the most aggressive advancement of GVT. More formally, the LP computes (and reports) a new LGVT value whenever:

$$GVT + \lceil K \rceil * \Delta GVT \geq LGVT \tag{4}$$

   holds. Informally, the factor $\lceil K \rceil * \Delta GVT$ denotes the expected increase in the GVT value over the real time interval required to send (and receive acknowledgment of) a message to the GVT manager. If the GVT value plus the expected increase exceeds the last reported LGVT value, a new value for LGVT should be calculated and reported. Failure to do so would likely inhibit the advancement of GVT.

[3] A LP is said to be on the critical path if its reported LGVT value is the minimum of all values thus becoming the new GVT update.

3 An Overview of Larch

Many formal specification languages could have been used to specify the pGVT algorithm. The alternatives considered included Z [25], Larch [11] and CSP [12]. Larch was selected due to tool availability, the two-tiered specification style, and local expertise. Specifications for the pGVT algorithm components were written in the Larch Shared Language (LSL) [11] and verified using the Larch Prover [10].

The Larch style of specification is described as a two-tiered approach because specifications are written using two languages. The lower tier is written using the Larch Shared Language (LSL). LSL is an algebraic specification language that is used to model abstract data types. The functional unit of a LSL specification is the trait. The first line of the trait gives the name of the specification and declares the trait. The reminder of the specification is given in three parts: (1) the `introduces` section defining operation signatures and sorts; (2) the `asserts` section defining axioms over operations; and (3) the `implies` section defining proof obligations.

The `introduces` section specifies the operators by their signatures. A signature defines the sorts for the operator's domain and range. The `asserts` section specifies relationships among the operators using equational logic and induction rules by specifying generators for sorts. Finally, the `implies` section specifies equations that should be provable from the introduces and asserts sections. LSL supports combining specifications through parameterized inclusion much like macro expansion.[4]

A Larch specification's upper tier is an interface specification describing the specified component's interface. Interface specifications are written using a Larch Interface Language (LIL) that is tailor made to represent the target application language's calling conventions and language structures. LSL structures are referenced from LIL specifications providing common structures and behaviors in an application language independent manner. Since the algorithm being specified is written in C++, the Larch/C++ LIL is used for the GVT interface specification. The pGVT algorithm's behavior is specified using LSL making it accessible to any LIL, not simply Larch/C++. As this work deals with the pGVT's correctness independent of the specific Larch/C++ implementation, the interface specifications are not presented here.

The Larch Prover [10] is a proof assistant compatible with the LSL specifications. The equations specified in an LSL asserts section are converted into rewrite rules, deduction rules and induction rules. The Larch Prover allows the user to make conjectures and applies the rules using either forward or backward inferencing techniques. The Larch Prover's primary uses include checking for consistency and theory containment.

[4] LSL contains a number of additional constructs not used in this specification.

4 The Specification of the pGVT Algorithm

The formal specification of the model consists of two parts defining the GVT manager and the simulation model from a logical process view point. This two part approach supports direct representation of the pGVT algorithm's two functional elements described in Section 2.2. The GVT Manager trait specifies GVT calculation and LGVT value update. The trait provides two operations representing these activities for use in the LP specification. The Model trait specifies the behavior of a logical process. This logical process can be any one of the LPs present in the system. The LP model processes messages and interacts with the GVT manager to update its LGVT entry and obtain new values of GVT.

4.1 The GVT Manager

The GVT manager trait defines a GVT manager's behavior. The GVT manager maintains a record of LGVT values for each LP. The interface to the GVT manager consists of function to: (a) update an LP's associated LGVT value and (b) calculate and return GVT.

```
Manager : trait
includes FiniteMap(LPRecords, LPName, LatestLGVT)
includes Natural(LatestLGVT)
introduces
        Mgr            : LPRecords → GVTmgr
        sendGVT        : GVTmgr, LPName, LatestLGVT → GVTmgr
        gvt            : GVTmgr → LatestLGVT
        empty          : → LPInfo
        range          : LatestLGVT, LPInfo → LPInfo
        getrange       : LPRecords → LPInfo
        min_in_range   : LPInfo → LatestLGVT
        min            : LPRecords → LatestLGVT
asserts
  LPInfo generated by empty, getrange
  ∀ LastReportLGVT : LPRecords,
        lgvt1, lgvt2 : LatestLGVT,
        lpname : LPName,
        lpinfo : LPInfo

  gvt(Mgr(LastReportLGVT)) == min(LastReportLGVT);
  sendGVT( Mgr(LastReportLGVT), lpname, lgvt1) ==
      Mgr(update(LastReportLGVT,lpname,lgvt1));
  getrange({}) = empty;
  getrange(update(LastReportLGVT,lpname,lgvt1)) ==
      range(lgvt1,getrange(LastReportLGVT));
  min(LastReportLGVT) == if getrange(LastReportLGVT) ¬= empty
    then
```

```
    min_in_range(getrange(LastReportLGVT))
  else
    0;
 min_in_range(range(lgvt1,lpinfo)) ==
  if lpinfo = empty then
    lgvt1
  else
    if lgvt1 < min_in_range(lpinfo) then
      lgvt1
    else
      min_in_range(lpinfo);
 update(update(LastReportLGVT,lpname,lgvt2),lpname,lgvt1)
   = update(LastReportLGVT,lpname,lgvt1);
 getrange(update(LastReportLGVT,lpname,lgvt1)) ¬= empty
implies
 ∀ LastReportLGVT : LPRecords, lgvt1 : LatestLGVT, lpname : LPName
 lgvt1 ≥ min(LastReportLGVT) ⇒
  gvt(sendGVT(Mgr(LastReportLGVT), lpname, lgvt1))
    ≥ gvt(Mgr(LastReportLGVT) );
```

Manager Trait Operators A GVT manager is represented by sort *GVTmgr* generated by the operator Mgr. Its principle data structure is a finite map from each LP name to that LP's most recently reported LGVT. This finite map is updated when a new LGVT is reported by any LP.

Two operators are specified to update the LGVT map and obtain a new GVT value from a GVT manager. The sendGVT operator updates the value of an LGVT value stored in the GVT manager. The operator's domain is a 3-tuple, $\langle GVTmgr, LPName, LatestLGVT\rangle$, where *GVTmgr* is the current state of the GVT manager, *LPName* represents the logical process in question and *LatestLGVT* represents the new LGVT. The gvt operator is used to get the current GVT value from a GVT manager. GVT is obtained by applying the operator gvt to the GVT manager (*GVTmgr*). These two operators define the external interface of a GVT manager allowing updates to stored LGVT values and GVT value retrieval.

GVT Manager Axioms Updating an LGVT value in the GVT manager is represented as a finite map update for the LP in question. The update function is defined in the finite map trait and simply referenced in the single sendGVT axiom:

```
sendGVT(Mgr(LastReportLGVT),lpname,lgvt1) ==
                    Mgr(update(LastReportLGVT,lpname,lgvt1));
```

The system GVT is simply the minimum LGVT in the finite map maintained by the GVT manager. Thus, gvt is defined:

```
gvt(Mgr(LastReportLGVT)) == min(LastReportLGVT);
```

The minimum value in the finite map is found by obtaining its range and searching it for the minimum value.

```
min(LastReportLGVT) == if getrange(LastReportLGVT) ¬= empty then
  min_in_range(getrange(LastReportLGVT))
else
  0;
```

The check for an empty range exists because it is possible to have no LPs, leading to an empty map with an empty range. In the case of an empty map, GVT will not change and remains equal to zero.

The operator **min_in_range** is recursively defined as follows:

```
min_in_range(range(lgvt1,lpinfo)) ==
  if lpinfo = empty then
    lgvt1
  else
    if lgvt1 < min_in_range(lpinfo) then
      lgvt1
    else
      min_in_range(lpinfo);
```

This simple specification does a linear search for the minimum value in *lpinfo*.

The operator **getrange** maps the domain of a finite map to a range set. An empty map results in an empty range.

```
getrange({}) = empty;
getrange(update(LastReportLGVT,lpname,lgvt1)) ==
  range(lgvt1,getrange(LastReportLGVT));
```

getrange builds the range set recursively stepping through the finite map entries. If the finite map is not empty, the range is the value of the mapping function (the map entry, lgvt1) and the range of the rest of the finite map.

The following two domain axioms are added to support the Larch Proof assistant.

1. If a range value in the finite map is updated, it can be replaced by only the new value.

   ```
   update(update(LastReportLGVT,lpname,lgvt2),lpname,lgvt1) =
     update(LastReportLGVT,lpname,lgvt1);
   ```

2. A finite map with at least one entry cannot be empty.

   ```
   getrange(update(LastReportLGVT,lpname,lgvt1)) ¬= empty
   ```

4.2 Modeling the LPs

The logical process model defines a logical process's behavior. Each logical process communicates with the GVT manager by: (a) sending a new LGVT value; or (b) receiving a new GVT value. Thus, the interaction between an LP and the manager is completely defined by the two interface operators defined in the Manager trait. Using the Manager trait is a simple matter of including the trait in the LP specification.

```
Model : trait
includes Manager

introduces
  LP : LatestLGVT, GVTmgr → LPName
  check: LPName → LPName
  work: LPName → LPName
  progress: SystemState → SystemState
  state: SystemState, LPName → SystemState
  start : → SystemState
  straggler : SystemState → Bool
  stragglertime : SystemState → LatestLGVT
  rollback : SystemState, LatestLGVT, GVTmgr → SystemState
  MGR : SystemState → GVTmgr
  time: SystemState → LatestLGVT
  delta :→ LatestLGVT
asserts
  SystemState generated by state, start
  ∀ lpname : LPName,
      lgvt1, lgvt2 : LatestLGVT,
      mgr,curmgr : GVTmgr,
      LastReportLGVT : LPRecords,
      systemstate : SystemState

    progress(start) == state(start, LP(gvt(mgr), mgr));
    progress(state(systemstate,lpname)) ==
      if straggler(state(systemstate,lpname)) then
        rollback(state(systemstate,lpname),
          stragglertime(state(systemstate,lpname)),
          MGR(state(systemstate,lpname)))
      else
        state(state(systemstate,lpname),check(work(lpname)));

    stragglertime(state(systemstate,LP(lgvt1,mgr))) < lgvt1;
    stragglertime(systemstate) ≥ gvt(MGR(systemstate));

    rollback(state(systemstate,LP(lgvt1,mgr)),lgvt2,curmgr) ==
      if lgvt1 > lgvt2 then
        rollback(systemstate,lgvt2, curmgr)
      else
        state(systemstate,LP(lgvt1,
              sendGVT(curmgr,LP(lgvt1,mgr), lgvt1)));
```

```
    work(LP(lgvt1,mgr)) == LP(succ(lgvt1),mgr);
    check(LP(lgvt1, mgr)) ==
      if (gvt(mgr)+delta) > lgvt1 then
        LP(lgvt1, sendGVT(mgr,LP(lgvt1,mgr),lgvt1))
      else
        LP(lgvt1, mgr);

    MGR(state(systemstate, LP(lgvt1, mgr))) = mgr;
    time(state(systemstate,LP(lgvt1, mgr))) = lgvt1;

    gvt(MGR(start)) = time(start);
    time(progress(start)) ≤ time(state(systemstate,lpname));
    gvt(MGR(start)) ≤  gvt(MGR(progress(start)));
implies
  ∀ systemstate1,systemstate2 : SystemState
    time(systemstate1) ≥ gvt(MGR(systemstate1))
    progress(systemstate1) = systemstate2 ⇒
      gvt(MGR(systemstate1)) ≤ gvt(MGR(systemstate2))
```

The LP Model Trait Operators The basic model construct is the logical process. It is obtained using the operator LP with range *LPName* and domain $\langle LatestLGVT, GVTmgr\rangle$, where *LatestLGVT* represents the current LGVT value of the logical process and *GVTmgr* represents the GVT manager.

To model the progress of the GVT algorithm, modeling system state and change of state is necessary. The sort state consists of the tuple ⟨*SystemState*, *LPName*⟩ and stores the history of a simulation. To allow a proof by induction on the states, the initial state, start, is defined. The operator progress allows reference to the history of simulation states.

The operator check is a mapping from one logical process to another. It checks the conditions for LGVT update and changes the GVT manager's value if necessary.

In order to specify logical process execution, the operator work is defined. It maps one logical process to another and abstractly represents the change in LP state resulting from execution. The specifics of the state change are immaterial to this verification effort — only that the state changes need be represented. The only assumption made is that work increases the LPs LGVT value representing "positive" work.

Additional operators are introduced to specify the special simulation properties. A straggler operator is a mapping from a system state to a boolean type. The boolean variable indicates whether a straggler message has been processed. The operator stragglertime accesses the straggler message's arrival time. This time is used in the rollback operator, along with the present state and a reference to the GVT manager, to model rollback to an earlier state. Rollback is the inverse of work. The state change it produces always causes LGVT to decrease.

Two operators are defined to access the fields of a logical process state. MGR relates the GVT manager with its current state. The operator time references the LGVT of the state.

Finally, the operator **delta** represents passage of a small simulation time interval that represents the value calculated by Equation 3.

Model Trait Axioms The system is represented by states described by the **state** sort. To prove characteristics over system progress, proof by induction over states is necessary. The following axiom specifies the initial state:

```
progress(start) == state(start, LP(gvt(mgr), mgr));
```

The initial condition occurs when the logical process's LGVT is equal to the GVT held by the GVT manager. A change in state (progress) is modeled as shown below:

```
progress(state(systemstate,lpname)) ==
  if straggler(state(systemstate,lpname)) then
    rollback(state(systemstate,lpname),
     stragglertime(state(systemstate,lpname)),
     MGR(state(systemstate,lpname)))
  else
    state(state(systemstate,lpname),check(work(lpname)));
```

Note that the LP changes state in two ways. Either a straggler message arrives and the state is rolled back, or a logical process proceeds with its task.

The operator **straggler** is used in the **progress** operator definition. The straggler operator is an abstraction used to denote the fact that, the LP under consideration could have received this straggler message from any other LP in the system. Thus the whole system is modelled, by just focussing on any LP. If a straggler occurs, the following two statements determine the rollback time.

```
stragglertime(state(systemstate,LP(lgvt1,mgr))) < lgvt1;
stragglertime(systemstate) ≥ gvt(MGR(systemstate));
```

If a straggler message arrives, the straggler's event time is less than the LP's LGVT. In addition the event time must be greater than or equal to the GVT. Because all states up to the state whose LGVT is equal to the GVT are stored, rollback to a previous state is possible. This characteristic is asserted in the following axiom:

```
rollback(state(systemstate,LP(lgvt1,mgr)),lgvt2,curmgr) ==
  if lgvt1 > lgvt2 then
    rollback(systemstate,lgvt2, curmgr)
  else
    state(systemstate,LP(lgvt1,sendGVT(curmgr,LP(lgvt1,mgr), lgvt1)));
```

Although this appears to be an extremely strong assertion, it simply states that if a straggler arrives and GVT is managed correctly, stored state information can reconstruct the state when the straggler message should have arrived.

As long as the time of the previous state is greater than straggler time, rollback continues. When the state time is less than the straggler time, processing can continue as a state prior to message arrival has been reconstructed. This state's time is the rollback time. As mentioned in the algorithm 2.2, the rollback time must be reported to the GVT manager as the LP's current LGVT.

The following axioms model the internal behavior of a logical process.

```
work(LP(lgvt1,mgr)) == LP(succ(lgvt1),mgr);
```

The operator **work** describes forward progress from the logical process's point of view. When a logical process has done work, it increases its LGVT. The operator **check**, however has to determine whether the LGVT has reached the boundary described in Equation 4.If the condition is true, the logical process must report its LGVT to the GVT manager. Otherwise the logical process simply advances:

```
check(LP(lgvt1, mgr)) ==
  if (gvt(mgr)+delta) > lgvt1
    then LP(lgvt1, sendGVT(mgr,LP(lgvt1,mgr),lgvt1))
    else LP(lgvt1, mgr);
```

As described before, two accessor operators are defined. **MGR** accesses the GVT manager for the current state and **time** accesses the current state's LGVT.

```
MGR(state(systemstate, LP(lgvt1, mgr))) = mgr;
time(state(systemstate, LP(lgvt1, mgr))) = lgvt1;
```

The following auxiliary axioms state basic truths necessary for the proof process. They define characteristics of **time** and **gvt** in the initial state. Specifically, **time** and **gvt** in the initial state represent minimum values for each. These assertions are necessary for proof by induction.

1. The system's initial condition asserts that GVT and LGVT are initially the same for all logical processes.

   ```
   gvt(MGR(start)) = time(start);
   ```

2. A state's time will never be less than the initial state's time:

   ```
   time(progress(start)) ≤ time(state(systemstate,lpname));
   ```

3. GVT is never less than GVT in the initial state:

   ```
   gvt(MGR(start)) ≤ gvt(MGR(progress(start)));
   ```

5 The Correctness Proof

The pGVT algorithm is operating correctly when GVT monotonically increases. Each increase in GVT value represents movement forward in simulation time and thus progress towards a completed simulation. Although individual LPs may rollback, GVT should never decrease as it represents a lower floor for LGVT values. Allowing GVT to decrease causes the entire system to rollback eliminating the guarantee that "progress" is being made. Furthermore, since GVT is used for fossil collection, allowing GVT to decrease violates the assumption that throwing away information from states earlier than GVT is desirable.

The proof for this obligation is decomposed into 3 subproofs: (1) prove that GVT always increases and is calculated correctly if new LGVT values exceed GVT; (2) prove that in any state, the LGVT is always higher than the last GVT; and (3) using results from (1) and (2), show that GVT increases monotonically. Formally, the three proof obligations become:

```
(1) lgvt1 ≥ min(LastReportLGVT) ⇒
      gvt(sendGVT(Mgr(LastReportLGVT), lpname, lgvt1))
         ≥ gvt(Mgr(LastReportLGVT));
(2) time(systemstate1) ≥ gvt(MGR(systemstate1));
(3) progress(systemstate1) = systemstate2 ⇒
      gvt(MGR(systemstate1)) ≤ gvt(MGR(systemstate2));
```

5.1 Proving Conditional Monotonic GVT Increase

The primary focus of this proof is showing that the GVT manager must either make progress or maintain GVT. This represents the overall proof obligation — unfortunately it cannot be proven directly. What is shown initially is that the GVT manager definition guarantees that GVT monotonically increases given that all new LGVT values are greater than GVT. This obligation is modeled by the following Larch proposition:

```
lgvt1 ≥ min(LastReportLGVT)  ⇒
  gvt(sendGVT(Mgr(LastReportLGVT), lpname, lgvt1))
     ≥  gvt(Mgr(LastReportLGVT));
```

The proof obligation states simply that if all reported LGVT values increase, then GVT also increases or stays the same.

The prover initially tries to prove the propositions using existing axioms, formulas and rewrite rules in combination with the default proof methods. In this case, the prover does not have enough knowledge to select a more powerful proof method. Thus, the following directives are supplied by the user to the Larch Proof Assistant:

1. To reduce the complexity of the current conjecture, the formula

   ```
   Manager.5: getrange(update(LastReportLGVT, lpname, lgvt1))
                = range(lgvt1, getrange(LastReportLGVT))
   ```

   was applied to the conjecture. The command issued by the user is

   ```
   rewrite conjecture with Manager.5
   ```

2. After analyzing the conjecture, two range cases were found - either the number of logical processes is equal to 0 or greater than 0. Hence the following command was used to continue using a proof by cases:

```
resume by cases getrange(LastReportLGVT) = empty
```

The prover continues by attempting to prove a conjecture representing each case. A third obligation, proving the two cases cover all possibilities, is discharged automatically by the prover.

3. Next, the proof continues by implication using the following LP command:

```
resume by ⇒
```

4. Finally another proof by cases is attempted. This time the proof is generated for the case when *lgvt1* is less than the minimum value. The subproof is generated by the statement:

```
resume by cases
  lgvt1c ⊖ min_in_range(getrange(LastReportLGVTc)) = 0
  ∧  ¬(lgvt1c = min_in_range(getrange(LastReportLGVTc)))
```

The final command causes the proof to complete and the original proposition becomes a theorem for use in later proofs. Thus, we know that GVT always increases if new LGVT values increase.

Larch Prover instructions for the complete proof have the following form:

```
% Conjecture:
%  lgvt1 ≥ min(LastReportLGVT) ⇒
%    gvt(sendGVT(Mgr(LastReportLGVT), lpname, lgvt1))
%       ≥ gvt(Mgr(LastReportLGVT) );
% Proof steps:

    rewrite con with Manager.5
      % (get rid of update
      %  transform getrange into the range )

    resume by cases
      % (Either LPs exist or they don't)
      %  getrange(LastReportLGVT) = empty)

    resume by ⇒
      % (Assuming that the input is correct then the result
      %  is also)

    resume by cases
      % (for send time
      %  lgvt1c ⊖ min_in_range(getrange(LastReportLGVTc)) = 0
      %  ∧  ¬(lgvt1c = min_in_range(getrange(LastRepcrtLGVTc)))
```

5.2 Proving LGVT Less Than GVT

The second subproof conjecture is that the LGVT of any state will always be greater than or equal to the present GVT. The Larch statement representing this hypothesis is:

```
time(systemstate1) ≥ gvt(MGR(systemstate1))
```

After the transformation into the Larch Prover, the following steps guide the Larch Prover:

1. Because the statement has to hold for all possible states of the logical process, a proof by induction over states is required. The Larch Prover command to attempt a proof by induction is as follows:

   ```
   resume by induction on systemstate1
   ```

2. A close examination of the new conjecture shows that the present set of rewrite rules should be enough to prove the conjecture. In order to repeatedly apply the rewrite rules, the critical-pairs command is used to apply Knuth-Bendix [14] completion over a subset of assertions:

   ```
   critical-pairs Model* with Model*
   ```

The result is that for all LP states, LGVT is greater than or equal to GVT. Using this result and properties of work and rollback, it will be shown that LGVT associated with every next state is also greater than GVT. Thus, successive GVT values are greater than or equal to old GVT values.

5.3 Proving GVT Progress

Progress from one state to another implies that the GVT of the new state must be greater than or equal to the GVT of the old state. Because progress is defined on the state of a logical process, logical processes that make progress guarantee the growth of the GVT. This is represented by the following Larch conjecture:

```
progress(systemstate1) = systemstate2 ⇒
  gvt(MGR(systemstate1)) ≤ gvt(MGR(systemstate2))
```

Two occurrences cause an LP to change state: (1) normal forward processing (or work); or (2) processing straggler messages (or rollback). Recall that the definition of progress indicates when work or rollback applies. In either case, progress generates a new state. Using a proof by cases, it is shown that regardless of how the state changes, GVT will either change positively or not at all. The steps to aid the Larch Proof Assistant are:

1. Stating the proof obligation over state transitions allows proof by induction over states. This is written as follows:

   ```
   resume by induction on systemstate1
   ```

2. A proof by cases is attempted to show that in any state the logical process can either move forward (work) or receive a straggler message (rollback). To achieve this proof, LP is given the following command:

```
resume by cases straggler(state(systemstate1c, lpname))
```

3. Careful evaluation of the conjecture reveals that existing rewrite rules can prove the conjecture directly. However the `critical-pairs` command needs to be applied twice, because it halts after a first partial proof.

```
critical-pairs Model* with Model*
```

Larch Prover code for the final two proof obligations has the following form:

```
% Conjecture time(systemstate1) ≥ gvt(MGR(systemstate1))
% Steps :
   resume by induction on systemstate1
   critical-pairs Model* with Model*
   qed

% After stating the above axiom as a theorem we prove the following.
% Conjecture: progress(systemstate1) = systemstate2 ⇒
%             gvt(MGR(systemstate1)) ≤ gvt(MGR(systemstate2))
% Steps :
   resume by induction on systemstate1
   resume by cases straggler(state(systemstate1c, lpstate))
   critical-pairs Model* with Model*
   critical-pairs Model* with Model*
   qed
```

This completes the proof of the desired conjecture. Specifically that GVT monotonically increases over a set of simulation states. Because GVT monotonically increases and represents a floor for LGVT, discarding LP state information prior to GVT is a legitimate and correct fossil collection algorithm.

6 Limitations and Assumptions

6.1 Perfect Communication

This model specifies a pGVT algorithm under the assumption that message passing between the GVT manager and the logical processes is a single, perfect message. The actual algorithm specifies a handshaking protocol implemented using acknowledgment messages. The current specification does not model the acknowledgment process. The assumption is made that when a logical process or the GVT manager sends a message to another logical process or GVT manager the sender waits until an acknowledgment is received.

6.2 Simulation Progress

It should be noted that successive values of GVT are guaranteed to be greater than or equal to the previous GVT value. There is no guarantee that GVT ever increases. It is possible for a simulation to maintain a single GVT value indefinitely. Showing that GVT always increases is a desirable result, but it is impossible without knowing the internal details of the LPs. It can be concluded that if all LPs' LGVT values increase, then GVT will increase. Thus, if LPs make progress, the overall system will make progress.

7 Conclusions

Parallel processing promises to deliver performance improvement needed for large modeling efforts using discrete event simulation. However, this promise requires solutions of distributed synchronization that can be difficult to deliver. This is especially true with optimistic synchronization techniques where algorithm developers must deal with non-repeatable behaviors and transient error situations. In such environments traditional testing and path analysis fails and the designer must turn to other methods for algorithm design and analysis. One possible solution is the application of formal methods for specification and proof. From this context, we have pursued the application of formal methods for two important subproblems of a time warp simulator. The first addressed the problem of demonstrating correct LP behavior and event commitment [22]. The second, described herein, addresses the problem of global time management — specifically the estimation of GVT advancement with the pGVT [7] algorithm.

In this paper, a formal specification for the pGVT algorithm has been presented with an automated formal proof that GVT increases monotonically. Although the specifications and proof are important results in themselves, this activity represents a pragmatic application of formal verification to a realistic algorithm. The pGVT algorithm is a commonly used parallel simulation algorithm and represents much more than a "toy" analysis problem. The specifications were written and verified by formal methods practitioners working with experts in parallel simulation.

One gain of this effort was the knowledge that a formal specification of an algorithm is not as daunting as it seems and as an end result, the specifiers and readers of the proof have a more precise understanding of the algorithm. The result of this exercise ultimately led to a clean interface and well structured implementation of the algorithm in the WARPED kernel [18].

Lastly, the chief final objective of this effort is the development for a proof infrastructure to support reasoning about various alternative algorithms for GVT estimation. More precisely, we hope to develop a framework for GVT proof that will support and simplify the work required by future designers of GVT algorithms.

References

1. Bauer, H., and Sporrer, C. Distributed logic simulation and an approach to asynchronous GVT-calculation. In *6th Workshop on Parallel and Distributed Simulation* (January 1992), Society for Computer Simulation, pp. 205–208.

2. Blank, T. A survey of hardware accelerators used in computer-aided design. *IEEE Design and Test of Computers 1*, 4 (August 1984), 21–39.
3. Chandy, K. M., and Misra, J. Asynchronous distributed simulation via a sequence of parallel computations. *Communications of the ACM 24*, 11 (April 1981), 198–206.
4. Chandy, K. M., and Sherman, R. Space-time and simulation. In *Distributed Simulation* (1989), Society for Computer Simulation, pp. 53–57.
5. Denneau, M., Kronstadt, E., and Pfister, G. Design and implementation of a software simulation engine. *Computer-Aided Design 15*, 3 (May 1983), 123–130.
6. D'Souza, L. M. Global virtual time estimation algorithms in optimistically synchronized distributed discrete event driven simulation. Master's thesis, University of Cincinnati, Cincinnati, Ohio, May 1994.
7. D'Souza, L. M., Fan, X., and Wilsey, P. A. pGVT: An algorithm for accurate GVT estimation. In *Proc. of the 8th Workshop on Parallel and Distributed Simulation (PADS 94)* (July 1994), Society for Computer Simulation, pp. 102–109.
8. Fishwick, P. A. *Simulation Model Design and Execution: Building Digital Worlds.* Prentice Hall, Englewood Cliffs, NJ, 1995.
9. Fujimoto, R. Parallel discrete event simulation. *Communications of the ACM 33*, 10 (October 1990), 30–53.
10. Garland, S. J., and Guttag, J. V. A guide to LP, the Larch Prover. Tech. rep., TR 82, DEC/SRC, December 1991.
11. Guttag, J. V., and Horning, J. J. *Larch: Languages and Tools for Formal Specification.* Springer-Verlag, New York, NY, 1993.
12. Hoare, C. A. R. *Communicating Sequential Processes.* Prentice-Hall, Englewood Cliffs, 1985.
13. Jefferson, D. Virtual time. *ACM Transactions on Programming Languages and Systems 7*, 3 (July 1985), 405–425.
14. Knuth, D. E., and Bendix, P. B. Simple word problems in universal algebras. In *Computational Problems in Abstract Algebra*, J. Leech, Ed. Pergamon Press, 1970.
15. Lin, Y.-B., and Lazowska, E. Determining the global virtual time in a distributed simulation. In *1990 International Conference on Parallel Processing* (1990), pp. III-201–III-209.
16. Lincoln, P., and Rushby, J. Formal verification of an algorithm for interactive consistency under a hybrid fault model. In *Computer-Aided Verification, CAV'93* (June/July 1993), C. Courcoubetis, Ed., vol. 697 of *Lecture Notes in Computer Science*, Springer-Verlag, pp. 292–304.
17. Martin, D. E., McBrayer, T., and Wilsey, P. A. warped: A time warp simulation kernel for analysis and application development, 1995. (available on the www at `http://www.ece.uc.edu/~paw/warped/`).
18. Martin, D. E., McBrayer, T. J., and Wilsey, P. A. warped: A time warp simulation kernel for analysis and application development. In *29th Hawaii International Conference on System Sciences (HICSS-29)* (January 1996). (forthcoming).
19. Mattern, F. Effecient algorithms for distributed snapshots and global virtual time approximation. *Journal of Parallel and Distributed Computing 18*, 4 (August 1993), 423–434.
20. Misra, J. Distributed discrete-event simulation. *Computing Surveys 18*, 1 (March 1986), 39–65.

21. Owre, S., Rushby, J., Shankar, N., and von Henke, F. Formal verification for fault-tolerant architectures: Prolegomena to the design of pvs. *IEEE Transactions on Software Engineering 27(2)* (February 1995), 107–125.
22. Penix, J., Alexander, P., Martin, D., and Wilsey, P. A. Formal specification and partial verification of LVT in a time warp simulation kernel, 1995.
23. Rushby, J. A formally verified algorithm for clock synchronization under a hybrid fault model. *13th ACM Symposium on Principles of Distributed Computing(PODC'94)* (August 1994), 304–313.
24. Samadi, B. *Distributed Simulation, Algorithms and Performance Analysis.* PhD thesis, Computer Science Department, University of California, Los Angeles, CA, 1985.
25. Spivey, J. M. *Understanding Z: A Specification Language and its Formal Semantics.* Cambridge University Press, Cambridge, 1988.
26. Tomlinson, A. I., and Garg, V. K. An algorithm for minimally latent global virtual time. In *Proc of the 7th Workshop on Parallel and Distributed Simulation (PADS)* (July 1993), Society for Computer Simulation, pp. 35–42.

Automatic Verification of a Hydroelectric Power Plant[1]

Rosario Pugliese
Dip. di Scienze dell'Informazione
Università di Roma "La Sapienza"
via Salaria, 113, 00198 Roma, Italy
`pugliese@dsi.uniroma1.it`

Enrico Tronci
Dip. di Matematica Pura ed Appl.
Università di L'Aquila
Coppito, 67100 L'Aquila, Italy
`tronci@univaq.it`

Abstract. We analyze the specification of a hydroelectric power plant by ENEL (the Italian Electric Company). Our goal is to show that for the specification of the plant (its control system in particular) some given properties hold.
We were provided with an informal specification of the plant. From such informal specification we wrote a formal specification using the CCS/Meije process algebra formalism. We defined properties using μ-calculus. Automatic verification was carried out using model checking. This was done by translating our process algebra definitions (the model) and μ-calculus formulas into BDDs.
In this paper we present the informal specification of the plant, its formal specification, some of the properties we verified and experimental results.

1 Introduction

Computer controlled systems are more and more widespread. In safety critical applications this situation calls for formal verification of correctness with respect to the given specifications. Because of the cost of modifying the finished product it is essential that design errors are detected as early as possible in the design process. For this reason formal verification is also used to guarantee that for the specification of the plant some given properties hold.

Development of formal methods should go hand in hand with realistic case studies. Case studies are useful to assess the applicability of a verification technique and to guide research on new verification techniques.

In this paper we report on the analysis of a hydroelectric power plant by ENEL (the Italian Electric Company). Our goal is to guarantee that for the specification of the plant some given properties hold. We were provided with an informal specification of the plant [ENEL 92]. From this we derived a formal specification written using the CCS/Meije [AB 84] process algebra formalism. A previous version of such a formal specification was given in [LP 94]. To define properties we used μ-calculus (see, e.g., [BCMDH 92]) since it is a clean and expressive logic. Automatic verification was carried out using model checking.

[1] This work has been partially supported by the EUROFORM network and MURST funds.

This was done by translating process algebra definitions (the model) and μ-calculus formulas into Binary Decision Diagrams (BDDs, see [Bry 86]).

In this paper we present the informal specification of the plant, part of its formal specification, some of the properties we verified and experimental results. A full version of the formal specification is in [PT 95].

The main difficulties we had to face were: ambiguities in the informal specification and state explosion (our system has about 10^{52} states).

We succeeded in automatically verifying relevant properties of the formal specification. Our experiments were carried out on a SUN Sparc LX with 72MB RAM. Verification required building BDDs with up to $2 \cdot 10^6$ vertices. We needed 174 boolean variables to code the state of the system and 15 boolean variables to code the actions of the system. Thus the transition relation *(present state, action, next state)* of the overall system had 363 boolean variables. We did not have problems in building such transition relation, but its size forced us to be very careful during verification. In particular to avoid running out of memory during automatic verification a careful choice of the logic formula representing the property we wanted to verify was necessary.

The rest of the paper is organized as follows. In section 2 we give an informal description of the plant. In section 3, using CCS/Meije, we present a formal description of part of the plant. In section 4 we give μ-formulas for some of the formal properties we verified. In section 5 we give experimental results. In appendix A we define the syntax and sketch the operational semantics of CCS/Meije.

2 The case study: an informal description

Our reactive system is composed of a hydroelectric power plant and its control system. The control system drives the engines producing electrical power, handles the basin sluices, checks for safe working of the plant and monitors the water level in the basin. Moreover the control system interacts with an operator which solves by hand critical situations arising in the plant administration. The informal specification of the overall system was provided by ENEL (the Italian Electric Company) in [ENEL 92]. Such informal specification was quite ambiguous and incomplete. Since we wanted to study the power of CCS/Meije as a specification methodology we simplified the original specification by using small abstract domains as data values. Ambiguities were also removed. Nevertheless the resulting case study is meaningful and nontrivial. In the rest of this section we present such simplified version of the original specification provided by ENEL.

The environment of the *control system* includes a *hydroelectric power plant*, an *operator* and the aspects of the *surrounding environment* that have a prominent influence on the plant. The plant is composed of a *catch basin* and a *power plant.* The power plant is composed of *energy production engines* and a *penstock* to ensure a pressurized water flow from the basin to the power plant. Each *energy production engine* has a *generator* and an embedded *controller.*

The power plant can be directed by the operator (*manual administration*) or by the control system (*automatic administration*). The main goals of the control system are:

- Managing hydraulic resources so that the plant produces as much power as possible;
- Obtaining the best efficiency from production engines during daily production periods (which, in turn, are transmitted by the operator);
- Saving up hydraulic power outside of daily production periods without violate plant constraints (e.g. do not exceed minimum and maximum levels in the basin).

The control system achieves these goals by interacting with the power production engines and the basin sluices. In the following, we will ignore the interaction with the sluices and we will only concentrate on interaction with the production engines.

2.1 The catch basin

The shape and dimensions of the basin are known and, for the sake of simplicity, we will suppose that the water volume fluctuation can be computed by means of the water level fluctuation, that, in turn, is evaluated by means of a *transducer*. Hence, in the following, we will make no distinction between water volume or level in the basin. Water level increases due to rain and inflow of water through affluents. It decreases due to overflow from barrages and outflow through the penstock connecting the basin to the engines. Some water levels have a particular importance for the working of the plant. They are:

VMS (*) overflowing level;
VML maximum working level;
INT_1 (*) maximum working level when the transducer is broken;
INT_2 (*) minimum working level when the transducer is broken;
Vml minimum working level;
VMIN (*) minimum capacity level.

Some *sensors* send signals to the control system when one of the levels labelled with * is reached by the surface of water. When the transducer is broken it is possible to control the plant, even if in a less accurate way, using such sensors.

2.2 The hydroelectric power plant

The hydroelectric power plant is formed by some energy production engines, each of which contains a generator and an embedded controller.

The generator A generator is characterized by a finite state automaton whose states can be partioned into two classes: stable states and unstable states. Here are the generator states accordingly to such partition.

- *stable states*:
  S (stopped): the generator is stopped;
  G (generating): the generator is working;
  Bt (temporary block): the generator is blocked because of a fault that can be automatically removed (i.e. without the intervention of the operator);
  Bp (persistent block): the generator is blocked because of a failure that only the operator can fix. After removing such failure the operator has to restart the generator and signal to the control system that recovery has taken place.
- *unstable states*:
  sTg: transition state from **S** to **G** (representing the situation in which the generator is going from state **S** (stopped) to state **G** (working));
  gTs: transition state from **G** to **S** (representing the situation in which the generator is going from state **G** (working) to state **S** (stopped));
  gTbt: transition state from **G** to **Bt** (representing the situation in which the generator is going from state **G** (working) to state **Bt** (temporary block));
  gTbp: transition state from **G** to **Bp** (representing the situation in which the generator is going from state **G** (working) to state **Bp** (persistent block)).

To each generator the control system can send two kind of commands:

- *state commands*: **start/halt** to change the state of the generator;
- *position commands*: **inc/dec** to increase/decrease electric power production.

During the generation phase (state **G**), a generator may produce different amounts of power at different times, accordingly to the energy production plan. The working point of a generator can be adjusted on different positions. Each position selects a different amount of water intake and thus a different amount of power that can be produced in a period of time.
A generator can make the following transitions:

- from **S** to **sTg** when it receives **start** and from **sTg** to **G** when the command is executed;
- from **G** to **gTs** when it receives **halt** and from **gTs** to **S** when the command is executed;
- from **G** to **gTbt** when a temporary fault occurs and from **gTbt** to **Bt** when the generator stops;
- from **G** to **gTbp** when a failure whose repairing needs the operator intervention occurs and from **gTbp** to **Bp** when the generator gets stuck because of such failure;
- from **Bt** to **S** when the trouble causing the block disappears;
- from **Bp** to **S** when the operator has repaired the blocked generator.

The controller The controller behaves as a transparent interface between the control system and the generator. Indeed, the control system sends a command to the controller and this one transmits the command to the related generator and sends to the control system one of the following signals:

- The generator state is changing (until the expected state is reached). This happens when the generator has received a command asking for a change of state.
- The generator has not correctly changed its generation position. This happens when the generator has received a command asking for a change in the generation position and the generator has not successfully executed it.

The controller accepts and sends one command at a time. Moreover, for hydraulic reasons, the control system can send only one kind of command (change state or change position) at a time. This means that at most one generator at a time may execute a command to change state and at most one generator at a time may execute a command to change position.

With respect to the control system, the controller appears in one of two possible states:

- *available*, when it is prepared to automatic administration: it accepts commands from the control system and transmits them to the generator;
- *nonavailable*, when the generator is directed by the operator or a (temporary or persistent) block happened: in such a case the controller will ignore the commands from the control system.

Interactions between power production engines, control system and operator The control system handles the generator and its controller as one single entity. That is the control system interacts only with the controller which then transmits commands to the generator.

A production engine goes from the state nonavailable to the state available when the controller receives an automatic administration signal and no block (temporary or persistent) occurred. A production engine goes from available to nonavailable when a manual administration signal arrives or a block occurs.

After a temporary block, a generator is available again as soon as a variation in the storage curve (see section 2.3: Governing task) is expected. After a persistent block, a generator is available again only if explicitly required by the operator (following recovery of the generator).

Handling of state commands The signal **busy** is the answer of the controller to a state command. If the control system does not receive such answer it tries again sending the command at most twice. If both trials fail, it sends **halt** without verifying its outcome and declares that generator is out of order by sending a signal **alarm_gr_bad** to the operator. After having received a signal **busy** (following a state command), each minute for at most five minutes, the control system checks if the generator has reached the expected state. If this is the case then the control system sends a position command accordingly to the storage curve (see section 2.3: Governing task), otherwise, at the end of the fifth minute, it sends **halt** without verifying the outcome and declares that generator is out of order by sending a signal **alarm_gr_bad** to the operator.

Handling of position commands Position commands are sent each sampling time (see section 2.3: Activities of the control system) or, if necessary, after a successful state command. A minute after a position command has been sent, the control system checks the actual position of the generator. If such position is not the one expected, the control system tries again sending the command for at most two times and waiting for a successful outcome each time. If the second trial also fails, the system sends **halt** without verifying the outcome and declares that generator is out of order by sending a signal **alarm_gr_bad** to the operator.

2.3 The control system

Activities of the control system All control system activities are timed: the operations are executed *each minute* or *each five minutes* or *each sampling time*. For example, each minute or each five minutes, the control system records the evaluations of some quantities, and, each sampling time, computes their expected values and takes the appropiate actions.

Parameters When the control system is activated, it receives the initialization values for parameters from the operator. These parameters are: *water level* in the basin, *sampling time*, *time*, *daily production periods* and *connection priorities* of generators.

Working The control system usually monitors the basin and the power plant; but, if it receives a *managing consent* from the operator, then it has also to actively manages them.

At any moment the control system can receive data from the operator (e.g. time and water level), a managing agreement or its annulment, and a signal saying that a bad generator has been repaired.

Monitoring task The monitoring task is reading and updating periodically data about water level, state and position of generators.

Governing task The governing task consists of the following operations:

- check if there exist available generators;
- check the state and position of each available generator;
- if there is at least a generator available then
  - compute the basin fluent discharge;

- recompute the production program by using the data previously acquired.

We now examine in more detail the above mentioned activities. When the control system is enabled to direct the plant, it computes a *production program* and then, conforming to such program, establishes the amount of power the plant must produce during the day and sends the appropriate commands to generators. Production program inputs are the initialization values for parameters and *fluent discharge*. Fluent discharge is the average value of the variation of water volume in the basin (owing to rain and affluents) as recorded in the previous 24 hours. Production program output is the *storage curve*, that is a set of pairs (*volume, time*) specifying the average value of water volume each sampling time. To each pair (*volume, time*) is associated information about the expected state and position of generators.

The production activity of the plant should maintain water level in the interval between **Vml** and **VML**. This is the normal working range. If fluent discharge deviates from the expected values and the water level is not in the normal range then the control system has to take measures in order to drive the level back into the normal range. In such a case, it sends a signal **alarm_level_bad** to the operator, leaves the daily program for power production and follows a program trying to comply with the expected variations of water volume. In particular the control system estimates volume fluctuation in the next time interval on the basis of fluent discharge in the previous sampling time. It does not use the average fluent discharge from the previous 24 hours since in this situation it is not a reliable forecast. Finally the control system establishes a power (not greater than the maximum one the plant admits) to drive the volume back into the normal working range and sends appropriate commands to the generators.

INT_2 and **INT_1** are used in place of, respectively, **Vml** and **VML** when the transducer is broken.

Timed activities There is a clock that sends periodic timeout signals to some of the processes forming the system. Such timeouts are sent: each minute, each five minutes and each sampling time.

Activities accomplished every minute

- Update the output buffer towards the operator. If such updating is not successful then send a signal **alarm_bo_broken** to the operator and go on with the administration.
- Read and update availability of generators.
- Check the result of possible state or position commands previously sent.

Activities accomplished every five minutes

- Read transducer and sensors.

- If water level is out of the normal working range, send **alarm_out_work_int** and recompute the storage curve (using the fluent discharge evaluated in the previous sampling time instead of the daily average value (see section 2.3: Governing task)).
- If the level fluctuation estimated by the transducer disagrees with the signals coming from sensors, send a signal **alarm_transducer_broken** and compute again the storage curve using **INT_2** and **INT_1** as minimum and maximum levels.
- If the level is **VMS** (overflow), order to all available generators to produce the maximum power.
- If the level is **VMIN** (minimum level) halt all generators.
- Obtain new parameter values from the operator.

Activities accomplished every sampling period

- Acquire the value of the level in the basin and behave accordingly to the storage curve (see section 2.3: Governing task).
- Send state and position commands to the available generators to obtain a situation in agreement with the one prescribed by the storage curve.
- Compute fluent discharge in the sampling time and update the mean flow in the last 24 hours.

3 Formal specification

In this section we present the CCS/Meije formal specification for the informal specification in section 2. A description of CCS/Meije is in appendix A. With respect to the informal description in sec. 2 we make the following assumptions.

- We assume that the number of production engines is 3 (no value is specified in the informal description in section 2).
- To simplify clocking we assume that the sampling time is *about* five minutes. Note that sampling time is not specified in the informal description in sec. 2.
- We assume that system components synchronize without exchanging values. This means that we are not considering value dependent computations. Note that no numerical value is defined in the informal description in section 2.

In the rest of this section we only present the CCS/Meije term we have used to formally define the specification for the generator in section 2.2. For the interested reader the complete formal specification is in [PT 95].

Process *Generator* in figure 1 models the generator described in section 2.2. Process *Generator* defines a finite state automaton (see figure 2) with initial state S. Transitions are defined with equations defining present-state, action, next-state. Actions have form a? (input action) or a! (output action). Processes communicate using synchronization. Thus a process can execute action a? (a!)

```
Generator = let rec {
        S = startGr?: sTg + stopped!: S + operator?: G
and     G = noise!: gTbt + lock!: gTbp + haltGr?: gTs + incGr?: G + decGr?: G
            + producing!: G + act_gr_pos!: G + repaired_generator?: S
            + operator?: S + operator?: Bt + operator?: Bp
and     Bt = noisegone!: S + broken!: Bt + τ: Bt
            + repaired_generator?: noisegone!: S + operator?: S
and     Bp = repaired_generator?: (lockgone!: S + operator?: S)
            + locked!: Bp + τ: Bp
and     sTg = startOk!: G + τ: sTg + repaired_generator?: S
and     gTbt = ko!: Bt
and     gTbp = ko!: Bp
and     gTs = haltOk!: S + τ: gTs + repaired_generator?: S
            } in S.
```

Fig. 1. Process *Generator*

only if some other process can execute action a! (a?). E.g. equation "gTbt = ko!: Bt", says that if we are in state gTbt then performing output action ko we reach state Bt. Nondetermininsm is also possible. E.g. equation "S = startGr?: sTg + stopped!: S + operator?: G" says that from state S we can: perform input action startGr and reach state sTg or perform output action stopped and reach state S or perform input action operator and reach state G. Action τ models an action that is internal to the process performing it. Thus it is *invisible* to the other processes. We usually use τ's to model stuttering.

In the following we show how the definition of process *Generator* in this section links to the informal specification in section 2.2 (The generator). The informal meaning of all states has been already given in section 2.2 (The generator). The intended meaning of the signals (actions) is defined in the following.

- **startGr** requires the generator to start. This happens via a synchronization between process *Generator* and the process modelling the control system.
- **haltGr** requires the generator to halt. This happens via a synchronization between process *Generator* and the process modelling the control system.
- **incGr** requires the generator to increase the amount of produced power. This happens via a synchronization between process *Generator* and the process modelling the control system.
- **decGr** requires the generator to decrease the amount of produced power. This happens via a synchronization between process *Generator* and the process modelling the control system.
- **startOk** signals to the process modelling the control system that the generator has begun producing power.
- **haltOk** signals to the process modelling the control system that the generator has stopped producing power.
- **noise** signals to the process modelling the control system that a temporary failure has occurred and that the generator is going to stop.

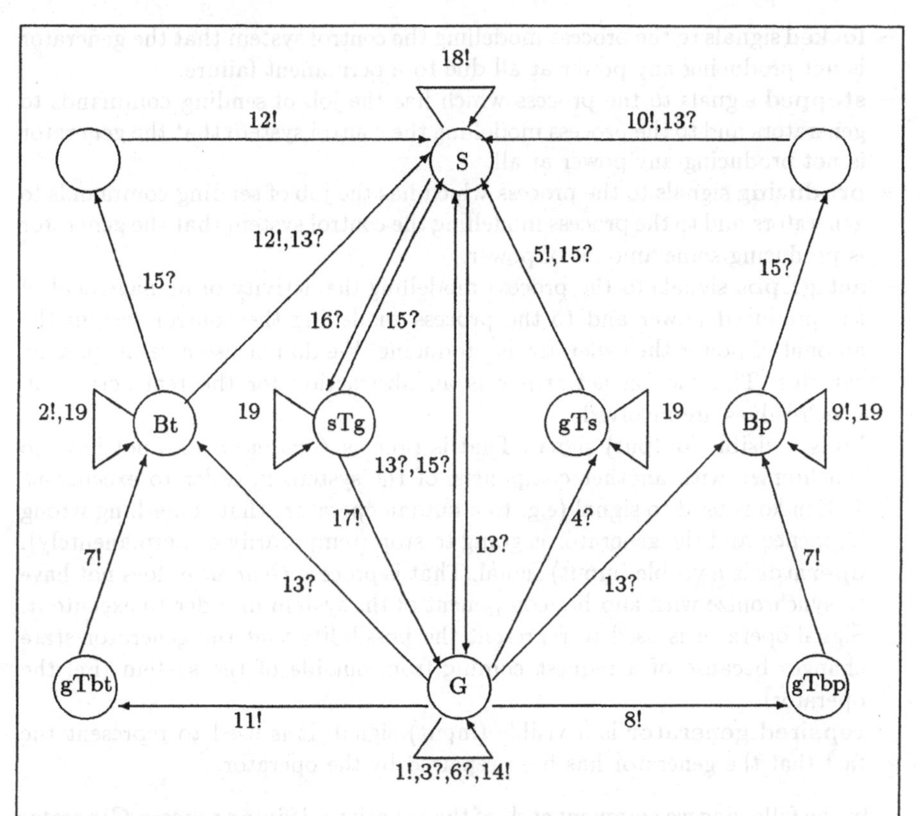

Legend: 1 ≡ act_gr_pos, 2 ≡ broken, 3 ≡ decGr, 4 ≡ haltGr, 5 ≡ haltOk, 6 ≡ incGr, 7 ≡ ko, 8 ≡ lock, 9 ≡ locked, 10 ≡ lockgone, 11 ≡ noise, 12 ≡ noisegone, 13 ≡ operator, 14 ≡ producing, 15 ≡ repaired_generator, 16 ≡ startGr, 17 ≡ startOk, 18 ≡ stopped, 19 ≡ τ.

An edge labelled $l_1, \ldots, l_k$ represents k edges labelled, respectively, $l_1, \ldots, l_k$.

Fig. 2. Process *Generator* Automaton

- **lock** signals to the process modelling the control system that a permanent (i.e. requiring operator's intervention) failure has occurred and that the generator is going to stop.
- **noisegone** signals to the process modelling the control system that temporary failure has disappeared and that the generator is ready to start producing power again.
- **lockgone** signals to the process modelling the control system that permanent failure has been repaired and the generator is ready to start producing power again.
- **broken** signals to the process modelling the control system that the generator is not producing any power at all due to a temporary failure.

- **locked** signals to the process modelling the control system that the generator is not producing any power at all due to a permanent failure.
- **stopped** signals to the process which has the job of sending commands to generators and to the process modelling the control system that the generator is not producing any power at all.
- **producing** signals to the process which has the job of sending commands to generators and to the process modelling the control system that the generator is producing some amount of power.
- **act_gr_pos** signals to the process modelling the activity of management of the produced power and to the process modelling the control system the amount of power the generator is producing. We do not use a value–passing calculus. Thus action act_gr_pos is an abstraction for the real actions in which values are involved.
- **ko** is a visible (output) signal. That is process *Generator* does not have to synchronize with another component of the system in order to execute it. Action ko is used to signal (e.g. to a human operator) that something wrong happened and the generator is going to stop (temporarily or permanentely).
- **operator** is a visible (input) signal. That is process *Generator* does not have to synchronize with another component of the system in order to execute it. Signal operator is used to represent the possibility that the generator state changes because of a request coming from outside of the system (i.e. the operator).
- **repaired_generator** is a visible (input) signal. It is used to represent the fact that the generator has been repaired by the operator.

In the following we comment each of the equations defining process *Generator* in figure 1.

From state S (stopped) the generator can perform the following actions.

- **startGr?** When this signal is received the generator goes to unstable state sTg.
- **stopped!** The generator can output signal stopped and go (i.e. stay) to state S.
- **operator?** When this signal is received (from the operator) the generator goes in state G.

From state G (generating) the generator can perform the following actions.

- **noise!** Due to a temporary failure the generator goes to unstable state gTbt.
- **lock!** Due to a persistent failure the generator goes to unstable state gTbp.
- **haltGr?** The generator is required to stop. Thus it goes to unstable state gTs.
- **incGr?** When signal incGr is received the generator has to increase the power which it is producing going to another generation state. Remember that we abstract away from any kind of value thus we represent this situation by using state G again.

- **decGr?** When signal incGr is received the generator has to increase the power which it is producing going to another generation state. Remember that we abstract away from any kind of value thus we represent this situation by using state G again.
- **producing!** The generator signals it is producing and stays in the same state.
- **act_gr_pos!** The generator signals the amount of power which it is producing and stays in the same state. Since we abstract away from any kind of value we represent this situation by using only a signal act_gr_pos.
- **repaired_generator?** The generator receives (from the operator) signal repaired_generator and goes to the state S.
- **operator?** This (input) signal represents the possibility that the generator is managed by the operator. After receiving this signal the generator can go in one of states G, Bt or Bp.

From state Bt (temporary block) the generator can perform the following actions.

- **noisegone!** The generator has recovered from a temporary failure and goes to state S.
- **broken!** The generator signals it is not producing due to a temporary failure and stays in the same state.
- τ The generator performs invisible action τ and stays in the same state.
- **repaired_generator?** The generator signals that it has been repaired (by the operator) and goes to an anonymous state from which it can perform only action noisegone! going to state S.
- **operator?** The generator can change state going to state S by performing the action operator? which represents the possibility the generator is managed by the operator.

From state Bp (permanent block) the generator can perform the following actions.

- **repaired_generator?** The generator has been repaired (by the operator) and goes to an anonymous state from which it can perform either action lockgone! going to state S or action operator? going to state S.
- **locked!** The generator signals it is not producing due to a persistent failure and stays in the same state.
- τ The generator performs invisible action τ and stays in the same state.

From unstable state sTg the generator can perform the following actions.

- **startOk!** The generator outputs signal startOk and goes to state G (generation).
- τ The generators performs invisible action τ and stays in the same state.
- **repaired_generator?** The generator receives (from the operator) signal repaired_generator and goes to the state S.

From unstable state gTBt the generator can perform only the output action ko! and go to state Bt.
From unstable state gTBp the generator can perform only the output action ko! and go to state Bp.
From unstable state gTs the generator can perform the following actions.

- **haltOk!** The generator signals it is going to halt and go to state S.
- τ The generator performs invisible action τ and stays in the same state.
- **repaired_generator?** The generator receives (from the operator) signal repaired_generator and goes to the state S.

4 Properties

4.1 Basic definitions

We carry out automatic verification using (BDD based) model checking on the Boolean Domain *Boole* $= \{0, 1\}$. Thus, as far as automatic verification is concerned, each property is represented with a computation on boolean functions (namely those defining the transition functions of the processes). One way of defining such computations is by using μ-calculus. Many temporal logics can be uniformly translated into μ-calculus (see [BCMDH 92]). E.g. temporal operators are just μ-terms. Thus temporal logics can also be used to define properties in our setting. Note, however, that in general there are many μ-terms representing the same temporal operator. Thus using directly μ-calculus rather then a temporal logic allows a finer control on the verification process. In our case this was essential to succesfully complete our verification task. To define properties we use μ-calculus as defined in [BCMDH 92]. Roughly speaking we can say that μ-calculus on a Boolean Domain can be seen as First Order Logic on a Boolean Domain augmented with the least fixpoint operator μ. In the following symbol $\equiv$ denotes syntactic equality.

We use vectors of boolean variables to represent actions and states. We usually denote boolean vectors with capital letters (e.g. X, Y). Let $X \equiv x_1, \ldots x_k$, and Q be a binding operator (e.g. $\exists$, $\forall$, λ). We write QX for $Qx_1, \ldots x_k$. Let $Y \equiv y_1, \ldots y_k$ and *op* be a binary boolean operator (e.g. $\vee$, $\wedge$, $=$). We write $(X \ op \ Y)$ for $((x_1 \ op \ y_1) \wedge \ldots (x_k \ op \ y_k))$. We write $F(x_1, \ldots x_m)$ to denote a formula which free variables are among $x_1, \ldots x_m$. Moreover we denote with $F(t_1, \ldots t_m)$ the formula obtained from $F(x_1, \ldots x_m)$ by simultaneosly substituting variables $x_1, \ldots x_m$ with terms $t_1, \ldots t_m$.

To use model checking we need to represent a process algebra as a μ-calculus model. We do this as in [EFT 91]. We use boolean vectors of size r ($= 15$) to represent actions and boolean vectors of size n ($= 174$) to represent states. We represent the initial state with a boolean vector having all components equal to 0. Thus the set of initial states (a singleton) is represented by the formula $S0(x_1, \ldots x_n) \equiv (x_1 = 0) \wedge \ldots (x_n = 0)$.

The transition relation of the overall system is represented with a predicate symbol S with arity $r + 2 * n$ ($= 363$). Thus $S(X, A, X')$ holds iff from state X performing action A it is possible to reach state X'.

Because of the size of the BDD representing S time/space performance of automatic verification of a property strongly depends on the logic formula we choose to represent such property. To speed up reachability analysis it was our intention to use the iterative squaring technique in [BCMDH 92]. However we could not follow such approach because of memory overflow. We saved memory space (at the expense of computation time) by representing our properties with carefully chosen logic formulas. In particular we avoided building fixpoints of predicate symbols with arity greater than, say, $r + n (= 15 + 174 = 189)$. Lack of space prevents us from illustrating all of the properties we verified. In the following we give the logic formulas we used to define and automatically verify some of the properties we studied. This should be sufficient to illustrate our approach.

It will be useful to consider the set of states reachable in one step from a given state. Such set can be represented with the formula $S1(X, X') \equiv \exists A\ S(X, A, X')$.

We will be interested in the set of states reachable from a given state without performing a given action, say B. Such set can be represented with the formula $S2(B, X, X') \equiv \exists A\ (\neg(A = B) \wedge S(X, A, X'))$.

Let $V(X)$ be a formula representing a set of states. The set of states reachable from a state satisfying $V(X)$ is the least solution to the fixpoint equation (unknown: G) $G(X) = (V(X) \vee \exists Z[G(Z) \wedge S1(Z, X)])$. Such solution can be denoted with the μ-calculus formula $G(X)$ defined as follows: $G(X) \equiv \mu g[\lambda X[V(X) \vee \exists Z[g(Z) \wedge S1(Z, X)]]](X)$. E.g. the set $V0$ of states reachable from the initial states can be represented with the formula $G0(X)$ defined as follows: $G0(X) \equiv \mu g[\lambda X[S0(X) \vee \exists Z[g(Z) \wedge S1(Z, X)]]](X)$.

Let A be an action. The set $H(A)$ of states from which action A will be performed on at least one computation can be described with the formula $S3(A, X) \equiv \mu g[\lambda X[\exists Z[S(X, A, Z) \vee (S1(X, Z) \wedge g(A, Z))]]](X)$.

We will need to observe synchronizations between processes. To this end we slightly extend CCS/Meije by considering actions of the following forms: $a\,!$, $a\,?$ and a_τ. Thus when two processes synchronize on action a we will be able to observe a_τ instead of just τ (as in CCS/Meije). In the following we represent actions $a\,!$, $a\,?$ and a_τ with, respectively, boolean vectors (of size r) **a_out**, **a_in** and **a_tau**.

4.2 A safety property

We are now ready to define the first property we will study here. It is a safety property. Its informal statement is:

> *If a generator is out of order because of a persistent block then that generator will not be used until the operator has repaired it.*

Using actions the above property (for generator 1) can be expressed as follows. If the system performs the following actions: **ko_1_in** (generator 1 is out of order), **locked_1_tau** (the system has detected that generator 1 is out of order) **noavilable_1_tau** (generator 1 is declared unusable for automatic administration) then action **available_1_tau** (generator 1 is available again for automatic administration) cannot be performed until action **repaired_generator_1_in** (the operator repaired generator 1) is performed.

In the following we build a formula describing such property.

The set $V0$ of states reachable from the initial state can be represented with the formula $G0(X)$ defined in section 4.1. The set $V1$ of states reachable from $V0$ by performing action **ko_1_in** is represented with the formula $G1(X)$ defined as follows: $G1(X) \equiv \exists Z[G0(Z) \wedge S(Z, \textbf{ko\_1\_in}, X)]$.

The set $V2$ of states reachable from $V1$ is represented with the formula $G2(X)$ defined as follows: $G2(X) \equiv \mu g[\lambda X[G1(X) \vee \exists Z[g(Z) \wedge S1(Z, X)]]](X)$.

The set $V3$ of states reachable from $V2$ by performing action **locked_1_tau** is represented with the formula $G3(X)$ defined as follows: $G3(X) \equiv \exists Z[G2(Z) \wedge S(Z, \textbf{locked\_1\_tau}, X)]$.

The set $V4$ of states reachable from $V3$ is represented with the formula $G4(X)$ defined as follows: $G4(X) \equiv \mu g[\lambda X[G3(X) \vee \exists Z[g(Z) \wedge S1(Z, X)]]](X)$.

The set $V5$ of states reachable from $V4$ by performing action **nonavailable_1_tau** is represented with the formula $G5(X)$ defined as follows: $G5(X) \equiv \exists Z[G4(Z) \wedge S(Z, \textbf{nonavailable\_1\_tau}, X)]$.

The set $V6$ of states reachable from $V5$ without performing action **repaired_generator_1_in** is represented with the formula $G6(X)$ defined as follows:

$G6(X) \equiv \mu g[\lambda X[G5(X) \vee \exists Z[g(Z) \wedge S2(\textbf{repaired\_generator\_1\_in}, Z, X))]](X)$.

The set $V7$ of states reachable from $V6$ by performing action **available_1_tau** is represented with the formula $G7(X)$ defined as follows: $G7(X) \equiv \exists Z[G6(Z) \wedge S(Z, \textbf{available\_1\_tau}, X)]$.

Our safety property requires that $V7$ be empty. This is expressed by the formula $G8$ defined as follows: $G8 \equiv \neg \exists X G7(X)$.

To verify our property we have to check that G8 holds. We do this by computing a BDD representation for G8 and testing that the result is the (unique) BDD representing the boolean function identically equal to 1.

4.3 A liveness property

The second property we study is a liveness property. Its informal statement is:

> *If the plant is managed by the control system and a persistent block occurs on generator 1 and the operator repairs it then generator 1 will become usable again.*

Using actions the above property can be expressed as follows. If the system performs the following actions: **consent_in** (the plant is managed by the control system), **locked_1_tau** (generator 1 is unusable because of a persistent block), **repaired_generator_1_in** (generator 1 has been repaired by the operator) then action **available_1_tau** (generator 1 is usable) will be performed on at least one computation.

In the following we build a formula describing such property.

The set $V0$ of states reachable from the initial state can be represented with the formula $G0(X)$ defined in section 4.1. The set $V1$ of states reachable from

$V0$ by performing action **consent_in** is represented with the formula $G1(X)$ defined as follows: $G1(X) \equiv \exists Z[G0(Z) \wedge S(Z, \textbf{consent\_in}, X)]$.

The set $V2$ of states reachable from $V1$ is represented with the formula $G2(X)$ defined as follows: $G2(X) \equiv \mu g[\lambda X[G1(X) \vee \exists Z[g(Z) \wedge S1(Z,X)]]](X)$.

The set $V3$ of states reachable from $V2$ by performing action **locked_1_tau** is represented with the formula $G3(X)$ defined as follows: $G3(X) \equiv \exists Z[G2(Z) \wedge S(Z, \textbf{locked\_1\_tau}, X)]$.

The set $V4$ of states reachable from $V3$ is represented with the formula $G4(X)$ defined as follows: $G4(X) \equiv \mu g[\lambda X[G3(X) \vee \exists Z[g(Z) \wedge S1(Z,X)]]](X)$.

The set $V5$ of states reachable from $V4$ by performing action **repaired_generator_1_in** is represented with the formula $G5(X)$ defined as follows: $G5(X) \equiv \exists Z[G4(Z) \wedge S(Z, \textbf{repaired\_generator\_1\_in}, X)]$.

The set $V6$ of states reachable from $V5$ is represented with the formula $G6(X)$ defined as follows: $G6(X) \equiv \mu g[\lambda X[G5(X) \vee \exists Z[g(Z) \wedge S1(Z,X)]]](X)$.

The set $V7$ of states from which action **available_1_tau** will be performed on at least one computation can be represented with the formula $S3(\textbf{available\_1\_tau}, X)$ (see section 4.1).

Our liveness property requires that if a state is in set $V6$ then it is also in set $V7$. This can be represented with the formula $G8 \equiv \forall X[G6(X) \rightarrow S3(\textbf{available\_1\_tau}, X)]$.

To verify our property we have to check that G8 holds. We do this by computing a BDD representation for G8 and testing that the result is the (unique) BDD representing the boolean function identically equal to 1.

4.4 One more property

The informal statement of this property is:

> *If the control system sends a signal to stop generator 1 then in at most 6 minutes either generator 1 is stopped or an alarm is sent to the operator.*

A logic formula for such property can be obtained as in the previous sections.

5 Experimental Results

In this section we describe our experimental results. We represent process P by representing, with BDDs, the transition relation of the automata defined by P. The BDD representing a process is obtained (manually) from the CCS/Meije syntax as illustrated in [EFT 91]. We only use standard BDD manipulation functions. Thus any BDD package can be used to carry out automatic verification. We used an in-house BDD package developed as part of a Boolean Functional Programming language [Tro 95]. Our BDD package is similar to the one described in [BRB 90], but we use shifted BDDs as in [MIY 90]. The main reason to use an in-house BDD package is source code availability. This allowed us to tune our package parameters to avoid running out of memory. We use a cache size of 19,997 and a hash table size of 200,003 with a load factor of 10. Garbage collection is called each time there is at least a deletable BDD vertex and BDD size is greater than 2,000,030. This is the main reason for our long verification times. In fact, after about half an hour of computation most of the computation time is spent doing garbage collection.

To convince ourselves that our formal specification was a faithful representation of the given informal specification we ran experiments on subsystems of the overall system. This was done by trying to verify suitable properties (e.g. of set of reachable states, of admissible traces, ...) for each subsystem. This allowed us to find errors in the formal specification (i.e. our formal specification did not correctly represent the considered subsystem) as well as in the formulations of the properties we expected to hold. On the base of such experiments we revised our formal specification. The formal specification thus obtained was used to carry out the verification experiments (for the overall system) reported in this paper.

We define properties with μ-calculus formulas. We carry out automatic verification via model checking. Our model is the transition relation S *(present state, action, next state)* of the overall system. We use 15 boolean variables $a_0, \ldots a_{14}$ to code actions. State coding requires 174 boolean variables: $x_0, \ldots x_{173}$. Thus S is a boolean function of 15 + 2*174 = 363 boolean variables and represents a system with about 10^{52} states. Variable ordering was as in [EFT 91], i.e.: $a_0, \ldots a_{14}, x_0, y_0, x_1, y_1, \ldots x_{173}, y_{173}$, where $y_0, \ldots y_{173}$ are boolean variables representing the "next state".

When using BDDs the state space size is not a good measure of complexity since BDD size depends on the (symmetries of the) system transition relation (not just on its arity). Nevertheless it is worth noting that our state space size (10^{52}) is quite big compared to usual academic examples and to other published case studies in the process algebras area. E.g.: an 18 process Milner scheduler has about $5 * 10^6$ states (e.g. see [DB 95]); the alternating bit protocol (with buffer capacity 4 x 2) has 18278 states (e.g. see [DB 95]); the security management system verified in [CRB 94] has 312 states. Moreover our system does not have a symmetric structure (e.g. as Milner scheduler). Note however that for hardware systems industrial applications larger than ours have been studied. E.g. see [BCLMD 94, CGHJLMN 95].

Given a BDD representation for S, verification of a μ-calculus formula F amounts to evaluation of F in model S. This is done as in [BCMDH 92].

Building a BDD representing S was possible for systems with up to 3 generators. Experimental results are in the left table of figure 3. However when we try to automatically verify a property on a system with more than one generator we run out of memory. Thus to automatically verify the properties we studied we simplify our system as follows. We assume that only one generator is present in the system and that the overall system is working in automatic administration mode. Note that our plant can only work in two administration modes: automatic and manual. However the safety critical one is the automatic administration mode.

Our experiments were carried out with a SUN Sparc LX with 72MB RAM.

Note that this is a relatively small (and easily affordable) machine when compared with 512MB machines often used for automatic verification. Experimental results for verification of the properties in section 4 are in the right table of figure 3. Column CPU gives the time spent verifying a property after a BDD representation for the system has been built. Note that beside the above mentioned semplification of the system our approach is completely automatic and does not require any user expertise on the verification tool.

clocked_sys	CPU	Max BDD size
1 generator	20	1,251,627
2 generators	41	2,000,031
3 generators	289	2,611,348

1 generator/automatic	CPU	Max BDD size
property section 4.2	10032	2,000,031
property section 4.3	8322	2,000,031
property section 4.4	14431	2,000,031

Fig. 3. Experimental results on SPARC LX with 72MB RAM. CPU times are in minutes.

6 Conclusions

We have shown a formal analysis of a specification for a hydroelectric power plant. Starting from the informal specification we developed a formal one written using the CCS/Meije process algebra. For such formal specification we automatically verified that some given properties hold. We defined properties using μ-calculus. Verification was carried out using model checking and BDDs.

Our experience shows that automatic verification of modest size plants is feasible. However the size of the BDDs we had to handle ($> 2 \cdot 10^6$ vertices) shows that if we want to study larger systems we need global optimization techniques to automatically transform a verification problem into an easier one. This is particularly true if values (data path) are to be considered. Studying the possibility of using global optimization techniques as in [Tro 95] to avoid state explosion will be our next step.

Acknowledgements

We are grateful to anonymous referees for helpful comments on a previous version of this paper.

References

[AB 84] D. Austry, G. Boudol, *Algebre de processus et synchronisation*, Theoretical Computers Science, 1(30), 1984.

[BCLMD 94] J.R. Burch, E.M. Clarke, D.E. Long, K.L. McMillan, D.L. Dill, *Symbolic Model Checking for Sequential Circuit Verification*, IEEE Trans. on Computer-Aided Design, Vol.13, N.4, pp. 401–424, Apr. 1994.

[BCMDH 92] J.R. Burch, E.M. Clarke, K.L. McMillan, D.L. Dill, L.J. Hwang, *Symbolic Model Checking: 10^{20} states and beyond*, Information and Computation, 98, (1992).

[Bry 86] R. Bryant, *Graph-Based Algorithms for Boolan Function Manipulation*, IEEE Trans. on Computers, Vol.C-35, N.8, Aug. 1986.

[BRB 90] K.S. Brace, R.L. Rudell, R.E. Bryant, *Efficient Implementation of a BDD Package*, 27th ACM/IEEE Design Automation Conference, 1995.

[CGHJLMN 95] E.M. Clarke, O. Grumberg, H. Haraishi, S. Jha, D.E. Long, K.L. McMillan, L.A. Ness, *Verification of the Futurebus+ Cache Coherence Protocol*, Formal Methods in System Design, Vol.6, N.2, pp. 217–232, Mar. 1995.

[CRB 94] O. Cherkaoui, N. Rico, A. Bernardi, *Specification and Analysis of a Security Management System*, FME 94, LNCS 873, Springer–Verlag.

[DB 95] A. Dsouza, B. Bloom, *Generating BDD Models for Process Algebra Terms*, CAV 95, LNCS 939, Springer–Verlag.

[EFT 91] R. Enders, T. Filkorn, D. Taubner, *Generating BDDs for Symbolic Model Checking in CCS*, Proceedings of CAV'91, Lecture Notes in Computer Science, 575, Springer–Verlag, 1991.

[ENEL 92] ENEL, *Descrizione informale di un caso di studio tratto dalle specifiche funzionali di un automatismo coordinatore delle manovre degli impianti idroelettrici*, Centro di Ricerca in Automatica, Rapporto Interno, Febbraio 1992.

[LP 94] S. Larosa, R. Pugliese, *Using the specification language CCS/Meije for a case study: a Software Control System of a Hydroelectric Power Plant*, Nota Interna B4-58, Istituto di Elaborazione dell'Informazione - CNR, Pisa, 1994.

[MIY 90] S. Minato, N. Ishiura, S. Yajima, *Shared Binary Decision Diagram with Attributed Edges for Efficient Boolean Function Manipulation*, 27th ACM/IEEE Design Automation Conference, 1995.

[PT 95] R. Pugliese, E. Tronci, *Automatic Verification of a Hydroelectric Power Plant*, Research Report SI/RR - 95/15, 1995.

[dSV 89] R. de Simone, D. Vergamini, *Aboard Auto*, Rapports Techniques 111, INRIA, Sophia Antipolis, 1989.

[Tro 95] E. Tronci, *Hardware Verification, Boolean Logic Programming, Boolean Functional Programming*, Proceedings of LICS 95, IEEE Computer Society.

A Meije: Syntax and Semantics

In this section, we give a brief presentation of the syntax and informal semantics of the CCS/Meije process algebra for reactive systems [AB 84]. More specifically we describe the subset of CCS/Meije we used in this paper to give our formal description of the ENEL Hydroelectric Power Plant in [ENEL 92]. We adopt the syntax used in the AUTO/MAUTO tools [dSV 89].

The syntax of the calculus is based on a set of elementary and uninterpreted actions that processes can perform and on a set of operators that permit to build complex processes from simpler ones. The syntax permits a two–layered design of *process terms.* The first level is related to *sequential regular terms,* the second one to *networks* of parallel sub–processes supporting communication and action renaming or restriction.

- *Act* is the set of atomic signal names ranged over by alphanumeric strings. Such names represent emitted signals if they are terminated by "!" or received ones if they are terminated by "?";
- τ denotes a special action not belonging to *Act.* Action τ representes the unobservable action (to model internal process communications);
- $Act_\tau = Act \cup \{\tau\}$, ranged over by a, denotes the full set of actions that a process can perform;
- $\mathcal{X}$, ranged over by X, is the set of term variables.

The following grammar generates all regular terms, ranged over by R, and all network terms, ranged over by P:

$$R ::= \mathbf{stop} \mid \mathrm{X} \mid a : R \mid R + R \mid \mathbf{let\ rec}\ \mathrm{X} = R\ [\mathbf{and}\ \mathrm{X} = R]\ \mathbf{in}\ \mathrm{X}$$

$$P ::= R \mid P//P \mid P\backslash a \mid P[a/b] \mid \mathbf{let}\ \mathrm{X} = P\ [\mathbf{and}\ \mathrm{X} = P]\ \mathbf{in}\ \mathrm{X}$$

where [...] denotes an optional and repeatable part of the syntax.

We give an intuitive semantics for the above constructs:

- **stop** is the process which does nothing;
- $a : R$ is the term that first executes action a and then behaves like R;
- $R + R$ is the nondeterministic composition between two regular terms;
- the construct $\mathrm{X} = R$ bounds the process variable X to the term R; then the **let rec** construct allows recursive definitions of processes;
- $P//P$ is the parallel composition between two network processes;
- $P\backslash a$ behaves like P apart from action a that can only be performed within a communication;
- $P[a/b]$ behaves like P apart from action b that is renaimed with a;
- the construct $\mathrm{X} = P$ bounds the process variable X to the network P; the let construct bounds nonrecursive definitions of process variables.

See [AB 84] for a more complete and formal description of Meije.

Experiences in Embedded Scheduling

David M. Jackson

Formal Systems Design & Development, Inc.
PO Box 3004, Auburn, AL 36831, USA, and
Formal Systems (Europe) Ltd
3 Alfred St, Oxford OX1 4EH, UK

Abstract. This paper summarises a number of features of several recent projects in the field of high-integrity embedded system design, and in particular in the design and verification of schedulers and schedules for such systems. It discusses the technical issues of modelling the timing requirements and features of such software with reference to the CSP language and the FDR model checking tool, and makes some observations about the choice and availability of data, re-use of modelling effort, and presentation of results. The technical work is illustrated by a small example, and shows a variety of useful modelling idioms rather than new mathematical results. The final section discusses the applicability of the present process, and attempts to draw conclusions regarding the wider application of formal methods.

1 Background

Over the last 2–3 years, both Formal Systems companies have taken part in projects aiming to increase confidence in the dependability of embedded real-time systems by using formal techniques. This paper attempts to summarize the technical and organizational issues encountered in these projects.

The applications considered come from a range of areas in which correct operation of a microprocessor-based controller is vital to the safe and reliable operation of some larger system or plant. Such systems are inevitably subject to critical timing and sequencing constraints. In addition, relatively limited resources must often be used to support a range of potentially distinct activities. The scheduling of such interacting tasks on a single processor is the main technical problem discussed here: this aspect of design is difficult to control and predict with historical software engineering methods.

The work described here was concerned principally with gaining confidence in scheduling policies and schedules produced manually as part of a conventional program development. Our project emphasis has been on producing useful results in an engineering environment as much as on formal proofs of correctness: our approach yields indications of the severity of a failure, or the margin of a success, where possible, and aims to use as little detailed information about the behaviour of the program in question as possible – such data is typically liable to change and may not, in any case, be available until late in the design process.

1.1 The Real-Time Environment

In the industries which provided the background to this paper, the design and construction of any system is often reviewed or controlled by external agencies and subject to rigorous audit and process management. Standards such as [9, 13] are typical of those enforced or proposed.

One consequence of this tight design control is that the implementation technologies available are tightly constrained by standards or by justifiable engineering conservatism. Programs for embedded systems of the type we are considering are commonly implemented in a distributed style: the software is structured as a series of distinct tasks, whose execution is triggered by a scheduler. Inter-task communication is usually implemented by the use of shared variables. As only a single task is executing at any instant, access control is typically not required for these variables. Input and output activities are implemented as tasks which are scheduled in the same way as computation. In the most critical systems preemptive scheduling is avoided and long low-frequency tasks are broken in to smaller sub-tasks if required.

The scheduling schemes are generally simple: many systems execute time-critical tasks in a fixed order in cycles synchronized with a single fixed period clock interrupt, although the techniques we will discuss here are rather more flexible, as will be discussed in Section 6.2. Task sequencing constraints are captured by the order of tasks in the list, and a variety of execution rates can be permitted by organizing the schedule into a series of minor cycles (frames) of fixed duration, each of which is executed in turn in a longer major cycle. For example, if a control system requires that certain outputs are updated every 2ms, while other status information need only be computed every 10ms, we might structure the execution schedule as shown in Figure 1.

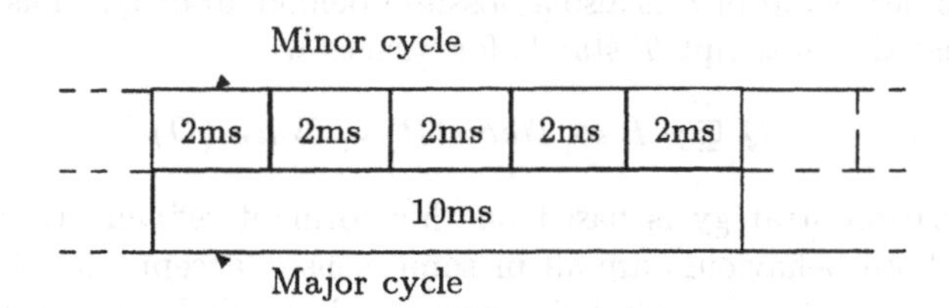

Fig. 1. Major and Minor Cycles in a Repetitive Schedule

Our work will concentrate on analysing and specifying the correctness and behavioural properties of schedulers of this type. Apart from specifically schedule related data, we will not consider the data flow or functional aspects of the software, but concentrate on the control flow. Critical embedded systems tend to have relatively limited data manipulation functions, and this is often already specified and analysed in detail within, say, the domain of control theory. This restriction also has the advantage of removing requirements for detailed information about the application program: simple timing estimates or budgets for principal tasks may be available early in design cycle, and are likely to change less frequently than functional requirements and design decisions determining data flow.

1.2 The CSP Formalism

The critical performance criteria of embedded systems are principally defined by the points at which external inputs are monitored and external outputs are provided. The Communicating Sequential Processes (CSP) theory [4] is an attractive base for the analysis of such systems because it treats observable external interaction, rather than structure or state, as the primary defining feature of a system. The CSP theory provides a an expressive process-algebraic programming language, a range of semantic models of varying abstraction, powerful notions of refinement and abstraction, and an extensive algebra of equality and refinement laws. Mechanical support for CSP refinement proofs is available in the form of Formal Systems' **FDR** refinement checker [11]. For readers unfamiliar with the language, a summary of notation is given in Appendix A.

Refinement and proof in CSP. A variety of complementary formal meanings can be given to a CSP program: the simplest model identifies just the sequences of events, or *traces* that a process can perform. For example, the traces of $open \rightarrow shut \rightarrow STOP$ are $\langle\rangle$ (the empty trace), $\langle open\rangle$, and $\langle open, shut\rangle$. More sophisticated models (see [4]) introduce additional information, such as refusal sets: sets of events which may be blocked by a process after executing a given trace.

We refer to one process, P, as a *refinement* of another, Q, written $Q \sqsubseteq P$, if any possible behaviour of P is also a possible behaviour of Q. Thus in the traces model (where the subscript T stands for 'traces'),

$$Q \sqsubseteq_T P \Leftrightarrow Traces(P) \subseteq Traces(Q)$$

Our specification strategy is based on this form of refinement. Suppose S is a process whose behaviours are all in some sense "acceptable": if P refines S ($S \sqsubseteq P$) then the same acceptability must apply to all P's behaviours and so P satisfies a requirement represented by S. This argument can be applied both to situations where S represents an abstract property (such as a safety or liveness condition) and where S represents some idealized model of a system's behaviour. In this paper we will often view S as a kind of observer who monitors and allows valid behaviours, while refusing to participate in invalid ones.

Modelling time-dependent behaviour. The questions which we seek to address clearly involve consideration of time-dependent effects and properties. While there is an established Timed CSP (TCSP) formalism [8], the work described here used the untimed theory and modelled the passage of time explicitly within the algebra. There were two main reasons for this decision. Firstly, the models of Timed CSP have a very rich structure, which makes them highly expressive, but tends to make proof complex and reduces the flexibility of the algebraic laws. Secondly, powerful tool support (in the form of **FDR**) is available for the untimed language, but not yet for the timed variant.

The representation of timing behaviour in our models is achieved by using an event *tock* which represent the passage of a constant time period. Our model of time is thus discrete, although the interval represented by *tock* is a parameter of our analysis. In this context, a process which simply terminates successfully after an interval of, say, three units is written

$$tock \rightarrow tock \rightarrow tock \rightarrow SKIP$$

and a process which offers event a but is willing to delay for any amount of time can be written

$$P = (tock \rightarrow P) \,\square\, (a \rightarrow \ldots)$$

This representation of time is not in itself novel; see, for example, [6]. The basis of this approach to CSP is principally the work of Roscoe [10].

Models in this style can be composed using the standard CSP operators and the resulting idiom has significant expressive power: renaming and parallel composition allow the effects of partially synchronized clocks to be investigated, and unsynchronized parallel offers an abstract model of time sharing computation. Not all such models maintain the clear physical intuition of these examples, however. In particular, we must show that our models never "stop time" by entering a state after which no timing events are possible or by insisting that infinite computation occurs between timing events. We may check these latter "well-formedness" conditions by verifying a single refinement in the more complex failures-divergence model:

$$RUN_{\{tock\}} \sqsubseteq_{FD} System \setminus (\Sigma - \{tock\}) \tag{1}$$

where Σ is the global set of all events and $RUN(A)$ is a process which accepts arbitrary sequences of events from A,

$$RUN_A = \mathop{\square}_{x:A} x \rightarrow RUN_A.$$

Once this is established, timing properties can be verified by considering only the *traces* of the processes involved, using refinement as above: we determine whether $Spec \sqsubseteq_T System$. It is important to note that although many of the requirements discussed would conventionally be thought of as liveness properties (tasks *will* be executed within bounds), the addition of quantitative timing constraints results in a property which can be expressed as a condition on allowable traces, coupled with the necessary proof of (1).

1.3 A Small Case-Study

As an example of the type of system which we plan to analyse, consider an automotive Engine Management System (EMS). We will assume that this microprocessor system is responsible for monitoring a range of inputs from the engine, the driver, and other vehicle systems. It will be required to produce outputs to various actuators and a range of informational and warning signals. We expect that some signals must be generated at a relatively high frequency and that the majority of the others are required less frequently. (The actual signals and timings are chosen to provide examples of the features of a range of systems rather than to give a realistic model of a particular application.) The time-critical tasks required by this application are listed in Table 1. The interactions between them are described in [5], which includes further information on all aspects of this example. The model described below assumes knowledge only of

Acronym	Function	Freq. Hz	Max Len. μs	Acronym	Function	Freq. Hz	Max Len. μs
RAA	Read Accel. Angle	80	300	DFP	Drive Fuel Pump	160	300
RSD	Read SpeeD	160	500	RXA	Read eXhaust Anal.	40	400
RFP	Read Fuel Pressure	160	300	AMX	Adjust MiXture	40	400
ROT	Read Oil Temp.	40	250	RWT	Read Water Temp.	40	250
CSD	Calc. Speed Demand	80	1000	CWT	Check Water Temp.	40	250
CIT	Calc. Injector Timing	160	700	DCP	Drive Cooling Pump	40	300
CFP	Check Fuel Pressure	160	300	LSS	Limit Speed Schedule	40	400
COT	Check Oil Temp.	40	250	IES	Indicate Eng. Status	40	800
DI	Drive Injector	160	500	DTM	Drive TachoMeter	40	250
AGT	Adjust iGniTion	80	800				

Table 1. Time-critical components of the EMS

a bound on the execution time of each task. This may be based on estimates or budgets rather than precise calculation, and our results will then indicate the consequences of the assumptions made.

2 Requirements

Requirements are placed on an embedded system by the external engineering disciplines governing the application. The functional requirements are often relatively simple and well-defined; timing and interfacing requirements may be much more complex. A system will typically be required to provide outputs at a specified rate, and to ensure that these outputs reflect a sufficiently 'fresh' set of input values. The majority of software timing requirements arise from these considerations. Time-independent requirements (including restrictions on valid orders of task execution) can be specified and verified using the established techniques of [4].

2.1 Iteration Rates

The simplest timing requirements are those which state that particular functions (such as providing an output) are executed regularly. Such requirements can express a variety of forms of constraint: repetition at a fixed rate, within specified timing tolerances; repetition at a nominal rate (placing a bound on the rate of timing deviation, but not an absolute maximum displacement), or perhaps long-term bounds on average execution rates. Requirements of this form provide one of the most important inputs to the design of a scheduler, and verifying these properties constitutes an important "sanity check" on a proposed design, although ensuring that such conditions are met is not usually a difficult task in itself.

2.2 Sequence Timing

A more sophisticated and more stringent requirement is necessary to capture overall response time conditions which are inevitable in embedded systems design. These typically take the form of constraints placed on sequences of task executions calls to ensure that the response to a particular input change is made in a timely fashion.

A typical requirement of this form will define a initial task, which is responsible for detecting some input condition, a list of subsequent tasks each of which derives a value from values provided by previous tasks, and a final task which generates the output. An associated time bound will define the maximum allowable delay between input and output, and is thus a maximum bound on the time from the start of the execution of the first procedure to the completion of the last specified. Any number of other operations could theoretically intervene, and several such conditions, or even several instances of the same condition, can be active at once. Some examples of sequence specifications for the EMS are shown in Table 3 (a more realistic example would have several dozen such conditions).

2.3 Quantitative Results

The final type of requirements which we might consider as having a direct impact on scheduler correctness are those which place quantitative bounds on the satisfaction of particular deadlines, or on the overall utilization of the system by time-critical tasks. It is common practice, for example, to insist that a specified proportion of processor time remains free for possible expansion, and to allow for the possible variations in clock frequency and interrupt latency. These conditions are not necessarily strictly enforced, and it is generally unreasonable to reject a design for missing a non-critical deadline by a small margin. We may attempt a rigorous verification, but accept the system anyway if it fails by a sufficiently "small" amount, or relax the specification initially and then *measure* the amount by which the weaker specification is satisfied. Both these approaches are discussed below (in Sections 3.2 and 3.4).

3 Specifications

This section is intended to give formal CSP characterizations of the properties discussed above. Our specifications will be based on trace refinement as described in Section 1.2. We give, as a formal description of the property we require, a CSP program which allows all the sequences of events we wish to consider as valid. A scheduling system will satisfy our requirements if all the possible behaviours of the system model are permitted by this specification process.

3.1 Observable events

Our correctness criteria concern the passage of time and the execution of software tasks. We will therefore assume that the following events may be used in representing the behaviour of our system:

tock indicates the passage of one unit of time, as discussed in Section 1.2. We usually make the unit of time a parameter to our model so as to investigate the effects of the approximation by varying the actual value used.

exec.i represents the start of execution of a task i. We do not need to model the completion of a task explicitly if it can be inferred to sufficient accuracy for our needs from the start of the next task.

cycle indicates the start of cycle of scheduler execution. *cycle* events are assumed to occur at intervals corresponding to the fastest execution period required by a program. In implementation terms, *cycle* might represent a timer interrupt.

3.2 Iteration Rates

We now present CSP processes capturing two of the possible interpretations of the informal requirement that a task "shall execute with period T_i". Our specifications are presented as observers which characterize the behaviour which the system should be permitted to perform. If all the system's behaviours are permitted by the observer, the requirement is satisfied; if not, the system is unacceptable.

Repetition at precise instants. In practice, we will never be able to achieve execution at exactly specified instants, but the following specification is a useful demonstration of the principles used by more realistic specifications. We first define a process which deterministically allows T *tock* events to occur between occurrences of *exec.i* events:

$$PERIOD(i, T, n) = \textbf{if } n = 0 \quad \textbf{then } exec.i \rightarrow PERIOD(i, T, T) \quad \textbf{else } tock \rightarrow PERIOD(i, T, n-1) \tag{2}$$

This process maintains n, the time allowed until the next occurrence of *exec.i*. When the count is zero, it will only allow this execution action to occur; when n is non-zero, the process will allow time to pass (represented by the *tock* action) and decrement the count accordingly. To allow the first execution to take place at any time between 0 and $T - 1$, we use a non-deterministic specification

$$\bigsqcap_{0 \leqslant t \leqslant T-1} PERIOD(i, T, t).$$

Should we wish to constrain the first occurrence more tightly, we can simply reduce the range of variation of t, or indeed specify its value precisely.

Allowing a tolerance. Now consider the a more practical requirement which places bounds $[Tmin_i, Tmax_i]$ on the interval between successive executions of a task. We will refer to this as a *bounded rate of drift* condition. The following process characterises such behaviour.

$$\begin{aligned} BRATE(i, n) = & \; (\textbf{if } n < Tmax_i \textbf{ then } tock \rightarrow BRATE(i, n+1) \textbf{ else } STOP) \\ & \; \Box \\ & \; (\textbf{if } Tmin_i \leqslant n \textbf{ then } exec.i \rightarrow BRATE(i, 0) \textbf{ else } STOP) \end{aligned}$$

The only information that need actually be retained from the history of the process is the time since the last execution, n. If this is greater than $Tmin_i$, the execution is allowed. Its initial value may be specified, or be permitted a non-deterministic variation.

Other conditions, such as that which allows a bounded deviation between the time of the actual execution and the desired time, can be expressed by a similar processes. Times relative to the system clock can be specified by referring to the *cycle* event. If our requirement refers to an average, rather than a bounded, execution rate our specification must maintain a more complex history of executions, but the principles remain the same.

Assisting analysis of errors. To augment these general specifications, we can employ a valuable practical insight which has arisen in recent work. When checking a refinement automatically, it is both usual and generally useful to insist that the shortest trace leading to an error is returned if the refinement fails to hold. In a timing requirement, this means that an error is reported when the execution of a task becomes overdue. In this application, however, it would be more useful to give some indication of the interval between a task becoming overdue and its actual execution time. (This is particularly the case with less-critical tasks, where some failure to meet deadlines may be permitted.) Specifications in the above style can provide this information if we change their action on the detection of an error.

Consider the *BRATE* process above; if a time limit is exceeded, this process will not let further *tock* events occur, and a delinquent implementation will fail to refine *BRATE* because it will allow *tock* but not the scheduling *exec* action. However we can weaken the specification slightly to give

$$\begin{aligned} BRATE(i,n) = {} & (\textbf{ if } n < Tmax_i \textbf{ then } tock \rightarrow BRATE(i, n+1) \\ & \qquad\qquad\qquad\qquad \textbf{else } IDLEFOR(2.Tmax_i)) \\ & \quad \Box \\ & (\textbf{ if } Tmin_i \leqslant n \textbf{ then } exec.i \rightarrow BRATE(i, 0) \textbf{ else } STOP) \end{aligned}$$

where

$$IDLEFOR(n) = \textbf{if } 0 \leqslant n \textbf{ then } tock \rightarrow IDLEFOR(n-1) \textbf{ else } STOP$$

This process allows some additional *tock* events to occur after a deadline has been missed, but prevents further task executions: if a task is scheduled late, the failure will be detected when it is actually executed, rather than when the deadline passed. Checking refinement of such a specification can have one of three outcomes:

- Successful refinement, indicating that the deadline is always met,
- A failure resulting from the implementation allowing an *exec* event which the specification did not permit. This indicates that a deadline has been missed, and allows the amount by which it was missed to be determined from the trace leading to the error.
- A failure resulting from the implementation allowing a clock tick (*tock*) which the specification did not permit. This indicates that the implementation missed the deadline by more than the amount specified ($2Tmax_i$ in the above example).

3.3 Sequence Timing

We can extend the style of specification used above to capture constraints on sequences of task execution. First consider the case when the task sequence we are considering is guaranteed to have completed before the next occurrence of the task which begins it. The specification process can be built in two parts: a timer, which records the time elapsed since the first task in the sequence began to execute, and a monitor which observes the remaining tasks being executed and resets the timer when the sequence is completed successfully. If the counter reaches the limit before all the desired executions have completed, the observer should indicate that the process violates the specification.

Suppose *trig* is the first task in the sequence, and that subsequently all the tasks in sequence *actions* must be scheduled within *Tlim*. The counter will start as a process *Limit* which simply awaits an occurrence of the first task:

$$\begin{aligned} Limit(trig, count) = {} & tock \rightarrow Limit(trig, count) \\ & \Box\, exec.trig \rightarrow Bound(trig, count, count) \end{aligned}$$

When this task has begun executing, the process will enter a state *Bound* in which the timer is active: each *tock* decrements the time remaining until zero is reached. At this point no further *tock*s are permitted by the specification, and if the implementation permits them, the trace refinement condition will fail to hold.

$$\begin{aligned} Bound(trig, count, curr) = \quad & (\,\mathbf{if}\ 0 < curr\ \mathbf{then} \\ & \quad tock \rightarrow Bound(trig, count, curr - 1) \\ & \quad \mathbf{else}\ STOP) \\ & \Box\ reset \rightarrow Limit(trig, count) \\ & \Box\ exec!trig \rightarrow Bound(trig, count, curr) \end{aligned} \tag{3}$$

The task monitor process is build as a sequential composition of processes which each wait for a specific task and terminate successfully when it is observed. This unit will be called $Await(f, X)$, where f is the required event and X is the set of possible events. Events in $X - \{f\}$ will be ignored.

$$Await(f, X) = \mathop{\Box}_{x:X} (x \rightarrow \mathbf{if}\ x = f\ \mathbf{then}\ SKIP\ \mathbf{else}\ Await(f, X))$$

The task execution sequence can be captured as a sequential composition of *Await* processes (*Events* records which events are possible):

$$\begin{aligned} & WaitingOn(current, Events, s) = \\ & \quad \mathbf{if}\ null(current)\ \mathbf{then}\ reset \rightarrow WaitingOn(s, Events, s) \\ & \quad \mathbf{else} \\ & \qquad (Await(head(current), Events); \\ & \qquad\ WaitingOn(tail(current), Events, s)) \end{aligned}$$

The following process shows how these elements may be combined. They synchronize on the *reset* signal and on *exec.trig*.

$$\begin{aligned} & (Limit(trig, Tlim) \\ & \quad \underset{\{exec.trig, reset\}}{\|} \\ & WaitingOn(s, ran(actions), s) \setminus \{reset\} \\ & \text{where } s = \langle exec.trig \rangle ^\frown \langle exec.i | i \leftarrow actions \rangle \end{aligned}$$

The *reset* event is not intended to be part of the specification, and thus is hidden from the environment. To use such a specification, we take a model of our system, and hide any events which do not directly appear in our specification, such as the *cycle* event marking the beginning of a frame, or executions of tasks not relevant to the requirement in question. We then simply require that this system model is a trace refinement of the specification.

This specification still makes two assumptions: that no more than one instance of any sequence is "active" at any one time, and that the triggering event of a sequence does not also occur in the list of triggered actions. The latter restriction seems rarely to be a problem in practice, because most specifications of this type start with a hardware related input task, while the remainder of the computation is concerned with updating state variables and producing output. The former is a somewhat greater restriction, but is may be relaxed by expanding our specification to include several concurrent instances of the process given above.

3.4 Quantitative Results

We now consider the problem of obtaining numerical estimates of properties of our system. Given that we may prove that a process *System* refines another, *Spec*, can we measure "how well" it actually meets the requirement thus represented? Our specification for a sequence timing constraint, for example, is already constructed as an observer, monitoring the tasks which are executed and maintaining a count of the time elapsed since the start of a sequence. The value of this counter at the point where the execution of the last task in the sequence is observed clearly gives an measure of the margin remaining before the deadline in a particular point in the execution. Every state of the specification in which the timing requirement has just been satisfied will have such a value associated with it. Thus if we can identify the set of states which our "observer" can reach while observing our system, we can find the set of possible margin values, and in particular we can identify the least.

Suppose that our specification is augmented to offer to transmit the value of this margin on some channel m which is not used in the actual system model. The set of all possible values of this margin can be obtained by examining all possible sequences of events which our system may perform. Call this set $Val(m)$:

$$Val(m) = \{t \mid \exists\, s \bullet s \in Traces(System) \text{ and } s^\frown\langle m.t\rangle \in Traces(Spec)\} \quad (4)$$

The minimum numerical value in this set represents the least timing margin which can be achieved after any trace of the process *System*. (Recall that if $Spec \sqsubseteq_T System$, then *Traces*(*Spec*) includes all the traces of *System*, by definition.) For the cases concerning us at present, *System* and *Spec* can be represented as finite-state machines, and it is thus theoretically possible to identify all the traces of *System*, and all the events which *Spec* may allow after them. When proving a refinement holds using the **FDR** tool, the set of all reachable specification states is necessarily maintained by the tool: it is a trivial matter to arrange that the tool return the set of events which the specification were ever willing to allow. This gives the value of $Val(c)$ for any channel c at negligible additional cost over proving that the refinement held in any case.

The necessary modification to the sequential execution specification (3) is simple: we replace the process $reset \rightarrow Limit(trig, count)$ with one which may output the margin after a reset:

$$reset \rightarrow (Limit(trig, count) \sqcap m!curr \rightarrow STOP)$$

As the only additional events are confined to a channel whose name can be chosen so as not to appear in the implementation model, this change equally does not accept any otherwise prohibited implementations, and the observer's behaviour after $m!curr$ is irrelevant – the channel is never used by the system, and thus never actually observed.

A similar construction can be used to determine parameters which are generated not by an external observer, but which are actually available within the system model itself. We will use processor slack time as a example, but the same technique applies to parameters (e.g. queue lengths) which are less easy to estimate by straightforward arithmetic. Provided that our design is adequate, when the processor completes the scheduled work within a cycle there will be some time remaining before the next cycle is due to start. In practice, the time between one frame and the next will be occupied with non-critical background tasks; similarly we may add a task to our formal model which is active over this interval and which simply counts the time periods which elapse until the next cycle start signal occurs. If this count is output over a channel not otherwise used in the model on commencement of the following cycle, the possible values of the processor slack time may be determined simply from the set of all events which the extended system may ever be observed to perform. This set is usually denoted $\sigma System$ in CSP and may be expressed as

$$\sigma P = \{a \mid \exists s \bullet s \in Traces(P) \text{ and } s^\frown\langle a\rangle \in Traces(P)\}$$

(The first conjunct is implied by the second, but this form serves to show the structural resemblance to (4).) Once again this information can be collected as during an automated refinement check with **FDR**. Indeed the results will be independent of the specification so long as the specification does not fail or diverge[1]. As the additional channel (*slack*, say) is an artifact of our modelling rather than a physical entity, other specifications can simply be expanded to ignore it:

$$SPEC' = SPEC \underset{\{\}}{\|} CHAOS_{\{slack\}}$$

4 Modelling Embedded Programs

4.1 Implementation structures

As discussed in Section 1.1, the type of system we are considered is usually programmed in an extremely conservative and simplistic style. Time critical activities are generally regulated by a single timer interrupt signal, which will cause the scheduler to be invoked at the beginning of each minor cycle. The scheduler will determine which tasks are to be executed, updating its internal state as necessary, and then execute the tasks in sequence. In the simplest cases, the relative order of in which the tasks are examined as candidates for execution is fixed. The scheduler maintains a count identifying the position of the current

[1] A situation in which all CSP refinements trivially hold, and which **FDR** thus does not examine further.

minor cycle within the major one, and simply examines each task in turn. Tasks are associated with the set of minor cycle numbers in which they are to execute, and if the current cycle is in this set, the task is run, otherwise it is skipped for the current minor cycle. This gives rise to a natural harmonic execution scheme: tasks active in every minor cycle run at the highest frequency; tasks active in every other minor cycle at half this frequency and so for slower repetition rates if necessary. This is reasonable restriction keeps the potential interactions between tasks executing at different frequencies to a minimum, which is important for both design and testing.

In the case of the EMS example, the highest frequency tasks are to be executed every 6.25ms, and the slowest frequency tasks at intervals of 25ms. We may thus arrange our schedule with a major cycle of 25ms containing four minor cycles (0...3) each 6.25ms long. A possible schedule to implement this scheme is given in Table 2. In our simple case-study the scheduling requirements have been

Order	Task	Cycles—	Order	Task	Cycles—	Order	Task	Cycles
1	RSD	0 1 2 3	8	COT	0	15	AGT	1 3
2	RFP	0 1 2 3	9	CSD	0 2	16	DCP	2
3	ROT	0	10	CIT	0 1 2 3	17	DFP	0 1 2 3
4	RAA	0 2	11	CWT	2	18	LSS	3
5	RWT	2	12	AMX	1	19	IES	3
6	RXA	1	13	DI	0 1 2 3			
7	DTM	1	14	CFP	0 1 2 3			

Table 2. A cyclic schedule for the EMS

assumed to be the same at all times; in more practical systems there are likely to be additional factors (such as a system operating mode) to be taken into account. In the majority of cases, relatively little information is used by the scheduler, and so maintaining and testing this information adds little complexity to either the program or its verification. Although the additional scheduling cases must be analysed, there are unlikely to be more than a small number of them. We may also make use of the abstraction supported by the CSP theory to replace a complex but constrained data structure by a process which is more nondeterministic but requires less information about the application or the environment (see Section 5).

4.2 CSP models

We use three major components to construct a CSP model of a scheduler system of this sort: a timing element, a state or memory element, and a process which represents the actual execution sequences. These are expressed as CSP processes and combined using parallel composition to give a complete model of the system.

Timing. A timer process is used which relates the occurrence of scheduler events (such as *cycle* events indicating the start of a minor cycle) to the physical passage of time. Our formal model will simply insist that a *cycle* events are separated by a fixed number of time intervals – the process has an exactly similar structure to Equation 2.

Memory. One or more store processes will keep track of the information which the scheduler uses to determine control flow. This will include both scheduler specific state, such as the frame and cycle counters, and any application-dependent data (such knowledge of any failures observed in a fault-tolerant network, system operating mode, etc.). Counters may be modelled simply as a process which maintains a number which is incremented periodically and which may be read by the scheduler when required. In modelling other state information, we may take any conservative non-deterministic approximation to the actual system behaviour and still be assured of the validity of our analysis. The correctness of such an approximation can be proved by refinement (see Section 5).

Execution sequencing The most complex process is that which represents the control flow through the actual program. In its simplest form, this may closely resemble the procedural code for the scheduler implementation, taking the form of a loop which indexes a data table including information about each task. One possible form for this component simply treats tasks as separate parallel components, and adds an additional scheduling process which repeatedly schedules a task, awaits its completion and schedules the next task. A typical task might take the form

$$\begin{aligned} TASK(id, max) &= exec.id \rightarrow Run(id, max, max) \\ &\qquad \Box \\ &\quad\; tock \rightarrow TASK(id, max) \\ Run(id, max, rest) &= \textbf{if } rest = 0 \textbf{ then } done \rightarrow TASK(id, max) \\ &\quad\; \textbf{else } (done \rightarrow TASK(id, max) \sqcap \\ &\qquad\quad tock \rightarrow Run(id, max, rest - 1)) \end{aligned}$$

The task switches from idle to running on receipt of an *exec* signal, and executes for a maximum of *max* time units. On completion it informs the scheduler via the *done* signal and returns to the idle state. This approach follows the conceptual model of the implementation and requires that the scheduler ensures that at most one task is active at any time.

An alternative approach which reflects the structural arrangement of the software is to represent each task by a process which terminates successfully on completion of a single cycle's execution. These processes can be arranged in sequence to represent the schedule:

$$TaskSet = Task(A, 30) \; ; \; Task(B, 45) \; ; \ldots ; \; TaskSet$$

This approach removes the need for a *done* signal, and makes explicit the fact the only one process is executing at any given time. Both these factors can simplify the mechanical verification of a refinement. In either case, the structure of all tasks is similar: changes in schedule or task sets require modification to the data and the instantiation of these process definitions, not to the definitions themselves.

5 Verification

The essence of verifying that a model of the form outlined above satisfies specifications as discussed in Section 3 is to prove that a refinement relation holds between the CSP specification process and the implementation model. As described in Section 1.2, once certain liveness obligations have been satisfied by the system model, we may demonstrate many properties solely by considering the traces of the processes involved.

The compositional nature of trace refinement and the CSP operators allow us to break verifications down into a number of separate cases. The CSP parallel operator $\underset{\Sigma}{\|}$ is identical to conjunction of trace specifications, and we may thus choose to prove one or more conditions with single refinement. Additionally if R is a trace specification which constrains only events in set X, and a process P satisfies R, the laws of CSP guarantee that any system whose behaviour on X is constrained by P will also satisfy R: we may "factor out" that part of our system model which enforces a particular condition and thus simplify our analysis further.

The relationship between trace refinement and parallel composition can be exploited further if we need to verify a condition which depends on assumptions about the environment: placing a deterministic process which enforces the condition in parallel with our system model will constrain the space of possible behaviours accordingly. We should note, however, that in order for this approach to be valid, the "well-formedness" property (1) must be shown to hold of the system and constraint together.

The complexity of any analysis of a cyclic system, either mechanical or by hand, will depend heavily on the length of the cycle being considered. To avoid the complexity of modelling long cycles, we can abstract away from the details of some infrequent tasks. Suppose the highest frequency tasks in our system were executed every 5ms, and the majority of tasks were repeated every 50ms. If one of these tasks in turn executed a sub-schedule and invoked relatively infrequent task with period 1s, say, then a full inductive proof would have to consider at least a possible 200 combinations. In many cases, however, the time occupied by infrequent tasks will be small, and we may make a conservative assumption that every invocation of the sub-scheduling task occupies a non-deterministic amount of time up to the actual worst case. If this approximation can be made, we need only consider (50ms/5ms =) 10 configurations. It may be that the schedule will not meet all its requirements under this assumption, but we can be sure that those it does meet hold of the actual system.

This is an example of an approach which has been found of use on a number of separate projects: the exploitation of the compositional nature of CSP refinement to allow piecewise simplification of a complex system while maintaining a formal guarantee of correctness. If a system S built up from a sub-component P using any of the standard CSP operators, the monotonicity of refinement with respect to these operations ensures that if S meets a requirement R when some simpler component P' is used in place of P, say $R \sqsubseteq S[P']$, and P' is a conservative approximation of P, $P' \sqsubseteq P$, then the whole system $S[P]$ is a refinement of R.

5.1 Extraction of quantitative data

Assuming that the refinement relations which need to be established are being verified mechanically by the **FDR** tool, extraction of the additional information required to give quantitative results is straightforward, and in the majority of cases causes no significant run-time penalties. As discussed earlier, the quantitative measure associated with a specification state can be encoded in the set of events which the state may permit. A simple modification to the **FDR** system allows the refinement checking process to record which specification states were visited in the course of a check, and to export this information at the end of a check. We then may examine which events on any nominated channel were possible, and so deduce the possible values of the timing margin. Processor slack time can be similarly extracted from the set of all events occurring in any trace of the implementation. In either of these cases we are most interested in the minimum values of the sets of (margin or slack) times returned by the modified tool. Table 3 shows the results obtained for the EMS example.

Input	Output	Limit/μs	Task sequence	Margin/μs
Accel. position	Injector timing	6250	⟨ RAA, CSD, CIT, DI ⟩	3000
Exhaust anal.	"	25000	⟨ RXA, AMX, LSS, CSD, CIT, DI ⟩	2250
Engine speed	"	6250	⟨ RSD, CIT, DI ⟩	2250
Engine speed	Tachometer	25000	⟨ RSD, DTM ⟩	4000

Table 3. Some sequence specifications for the EMS, with margins

6 Extensions, Prospects and Related Work

6.1 Inter-processor communications & fault-tolerance

While establishing the properties described above can give significant confidence in the basic correct operation of a scheduler, when we consider more complex issues, the benefits of formal analysis over informal inspection become still more apparent. Embedded systems need to communicate for a variety of reasons, including the implementation of distributed control, instrumentation and testing, or to exchange information with peer systems providing a fault-tolerant multiprocessor. The design of such systems must address a number of complexities including the architectural and algorithmic arrangement of suitable communication patterns, and the lower level issues of synchronization, timing, and data flow. The CSP formalism can be used to specify and verify system-wide properties such as deadlock-freedom, or fault-tolerant agreement.

Models build from the implementation structure in the manner of Section 4 are generally unwieldy for such verification, but the compositional and symmetric nature of CSP refinement provides a useful approach. Suppose two processors are communicating via shared memory: to ensure reliable communication we must maintain timing constraints on the reading and writing tasks. Specifications based on (3) can be produced for the reader and writer, and each processor verified independently. These specifications abstract from all but the crucial communications related events, and are consequently much simpler than the full processor models. We may now build a model of the system replacing each processor by the specification which we know it to satisfy, and verify system-wide properties using this simpler model.

6.2 Prospects

The scheduler scheme modelled in Section 4 is simple, easy to implement, and consequently widely used in practice. It does have significant disadvantages, however, in that providing a flexible response to a variety of loading conditions and functions can be difficult to achieve with a single order of execution, and the time at which tasks later in the cycle are executed can vary widely. Where the authoritative bodies permit, we may ease these problems by adopting a more flexible scheduling policy. Systems based on priority queues are common, for example. Extension of the analysis given here to such systems is not difficult, and simple examples using a pre-emptive scheduler have also been examined. The same analysis techniques can be applied to automatically generated schedules: the confidence gained by using a verification technique separate from the program which generates a schedule is a valuable asset in some markets.

6.3 Related Work

Many languages [1] and notations [3] have been proposed and adopted for describing real-time systems. The encoding of time used in this work is particularly close to the synchrony hypothesis of ESTEREL [1], which assumes that elementary computation and communication take negligible time. Verification work based on these languages, however, tends to use different notations to express properties and system models: our use of CSP for both purposes not only enables partial abstraction as described in Section 5, but also removes the practical barriers of introducing and maintaining two distinct languages. This also applies to the work in [2], which uses the SMV model-checker to yield similar results to those described here. The modelling of time used in that work, however, depends on a synchronous transition relation: time is measured in terms of the number of state-transitions undergone by the system. Our encoding of time as an event, in contrast, provides a more flexible interpretation: different events may encode different clocks (an important feature of multi-processor analysis), and relationships between them can be flexibly expressed as concurrent processes.

Much work on the formalization and verification of fault-tolerance has been done by Rushby *et al.* [12, 7]. Their approach differs in using a logical rather than process algebraic expression of properties and in concentrating on the correctness of the fundamental algorithms rather than on a particular implementation.

7 Summary

As a technical exercise, this work shows how formal specification can be used to verify key properties of embedded scheduling systems taken directly from production software. The results show that all tasks complete before the next cycle is due and demonstrates that tasks are executed with specified frequencies and "jitter". We also produce quantitative estimates of process slack time and the margins associated with input-to-output timing bounds. Variation of the discrete time step used shows that the results are largely independent of this modelling parameter.

The analysis requires only a single model of the software system, which can support both straightforward safety property tests and timing analysis. In practice, a great many timing requirements will be either a repetition constraint or a sequence timing condition. This regularity means that a great many requirements can be expressed in terms of a few basic definitions. The ability of the theory to support compositional verification means that checking these properties is then a mechanical task, involving little human input once the data entry is complete. Further, the systems to be modelled tend to exhibit similar regularity: once we have defined the process structures and models which characterize a class of schedulers or policies, changes to the actual system implementation require modification of the parameters of the model, not its structure.

In terms of the engineering process, we feel that the results are similarly encouraging: we have used this approach on practical problems taken from important application areas, and have had little difficulty in obtaining useful results. Even "real-world" schedulers produced without the intention of applying a formal model seem amenable to capture in CSP, and the models that result are not overly complex for analysis using existing tools. Among the issues highlighted by these projects are:

- Choice of formalism: where practical results in a short time-scale are required a mature theory with simple models and theoretical and practical support (such as CSP) may prove a better choice than a more expressive but more complex theory (such as real-time TCSP).
- Understanding the engineering environment is important. Theorems asserting correctness with respect to given assumptions may not be as useful as cheap investigations of the consequences of a set of approximations.

- Modelling effort should be independent of actual implementations where practical: details of system requirements and designs change far more often than the basic structure.
- Formal methods practitioners need to be open to suggestions: the quantitative results and the modified specification of Section 3.2 were devised in direct response to user queries.

If the application of formal methods is to have a future, we must remember that providing the customer with results is the goal; as with any other engineering discipline, delivering the required information or assurance is more important than the methods used to provide it.

Acknowledgements

Specific thanks are due to: Mike Bardill, Stuart Dootson and Peter Summers of Rolls-Royce Aerospace; Eddie Williams and Paul Jackson of Rolls-Royce & Associates; Neil Brock, Rick Harper, Beth Stanford and Sharon Donald of C.S. Draper Laboratories; Trevor King and Janet Barnes of Praxis Critical Systems; and colleagues at both Formal Systems companies. This work has been supported by the US Office of Naval Research, contract number N00014–91–C–0054. Thanks also to the anonymous referees for their many useful comments.

A The CSP language.

The CSP language is a means of describing components or systems, *processes*, whose external actions are the communication or refusal of instantaneous atomic *events*. All the participants in an event must agree on its performance. The CSP processes we use will be constructed from the following:

$STOP$ is the simplest CSP process: it never engages in any action, and never terminates.

$SKIP$ similarly never performs any action, but instead terminates successfully, passing control to the next process in sequence (see ; below).

$CHAOS_A$ is another simple process: it may perform, or refuse, any actions from the set A at any time.

$a \rightarrow P$ is the most basic program constructor. It waits to perform the event a and after this has occurred subsequently behaves like process P. The same notation is used for outputs ($c!v \rightarrow P$) and inputs ($c?x \rightarrow P(x)$) of values along named channels.

$P \sqcap Q$ represents *nondeterministic* or internal choice. It may behave like P or Q arbitrarily.

$P \Box Q$ represents external or *deterministic* choice. It will offer the initial actions of both P and Q to its environment at first; its subsequent behaviour is like P if the initial action chosen was possible only for P, and like Q if the initial action selected Q. If P and Q have common initial actions, its subsequent behaviour is nondeterministic (like $\sqcap$). A deterministic choice between $STOP$ and another process, $STOP \sqcap P$, is identical to P.

$P \parallel_A Q$ represents parallel (concurrent) composition. P and Q evolve separately, except that events in A occur only when P and Q agree to perform them.

$P ; Q$ is a sequential, rather than parallel, composition. It behaves like P until and unless P terminates successfully; its subsequent behaviour is that of Q.

$P \setminus A$ is the CSP abstraction or hiding operator. This process behaves as P except that events in set A are hidden from the environment and are solely determined by P: the environment can neither observe nor influence them.

We also use the obvious generalizations of the choice operators over non-empty sets, written $\sqcap_{x:X}$ and $\square_{x:X}$.

References

1. G. Berry and G. Gonthier. The ESTEREL synchronous programming language: design, semantics, implementation. *Science of Computer Programming*, 1992.
2. S. Campos, E. Clarke, W. Marrero, and M. Minea. Timing analysis of industrial real-time systems. In *Workshop on Industrial-Strength Formal Specification Techniques (WIFT'95)*, pages 97–107. IEEE, 1995.
3. D. Harel. STATECHARTS: A visual formalism for complex systems. *Science of Computer Programming*, 1987.
4. C.A.R. Hoare. *Communicating Sequential Processes.* Prentice-Hall, 1985.
5. David M. Jackson. Verifying Timing Properties of Static Schedulers. Contractors report to U.S. ONR SBIR N00014-93-C-0213, Formal Systems Design and Development, Inc., P.O. Box 3004, Auburn, AL 36831-3004, 1995.
6. X. Nicollin, J.L. Richier, J. Sifakis, and J. Voiron. ATP: an algebra for timed processes. In *Proceedings IFIP Working Group Conference on Programming Concepts and Methods*, pages 402–429. Springer-Verlag, 1990.
7. Sam Owre, John Rushby, Natarajan Shankar, and Friedrich von Henke. Formal verification for fault-tolerant architectures: Prolegomena to the design of PVS. In *Transactions on Software Engineering Vol. 21*, pages 107–125. IEEE, 1995.
8. Oxford TCSP Group. Timed CSP: Theory and practice. In *Proceedings of REX Workshop, Nijmegen.* Springer-Verlag, 1991.
9. Requirements and Technical Concepts for Aviation, Washington, DC. *DO-178B: Software Considerations in Airborne Systems and Equipment Certification*, 1992.
10. A.W. Roscoe. Modelling discrete time in untimed CSP. Contractors report to U.S. ONR SBIR N00014-93-C-0213, Formal Systems Design and Development, Inc., P.O. Box 3004, Auburn, AL 36831-3004, 1995.
11. A.W. Roscoe et al. Hierarchical Model-checking for CSP. In *Proceedings of TACAS '95.* Springer-Verlag, 1995.
12. John Rushby. Formal Methods and their Role in the Certification of Critical Systems. Technical report SRI-CSL-95-01, SRI International, 1995.
13. UK Ministry of Defence. *Interim Defence Standard 00-55: The Procurement of Safety Critical Software in Defence Equipment*, April 1991.

Model Checking in Practice: An Analysis of the ACCESS.bus™ Protocol using SPIN

Bernard Boigelot[1]* and Patrice Godefroid[2]**

[1] Université de Liège
Institut Montefiore, B28
B-4000 Liège Sart-Tilman, Belgium
boigelot@montefiore.ulg.ac.be

[2] AT&T Bell Laboratories
1000 E. Warrenville Road
Naperville, IL 60566, U.S.A.
god@research.att.com

Abstract. This paper presents a case study of the use of model checking for analyzing an industrial protocol, the ACCESS.bus™ protocol. Our analysis of this protocol was carried out using SPIN, an automated verification system which includes an implementation of model-checking algorithms. A model of the protocol was developed, and properties expressed by linear-time temporal-logic formulas were checked on this model. This analysis revealed subtle flaws in the design of the protocol. Developers who worked on implementations of ACCESS.bus™ were unaware of these flaws at a very late stage of their development process. We also present suggestions for solving the detected problems.

1 Introduction

State-space exploration techniques are increasingly being used for debugging and proving correct finite-state concurrent reactive systems (cf. [Rud87, Liu89, HK90, Hol91, DDHY92, FGM+92]). These techniques consist of exploring a global state graph, called the *state space*, representing the combined behavior of all concurrent components in the system. This is done by recursively exploring all successor states of all states encountered during the exploration, starting from a given initial state, by executing all enabled transitions in each state. Many different types of properties of a system can be checked by exploring its state space: deadlocks, dead code, unspecified receptions, buffer overruns, etc. Moreover, the range of properties that state-space exploration techniques can verify has been substantially broadened during the last decade thanks to the development of

* "Aspirant" (Research Assistant) for the National Fund for Scientific Research (Belgium). The work of this author was done in part while visiting AT&T Bell Laboratories.

** This work was carried out in part while this author was with the University of Liège.

model-checking methods for various temporal logics (e.g., [CES86, LP85, QS81, VW86]).

In this paper, we present an application of model checking for the analysis of the ACCESS.bus™protocol. The ACCESS.bus™ protocol is a serial communication protocol aimed at providing a simple, uniform, and inexpensive way to connect peripheral devices (such as keyboards, mice, modems, monitors, and printers) to a host computer. It has been developed and standardized by an industrial consortium of computer and peripheral manufacturers, referred to as the *ACCESS.bus™ Industry Group* [ACC94]. At the time of this writing, implementations of the ACCESS.bus™ protocol already exist, and are expected to be commercialized soon.

Our analysis of the correctness of the ACCESS.bus™protocol was performed using the automated protocol verification system *SPIN* [Hol91]. SPIN checks properties of communication protocols, modeled in the *Promela* language, by exploring their state space. Promela is a nondeterministic guarded-command language for modeling systems of concurrent processes that can interact via shared variables and message channels. Interaction via message channels can be either synchronous (i.e., by rendez-vous) or asynchronous (buffered) with arbitrary (user-specified) buffer capacities, and arbitrary numbers of message parameters. Given a concurrent system modeled by a Promela program, SPIN can check for deadlocks, dead code, violations of user-specified assertions, and temporal properties expressed by linear-time temporal-logic formulas. When a violation of a property is detected, SPIN reports a scenario, i.e., a sequence of transitions, violating this property.

Our analysis of the ACCESS.bus™protocol pointed out several ambiguities in the standardized document specifying the protocol. Moreover, it revealed subtle and potentially harmful flaws in the design of the protocol itself. Developers who worked on implementations of ACCESS.bus™ were still unaware of these flaws at a very late stage of their development process.

This paper is organized as follows. In the next section, we present an overview of the ACCESS.bus™ protocol. Next, we describe our model for this protocol, and discuss our assumptions. In Section 4, we specify two basic properties that the protocol has to satisfy. Then, we turn to the verification of these properties. For both of these properties, SPIN reported scenarios violating the property. These scenarios are presented in Sections 5 and 6. By analyzing these scenarios, causes of errors have been identified, and suggestions for solving the detected problems are presented.

2 ACCESS.bus™ Protocol

The ACCESS.bus™ protocol is a serial communication protocol. Its purpose is to provide a simple, uniform and inexpensive way to connect peripheral devices to a host computer. The analysis presented in this paper is based on release 2.2 of the protocol specifications [ACC94].

An important feature of ACCESS.bus^{TM} is that it supports dynamic reconfiguration, which means that devices can be connected to the bus while the system is operating, and can become operational without the system being rebooted. The overall structure of ACCESS.bus^{TM} is illustrated in Figure 1. The protocol is composed of a hardware layer based on the I^{2}C protocol developed by Philips, and of two software layers referred to as "Base Protocol" and "Device Drivers". Device Drivers are controlled by user applications running on the host.

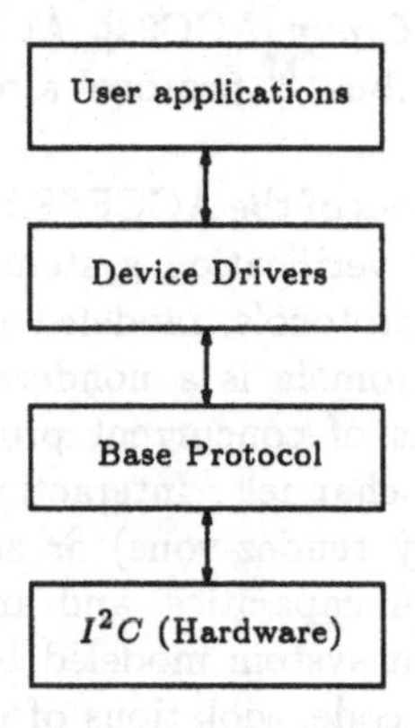

Fig. 1. **Structure of ACCESS.bus^{TM}.**

The I^{2}C protocol is a serial protocol that is used for interconnecting IC's inside electronic appliances such as TV's and VCR's. It uses a *bus* composed of two wires, *serial data* (SDA) and *serial clock* (SCL), which connects the host and the devices together. Each *component* (i.e., device or host) has an 8-bit I^2C *address* which is not necessarily unique and may change over time. When a component is plugged in, its address becomes the *default I^2C address.* Information is transmitted on the I^{2}C bus by means of *messages* composed of an *address part* and a *data part.* Since the bus is synchronous, there is no propagation delay. Any I^{2}C component may try to send a message at any time over the bus. Although a *same* message can be sent simultaneously by several components, an *arbitration mechanism* ensures that two *different* messages are never sent at the same time. This mechanism is deterministic: whenever two or more components attempt to simultaneously send different messages over the I^{2}C layer, the conflict is resolved in favor of the same message. A transmitted message is received by a component if and only if the address of the component matches the address part of the message, and the component is not simultaneously transmitting the same message over the bus. A message can thus be *lost* if its recipient is simultaneously transmitting the same message, or if there is no recipient. Each time a message is sent over the I^{2}C layer, its sender receives a *Positive Acknowledgment* from the I^{2}C layer if the message is received by another component, and a *Negative Acknowledgment* otherwise.

The Base Protocol aims at ensuring that every device will always be recog-

Message Types	Purpose
Reset()	**Force a device to its power-up state and to the default I^2C address. This message is sent by the host on power-up to all the I^2C addresses. A device also sends this message to its address right after being assigned a new address.**
Attention()	**Inform the host that a device has finished its power-up/reset test and needs to be configured.**
IdentificationRequest()	**Ask a device for its *identification string*, which is a sequence of bytes describing the hardware composing the device. This message is issued by the host after reception of an *Attention* message from a device.**
IdentificationReply(Id)	**Reply to *IdentificationRequest* with the identification string *Id* of the device.**
AssignAddress(Id, Addr)	**Ask all the devices with a matching identification string *Id* to turn their address into *Addr*.**
PresenceCheck()	**Check if a device is present on the bus at a specific address (specified in the address part of the message). This message is sent by the host at regular intervals of time in order to detect new and missing devices.**
CapabilitiesRequest(Offset)	**Ask a device to send a fragment (specified by *Offset*) of its *capabilities string*, which is a sequence of bytes describing the functional characteristics of the device.**
CapabilitiesReply(Offset, Data)	**Reply to *CapabilitiesRequest* with a fragment of the capabilities string of the device.**
EnableApplicationReport()	**Enable or disable a device to send application reports, that is, device-dependent functional information, to the host.**
ApplicationReport(Data)	**Send device-dependent functional information.**

Fig. 2. Base Protocol Message Types.

nized by the host within a finite amount of time after being plugged in, that it will be assigned a unique I^2C address, and that its Device Drivers will be able to send and receive device-dependent functional data (such as mouse moves). The Base Protocol defines a set of message types that can be sent over the I^2C layer. These message types are listed in Figure 2. When a device is plugged in, it sends an *Attention* message to the host, which should reply with an *Identification-Request* message, which should itself be replied to with an *IdentificationReply* message from the device. Then, the host should send an *AssignAddress* message containing a new I^2C address for the device. When processing this message, the device updates its address, and sends a *Reset* message to this address.

3 Design of the Model

Our analysis of ACCESS.bus™ focused on the power-up/reset and identification phases, that is, the part of the Base Protocol dealing with *Reset, Attention, IdentificationRequest, IdentificationReply, AssignAddress* and *PresenceCheck* messages. We made the following assumptions in order to resolve ambiguities in the specification document.[3]

- At the Base Protocol layer, every message received from the I^2C layer is stored in a bounded fifo buffer while waiting to be processed. If the buffer is full, new incoming messages are lost.
- The processing of a *Reset* message by a Base Protocol entity empties its associated fifo buffer.

Moreover, the following features of ACCESS.bus™ were not modeled:

- the deterministic nature of the I^2C arbitration mechanism,
- the timing constraints defined in the specification document, and
- the possible corruption of messages sent over the I^2C bus.

Consequently, if a message is sent over the I^2C layer at the same time by one or more components, it is always correctly received exactly once by every component with a matching address that does not belong to the set of the senders.

The overall structure of the model is shown in Figure 3. Each component is modeled by two processes: a *microcontroller* and an *Upper Base Protocol* (UBP). The I^2C bus is modeled by shared variables, since message broadcasting is not a basic communication primitive in Promela. A set of semaphores is used to control the access to the bus.

Each microcontroller continually listens to the bus, grabs messages destined to its corresponding UBP, and appends them to a bounded fifo buffer, which is a basic Promela data type. Each UBP takes messages from its associated fifo buffer, and processes them according to the protocol rules (cf. Figure 2). It can send messages directly (without queuing) over the I^2C layer. Moreover, it can nondeterministically switch between two modes, plugged and unplugged,

[3] These assumptions match those made by the developers we had contacts with.

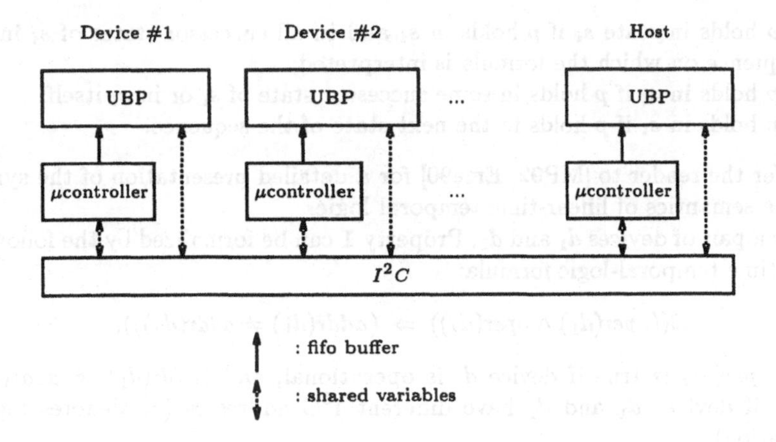

Fig. 3. Structure of the model.

in order to simulate repeated pluggings and unpluggings of the corresponding component.

Initially, all devices are assumed to be unplugged. To keep the state space of the Promela model as small as possible, the maximum size of each fifo buffer was set to two elements, and the number of devices was limited to two. The complete Promela model contains about 200 lines of code.

4 Properties

The specification document [ACC94] does not contain a precise and complete description of the service provided by the Base Protocol to the Device Drivers. Two basic properties that have to be satisfied by the Base Protocol were extracted from the document.

Property 1. A device d_i is said to be *operational* when it has an I^{2}C address $addr(d_i)$ different from the default I^{2}C address, and it has sent a *Reset* message to the address $addr(d_i)$. At any time, all devices that are operational must have different I^{2}C addresses.

This property can be formalized by using linear-time propositional temporal logic [MP92]. Linear-time temporal logic can be used for specifying properties of infinite sequences of states. Propositions in the logic correspond to boolean conditions on variables and process states of the program. Formulas are constructed over propositions using the classical boolean connectives ($\neg$, $\vee$, ...) and the temporal operators $\Box$ (always), $\Diamond$ (eventually), and $\bigcirc$ (next). Formulas are interpreted on *infinite* sequences $s_0 s_1 s_2 \ldots$ of states: given a particular infinite sequence of states, the formula is either satisfied or falsified by this sequence. Informally, one has:

- $\Box p$ holds in state s_i if p holds in s_i and in all successor states of s_i in the sequence on which the formula is interpreted;
- $\Diamond p$ holds in s_i if p holds in some successor state of s_i or in s_i itself;
- $\bigcirc p$ holds in s_i if p holds in the next state of the sequence.

We refer the reader to [MP92, Eme90] for a detailed presentation of the syntax and the semantics of linear-time temporal logic.

For a pair of devices d_1 and d_2, Property 1 can be formalized by the following linear-time temporal-logic formula:

$$\Box((oper(d_1) \wedge oper(d_2)) \Rightarrow (addr(d_1) \neq addr(d_2))),$$

where $oper(d_i)$ is true if device d_i is operational, and $(addr(d_1) \neq addr(d_2))$ is true if devices d_1 and d_2 have different I^2C addresses ($\Rightarrow$ denotes logical implication).

The second property of the Base Protocol we consider is the following.

Property 2. Whenever a device is plugged in, it will eventually become operational, provided that it remains plugged.

This property can be formalized by the following linear-time temporal-logic formula:

$$\Box(plugged(d_1) \Rightarrow \Diamond(oper(d_1) \vee \neg plugged(d_1))),$$

where $plugged(d_1)$ is true if device d_1 is plugged.

Given the finite state space A_G of a system and a linear-time temporal-logic formula f, checking that all infinite sequences of states defined by transitions in A_G satisfy f is known as the *model-checking problem*. Various techniques have been proposed for solving this problem [LP85, VW86, CVWY90, GH93, GPVW95]. SPIN includes an implementation of the algorithms presented in [GH93] and [GPVW95], which are based on a depth-first search in the state space of the system (see [GH93] for details). When SPIN detects a sequence of states that violates the property to be checked, it stops its search, and exhibits this scenario (formed by all states and transitions currently stored in the depth-first-search "stack") to the user.

Let us now turn to the results obtained by SPIN with the Promela model described in the previous section and the two properties defined above.

5 Verification of Property 1

5.1 First Flaw

After a few seconds of computation, SPIN detected that the first property was not satisfied.

Figure 4 depicts a first sequence of transitions leading to a state where two devices are operational while having been assigned the same I^2C address. In this diagram, a thin vertical *time line* is associated with each plugged component. Time increases from the top to the bottom of the time lines. The sending of a

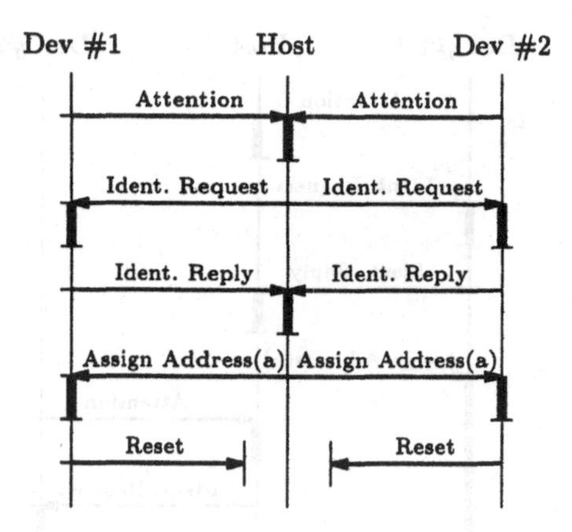

Fig. 4. First flaw.

message through the I^2C layer is represented by an horizontal arrow drawn from the time line of the sender to the time line of the receiver. (Indeed, there is no delay between the sending and the reception of a message.) The head and the tail of the arrow correspond to the exact moment when the message starts to be transmitted on the I^2C bus. If a message is lost (i.e., is not received by any component), the corresponding arrow does not reach any time line. A message is lost when its recipient does not exist, when its recipient is sending the same message over the bus, or when the fifo buffer of the recipient is full. Thick vertical lines represent the delay between the moment when the message is appended to the input buffer of its recipient and the moment when the message is actually processed by its recipient.

In the scenario of Figure 4, two devices with the same identification string are plugged in at the same time. If both devices send and receive simultaneously all the messages shown in Figure 4, it is impossible for the host to distinguish them. Moreover, the self-addressed *Reset* message is not received by any device if they both send this message at the same time.

This problem is a direct consequence of the properties of I^2C, and is not surprising. However, it is worth noticing that having two devices sending the same message at exactly the same time is not an unlikely event. Two devices that wait for sending a message will synchronize on the message frame currently being transmitted on the I^2C bus, and will both start trying to transmit their message at the exact end of this frame.

5.2 Second Flaw

A more complex sequence of events violating Property 1 is given in Figure 5. As in the previous scenario, two devices are plugged in and have the same identification string. The first device finishes its internal initialization process, and sends an *Attention* to the host at time t_0. At time t_1, the host assigns the address a to this device by sending an *AssignAddress* message, which is stored in the input

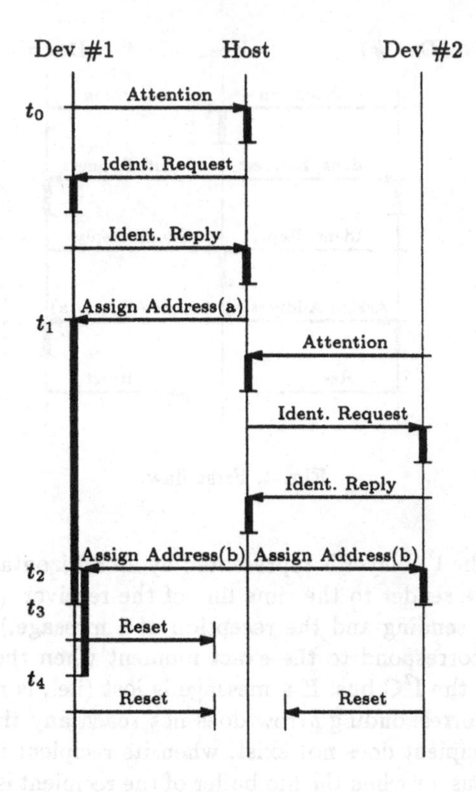

Fig. 5. Second flaw.

fifo buffer of the device. Then the second device sends an *Attention* to the host, and enters its identification phase. When the host assigns the address b to the second device at time t_2, the *AssignAddress* message is also received by the first device, since its address is still the default address at that time, because the request to change its address to a is still waiting in its buffer and has not been processed yet. When the first device finally processes its incoming messages, it changes its address to a at time t_3, sends a self addressed *Reset*, and sets its address to b at time t_4. The self addressed *Reset* messages are then sent simultaneously by both devices, and are thus lost, allowing the two devices to become operational with the same address b.

This scenario reveals another problem in the protocol: here, the erroneous situation results not only from losing two *Reset* messages, but also from delaying an *AssignAddress* in a fifo buffer.

5.3 Third Flaw

When observing the first two flaws, one could wonder if Property 1 is violated only when two devices may share the same identification string. SPIN can easily show that this is not the case. A scenario resulting in the assignment of the same

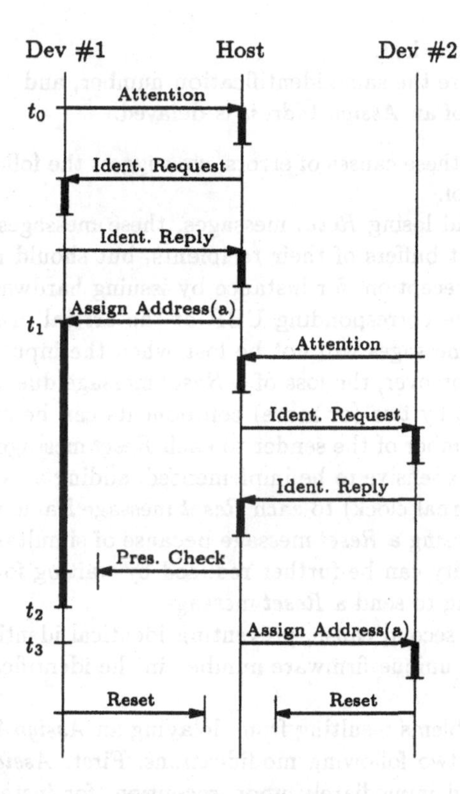

Fig. 6. Third flaw.

address to two devices with different identification strings is given in Figure 6. As in the previous scenario, the first device starts its identification phase at time t_0, and the processing of the *AssignAddress* message received from the host at time t_1 is delayed until time t_2. In the meantime, the second device sends an *Attention* to the host, and proceeds with its identification phase. On reception of an *IdentificationReply* from the second device, the host issues a *PresenceCheck* aimed at checking if the first device is still plugged. The first device does not receive this *PresenceCheck* message, since it is still using the default bus address. Therefore, the host receives a *Negative Acknowledgment* from the I^2C layer. It concludes that the first device is not present anymore, and that address a is available. It then assigns address a to the second device at time t_3. Again, if the self-addressed *Reset* messages are sent simultaneously by the two devices, they are lost, and both devices become operational with the same address a, thus violating the first property.

5.4 Suggestions

The three scenarios presented in Figures 4, 5, and 6 reveal the existence of three causes of errors for Property 1 in the Base Protocol:

- a *Reset* message is lost,
- two devices share the same identification number, and
- the processing of an *AssignAddress* is delayed.

For eliminating these causes of errors, we suggest the following modifications to the Base Protocol.

In order to avoid losing *Reset* messages, these messages should not be appended to the input buffers of their recipients, but should rather be processed immediately upon reception, for instance by issuing hardware interrupts to notify immediately the corresponding UBP of the arrival of such a message. In such a way, *Reset* messages will not be lost when the input buffers of their recipients are full. Moreover, the loss of a *Reset* message due to the fact that it is simultaneously sent by two (or more) components can be avoided by adding a unique firmware number of the sender to each *Reset* message frame. If this radical solution is too expensive to be implemented, adding a random number (e.g., the value of an internal clock) to each *Reset* message frame will strongly reduce the probability of losing a *Reset* message because of simultaneous transmissions of it. This probability can be further reduced by waiting for a random amount of time before trying to send a *Reset* message.

Concerning the second cause, preventing identical identification strings can be done by using a unique firmware number in the identification string of each device.

Finally, the problems resulting from delaying an *AssignAddress* message can be avoided by the two following modifications. First, *AssignAddress* messages should be processed immediately upon reception, for instance by using hardware interrupts as indicated above. Second, whenever a component receives an *AssignAddress* message requesting a modification of its current I^2C address, its fifo buffer should be emptied.

Once we have modified our Promela model by following the above suggestions, SPIN proved in about 30 minutes of computation on a SPARC20 workstation with 256 Megabytes of RAM that Property 1 was satisfied by all possible executions of the model. Note that the correctness proof of our model does not guarantee that the modifications suggested above are sufficient for avoiding the reported problems in practice.

It is worth noticing that the timing constraints defined in the specification document do not prevent any of the three scenarios discussed in this section from occurring. Indeed, each of these scenarios can easily be annotated with timestamps satisfying these timing constraints.

6 Verification of Property 2

6.1 Fourth Flaw

SPIN quickly found scenarios violating Property 2 as well. Indeed, two or more devices can hold the I^2C bus for an unbounded amount of time, and thus prevent other components from sending messages. The timing constraints described in the protocol specification help to prevent such situations, but it is easy to show that these constraints are not sufficient to completely solve the problem. Moreover, the deterministic nature of the I^2C arbitration mechanism (which we did not model) does not help to solve this problem. Indeed, if two devices alternatively send *ApplicationReport* messages over the bus, it can be deduced from the arbitration rules that, if their addresses have high-priority values (i.e., 02 and 03), it is impossible for a third device with an address of lower priority (i.e., FE) to be granted the bus at any time. In this scenario, the third device will never be able to send an *Attention* message to the host to signal its presence in the system, and hence will never become operational.

6.2 Suggestions

The probability of occurrence of such scenarios can be reduced by modifying the structure of the message frames in order to give a higher priority to protocol messages, as opposed to application reports, with respect to the I^2C arbitration mechanism. One could use for this purpose the least significant bit of the first byte of the frame (0 for protocol message frames, 1 for application reports). The protocol specification also includes an optional *Device Bandwidth Management* system, which could help avoiding the problem.

7 Conclusions

We have presented the main stages and the results of an analysis of an industrial protocol, the ACCESS.bus^{TM} protocol. The analysis of this protocol was performed using SPIN, an automated protocol verification system including state-space exploration and model-checking algorithms. Our analysis revealed subtle flaws in the design of this protocol, which were not found by simulating or testing the existing prototype implementations. We have also presented suggestions for solving the detected problems. During this work, SPIN repeatedly proved to be a powerful and efficient verification tool.

Model checking is an effective and simple method for verifying that a concurrent reactive system satisfies a temporal logic formula. It makes it possible to reason about programs without having the burden of carrying out correctness proofs by hand. Indeed, model checking is *fully automatic*: no intervention of the user is required. This is a crucial feature for a verification technique to be used in industry, since products are often (read always) developed under time pressure, and therefore verification steps that would be too time consuming are likely to be skipped.

Although model checking is fully automatic, applying model checking for the analysis of communication protocols is not yet a systematic activity. The ability of quickly modeling a system at the "right" level of abstraction requires training, experience, and some knowledge of how model-checkers work: oversimplifying the model of the system should be avoided in order to be able to detect potential problems in the actual system, while abstracting enough irrelevant details is needed in order to keep automatic verification computationally tractable. Moreover, ingenuity and tenacity are often necessary for expressing interesting properties (i.e., those that might reveal significant errors) and for filtering error traces when looking for plausible scenarios (i.e, those that may occur in a realistic environment). In summary, verification is and remains a discipline in itself, even with the help of powerful verification tools such as model-checkers. Therefore, we believe that the most promising and pragmatic way for introducing formal verification in existing development processes is by forming groups of "validation engineers" who are specially trained for this task.

Another analysis of the Base Protocol can be found in [Hoo95]. It was carried out by using an assertional method with the help of the interactive proof checker included in the verification system PVS [ORS92]. Hooman proved manually that the Base Protocol satisfies Property 1 and 2 provided that all the devices have a different identification string, that messages between base-protocol components are not buffered, and that whenever a component wants to transmit a message over the I^2C layer, this message is transmitted within a bounded amount of time. If one of these (strong) assumptions is not satisfied, no information about the correctness of the protocol is provided. In contrast, our analysis was based on a more detailed model, i.e., on weaker assumptions, and produced counter-examples violating Property 1 and 2. This enabled us to precisely identify the causes of these errors, and to suggest implementable solutions for these problems. Finally, all counter-examples mentioned above and the proof of correctness of our modified model were produced automatically by SPIN.

8 Acknowledgments

We wish to thank Didier Pirottin, who contributed to the results presented in this paper. We are also grateful to Ron Koymans (Philips Research) for challenging us to analyze the ACCESS.bus™ protocol and for fruitful discussions, and to Mark Staskauskas for helpful comments on a preliminary version of this paper.

References

[ACC94] ACCESS.bus Industry Group. Access.bus specifications, version 2.2. 370 Altair Way, Suite 215, Sunnyvale, California 94086, USA, 1994.

[CES86] E.M. Clarke, E.A. Emerson, and A.P. Sistla. Automatic verification of finite-state concurrent systems using temporal logic specifications. *ACM Transactions on Programming Languages and Systems*, 8(2):244–263, January 1986.

[CVWY90] C. Courcoubetis, M. Vardi, P. Wolper, and M. Yannakakis. Memory efficient algorithms for the verification of temporal properties. In *Proc. 2nd Workshop on Computer Aided Verification*, volume 531 of *Lecture Notes in Computer Science*, pages 233–242, Rutgers, June 1990.

[DDHY92] D. L. Dill, A. J. Drexler, A. J. Hu, and C. H. Yang. Protocol verification as a hardware design aid. In *1992 IEEE International Conference on Computer Design: VLSI in Computers and Processors*, pages 522–525, Cambridge, MA, October 1992. IEEE Computer Society.

[Eme90] E. A. Emerson. Temporal and modal logic. In J. van Leeuwen, editor, *Handbook of Theoretical Computer Science*. Elsevier/MIT Press, Amsterdam/Cambridge, 1990.

[FGM+92] J.C. Fernandez, H. Garavel, L. Mounier, A. Rasse, C. Rodriguez, and J. Sifakis. A toolbox for the verification of LOTOS programs. In *Proc. of the 14th International Conference on Software Engineering ICSE'14*, Melbourne, Australia, May 1992. ACM.

[GH93] P. Godefroid and G. J. Holzmann. On the verification of temporal properties. In *Proc. 13th IFIP WG 6.1 International Symposium on Protocol Specification, Testing, and Verification*, pages 109–124, Liège, May 1993. North-Holland.

[GPVW95] R. Gerth, D. Peled, M. Vardi, and P. Wolper. Simple on-the-fly automatic verification of linear temporal logic. In *Protocol Specification Testing and Verification*, pages 3–18, Warsaw, Poland, 1995. Chapman & Hall.

[HK90] Z. Har'El and R. P. Kurshan. Software for analytical development of communication protocols. *AT&T Technical Journal*, 1990.

[Hol91] G. J. Holzmann. *Design and Validation of Computer Protocols*. Prentice Hall, 1991.

[Hoo95] J. Hooman. Verifying part of the ACCESS.bus protocol using PVS. To appear in the Proceedings of Foundations of Software Technology and Theoretical Computer Science, December 1995.

[Liu89] M.T. Liu. Protocol engineering. *Advances in Computing*, 29:79–195, 1989.

[LP85] O. Lichtenstein and A. Pnueli. Checking that finite state concurrent programs satisfy their linear specification. In *Proceedings of the Twelfth ACM Symposium on Principles of Programming Languages*, pages 97–107, New Orleans, January 1985.

[MP92] Z. Manna and A. Pnueli. *The Temporal Logic of Reactive and Concurrent Systems: Specification*. Springer-Verlag, 1992.

[ORS92] S. Owre, J. Rushby, and N. Shankar. PVS: A prototype verification system. In *Proc. 11th Conference on Automated Deduction*, volume 607 of *Lecture Notes in Artificial Intelligence*, pages 748–752. Springer-Verlag, 1992.

[QS81] J.P. Quielle and J. Sifakis. Specification and verification of concurrent systems in CESAR. In *Proc. 5th Int'l Symp. on Programming*, volume 137 of *Lecture Notes in Computer Science*, pages 337–351. Springer-Verlag, 1981.

[Rud87] H. Rudin. Network protocols and tools to help produce them. *Annual Review of Computer Science*, 2:291–316, 1987.

[VW86] M.Y. Vardi and P. Wolper. An automata-theoretic approach to automatic program verification. In *Proceedings of the First Symposium on Logic in Computer Science*, pages 322–331, Cambridge, June 1986.

The Incremental Development of Correct Specifications for Distributed Systems

Stephan Kleuker[1] and Hermann Tjabben[2]

[1] FB Informatik, University of Oldenburg
P.O. Box 2503, 26111 Oldenburg, Germany
E-mail: kleuker@informatik.uni-oldenburg.de

[2] Philips Research Laboratories Aachen
Weißhausstraße 2, 52066 Aachen, Germany
E-mail: tjabben@pfa.philips.de

Abstract. Provably correct software can only be achieved by basing the development process on formal methods. For most industrial applications such a development never terminates because requirements change and new functionality has to be added to the system. Therefore a formal method that supports an incremental development of complex systems is required. The project CoCoN (Provably Correct Communication Networks) that is carried out jointly between Philips Research Laboratories Aachen and the University of Oldenburg takes results from the ESPRIT Basic Research Action ProCoS to show the applicability of a more formal approach to the development of correct telecommunications software. These ProCoS-methods have been adapted to support the development of extensible specifications for distributed systems. Throughout this paper our approach is exemplified by a case study how call handling software for telecommunication switching systems should be developed.

keywords: extension of existing formal methods, combination of methods, incremental development

1 Introduction

During the last few years there has been an ever increasing demand for the fast and flexible introduction of value-added services and new features into private as well as into public telecommunications networks. Intelligent networks (IN), personal communications, computer-supported telecommunications applications (CSTA) are just a few areas from which these services are emerging. Adding more and more services to the telecommunications network leads to a situation where not only the software part of the separate network components but also the structure of the network is becoming increasingly complex. Today, it is already difficult to maintain and to extend the systems. It becomes more and more difficult to understand and to predict the behaviour of the system, e.g. in situations when interactions between services occur.

Therefore it becomes a key issue to design communications system software that provably — not only arguably — meets its requirements. Aim of the project CoCoN (Provably Correct Communication Networks) is to support a stepwise and verified development of communications systems from the requirement phase over the specification phase to an implementation. The vision that we have in mind is an engineering approach for the development of correct communications networks.

The method presented here results from the project CoCoN, carried out jointly by Philips Research Laboratories Aachen and the Department of Computer Science at the University of Oldenburg since April 1993. CoCoN is based on the ESPRIT Basic Research Action ProCoS (Provably Correct Systems) where formal methods for the design of embedded, distributed real-time systems are developed. CoCoN thus aims to show that ProCoS methods — suitably adapted — can contribute to solve problems of industrial relevance.

CoCoN extends the ideas of ProCoS [1, 2, 5] with a method for the development of *extensible* systems. An approach for the reuse and extension of proofs (produced by model-checking or an interactive verification tool) is suggested.

In this paper we identify steps of a general methodology for the incremental development of correct specifications for distributed systems. We show how several individual results and techniques can be combined to a method. Full details are suppressed in favour of an overview of the methodology. However, the formal background is outlined in 14 figures.

To illustrate the typical design steps, a system which describes a simple version of call handling is developed throughout the main text. A more detailed elaboration of our approach can be found in [14]. At the top-level view the system in our example consists of n telephones which are connected by a basic switch (see figure 1). Each call shall be represented by a different process in the network.

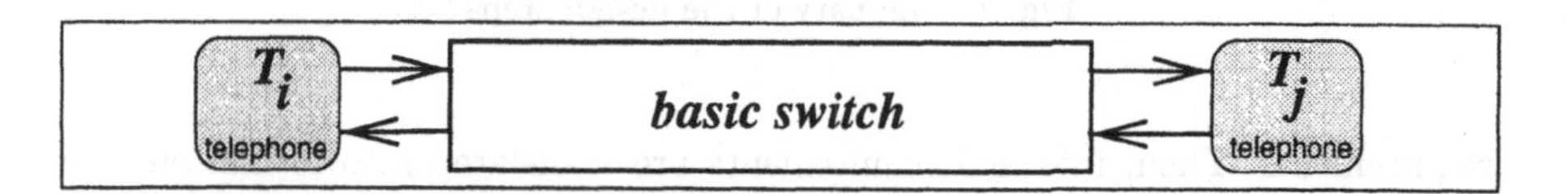

Fig. 1. Architecture of the network

The next section gives a survey of the applied methods. Section 3 describes the development of a first provably correct specification. The sections 4 and 5 describe how verified specifications can be decomposed and extended. The conclusions contain a short summary and possible further steps.

2 Approach

The main steps of the design are sketched in figure 2 and can be described as follows: The complete development begins with describing the main task of the desired system. This task is analyzed and split into subtasks. Tasks can be described in natural language. These tasks are structured as a set of informal

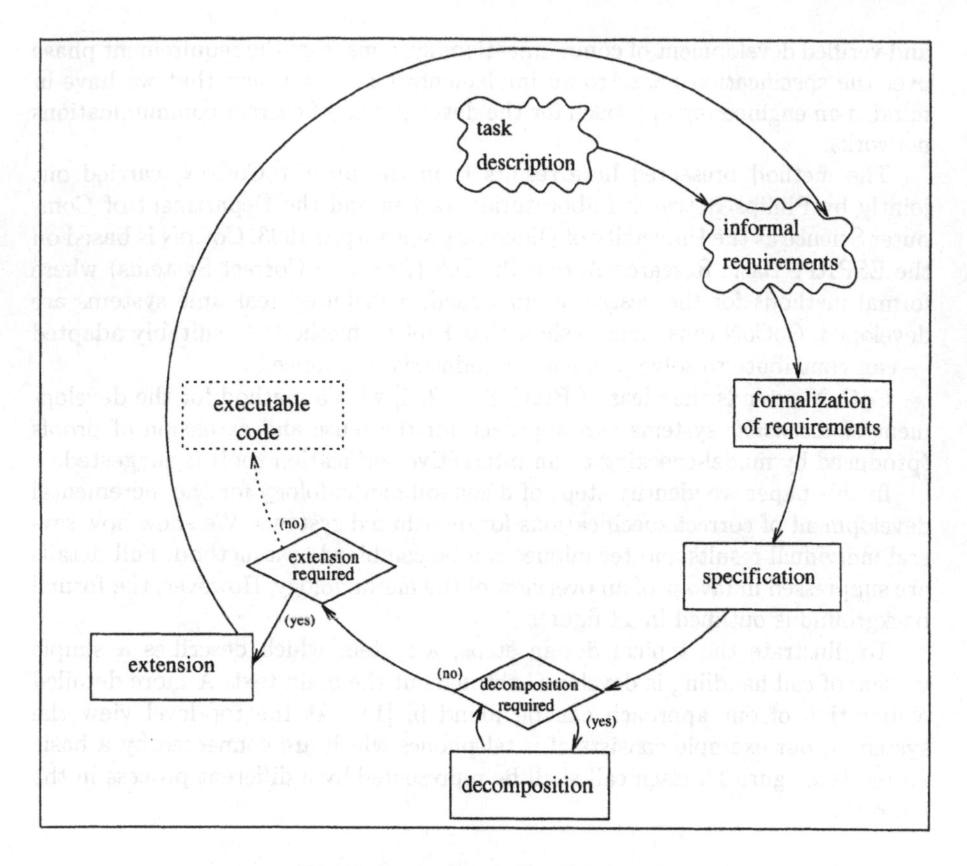

Fig. 2. Summary of the design steps

requirements. Then, informal requirements are translated into formal ones. A system (or specification) is provably correct if and only if the system fulfils these formal requirements.

The next step is the development of a first specification which already takes into account the architectural idea, i.e. it specifies the components and the interfaces between them. It is then proven that this specification fulfils the requirements and is therefore provably correct.

At this point two cases have to be considered. Either this specification is the final desired result and no changes are needed. Then this specification can be transformed into correct code. Or the specification is an intermediate result. Then, next possible steps are a decomposition of the components into sets of smaller ones or an extension of the functionality. An extension begins with an informal description of the changed behaviour of the system or one component. Typical extension tasks have the form "The following sequence of actions shall be possible, too". Here, the loop of the development from informal requirements to a verified specification begins again. This loop leads to an incremental design and therefore it is possible to start with the development of a very simple system and to finish with a complex specification of a distributed system. Note that an extension may also include that old requirements have to be changed.

The most time consuming part of the development is the verification of the specifications against the formal requirements. Therefore a method is needed which guarantees that not each new specification has to be verified again. This is the basic idea of the so called ***transformational approach.*** Verified transformation rules (i.e. rules that preserve the correctness w.r.t. the requirements) are used for the system development (e.g. decomposition and extension). If such a rule is applied it is guaranteed that the result of the application fulfils the same requirements as the initial specification. Therefore, we only have to prove the application conditions of the transformation rules and need not repeat the complete verification. This approach is studied in the project ProCoS which is the foundation of CoCoN. ProCoS emphasizes a constructive approach to correctness, using verified transformations between requirements, specifications, programs and machine code.

In CoCoN two different kinds of transformation rules are used. The first ones are the fully behaviour (or semantics) preserving rules from ProCoS [29, 30]. The other transformation rules preserve only certain important requirements like deadlock-freedom. Proofs that other requirements are fulfilled have to be done again. But old proofs can be reused to a large extent because our proofs annotate the specifications. Therefore it is possible to calculate the changes that are needed for the proofs if the changes for the specifications are known.

The main reason why it is impossible to use only rules of the first kind is that we are interested in extending the system in a way that changes its behaviour. This paper demonstrates how the transformational approach is used in a stepwise design from an informal task description to the desired system.

We summarize the application of different kinds of transformation rules together with the technique of reusing proofs under the term *Specification Engineering.*

3 A First Verified Specification

3.1 From Informal Requirements to Formal ones

A correct program shall always be the final result of the development process. But, what does correct or verified mean? To be more precise: a system or specification is *correct* with respect to certain requirements, if it is *verified* that the program fulfils each requirement. So, the most important part in a formal system development is the question how to get the right formal requirements to begin with.

The following tasks are identified to come to an appropriate initial set of requirements. First, we have to specify which kind of process structure is used. This architecture is a basis for the informal requirements. Then the interfaces (set of possible communications between the processes) are fixed. The informal requirements are given in natural language and describe e.g. the interplay of the processes. The next step is the translation of the informal requirements into formal ones. Note that the initial set of requirements is changed in the subsequent decomposition and extension steps.

It must also be taken into account that a bad set of requirements may lead to a very complex development process or, even worse, to software with undesired behaviour (if an important requirement is forgotten or formalized in the wrong way). Therefore the requirement step is the part in the development process where human faults occur most easily.

An important correctness criterion for requirements is also that of *consistency.* A set of requirements is inconsistent if it is impossible for a specification to fulfil the set. Informal requirements can be investigated by a human being whether an inconsistency exists. For formal requirements it can be proven that the requirements are consistent.

The process of finding requirements, called *requirement engineering* (see also [27]), starts with an informal description of the desired system. Any kind of description of the desired system ranging from oral descriptions to documents from related projects can be important. Requirements of the form 'if this happens then this must not (has to or might) happen' and many more have to be described. An intensive discussion is needed to come from an informal description to informal requirements. Informal requirements are simple sentences in a reduced natural language that can be understood by customers and developers. These requirements shall give a description of the initial system that we have in mind as precisely as possible. They are developed by customer and developer together.

For our example, based on the system components a first architectural concept is fixed (see e.g. figure 1) which will be decomposed into more realistic subsystems later. Our first simple system shall consist of n telephones connected by one process, called basic switch.

A typical informal requirement for our call handling system is:

- If user i dials the number of j and gets a connect signal then he or she cannot be connected with others than j.

In the next step we need to know which events are observed to formalize the requirements. Our communications are related to messages from protocols like DSS.1 (Digital Subscriber Signaling System No. 1). Table 1 lists the set of communications for the originating site (the first letter of these communications is therefore an 'O') and their informal meaning. The corresponding communications for the terminating part (starting with the letter 'T') are omitted.

The developer formalizes the requirements in a formal language which allows the verification of the derived specifications. The customer needs to understand the formal language to the extent that it can be guaranteed that customer and developer are sure of an appropriate set of requirements. A requirement language is needed that is easy to understand and in which it is possible to formalize complex parts in small formulas. We use *trace logic* [32] (traces are finite sequences of communications) as our requirement language. Trace logic is used because it is

from an originating site $T_{i_{orig}}$ to a process $Call_{i-j}$ that represents a call from i to j inside the process *network*:	
$Osetup_i$	(capital letter O for originating) initial message to the network
$Oinformation_i$	transmission of the complete number of the called party
$Odiscon_i^u$	originating site initiates call termination (^{u} for "from user")
$Odiscompl_i^n$	originating site acknowledges a call termination signal from network (indicated by ^{n})
from $Call_{i-j}$ to $T_{i_{orig}}$:	
$Oabort_i$	call is aborted by some reason like no free line or called site is busy
$Oalerting_i$	network indicates that it rings at terminating site
$Oconnect_i$	terminating site has gone off-hook
$Odiscon_i^n$	network indicates that terminating site has gone on-hook
$Odiscompl_i^u$	network acknowledges a call termination signal from originating site
From $T_{j_{term}}$ to $Call_{i-j}$ and vice versa the dual communication to the explained one.	

Table 1. Communications of the first specification

quite easy to formalize given requirements about relations between communications in such an expressive language. It is another advantage that the semantics of our specification language (introduced in a following subsection) is also based on trace logic. Verification boils down to reasoning in trace logic. An example of a formalized requirement is given in figure 3.

$$\forall t_1, t_2, i, j \bullet \; (([\![X]\!][t_1.(Oinformation_i, j).t_2.Oconnect_i/tr] \quad (1)$$
$$\wedge\; t_2 \downarrow Comm(T_i) \in \{\varepsilon, Oalerting_i\}) \quad (2)$$
$$\Rightarrow t_2 \downarrow \{Tconnect_j\} \neq \varepsilon) \quad (3)$$

This is a second order trace logic predicate with free variable X which stands for a simple trace predicate with one free variable tr, $[t/tr]$ denotes the substitution of tr with t, $\cdot \downarrow \cdot$ denotes the projection, $Comm(T_i)$ denotes the set of communications of T_i, ε denotes the empty word (sequence).
The variables tr, t_1 and t_2 range over traces, i.e. sequences of communications. The predicate formalizes that (1) if terminal i calls terminal j after a trace t_1 and i gets a connect signal after t_2 and (2) there is at most one alert signal in between these two communications w.r.t. terminal i then (3) terminal j has gone off-hook in between these two communications. (The ε in the second line denotes the possibility that j goes immediately off-hook without alert signal.)
The typical structure of a requirement looks like:

$$\forall t_1, \ldots, t_k \bullet \; (([\![X]\!][t_1.t_2.\ldots.t_k/tr]$$
$$\wedge\; side\_conditions(t_1, \ldots, t_k))$$
$$\Rightarrow desired\_behaviour(t_1, \ldots, t_k))$$

Fig. 3. An informal requirement formalized in trace logic

If the kind of requirements engineering as described in this paper should be applied by engineers then it must be easy for *them* to write requirements. Trace logic uses many mathematical symbols which look at the first glance quite strange. It is necessary to change some parts of the syntax and/or to add a graphical representation to make the formulae more readable. Our approach will be a 'semi-graphical' representation to support engineers. As mentioned by Lamport [19] and others it seems to be impossible to describe each kind of set of requirements and their combination with a graphical representation. The graphics are either not powerful enough or one has to use too many different symbols. Therefore we want to choose a presentation which supports the reader to understand a requirement, but describes maybe only a subset of the expressed behaviour. For the requirement explained in figure 3 a graphical presentation can look like the diagram presented in figure 4.

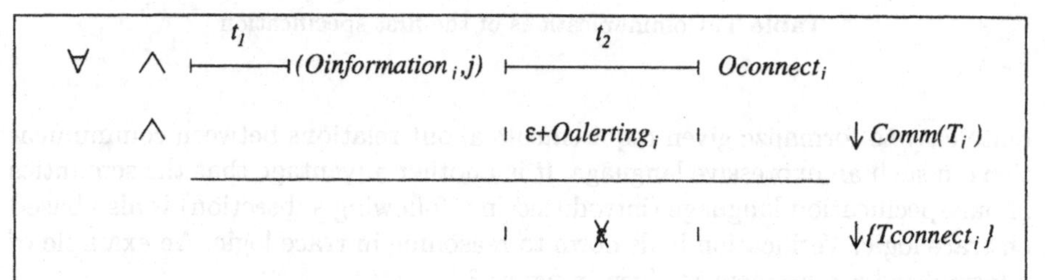

The figure shows the trace variables and their relation. The long horizontal line is used to express implication ('⇒'). The left margin is used to describe the relations and the right margin to describe the projections.

Fig. 4. Graphical representation of a requirement

3.2 First Specification

Our approach for this step can be summarized as follows: A superset of the possible system behaviour is described with *finite automata* and is reduced by examining the requirements to disable undesired behaviour. Finally, it is verified that our specification fulfils the requirements. The following text explains these steps in detail and shows how to come to a first specification for our example. It also includes an introduction to the ProCoS-specification language SL [23, 25].

We start with a description of a superset of all possible traces for all processes. Note that automata can only be used to describe a superset because their expressive power (regular languages) are not powerful enough. Finite automata (related to approaches like [11, 21]) are used to describe the behaviour of each telephone and the switch. The automata are given in figure 5. Each communication is marked to show whether it is an input ($> c$) or an output ($c >$).

Every automaton starts in its initial state, marked by an initial arrow at the top. A communication can only happen if it is possible as the next communi-

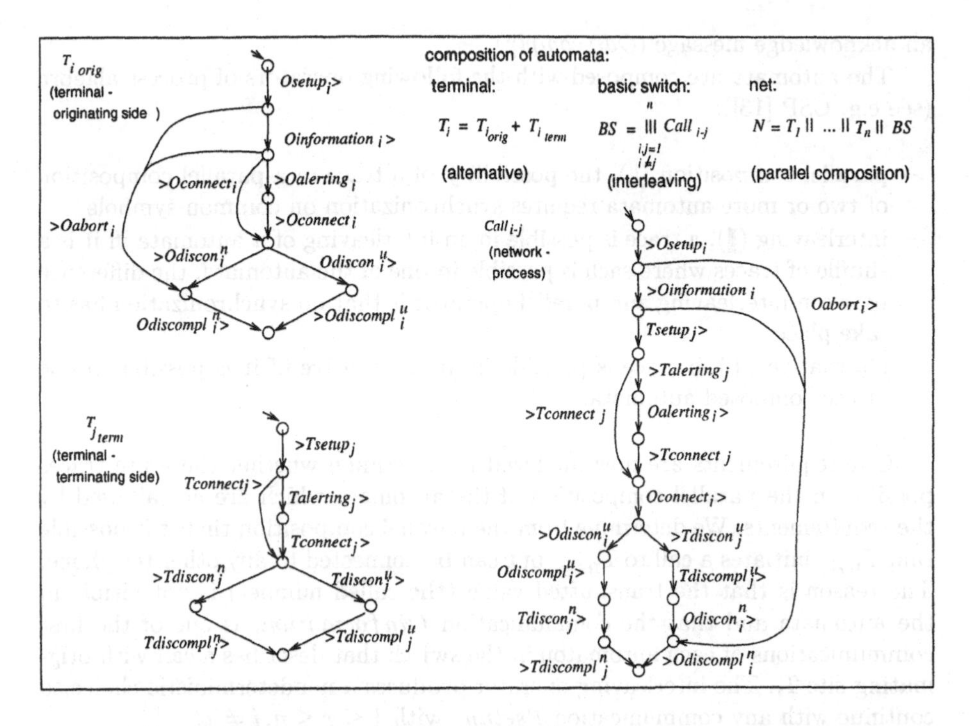

Fig. 5. Automata for each component of a call and the composition

cation by the sender and the receiver (fully synchronized communication). The automaton changes its state to the following state after performing a communication. If a process described by an automaton terminates (no communication can follow) it returns immediately to its initial state. These final states and the first state can be seen as equal or connected by an ε-arc denoting a silent transition. There is no graphical presentation of this fact in our representation because it would be the same for each automaton and because in this way we can emphasize that one cycle of the protocol has terminated.

There exists one automaton for each possible call in the specification of the network, called $Call_{i-j}$ $(i \neq j, 1 \leq i, j \leq n)$. This is a possibility to represent a dynamic number of processes (calls) in a static model.

A typical call can be described with the following sequence of actions: User i goes off-hook (an $Osetup_i$ message is sent to the basic switch). User i dials the number j (the number is transmitted with $(Oinformation_i, j)$). The terminating site is informed $(Tsetup_j)$. The switch is informed that it rings at the terminating site $(Talerting_j)$. The originating site is informed about that $(Oalerting_i)$. The terminating site goes off-hook $(Tconnect_j)$ and the originating site is informed $(Oconnect_i)$. Now, it is possible for both sites to terminate the call, e.g. the terminating site goes on-hook $(Tdiscon_j^u)$. This is acknowledged by the switch $(Tdiscompl_j^u)$. The originating site is informed $(Odiscon_i^n)$ and sends an acknowledge message ($Odiscompl_i^n$).

The automata are composed with the following operators of process algebra (see e.g. CSP [13]):

- parallel composition (||), the possibility of a trace in a parallel composition of two or more automata requires synchronization on common symbols
- interleaving (|||), a trace is possible in an interleaving of n automata iff it is a shuffle of traces where each is possible in one of the automata, the difference between interleaving and parallel operator is that no synchronization has to take place
- alternative (+), a trace is possible in an alternative iff it is possible in one of the composed automata.

Our requirements are now analyzed to determine whether there are traces possible in the parallel composition of the automata which are not allowed by the requirements. We determine from the parallel composition that it is possible that $T_{i_{orig}}$ initiates a call to $T_{j_{term}}$ but can be connected to any other telephone. The reason is that the transmitted value (the called number) is not visible in the automata and that the communication $Oinformation_i$ is one of the first communications of each automaton in the switch that describes a call with originating site T_i. The interleaving operator produces a nondeterministic choice to continue with any communication $Tsetup_x$ with $1 \leq x \leq n, i \neq x$.

The number of the terminating site j is transmitted with the communication $Oinformation_i$. The next communication w.r.t. this call shall be $Tsetup_j$. The value j has to be stored and $Tsetup_j$ activated (i.e. $Tsetup_j$ has to become the only possible next $Tsetup$ communication).

For this reason local variables are added to our specification. We then can formulate that a communication can happen only if a certain pre-condition over the local variables (an *enable-predicate*) is fulfilled. After the execution of a communication a post-condition (an *effect-predicate*) in which values of local variables may change must be fulfilled. Local variables are introduced for each process to formulate these predicates. Altogether a communication can happen if and only if

(a) it is the next possible communication of the related automata (the automata where the communication belongs to)
and
(b) the enable-predicate for this communication of each related automaton is fulfilled.

The enable- and effect-predicate for a communication are summarized in a *communication assertion*. Possible communication assertions for our example are given in figure 6.

We summarize the specification and describe it in the syntax of the specification language SL [23, 25] developed in the ProCoS project:

```
var set[1..n] of bool init false
com Oinformation_i write set
    when true then set[@Oinformation_i]'
com Tsetup_j write set[j]
    when set[j] then ¬set[j]'
```

In our example Boolean variables *set*[*i*], $1 \leq i \leq n$, are used, one for each telephone inside the basic switch. Their initial values are *false*. If a communication $(Oinformation_i, j)$ happens (we refer to the communicated value as $@Oinformation_i$), the value of *set*[*j*] is set to *true*. The communication $Tsetup_j$ is possible only if the value of *set*[*j*] is *true*. The value of *set*[*j*] is reset to *false* after the communication $Tsetup_j$ is executed.

Fig. 6. Communication assertions

```
BS = spec
        <interface>
        <trace assertions>
        <local variables>
        <communication assertions>
     end
```

The interface consists of the communications explained above together with the type of the communicated values. The trace assertions are simple regular expressions over a subset of communications of the interface. Together they describe a superset of all possible traces. An automaton is an equivalent representation of a trace assertion. Therefore we can say that the derived automata describe the trace assertions. The local variables represent the local state. They are used inside the communication assertions in the enable and effect predicates. Trace assertions, local variables and communication assertions are optional parts.

3.3 Verification

The verification that a specification fulfils the given requirements is usually the most complicated part in the formal development. The result of this effort is that verified properties needs not to be tested for the final implementation. If formal steps are applied then the correctness of the implementation w.r.t. to the formalized requirements follows immediately from the correctness of the specification. Therefore time spent with the verification is at least regained in a test phase.

Several techniques have been developed as support for a verifier. The verification of complex specifications has to be supported by computers. Two main approaches are studied in this field:

- The fully automatic approach. The specification and the requirements are the input to a computer program which checks whether the requirements are fulfilled or not. If the requirements are not fulfilled then a counter example is presented. The advantage of this *model checking* [6, 8, 9] approach is that the verifier needs no detailed knowledge of the applied verification technique. The disadvantage is that model checking usually only works for systems with a small state space because time (and storage) which is needed for the verification usually grows exponentially in the number of components (states of the automata, numbers of variables). This ***state space explosion*** problems lead also to the fact that the verifier has to decide in which way he or she prepares the specification and requirements as input for the verification algorithm. This is a big restriction of the advantage mentioned before.

– The interactive approach by using an interactive verification tool like LAMDBDA [3, 4, 10]. The verifier develops a proof for a requirement step by step supported by the verification tool. The tool checks automatically whether preconditions for verification steps are fulfilled and offers suggestions for next verification steps. The verifier needs explicit knowledge about the verification techniques and needs experiences to become an effective verifier. On the other hand, it is shown in that this approach works for more complex specifications.

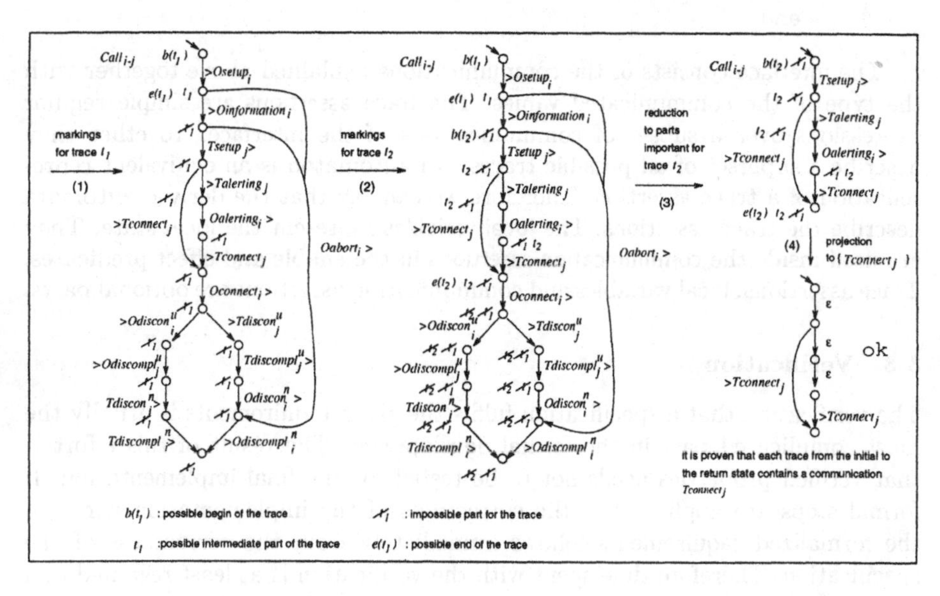

Fig. 7. Verification of the requirement in figure 3 in four steps

A third approach is the combination of the two other approaches [12, 22]. A model checker can be integrated in an interactive verification tool. The model checker solves problems of an appropriate size and the results are combined to a more complex proof.

CoCoN uses the third approach. A model checking algorithm is developed which can be used for the automatic verification of a subclass of trace logic formulae. For formulae outside of this subclass the algorithm calculates the part of the specification which has to be treated an interactive verification.

A *marking algorithm* is used in which proofs annotate the states of the automata. These annotated states can be reused if the same requirement has to be checked for an extended version of the specification. The idea of marking a specification is well-known from the model-checking approach or more general from program verification [26].

The verification of the requirement in figure 3 is sketched in figure 7. Parts of a proof which are not successful do also annotate the states. This information can be used later on for the verification of extensions.

The verification follows the schema: First, it is calculated which parts of the automata can be chosen for the trace variables t_1 and t_2 of the formal requirement in figure 3. Then the side conditions and finally the desired behaviour are checked. (For full details see [18].)

4 Decomposition

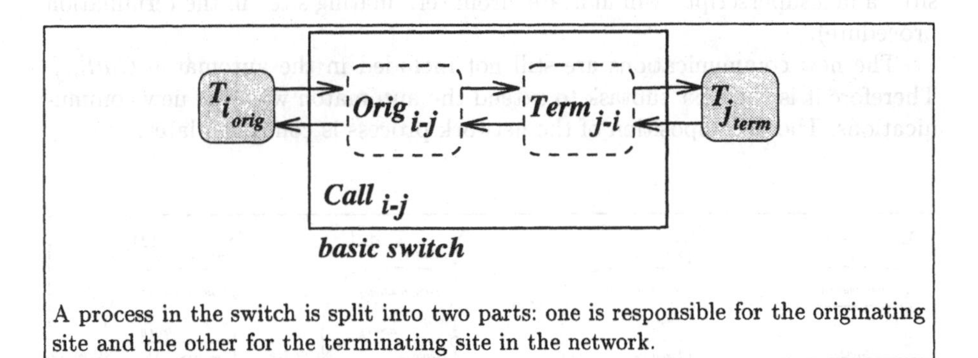
$T_{i\,orig}$
$Orig_{i\text{-}j}$
$Term_{j\text{-}i}$
$T_{j\,term}$
$Call_{i\text{-}j}$
basic switch
A process in the switch is split into two parts: one is responsible for the originating site and the other for the terminating site in the network.

Fig. 8. Architecture after decomposition

After verifying the simple system, the question arises how to use our specification for the next steps. Our intention is to split up the network process in a distributed system where originating and terminating site are represented separately by local processes. These processes could then be allocated at different switches inside the network.

Decomposition is usually done in 3 steps:

(1) determining the *new local communications* for the interface between the desired components,
(2) *augmenting (extending)* the automaton by these local channels,
(3) *parallel decomposition* of the augmented automaton.

Suppose that in the example we add a requirement that each process $Call_{i-j}$ should consist of two parts, one related to the originating and one to the terminating site (see figure 8).

Before we decompose $Call_{i-j}$ into two separate processes we have to think about the new local communications between the new processes. We observe every state of $Call_{i-j}$ and try to find out which protocol is useful between the new processes.

$setup_{ij}$	initial message between new processes
$abort_{ij}$	for an abort of a call
$alert_{ij}$	for ringing at the terminating site
$connect_{ij}$	for a completed connection
$discon_{ij}$	for disconnect initiated
$discompl_{ij}$	for disconnect complete (acknowledge)

Table 2. Communications between originating and terminating part in the network

The interface of table 2 is introduced (a subscript ij indicates that this is a communication from site i to site j, a superscript ^{o} will indicate "from originating site" and a superscript ^{t} will indicate "from terminating site" in the termination procedure).

The new communications are still not included in the automaton $Call_{i-j}$. Therefore it is the next subtask to extend the automaton with the new communications. The decomposition of the network process is continued later.

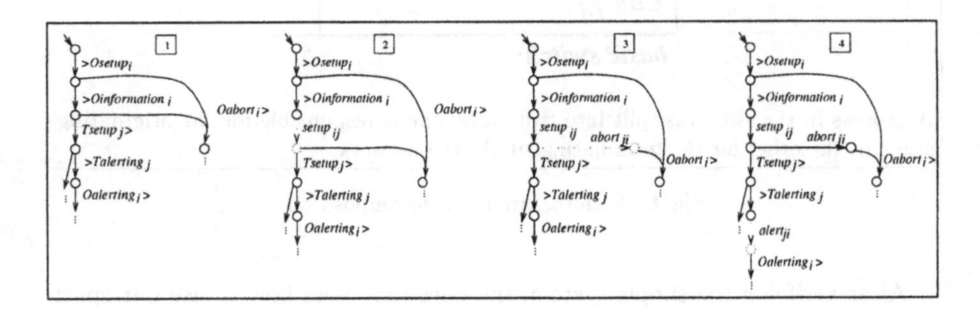

Fig. 9. Extension with local channels

The new communications are local ones. They do not have to be synchronized with the other processes. A local communication of a subprocess of a parallel composition can happen if it is a next possible communication.

The new automaton for $Call_{i-j}$ is the result of applying a transformation rule for adding new local communications several times. The first three applications are described in figure 9.

A local *setup* communication is added in part 2 of figure 9 between the transmission of the dialed number and informing the terminating site. Then, a local communication is added for a local *abort* after the *setup* communication. Finally, a local *alert* communication is added between the communication indicating that it rings at the terminating site and informing the originating site about that.

The new specification is deadlock-free because transformation rules are used which preserve deadlock-freedom. (The application criteria which have to be checked are omitted here.) The old requirements are still fulfilled because no changes are done that are relevant for these requirements.

Now, we have the possibility to use a verified semantics-preserving SL-Transformation rule to decompose the process. The processes after decomposition are described in figure 13 (with ignoring the dotted parts). The process $Call_{i-j}$ is split into $Orig_{i-j}$ and $Term_{j-i}$.

5 Extension

The previous sections described a complete path from informal requirements to a provably correct specification of a distributed system. But this specification is not likely to be a final result because the development process for large distributed systems like telephone networks never comes to an end. One important point is the extension of the existing specification. An approach is needed that takes verified specifications and the desired extensions as an input and produces a verified extension of the specification.

Let $\rightarrow_{A_i}$ be the transition relation of an automaton A_i, let A_i and A_j be two automata that are directly connected, with initial states q_{0_i} and q_{0_j}. Let q_i be a state of A_i and q_j be a state of A_j. Then q_i is in *K-relation* (*K* for german "Kommunikation") to q_j (abbreviated $q_i\ {}^{A_i}\mathsf{K}^{A_j}\ q_j$) iff

$$\exists t,t' : (q_{0_i} \xrightarrow{t}_{A_i} q_i \wedge q_{0_j} \xrightarrow{t'}_{A_j} q_j \wedge t \downarrow (Comm(A_i) \cap Comm(A_j)) = t' \downarrow (Comm(A_i) \cap Comm(A_j))$$

Informally, q_i is in K-relation to q_j iff there exists a possible trace t to q_i in A_i and a possible trace t' to q_j in A_j such that the same sequence of communications w.r.t. $Comm(A_i) \cap Comm(A_j)$ is used. Communications outside of $Comm(A_j) \cap Comm(A_i)$ can be added everywhere in t and t'.

Fig. 10. The K-relation

For the formalization of the effects of an extension and for the calculation of necessary changes an auxiliary relation between states of different processes is defined. It formalizes that if a certain subprocess is in the state p another subprocess might be in the state q (formalized in figure 10). This K-relation is used e.g. to describe how an existing specification can be extended with preserving deadlock freedom.

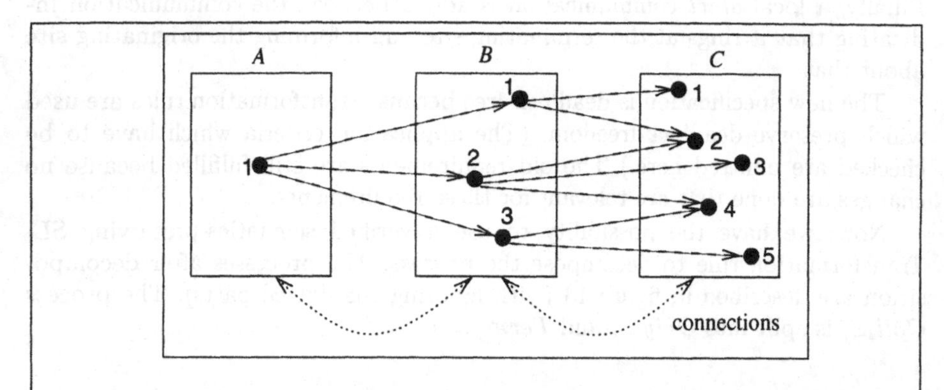

The change of the behaviour of the subautomata A at state 1 can influence many states in B and C. These states are calculated by the K-relation (The dashed arrows denote K-related states, e.g. $1\ {}^{A}\mathsf{K}^{B}\ 2$). Thus a small change in one small component can have a big influence in a component that is far away from the original change.

Fig. 11. A small system with an example of K-related states

Figure 11 shows an informal example for the fact that the change of the behaviour at one state can have substantial influences to many other states of the system. The system in figure 11 consists of three connected processes. The dotted arrows describe the connections between the components. Dashed arrows represent the K-relation and therefore possible states where a change in one component may lead to a different behaviour in another component. A change at state 1 of subautomaton A may lead to a new behaviour at the states $\{1,2,3,4,5\}$ of subautomaton C.

Now, we explain the extension of a system where the result is deadlock-free, too. The requirement 'deadlock freedom' is emphasized because we have observed the following: if deadlock freedom is guaranteed it can be easily shown in many cases that other requirements are fulfilled.

Let us take the example that another requirement is added to the system: we allow that the originating site can terminate a call after dialing a number. The new call termination can be described by a trace t that shall be possible in the new system. The idea is to extend each automaton A with the part of the trace which belongs to the automaton ($t \downarrow Comm(A)$).

Such a trace is added to the automaton by taking two existing states and connecting them with the new (added) trace. Then each related state of the other automata of other subprocesses is calculated. These states are also extended to make the new trace possible in the presence of synchronization and to guarantee that no new deadlocks are introduced. This idea is sketched in figure 12 and an

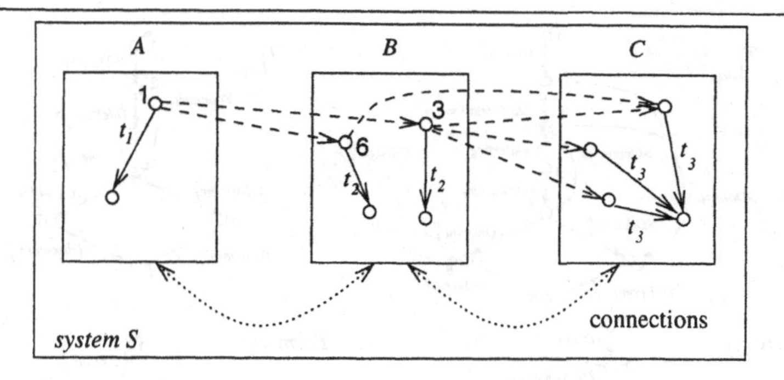

This figure sketches the general idea of extension. First, we choose a state (here state 1 of A) where a new trace t shall be possible, a trace $t_1 = t \downarrow Comm(A)$ is added from this state to a final state. Then, the K-related states of the extended state in B are calculated (here 3 and 6, the K-relation is painted as dashed arrows). These states are extended with $t_2 = t \downarrow Comm(B)$ to final states of B. Finally the K-related states of 3 and 6 are calculated in C and these states are extended with $t_3 = t \downarrow Comm(C)$. If S is deadlock free before the extension then it is deadlock-free afterwards, too.

Fig. 12. Extension of a distributed system with a new trace

example is presented in figure 13. The task is to extend the system in such a way that it is possible for the user to go on-hook after dialing a number. The state 3 of $T_{i_{orig}}$ has to be extended. The new termination is described with a new trace which is added stepwise to the automata. The extension algorithm which is used here is described with optimizations in [16].

The new specification is deadlock free because a deadlock freedom preserving transformation rule is used. The new trace is possible because the extended state is reachable. If we want to prove the other requirements we can reuse the old proofs. The markings of the old proofs are used to calculate the markings for the added part. In most cases, the old markings need not be changed. If changes for these markings are needed, they are calculated by a back-tracking algorithm.

The idea to reuse (parts of successful) proofs is adopted from approaches for sequential programs (like [28] and related to the work of summarizing small proof steps to a large step or tactics). An example for the extension of an existing proof is given in figure 14. (The formal requirement described in figure 3 is decomposed into two requirements, the K-relation is used as auxiliary information in the proof.)

6 Conclusions and Final Remarks

The previous sections describe a general methodology based on several individual approaches for the incremental development of distributed systems. Specification

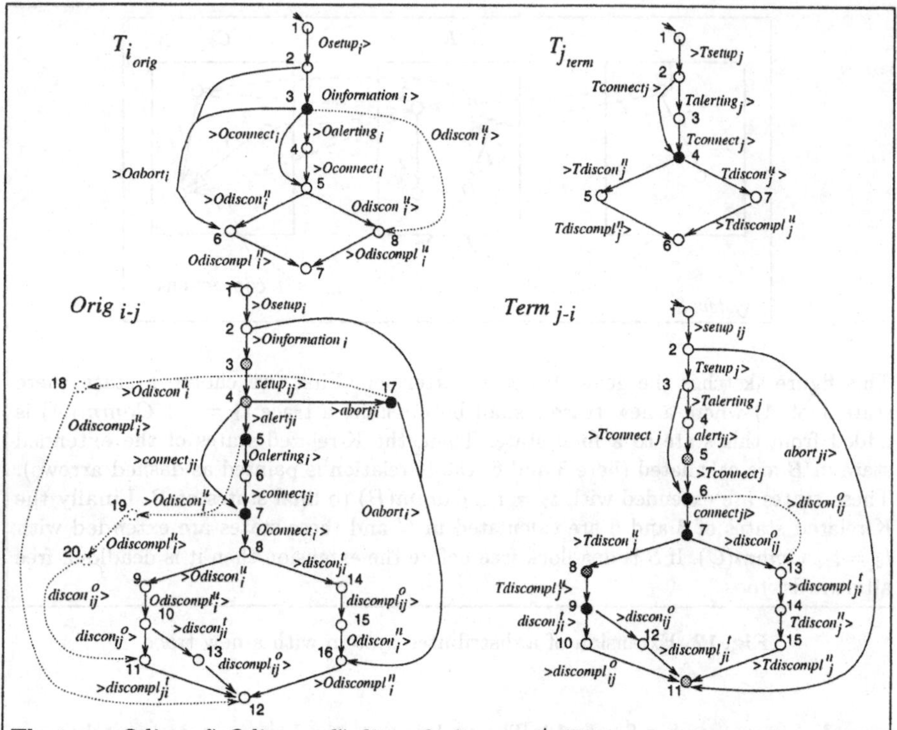

The trace $Odiscon^u_i.Odiscompl^u_i.discon^o_{ij}.discompl^t_{ij}.Tdiscon^n_j.Tdiscompl^n_j$ is added to the system. Black and gray states show K-related states that are used during the extension. The extension is described by the dotted parts. Gray states are not extended because an optimization algorithm is applied.

Fig. 13. Extension of the system

engineering is shown as a way to come to large verified specifications by small intuitive steps. It offers solutions to typical problems like system decomposition and extension of distributed systems. In contrast to other formal methods where only static systems can be developed, our approach enables us to develop extensible systems. Other approaches for an incremental design of systems like [7, 31] describe only the development of asynchronous protocols with the restriction that new communications are added one at a time.

The basic ideas of specification engineering can be transferred to other languages that are based on extended finite state machines (like LOTOS [20]). Future research will cover possibilities and limitations of this idea. Typical phases of the development of extensible systems are summarized in table 3. The way to come to a first verified specification are steps 1 and 2. An extension of a system deals with a sequence of steps 1 and 3. Note that not every typical task must be performed, e.g. in step 3 we can decide for a decomposition or an extension of

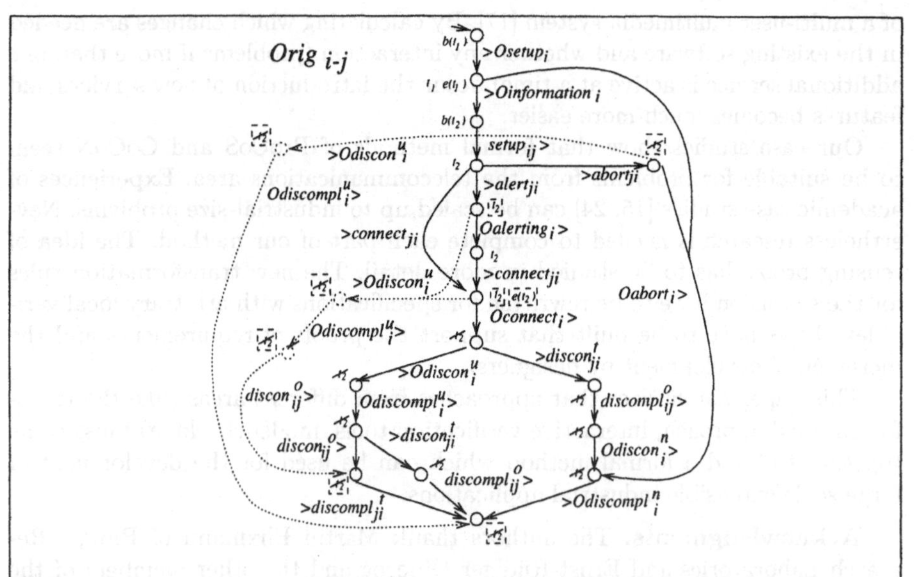

This figures shows the necessary extensions of a proof after the extension of the specifications. Markings in dashed boxed are re-calculated or new markings as a result of the marking algorithm.

Fig. 14. Extending an old proof

the functionality and if we use semantics-preserving transformation rules then no additional verification needs to be done. Otherwise requirements that are not guaranteed by the rule need to be proven again.

step	name of phase	related subjects
1	requirement engineering	informal description informal requirements formal requirements
2	initial specification	typical system behaviour superset of all possibilities restriction verification
3	specification engineering	decomposition extension of functionality transformation verification of new parts

Table 3. Phases in the development of extendable systems

We applied our approach to show the extensibility of a given Private Automatic Branch Exchange (PABX)-specification and are working on a specification of a multi-user multimedia system [17]. By calculating which changes are needed in the existing software and whether any interaction (problems if more than one additional service is active at a time) occur the introduction of new services and features becomes much more easier.

Our case studies show that formal methods of ProCoS and CoCoN seem to be suitable for problems from the telecommunications area. Experiences of academic case studies [15, 24] can be scaled up to industrial-size problems. Nevertheless research is needed to complete each part of our method. The idea of reusing proofs has to be studied in more detail. The new transformation rules for the extension have to be rewritten for specifications with arbitrary local variables. Tools have to be built that support the proofs of requirements and the incremental development by designers.

This paper emphasizes that approaches from different areas (like the transformational approach, interactive verification tools, model-checking) must come together to build a formal method which can be used for the development of large scale extensible industrial applications.

Acknowledgments. The authors thank Martin Elixmann of Philips Research Laboratories and Ernst-Rüdiger Olderog and the other members of the ProCoS Group in Oldenburg for helpful and detailed discussions.

References

1. D. Bjørner, H. Langmaack, C.A.R. Hoare, ProCoS I Final Deliverable, ProCoS Technical Report ID/DTH db 13/1, January 1993
2. D. Bjørner et al., A ProCoS project description: ESPRIT BRA 3104, Bulletin of the EATCS, 39:60-73, 1989
3. J. Bohn, H. Hungar, TRAVERDI - Transformation and Verification of Distributed Systems, in M. Broy, S. Jähnichen, (eds.): KORSO: Methods, Languages, and Tools for the Construction of Correct Software, LNCS 1009 (Springer-Verlag), 1995
4. J. Bohn, S. Rössig, On Automatic and Interactive Design of Communicating Systems, in B. Steffen (ed.): Proc. TACAS '95, LNCS 1019 (Springer Verlag), 1995
5. J. Bowen et al., Developing Correct Systems, Bulletin of the EATCS, June 1993
6. J.R. Burch et al., Symbolic Model Checking: 10^{20} States and Beyond, in Proceedings of the Fifth Annual Logic in Computer Science, June 1990
7. D. Y. Chao, D. T. Wang, An Interactive Tool for Design, Simulation, Verification, and Synthesis of Protocols, Software - Practice and Experience, Vol. 24(8), 1994
8. E.M. Clarke et al., Automatic Verification of Finite State Concurrent Systems Using Temporal Logic Specifications, ACM TOPLAS 8, 1986
9. E.M. Clarke, O. Grumberg, D. Long, Verification Tools for Finite-State Concurrent Systems, in J.W. de Bakker, W.-P. de Roever, G. Rozenberg (eds.): Decade of Concurrency, LNCS 803 (Springer-Verlag), 1995
10. M. Francis et al., LAMBDA Version 4.3, Documentation Set, 1993
11. D. Harel, Statecharts: A Visual Formalism for Complex Systems, Science of Computer Programming 8, 1987
12. H. Hungar, Combining Model Checking and Theorem Proving to Verify Parallel Processes, in C. Courcoubetis (ed.): Computer Aided Verification, LNCS 697 (Springer-Verlag), 1993

13. C.A.R. Hoare, Communicating Sequential Processes, Prentice-Hall, London, 1985
14. S. Kleuker, A. Kehne, H. Tjabben, Provably Correct Communication Networks (CoCoN), Philips Research Laboratories Aachen, Technical Report, 1123/95, 1995 available by ftp: ftp.informatik.uni-oldenburg.de: /pub/procos/cocon/lab1123.ps.Z
15. S. Kleuker, Case Study: Stepwise Development of a Communication Processor using Trace Logic, in D.J.Andrews et al. (eds.): Workshop on Semantics of Specification Languages, Utrecht 1993, Workshops in Computing (Springer-Verlag), 1994
16. S. Kleuker, A Gentle Introduction to Specification Engineering Using a Case Study in Telecommunications, in P.D. Mosses, M. Nielsen, M.I. Schwartzbach (eds.): Proc. TAPSOFT '95, LNCS 915 (Springer-Verlag), 1995
17. S. Kleuker, H. Tjabben, A Formal Approach to the Development of Reliable Multi-User Multimedia Applications, in R. Gotzhein, J. Bredereke, (eds.): Proc. of the 5th GI/ITG-Fachgespräch "Formale Beschreibungstechniken für verteilte Systeme", University of Kaiserslautern, 1995
18. S. Kleuker, Model Checking with Trace Logic (Draft), University of Oldenburg, internal paper, 1995
19. L. Lamport, TLA in Pictures, technical research report, Digital Equipment Corporation, in http://www.research.digital.com/SRC/tla/,1994
20. L. Logrippo, M. Faci, M. Haj-Hussein, An Introduction to LOTOS, Computer Networks and ISDN Systems 23 (1992) 325-342, North-Holland
21. N.A. Lynch, M.R. Tuttle, An Introduction to Input/Output Automata, Technical Report CWI-Quarterly 2(3), CWI, 1989
22. O. Müller, T. Nipkow, Combining Model Checking and Deduction for I/O-Automata, in B. Steffen (ed.): Proc. TACAS '95, LNCS 1019 (Springer Verlag), 1995
23. E.-R. Olderog, Towards a Design Calculus for Communicating Programs, LNCS 527 (Springer-Verlag), p. 61-77, 1991
24. E.-R. Olderog, S. Rössig, A Case Study in Transformational Design on Concurrent Systems, in M.-C. Gaudel, J.-P. Jouannaud (eds.): Proc. TAPSOFT '93, LNCS (Springer-Verlag), 1993
25. E.-R. Olderog, S. Rössig, J. Sander, M. Schenke, ProCoS at Oldenburg: The Interface between Specification Language and OCCAM-like Programming Language. Technical Report Bericht 3/92, Univ. Oldenburg, Fachbereich Informatik, 1992.
26. S. Owicki, D. Gries, An Axiomatic Proof Technique for Parallel Programs, Acta Informatica, 16, 1976
27. H.A. Partsch, Specification and Transformation of Programs, Springer-Verlag, 1990
28. W. Reif, K. Stenzel, Reuse of Proofs in Software Verification, in Shyamasundar (ed.): Foundations of Software Technology and Theoretical Computer Science, Bombay, LNCS 761 (Springer-Verlag), 1993
29. S. Rössig, A Transformational Approach to the Design of Communicating Systems, PhD thesis, University of Oldenburg, 1994
30. S. Rössig, M. Schenke, Specification and Stepwise Development of Communicating Systems, LNCS 551 (Springer-Verlag), 1991
31. P. Zafiropulo et al., Towards Analyzing and Synthesizing Protocols, IEEE Transactions on Communications, Vol COM-28, No. 4, April 1980
32. J. Zwiers, Compositionality, Concurrency and Partial Correctness - Proof Theories for Networks of Processes and Their Relationship, LNCS 321 (Springer-Verlag), 1989

A Theory of Distributing Train Rescheduling

Chris George

United Nations University International Institute for Software Technology (UNU/IIST), Macau

Abstract. We outline the formal modelling of a software system to support the scheduling and rescheduling of trains. The current (prototype) system supports only centralized rescheduling, but in practice rescheduling is done on an area basis, and a distributed system is required. Developing a distributed system involves the notions of *delegability* of functions to adjust schedules and *distributability* of functions to analyse them for conformance to regulations. We formalize these notions in terms of a more abstract, generic specification and then instantiate this to generate a specification of the distributed system.

1 Introduction

The PRaCoSy (Peoples Republic of China Railway Computing System) project [2] is a collaborative project between the Chinese Ministry of Railways and UNU/IIST. The main purpose is to produce software to assist in the dispatching of trains. Efficient dispatching, especially rescheduling to take account of disturbances to the timetable such as train delays, is critical to optimize the use of the railway resources — track, rolling stock and staff.

In the first phase of the project a formal model of the railway network and of a railway timetable [7, 8] were produced in the RAISE Specification Language (RSL [9]). These were developed (by hand) into a prototype *running map* tool [6] that allows train dispatchers to enter a timetable, graphically display it (figure 1) and graphically or textually edit it. This software is currently under evaluation in China.

To illustrate the problem of rescheduling, note in figure 1 that train Y1 overtakes the slower, stopping train K542 in Danyan. On this route, as is common, trains can only overtake at stations, where there are additional tracks. Now, suppose train Y1 leaves Nanjing 10 minutes late. If we adjust Y1's display accordingly it will be scheduled to leave Danyan at the same time as K542. The tool will report this conflict to the dispatcher, who then has to further adjust the timetable to remove the conflict. One option is to delay K542 in Danyan until Y1 has passed through; another is to delay Y1 a little more and let it overtake K542 in the next station, Changzhou.

In China, dispatching of trains is handled at several levels (figure 2). A *dispatch centre* is in charge of the trains over a large area. Beneath that are several *dispatch units*; each deals with part of the area and is in charge of a number of *stations* that actually dispatch trains according to instructions from their

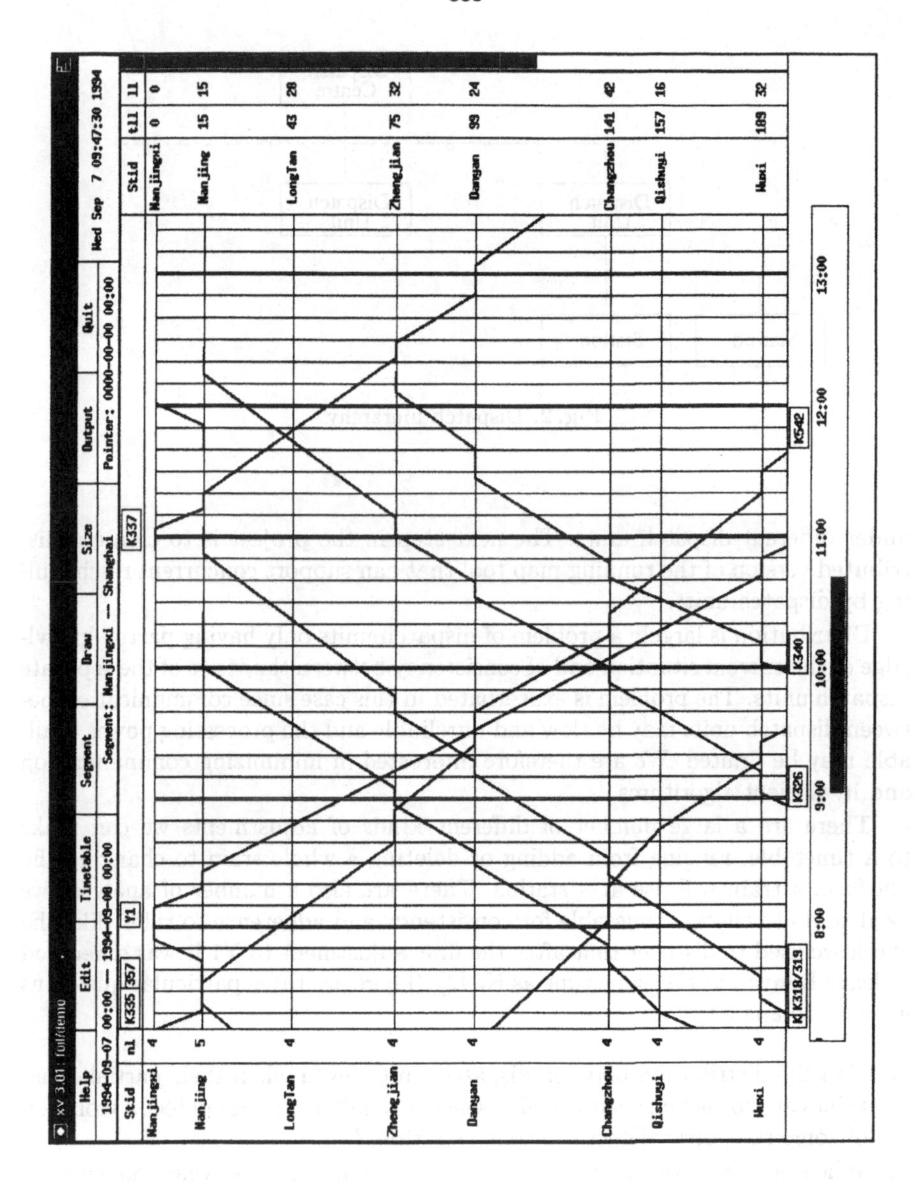

Fig. 1. Running map tool display

dispatch units. The term "station" includes both passenger stations and marshalling yards for the handling of freight trains.[1]

Dispatching is more complicated when there is more than one dispatch unit involved. The discussion earlier about whether train Y1 should overtake K542 in Danyan or Changzhou would be more complicated if these two stations were

[1] In this paper we will for simplicity use only the terminology relevant to passenger trains and passenger stations.

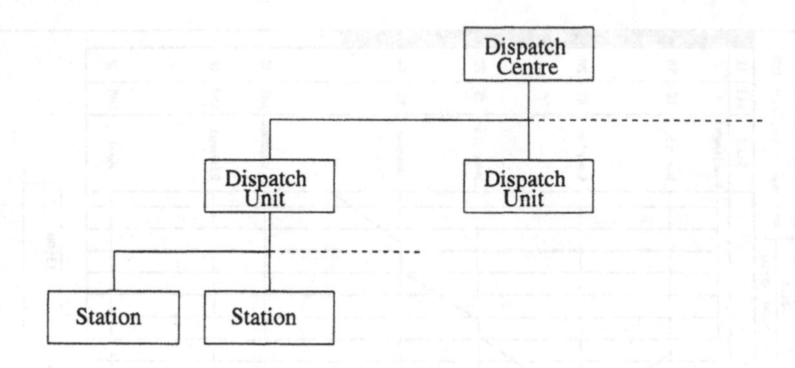

Fig. 2. Dispatch hierarchy

under different dispatch units. The next step in the project is to create a distributed version of the running map tool that can support concurrent rescheduling by dispatch units.

Distribution is largely a problem of dispatch units only having partial knowledge of the current situation and of consistency between the views of the separate dispatch units. The problem is exacerbated in this case since communication between dispatch units may be slow and unreliable and the processing power available may be limited. We are therefore interested in minimizing communication and in efficient algorithms.

There are a large number of different kinds of adjustments we can make to a timetable, ranging from adding or deleting a whole train to changing the platform a train will use at a station. There are also a number of analyses we need to do to check a timetable for consistency and adherence to rules (like the check we used to discover that after the first adjustment to Y1 it was scheduled to leave Danyan at the same time as K542). There are three particular questions we need to answer:

1. Can the distribution between dispatch units (even when their partial timetables are consistent) cause analysis either to fail, i.e. to not detect a violation of some rule, or to detect spurious violations?
2. When does an adjustment affect other dispatch units, i.e. when do we need to communicate to achieve consistency between dispatch units?
3. What analyses need to be redone after an adjustment?

If we can formalize these questions we have a theory of distributing adjustment and analysis functions that we can then apply to the actual ones to be used. We can then be sure that distributed analysis is effective, that after adjustments we communicate sufficient data between dispatch units to achieve consistency, and that we minimise the time taken to analyse adjustments. We achieve this by producing a theory of an abstraction of a timetable and its distribution.

The structure of the rest of this paper is as follows. Section 2 presents the formal model of the railway network and timetables, and the adjustment and analysis functions on timetables needed for dispatching. In particular, it shows how timetables are modelled as maps. Section 3 presents a generic theory of distributing maps and defines a number of functions that model criteria for distributing adjustment and analysis functions over maps. In section 4 the distributed timetable is then defined by instantiating the generic map. Section 5 draws some general conclusions and indicates directions for further work.

2 The railway network and timetables

In this section we present a formal model in RSL of the railway network and timetables, plus the adjustment and analysis functions needed to support the activities of scheduling and rescheduling.

2.1 The railway network

The network consists essentially of stations and lines connecting them. Stations have tracks (usually referred to as platforms in the case of passenger stations). A line goes from one station to another. For any track, there is a set of lines from which it is possible to get to the track, and a set of lines it is possible to reach from the track.

type
  Network, Line, Station, Track,
  Line_type == *up* | *down* | *both*
value
  lines : Network → *Line*-**set**,
  stations : Network → *Station*-**set**,
  tracks : Station → *Track*-**set**,
  from_station : Line → *Station*,
  to_station : Line → *Station*,
  lines_in : Track → *Line*-**set**,
  lines_out : Track → *Line*-**set**

The first four types defined here are *sorts*, abstract types. The functions defined (by signature) in the **value** declaration are all *observers* or attributes of these sorts. This style allows us to add later, if we need to, other attributes, such as the length of a track or the possible routes (through switches) between a track and each line it connects to.

The complete model includes more details. The rails are modelled in terms of *units*, the smallest portion of rails controlled by signals. Units may be linear or may model various kinds of switches (points) or crossovers. Lines and tracks are sequences of connected linear units; they may be connected to each other by connected sequences of possibly non-linear units.

We need to add to these type definitions and function signatures a number of constraints to state, for example, that lines do connect actual (different) stations. These are written as axioms, such as:

axiom
[*lines_connect_stations*]
$\forall$ *net : Network, line : Line* •
line $\in$ *lines(net)* $\Rightarrow$
  from_station(line) $\neq$ *to_station(line)* $\wedge$
  {*from_station(line), to_station(line)*} $\subseteq$ *stations(net)*

Similarly, if a track in a station is reachable from a line (in *lines_in(track)*) then that line must be a line to the track's station (in the right direction if the line is *up* or *down*). And so on.

2.2 Timetables

Timetables are usually presented to passengers as tables indexed vertically by station and horizontally by train with entries giving the times of stops at stations. Timetables needed by railway staff will have more information: the time of trains passing through stations, both arrival and departure times for trains that stop, the tracks trains will use, the lines trains will use, etc.

In addition (and usually implicitly) passenger timetables indicate possible *connections* between trains: possibilities for passengers to change from a train to another one. For railway staff, connections are needed to allow the possibility also of transfer of staff, freight or rolling stock between trains.

Connections are related to particular stations, and we will model the information needed about a train's visit to (or passage through) a station as a *visit*. A map seems a natural data structure for a timetable, but there are several possibilities:

1. The passenger or train driver's view might be

   type *TT* = *(Train* $\overrightarrow{m}$ *Station* $\overrightarrow{m}$ *Visit)* × *(Station* $\overrightarrow{m}$ *Connection*-**set**)

2. The station staff's view might be

   type *TT* = *Station* $\overrightarrow{m}$ *(Train* $\overrightarrow{m}$ *Visit)* × *Connection*-**set**

3. Or we can flatten the nested maps in the first two possibilities:

   type *TT* = *(Station* × *Train* $\overrightarrow{m}$ *Visit)* × *(Station* $\overrightarrow{m}$ *Connection*-**set**)

In the above definitions note that × binds more tightly than $\overrightarrow{m}$ and that $\overrightarrow{m}$ associates to the right. How do we choose between these three? The usual criteria are:

– reducing any ***invariants*** needed to express consistency
– simplifying the functions to read or change the data structure.[2]

The consistency between the connections and visits (a connection may only mention stopping visits) is needed in all three; only the second avoids the need to express consistency between the domains of two maps. For ease of specifying functions on timetables, however, it turns out that the first and third are more convenient.

But we will also need to consider the distribution of timetables. This distribution, as we shall see, is by partitioning the stations according to what dispatch unit they belong to, and the first is not very suitable for this. The second is convenient for distribution but the depth of nesting makes the justifications very complicated. On balance the third version is best.

2.3 Scheduling and rescheduling

Before we can finalize the data structures of timetables we need to consider what functions are required by users, in particular dispatch staff. They have two essential tasks: scheduling and rescheduling.

Scheduling is the construction of a timetable for a particular shift (part of a day). Its inputs are the basic timetable (perhaps the summer timetable for a Saturday) plus additional information relevant to that day: extra trains required, trains affected by shortages or wrong positioning of rolling stock or staff, repair work affecting the network etc. It is done by dispatch centres. Essentially the task is to create and disseminate to dispatch units (and from them to stations) a timetable that is ***feasible***. A feasible timetable is one that

– corresponds to the network in using existing and connected lines and tracks that are actually available
– corresponds to timing restrictions like allowing trains sufficient time to travel between stations
– corresponds to physical restrictions like not putting two trains in the same track or in opposite directions on lines usable in *both* directions in overlapping time intervals, or not putting more trains in the same direction on a line in any time interval than the signaling equipment available allows that line to contain
– does not violate various ***regulations*** like the minimum time allowed between arrivals at the same station.

There is also a requirement that a feasible timetable should generate minimal ***disruption*** when compared to the basic timetable plus any additional trains. Disruptions are the late arrival of trains and the breaking of connections.

[2] Here simplicity does not mean efficiency when implemented as code. We are concerned with specification, not execution. So simplicity means simplicity and clarity of expression (so that correctness may be checked effectively manually) and giving ease of proof (where correctness is checked formally). The data structure used in the final implemented code may be different.

Rescheduling is the changing of a timetable for a shift during that shift. Its inputs are the current timetable for the shift and actual events like arrivals and departures of trains. Such events may be normal (according to the timetable) or abnormal but anticipated, such as late arrivals or departures, breakdowns, etc. They do not include the abnormal and unanticipated, because physically impossible, like the sudden appearance of a train from nowhere, or the overtaking of one train by another on the same line, or the departure of a train that has not arrived.

It is apparent that scheduling and rescheduling are essentially the same: they start with inputs which include a timetable that may or may not be currently feasible and try to construct a timetable that is feasible with minimal disruption. The time constraints may be tighter for rescheduling, but scheduling is also time constrained: it has to be constructed before the shift starts. It would therefore be convenient if we could use the same data structure and as far as possible the same functions for both tasks; then we can use the same tools for both. This also means that the timetable is the output from both; we do not produce some other "schedule" type. This leads to two requirements for timetables:

1. Rescheduling requires that we can distinguish actual (occurred) events (like arrivals and departures) from scheduled events. Only scheduled events can be subject to rescheduling.
2. Rescheduling requires rapid responses (part of the purpose of introducing computer support) and it must be possible to make decisions about scheduled events in the immediate future while deferring decisions about later ones, even though after making the first change the resulting timetable may be infeasible. This may be unwise on some occasions, but the tools should allow dispatchers to make judgements about what they can sort out later.

The second requirement means that we must not constrain the type *TT* to be always feasible. So we cannot use the style we did with the network of imposing constraints as axioms (which must always hold). Instead we define some analysis functions that can check if a timetable is feasible and, if not, inform the user why. For example, we must be able to record in the timetable the arrival of a train even if it is later than the (scheduled) departure time. We see that the timetable (and its visual tool the running map) is a means of both (re)scheduling the movement of trains and also analysing the evolving state of the movements for potential problems.

3 Distribution

In this section we present a general theory of distribution of a map. Then we show how this may be applied to a map representing a timetable in section 4.

3.1 Distributing a map

We have already used the notation for maps. A type *Map* mapping elements from a domain type *D* to a range type *R*, both sorts, is defined by

type
  D, R,
  $Map = D \xrightarrow[m]{} R$

The main operations available for the type *Map* are the prefix operator **dom** (giving the set of elements in the domain of a map) and application (giving the range value corresponding to a domain value). Application is written like function application; it is only (necessarily) defined for a value in the set returned by **dom**.

We take the idea of distributing a map to mean partitioning the domain into a set of disjoint subsets and then forming a submap for each subset. Thus a map is partitioned into disjoint maps.

We can partition the domain type *D* by means of a total function *p_of* from *D* to some "partitioning" type (another sort) *P*:

type
  P,
  $Dist\_Map = P \xrightarrow[m]{} Map$

value
  $p\_of : D \rightarrow P$,

  $distribute : Map \rightarrow Dist\_Map$
  $distribute(m) \equiv [\ p \mapsto m \ / \ partition(p) \mid p : P\ ]$,

  $partition : P \rightarrow D\textbf{-set}$
  $partition(p) \equiv \{\ d \mid d : D \bullet p\_of(d) = p\ \}$

The operator "/" is the "restriction to" operator. "m / s" is the restriction of the map m to those domain elements in the set s.

For example, we can see the telephone directories (maps from names to telephone numbers) for different areas of a country as a distribution of a national directory partitioned by "area" according to the function "lives in". For a division into "white" and "yellow" pages the partition type would contain the two elements "private" and "business".

There is an obvious "inverse" to *distribute*, *merge*:

  $merge : Dist\_Map \rightarrow Map$
  $merge(dm) \equiv$
    $[\ d \mapsto dm(p\_of(d))(d) \mid d : D \bullet p\_of(d) \in \textbf{dom}\ dm \wedge d \in \textbf{dom}\ dm(p\_of(d))\ ]$

and it is then simple to justify[3] the theorem that *merge* is the (left) inverse of *distribute*:

$$\forall\ m : Map \bullet merge(distribute(m)) = m \qquad (1)$$

[3] This and the other theorems mentioned in this paper have been justified using the RAISE justification editor [4].

3.2 Delegability

We now consider functions on a distributed map. Suppose we have some function *f* that can be applied to a global map (and generating a new map), and propose to apply instead a function *df* to the distributed map. We can define a notion of *df* being a "correct" version of *f* if the diagram in figure 3 "commutes".

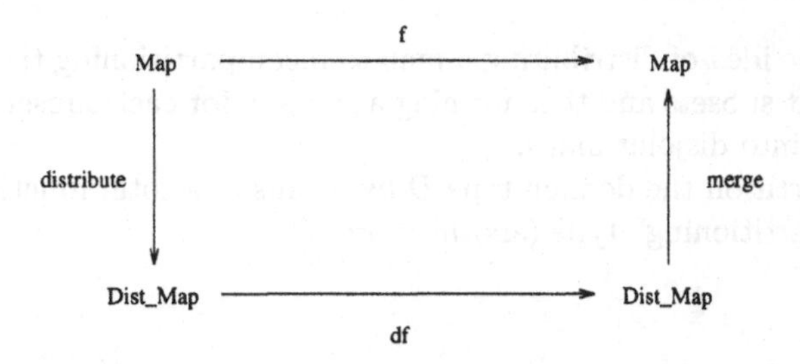

Fig. 3. Correctness of distributed function

That is, we require that

$$\forall\, m : Map \bullet merge(df(distribute(m))) = f(m) \qquad (2)$$

From (1) we can see that (2) will hold if

$$\forall\, m : Map \bullet distribute(f(m)) = df(distribute(m)) \qquad (3)$$

and it is condition (3) that we shall employ in the following discussion of "delegable" functions.

If there is no means of identifying a single value of *P* from the arguments of the function *f*, then distributing *f* must in general involve applying it to all the component maps of the distributed map. Consider, for example, prefixing all telephone numbers with a digit. But to change the number of a particular subscriber we can apply *p_of* to the subscriber's name to get the area and then change just the appropriate area directory.

We call a function that can be in effect applied to the complete map by being applied to just one component map "delegable" since it is possible to "delegate" the responsibility for applying it to just one component.

"Lookup" functions will usually be delegable. Such a function will typically have type

$$D \times Map \rightarrow T$$

where *T* is the result type of the lookup (and does not involve *Map*). Such a function is delegable if we get the same result when we calculate a *P* value from the first argument and apply the lookup to the component of the map as we would if we applied the lookup to the complete map. That is, we can define a test:

$$
\begin{array}{l}
\mathit{is\_delegable\_lookup} : (D \times \mathit{Map} \to T) \to \mathbf{Bool} \\
\mathit{is\_delegable\_lookup}(f) \equiv \\
\quad (\forall\ d : D,\ m : \mathit{Map} \bullet f(d,m) = f(d,\ \mathit{distribute}(m)(\mathit{p\_of}(d))))
\end{array}
$$

We shall return to lookup functions (in a general form) later. We first consider functions that change maps. Such a function will typically have a type

$$\mathbf{type}\ \mathit{Fun} = D \times \mathit{Map} \xrightarrow{\sim} \mathit{Map}$$

The symbol "$\xrightarrow{\sim}$" indicates that *Fun* is the type of partial functions, i.e. functions for which application may not be defined for some arguments. A function in *Fun* will typically be associated with a precondition which we can express as a function with type

$$\mathbf{type}\ \mathit{Pre\_Fun} = D \times \mathit{Map} \to \mathbf{Bool}$$

We describe such a function as "weakly" delegable if truth of the precondition applied to one component map implies

- truth of the precondition for the global map
- that distributing and applying the function only to one component gives the same map as applying the function to the global map and then distributing.

The first condition ensures that if we can apply a function locally we could have applied it globally; the second (condition (3) above) says we get the same result from local or global application. Here are the formal definitions:

$$
\begin{array}{l}
\mathit{delegate} : \mathit{Fun} \to D \times \mathit{Dist\_Map} \xrightarrow{\sim} \mathit{Dist\_Map} \\
\mathit{delegate}(f)(d,\ dm) \equiv \mathbf{let}\ p = \mathit{p\_of}(d)\ \mathbf{in}\ dm \dagger [p \mapsto f(d,\ dm(p))]\ \mathbf{end},
\end{array}
$$

$$
\begin{array}{l}
\mathit{delegate} : \mathit{Pre\_Fun} \to D \times \mathit{Dist\_Map} \to \mathbf{Bool} \\
\mathit{delegate}(\mathit{pre\_f})(d,\ dm) \equiv \mathbf{let}\ p = \mathit{p\_of}(d)\ \mathbf{in}\ \mathit{pre\_f}(d,\ dm(p))\ \mathbf{end},
\end{array}
$$

$$
\begin{array}{l}
\mathit{weakly\_delegable} : \mathit{Fun} \times \mathit{Pre\_Fun} \to \mathbf{Bool} \\
\mathit{weakly\_delegable}(f,\ \mathit{pre\_f}) \equiv \\
\quad \mathbf{let}\ \mathit{df} = \mathit{delegate}(f),\ \mathit{pre\_df} = \mathit{delegate}(\mathit{pre\_f})\ \mathbf{in} \\
\quad\quad \forall\ d : D,\ m : \mathit{Map} \bullet \\
\quad\quad\quad \mathit{pre\_df}(d,\ \mathit{distribute}(m)) \Rightarrow \\
\quad\quad\quad \mathit{pre\_f}(d,\ m) \wedge \mathit{df}(d,\ \mathit{distribute}(m)) = \mathit{distribute}(f(d,\ m)) \\
\quad \mathbf{end}
\end{array}
$$

(Note that we have overloaded "delegate".) We use the description "weakly" delegable because it may be that the pre-condition calculated for only one component map is stronger than that calculated for the global map. That is, it might be possible to apply the function to the global map but not to one component only. If this is not so, i.e. truth of the precondition for the global map implies truth for the component (and the function is weakly delegable) then we say the function is "strongly" delegable:

strongly_delegable : Fun × Pre_Fun → **Bool**
strongly_delegable(f, pre_f) ≡
  weakly_delegable(f, pre_f) ∧
  let *pre_df = delegate(pre_f)* **in**
    ∀ d : D, m : Map • pre_f(d, m) ⇒ pre_df(d, distribute(m))
  end

It should be apparent that (ignoring preconditions for the present) a function will be delegable if

- the changed relevant component map is the same as the extraction of the component after applying the function to the global map
- all other components are unchanged if extracted after applying the function to the global map.

Since two maps are equal if they have equal domains and give the same results on application to domain values, this allows us to define a function (in the weak case) that expresses this more algorithmic view of the check for a function being delegable:

weakly_delegable1 : Fun × Pre_Fun → **Bool**
weakly_delegable1(f, pre_f) ≡
  (∀ d : D, m : Map • pre_f(d, m) ⇒ (f(d, m) **post true**)) ∧
  (∀ d : D, m : Map •
    let *ds = partition(p_of(d))* **in**
      pre_f(d, m / ds) ⇒
      pre_f(d, m) ∧
      let *(m1, m2) = (f(d, m / ds), f(d, m))* **in**
        dom *m1 =* **dom** *m2 ∩ ds ∧*
        (∀ d′ : D • d′ ∈ **dom** *m1 ⇒ m1(d′) = m2(d′)) ∧*
        (∀ p : P • p ≠ p_of(d) ⇒
          dom *m ∩ partition(p) =* **dom** *m2 ∩ partition(p)) ∧*
        (∀ d′ : D • d′ ∈ **dom** *m ∧ d′ ∈* **dom** *m2 ∧ d′ ∉ ds ⇒*
          m(d′) = m2(d′))
      end
    end)

The expression *f(d, m)* **post true** above says that *f(d, m)* is (uniquely) defined.

Having formulated this it is possible to justify the expected theorem

∀ f : Fun, pre_f : Pre_Fun •
  weakly_delegable1(f, pre_f) ⇒ weakly_delegable(f, pre_f)   (4)

weakly_delegable1 provides us with a more convenient test than *weakly_delegable* for checking that a function is weakly delegable (and for strongly delegable we have only an additional relation between preconditions to justify). We can see theorem (4) as providing a partial decomposition of any proof of a function being delegable.

3.3 Analysis functions

As mentioned above, lookup functions are generally fairly easy to deal with. Of rather more interest in our case will be functions that "analyse" a map (in particular functions that check for well-formedness).

An analysis function may be one that simply returns **true** or **false**, but of rather more usefulness is one that returns some information, say a set of "messages". The question is whether we can analyse the component maps and merge the messages that result into the same set of messages as we would get if we analysed the global map. The same set of messages implies that when checking each component separately

- no messages are lost
- no "spurious" messages are generated.

We have another commuting diagram, figure 4.

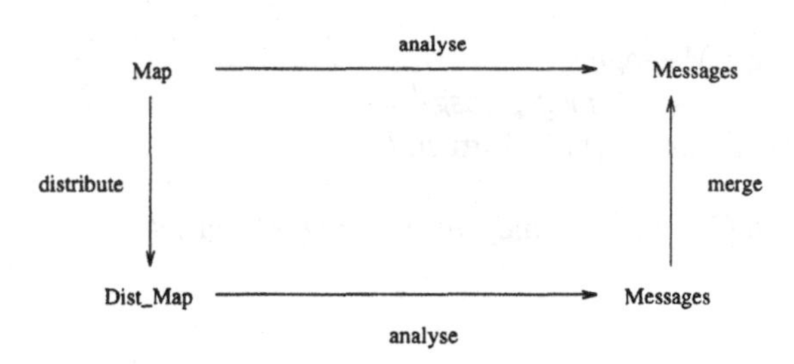

Fig. 4. Distributed analysis

We provide a function *analyse_distributable* to check this requirement:

type
  Message,
  Analyse = *Map* → *Message*-**set**
value
  analyse_distributable : *Analyse* → **Bool**
  analyse_distributable(analyse) ≡
    ($\forall$ *m* : *Map* • *analyse(m)* = *merge*({ *analyse(distribute(m)(p))* | *p* : *P* })),

$$
\begin{array}{l}
\mathit{merge} : (\mathit{Message}\textbf{-set})\textbf{-set} \rightarrow \mathit{Message}\textbf{-set} \\
\mathit{merge}(\mathit{mss}) \equiv \\
\quad \{\, m \mid m : \mathit{Message} \bullet \exists\, \mathit{ms} : \mathit{Message}\textbf{-set} \bullet \mathit{ms} \in \mathit{mss} \wedge m \in \mathit{ms} \,\}
\end{array}
$$

Suppose we have a current map and a distributable analysis function. We apply a delegable function to the appropriate component map of the distributed map. Under what circumstances can we update our set of global messages by applying the analysis function only to the changed component?

It should be apparent that if the analysis applied to the changed component does not cause any messages to be deleted that were also produced by another component then we will get the correct global change in messages by analysing only the changed component. That is, we have a theorem

$$
\begin{array}{l}
\forall\, f : \mathit{Fun},\ \mathit{pre\_f} : \mathit{Pre\_Fun},\ \mathit{analyse} : \mathit{Analyse} \bullet \\
\quad (\forall\, d : D,\ m : \mathit{Map} \bullet \mathit{pre\_f}(d, m) \Rightarrow (f(d, m)\ \textbf{post true})) \wedge \\
\quad \mathit{weakly\_delegable}(f, \mathit{pre\_f}) \wedge \mathit{analyse\_distributable}(\mathit{analyse}) \Rightarrow \\
\quad (\forall\, d : D,\ m : \mathit{Map} \bullet \\
\qquad \textbf{let}\ \mathit{pre\_df} = \mathit{delegate}(\mathit{pre\_f})\ \textbf{in} \\
\qquad\quad \mathit{pre\_df}(d, \mathit{distribute}(m)) \Rightarrow \\
\qquad\quad \textbf{let} \\
\qquad\qquad \mathit{md} = \mathit{distribute}(m)(\mathit{p\_of}(d)), \\
\qquad\qquad \mathit{msgs} = \mathit{analyse}(\mathit{md}), \\
\qquad\qquad \mathit{md'} = f(d, \mathit{md}), \\
\qquad\qquad \mathit{msgs'} = \mathit{analyse}(\mathit{md'}) \\
\qquad\quad \textbf{in} \\
\qquad\qquad (\forall\, \mathit{msg} : \mathit{Message} \bullet \\
\qquad\qquad\quad \mathit{msg} \in \mathit{msgs} \wedge \mathit{msg} \notin \mathit{msgs'} \Rightarrow \\
\qquad\qquad\quad \mathit{msg} \notin \mathit{analyse}(m \setminus \textbf{dom}\ \mathit{md}) \\
\qquad\qquad) \Rightarrow \\
\qquad\qquad \mathit{analyse}(f(d, m)) = \mathit{analyse}(m) \setminus \mathit{msgs} \cup \mathit{msgs'} \\
\qquad\quad \textbf{end} \\
\qquad \textbf{end})
\end{array}
$$

In particular, an analysis function may be *analyse_disjoint*, i.e. it cannot generate the same message from two different components:

$$
\begin{array}{l}
\mathit{analyse\_disjoint} : \mathit{Analyse} \rightarrow \textbf{Bool} \\
\mathit{analyse\_disjoint}(\mathit{analyse}) \equiv \\
\quad (\forall\, m : \mathit{Map},\ p1, p2 : P \bullet p1 \neq p2 \Rightarrow \\
\qquad \mathit{analyse}(\mathit{distribute}(m)(p1)) \cap \mathit{analyse}(\mathit{distribute}(m)(p2)) = \{\})
\end{array}
$$

Then we know that if a function f is delegable and we apply f to a component map only, then we may apply a distributable and disjoint function *analyse* by applying *analyse* to the component only.

3.4 Partial analysis

When we apply a function to a map it is likely only to change part of it. It may then be possible to "update" an analysis by repeating only a part of it. We can formalize this notion:

is_adequate_partial_analysis : Analyse × Fun × Pre_Fun × Analyse → **Bool**
is_adequate_partial_analysis(analyse, f, pre_f, part_analyse) ≡
  (∀ d : D, m : Map • pre_f(d, m) ⇒
    let
      msgs = analyse(m),
      old_msgs = part_analyse(m),
      m′ = f(d, m),
      new_msgs = part_analyse(m′)
    in
      analyse(m′) = msgs \ old_msgs ∪ new_msgs
    end*)*

Note that there is some interplay here between the precondition *pre_f* and the partial analysis function *part_analyse*. Suppose, for example, that *f* is inserting some new data into a map. Then by strengthening *pre_f* (in particular by checking the new data to be inserted) it will typically be possible to do less checking in *part_analyse*. This suggests one extreme possibility: for some functions it may be possible to define *pre_f* so that analysing the resulting map generates exactly the same messages as before the function was applied. In this case we can take *part_analyse* as the constant function returning the empty set of messages. In practice we need to balance the amount of computation in *pre_f* (and also the resulting restrictiveness of possible applications of *f*) against the amount of computation in *part_analyse*. Then applying *is_adequate_partial_analysis* is a means of checking we have not missed anything.

In section 1 we posed three questions for distributed timetables:

1. Can the distribution between dispatch units (even when their partial timetables are consistent) cause analysis either to fail, i.e. to not detect a violation of some rule, or to detect spurious violations?
2. When does an adjustment affect other dispatch units, i.e. when do we need to communicate to achieve consistency between dispatch units?
3. What analyses need to be redone after an adjustment?

It should be apparent that the notions of distributability of analysis functions, of delegability of change functions, and of adequacy of partial analysis are formalizations of these questions applied to maps. We have also, implicitly, stated what we mean by a consistent distributed map — one that is a distribution of a global map.

Now we need to instantiate the theory for timetables.

4 Distributing timetables

We earlier decided to use a pair of maps to model a timetable, one for visits and one for connections. We distribute these separately, by instantiating the generic distributed map twice. This generic distributed map is defined in an RSL module *DIST_MAP* which is parameterized by the types *D*, *R*, *P* and *Message*, plus the function *p_of*. For each instantiation we need to provide a parameter object defining these four types and one value.

```
type
  Dispatch_Unit, Message,
  TT :: visits : Visits   connections : Connections,
  Visits = Station × Train ⇸ Visit,
  Connections = Station ⇸ Connection-set
value
  du_of : Station → Dispatch_Unit
object
  A :
    class
      type
        D = Station × Train, R = Visit, P = Dispatch_Unit, M = Message
      value
        p_of : D → P
        p_of((st, tn)) ≡ du_of(st)
    end,
  V : DIST_MAP(A),
  B :
    class
      type
        D = Station, R = Connection-set, P = Dispatch_Unit, M = Message
      value
        p_of : D → P = du_of
    end,
  R : DIST_MAP(B)
type Dist_TT = V.Dist_Map × R.Dist_Map
```

We have used a short record for the type *TT* of timetables rather than the (isomorphic) Cartesian product discussed earlier.

We need a theory of which adjustment functions are delegable. Adjustment functions on timetables will apply to one or both of the *visits* and *connections* parts, and we can define the predicate *weakly_delegable* as follows:

```
value
  weakly_delegable :
    (Station × Train × TT ⥲ TT) × (Station × Train × TT → Bool) → Bool
  weakly_delegable(f, pre_f) ≡ true
  pre (∃ vf : V.Fun, rf : R.Fun, pre_vf : V.Pre_Fun, pre_rf : R.Pre_Fun •
```

$\forall\, st : Station,\ tn : Train,\ tt : TT \bullet$
$\quad pre\_f(st, tn, tt) =$
$\quad (pre\_vf((st, tn), visits(tt)) \wedge pre\_rf(st, connections(tt))) \wedge$
$\quad (pre\_f(st, tn, tt) \Rightarrow$
$\qquad f((st, tn, tt)) = mk\_TT(vf((st, tn), visits(tt)), rf(st, connections(tt)))) \wedge$
$\quad V.weakly\_delegable(vf, pre\_vf) \wedge R.weakly\_delegable(rf, pre\_rf))$

strongly_delegable is defined similarly.

Note that this definition is only partial; the precondition gives a sufficient but not necessary condition for delegability when the adjustment function is defined in terms of two functions applied separately to the *visits* and *connections* of a timetable. This is true for all the functions currently defined on timetables,[4] but we allow for the possibility of functions not defined in this manner, when we would define the appropriate *delegable* function from first principles in a manner analogous to the definition in *DIST_MAP*.

Some adjustment functions change only the *visits* or *connections* of a timetable. We can consider such functions as defined in terms of a function on each part, one of which is the identity function (with precondition true). It is easy to justify the theorem for *DIST_MAP* (and hence for both the *visits* and the *connections* of the distributed timetable) that an identity function is strongly delegable.

For analysis functions to be distributable and disjoint we proceed similarly:

$analyse\_distributable : (TT \rightarrow Message\textbf{-set}) \rightarrow \textbf{Bool}$
$analyse\_distributable(analyse) \equiv \textbf{true}$
$\textbf{pre}\ (\exists\, vanalyse : V.Analyse,\ ranalyse : R.Analyse \bullet$
$\quad \forall\, tt : TT \bullet$
$\qquad analyse(tt) = vanalyse(visits(tt)) \cup ranalyse(connections(tt)) \wedge$
$\qquad V.analyse\_distributable(vanalyse) \wedge R.analyse\_distributable(ranalyse)),$

$analyse\_disjoint : (TT \rightarrow Message\textbf{-set}) \rightarrow \textbf{Bool}$
$analyse\_disjoint(analyse) \equiv \textbf{true}$
$\textbf{pre}\ (\exists\, vanalyse : V.Analyse,\ ranalyse : R.Analyse \bullet$
$\quad \forall\, tt : TT \bullet$
$\qquad analyse(tt) = vanalyse(visits(tt)) \cup ranalyse(connections(tt)) \wedge$
$\qquad vanalyse(visits(tt)) \cap ranalyse(connections(tt)) = \{\} \wedge$
$\qquad V.analyse\_disjoint(vanalyse) \wedge R.analyse\_disjoint(ranalyse))$

Again the analysis may be calculated from one part only, and we take the other to be the constant function returning the empty set. It is easy to justify that this constant function is both distributable and disjoint.

The need for sufficient but not necessary conditions for distributability and disjointness for analysis functions is more apparent than for adjustment functions. We will, for example, have an analysis function to report inconsistencies between connections and visits. It will report if either of the trains mentioned in a connection for a station does not visit the station, or if the arrival and

[4] This is one of the things that made us choose the pair of maps model.

departure times of the trains do not satisfy the time requirement of the connection. We cannot define this analysis function in terms of separate analyses of the *visits* and the *connections*.[5] We can instead define it for the distributed timetable as the union of the messages for the corresponding function applied to the local timetables. The analysis function is then immediately distributable by definition. It will also be disjoint if each message mentions the station involved.

Examples Consider first some examples of adjustment functions. One function we will need is *report_arrival* to record an actual arrival of a train at a station. This function is delegable, since it only affects one visit and it is possible to find the local map corresponding to the station involved. In fact it is strongly delegable; the precondition will be that the train does in fact visit the station and if this is true globally it is true locally. The precondition is expressed by the function *includes_visit*, so to justify the assertion that *report_arrival* is strongly delegable we assert and then justify the theorem

$$\forall\, t : T.Time \bullet$$
$$strongly\_delegable($$
$$\lambda\ (st, tn, tt) : Station \times Train \times TT \bullet report\_arrival(st, tn, t, tt),$$
$$\lambda\ (st, tn, tt) : Station \times Train \times TT \bullet includes\_visit(st, tn, visits(tt)))$$

Now consider an adjustment function *append_visit* to append a visit to a train journey. This involves adding the new visit and also changing the previous visit to show that the train is scheduled to leave at some time on the appropriate line. Therefore its precondition implies that both stations are in the domain of the map. This function is delegable, but only weakly: the two stations may be in the domain of the global map but not the local one.

An example of an analysis function that is distributable is one that reports inconsistencies between station visits and the network, such as tracks not being in the relevant station, arrival or departure lines not leading to or from the station, or not being connected to the track. It will also be disjoint if the messages mention the station involved.

An example of an analysis function that is not distributable is one that reports if there is no following visit for a non-final visit. If the two stations involved belong to different dispatch units then no message can be generated for the distributed analysis but one might be generated by analysing a global timetable.

5 Conclusions

At the point where this piece of the PRaCoSy project began we had a prototype running map tool to support train dispatchers, and hence had specified and implemented a model of railway network and timetables, together with a

[5] This is a cost of the pair of maps model.

large number of adjustment and analysis functions for timetables. The complete specification, excluding theorems and proofs, is some 1400 lines in 15 modules of RSL, all produced using the RAISE tools [1]. The running map tool does not support the distribution of dispatching across dispatch units, and developing this distribution capacity is the aim of the next part of the project.

The requirements analysis for distribution led to some requirements on the adjustment and analysis functions. We could have formalized these requirement in terms of the full specification, but this would be complicated and tend to obscure the issues in the detail. We chose instead to formalize the requirements in terms of an abstraction, a map, and then to re-specify the timetable as an instantiation of the abstraction. The notions of "delegability", "distributability" and "adequacy of partial analysis" were therefore simply and clearly defined for maps and immediately available for timetables, as they instantiate maps. In particular, we have predicates to check these properties, and are thus able to justify whether a particular timetable adjustment or analysis function satisfies them or not. The full details may be found in [3].

The further steps towards a distributed software system to support scheduling and rescheduling are listed in the following sections.

5.1 Validation of (re)scheduling functions

The adjustment and analysis functions defined for timetables need to be validated against the requirements of train dispatchers and amended or augmented as necessary. Much of this was done in the earlier stages of the PRaCoSy project (by engineers from the Chinese Railways who have worked or are working on the project). We have a number of data flow diagrams showing the communications between dispatch units, dispatch centres and stations; we have definitions of terms that we use (translated into Chinese); etc. And the current prototype has been installed in the first target area for the final system to give us feedback. But it is always essential to review specifications with the customers and, if possible, with future users to validate that what is being produced is what is wanted. Few of these users will be able to read RSL in sufficient detail (though those working at UNU/IIST certainly can). For others we need to "replay" the specification, by writing natural language documents describing them (a kind of "reverse engineering" of requirements) and/or by constructing prototypes.

5.2 Delegable and distributable functions

All adjustment functions need to be checked for the conditions (if any) for which they are delegable and the analysis functions checked for the conditions (if any) for which they are distributable and disjoint. This involves writing the appropriate theorems and then justifying them with the tools. The results need to be compared with the current railway practices and suitable protocols devised for communicating between dispatch centres, and dispatch units when functions are applied locally but do not meet the requirements for local application.

5.3 Concurrent system

The specification can then be developed into a concurrent system with server processes for each dispatch unit and a means, by incorporating the protocols devised in section 5.2, of communication between dispatch units, dispatch centres and stations. An architecture for a concurrent version of the generic distributed map has already been produced [5] using the RAISE method [10] and is expected to be instantiated for the complete system just as the distributed map was instantiated for the timetable.

6 Acknowledgements

This work relies heavily on the earlier work done by UNU/IIST staff Dines Bjørner and Søren Prehn and the Fellows from the Chinese Railways: Dong Yulin, Jin Danhua, Liu Xin, Ma Chao and Sun Guoqin. Hong Mei also contributed during her brief Fellowship.

Useful comments on an earlier draft of this paper were made by Liu Liansuo, Yang Dong and Tomasz Janowski.

References

1. Peter Michael Bruun et al: RAISE tools user guide. Technical report LACOS/-CRI/DOC/4, CRI A/S (1995)
2. Dong Yulin and Dines Bjørner: PRaCoSy: Document deliverables. Technical report dyl/deliv/1, UNU/IIST (1994)
3. Chris George: Distributed train rescheduling. Technical report 42, UNU/IIST (1995)
4. Chris George and Søren Prehn: The RAISE Justification Handbook. Technical report LACOS/CRI/DOC/7, CRI A/S (1995)
5. Hong Mei: Distributed concurrent architecture for rescheduling. Technical report hm/arch/1, UNU/IIST (1995)
6. Liu Xin: A simple running map display tool. Technical report lx/tool/01, UNU/IIST (1994)
7. Søren Prehn: A formal model of the railway application domain system. Technical report sp/5, UNU/IIST (1994)
8. Søren Prehn: A railway running map design. Technical report sp/12, UNU/IIST (1994)
9. The RAISE Language Group: The RAISE Specification Language. Prentice Hall BCS Practitioners Series (1992)
10. The RAISE Method Group: The RAISE Development Method. Prentice Hall BCS Practitioners Series (1995)

An Improved Translation of SA/RT Specification Model to High-Level Timed Petri Nets

Lihua Shi[1] and Patrick Nixon[2]

[1] Dept. of Computing, Manchester Metropolitan University, M1 5GD, UK
[2] Dept. of Computer Science, Trinity College, Dublin 2, Ireland
Email:L.Shi@doc.mmu.ac.uk or Paddy.Nixon@cs.tcd.ie

Abstract. Structured analysis methods for real-time systems (SA/RT) are widely accepted by the industrial world as a mature approach to real-time systems design. These methods use highly expressive graphical specification languages to specify system requirements. Giving semantics to SA/RT specifications via selected formal models has the advantage of not only retaining their user-friendly and problem-oriented characteristics, but also making good use of the existing results of formal models for easier simulation and more powerful analysis. An automatic translation from SA/RT specification models to high-level timed Petri nets has recently been reported in [5]. But this translation suffers from some drawbacks, especially that it is not compositional, and the resulting subnets, in some cases, can be of at least exponential complexity. In this paper, we propose an improved translation, which is compositional and the resulting nets are of much lower complexity, e.g. the number of transitions is linear with respect to the scale of the original model. The efficient translation will benefit the simulation and analysis of specifications, and the compositionality of the translation process will support their incremental or modular development and compositional analysis.

1 Introduction

Tom DeMarco structured analysis and system specification (SASS) method with the data flow diagram has always been one of the most important methods used in the development of software systems since its emergence. But for real-time systems, it is still not powerful enough to describe the timing information and dynamic behaviour. In order to address this problem, different ways have been proposed to extend the data flow diagram to capture control and timing information, among which, Ward–Mellor[18, 19] and Hatley–Pirbhai[9] extensions are two of the most popular ones. Each is used by 1/6 of all real-time system analysts in USA according to [20]. Structured analysis for real-time systems (SA/RT), is usually used to refer to these kinds of extensions to SASS. In [14] the Extended Systems Modeling Language (ESML) was proposed by Rruyn et al., which was based on the above two techniques. The combined notation has a more comprehensive and flexible set of constructs for representing control logic than either of the original notations.

SA/RT methods use highly expressive graphical specification languages, allowing the developer to concentrate on the clear understanding of the nature of problems, rather than the handling of formalisms, and also supports communication among the people involved with the development, which is very important in early stages of the system development process. On the other hand, these specification languages are not formal in that they lack appropriate formal semantics. Different understandings to the same symbol or combination of symbols may occur, and it is hard to analyze the completeness and consistency of the specification, which may result in flaws in the design and implementation. This can be very harmful for the development of complex real-time systems, since those flaws remaining from specifications are the most difficult to detect and need more efforts to correct[15].

In order to make full use of the existing highly expressive graphical languages of SA/RT, some work has been done to give semantics to them, either directly or indirectly.

1. Direct way :
   At Deutsche System-Technik, a project has been undertaken to make the specification used in the Ward–Mellor structured method automatically analyzable and suitable for applications in the field of safety-critical systems[12]. By using techniques developed for defining the semantics of statecharts[8], a family of semantics (i.e. recursive casual-chain semantics, weakly-fair interleaving semantics, and full interleaving semantics) are given to *transformation schema* (TS), the specification language in Ward–Mellor method. And a number of ambiguities and inconsistencies in Ward–Mellor's original definition are resolved.
2. Indirect way, i.e. translating SA/RT specification into formal models :
   (a) In [12], CSP semantics for transformation schema is given by translating TS into CSP according to a set of rules.
   (b) In [13], a rigorous interpretation of Extended Systems Modeling Language (ESML) is given by translating ESML into Petri nets.
   (c) In IPTES (Incremental Prototyping Technology for Embedded Real-Time Systems) project, a tool is implemented to translate SA/RT models automatically into high-level timed Petri nets[5].

To give formal semantics directly to informal graphical languages can result in rather complicated semantics[11, 5] which are difficult to analyze; while translating them into a selected formal model has the advantage of not only retaining their user-friendly and problem-oriented characteristics, but also making good use of the existing results of the corresponding formal model for easier simulation and more powerful analysis.

The main formal models for real-time systems can be classed into three categories : temporal logics, process algebras, and Petri nets. Process algebras, eg. CSP, CCS, lead to methods for compositional verification, which is desirable for complex systems. But they are not appropriate for specifying inherently global properties, such as safety, liveness, fairness, and real-time response, which involve the global computation. While Petri nets and temporal logic are good at describing properties that pertain to the complete systems, however, they are relatively unstructured and not ideal for compositional verification[11]. Recent work on the compositionality or modularity of Petri nets[6, 2, 3, 10] and the emergence of high-level timed Petri nets[7, 17] has made them more attractive to the specification and analysis of complex real-time systems.

Although some work has been reported to give rigorous interpretation to the SA/RT requirement model via Petri nets, *time* has been taken into consideration only by Elmstrom et al.[5]. This work suffers from the following drawbacks:

1. Lack of compositionality in the translation process: For example, the translation of a control transformation should depend on the type and sometimes even internal structure of all the controlled transformations. We believe that compositionality is essential for the translation to assist the incremental or modular development of SA/RT specifications and their compositional analysis.
2. High complexity of the resulting nets: In many cases the growth of transitions and arcs is intolerably fast. Especially in the case of state/transition diagrams, the complexity of the resulting subnets relating to one *state* becomes at least exponential with respect to the scale of the subdiagram. The high complexity of translation results is a severe problem to efficient simulation and analysis.

The general aim of our work is to solve the above problems. In addition, our work is based on the latest SA/RT model [14] which is more powerful than that used by [5] in that it allows the description of more control activities in a succinct way. We have proposed a translation which is compositional, and the resulting nets have much lower complexity, e.g. the number of transitions is linear with respect to the scale of the original model. Due to the space limit, this paper will only discuss the main improvement to the translations given in [5, 4]. A detailed description of our translation rules can be found in [16].

First, a brief description of the STER nets, i.e. the Petri net model we use, is given in the next section.

2 ER nets – high-level timed Petri nets

Environment/Relationship (ER) nets[7] are a kind of high-level timed Petri nets, where both time and functional aspects can be modelled in a semantically coherent way. It was shown in [7] that ER nets are the most powerful model among all the existing timed versions of Petri nets. On the one hand, the more general the model, the less amenable it is to analysis. While on the other hand, if a model lacks modeling power or flexibility, it forces the specifier to add new features informally, or specify things in an unnatural way, which inhibits the discovery of system properties of interest. For large real-time systems, due to the complexity of the applications, not many choices exist. Some control and timing properties in SA/RT cannot be specified in any of the existing timed models except ER nets[16].

ER nets: An ER net is a net where,

- Tokens are environments on ID and V, i.e. partial functions : $ID \rightarrow V$, where ID is a set of identifiers and V a set of values.
- Each transition t is associated with an action $\alpha(t) \subseteq ENV^{k(t)} \times ENV^{h(t)}$, where ENV is the set of all environments, $k(t)$ and $h(t)$ denote the cardinalities of the preset and the postset of transition t, respectively. The projection of $\alpha(t)$ on $ENV^{k(t)}$ is denoted by $\pi(t)$ and is called the preconditions of transition t.
- A marking m is an assignment of multisets of environments to places.
- A transition t is enabled in a marking m iff for every input place p_i of t, there exists at least one token env_i such that $< env_1, \ldots, env_{k(t)} > \in \pi(t)$.
- A firing is a triple $x =< enab, t, prod >$, such that $< enab, prod > \in \alpha(t)$; and the occurrence of the firing changes a marking m to $m' = m - enab + prod$.

Time ER (TER) nets: A TER net is an ER net where all tokens contain a variable *chronos*, which represents the timestamp, and for any firing $x =< enab, t, prod >$, the following axioms are satisfied: (1) constraint on timestamps: all elements of the tuple *prod* have the same value of *chronos*, called the time of the firing; (2) local monotonicity: the time of the firing cannot be less than the value of *chronos* of any token in *enab*.

Strong TER(STER) nets: ER nets allow both the *strong* and *weak* time semantics. With strong time semantics, if a transition is enabled and remains enabled for all possible time values at which it can fire, then it must fire; with weak time semantics, a continuously enabled transition may not fire during the specified timing points/duration. For the interpretation of SA/RT specifications, the STER model, i.e. the TER model with strong time semantics, applies. The formal definition of STER nets [7] is omitted here.

An example: Figure 1 illustrates a TER net, where $ID = \{a, b, chronos\}$, and $V = N$. According to the definition of the actions[3], $t1$ and $t2$ are enabled, and $t3$ is not. Given the tokens (of $P3$) $tok4 = \{(a, 1)(chronos, i)\}$, $tok5 = \{(a, 2)(chronos, j)\}$ where $10 \leq i \leq 15$, $3 \leq j \leq 6$, $< tok1, t1, tok4 >$ and $< tok2, t2, tok5 >$ are possible firings.

The data type of a place P can be defined as all the possible tokens in P. The data type of $P1$, for example, can be defined as:[4] $P1 :: \{a, chronos\} \rightarrow N$, or written as $P :: a, chronos : N$. Also, for the definition of an action to be more intuitive, we can express it in three parts as in [5], i.e.

time : predicates relating to chronos fields of all the preset/postset places
precondition : other pre-conditions
action : assignments to postset places to make other post-conditions hold

For example, *act*1 in figure 1 can be rewritten as:

$time : p1.chronos + 10 \leq p3.chronos \leq p1.chronos$
$precondition : p1.a < 10$
$action : p3.a := p1.a$

[3] Note for the Petri nets discussed in this paper, the weight of any arc is 1, so we can use P_i to denote the token in place P_i in describing the actions.

[4] It can be assumed that all the possible tokens in the same place have the same domain.

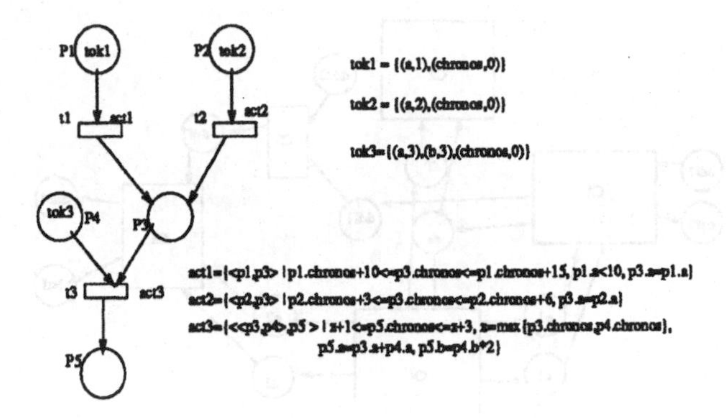

Fig. 1. an ER net considering time

3 Compositionality of the Translation

The development of an SA/RT model is a hierarchical process, and it is the flattened SA/RT model we are mainly concerned with, since an upper level of an SA/RT model is not considered in enough detail, and its information may be incomplete for it to be interpreted in a rigorous way. The most important principle of our translation with the flattened level is *compositionality* (or say, *locality*), i.e. the translation of each *component* is independent of other components.

3.1 Compositional Principle of the Translation

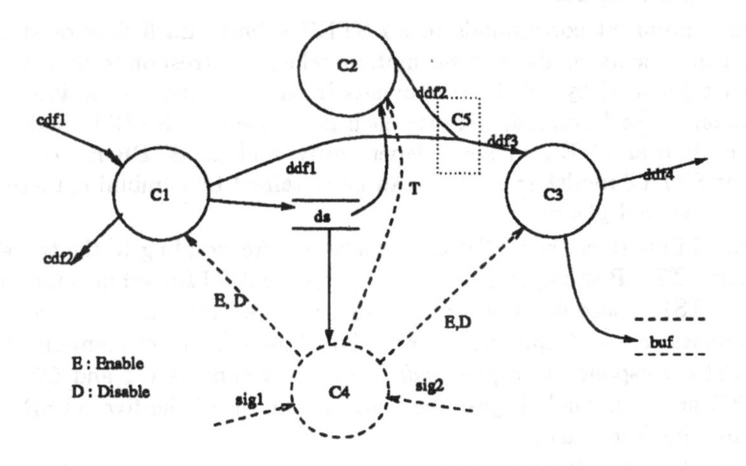

Fig. 2. The concept of *component* in transformation schema TS1

A *component* is either a data or control transformation together with all its inputs and outputs, or, a merging or splitting structure representing flows from

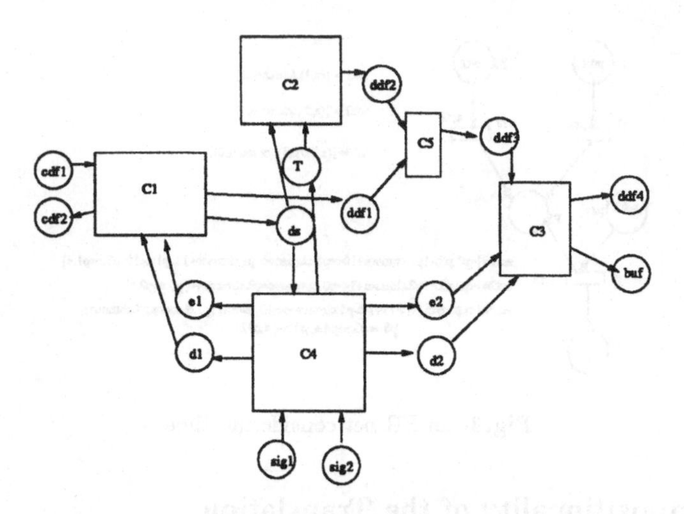

Fig. 3. The compositional principle of translation for TS1

multiple sources or to multiple destinations[18]. Figure 2 illustrates a transformation schema TS1 with five components $C1$-$C5$, where $C1$-$C3$ are data transformations, $C4$ is a control transformation, and $C5$ is a merging structure which merges *ddf*1 and *ddf*2 to *ddf*3. The interface of a component includes all the data/control flows to/from it. For example, $C3$ is a data transformation with *ddf*3, *Enable* and *Disable* as input interface, and with *ddf*4, *buf* as output interface; $C5$ is a merging structure with *ddf*1 and *ddf*2 as input interface, and with *ddf*3 as output interface.

Each component corresponds to an STER subnet. Each flow or store connecting components in the transformation schema corresponds to a place (or some places) shared by STER components in the net. The translation rules are *compositional* (or *localized*) because each component in SA/RT model can be translated into an STER subnet independently, and the STER net corresponding to the SA/RT model as a whole can be obtained by combining these STER subnets via shared places.

Figure 3 illustrates the STER net structure corresponding to the transformation schema TS1. Rectangles $C_i (1 \leq i \leq 5)$ represent STER subnets for components C_i of TS1. Those flows in TS1 are all translated into shared places outside the rectangles. For example the discrete data flow *ddf*1 from component $C1$ to $C5$ in TS1 corresponds to a place *ddf*1 shared by subnets $C1$ and $C5$ here. So the STER net as a whole is just the composition of all the five STER subnets that share interface places.

To simplify the situation, it is assumed in the above example that each data/control flow corresponds to one place. The same principle follows if some flow corresponds to more than one place, or some group of flows share one place. The translation strategies of data flows and stores are illustrated in figure 4 (the translation of control prompts will be discussed in the next subsection). Each flow f corresponds to place P_f, and when f is not connected with a data store, there is also a complementary, or say, an "empty" place P'_f (i.e. a token in P'_f represents that no value is attached to the flow f). Suppose the value of f is produced by component C1 and consumed by C2. Then the STER subnet of C1 should have transition *write* (and also *write'* if f is not a data store) that produce(s) a token to place P_f; similarly the STER subnet of C2 should have transition *read* (and also *read'* if f is from a buffer) that consume(s) a token from place P_f. Note that for buffer *buf* in figure 4(d), *read* and *read'* represent that after one item of *buf* is consumed by $C2$, *buf* is non-empty and empty respectively. Detailed explanations are given in [16].

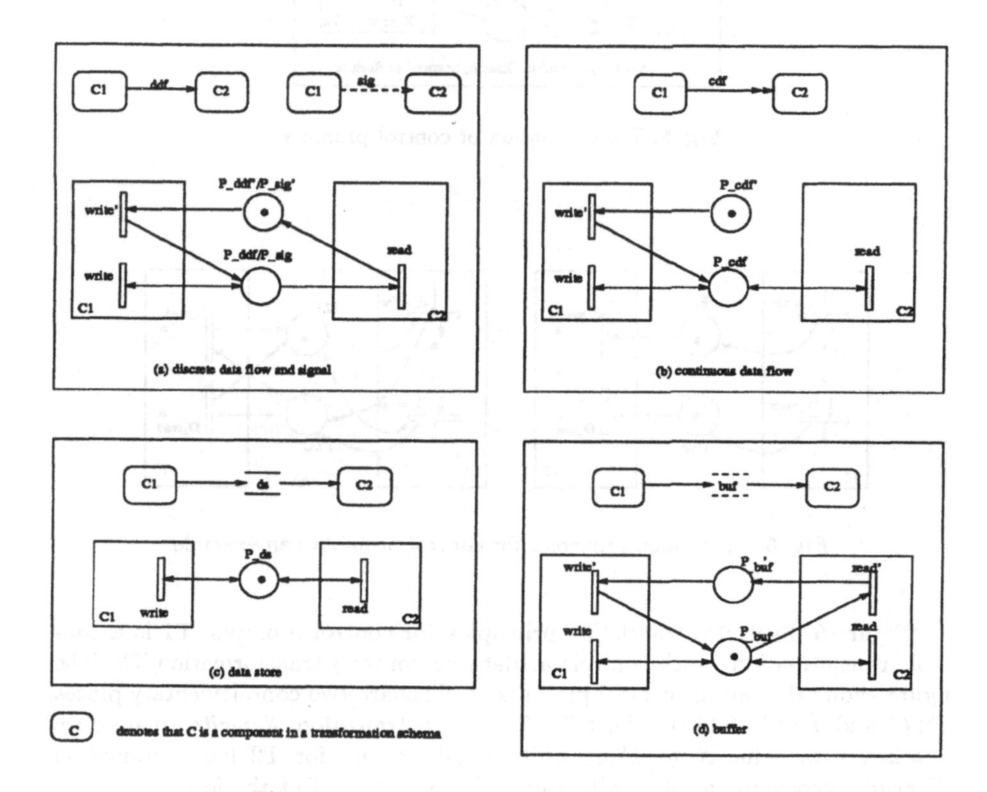

Fig. 4. The translation of data flows and stores

3.2 Localizing the Translation for Control Prompts

The translation in [5] is not compositional since some SA/RT constructs can not be translated independently. The main problem lies in the translation of control prompts, which are translated as transitions, and depend on the types, and even internal structures of all the transformations that receive them. We solve this problem by translating all control prompts going to the same transformation as two complementary shared places, and making the translation of the controlling and controlled transformations independent of each other.

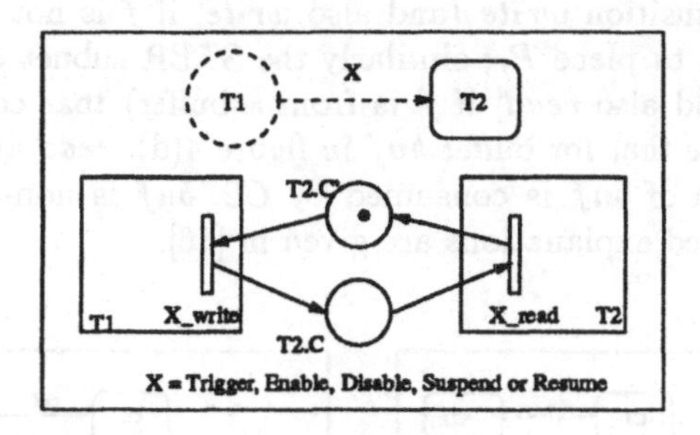

Fig. 5. The translation of control prompts

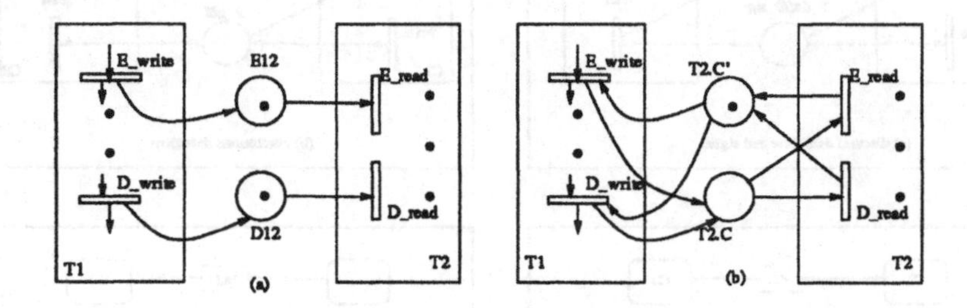

Fig. 6. Translation principles for control prompts : an example

Figure 5 illustrates translation principles for control prompts. T1 is a control transformation which controls a (data or control) transformation T2. The figure shows that all the control prompts of T2 share two complementary places *T2.C* and *T2.C'*. STER subnet for T1 has a transition *X_write* to produce a token with value X to T2.C; while STER subnet for T2 has a transition *X_read* to consume a token with value X from T2.C. But the form and number of such *X_write* or *X_read* transitions may vary, and they depend *only* on transformation T1 or T2. Some definitions are given as follows (where $X \in \{Trigger, Enable, Disable, Suspend, Resume\}$):

T2.C' :: *chronos* : *data_type_of_time*
T2.C :: *chronos* : *data_type_of_time*
data : $\{Trigger, Enable, Disable, Suspend, Resume\}$
X_write :: *time* :
precondition :
action : $T2.C.data = X$

X_read :: *time* : $time_0(X\_read)$
precondition : $T2.C.data = X$
action :

Where for transition t, $time_0(t)$ is defined as :
$\forall p \in t.postset, p.chronos := max\{pre.chronos | pre \in t.preset\}$

We omit the parameter t when there is no ambiguity. So the transition specified with $time_0$ should fire immediately when its *precondition* holds.

Note here we do not use separate places for different control prompts as for data flows. Consider the simple example as illustrated in figure 6(a), where two places $E12$ and $D12$ are used to represent the two prompts *Enable* and *Disable* sent by T1 to T2 respectively. When *Enable* and *Disable* are generated by the automaton of T1 sequentially, yet with the same timestamp; or when *time* is simply not considered in the analysis of some properties, usually it is required that the prompts be consumed in the same order as they are produced. But with transitions *E_read* and *D_read*, it is indeterminate which one fires first when their preset places have the same value in *chronos*, or when *time* is not considered. Thus the control prompts may not be consumed in the same order as they are produced. This problem can be solved in our method by using shared places for all control prompts, as in figure 6(b), where $T2.C$ is $safe$ by initially putting one token in its complementary place $T2.C'$. So we can guarantee that all the control prompts are accepted and consumed in an orderly manner.

3.3 Benefits of Compositional Translation

The compositionality of the translation process benefits the development of SA/RT specifications in the following aspects:

- Assisting the interactivity of the development process of SA/RT specifications. The development of SA/RT specification is quite an interactive process. The users modify the specification, and expect a *responsive* change in the corresponding animation and analysis. The compositional translation localizes the modification of the underlying subnets, thus improving the efficiency and interactivity.
- Assisting the incremental development of specifications. In many occasions, the development process of a specification can be incremental. For example, a critical part of the model may be developed and its critical properties need to be analyzed first. Compositional translation allows the translation and analysis of part of the model, thus supporting the incremental development of specifications.
- Assisting modular development and analysis of specifications. Any module in transformation schema can be translated independently into a Petri net module; Petri net modules can be combined just by shared places. Modifying of any part of the specification only results in *localized* modification of the underlying net and other parts, including their properties, will be kept intact. Thus compositional translation is essential to the compositional/modular development and analysis of specifications.

4 Improved Efficiency to the Resulting Nets

It is mainly for the benefit of analysis that formal models are used to interpret SA/RT specifications. As pointed out in [7], STER nets are general enough for the requirement specification of most complex real-time systems; on the other hand, most of the usual temporal properties are undecidable in STER nets. Generally, the STER nets can be analyzed in the following ways[7]:

- to restrict the analysis to special decidable subcases corresponding to special classes of applications;
- to derive approximate solutions : by ignoring token values, STER nets are reduced into low-level (timed) Petri nets. So in general, all known techniques for analyzing (timed) Petri nets can be used as approximate analysis aids in the case of STER net;
- to provide interactive decision-support systems to assess them;
- to test specifications by simulation.

Whatever method is used, the complexity of simulation and analysis of Petri nets grows with their sizes, especially the numbers of transitions and arcs, that is, the efficiency of translations in our case.

In [5], the growth of transitions and arcs in the resulting nets is very fast in some cases. Our strategies can greatly decrease the complexity. In this section we illustrate this improvement via state/transition diagrams, where the size of the nets grows the fastest in [5].

4.1 An Efficient Translation for State/Transition Diagrams

Figure 7 shows a typical example of a state/transition diagram STD, with two states and three transitions. In order to distinguish between a transition in Petri nets and a (state) transition in state/transition diagrams, in the following we use *Stransition* to denote the latter. The translation for state/transition diagrams is localized in the sense that the subnet for each state is decided only on this state and Stransitions from it. For the ease of description, we consider the input and output part of Stransitions separately.

The translation for inputs of Stransitions. In this part we ignore the Stransition outputs in order to concentrate on the rules of the inputs.

Consider first a specious solution in figure 8(a)(note that only Stransitions from *state1* to *state2* of STD are considered at this moment), where each state corresponds to one place, and each Stransition corresponds to one transition. It has problems when *sig1* and *sig2* arrive at *state*1 simultaneously, and both the input conditions of Stransition 1 and 2 are satisfied. In this situation, only one transition will fire, thus only one of the two signals is consumed. So the other signal remains, and will be consumed by some transition later. But this violates the requirement that an Stransition occurs only if its signal input comes *when* or *after* the origin state is reached[14].

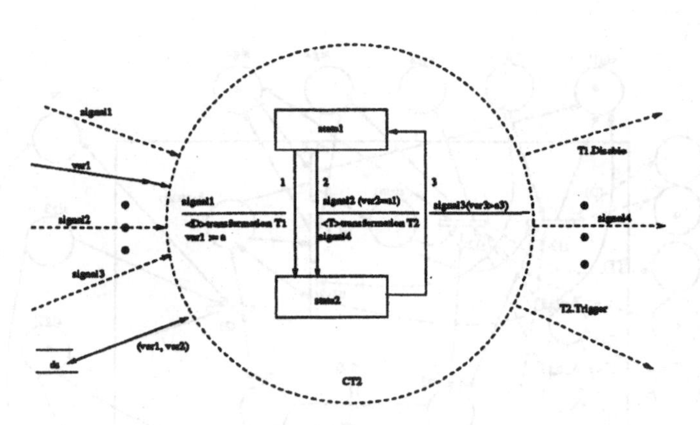

Fig. 7. STD : a state/transition diagram

Another possible method which is used in [5] is illustrated in figure 8(b). It considers all the combinations of input signals, and if more than one signal arrive at the same time, only one of the Stransitions whose input conditions are satisfied is selected (nondeterministically) to occur, but all the signals are consumed. So four transitions are used to represent two Stransitions:

- t12-1a, t12-2a : Stransition1 or 2 occurs when *sig*2 or *sig*1 is empty.
- t12-1b, t12-2b : Stransition1 or 2 occurs when both *sig*1 and *sig*2 are non-empty, and both are consumed after the firing.

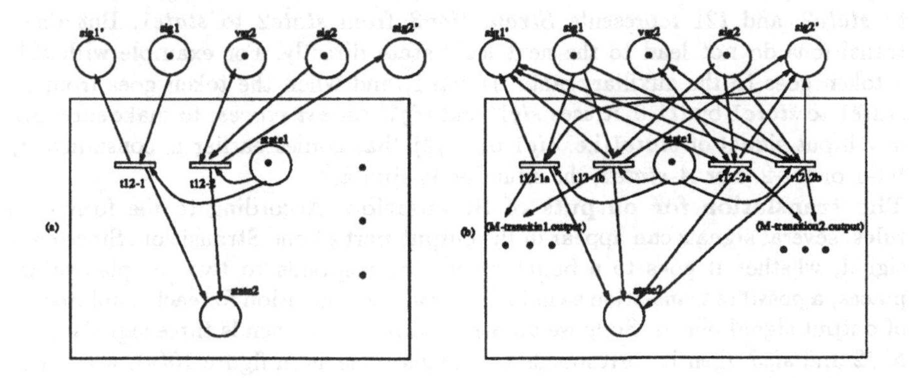

Fig. 8. Possible STER subnets for STD

With this translation, any signal that comes at *state1* will not remain and thus will not be used later, but the number of transitions needed increases rapidly with the number of Stransitions. Suppose there are n Stransitions from $state_i$ to $state_j$, each with a signal event, the number of corresponding transitions (when outputs are not considered) will be $n \times 2^{n-1}$(A proof can be found in [16]).

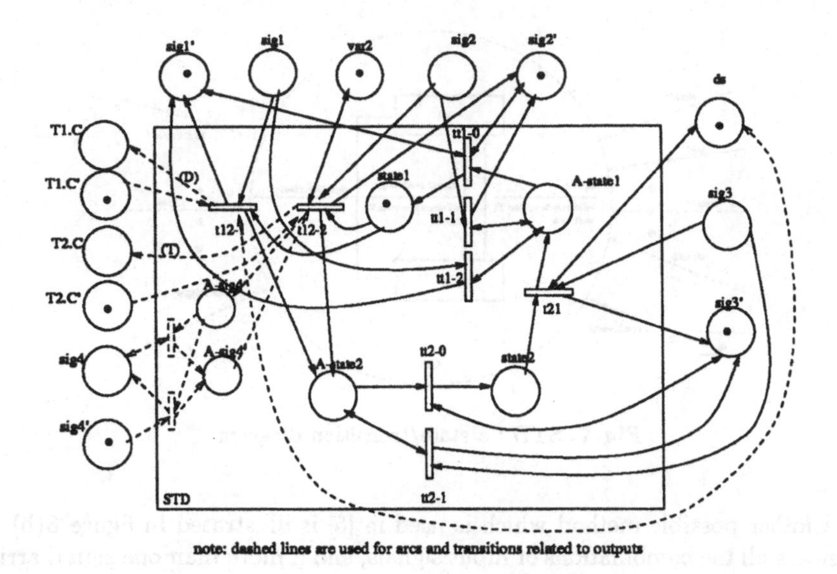

Fig. 9. STER subnet for STD

To solve this problem of "*transition explosion*", we use an auxiliary place for each state to consume all the possible signal inputs of that state before it is reached, so no state will consume any signal that comes earlier. Figure 9 illustrates our translation of STD. *A_state*1, 2 are auxiliary places for *state*1, 2 respectively. Transitions *t*12-1 and *t*12-2 represent *Stransition*1, 2 from *state*1 to *state*2, and *t*21 represents *Stransition*3 from *state*2 to *state*1. But these transitions do not lead to the next legal state directly. For example with *t*21, a token goes to the auxiliary state *A-state*1, and when the token goes from *A-state*1 to *state*1 by *tt*1-0, it uses *sig*1$'$ and *sig*2$'$ as ***test places***, to make sure that any input signal of *state*1(i.e. *sig*1 or *sig*2) that comes earlier is consumed by *tt*1-1 or *tt*1-2. For *A-state*2, the situation is similar[5].

The translation for outputs of Stransition. According to the formation rules, several signals can appear in the output part of one Stransition. Since each signal, whether it goes to a buffer or not, corresponds to two complementary places, a possible translation as in [5] is to use one transition for each combination of output signal places. Suppose an Stransition *Stran*1 sends three signals, *sig1*, *buf*2 and *sig3*, then it corresponds to 8 transitions as in figure 10(a), where e.g. transition t_{011} corresponds to the situation when *sig1* is empty, *buf*2 and *sig3* are non-empty, etc. Generally if the number of output signals in an Stransition is n, then 2^n transitions are needed, and the number of related arcs is $n(2^n + 2^{n-1})$.

[5] There are some differences if the input signal of a Stransition comes from a buffer. Firstly a data item in a buffer will not be removed unless it is used as the event of some Stransition. Secondly, two transitions are needed for each Stransition with a buffer input, which correspond to *read* and *read'* in figure 4(d) respectively. An example can be found in [16]

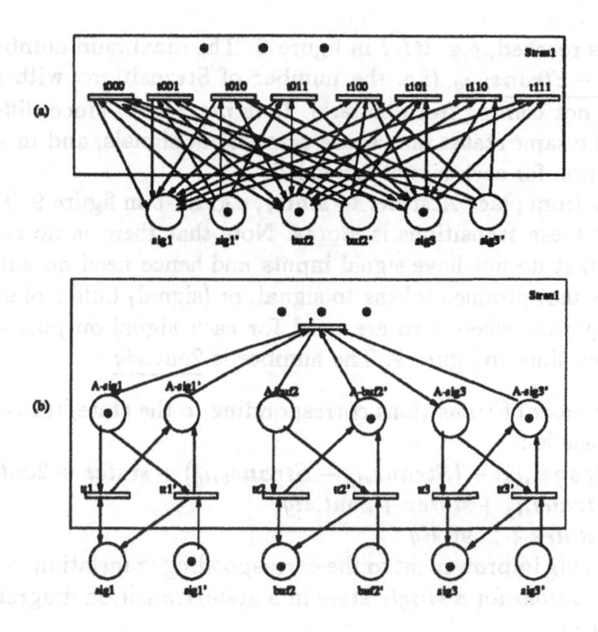

Fig. 10. Possible translations for a Stransition *Stran*1 with 3 active outputs

Our translation for *Stran*1 is illustrated in figure 10(b). Two complementary auxiliary places are used for each of the signals, e.g. *A-sig1* and *A-sig1′* are auxiliary places for *sig*1. Transition *t* corresponds to *Stran*1, consuming its inputs and producing outputs, but the tokens for signal outputs are sent to *auxiliary* places. With transitions tt_i and $tt'_i (1 \leq i \leq 3)$, tokens in auxiliary places are sent to actual output shared places. Note that the *time* part of each transition tt_i or tt'_i is defined as $time_0$, i.e. they fire immediately when they are enabled. This means the outputs to places *sig1*, *buf*2 and *sig3* will be produced with the same timestamp, although may be sequentially.

According to this strategy, we use auxiliary places for the output signal *sig*4 in STD. The transitions and arcs related to the outputs in STD are represented by dashed lines in figure 9.

The complexity of the resulting nets. Suppose for a state/transition diagram, the total number of Stransitions is *Strans*, and the number of those with signal inputs is $Strans_{sig}$, of which the number of those with signals coming from buffers is $Strans_{bsig}$; the number of all the output signals is *out.sig*, and the number of states is *states*, then all the transitions in the corresponding STER subnet consists of:

1. transitions from place $state_i$ to A_state_j(or $state_j$) corresponding to the Stransition from $state_i$ to $state_j$, e.g. *t12-1* in figure 9. The number is $Strans + Strans_{bsig}$, since two transitions are used for an Stransition with an input signal coming from a buffer.
2. transitions that make sure all input signals of the next legal state are empty

before it is reached, e.g. *tt1-1* in figure 9. The maximum number is $\underline{Strans_{sig} - Strans_{bsig}}$ (i.e. the number of Stransitions with signal inputs which are not coming from buffers). It is *maximum* since different Stransitions to the same states may share same input signals, and in this case only one transition for each signal is needed.

3. transitions from place *A_state$_i$* to *state$_i$*, e.g. *tt1-0* in figure 9. The maximum number of these transitions is $\underline{states}$. Note that there is no such transition for states that do not have signal inputs and hence need no auxiliary place.
4. transitions that produce tokens to signal, or (signal) buffer places from their auxiliary places, where two are used for each signal output, as transitions with dashed lines in figure 9. The number is $\underline{2out.sig}$.

So the total number of transitions corresponding to the state/transition diagram in the worst case is :

$(Strans + Strans_{bsig}) + (Strans_{sig} - Strans_{bsig}) + states + 2out.sig$
$= Strans + Strans_{sig} + states + 2out.sig$
$\leq 2Strans + states + 2out.sig$

This result is a big improvement to the corresponding translation in [5], where the number of transitions for a *single* state in a state/transition diagram is analyzed in [5] as follows :

> ...(Suppose) n denotes the number of input signals (not coming from buffers) and B denotes the number of input signals (coming from buffers) in the condition of the state transitions from a specific state, (then the number of transitions corresponding to this state is[6]:)
>
> $$\sum_{i=1}^{2^n}\left(\sum_{j=1}^{n} g(i,j)\right) + \sum_{b=1}^{B}\left(\sum_{st\_tr=1}^{l}\left(\prod_{st\_tr\_out=1}^{N} h(st\_tr\_out)\right)\right)$$
>
> where g is an auxiliary function defined as :
>
> $$g(i,j) = \begin{cases} \sum_{st\_tr=1}^{l}(\prod_{st\_tr\_out=1}^{N} h(st\_tr\_out)) & if\ odd(i-1\ div\ 2^{j-1}) \\ 0 & if\ even(i-1\ div\ 2^{j-1}) \end{cases}$$
>
> where l denotes the number of state transitions which have signal j or b as incoming signal, N denotes the number of output flows in state transition *st_tr*, and *st_tr_out* denotes a specific output flow in state transition *st_tr*. h is an auxiliary function ...

The definition of h is omitted here, but we must point out that $\forall i, h(i) \geq 2$.

[6] The result the authors get is:

$$\sum_{i=1}^{2^n}\left(\sum_{j=1}^{n} g(i,j)\right) + \left(\sum_{b=1}^{B}\left(\sum_{st\_tr=1}^{l}\left(\prod_{st\_tr\_out=1}^{N} h(st\_tr\_out)\right)\right)\right) \times 2^n$$

which is different to the above result in the number of transitions for buffers.

5 An Example

Figure 11(a) illustrates a simple case of a control transformation CT with a state/transition diagram given in [5]. The translation for CT in [5] depends on the information of transformation $T1$ that it disables: (1)$T1$ is a discrete data

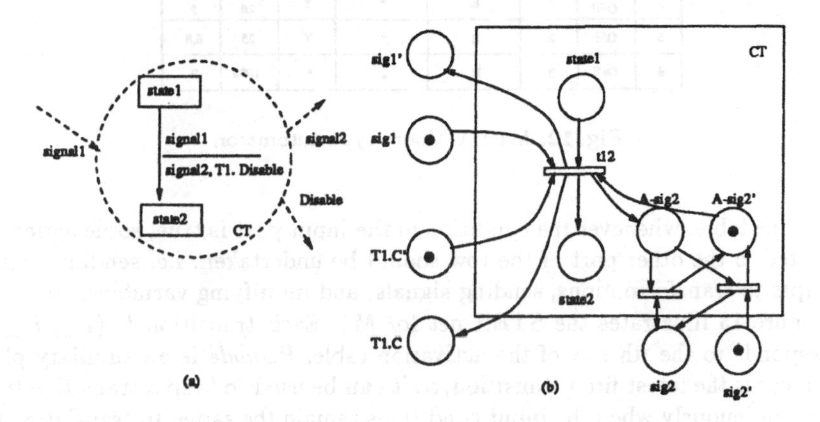

Fig. 11. CT: a simple example of control transformation

transformation. The High-level timed Petri net(HLTPN) for CT has 7 transitions and 46 arcs(figure 29 of [5]); (2)$T1$ is a continuous data transformation. The HLTPN for CT has 11 transitions and 76 arcs(figure 30 of [5]); (3)$T1$ is a control transformation. In this case, the HLTPN for CT will depend on the internal information of T1, e.g. the number of states in the case of state/transition diagram. The HLTPN for CT has 7 transitions and 46 arcs (figure 31 of [5]) when T1 has *two* states.

But with our strategies, the STER subnet for CT with only 3 transitions and 15 arcs can be derived independently. It only shares those places outside the rectangle with other components, e.g. $T1.C$ and $T1.C'$ are places it shares with transformation T1. Note that t12.action includes $T1.C.data := Disable$.

6 Other Improvements

6.1 Moore-type automata

Moore-type automata are not used in [18, 19], and they are not considered in [5]. But since they succinctly describe the combinational control logic, they are used in [9], and adopted in [14].

A Moore-type automaton is used if the logic of a control transformation is purely combinatorial – the control exerted during a time period depends only on a combination of continuous input or stored variable values that hold during the period. It can be represented as an activation table as M1 in figure 12. For each

row no.	INPUT		TRANSFORMATIONS		OUTPUT		
	ds1.var1	var2	T1	T2	sig1	var3	var4
1	ON	1	D	•	Y	5	9.5
2	ON	2	D	•	•	10	8
3	ON	3	E	T	•	15	7.6
4	OFF	1	E	•	Y	20	5
5	OFF	2	E	•	Y	25	6.8
6	OFF	3	E	•	•	1000	2

Fig. 12. M1 : A Moore-type automaton

row of the table, whenever the condition in the input part is true, some actions as indicated in the other part of the row should be undertaken, i.e. sending control prompts to transformations, sending signals, and modifying variables, etc.

Figure 13 illustrates the STER net for M1. Each transition t_i $(1 \leq i \leq 6)$ corresponds to the *i*th row of the activation table. *P_mode* is an auxiliary place that records the latest fired transition, so it can be used to keep a transition from firing continuously when the input conditions remain the same. In translating the signal outputs, the same method as for state/transition diagrams is used, i.e. two auxiliary complementary places are used for each signal output. For continuous data flow outputs, i.e. *var3* and *var4*, they are all empty or non-empty at the same time, so they can share one *empty* place *cdf'*, and also share two auxiliary places *A-cdf* and *A-cdf*. Note that for each transition $t_i(1 \leq i \leq 6)$, there are an arc from $T1.C'$ and an arc to $T1.C$ sending either *Enable* or *Disable* prompt to transformation T1. We do not draw these arcs in detail for the net to be more readable. Some of the definitions are:

P_mode :: $chronos : data\_type\_of\_time$
$data$: 0..6 *0 is used when M1 is just enabled *\

A-cdf :: $chronos : data\_type\_of\_time$
$var3 : data\_type\_of\_var3;$
$var4 : data\_type\_of\_var4)$

$t1 :: time : time_0$
$precondition : (ds1.data.var1 = ON) and (var2.data = 1)$
$and (P\_mode.data \neq 1)$
$action : T1.C.data := Disable, P\_mode.data := 1,$
$A\_cdf.var3 := 5, A\_cdf.var4 := 9.5$

Other transitions *t2-t6* can be similarly defined.

Suppose the number of signal outputs is n, and the number of rows in the activation table is $rows$, then the number of transitions is : $rows + 2(n + c)$, where $c = 1$ when there is continuous output, and $c = 0$ otherstate/transition diagramControl Prompts *Suspend* and *Resume Suspend* and *Resume* prompts are not incorporated in [18] and [19], and they are not considered in [5]. But they permit more detailed modeling of certain implementation situations, and are useful for the design of real-time systems.

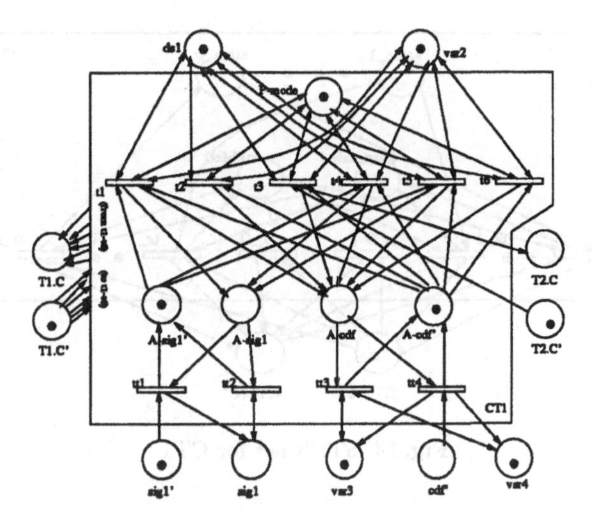

Fig. 13. STER net for M1

Suspend and *Resume* prompts are similar to *Enable* and *Disable*, except that a suspended transformation remembers its intermediate results and the system context and picks up where it left off when resumed. For a control transformation that has *Pause* (i.e. *Suspend* and *Resume*) as outputs, the related translation is similar to that for CT with *T*1.*Disable* as output in figure 11(b). For a transformation with *Pause* as inputs, the translation rule varies with its type. We illustrate them by the following two cases.

1. *Pause* for a control transformation CT1, which is described by STD, a state/transition diagram without terminal states
   Suppose STD has n states, denoted by $state_i (1 \leq i \leq n)$. The corresponding net is shown in figure 14. Places *suspended* and *enabled* represent the two complementary states of CT1, and when a token is in place *enabled*, another token should also be in one of places $state_i$(or their auxiliary state $A\text{-}state_i$, which we omit in this figure, since they are irrelevant for the translation here). We have the following definitions:

   suspended :: *chronos* : *data_type_of_time*
   data : 1..n
   ts_0 :: **Suspend comes at suspended state, nothing happens**\\
   $ts_i (1 \leq i \leq n)$:: **transitions consume Suspend prompt at* $state_i$ *\\
   time : $time_0$
   precondition : $CT1.C.data =$ *Suspend*
   action : *suspended.data* := i
   tr_0 :: **Resume comes when CT1 is in enabled state, nothing happens**\\
   $tr_i (1 \leq i \leq n)$ :: **transitions consume Resume prompt at* $state_i$ *\\
   time : $time_0$
   precondition : $CT1.C.data =$ *Resume*, *suspended.data* $= i$

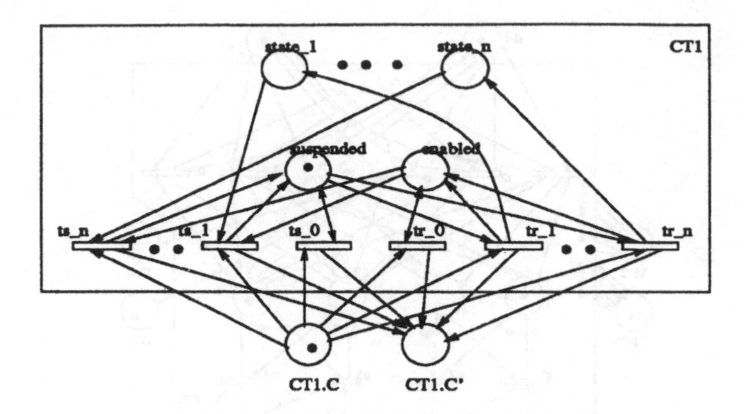

Fig. 14. STER net for CT1

action :

2. *Pause* for data transformations
   For a data transformation, say DT, there are two internal *enabled* states, i.e. *idle* or *executing*. For place *executing*, the *start_time* field is used to record the time when DT begins to process the inputs, and the temporal requirements of DT (e.g. output delay) are usually calculated with respect to its value. When *Pause* is used, the temporal requirements depend not only on *start_time*, but also on the suspended time period. So to obtain correct temporal properties of DT, the suspended time should be counted to *start_time* of the place *executing*. The corresponding subnet is the same as figure 14 except that (1) $n = 2$, and $state_1 = idle$, $state_2 = executing$; (2) the data type of *suspended* should include the field *start_time* : *data_type_of_time*; and (3) the action part of ts_2, which accepts a *Suspend* prompt at *executing* state, should include: *suspended.start_time* := $CT1.C.chronos$; and the action part of tr_2, which accepts a *Resume* prompt at (*executing_*)*suspended* state, should include the following:
   executing.start_time := *executing.start_time*+
   ($CT1.C.chronos$ − *suspended.start_time*)
   \∗ ($CT1.C.chronos$ − *suspended.start_time*) is the suspended time∗\

Pause can also interact with other control prompts, i.e. *Trigger* or *Activate*. See [16] for detailed descrstate/transition diagramThe Inheritance of "Disabling" Control According to [18], [19] and [14], when a control transformation is disabled, all the transformations it controls should be disabled as well. An example of controlling structure of a transformation schema is given in figure 15(a), where CT3 and DT1 should be disabled at the moment CT2 is disabled by CT1. But this requirement is not considered in [5], because the translation of a control transformation depends on the type and the internal structure of the disabled transformations, and that means in this example, the translation of CT1 would depend on all its *decending* transformations, i.e. CT2, CT3 and DT1, to meet the "*disabling transitivity*" requirement above, which would be impractical.

This requirement can be easily implemented in our translation, as illustrated in figure 15(b). Note that transition t is the abstract form of all the transitions in the STER subnet of CT2 that make CT2 go to *disabled* state on receiving a *Disable* prompt. It can be defined as follows:

time : $time_0$

precondition : $CT2.C.data = Disable$

action : $CT3.C.data := Disable,\ DT1.C.data := Disable$

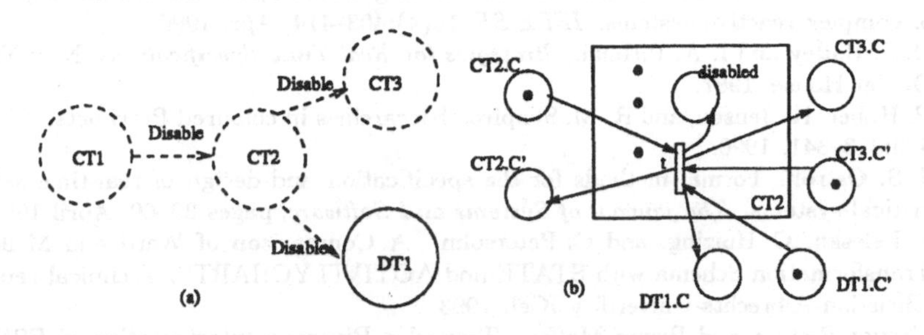

Fig. 15. Translation of disabling control

7 Conclusions

This paper has presented a new method for translating SA/RT models to high-level timed Petri nets; this can greatly improve the efficiency of the resulting nets with respect to their numbers of transitions and arcs, and thus facilitate the simulation and analysis of specifications. Also the introduction of compositional principles into the translation process supports the incremental or modular development of specifications and their compositional analysis. The resulting nets can be analyzed at different levels of abstraction as described in §4. Despite the previous efforts on such analysis[7, 6, 1], more work needs to be done for efficient analysis methods of high-level timed Petri nets and especially their modular/compositional analysis.

References

1. C. Bellettini, M. Felder, and M. Pezzé. A Tool for Analysing High-Level Timed Petri Nets. Technical Report IPTES-PDM-41-V2.0, Politecnico di Milano, 1993.
2. L. Bernardinello and F. De Cindio. A Survey of Basic Net Models and Modular Net Classes. In *LNCS 609: Advances in Petri nets*, pages 304–351. 1992.
3. Wilfried Brauer, Robert Gold, and Walter Vogler. A survey of behaviour and equivalence preserving refinements of Petri Nets. *LNCS*, 483:1–46, 1990.

4. R. Elmstrøm, R. Lintulampi, and M. Pezzé. Giving semantics to SA/RT by means of high-level timed Petri nets. *Real-Time Systems Journal*, 5(2-3):249–271, May 1993.
5. R. Elmstrøm, R. Lintulampi, and M. Pezzé. Automatic translation of SA/RT to high-level timed Petri nets. Technical Report IPTES-PDM-17-V2.3, Jan 1994.
6. M. Felder, C. Ghezzi, and M. Pezzé. Hierarchical Decomposition of High Level Timed Petri Nets. Technical Report IPTES-PDM-54-V2.0, Politecnico di Milano, Dec 1993.
7. C. Ghezzi, D. Mandrioli, S. Marasca, and M. Pezzé. A unified high-level Petri net formalism for time-critical systems. *IEEE SE*, 17(2):160–172, Feb. 1991.
8. D. Harel, H. Lachover, A. Naamad, A. Pnueli, M. Politi, R. Sherman, and M. Trachtenbrot. STATEMATE : A working environment for the development of complex reactive systems. *IEEE SE*, 16(4):403–414, Apr. 1990.
9. D. J. Hatley and I. A. Pirbhai. *Strategies for Real Time Specifications*. New York, Dorset House, 1987.
10. P. Huber, K. Jensen, and R. M. Shapiro. Hierarchies in coloured Petri nets. *LNCS*, 483:313–341, 1990.
11. J. S. Ostroff. Formal methods for the specification and design of real-time safety critical systems. *The journal of Systems and Software*, pages 33–60, April 1992.
12. J. Peleska, C. Huizing, and C. Petersohn. A Comparison of Ward and Mellor's Transformation Schema with STATE-and ACTIVITYCHARTS. Technical report, Christian-Albrechts-Univerdity Kiel, 1993.
13. Gernot Richter and Bruno Maffeo. Toward a Rigorous Interpretation of ESML–Extended Systems Modeling Language. *IEEE-SE*, 19(2):165–180, Feb 1993.
14. W. Rruyn, R. Jensen, D. Keskar, and P. Ward. ESML : An extended systems modeling language based on the data flow diagram. *ACM SIGSOFT, Software Engineering Notes*, 13(1):58–67, Jan. 1988.
15. J. Rushby. Formal Methods and the Certification of Critical Systems. Technical report, ACAA, Dec. 1993.
16. L. Shi. Uniting formal and structured design methods for real-time systems. Transfer report, Department of Computing, Manchester Metropolitan University, 1995.
17. W. M. P. van der Aalst. Interval Timed Coloured Petri Nets and their Analysis. In *LNCS 691: Application and Theory of Petri nets*, pages 453–472. 1993.
18. P. Ward and S. Mellor. *Structured Development for Real-Time Systems*, volume 1-3. New Jersey: Prence Hall, 1985.
19. Paul T. Ward. The transformation schema: an extension of the data flow diagram to represent control and timing. *IEEE SE*, 12(2):198–210, Feb 1986.
20. D. P. Wood and W. G. Wood. Comparative Evaluations of Specification Methods for Real-Time Systems. Technical report, SEI, CMU, Dec 1989.

From Testing Theory to Test Driver Implementation

Jan Peleska and Michael Siegel

JP Software-Consulting* and Christian-Albrechts-Universität zu Kiel**

Abstract. In this article we describe the theoretical foundations for the VVT-RT test system *(Verification, Validation and Test for Reactive Real-Time Systems)* which supports automated test generation, test execution and test evaluation for reactive systems. VVT-RT constructs and evaluates tests based on formal CSP specifications [6], making use of their representation as labelled transition systems generated by the CSP model checker FDR [3]. The present article provides a sound formal basis for the development and verification of high-quality test tools: Since, due to the high degree of automation offered by VVT-RT, human interaction becomes superfluous during critical phases of the test process, the trustworthiness of the test tool is an issue of great importance. The VVT-RT system will therefore be formally verified so that it can be certified for testing safety-critical systems. The present article represents the starting point of this verification suite, where the basic strategies for test generation and test evaluation used by the system are formally described and verified. VVT-RT has been designed to support automation of both untimed and real-time tests. The present article describes the underlying theory for the untimed case. Exploiting these results, the concepts and high-level algorithms used for the automation of real-time tests are described in a second report which is currently prepared [14]. At present, VVT-RT is applied for hardware-in-the-loop tests of railway and tramway control computers.

Keywords: CSP — FDR — may tests — must tests — reactive systems — refinement — test evaluation — test generation

1 Introduction

Design, execution and evaluation of trustworthy tests for safety-critical systems require considerable effort and skill and consume a large part of today's development costs for software-based systems. It has to be expected that with conventional techniques, the test coverage to be required for these systems in the near future will become technically unmanageable and lead to unacceptable costs. This hypothesis is supported by the growing complexity of applications

* Goethestraße 26, D-24116 Kiel, e-mail: jap@informatik.uni-kiel.d400.de

** Institut für Informatik und Praktische Mathematik, Preusserstrasse 1-9, 24105 Kiel, Germany, Email: mis@informatik.uni-kiel.d400.de

and the increasingly strict requirements of certification authorities with respect to the verification of safety issues. For these reasons methods and tools helping to automize the test process gather wide interest both in industry and research communities. *"Serious"* testing – not just playing around with the system in an unsystematic way – always has to be based on some kind of specification describing the desired system behaviour at least for the situations covered by the test cases under consideration. As a consequence, the problem of test automation is connected to formal methods in a natural way, because the computer-based design and evaluation of tests is only possible on the basis of formal specifications with well-defined semantics.

Just as it is impossible to build theorem provers for the fully mechanized proof of arbitrary assertions, the general problem of testing against arbitrary types of specifications cannot be solved in a fully automized way. The situation is much more encouraging, however, if we specialize on well-defined restricted classes of systems and test objectives. This strategy is pursued in the present article, where we will focus on the test of *reactive systems.*

The idea to apply the theoretical results about testing in process algebras to practical problems was first presented by Brinksma, with the objective to automize testing against LOTOS specifications. His concept has been applied for the automation of *OSI conformance tests*; see [1] for an overview. Today, testing against different types of formal specifications has gained wide interest both for engineers responsible for the quality assurance of safety-critical systems and in the formal methods community: To name a few examples, Gaudel [4] investigates testing against *algebraic specifications*, Hörcher and Mikk in collaboration with the author [7, 8, 9] focus on the automatic test evaluation against *Z specifications* and Müllerburg [11] describes test automation in the field of *synchronous languages*.

Rather than presenting a new testing theory for reactive systems, we investigate how to construct *implementable* and *provably correct test drivers* on the basis of results from testing theory. Our approach is based on the untimed CSP process algebra and uses Hennessy's testing methodology [5] as starting point. To apply the concepts in practice, the VVT-RT tool *(Validation, Verification and Test for Reactive Real-Time Systems)* offers the following possibilities:

- symbolic execution of CSP specifications
- formal validation and verification of the specification
- automized generation of test cases based on the CSP specification
- automized test execution
- automized test evaluation, including the check of real-time properties
- automized test documentation

Typical applications addressed by our approach are systems with discrete interfaces and an emphasis on possibly complex control functionality. Examples are railway control systems, telephone switching systems and network protocols. At present the VVT-RT system is used for the test of computers controlling components of railway interlocking systems. The first application was the automized test of a PLC system controlling signals, traffic lights and train detection sensors for a tramway crossing, documented in [2, 12, 13]. VVT-RT makes use of the model checker FDR developed by Formal Systems Ltd [3].

This article focuses on theoretic results that are essential for the trustworthy practical application of our testing approach. Examples, industrial applications and a summary of the benefits to be expected from such a test automation concept are described in [16].

The article is structured as follows. In Section 2 we introduce notations and conventions used in subsequent sections. Section 3 introduces transition graphs and results from Hennessy's testing theory. Section 4 contains the main results, where we investigate implementable, minimal test classes and trustworthy test drivers. The full proofs of the theorems discussed in this paper are contained in a technical report [15] which may be obtained from the authors. Section 5 contains conclusions.

2 Preliminaries

2.1 CSP Operators, Semantics and Refinement

In this section we introduce some notation and conventions used throughout the paper.

Tests and test drivers will be specified in the process algebraic framework of *Communicating Sequential Processes (CSP)* [6]. We use the following set of *CSP* operators: *STOP* (deadlock process), *SKIP* (terminating process), $\rightarrow$ (prefixing), $\sqcap$ (internal choice), $\Box$ (external choice), $\|$ (parallel composition with synchronization on common events), $|||$ (interleaving operator without synchronization), $\setminus$ (hiding), and $\hat{}$ (interrupt). Operator $(x : \{a_1, \ldots, a_n\} \rightarrow P(x))$ abbreviates $a_1 \rightarrow P(a_1) \Box \ldots \Box a_n \rightarrow P(a_n)$, and $\sqcap_{x:\{a_1,\ldots,a_n\}}(x \rightarrow P(x))$ is an abbreviation for $a_1 \rightarrow P(a_1) \sqcap \ldots \sqcap a_n \rightarrow P(a_n)$. As basic programming operators we use **if then else**, $c?$ (input from channel c) and $g \& B$ (guarded command, g is the guard and B the body).

For the specification of recursive processes we use sets of recursive equations rather than an explicit μ-operator. The alphabet of a process P is denoted by $\alpha(P)$.

We use the standard semantics for *CSP* processes: $Traces(P) \subseteq \alpha(P)^*$ (trace semantics), $Fail(P) \subseteq \alpha(P)^* \times \mathbb{P}\,\alpha(P)$ (failure semantics, $\mathbb{P}$ denotes the power set operator), and $Div(P) \subseteq \alpha(P)^*$ (divergences of process P). The elements $s \in Traces(P)$ are the observable traces generated by P. A failure $(s, A) \in Fail(P)$ records the fact that process P may refuse to engage in any action of set A after having performed trace s. Due to nondeterminism there may be several $A, A' \subseteq \alpha(P)$ with $(s, A) \in Fail(P)$ and $(s, A') \in Fail(P)$. The *refusals* of a process P are defined by $Ref(P) =_{df} \{A \mid (\langle\,\rangle, A) \in Fail(P)\}$, where $\langle\,\rangle$ denotes the empty trace. A divergence $s \in Div(P)$ denotes the situation that process P may diverge after having engaged in trace s. Diverging processes show completely unpredictable behaviour, denote by *CHAOS* in *CSP*.

Infinite behaviours are defined as limites of prefix closed sets of finite behaviours [6, p. 132]. We use the standard fixpoint semantics for recursive processes. The set *maxTraces*(P) denotes the union of the set of all terminated behaviours and the set of infinite behaviours of P.

In this paper we consider the following refinement relations:

- trace refinement: $P \sqsubseteq_T Q$ iff $\mathit{Traces}(Q) \subseteq \mathit{Traces}(P)$
- failures refinement: $P \sqsubseteq_F Q$ iff $\mathit{Fail}(Q) \subseteq \mathit{Fail}(P)$
- failure–divergence refinement: $P \sqsubseteq_{FD} Q$ iff $\mathit{Fail}(Q) \subseteq \mathit{Fail}(P) \wedge \mathit{Div}(Q) \subseteq \mathit{Div}(P)$.

For $x \in \{T, F, FD\}$ we define process equivalence $P =_x Q$ by $P \sqsubseteq_x Q \wedge Q \sqsubseteq_x P$.

For $s \in \mathit{Traces}(P)$ P/s denotes the process that behaves like process P after having engaged in trace s. For arbitrary (finite) sequences $s = \langle a_1, \ldots, a_n \rangle$ the function $\mathit{first}(s)$ returns a_1 and $\mathit{last}(s)$ returns a_n. The functions $\mathit{tail}(s), \mathit{front}(s)$ are defined by $s = \langle \mathit{first}(s) \rangle ^\frown \mathit{tail}(s)$ and $s = \mathit{front}(s) ^\frown \langle \mathit{last}(s) \rangle$, where $^\frown$ denotes concatenation on sequences. Function $\#$ returns the length of a sequence, function $\lceil A$ projects traces to set A, e.g. $\langle a, b, b, a, c \rangle \lceil \{b, c\} = \langle b, b, c \rangle$. The set $[P]^0$ is defined as $[P]^0 =_{df} \{e \in \alpha(P) \mid (\exists\, u \in \mathit{Traces}(P/s) \bullet \mathit{head}(u) = e)\}$. Predicate a **in** $\langle a_1, \ldots, a_n \rangle$ is true iff there exists $i \in \{1, \ldots, n\}$ with $a = a_i$. Relation $s \leq t$ denotes the prefix relation on sequences. Operator $\setminus$ stands for minus on sets.

2.2 Alternative Refinement Definitions

The notion of correctness of an implementation *IMP* w.r.t. a specification *SPEC* is given by the different refinement relations introduced above, depending on the semantics which is currently investigated. However, in this paper we will slightly re-phrase these refinement notions in order to emphasize their relationship to the test classes introduced by Hennessy. (We assume without loss of generality that *IMP* and *SPEC* use the same set of visible interface events, while their internal hidden events may differ).

1. **Safety:** The implementation only generates traces alowed by the specification. This corresponds to the notion of trace refinement:

   $$\mathit{SPEC} \sqsubseteq_S \mathit{IMP} \text{ iff } \mathit{Traces}(\mathit{IMP}) \subseteq \mathit{Traces}(\mathit{SPEC})^3$$

2. **Requirements Coverage:** After having engaged in trace s, the implementation never refuses a service which is guaranteed by the specification.

   $$\mathit{SPEC} \sqsubseteq_C \mathit{IMP} \text{ iff } (\forall\, s : \mathit{Traces}(\mathit{SPEC}) \cap \mathit{Traces}(\mathit{IMP}) \bullet \mathit{Ref}(\mathit{IMP}/s) \subseteq \mathit{Ref}(\mathit{SPEC}/s))$$

[3] We have introduced a new subscript for trace to indicate the correspondence to the safety notion

Since $\langle\ \rangle \in Traces(SPEC) \cap Traces(IMP)$, this implies that a trace which can never be refused by *SPEC* will also be guaranteed by *IMP*.

3. **Non-Divergence:** The implementation may only diverge after engaging in trace s if also the specification diverges after s.

$$SPEC \sqsubseteq_D IMP \text{ iff } Div(IMP) \subseteq Div(SPEC)$$

4. **Robustness:** An implementation is robust w.r.t. a specification if every traces that can be performed by the specification is also a valid trace of the implementation.

$$SPEC \sqsubseteq_R IMP \text{ iff } Traces(SPEC) \subseteq Traces(IMP)$$

The notion of robustness, introduced in [1], can also be expressed as $IMP \sqsubseteq_T SPEC$. This relation has not received much attention in the literature about CSP refinement, though it is a common requirement in practical applications: For example, robustness covers the situation where the specification contains nondeterminism for exception handling. Failures refinement only requires that every guaranteed behaviour of the specification will also be performed by the implementation. Robustness additionally requires that exceptional behaviours of the specification are also covered by the implementation.

The advantage of the new refinement notions is the possibility to give elegant alternative characterizations of these notions by means of mutually distinct test classes. Before introducing these test classe we state the following obvious relations between the standard and the new refinement notions.

Lemma 1.

1. $\sqsubseteq_S \; = \; \sqsubseteq_T$
2. $\sqsubseteq_S \cap \sqsubseteq_C = \sqsubseteq_F$
3. $\sqsubseteq_S \cap \sqsubseteq_C \cap \sqsubseteq_D = \sqsubseteq_{FD}$

□

Furthermore we define $\sqsubseteq_{FDR} =_{df} \sqsubseteq_S \cap \sqsubseteq_C \cap \sqsubseteq_D \cap \sqsubseteq_R$ (failure-divergence refinement plus robustness) .

3 Transition Graphs and Test Classes

In this section we describe an implementable encoding of the semantics of *CSP* processes by means of transition graphs. Afterwards we discuss those results of Hennessy's testing theory [5] that are relevant for the development of implementable test drivers.

3.1 Transition Graphs

Automated test generation will be performed by mechanized analysis of the specification, which results in a choice of traces and possible continuations to be exercised as test cases on the target system. *Automated test evaluation* will be performed by observing traces and their continuations in the target system and checking mechanically, if these behaviours are correct with respect to the specification. Obviously, these tasks are fundamentally connected to the problem of mechanized *simulation* of the specification which is in general based on the following theorem [5, p. 94].

Theorem 2 (Normal Form Theorem). *Let P be a CSP process, interpreted in the failures-divergence model.*

1. *If* $\langle\,\rangle \notin Div(P)$, *then* $P =_{FD} \sqcap_{R:Ref(P)} (x : ([P]^0 \setminus R) \rightarrow P/\langle x\rangle)$
2. *If* $Div(P) = \emptyset$, *then* $P/s =_{FD} P(s)$ *with* $P(s) =_{df} \sqcap_{R:Ref(P/s)} (x : ([P/s]^0 \setminus R) \rightarrow P(s ^\frown \langle x\rangle))$
3. *For arbitrary* P, $P \sqsubseteq_{FD} P(\langle\,\rangle)$ *holds.*

□

This theorem shows how *CSP* specifications can be symbolically executed: choose a valid refusal set R of P/s at random, engage into any one of the remaining events $e \in [P/s]^0 \setminus R$ and continue in state $P/s ^\frown \langle e\rangle$. Given an implementation of a simulator, the problem of test generation for a given specification can be related to the task of finding executions performable by the simulator. Test evaluation can be performed by determining whether an execution of the real system is also a possible execution of the simulator.

With these general ideas in mind, the first problem to solve is how to retrieve the semantic representation – i. e., the failures and divergences – of a specification written in CSP syntax. This has been solved by Formal Systems Ltd and implemented in the FDR system [3], for the subset of CSP specifications satisfying:

- The specification only uses a *finite* alphabet. As a consequence, each channel admits only a finite range of values.
- Each sequential process which is part of the full specification can be modelled using a finite number of states.
- The CSP syntax is restricted by a separation of operators into two levels: The *lower-level process language* describes isolated communicating sequential processes by means of the operators $\rightarrow, \sqcap, \Box, ;, X = F(X)$. The *composite process language* uses the operators $\|, |||, ^\frown, \setminus, f^*$ to construct full systems out of lower-level processes.

Under these conditions the CSP specification may be represented as a *labelled transition system* [10] which can be encoded as a *transition graph* with only a finite number of nodes and edges. Basically, the nodes of this directed graph are constructed from Hennessy's *Acceptance Tree* representation [5] by identifying semantically equivalent nodes of the tree in a single node of the transition graph. The edges of the graph are labelled with events, and the edges leaving one node carry distinct labels. Therefore, since the alphabet is finite, the number of leaving edges is also finite. A distinguished node represents the equivalence class of the initial state of the process P. A directed walk through the graph, starting in the initial state and labelled by the sequence of events $\langle e_1, \ldots, e_n \rangle$ represents the trace $s = \langle e_1, \ldots, e_n \rangle$ which may be performed by P. The uniquely determined node reached by the walk s represents the equivalence class of process state P/s. The labels of the edges leaving this node in the graph correspond to the set $[P/s]^0$ of events that may occur for process P after having engaged in s. The set of internal states reachable in process P after s is encoded in one node of the transition graph as the collection of their refusal sets, one for each internal state. If two directed walks s and u lead to the same node in the transition graph, this means that $P/s = P/u$ holds in the failures model.

The problem of automatic test evaluation now can be re-phrased as follows: A test execution results in a trace performed by the implementation. Evaluating the transition graph, it may be verified whether this execution is correct according to the specification. The problem of test generation is much more complex: Theoretically, the transition graph defines exactly the acceptable behaviours of the implementation. But at least for non-terminating systems, this involves an infinite number of possible executions. Therefore the problem how to find relevant test cases and how to decide whether sufficiently many test executions have been performed on the target system has to be carefully investigated.

3.2 Test Classes

Tests to Characterize Refinement In this section we recall results of Hennessy's testing theory [5] that are relevant for the construction of the test drivers in Section 4.3.

Hennessy introduced processes U, so-called *experimenters*, with $\alpha(SPEC) = \alpha(U) \setminus \{w\}$, where w is a specific event denoting successful execution of the experiment which consists of U running in parallel with the process to be tested[4]. Experimenters coincide with our notion of *test cases*, so we will only use the latter term. An execution of the test case U for the test of some system P is a trace $s \in Traces(P \,||\, U)$. The execution is successful if $\langle w \rangle$ **in** s. Depending on U and P, two satisfaction relations may be distinguished with respect to the outcome of test executions:

Definition 3. For a process P and an associated test case U we say

1. $P \; \underline{may} \; U \equiv_{df} (\exists\, s : Traces(P \,||\, U) \bullet \langle w \rangle \textbf{ in } s)$
2. $P \; \underline{must} \; U \equiv_{df} (\forall\, s : maxTraces(P \,||\, U) \bullet \langle w \rangle \textbf{ in } s)$

□

[4] In [5] also another local experimenter event '1' has been introduced which enables the experimenter to control the course of a test execution. However, for the specific Hennessy test classes referenced in this article, this event is not needed.

$P\ \underline{may}\ U$ holds if there exists at least one successful execution of $(P \,||\, U)$. Only if every execution of $(P \,||\, U)$ leads to success $P\ \underline{must}\ U$ holds.

Note that in general we cannot construct test cases that indicate *failure* in addition to success, because the failure may materialize as a situation where the test execution is blocked or diverges. Even if only non-diverging processes are tested we would need a priority concept for transitions. We are currently elaborating a corresponding theory for reactive real-time systems. Here, expected events always have to occur within certain time bounds, so failures may be detected by means of timeouts.

Based on the introduced refinement notions we classify test according to their capability to detect certain implementation faults.

Definition 4. Let U be a test case.

1. U detects *safety failure* s iff $(\forall P \bullet P\ \underline{must}\ U \Rightarrow s \notin Traces(P))$
2. U detects *requirements coverage failure* (s, A) iff $(\forall P \bullet P\ \underline{must}\ U \Rightarrow (s, A) \notin Fail(P))$
3. U detects *divergence failure* s iff $(\forall P \bullet P\ \underline{must}\ U \Rightarrow s \notin Div(P))$
4. U detects *robustness failure* s iff $(\forall P \bullet P\ \underline{may}\ U \Rightarrow s \in Traces(P))$

□

A main result of [5] is the definition of test classes which detect exactly the failures introduced in the previous definition.

Definition 5. For a given specification $SPEC$, let $s \in \alpha(SPEC)^*$, $a \in \alpha(SPEC)$, and $A \subseteq \alpha(SPEC)$. The class of *Hennessy Test Cases* is defined by the following collection of test cases:

1. *Safety Tests* $U_S(s, a)$:

$$\begin{aligned} U_S(s,a) =_{df}\ & \textbf{if}\ s = \langle\,\rangle \\ & \textbf{then}\ (w \rightarrow SKIP \,\square\, a \rightarrow SKIP) \\ & \textbf{else}\ (w \rightarrow SKIP \,\square\, (head(s) \rightarrow U_S(tail(s), a)) \end{aligned}$$

2. *Requirements Coverage Tests* $U_C(s, A)$:

$$\begin{aligned} U_C(s,A) =_{df}\ & \textbf{if}\ s = \langle\,\rangle \\ & \textbf{then}\ (a : A \rightarrow w \rightarrow SKIP) \\ & \textbf{else}\ (w \rightarrow SKIP \,\square\, head(s) \rightarrow U_C(tail(s), A)) \end{aligned}$$

3. *Divergence Tests* $U_D(s)$:

$$\begin{aligned} U_D(s) =_{df}\ & \textbf{if}\ s = \langle\,\rangle \\ & \textbf{then}\ w \rightarrow SKIP \\ & \textbf{else}\ (w \rightarrow SKIP \,\square\, head(s) \rightarrow U_D(tail(s))) \end{aligned}$$

4. ***Robustness Tests*** $U_R(s)$:

$$U_R(s) =_{df} \textbf{if } s = \langle\,\rangle \; \textbf{then } w \rightarrow SKIP \; \textbf{else } head(s) \rightarrow U_R(tail(s))$$

□

Definition 5 is motivated by the following lemma:

Lemma 6.

1. *$U_S(s, a)$ detects safety failure $s^\frown\langle a\rangle$.*
2. *$U_C(s, A)$ detects requirements coverage failure (s, A).*
3. *$U_D(s)$ detects divergence failure s.*
4. *$U_R(s)$ detects robustness failure s.*

□

Note that the Hennessy test classes even *characterize* the associated failure types: If $s^\frown\langle a\rangle \notin Traces(P)$ then P <u>must</u> $U_S(s, a)$ follows. Analogous results hold for $U_C(s, A)$, $U_D(s)$, $U_R(s)$. However, we are less interested in this property, because test cases of practical relevance should be able to detect more than one failure type during test execution.

In our context $s \in Div(P)$ means $P/s = CHAOS$ in the sense of [6], that is, P/s may both *diverge internally (livelock)* and produce and refuse arbitrary *external* events. The tests $U_D(s)$ have been designed by Hennessy to detect internal divergence only. Conversely, the tests $U_S(s, a)$ and $U_C(s, A)$ can detect external chaotic behaviour but cannot distinguish internal divergence from deadlock. However, using the three test classes together enables us to distinguish deadlock, livelock and external chaotic behaviour. Note that P <u>must</u> $U_S(s, a)$ also implies $s \notin Div(P)$, because divergence along s would imply that every continuation of s, specifically $s^\frown\langle a\rangle$ would be a trace of P. P <u>must</u> $U_C(s, A)$ implies $s \notin Div(P)$, because divergence along s implies the possibility to refuse every subset of $\alpha(P)$ after s.

Hennessy's results about the relation between testing and refinement can be re-phrased for our context as follows:

Theorem 7.

1. *If SPEC <u>must</u> $U_S(s, a)$ implies IMP <u>must</u> $U_S(s, a)$ for all $a \in \alpha(SPEC)$, $s \in \alpha(SPEC)^*$, then $SPEC \sqsubseteq_S IMP$.*
2. *If SPEC <u>must</u> $U_C(s, A)$ implies IMP <u>must</u> $U_C(s, A)$ for all $s \in Traces(SPEC)$ and $A \subseteq \alpha(SPEC)$, then $SPEC \sqsubseteq_C IMP$.*
3. *If SPEC <u>must</u> $U_D(s)$ implies IMP <u>must</u> $U_D(s)$ for all $s \in \alpha(SPEC)^*$, then $SPEC \sqsubseteq_D IMP$.*
4. *If SPEC <u>may</u> $U_R(s)$ implies IMP <u>may</u> $U_R(s)$ for all $s \in \alpha(SPEC)^*$, then $SPEC \sqsubseteq_R IMP$.*

□

If $SPEC \sqsubseteq_D IMP$ holds, the four implications of the theorem become equivalences. Theorem 7 shows that only *requirements-driven* test design is needed: It is only necessary to execute test cases that will succeed for the specification. Due to possible nondeterminism in $SPEC, IMP$ and U the properties covered by Theorem 7 cannot be verified by means of black-box tests alone, because they require the analysis of *every* possible execution of $SPEC \parallel U$ and $IMP \parallel U$. Therefore a ***test monitor*** collecting information about the executions performed so far is, in general, unavoidable. Note, that this is no disadvantage of the defined classes of tests but inherent in every testing approach that is sensitive to nondeterminism.

4 Minimal Test Classes and Test Drivers

The previous section summarized the relevant *theoretical* aspects of testing for our approach. However, when constructing test drivers one is also confronted with *pragmatical* concerns, such as implementability. Moreover, pragmatics include the definition of *minimal* test classes to avoid redundancy, characterization of test strategies that eventually reveal every possible implementation failure, and last but not least the implementation of such strategies by test drivers that simultaneously simulate the operational environment of the process to be tested. These topics will be discussed in this section.

4.1 Admissible Tests

First of all we characterize a class of tests that is particularly well-suited for implementation. These tests satisfy the following requirements: 1) If the test execution is successful success will be indicated within a bounded number of events, 2) as test drivers have to know when a test execution has been successfully completed, these tests perform a termination event after signalling success, 3) success is signalled at most once during a test execution, and 4) the tests can be successfully passed (according to the <u>must</u> interpretation) by at least one process.

This leads to the following definition:

Definition 8. An *admissible test case* for the test against $SPEC$ is a CSP process U satisfying

1. $\alpha(U) = \alpha(SPEC) \cup \{w\}$, $w \notin \alpha(SPEC)$
2. U **sat** $S_U(s, R)$ with

$$
\begin{aligned}
&S_U(s,R) \equiv \\
&\quad (\exists\, n \in \mathbb{N} \bullet \forall\, s \in Traces(SPEC) \bullet \forall\, R \in Ref(SPEC/s) \bullet \\
&\qquad w \in [U/s]^0 \Rightarrow \\
&\qquad\quad w \notin R \wedge \#s \leq n \wedge \neg\,(\langle w\rangle \ \mathbf{in}\ s) \wedge U/s^\frown\langle w\rangle = SKIP)
\end{aligned}
$$

where $n \in \mathbb{N}$ is a constant not depending on s or R.

3. There exists a process P such that $P\ \underline{must}\ U$.

□

The following examples illustrate the intuition standing behind the above definition by presenting test cases that are *not* admissible.

Example 1. The test case $U = a \rightarrow SKIP \,\Box\, b \rightarrow (w \rightarrow SKIP \sqcap U)$ would not be admissible in the sense of Definition 8, because it is uncertain whether success will be indicated after event b.
□

Example 2. The test case $U = a \rightarrow w \rightarrow SKIP \sqcap STOP$ would not be admissible in the sense of Definition 8, because no process can satisfy U as a $\underline{must}$-test.
□

Example 3. The test case

$$U = \sqcap_{n:\mathbb{N}} U(n)$$
$$U(n) = (n > 0) \& a \rightarrow U(n-1) \,\Box\, (n = 0) \& w \rightarrow SKIP$$

would be well-defined in the infinite traces model of Roscoe and Barret [17], and $P\ \underline{must}\ U$ holds for process $P = a \rightarrow P$. Moreover, if success w is possible after U/s it will never be refused. However, U would not be admissible in the sense of Definition 8, because no global upper bound exists after that every execution of $(P \parallel U)$ would show success.
□

Lemma 9. *The Hennessy tests specified in Definition 5 are admissible in the sense of Definition 8.*
□

4.2 Minimal Test Classes

When performing a test suite to investigate the correctness properties of a system, a crucial objective is to perform a *minimal* number of test cases. The following definition specifies minimal sets of Hennessy test, which are still trustworthy in the sense that if the implementation passes these tests then it is a refinement of the specification w.r.t. the currently chosen semantics.

Definition 10. For a given specification *SPEC*, we define the following collections of test cases:

1. $\mathcal{H}_S(SPEC) = \{U_S(s,a) \mid s \in Traces(SPEC) - Div(SPEC) \wedge a \notin [SPEC/s]^0\}$
2. $\mathcal{H}_C(SPEC) = \{U_C(s,A) \mid s \in Traces(SPEC) - Div(SPEC) \wedge$
$A \subseteq [SPEC/s]^0 \wedge$
$(\forall R : Ref(SPEC/s) \bullet A \not\subseteq R) \wedge$
$(\forall X : \mathbb{P} A - \{A\} \bullet (\exists R : Ref(SPEC/s) \bullet X \subseteq R))\}$

3. $\mathcal{H}_D(SPEC) = \{ U_D(s) \mid s \in Traces(SPEC) - Div(SPEC) \wedge$
$(\forall u : Traces(SPEC) - Div(SPEC) \bullet$
$s \leq u \wedge [SPEC/u]^0 = \varnothing \Rightarrow s = u)\}$
4. $\mathcal{H}_R(SPEC) = \{ U_R(s) \mid s \in Traces(SPEC) \wedge$
$(\forall u : Traces(SPEC) \bullet$
$s \leq u \wedge [SPEC/u]^0 = \varnothing \Rightarrow s = u)\}$

□

The following theorems state that in order to characterize the refinement notions addressed by Theorem 7, it suffices already to exercise the tests specified in Definition 10 on the implementation. Compared to the full set of Hennessy tests, defined for *all* sequences $s \in \alpha(P)^*$ of events and sets $A \subseteq \alpha(P)$, this represents a considerable reduction of the test cases to be considered.

Theorem 11. *If*

$$\mathcal{H}(SPEC) =_{df} \mathcal{H}_S(SPEC) \cup \mathcal{H}_C(SPEC) \cup \mathcal{H}_D(SPEC) \cup \mathcal{H}_R(SPEC)$$

for a given specification SPEC, then SPEC <u>*must*</u> *U holds for all* $U \in \mathcal{H}(SPEC)$.
□

Theorem 12. *Given SPEC and the corresponding test classes* $\mathcal{H}_x(SPEC), x \in \{S, C, D, R\}$, *the following properties hold:*

1. *If IMP* <u>*must*</u> *U for all* $U \in \mathcal{H}_S(SPEC)$ *, then SPEC* $\sqsubseteq_S$ *IMP.*
2. *If IMP* <u>*must*</u> *U for all* $U \in \mathcal{H}_C(SPEC)$, *then SPEC* $\sqsubseteq_C$ *IMP.*
3. *If IMP* <u>*must*</u> *U for all* $U \in \mathcal{H}_D(SPEC)$, *then SPEC* $\sqsubseteq_D$ *IMP.*
4. *If IMP* <u>*may*</u> *U for all* $U \in \mathcal{H}_R(SPEC)$, *then SPEC* $\sqsubseteq_R$ *IMP.*

□

This theorem shows that for terminating systems, refinement properties can be verified by performing a finite number of tests. (Note, that all processes have only *finite* internal nondeterminism.)

The definitions of $\mathcal{H}_S, \mathcal{H}_C, \mathcal{H}_D$ indicate further that it is not necessary to perform any tests for traces s after which *SPEC* diverges[5], since in such a case $SPEC/s$ will allow chaotic behaviour which does not restrict the admissible behaviours of IMP/s. For the test of safety properties, the definition of $\mathcal{H}_S$ states that we only have to use those test cases $U_S(s, a)$, where s is a trace of *SPEC*, but $SPEC/s$ does not admit event a. For the requirements coverage tests $U_C(s, A)$, $\mathcal{H}_C$ indicates that only the smallest sets A, such that $SPEC/s$ can never refuse A completely, have to be tested. As a consequence, it is not necessary to exercise any tests $U_C(s, A)$, if $SPEC/s$ may refuse the full alphabet.

The definitions of $\mathcal{H}_D$ and $\mathcal{H}_R$ are motivated by the fact that for the test of divergence and robustness properties we only have to analyze *maximal* traces:

[5] Of course, it is questionable if specifications allowing divergence will be used in practice at all.

If *SPEC* terminates or blocks after a trace u, the tests corresponding to proper prefixes of u are covered by $U_D(u)$ and $U_R(u)$, so only the latter are contained in $\mathcal{H}_D$ and $\mathcal{H}_R$ respectively.

The next theorem investigates minimality of the test classes $\mathcal{H}_S$ and $\mathcal{H}_C$ defined above.

Theorem 13. *Given SPEC and the corresponding test classes $\mathcal{H}_S, \mathcal{H}_C$, the following properties hold:*

1. *If $\mathcal{H} \subset \mathcal{H}_S$ there exists a process P satisfying P $\underline{must}$ U for all $U \in \mathcal{H}$ but not refining SPEC in the trace model.*
2. *If $\mathcal{H} \subset \mathcal{H}_C$ there exists a process P satisfying P $\underline{must}$ U for all $U \in \mathcal{H}_S \cup \mathcal{H}$ but not refining SPEC w.r.t. requirements coverage.*
3. *If $U_C(s, A) \in \mathcal{H}_C$ and $B \subset A$ then $\neg$ (SPEC $\underline{must}$ $U_C(s, B)$).*

□

Theorem 13 shows that $\mathcal{H}_S$ and $\mathcal{H}_C$ are indeed minimal: If one test $U(s, a)$ is removed from $\mathcal{H}_S$, a process with safety failure $s^\frown\langle a \rangle$ could be constructed, for which all the remaining tests would succeed. Removing a test $U_C(s, A)$ from $\mathcal{H}_C$ would admit processes P satisfying the remaining tests without refining *SPEC* in the failures model. Moreover, the set A cannot be reduced in $U_C(s, A)$ in $\mathcal{H}_C$, since otherwise *SPEC* would no longer pass this test.

The test collections $\mathcal{H}_D$ and $\mathcal{H}_R$, however, cannot be defined as minimal sets, as soon as *SPEC* describes a non-terminating system: If $s \in maxTraces(SPEC)$ is an infinite computation of *SPEC*, $\mathcal{H}_D$ and $\mathcal{H}_R$ must contain infinitely many tests associated with prefixes $s_1 < s_2 < s_3 < \ldots$ of s, and each infinite subset of these tests would suffice to verify correct behaviour along s. At least we can state that any $\mathcal{H}_D^0 \subseteq \mathcal{H}_D$ satisfying

$$(\forall\, u : Traces(SPEC) - Div(SPEC) \bullet \exists\, s : \mathcal{H}_D^0 \bullet u \leq s)$$

is sufficient to detect divergence failures against *SPEC* and any $\mathcal{H}_R^0 \subseteq \mathcal{H}_R$ satisfying

$$(\forall\, u : Traces(SPEC) - Div(SPEC) \bullet \exists\, s : \mathcal{H}_R^0 \bullet u \leq s)$$

is sufficient to detect robustness failures.

4.3 Test Drivers

The Concept of Test Drivers *Test Drivers* are hardware and/or software devices controlling the executions of test cases for a target system. To formalize this notion, recall that a *context* in CSP is a term $\mathcal{C}(X)$ with a free identifier X. Apart from the free identifier X, $\mathcal{C}(X)$ may contain other CSP processes as parameters.

Definition 14. A *Test Driver for the test against SPEC* is a context $\mathcal{D}(X)$ using admissible test cases U_i satisfying $\alpha(SPEC) = \alpha(U_i) \setminus \{w\}$ as parameters.
□

We will focus on test drivers of the form

$$\mathcal{D}(X) = (i := 0);\ *\,(U_i \parallel X\widehat{\ }(w \rightarrow monitor?next \rightarrow (\textbf{if } next \textbf{ then } i := i + 1;\ SKIP \textbf{ else } SKIP)));$$

with admissible test cases U_i. A test driver of this type will execute the test cases in a certain order $U_1, U_2, \ldots$; one test case at a time and with only one copy of the target system $X = IMP$ running. As soon as a test case signals success w, the execution will be interrupted. An input *monitor?next* will be required from a process monitoring the test coverage achieved so far with the actual test U_i[6]. If the monitor signals $next = true$, the next test case U_{i+1} will be performed, otherwise U_i will be repeated. If U_i is a <u>may</u>-test, *next* is always set to *true*.

The main criterion that test drivers have to satisfy is given in the next definition.

Definition 15. Let $\mathcal{D}(X)$ be a test driver for the test against *SPEC*, performing test cases of a collection $\mathcal{U}$ in the order $U_1, U_2, U_3, \ldots$. Let $\sqsubseteq \in \{\sqsubseteq_T, \sqsubseteq_F, \sqsubseteq_{FD}, \sqsubseteq_R\}$. Then $\mathcal{D}(X)$ is called *trustworthy for* $\sqsubseteq$*-test against SPEC*, iff the following conditions hold:

1. $\mathcal{U}$ contains a subset $\mathcal{U}_\sqsubseteq$ which characterizes $\sqsubseteq$-refinement against *SPEC*.
2. For every safety-, requirements coverage-, divergence- or robustness-failure violating $\sqsubseteq$, there exists an $n \in \mathbb{N}$ such that $U_n \in \mathcal{U}_\sqsubseteq$ can detect this failure in the sense of Definition 4.

□

Definition 15 covers the intuitive understanding of trustworthiness in a formal way: whenever a fault may occur for *IMP*, this can be uncovered by a test case which is guaranteed to be chosen by the driver after having selected a finite number of other test cases.

Theorem 16.

$$\mathcal{D}(X) = (i := 0);\ *\,(U_i \parallel X\widehat{\ }(w \rightarrow monitor?next \rightarrow (\textbf{if } next \textbf{ then } i := i + 1;\ SKIP \textbf{ else } SKIP)));$$

applying the tests $U \in \mathcal{H}$ according to Definition 10, ordered by the length of the defining traces, is trustworthy for $\sqsubseteq_{FDR}$-refinement.
□

Analogous results hold for the other refinement notions $\sqsubseteq_S$, $\sqsubseteq_C$, $\sqsubseteq_R$, $\sqsubseteq_D$, $\sqsubseteq_F$, $\sqsubseteq_{FD}$.

[6] The implementation of test monitors is not addressed in this paper.

Test Drivers for Reactive Systems The testing methodology presented so far will now be specialized on the development of test drivers for the automated test of *reactive systems.*

In the context of reactive systems it is useful to distinguish between the target system and its operational environment in an explicit way, when investigating properties of a specification *SPEC* and implementation *IMP*. The very paradigm of reactive systems is to interact continuously with their environment. In many applications certain hypotheses are made about the environment behaviour. This means that the target system is not expected to act properly in *every* context. Indeed, the objective of the test suite is to ensure the correct behaviour of the target system when running in an operational environment satisfying these hypotheses. Therefore test drivers have to *test* the target system behaviour while simultaneously *simulating* the operational environment.

To formalize the notion of an operational environment we consider expressions of the type

$$SPEC = \mathcal{E}(ASYS) \setminus (\alpha(\mathcal{E}(ASYS)) - I)$$

with the following interpretation: $\mathcal{E}(X)$ is a context and $ASYS$ is the abstract specification of the target system to be developed. The processes appearing as parameters in $\mathcal{E}$ represent the operational environment. The correctness of a reactive system implementation will only be decided with respect to a subset I of interface events. Therefore the specification consists of $\mathcal{E}(ASYS)$ with all events apart from I concealed. The implementation can be described by the term

$$IMP = \mathcal{E}(SYS) \setminus (\alpha(\mathcal{E}(SYS)) - I)$$

where SYS is the target system plugged into environment $\mathcal{E}$. It is natural to require that $I \subseteq \alpha(\mathcal{E}(ASYS)) \cap \alpha(\mathcal{E}(SYS))$.

In many applications, the configuration of a reactive system and its environment will be appropriately described by the following definition:

Definition 17. A *standard configuration* $(E, ASYS, SYS, I)$ *(for reactive systems)* consists of CSP processes $E, ASYS, SYS$ and a set I of events such that $I = \alpha(E) \cap \alpha(ASYS) = \alpha(E) \cap \alpha(SYS)$. Context $\mathcal{E}_0(X) = (E \,||\, X)$ is called the *environment*. $SPEC = \mathcal{E}_0(ASYS) \setminus (\alpha(\mathcal{E}_0(ASYS)) - I)$ is called the *specification*, and $IMP = \mathcal{E}_0(SYS) \setminus (\alpha(\mathcal{E}_0(SYS)) - I)$ the *implementation*. For $\sqsubseteq \in \{\sqsubseteq_T, \sqsubseteq_F, \sqsubseteq_{FD}, \sqsubseteq_{FDR}, \sqsubseteq_R, \sqsubseteq_C, \sqsubseteq_D\}$, a standard configuration is called $\sqsubseteq$*-correct*, if $SPEC \sqsubseteq IMP$ holds.
□

In the following we use the abbreviation $P_I = P \setminus (\alpha(P) \setminus I)$. Note that in a standard configuration $(E \,||\, ASYS)_I = (E_I \,||\, ASYS_I)$ and $(E \,||\, SYS)_I = (E_I \,||\, SYS_I)$ holds, because the hiding operator distributes through $||$, if none of the interface events shared between the parallel components are concealed [6, p. 112].

4.4 A Trustworthy $\sqsubseteq_{FD}$-Test Driver for Reactive Systems

Now we are prepared to state the main result of this article, an implementable test driver that is trustworthy for $\sqsubseteq_{FD}$-refinement. The test driver uses test cases derived from the Hennessy Test Cases introduced in Definition 10 and simultaneously simulates the operational environment of the process to be tested. The properties of these test cases are formally expressed by Theorem 18. Their main advantage when compared to the Hennessy Test Cases is that they allow to investigate safety, requirements coverage and non-divergence at the same time, while the Hennessy Cases require to perform different test suites for each correctness feature. Therefore our test cases are more efficient in practical applications.

Theorem 18. *Let $(E, ASYS, SYS, I)$ be a standard configuration of a reactive system. Define a collection $\mathcal{U} = \{U(n) \mid 0 \leq n\}$ of test cases by*

$$
\begin{aligned}
U(n) &= U(n, \langle\,\rangle) \\[1ex]
U(n,s) &= (e : ([E_I/s]^0 \setminus [ASYS_I/s]^0) \rightarrow \dagger \rightarrow SKIP) \\
&\quad \Box \\
&\quad (\mathbf{if}\ \#s < n \\
&\quad\quad \mathbf{then}\ \sqcap_{R:Ref(E_I/s)} U(n, s, [E_I/s]^0 \setminus R) \\
&\quad\quad \mathbf{else}\ (\mathbf{if}\ A(s) = \varnothing \\
&\quad\quad\quad \mathbf{then}\ (w \rightarrow SKIP) \\
&\quad\quad\quad \mathbf{else}\ \sqcap_{R:Ref(E_I/s), A:A(s)} U(n, s, A \setminus R))) \\[1ex]
U(n,s,M) &= (M = \varnothing)\&(w \rightarrow SKIP) \\
&\quad \Box \\
&\quad (e : M \rightarrow (\mathbf{if}\ e \in [ASYS_I/s]^0 \\
&\quad\quad\quad \mathbf{then}\ (\mathbf{if}\ \#s = n \\
&\quad\quad\quad\quad \mathbf{then}\ (w \rightarrow SKIP)\ \mathbf{else}\ U(n, s^\frown\langle e\rangle)) \\
&\quad\quad\quad \mathbf{else}\ (\dagger \rightarrow SKIP)))
\end{aligned}
$$

where

$$
\begin{aligned}
A(s) = \{A : \mathbb{P}\, I \mid\ & A \subseteq [(E \,\|\, ASYS)_I/s]^0 \wedge \\
& (\forall R : Ref((E \,\|\, ASYS)_I/s) \bullet A \not\subseteq R) \wedge \\
& (\forall X : \mathbb{P}\, A - \{A\} \bullet (\exists R : Ref((E \,\|\, ASYS)_I/s) \bullet X \subseteq R))\}
\end{aligned}
$$

Then

1. *If SYS_I must $U(n)$ for all test cases in $\mathcal{U}$, then $(E \,\|\, ASYS)_I \sqsubseteq_{FD} (E \,\|\, SYS)_I$ follows.*
2. *If $(E \,\|\, ASYS)_I \sqsubseteq_{FD} (E \,\|\, SYS)_I$ and $Div(SYS) = \varnothing$ then SYS_I must $U(n)$ for all test cases in $\mathcal{U}$.*
3. *If $Div(ASYS) = \varnothing$ then $ASYS_I$ must $U(n)$ for all test cases in $\mathcal{U}$.*
4. *For all $n \in \mathbb{N}$, test $U(n)$ is admissible.*

□

Each test case $U(n)$ explores the behaviour of the target system for traces s of length $\#s \leq n$. The basic idea of the structure of $U(n)$ is to simulate the environment E_I with respect to traces and refusals, in parallel with a combination of test cases $U_S(s,a)$ and $U_C(s,A)$. $U(n,s)$ represents the state of a test execution where trace s has already been successfully performed. At each execution step, $U(n,s)$ will detect any event $e \in ([E_I/s]^0 \setminus [ASYS_I/s]^0)$, which is acceptable according to the environment but corresponds to a failure of the target system SYS. Such a safety failure will be indicated by a special event $\dagger$, if the target system does not diverge before indication becomes possible. Note that the first alternative $(e : ([E_I/s]^0 \setminus [ASYS_I/s]^0) \rightarrow \dagger \rightarrow SKIP)$ in the definition of $U(n,s)$ is redundant, since a safety failure $s^\frown\langle a\rangle$ would also be detected by the tests $U(n), n \geq \#s$ in the last branch of a process $U(n,s,M)$ satisfying $a \in M$. However, for practical reasons it is desirable to detect safety violations as soon as possible, therefore $U(n)$ never refuse a safety failure which might be accepted by the environment E in the actual state of the test execution. As long as $\#s < n$, $U(n,s)$ will behave as E_I/s with respect to the refusal of events. For $\#s = n$, $U(n,s)$ will only admit events contained in a minimal acceptance set $A \in A(s)$, so that $U(n)$ can detect requirement coverage failures of SYS occurring after traces of length n, when running in environment E. The nondeterministic $\sqcap$-operator used in the definition of $U(n,s)$ shows where internal decisions with respect to the control of the test execution may be taken: At each execution step $U(n,s)$, the refusals R or the sets A may be selected according to a test coverage strategy implemented in the test driver. Since there are many possibilities for suitable strategies, these are hidden in the definition of $U(n)$. Any strategy covering all possible executions of $U(n)$ is valid. Using LTS representations for the CSP specifications of E_I and $ASYS_I$, test $U(n)$ is implementable in a straight forward way: $U(n)$ is determined by the traces and refusals of E_I and $ASYS_I$; and these are contained in the corresponding LTS representations.

Using the results of Theorem 16 and Theorem 18, now we can state that test drivers using the test cases $U(n)$ have the desired correctness properties:

Theorem 19. *For a given standard configuration $(E, ASYS, SYS, I)$ of a reactive system, let the associated tests $U(n)$ be defined as above. Then the test driver*

$$\mathcal{D}(X) = (n := 0);\ *\,(U(n) \,\|\, X^\frown(w \rightarrow monitor?next \rightarrow (\textbf{if } next \textbf{ then } i := i + 1;\ SKIP \textbf{ else } SKIP)));$$

is trustworthy for $\sqsubseteq_{FD}$-test.

□

5 Conclusion

This article focused on the development of test drivers performing automized generation, execution and evaluation of tests for reactive systems against CSP specifications. Given a correctness relation between specifications and implementations, a test driver should be capable of

- generating test cases for every possible correctness violation,
- exercising test cases on the target system, at the same time simulating proper environment behaviour,
- detecting every violation of the correctness requirements during test execution.

To obtain test drivers which are *provably correct* with respect to these objectives, we analyzed Hennessy's testing theory in the framework of untimed CSP. Hennessy's test classes are suitable for the detection of safety failures, insufficient requirements coverage, divergence failures and insufficient robustness in an implementation and characterize the corresponding refinement notions. As a result of this analysis we determined minimal subsets of Hennessy's test classes that are still sufficient for the detection of safety failures and insufficient requirements coverage. Furthermore we presented the top-level specification of a test driver as implemented in the VVT-RT system. It was demonstrated that a test driver implementing this specification possesses the three capabilities listed above, with respect to testing safety and requirements coverage.

The work presented in this article reflects a "building block" of a joint enterprise of ELPRO LET GmbH, JP Software-Consulting, Bremen University and Kiel University in the field of test automation for reactive real-time systems. An overview of these activities is given in [16].

References

1. E. Brinksma: A theory for the derivation of tests. In P. H. J. van Eijk, C. A. Vissers and M. Diaz (Eds.): *The Formal Description Technique LOTOS.* Elsevire Science Publishers B. V. (North-Holland), (1989), 235-247.
2. ELPRO LET GmbH: *Programmablaufplan – Bahnübergang.* ELPRO LET GmbH (1994).
3. Formal Systems Ltd.: *Failures Divergence Refinement.* User Manual and Tutorial Version 1.4. Formal Systems (Europe) Ltd (1994).
4. M.-C. Gaudel: Testing can be formal, too. In P. D. Mosses, M. Nielsen and M. I. Schwartzbach (Eds.): *Proceedings of TAPSOFT '95: Theory and Practice of Software Development.* Aarhus, Denmark, May 1995, Springer (1995).
5. M. C. Hennessy: *Algebraic Theory of Processes.* MIT Press (1988).
6. C.A.R. Hoare. *Communicating sequential processes.* Prentice-Hall International, Englewood Cliffs NJ (1985).
7. H. M. Hörcher and J. Peleska: The Role of Formal Specifications in Software Test. Tutorial, held at the FME '94.
8. H. M. Hörcher: Improving Software Tests using Z Specifications. To appear in J. P. Bowen and M. G. Hinchey (Eds.): *ZUM '95: 9th International Conference of Z Users*, LNCS, Springer (1995).
9. E. Mikk: Compilation of Z Specifications into C for Automatic Test Result Evaluation. To appear in J. P. Bowen and M. G. Hinchey (Eds.): *ZUM '95: 9th International Conference of Z Users*, LNCS, Springer (1995).
10. R. Milner: *Communication and Concurrency.* Prentice-Hall International, Englewood Cliffs NJ (1989).

11. M. Müllerburg: Systematic Testing: a Means for Validating Reactive Systems. In *EuroSTAR'94: Proceedings of the 2nd European Intern. Conf. on Software Testing, Analysis&Review*. British Computer Society, (1994).
12. J. Peleska: *Bahnübergangssteuerung Straßenbahn — ELPRO LET GmbH: Prüfspezifikation für formale Verifikation und automatisierte Testdurchführung.* JP Software-Consulting (1994).
13. J. Peleska: *Bahnübergangssteuerung Straßenbahn — ELPRO LET GmbH: Sicherheitsspezifikation und BUE-Spezifikation.* JP Software-Consulting (1994).
14. J. Peleska: *Trustworthy Tests for Reactive Systems — Automation of Real-Time Testing.* In preparation, JP Software-Consulting (1995).
15. J. Peleska and M. Siegel: From Testing Theory to Test Driver Implementation. Technical Report, JP Software-Consulting (1995).
16. J. Peleska: Test Automation for Safety-Critical Systems: Industrial Application and Future Developments. To appear in *Proceedings of the Formal Methods Europe Conference, FME '96.*, LNCS, Springer (1996).
17. A. W. Roscoe and G. Barret: Unbounded Nondeterminism in CSP. In *MFPS '89*, volume LNCS 298, Springer-Verlag, (1989).

Program Slicing Using Weakest Preconditions

Joseph J. Comuzzi and Johnson M. Hart

Peritus Software Services, Inc.
304 Concord Road
Billerica, MA 01821-3485, U.S.A.

Abstract. Program slices have long been used as an aid to program understanding, especially in maintenance activities. Most slicing methods involve data and control flow analysis to determine what statements might affect a set of variables. Here, we develop a more precise slicing concept, called *p-slices*, defined using Dijkstra's weakest precondition (wp), to determine which statements will affect a specified predicate. Weakest preconditions are already known to be an effective technique for program understanding and analysis, and this paper unifies wp analysis and slicing and simplifies existing slicing algorithms. Slicing rules for assignment, conditional, and repetition statements are developed. The authors are currently using these techniques in their work with software maintenance teams and are incorporating p-slice computation into a program analysis tool.

1 Introduction

The concept of *slicing* a program in order to aid understanding, maintenance, and resuse goes back to Weiser [13, 14]. The basic idea is to create a reduced program consisting of only those statements that affect a given variable or set of variables. In this way, the software engineer can concentrate on the relevant parts of the code. Livadas and Croll [11] review the case for slicing and the related techniques of *dicing* and *ripple analysis*, showing the benefits for code understanding, code simplification, reuse, maintenance, and other tasks. [11] then proceeds to present an improved slicing algorithm based on program and system dependence graphs.

The present authors have become convinced of the value of *logical code analysis* (LCA) in all aspects of software maintenance [8, 9] as well as in earlier phases of the software life-cycle. LCA applies the theory of *weakest precondition program semantics* (wp) as developed by Dijkstra [4] and extended in such works as [3, 5, 7]. wp theory was originally developed for *program synthesis* and *proofs of correctness*, but, as mentioned above, we have found that the wp theory, or what we call LCA, is extremely effective for program understanding and maintenance. There are a number of reasons for this, one of which is that LCA efficiently represents control and data flow and precisely captures the relevant information that the slicing algorithms capture with dependence graphs.

The wp-based definition of a slice (called a *p-slice* or *predicate slice*) gives a desirable alternative to the classical slice concept, and, in addition, p-slices can be computed quickly, assuming reasonable constraints.

The paper starts by giving a background in slicing and weakest precondition semantics. Following that, we define the p-slice and show why it is a valuable alternative to Weiser's classical slice definition. Next, we develop some p-slice theorems for alternation and repetition statements and proceed to use the theorems to compute p-slices in some examples. We conclude with some comments on directions for future work.

2 Comments on the Relationship to Formal Methods

This work can be placed in the context of a much larger subject; namely formal methods. Frequently, the goal of formal methods research is the formal specification, development, and verification of programming systems. These systems may be very large and are often mission-critical or even real-time. Formal methods emphasize a program's logical properties as opposed to its operational behavior. The goal of creating error free software requiring minimal testing is, of course, ambitious. Furthermore, the debates on the value of formal methods are frequently polarized between advocates and opponents.

Our goals are less ambitious, as are our claims. We do claim, however, based on [8, 9] and our own experience in software maintenance, that LCA is indispensable in analyzing and understanding the code produced by real programmers. Many examples show the value, even the necessity, of this sort of analysis even for very small (a few lines) code segments. While one critique of formal methods targets scaling problems, it is difficult to comprehend how one could claim to understand and trust a large system that contains unreliable short code segments that no one comprehends. Furthermore, while many formal systems use different semantic models, we feel that Dijkstra's wp is a precise and sharp analytical tool. [5] makes the wp argument effectively.

In turn, classical program slicing as developed in [13, 14, 6, 11] should be considered a "formal method" as it, too, is based on code analysis rather than its actual execution. Therefore, it is not surprising that we are able to treat slicing in terms of wp semantics. Furthermore, the early slicing papers [13, 14] refer to analyzing programs backwards from the point of interest, just as wp analysis depends on backward analysis. Finally, slicing partially addresses the scaling issue by reducing the amount of code under consideration so that other forms of logical analysis are more practical.

3 Program Slices

The objective of slicing program S at some location, p, is to create a smaller program, S', that has exactly the same effect as S (at point p) on a predicate relating a set of variables, or *slicing criterion*. S' is formed from S by removing statements so that every statement in S' is also in S, and statement order remains unchanged. Declaration statements can also be removed, but S' should be syntactically correct and executable.

Livadas and Croll [11] give the following "classical" definition, which they say is less general than Weiser's definition [13, 14] but is sufficient for practical purposes.

> Let S be a program, let p be a point in S, and let v be a variable of S that is either defined (Author Note: "defined" means "assigned a value" rather than "declared") or used at p. A static slice or simply a slice of S relative to the slicing criterion $\langle p, v\rangle$ is defined as the set of all statements and predicates of S that *might* affect the value of variable v at point p.

Weiser's definition [14] allows for a set of variables, V, and *slicing criteria* $\langle p, V\rangle$. The definition is ambiguous in referring to statements that *might* affect the variable, and our p-slices will differ from classical slices by tightening up the definition. In this way, we will be able to create smaller slices than those produced by the classical method.

Gallagher and Lyle [6] have an interesting example based on the source code for the UNIX wc utility, which counts characters, words, and lines in text files. Using different slicing criteria, they produce separate word counter, character counter, and line counter programs.

4 Weakest Precondition Semantics

The weakest precondition predicate transformer can be regarded as a function of two arguments. The first argument is a program, S, the second is a logical predicate, P, and the arguments are separated by periods. The value of the predicate transformer is, of course, another predicate. We say:

$$wp.S.P = Q$$

to mean that it is necessary and sufficient that program S start in state Q (that is, the predicate Q is *true*) to reach state P. (Note: We will confine our attention to deterministic programs.)

A few examples and wp calculation rules will help and will also hint at the p-slice definition. In all our examples we will use the following conventions, often with subscripts:

S, T, ... denote programs (statements), possibly compound statements.

P, Q, ... denote predicates, often in simple propositional calculus and occasionally in first order predicate calculus with quantifiers. These predicates are not part of a program; rather they are used to express the state of program variables.

B will denote a predicate, or logical expression, that is part of a program and is evaluated as part of the execution of alternation and repetition statements.

Sample programs are written in ANSI C [10], much as they might appear to a software engineer.

Dijkstra's language of *guarded commands* (DGC) [3, 4, 5, 7] is used as an *intermediate language* as the wp is defined in this language. This conforms to the operation of our analysis tool which converts the program source (C, PL/I, COBOL, FORTRAN, ...) into DGC as an intermediate language. We will explain DGC as required.

Initially, we will compute the wp on DGC programs, but, later in the paper, we will go directly from C source language to the wp predicate.

We will use the terms "statement" and "program" interchangeably in most cases. Therefore, a statement can be a compound of many other statements. Where there is a difference, we imply that a program has all the required declarations and other features to make it completely executable.

Except where explicitly stated, we will ignore overflow and other issues associated with computer arithmetic, but one example indicates how to treat these issues.

Example 1: S_1 is the single statement program:

In C: `x = x + 1;` or `x++;`

In DGC: $x := x + 1$

Note: := is the DGC assign operator

Here are the weakest preconditions for two predicates:

$$wp.S_1.(x = 2) = (x = 1)$$

$$wp.S_1.(x > 0) = (x > -1)$$

In words, program S will terminate in the state $(x = 2)$ if and only if it starts in the state $(x = 1)$, and it will terminate with x greater than 0 if and only if it starts with x greater than -1. While these results are obvious for these simple examples, it is necessary to have a more general rule.

wp Assignment Statement Semantics: The semantics of the assignment statement $x := e$, for any expression e, is defined to be:

$$wp.(x := e).P = P(x \leftarrow e)$$

where the notation $P(x \leftarrow e)$ means that all occurrences of the variable x in predicate P are textually replaced by (e). The parentheses are required to resolve operator precedence issues. It could be, of course, that the variable does not occur in the predicate so the predicate is unchanged by the wp predicate transformer. The next example is an instance of this.

Note: Assignment statement semantics assume that Hoare's axiom (see below) holds, which causes problems in certain situations involving pointers, variable aliasing, and the like. Bijlsma [2] and Manna and Waldinger [12] discuss this problem. For now, assume that we can use assignment statement semantics as defined above.

Hoare's axiom is stated in [12] as a state transition, but it is essentially equivalent to the wp assignment semantics.

Example 2: S_2 is the composition of two statements (all variables are signed integers):

In C:
```
x = x + 1;
y = y * y;
```

In DGC: $x := x + 1;$
$y := y * y;$

First, here is the rule for the composition of statements:

wp Composition Semantics: For any two statements S_a and S_b, the semantics of the composition of the two statements, $S_a; S_b$ is:

$$wp.S_a;\ S_b.P = wp.S_a.(wp.S_b.P)$$

This is the "backward computation." The wp of the last statement is the predicate used in the wp computation of the first statement.

Continuing with Example 2 for several predicates:

$$wp.(x := x + 1;\ y := y * y).(x > 1) = (x > 0)$$

$$wp.(x := x + 1;\ y := y * y).(y > 4) = (y > 2 \vee y < -2)$$

$$wp.(x := x + 1;\ y := y * y).(x > 1 \wedge y > 4) = (x > 0 \wedge (y > 2 \vee y < -2))$$

Example 3: S_3 is the program:

In C:
```
if (x > 0) x = x - 1;
```

In DGC: *if* $x > 0 \rightarrow x := x - 1;$
$[]\ x \leq 0 \rightarrow$ *skip*;
fi

This example introduces the *(guarded) alternation statement*. In general, a list of *guards* (arbitrary predicates) and statement pairs are separated by [] ("fat bar") and surrounded by *if...fi*. A statement will be executed only if its guard is true; if more than one guard is true, a single statement is selected nondeterministically. If no guards are true, the program aborts and no postcondition is possible since the program never reaches the end of the statement. We will define guarded command semantics in a later section; for the time being, it is fairly straightforward to verify the following. (For several of these examples, the fact that x is an integer is important.)

$wp.S_3.(x > 2) = (x > 3)$

$wp.S_3.(x > 0) = (x > 1)$

$wp.S_3.(x \geq 0) = (x \geq 0)$

$wp.S_3.(x < 0) = (x < 0)$

The only remaining DGC construct is the repetition (loop), which is described later. There are also two important special DGC statements: *skip* (used above) and *abort*. They are defined by their *wp* semantics.

$wp.abort.P = false$

for any P because the program never reaches the end.

$wp.skip.P = P$

for any P because the *skip* does not change anything.

Here are several other simple but important *wp* facts that we will use from time to time.

$wp.S.false = false$ for any program S.

This is the "law of the excluded miracle."

$wp.S.true = true$ for any program S, if S contains no *abort* and all repetitions are assured of termination

Program S and program T are semantically equivalent if and only if, for all predicates, P,

$wp.S.P = wp.T.P$

Equivalent programs need not be textually equal, of course; they simply are equivalent as predicate transformers.

For any program S, the following three programs are semantically equivalent:

S

skip; S and

S; *skip*

skip, then, by itself, is the null program. We will eliminate extra *skip* statements without comment.

In summary, the language of DGC statements can be defined recursively, as follows:

- Assignment statements, *skip*, and *abort* are DGC statements, sometimes called *primitive statements*.
- *Compound DGC statements* can be formed from other DGC statements by composition, alternation statements, and repetition statements.

- Nothing else is a DGC statement.

This definition corresponds to the way in which statements in C and other languages are defined recursively with BNF or some other grammar; see, for instance, Aho, Sethi, and Ullman [1]. Whenever we use the term *statement*, we mean it in this sense, regardless of whether we are discussing C or DGC programs.

We will complete the semantic definitions as required, and, what is more, we will define the p-slice for each type of DGC statement.

5 Weakest Precondition Slices

The examples above give a good hint as to how to define slices in terms of the weakest preconditions. Our definition slices code that does not affect a predicate, rather than on the basis of potential effect on a variable, as in the classical definition. First, it is necessary to define a partial order on statements so that we have a concept of removing statements from a compound statement or program.

Definition (Statement Portion): Let S be a statement and let S' be the same as S except that a single statement (not necessarily primitive) in S is replaced by *skip*. Then S' is a *reduction of* S. Let $\subseteq$ be the transitive, reflexive closure of the reduction relation. If T is a statement with $T \subseteq S$, we say that T is a *portion* of S. $T \subset S$ is used to indicate the additional fact that the two statements are not the same.

A slice can now be defined as a portion that has the exact same behavior (semantics) with respect to a given predicate.

Definition (p-slice): Let P be a predicate and S and T be programs. If $T \subset S$ and $wp.T.P = wp.S.P$, then T is a *p-slice of* S with respect to P.

It will turn out that there can more than one p-slice, so we write:

$$T \in PSlice(S, P)$$

A p-slice of S is simply a statement with some statements replaced by *skip* without changing the behavior with respect to P. Again, redundant *skip*s are omitted without comment.

It follows immediately from the definition that:

$skip \in PSlice(S, P)$	if and only if $wp.S.P = P$
$skip \in PSlice(S, true)$	for any statement S, if S contains no *abort* and all repetitions are assured of termination
$skip \in PSlice(S, false)$	for any statement, S

Example 4: Let S_4 (in DGC) be $x := 2 * x$ where $*$ denotes multiplication and x is an integer. Then:

$$skip \in PSlice(S_4, x > 0)$$

However, S_4 has no slices at all with respect to the predicate $(x > 2)$.

This example immediately shows that the p-slice is not the same as the classical slice, which would not slice the statement if x were part of the slicing criteria. Example 4 shows that a statement can sometimes be eliminated even if it assigns a value to a variable in the slicing predicate.

Note: This result ignored the realities of computer arithmetic; i.e., we made the implicit assumption that x was relatively small. Removing this assumption on a machine with 16-bit signed (2's complement) arithmetic gives:

$$wp.S_4.(x > 0) = (x > 0 \wedge x < 16384)$$
$$\vee (x > -32767 \wedge x < -16384)$$

Therefore, the slice really could not be performed in Example 4 without the underlying assumption that x is small. Programmers, of course, commonly make such assumptions, and programs often break when the hidden assumptions no longer hold.

It is tempting to expect that there would be a unique *minimal slice* (in the sense of the portion relation) for any statement and predicate. Weiser [14] argues that there is no minimal slice on decidability grounds. A simple example will also suffice to show that there are local minimum slices, but no unique minimum slice.

Example 5: Consider the DGC statement:

$$S_5\!: x := x - 1;\ x := x + 1;\ x := -1 + x$$

Two statements, $x := x - 1$ and $x := -1 + x$ are both minimal slices with respect to any predicate involving x.

Example 6: Recall Example 2 where we had:

$$S_2\!: x := x + 1;\ y := y * y$$

Using the predicates in Example 2, we have:

$$x := x + 1 \in PSlice(S_2, x > 0)$$

$$y := y * y \in PSlice(S_2, y > 4)$$

However, S_2 has no slices with respect to the predicate $(x > 0 \wedge y > 4)$.

Example 6 is typical of the situation that slicing was probably intended to address originally where program statements can be clearly distinguished by the variables that they affect. Slicing removes those statements that do not affect variables in the slicing predicate.

Classical Slices and P-slices: Example 4 showed how predicate slices can differ from the classical slices which are defined in terms of statements that *might* affect a variable. There is no straightforward way to obtain classical slices from p-slices, even by using free variables (which show all statements that affect a variable in any way at all). A free variable is one that does not occur in the program and is usually denoted by a Greek letter, as in the next example.

Example 7: Consider (in C)

S_7: `y = 2 * y; if (y > 0) x = 2 * x;` Then:

$wp.\ S_7.(x = \eta) = (y > 0 \wedge 2 * x = \eta) \vee (y \leq 0 \wedge x = \eta)$

The *wp* is exactly the same without the first assignment statement (`y = 2 * y`), so this statement can be sliced (using p-slicing), even though it *might* affect variable **x**. Classical slicing would not remove this assignment.

The next step is to complete the semantic definitions of *alternation* and *iteration* statements and then show our principal *slicing theorems*. Following that, we will give an algorithm to obtain a minimal p-slice for any predicate.

6 Alternation Semantics And Slicing

Following Dijkstra [4], Cohen [3] and Gries [7], the "if" or *alternation* statement takes the form:

$$
\begin{array}{l}
\textit{if } B_1 \rightarrow S_1 \\
[]\ B_2 \rightarrow S_2 \\
[]\ \ldots \\
[]\ B_n \rightarrow S_n \\
\textit{fi}
\end{array}
$$

Each B_i is a *guard*, that is, an arbitrary predicate, and each S_i is a *guarded statement*. Operationally speaking, a statement is executed for some *true* guard, and the statement aborts if the guards are all *false*. The alternation is nondeterministic as several guards may hold, but only one statement is executed.

Alternation semantics are then defined as:

$$
\begin{array}{l}
wp.(\textit{if} \ldots \textit{fi}).P \equiv \\
\exists i\!: 1 \leq i \leq n\!: B_i \wedge (\forall i\!: 1 \leq i \leq n\!: B_i \Rightarrow wp.\ S_i.P)
\end{array}
$$

That is, to obtain the postcondition, the necessary and sufficient precondition requires that at least one guard must hold (or else the alternation aborts) and, for every guard that is *true*, the wp of the guarded statement must hold.

In the practical, but special, case of deterministic programs derived from syntactically correct compound *if...then...else* statements (in C or nearly any other programming language), the guards are mutually exclusive and exactly one will hold. Be certain, however, to include *skip* statements for missing *else* clauses, as we did in Examples 3 and 7. Dijkstra and Scholten [5, p. 144] prove what we call the "ITE" (*if...then...else*) rule; namely, if the alternation is derived from compound conditional statements in a deterministic language, then:

$wp.(if...fi).P \equiv$
$(\exists i{:}\ 1 \le i \le n{:}\ (B_i \wedge wp.\ S_i.P))$

That is, to obtain the postcondition, it is necessary and sufficient that there is at least one *true* guard (in fact, there is only one) and the wp of the guarded statement holds (for the postcondition). We implicitly used the ITE rule in Examples 3 and 7.

Note: PL/I is the only common language that implements a deterministic conditional statement that resembles the DGC alternation. The C *switch* statement is much different as the *cases* are not general predicates and, unless there is a *break* after every *case* group, the semantics are different.

There are two possibilities when determining p-slices of an alternation statement (in the standard form at the start of this section) with respect to a slicing predicate, P. The first possibility is that one of the conditionally executed statements, S_i, can be sliced, even though the entire alternation cannot be sliced. This gives:

Alternation Slicing Theorem: For an alternation, if, for some j, $B_j \Rightarrow (wp.\ S_j.P \equiv P)$, then S_j may be sliced (replaced with a *skip*). This is immediate, since:

$$
\begin{aligned}
& wp.(if...fi).P \\
\equiv & \langle \textit{WP of alternation} \rangle \\
& \exists i{::}\ B_i \wedge (\forall i{::}\ B_i \Rightarrow wp.\ S_i.P) \\
\equiv & \langle p.c. \rangle \\
& \exists i{::}\ B_i \wedge (\forall i{:}\ i \neq j{:}\ B_i \Rightarrow wp.S_i.\ P) \wedge (B_j \Rightarrow wp.S_j.P) \\
\equiv & \langle p.c., B_j \Rightarrow (wp.S_j.P \equiv P) \rangle \\
& \exists i{::}\ B_i \wedge (\forall i{:}\ i \neq j{:}\ B_i \Rightarrow wp.S_i.\ P) \wedge (B_j \Rightarrow P)
\end{aligned}
$$

This later expression is readily seen to be the wp of the alternation with S_j replaced with *skip*.

Note: We have used the calculational proof style developed and advocated by Dijkstra and Scholten [5]. The bracketed comments are an aid to understanding the calculation step, and when we write "p.c." we have used common predicate calculus identities.

Alternation Slicing Corollary: If all the S_j can be sliced, then the entire alternation can be sliced if $P \Rightarrow \exists i{::}\ B_i$. That is, if P implies the disjunction of the guards (equivalently, at least one guard is *true*, which is always the case when starting from compound conditionals in languages such as C).

This is immediate, since:

$$
\begin{aligned}
& wp.(if...fi).P \\
\equiv & \langle \textit{WP of alternation} \rangle \\
& \exists i{::}\ B_i \wedge (\forall i{::}\ B_i \Rightarrow wp.\ S_i.P) \\
\equiv & \langle \forall i{::}\ B_i \Rightarrow (wp.\ S_i.P \equiv P) \rangle \\
& \exists i{::}\ B_i \wedge (\forall i{::}\ B_i \Rightarrow P)
\end{aligned}
$$

$\equiv \langle\, p.c. \,\rangle$

$\exists i{::}\ B_i \wedge P$

$\equiv \langle\, P \Rightarrow \exists i{::}\ B_i \,\rangle$

P

Thus, we may cut an alternation entirely if:

$$P \Rightarrow \exists i{::}\ B_i \wedge \{\ (\forall i{::}\ B_i \Rightarrow (wp.\ S_i.P \equiv P)\ \}$$

This latter result is not that important in practice since it is usually simple enough to directly check whether:

$$wp.(if..fi).P \equiv P$$

7 Repetition Semantics and Slicing

The DGC repetition statement (or "do loop," or, in C, the "while loop") is of the form:

$$do\ B \rightarrow S\ od$$

B guards the "loop body," S, which is repeated so long as B evaluates to *true*. If B is initially *false*, then S is never executed. To be useful, of course, S must have "progress properties" that assure that B will eventually be *false* (although many systems, such as an operating system, loop forever without any progress).

Repetition semantics must be defined in terms of a "loop invariant" which is a predicate that holds before and after S; that is, S does not transform the invariant predicate. A necessary and sufficient condition for predicate P_I to be an invariant of S is that:

$$B \wedge P_I \Rightarrow wp.S.P_I$$

This states that, once past the guard, we know that both B and the invariant hold, and, if the invariant is to hold after the loop body, we must have the wp.

When the statement terminates, the guard will be *false*, but the invariant must still hold. Furthermore, the invariant must hold initially. These observations lead to the semantics (wp) of the repetition statement in the special case of loops that make progress and are therefore guaranteed to terminate:

$$wp.(\ do\ B \rightarrow S\ od\ ).(\neg B \wedge P_I) \equiv P_I$$

Invariants are not unique. If a loop body does not contain any *abort* statements or non-terminating loops, then *true* is a trivial invariant. Furthermore, the conjunction of two invariants is also an invariant. In order to understand a loop completely, it is necessary to determine the "strongest" invariant. Needless to say, this is not always an easy, or even possible, task (computational complexity and decidability issues can come into play). In many practical situations, such as isolating defects, partial invariants are sufficient [8, 9].

In the following theorem about repetition statements, S is the repetition body. We also use Gries' $H_k(P)$ [7], which is defined recursively by:

$$H_0(P) \equiv \neg B \wedge P$$
$$H_k(P) \equiv H_0(P) \vee B \wedge wp.S.H_{k-1}(P)$$

$H_k(P)$ holds if and only if the repetition terminates with P *true* in k or fewer iterations.

These definitions permit a more general expression of repetition statement semantics, $wp.(\, do\ B \rightarrow S\ od).P$.

Specifically:

$$wp.(do\ B \rightarrow S\ od).P \equiv \exists k\colon 0 \le k\colon H_k(P)$$

We first prove a Lemma that will be fundamental to subsequent work.

Iteration Termination Lemma:

$$\{\, B \wedge wp.S.P \equiv B \wedge P \,\} \Rightarrow \{\, \forall k\colon 0 \le k\colon (H_k(P) \equiv (P \wedge H_k(true))) \,\}$$

Note: $\wedge$ is a higher precedence operator than $\equiv$. Also notice that $wp.S.P \equiv P$ is a stronger form of the left side of this implication. Saying that P is an invariant is a weaker statement than the left hand side of the implication.

We prove this by induction. First, we have:

$$H_0(true) \wedge P$$
$$\equiv \langle\, Def\ of\ H_0,\ p.c.\, \rangle$$
$$\neg B \wedge P$$
$$\equiv \langle\, Def\ of\ H_0 \,\rangle$$
$$H_0(P)$$

Next we have:

$$H_k(true) \wedge P$$
$$\equiv \langle\, Def\ of\ H_k \,\rangle$$
$$(H_0(true) \vee B \wedge wp.S.H_{k-1}(true)) \wedge P$$
$$\equiv \langle\, p.c.,\ B \wedge wp.S.P \equiv B \wedge P \,\rangle$$
$$H_0(true) \wedge P \vee B \wedge wp.S.H_{k-1}(true) \wedge wp.S.P$$
$$\equiv \langle\, H_0(true) \wedge P \equiv H_0(P),\ Conjunctivity\ of\ WP \,\rangle$$
$$H_0(P) \vee B \wedge wp.S.(H_{k-1}(true) \wedge P)$$
$$\equiv \langle\, Induction\ step \,\rangle$$
$$H_0(P) \vee B \wedge wp.S.(H_{k-1}(P))$$
$$\equiv \langle\, Def\ of\ H_k \,\rangle$$
$$H_k(P)$$

Armed with this Lemma, we immediately have:

$$\{ B \wedge wp.S.P \equiv B \wedge P \} \Rightarrow$$
$$\{ wp.(do\ B \rightarrow S\ od).P \equiv P \wedge wp.(do\ B \rightarrow S\ od).(true) \}$$

Since:

$$\begin{aligned}
& wp.(do\ B \rightarrow S\ od).P \\
\equiv & \langle\ \textit{Def of } wp.(do\ldots od) \textit{ in terms of } H_k \rangle \\
& \exists k{:}\ 0 \leq k{:}\ H_k(P) \\
\equiv & \langle\ B \wedge wp.S.P \equiv B \wedge P, \textit{Lemma}\ \rangle \\
& \exists k{:}\ 0 \leq k{:}\ (H_k(true) \wedge P) \\
\equiv & \langle\ p.c.\ \rangle \\
& P \wedge \exists k{:}\ 0 \leq k{:}\ H_k(true) \\
\equiv & \langle\ \textit{Def of } wp.(do\ B \rightarrow S\ od) \textit{ in terms of } H_k \rangle \\
& P \wedge wp.(do\ B \rightarrow S\ od).(true)
\end{aligned}$$

From this last result, we immediately have:

$$\{ B \wedge wp.S.P \equiv B \wedge P \} \Rightarrow \{ wp.(do\ B \rightarrow S\ od).P \Rightarrow P \}$$

In words, if P isn't changed by the repetition body, then the wp of the entire repetition implies P. From the above Lemma we can also derive:

Repetition Slice Theorem:

$$\{ (B \wedge wp.S.P \equiv B \wedge P) \wedge P \Rightarrow (wp.(do\ B \rightarrow S\ od).(true)) \} \Rightarrow$$
$$\{ wp.(do\ B \rightarrow S\ od).P \equiv P \}$$

Again, in words, if P isn't changed by the repetition body, and P implies the repetition terminates, then the repetition may be eliminated (sliced with respect to P).

Note: An important way to have $P \Rightarrow (wp.(do\ B \rightarrow S\ od).(true))$ is to have $wp.(do\ B \rightarrow S\ od).(true)$ always *true*; that is, if the repetition is guaranteed to terminate. This is the

Bounded Repetition Slice Theorem:

$$\{ (B \wedge wp.S.P \equiv B \wedge P) \wedge wp.(do\ B \rightarrow S\ od).(true) \} \Rightarrow$$
$$\{ wp.(do\ B \rightarrow S\ od).P \equiv P \}$$

This theorem is helpful when we are certain that a repetition terminates, as would be the case in a C repetition of the common form:

```
for (i=0; i < MAX; i++) { /* Loop Body */ }
```

8 Computing a p-Slice

Practical use of p-slices requires an algorithm to find at least one p-slice for a given predicate. Also, in practice, users do not want to slice an entire program, but, rather, want to examine a sequence of syntactically complete statements. With this requirement in mind, let:

$$S: \quad S_1; S_2; \ldots; S_N$$

be a composition of individual statements, S_i, each of which is a primitive statement (assignment, *skip*, or *abort*), an alternation, or a repetition. Further, suppose that we want to slice S with respect to the slicing predicate P. That is, we want to compute a member of the set *PSlice* (S, P).

Our current implementation (in the code analysis tool) proceeds as follows:

1. Slice (i.e., replace with *skip*) all statements that do not make assignments to variables in P. This assumes, of course, that there is no potential aliasing so that Hoare's axiom holds. (Caution: Also, do not slice statements affecting loop progress.)
2. Compute $P_i \equiv wp.(S_i; S_{i+1};\ldots; S_N).P$ for $1 \leq i \leq N$. Set $P_{N+1} \equiv P$.
3. Starting with $j = N+1$, find the smallest $i \leq j$ such that $P_i \equiv P_j$ and slice all the statements from S_i to S_j inclusive. (Note: If $i = j$, there is nothing to slice.)
4. Set $j = i-1$ and repeat from step (3) while j is positive.
5. Next, examine all remaining alternation and repetition statements, performing steps (1) to (4) to slice each guarded statement and loop body. If you are examining statement S_i (in the original labeling), then P_{i+1} plays the role of P (the slicing predicate). In simplifying alternations, combine guard predicates where the guarded statements are the same.

We have found this algorithm to be effective for moderately sized code sequences, although its time complexity is, of course, $O(N^2)$. The first step (removing all obviously irrelevant statements) helps in the processing of larger programs.

Note: By modifying Step 3 to test only whether $P_{j-1} = P_j$, we get a weaker, but faster, linear time algorithm.

9 An Extended Example

The following code is a simplification of some code that we actually encountered in tracing a defect. While one might object that good programmers would never write such code, it is an unfortunate fact that they do. Our experience with maintenance teams dealing with day-to-day problems shows that there is no need to contrive examples.

```
typedef struct connect_table {
  int entry;
  int srce;
  int dest;
  } CTABLE;

#define  TSIZE 100
#define  TRUE  1
#define  FALSE 0

main ( )
{
CTABLE list [TSIZE];
   int count, oldc;
   char found;
   int s_target, d_target;
   count = 0;
   oldc = -1;
   found = FALSE;

   while (count < TSIZE && !found) {
       if (list[count].srce == s_target) {
           if (list[count].dest == d_target)
               found = TRUE;
       } else {
           if (list[count].entry > 0) list[count].entry--;
           oldc++;
       }
       count++;
   }
   if (found) {
       list[count-1].entry++;
   }
}
```

Fig. 1. Code Fragment Before Conversion to DGC

In dealing with this code and the defects associated with it, we were interested in a predicate which we had inferred to be necessary for correct operation.

$$P \equiv (\texttt{count == oldc + 1})$$

Putting this code into a form approximating DGC (our code analyzer does this conversion) gives the code in Figure 2 (the declarations are omitted here). Many programmers quickly note the defects once the code is put into this form, and we consider this to be evidence of the clarity of DGC. It is unfortunate that most programming languages allow, indeed encourage, coding such as Figure 1.

```
count = 0;
oldc = -1;
found = FALSE;

while (count < TSIZE && !found) {
    if (list[count].srce == s_target
        && list[count].dest == d_target)
            { found = TRUE; }
    else if (list[count].srce == s_target
        && list[count].dest != d_target)
            { /* skip */ }
    else if (list[count].srce != s_target
        && list[count].entry > 0)
            { list[count].entry--; oldc++; }
    else if (list[count].srce != s_target
        && list[count].entry <= 0)
            { oldc++; }
    count++;
}
if (found)
    { list[count-1].entry++; }
else if (!found)
    { /* skip */ }
```

Fig. 2. Code Fragment in a DGC-Like Form

It is now possible to determine the p-slice slices, shown in Figure 3. The defect (with respect to maintaining the slicing predicate) is now clear.

```
count = 0;
oldc = -1;
found = FALSE;

while (count < TSIZE && !found) {
    if (list[count].srce == s_target
        && list[count].dest == d_target)
            { found = TRUE; }
    else if (list[count].srce == s_target
        && list[count].dest != d_target)
            { /* skip */ }
    else if (list[count].srce != s_target)
            { oldc++; }
    count++;
}
/* Slicing Predicate: count == oldc + 1  */
```

Fig. 3. A Member of *Slice* (Figure 2, `count == oldc + 1`)

Another interesting slicing predicate is one that asserts that all `entry` fields are positive.

10 A Repetition Example

The following simple loop illustrates one of many useful applications of the *Repetition Slice Theorem*. Consider the following code fragment (in C):

```
int c;
char exit;
    . . . . . .
while (!exit) {
    c = c - 1;
    /* . . . code that does not affect c . . . */
    c = c + 1;
}
```

Fig. 4. A Loop with a Positive Counter

Using the slicing predicate:

$$c \geq 0$$

the entire loop can be sliced. Generalizing, suppose that instead of incrementing and decrementing `c` (a counter), we instead allocate and free a resource or enter and leave a critical section. Alternatively, a data structure (such as a search tree) is manipulated at the top of the loop and re-assembled at the bottom (consider an insertion operation).

In all these cases, the slicing predicate states a "safety property." The fact that the loop can be sliced with respect to this property shows that the loop is correct with respect to this safety property, which is useful information. Classical slicing would not yield this information.

Alternatively, consider the following variation, which has a bug with respect to the safety property:

```
while (!exit) {
    c = c - 1;
    if (. . .) {
        exit = true;
    } else {
        c = c + 1;
        /*   other code   */
    }
}
```

Fig. 5. A Defective Loop

This loop would not be sliced using the slicing, or safety, predicate, $c \geq 0$, highlighting the defect.

11 Conclusions and Future Work

Predicate slicing is a useful logical code analysis technique during software maintenance. We also feel that it can be useful during other parts of the software life cycle, including code inspections and quality assurance. We have used this form of slicing successfully to isolate code defects and expect to deploy automated, tool-based slicing in the near future.

There are a number of challenging additional problems that we will need to address in the future in order to realize the full powers of these techniques. These problems appear, in fact, in any use of formal methods to aid program understanding and maintenance. These problems include:

1. Aliasing is a significant problem, and C's liberal use of pointers aggravates the problem beyond the issues examined by Bijlsma [2]. We have found Bijlsma's approach, however, to be effective. The problem also occurs with arrays, especially where indices can go out of bounds.
2. It can be useful to include assertions in the slicing predicates. These assertions typically state "safety properties" to the effect that an array index is within bounds, that a pointer only contains addresses of one type of object, that a counter is always positive, that an array is sorted, and so on. Then, predicate slicing will expose statements that could violate these safety properties. For example, the following assertion could be useful in slicing the code of Figure 1.

   $$0 \leq count \leq N \; \&\& \; -1 \leq oldc \leq N$$

3. Currently, procedures are processed by including the procedure code in-line, as in Gries [7]. We would like to extend our analysis tool to allow the use of procedure specifications (in terms of weakest precondition semantics), possibly extracted from a library.

References

1. Aho, Sethi & Ullman, *Compilers: Principles, Techniques, and Tools.* Addison-Wesley, 1986.
2. A. Bijlsma, "Calculating with pointers," *Sci. Comput. Programming*, vol. 12, pp. 191-205, 1989.
3. E. Cohen, *Programming in the 1990s*. NY: Springer-Verlag, 1990.
4. E. W. Dijkstra, *A Discipline of Programming*. Englewood Cliffs, NJ: Prentice-Hall, 1976.
5. E.W. Dijkstra and C.S. Scholten, *Predicate Calculus and Program Semantics.* NY: Springer-Verlag, 1989.

6. K. B. Gallagher and J. R. Lyle, "Program slicing in software maintenance," *IEEE Trans. Software Eng.*, vol. 17, no. 8, Aug. 1991.
7. D. Gries, *The Science of Programming*. NY: Springer-Verlag, 1981.
8. J. M. Hart, "Experience with logical code analysis in software reuse and re-engineering," in *AIAA Computing in Aerospace 10* (San Antonio, TX), Mar. 28-30, 1995, pp. 549-558.
9. J. M. Hart, "Experience with logical code analysis in software maintenance," *Software Practice and Experience*, vol. 25, no. 11, pp. 1243-1262, 1995.
10. B. Kernighan and D. Ritchie, *The C Programming Language*. Englewood Cliffs, NJ: Prentice-Hall, 1978.
11. P. E. Livadas and S. Croll, "A new algorithm for the calculation of transitive dependencies," *Software Maintenance: Research and Practice*, vol. 7, pp. 151-176, May-June 1995.
12. Z. Manna and R. Waldinger, "Problematic features of programming languages: A situational-calculus approach," *Acta Informatica*, vol. 16, pp. 371-426, 1981.
13. M. Weiser, "Programmers use slices when debugging," *Commun. Assoc. Comput. Mach.*, vol. 25, pp. 446-452, July 1982.
14. M. Weiser, "Program slicing," *IEEE Trans. Software Eng.*, vol. SE-10, pp. 352-357, July 1984.

A Formal Approach to Architectural Design Patterns

P.S.C. Alencar[1], D.D. Cowan[1], C.J.P. Lucena[2]

[1] Computer Science Department, University of Waterloo, Waterloo, Ontario, Canada
[2] Departamento de Informática, Pontifícia Universidade Católica do Rio de Janeiro, Rio de Janeiro, Brazil

Abstract. In this paper we introduce a formal approach to architectural design patterns based on an object-oriented model integrated with a process-oriented method for describing the patterns. The object-oriented model is based on the Abstract Data View (ADV) concept, which is a formal model for subjectivity in that it explicitly distinguishes between two kinds of objects, namely application objects and object views. The formalism allows the definition and application of design patterns by considering both the process program for the pattern tasks and the interconnected objects and views resulting from a particular pattern instantiation. The approach can be used to describe design patterns at many different architectural levels, and this is illustrated by presenting patterns for the master-slave, pipes-and-filters, layered systems, adapter, observer, and composite.

1 Introduction

Design patterns can be viewed as a means to achieve large-scale reuse by capturing successful software development design practice within a particular context [12, 7, 6]. Patterns should not be limited in what they can describe and can be used to encapsulate good design practices at both the specification and implementation levels. Thus, design patterns can be applied at many different levels of abstraction in the software development life-cycle, and can focus on reuse within architectural design as well as detailed design and implementation. In fact, a system of patterns for software development should include patterns covering various ranges of scale, beginning with patterns for defining the basic architectural structure of an application and ending with patterns describing how to implement a particular design mechanism in a concrete programming language.

Most published research [12, 6] in design patterns has been described in a structured but informal notation, and has focused on implementation-oriented patterns rather than architectural ones. For example, one publication [12] contains descriptions of patterns using text and diagrams, and has grouped patterns into three major categories. These descriptions can be viewed as an informal recipe or process for producing instantiations of specific patterns in languages such as Smalltalk or C++. Even when architectural issues are considered [7], the software architectural design is expressed only through informal patterns.

An architectural pattern is based on selected types of components and connectors, together with a control structure that governs their execution.

In this paper we describe a formal approach to design patterns which encompasses patterns at different levels of granularity ranging from architectural to implementation descriptions. There are two aspects to design patterns that are considered in this presentation: the process of producing specific instantiations of a design pattern, and the use of formally defined components or objects to substitute in these instantiations.

If the process is defined through a process language with formal syntax and semantics, then any ambiguities in the process of design pattern instantiation should be eliminated. Reducing or even eliminating ambiguity should make it easier to derive code consistently and perhaps even lead to some automation of the code production for the particular instantiation of a design pattern [1]. Substituting formally defined components into an instantiation could permit a formal reasoning process about the resulting system. We currently have established two different frameworks for reasoning about designs[3, 5] of this type.

Recent investigations[5] have shown how both a formal model and a prototype can be derived from a single component-based specification, thus providing a strong link between formalism and implementation.

The formally defined components are based on the Abstract Data View (ADV) approach[8, 9, 10] which uses a formal model [3, 4] to achieve separation by dividing designs into two types of components: objects and object views, and by strictly following a set of design rules. Specific instantiations of views as represented by Abstract Data Views (ADVs) and objects called Abstract Data Objects (ADOs) are substituted into the design pattern realization while maintaining a clear separation between view and object. Currently the ADV and ADO components are specified using temporal logic and the interconnection between components is described in terms of category theory.

Each design pattern has an associated process program that describes how to substitute these components to create a specific instantiation. In fact, this framework can be seen as a formal approach for a system of design patterns.

2 Abstract Data Views: the Model and Its Schema

In this section we describe the Abstract Data View (ADV) model and associated schema. This model allows us to create design patterns at various levels of granularity ranging from program design to software architectures, while maintaining a clear separation of concerns among the components.

A model of the ADV/ADO concept showing how these two types of objects interact is presented in Figure 1. An ADO is an object in the object-oriented sense, but has no direct contact with the "outside" world. As an object, an ADO has state and a public interface that can be used to query or change this state. An ADO is abstract since we are only interested in the public interface. An ADV is an ADO augmented to support the development of general "views" of ADOs, where a view could include a user or network interface or an adaptation of the

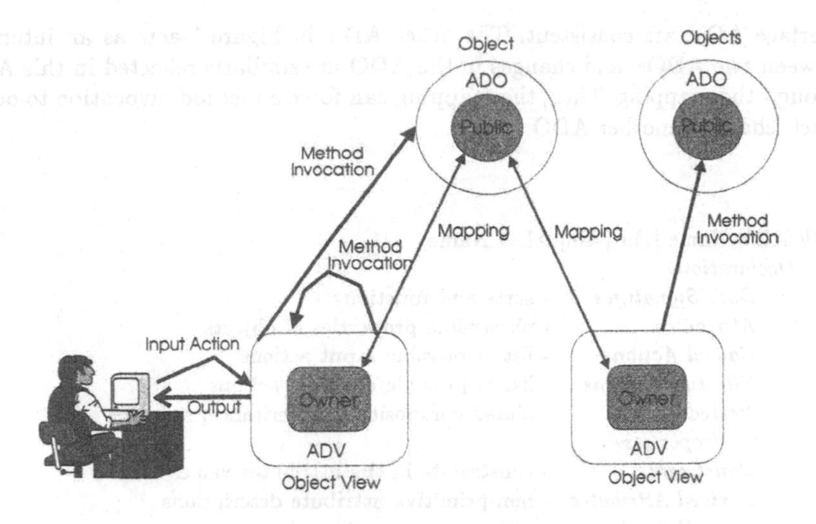

Fig. 1. An ADV/ADO interaction model

public interface of an ADO to change the way the ADO is "viewed" by other ADOs. A view may change the state of an associated ADO either through an input action (event) as found in a user interface, or through the action of another ADO.

Since an ADV is conceived to be separate from an ADO and yet specify a view of an ADO, the ADV should incorporate a formal association with its corresponding ADO. The formal association consists of: a naming convention, a method of ensuring that the ADV view and the ADO state are consistent, and a method of changing the ADO state from its associated ADV. Because an ADV is an object with properties which assist the designer in maintaining a clear separation of concerns we have chosen to give this "special" object a unique identity.

In order to maintain a separation of concerns, an ADV knows the name of any ADO to which it is connected, but an ADO does not know the name of its attached ADVs. The name of the ADO connected to an ADV is represented in the ADV by a placeholder variable called "owner" which is shown in Figure 1.

If the state of an ADO is changed then any part of the state that may be viewed by a connected ADV through the ADO's public interface must be consistent with that change. A morphism or mapping is defined between the ADV and ADO that expresses this invariant, and of course, uses the naming convention previously described. In addition, an ADV may query or change the state of a connected ADO through its normal public interface.

Figure 1 illustrates many of these concepts. The user depicted in the Figure causes an input action that is received by the ADV acting as a user interface. This action can cause a method invocation in which the ADV changes or queries its own state or the state of its associated ADO. If the state of the ADO changes through some other action, then the mapping ensures that the ADO and the user interface ADV are consistent. The other ADV in Figure 1 acts as an interface between two ADOs, and changes in the ADO are similarly reflected in this ADV through the mapping. Thus, the mapping can force a method invocation to occur which changes another ADO.

ADV ADV_Name [*For* | *On*] ADO_Name
- *Declarations*
  - *Data Signatures* - sorts and functions
  - *Attributes* - observable properties of objects
  - *Causal Actions* - list of possible input actions
  - *Effectual Actions* - list of possible effectual actions
  - *Nested ADVs* - allows composition, inheritance, sets, ...
- *Static Properties*
  - *Constraints* - constraints in the attributes values
  - *Derived Attributes* - non-primitive attribute descriptions
- *Dynamic Properties*
  - *Interconnection* - description of the communication process among objects
  - *Valuation* - the effect of events on attributes
  - *Behavior* - behavioral properties of the ADV

End ADV_Name

Fig. 2. A descriptive schema for an ADV.

In summary we observe that there are two types of ADVs: an ADV which acts as an interface between two different media, and an ADV which acts as an interface between two ADOs operating in the same medium. Although there are two types of ADVs, they are natural extensions of each other.

The ADV/ADO model was originally conceived to address the same concerns as the MVC [19] paradigm. However, the ADV/ADO model is more general in its approach in that it explicitly models both interfaces to the external world and interfaces between objects. Emphasis on the interface as a special type of object encourages the designer to address separation of concerns explicitly in a design. In addition, the ADV/ADO model is formally defined and can support both reasoning and implementation with the same model.

The separation between views and objects makes it possible to use several ADVs to create different views for a single collection of ADOs. In this case, both ADOs and their associated views must be consistent. For example, a clock ADO could have a digital view, an analog view, or both. We call consistency among the different ADVs *horizontal consistency,* while consistency between the visual object (ADV) and its ADO is called *vertical consistency.* These consistency properties must be guaranteed by the specification of ADVs, ADOs, and their environment.

ADVs and ADOs have distinct roles in a software system. As a consequence, they are described by different schemas. These schemas are not the actual objects of the system, but rather provide descriptions of their static and dynamic properties and declarations of entities that are used within the scope of the object. Such schemas are presented in detail in [4].

The specification syntax of the whole schema which is based on ones described in [13] is presented essentially through a temporal logic formalism [4, 22]. Every ADV or ADO structure is subdivided into three sections. A declaration part contains a description of all of the elements that compose the object including sorts, functions, attributes, and actions. The static properties part defines all the properties which do not affect the state of the object. Dynamic properties establish how the states and attribute values of an object are modified during its lifetime.

Figure 2 shows the structure of the schemas to be used in the specification of ADVs. Causal actions correspond to input events while effectual actions correspond to method invocations. The header of the schema has the name of the ADV and the name of its associated ADO. ADO schemas, which are not illustrated here, have a similar structure to ADVs, except that ADOs do not support causal actions, and they do not contain references to any ADVs.

These formal ADV/ADO schemas are based on temporal logic and some tools from category theory (institutions). This approach is strongly based on Maibaum and Fiadeiro's combination of temporal logic and category theory [11] that was initially developed for the purpose of formalizing modularization techniques for reactive systems. We capture the ADV semantics in logic by using temporal logic to describe the ADV and ADO components and their properties, morphisms (or mappings) to describe the relationship between these components (through a concept related to interpretation between theories), and tools from category theory (institutions) to specify systems of interconnected ADVs and ADOs (the structuring mechanisms). For more details on the issues treated in this section see [3].

The formal category theory tool used here, called the theory of institutions (and its associated tools), was introduced by Goguen and Burstall [15] and allows the theories of a logic to be shown to constitute a category whose morphisms correspond to property preserving translations between their languages. These translations or mappings are also known as interpretations between theories, and have been used to model relationships between abstract and concrete specifications [25], or to model mappings between different notions of software architecture [23].

We adopt a temporal logic with a (global) discrete linear time structure similar to those used in [21], since this allows easier assessment of the support for modular specification that is described. We also use the fact that temporal logics may be defined that satisfy, to some extent, institution [14], and hence, that temporal theories may be used as modularization units for concurrent system specification.

The formal specifications of ADVs and ADOs are provided as theory presentations [3] and a categorical account of the ADV/ADO specifications is provided through a category of temporal theories. A morphism or mapping of theory presentations is a signature morphism that defines a theorem preserving translation between the two theory presentations and a locality property. Morphisms capture the relationship that exists between two ADV/ADO theory presentations. Thus, morphisms can be used to express a system as a diagram showing an interconnection of its parts. Formally, this diagram is a directed multigraph in which the nodes are labeled by ADV/ADO specifications, and the edges by the specification morphisms.

3 A Formal Description of Design Patterns

The ADV model supports reuse since it divides an application into a set of specialized objects (separation of concerns) each of which may be used in other designs. However, we would like to "glue" these objects into reusable systems, that is, systems which are easily maintained over time. Design patterns as proposed in [12] support this form of reuse. Each design pattern is a meta-description of a solution for a problem that occurs frequently in software design. The application of the meta-description results in several objects connected together to form a specific instantiation of such a design solution.

Operator **Pattern Name**
  Objective - description of the intent of the pattern
  Parameters - external elements used in the pattern definition
  Subtasks - description of pattern in primitive constructors
  Consequences - how the pattern supports its objective
  Product Text - language-dependent specification of pattern
End Operator

Fig. 3. Development constructor structure for a design pattern.

The acceptance of reusable descriptions, such as design patterns, is highly dependent on easily comprehensible definitions and unambiguous specifications. We address both issues in a single formalism for design pattern application.

In order to formalize the application of design patterns we introduce development constructors which are based on schemas that indicate how to apply a pattern. We define design pattern constructors to consist of a language-independent part and a product text specification, where a specific language is adopted; this approach is similar to that described in [20].

The language-independent part of the structure should clearly define the characteristics of a design pattern. According to [12], a pattern is composed of four essential elements: *pattern name*, *problem statement*, *solution*, and *consequences*.

Appropriate pattern names are usually important factors to assist developers in the specification of a system. In the case of reusable modules, the vocabulary of patterns could be one way of guiding the user to choosing suitable modules for the solution of particular problems.

A problem statement is a description of the circumstances in which to apply a design pattern, and clarifies the pattern objectives. In the development constructor structure shown in Figure 3, such a statement is described by an *Objective* section.

Applying a pattern in the context of a specific problem requires a process description, and so we specify this process in terms of primitive development constructors and parameters. The primitive constructors applied to pattern construction are organized in a section of the schema called *Subtasks*, while input parameters used in this process are declared in the *Parameters* section.

The consequences of an application of a pattern provide a description of the results of using such structure in a software system. The roles of the components within the pattern objectives are also illustrated. This section may be helpful in evaluating the suitability of a pattern in a specific context. These ramifications are specified in the *Consequences* section of a pattern schema.

The language-dependent part of the pattern constructors describes the result of the application of a pattern as a specific formal representation. Since design patterns are solution abstractions, a template of the pattern should be a helpful instrument in guiding the user to a particular specification. Such templates are illustrated in the pattern development constructors using the formalism of ADV/ADO schematic representations described in Section 2.

4 Formal Design Patterns

In this section we provide a formal description of some design patterns at both the program design and architectural levels. We have chosen the adapter, observer, and composite design patterns to illustrate formal descriptions of patterns used to support program designs and the master-slave, pipes and filters, and layers as typical patterns that are used to describe system architectures. In this way we illustrate how the same basic formalism may be used to specify software at two different levels of abstraction. We present the implementation patterns first, since they have appeared elsewhere [12], and the interested reader may wish to compare the two different styles of presentation.

4.1 Program Design Patterns

We have chosen the adapter, observer and composite patterns from [12], to illustrate how the pattern constructor described in Figure 3 is applied. There is a substantial difference between the pattern specifications presented in [12], and the specifications introduced in this paper. The patterns in [12] are based on OMT diagrams, informal descriptions in English and C++ templates, and are much closer to the implementation level than the version of the pattern

Operator Design Pattern Adapter
Objective Modify the interface of an object
Parameters Objects: ADAPTEE, TARGET;
Subtasks 1 - Specify Adaptation Object: ADAPTEE, TARGET → ADAPTER
1.1 - Create Object: → ADAPTER
1.2 - Compose Objects: ADAPTEE, ADAPTER → ADAPTER
1.3 - Inherit Objects: TARGET, ADAPTER → ADAPTER
1.4 - Specify Links: ADAPTEE, ADAPTER → ADAPTER

Consequences ADAPTER will contain most of ADAPTEE functionality available through the TARGET object interface

Product Text *ADV/ADO* ADAPTER
Declarations
...
Nested ADVs/ADOs
Compose ADAPTEE;
Inherit TARGET;
...
Dynamic Properties
...
Interconnection
With ADV/ADO ADAPTEE
TargetActions ⟼ *AdapteeActions*;
End ADAPTER
End Operator

Fig. 4. Specification of adapter pattern constructor.

descriptions we present in this paper. Our version of the patterns is based on the pattern constructors and the specification formalism associated with the ADV design approach. Although we only present three patterns from [12] in this paper, our notation can handle a much broader range of patterns at the program design level as illustrated in [1].

In the following design pattern examples, the pattern specifications provide explanations and directions to instantiate a design through the use of well-defined development operators and incomplete object schemas. The development operators are sequentially numbered in a section called *Subtasks*, while the object schemas are defined in the language-dependent section called *Product Text*, which provides reusable patterns for the program design. Other sections complete the design pattern specifications by providing additional information.

The first pattern we describe is the *adapter*, and its corresponding specification schema is shown in Figure 4. The objective of the *adapter* is to modify

Operator Design Pattern Observer
Objective Define dependency between objects
Parameters Objects: SUBJECT;
Subtasks 1 - Specify Observers to Objects: SUBJECT → OBSERVERs
1.1 - Create Object: → OBSERVERs
1.2 - Compose Objects: SUBJECT, OBSERVERs → OBSERVERs
1.3 - Specify Links: OBSERVERs → OBSERVERs
Consequences OBSERVERs monitor changes in the state of SUBJECT to update its own state
Product Text *ADV* OBSERVERs for ADO SUBJECT
Declarations
...
Attributes
ObserverAttributes;
Actions
ObserverQueryActions;
ObserverChangeActions;
...
Dynamic Properties
Interconnection
With ADO SUBJECT
SubjectAttributes ⟼ *ObserversAttributes*;
SubjectQueryActions ⟼ *ObserversQueryActions*;
SubjectChangeActions ⟼ *ObserversChangeActions*;
...
End OBSERVERs
End Operator

Fig. 5. Specification of observer pattern constructor.

the interface of a given object to conform to the needs of a client object. It is generally used to produce compatibility between two objects. The adapter might be seen as an object which is a wrapper for another object, and it can be used for adaptations of interface objects (ADVs) as well as application objects (ADOs). An adapter object could also be regarded as a view (ADV) for an application object (ADO).

The subtasks which specify how to instantiate a pattern are given in a task or function notation of the form: "$f : x \rightarrow y$" where f is a function, x is a list of parameters for the function f, and y is the result of applying the function f. In the *adapter* pattern the function "Create Object" returns a copy of the ADAPTER Product Text while the function "Inherit Objects" takes the two arguments TARGET and ADAPTER and returns the modified Product Text for ADAPTER. In the context of C++ the ADAPTER text would have the

Operator Design Pattern Composite

Objective	Compose objects into tree structures to represent part-whole hierarchies
Parameters	Objects: COMPONENT;
Subtasks	1 - Create a Tree Structure. 1.1 - Instantiate Concrete Object: COMPONENT → COMPOSITE 1.2 - Instantiate Concrete Object: COMPONENT → LEAFs 1.3 - Compose Objects: LEAFs, COMPOSITE → COMPOSITE 1.4 - If Subtree is needed: 1.4.1 - Recursively Create SubTrees (Step 1) 1.4.2 - Compose Objects: SubCOMPOSITE, COMPOSITE → COMPOSITE
Consequences	A tree structure composed of LEAF objects and COMPOSITE objects is created, where the last ones represent the internal nodes of the tree
Product Text	*ADV/ADO* COMPOSITE *Declarations* ... *Attributes* ComponentType: ADO COMPONENT; *Nested ADVs/ADOs* Set CompSet of ComponentType; Inherit Component; ... *End* COMPOSITE *ADV/ADO* LEAF *Declarations* ... *Nested ADVs/ADOs* Inherit Component;

Fig. 6. Specification of composite pattern constructor.

words "inherit from TARGET" inserted in the appropriate location.

The *observer* design pattern, illustrated in Figure 5, is an example of a connecting pattern. The main objective of this pattern is to define a one-to-many dependency between objects, so that the dependent objects can monitor changes in one object. In the specification introduced here, we assume that *observer* objects are views (ADVs) of application objects, which we call *subject* in the pattern constructor.

The current specification approach differs from the design proposed in [12], in that the link between a view and its application object is represented by the ADV *mapping* design mechanism, which was explained in Section 2. This approach does not describe the implementation of the link, but indicates a mapping or morphism between elements of the objects involved. In contrast, the design described in [12] proposes a design technique that is closer to the implementation than the proposed *mapping*.

Figure 6 describes the specification of the *composite* design pattern. This pattern defines a hierarchical structure of objects sharing part-whole relationships. In such a relationship between objects, a composite object performs the "whole" role, while *leaf* and other *composite* objects represent the "parts."

The elements composing the resulting tree structure have uniform interfaces, since all of them inherit the tree interface from the abstract class called *component*. Additionally, these elements might be defined by ADVs or ADOs, since the *composite* design pattern might be used to structure both user interface objects and application objects.

The product text in Figure 6 has an attribute that contains the name of an ADO. Thus, it is possible to specify dynamic object structures where the names change over time.

4.2 Architectural Design Patterns

There are situations in a software system in which it is necessary to replicate a particular service in order to achieve fault tolerance, safety, and correctness. The redundant services are needed because in these situations it is not desirable to have a single supplier for a critical service. In these cases a design pattern called Master-Slave can be used. This pattern consists of a master component and a set of at least two slave components. The slaves are independent components that each provide the same service, but may use different solution strategies for providing that service. The master is the only component to which the clients of the service communicate, and the service is only accessible through the master's public interface. The master is responsible for invoking the slaves and for producing the final result which is computed from the results returned by the slaves. Thus, the master does not provide the service directly, but delegates the same task (the particular service) to several independent suppliers, and then returns the selected result to its clients.

From this discussion we can see that the Master-Slave design pattern has three kinds of participants: the client, the master and the slaves. The client requires a certain service in order to complete its own task. The master organizes the invocation of replicated services and decides which of the results returned by its slaves is to be passed to its clients, while the slaves are responsible for implementing the critical service. The Master-Slave Design Pattern is specified in Figure 7 with the *Product Text* for the Client and Master shown in Figure 8 and the *Product Text* for the Slave shown in Figure 9.

Pipes-and-filters is another important architectural pattern which is often used when software systems are composed of several independent complete sub-

Operator **Design Pattern Master-Slave**

Objective	**Handle the computation of replicated services**
Parameters	**Objects: CLIENT;**
Subtasks	**1 - Specify Master Object: CLIENT → MASTER**
	1.1 - Create Object: → MASTER
	1.2 - Compose Objects: CLIENT, MASTER → MASTER
	1.3 - Specify Links: MASTER → MASTER
	2 - Specify Slave Objects: MASTER → SLAVE$_i$ $i = 1, \ldots, N$
	2.1 - Create Objects: → SLAVE$_i$ $i = 1, \ldots, N$
	2.2 - Compose Objects: MASTER, SLAVE$_i$ → MASTER $i = 1, \ldots, N$
	2.3 - Specify Links: MASTER → MASTER
Consequences	**The replicated service provided by the SLAVE$_i$ (the slaves) is offered to CLIENT through the MASTER after selection**
Product Text	*ADV/ADO* CLIENT
	...
	End CLIENT
	ADV/ADO MASTER
	...
	End MASTER
	ADV/ADO SLAVE$_i$ $i = 1, \ldots, N$
	...
	End SLAVE$_i$

Fig. 7. Specification of the Master-Slave pattern constructor.

tasks. The subtasks are performed in a sequential or parallel order, and communicate with each other only by exchanging streams of data. The objective is to obtain highly reusable, interchangeable, and maintainable applications. This pattern consists of filter and pipe components. The filter components transform data and are responsible for a particular, independent, complete subtask of an application. The filter's interface consists of an input and output stream only. A filter reads streams of data from its inputs, processes this data, and produces streams of data as its outputs. The filter preserves any ordering relationship between the input and output data. The transformation of input is usually done locally and incrementally, and thus the output may begin before the input is completely read. A filter should not know the identity of the filters preceding or following it in the computation sequence, and so filters may not share state in order to preserve this independence. The pipe components (the pipes) are the connections between the filters that transmit data. There are normally two different ways to realize pipes: they may be links between filters (such as message calls) or they may be separate components (such as repositories or sensors). The responsibility of a pipe is to transmit data between filters, possibly converting the data format between the inout and output filter.

Product Text ADV/ADO CLIENT
Declarations
...
Nested ADVs/ADOs
...
Attributes
ClientAttributes;
Actions
ComputeTask;
...
End CLIENT
ADV/ADO MASTER
Declarations
...
Nested ADVs/ADOs
...
Attributes
MasterAttributes;
Actions
OutCom; Service; $\overline{Service}$;
SelectResult($Res_1, \ldots, Res_N$);
...
Dynamic Properties
...
Interconnection
With ADV/ADO CLIENT
Service $\longmapsto$ *ComputeTask;*
With ADV/ADO SLAVE_i $i = 1, \ldots, N$
$\overline{Service} \longmapsto ServiceSlave_1$;
...
$\overline{Service} \longmapsto ServiceSlave_N$;
Behavior
$s_1 \wedge \overline{Service} \rightarrow s_2$
$s_2 \wedge \overline{Service} \rightarrow s_3$
...
End MASTER

Fig. 8. The Master and Client product text for the Master-Slave pattern constructor.

The Pipes-and-Filters Architectural Pattern is specified in Figure 10 where the product text is shown in Figure 11. The Pipe-and-Filter architectural pattern can be viewed as an arrangement of producer-consumer structures. Each filter can be seen as a consumer of input, either from a user or from the output of some other filter, and as a producer of output, either for the user or as input to some other filter.

Another important architectural design pattern is the layered architecture.

Product Text ...

ADV/ADO SLAVE_i $i = 1, \ldots, N$

Declarations

...

Attributes

$Slave_i Attributes$;

Actions

$ServiceSlave_i$;

...

Dynamic Properties

...

End SLAVE_i

End Operator

Fig. 9. The Slave product text for the Master-Slave pattern constructor.

Operator Design Pattern Pipes-and-Filters

Objective Structure applications that can be divided into several completely independent subtasks performed in a strongly determined sequential or parallel order

Subtasks
1 - Specify Filter Objects: $\rightarrow$ FILTER_i $i = 1, 2$
   1.1 - Create Objects: $\rightarrow$ FILTER_i $i = 1, 2$
2 - Specify Pipe (Object): $\rightarrow$ PIPE
   2.1 - Create Object: $\rightarrow$ PIPE
   2.2 - Compose Objects: FILTER_1,FILTER_2,PIPE $\rightarrow$ PIPE
   2.4 - Specify Links: PIPE $\rightarrow$ PIPE

Consequences The subtasks are connected through the PIPEs

Product Text *ADV/ADO* FILTER_1

...

End FILTER_1

ADV/ADO FILTER_2

...

End FILTER_2

ADV/ADO PIPE

...

End PIPE

Fig. 10. Specification of the Pipes-and-Filters pattern constructor.

This pattern can be used to structure applications that can be organized hierarchically, and its use implies that each layer provides services to the layer above and serves as a client to the layer below. The specification in Figure 12 considers the particular case in which we have one layer object built on the top of the object $LAYER_i$. The top layer object, referred to as $LAYER_{i+1}$, is connected to $LAYER_i$ by the object view $CONNECTOR_i$.

```
Product Text ADV/ADO FILTER₁
        Declarations
            Attributes
                FILTER₁ Attributes;
            Actions
                SubTask₁; ActCom_out; ActCom_in; ‾ActCom_in‾;
        ...
        Dynamic Properties
            ...
            Interconnection
                With ADV/ADO OUTCOMPONENT
                    ‾ActCom_in‾ ⟼ OutCompAction;
            Behavior
                s₁ ∧ ‾ActCom_in‾ → s₂
                s₂ ∧ ActCom_in → s₃
                ...
    End FILTER₁
    ADV/ADO FILTER₂
        Declarations
            ...
            Nested ADVs/ADOs
            ...
            Attributes
                FILTER₂ Attributes;
            Actions
                SubTask₂;
        ...
    End FILTER₂
    ADV/ADO PIPE
        Declarations
            ...
            Nested ADVs/ADOs
            ...
            Attributes
                PIPEAttributes;
            Actions
                AddResult; RetrieveResult;
        ...
    End PIPE
```

Fig. 11. The Filter and Pipe product text for the Pipes-and-Filters pattern constructor.

Operator Design Pattern Layered-System

Objective Used to structure applications organized hierarchically

Subtasks
1 - Specify First Layer Object: $\rightarrow$ LAYER$_i$
  1.1 - Create Object: $\rightarrow$ LAYER$_i$
2 - Specify Second Layer Object: $\rightarrow$ LAYER$_{i+1}$
  2.1 - Create Object: $\rightarrow$ LAYER$_{i+1}$
  2.2 - Create Connector Object: $\rightarrow$ CONNECTOR$_i$
  2.3 - Specify Links: LAYER$_i$,LAYER$_{i+1}$,CONNECTOR$_i$ $\rightarrow$ CONNECTOR$_i$

Consequences Each layer provides services to the layer above and serves as a client to the layer below

Product Text

ADV/ADO LAYER$_i$
  Declarations
    Attributes
      LAYER$_i$ Attributes
    Actions
      LAYER$_i$ Action
  ...
End LAYER$_i$
ADV/ADO LAYER$_{i+1}$
  Declarations
    Attributes
      LAYER$_{i+1}$ Attributes
    Actions
      LAYER$_{i+1}$ Action
  ...
End LAYER$_{i+1}$
ADV/ADV CONNECTOR$_i$
  Declarations
    Attributes
      CONNECTOR$_i$ Attributes
    Actions
      CONNECTOR$_i$ Action
  Dynamic Properties
    ...
    Interconnection
      With ADO LAYER$_i$
        CONNECTOR$_i$ *Action* $\longmapsto$ LAYER$_i$ Action
      With ADO LAYER$_{i+1}$
        CONNECTOR$_i$ *Action* $\longmapsto$ LAYER$_{i+1}$ Action
End CONNECTOR$_i$

Fig. 12. Specification of the Layered System pattern constructor.

This pattern indicates how the ADV model can be viewed as a formalism [3] supporting the integration of subject-oriented programming [16, 17] and design patterns [12, 7, 6], establishing the relationship of object views and objects with subjects and subject activations. The object $LAYER_1$ can be, for example, an ADO House and the object $LAYER_2$ and its associated $CONNECTOR_1$ can be thought of as the subject activation related to a buyer view of the House. In this case, an extrinsic value of the House (an attribute of the ADO Buyer) can be computed by an action or method defined in the $CONNECTOR_1$ using the intrinsic attributes of the ADO House such as the size and number of rooms. Besides allowing the specification of layered systems, we can also formalize in principle other applications of the subject model such as, for example, the specification of multiple views of data, code debugging from a stable or a temporary perspective, and the management of the versions of a system by introducing subjects as a mechanism to associate different state with a single object.

5 Conclusions

In this paper we describe a formal approach for capturing software designs expressed by design patterns, and have demonstrated our techniques by describing design patterns at both the architectural and program design levels of software description. Our process programming approach to design patterns allows us to define primitive design pattern tasks or constructors that can then be used to produce specific instantiations of a design. We believe that this approach clarifies both the application and structure of the design patterns. In addition, the patterns have been specified so as to incorporate the concept of objects (ADOs) and object views (ADVs).

Using this formal approach including objects and object views directs us toward several important results. By using formally defined components we are able to reason about the design and prove properties as shown in [3, 5]. Of course systems often do not yield to formal approaches because of their size and complexity. However, the formal approach could still produce useful results in that the models generated could be used to aid in the testing process [5] by serving as a basis for test case generation [18], or by providing a means for measuring test coverage.

We are also investigating code generation from design patterns incorporating ADO and ADV schemas. Experiments based on the process program description have shown that design patterns can yield corresponding C++ schemas which can be completed by the designer through an interactive dialogue. In fact, we are currently experimenting with C++ code generation by constructing an interactive tool to generate and complete the schemas [2]. Thus, we should be able to produce a single design representation from which we can both reason about formally specified properties, and generate most of the code.

In addition to providing a basis for code generation and reasoning, this formal approach can be used to address several other important issues. This approach can indicate possible steps towards the definition of a unique process language vocabulary that can describe the interconnection mechanisms at the object, module, and architectural description levels. It can also provide a foundation for the definition of an integrated formal approach to software system specification and design that considers various levels of abstraction [23, 24]. The formal components can be specified at different levels of detail and thus various program/system/architecture features such as data, control, functionality, behavior, communication, concurrency/distribution/timing concerns can be included in the description as it is developed. Such an approach using ADVs has been briefly described in [10]. Using a uniform formal approach similar to the one we describe in this paper can enhance the quality of a design as the architects and designers work from a single system description.

6 Note to the Reader

The technical reports mentioned in this paper are available through our World Wide Web site at http://csg.uwaterloo.ca/.

References

1. P.S.C. Alencar, D.D. Cowan, D.M. German, K.J. Lichtner, C.J.P. Lucena, and L.C.M. Nova. A Formal Approach to Design Pattern Definition & Application. Technical Report CS-95-34, University of Waterloo, Waterloo, Ontario, Canada, August 1995.
2. P.S.C. Alencar, D.D. Cowan, K.J. Lichtner, C.J.P. Lucena, and L.C.M. Nova. Tool Support for Formal Design Patterns. Technical Report CS-95-36, University of Waterloo, Waterloo, Ontario, Canada, August 1995.
3. P.S.C. Alencar, D.D. Cowan, and C.J.P. Lucena. A Logical Theory of Interfaces and Objects. Technical Report CS-95-15, University of Waterloo, Waterloo, Ontario, Canada, 1995.
4. P.S.C. Alencar, D.D. Cowan, C.J.P. Lucena, and L.C.M. Nova. Formal specification of reusable interface objects. In *Proceedings of the Symposium on Software Reusability (SSR'95)*, pages 88–96. ACM Press, 1995.
5. P. Bumbulis, P.S.C. Alencar, D.D. Cowan, and C.J.P. Lucena. Combining Formal Techniques and Prototyping in User Interface Construction and Verification. In *2nd Eurographics Workshop on Design, Specification, Verification of Interactive Systems (DSV-IS'95)*. Springer-Verlag Lecture Notes in Computer Science, 1995. to appear.
6. P. Coad. *Object Models: Strategies, Patterns & Applications.* Yourdon Press, 1995.
7. J.O. Coplien and D.C. Schmidt, editors. *Pattern Languages of Program Design.* Addison-Wesley, 1995.
8. D. D. Cowan, R. Ierusalimschy, C. J. P. Lucena, and T. M. Stepien. Abstract Data Views. *Structured Programming*, 14(1):1–13, January 1993.
9. D. D. Cowan, R. Ierusalimschy, C. J. P. Lucena, and T. M. Stepien. Application Integration: Constructing Composite Applications from Interactive Components. *Software Practice and Experience*, 23(3):255–276, March 1993.
10. D.D. Cowan and C.J.P. Lucena. Abstract Data Views: An Interface Specification Concept to Enhance Design. *IEEE Transactions on Software Engineering*, 21(3):229–243, March 1995.
11. J. Fiadeiro and T. Maibaum. Temporal Theories as Modularization Units for Concurrent System Specification. *Formal Aspects of Computing*, 4(4), 1992.

12. E. Gamma, R. Helm, R. Johnson, and J. Vlissides. *Design Patterns - Elements of Reusable Object-Oriented Software*. Addison-Wesley Publishing Company, Reading, Massachusetts, 1995.
13. Martin Gogolla, Stefan Conrad, and Rudolf Herzig. Sketching Concepts and Computational Model of TROLL Light. In *Proceedings of Int. Conf. Design and Implementation of Symbolic Computation Systems (DISCO'93)*, Berlin, Germany, March 1993. Springer.
14. J. Goguen and R. Burstall. *Introducing Institutions*, volume 164 of *Lecture Notes in Computer Science*. Springer-Verlag, 1984.
15. J. Goguen and R. Burstall. Institutions: Abstract Model Systems Theory. *Journal of the ACM*, 39(1):95–146, 1992.
16. William Harrison and Harold Ossher. Subject-Oriented programming (A Critique of Pure Objects). In *OOPLSA'93*. ACM, 1993.
17. William Harrison, Harold Ossher, Randal B. Smith, and Ungar David. Subjectivity in Object-Oriented Systems, Workshop Summary. In *OOPLSA'94*. ACM, 1994.
18. Bogdan Korel. Automated software test data generation. *IEEE Transactions on Software Engineering*, 16(8):870–879, August 1990.
19. Glenn E. Krasner and Stephen T. Pope. A Cookbook for Using the Model-View-Controller User Interface Paradigm in Smalltalk-80. *JOOP*, pages 26–49, August September 1988.
20. N. Levy and G. Smith. A Language Independent Approach to Specification Construction. In *Proceedings of the SIGSOFT'94*, New Orleans, LA, USA, December 1994.
21. Z. Manna and A. Pnueli. *The Temporal Logic of Reactive and Concurrent Systems*. Springer-Verlag, 1991.
22. Zohar Manna and Amir Pnueli. *The temporal logic of reactive systems: Specification*. Springer-Verlag, 1992.
23. M. Moriconi, X. Qian, and R. A. Riemenschneider. Correct Architecture Refinement. *IEEE Transactions on Software Engineering*, 21(4):356–372, 1995.
24. Y. V. Srinivas and R. Jullig. Specware: Formal Support for Composing Software. In *Proceedings of the Conference on Mathematics of Program Construction*, Kloster Irsee, Germany, 1995.
25. W. M. Turski and T. S. E. Maibaum. *The Specification of Computer Programs*. Addison-Wesley, 1987.

Modular Completeness: Integrating the Reuse of Specified Software in Top-down Program Development*

Job Zwiers[1], Ulrich Hannemann[2], Yassine Lakhneche[2], Willem-Paul de Roever[2], Frank Stomp[3]

[1] Twente University, P. O. Box 217, 7500 AE Enschede, The Netherlands.
Email: zwiers@cs.utwente.nl.

[2] Institut für Informatik und praktische Mathematik, Christian-Albrechts-Universität zu Kiel, Preußerstraße 1-9, 24105 Kiel, Germany.
Email: {uha, yl, wpr}@informatik.uni-kiel.d400.de.

[3] AT&T Bell Laboratories, 600 Mountain Avenue, Murray Hill, NJ 07974, USA.
Email: frank@research.att.com.

Abstract. *Reuse* of correctly specified software is crucial in bottom-up program development. Compositional specification formalisms have been designed to reduce the specification of a syntactically composed construct to specifications of its components, and therefore support top-down development methodology. Thus, the integration of reuse of correctly specified software components in a compositional setting calls for adaptation of a given specification to specifications needed in particular circumstances (depending on their application). Proof systems in which such adaptation steps can be performed whenever they are valid are called *modular complete* [Z89]. We present a generic way of constructing such systems for sequential and concurrent Hoare logics.

1 Introduction

Within software development, *reuse* of correctly specified software modules contributes to the efficiency of the programming process while at the same time improving its reliability. Obviously, such reuse belongs to bottom-up program development. Equally obvious, top-down development is supported best by compositional formalisms which have been designed to reduce the specification of a syntactically composed construct to specifications of its components. Thus, their combination with reuse of correctly specified software components calls for an *integrated* specification methodology in which top-down decomposition is combined with bottom-up composition of given specifications for already developed systems, "residing on the shelf of one's software library". The additional property which such an integrated methodology should satisfy is called *the adaptation*

* The collaboration of the authors has been partially supported by the European Community ESPRIT Basic Research Action Project 6021 (REACT).

property [H71]: whenever satisfaction of a fixed, given, specification implies satisfaction of an alternative specification, *this can be deduced within that methodology.* Such formalisms embody the realization of Lamport's concept of a specification *as a contract between a client and the implementation* [L83], because that specification can now be adapted to any context in which such implied specifications are needed, and hence programming with such specifications becomes possible. Compositional formalisms which additionally satisfy this property are called *modular complete* in [Z89] and represent a formal counterpart of such integrated top-down/bottom-up development methodologies. We present a generic way of constructing modularly complete proof systems for Hoare logics, which especially applies to capturing parallelism, and illustrate this technique for Hoare logics in which the interaction between a process and its parallel environment is characterized by a pair of assumption/commitment in [MC81, ZBR83]. The same technique applies to the rely-guarantee formalism of [J81, Q92] and the presupposition/affirmation style of [P88, PJ91].

Recently the interest in modularly complete formal methods has been revived. In [deB94] a semantic analysis of such logics in compositional settings for distributed communication and shared variable parallelism is presented, [M94] identifies a subset of his temporal interval logic formalism as modular complete, and in [AL94] such a formalism is developed for Lamport's TLA [L91]. Ramesh [R90] also studies the notion of modular *completeness.*

Technically the problem of adaptation is a fundamental one, and emerges already in the context of Hoare style pre/post specifications, where transitions are characterized by pairs of predicates. Where top-down development meets bottom-up, there is in general a gap between a required specification $(\tilde{pre}, \tilde{post})$ and a provided specification $(pre, post)$ in such formalisms. For instance, the bottom up specification might be a translation of a VDM or Z style specification. In that case, the $(pre, post)$ specification is of the form $(\bar{x} = \bar{v}, post(\bar{v}, \bar{x}))$, thus relating the program variables $\bar{x}$ explicitly to so-called *freeze* variables $\bar{v}$. Most likely this does not directly match the required $(\tilde{pre}, \tilde{post})$ specification, and one needs proof rules like the rule of consequence [H69] as well as various substitution rules [G75] in order to derive $(\tilde{pre}, \tilde{post})$ from $(pre, post)$. The adaptation rule from [H71], and also the stronger rules proposed in [O83, D92], look rather complicated, certainly when compared to other rules of Hoare's logic (These adaptation rules apply to *arbitrary* preconditions, whereas [G75] is limited to preconditions of the form $\bar{x} = \bar{v}$.) The same remark applies to the adaptation rules put forward in this paper. Now the way we arrive at these adaptation rules indicates an alternative way to achieve adaptation. The idea is to switch back and forth between a given specification formalism and an alternative formalism, with adaptation carried out in the latter one. In order to do so, we propose here rather simple rules for translating back and forth between Hoare's logic and single predicate specifications in the style of VDM or Z. Adaptation of single predicates boils down to showing logical implication between two predicates, which is easier than adaptation of Hoare style formulae.

We present similar translation rules for the assumption/commitment framework. Here we translate specifications that consist of a pre/post condition together with an assumption/commitment pair to single predicates on traces. Again this reduces the adaptation problem to showing logical implication between predicate logic formulae.

Given the complexity of these adaptation rules, one might wonder whether it wouldn't make sense to stick to single predicate specification formalisms such as VDM. The problem is that such formalisms don't cope conveniently with sequential constructs, and that application of their parallel composition rules requires complicated induction arguments which are rendered superfluous in case of assumption/commitment and rely/guarantee based formalisms.

Section 2 describes a single, unified formalism which is essentially a variation of second order predicate logic. In Sect. 3 a generic solution of the adaptation problem is presented in a sequential setting, which is extended in Sect. 4 to parallelism. Section 5 draws some conclusions.

2 A Uniform Framework

We discuss specification adaptation and modularity for a variety of specification formalisms, both for sequential and concurrent systems. Think of specification of states, specification of state transitions, specification of communication histories etc. Despite this variety of applications we have a single, unified, logic formalism which is essentially a variation of second order predicate logic. Languages for programs, mixed terms, pre/postconditions and correctness formulae are defined as sub-languages of the unified language. One of the advantages of using a unified formalism is that it becomes possible to translate back and forth between sublanguages, where the translation can be carried out fully within the formalism. This is used to ease the adaptation of specifications. A second advantage is that it becomes easier to relate our results to other formalisms based on logic, such as TLA [L91], VDM [J86], Z [S92]. After defining the predicate logic we show how the embedding works out for VDM, Z and Hoare style pre-postcondition specifications, and for trace based CSP specifications.

2.1 Predicate Formulae

We assume given sets of typed first order variables $x \in Var$, and of (second order) relation variables $X \in VAR$. The exact typing scheme is not important for our goal; we only assume that each variable x has an associated type τ and that the type of a relation variable is a pair of lists of first order variables. Variables x can be *decorated*, for instance by means of primes like x', x'', $\overleftarrow{x}$. Such decorated versions are considered to be different variables, of the same type as the undecorated version. Expressions e are built from first order variables x and constants c by means of operations f, where appropriate typing constraints are to be observed, as usual. Relation constants and relation variables are interpreted as $n-ary$ typed relations, where both an arity and a typing are assumed to be associated with each constant R and variable X. We assume that among these relational constants we have at least the equality relation "=", for each first order type τ. Within the syntax of formulae below, it is tacitly assumed that typing constraints are satisfied.

The class of predicate formulae $\phi \in Pred$ is defined by:

$$\phi ::= e_0 = e_1 \mid R(e_0, \ldots, e_{n-1}) \mid X(e_0, \ldots, e_{n-1}) \mid \phi_0 \wedge \phi_1 \mid \neg\phi \mid \forall x.(\phi) \mid \forall X.(\phi)$$

Formulae like $\phi_0 \rightarrow \phi_1$, where $\rightarrow$ denotes implication, are seen as standard abbreviations of *Pred* formulae, and will be used freely. $FV(\phi)$ denotes the free first order variables of ϕ. A more substantial abbreviation that we use is $\mu X.\phi(X)$, denoting the smallest predicate Y such that $\phi(Y)$ is valid.

2.2 The Satisfaction Relation

Below we explain how to embed VDM, Z, Hoare style formulae and trace based CSP specifications in the predicate logic. All these embeddings have in common is that they are based on a general ***satisfaction relation*** "**sat**". A formula of the form ϕ **sat** ψ is defined here as a predicate formula $\forall \bar{x}.(\phi \rightarrow \psi)$. The variables $\bar{x}$ are the so-called ***base variables***, denoted by $base(\phi, \psi)$, of the specifications ϕ and ψ; they are the subset of $FV(\phi, \psi)$ consisting of those variables that refer to the ***observable behavior***. For typical sequential systems, the base of a system or specification is a set of state variables, possibly decorated to distinguish between initial and final state values. On the other hand, trace based specifications for communicating processes are predicates with a single base variable "h" that denotes the communication history of a process. Ready-trace specifications for CSP have a base consisting of a history "h" and a ready set "R". In [Z89] the base of process specifications includes a history h as well as (decorated) local state variables.

The remaining first order variables, i.e. the non-base ones, are denoted by $lvar(\phi)$, and are called the ***logical variables*** of ϕ; in the literature one also refers to these as "freeze variables", or "rigid variables". We assume that syntactic conventions are used to distinguish base variables from logical variables. When relation variable Y occurs within a system S with base $\{\bar{x}, \bar{x}'\}$, then Y without explicit arguments abbreviates $Y(\bar{x}, \bar{x}')$.

2.3 Decorated Identifiers

Sequential programs and ***state transitions*** are relations on states; relations in turn are regarded as predicate formulae where certain variables relate to inputs and other variables relate to outputs. Together these variables constitute the *base* of a specification. In concrete specification languages one employs declarations and suitable syntactic conventions for indicating which variables x are inputs and which are outputs, usually by means of ***decorated identifiers*** like $\overleftarrow{id}$, id', or id°. Here we only assume that $base(\phi)$ is the disjoint union of ***input variables*** $in(\phi)$, ***output variables*** $out(\phi)$. If x is some state variable then we use $\underline{x}$ to denote the undecorated version of x, x' to denote the corresponding output version, and $`x$

to denote the corresponding input version. Note that we employ $\underline{x}$, $\grave{x}$ and $x\acute{}$ not as decorations as such but rather as meta operations on decorated identifiers, that will work out differently for particular formalisms. A few concrete examples:

- For VDM specifications, undecorated identifiers *id* denote outputs, whereas "hooked" identifiers like $\overleftarrow{id}$ denote inputs. So for this case, $\underline{(\overleftarrow{id})}$ as well as $(id)'$ equal *id*, and $\grave{}(id)$ is $\overleftarrow{id}$.
- For Z schemes and TLA formulae, undecorated identifiers *id* denote inputs, whereas "primed" identifiers like *id'* denote outputs. For this case $(id)'$ is *id'*, and $\underline{(id')}$ as well as $\grave{}(id')$ equal *id*.
- In [He84], our notation $\grave{x}$ and $x\acute{}$ is employed, not on the meta level but rather as actual decoration for input and output variables. So, with slight abuse of notation, $(\grave{}(id))\acute{}$ is $id\acute{}$ and $\grave{}(id\acute{})$ is $\grave{id}$.

Decoration applied to predicates ϕ denotes that all relevant variables occurring free in ϕ are decorated.

2.4 Sequential Programs

Sequential ***programs*** can be translated into predicates, too. That is, assume that we have a program S that reads and writes a set of state variables $\bar{x}$. (One says that S is based on $\bar{x}$.) Then one can construct a predicate formulae ϕ_S with base $\grave{\bar{x}}, \bar{x}\acute{}$ that captures the input-output behavior of S. The translation can be given in a compositional style. As an example, if programs S and T can be translated into ϕ_S and ϕ_T, then $S\ ;T$ can be translated into: $\phi_S\ ;\phi_T \stackrel{\text{def}}{=} \exists \bar{z}.(\phi_S[\bar{z}/\bar{x}\acute{}] \wedge \phi_T[\bar{z}/\grave{\bar{z}}])$, where $\bar{z}$ is a list of undecorated identifiers such that $out(\phi_S) \subseteq \{\bar{z}\acute{}\}$, and $in(\phi_T) \subseteq \{\grave{\bar{z}}\}$. In the sequel, we treat programs as (abbreviations of) predicate formulae.

2.5 Predicate Transformers and Hoare's Logic

Let p, q be predicates with $base(p, q) \subseteq \{\bar{x}\}$, and let S be a predicate with $base(S) \subseteq \{\grave{\bar{x}}, \bar{x}\acute{}\}$. Let $\grave{p}$ denote the predicate $p[\grave{\bar{x}}/\bar{x}]$ and let $q\acute{}$ denote the predicate $p[\bar{x}\acute{}/\bar{x}]$. We introduce Hoare formulae, weakest preconditions and strongest postconditions as abbreviations:

$$\{p\}\ S\ \{q\} \text{ abbreviates: } S \textbf{ sat } (\grave{p} \rightarrow q\acute{}).$$

$$wp(S, q) \text{ abbreviates: } \underline{\forall \bar{x}\acute{}.(S \rightarrow q\acute{})}$$

$$sp(p, S) \text{ abbreviates: } \underline{p\acute{}\ ;\ S} \text{ or, equivalently: } \underline{\exists \grave{\bar{x}}.(\grave{p} \wedge S)}$$

Note that the definitions are not limited to predicates S that result from translating a program text. So one can, for instance, calculate $wp(\grave{p} \rightarrow q\acute{}, r)$. This aspect is of vital importance for our results on modular completeness for Hoare's logic.

2.6 Trace Logic and CSP

Trace based specifications are assertions of the form $S(h)$ with free occurrences of a trace typed variable h. A *trace* is a finite sequence of communications, as usual [CH81]. We employ standard notations and operations for traces, such as *concatenation* $t_0 \hat{} t_1$ of traces t_0 and t_1, and *projection* $t \,|\, \alpha$ of trace t onto alphabet α. For a non-empty trace t, i.e. of the form $t_f \hat{} \langle a \rangle$, we denote communication a by $last(t)$ and the remaining sequence t_f by $rest(t)$. The special communication symbol "$\surd$", is used to signal that a process has terminated. We define *sequential composition* $t_0 \,;\, t_1 = t_0$ if $last(t_0) \neq \surd$, and $t_0 \,;\, t_1 = rest(t_0) \hat{} t_1$ if $last(t_0) = \surd$.

It is known from the literature [CH81, Z89] how to assign to a CSP process a trace specification $S(h)$. Within our uniform framework we can thus regard CSP processes as abbreviations of certain trace specifications. The special variable h is the only base variable of such process specification, i.e. all other free variables are logical variables. This implies that a refinement relation of the form "P **sat** Q" must be read as "$\forall h.(P(h) \rightarrow Q(h))$". Depending on whether P and Q are structured as CSP processes or as logical formulae, we call "**sat**" a *refinement relation*, an *implementation relation*, or a *specification adaptation.*

Composition operations for processes fit easily in this approach. As an example, sequential composition $P \,;\, Q$ is defined by: $(P \,;\, Q)(h) = \exists t_0 \exists t_1.(P(t_0) \wedge Q(t_1) \wedge h = t_0 \,;\, t_1)$.

3 Modularity and Specification Adaptation

We now present a generic solution of the adaptation problem in a sequential setting.

3.1 Specification Adaptation: The Problem

Modular design of systems is often a combination of top-down global design and bottom-up reuse of existing modules. A pure top-down approach starts with a first specification S_0, which is then transformed gradually, via a series of intermediate designs $S_1, \ldots S_{n-1}$, into a final program text S_n. An intermediate design, say S_i, is built up from a number of (logical) specifications $\phi_0, \ldots, \phi_m$ by means of programming language constructs, such as sequential composition and iteration. Since they combine programming constructs with logical specifications, the S_i are called *mixed terms*. Mixed term S_i is obtained from S_{i-1} by replacing some sub-term T in S_{i-1} by an implementing mixed term R, i.e. R must be such that R **sat** T is the case. When T actually has the form of a logical specification and R the form of a program, then this describes a classical, top-down development step. When both T and R are programs, then we have a classical program transformation step.

Finally, when both T and R are logical specifications, we are dealing with specification adaptation. Such an adaptation step in the development can become necessary when one would like to implement by some already available module M, where M is known to satisfy specification R. We do not want to verify *directly* that M **sat** T, as this would force us to inspect the internal structure of M. Our programming language might even include encapsulation constructs that does not allow us to inspect this internal structure. Therefore, we have to check indirectly that M **sat** T, by showing that R **sat** T. Because T and R are specifications created by different designers, there might be a substantial "gap" between the two, and consequently verifying that R **sat** T then becomes a non-trivial design step. This is especially the case when at least one of T and R is a pre/post specification.

3.2 Specification Adaptation for Pre/post Specifications

We consider the case where both are pre/post specifications: Assume that T is determined by a pre/post condition pair $pre_T, post_T$, that is, we seek a module "X" such that $\forall \bar{v}.(\{pre_T\}\ X\ \{post_T\})$, where $\bar{v}$ are the logical variables of $pre_T, post_T$. Assume that R is a similar pair of assertions $pre_R, post_R$, with logical variables $lvar(pre_R, post_R) = \bar{u}$. The check "$R$ **sat** T" now boils down to checking that $\forall \bar{u}.(\{pre_R\}\ X\ \{post_R\})$ implies $\forall \bar{v}.(\{pre_T\}\ X\ \{post_T\})$.

This is the problem of specification adaptation, for the case of pre/post specifications. Already in [G75] this problem was considered for proof systems for (parameterless) recursive procedures. In this case pre_R is restricted to be of the form $\bar{x} = \bar{u}$. (A so-called "freeze" predicate.) It was shown that the following set of rules suffices, where we have reformulated the rules in [G75] to fit in our framework:

$$\frac{\tilde{p} \rightarrow p,\ \{p\}\ S\ \{q\},\ q \rightarrow \tilde{q}}{\{\tilde{p}\}\ S\ \{\tilde{q}\}} \quad \text{(Rule of consequence)}$$

$$\frac{\forall v.(\{p\}\ S\ \{q\})}{\forall u.((\{p[u/v]\}\ S\ \{q[u/v]\})}, \text{ provided } v \text{ not free in } S \quad \text{(Substitution)}$$

$$\frac{\{p_i\}\ S\ \{q_i\},\ \text{for } i = 0, 1}{\{p_0 \wedge p_1\}\ S\ \{q_0 \wedge q_1\}} \quad \text{(Conjunction)}$$

$$\frac{\{p(v)\}\ S\ \{q\}}{\{\exists v.(p(v))\}\ S\ \{q\}}, \text{ provided } v \text{ not free in } q, S \quad \text{(Elimination)}$$

$$\{p\}\ S\ \{p\} \quad \text{(Invariance)},$$

provided that p contains no free occurrences of state variables. (Only logical variables are allowed.)

An interesting alternative to this set of rules are the so-called *rules of adaptation*, proposed by Hoare [H71], Dahl [D92], and Olderog [O83]. Each of these three rules can, together with the rule of consequence, replace the set of rules proposed by [G75]. We have listed the rules below, where we have used explicit quantifiers for logical variables around Hoare formulae. (Within pure Hoare logics such quantifiers are left implicit). Let $\{\bar{x}\} = base(p, q, r)$, $\{\bar{u}\} = lvar(p, q)$,

$\{\bar{v}\} = lvar(r)$, $\{\bar{z}\} = \{\bar{u}\} - \{\bar{v}\}$, $\{\bar{w}\} = \{\bar{v}\} - \{\bar{u}\}$, and assume that $lvar(S) \cap lvar(p, q, r) = \emptyset$, and let $\tilde{u}$ be a fresh list of logical variables

$$\frac{\forall \bar{u}.(\{p\}\ S\ \{q\})}{\forall \bar{w}.(\{\exists \bar{z}.(p \wedge \forall \bar{x}.(q \rightarrow r))\}\ S\ \{r\})} \quad \text{(Hoare's rule of adaptation)}$$

$$\frac{\forall \bar{u}.(\{p\}\ S\ \{q\})}{\forall \bar{v}.(\{\exists \tilde{u}.(p[\tilde{u}/\bar{u}] \wedge \forall \bar{x}.(q[\tilde{u}/\bar{u}] \rightarrow r))\}\ S\ \{r\})} \quad \text{(Dahl's rule of adaptation)}$$

$$\frac{\forall \bar{u}.(\{p\}\ S\ \{q\})}{\forall \bar{v}.(\{\forall \bar{x}'.(\forall \bar{u}.(`p \rightarrow q') \rightarrow r')\}\ S\ \{r\})} \quad \text{(Olderog's rule of adaptation)}$$

As analyzed in [O83], the precondition in Olderog's rule is actually the weakest precondition $wp(\forall \bar{u}.(`p \rightarrow q'), r)$. As pointed out in [O83] the precondition in Hoare's rule is not the weakest precondition. As pointed out by [D92], the precondition in Dahl's rule, although weaker than the Hoare's, appears to be the weakest precondition only when a total correctness interpretation for Hoare formulae is assumed.

We present a fourth rule of adaptation, based on the observation that the strongest postcondition $sp(r, \forall \bar{u}.(`p \rightarrow q'))$ is equivalent to the predicate formula $\exists `\bar{x}(`r \wedge \forall \bar{u}(`p \rightarrow q))$.

$$\frac{\forall \bar{u}.(\{p\}S\{q\})}{\forall \bar{v}.(\{r\}S\{\exists `\bar{x}(`r \wedge \forall \bar{u}(`p \rightarrow q))\})} \quad \text{(SP version of rule of adaptation)}$$

The rules of adaptation are somewhat complicated to work with. We therefore propose an alternative set of adaptation rules that cannot be formulated within Hoare logics. Rather they allow one to switch between Hoare style pre/post specifications and VDM or Z style specifications. By switching back and forth, one obtains Olderog's rule of adaptation or our SP version as derived rules. Again we have formulated the rules with explicit quantifiers for logical variables $\bar{u}, \bar{v}$ around Hoare formulae.

$$\frac{\forall \bar{u}.(\{p\}\ S\ \{q\})}{S \textbf{ sat } \forall \bar{u}.(`p \rightarrow q')} \quad \text{(Hoare-SAT)}$$

$$\frac{S \textbf{ sat } \psi}{\forall \bar{v}.(\{wp(\psi, r)\}\ S\ \{r\})} \quad \text{provided } \bar{v} \text{ not free in } S \qquad \text{(SAT-WP)}$$

$$\frac{S \textbf{ sat } \psi}{\forall \bar{v}.(\{r\}\ S\ \{sp(r, \psi)\})} \quad \text{provided } \bar{v} \text{ not free in } S \qquad \text{(SAT-SP)}$$

Actually, the Hoare-SAT rule is an equivalence, that is, $\forall \bar{u}.(\{p\}\ S\ \{q\})$ iff S **sat** $\forall \bar{u}.(`p \rightarrow q')$. This suggests (yet) another way for adaptation of Hoare formulae: If $\forall \bar{u}.(`p \rightarrow q')$ implies $\forall \bar{v}.(`r \rightarrow t')$, then from $\forall \bar{u}.(\{p\}\ S\ \{q\})$ it follows that $\forall \bar{v}.(\{r\}\ S\ \{t\})$. A Hoare style rule along these lines was formulated by Cartwright and Oppen [CO81, O83].

3.3 Modular Completeness

The classical notion of (relative) completeness does not suffice for proof systems aiming at modular verification. This sort of completeness, that we will call *compositional completeness* of a given proof system asserts the following: Assume we have a structured system S, of the form $C(S_1, \ldots, S_n)$ where $n \geq 0$. If $C(S_1, \ldots, S_n)$ **sat** *spec* is a *valid* formula, then *there exist* specifications $spec_i$, such that S_i **sat** $spec_i$ is valid for $1 \leq i \leq n$, and moreover, the proof system allows a *derivation* of $C(S_1, \ldots, S_n)$ **sat** *spec* from the premisses S_i **sat** $spec_i, 1 \leq i \leq n$. Note that the specifications of the S_i can be chosen such as to suit the derivation. For this reason, compositional completeness is the appropriate completeness notion for *top-down* development.

A stronger notion is *modular completeness*. Here one considers systems of the form $S(X_1, \ldots, X_n)$, where the X_i represent modules with a priori given specifications. The idea is that the X_i will be replaced by implementations S_i that satisfy these specifications, but we may neither inspect the internals of the S_i, nor can we design or otherwise influence the given specifications. Modular completeness asserts the following: If $(\bigwedge_{i=1}^{n} X_i \textbf{ sat } spec_i) \rightarrow S(X_1, \ldots, X_n) \textbf{ sat } spec$ is a *valid* formula, the proof system allows a *derivation* of $S(X_1, \ldots, X_n)$ **sat** *spec* from the premisses X_i **sat** $spec_i$. In full generality, we also allow for the case where one module X_i has several (complementary) specifications. We call a proof system *strong adaptation complete* if whenever a formula of the form

$$(\bigwedge_{1 \leq j \leq n} X_{i_j} \textbf{ sat } spec_j) \rightarrow X \textbf{ sat } spec$$

is valid, then it is *derivable* within the proof system. In this definition, X_{i_j} is the variable Y such that X_j and Y are syntactically the same, $1 \leq i_j \leq n$, and X is any of the variables $X_1, \ldots, X_n$. *Adaptation completeness* is defined as strong adaptation completeness but with $n = 1$.

Lemma 1. *A proof system that is both compositionally complete and strong adaptation complete is modularly complete.*

The adaptation rules for Hoare's logic presented in previous sections aim at adaptation completeness. It is easy to change them into rules that achieve *strong* adaptation completeness. For instance, our SP-adaptation rule becomes:

$$\frac{\bigwedge_{i=1}^{n} \forall \bar{u}.(\{p_i\}S\{q_i\})}{\forall \bar{v}.(\{r\}S\{\exists \grave{\bar{x}}(\grave{r} \wedge \forall \bar{u}(\bigwedge_{i=1}^{n}(\grave{p}_i \rightarrow q_i))))\}} \quad \text{(Strong SP adaptation)}$$

We end this section with two lemmata which formalize the relationship between modular completeness and top-down program development.

Lemma 2. *Let $S(X_1, \cdots, X_n)$ be a system. Consider pairwise distinct variables $Y_1, \cdots, Y_m$ all in $\{X_1, \cdots, X_n\}$, and sets of indices $I_j = \{i \mid 1 \leq i \leq n$, and Y_j and X_i denote the same variable$\}$, $j = 1, \cdots, m$. If the formula $\bigwedge_{1 \leq i \leq n} X_i \textbf{ sat } spec_i$ is valid, then (a) and (b) are equivalent:*

*(a) $S(X_1, \cdots, X_n)$ **sat** spec is valid.*
(b) For all formulae $S_1, \cdots, S_m$ whose relation variables are all among $X_1, \cdots, X_n$, the formula $((\bigwedge_{1 \leq j \leq m} \bigwedge_{k \in I_j} S_k \textbf{ sat } spec_j) \rightarrow S' \textbf{ sat } spec)$ is valid. Here, S' is the formula obtained from $S(X_1, \cdots, X_n)$ by substituting S_j for every variable Y_j, $1 \leq j \leq m$.

As an immediate consequence we of this lemma we obtain its proof theoretic counterpart:

Corollary 3. *Let T be a modularly complete proof system. Using the same notation as in the previous lemma, and assuming that* $\bigwedge_{1\leq i\leq n} X_i$ **sat** *spec*$_i$ *is derivable in T, (a) and (b) are equivalent:*

(a) S **sat** *spec is derivable in T.*
(b) For all formulae $S_1, \cdots, S_m$ *whose relation variables are all among* $X_1, \cdots, X_n$, $((\bigwedge_{1\leq j\leq m} \bigwedge_{k\in I_j} S_k$ **sat** *spec*$_j) \rightarrow S'$ **sat** *spec) is derivable in T.*

4 Modular Completeness for Concurrent Processes

For CSP processes various specification and verification styles are known. We discuss some of these, in particular the issue of specification adaptation for such formal systems.

4.1 "SAT" Proof Systems and Generalized Hoare Logic

Simple proof systems have been built around the "sat" relation. [H71, Z89, O83] Specification adaptation is rather straightforward here, which is certainly one of the advantages of such "SAT" systems: Let $P(h)$ and $Q(h)$ be logical specifications. Then it is clear that $\forall X.((X \textbf{ sat } P) \rightarrow (X \textbf{ sat } Q))$ iff P **sat** Q. The latter formula abbreviates $\forall h.(P(h) \rightarrow Q(h))$, which is a simple verification condition. Proof rules for "**sat**" formulae are easily formulated, but the rules for sequential constructs are not very helpful. For example, in the conclusion of:

$$\frac{P_0 \textbf{ sat } Q_0 \,,\; P_1 \textbf{ sat } Q_1}{P_0 \,;\, P_1 \textbf{ sat } Q_0 \,;\, Q_1} \qquad \text{(Sequential Composition)}$$

the specification $Q_0 \,;\, Q_1$ still contains a sequential operator, that can be eliminated only at the expense of introducing an existential quantifier. A "nicer" rule can be obtained by mimicking Hoare's logic within the SAT system. For any trace predicate S, define a *relation* on traces "$;\, S$" as follows:

$$(\,;\, S)(h, h') = \exists h''.(S(h'') \wedge h' = h \,;\, h'').$$

Note that $;\, S$, as any relation, can be specified by Hoare formulae or predicate transformers. A novel aspect is that within $\{P\} \;;\, S\;\{Q\}$ the pre and postconditions P and Q are *trace* specifications and so, could be CSP processes themselves. The Hoare formula above is equivalent to the "**sat**" formula $P\,;\, S$ **sat** Q; a correspondence between a SAT formula and a Hoare formula that resembles the concept of *weakest prespecifications* [HHS87]. Simplicity of this specification style shows up clearly with the rules for sequential composition and iteration; for example:

$$\frac{\{P\} \;;\, S_0\;\{R\}, \{R\} \;;\, S_1\;\{Q\}}{\{P\} \;;\, (S_1 \,;\, S_2)\;\{Q\}} \qquad \text{(Sequential composition)}$$

The adaptation rules for Hoare's logic apply here too. Yet it appears simpler to *specify* reusable modules by means of **sat** specifications. Then, when placed within a sequential context, a **sat** specification S *sat* T can be adapted to a Hoare formulae $\{P\}$; S $\{P\,;\,T\}$, for any precondition P.

4.2 Extensions of the Hoare Style System for CSP Processes

For practical verification purposes, the Hoare style system for CSP is still not very convenient. Consider a formula $\{P\}\ S\ \{Q\}$. The postcondition Q is required to hold for all traces of the system $P\,;\,S$, that is, both for traces that end in a "$\surd$" and for those that do not. Intuitively, the traces ending with a "$\surd$" correspond to executions in which control is after process S, whereas traces without such a "tick" correspond to intermediate stages of the execution of process S. In [ZRE84] a class of formulae was introduced where pre/postconditions describe only traces ending with "$\surd$", corresponding to snapshots before and after execution of S, and where the specification of traces without "$\surd$" is delegated to a *trace invariant* I. Let "FIN" be the predicate "$last(h) = \surd$". Then we define $(I\ :\ \{P\}\ S\ \{Q\})$ as an abbreviation for $\{I \wedge (FIN \rightarrow P)\}\ ;\ S\ \{I \wedge (FIN \rightarrow Q)\}$.

This specification style separates local conditions, such as pre- and postcondition, from the interface towards the entire system without losing the simplicity of the rules of Hoare's logic. Moreover, we can restrict ourselves to assertions for I, P and Q, where these special FIN predicates do not occur anymore in contrast to the Hoare style where they are inevitable [Z89]. Typical proof rules in this style are (details concerning side conditions omitted):

$$\frac{I_0 : \{P_0\}\ S_0\ \{Q_0\},\ I_1 : \{P_1\}\ S_1\ \{Q_1\}}{I_0 \wedge I_1 : \{P_0 \wedge P_1\}\ S_0 \| S_1\ \{Q_0 \wedge Q_1\}} \quad \text{(provided } chanbase(I_i, Q_i) \subseteq \alpha(S_i))$$

$$\frac{I : \{P\} S_0 \{R\}\ ,\ \{R\} S_1 \{Q\}}{I : \{P\} S_0\ ;\ S_1 \{Q\}}$$

An invariant formula $I : \{\ P\ \}\ S\ \{\ Q\ \}$ is equivalent to S **sat** $I : P \leadsto Q$, where $(I : P \leadsto Q)(h)\ \equiv\ \forall t.((FIN(t) \wedge P(t)) \rightarrow (I(t\,;\,h) \wedge (FIN(t\,;\,h) \rightarrow Q(t\,;\,h))))$
This allows for a straightforward adaptation rule:

$$(I : \{P\}\ X\ \{Q\})\ \rightarrow\ (J : \{R\}\ X\ \{T\}) \quad \text{iff} \quad (I : P \leadsto Q)\ \mathbf{sat}\ (J : R \leadsto T).$$

It is possible to present a direct adaptation rule, without switching to "**sat**" formulae, along similar lines as for the case of Hoare formulae:

$$\frac{I : \{\ P\ \}\ S\ \{\ Q\ \}}{sinv(R, (I : P \leadsto Q)) : \{\ R\ \}\ S\ \{\ sp(R, (I : P \leadsto Q))\ \}} \quad \text{(Adaptation)}$$

where $sinv(R, (I\!: P \leadsto Q)) = R; ((I\!: P \leadsto Q)[\mathbf{true}/FIN(t),\ \mathbf{false}/FIN(t;\,h)])$
$sp(R, (I : P \leadsto Q))\ = R\,; ((I : P \leadsto Q)[\mathbf{true}/FIN(t),\ \mathbf{true}/FIN(t\,;\,h)])$.

4.3 Misra/Chandy Specification Style

An *Assumption/Commitment* style was introduced by Misra and Chandy [MC81] to ease inductive forms of reasoning for distributed processes. An *assumption* A refers to the expected communication behavior of the environment and a *commitment* C refers to the communications of the specified module. Proof rules for a state-trace based model were given in [ZBR83] and [ZRE84] as derivations of rules of the invariant system. A compositional complete proof system in this Assumption/Commitment style has been given in [P88], called *P-A Logic*. Here, we introduce assumption/commitment pairs as abbreviations:

Definition 4 A/C Invariants. Let A, C be trace assertions. We abbreviate $(h \neq \langle\rangle \rightarrow A(rest(h)))$ by $\bullet A(h)$; $\forall h'(h' \leq h.(P(h')))$ by $\mathcal{K}ern(P)(h)$; and $\mathcal{K}ern(\mathcal{K}ern(\bullet A(h)) \rightarrow C(h))(h)$ by $(A, C)(h)$.

An assumption/commitment specification is a formula of the form: (A, C) : $\{P\}\ S\ \{Q\}$. Since this is just a special case of the formulae we discussed above, rules like the one for parallel composition remain valid. For example, if we have specifications of the form (A_i, C_i) : $\{P_i\}\ S_i\ \{Q_i\}$, for $i = 0, 1$, then the rule yields a specification for $S_0 \parallel S_1$ of the form:

$$(A_0, C_0) \wedge (A_1, C_1)\ :\ \{P_0 \wedge P_1\}\ S_0 \parallel S_1\ \{Q_0 \wedge Q_1\}.$$

The invariant of this formula can be rewritten into assumption/commitment style again provided that, for some assertion A, $(A \wedge C_i) \rightarrow A_{i-1}$ for $i = 0, 1$. For, under these assumptions, a proof by induction on the length of traces shows that $((A_0, C_0) \wedge (A_1, C_1))$ **sat** $(A, C_0 \wedge C_1)$.

It will be clear that *adaptation* of assumption/commitment formulae can be achieved by translating such formulae to corresponding "**sat**" formulae [Ha94]. Finally, one can even formulate a, rather complex, adaptation rule within the Assumption/Commitment formalism itself:

Rule 1 (Adaptation Rule)

$$\frac{(A,C) : \{\ P\ \}\ S\ \{\ Q\ \}}{\begin{array}{c}(A', \bullet(\mathcal{K}ern(A')) \wedge (sinv(R, ((A,C) : P \leadsto Q)))) : \\ \{\ R\ \}\ S\ \{\ \mathcal{K}ern(\mathcal{K}ern(A')) \wedge sp(R, ((A,C) : P \leadsto Q))\ \}\end{array}}$$

The derivation of this rule within the assumption/commitment framework follows the same pattern as before as indicated by the close relationship to the invariant system.

5 Conclusion

We have shown how to approach the problem of specification adaptation for a variety of formal proof systems, both for sequential and for parallel programs. Basically, there are two approaches:

1. Formulate special adaptation rules *within the formal system itself*
2. Formulate transformation rules for *switching back and forth between the given formalism and other, more basic, formalisms.* Adaptation is then carried out in the more basic formalism.

We have illustrated our theory for the sequential case by showing how to translate between Hoare logic, predicate transformers and VDM or Z style specifications. For CSP processes we reduced Misra/Chandy style specifications to invariant formulae, then invariant formulae to (generalized) Hoare formulae, and finally Hoare formulae to SAT formulae. It is interesting to see that on the most basic level, both sequential and concurrent processes can be formalized in essentially the *same* SAT formalism. Moreover, the adaptation problem for SAT systems boils down to showing logical implication between predicates.

To carry out our programme we relied on a *uniform logical framework*. This framework makes it easy to combine, and to translate between, different formalisms.

References

[AL94] Abadi, M., and Lamport L.: *Conjoining Specifications*, DEC Systems Research Center, Research report (1994)

[A81] Apt, K. R.: *Ten Years of Hoare's Logic, A Survey, Part I*, ACM Transactions on Programming Languages and Systems **3**:4 (1981) 431–483

[deB94] de Boer, F.: *Compositionality in the Inductive Assertion Method for Concurrent Systems*, IFIP TC 2 Working Conference on programming concepts, methods and calculi (1994)

[CO81] Cartwright, R., and Oppen, D.: *The logic of aliasing*, Acta Informatica **15** (1981) 365–384

[CH81] Chen, Z. C., and Hoare, C. A. R.: *Partial correctness of CSP*, Conf. on Distr. Comp. Sys. (1981)

[D92] Dahl Ole-Johan: *Verifiable Programming*, Prentice Hall (1992)

[D76] Dijkstra, E. W.: *A discipline of programming*, Prentice-Hall (1976)

[G94] Gibbs, W. W.: *Software's Chronic Crisis* Scientific American **9** (1994)

[GM93] Gordon, M. J. C., and Melham, T. F.: *Introduction to HOL – A theorem proving environment for higher order logic*, Cambridge University Press (1993)

[G75] Gorelick, G. A.: *A complete axiomatic system for proving assertions about recursive programs and non-recursive programs*, TR **75**, University of Toronto (1975)

[H69] Hoare, C. A. R.: *The axiomatic basis of programming*, Communications of the ACM (1969)

[H71] Hoare, C. A. R.: *Procedures and parameters: An axiomatic approach*, Lecture Notes in Mathematics (1971) 102–116

[HHS87] Hoare, C. A. R., He Jifeng, and Sanders, J. W.: *Prespecification in Data Refinement*, Information Processing Letters **25** (1987)

[He84] Hehner, E. C. R.: *Predicative Programming, part I and II*, Communications of the ACM **27** (1984)

[Ha94] Hannemann, U.: *Modular complete proof systems for distributed processes*, M. Sc. thesis, University of Kiel (1994)

[J81] Jones, Cliff B.: *Development methods for computer programs including a notion of interference*, Oxford (1981)

[J86] Jones, Cliff B.: *Systematic software development using VDM*, Prentice-Hall (1986)

[L83] Lamport, L.: *Specifying concurrent program modules*, ACM Transactions on Programming Languages and Systems **6**(2) (1983)

[L91] Lamport, L.: *The Temporal Logic of Actions*,DEC Systems Research Center (1991)

[MP91] Manna, Z., and Pnueli, A.: *The Temporal Logic of Reactive and Concurrent Systems*, Springer Verlag (1991)

[M88] Meyer, B.: *Object-Oriented Software Construction*, Prentice-Hall (1988)

[MC81] Misra, J., and Chandy, K. M.: *Proofs of networks of processes*, IEEE Transactions on Software Engineering **7**:4 (1981)

[M94] Moszkowski, B.: *Some very compositional temporal properties*, IFIP TC 2 Working Conference on programming concepts, methods and calculi (1994)

[O83] Olderog, E. R.: *On the Notion of Expressiveness and the Rule of Adaptation*, Theoretical Computer Science **24** (1983) 337–347

[P88] Pandya, P: *Compositional Verification of Distributed Programs*, Ph. D. thesis, Tata Institute of Fundamental Research, Bombay (1988)

[PJ91] P. Pandya, and M. Joseph: *P-A logic – a compositional proof system for distributed programs* Distributed Computing **5** (1991)

[R90] Ramesh, S.: *On the Completeness of Modular Proof Systems*, Information Processing Letters **36** (1990) 195–201

[S92] Spivey, Mike: *The Z notation: A reference manual*, Prentice-Hall (1992)

[Q92] Xu Qiwen: *A theory of state-based parallel programming*, Oxford (1992)

[Z89] Zwiers, J.: *Compositionality, Concurrency and Partial Correctness*, Lecture Notes in Computer Science **321** (1989)

[ZBR83] Zwiers, J., de Bruin, A., and de Roever, W. -P.: *A proof system for partial correctness of Dynamic Networks of Processes*, Lecture Notes in Computer Science **164** (1984)

[ZRE84] Zwiers, J., de Roever W. -P., and van Emde Boas, P.: *Compositionality and concurrent networks: soundness and completeness of a proof system.* TR **57**, Nijmegen (1984)

[ZRE85] Zwiers, J., de Roever, W. -P., and van Emde Boas, P.: *Compositionality and concurrent networks: soundness and completeness of a proof system*, Lecture Notes in Computer Science **194** (1985)

A Strategic Approach to Transformational Design

Jürgen Bohn & Wil Janssen *
University of Oldenburg **

Abstract. Designing parallel systems in a correct way is difficult. Transformational design of systems guarantees correctness by the correctness of the transformations, but is often tedious and complicated. We discuss different *transformation strategies* to guide the designer from the initial specification to different implementations, tailored to different architectures. Strategies give rise to simpler transformation rules, point the way in the design trajectory, and allow for the reuse of proofs and transformation steps when deriving optimizations and variants of algorithms.

1 Introduction

Correct design of parallel and distributed algorithms and protocols is a difficult task. Such algorithms are often the result of numerous design decisions and architectural optimizations, and are therefore very hard to prove correct. When designing such systems in a *transformational way* from a specification, correctness with respect to the initial specification is obtained for free due to the correctness of the transformation steps.

Although transformational design in principle solves the correctness issue, it is very hard to apply to larger systems. In developing systems transformationally one often has an abundance of choices between different transformation rules. It is difficult to decide which way to go, and decisions taken at an early stage can have severe influences in the rest of the design trajectory. Thus it is very easy to "get lost" in the design process. Moreover, transformation rules are often rather complicated as they are designed for a general setting. Also they often concern only small steps, leading to a very long design trajectory. Finally, having derived one algorithm, it would be desirable to be able to reuse the proofs and steps used in other derivations of similar systems.

In such a transformational design process the design engineer needs guidance in order to keep him or her from getting lost. We propose the use of *strategies* for this purpose. A strategy describes *what type of transformation should be applied at what stage of the design process.* One can think of many different strategies for developing parallel systems. A first strategy is called the *layered strategy.* In this strategy the first steps in the design are restricted to *sequential* or layered program development. After having obtained a sufficient level of detail the resulting design is then parallelized to

* This work was partially supported by the Deutsche Forschungsgemeinschaft under grant No. Ol 98/1-1.

** Fachbereich Informatik, P.O. Box 2503, D-26111 Oldenburg, Germany. E-mail: {Juergen.Bohn,Wil.Janssen}@informatik.uni-oldenburg.de

meet the desired architecture, and finally implemented. Examples of this approach are the work by Elrad and Francez [8], by Chou and Gafni [7], Stomp [23], and by Janssen, Poel and Zwiers [14, 13].

A second strategy is the *parallel* strategy, where at the initial stages one is not concerned about architectural issues but simply views the system as a set of continuously executing actions. In the later stages one then introduces architectural decisions as optimizations, leading to an implementable algorithm. The most prominent example of this approach is the UNITY approach as developed by Chandy and Misra [6]. The work by Back and Sere on action systems [1, 2] also takes this viewpoint.

A third strategy is called the *architectural strategy,* where one aims at a specific architecture already at the very initial design stages, thus giving a more direct design trajectory. This approach has been employed by Olderog et al. in the ProCoS project [18, 19, 20].

Having recognized a certain strategy one can develop specialized rules that are tailored for certain design stages and therefore can be much more restricted and thus simpler. Due to the simplicity, such strategies can be amenable for tool support. Also, if a certain strategy applies nicely to a class of algorithms, the derivations of the different algorithms in that class often share large parts and have similar steps at similar stages. Thus strategies encourage reuse of proofs.

In this paper we discuss the three strategies mentioned above, and use them to derive different implementations of *atomic commit protocols* for different architectures, such as Centralized Two-Phase Commit, Linear Two-Phase Commit, and Decentralized Two-Phase Commit (see Bernstein, Hadzilacos and Goodman [3] for a discussion of these protocols). Atomic commit protocols are used in distributed database systems to guarantee consistent termination of transactions that are executed at different sites in a database network.

As a vehicle for transformational design we use the mixed terms approach as has been developed in the ProCoS project [19]. There a specification language SL has been developed that allows to specify reactive behavior by means of regular expressions, as well as state transitions in Z style. Such specifications are also part of a mixed terms language `MIX` which allows to transform specifications up to a point where they correspond to CSP style language constructs [12] and can be implemented in OCCAM. As SL allows to specify both aspects, reactive behavior and state transitions, it is very well suited to handle the different aspects of the different strategies. Besides that, the transformational theory for SL and `MIX` is well developed [5, 20, 19].

For a detailed account of the different transformations and a discussion of the derivations of other architectures we refer to [4].

2 Strategies and Their Ingredients

In the introduction we mentioned three different strategies to develop parallel and distributed systems transformationally. In this section we discuss these strategies in more detail, and list what types of transformations are needed for such strategies to work out nicely. Different strategies also have different application areas they are most suited for.

By no means we want to claim that these three are the *only* strategies one can think of, but they are three well-known approaches to program development and therefore we restrict ourselves to these three.

2.1 The layered approach

The design and analysis of sequential programs is inherently much simpler than of parallel programs. One does not have to take interference of other components into account, and no deadlock can occur due to synchronization. For parallel and distributed systems it has been observed that they often can be analyzed in a sequential or *layered* fashion as well. This is already obvious from the terminology used: one talks about "two-phase" or "three-phase" commit protocols, termination "phases" or connection "phases" in communication protocols etcetera. Such "phases" are also sometimes called *layers*, which should not be mistaken for the term "layers" as used in the OSI reference model.

Elrad and Francez [8] used this observation to formulate the so-called *communication closed layers principle* that states that under certain circumstances a layered and a parallel program are equivalent. This principle has later been used in a transformational setting by, amongst others, Stomp [23] and by Janssen, Poel and Zwiers [14, 13]. Similar ideas of independence also play a crucial role in parallelization of loops in conventional programs (see, for example, Lengauer [16]). Also in the work by Back and Sere [2] one uses transformations to go from initial a sequentially structured solution to parallel implementations. Their work is formulated using *action systems.*

Based on these ideas we can formulate the following layered strategy.

(L1) Given a specification or initial design (that is correct by definition), repeatedly decompose the specification in sequence of (abstract) actions, using standard techniques as known for sequential program development.

(L2) If one arrives at a sufficient level of detail, for example at an implementable level, the resulting algorithm is analyzed for possible parallelization: Independence of actions indicates potential parallelism, where independence is determined on syntactic grounds or on semantic grounds in the most general case.

(L3) Finally, the resulting system consisting of the parallel composition of sequential components is transformed into a real, fine-tuned implementation.

Note that in this strategy there is not explicit reasoning on parallelism, only independence analysis is needed. For this strategy to be applicable one requires easy laws for sequential decomposition and independence analysis. It has been shown in the work mentioned above that this strategy is applicable to a large class of systems, although it is by no means a complete strategy.

2.2 The parallel approach

A similar idea of avoiding architectural bias also is the basis of the parallel approach. In this strategy, as for example employed in the work on UNITY [6] by Chandy and Misra, or by Back and Sere using *action systems* [2], one first derives an unstructured but complete implementation, after which one defines a mapping of actions and variables to processes satisfying the constraints induced by the desired architecture.

This approach goes through the following phases.

(P1) Given a certain specification of the problem, develop a set of actions as basic ingredients of the eventual implementation.

(P2) Prove that all runs consisting of the actions in the set under a weakly fair scheduling policy lead to a stable state satisfying the desired end state.

(P3) Define a mapping of variables to processors, and define sequences of actions from the initial action set that are weakly fair for each processor, satisfying constraints induced by the communication structure between the processors.

(P4) Rewrite the initial unstructured solution under the mappings defined in a previous step to an actual implementation.

The most difficult part in this is proving that the actions indeed lead to the desired stable state. For this one can use, for example, the UNITY logic as introduced in [6]. Also, depending on the desired architecture, the definition of the mappings can require encoding of channels or buffers, which is not always as natural as one would hope for. In general however, the application area of this approach is not limited to a specific class of algorithms.

2.3 The architectural approach

In the layered and parallel strategies the architectural decisions are postponed to as late as possible, allowing different implementations. However, often one has a very clear idea of the architecture the system should function in, for example a fully connected network with n nodes, or a two processor shared memory architecture. Incorporating such information at a very early stage might allow to simplify intermediate specifications or systems to a large extent.

This approach has been taken in the ProCoS project to design synchronously operating parallel CSP style systems [18, 5]. The architectural approach goes through the following four phases:

(A1) Given an initial specification, one adds to this specification the synchronization skeleton of the system one is aiming at, so for each process the sequence of synchronizing actions is specified.

(A2) The state space of each process is extended with the required local variables.

(A3) For every action, the corresponding state transformation part of the initial specification is moved to it, making the initial specification redundant.

(A4) Analogously as for the layered approach, the resulting system is transformed into an implementation.

Addition of synchronization skeletons and moving (parts of) state transformations are two important ingredients here. Both transformations can be performed very nicely in the mixed terms language MIX, as is discussed in section 4. Moreover, this approach is not bound to a certain class of algorithms, although due to its directness, reuse and structuring of proofs seems to be more difficult.

3 Atomic Commit Protocols

Distributed systems consist of a collection of *sites* that are connected by means of some network. In a distributed database system an important concept is maintaining *consistency* of the different sites. Each site has a local database system that maintains a part of the distributed database. A *distributed transaction* consists of a sequence of reads and writes to database items. We assume every transaction T has a "home site" where it originated. Termination of a transaction T is intricate, as it concerns *all* sites that participated in T. Simply sending a message to a site stating that it should commit is not sufficient: it is possible that — for example due to failures of storage media or volatile memory — a site cannot store the changes to the database, and therefore cannot commit. The fact that a single site is not able to commit should result in aborting the transaction, which implies aborting at all sites involved in order to keep the distributed database consistent.

An algorithm that guarantees consistent termination of distributed transactions is called an *Atomic Commit Protocol* (ACP). We assume the transaction involves a coordinator process C at the home site, and a set of participating processes P for all sites that were accessed. Every participating process has one vote: YES or NO, and every process can reach one of two decisions: COMMIT or ABORT. An ACP should guarantee that every process votes, and eventually makes a decision, where the decision should be COMMIT iff every process voted YES, and ABORT otherwise. (See [3] for details.)

A well-known example of an ACP is the *Two-Phase Commit Protocol* (TPC), which operationally behaves as follows. After the process at the home site (the *coordinator*) has received a signal it requests all participating processes to send their votes. When it has gathered all votes it decides according to these votes and sends the decision back to all participants, which decide accordingly. This protocol is formulated for a system with a coordinator that can communicate with all participants, which is called *centralized* TPC. There exist also solutions for other network architectures. For example, if we have a fully connected network, all processes can send their votes to all other processes, after which every process can make the decision itself. This is called *decentralized* TPC.

4 Specifications and Implementations

The ESPRIT Basic Research Actions ProCoS I and II investigate the trustworthy design of embedded systems over the whole development process ranging from requirements capture over specification and programming level down to transputer machine code [9]. As part of this project a refinement calculus for communicating systems was developed in order to provide a constructive and mathematically sound way for bridging the gap between specifications and programs [17, 20]. From ProCoS we take the specification language SL [20] for communicating systems. SL combines regular expressions, process algebra and action systems.

Simple specifications in SL consists of an interface Δ, a set *TA* of trace assertions, a set *IV* of local variables and a set *CA* of communication assertions, written as

$$\texttt{system}\ \Delta\ TA\ IV\ CA\ \texttt{end}.$$

The interface provides a static view of the specified system. Components from Δ are directed channels (input or output) and global typed variables (read or write).

Trace assertions have the form "`trace on` α `in` re," where the alphabet α is a set of channels from Δ and re is a regular expression over α. They define sequencing constraints on the global communication order using regular expressions over channel names, that is any sequence of communications projected to α has to be a word in the language defined by re. Using more than one trace assertion allows to focus on different aspects concerning different channel sets separately.

The state part of a specification encompasses local variable declarations and communication assertions. In the style of Z [21] and TLA [15], the latter specify what the values are that are communicated and how the single communication actions will change the system state. Such communication assertions are of the form

$$\texttt{com}\ a\ \texttt{read}\ \bar{x}\ \texttt{write}\ \bar{y}\ \texttt{when}\ wh(\bar{x},\bar{y})\ \texttt{then}\ th(\bar{x},\bar{y},\bar{y}'),$$

where $\bar{x}$ and $\bar{y}$ are lists of variables read and written respectively, and wh is a predicate defining when action a is enabled, and where th specifies the result of the action. As in, for example, Z we use primed versions of variables to refer to their new values after the communication. We use the channel or action names prefixed by the symbol "@" as logical variables referring to the values communicated on these channels. Simple specifications may be enriched by local channels and state restrictions such as initializations and invariants.

As the target programming language we consider an OCCAM-like language PL, with basic processes SKIP, STOP, assignment, input and output communications, WHILE loops and compositional operators for sequences, alternatives, conditionals and concurrency.

To perform transformations from SL to PL we work in a "combined language" MIX which contains SL and PL as subsets. MIX consists of so-called *mixed terms* that may apply program operators to specifications. The transformational approach is based on a common semantic model for SL, PL and MIX. It is a *trace-state-readiness* model [20], which is well suited for describing all features such as synchronous communication, parallelism, nondeterminism and states.

Starting from a given SL specification *Spec*, a correct implementation *Prog* is derived by iterated application of transformation rules such that the specification notation is gradually replaced by PL constructs.

$$Spec \equiv S_1 \Lleftarrow \cdots \Lleftarrow S_n \equiv Prog$$

Typically a transition step from mixed term S_i to S_{i+1} is performed by replacing some specification expression S in S_i by a mixed term T where the refinement $T \Rrightarrow S$ or even $T \equiv S$ is guaranteed by a transformation rule. Then the overall implementation correctness follows from the transitivity of "$\Rrightarrow$" and the monotonicity of all operators with respect to "$\Rrightarrow$."

4.1 Specifying Atomic Commit

Let us now explain the concepts of SL by the starting specification of the *ACP*. The idea is that the protocol performs a state transformation that we model by a single action *ACP*. Thus the only trace assertion is

$$\texttt{trace on } ACP \texttt{ in } ACP,$$

where *ACP* is an local channel/action and the regular expression ACP states that the protocol is executed once only.

To describe the state space of the system we use local variables as follows: The vote given by every process is stored in a variable $vote_i$ and the decision taken by every process in dec_i. The fact that every process has a way of checking whether or not it can COMMIT if needed is modeled by a boolean flag $stable_i$ for each process i. Since this decision is not done by the protocol but by the environment $stable_i$ is a read variable in the interface (for all $i = 1..n$). The state transformation is specified by a single communication assertion for *ACP*.

The result is the specification presented in figure 1. In particular it states that from

$$
\begin{array}{l}
ACP = \texttt{system} \\
\quad\quad \texttt{chan } ACP \\
\quad\quad \texttt{trace } ACP \\
\quad\quad \texttt{read } stable_1, \ldots, stable_n \texttt{ of Bool} \\
\quad\quad \texttt{write } vote_1, \ldots, vote_n \texttt{ of } \{\text{YES}, \text{NO}\} \\
\quad\quad\quad\quad dec_1, \ldots, dec_n \texttt{ of } \{\text{COMMIT}, \text{ABORT}\} \\
\quad\quad \texttt{com } ACP \texttt{ when true} \\
\quad\quad\quad\quad \texttt{then } \bigwedge_{i=1..n} (vote'_i = \text{YES} \Leftrightarrow stable_i \wedge \\
\quad\quad\quad\quad\quad\quad vote'_i = \text{NO} \Leftrightarrow \neg stable_i \wedge \\
\quad\quad\quad\quad\quad\quad dec'_i = \text{COMMIT} \Leftrightarrow \bigwedge_j vote'_j = \text{YES} \wedge \\
\quad\quad\quad\quad\quad\quad dec'_i = \text{ABORT} \Leftrightarrow \bigvee_j vote'_j = \text{NO}\,) \\
\quad \texttt{end}
\end{array}
$$

Fig. 1. Starting specification of *ACP*.

any initial state the protocol should terminate in a state where the decision for each process is COMMIT iff every process voted YES. Furthermore a process shall vote YES iff $stable_i$ was true. Depending on the requirements of the environment the specification may terminate after an application or reach a stable state where it is ready for another protocol run.

4.2 A transformation rule

In a transformational setting we use decomposition rules to refine systematically specifications like ACP. Decomposition means here that a more complex specification is replaced by a mixed term where some composition operator is applied to several simpler subsystems. As a typical example supporting this kind of refinements, figure 2 shows a

SYN: Parallel decomposition of specifications	

`system` Δ TA CA `end` $\equiv$	`SYN[ system` Δ_1 TA_1 CA_1 `end,`
	`...,`
	`system` Δ_n TA_n CA_n `end ]`

Provided $\Delta = \bigcup_{\Vert} \Delta_i$, $TA = \bigcup TA_i$, and $CA = \bigcup CA_i$ with $n \geq 1$ and	

Fig. 2. Transformation rule SYN decomposition.

general transformation rule which introduces the synchronization operator SYN. Generally a side condition "provided..." restricts the applicability of the transformation rule and describes how the new mixed term is derived by syntactic modifications from the given one.

At the end of the design process simple specifications are replaced in transformation steps by basic PL statements as for example input or output communications or assignments. Figure 3 shows appropriate equivalences of specification and programming constructs. Other simple specifications can be transformed into these patterns and are therefore automatically implementable.

```
c?v ≡ system                    c!e ≡ system
        input c write v                 output c read free(e)
        trace on c in c                 trace on c in c
        com c write v                   com c read free(e)
          then v' = @c                    then @c = e
      end                             end
```

Fig. 3. Meaning of input and output communication statements in PL

5 A Layered Derivation of TPC

As a first derivation we will use the layered strategy to go from the initial specification ACP to an implementation. The protocol we will aim at will be centralized TPC where a single coordinator process communicates with a set of participating processes.

The layered strategy uses two important ingredients: sequential decomposition and independence analysis. We first define specialized transformation rules to do so.

5.1 Decomposition and independence rules

The general idea for sequential decomposition is rather simple. Assume we have a complicated action a. If we can split a into two actions a_1 and a_2 such that the combined effect of executing a_1 and a_2 after one another is equivalent to a, then we would like to replace a by the sequence $a_1.a_2$. The general rule to do so is rather complicated: one has to ensure atomicity of $a_1.a_2$ and also that no new actions become enabled by the extra intermediate state between a_1 and a_2. (See [20],**T 5.19**, page 103.) In a sequential setting atomicity however is immediate, and no other actions can become enable as their order is fully specified.

The notion of "combined effect" is formalized by a contraction function *contr* that maps non-empty sequences of (local) actions to a single (local) action with the combined effect. Roughly speaking this amount to joining read and write lists of actions and combining the enable and effect predicate to a single enable and effect predicate. For the full definition we refer to [4]. All these simplifying circumstances lead to the rule given in figure 4, where $\bar{v}$ is a (possibly empty) set of local variables to store intermediate results, and $a\backslash\bar{v}$ is the action resulting from hiding the variables $\bar{v}$ from a. Moreover $t(c)$ denotes a trace expression where c occurs as a subexpression in t.

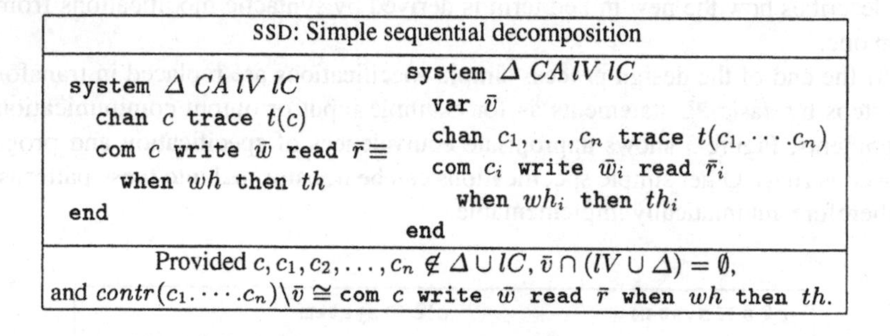

SSD: Simple sequential decomposition
system Δ CA IV IC
chan c trace $t(c)$
com c write $\bar{w}$ read $\bar{r}\equiv$
when wh then th
end
system Δ CA IV IC
var $\bar{v}$
chan $c_1,\ldots,c_n$ trace $t(c_1.\cdots.c_n)$
com c_i write $\bar{w}_i$ read $\bar{r}_i$
when wh_i then th_i
end
Provided $c, c_1, c_2, \ldots, c_n \notin \Delta \cup IC, \bar{v} \cap (IV \cup \Delta) = \emptyset$,
and $contr(c_1.\cdots.c_n)\backslash\bar{v} \cong$ com c write $\bar{w}$ read $\bar{r}$ when wh then th.

Fig. 4. A rule for sequential decomposition

To derive parallel programs more is needed than sequential decomposition. Independence analysis and rules to introduce parallel components are needed. The latter was already introduced in section 4. For this to apply we have to rewrite the single trace that is the result of the sequential decomposition into a set of (synchronizing) traces.

The simplest notion of independence is *syntactic independence*. Two actions a and b are syntactically independent, denoted by $a \not\leftrightsquigarrow b$, iff every variable they share is only read by them and not written. This can be determined from the communication assertions as they specify the lists of variables read and written. A more general notion of independence can be defined if we take states into account. For example, two actions both increasing x by one are independent in the sense that in what ever order they are performed, the overall effect remains the same. This however will not be used in this paper (see [4] for an application thereof). We say that a and b are *dependent*, denoted by $a \leftrightsquigarrow_S b$, iff they are not independent. Note that both dependence and independence are symmetric relations. A rule for parallelizing independent actions is given in figure 5. If

PAR: Syntactic independence parallelization		

system Δ *CA IV IC*
  chan $a_1, \ldots, a_n$
  trace $t(a_1 \cdot \cdots \cdot a_n)$
end
	$\equiv$	**system** Δ *CA IV IC*
		  chan $a_1, \ldots, a_n$
		  trace $t(a_1), \ldots,$ **trace** $t(a_n)$
		end

Provided $a_i \not\leftrightsquigarrow a_j$ for all $1 \leq i < j \leq n$.		

Fig. 5. A rule for parallelizing independent actions

besides independence also the side conditions for write accesses to shared variables are fulfilled and so on (as required for SYN decomposition) we can indeed replace the above specification by the synchronization of the sub specifications. In the case of other interfering trace assertions this last step cannot be taken as then no suitable decomposition of the different parts exists.

5.2 The first decomposition steps

We now have the ingredients for the derivation. As a first derivation step we decide to split the single action *ACP* into a sequence of two abstract *phases*. The idea is that after the first phase the decision to be taken by the protocol should be known. To store this decision we introduce a local variable *dec*. The result is TPC_1 in figure 6.

$TPC_1 =$ **system**
  chan $Phase_1, Phase_2$ **trace** $Phase_1.Phase_2$
  read $stable_i$ **of Bool**
  write $vote_i$ **of** $\{\text{YES}, \text{NO}\}$
    dec_i **of** $\{\text{COMMIT}, \text{ABORT}\}$
  var dec **of** $\{\text{YES}, \text{NO}\}$
  com $Phase_1$ **read** $stable_i$ **write** $vote_i, dec$
    then $\wedge_i ((vote'_i = \text{YES} \Leftrightarrow stable_i) \wedge (vote'_i = \text{NO} \Leftrightarrow \neg stable_i)) \wedge$
     $dec' = \text{COMMIT} \Leftrightarrow \wedge_j vote'_j = \text{YES} \wedge$
     $dec' = \text{ABORT} \Leftrightarrow \vee_j vote'_j = \text{NO}$
  com $Phase_2$ **read** dec **write** dec_i **then** $\wedge_i\, dec'_i = dec$
end

Fig. 6. The specification after the first decomposition step

The correctness of this step follows from the fact that the effect of $Phase_1.Phase_2$ is the same as that of ACP. We now take a closer look at the first phase. There are several ways to split this action again. We split it into a voting action and an action where the decision is taken based on the votes.

$TPC_2 =$ **system**
    chan $Vote, Decide, Phase_2$ **trace** $Vote.Decide.Phase_2$
    ...
    com $Vote$ **read** $stable_i, vote_i, dec_i$ **write** $vote_i$
      then $\wedge_i\, ((vote_i' = \text{YES} \Leftrightarrow stable_i) \wedge (vote_i' = \text{NO} \Leftrightarrow \neg stable_i))$
    com $Decide$ **read** $vote_i$ **write** dec
      then $dec' = \text{COMMIT} \Leftrightarrow \wedge_j vote_j = \text{YES} \wedge$
      $dec' = \text{ABORT} \Leftrightarrow \vee_j vote_j = \text{NO}$
    com $Phase_2$ **read** dec **write** dec_i **then** $\wedge_i\, dec_i' = dec$
end

In the next step we make two design decisions. First of all we want to have that the votes are triggered by a request action. Secondly, we want to model that the second phase consist of an information part and an effectuation part. In the first part the participants are informed of the decision, and in the second part some (internal) action is performed to effectuate the decision to be taken. Although this has no visible effect we introduce it to model that in the actual algorithm there is more activity than is specified by the simple input/output specification ACP.

The introduction of such internal actions is even simpler than the other two steps: any **then** relation can be viewed as the composition of the identity relation and itself. The result is a specification with the following trace.

$TPC_3 =$ **system** ... **trace** $Req.Vote.Decide.Inform.Eff...$ **end**

In the system above the structure and distribution of processes is not visible as yet. In the next step we want to introduce such information. We decide that all actions but $Decide$ should be split into n different actions, one for every process. This is done in order to allow parallelization later on. The decision should be taken by a single process. Note that this is also a design decision: a different decision would be to split dec again and let *all* processes decide themselves.
We split all actions into a *sequence* of n actions, similarly as would be done in ordinary sequential program development in the style of Dijkstra. All conjunctive relations allow to do so. The result is given in figure 7.

5.3 Distributing actions

In the system TPC_4 there is a lot of superfluous ordering. Many actions are independent, even at a syntactic level. At this stage we exploit these independencies to parallelize the system. In principle all Req_i actions are independent, all $Vote_i$ actions are independent, all $Inform_i$ actions are independent, and all Eff_i actions are independent. In fact, all Req_i actions are independent with respect to any other action, but these were introduced to model triggering of the protocol, and therefore we want to have that first the coordinator is triggered (process 1, using Req_1) and thereafter the rest is triggered. Obviously this is not a formal interpretation of the specification, but only interpretation of the way the system should function in an environment.
We repeatedly apply the transformation rule PAR to arrive at the following system, where all actions for the coordinator have been grouped into a single sequence as we

```
TPC_4 = system
        chan Req_i, Vote_i, Decide, Inform_i, Eff_i
        trace Req_1.···.Req_n.Vote_1.···.Vote_n.Decide.
              Inform_1.···.Inform_n.Eff_1.···.Eff_n
              ...
i : 1..n   com Req_i
i : 1..n   com Vote_i read stable_i write vote_i
              then (vote'_i = YES ⇔ stable_i) ∧ (vote'_i = NO ⇔ ¬stable_i)
           com Decide read vote_i write dec
              then dec' = COMMIT ⇔ ∧_j vote_j = YES ∧
                   dec' = ABORT ⇔ ∨_j vote_j = NO
i : 1..n   com Inform_i read dec write dec_i then dec'_i = dec
i : 1..n   com Eff_i read dec_i
        end
```

Fig. 7. Structure of TPC_4

want to arrive at a system consisting of n *sequential* processes. Thus we do not exploit the full potential of parallelism in the system.

```
TPC_5 = system ...
  i : 2..n  trace Req_i.Vote_i.Inform_i.Eff_i
            trace Req_1.···.Req_n.Vote_1.···.Vote_n.Decide.
                  Inform_1.···.Inform_n.Eff_1
            ...
        end
```

For the above system to be parallelized completely, we have to split the different communication assertions of actions that are used to synchronize components into two parts, one for each of the synchronizing components. For example, a $Vote_i$ action is split into two communication assertions, one modeling sending of a value, the other modeling reception of a value. Recall that @a represents the communicated value. For $Vote_i, i \neq 1$ this results in:

```
com Vote_i read stable_i then
      (@Vote_i = YES ⇐ stable_i) ∧ (@Vote_i = NO ⇐ ¬stable_i)
com Vote_i write vote_i then vote'_i = @Vote_i
```

The *Decide* action and other non-synchronizing actions need not to be split.

5.4 Final steps

The system that is the result of the above transformations is now decomposed to the parallel composition of specifications using the SYNC rule, resulting in the structure

$$TPC_6 \;=\; \mathbf{chan}\ \alpha\ \mathtt{SYNC}[S_1, \ldots, S_n],$$

where α is the set of all synchronizing channels and every S_i is the specification of a component, S_1 is the coordinator and S_2 through S_n are the participants. For example, for $2 \leq i \leq n$,

$$
\begin{array}{l}
S_i = \texttt{system} \\
\qquad \texttt{input } \mathit{Req}_i, \mathit{Inform}_i \texttt{ output } \mathit{Vote}_i \texttt{ chan } \mathit{Eff} \\
\qquad \texttt{trace } \mathit{Req}_i.\mathit{Vote}_i.\mathit{Inform}_i.\mathit{Eff} \\
\qquad \texttt{read } \mathit{stable}_i \texttt{ of Bool write } \mathit{dec}_i \texttt{ of } \{\mathrm{COMMIT}, \mathrm{ABORT}\} \\
\qquad \texttt{com } \mathit{Req}_i \\
\qquad \texttt{com } \mathit{Vote}_i \texttt{ read } \mathit{stable}_i \\
\qquad\quad \texttt{then } (@\mathit{Vote}_i = \mathrm{YES} \Leftarrow \mathit{stable}_i) \wedge (@\mathit{Vote}_i = \mathrm{NO} \Leftarrow \neg\mathit{stable}_i) \\
\qquad \texttt{com } \mathit{Inform}_i \texttt{ write } \mathit{dec}_i \texttt{ then } \mathit{dec}_i' = @\mathit{Inform}_i \\
\qquad \texttt{com } \mathit{Eff} \texttt{ read } \mathit{dec}_i \\
\texttt{end}
\end{array}
$$

Every specification S_i has a single trace assertion only. Since all the communication assertions are implementable, the systems can directly—even automatically—be translated into a sequential implementation [5]. This automatic translation, called *Syntax Directed Transformation,* results in an OCCAM like implementation, given in figure 8. In this program we have left *Eff* unspecified, but besides that it can directly be in-

$$
\mathit{TPC}_7 = \texttt{PAR } [S_1', S_2', \ldots, S_n'],
$$

$$
\begin{array}{ll}
S_1' = \texttt{SEQ}[\,\mathit{Req}_1\,?\,, \mathit{Req}_2\,!, \ldots, \mathit{Req}_n\,!, & 1 < i \leq n: \\
\qquad \texttt{IF}[\mathit{stable}_1 \rightarrow \mathit{vote}_1 := \mathrm{YES}, & S_i' = \texttt{SEQ}[\,\mathit{Req}_i\,?\,, \\
\qquad\quad \neg\mathit{stable}_1 \rightarrow \mathit{vote}_1 := \mathrm{NO}], & \qquad \texttt{IF}[\mathit{stable}_i \rightarrow \mathit{Vote}_i\,!\,\mathrm{YES}, \\
\qquad \mathit{Vote}_2\,?\,\mathit{vote}_2, \ldots, \mathit{Vote}_n\,?\,\mathit{vote}_n, & \qquad\quad \neg\mathit{stable}_i \rightarrow \mathit{Vote}_i\,!\,\mathrm{NO}], \\
\qquad \texttt{IF}[\wedge_i \mathit{vote}_i = \mathrm{YES} \rightarrow \mathit{dec} := \mathrm{COMMIT}, & \qquad \mathit{Inform}_i\,?\,\mathit{dec}_i, \mathit{Eff}\,]\texttt{ od} \\
\qquad\quad \vee_i\, \mathit{vote}_i = \mathrm{NO} \rightarrow \mathit{dec} := \mathrm{ABORT}], & \\
\qquad \mathit{dec}_1 := \mathit{dec}, & \\
\qquad \mathit{Inform}_2\,!\,\mathit{dec}, \ldots, \mathit{Inform}_n\,!\,\mathit{dec}, & \\
\qquad \mathit{Eff}\,]\texttt{ od} &
\end{array}
$$

Fig. 8. Centralized Two-Phase Commit

terpreted as an OCCAM program and it is suited for the architecture we had in mind. Concludingly, we have derived an implementation for the atomic commit protocol that satisfies our needs.

6 The Parallel Approach

In the parallel strategy one tries to obtain a first solution that is free of any architectural bias. We assume we have a "single step" specification modeling input/output behavior only, such as in the case of *ACP*. The idea is to find a set of actions that, given an initialization and a weakly fair scheduling policy, evolves to a stable state satisfying the desired final state [6]. To prove that such an initial solution is indeed a solution to the problem we have to define an invariant $\mathcal{I}$ that is invariant for all actions, which is established by the initialization. Together with the fix point predicate FP of the computation this invariant should establish the postcondition of the specification. In UNITY this fix point is defined as the condition such that no action leads to any changes anymore. In our MIX context this condition changes to the predicate that states that no action is enabled anymore, as only in terminating runs the end state is defined. To show termination we moreover have to specify a metric τ that decreases under a weakly fair scheduling of the actions, analogously to bound functions in sequential programming. We refer to Chandy and Misra [6] for more details on these ideas.

For this strategy one has a number of proof obligations for the first solution, as was mentioned above. This is due to the fact that there is a rather large "gap" between the initial specification and the first refinement. The larger the distance, the more complicated the proof usually is.

6.1 An initial solution

As a first solution we take a set of actions assigning values to the variables $vote_i$ and dec_i. Initially these variables are assigned the value NONE, so we slightly extend the types of the variables. The solution is given in figure 9. (We continue with TPC_8 in order to have unique names of specifications.)

```
TPC8 = system
         chan Init, Vote_i, Decide_i
         trace Init.(Σ_i Vote_i + Σ_i Decide_i)*
           ...
         com Init write vote_i, dec_i
           then ∧_i (vote'_i = NONE ∧ dec'_i = NONE)
i : 1..n com Vote_i read stable_i write vote_i
           then (vote'_i = YES ⇔ stable_i) ∧ (vote'_i = NO ⇔ ¬stable_i)
i : 1..n com Decide_i read vote_j write dec_i
           then dec'_i = COMMIT ⇔ ∧_j vote_j = YES ∧
                dec'_i = ABORT ⇔ ∨_j vote_j = NO
       end
```

Fig. 9. Structure of TPC_8

To prove that this program indeed is a refinement of ACP we choose as an invariant $\mathcal{I}$ and have the termination predicate FP:

$$\begin{aligned} \mathcal{I} = \wedge_i\, ((&vote_i = \text{YES} \Rightarrow stable_i) \wedge (vote_i = \text{NO} \Rightarrow \neg stable_i) \wedge \\ &(dec_i = \text{COMMIT} \Rightarrow \wedge_j vote_j = \text{YES}) \wedge \\ &(dec_i = \text{ABORT} \Rightarrow \vee_j vote_j = \text{NO})), \\ FP = \wedge_i\, (&vote_i \neq \text{NONE} \wedge dec_i \neq \text{NONE}). \end{aligned}$$

The bound function is given by the number of variables $vote_i$ and dec_i that (still) have the value NONE. The initialization trivially ensures $\mathcal{I}$ as no left hand side of any implication holds. Also, all actions may change the value of one variable only, which is changed in the correct way if it changes, preserving $\mathcal{I}$. Finally, given the possible values of the variables and FP, we obtain the post condition of ACP.

6.2 Mapping to an architecture

The above solution is a general solution. We now have to tune it to a certain architecture, that is, n processes with point to point communication. For point to point communication no action may involve variables that are assigned to more than two processors, and may only write a single variable. So we can assign actions to processors, and then have to refine in such a way that the above is indeed satisfied. For a shared variables implementation we would only have to assign actions to processors, without having to both about variables. The variable distribution will be as in the previous protocol, so, for example, the actions $Decide_i$ in TPC_8 are not implementable.

In UNITY one has the concept of *superposition* that allows to modify actions to a certain extent and to add variables and actions. Here we add an action *Decide*, that assigns a value to a new, local variable *dec*. The addition of such an action that simply writes a new variable and does not change the flow of control can always be done.

Besides that superposition we would like to modify the $Decide_i$ actions such that they no longer read the $vote_j$ variables but *dec*. Otherwise the previous modification would not make much sense. To prove the correctness thereof we have to give a strengthened invariant and FP and prove correctness again.

Finally, the *Init* action is split in a parallel composition of n actions initializing the variables for every process. The result is a (still unstructured) algorithm that however can be mapped to a point to point architecture.

To map the result of the above steps to a sequential program, we need something extra. We can deduce that every action changes the state exactly once: every $Vote_i$ the first time it is executed, *Decide* as soon as all votes are known or at least one vote is NO etcetera. All other executions of the actions do not change the state. Based on this, we can define a bijective mapping $s : |A_i| \rightarrow A_i$ that defines the order in which the set of actions A_i for process i is executed. This mapping should be such that the state after the j-th action ensures that $s(j+1)$ is enabled and changes the state. In our case, the mapping (obviously) corresponds to the order in which the actions are executed in TPC_4, modulo some renaming. The rule to introduce such ordering is given in [4], we here restrict ourselves to showing the result. Finally, we have to add actions Eff_i as well, which can be done without any problems in this case, as these are local actions that do not change the state. The result is given in figure 10. If we rename the actions $Init_i$ into Req_i and $Decide_i$ into $Inform_i$ the rest of the derivation is the same as in section 5, but for the implementation of Req_i which now does change the state. This concludes the sketch of the derivation.

$$
\begin{array}{lll}
TPC_9 = \texttt{system} & & \\
 & \texttt{chan} & Init_i, Vote_i, Decide, Decide_i, Eff_i \\
 & \texttt{trace} & Init_1.\cdots.Init_n.Vote_1.\cdots.Vote_n.Decide. \\
 & & \quad Decide_1.\cdots.Decide_n.Eff_1.\cdots.Eff_n \\
i: 2..n & \texttt{trace} & Init_i.Vote_i.Decide_i.Eff_i \\
 & & \ldots \\
i: 1..n & \texttt{com} & Init_i \ \texttt{write} \ vote_i, dec_i \ \texttt{then} \ vote_i' = \text{NONE} \land dec_i' = \text{NONE} \\
i: 1..n & \texttt{com} & Vote_i \ \texttt{read} \ stable_i \ \texttt{write} \ vote_i \\
 & & \quad \texttt{then} \ (vote_i' = \text{YES} \Leftrightarrow stable_i) \land (vote_i' = \text{NO} \Leftrightarrow \neg stable_i) \\
 & & \ldots \\
 & \texttt{end} &
\end{array}
$$

Fig. 10. Structure of TPC_9

7 Using the Architectural Strategy

The two previous sections used strategies that delay architectural decisions to as late stage as possible. In the architectural approach we do the opposite: the synchronization skeleton of the system one is aiming at is introduced as a first step, and only thereafter state transitions are analyzed. This can have the advantage that certain simplifications due to the architecture can be exploited already at an early stage. Here we give a sketch of how to apply this strategy to *ACP*.

Following the architectural strategy as described in section 2 we first introduce new local channels *Req*$_i$, *Vote*$_i$, *Decide*, *Inform*$_i$ and *Eff*$_i$ and define in what way the different communications synchronize, the so-called synchronization skeleton. This introduction doesn't change the specified state transitions. Only the ordering of the new channels is constraint by integrating them into the trace assertions. Such introduction is therefore allowed as long as the language generated projected on ACP doesn't change. The result is given in figure 11.

The next step in this strategy is the extension of the state space as required. Here we introduce the local variable *dec* and give the ACP action the right to write into it. For the third part of the strategy we need a rule that allows to shift state transitions over actions. Informally this rule states that, if an action c is always followed by an action d, then we can move part of the effect of c to d, provided certain restrictions on variables accesses are fulfilled. To apply this rule we must partition the set of actions into three sets Ch_1, Ch_2 and $\{c, d\}$, where d is the channel we want to move part of c to, Ch_1 is the set of channels that might interfere with c or d, and Ch_2 all other channels. The trace language should be such that we can add the trace assertion $\texttt{trace}\ (Ch_1^*.c.d)^*$ without changing the language. Usually we can take Ch_1 to be the set of actions we can ensure to be ordered to the left or to the right of both c and d. This set should then contain all interfering actions for c and d. The rule is given in figure 12, where $P\ ;_{\bar{y}} Q$ is the relational composition of predicates P and Q, defined as

$$P\ ;_{\bar{y}} Q \stackrel{\text{def}}{=} \exists \bar{y}''.\ P[\bar{y}''/\bar{y}'] \land Q[\bar{y}''/\bar{y}].$$

```
TPC_10 = system
           chan ACP
           chan Req_1, ..., Req_n, Vote_1, ..., Vote_n, Decide,
                Inform_1, ..., Inform_n, Eff_1, ..., Eff_n
           trace ACP.Req_1. ··· .Req_n.Vote_1. ··· .Vote_n.Decide.
                 Inform_1. ··· .Inform_n.Eff_1
  i : 2..n trace ACP.Req_i.Vote_i.Inform_i.Eff_i
           read stable_i of Bool
           write vote_i of {YES, NO}
                 dec_i of {COMMIT, ABORT}
           com ACP write vote_i, dec_i read stable_i ...
         end
```

Fig. 11. After adding the synchronization skeleton, TPC_{10}

In this case applying the SHIFT rule is rather simple, as there is only a limited amount

SHIFT: Shift effects		
system Δ *TA CA lV lC* **chan** c, d **trace** $(Ch_1^*.c.d)^*$ **com** c **write** $\bar{w}$ **read** $\bar{r}$ **when** wh_c **then** $P ;_{\bar{w}} Q$ **com** d **write** $\bar{w}$ **read** $\bar{r}$ **when** wh_d **then** R **end**	$\equiv$	**system** Δ *TA CA lV lC* **chan** c, d **trace** $(Ch_1^*.c.d)^*$ **com** c **write** $\bar{w}$ **read** $\bar{r}$ **when** wh_c **then** P **com** d **write** $\bar{w}$ **read** $\bar{r}$ **when** wh_d **then** $(Q ;_{\bar{w}} R)$ **end**
Provided all channels are partitioned into Ch_1, Ch_2 and $\{c, d\}$ such that $\{\bar{w}, \bar{r}\} \cap Vars(Ch_2) \subseteq Reads(Ch_2) \backslash \bar{w}$ and $free(wh_d) \cap \bar{w} = \emptyset$.		

Fig. 12. Shifting effects

of parallelism in the algorithm due to the sequential structure of the coordinator. So we iteratively rewrite the **then** predicate belonging to ACP to the composition of two predicates. Of course this is not possible in general: we should carefully select the order in which to apply the SHIFT rule. For example, take the action $Inform_i$. One can rewrite the predicate corresponding to ACP, that is, the full specification, as

$$P ;_{dec} \wedge_i (dec_i' = dec).$$

Moreover, this conjunction can be rewritten as

$$dec_1' = dec ;_{\emptyset} dec_2' = dec ;_{\emptyset} \cdots ;_{\emptyset} dec_n' = dec,$$

as " $;_{\emptyset}$" simply *is* conjunction due to the definition of " $;_{\bar{y}}$." Therefore we can move the predicate $dec_i' = dec$ to its place, starting with $i = n$ using SHIFT with the channel set

$Ch_1 = \{Inform_{i+1}, \ldots, Inform_n\}$ and the channel set Ch_2 is everything but ACP and $\{Inform_i, \ldots, Inform_n\}$, and iteratively removing the whole of the conjunction. As only the channels $Inform_i$ and ACP access any variables the side conditions for the SHIFT rule are obviously fulfilled. Thereafter we can shift making the decision to *Decide*. The part for the *Vote* actions is then analogous to the *Inform* part. Finally, we arrive at an algorithm that is almost the same as TPC_5, but for the fact that all traces start with ACP. As ACP now has become a local channel with empty effect and is always enabled, we can remove it from the traces without changing the effect of the system as a whole. The result is exactly TPC_5 and we can proceed as in section 5.

8 Implementations for alternative architectures

Having developed a first implementation of the atomic commit problem for a certain architecture in different ways, it is an interesting question to see how this helps when developing solutions for other architectures. It would be nice if one could reuse parts of the proof due to overlapping development strategies. In doing so one also gets insight in the design decisions that are taken during the development and how they relate to the eventual implementations.

In [4] we derived different versions of the Two-Phase Commit protocol, such as *Linear TPC* for chain networks, a *Tree based* version, assuming a tree network, a solution for a *Ring* network, and finally a *Decentralized TPC* for fully connected networks. For the latter also an optimized version was derived.

In figure 13 we have sketched how the different transformation steps of the protocols relate. Arrows denote transformation steps, and dotted regions denote sets of highly related algorithms, in the sense that the transformation steps going from one region to another are completely analogous. All derivations were performed using the layered strategy. Each number in the graph correspond to the numbers of the specifications in

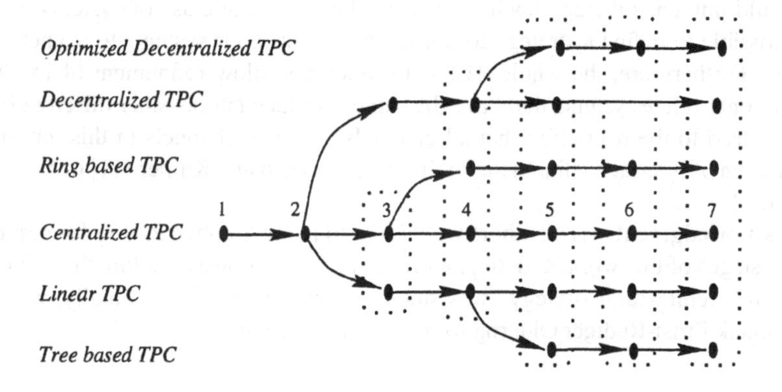

Fig. 13. Relations between different derivations

this paper. Many derivations share large parts of their paths, either almost literally, or by analogy in steps. The extra derivations were thus even easier than the derivations given in the previous sections.

9 Conclusion

In this paper we studied and compared three different strategies for transformational design of parallel systems: the layered strategy, the parallel strategy, and the architectural strategy. All three strategies were employed within a single formalism, resulting in a comparison of strategies on a non-trivial example. In this example it has been shown that the use of strategies helps in designing systems and designing variants of systems. Proofs of alternative implementations were lead by the first proof, and different proofs could reuse large parts of each other. The similarities in these proofs were induced by the strategy.

Also the derivation of optimizations is supported by the use of strategies. Optimizations can also be seen as variants, often variants that differ to a rather small extent. It is however not yet clear whether we have the right set of rules for such applications.

Having a single formal basis for all strategies enables the integration within existing or future tools, such as the tools supporting `MIX` transformations that are being built at the University of Oldenburg. The idea is to add strategies as *meta-level transformations* with user interaction to guided developers through the long and complicated design trajectory as smoothly as possible.

A question to be answered in the near future is how to *formalize* strategies. For theorem provers strategies can either be formalized on a meta-level or using the underlying logic, as has been studied in [5]. In the context of automatic tool synthesis there is interesting work by Steffen and Margaria [22] using a modal (dynamic) logic to specify similar constraints.

Another interesting topic is the introduction of asynchronous message passing. Some work in this direction has already been done by Fischer [10]. This would also allow to model things like duplication, loss, or corruption of messages. It is not yet clear how this would influence the approach taken here. For a certain class of systems it seems to be possible to define a strategy to transform synchronous systems to asynchronous systems. Furthermore, the whole `MIX` setup does not allow refinement of interfaces. One can only relate systems that have the same interface but possibly different behavior. This lead to the restriction that all channels are local channels in this report. The introduction of interface refinement, in the style of Gerth and Kuiper [11] or Stomp and Siegel [24].

Acknowledgments. The authors would like to thank Stephan Rössig for comments in early stages of this work, and Stephan Kleuker for rigorously reading the full report. The term "architectural strategy" was suggested by Anders Ravn. Finally, we would like to thank Ernst-Rüdiger Olderog for useful suggestions.

References

1. R. Back. Refinement calculus, Part II: Parallel and Reactive Programs. In de Bakker, de Roever, and Rozenberg, editors, *Stepwise Refinement of Distributed Systems, LNCS 430*, pages 67–93. Springer-Verlag, 1990.

2. R. Back and K. Sere. Stepwise refinement of action systems. *Structured Programming*, 12:17–30, 1991.
3. P. Bernstein, V. Hadzilacos, and N. Goodman. *Concurrency Control and Recovery in Database Systems*. Addison-Wesley, 1987.
4. J. Bohn and W. Janssen. From a single specification to many implementations — many roads lead to parallelism. Technical report, University of Oldenburg, 1995. Available at `ftp://ftp.informatik.uni-oldenburg.de/pub/procos/`.
5. J. Bohn and S. Rössig. On automatic and interactive design of communicating systems. In E. Brinksma, W. Cleaveland, K.G. Larsen, T. Margaria, and B. Steffen, editors, *Proceedings of the First TACAS workshop, LNCS 1019*, pages 216–247. Springer-Verlag, 1995.
6. R. Chandy and J. Misra. *Parallel Program Design: A Foundation*. Addison-Wesley, 1988.
7. C. Chou and E. Gafni. Understanding and verifying distributed algorithms using stratified decomposition. In *Proceeding 7th ACM Symposium on Principles of Distributed Computing*, 1988.
8. T. Elrad and N. Francez. Decomposition of distributed programs into communication closed layers. *Science of Computer Programming*, 2:155–173, 1982.
9. J. P. Bowen et al. A ProCoS II project description: ESPRIT Basic Research project 7071. *Bulletin of the EATCS*, 50:128–137, 1993.
10. C. Fischer. Transformation von synchronen SL-Specifikationen von Telekommunikation-ssytemen in asynchrone SL-Specifikationen. Master's thesis, University of Oldenburg, 1995. In German.
11. R. Gerth, R. Kuiper, and J. Segers. Interface refinement in reactive systems. In *Proceedings CONCUR '92, LNCS 630*, pages 77–94. Springer-Verlag, 1992.
12. C.A.R. Hoare. *Communicating Sequential Processes*. Prentice-Hall, 1985.
13. W. Janssen. *Layered Design of Parallel Systems*. PhD thesis, University of Twente, 1994.
14. W. Janssen, M. Poel, and J. Zwiers. Action systems and action refinement in the development of parallel systems. In *Proceedings of CONCUR '91, LNCS 527*, pages 298–316. Springer-Verlag, 1991.
15. L. Lamport. The Temporal Logic of Actions. *ACM TOPLAS*, 16(3):872–923, 1994.
16. C. Lengauer. Loop parallelization in the polytope model (invited talk). In Eike Best, editor, *Proceedings CONCUR '93, LNCS 715*, pages 398–416. Springer-Verlag, 1993.
17. E.-R. Olderog. Towards a design calculus for communicating programs (invited paper). In *Proceedings of CONCUR '91, LNCS 527*, pages 61–77. Springer-Verlag, 1991.
18. E.-R. Olderog and S. Rössig. A case study in transformational design of concurrent systems. In M.-C. Gaudel and J.-P. Jouannaud, editors, *TAPSOFT '93, LNCS 668*, pages 90–104. Springer-Verlag, 1993.
19. E.-R. Olderog, S. Rössig, J. Sander, and M. Schenke. ProCoS at Oldenburg: The interface between specification language and occam-like programming language. Berichte aus dem Fachbereich Informatik 3, University of Oldenburg, 1992.
20. S. Rössig. *A Transformational Approach to the Design of Communicating Systems*. PhD thesis, University of Oldenburg, 1994.
21. J. Spivey. *The Z Notation: A Reference Manual*. Prentice Hall, 1989.
22. B. Steffen, T. Margaria, and A. Claßen. Heterogeneous analysis and verification for distributed systems. Technical Report MIP-9509, University of Passau, 1995.
23. F. Stomp. A derivation of a broadcasting protocol using sequentially phased reasoning (extended abstract). In L. Logrippo, R. Probert, and H. Ural, editors, *Proceedings 10th IFIP symp. on Protocol Specification, Testing and Verification*, pages 19–32. Elsevier Science Publishers, 1990.
24. F. Stomp and M. Siegel. Extending the limits of sequentially phased reasoning. In P. Thiagarajan, editor, *Proceedings FST & TCS 14, LNCS 880*. Springer-Verlag, 1994.

Correct and User-Friendly Implementations of Transformation Systems[1]

Kolyang[†], **T. Santen**[‡], **B. Wolff**[†]

[†]Universität Bremen , FB3
P.O. Box 330440
D-28334 Bremen
{bu,kol}@informatik.uni-bremen.de

[‡]GMD FIRST Berlin
Rudower Chaussee 5
D-12489 Berlin
santen@first.gmd.de

Abstract. We present an approach to integrate several existing tools and methods to a technical framework for correctly developing and executing program transformations. The resulting systems enable program derivations in a user-friendly way.
We illustrate the approach by proving and implementing the transformation Global Search on the basis of the tactical theorem prover Isabelle. A graphical user-interface based on the X-Window toolkit Tk provides user friendly access to the underlying machinery.

1 Introduction

Development by transformation is a prominent approach in formal program development (CIP [Bau+85], PROSPECTRA [HK 93], KIDS [Smi 90]). Many case studies have proven its feasibility and demonstrated how much more abstract and user-oriented developments could be achieved than using usual post-verification approaches (fundamental for systems like PVS [OSR 93]). One recent case study is [KW 95]; and a prominent one is [SPW 95] where a strategic transportation scheduling algorithm is developed which is 200 times faster than the ones in practical use today. Unfortunately, implementations of transformation systems tend to be complicated and insecure. The correctness issue of transformation rules is usually not treated at the implementation level of existing systems.

In contrast to this, there is a family of "tactical theorem provers" in the tradition of LCF available with systems like *HOL* [GM 93] and *Isabelle* [Pau 94a], that are both well-designed and powerful. Coming with an open system-design going back to Milner, they allow for user-programmed extensions in a logically sound way. But there is recent prominent criticism that these provers, because of their "academic (ivory tower) origins", have "historically placed more emphasis on logical foundations and less on usability" [Gor 95]. This is clearly one of the reasons for the small acceptance of these provers in industry up to now.

In this paper, we demonstrate a technique to combine these two approaches. It results in a *simple* implementation design, in proven correct transformations which are easy to extend and to modify, and in a graphical user-interface that allows developers to profit from the abstraction of the transformational approach. We claim that our

---

1 This work has been supported by the BMBF projects **UniForM** [Kri+95] and **ESPRESS**.

technique is applicable in a fairly wide range of problems, simply by modifying and extending our prototype implementation.

Our work integrates three existing and well documented public domain tools — the tactical theorem prover Isabelle based on *Standard ML* [HMM 86] and the X-Window toolkit *Tk* [Ous 94]. As object-language, we chose higher-order logic (HOL) which is one instantiation of the generic system Isabelle with an object logic and is delivered with the standard package. A subset of HOL formulas can easily be translated into functional programs (e.g. ML).

The basic idea of our approach is to separate the *logical core* of a transformation from the pragmatics of its application. As a *synthesis theorem* it can be proven correct independently in the logics of the object language, while the *tactical sugar,* which often highly system dependent, is concerned with the concrete application in a development context, i.e. the construction of suitable substitutions, "hard-wired" quantifier eliminations and standard simplifications, together with user interaction to control this process. The distinction between synthesis theorem and tactical sugar establishes an important separation of concerns.

We illustrate our approach by the transformation *Global Search* [Smi 87] that converts a non-constructive specification into a constructive one. This complex transformation has the character of a "design tactic" [Smi 90] or "design method" [HK 93]. Other transformations like *Divide-and-Conquer* or *Split of Postcondition* and elementary transformations like *recursion removal* or *fusion* also fit into our framework.

We proceed as follows: after introducing the idea of synthesis theorems and a brief presentation of Isabelle, we present Global Search as a synthesis theorem and prove it correct within Isabelle/HOL. We sketch several possibilities of tactical programs for our synthesis theorem. The resulting system is embedded into a user interface. Lastly, a small application example demonstrates the use of the resulting prototype system.

2 Transformations as Synthesis Theorems

2.1 The Concept

The core of our presentation is a general scheme of synthesis theorems, i.e. of logical formulas. The automatic construction of substitutions and other deduction-technical machinery, for short — the tactical sugar — is discussed in section 3.5.

Our intuition of "performing a program transformation" motivates several key notions (cf. [HK 93]). A transformation is composed of an *input pattern I* which is matched against an application context of a specification. This pattern is designed to be as general as possible and at the same time to be best supportable by automatic matching procedures (which belong to the tactical sugar). From the result of matching *I* against the specification at a specific position, an instance of the *output pattern O* is constructed automatically. All side conditions that can not be treated by automatic procedures and require theorem proving are collected in the *applicability condition V*. Usually, the output pattern contains function symbols that are introduced by the application of the transformation. They represent the design decisions of the whole transformation step, i.e. auxiliary functions whose definitions have to be provided by the user. These items are called the *parameters* $P_1 \ldots P_n$ of the transformation.

On the logical side, these items can be organised as a conditional equation:

$$\forall P_1 \,..P_n.\, V \Rightarrow I \rightsquigarrow O$$

where $\rightsquigarrow$ is a transitive binary operator that typically stands for

- logical equality or equivalence in case of symmetric transformations or
- the implication $\Leftarrow$ in case of classical refinement (the input pattern has to follow from the output; in algebraic jargon: the model class of the output specification is included in the model class of the input specification) or
- the Scott-definedness ordering $\sqsubseteq$ in case of "robust implementations" using object-logics like LCF (see [Pau 94a]).

This scheme is strong enough to capture a large variety of transformations — from "Filter Fusion" [BM 93] to "Split of Postcondition" [HK 93]. These have been presented in [KW 95]. The synthesis theorem for Global Search is discussed later.

The separation into synthesis theorem and tactical sugar has the following consequence for the soundness of a transformation: The logical core can be proven *within* the logic in which it is represented. This can be done by showing that the synthesis theorem follows from the basic axioms of the logic — or, in other words, the synthesis theorem follows from a *conservative extension of the core logic* (see below).

2.2 Introduction to Isabelle

Isabelle is a *generic* theorem prover that supports a family of logics, e.g. first-order logic (FOL), Zermelo-Fränkel set theory (ZF), constructive type theory (CTT), the Logic of Computable Functions (LCF), and others. We only use its set-up for higher-order logic (HOL). Isabelle supports natural deduction style. Its principal inference techniques are resolution (based on higher-order unification) and term-rewriting. Isabelle provides syntax for hierarchical theories (containing signatures and axioms).

As an example, let us create the theory List0 from the theory HOL that contains the basic rules of the logic. All input in the form of UNIX files or user input will be denoted with this FONT — enriched by the usual mathematical notation for ∀, ∃,... instead of ASCII-transcriptions.[2] We define the unary type constructor list, its constructors ([], #) and the concatenation @:

```
List0 = HOL +
      types     list     1
      arities   list     :: (term)term
      consts    "[]"     :: "α list"                       ("[]")
                "#"      :: "[α, α list] → α list"         (infixr 70)
                "@"      :: "[α list, α list] → α list"    (infixl 60)
rules
      app_mt             "[]@m = m"
      app_cons           "(a#n)@m = a#(n@m)"
end
```

Here, list belongs to the type universe term of HOL and accepts types from term. This construct is a tribute to the genericity of Isabelle. "→" is the function space constructor, and the brackets denote curried functions: [α, α list] → α list is equivalent to α→α list→α list. The equality "=" stems from HOL, while "≡" is

---

2 We do not distinguish quantifications and implications at the different logical levels throughout this paper; see [Pau 94a].

used to denote the definitional equality. The comments ("[]") and (infixl 70) are pragmas setting up the parsing and pretty-printing machinery of Isabelle.

2.3 The Logic HOL

In this section, we will give a short overview of the concepts and the syntax. Our object-language HOL goes back to [Chu 40]; a more recent presentation is [And 86]. In the formal methods community, it has achieved some acceptance, especially in hardware-verification. HOL is a classical logic with equality. It is based on total functions denoted by λ-abstractions like "$\lambda x.x$". Function application is denoted by $f\,a$. Although its type discipline incorporates polymorphism with type-classes (as in Haskell), in this paper we only use Milner-Polymorphism (as in ML).

Logical rules of HOL like:

$$\frac{P \quad Q}{P \wedge Q}\ (\text{conjI}) \qquad\qquad \frac{P \wedge Q}{P}\ (\text{conjunct1})$$

will be represented in Isabelle by

[| ?P ; ?Q |] ⇒ ?P ∧ ?Q   ?P ∧ ?Q ⇒ ?P

where variables prefixed by a question mark are called *meta-variables*. Their exact meaning in the deduction process is discussed later.

2.4 Proving in Isabelle

Isabelle as a system is a set of function definitions in the ML-environment (or: "database"). They represent a collection of function- and data type definitions. Most notable are the three mutually dependent data types: tactic, thm and (internal) proof_state.

Isabelle supports two styles of theorem proving: forward proof and backward proof.

Backward proving in Isabelle. The general scheme of a backward proof consists of three steps:

(1) The initialisation of the internal "proof-state" with the formula to be proven (the "goal"). It is done by the operation:

    goal: theory -> string -> thm list

    where the string contains the textual representation of the formula to be type-checked and proved within theory.

(2) A refinement of the proof-state. It is performed with the operation:

    by : tactic -> unit

    This refinement can be seen as a transformation of the proof-state by means of tactics and already proven theorems. Two of these are the following pivotal *built-in* tactics

    atac: int -> tactic   rtac: thm -> int -> tactic

    The integer parameters specify the subgoal to which the tactic is applied. They encapsulate the Isabelle meta-inferences *assumption* (basically "A" implies "A" modulo unification) and *resolution* (essentially "A ⇒ B" and "B ⇒ C" implies "A ⇒ C" modulo unification)

(3) The extraction of a theorem produced out of a proof-state with no subgoals:

```
result: unit -> thm;
```

returns a value that can be bound to an arbitrary ML-identifier.

By composition of these operations on the proof-state, large proof-scripts can be organised in the *.ML files that are executed automatically when loading a theory.

Forward proving in Isabelle. Forward reasoning mimics the classical way of constructing proof trees. The combination of two rules, say conjI and conjunct1 given above, can be done by using the resolution combinator (involving unification):

```
RS : thm * thm -> thm
```

in the form:

```
conjI RS conjunct1
```

which is evaluated by Isabelle to the derived rule:

$[|\ ?P;\ ?Q\ |] \Longrightarrow\ ?P$

As simple example for higher-order unification, we consider the specialisation rule:

$\forall x.\ ?P\ x \Longrightarrow\ ?P\ ?x$ (spec)

With this HOL rule it is possible via forward proving in a theorem, say $\forall y.\ y = a$, to eliminate the quantification and to replace the bound variable y by the *meta-variable* ?x. The resulting formula would be ?x = a. We can interpret the meta-variable ?x as a "hole" in the formula that can be filled later by substitutions (usually produced as a consequence of unification inside atac and rtac). This possibility of "postponing substitutions" and of transforming theorems in a programmed, but logically sound way, is important for our approach.

Isabelle provides substantially more machinery, especially for people who want to set-up their own logic or who yearn for a higher degree of automatisation. However, with the subset presented here, extended by some variants, it is already possible to perform substantial proofs and to describe the relevant operations in this paper.

2.5 Conservative Extension in HOL

The introduction of new axioms ("rules" in case of List0) while building a new theory is an extremely dangerous method, since the resulting theory may easily be inconsistent. Hence it is necessary to recall that there is a number of syntactic schemes for specification-extension that maintain the consistency of the extended one. (For a more formal and very readable account on "conservative extensions schemes" the reader is referred to [GM 93]). Some schemes are:

- the *constant definition* "$c \equiv t$" or "$c\ x \equiv t\ x$" of a fresh constant symbol c by a closed expression t not containing c,
- the *type definition* (a set of axioms stating an isomorphism between a non-empty subset of a base-type and the new type to be defined),
- a set of equations forming a *primitive recursive scheme* over a fresh constant symbol f,
- a set of equations forming a *well-founded recursive scheme* over a fresh symbol f.

The basic idea of these extension schemes is to avoid general recursion. Instead, they introduce axioms only in a controlled way. The desired properties have to be derived from these. Building up large theories by methodically using conservative extensions used to be a quite tedious enterprise, but recent advances in the Isabelle implementation have substantially improved the support for this approach [Pau 94b].

3 Global Search Transformation

We use the approach sketched in section 2 to implement a transformation based on the theory of *Global Search* algorithms that has been developed at Kestrel Institute and implemented in the *Kestrel Interactive Development System* (KIDS) [Smi 87, Smi 90]. After presenting the basic idea of global search, we show how the theory can be formalised in Isabelle/HOL. We prove a synthesis theorem under the resulting theory, and finally provide a tactic program (the sugar) converting the synthesis theorem into an executable transformation.

3.1 The Algorithm Design Theory *Global Search*

The global search theory characterises a large class of algorithmic problems that are solvable by search or optimisation algorithms. It covers problems typically solved, e.g., by backtracking, branch-and-bound, or simplex algorithms.

For the purpose of this paper, we closely stick to the notation used in [Smi 87]. There, algorithms are described by input / output predicates. A *problem specification* is a quadruple $P = \langle D,R,I,O \rangle$ where D is the input domain and R is the output range of the function f to synthesise. The predicate I describes the admissible inputs, and O describes the input / output behaviour of f. Hence, f is a solution to P if

$$\forall\, x{:}D.\ I(x) \wedge y = f(x) \Rightarrow O(x, f(x))$$

A *design theory* extends a problem specification by additional functions. It states sufficient properties of these functions to formulate a schematic algorithm that solves the problem correctly. The basic idea of global search is to associate inputs x with *search spaces* that initially contain all solutions z with $O(x,z)$. Search is then performed by splitting search spaces into "smaller" ones until solutions are directly extractable. This idea is captured in the design theory of Figure 3.1.1.

sorts D, R, R'
operations

$I : D \to \text{Bool}$	$Satisfies : R \times R' \to \text{Bool}$
$O : D \times R \to \text{Bool}$	$Split : D \times R' \times R' \to \text{Bool}$
$I' : D \times R' \to \text{Bool}$	$Extract : R \times R' \to \text{Bool}$
$r'_0 : D \to R'$	$< : R' \times R' \to \text{Bool}$

axioms

GS0 $I(x) \Rightarrow I'(x, (r'_0(x))$

GS1 $I(x) \wedge I'(x,r') \wedge Split(x,r',s') \Rightarrow I'(x,s') \wedge s' < r'$

GS2 $I(x) \wedge O(x,z) \Rightarrow Satisfies(z, r'_0(x))$

GS3 $I(x) \wedge I'(x,r') \Rightarrow Satisfies(z,r') = (\exists\, s'.\ Split^*(x,r',s') \wedge Extract(z,s'))$

GS5 $<$ is a well-founded ordering on R'

Figure 3.1.1: Global Search Theory.[3]

The sort R' is the type of search space descriptors, I' defines legal descriptors. For an input x, r'_0 and $Split$ describe the search tree for solutions z with $O(x,z)$: its root is

---

[3] In [Smi 87], axiom GS4 deals with necessary filters, which we do not consider in this paper. Still, we call our last axiom GS5 to stay consistent with the literature.

$r'_0(x)$, the initial search space; a descendant relation on nodes is given by *Split*: *Split*(x,r',s') is true if s' is a (direct) subspace of r' for an input x. *Split** is defined by

$$Split^*(x,r',s') = (\exists\ k{:}\mathbb{N}.\ Split^k(x,r',s'))$$
$$Split^0(x,r',s') = (r' = s')$$
$$Split^{k+1}(x,r',s') = (\exists\ t'.\ Split(x,r',t') \wedge Split^k(x,t',s'))$$

The possible solutions that can be extracted from a node r' are *Extract*(z,r').

Axioms GS0 and GS1 ensure that all considered search spaces are legal. Axiom GS1 additionally ensures that search spaces can be split only finitely often, i.e. that the search tree has a finite depth. GS2 requires the initial search space to contain all feasible solutions.

By axiom GS3, *Satisfies*(z,r') describes the solutions z contained in a search space r' that can be found with finite effort: there must exist a finite path in the search tree from r' to a search space s' from which z can be extracted.

Under the global search theory, we can use *Split* and *Extract* to get an algorithm schema satisfying the problem specification $\langle D,R,I,O\rangle$. Following [Smi 87], we express the algorithm by input / output predicates.

$$I(x) \wedge I'(x,r') \Rightarrow Fgs(x,r',z) = (Extract(z,r') \wedge O(x,z)$$
$$\vee\ (\exists\ s'.\ Split(x,r',s') \wedge Fgs(x,s',z)))$$
$$I(x) \Rightarrow F(x,z) = Fgs(x,r'_0(x),z)$$

F computes a solution z for some admissible input x by searching in the initial search space $r'_0(x)$. Searching is performed by the auxiliary function *Fgs*: if z is not directly extractable from r' this search space is split and its subspaces are searched.

The global search theory described above is relatively simple. More refined ones incorporate filters to prune search spaces. The most elaborate one stated in [SPW 95] uses a refinement relation on search spaces and cutting constraints to profoundly exploit the problem domain and synthesise highly efficient search algorithms.

3.2 Formalisation in Isabelle/HOL

How do we know that a particular application of Global Search is correct, i.e. how can we be sure that we get a correct implementation of our problem specification when we instantiate the abstract global search algorithm on the basis of particular I', r'_0, *Satisfies*, *Split*, *Extract* and < defined in our problem domain? There are two reasons why correctness might be spoiled: we may make a mistake in the particular application, e.g. choosing components that do not fulfil the global search axioms, or, more fundamentally, the implementation of the transformation may be faulty, i.e. the actually implemented transformation may be unsound. It is not in question here that "something" like the theory presented in section 3.1 describes a mathematically sound transformation. But it is a long way from a paper-and-pencil proven "idea" of a transformation to its actual implementation and application. We must make sure that the transition from idea to implementation is traceable and based on well-understood principles, and that it leads to a *soundly implemented* transformation.

In contrast to the KIDS system which is not based on a general logical framework but implements transformations like Global Search directly, we have chosen higher-order logic as implemented in Isabelle. Implementing the transformation in our system first of all means formalising the description of global search given in section 3.1 in a Isabelle/HOL theory. The Isabelle theory is sketched in the following. It is based on the HOL theories of natural numbers and sets.

```
GlobalSearch = Nat + Set +
consts
    ...
    GS3 ::        "[δ → bool,[δ, ρ'] → bool,
                  [δ, ρ', ρ']→ bool,
                  [ρ, ρ'] → bool,[ρ, ρ'] → bool] → bool"
    ...
defs
...
REC_def "REC Fgs I I' Extract Out Split ≡
              ∀ x r z . I x ∧ I' x r ⇒
              Fgs x r z = (Extract z r ∧ Out x z ∨
                         (∃ s'.Split x r s' ∧ Fgs x s' z))"

GS3_def "GS3 I I' Split Satisfies Extract ≡
              ∀ x z r'. I x ∧ I' x r' ⇒
                 Satisfies z r' = (∃ s'. rep_s Split x r' s' ∧ Extract z s')"
...
GSA_def "GSTHEORY I Out I' r0 Split Extract subspace Satisfies ≡
              GS0 I I' r0                         ∧
              GS1 I I' Split subspace             ∧
              GS2 I Out Satisfies r0              ∧
              GS3 I I' Split Satisfies Extract    ∧
              GS5 subspace"
```

Figure 3.2.1: Isabelle theory of Global Search.

Using the definitional equality ≡, we define higher-order predicates GS1 through GS5 for the global search axioms. Their conjunction GSTHEORY gives us a predicate that represents the global search axiomatization. We chose to formalise the parameter sorts D, R and R' of Figure 3.1.1 by making GS1 through GS5 polymorphic and use the type variables δ, ρ and ρ', respectively. In this way, we need not explicitly instantiate parameter sorts when applying the Global Search transformation: Isabelle's type inference system will find suitable sorts for us. The predicates rep_n and rep_s are defined as primitive recursors on Nat, which construct $Split^k$ and $Split^*$ from a given *Split*. REC provides an abbreviation of the characteristic equation for *Fgs*.

Building the theory in this way ensures consistency since each axiom is formalised as a conservative constant definition. We indicate this by the keyword defs, and the system checks for conservativity of these axioms as sketched in section 2.5.

3.3 The Global Search Synthesis Theorem

The following synthesis theorem for global search is based on theory GlobalSearch:

```
       ∀ I' r0 Split Extract subspace Satisfies.
         GSTHEORY I Out I' r0 Split Extract subspace Satisfies ⇒
           (I x ⇒ F x z = Out x z)
(GS)       =
           (I x ⇒ (∃ Fgs. REC Fgs I I' Extract Out Split ∧ F x z = Fgs x (r0 x) z ))
```

Assuming a global search theory, (GS) relates the problem specification to the schematic search algorithm. The function Fgs we get when composing I, I', Extract, Out, and Split according to REC finds exactly the solutions z that are specified by Out if the search starts with the initial search space r0(x) for some legal input x.

Note that (GS) has the form of synthesis theorems introduced in section 2.1. The components of the problem specification are free variables, while the bound variables I' through Satisfies serve as parameters to the transformation obtained from (GS).

What are axioms in the theory of Figure 3.1.1 appears as the premise (GSTHEORY ...) in the implication of (GS). Therefore, an inconsistency in Figure 3.1.1 can not affect the "global" consistency of the Isabelle theory we are working in. If the theory of global search algorithms were inconsistent, this would only affect the applicability of the global search transformation: the synthesis theorem would trivially hold but the corresponding transformation could never be applied.

3.4 Mechanical Proof of the Synthesis Theorem

Figure 3.4.1 shows the structure of the proof of (GS) that we have carried out in Isabelle. To keep the picture readable, we omit most of the functions' parameters.

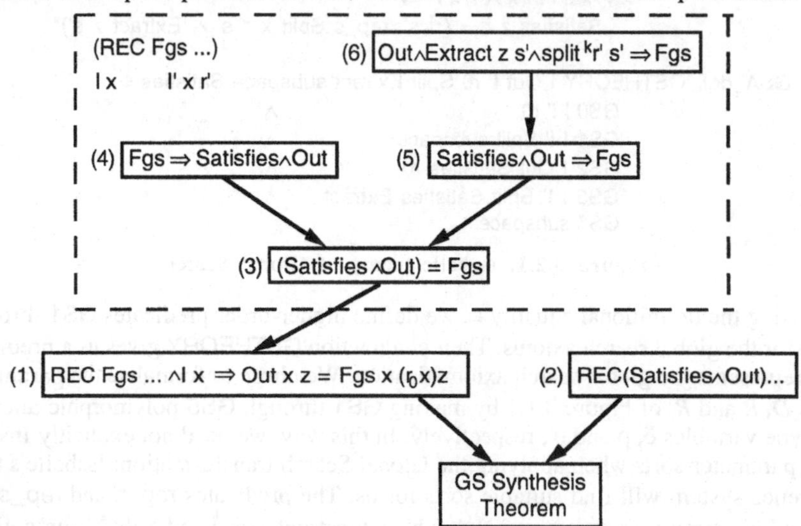

Figure 3.4.1: Proof Structure

The proof proceeds backwards in a goal-directed fashion. The first steps are to apply the introduction rules for universal quantification and implication and exhibit the equality

$$(I\ x \Rightarrow F\ x\ z = Out\ x\ z)$$
$$=$$
$$(I\ x \Rightarrow (\exists\ Fgs.\ REC\ Fgs\ I\ I'\ Extract\ Out\ Split \wedge F\ x\ z = Fgs\ x\ (r0\ x)\ z\ ))$$

We prove this equality by mutual implication. The "right-to-left" direction is the hard one, which after some simplification reduces to Lemma (1):

(1) $I\ x \wedge REC\ Fgs\ I\ I'\ Extract\ Out\ Split \Rightarrow Out\ x\ z = Fgs\ x\ (r0\ x)\ z$

The central proof-idea is to find a closed form for the recursively defined Fgs.

(3) REC Fgs ... ∧ ... ⇒ (Satisfies z r' ∧ Out x z) = Fgs x r' z

This lemma says that any function Fgs satisfying the recursive equation REC behaves like the conjunction of Satisfies and Out. By GS3, Satisfies z r' means that we only need finitely many applications of Split to find a subspace of r' where we can extract z from. On the other hand, Fgs x r' z is defined by recursively splitting r' and extracting solutions z that additionally fulfil Out x z — the latter condition being the only intuitive difference between the two predicates. Once we have proved (3), we can use GS2 to specialise it and show (1).

With Lemma (3) in mind, it is easy to prove the "left-to-right" direction of (GS). Here, we basically have to show that there exists a function Fgs fulfilling REC. From (3) we know that *if* a function Fgs satisfies REC then it behaves like the conjunction of Satisfies and Out. So we use this conjunction — suitably abstracted — as a witness for the existential quantification and show that it indeed satisfies REC.

The proof of (3) does the real work. Here, we generally assume that Fgs satisfies REC, and that the input x and search space r' are admissible, which is indicated by the dashed frame in Figure 3.4.1. Again, we prove the equality by mutual implication and reduce (3) to (4) and (5). Both can be interpreted computationally. Lemma (4) deals with termination and correctness of solutions produced by Fgs.

(4) Fgs x r' z ⇒ (Satisfies z r' ∧ Out x z)

We not only have to show that all output z produced by Fgs is a feasible solution, i.e. Out x z holds, but also that it can be extracted from the input search space r' by finitely many Split's, i.e. Satisfies z r' holds. Here it is crucial that Split produces a decreasing chain of search spaces with respect to a well-founded ordering (cf. GS1 and GS5). Only this requirement allows us to interpret REC as a definition of a recursive function. Otherwise predicates that are true on cycles of Split's where Extract is false would satisfy REC. GS5 allows us to use a theory of well-founded sets that comes with Isabelle/HOL: we prove (4) by well-founded induction on r'.

Lemma (5) deals with completeness of the set of solutions produced by Fgs: all feasible solutions are indeed found by Fgs.

(5) (Satisfies z r' ∧ Out x z) ⇒ Fgs x r' z

The proof idea for (5) is induction on the length of search paths, i.e. the number k of Split's leading to the search space from which the solution z can directly be extracted. Lemma (6) formally captures this idea. It is gained from (5) by unfolding the definitions of Satisfies and rep_s, i.e. *Split**.

Global search is an example of a non-trivial transformation. The entire proof script for (GS) consists of about 140 tactics' applications. Isabelle under Standard ML of New Jersey takes about 60 CPU seconds to execute it on a Sun Sparc 5 workstation. We needed several attempts to develop the global search theory and the proof of the synthesis theorem in Isabelle. The first version of the theory was non-conservative and explicitly introduced parameter sorts D, R and R'. We then abolished these sorts and used polymorphism. The next stage in the theory development was to come to the conservative theory sketched in Figure 3.2.1.

The proofs had to be adapted to each rephrasal of the theory. The structure of the proofs also changed several times due to new proof ideas — the latest being to introduce Lemma (3) – and due to changes in the formulation of the synthesis theorem: the first version only was an implication from the algorithm schema to the problem specification. In this version, we also left out the precondition I x ∧ I' x r in the definition of REC. This formulation of the theorem was still correct but its premises would have been too strong to be practically useful. Only after we introduced Lemma (3) and tried to prove equality instead of implication, we became aware of the missing precondition.

Despite of all these changes to the theory, it was relatively easy to adapt the proof scripts. Simple "replay until failure" was usually sufficient to find the points were changes had to be made, and these were mostly local ones like inserting a tactic to re-establish some syntactic structure, that the next tactic depended on.

3.5 Tactical Sugar for Global Search

Global Search is used in algorithm construction by providing a mapping from GlobalSearch to an extension of the concrete problem theory such that the global search axioms are theorems under the extended problem theory. We can apply the same mapping to the schematic algorithm and get a solution for our problem, i.e. we have transformed the non-constructive problem specification into a constructive form. This algorithm is usually inefficient and has to be optimised by further transformations.

In [Smi 90, SPW 95], elaborate techniques to find a global search algorithm for a given problem specification are described. They are based on a library of global search theories that basically describe the structures of search trees for various data structures.

While it is certainly possible to implement these techniques in our framework, we focus on the description of the basics of our approach and restrain ourselves to much simpler tactical sugar: the proven synthesis theorem is used to define an ML function

```
fun GLOBAL_SEARCH : nat * string list → tactic
```

that takes the subgoal number and the list of parameters to produce a tactic. This function successively removes the universal quantification via forward proof and rule spec (see section 2.4). Similarly, the implication and the equality are converted by application of the modus ponens and substitutivity rule. These operations convert the synthesis theorem into the following version:

```
[| GSTHEORY ?I ?Out ?I' ?r0 ?Split ?Extract ?subspace ?Satisfies ;
   ?I ?x ⇒ (∃ Fgs. REC Fgs ?I ?I' ?Extract ?Out ?Split ∧
                                ?F ?x ?z = Fgs ?x (?r0 ?x) ?z) |]
⇒ (?I ?x ⇒ ?F ?x ?z = ?Out ?x ?z)
```

Furthermore, GLOBAL_SEARCH successively substitutes the parameters (after parsing and typechecking the string list) into the meta-variables. Finally, the result is applied via rtac to a particular subgoal — this will set the remaining variables (?F, ?x and ?z) and complete the mapping to the problem theory.

There are different versions of tactical sugar conceivable — one could leave more parameters uninstantiated or massage the conclusion into a different syntactical form using more forward resolution steps. More complex tactics based on the synthesis theorem could employ the substitution rule for equality of higher-order logic. We would not break up the equality in (GS) but apply it to a subterm of a possibly complex goal. The choice how to come to the parameters of the global search theory would remain the same as before.

Note that the process of transforming the synthesis theorem into a logical rule which is applied by some ML function is "safe". The transformations used there are all based on proven correct rules and the primitive theorem manipulating functions of Isabelle, so nothing incorrect can happen — assuming the core of Isabelle is sound.

Proving the correctness of tactical sugar is not necessary in the sense that it simply controls the application of basic axioms and lemmas. This control may lead to a dead end and *fail,* or it might prove something that we did not want to prove, but it can never produce a proof for something that would not be provable in the theorem prover without this tactical program. Of course, the *implementation* for "apply an axiom" which represents the atoms of our tactical control programs might be incorrect or the basic rules of the logic might be unsound. But proving the correctness of "apply an axiom" in the absolute sense would require a formalisation and verification of the core theorem prover. As a consequence, this "meta-encoding" can not fully solve the problem since it raises the same problems of correctness on the meta-level.

4 YATS — the System

YATS can be regarded as a step towards an IFDSE (Integrated Formal Development Support Environment) following the philosophy of [BH 95] or [Kri+95]. Such systems support many stages of the formal development, from initial functional specifications, through design specifications and refinement. More elaborated systems will also provide a support for specification animation, version-management etc.

We believe that a high-quality graphical user interface (GUI) plays a key role for both the acceptance and productivity of an IFDSE. To date, there is no common agreement on what could be a good design of a GUI for a theorem prover or an IFDSE (we admit that we have not found the definite answer either), although there are recent remarkable efforts in this direction.

Our GUI should be completely independent from Isabelle and as independent as possible from our system environment and our hardware-platform. In the past, the development of many systems (PROSPECTRA, for example) has been trapped by their complex and monolithic design. An answer to this dilemma of monolithic designs can be a *heterogeneous* one with few complementary components that are systems in their own right. This way it is possible to integrate work of independent research groups. The main task of an heterogeneous design is to provide suitably abstract and flexible interfaces in order to enable an easy and stable integration of new versions of its components.

For our GUI, we chose the toolkit *Tk* [Ous 94] to achieve this goal. Although we wish to profit from Tk as a highly portable interface to X-Windows, we do not believe that the command-language Tcl on top of Tk should be used for larger software developments. The major reason is that Tcl supports only one data-structure — text — in a way similar to LISP and its lists. Tcl is an untyped language without data structures and lacks higher modularisation concepts.

For this reason, we implemented an SML interface for Tk, called *sml_tk.* It is a component in its own right and provides a toolkit for standard windows, e.g. a substitution window, that can be reused by research groups working on, e.g., another theorem prover interface. Based on sml_tk, the GUI itself is implemented as an SML functor, called *isawin*, which is parametrised by a list of tactical-sugar functions. The system YATS is an instantiation of this functor with a list containing the function

GLOBAL_SEARCH (see section 3.5). According to the instantiation, isawin automatically produces new interface components and new dialogues with the user — the implementor of a transformation has only to provide its proof and its tactical sugar.

The following diagram gives a short overview over the stack of main components (the size of the blocks roughly corresponds to their implementation size):

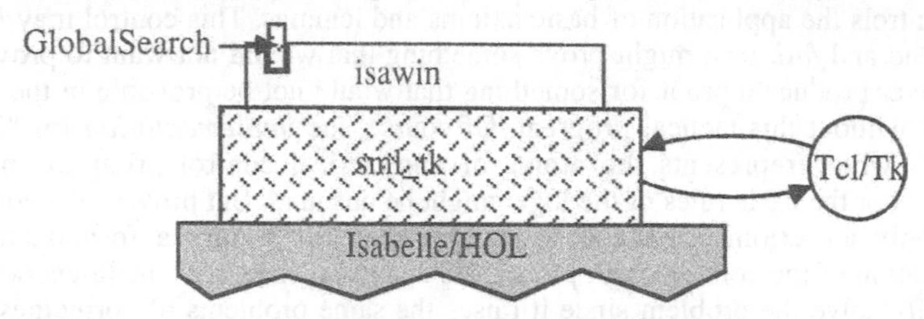

Figure 4.0.1: The System architecture

Note that the formal proof of Global Search and its integration into the system contributes only to a very small part to the whole system. This justifies our claim that the design allows the implementors to concentrate on the real intellectual problem of designing and verifying new transformations. Moreover, the instantiation of isawin with a new transformation is a question of a few seconds. Even if a very different state of technology (hardware and software) has to be taken into consideration, in comparison to PROSPECTRA, for example, where a complete recompilation was necessary that took 2 hours [GL 93], this is quite remarkable.

4.1 The interface sml_tk

Our interface evolved from an imperative version of a purely functional, monad-style encapsulation of Tk in Gofer [VTS 95]. It has a more functional flavour than the interface available for caml/light [PR 95]. It is characterised by the following features:

- abstract data-types for options, configurations, packing information
- abstract data-type for graphical objects, called *widgets*
- events on the interface (mouse clicks, key strokes, etc) are mapped to SML functions associated to widgets via *bindings*.
- a toolkit for defining a problem specific set of window types.

To give a flavour of programming in sml_tk, let us have a brief look at a fragment of the essential tree-like data type for widgets used to describe the content of windows:

```
datatype  Widget =
        Frame of WidId * Widget list * Pack list * Configure list * Binding list
      | Label of WidId * Pack list * Configure list * Binding list
      | Entry of WidId * Pack list * Configure list * Binding list
      ...

type Window   = (WinId * Title * (Widget)list * Action);
```

The following fragment is taken from the description of a small standard-window of the toolkit:

```
fun input enteraction =
      let fun mrs () = let val nm = selectTextAll "e1"
                       in   enteraction nm ();closeWindow "enter" end
      in  Entry("e1",[],[Width  20],  [Bind("<Return>",mrs)])  end;
```

The function input yields an Entry-Widget [Ous 94], that represents a graphical field allowing to enter a string. It has the name e1 and a width of 20 characters. Associated to e1, there is a function mrs that is evaluated whenever the event <Return> happens. mrs selects the inserted text, passes it to the parameter function enteraction and closes the surrounding window called enter.

4.2 The GUI of YATS

The main window of YATS (as well as any other instance of isawin) consists of two major components: An edit-window (where the editing facilities like Cut-Copy-Paste are already provided by Tk without writing any additional line of code in the interface) and a prover-window to which the transformation facilities (a result of the instantiation of isawin) and the operations controlling Isabelle are associated. It is possible to browse theories and ML files in suitable subwindows with their associated axioms and theorems (see Figure 4.2.1 below). The user-interface for the prover part is not in the focus of this paper.

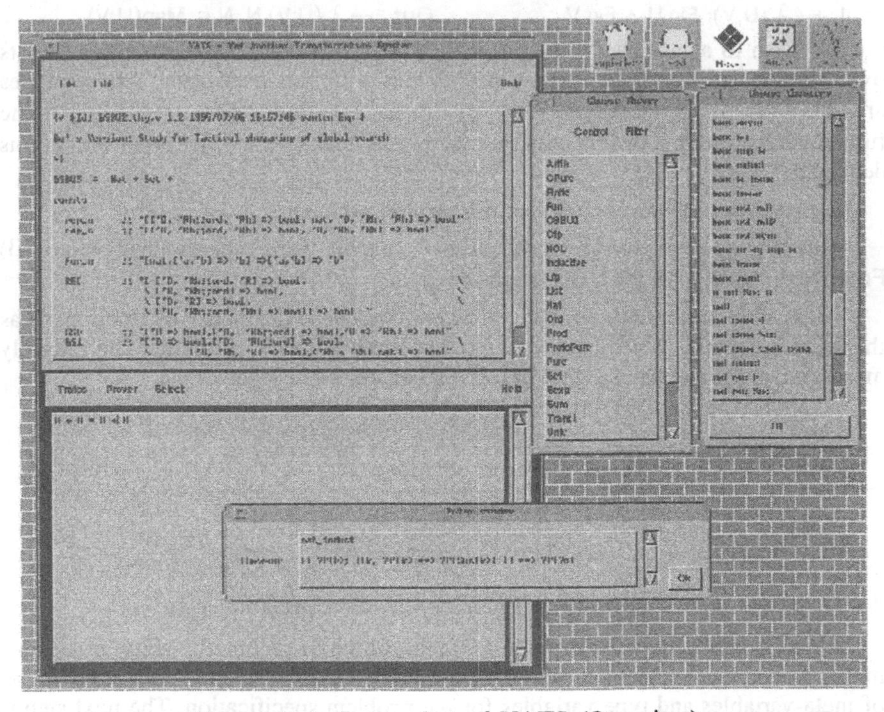

Figure 4.2.1: Screenshot of YATS (Overview)

Usually, by double-click on an arbitrary widget of the interface, the user can get more information, and by triple-clicks suitable operations on the activated unit are executed. For example, when pointing to a subgoal in the prover-state-widget, a double-click will inform the user on what transformation or Isabelle-command will be executed (due to settings and other information inferred by the system), while a triple-click performs this command.

4.3 An Application Example

In this section we use our system to develop a global search algorithm that enumerates all maps from a finite set U to a finite set V. We take the global search theory for this algorithm, *gs_finite_mappings*, from [Smi 87]. In KIDS, abstract and simple theories like *gs_finite_mappings* are used to describe search patterns on particular data structures. To develop a search algorithm for a particular problem with KIDS means to *specialise* such a "pattern theory" to the given problem specification (see [Smi 90]). Since the specialisation procedure as well as the pattern theories are hard-wired into KIDS, their correctness can not be guaranteed within the system. The development of "pattern theories" can not rely on specialisation but must use different tactical sugar like we have implemented in YATS.

The problem specification for *gs_finite_mappings* is based on a library theory of finite maps:

$F \mapsto$ fin_maps

$\delta \mapsto \alpha$ set $\times\ \beta$ set $\qquad\qquad \rho \mapsto (\alpha, \beta)$ Fmap

$I \mapsto \lambda\,(U,V).\ \mathrm{Fin}\ U \wedge \mathrm{Fin}\ V \qquad\qquad \mathrm{Out} \mapsto \lambda\,(U,V)\ N.\ N \in \mathrm{Map}(U,V)$

We wish to synthesise a function called fin_maps that transforms pairs of sets over types α and β to finite maps whose domains are sets over α and whose ranges are sets over β, i.e. members of (α, β) Fmap. For finite input sets U and V the function must return a map N with domain U and a range in V. The predicate Map is defined by

$$\mathrm{Map}(U,V) \equiv \{\ M \mid \mathrm{dom}\ M = U \wedge \forall\, b \in \mathrm{dom}\ M.\ M \wedge b \in V\ \}$$

Note that we need an explicit operation ^ to apply maps because their type (α, β) Fmap is different form the HOL function type.

To develop an algorithm for the problem, we chose the theory of finite maps as the logical context (just by activating it via a mouse-click) and enter the (slightly massaged) specification as a goal into YATS as shown in Figure 4.3.1.

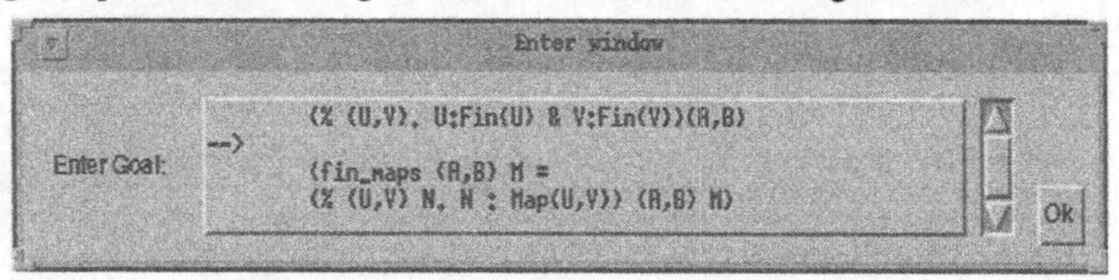

Figure 4.3.1: Entering the transformation goal

We now apply the transformation Globalsearch of section 3.5. First of all, this makes Isabelle match the goal with the transformation rule and set up the substitution of meta-variables and type variables for the problem specification. The next step is the creative part of the transformation: we have to provide the parameters that establish a global search theory. To date, as Figure 4.3.2 shows, this is done by explicitly entering a substitution for the parameters.

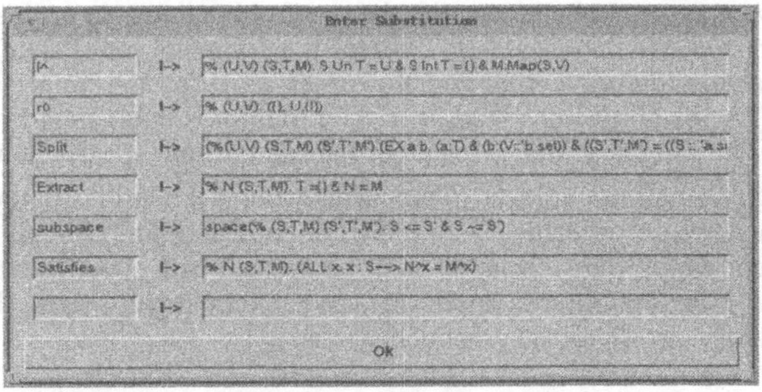

```
Enter Substitution

I^          I->  % (U,V) (S,T,M). S Un T = U & S Int T = {} & M:Map(S,V)
r0          I->  % (U,V). ({}, U,{|})
Split       I->  (% (U,V) (S,T,M) (S',T',M'). (EX a b. (a:T) & (b:(V::'b set)) & ((S',T',M') = ((S :: 'a s
Extract     I->  % N (S,T,M). T ={} & N = M
subspace    I->  space(% (S,T,M) (S',T',M'). S <= S' & S ~= S')
Satisfies   I->  % N (S,T,M). (ALL x. x : S--> N^x = M^x)
            I->

Ok
```

Figure 4.3.2: Entering parameter substitution

In mathematical notation, the substitution looks as follows:

I'	$\mapsto \lambda\,(U,V)\,(S,T,M).\ S \cup T = U \wedge S \cap T = \emptyset \wedge M \in \text{Map}(S,V)$
r'_0	$\mapsto \lambda\,(U,V).\ (\emptyset, U, \{\|\})$
Split	$\mapsto \lambda\,(U,V)\,(S,T,M)\,(S',T',M').\ (\exists\ a\,b.\ a \in T \wedge b \in V$ $\wedge\ (S',T',M') = (S \cup \{a\}, T - \{a\}, M \oplus \{a \mapsto b\}))$
Extract	$\mapsto \lambda\,N\,(S,T,M).\ T = \emptyset \wedge N = M$
subspace	$\mapsto \text{space}(\lambda\,(S,T,M)\,(S',T',M').\ S \subset S')$
Satisfies	$\mapsto \lambda\,N\,(S,T,M).\ (\forall\ x \in S.\ N \wedge x = M \wedge x)$

The crucial part here is to find a representation of search spaces and a suitable Split based on that representation. Our search idea is to successively extend a partial map until its domain encompasses all of U. Therefore, we model search spaces by triples (S,T,M) where S and T partition U and M is a map to V with domain S. Splitting a search space means to extend M by a new pair mapping a not yet used member a of U to some arbitrary value b of V. The operation $\oplus$ overwrites the first map on the domain of the second, and $\{a \mapsto b\}$ maps a exactly to b. The subspace relation on search spaces is induced by the strict subset relation on S, which we for–malise using the library function space that converts an ordering function into its graph. Given the transformation above, Isabelle computes the type of search spaces auto–matically.

$\rho' \mapsto \alpha\ \text{set} \times \beta\ \text{set} \times (\alpha, \beta)\ \text{Fmap}$

After type checking the parameter substitution, YATS responds with the following proof state, containing the proof obligations and the synthesised "program":

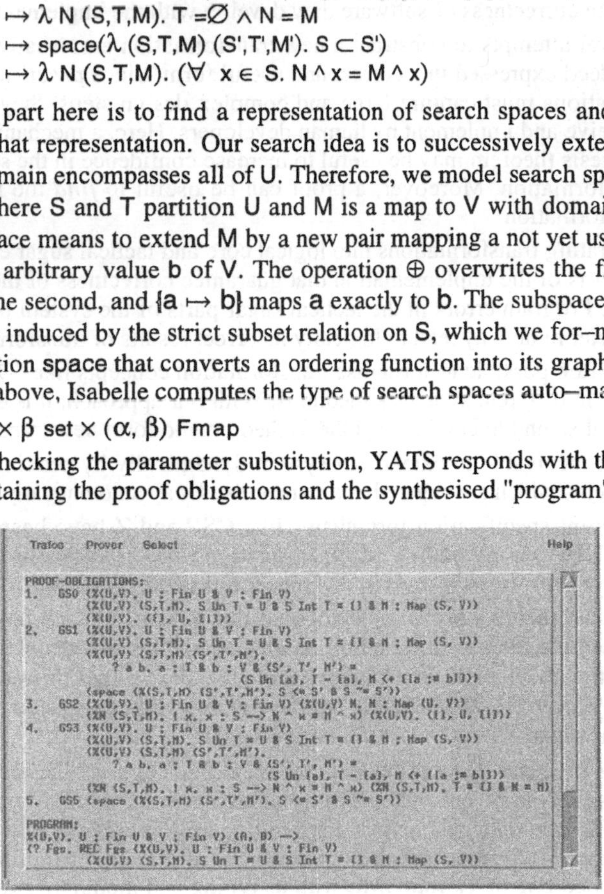

```
Trafoo   Prover   Select                                          Help

PROOF-OBLIGATIONS:
1.   GS0 (%(U,V). U : Fin U & V : Fin V)
         (%(U,V) (S,T,M). S Un T = U & S Int T = {} & M : Map (S, V))
         (%(U,V). ({}, U, {|}))
2.   GS1 (%(U,V). U : Fin U & V : Fin V)
         (%(U,V) (S,T,M). S Un T = U & S Int T = {} & M : Map (S, V))
         (%(U,V) (S,T,M) (S',T',M').
              ? a b. a : T & b : V & (S', T', M') =
                                  (S Un {a}, T - {a}, M <+ {|a := b|}))
         (space (%(S,T,M) (S',T',M'). S <= S' & S ~= S'))
3.   GS2 (%(U,V). U : Fin U & V : Fin V) (%(U,V) N. N : Map (U, V))
         (%N (S,T,M). ! x. x : S --> N ^ x = M ^ x) (%(U,V). ({}, U, {|}))
4.   GS3 (%(U,V). U : Fin U & V : Fin V)
         (%(U,V) (S,T,M). S Un T = U & S Int T = {} & M : Map (S, V))
         (%(U,V) (S,T,M) (S',T',M').
              ? a b. a : T & b : V & (S', T', M') =
                                  (S Un {a}, T - {a}, M <+ {|a := b|}))
         (%N (S,T,M). ! x. x : S --> N ^ x = M ^ x) (%N (S,T,M). T = {} & N = M)
5.   GS5 (space (%(S,T,M) (S',T',M'). S <= S' & S ~= S'))

PROGRAM:
%(U,V). U : Fin U & V : Fin V) (A, B) -->
(? Fgs. REC Fgs (%(U,V). U : Fin U & V : Fin V)
         (%(U,V) (S,T,M). S Un T = U & S Int T = {} & M : Map (S, V))
```

Figure 4.3.3: The resulting proof state

Now, we may use Isabelle to verify the proof obligations. At an arbitrary point of the development, we may decide to "freeze" the complete proof state i.e. convert it into an Isabelle theory containing the proof state as the implication: "if the (remaining) proof obligations hold, then the program is equivalent to the specification". Later, we can reload the frozen proof state and resume the development.

Although a small example, fin_maps demonstrates the virtues of top-down development via stepwise refinement in a transformational setting. Simply by indicating to the system which transformation shall be applied to a specification, YATS can check if the transformation is applicable, and systematically leads the user to the necessary design decisions and proof obligations.

5 Discussion

We have shown how to implement transformation systems in a systematic way that clearly separates the *soundness* issues of transformations, the *pragmatics* of their application, and their *presentation* to developers at the user interface.

For several reasons, representing the logical content of transformations by synthesis theorems highly increases the users' confidence in single transformation steps and thereby in the correctness of software they develop with the implemented system.

- Several attempts to construct a new transformation are usually needed until it is indeed expressed in a correct and useful form. Since *practically useful* transformations must capture large and complex design steps, they are difficult to conceive and implement by human developers. Here, a mechanical proof of the synthesis theorem may be useful to increase confidence in the soundness of the transformation. Moreover, a proof can be useful to *find* the final shape of a transformation.
- Separating transformations into logical core and tactical sugar clearly identifies the parts of the implementation that guarantee correctness of the resulting software. Program errors in the tactical sugar parts of the system or the user interface can in no way lead to logically incorrect results of transformations.
- It is often possible to formalise transformation concepts like "Divide-and-Conquer" in different synthesis theorems. With our approach, it is easy to relate, to specialise and to combine synthesis theorems to form new transformations.
- It is conceivable to extend our system dynamically by proving the synthesis-theorems which are sugared in a standardised way automatically.
- Different specification formalisms like CSP and Z have been represented in HOL. The representation of transformation rules as synthesis theorems provides a means to study rules in combined multi-formalism environments.

The tactical theorem prover is the core of our system. It is not only used to prove synthesis theorems but also, based on its meta-variables and deduction facilities, to implement transformation applications. We have shown that this can be done with little effort. Moreover, in [HSZ 95], we have demonstrated a systematic approach to build tactical sugar.

The user-interface description and command language Tcl/Tk has seen a tremendous success in the recent years. From our experience, the X-Window toolkit Tk seems to offer "the right abstraction" for building user interfaces. However, the design of our parameterized interface and our productivity to code it profited substantially from the embedding of Tk into SML with its typing and modularisation concepts.

5.1 Related Work

The transformational approach to program development has a long tradition. Starting from the Munich CIP project [Bau+85], many studies have stressed the importance of the approach. During the PROSPECTRA project [HK 93], a system has been developed that enabled the formalisation of transformation rules and their use during the software development process.

In KIDS [Smi 91], programs are developed by transforming *problem specifications* to programs. First, high-level transformations such as global search are used to come from the problem specification to a (inefficient) program. This program is then optimised by low-level program transformations like finite differencing or case distinction.

While the research in the context of KIDS has contributed much in the area of mathematically describing complex transformations and tactical sugar for their successful application, a shortcoming of the implemented system is that there is no easy way to convince oneself of the soundness of the implemented transformations. Our work focuses on this aspect and may thus be regarded complementary to the KIDS work.

Kreitz [Kre 93] gives mechanical proofs of global search theories in a constructive type theory, namely Nuprl [Con 86]. He aims at capturing even the pragmatics of transformation applications in a logical framework and attempts to extract synthesis tactics from the computational content of constructive proofs. In our approach, formal logic is used only to treat the soundness of transformations. This admits varying degrees of sophistication of tactical sugar: we can easily have different tactics for the same synthesis theorem. To achieve the same effect, Kreitz would have to provide different *proofs* of the theorem, each encoding a different approach to its application.

Basin's work [Bas 94] represents an approach to logic program synthesis also implemented in Isabelle. It is based on the Whelk logic that has been proposed as foundation. The rules of Whelk are derived in Isabelle. This work focuses on foundational issues rather than on a practical system implementation.

The recent formation of new workshops show a growing interest in the design and implementation of graphical user interfaces for both theorem provers and IFDSEs. A notable implementation is the TkHOLWorkbench currently developed in Cambridge [Sym 95], another one is [CO 95] for Isabelle. Although these interfaces currently are clearly superior to ours it is predominantly implemented in Tcl and not in ML. For this reason, we believe that our approach offers a higher potential of growth and reusability for similar systems.

5.2 Future Work

Our implementation to date is a prototype to illustrate the approach. To make it practically usable, two improvements have to be made: we need to extend the library of transformations and we need to incorporate a standard specification language which is used in practice.

Incorporating more standard transformations from the literature is easy. The standardised form of synthesis theorems even allows us to develop a set of "meta-transformations" — as ML functions — yielding transformations from synthesis theorems automatically. Meta-transformations might implement different ways to deal with application conditions and parameters. As we have mentioned in section 3.5, verificational approaches supplying the parameters directly and leaving application conditions as subgoals to verify are as well as possible as constructive approaches that — automatically or interactively — synthesise parameters while proving application conditions. Different techniques to match an input pattern against a goal are possible.

As for the use of a standard specification language, research is going on to implement support for, e.g., Z in Isabelle. Proving suitable synthesis theorems in the logical representation of such a specification language makes our approach immediately applicable to that language. This work is partly an objective of the project UniForM [Kri+95].

Acknowledgement. We would like to thank Maritta Heisel for many discussions on synthesis theorems, and two anonymous referees for very extensive and constructive comments.

References

[And 86] Andrews, P.B., *An Introduction to Mathematical Logic and Type Theory: To Truth Through Proof*, Academic Press, 1986.

[Bas 94] Basin, D., Isawhelk: Whelk interpreted in Isabelle. Abstract accepted at the *11th International Conference on Logic Programming* (ICLP 94). Full version available via http://www.mpi-sb.mpg.de/guide/staff/basin/-pubs/iclp11.ps.Z.

[Bau+85] Bauer et al. (The CIP Language Group): *The Munich Project CIP. Volume I: The wide spectrum language CIP-L.* LNCS 183. 1985.

[BH 95] Bowen, J. P., Hinchey, M. J., Seven more Myths of Formal Methods: Dispelling Industrial Prejudices, in *FME'94: Industrial Benefit of Formal Methods*, proc. 2nd Int. Symposium of Formal Methods Europe, LNCS 873, Springer Verlag 1994, pp. 105-117.

[BM 93] Bird, R., de Moor, O.: Solving Optimisation Problems with Catamorphisms, in Proc. *Second Conference on the Mathematics of Program Construction*, LNCS 669, Springer Verlag 1993, pp. 49-56.

[Chu 40] Church, A., A formulation of the simple theory of types. *Journal of Symbolic Logic*, 5, 1940, pp. 56-68.

[CO 95] Cant, A., Ozohls, M.A. XIsabelle: A graphical User Interface to the Isabelle Theorem Prover. ftp://ftp.cl.cam.ac.uk/ml/XIsabelle-2.0.tar.gz

[Con 86] Constable, R. S. et al. *Implementing Mathematics with the Nuprl Proof Development System.* Prentice Hall, 1986.

[GL 93] Gersdorf, B., Liu, J. personnal communication.

[GM 93] Gordon, M.J.C., Melham, T.M.: *Introduction to HOL: a theorem proving environment for higher order logics*, Cambridge University Press, 1993.

[Gor 95] Gordon. M: Notes on PVS from a HOL perspective. Available via Internet http://www.cl.cam.ac.uk/users/mjcg/PVS.ps.gz, 1995.

[HK 93] Hoffmann, B., Krieg-Brückner, B. (eds.): *PROgram Development by Specification and Transformation, The PROSPECTRA Methodology, Language Family, and System.* LNCS 680, Springer-Verlag 1993.

[HMM 86] Harper, R., MacQueen, R., Milner, R: Standard ML. Technical Report ECS-LFCS-86-2. 1986.

[HSZ 95] Heisel, M., Santen, T., Zimmermann, D.: Tool Support for Formal Software Development: A Generic Architecture, in *Software Engineering — ESEC '95*, LNCS 989, Springer Verlag, 1995, pp. 272-293.

[Kre 93] Kreitz, C.: Meta-Synthesis. Deriving Programs that Develop Programs. Technische Hochschule Darmstadt, 1993.

[Kri+95] Krieg-Brückner, B., Peleska, J., Olderog, E.-R., Balzer, D., Baer, A.: Uniform Workbench — Universelle Entwicklungsumgebung für formale Methoden. Technischer Bericht 8/95, Universität Bremen, 1995.

[KW 95] Kolyang, Wolff, B.: Development by Refinement Revisited: Lessons learnt from a case study. Proc. *Softwaretechnik '95*. Software-Technik Trends, Gesellschaft für Informatik, 1995, pp. 55-66 .

[OSR 93] Owre, S., Shankar, N., Rushby, J.M.: The PVS Specification Language (Beta Release). Comp. Sci. Lab., SRI International, Menlo Park, 1993.

[Ous 94] Ousterhout, J.K.: *Tcl and the Tk Toolkit.* Addison Wesley, 1994.

[Pau 94a] Paulson, L. C.: *Isabelle - A Generic Theorem Prover.* LNCS 828, Springer Verlag, 1994.

[Pau 94b] Paulson, L. C.: A fixedpoint approach to implementing (co)inductive definitions, in Alan Bundy (ed), *12th International Conference on Automated Deduction,* LNAI 814, 1994, Springer Verlag, pp. 148-161.

[PR 95] Pessaux, F., Rouaix, F.: The Caml/Tk interface, Projet Cristal, INRIA Rocquencourt, July 1995 ftp://ftp.inria.fr/lang/../INRIA/Projects/cristal/caml-light/camltk.dvi.tar.gz

[Smi 87] Smith, D. R.: Structure and Design of Global Search Algorithms, Technical Report Kes.U.87.12, Kestrel Institute, Palo Alto, 1987.

[Smi 90] Smith, D. R.: KIDS – a semi-automatic program development system. *IEEE Transactions on Software Engineering* Special Issue on Formal Methods in Software Engineering, 16(9), 1990, pp. 1024–1043.

[SPW 95] Smith, D. R., Parra, E. A., Westfold, S. J.: Synthesis of High-Performance Transportation Schedulers, Technical Report, Kestrel Institute, Palo Alto, 1995.

[Sym 95] Syme, D.: A New Interface for HOL – Ideas, Issues and Implementation in *Higher Order Logic: Theorem Proving and its Applications*, LNCS 971, Springer Verlag 1995. pp 325-339.

[VTS 95] Vullinghs,T., Tuijnman, D., Schulte, W., Lightweight GUI's for functional programming. PLILP 95, Utrecht, The Netherlands, 1995.

An Example of Use of Formal Methods to Debug an Embedded Software

André Arnold[1], Didier Bégay[1], Jean-Pierre Radoux[2]

[1] LaBRI, Université Bordeaux I
351, cours de la Libération
F-33405 Talence, France
[2] SERLI-Informatique,
avenue du Téléport
F-86960 Futuroscope, France

Abstract. This article releases an industrial experiment of using formal methods to analyze and to debug a system that was shown erroneous by testing. After presenting the industrial context of the experiment, it details the modelling process and the interpretation of the results, in conjunction with the designers of the system.

1 Introduction

1.1 The EUROTRI project

The EUROTRI project was aimed by Schlumberger-Industries to define, conceive, design and develop a static electricity meter with large abilities of tariff programming and distant measuring. For commercial and industrial reasons, short time of development and low cost of production (through the use of components at frontier of their technical limits) were the challenges. It was also the first time a software-based product was designed and developped in this industrial center: the previous products had been conceived as electronical, even if they used some software.

The main idea was to avoid iteration of any development step, and to meet the deadlines by a straightforward way. This implied to use at every step of design and development all possible means to validate it definetely. This process was usual for the electronics engineers, and we convinced them easily that an equivalent for the software would be formal methods. So it has been decided at the very beginning of the project to use formal methods in most steps of it, from feasability study to reception testing.

For different reasons, including readability of transition systems by electronic engineers and availability of a powerful model-checker, the Arnold-Nivat model and the MEC tool have been selected, in conjunction with the language Ada and the Rate Monotonic Analysis.

The "Concurrency Semantics" team of LaBRI became involved in the design and development process as an extra team among the usual industrial ones: hardware, software, marketing and industrialization, with a general interest on the use of formal methods along the project.

The different aspects of this collaboration, and peculiarly the different ways formal methods have been combined and applied in the project, have been presented in [4].

The study we present here is illustrative of the power of the formal methods. The application described here had been thought simple enough not to deserve formal methods in its design (furthermore, this would spare academy resource in the project). On the bench the application did not work properly, although not clearly enough to point out where the default was lying. The lack of rational explanation made the engineers report the phenomenon to our team. Happily we happened to explain "intellectually" what was going on, as it is described hereby, but *during the project, this has been the only solution to this important problem related to security.* This emphasizes the ability of formal methods to intervene successfully and a posteriori in an application developped without them, in the tests step.

So this is a real industrial application, solved by academy people.

A part of the project, related to electronics, the study of the physical layer of the two processors, at the interface of hardware and software, has been released in [5].

The interesting way the Synchronized Transition Systems approach and the Rate Monotonic Analysis have been coupled to study the temporal aspects of the embedded system has been explained in [1].

The whole work has been presented as a thesis by Jean-Pierre Radoux [8].

The consequences of this project on the way Schlumberger-Industries considers system development will certainly impact its R&D structure.

1.2 The OUCABO system

The detailed design of this system, and some informations related to implementation details, were the basis of our approach of the OUCABO system.

Dealing with an electricity meter, it is a basic feature to iteratively measure N numerical values (such as voltage, intensity and phase) and to process them in the flow. At a given time t, one among the N analog signals is input in the measuring software, by the mean of a 1-in-n multiplexer, driven by an external (external to the software) counter. So we have two counters referring to the same value: an *external* (hardware) counter, selecting the input signal, an *internal* (software) counter, processing the input signal, both of them being controled by the same clock.

The first problem we have to deal with is that parasites can impact the links between the common clock and both devices, and thus desynchronize both counters, making the software process erroneously input values.

This can be handled either by identifying each sample transmitted to the software or by periodically synchronizing both counters. The first solution was not relevant for technical reasons, and it has been designed that an output port would be used by the software counter to reset the hardware counter.

In such an embedded system as the electricity meter, various processes have to be activated to ensure the fiability of the apparatus. One of them is the OUCABO system. This system requires a device to be periodically activated and tested. *The second problem is that the solution to first problem left no output port available to activate this secondary device, nor input port to test it.* The situation on the output port has been handled using the leftmost carry bit of the hardware counter to activate the device : if the software counter does not reset the hardware counter in due time, there occurs an arithmetic overflow and the device is activated.

This solution had been conceived and implemented ignoring formal methods, as an electronic hack to answer a very simple, low-level problem.

1.3 Debugging the OUCABO system

This part of the system had been developped and implemented, and tested using laboratory equipment: same signals were simultaneously measured by the system and the testers. Unfortunately, it happened that a very seldom measure difference occurred between both measures; at first glance, the origin could be hardware, software or a *testing protocol error*.

Testing such rare behaviours may last a long time, and in order to spare time, a model-checking approach was accepted. Then, using the detailed design and some implementation details, * the system has been modelled using synchronized labeled transition systems. The error and the error rate could be confirmed on a study of synchronized transitions, thus identifying the source of the erroneous behaviour. The bug was fixed in the model and after verification, the system could be efficiently and safely corrected.

1.4 Content of the paper

Instead of reporting the experience as it was, we choose in this paper to construct step by step, in a pedagogical order, the system to model.

2 Synchronized products of transition systems

We model any behaviour using labeled transition systems (LTS), ie: uniquely named states linked by transitions, each of them wearing a non-null string of characters called its label, and due to model what triggers the transition from source state to target state. As same phenomenon can trigger different transitions depending of current state, different transitions can wear same label.

A parameterized LTS is a LTS where boolean properties are defined on states and transitions, and operators allow computation of such properties as deadlocks of loops, etc... using an adapted version of Tarjan's algorithm and a μ-calculus engine ([6, 7]).

Interactions between behaviours is expressed in our synchronous model using correlation of labels: behaviours triggers freely, provided they respect a set of synchronization constraints, expressed as a set of vectors of firing configurations of labels. So we construct the synchronized product of original LTS's as a LTS where states are vectors of original states, and transitions are labeled by vectors of original labels, restricted to the synchronization constraints. This synchronized transition system models the global behaviour under study. We can apply on it the usual computing of boolean properties.

Both construct of the synchronized product and computing of boolean properties are implemented in the MEC tool.

A complete description of our model and of the power of expression of the properties will be found in [2], and a shorter one illustrated by some demonstrative examples using MEC is given in [3].

3 Hard and soft counters

The system contains a hardware counter modulo N activated by ticks of a clock and able to be reset to 0 by an input signal. If N ticks occur without any reset, a carry bit is set. Each tick of the clock generates an interruption: the interruption routine increments a counter, called **channel** and initialized to 0, when its value is strictly less than $N-1$, and resets it to 0 and sends a reset signal to the hardware counter when it has value $N-1$. The code of this interruption routine is thus
if channel $<N-1$ **then increment(channel) else send(reset); channel:=0; endif**

3.1 Modeling the hardware counter

The first thing to do is to give a definite value to N. Recall this value is inversely related to the error ratio. We assume that N has a lesser value than the actual value, say 4, and it will not be difficult to convince oneself that is a quite admissible simplification with respect to the verifications to be done. The hardware counter can have its carry bit set or not. In order to make things easier, we model activity of the carry bit during $3 \times N$ ticks.

Therefore, the hardware counter can be modeled by a transition with thirteen states. A state of the counter is encoded by a two-digit number: the second digit (0,1,2, or 3) represents the value of the counter and the fist digit counts the number of carries since its last reset. Two actions can change the state of the counter:

- a tick of the clock, denoted by `t`,
- a reset signal, denoted by `reset`.

We also use the null action denoted by `e` to express that something else may occurs that has no effect on the counter.

In MEC, such a transition system is described by

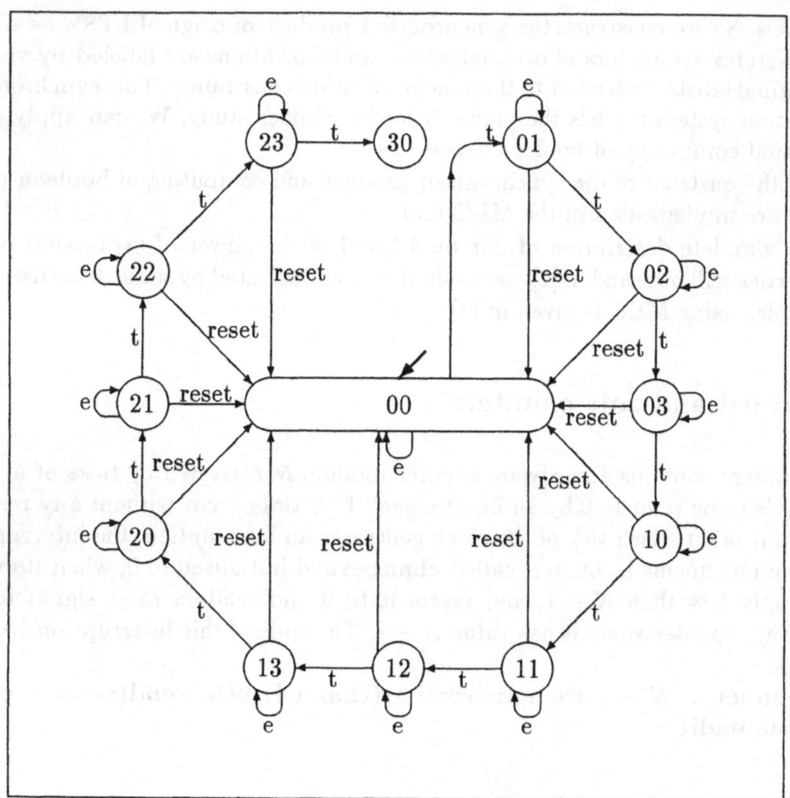

Figure 1: Counter

3.2 Modeling the software counter

The software counter is similar to the hardware counter: its states are the values of **channel** and when a tick occurs (action denoted by **t**) this value changes. However, when this value is 3, a reset signal is immediately sent to the hardware counter before the value becomes 0 (action denoted by **reset**). Therefore, we get the following system.

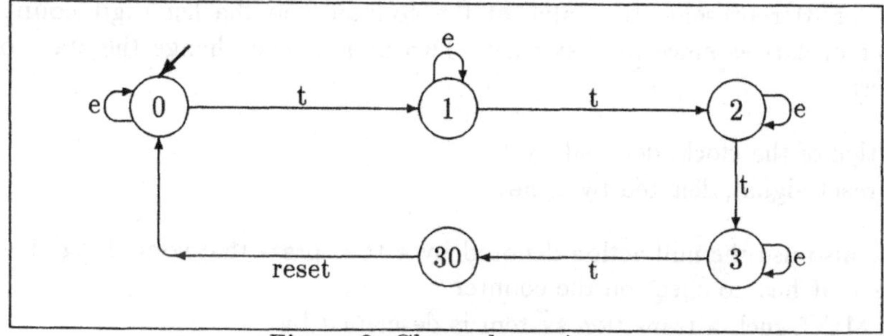

Figure 2: Channel, version 1

Remark that when the channel receives a tick in state `3`, it goes into an intermediate state `30`. In this state it is not allowed to wait (there is no "e-loop"), it has to immediately execute **`reset`** and to go into state `0`.

3.3 Synchronization constraint

We consider the system composed of the counter and the channel. When a tick occurs, both components react simultaneously by executing a transition labeled by the action **`t`**. When the interruption routine sends a reset signal by **`reset`**, the counter simultaneously receives this signal and executes **`reset`** too. Finally both components can stay idle together. This synchronization constraint is described :

counter	*channel_v1*
t	t
reset	reset
e	e

The synchronized product of this system is

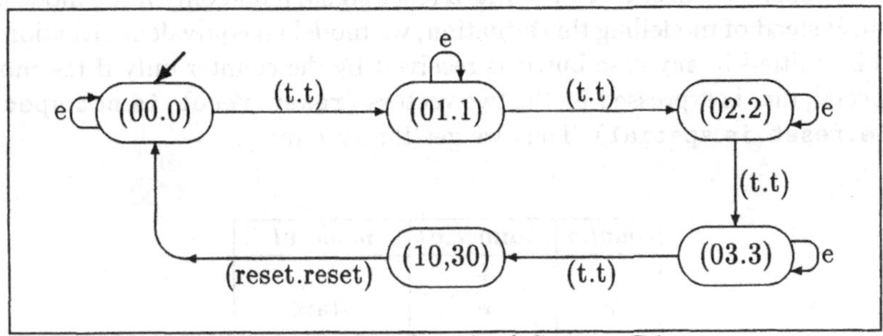

Figure 3: Synchronized System R1

and one can see that, excepted when the channel is in its intermediate state `30`, the values of the counter and of the channel are the same.

4 Introduction of a mode

Actually, for some reasons relating to the activity of the secondary device via the carry bit, the above system can be in two modes, special and non special. The mode becomes special when an external and uncontrollable event, called **`start`**, is generated by the environment of the system. The only difference between the two modes is that no reset signal is emitted when in special mode, and thus the carry bit will be set to activate the secondary device:

if channel $< M - 1$ **then increment(channel)**
else if mode is not special then send(reset); channel:=0; endif

We model the mode by the transition system:

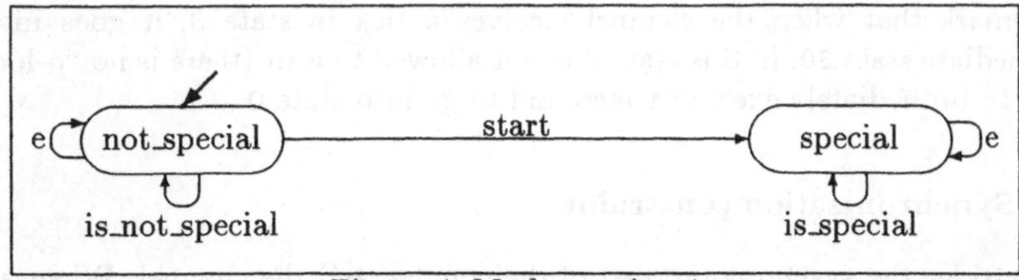

Figure 4: Mode, version 1

The action **start** switches the mode from non special to special. The actions **is_not_special** and **is_special** allows to know what the mode of the system is.

We now have a system with three components: **counter**, **channel_v1**, **mode_v1**. Let us describe the interactions between these components.

When a tick occurs it is received by **counter** and **channel** and has no effect on **mode**; this is expressed by the synchronisation vector **(t.t.e)**. When the mode becomes special, nothing happens to the counter and the channel: **(e.e.start)**. When the channel is in state **30** it emits a reset signal if and only if the mode is not special. Instead of modelling this situation, we model an equivalent situation: this signal is emitted in any case but it is received by the counter only if the mode is not special, that is expressed by the two vectors **(reset.reset.is_not_special)** and **(e.reset.is_special)**. Thus we get the system:

counter	*channel_v1*	*mode_v1*
t	t	e
e	e	start
reset	reset	is_not_special
e	reset	is_special
e	e	e

whose synchonized product is:

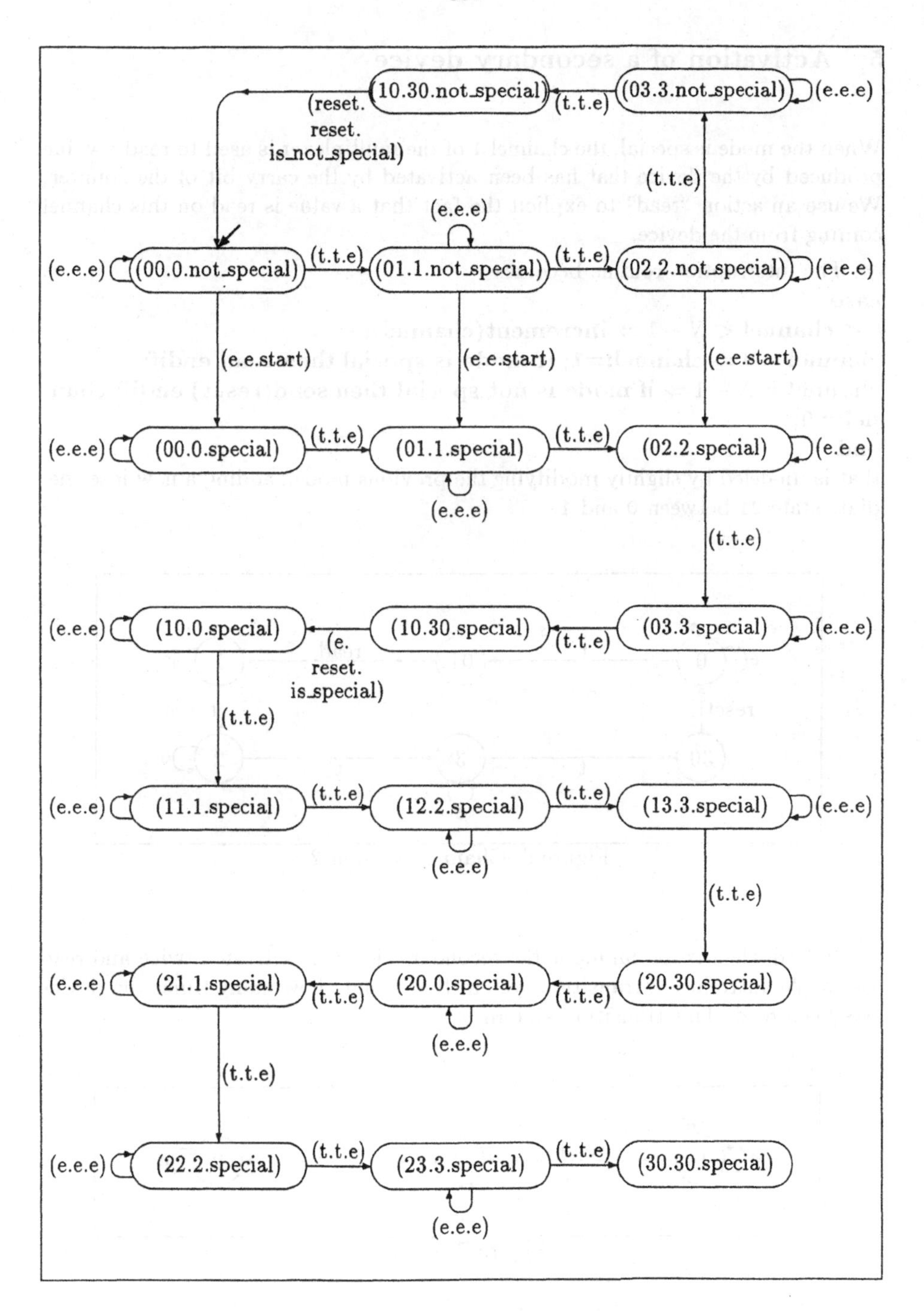

Figure 5: Synchronized Product R2

5 Activation of a secondary device

When the mode is special, the channel 1 of the multiplexer is used to read a value produced by the device that has been activated by the carry bit of the counter. We use an action "read" to explicit the fact that a value is read on this channel coming from the device.

The interruption routine becomes
case
$0 <$ **channel** $< N - 1 \Rightarrow$ **increment(channel);**
channel $= 0 \Rightarrow$ **channel:=1; if mode is special then read endif;**
channel $= N - 1 \Rightarrow$ **if mode is not special then send(reset) endif; channel:=0;**
end
that is modeled by slightly modifying the previous model: adding a new intermediate state `01` between `0` and `1`.

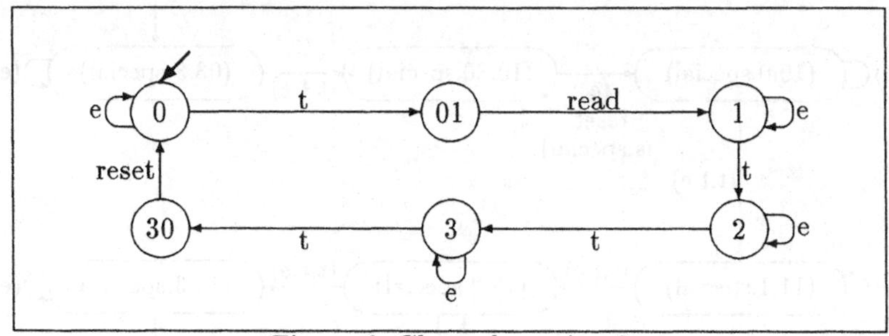

Figure 6: Channel, version 2

Indeed when is special mode the secondary device is activated twice and read twice. We introduce a transition system that counts how many times the device has been read. This transition system is:

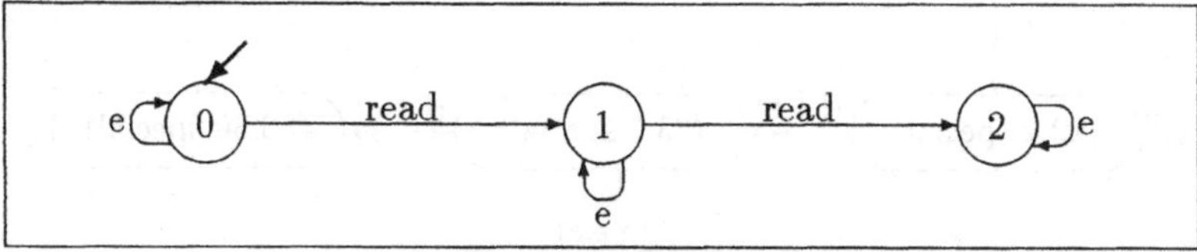

Figure 7: Device

As for the reset signal, the "read" action will be taken into account depending on the mode is special or not. Thus our system now is:

device	*counter*	*channel_v2*	*mode_v1*
e	t	t	e
e	e	e	start
e	reset	reset	is_not_special
e	e	reset	is_special
e	e	read	is_not_special
read	e	read	is_special

The corresponding synchronized product has 36 states and 38 transitions.

6 Fixing a bug

To behave correctly the system must meet the following property:

> Just after any reading of the device, the number of activations of the device (i.e., the first digit of the state of the hardware counter) must be equal to the number of readings (i.e., the state of **device**).

The designers of the code were almost sure that this property was true. Experiments showed that indeed it was not, and we introduced the modelling above just to understand how and why it happened.

6.1 Finding the cause of the errors

First, we look at the states reached after any reading of the device by computing

```
s := tgt(!label[1]="read");
```

This set contains four states: **e(1.01.1.special)**, **e(1.11.1.special)**, **e(2.11-.1.special)**, and **e(2.21.1.special)**. The second and the fourth ones satisfy the above requirement, while the first and the third do not. This is indeed the bug in the system and is consistent with the experimental observations.

Looking at a path leading to one of those states, one finds the one:

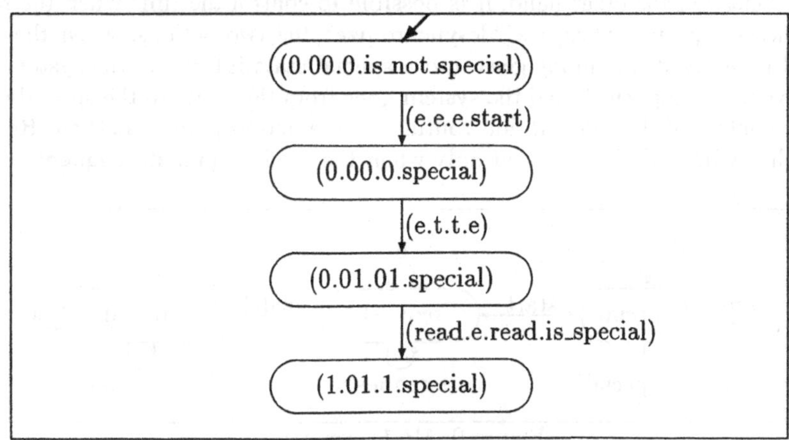

Figure 8: Path

Then one guesses that the problem is probably caused by the mode switching from non special to special while the channel has value 0. To check this guess we define the set of transitions where the mode changes and the channel is 0,

```
cause := !label[4]="start"/\rsrc(!state[3]="0");
```

and we compute the set of states that can be reached without using these transitions (indeed, there is only one)

```
reachable:=reach(initial,*-cause);
```

The intersection of the sets **s** and **reachable** contains only two states, **e(1.11.1.-special)** and **e(2.21.1.special)**, and the two incorrect states become unreachable.

6.2 Some predictions

We know that the observed errors are due to the fact that the system switches to special mode when the channel has value 0. Since the start event is randomly distributed, the probability it occurs when channel has value 0 is 1/4 and the misbehaviour of the system should be observed with a frequency of 1/4. The frequency $1/N$ was experimentally observed, with respect to the actual value N of the software counter. What is more, the fact that the incorrect result of the actual system is caused by one additionnal reading of the inactivated device (when start event arrives on channel 0) was also experimentally confirmed.

6.3 The correction

A solution for avoiding the problem is to force the system to switch to special mode when the channel has not value 0. But there is no possible control on the start event. On the other hand, it is possible to control the time when the mode switches to special. Thus, we "desynchronize" the two actions: when the start signal is received, the mode goes into a special state informing the system that this event has happened, and the system goes from this state to the special mode under control of the interruption routine by the action named **switch**. Remark that this action can be executed only when the mode is in state **request**.

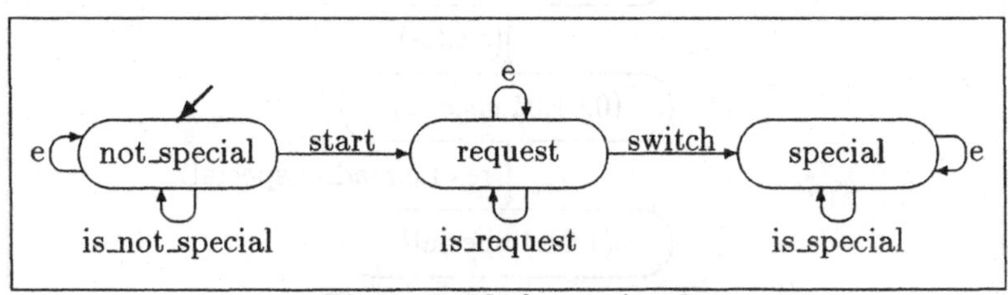

Figure 9: Mode, version 2

When setting the channel from 0 to 1 the interruption routine makes the device to be read if the mode is special and do nothing if the mode is not special. If the mode is in the intermediate state `request` it switches the mode to `special`. That new value of the mode will have effect at the next `activate`, as if the start event has occurred when the channel has value 1, 2, or 3! Of course, this cause a delay of four additionnal ticks before switching to the special mode, but engineers found it quite acceptable.

The new constraint is:

device	*counter*	*channel_v2*	*mode_v2*
e	t	t	e
e	e	e	start
e	reset	reset	is_not_special
e	e	reset	is_special
e	reset	reset	is_request
e	e	read	is_not_special
read	e	read	is_special
e	e	read	switch

The corresponding system has 28 states and 31 transitions. Now, the set

```
s := tgt(!label[1]="read");
```

contains only the two correct states `e(1.11.1.special)` and `e(2.21.1.special)`.

Finally it is easy to rewrite the interruption routine so that it conforms to the model above:

case
$0 < \text{channel} < N-1 \Rightarrow$ **increment(channel)**
channel $= 0 \Rightarrow$ **channel** $:=$ **1;**
  if mode $=$ **special then read;**
  elsif mode $=$ **request then mode** $:=$ **special;**
  endif;
channel $= N-1 \Rightarrow$ **if mode is not special then send(reset)**
  endif;
  channel $:=$ **0;**
end

7 Conclusion

We presented a use of formal methods in an unusual context: at testing time, to find out the cause of an error in a system, with respect to the difficulty to show up some very seldom behaviours on the bench. As model-checking aims to exhibit all possible behaviours, whatever their individual probability may be, this approach is extremely powerful in applications showing very seldom misbehaviours. The fault of the system was confirmed, and a precise diagnostic set. This would not have been possible (and they tried to do so) in a reasonable delay using testing techniques.

Notice however we did not intend to model and verify an implementation: we specified *a posteriori* the system by abstracting relevant elements with respect to the observed misbehaviour.

The efficiency of the use of synchronized labeled transition systems for modelling and checking electronic components has been widened to debugging the system in a way efficient for the developpers.

Using formal modelling techniques in the development can not guarantee systems are error-free, for this is impeded by the necessary abstraction made to build the model. This experience shows that formal methods can be used at any stage of development to reinforce the quality of the product.

This has been the conclusion of Schlumberger-Industries as well; and the R&D center is under works to internalize this new way of engineering.

References

1. M. Alabau, D. Bégay, J.-P. Radoux. *Formal Methods and Real-Time: design and validation of a Real-Time embedded System.* Real-Time Systems conference, Paris, january 1996.
2. A. Arnold. *Finite transition systems. Semantics of communicating sytems.* Prentice-Hall, 1994.
3. A. Arnold, D. Bégay, P. Crubillé. *Construction and analysis of transition systems with MEC.* World Scientific Pub., 1994.
4. A. Arnold, D. Bégay, J.-P. Radoux. *The embedded software of an electricity meter: An experience in using formal methods in an industrial project.* In a Special issue of Sci. Comp. Prog., to appear 1996.
5. D. Bégay, J. Dormoy, P. Félix. An experiment in developing real-time systems using Mec. In Teodor Rus and Charles Rattray, editors, *Theories and experiences for real-time system development*, volume 2 of *AMAST series in Computing*, chapter 14, pages 363–388. World Scientific Pub., 1994.
6. P. Crubillé. *Réalisation de l'outil Mec : spécification fonctionnelle et architecture.* PhD thesis, Université de Bordeaux I, novembre 1989.
7. A. Dicky. *Une approche algébrique et algorithmique de l'analyse des systèmes de transition.* PhD thesis, Université de Bordeaux I, février 1985.
8. J.-P. Radoux. *Utilisation de systèmes de transitions finis pour la conception et le développement d'un système embarqué.* PhD thesis, Université de Bordeaux I, mars 1995.

This article was processed using the LaTeX macro packages with LLNCS style,
and with automata graphical style by A. Griffault from LaBRI.

Experiments in Theorem Proving and Model Checking for Protocol Verification*

Klaus Havelund[1]** and Natarajan Shankar[2]***

[1] LITP, Institut Blaise Pascal, 4 place Jussieu, 75252 Paris, France
Email: havelund@litp.ibp.fr URL: http://cadillac.ibp.fr:8000/~havelund
[2] Computer Science Laboratory, SRI International, Menlo Park CA 94025, USA
Email: shankar@csl.sri.com URL: http://www.csl.sri.com/~shankar/shankar.html

Abstract. Communication protocols pose interesting and difficult challenges for verification technologies. The state spaces of interesting protocols are either infinite or too large for finite-state verification techniques like model checking and state exploration. Theorem proving is also not effective since the formal correctness proofs of these protocols can be long and complicated. We describe a series of protocol verification experiments culminating in a methodology where theorem proving is used to abstract out the sources of unboundedness in the protocol to yield a skeletal protocol that can be verified using model checking.

Our experiments focus on the Philips bounded retransmission protocol originally studied by Groote and van de Pol and by Helmink, Sellink, and Vaandrager. First, a scaled-down version of the protocol is analyzed using the Murϕ state exploration tool as a debugging aid and then translated into the PVS specification language. The PVS verification of the generalized protocol illustrates the difficulty of using theorem proving to verify infinite-state protocols. Some of this difficulty can be overcome by extracting a finite-state abstraction of the protocol that preserves the property of interest while being amenable to model checking. We compare the performance of Murϕ, SMV, and the PVS model checkers on this reduced protocol.

* Sam Owre (SRI) has assisted with the use of PVS and suggested several improvements to the paper. Sreeranga Rajan (SRI) was instrumental in integrating the mu-calculus model checker (built by Geert Janssen of Eindhoven University of Technology) into PVS. SeungJoon Park of Stanford University implemented the Murϕ-to-PVS translator. David Cyrluk (SRI and Stanford University) sped up parts of the PVS equality decision procedure. Ken McMillan (Cadence Labs) suggested that we examine forward reachability as a way of obtaining efficiency from the PVS model checker. We are also grateful to John Rushby (SRI) for facilitating Klaus Havelund's visit to SRI, and to Therese Hardin (LITP) for providing a stimulating environment at LITP in Paris.

** Supported by a European Community HCM grant, with origin institution being DIKU, Institute of Computer Science, University of Copenhagen, Denmark.

*** Supported by NSF Grant CCR-930044 and by ARPA through NASA Ames Research Center under Contract NASA-NAG-2-891 (ARPA Order A721).

1 Introduction

Communication protocols are an important class of concurrent algorithms that pose a difficult challenge for existing verification technologies [11]. Tools based on model checking and state exploration are effective and widely used for protocol verification, but many real-life protocols are not finite state and cannot be fully analyzed by these methods. In these instances, verification techniques based on theorem proving can be applied, but these have the disadvantage that they are not automatic and the verification effort involved can be substantial. In this paper, we examine the relative efficacy of finite-state and theorem proving approaches to verification when applied to a non-academic example of a communication protocol. We show how it is possible to combine the two techniques to create a useful methodology for protocol verification.

The specific protocol we examine is the socalled bounded retransmission protocol (BRP) from Philips Electronics. This variant of the alternating bit protocol transmits files each consisting of a sequence of individual messages. File transmission is aborted if any message in the file remains unacknowledged after a fixed number of retransmissions. This protocol has already been verified by researchers at Philips and CWI [10] using the Coq proof checker [5] using the framework of Lynch and Tuttle's I/O automata [16]. Their hand proof effort occupied two man-months, and it took them three man-months to mechanize this proof using Coq. The protocol has also been formalized in the process algebra μCRL and similarly checked using Coq [9]. This proof also required a serious amount of effort.

The interesting question therefore is whether this verification effort can be dramatically reduced, perhaps by using a combination of finite state and theorem proving techniques. To explore this question, we first consider a scaled-down version of the protocol BRP-M and show that it can be quickly analyzed and debugged using the Murϕ state exploration tool from Stanford University. This Murϕ specification can be converted into PVS [20] using a mechanical translator. The PVS description of the protocol is then generalized to the full protocol BRP-PVS, and the main safety property of the protocol is proved in a conventional manner as an invariant. Our initial PVS proof attempt of BRP-PVS took about three months to develop and verify, and this is roughly similar to the Philips/CWI effort. By employing a more finely tuned proof methodology and by taking further advantage of the automation provided by PVS, the verification has been redone in about one man-month.

Since this level of effort is still very large, we investigate techniques for reducing the verification effort without compromising the generality of the protocol. The PVS theorem prover has recently been extended with mu-calculus based model checking [21] so it is natural to ask whether model checking can somehow be applied to BRP-PVS. We answer this question in the affirmative by using theorem proving to construct a property-preserving finite-state abstraction BRP-mu that can be verified using model checking. There are three sources of unboundedness in the state space of the protocol: the message data, the retransmission bound, and the file length. Each of these sources of unboundedness can be eliminated by means of abstraction. The correspondence between BRP-PVS and BRP-mu is verified using PVS. The resulting finite-state protocol BRP-mu can be verified using a model checking or state exploration tool. We have successfully applied and can compare the PVS model checker [12], Murϕ [18], and SMV [17] on this example. The model checking part is automatic, but our initial attempts with the PVS model checker were unsuccessful until the mu-calculus definition of invariance was revised to compute fixpoints differently.

The general lesson from this is that the correctness of communication protocols is primarily control-sensitive, and the most effective verification approach is to use theorem proving to abstract out the control skeleton which can then be verified by finite-state techniques. We believe that the above verification paradigm can be generalized to apply to other protocols of industrial relevance. The main contribution of the paper is a mechanized methodology for industrial-strength protocol verification where:

1. A scaled-down version of the protocol is debugged using state exploration
2. This scaled-down version is generalized to recover the full version of the protocol for verification using theorem proving
3. Theorem proving is used to abstract out a finite-state protocol whose correctness (when established by model checking) implies the correctness of original protocol.

The work reported here is very much in progress. The effort saved by combining theorem proving and model checking is still quite modest at this point, but we believe that such savings can indeed be achieved through a more aggressive application of our proposed methodology.

The main difference between our work and previous work is that we develop a mechanized verification methodology for communication protocols where theorem proving is used to compute finite abstractions that can be verified by model checking. The closest related work is obviously the earlier verification of Helmink, Sellink, and Vaandrager [10]. The bulk of their verification is in proving various invariance properties but their main result is a refinement argument showing that one I/O automaton specification implements another more abstract one. We have employed a formalization that is closer to the state-transition model of Unity [3] and TLA [14]. By superposing the abstract and concrete state machines, we reduce the refinement demonstration to that of invariance. While the manual effort required by both their proof and by our initial proof attempt with BRP-PVS is comparable, PVS seems to provide greater and more efficient automation in the verification process particularly through the use of highly optimized rewriting and BDDs [6]. Our use of the abstracted protocol BRP-mu yields a simplification in the proof and a valuable technique for other protocol correctness proofs.

Groote's and van de Pol's specification [9] in μCRL is notationally compact, but their computer aided verification in Coq requires detailed encoding, and the resulting Coq description is fairly large and their verification is not mechanized to the degree achieved in PVS.

Müller and Nipkow [19] use a clever abstraction for reducing the alternating bit protocol to an infinite-state system with only a finite number of reachable states. Most finite-state model checking tools cannot cope with potentially infinite but reachably finite state spaces and therefore cannot exploit such an abstraction. Cardell-Oliver [2] has used the HOL proof checking system [8] to verify the sliding window protocol. It would be an interesting challenge to obtain a finite-state abstraction of the sliding window protocol.

Lam and Udaya Shankar [13] present a systematic method of projecting images of protocols by applying stepwise refinement to the protocol with respect to the property being verified. Their abstractions preserve the property so that protocol M has property P if and only if the abstract protocol M' has the property P. Our abstractions only preserve the property in one direction, i.e., if the abstract protocol M' has property P' (which in our case need not be P), then the concrete protocol M has property P. This means that we have much more freedom in our choice of abstractions, and in particular, we can introduce more nondeterminism into the abstract protocol. Some of the specific abstractions proposed here cannot be obtained by Lam and Shankar's technique. We do not provide a systematic method for obtaining abstractions; this is a topic for future research. The theoretical ideas underlying our use of abstraction have been previously studied [4, 7, 15].

2 The Bounded Retransmission Protocol

The bounded retransmission protocol developed at Philips Research Laboratory communicates messages from a *producer* to a *consumer* over an unreliable physical medium that can lose messages. The protocol is a nontrivial extension of the alternating bit protocol [1] that uses timeouts and aborts transmission following a bounded number of retransmission attempts. The *environment* to the protocol consists of the producer and the consumer. The black box view of the system is that it accepts requests REQ(f) from the producer to transmit the file f. When transmission of a file has been either completed or aborted, the producer receives a confirmation CONF(c), where c is either OK, NOT_OK, or DONT_KNOW, respectively indicating that the file was successfully transmitted, aborted, or that the last message in the file was not acknowledged but might have been received by the consumer. The consumer either receives an IND_ERR signal indicating that the file transmission was aborted, or an IND(m, i) signal where m is the message and i is either FIRST, LAST, or INCOMPLETE corresponding to the first, last, or an intermediate message in the file.

The protocol consists of a *sender* program at the producer side; a *receiver* program at the consumer side, and two channels (one-place buffers): a message channel K, and an acknowledgment channel L. Both channels are unreliable in that they can lose messages or acknowledgments. The protocol is pictured in figure 1. The sender sends each message over the channel K and then waits for an acknowledgment on channel L. If there is no acknowledgment, the sender times out and retransmits the message. There is a fixed upper bound on the number of such retransmissions.

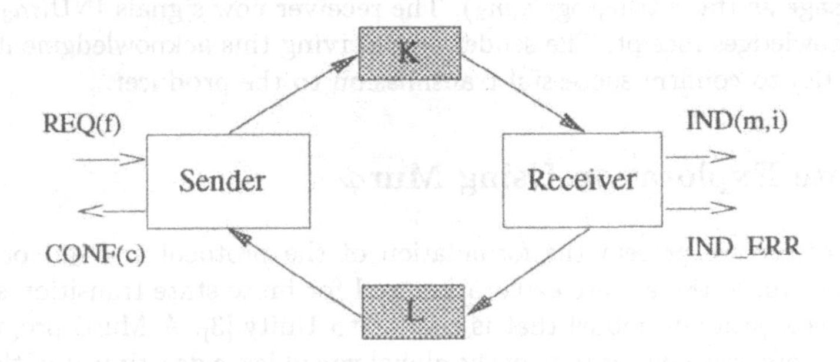

Fig. 1. The BRP Protocol

The protocol uses three timers to deal with loss of messages and acknowledgments. A timer has a fixed period T of time associated. When it is *set*, a *timeout* occurs T time units or more later. The first timer in the sender is used to detect the loss of a message or an acknowledgement. It is used as follows: when the sender sends a new message over K, timer 1 is set. The time associated with this timer exceeds the time it takes from when a message has been sent over K until the corresponding acknowledgment is received over L. If an acknowledgment comes back within this time, the timer is *cleared* (and the next message is sent). If not, a timeout occurs whereupon the message is retransmitted, and the timer is set again. When the retransmission bound has been reached, the sender aborts transmission and confirms that the transmission failed. Either it confirms CONF(NOT_OK) or it confirms CONF(DONT_KNOW). Two other timers are used to bring the sender and the receiver back in synchrony after a file transmission has been aborted by the sender. We do not model the real-time aspects of the protocol but instead represent the timers by timer events. For example, the timeout event which is supposed to detect message loss is instead defined to occur when a message is lost. This simplification is also present in Helmink, *et al* [10].

The receiver may also retransmit acknowledgments. This happens when the receiver gets a message that it has already received once. The receiver distinguishes between an old message and a new message via the alternating bit (the toggle) which is part of the message.

We can now examine the behavior of the protocol for the case when no messages or acknowedgments are lost. The sender sends each individual message in the file to the receiver over the channel K in the form (first,last,toggle,m). If the producer signals REQ(f) where f is $[m_1, m_2, m_3]$, then the sender first sends the tuple (true,false,toggle,m_1) on channel K. Upon receipt of this message, the receiver signals IND(m_1,FIRST) to the consumer and sends an acknowledgement on channel L. The sender then sends the second message as (false,false,¬ toggle,m_2). The receiver correspondingly signals IND(m_2,INCOMPLETE) and acknowledges receipt. The sender then sends the last message as (false,true,toggle,m_3). The receiver now signals IND(m_3,LAST) and acknowledges receipt. The sender on receiving this acknowledgment signals CONF(OK) to confirm successful transmission to the producer.

3 State Exploration Using Murϕ

In this section we present the formulation of the protocol and its correctness criteria in Murϕ [18], a state exploration tool for finite state transition systems. Murϕ uses a program model that is similar to Unity [3]. A Murϕ program has three components: a declaration of the global variables, a description of the initial state, and a collection of transition rules. Each transition rule is a guarded command that consists of a boolean guard expression over the global variables, and a deterministic statement that changes the global variables. Transition rules can include `Assert` statements that terminate execution when the asserted condition is falsified. We use Murϕ as an effective debugging tool for testing invariance assertions.

An execution of a Murϕ program is obtained by repeatedly *(1) arbitrarily selecting one of the transition rules where the boolean guard is true in the current state; (2) executing the statement of the chosen transition rule.* The statement is executed atomically: no other transition rules are executed in parallel. Thus state transitions are interleaving and processes communicate via shared variables. The notion of process is not formally supported, but may be thought of as a subset of the transition rules. The Murϕ verifier tries to explore all reachable states in order to ensure that all `Assert` statements hold. If a violation is detected, Murϕ generates a violating trace.

Programming the Protocol. The protocol we have described in the previous section takes three parameters: the kind of data transmitted, the size of files (how many messages in each file), and finally the number of retransmissions (max) performed by the sender before it aborts file transmission. It turns out that when we choose the data domain to be finite, bound the size of files, and choose some fixed value for max, then the protocol state space is bounded and it can be formulated and verified in Murϕ. We therefore choose the data domain to be boolean, fix the size of files at 3, and set the retransmission limit to 2:

Const	Type	Var

`last : 3;`
`max  : 2;`
	`Data : boolean;`
	`File : Array[1..last] Of Data;`
		`file : File;`
		`head : 1..last+1;`
		`rn   : 0..max;`

A file is modeled as an array of data, of length 3, where the `head` variable points to the current message being sent, exceeding the domain of the array if the file is empty. The variable **rn** contains the current number of retransmissions tried. Recall that channel K carries tuples containing a **first**, **last**, **toggle** and **data** field:

```
Type                                    | Var
  Msg : Record                          |   K : Msg;
        first,last,toggle : boolean;    |   K_full : boolean;
        data : Data                     |
      End;                              |
```

When the sender sends a message, it just writes to K, and when the receiver reads this message it just reads K. The flag **K_full** is raised when some message has been written to K, i.e., the sender sets it to true when writing to K, and the receiver sets it to false when reading from K. Similar flags are used for other variables that play the role of "channels." The sender control is managed via a sender program counter **spc** of type **Spc**:

```
Type                                    | Var
  Spc : Enum{WR, SF, WA, SC, WT2};      |   spc : Spc;
```

When, for example, the sender is waiting for a new file, **spc** is **WF**. We only explain a few of the rules in the Murϕ specification. Assume that the environment writes new files to a **req** channel. The following sender rule reads a new file to be transmitted from the **req** channel into the **file** variable.

```
Rule "read_req"
  spc = WR & req_full ==>
    req_full := false; file := req; head := 1; spc := SF;
    verify_REQ(req)
End;
```

The rule is named **read_req**. The precondition requires that the sender's program counter is **WR**: "wait for a request". Also, the **req_full** flag must be true – the environment must have written some file into **req**. The **head** is set to point to the first message in the new file, and the program counter is set to **SF**: "send the file." The **verify_REQ** procedure contains part of the abstract specification of the protocol. The call will verify certain assertions in the abstract protocol, and if they fail to hold, program execution will terminate. The abstract protocol thus "polices" the behavior of the protocol; this will be explained in the next section. Note that the "policing" only takes place for so called *external* transition rules: the ones that model externally visible events according to a black box view. Communications on channels K and L are, for example, not external.

The next rule models how the sender sends a message to the receiver on K:

```
Rule "write_K"
  spc = SF & !K_full ==>
    K_full := true; K.first := sfirst; K.last := (head = last);
    K.toggle:= stoggle; K.data := file[head];
    spc:= WA; rn := rn+1; stimer1_on := true;
End;
```

The program counter is updated so that the sender now waits for an acknowledgment to arrive. The number `rn` of retransmissions is incremented, and finally, a timer `stimer1` is set: if an acknowledgment does not arrive within a certain time period, a timeout will occur.

There are other sender rules, and there are similar rules for the receiver, seventeen in total. The complete program is included in appendix B.

The Correctness Criteria. The abstract protocol specification is written as part of the Murϕ program and uses its own local variables. For example, the following three variables are declared:

```
Var
  abusy : boolean; afile : File; ahead : 1..last+1;
```

The `abusy` variable is true whenever a file is being transmitted. The variables `afile` and `ahead` will together at any time model which message the abstract protocol is prepared to transmit (by an `IND` action).

Now we are ready to define the abstract protocol. We do this in terms of a collection of procedures, one for each of the four external activities of the protocol: `REQ`, `IND`, `IND_ERR`, and `CONF`. For example, we saw previously the call `verify_REQ(req)`. This procedure is defined as follows:

```
Procedure verify_REQ(f:File);
Begin
  Assert !abusy;
  abusy := true; afile := f; ahead := 1;
End;
```

So these procedures are supposed to model the same external behavior as the protocol, ignoring channels `K` and `L`. Note how the `Assert` statements function as "pre-conditions": when the protocol calls the procedure, the `Assert` condition is evaluated, and if it evaluates to false, the Murϕ verification terminates, printing the trace of states that leads to the falsified assertion. In the above case, `abusy` must be false. The complete specification is included in appendix A. When we verified the protocol, no such error states occurred: the downscaled protocol was verified "correct" in 784 seconds on a Sun Sparc station.

4 Theorem Proving: Proving Safety with PVS

In the previous section, we verified a scaled down finite-state version of the protocol using Murϕ. The advantage of the verification was that it was automatic. In this section, we shall describe the use of PVS to construct a full-scale proof for the complete infinite state protocol. In order to obtain an infinite state protocol in PVS we apply a Murϕ-to-PVS translator. That is, we apply this translator to the Murϕ program in the previous section, and get a corresponding PVS specification. This is still a finite-state specification and to obtain the infinite state specification, we manually modify a few of the PVS declarations.

Applying the translator to the Murϕ program yields two PVS theories. The first one (protocol) contains the protocol itself. The second theory (protocol_safe) contains the statement of the correctness criteria. This correctness criteria was implicit in the Murϕ program: whenever an Assert evaluated to false, the verifier would terminate. We have to find a way of modeling this in the PVS-specification.

The Protocol. The Protocol (obtained by the translation, and some modification) is represented as a theory in PVS, a portion of which is shown below.

```
protocol : THEORY
BEGIN
  last     : posnat
  max      : posnat
  Data     : NONEMPTY_TYPE
  Position : TYPE = {i: int | 1 <= i AND i <= last+1}
  File     : TYPE = ARRAY[Position -> Data]
  Msg      : TYPE = [# first,last,toggle : bool, data: Data #]
  Spc      : TYPE = {WR, SF, WA, SC, WT2}
  State    : TYPE = [# file  : File, head  : Position, spc : Spc ...
                       afile : File, ahead : Position, SAFE : bool #]
  ...
END protocol
```

The theory contains definitions of constants, types, functions, relations, etc. We have modified the first three declarations (i.e., last, max, and Data) in order to get an inifinite state protocol. The Murϕ state is modeled as a record. The additional state component SAFE captures the effect of an Assert command. It is initially TRUE, and can only be affected by the Assert commands in the abstract specification which checks the externally observable behaviour of the protocol.

We first look at the PVS definition of the abstract specification. Murϕ transitions are translated into PVS as functions over state. The abstract specification is defined as a function which takes an input state and the external action and returns an output state which is the same as the input state except that the abstract state variables may have changed and the SAFE variable may have been falsified as a result of a failed Assert. The action argument is constructed as an element of the abstract datatype Action shown below. This datatype definition uses two enumerated types Conf and IndT and has four constructors: REQ, IND, IND_ERR, and CONF. There is a recognizer corresponding to each constructor, and some of the constructors have associated accessors, e.g., the accessor req corresponds to the constructor REQ.

```
Conf : TYPE = {OK,NOT_OK,DONT_KNOW}
IndT : TYPE = {FIRST,INCOMPLETE,LAST}

Action : DATATYPE
  BEGIN
    REQ(req:File):REQ?
    IND(data:Data,ind:IndT):IND?
    IND_ERR:IND_ERR?
    CONF(conf:Conf):CONF?
  END Action
```

With this type, the abstract protocol can be defined as the function **automaton** shown below. The body is a case-expression over the constructors of the action data type. In the `REQ(f)` case, `f` is bound, the `SAFE` variable is set to denote the value of the condition `NOT abusy(st)` — exactly the `Assert` condition in the Murϕ program. The state is then "updated" corresponding to the Murϕ assignment statements where sequencing is enforced by the `LET` construct.

```
automaton(st:State,action:Action):State =
  CASES action OF
    REQ(f) :
      LET
        st = st WITH [SAFE := NOT abusy(st)],
        st = st WITH [abusy := TRUE],
        st = st WITH [afile := f],
        st = st WITH [ahead := 1]
      IN st,
    IND(d,i) : ...
    IND_ERR  : ...
    CONF(c)  : ...
  ENDCASES
```

The Murϕ transition rule **read_req** is translated as the function **Rule_read_req** shown below.

```
Rule_read_req(st:State):State =
  IF spc(st) = WR AND req_full(st) THEN
   LET
     st = st WITH [req_full := FALSE],
     st = st WITH [file := req(st)],
     st = st WITH [head := 1],
     st = st WITH [spc  := SF],
     st = automaton(st,REQ(req(st)))
   IN st
  ELSE
   st
  ENDIF
```

Another perhaps more interesting rule is:

```
Rule_write_K(st:State):State =
  IF spc(st) = SF AND NOT K_full(st) THEN
    LET
      st = st WITH [K_full := TRUE],
      st = st WITH [(K)(first) := sfirst(st)],
      st = st WITH [(K)(last) := head(st) = last],
      st = st WITH [(K)(toggle) := stoggle(st)],
      st = st WITH [(K)(data) := file(st)(head(st))],
      st = st WITH [spc := WA],
      st = st WITH [rn := incr_rn(rn(st))],
      st = st WITH [stimer1_on := TRUE]
    IN st
  ELSE
    st
  ENDIF
```

We have seen that rules are modeled as functions of type `[State -> State]` since they are deterministic. The program which features nondeterminism in the selection of the transition rule is modeled with the help of a transition relation `transition : [[State,State] -> bool]` between states. That is, `transition(s1,s2)` holds between two states `s1` and `s2`, if one of the rules can bring us from state `s1` to `s2`. The relation is defined as follows:

```
transition(st1,st2:State):bool =
  ...
  OR st2 = Rule_read_req(st1)
  OR st2 = Rule_write_K(st1)
  ...
```

A program is a predicate that holds of a sequence of states `aa` if and only if the initial state of `aa` is `startstate` and each pair of successive states is related by the `transition` relation.

```
Behavior : TYPE = sequence[State]

program(aa:Behavior):bool =
  aa(0) = startstate
    AND
  FORALL (n:nat): transition(aa(n),aa(n+1))
```

Sequences are infinite lists of elements, represented as functions of type: `[nat -> State]`. The protocol theory contains a definition of the `startstate` (a particular record not shown).

The Correctness Criteria in PVS. We mentioned earlier that the Murϕ-to-PVS translator generates two theories: `protocol` above, and the theory `protocol_safe` containing the correctness criteria to be proved. The theory defines two predicates and a theorem: the correctness criteria. The predicate `invariant` takes as argument a predicate `p` on states (`pred[State]` is short for the function space [State -> bool]). It returns TRUE if for all execution traces aa of the program: the predicate p holds in every position of that trace. Note that the program referred to here is the one defined in protocol.

```
protocol_safe : THEORY
BEGIN
  IMPORTING protocol

  invariant(p:pred[State]):bool =
    FORALL (aa:Behavior):
      program(aa) IMPLIES
        FORALL (n:nat): p(aa(n))

  safe(st:State):bool =
    SAFE(st)

  correct : THEOREM invariant(safe)
END protocol_safe
```

The safety property we want to verify for each reachable state is defined by the predicate safe, which again states that the variable SAFE evaluates to TRUE. The correctness criteria is defined by the formula named correct. Obviously, the invariant safe in formula correct needs to be greatly strengthened in order to be provable, and this invariant strengthening is the real challenge of the proof.

57 invariants were needed in the proof. Their formulation in Murϕ is included in appendix C. In a second proof attempt, several proof optimizations led to a significant reduction in effort. In comparison with the work of Helmink, *et al* [10], the invariants used are roughly the same but their invariants were discovered by hand in advance of a mechanical proof, whereas we used the PVS proof to guide the discovery of invariants. Rerunning the proof takes 5 hours.

The verification of the protocol has been automated as far as possible by defining a set of tactics (occupying five pages). This level of automation could be achieved primarily because of the flexibility afforded by the PVS decision procedures.

5 Abstraction: Reduction to Finite State Using PVS

In recent work [21] a Boolean mu-calculus model checker [12] has been integrated into PVS as a decision procedure. This integration uses a relational mu-calculus (quantified Boolean formulas with least and greatest fixpoints of monotone Boolean predicate transformers) as a medium for communicating between PVS and the model checker for the Boolean mu-calculus. In this section we shall see how to apply this integration to our protocol.

The mu-calculus of a given state type can be formalized within the higher-order logic by defining least and greatest fixpoint operators for monotone predicate transformers. More usefully, the temporal operators of the branching time logic CTL can be defined using this mu-calculus. In particular, we can define the

CTL `AG` operator which represents the modality: "for every path, and for every state along that path" of CTL. The assertion `AG(i,n)(p)`, where `i` is the initialization predicate and `n` is the next-state relation, holds if `p` holds in all reachable states; the latter notion is defined in terms of the least fixpoint operator `mu`.

When the state type is finite, i.e., constructed inductively from the booleans and scalar types using records, tuples, or arrays over subranges, the PVS mu-calculus (and the corresponding CTL) can be translated into the Boolean mu-calculus and model checking can be used as a decision procedure for this fragment, using just boolean variables and BDDs. The PVS proof command `model-check` carries out these verification steps automatically. The resulting model checker by itself has few advantages over a conventional model checker. The main advantage is when it is combined with theorem proving to exploit the use of abstraction to reduce unbounded state spaces to finite ones. Abstraction is well studied in the literature [4, 7, 15], but the reasoning is usually carried out informally.

In order to prove an `AG` property, there is a simple way to define an abstraction, as shown in [4] and recalled in [21]. Suppose we are given a concrete, possibly infinite state, system S_c (like our protocol) defined by a state type, an initialization predicate and a next-state transition relation over the state. That is: $S_c = \langle \Sigma_c, I_c, N_c \rangle$, where $I_c : \Sigma_c \rightarrow B$ and $N_c : (\Sigma_c \times \Sigma_c) \rightarrow B$. Suppose further that we want to verify the property $p_c : \Sigma_c \rightarrow B$ about the concrete system, that is, $AG(I_c, N_c)(p_c)$. We define an abstract system: $S_a = \langle \Sigma_a, I_a, N_a \rangle$ and an abstract property p_a, together with an abstraction mapping $h : \Sigma_c \rightarrow \Sigma_a$. We then show that the abstract system satisfies the abstract property, and that the mapping preserves the initialization predicate, the next-state relation and the property. This is expressed by the following theorem which has been proved using PVS:

Theorem 1. *In order to prove $AG(I_c, N_c)(p_c)$ it is sufficient to prove that:*

1. $\forall s : \Sigma_c.\ I_c(s) \Rightarrow I_a(h(s))$
2. $\forall s_1, s_2 : \Sigma_c^r.\ N_c(s_1, s_2) \Rightarrow N_a(h(s_1), h(s_2))$ *where Σ_c^r denotes all the concrete states reachable from an initial state via the next-state relation.*
3. $\forall s : \Sigma_c.\ p_a(h(s)) \Rightarrow p_c(s)$
4. $AG(I_a, N_a)(p_a)$

We saw that there were three sources of unboundedness in BRP: the file size, the message data, and the retransmission bound. These can be abstracted away to obtain a property-preserving abstraction. The main trick is that since we are dealing with ACTL properties, i.e., those that involve only universal path quantification, it is okay to introduce additional nondeterminism at the abstract level. In particular, the size of the as yet untransmitted portion of the file can be abstracted to one of `NONE`, `ONE`, or `MANY`, the message data is irrelevant and can be eliminated, and the retransmission bound can be replaced by a nondeterministic choice between the continuation and termination of retransmission. As a result, the type `Data` is removed. A file is no longer an array of `Data` but an element of the enumerated type `{NONE,ONE,MANY}`, indicating whether the file has no elements, one element or more than one element. The constant **max** is removed: there is no longer an upper bound for the number of retransmissions. This is possible since we just require that whenever the concrete protocol can make a transition, the abstract protocol must also be able to, and surely, if we remove the upper bound, then this is guaranteed. The counter **rn** itself that counts the number of retransmissions is turned into a single boolean: it is true only if a message has been sent at least once. The file component (**afile**) in the **automaton** is just a boolean, indicating whether it is empty or not: whether there is more to send or not.

```
abstract_protocol : THEORY
  BEGIN
    File  : TYPE = {NONE,ONE,MANY}
    Msg   : TYPE = [# first: bool, last: bool, toggle: bool #]
    State : TYPE = [# file : File, rn : bool, afile : bool, ... #]
```

The **automaton** specification also changes, but we omit the details of this new automaton specification. Concerning the program itself, in the abstract version of f.ex. the transition rule **Rule_write_K**, the update of **K(last)** has been changed from **K(last) := (head(st)=last)** to **K(last) := (file(st)=ONE)**. The update of **rn** has changed, and the update of **K(data)** has now disappeared.

The abstraction mapping between the concrete state type and the abstract state type is then given by the function **abs** defined below.

```
abstraction : THEORY
BEGIN
  A  : THEORY = abstract_protocol
  C  : THEORY = protocol

  abs(s:C.State):A.State =
    (# file  := IF    head(s)=nil  THEN NONE
                ELSIF head(s)=last THEN ONE ELSE MANY ENDIF,
       rn    := rn(s)/=0,
       afile := ahead(s)/=nil, ... #)
  ...
END abstraction
```

Theorem 1 can now be used to prove the invariant asserted in the theorem **concrete_correct** shown below.

```
concrete_correct : THEOREM
  AG(C.initial,C.transition)(safe)
```

Recall that Theorem 1 was defined in the context of a concrete system S_c (**protocol** in our case), an abstract system S_a (**abstract_protocol**) and an abstraction mapping h (**abs**) between the two. Theorem 1 tells us that it is sufficient to prove the propositions corresponding to items 1–4 in the theorem. The first and third of these are easily proved by the **grind** proof strategy of PVS. The fourth is proved by the **model-check** proof strategy of PVS. The second proof obligation is the only nontrivial one and it is shown below as transition_preserves.

```
transition_preserves : PROPOSITION
  FORALL (s1,s2:C.State):
    (I(s1) AND I(s2) AND C.transition(s1,s2))
      IMPLIES
    A.transition(abs(s1),abs(s2))
```

The proof obligation transition_preserves only requires the abstract system to simulate a step of the concrete system when a concrete invariant I holds of the initial and final states of the transition. Indeed, we do require the use of a specific concrete invariant in justifying the abstraction, and this is currently proved directly in PVS without the aid of abstraction. We, in fact, reuse this invariant from the proof of BRP-PVS in the Section 4.

It took two weeks to define the abstract protocol and the abstraction mapping, and to carry out the proof of the main lemma: transition_preserves. It takes two hours to rerun the proof of this lemma. However, this lemma again uses a number of invariants about the concrete protocol; we need 45 of the 57 invariants invented in the original invariant proof in Section 4. Considering the extra two-week effort in carrying out this abstraction proof, one may conclude that no essential work effort has been saved by doing the abstraction with model checking in comparison with the pure invariant proof. We claim, however, that the abstraction gives a good intuition about the functioning of the protocol, since it focuses on control. Also, it is likely that many of the prior invariance proofs can also be proved via abstraction and model checking.

The final proof obligation corresponding to item 4 of theorem 1 is proved by means of model checking. Using the PVS command model-check, this lemma is proved in 36.7 minutes. Our initial experiences in applying the PVS model checker to this example were not satisfactory. This led us to reformulate the abstract protocol in Murϕ and in the CTL model checker SMV, in order to compare execution times. In Murϕ, the verification took 28.51 seconds. The main source of efficiency in Murϕ with respect to this example is that it uses an explicit (not symbolic) representation of the state space and only explores the reachable states. Our initial definition of the AG operator was such that it explored all those states that could potentially lead to a state violating the invariant in order to check if these states included the start state. Obviously, many more states were explored in this manner.

When we apply the SMV model checker [17] to the example, it takes 2.5 hours to verify the abstract protocol. When SMV is used with the option '-f', only the 'forward' reachable states are examined, and this gives an impressive improvement in efficiency taking only 24 seconds — an improvement factor of nearly 400.

6 Observations

As a general remark, we want to stress a basic result of the work: to provide a nontrivial example/methodology for reasoning about protocols using theorem proving and model checking. Our framework is adequate for deeper studies of the problems we have encountered, such as the identification of suitable invariants and the design of useful finite-state abstractions.

We have found it useful and productive to employ a state exploration tool such as Murϕ as a prelude to full theorem proving. Murϕ was also useful for checking putative invariants.

In [10] a refinement between the protocol and an abstract protocol was defined and verified. Our contribution has been to reformulate refinement as a safety property by superposing the implementation and specification of the protocol. This technique seems simple and yet useful.

The infinite state PVS specification initially took three man-months to verify. This is comparable to the work in Coq [10] where they were starting from a hand-written proof. We believe though that our proof is more automated than the Coq proof: for any invariant proof, once we had identified (and included as assumptions) which other sub-invariants it depended on, the proof was automatic using a specially designed tactic based on decision procedures. With our improved approach of strengthening invariants on the fly, we were able to reduce the proof effort to four weeks.

Our use of abstraction yields a better understanding of the protocol since it extracts out the relevant control skeleton. We hope that a deeper study will reveal systematic techniques for obtaining such abstractions.

References

1. K. A. Bartlett, R. A. Scantlebury, and P. T. Wilkinson. A note on reliable full-duplex transmission over half-duplex links. *Communications of the ACM*, 12(5):260, 261, May 1969.
2. Rachel Mary Cardell-Oliver. The formal verification of hard real-time systems. Technical Report 255, University of Cambridge Computer Laboratory, 1992.
3. K.M. Chandy and J. Misra. *Parallel Program Design: A Foundation.* Addison Wesley, 1988.
4. E.M. Clark, O. Grumberg, and D.E. Long. Model checking and abstraction. *ACM Transactions on Programming Languages and Systems*, 16(5):1512–1542, September 1994.
5. C. Cornes, J. Courant, J.C. Filliatre, G. Huet, P. Manoury, C Paulin-Mohring, C. Munoz, C. Murthy, C. Parent, A. Saibi, and B. Werner. The Coq proof assistant reference manual, version 5.10. Technical report, INRIA, Rocquencourt, France, February 1995. This version is newer than the version used to verify the BRP-protocol in [10].
6. D. Cyrluk, S. Rajan, N. Shankar, and M. K. Srivas. Effective theorem proving for hardware verification. In Ramayya Kumar and Thomas Kropf, editors, *Theorem Provers in Circuit Design (TPCD '94)*, volume 910 of *Lecture Notes in Com-*

puter Science, pages 203–222, Bad Herrenalb, Germany, September 1994. Springer-Verlag.

7. Dennis Dams, Orna Grumberg, and Rob Gerth. Abstract interpretation of reactive systems: Abstractions preserving ∀CTL*, ∃CTL* and CTL*. In Ernst-Rüdiger Olderog, editor, *Programming Concepts, Methods and Calculi (PROCOMET '94)*, pages 561–581, 1994.
8. M. J. C. Gordon. HOL: A proof generating system for higher-order logic. In G. Birtwistle and P. A. Subrahmanyam, editors, *VLSI Specification, Verification and Synthesis*, pages 73–128. Kluwer, Dordrecht, The Netherlands, 1988.
9. J. F. Groote and J. C. van de Pol. A bounded retransmission protocol for large packets. A case study in computer checked verification. Logic Group Preprint Series 100, Utrecht University, 1993.
10. L. Helmink, M.P.A. Sellink, and F.W. Vaandrager. Proof-checking a data link protocol. Technical Report CS-R9420, Centrum voor Wiskunde en Informatica (CWI), Computer Science/Department of Software Technology, March 1994.
11. G. J. Holzmann. *Design and Validation of Computer Protocols*. Prentice-Hall, 1991.
12. G. Janssen. ROBDD software. Department of Electrical Engineering, Eindhoven University of Technology, October 1993.
13. Simon S. Lam and A. Udaya Shankar. Protocol verification via projections. *IEEE Trans. on S.W. Engg*, SE-10(4):325–342, July 1984.
14. L. Lamport. The Temporal Logic of Actions. Technical report, Digital Equipment Corporation (DEC) Systems Research Center, Palo Alto, California, USA, April 1994.
15. C. Loiseaux, S. Graf, J. Sifakis, A. Bouajjani, and S. Bensalem. Property preserving abstractions for the verification of concurrent systems. *Formal Methods in System Design*, 6:11–44, 1995.
16. N.A. Lynch and M.R. Tuttle. Hierarchical correctness proofs for distributed algorithms. In *Proceedings of the sixth Annual Symposium on Principles of Distributed Computing, New York*, pages 137–151. ACM Press, 1987.
17. K.L. McMillan. *Symbolic Model Checking*. Kluwer Academic Publishers, Boston, 1993.
18. R. Melton, D.L. Dill, and C. Norris Ip. Murphi annotated reference manual, version 2.6. Technical report, Stanford University, Palo Alto, California, USA, November 1993. Written by C. Norris Ip.
19. O. Müller and T. Nipkow. Combining model checking and deduction for i/o-automata. Technical University of Munich. Draft manuscript, 1995.
20. S. Owre, J. Rushby, N. Shankar, and F. von Henke. Formal verification for fault-tolerant architectures: Prolegomena to the design of PVS. *IEEE Transactions on Software Engineering*, 21(2):107–125, February 1995.
21. S. Rajan, N. Shankar, and M.K. Srivas. An integration of model-checking with automated proof checking. In *Computer-Aided Verification (CAV) 1995, Liege, Belgium, Lecture Notes in Computer Science, Volume 939*, pages 84–97. Springer Verlag, July 1995.

A Specification Automaton In Murϕ

Note that certain constants and types are defined in the implementation automaton below.

```
Var
  abusy : boolean; afile : File;
  ahead  : 1..last+1;
  afirst : boolean; aerror : boolean;

Procedure verify_REQ(f:File);
Begin Assert !abusy;
  abusy := true; afile := f; ahead := 1;
End;

Procedure verify_IND(d:Data;i:IndT);
Begin Assert
        abusy & !aerror & ahead != nil &
        d = afile[ahead] &
        i = (ahead=last ? LAST :
               (afirst ? FIRST :
                         INCOMPLETE));
  afirst := (ahead=last);
  ahead := ahead + 1;
End;

Procedure verify_IND_ERR();
Begin Assert aerror;
  afirst := true; aerror := false;
End;

Procedure verify_CONF(c:Conf);
Begin Assert
        abusy & !aerror &
        (c=OK -> ahead=nil) &
        (c=DONT_KNOW  ->
           (ahead=nil|ahead=last)) &
        (c=NOT_OK  -> ahead != nil);
  abusy := false; aerror := !afirst;
  ahead := nil;
End;
```

B Implementation Automaton in Murϕ

```
Type
  Data : boolean;
  Msg  : Record
           first, last, toggle : boolean;
           data : Data
         End;
  Spc  : Enum{WR,SF,WA,SC,WT2};
  Conf : Enum{OK,NOT_OK,DONT_KNOW};
  File : Array [1..last] Of Data;
  Rpc  : Enum{WF,SI,SA,RTS,NOK};
  IndT : Enum{FIRST,INCOMPLETE,LAST};

Const
  max  : 2; last : 3; nil : last+1;

Var
  K : Msg; K_full : boolean; L : boolean;
  req : File; req_full : boolean;
  conf : Conf; conf_full : boolean;
  spc : Spc; sfirst : boolean;
  stoggle : boolean; file : File;
  head : 1..last+1; rn : 0..max;
  stimer1_on : boolean;
  stimer1_enabled : boolean;
  stimer2_on : boolean;
  stimer2_enabled : boolean;
  ind_data : Data; ind_indication : IndT;
  ind_full : boolean; ind_error : boolean;
  rpc : Rpc; rfirst : boolean;
  rtoggle : boolean; ctoggle : boolean;
  msg : Msg;
  rtimer_on : boolean;
  rtimer_enabled : boolean;

Ruleset d1 : Data; d2 : Data; d3 : Data Do
  Rule "write_req" !req_full ==>
    req_full := true;
    req[1] := d1; req[2] := d2; req[3] := d3;
  End;
End;

Rule "read_conf" conf_full ==>
  conf_full := false;
End;

Rule "read_ind" ind_full ==>
  ind_full := false;
End;

Rule "read_ind_error" ind_error ==>
  ind_error := false;
End;

Rule "lose_msg" K_full ==>
  K_full := false;
  stimer1_enabled := true;
End;

Rule "lose_ack" L ==>
  L := false; stimer1_enabled := true;
End;

Rule "read_req" spc = WR & req_full ==>
  req_full := false;
  For i := 1 To last Do file[i] := req[i] End;
  head := 1; spc := SF;
  verify_REQ(req);
End;

Rule "write_K" spc = SF & !K_full ==>
  K_full := true; K.first := sfirst;
  K.last := (head = last);
  K.toggle:= stoggle; K.data := file[head];
  spc:= WA; rn := rn+1; stimer1_on := true;
```

```
End;

Rule "read_L" spc = WA & L ==>
  L := false;
  If head = last Then
    spc := SC;
  Else
    spc := SF;
  End;
  sfirst := (head = last);
  If !(head = last) Then rn := 0 End;
  head := head + 1; stoggle := !stoggle;
  stimer1_on := false;
  stimer1_enabled := false;
End;

Rule "write_conf" spc = SC & !conf_full ==>
  conf_full := true;
  If head = nil Then conf := OK
  Elsif head = last & rn != 0 Then
    conf := DONT_KNOW;
  Else conf := NOT_OK; End;
  If head = nil Then spc := WR; Else
    spc := WT2;
    sfirst := true; stoggle := !stoggle;
    stimer2_on := true;
    rtimer_enabled := true;
  End;
  head := nil; rn := 0;
  verify_CONF(conf);
End;

Rule "stimer1" stimer1_on & stimer1_enabled
  ==>
  If rn = max Then
    spc := SC;
  Else
    spc := SF;
  End;
  stimer1_on := false;
  stimer1_enabled := false;
End;

Rule "stimer2" stimer2_on & stimer2_enabled
  ==>
  spc := WR; stimer2_on := false;
  stimer2_enabled := false;
End;

Rule "read_K" rpc = WF & K_full ==>
  K_full := false;
  msg.first := K.first; msg.last := K.last;
  msg.toggle := K.toggle; msg.data := K.data;
  If !ctoggle | (msg.toggle = rtoggle) Then
      rpc := SI; rtimer_on := false;
      rtimer_enabled := false;
  Else
    rpc := RTS;
  End;
End;

Rule "write_ind" rpc = SI & !ind_full ==>
  ind_full := true; ind_data := msg.data;
  If msg.last Then ind_indication := LAST;
  Elsif msg.first Then
    ind_indication := FIRST;
  Else ind_indication := INCOMPLETE;
  End;
  rpc := SA; rfirst := msg.last;
  ctoggle := true; rtoggle := !msg.toggle;
  verify_IND(ind_data,ind_indication);
End;

Rule "write_L" (rpc = SA | rpc = RTS) & !L
  ==>
  L := true;
  If rpc = SA Then rtimer_on := true; End;
  rpc := WF;
End;

Rule "write_ind_error" rpc = NOK & !ind_error
  ==>
  ind_error := true; rpc := WF; rfirst := true;
  rtimer_on := true; stimer2_enabled := true;
  verify_IND_ERR();
End;

Rule "rtimer" rtimer_on & rtimer_enabled ==>
  ctoggle := false;
  If !rfirst Then
    rpc := NOK; rtimer_on := false;
  Else
    stimer2_enabled := true;
  End;
  rtimer_enabled := false;
End;
```

C Invariants

```
Invariant "ref_abusy"
  abusy = (spc = SF | spc = WA | spc = SC);

Invariant "ref_afirst"
  afirst = rfirst;

Invariant "ref_aerror"
  aerror = ((rpc = NOK) |
            (spc = WT2 & rtimer_on & !rfirst));

Invariant "ref_afile"
  Forall i:1..last Do afile[i]=file[i] Endforall;

Invariant "ref_ahead"
  ahead =
   ((spc = WT2 |
    (ctoggle -> stoggle=rtoggle)) ? head : head+1);

Invariant "spc_1"
  (spc = WR | spc = SF | spc = SC) -> rpc = WF;

Invariant "spc_2"
  (spc = SF & rn = 0) ->
    (ctoggle -> stoggle = rtoggle);

Invariant "spc_3"
  spc = WA -> rn != 0;

Invariant "spc_4"
  spc = WT2 & !rtimer_enabled -> !ctoggle;

Invariant "spc_5"
  spc=SC & head = nil ->
   (ctoggle & stoggle = rtoggle);

Invariant "spc_6"
  spc = SC & head = nil -> rfirst;
```

```
Invariant "spc_7"
  spc = WR -> (ctoggle -> stoggle = rtoggle);

Invariant "spc_8"
  spc = WT2 -> rn = 0;

Invariant "spc_9"
  (spc = SC & rn = 0) ->
    (ctoggle -> stoggle = rtoggle);

Invariant "spc_10"
  spc = SF ->
   ((ctoggle -> stoggle = rtoggle) ->
    sfirst = rfirst);

Invariant "spc_11"
  spc = WR ->
   ((ctoggle -> stoggle = rtoggle) ->
    sfirst = rfirst);

Invariant "spc_12"
  spc = WA ->
   ((ctoggle -> stoggle = rtoggle) ->
    sfirst = rfirst);

Invariant "spc_13"
  spc = SC ->
   ((ctoggle -> stoggle = rtoggle) ->
    sfirst = rfirst);

Invariant "spc_14"
  spc = WT2 -> sfirst;

Invariant "spc_15"
  spc = WA -> head != nil;

Invariant "spc_16"
  spc = SF -> head != nil;

Invariant "rpc_1"
  (rpc =  SI | rpc =  SA | rpc =  RTS)
    ->
  spc  =  WA;

Invariant "rpc_2"
  rpc  =  NOK -> spc  =  WT2;

Invariant "rpc_3"
  rpc = SI -> msg.last = (head = last);

Invariant "rpc_4"
  rpc = NOK -> !ctoggle;

Invariant "rpc_5"
  rpc = SI -> stoggle = msg.toggle;

Invariant "rpc_6"
  (rpc = SA | rpc = RTS) -> stoggle = msg.toggle;

Invariant "rpc_7"
  (rpc = SA | rpc = RTS) ->
   (ctoggle & msg.toggle != rtoggle);

Invariant "rpc_8"
  (rpc = WF | rpc = RTS) -> rtimer_on;

Invariant "rpc_9"
  rpc = SI -> (ctoggle -> msg.toggle = rtoggle);

Invariant "rpc_10"
  rpc = SI -> msg.data = file[head];

Invariant "rpc_11"
  rpc = SI -> rfirst = msg.first;

Invariant "K_1"
  K_full
    ->
  (spc  =  WA & rpc  =  WF & !L);

Invariant "K_2"
  K_full -> K.last = (head = last);

Invariant "K_3"
  K_full -> K.toggle = stoggle;

Invariant "K_4"
  K_full -> K.data = file[head];

Invariant "K_5"
  K_full -> ((ctoggle -> K.toggle = rtoggle) ->
          K.first = rfirst);

Invariant "L_1"
  L
    ->
  (spc  =  WA & rpc  =  WF & !K_full);

Invariant "L_2"
  L -> ctoggle & (!rtoggle) = stoggle;

Invariant "stimer1_1"
  stimer1_enabled
    ->
  (spc  =  WA & rpc  =  WF & !K_full & !L);

Invariant "stimer2_1"
  stimer2_enabled
    ->
  (spc  =  WT2 & rpc  =  WF & !K_full & !L);

Invariant "stimer2_2"
  stimer2_enabled -> rfirst;

Invariant "stimer2_3"
  stimer2_enabled -> rfirst;

Invariant "rtimer_1"
  rtimer_enabled
    ->
  (spc  =  WT2 & rpc  =  WF &
   !K_full & !L & !stimer2_enabled);

Invariant "rn_1"
  rn !=  0 -> spc != WR;

Invariant "rn_2"
  (rn !=  0 & ctoggle & stoggle !=  rtoggle) ->
    rfirst = (head = last);

Invariant "head_1"
  head = nil -> (spc = WR | spc = WT2 | spc = SC);

Invariant "safe_1"
  spc = WR -> !abusy;

Invariant "safe_2"
  spc = SC -> abusy;

Invariant "safe_3"
  spc = SC -> !aerror;

Invariant "safe_4"
  spc = SC ->
    (head = nil -> ahead = nil)
      &
    ((head = last & rn !=  0) ->
     (ahead = nil | ahead = last))
      &
    ((head = last & rn = 0) -> ahead !=  nil)
      &
    ((head < last) -> ahead !=  nil);

Invariant "safe_5"
  rpc = SI -> abusy;

Invariant "safe_6"
  rpc = SI -> !aerror;

Invariant "safe_7"
  rpc = SI -> ahead !=  nil;

Invariant "safe_8"
  rpc = SI -> msg.data = afile[ahead];

Invariant "safe_9"
  rpc = SI ->
   ((msg.last = (ahead = last)) &
    (msg.first = afirst));

Invariant "safe_10"
  rpc = NOK -> aerror;
```

Procedure-Level Verification of Real-time Concurrent Systems*

Farn Wang Chia-Tien Lo

Institute of Information Science, Academia Sinica, Taipei, Taiwan 115, Republic of China

+886-2-7883799 ext. 2420; FAX +886-2-7824814; farn@iis.sinica.edu.tw

Abstract. We want to develop verification techniques for real-time concurrent system specifications with high-level behavior structures. Nowadays, there is a big gap in between the classical verification theories and the engineering practice in real-world projects. This work identifies two common engineering guidelines respected in the development of real-world software projects, structured programming and local autonomy in concurrent systems, and experiments with special verification algorithm based on those engineering wisdoms. The algorithm we have adopted respects the integrity of program structures, treats each procedure as an entity instead of as a group of statements, allows local state space search to exploit the local autonomy in concurrent systems without calculating the Cartesian products of local state spaces, and derives from each procedure declaration characteristic information which can be utilized in the verification process anywhere the procedure is invoked. We have endeavored to implement our idea, test it against an abstract version of a real-world protocol in a mobile communication environment, and report the data.

1 Introduction

There is a great disparity between the engineering practice and the classical theories in verifying sophisticated computer systems. It is the goal of this work to investigate this disparity and experiment with verification techniques which combine the engineering wisdom with the classical verification theories.

Facing each nontrivial industrial problem human has encountered, there are in general two types of approaches used to surpass it and push the technology frontier forward. The first is engineering and the second is scientific. With the engineering approach, people strive to solve the problem using common wisdoms derived from their experiences in the field. With the scientific approach, people emphasize understanding the nature of the problem, by building mathematical models which simulate the problem, and design solution techniques based on

* The work is partially supported by NSC, Taiwan, ROC under grant NSC 85-2213-E-001-005 and by the Communication Technology Division, Computer & Communication Research Laboratories, Industrial Technology Research Institute, Taiwan, ROC under a new grant for 1995-1996.

the models. In the evolution of industry, these two approaches usually benefit from each other. On one hand, engineering wisdom reveals the true nature of the problem and inspires people to build better models. On the other hand, better understanding of the problem nature corroborates the engineering wisdom and may eventually lead to better solution.

As the computer systems we would like to build become more and more sophisticated, nowadays these two types of approaches are also employed in the task of system verification. On the engineering side, people have developed various engineering guidelines from their experience in the field and have been successful in constructing some really big real-world systems with complex high-level behavior [28, 18, 30]. Examples of those successes include network layer communication protocols, software systems with abstract data types, parallel databases. On the theoretical side, basic mathematical models have been proposed to help people better understanding the intrinsic nature, e.g. complexities, of the problem [1, 4, 9, 10, 12, 14, 15, 25, 31]. Indeed, it has been reported that the advancement in the classical theory has led to the successful verification of several small real-world products, including physical layer communication protocols[7] and integrated circuit design[4, 23].

But ironically, if we look at the common guidelines respected by computer system engineers, we find that they are very hard to mechanize and really do not fit into the classical verification theories. For example, in building sophisticated system, people adopt the guideline of ***structured programming*** to structurally divide the design into smaller functional parts like procedures and loops and to refrain themselves from using arbitrary connection among the parts. But in the classical theories, basic models are usually assumed to be equivalent to random graphs. If there is a procedure, the standard treatment is just to use it as a macro expansion regardless of its functional integrity.

Another example of the disparity regards the practice in using clocks. For engineers, clocks sometimes serve as convenient devices in simplifying interaction among different threads in concurrent systems. Here is a hypothetical example. A gentleman named Mike drives his friend Frank to a shopping mall and tells Frank that he will come back to pick him up at 5pm. In this case the interaction gets simplified to a number, i.e. the deadline to meet. Both of them do not care what the other party plans to do before 5pm as long as the deadline is met. But from the viewpoint of the verification theory, clock is really not so pleasant a device because it always blows up the worst case complexities by an exponential factor. Also interestingly enough, even clock readings are intuitively numbers, the most, if not the only, used property of clock readings in real-time system verification theories is that if you increment a clock reading by noninfinitesimal amount for enough number of times, it will eventually be bigger than any given finite constant.

The third example of the disparity concerns with the way people use concurrency. In the design of sophisticated systems involving the interaction of several parties, it is the common engineering wisdom to localize the design consideration so that the reliability and safety of the whole systems can be derived from the verification of local properties of each party. But in the classical verification theory, calculation of Cartesian products of the local state spaces is usually adopted as the safe and complete technique. One exception is the composition and hiding operation proposed in process algebra [15, 25]. But still successful application to a real-world project with high-level behavior structure is yet to be observed.

This work integrates the two engineering guidelines cited in the above, i.e. structured programming and local autonomy in concurrent systems, into the design of verification algorithm which can be efficient in verifying well-designed computer systems. We target our research on real-time concurrent systems with timed atomic actions, synchronization primitives, procedures, loops, nondeterminism, and concurrency. A real-time system performs by giving out correct response at the correct moment. A concurrent system may allow several *threads*[11] (basic autonomous sequential executions) running concurrently. Recently, a theoretical framework for this purpose was proposed in [33] in which the verification complexities for both recursive and nonrecursive real-time concurrent systems are discussed and an algorithm is developed for the nonrecursive ones. One desirable feature of the algorithm is that it respects the procedure and loop structures of the systems by treating a rendezvousless execution of a procedure (loop) as a numerical entities, i.e. its execution time, which once analyzed, can be used in the verification process anywhere the procedure (loop) is invoked. Local autonomy of concurrent systems is utilized by a technique called *timing coincidence analysis* which determines the coincidibility of two states by telling if there are two synchronization-less local state sequences with the same execution time leading to the two states respectively. Such a technique enables us to construct global analysis from local state space search outcomes and is supposed to work well in systems with long autonomous executions and procedure invocations in between synchronization among the concurrent threads.

In this paper, we report the implementation of the algorithm proposed in [33]. However, we shall redesign the specification language to make it look like a traditional programming language. Several techniques to improve the average-case performance of the algorithm are incorporated which make the analysis of an abstract version of a general session setting control protocol (GSSC) in a wireless communication environment feasible. First, some related work will be discussed in section 2. We then formally introduce our new specification language and review the complexity issues in section 3. The reachability analysis algorithm proposed in [33] is then rewritten to fit our specification language in section 4. The important techniques we employed in the implementation are discussed in section 5. GSSC is discussed in section 6 with the performance on the reachability analysis of two states, one consistent and one inconsistent, reported. Section 7 discusses some extension to the implementation on the way and some future work.

We shall adopt the following notations. Given a set or sequence K, $|K|$ is the number of elements in K. We let $\mathcal{N}$ be the set of nonnegative integers, $\mathcal{Z}$ the set of integers, $\mathcal{N}^{\{\infty\}} = \mathcal{N} \cup \{\infty\}$, and $\mathcal{N}^{\{*\}} = \mathcal{N} \cup \{*\}$.

2 Related work

With the theoretical development of real-time and hybrid automata[1, 14, 21, 26, 27, 32] and the successful engineering of automated verification tools[2, 8, 4, 23], the research of computer-aided verification has received much attention. At this moment, various state-based [1, 4, 9, 10, 12, 14, 31] or event-based[20] model description languages are available, to which the standard verification technique of global space reachability analysis is usually applied. So far, several small real-world examples have been verified using this approach [4, 7, 23]. However such abstractions, although very elegant, may be at too low a level to make automatic verifiers efficiently uncover the behavior structures hidden in big system model descriptions.

Process algebra[15, 25] takes advantage of hiding and composition operators to construct complex systems from submodules. Since the verification algorithms for process algebra take care of general specifications without special program structure in mind, it may not be able to exploit the regularity of high-level behavior structure resulted from the observance of engineers to those guidelines.

People also use first-order logic or even higher-order logics to verify system designs. In those cases, very high-level behavior structures can be specified and verified[6, 13, 29]. For example, in [19], it was proposed to use positive cycles as intuitive refutation units in verifying real-time systems. The drawback is that the verification software can only do as much as proof checking and the engineers are pretty much left to their own. Still several remarkable benchmarks have been passed because of the industrious ingenuity of researchers in the community[6].

A good integration of engineering wisdom and scientific principles is formal methods in the line of VDM[18] and Z[30]. In that approach, a set of guidelines for system construction and a set of rules for verification are proposed and have been successfully applied in several real-world projects with benefits recorded. For example, in 1992, a Queen's Award of Britain was given to Oxford University Computing Laboratory and IBM UK Laboratories at Hursley Park for the development of IBM CICS using Z notation.

3 Real-time concurrent systems

3.1 Syntax

The underlying concept of our approach is *DAG_1^1 procedure*, defined in [33], which is a single-source single-destination directed acyclic graph in which each node represents a compound statement of procedure-call and atomic operation. Here we shall redefine DAG_1^1 procedure in the concept of traditional programming languages. As in the traditional imperative languages, a DAG_1^1 procedure is constructed from three types of statements, *timed atomic, rendezvous, procedure-calling*, and two types of *statement structures, switch, concatenation.* A timed atomic statement is executed with a prespecified earliest starting time and deadline. Unlike in Ada, here rendezvous is fulfilled by having all the participating parties executing the same rendezvous type at the same time. A procedure-call represents either a fixed or a nondeterministic number of sequential execution of a DAG_1^1 procedure. A switch statement structure represents a nondeterministic choice, while a concatenation statement structure represents a successive execution of two statement structures. We use the following example to give intuition to the readers before the formal definition.

Example 1. In Figure 1, we illustrate three procedures, P, Q, R. P may loop nondeterministically many times to invoke R. Q invokes R also as the body of a 2-iteration loop. σ is a rendezvous type. An interval, like [4, 9], represents a

```
P {
    [3,5];
    switch {
        case [0,2];
        case [3,7]; σ;
    }
    R *;
}
```

```
Q {
    [4,9];
    R 2;
}
```

```
R {
    σ;
}
```

Fig. 1. Several simple procedures

timed atomic statement with the earliest starting times and deadlines. ||

Definition 1 : DAG_1^1 procedure. A DAG_1^1 *procedure* P is constructed from finite application of the following rules.

$P ::= w\{B\}$
$B ::= [i,j]; \mid \sigma; \mid w_1 n; \mid w_1 *; \mid B_1 B_2 \mid \mathbf{switch}\{\mathbf{case} B_1 \mathbf{case} B_2 \ldots \mathbf{case} B_n\}$

Here w, w_1 are procedure names (character strings) and B, B_1, B_2, B_n are statement structures. $i \in \mathcal{N}$, $j \in \mathcal{N} \cup \{\infty\}$, and n is a nonnegative integer. σ is a rendezvous type. Given $P = w\{B\}$, we shall use $\bar{P}$ as the notation for the name w of P. ||

Given a set Π of DAG_1^1 procedures, we treat each statement position as the true identity of the corresponding statement. That is given two statement positions which both execute a syntactically identically statement (say a rendezvous "σ;," or a procedure-calling "$\bar{P}n$;," or a timed atomic statement "$[i,j]$;"), we shall still treat these two positions as two different statements. Given a DAG_1^1 procedure P, we let $S(\bar{P})$ be the set of statements used in P. We also define $S_0(\bar{P})$ and $S_f(\bar{P})$ to be the set of first and final statements in P respectively in the following.

- If $\bar{P}\{B\}$ is defined, then $S_0(\bar{P}) = S_0(B)$
- If B is a statement, then $S_0(B) = \{B\}$.
- $S_0(B_1 B_2) = S_0(B_1)$.

• $S_0(\textbf{switch}\ \{\textbf{case}\ B_1 \ldots \textbf{case}\ B_n\}) = S_0(B_1) \cup \ldots \cup S_0(B_n)$
Similarly, we have the following definition for $S_f(\bar{P})$.
• If $\bar{P}\{B\}$ is defined, then $S_f(\bar{P}) = S_f(B)$
• If B is a statement, then $S_f(B) = \{B\}$.
• $S_f(B_1B_2) = S_f(B_2)$.
• $S_f(\textbf{switch}\ \{\textbf{case}\ B_1 \ldots \textbf{case}\ B_n\}) = S_f(B_1) \cup \ldots \cup S_f(B_n)$
Given a concatenation statement structure B_1B_2 in a DAG_1^1 procedure P, for each $s_1 \in S_f(B_1)$ and $s_2 \in S_0(B_2)$, we call s_2 a successor of s_1.

Notice that the looping in DAG_1^1 procedures are restrained as a special type of procedure calls. Conceptually, a real-time concurrent system allows many threads running concurrently. By giving additional information on the starting statement of each thread and the participating parties of each rendezvous type, a set of procedure definitions can be grouped to define a real-time concurrent system.

Definition 2 : Real-time concurrent system. Given a set Π of DAG_1^1 procedures, we let Σ^Π be the set of rendezvous types used in procedures in Π. A *real-time concurrent system* is a tuple $\langle \Pi, \Omega, \tau \rangle$ satisfying the following properties.

- Π is a set of DAG_1^1 procedure definitions such that for every procedure P defined in Π, any procedure referenced in P is also defined in Π.
- Ω is a sequence $\langle \bar{P}_1, \ldots, \bar{P}_m \rangle$ of procedure names in $\overline{\Pi}$ and declares the m threads in the system. For each $1 \leq i \leq m$, thread i starts by invoking P_i.
- $\tau : \Sigma^\Pi \mapsto 2^{\{1,\ldots,|\Omega|\}}$ defines the set of parties participating in each rendezvous. For each $i \in \tau(\sigma)$, thread i is expected to participate in each instance of rendezvous σ.

A real-time concurrent system is *recursive* iff its procedure-calls are recursive. ||

Example 2. Assume we have the four procedure definitions in example 1. Then $R = \langle \{P, Q, R\}, \langle \bar{P}, \bar{Q} \rangle, \{\alpha \to \{1,2\}\} \rangle$ is a legitimate nonrecursive and unambiguous real-time concurrent system. ||

3.2 An operational semantics for systems with single discrete clock

Given a real-time concurrent system with m threads, the *states* of the system can be described by an array of *local states* of the m threads. The procedure-calling scheme for the threads in our real-time concurrent systems resembles the push-pop operation of stacks[17] which have often been used as theoretical abstraction of nested procedure-callings. The *local state* of a thread can be conceptually recorded in a structure like the *control stack* (the name we shall adopt henceforth) in [3] and the *activation record* in [16, 34]. All possible executions of a thread from a moment can be deduced from the contents of the corresponding control stack.

Given a real-time concurrent system R, we let $S^{(R)}$ be the set of statements used in procedures defined in R. Given a thread local state (control stack) Γ represented as the following sequence

bottom					top
(s_0, t_0)	(s_1, t_1)	(s_2, t_2)	......	(s_{m-1}, t_{m-1})	(s_m, t_m)

we let (s_0, t_0) and (s_m, t_m) be the *bottom* and *top* respectively of Γ. A control stack, say the above-mentioned Γ, must satisfy the following conditions.

- For each $0 \leq i < m$, either
  - for some P and n, s_i is a procedure-calling statement "$\bar{P}n$;" with $0 \leq t_i < n$; or
  - for some P, s_i is a procedure-calling statement "$\bar{P}*$;" with $t_i = 0$.
- One of the following must be true for the top (s_m, t_m) of Γ.
  - s_m is a procedure-calling statement "$\bar{P}n$;" and $0 \leq t_m \leq n$.
  - s_m is a procedure-calling statement "$\bar{P}*$;" and $t_m = 0$.
  - s_m is a timed atomic statement "$[i, j]$;" and either $0 \leq t_m \leq j \neq \infty$ or $0 \leq t_m \leq i \vee t_m = j = \infty$.
  - s_m is a rendezvous statement "σ;" and either $t_m = 0$ or $t_m = \sigma$.

Given a control stack Γ, we let top(Γ) symbolically denote the top of Γ. $\Gamma\gamma$ is a new control stack obtained by pushing γ into Γ. pop(Γ) is a new control stack obtained by popping the top element from Γ. Given top(Γ) $= (s, t)$ with $t, c \in \mathcal{Z}$, we let Γ^{+c} be an abbreviation of pop(Γ)$(s, t + c)$, i.e. the local state obtained by incrementing the top counter value by c.

Suppose we are given a local state $\Gamma = (s_0, t_0)(s_1, t_1) \ldots (s_m, t_m)$. For each $0 \leq i \leq m$, when s_i is a procedure-calling statement "Pn;," it means the thread is now in the middle of executing procedure P and is going to invoke P consecutively for $|n - t_i|$ more times.

Similar to [17], we can define the succession of local states which follows the intuition of control stack evolution during procedure-calling and strongly matches the relation among paths in activation trees as discussed in [3]. However, for the convenience of our algorithm design, we shall present the following concept of local state successions.

Definition 3 : Succession of thread local states. The succession relation, $\vdash$, between local states are defined in the following way. Suppose we are given a local state Γ whose top is (s, t).

- **Fixed-loop procedure-call :** Suppose s is a procedure-calling statement "$\bar{P}n$;." If $t < n$, then for each $s_0 \in S_0(\bar{P})$, $\Gamma \vdash \Gamma^{+1}(s_0, 0)$. If $t = n$, then for each successor statement s' of s, $\Gamma \vdash$ pop(Γ)$(s', 0)$.
- ***-loop procedure-call :** If s is a procedure-calling statement "$\bar{P}*$;," then for each $s_0 \in S_0(\bar{P})$, $\Gamma \vdash \Gamma(s_0, 0)$ and for each successor statement s' of s, $\Gamma \vdash$ pop(Γ)$(s', 0)$.
- **Return from procedure-call :** When $s \in S_f(\bar{P})$, if one of the following three condition is true,
  - s is a timed statement "$[i, j]$" and $i \leq t \leq j$.
  - $t = \sigma$ form some rendezvous type σ.
  - s is a procedure-calling statement "$\bar{Q}n$;" and $t = n$.
  - s is a procedure-calling statement "$\bar{Q}*$;."

  $\Gamma \vdash$ pop(Γ)

- **Timed statement :** Suppose s is a timed atomic statement "$[i, j]$;."
  - If $t < i$, then $\Gamma \vdash \Gamma^{+1}$.
  - If $i \leq t < j \neq \infty$, then $\Gamma \vdash \Gamma^{+1}$.
  - If $i \leq t < j = \infty$, then $\Gamma \vdash \text{pop}(\Gamma)(s, \infty)$.
  - If $i \leq t \leq j$, then for each successor statement s' of s, $\Gamma \vdash \text{pop}(\Gamma)(s', 0)$.
- **Rendezvous statement :** If s is a rendezvous statement and $t = 0$, then for each successor statement s' of s, $\Gamma \vdash \text{pop}(\Gamma)(s, \sigma) \vdash \text{pop}(\Gamma)(s', 0)$. ||

Based on the concept of local state succession, we are now ready to define the computation in multi-thread real-time concurrent systems.

Definition 4 : States and runs. Suppose we are given a real-time concurrent system $R = \langle \Pi, \Omega, \tau \rangle$. A *state* of R is a sequence of $|\Omega|$ local states. A finite sequence $(\Delta_0, g_0)(\Delta_1, g_1) \ldots (\Delta_m, g_m)$ is called a Δ_0-*run* of R, where for each $0 \leq k \leq m$, Δ_k is a state and $g_k \in \{0, 1\}$ indicates the presence of a global clock tick. Assume, for each $0 \leq k \leq m$, $\Delta_k = \langle \Gamma_k^{(1)}, \ldots, \Gamma_k^{(n)} \rangle$. The following requirements are imposed on a Δ_0-run.

- For each $0 \leq k < m$ and $1 \leq i \leq n$, either $\Gamma_k^{(i)} \rightarrow \Gamma_{k+1}^{(i)}$ or $\Gamma_k^{(i)} = \Gamma_{k+1}^{(i)}$.
- **Enforcement of synchrony to global clock** : For each $0 \leq k < m$, $g_k = 1$ iff every thread increments its time reading by 1, that is for each $1 \leq i \leq n$ such that $\text{top}(\Gamma_k^{(i)}) = (s, t)$ and $\text{top}(\Gamma_{k+1}^{(i)}) = (s', t')$, $s = s'$ and either $t + 1 = t'$ or $t = t' = \infty$.
- **Enforcement of rendezvous** : For each $\sigma \in \Sigma^{\Pi}$ and each $0 \leq k \leq m$, if $\text{top}(\Gamma_k^{(i)}) = (s, \sigma)$ for some s and $i \in \tau(\sigma)$, then for each $j \in \tau(\sigma)$, $\text{top}(\Gamma_k^{(j)}) = (s', \sigma)$ for some s'.

Given a state Δ and a Δ-run $\Psi = (\Delta_0, g_0)(\Delta_1, g_1) \ldots (\Delta_m, g_m)$, for each $0 \leq k \leq m$, the time of the k-th state in Ψ, in symbols $time_{\Psi}(k)$, is defined inductively by two cases : (1) $time_{\Psi}(0) = 0$. (2) For each $0 \leq k < m$, $time_{\Psi}(k + 1) = time_{\Psi}(k) + g_k$. ||

Example 3. Assume that we have the real-time concurrent system in example 2. It can be seen that while thread 1 may loop nondeterministically many times, thread 2 terminates after executing two instances of rendezvous α. Thus the whole system only has runs with two rendezvous instances. ||

3.3 Complexities of reachability analysis

We shall introduce a basic version of the reachability problem here. Such a version is instrumental in constructing other interesting versions.

Definition 5 : State reachability. Given a real-time concurrent system $R = \langle \Pi, \Omega, \tau \rangle$, a state Δ' is said *reachable from* another state Δ in R iff there is a Δ-run $(\Delta_0, g_0)(\Delta_1, g_1) \ldots (\Delta_m, g_m)$ such that $\Delta' = \Delta_m$. ||

The reachability problem in our real-time concurrent systems can then be formulated in the following way. Given a real-time concurrent system R and two of its states Δ, Δ', the corresponding *state reachability problem* instance asks if Δ' is reachable from Δ in R. We cite the following theorem and lemmas from [33] to show the complexities of the problem for recursive and nonrecursive systems.

Theorem 6. *Two-counter machine halting problem[22] is reducible to the reachability problem of real-time concurrent systems.* ||

Lemma 7. *QBF[17] is reducible in PTIME to the state reachability problem for nonrecursive real-time concurrent systems.* ||

Lemma 8. *The state reachability problem of nonrecursive real-time concurrent systems is in PSPACE.* ||

4 Reachability analysis for nonrecursive systems

Our algorithm will be presented in two steps. First, we shall give a skeleton view of the algorithm in subsection 4.1 in which the implementation of one particular code line is not detailed. The skeleton describes how we exploit the autonomy of each thread in between hitting rendezvous to reduce the size of state space. Second, details about that one code line will be supplemented in subsection 4.2 and 4.3.

4.1 Skeleton view of the algorithm

We formalize the concept of thread autonomy in between hitting rendezvous with the following definition.

Definition 9 : Successor through rendezvous-less run. Given a real-time concurrent system R, and two states Δ and Δ', we say Δ' is a *successor through rendezvous-less run (or $\neg r$-successor)* of Δ iff there is a finite Δ-run $\Psi = (\Delta_0, g_0) \ldots (\Delta_m, g_m)$ of R such that

- Ψ ends at Δ', i.e. $\Delta' = \Delta_m$; and
- for each $0 < k < m$, Δ_k does not mark the completion of a rendezvous, that is, assuming $\Delta_k = \langle \Gamma_k^{(1)}, \ldots, \Gamma_k^{(n)} \rangle$, for each $1 \leq i \leq n$, there is no $\sigma \in \Sigma^{\Pi}$ s.t. $\text{top}(\Gamma_k^{(i)}) = (s, \sigma)$ for some s. ||

In between hitting rendezvous, each thread executes in an independent way. We say a state $\langle \Gamma^{(1)}, \ldots, \Gamma^{(n)} \rangle$ is *at the stage of completion of rendezvous σ* iff for some $1 \leq i \leq n, s$, $\text{top}(\Gamma^{(i)}) = (s, \sigma)$. A major source of efficiency of our algorithm comes from the fact that we only work with states which are at the completion stage of rendezvous. The algorithm in table 1 takes this characteristic of real-time concurrent systems into consideration to answer instances of state reachability problem. Succession relation among such states is figured out by manipulation of arithmetic set expressions as defined in subsection 4.2 The correctness of procedure Reachable() has been proven in [33] and restated in the following lemma.

Lemma 10. *Given two states Δ, Δ' of a nonrecursive real-time systems R, with the oracle for $\neg r$-successorship, Δ' is reachable from Δ in R iff Reachable(R, Δ, Δ') is TRUE.* ||

```
Reachable(R, Δ, Δ')
/* R = ⟨Π, Ω, τ⟩, is a nonrecursive real-time concurrent system. */ {
    (1) Generate the set X of all states in which a rendezvous is at the stage of
        completion.
    (2) Determine the pairwise ¬r-successor relation in X ∪ {Δ, Δ'} and call it Y.
    (3) If Δ' is reachable from Δ in (X ∪ {Δ, Δ'}, Y), answer TRUE; else answer
        FALSE.
}
```

Table 1. Algorithm for state reachability problem

All but the second code line in table 1 are obvious. In subsection 4.2, we shall introduce arithmetic set expressions, as the abstraction tool used to construct a solution for the second code line. In subsection 4.3, we shall use the technique of timing coincidibility analysis to determine the $\neg r$-successor relation between two states.

4.2 Arithmetic set expressions and their operations

The transitions in our system models are carried out within intervals bounded by earliest starting times and deadlines. Since earliest starting times, and deadlines alike, of a sequence of consecutive transitions can be accumulated during the analysis of thread behavior, it is natural to define the addition and integer multiplication of integer intervals. And indeed our reachability analysis algorithm is presented based on this kind of arithmetic set operations.

Our arithmetic set expression is constructed by the following rules.

$$H ::= \{c\} \mid H_1 \cup H_2 \mid H_1 \cap H_2 \mid H_1 + H_2 \mid H_1 k \mid H_1 *$$

c, k are natural numbers. $\{c_1, \ldots, c_n\}$ is a shorthand for $\{c_1\} \cup \ldots \cup \{c_n\}$. Conceptually, we treat an integer interval $[a, b)$ as a shorthand for the set $\{a, a+1, \ldots, b-1\}$. Especially, $[a, \infty)$ is a shorthand for $\{a\} + \{1\}^*$. The meaning of these set expression is inductively given in the following.

- Case $H = \{c\}$, H is the set of integer c.
- Case $H = H_1 \cup H_2$ ($H = H_1 \cap H_2$), H is the union (intersection) of H_1 and H_2.
- Case $H = H_1 + H_2$, $H = \{a + b \mid a \in H_1; b \in H_2\}$.
- Case $H = H_1 k$, (1) when $k = 0$, then $H = \{0\}$; (2) otherwise $H = H_1(k-1) + H_1$.
- Case $H = H_1 *$, $H = \bigcup_{k \geq 0} H_1 k$.

Note $\emptyset$ acts as a nullifier in arithmetic set addition, i.e. for all integer set expression H, $H + \emptyset = \emptyset$. Also, we allow distribution of addition against union and intersection.

An arithmetic set expression H is said to be in *periodical normal form (PNF)* iff $H = \bigcup_{1\le i\le m}(\{a_i\} + \{c_i\}*)$. In the following, we give a set of rewriting rules to transform arithmetic set expressions into PNF arithmetic set expressions.

1) $\left(\bigcup_{1\le i\le m}(\{a_i\} + \{c_i\}*)\right) \cap \left(\bigcup_{1\le j\le n}(\{b_j\} + \{d_j\}*)\right)$
$= \bigcup_{1\le i\le m; 1\le j\le n} K_\cap(\{a_i\} + \{c_i\}*, \{b_j\} + \{d_j\}*)$
where $K_\cap(\{a\} + \{c\}*, \{b\} + \{d\}*)$ is defined by the following two cases.
   - If there is no integer solution i, j to $a + ci = b + dj$, then $K_\cap(\{a\} + \{c\}*, \{b\} + \{d\}) = \emptyset$
   - Otherwise, let $\bar{i}, \bar{j}$ be the minimum integer solution. $K_\cap(\{a\} + \{c\}*, \{b\} + \{d\}*) = \{a + c\bar{i}\} + \{\mathrm{lcm}(c, d)\}*$

2) $\left(\bigcup_{1\le i\le m}(\{a_i\} + \{c_i\}*)\right) + \left(\bigcup_{1\le j\le n}(\{b_j\} + \{d_j\}*)\right)$
$= \bigcup_{1\le i\le m; 1\le j\le n} \left(\begin{array}{l} \{a_i + b_j + \mathrm{lcm}(c_i, d_j)\} + \{\gcd(c_i, d_j)\}*) \\ \cup \{a_i + b_j + c_i h + d_j k \,|\, h, k \in \mathcal{N}; c_i h + d_j k < \mathrm{lcm}(c_i, d_j)\} \end{array} \right)$

3) $\left(\bigcup_{1\le i\le m}(\{a_i\} + \{c_i\}*)\right) k$
$= \begin{cases} \{0\} & \text{if } k = 0 \\ \left(\bigcup_{1\le i\le m}(\{a_i\} + \{c_i\}*)\right)(k-1) + \bigcup_{1\le i\le m}(\{a_i\} + \{c_i\}*) & \text{if } k > 0 \end{cases}$
After application of the rule, rule 2 should be used immediately.

4) $\left(\bigcup_{1\le i\le m}(\{a_i\} + \{c_i\}*)\right)* = \sum_{1\le i\le m}(\{a_i\} * + \{c_i\}*)$
After application of the rule, rule 2 and distribution of addition against unions should be used iteratively to transform the formula to its PNF.

4.3 Timing coincidibility analysis

The technique of *timing coincidibility analysis* is based on the following observation. Given two concurrent threads starting their execution simultaneously, after running without interaction (rendezvous) for t time units according to the global clock, they may get to local states Γ, Γ' respectively. Then due to the strong synchrony in global clock systems, we can conclude that Γ, Γ' may happen at the same time during the two threads rendezvous-less executions respectively. This implies that we can separately work with the subtasks of searching in the local state space of each thread while analyzing the reachability between states. By figuring out the general time patterns between pairs of local states in the local state spaces, we can tell the $\neg r$-successor relations by intersecting those time representations. In this approach, time representations are often very concise since it tends to ignore the difference among different state sequences as long as they have the same time values.

The following definition formalizes the concept of local state space search.

Definition 11 : Local state sequence. Given a real-time concurrent system $R = \langle \Pi, \Omega, \tau \rangle$, a finite local state sequence $\Phi = \Gamma_0 \Gamma_1 \ldots \Gamma_m$, with $\Gamma_k \vdash \Gamma_{k+1}$ for each $0 \le k < m$, defines a legitimate thread execution in R from Γ_0 and is called a *Γ_0-sequence. Φ* is *rendezvous-less* iff for every $0 < k < m$, Γ_k is not at the completion stage of a rendezvous, i.e. $\forall \sigma \in \Sigma^\Pi \forall s(\mathrm{top}(\Gamma_k) \ne (s, \sigma))$. ||

Definition 12 : Rendezvous-less time expressions. Given a DAG_1^1 procedure $\bar{P}\{B\}$, the *rendezvous-less time expression* of P, $texp_{\neg r}(\bar{P})$, is defined inductively as follows.

- then $texp_{\neg r}(\bar{P}) = texp_{\neg r}(B)$.
- $texp_{\neg r}([i,j];) = [i,j]$
- $texp_{\neg r}(\sigma) = \emptyset$
- $texp_{\neg r}(\bar{P}_1 n;) = (texp_{\neg r}(\bar{P}_1))n$
- $texp_{\neg r}(\bar{P}_1 *;) = (texp_{\neg r}(\bar{P}_1))*$
- $texp_{\neg r}(B_1 B_2) = texp_{\neg r}(B_1) + texp_{\neg r}(B_2)$
- $texp_{\neg r}(\mathbf{switch}\{\mathbf{case}B_1 \ldots \mathbf{case}B_n\}) = texp_{\neg r}(B_1) \cup \ldots \cup texp_{\neg r}(B_n)$

Suppose we are given a finite rendezvous-less local state sequence $\Phi = \Gamma_0 \ldots \Gamma_m$ with $\mathrm{top}(\Gamma_i) = (s_i, t_i)$ for each $0 \leq i \leq m$. We conveniently let $texp_{\neg r}(\Phi)$ equal to

$$\sum_{0\leq i<m; s_i=[i,j]; 0\leq t_i \neq \infty; 0 \leq t_{i+1} \neq \infty} (t_{i+1} - t_i) + \delta_\Phi * + \sum_{0 \leq i < m; s_i = \text{“}\bar{Q}*;\text{”}} ((texp_{\neg r}(\bar{Q}))*)$$

be our notation for the time expression for rendezvous-less local state sequence Φ. Here δ_Φ is $\{1\}$ when $\exists 0 \leq i \leq m(t_i = \infty)$; $\{0\}$ otherwise. Also we let

$$texp_{\neg r}(\Gamma, \Gamma') = \bigcup_{(\ \Phi \text{ is a finite simple rendezvous-less } \Gamma\text{-sequence of } R \text{ ends at } \Gamma'\ )} texp_{\neg r}(\Phi)$$

where “simple” means no two local states are the same. ||

The execution times of all rendezvous-less execution sequences between two local states can be figured out by doing some arithmetic on time expressions. The meaning of the time expression is given by the following lemma proven in [33].

Lemma 13. *Given two local states Γ, Γ' of a nonrecursive real-time concurrent system, there is a rendezvous-less execution sequence of time t from Γ to Γ' iff $t \in \mathrm{texp}_{\neg r}(\Gamma, \Gamma')$ which is computable.* ||

With definition 11, 12, and lemma 13, we have made the concept of autonomous execution of a single thread precise and proven our derivation of rendezvous-less thread execution time expression correct. Now all these can be readily combined to prove the correctness of the technique of timing coincidibility analysis.

Lemma 14. *Given $t \in \mathcal{N}$ and two states of a nonrecursive real-time concurrent system R, $\Delta = \langle \Gamma^{(1)}, \ldots, \Gamma^{(n)} \rangle$ and $\Delta' = \langle \Gamma'^{(1)}, \ldots, \Gamma'^{(n)} \rangle$, Δ' is a successor of Δ through rendezvous-less run of t time units in R iff $t \in \bigcap_{1\leq i \leq n} \mathrm{texp}_{\neg r}(\Gamma^{(i)}, \Gamma'^{(i)})$.*

Proof. According to definition 9, 11, 12, and lemma 13. ||

5 Implementation techniques

We have employed several techniques to take advantage of the behavior structure of procedure-callings and local autonomy to make the reachability analysis more efficient. As we have observed, such techniques are valuable and often result in orders of magnitude in verification performance improvement.

5.1 Nonpeak execution path

Given a stack Γ, remember that we use $|\Gamma|$ to denote the height of Γ. A local state sequence $\Gamma_0\Gamma_1\ldots\Gamma_m$ is called a peak local state sequence iff there are integers i, j, k with $0 \leq i < j < k \leq m$ such that $|\Gamma_i| < |\Gamma_j|$ and $|\Gamma_j| > |\Gamma_k|$.

In an interval of the rendezvous-less execution of a thread, a peak in its execution sequence represents a procedure-call which does not incur any rendezvous. The effect of the rendezvous-less procedure-call can be treated as purely numerical values, i.e. its rendezvous-less time expressions. Thus we introduce the following new concept of local state succession involving encapsulated procedure-calls.

Definition 15 **Successors of local states with encapsulated procedure-call.** If s is a procedure-calling statement "$\bar{P}n$;" with $t < n$, then for each $1 \leq c \leq n-t$, $\Gamma \vdash \Gamma^{+c}$. ||

We have observed that while calculating the rendezvous-less time expressions between two local states, we only have to consider nonpeak path. While calculating the time expression of a rendezvousless local state sequence Φ between two local states, if we find out that two consecutive local states along Φ are connected by the above-defined successor relations, we shall include $(texp_{\neg r}(\bar{P}))c$ in $texp_{\neg r}(\Phi)$.

5.2 Starting timed atomic local states

While computing the time expression of rendezvousless local state sequence, we ignore those local states which mark the execution in the middle of timed atomic statements. That is we can ignore all local states Γ with $\text{top}(\Gamma) = (s, t)$, $s = [i, j];$, and $t \neq 0$ by introducing the following new local state successor relationship.

Definition 16 **Successors from starting timed atomic local states.** If $\text{top}(\Gamma) = (s, 0)$ and s is a timed statement $[i, j];$, then for each successor statement s' of s, $\Gamma \vdash \text{pop}(\Gamma)(s', 0)$. ||

Suppose we are given a rendezvousless local state sequence $\Phi = \Gamma_0 \ldots \Gamma_m$, if $\text{top}(\Gamma_0) = (s, t)$ and $\text{top}(\Gamma_m) = (s', t')$ with $s = [i, j];$, $s' = [i', j'];$, $t \neq 0$, and $t' \neq 0$. Let $\bar{\Phi}$ be the local state sequence identical to Φ except that

- $\bar{\Phi}$ starts t time units earlier than Φ in s; and
- $\bar{\Phi}$ ends t' time units earlier than Φ in s'.

Then we can compute $texp_{\neg r}(\Phi)$ to be $texp_{\neg r}(\bar{\Phi}) - [t, t] + [t', t']$. Note however that our original time expression definition does not deal with subtraction. But since we always reduce time expression to PNF, a time expression like $[a, b] + [c, c] * - [t, t]$ is equivalent to $[a + cg - t, b + cg - t] + [c, c]*$ where g is the smallest integer solution for x to $a + cx \geq t$.

5.3 Local state space segmentation

Given a real-time concurrent system with m threads, a naive approach in calculating states is to calculate all the Cartesian products of m local states. This usually results in huge number of pseudo states most of which can never be reached from the system initial state. The trick we use in the implementation is to segment the local state space of each thread by rendezvous local states. Thus given a state $\Delta = \langle \Gamma_1, \ldots, \Gamma_m \rangle$, while calculating the states reachable from Δ through rendezvous-less runs, we only compute the Cartesian product of the local state subspaces $K_1, \ldots, K_m$ defined in the following way. For each $1 \leq i \leq m$, if Γ_i is a rendezvous local state, then K_i is the next segment reachable from local states in the segment where Γ_i is in. Otherwise it is the present segment where Γ_i is in.

6 General Session Setup Control protocol

We have tested our implementation against an abstract version of a real-world project which deals with the communication link setup in a mobile phone environment. The test example GSSC comes from the Wireless Communication Department, Computer & Communication Research Laboratories, Industrial Technology Research Institute, Taiwan, ROC. It deals with setting up and later releasing a communication channel between a client and a server. Five threads are involved in the system, the client, the system service for client (SS_C), the line control unit (LCU), the system service form server (SS_S), and the server. The protocol must take care of communication failure incurred by, e.g. timeout, server busy, ...

In our experiment, we test two cases, one for the reachability of an inconsistent states and one for that of a consistent one. We thus give a brief description to all these five threads. After this, we shall then present part of the protocol in our description language.

- Reaction sequence from the client's viewpoint :
  1) The client starts the whole session by sending an SS_SETUP_req message to SS_C.
  2) If an SS_RELEASE_ind message is received from SS_C, quit the session. If an SS_FACILITY_ind message is received, send an SS_FACILITY_req message to SS_C to request for the facility and wait for further response from SS_C.
  3) If an SS_RELEASE_ind message is received from SS_C, quit the session. If an SS_FACILITY_ind message is received, then send an SS_RELEASE_req message to release the resources and quit.
- Reaction sequence from SS_C's viewpoint :
  1) When an SS_SETUP_req message is received from the client, send an LCU_DATA_req message with identifier 4 to LCU and starts a timer which timeouts at 10 time units later.

2) If an LCU_RELEASE_ind message is received from LCU within 10 time units, send an SS_RELEASE_ind message to the client and quit the session.
   If a timeout occurs, send an SS_RELEASE_ind message to the client and an LCU_RELEASE_req message with identifier 4 to LCU to quit the session.
   If an LCU_DATA_ind message is received from LCU within 10 time units, send an SS_FACILITY_ind message back to the client and wait for its further response.
3) If an SS_RELEASE_req message is received from the client, send an LCU_RELEASE_req message with identifer 4 to LCU to quit.
   If an SS_FACILITY_req message is received from the client, send an LCU_DATA_req message with identifier 4 to LCU and starts a timer which timeouts at 10 time units later.
4) If an LCU_RELEASE_ind message is received from LCU within 10 time units, send an SS_RELEASE_ind message to the client and quit.
   If a timeout occurs, send an SS_RELEASE_ind message to the client and an LCU_RELEASE_req message with identifier 4 to LCU to quit the session.
   If an LCU_DATA_ind message is received from LCU within 10 time units, send an SS_FACILITY_ind message back to the client and wait for its further response.
5) Upon the reception of an SS_RELEASE_req message from the client, send an LCU_RELEASE_req message with identifier 4 to LCU to quit the session.

- Reaction sequence from LCU's viewpoint :
  1) If an LCU_DATA_req message is received with identifier 4, send an LCU_DATA_ind message to SS_S. Go back to initial state.
  2) If an LCU_DATA_req message is received with identifier 132, send an LCU_DATA_ind message to SS_C. Go back to initial state.
  3) If an LCU_RELEASE_req message is received with identifier 4, send an LCU_RELEASE_ind message to SS_S. Go back to initial state.
  4) If an LCU_RELEASE_req message is received with identifier 132, send an LCU_RELEASE_ind message to SS_C. Go back to initial state.
- Reaction sequence from SS_S's viewpoint :
  1) When an LCU_DATA_ind message is received from LCU, if it is an SS_START message, then send an SS_SETUP_ind message to the server and wait its response; otherwise quit.
  2) If an SS_RELEASE_req message is received from the server, send an LCU_RELEASE_req message with identifier 132 to LCU to quit.
     If an SS_FACILITY_req message is received from the server, send an LCU_DATA_req message with identifier 132 to LCU and starts a timer which timeouts at 10 time units later.
  3) If an LCU_RELEASE_ind message is received from LCU within 10 time units, send an SS_RELEASE_ind message back to the server and quit.

If a timeout occurs, send an SS_RELEASE_ind message to the server and an LCU_RELEASE_req message with identifier 132 to LCU to quit. If an LCU_DATA_ind message is received from the LCU within 10 time units, send an SS_FACILITY_ind message to the server and wait for its further response.

4) If an SS_RELEASE_req message is received from the server, then send an LCU_RELEASE_req message with identifier 132 to LCU to quit. If an SS_FACILITY_req message is received from the server, send an LCU_DATA_req message with identifier 132 to LCU and starts a timer which timeouts at 10 time units later.
5) If an LCU_RELEASE_ind message is received from LCU within 10 time units, send an SS_RELEASE_ind message back to the client and quit the session.
6) If a timeout happens, send an SS_RELEASE_ind message to the server and an LCU_RELEASE_req messge with identifer 132 to LCU to quit.

- Reaction sequence from the server's viewpoint :
  1) Upon receipt of an SS_SETUP_ind message from SS_S, the server either sends an SS_RELEASE_req message back to SS_S if the service is not available and goes back to the initial state, or sends an SS_FACILITY_req message to SS_S to notify that the service is available and waits for further response from SS_S.
  2) Upon receipt of the an SS_RELEASE message, the server knows that the the service is no longer needed and go back to the initial state. On the other hand, if an SS_FACILITY_ind message is received from SS_S, the server may either send an SS_RELEASE_req message to SS_S in case the server has to abort the service, or an SS_FACILITY_req message to provide the service and wait for further response from SS_S.
  3) Upon receipt of the an SS_RELEASE message, the server knows that the the service has completed and goes back to the initial state.

In our specification, we treat each message as a rendezvous. Message to and from LCU with different identifiers are also treated as of different message types for convenience. Messages between the client and SS_C all begin with prefix SS_C_. Messages between the server and SS_S all begin with prefix SS_S_. In table 2 and 3. we list our specifications for thread LCU, and SS_C. Because of page limit, we shall not present the specification for the client, SS_S, and the server. Also in table 4, we list the thread and rendezvous type declaration.

We have performed two reachability analyses. One is for an unreachable state which says that the server has aborted the service while the client is still using the service. The total number of states generated is 3675 and the CPU time is 5075 seconds on a Sparc 10 clone.

The second is for a reachable state which says that the client is using the service provided by the server. The total number of states generated is 3676 and the CPU time is 6649 seconds on a Sparc 10 clone.

```
/* Line Control Unit */
LCU {
    LCU_body *;
}

LCU_body {
    [0,\infty]; /* NULL */
    switch {
        case LCU_DATA_req_132;     /* LCU_DATA_req */
             LCU_DATA_ind_132;
        case LCU_DATA_req_4;  /* LCU_DATA_req */
             LCU_DATA_ind_4;
        case LCU_RELEASE_req_4;
             LCU_RELEASE_ind_4;  /* LCU_RELEASE_ind */
        case LCU_RELEASE_req_132;
             LCU_RELEASE_ind_132;  /* LCU_RELEASE_ind */
    }
}
```

Table 2. Thread LCU, Line Control Unit

7 The challenge ahead

It is easy to see that given an unstructured real-time system specification, its timing behavior structure can be horribly difficult to analyze. But this kind of input assumption usually contradicts the common practice of structured programming in software engineering, the high-level semantics of programming languages, and the design rules in real-time systems. We advocate procedure-level model descriptions and verifications for real-time concurrent systems for their potentially better average-case performance in automated verification. At the current stage, we have implemented an verification system which respects and utilizes the high-level behavior structures demonstrated in the program structures and local autonomy of real-time concurrent system specifications. An abstract version of a real-world protocol is tested with performance reported. However, we are still looking for test examples which exhibit more program structures like nested procedure-calling.

The concept of statements with earliest starting times and deadlines was also adopted in formal frameworks like [20, 24]. Special techniques for reachability analysis has also been reported under this kind of framework[20, 5]. However, we do not know if there is any previous formal framework for real-time concurrent systems aimed at taking advantage of local autonomy and program structures to improve the verification performance.

```
/* Supplementary Service A */
/* Any service request to LCU is with identifier 4 */
SS_C  {
    SS_C_body *;
}

SS_C_body  {
    [0,\infty]; /* NULL */
    SS_C_SETUP_req;
    [0,0]; /* PD_TI := 4 */
    LCU_DATA_req_4;
    [0,0];  /* set timer = 10; Initiated  */
    switch {
    case  [0,10]; LCU_RELEASE_ind_132; SS_C_RELEASE_ind;
    case  [0,10]; LCU_DATA_ind_132; SS_C_FACILITY_ind; [0,\infty];
          switch {
          case  SS_C_RELEASE_req;
                [0,0];  /* PD_TI := 4 */
                LCU_RELEASE_req_4;
          case  SS_C_FACILITY_req;
                [0,0]; /* PD_TI := 4 */
                LCU_DATA_req_4;
                [0,0]; /* set timer = 10 */
                switch  {
                case  [0,10]; LCU_RELEASE_ind_132; SS_C_RELEASE_ind;
                case  [0,10]; LCU_DATA_ind_132; SS_C_FACILITY_ind;
                      [0,\infty]; SS_C_RELEASE_req;
                      [0,0]; /* PD_TI := 4 */
                      LCU_RELEASE_req_4;
                case  [10,10]; SS_C_RELEASE_ind; LCU_RELEASE_req_4;
                }
          }
    case  [10,10]; [0,0]; SS_C_RELEASE_ind; LCU_RELEASE_req_4;
    }
}
```

Table 3. Thread SS_C, System Service for the Client

Acknowledgments

We thanks Professor Clarke and his crew at CMU for offering SMV[4, 23], which were used in our reachability analysis part of our implementation, and the associated technical advice. SMV is used as a routine for calculating the transitive closure in the rendezvous state graph in table 1.

```
/*=Thread description========================================================*/
<C, SS_C, LCU, SS_S, S>

/*=Rendezvous description====================================================*/

/* Between SS_C and LCU */
LCU_DATA_req_4 : 1,2;          LCU_RELEASE_req_4 : 1,2;
LCU_DATA_ind_132 : 1,2;        LCU_RELEASE_ind_132 : 1,2;

/* Between Client and SS_C */
SS_A_SETUP_req : 0,1;          SS_A_RELEASE_ind : 0,1;
SS_A_FACILITY_ind : 0,1;       SS_A_RELEASE_req : 0,1;
SS_A_FACILITY_req : 0,1;

/* Between SS_S and LCU */
LCU_RELEASE_req_132 : 2,3;     LCU_DATA_req_132 2,3;
LCU_RELEASE_ind_4 : 2,3;       LCU_DATA_ind_4 : 2,3;

/* Between Server and SS_S */
SS_B_SETUP_ind : 3,4;          SS_B_RELEASE_req : 3,4;
SS_B_FACILITY_req : 3,4;       SS_B_RELEASE_ind : 3,4;
SS_B_FACILITY_ind: 3,4;
```

Table 4. Thread and rendezvous type declaration

References

1. R. Alur, C. Courcoubetis, D.L. Dill. Model Checking for Real-Time Systems, IEEE LICS, 1990.
2. R. Alur, T.A. Henzinger, P.-H. Ho. Automatic Symbolic Verification of Embedded Systems. in Proceedings of 1993 IEEE Real-Time System Symposium.
3. A.V. Aho, R. Sethi, J.D. Ullman. *Compliers - Principles, Techniques, and Tools*, pp.393-396, Addison-Wesley Publishing Company, 1986.
4. J.R. Burch, E.M. Clarke, K.L. McMillan, D.L.Dill, L.J. Hwang. Symbolic Model Checking: 10^{20} States and Beyond, IEEE LICS, 1990.
5. B. Berthomieu, M. Diaz. Modeling and Verification of Time Dependent Systems Using Time Petri Nets. IEEE TSE, Vol. 17, No.3, March 1991.
6. Boyer, Moore. A Computational Logic Handbook, Academic Press, 1988.
7. D. Bosscher, I. Polak, F. Vaandrager. Verification of an Audio Control Protocol. Proceedings of Symposium on Formal Techniques in Real-Time and Fault-Tolerant Systems, 1994; in LNCS, Springer-Verlag.
8. R.E. Bryant. Graph-based Algorithms for Boolean Function Manipulation, IEEE Trans. Comput., C-35(8), 1986.
9. E. Clarke and E.A. Emerson. Design and Synthesis of Synchronization Skeletons using Branching-Time Temporal Logic, Proceedings of Workshop on Logic of Programs, Lecture Notes in Computer Science 131, Springer-Verlag, 1981.

10. E. Clarke, E.A. Emerson, and A.P. Sistla. Automatic Verification of Finite-State Concurrent Systems Using Temporal Logic Specifications, ACM Transactions on Programming Languages and Systems 8(2), 1986, pp. 244-263.
11. H.M. Deitel. An Introduction to Operating Systems, pp.110-115, Addison-Wesley, 1984.
12. E.A. Emerson, C.-L. Lei. Modalities for Model Checking: Branching Time Logic Strikes Back, Science of Computer Programming 8 (1987), pp.275-306, Elsevier Science Publishers B.V. (North-Holland).
13. M.J.C. Gordon. HOL - A Proof Generating System for Higher-Order Logic. Cambridge University, Computer Laboratory, 1987.
14. T.A. Henzinger, X. Nicollin, J. Sifakis, S. Yovine. Symbolic Model Checking for Real-Time Systems, IEEE LICS 1992.
15. C.A.R. Hoare. Communicating Sequential Processes, Prentice Hall, 1985.
16. E. Horowitz. Fundamentals of Programming Languages, Computer Science Press, 1984.
17. J.E. Hopcroft, J.D. Ullman. Introduction to Automata Theory, Languages, and Computation, Addison-Wesley, 1979.
18. C.B. Jones. Systematic Software Development using VDM, 2nd ed., Prentice Hall, 1990.
19. F. Jahanian and A.K. Mok. Safety analysis of timing properties in real-time systems, IEEE Transactions on Software Engineering, Vol.SE-12, No9, 1986, pp. 890-904.
20. F. Jahanian, D.A. Stuart. A Method for Verifying Properties of Modechart Specifications. IEEE RTSS 1988.
21. Y. Kesten, A. Pnueli, J. Sifakis, S. Yovine. Integration Graphs: a Class of Decidable Hybrid Systems. In Proc. Workshop on Theory of Hybrid Systems, LNCS 736, Springer-Verlag, 1993.
22. H.R. Lewis. Unsolvable Classes of Quantificational Formulus, 1979, Addison-Wesley Pub. Co.
23. K.L. McMillan, "Symbolic Model Checking", Kluwer Academic Publishers, Boston, MA, 1993.
24. P. Merlin, D.J. Faber. Recoverability of Communication Protocols. IEEE Trans. Commun, Vol. COM-24, no. 9, Sept. 1976.
25. R. Milner. Communication and Concurrency. Prentice Hall, 1989.
26. O. Maler, Z. Manna, A. Pnueli. From Timed to Hybrid Systems. In Real Time : Theory in Practice, LNCS 600, pp. 447-484, Springer-Verlag, 1991.
27. Z. Manna, A. Pnueli. Verifying Hybrid Systems. In Proc. Workshop on Theory of Hybrid Systems, LNCS 736, Springer-Verlag, 1993.
28. R.S. Pressman. Software Engineering, A Practitioner's Approach. McGraw-Hill, 1982.
29. K. Slind. HOL90 Users Manual. Technical report, 1992.
30. J.M. Spivey. The Z Notation, A Reference Manual, second edition. Prentice Hall, 1992.
31. F. Wang, A.K. Mok, E.A. Emerson. Real-Time Distributed System Specification and Verification in APTL. ACM TOSEM, Vol. 2, No. 4, Octobor 1993, pp. 346-378.
32. F. Wang. Timing Behavior Analysis for Real-Time Systems. IEEE LICS 1995.
33. F. Wang. Reachability Analysis at Procedure Level through Timing Coincidence. in Proceedings of the 6th CONCUR, Philadelphia, USA, August 1995, LNCS 962.
34. W. Wulf, M. Shaw, P. Hilfinger, L. Flon. Fundamentals of Computer Science, Addison-Wesley, Reading, Mass., 1981.

Authors' Index

Springer-Verlag and the Environment

We at Springer-Verlag firmly believe that an international science publisher has a special obligation to the environment, and our corporate policies consistently reflect this conviction.

We also expect our business partners – paper mills, printers, packaging manufacturers, etc. – to commit themselves to using environmentally friendly materials and production processes.

The paper in this book is made from low- or no-chlorine pulp and is acid free, in conformance with international standards for paper permanency.

Lecture Notes in Computer Science

For information about Vols. 1–975

please contact your bookseller or Springer-Verlag

Vol. 976: U. Montanari, F. Rossi (Eds.), Principles and Practice of Constraint Programming — CP '95. Proceedings, 1995. XIII, 651 pages. 1995.

Vol. 977: H. Beilner, F. Bause (Eds.), Quantitative Evaluation of Computing and Communication Systems. Proceedings, 1995. X, 415 pages. 1995.

Vol. 978: N. Revell, A M. Tjoa (Eds.), Database and Expert Systems Applications. Proceedings, 1995. XV, 654 pages. 1995.

Vol. 979: P. Spirakis (Ed.), Algorithms — ESA '95. Proceedings, 1995. XII, 598 pages. 1995.

Vol. 980: A. Ferreira, J. Rolim (Eds.), Parallel Algorithms for Irregularly Structured Problems. Proceedings, 1995. IX, 409 pages. 1995.

Vol. 981: I. Wachsmuth, C.-R. Rollinger, W. Brauer (Eds.), KI-95: Advances in Artificial Intelligence. Proceedings, 1995. XII, 269 pages. (Subseries LNAI).

Vol. 982: S. Doaitse Swierstra, M. Hermenegildo (Eds.), Programming Languages: Implementations, Logics and Programs. Proceedings, 1995. XI, 467 pages. 1995.

Vol. 983: A. Mycroft (Ed.), Static Analysis. Proceedings, 1995. VIII, 423 pages. 1995.

Vol. 984: J.-M. Haton, M. Keane, M. Manago (Eds.), Advances in Case-Based Reasoning. Proceedings, 1994. VIII, 307 pages. 1995.

Vol. 985: T. Sellis (Ed.), Rules in Database Systems. Proceedings, 1995. VIII, 373 pages. 1995.

Vol. 986: Henry G. Baker (Ed.), Memory Management. Proceedings, 1995. XII, 417 pages. 1995.

Vol. 987: P.E. Camurati, H. Eveking (Eds.), Correct Hardware Design and Verification Methods. Proceedings, 1995. VIII, 342 pages. 1995.

Vol. 988: A.U. Frank, W. Kuhn (Eds.), Spatial Information Theory. Proceedings, 1995. XIII, 571 pages. 1995.

Vol. 989: W. Schäfer, P. Botella (Eds.), Software Engineering — ESEC '95. Proceedings, 1995. XII, 519 pages. 1995.

Vol. 990: C. Pinto-Ferreira, N.J. Mamede (Eds.), Progress in Artificial Intelligence. Proceedings, 1995. XIV, 487 pages. 1995. (Subseries LNAI).

Vol. 991: J. Wainer, A. Carvalho (Eds.), Advances in Artificial Intelligence. Proceedings, 1995. XII, 342 pages. 1995. (Subseries LNAI).

Vol. 992: M. Gori, G. Soda (Eds.), Topics in Artificial Intelligence. Proceedings, 1995. XII, 451 pages. 1995. (Subseries LNAI).

Vol. 993: T.C. Fogarty (Ed.), Evolutionary Computing. Proceedings, 1995. VIII, 264 pages. 1995.

Vol. 994: M. Hebert, J. Ponce, T. Boult, A. Gross (Eds.), Object Representation in Computer Vision. Proceedings, 1994. VIII, 359 pages. 1995.

Vol. 995: S.M. Müller, W.J. Paul, The Complexity of Simple Computer Architectures. XII, 270 pages. 1995.

Vol. 996: P. Dybjer, B. Nordström, J. Smith (Eds.), Types for Proofs and Programs. Proceedings, 1994. X, 202 pages. 1995.

Vol. 997: K.P. Jantke, T. Shinohara, T. Zeugmann (Eds.), Algorithmic Learning Theory. Proceedings, 1995. XV, 319 pages. 1995.

Vol. 998: A. Clarke, M. Campolargo, N. Karatzas (Eds.), Bringing Telecommunication Services to the People – IS&N '95. Proceedings, 1995. XII, 510 pages. 1995.

Vol. 999: P. Antsaklis, W. Kohn, A. Nerode, S. Sastry (Eds.), Hybrid Systems II. VIII, 569 pages. 1995.

Vol. 1000: J. van Leeuwen (Ed.), Computer Science Today. XIV, 643 pages. 1995.

Vol. 1001: M. Sudan, Efficient Checking of Polynomials and Proofs and the Hardness of Approximation Problems. XIV, 87 pages. 1995.

Vol. 1002: J.J. Kistler, Disconnected Operation in a Distributed File System. XIX, 249 pages. 1995.

VOL. 1003: P. Pandurang Nayak, Automated Modeling of Physical Systems. XXI, 232 pages. 1995. (Subseries LNAI).

Vol. 1004: J. Staples, P. Eades, N. Katoh, A. Moffat (Eds.), Algorithms and Computation. Proceedings, 1995. XV, 440 pages. 1995.

Vol. 1005: J. Estublier (Ed.), Software Configuration Management. Proceedings, 1995. IX, 311 pages. 1995.

Vol. 1006: S. Bhalla (Ed.), Information Systems and Data Management. Proceedings, 1995. IX, 321 pages. 1995.

Vol. 1007: A. Bosselaers, B. Preneel (Eds.), Integrity Primitives for Secure Information Systems. VII, 239 pages. 1995.

Vol. 1008: B. Preneel (Ed.), Fast Software Encryption. Proceedings, 1994. VIII, 367 pages. 1995.

Vol. 1009: M. Broy, S. Jähnichen (Eds.), KORSO: Methods, Languages, and Tools for the Construction of Correct Software. X, 449 pages. 1995. Vol.

Vol. 1010: M. Veloso, A. Aamodt (Eds.), Case-Based Reasoning Research and Development. Proceedings, 1995. X, 576 pages. 1995. (Subseries LNAI).

Vol. 1011: T. Furuhashi (Ed.), Advances in Fuzzy Logic, Neural Networks and Genetic Algorithms. Proceedings, 1994. (Subseries LNAI).

Vol. 1012: M. Bartošek, J. Staudek, J. Wiedermann (Eds.), SOFSEM '95: Theory and Practice of Informatics. Proceedings, 1995. XI, 499 pages. 1995.

Vol. 1013: T.W. Ling, A.O. Mendelzon, L. Vieille (Eds.), Deductive and Object-Oriented Databases. Proceedings, 1995. XIV, 557 pages. 1995.

Vol. 1014: A.P. del Pobil, M.A. Serna, Spatial Representation and Motion Planning. XII, 242 pages. 1995.

Vol. 1015: B. Blumenthal, J. Gornostaev, C. Unger (Eds.), Human-Computer Interaction. Proceedings, 1995. VIII, 203 pages. 1995.

VOL. 1016: R. Cipolla, Active Visual Inference of Surface Shape. XII, 194 pages. 1995.

Vol. 1017: M. Nagl (Ed.), Graph-Theoretic Concepts in Computer Science. Proceedings, 1995. XI, 406 pages. 1995.

Vol. 1018: T.D.C. Little, R. Gusella (Eds.), Network and Operating Systems Support for Digital Audio and Video. Proceedings, 1995. XI, 357 pages. 1995.

Vol. 1019: E. Brinksma, W.R. Cleaveland, K.G. Larsen, T. Margaria, B. Steffen (Eds.), Tools and Algorithms for the Construction and Analysis of Systems. Selected Papers, 1995. VII, 291 pages. 1995.

Vol. 1020: I.D. Watson (Ed.), Progress in Case-Based Reasoning. Proceedings, 1995. VIII, 209 pages. 1995. (Subseries LNAI).

Vol. 1021: M.P. Papazoglou (Ed.), OOER '95: Object-Oriented and Entity-Relationship Modeling. Proceedings, 1995. XVII, 451 pages. 1995.

Vol. 1022: P.H. Hartel, R. Plasmeijer (Eds.), Functional Programming Languages in Education. Proceedings, 1995. X, 309 pages. 1995.

Vol. 1023: K. Kanchanasut, J.-J. Lévy (Eds.), Algorithms, Concurrency and Knowlwdge. Proceedings, 1995. X, 410 pages. 1995.

Vol. 1024: R.T. Chin, H.H.S. Ip, A.C. Naiman, T.-C. Pong (Eds.), Image Analysis Applications and Computer Graphics. Proceedings, 1995. XVI, 533 pages. 1995.

Vol. 1025: C. Boyd (Ed.), Cryptography and Coding. Proceedings, 1995. IX, 291 pages. 1995.

Vol. 1026: P.S. Thiagarajan (Ed.), Foundations of Software Technology and Theoretical Computer Science. Proceedings, 1995. XII, 515 pages. 1995.

Vol. 1027: F.J. Brandenburg (Ed.), Graph Drawing. Proceedings, 1995. XII, 526 pages. 1996.

Vol. 1028: N.R. Adam, Y. Yesha (Eds.), Electronic Commerce. X, 155 pages. 1996.

Vol. 1029: E. Dawson, J. Golić (Eds.), Cryptography: Policy and Algorithms. Proceedings, 1995. XI, 327 pages. 1996.

Vol. 1030: F. Pichler, R. Moreno-Díaz, R. Albrecht (Eds.), Computer Aided Systems Theory - EUROCAST '95. Proceedings, 1995. XII, 539 pages. 1996.

Vol.1031: M. Toussaint (Ed.), Ada in Europe. Proceedings, 1995. XI, 455 pages. 1996.

Vol. 1032: P. Godefroid, Partial-Order Methods for the Verification of Concurrent Systems. IV, 143 pages. 1996.

Vol. 1033: C.-H. Huang, P. Sadayappan, U. Banerjee, D. Gelernter, A. Nicolau, D. Padua (Eds.), Languages and Compilers for Parallel Computing. Proceedings, 1995. XIII, 597 pages. 1996.

Vol. 1034: G. Kuper, M. Wallace (Eds.), Constraint Databases and Applications. Proceedings, 1995. VII, 185 pages. 1996.

Vol. 1035: S.Z. Li, D.P. Mital, E.K. Teoh, H. Wang (Eds.), Recent Developments in Computer Vision. Proceedings, 1995. XI, 604 pages. 1996.

Vol. 1036: G. Adorni, M. Zock (Eds.), Trends in Natural Language Generation - An Artificial Intelligence Perspective. Proceedings, 1993. IX, 382 pages. 1996. (Subseries LNAI).

Vol. 1037: M. Wooldridge, J.P. Müller, M. Tambe (Eds.), Intelligent Agents II. Proceedings, 1995. XVI, 437 pages. 1996. (Subseries LNAI).

Vol. 1038: W: Van de Velde, J.W. Perram (Eds.), Agents Breaking Away. Proceedings, 1996. XIV, 232 pages. 1996. (Subseries LNAI).

Vol. 1039: D. Gollmann (Ed.), Fast Software Encryption. Proceedings, 1996. X, 219 pages. 1996.

Vol. 1040: S. Wermter, E. Riloff, G. Scheler (Eds.), Connectionist, Statistical, and Symbolic Approaches to Learning for Natural Language Processing. Proceedings, 1995. IX, 468 pages. 1996. (Subseries LNAI).

Vol. 1041: J. Dongarra, K. Madsen, J. Waśniewski (Eds.), Applied Parallel Computing. Proceedings, 1995. XII, 562 pages. 1996.

Vol. 1042: G. Weiß, S. Sen (Eds.), Adaption and Learning in Multi-Agent Systems. Proceedings, 1995. X, 238 pages. 1996. (Subseries LNAI).

Vol. 1043: F. Moller, G. Birtwistle (Eds.), Logics for Concurrency. XI, 266 pages. 1996.

Vol. 1044: B. Plattner (Ed.), Broadband Communications. Proceedings, 1996. XIV, 359 pages. 1996.

Vol. 1045: B. Butscher, E. Moeller, H. Pusch (Eds.), Interactive Distributed Multimedia Systems and Services. Proceedings, 1996. XI, 333 pages. 1996.

Vol. 1046: C. Puech, R. Reischuk (Eds.), STACS 96. Proceedings, 1996. XII, 690 pages. 1996.

Vol. 1047: E. Hajnicz, Time Structures. IX, 244 pages. 1996. (Subseries LNAI).

Vol. 1048: M. Proietti (Ed.), Logic Program Syynthesis and Transformation. Proceedings, 1995. X, 267 pages. 1996.

Vol. 1049: K. Futatsugi, S. Matsuoka (Eds.), Object Technologies for Advanced Software. Proceedings, 1996. X, 309 pages. 1996.

Vol. 1050: R. Dyckhoff, H. Herre, P. Schroeder-Heister (Eds.), Extensions of Logic Programming. Proceedings, 1996. VII, 318 pages. 1996. (Subseries LNAI).

Vol. 1051: M.-C. Gaudel, J. Woodcock (Eds.), FME'96: Industrial Benefit and Advances in Formal Methods. Proceedings, 1996. XII, 704 pages. 1996.